Encyclopedia of

ROMANTICISM

Culture in Britain, 1780s–1830s

Garland Reference Library of the Social Sciences
(Vol. 1299)

Encyclopedia of

ROMANTICISM

Culture in Britain, 1780s–1830s

Laura Dabundo

Editor

Pamela Olinto, Greg Rider, Gail Roos
Editorial Assistants

Garland Publishing, Inc.
New York & London
1992

Library of Congress Cataloging-in-Publication Data

Encyclopedia of Romanticism: Culture in Britain, 1780s–1830s /
    Laura Dabundo, editor; Pamela Olinto, Greg Rider, Gail Roos, editorial assistants.
        p. cm.—(Garland reference library of social science; v. 1299)
    Includes index.
    ISBN 0-8240-6997-8
    1. Great Britain—Civilization—19th century—Encyclopedias. 2. Great Britain—Civilization—18th century—Encyclopedias. 3. Romanticism—Great Britain—Encyclopedias. I. Dabundo, Laura Susan.
II. Series.
DA529.E53   1992
941.07'3—dc20   92-2682
              CIP

Printed on acid-free, 250-year-life paper
Manufactured in the United States of America

Book and cover design by Julia Threlkeld

Jacket illustration: George Morland, "The Industrious Cottager."
Stipple engraving by William Blake, published by J.R. Smith,
London, 1788. 21.3 x 26 cm. Third state. From the collection
of Jenijoy La Belle.

I live not in myself, but I become
Portion of that around me . . .
—Byron, *Childe Harold*

Preface

The *Encyclopedia of Romanticism* is designed to survey the social, cultural, and intellectual climate of English Romanticism from approximately the 1780s and the French Revolution to the mid-1830s and the First Reform Bill, Scott's death (the traditional point of closure), and Victoria's accession, all of which marked a sea change in the temper of the times.

This book focuses on what Hazlitt called "the spirit of the age," not just the esthetic but also the scientific, the socioeconomic—indeed the human—environment in which flourished, at least poetically and at least for a time, not just the six canonized male poets of Romanticism, but many other artists, thinkers, and agents of change. This book considers poets, playwrights, and novelists; critics, editors, and booksellers; painters, patrons, and architects; as well as ideas, trends, fads, and conventions, the familiar and the newly rediscovered. As an embassy of change, moreover, Romanticism in many ways prepared its own overthrow, that is, its succession by Victorian and ultimately modern times. All of this, this book attempts to chart. As the eminent critic Thomas McFarland noted in *Romanticism and the Forms of Ruin*, "great poems are possible only in contexts," so this book, then, attempts to scan Romanticism's context—hence, the book's Byronic epigraph.

How to Use It

The *Encyclopedia of Romanticism* is organized alphabetically with some cross references. I kept them to a minimum for fear of drowning the content in such references. People from the period who are identified *only by last name* in articles on subjects other than themselves have their own separate entries and so are not cross referenced. For additional information, readers are directed to the Index. Also, the list of publications at the end of almost every entry constitutes works consulted by the author and is not necessarily an exhaustive bibliography or even recommended reading, which is not to say that you might not benefit from them.

Why Use It?

The *Encyclopedia of Romanticism* is for everyone from undergraduate English majors through thesis- or dissertation-driven graduate students to teaching faculty and scholars. And, as it happens, individuals from all of those levels have contributed to the making of this book, which thereby assured some awareness of their needs, expectations, or desires.

Romantic studies have typically been in the vanguard of scholarship, so that this book attempts to steer a middle course by acknowledging and profiting from the prevailing wealth in the field—the substance, for instance, of the work on the six traditionally central male poets—while reaching out to current and innovative explorations, such as the insights of feminist and new-historicist critics. Consequently, this book attempts to take the measure of the breadth and depth of the academy's Romanticism. To that end, I have not ruthlessly edited out all opinions contrary to my own; the articles reflect the research and conclusions of their authors. I have attempted to preserve the diversity of voices in this text, both on the part of the subjects as well as of the authors, while striving to present a unified vision of the diversity of Romantic culture and Romantic studies.

What to Expect From It

While the *Encyclopedia of Romanticism* has comprehensive aspirations, there are surely other topics to be noted, especially given the grand eclecticism of the period. Several of this book's characteristics should be pointed out: Unlike encyclopedias in other fields, this book eschews the unabridged approach (and therefore the cursory or summary entry) in order to permit entries that do justice to their subjects and are not telegraphic. Less is more? In general, the controlling principle has been to hew to the perspective of literary English Romanticism. Moreover, single essays on American, French, Russian, and Spanish Romanticism appear, while the German one is supplemented by articles on German fairytales, Baron Münchausen, the Grimm Brothers, and two pieces on aspects of German Idealism to account for the considerable influence and intersection with German culture.

Similarly, at times, the books strays to poach in other fields: Burns, Burnet, Carlyle, Cowper, Crabbe, Mitford, Montagu, Percy, and Piranesi were deemed of sufficient related interest to merit consideration. And, one of the delights in constructing the text was to include novel topics volunteered by their discoverers, such as hymnody, puns, satanism, vegetarianism, to name a few. One of Romanticism's strengths is that it is a melange. Lastly, there is occasionally an overlap among related essays, which I decided to retain when the scope, shape, and treatment of each essay rendered the content unique and that to view similar matter differently might be provocative.

In conclusion, as the now much abandoned "General Confession" in the *Book of Common Prayer* directs: "We have left undone those things which we ought to have done; And we have done those things which we ought not to have done." It is my hope that you will find what you seek, and more!

Laura Dabundo
Kennesaw State College

For Linda Jordan Tucker

Friendship is a sheltering tree . . .
— Coleridge

Contents

Foreword

Because the Romantic period was so learned, diverse, and intellectually aware, an encyclopedia is an especially appropriate form for representing Romanticism in England. Indeed, it was during the English Romantic period that the encyclopedia acquired the form and even the function now associated with it: an eclectic, popular, and authoritative compilation of knowledge or information.

Perhaps what is the most familiar encyclopedia, the *Britannica*, began its long evolution in 1771 as a three-volume entrepreneurial venture produced by Andrew Bell, a Scot. Although he was inspired by the French Encyclopédistes, who published 35 volumes between 1751 and 1772, he and his colleagues wanted to avoid the scandal, notoriety, censorship, and political and religious reprisals that Diderot, the editor, endured for his critical approach to ideas and institutions, a criticism so pointed and effective that some say it contributed to the French Revolution. Consequently, *Britannica,* like all encyclopedias that followed, reflected rather than shaped conventions; it was produced on largely historical principles, a conservative representation of contemporary human knowledge, including its limitations—the tendency of the *Britannica,* for example, was to mix, not always consciously, popular superstition along with actual information, providing access to the interesting misconceptions of the period.

Over the years, it became more factual, more comprehensive, and more popular, one of the most successful publishing ventures in the Western world. Spanning Wordsworth's lifetime, for example, it went through eight editions. Nor was it the only encyclopedia: the lesser but equally popular *Perthensis* was published in 12 volumes from 1796 to 1806, and the *Pantalogia* also ran to 12 volumes between 1802 and 1813. Coleridge objected to the alphabetical arrangement of encyclopedias and designed a complicated philosophical system which he believed more nearly represented the categories and relationships of human knowledge, which he explained in an essay called *On Method*. It was adapted as the Introduction to *Encyclopedia Metropolitan,* which took 28 years to produce, from 1817 to 1845, so that many of the entries were outdated by the time it appeared and the system too complicated to use. It was one of the few that failed.

From the speed at which these encyclopedias appeared, their range, and their diversity, it was clear that not only was knowledge expanding but so was the reading public, the publishing industry that served it, its marketing skills, and the capacity for distribution. It was essentially the same reading public that made Scott wealthy, Byron famous, and Southey, who could write in almost any form, productive. But it was also a public that depended on encyclopedias because there was no universal system of education and the existing institutions were so poor that people graduated from universities with little education. Even in its mix of folklore and fact, the encyclopedias, appearing frequently and often updated, offered the best education there was, in the form of self-education, with bibliographic citations enabling the reader to consult the original authorities. (See also Richard Altick, *English Common Reader,* and Robert Lewis Collison, *Encyclopedias: Their History Throughout the Ages.*)

To us now, the encyclopedias produced during the Romantic period offer a rare insight into the minds of literate people during the period, their biases, assumptions, tastes, perspectives, priorities, as well as what they knew. Similarly, this encyclopedia, assembled so resourcefully and carefully by Laura Dabundo, is as much a reflection of our age, the way it views the Romantic tradition, as it is a reflection of the English Romantic period. Topics such as Jeremy Bentham, pantomime, and geology probably would not have appeared even 20 years ago, when the primary scholarly effort was devoted to defining Romanticism and finding single unifying characteristics or ideas limited to certain major poetic figures. Fortunately, a more historically oriented criticism has required us to know more, and new historical concerns with previously forgotten events, neglected individuals, and overlooked ideas have produced more information for us from untapped sources. The contemporary approach to Romanticism recognizes that it is a far more complex movement than merely a return to nature or a revival of interest in the Middle Ages, as it was characterized, say, 30 years ago, that it contains contradictions, diversity, and fragmentation. When the information, the organization, and the topics in this encyclopedia are themselves transcended by time and taste, the work itself, I believe, will remain a monument to this period in Romantic studies.

Marilyn Gaull

Acknowledgments

This volume was virtually a companion to me for several months—when a tornado threatened northern Georgia, I gathered up the two-foot pile of manuscript and headed for the basement. However, it has been not only a companion but also the kind of good friend that, while certainly taxing and recalcitrant at times, has introduced me to many of the "joint labourers" whom Wordsworth sought. That is to say, more pedestrianly, I am grateful to my contributors, from seven countries, who have written learned, wonderful, exciting entries on all aspects of Romanticism. How vigorous and vital Romanticism is! Their efforts are a tribute to the comradeship of Romantic studies. I am thankful, as well, for the sage counsel on topics, contributors, scope, content, and focus from the Advisory Board, especially Marilyn Gaull, who reviewed the entire manuscript critically and carefully. Thanks, too, goes to Gary Kuris, my ever-encouraging, ever-supportive editor at Garland. I am appreciative, as well, of the efforts of Kevin Bradley at Garland.

Closer to home, I would like to acknowledge the support, both institutional and personal, from George H. Beggs, Dean of the School of Arts and Behavioral Sciences, and Robert W. Hill, Chair of the Department of English, both at Kennesaw State College. I am most appreciative of the diligent and fruitful labors of my editorial assistants in Georgia: Gail Roos, Pamela Olinto, Greg Rider, Debra Taylor, Maggie Riley, and Cathy Anderson. I could not have done this work in terms of sheer mass or volume without the secretarial aid of the English Department's splendid, indispensable Shirley Dean and the industrious and invaluable Lori Krise. And I am glad to recognize my indebtedness to Linda Jordan Tucker, whose friendship has been a bulwark throughout this project as the dedication implies, but who has also been actively involved in it and has provided sound ideas, much assistance, and welcome energy.

Thank you, thank you, thank you.

You are all true friends—

> *Joy lift your spirits, joy attune your voice;*
> *To you may all things live, from pole to pole,*
> *Their life the eddying of your living soul!*
>
> . . .
>
> *Friends devoutest of my choice,*
> *Thus mayest thou ever, evermore rejoice!*
> —Coleridge

Contributors

Carol J. Adams
Richardson, TX

Karla Alwes
State University College at Cortland

John M. Anderson
Boston College

Phillip B. Anderson
University of Central Arkansas

Linda A. Archer
Eastern New Mexico University

Bryan Aubrey
Fairfield, IA

John Axcelson
Columbia University

Kit Ayars
University of Pittsburgh

Susan Taylor Baltimore
Kennesaw State College

James E. Barcus
Baylor University

Martha Watson Bargo
Kennesaw State College

Samuel I. Bellman
California State Polytechnic University

Toby Benis
Columbia University

Shelley M. Bennett
The Huntington

G. Kim Blank
University of Victoria
Canada

William D. Brewer
Appalachian State University

Monika Brown
Pembroke State University

Robert W. Brown
Pembroke State University

Hallman B. Bryant
Clemson University

Miranda Burgess
Boston University

Catherine Burroughs
Cornell College

Frederick Burwick
University of California, Los Angeles

Jo-Anne Cappeluti
California State University

Henry L. Carrigan, Jr.
Otterbein College

Anne T. Ciecko
University of Pittsburgh

Timothy J.A. Clark
Elvet Riverside
England

Doris A. Clatanoff
Texas A & I University

Marilyn Clay
The Regency Plume

Thomas L. Cooksey
Armstrong State College

John Michael Crafton
West Georgia College

Lisa Plummer Crafton
West Georgia College

William Crisman
Pennsylvania State University—Altoona

Thomas C. Crochunis
Rutgers University

Laura Dabundo
Kennesaw State College

Paul Davies
Universität Passau
Germany

Patricia Elizabeth Davis
Kennesaw State College

Frank Day
Clemson University

Joseph Duemer
Clarkson University

Gary Dyer
University of Pennsylvania

Ann W. Engar
University of Utah

Angela Esterhammer
University of Western Ontario
Canada

Lynn Fedeli
Kennesaw State College

Jo Ann Ferguson
Attleboro, MA

Donna Ferrantello
Lawrenceville, NJ

Louise Flavin
University of Cincinnati

Norma W. Goldstein
Mississippi State University—Meridian

Alexander S. Gourlay
Rhode Island School of Design

Dorothy H. Graham
Kennesaw State College

Kyle Grimes
University of Alabama at Birmingham

Jonathan Gross
Columbia University

David Groves
Social Sciences and Humanities Research
Council of Canada

Joel Haefner
Illinois State University

R.M. Healey
University of London
England

Jonathan E. Hill
St. Olaf College

Robert W. Hill
Kennesaw State College

Brenda Hutchingson
National Defense University

Gregory S. Jackson
London, England

Gregg Johnson
Kennesaw State College

Mary Susan Johnston
Mankato State University

Marilyn Jurich
Suffolk University

Deborah Kennedy
Mount Saint Vincent University
Canada

Gary Kerley
Brenau Academy

Kathryn Kirkpatrick
Appalachian State University

J. Douglas Kneale
University of Western Ontario
Canada

Jenijoy La Belle
Claifornia Institute of Technology

Jackie Labbe
University of Pennsylvania

Shirley Laird
Tennessee Technological University

Jennifer Lawler
University of Kansas

Raymond Lister
University of Cambridge
England

Leon Litvack
The Queen's University of Belfast
Northern Ireland

Mark Lussier
Western Illinois University

Stephen J. Lynch
University of North Carolina at Asheville

Elaine McAllister
Kennesaw State College

Len McCall
Clemson University

John F. McElroy
New York, NY

Richard D. McGhee
Arkansas State University

Gayla S. McGlamery
Loyala College in Maryland

Karen McGuire
Pasadena City College

Carol McGuirk
Florida Atlantic University

Raymond N. MacKenzie
College of St. Thomas

Kenneth McNamee
Temple University

Martin P. McNamee
University of North Carolina
    at Chapel Hill

Harmon Droge Maher
University of Nebraska at Omaha

Susan N. Maher
University of Nebraska at Omaha

John L. Mahoney
Boston College

Susan Meisenhelder
California State University

David S. Miall
University of Alberta
Canada

Elizabeth Mihaly
Kent State University

Walter S. Minot
Gannon University

John V. Murphy
Bucknell University

James Najarian
Yale University

Guin A. Nance
Auburn University

Ashton Nichols
Dickinson College

Elsa A. Nystrom
Kennesaw State College

Robert O'Connor
North Dakota State University

Brennan O'Donnell
Loyola College in Maryland

Pamela Olinto
Kennesaw State College

Louis J. Parascandola
Long Island University—Brooklyn

Jeffrey D. Parker
North Carolina A & T State University

Mark Parker
Randolph-Macon College

Paxman
London, England

Constance Pedoto
Samford University

Vincent F. Petronella
University of Massachusetts—Boston

Alan Rauch
Georgia Institute of Technology

Alan Richardson
Boston College

Greg Rider
Georgia State University

Samuel J. Rogal
Illinois Valley Community College

Kinsley G. Romer
Kennesaw State College

Gail M. Roos
Kennesaw State College

Joseph Rosenblum
University of North Carolina
   at Greensboro

Andrea Rowland
University of Virginia

William Ruddick
University of Manchester
England

D.C. Saxena
Panjab University
India

Matthew T. Schneider
University of California, Los Angeles

Beverly Schneller
Millersville University

Peter A. Schock
University of New Orleans

Carol A. Senf
Georgia Institute of Technology

Scott Simpkins
University of North Texas

Hartley S. Spatt
State University of New York
   —Maritime College

Sheila Spector
Kennesaw State College

Sue Starke
Rutgers University

John A. Stoler
University of Texas at San Antonio

Jack Truten
Lafayette College

Linda Jordan Tucker
Kennesaw State College

David W. Ullrich
Birmingham-Southern College

Heidi Van de Veire
Victoria University of Wellington
New Zealand

Jack Voller
Southern Illinois University at
Edwardsville

Gail Walker
Kennesaw State College

Kenneth Watson
University of Southern Mississippi

Paul M. Wiebe
Morehouse College

Albert E. Wilhelm
Tennessee Technological University

Carol Shiner Wilson
Lafayette College

D.C. Woodcox
Northeast Missouri State University

Kathryn Young
Coppell, TX

Paula P. Yow
Kennesaw State College

Mary D. Zoghby
Kennesaw State College

●

Encyclopedia of

ROMANTICISM

Culture in Britain, 1780s–1830s

Ackermann, Rudolph
(1754–1834)

Rudolph Ackermann was born at Stolberg in Saxony and educated at Scheeberg. He learned coach building and harness making from his father before moving, first, to Paris and then to London, where for 10 years he worked designing coaches. In 1795, he married an Englishwoman and opened a print shop on the Strand.

Instrumental in establishing lithography as a fine art in England, in 1817, Ackermann set up his Lithographic Press in London. Its first important production was a facsimile of the 1808 Munich volume of illustrations from Albrecht Durer's 1515 Prayer Book. Partial to lithography, he later popularized aquatint by using it to interpret the work of the artists who drew for his books. In fact, the decline of aquatint in book illustration may be dated from his death in 1834. Among the artists with whom Ackermann collaborated were Nash, Prout, Pugin, and Rowlandson.

Ackermann's *Repository of Arts, Literature, Commerce, Manufactures, Fashions and Politics* (1809–28) contains 1,500 colorplates of costumes, furniture, London shops, and carriages, as well as papers from such sources as the Royal Society and Natural History Society; it is an excellent guide to the appearance of Regency life. From 1809 until 1811, Ackermann's periodical *Poetical Magazine* was sustained by the lengthy parody *The Schoolmaster's Tour*, thereafter published as *Dr. Syntax's Tour in search of the Picturesque* (1812), written by William Combe and illustrated by Rowlandson. Ackermann's *The Forget-Me-Not*, published from 1823 onward, set the fashion for annuals, a periodical, normally designed as a gift, including samples of literature, art, fashion, and noncontroversial topical subjects representative of contemporary life. His other publications include the *The Microcosm of London* (three volumes) (1808–10); *The History of . . . Westminster* (two volumes) (1812); *A History of the University of Oxford* (two volumes) (1814); *A History of the University of Cambridge* (two volumes) (1815); *The Colleges of Winchester, Eton, Westminster, &c.* (1816). (*See also* also Publishing, Topographical and Travel Prints.)

Martin P. McNamee

Works Consulted
Dictionary of National Biography, s.v. "Ackermann, Rudolph."

Burch, R.M. *Colour Printing and Colour Printers*. 1910. New York: Garland, 1981.

Plant, Majorie. *The English Book Trade*. 1939. London: Allen, 1974.

Aikin, Lucy

(1781–1864)

Famous as the niece of Anna Laetitia Barbauld and as the editor of her aunt's poetry, Lucy Aikin, like Barbauld, enjoyed an education that included fluency in French, Italian, and Latin, and wrote books for children. Aikin was the daughter of John Aikin, who, with Barbauld, compiled a popular collection of essays for family reading, *Evenings at Home* (1792). Lucy wrote a handbook on letter writing, *Juvenile Correspondence* (1811), and edited a popular anthology of short verse, *Poetry for Children* (1801). The anthology draws mainly on the poetry of the Enlightenment, which also influenced Aikin's own poetry, notably her *Epistles on Women* (1810), a history of women, written in Neoclassical heroic couplets. As the title of her poem suggests, Aikin was more of a feminist than her famous aunt, and where Barbauld argued that girls should be educated to be good wives and mothers, Aikin held that it was necessary to augment the prose of their lives with poetry.

But during her career, Aikin turned from poetry to prose. First trying fiction in 1814, with a novel of sensibility (*Lorimer, A Tale*), she soon turned to history. *Memoirs of the Court of Queen Elizabeth* (1818) anecdotally combines biography, domestic history, and remarks on the manners and literature of the period (though Shakespeare receives only a single mention in the index, he is far surpassed there by the courtlier Raleigh and Sidney). This book was so successful that she followed it with *Memoirs of the Court of James I* (1822) and *Memoirs of*

Charles I (1833). She also wrote biographies of her father (1823) and of Joseph Addison (1843), and biographical sketches of Barbauld, and of Baillie, and Elizabeth Benger, the latter two among her many scholarly and literary friends.

John Anderson

Works Consulted

Blain, Virginia, Isobel Grundy, and Patricia Clements, eds. *The Feminist Companion to Literature in English*. London: Batsford, 1990.

Todd, Janet, ed. *British Women Writers*. New York: Bedrick, 1989.

American Romanticism

(1820–60)

American Romanticism, like English Romanticism, characterized not only literature and art, but also influenced an entire culture. In America as in Britain, Romanticism left its mark on the political scene, human suffrage (in the forms of abolitionist and feminist movements), the labor movement, religion (Unitarianism and Universalism), and experiments in communal living (Brook Farm).

In terms of literature, the Romantic period was America's first great creative flowering. The three major literary figures of the previous or Federalist age—William Cullen Bryant, James Fenimore Cooper, and Washington Irving—continued to be influential. The new writers of distinction who emerged during the period were novelists Nathaniel Hawthorne, Herman Melville, and Harriet Beecher Stowe; poets Henry Wadsworth Longfellow, Walt Whitman, and John Greenleaf Whittier; essayist poets Ralph Waldo Emerson, Oliver Wendell Holmes, and Henry David Thoreau; poet critics James Russell Lowell and Edgar Allan Poe, and novelist essayist William Gilmore Simms.

In American literature, the Romantic

movement was characterized by sentimentalism, the celebration of nature and the simple life, primitivism and the concept of the noble savage, political liberalism, humanitarianism, individualism, idealization of the common person, self-inquiry, interest in the picturesque past, interest in exotic locales, medievalism, antiquarianism, the Gothic romance, the world of mystery, melancholy, native legend, the historical romance, and technical innovation. The most clearly defined Romantic literary movement in American literature was Transcendentalism, centered at Concord, Massachusetts (c. 1836–60).

The New England Transcendentalists (i.e., Bronson Alcott, Emerson, Margaret Fuller, and Thoreau) carried the literary expression of religious and philosophic ideas to a high level in essays and on the lecture platform. Until 1850, the American novel, especially in the hands of Cooper and Simms, continued to be patterned after the model of Scott. During the 1850s, however, Hawthorne and Melville produced their great symbolic novels and Stowe developed her effective propaganda novels. The writing of the short story was further developed by Hawthorne, Melville, Poe, and Simms throughout the period, advancing beyond Irving's initial cultivation of the form in America.

The basis for a realistic literature in the language of the common people was initially established in the humorous writings of Josh Billings, George W. Harris, A.B. Longstreet, Artemus Ward, and the early Mark Twain, although the literature did not, at this time, receive the critical attention it was later to enjoy.

These writers found literary outlets in contemporary periodicals. Three important periodicals, the *Southern Review*, the *Southern Literary Messenger*, and the *Southern Quarterly Review*, advanced a movement toward Southern literary independence. In the North, the *Knickerbocker Magazine, Democratic Review*, and the *North American Review* (perhaps the most influential of all) were followed by *Harper's Magazine*, in 1850, and the *Atlantic Monthly*, in 1857. Throughout the period, essays and stories appeared in annuals and gift-books, which were profitably marketed.

In the American theater of the day, the imitation of English "spectacle" drama, the "star" system, and Romantic tragedy modeled on Shakespeare dominated the stage. The most successful native dramatists were N.P. Willis, R.M. Bird, and George Henry Boker, whose *Francesca da Rimini* displayed the most notable literary talent. Both *Uncle Tom's Cabin* and *Rip Van Winkle* were very successfully produced for the stage. (*See also* Theater.)

The Romantic characteristics that appeared in the literature of the period were also evident in other arts. The impulses that created the Gothic Romance also created the architectural movement of the Gothic Revival, which was based on medieval styles and designs that carried the eye above the form itself and sought to engender imaginative associations. In painting, these Romantic qualities brought about the change from the severe portraiture of the 18th century to the work of the Hudson River School artists, who sought to portray the wonder and grandeur of the national landscape. American music echoed European Romanticism in the works of such composers as Edward MacDowell.

After the passing of the period, many of its Romantic characteristics continued to be evident until the end of the century. While the later local-color movement eventually gave rise to realism, it also maintained the Romantic's interest in exotic places and unusual customs. Sentimentalism was a significant element in the stories of Bret Harte, and exoticism in those of G.W. Cable and Lafcadio Hearn. Even Twain, for the most part a realistic author, moved from the accurate representation of contemporary scenes to historical romancing and idealized depictions of youth. Lesser writers like Lew Wallace continued to present Romantic ideas to the general public. Minor poets like Nelson Aldrich, G.H. Boker, E.C. Stedman, R.H. Stoddard, and Bayard Taylor imitated earlier Romantic poets and relied on ameliorated Romantic conventions. The echoes of the period persisted until the early 20th century, when the remnants of this Romantic traditional encountered modern psychology, as seen in the works of numerous American writers during the 1920s and beyond.

The new nation that emerged after the Civil War required and received a literature less idealistic, exalted, and consciously artistic and more practical and direct. The works of the American Romantic period were produced at an earlier time when the American dream was viewed with greater optimism and enthusiasm.

Kenneth McNamee

Works Consulted

Chai, Leon. *The Romantic Foundations of the American Renaissance*. Ithaca: Cornell UP, 1987.

Weisbuch, Robert. *Atlantic Double-Cross*. Chicago: U of Chicago P, 1986.

Ancients, The

The "Ancients" were a group of artists who, with Palmer as the leading figure, gathered around the poet/artist Blake during his last years. The wood engravings Blake made to illustrate the first Eclogue in Thornton's *Virgil* enormously influenced the artistic outlook of these young men, as did, especially, his line-engraved *Illustrations of the Book of Job* (1826) and his relief etchings for *Songs of Innocence and Experience*

(1789, 1794). Apart from these, they understood little of Blake's mind and were especially baffled by his prophetic writings. But they did appreciate his lyric poems and valued him personally. One of the Ancients claimed that talking with Blake was like talking to the Prophet Isaiah, and the young men would kiss the bell-pull of his poor home in Fountain Court, Strand, London, before ringing.

The Ancients assembled in London, but also visited Palmer at his rural retreat at Shoreham in Kent. There, with "Poetry and Sentiment" as their motto, they lived on simple fare, such as bread and apples (with occasional green tea for a treat), bathed each morning in the River Darent, walked in the countryside, particularly during thunderstorms, and recited poetry. They carried campstools during their walks, which the villagers thought were some kind of astronomical instrument. The villagers dubbed the Ancients "extollagers" (derived perhaps from "ecstasy" and "astrology").

Despite their eccentric behavior, the artists in the group were serious workers, and some produced convincing evocations of the pastoral.

Their formal association lasted about six years, after which they separated, some to marry and raise families. They continued to meet monthly to discuss their work, and to sing, play the piano and violin, and recite poetry.

In addition to Palmer, the Ancients were Edward Calvert, Francis Oliver Finch, John Giles, George Richmond, Welby Sherman, the brothers Frederick and Arthur Tatham, and Henry Walter.

Edward Calvert (1799–1883) was enamored of the sea and ships from an early age and joined the Navy, spending many of his off-duty hours in drawing. Some of his early work has a jewel-like brilliance comparable to the best miniatures in illuminated manuscripts. Such is the tiny *Primitive City* (1822), similar to much of the work of the Ancients which is visualized on a small scale.

Once settled in London and attending the Royal Academy schools, Calvert quickly became a highly skilled engraver. Between 1827 and 1831, he made exquisite wood engravings, line engravings, and pen lithographs. None is much larger than a visiting card. In one work, *The Chamber Idyll*, he depicts the initial bliss of a bucolic honeymoon, combining in it his classical learning, what he derived from the work of his fellow Ancients and from Blake's *Virgil* wood engravings, and a very refined technique. Thereafter, he painted somewhat dreamy oil and watercolor evocations of classic landscapes and legends. As he grew older, he became a recluse and developed impenetrable theories about color and music.

Francis Oliver Finch (1802–62) studied painting under John Varley (1778–1842), a friend of Blake, and possibly attended Fuseli's lectures. Finch's work is influenced to a small extent by Blake and by the Ancients, but above all it is dominated by the vision of Claude Lorrain, expressed in a watercolor technique reminiscent of Varley. Finch was a devout Swedenborgian, and he believed firmly that to paint well, the artist must purify his spirit.

George Richmond (1809–96) was the youngest of the Ancients. For a few years, he shared their intense vision, which is evident in works such as the tempera *Abel the Shepherd* (1825), the engravings *The Shepherd* and *The Fatal Bellman* (both 1827), a miniature portrait of Palmer (1829), and the mixed media *The Eve of Separation* (1830). The influence of Blake is apparent, as is the influence of the German Nazarenes (i.e., painters of religious subjects similar to the British Pre-Raphaelites).

In 1831, following his elopement, Richmond concentrated on portraiture. Although he became a fashionable portrait painter and a rich man, he was unhappy in his work, relieving some of his frustration by painting landscapes in oil and watercolor. Richmond was elected a Royal Academician in 1866.

Frederick (1805–78) and *Arthur Tatham* (1809–74) were sons of the architect Charles Heathcote Tatham. Arthur was later an eminent clergyman.

Frederick was a sculptor and painter, especially of miniatures. A controversial figure, he employed Catherine Blake as a housekeeper after her husband's death. After her death in 1831, he claimed that she had bequeathed to him Blake's plates, drawings, and prints in her possession before she died. Blake's sister was unsuccessful in getting them from him. It is claimed, though never proven, that Tatham destroyed much of this material on religious grounds.

Raymond Lister

Works Consulted

Bentley, Gerald E., Jr., et al. *Essays on the Blake Followers*. San Marino: Huntington Library, 1983.

Gleeson, Larry, ed. *Followers of Blake*. Santa Barbara: Santa Barbara Museum of Art, 1976.

Lister, Raymond. *Edward Calvert*. London: Bell, 1962.

———. *George Richmond*. Montclair: Abner Schram, 1981.

———. *Samuel Palmer and "The Ancients."* Cambridge: Cambridge UP, 1987.

Viscomi, Joseph. *Prints by William Blake and His Followers*. Ithaca: Office of University Publications, Cornell U, 1983.

Androgyny

European Romanticism was marked by the pervasive desire to trace the progress of humanity through universal history back to the primal Adam, who, as a representation of cosmic wholeness, was an androgyne. Much Romantic post-Kantian philosophy and literature can be read as versions of Neoplatonic metaphysics. Recalling Plato's mythic ideal of art and beauty, the androgyne is an absolute or a composite, traditionally assigned classical and male attributes. (*See also* Classicism, Neoplatonism.)

In Romanticism, however, the term "androgyne" is often conflated with "hermaphrodite," a word with suggestions of mutability and the 19th-century preoccupation with the problem of evil, a Judeo-Christian view of the rupture of primitive unity as a result of the Fall. (*See also* Satanism.) Thus, the Romantic view of woman was both that of the "other" (i.e., a desired object of both beauty and corruption) and that of a more sentimental configuration as emotional, empathic, and nurturing.

English Romantic literature has often been described as a literature of movement—an individual life journey as personal exile or a journey in search of the unknown point of origin, toward apocalyptic reintegration. Although Coleridge was much more familiar with Continental philosophical discussions of human consciousness than were Wordsworth, Shelley, and Blake, their common themes reflect a shared post-Revolutionary body of intellectual materials, especially biblical interpretations of Protestant visionaries influenced by Neoplatonism.

Androgyny is thus a highly ambiguous and contested concept in the intellectual and artistic discourse of English Romanticism. Coleridge's often-quoted assertion that "a great mind must be androgynous," as well as his many inquiries into the (en)gendering of the imagination, illustrates the association made in Romantic thought

between the feminine and the nonrational and the desire for unity of masculine reason with feminine intuition, the myth of reconciliation of the symmetrical binaries, and a utopian ideal of wholeness.

The androgyne is conceived as a female type in Romantic literature and art (i.e., as a figure of horror in Coleridge's *Christabel*). Most often, however, it is an expression of the male Romantic ego. Shelley defines the feminine in his *Essay on Love* as "a miniature as it were of our entire self, yet deprived of all that we condemn or despise, the ideal prototype of everything excellent or lovely that we are capable of conceiving as belonging to the nature of man." According to Anne K. Mellor, the image of the desired woman as elusive yet necessary recurs again and again in Shelley's poetry, in his veiled maidens of *Alastor* and *The Witch of Atlas*, in the fleeting glimpses of Intellectual Beauty, as Asia in *Prometheus Unbound* and as Cythna in *The Revolt of Islam*—as a female form of her dead lover.

For Blake, the imagination is male, and the female is an emanation of the Zoas, faculties or powers of the integral mind, the human form divine as male. He writes at the end of his long poem *Jerusalem* that "Sexes must vanish and cease." Since feeling is inscribed as female in Romanticism, Keats's negative capability, Shelley's notion of sympathy in *A Defence of Poetry* and Wordsworth's "spontaneous overflow" described in his Preface to the *Lyrical Ballads* might all be taken to reflect feminine qualities in a masculine mind.

Byron is often cited by Freudians as an exemplar of Romantic narcissism or ego-projection. In his dramatic poem, *Manfred*, the title character describes his sister as an idealized version of himself. (Freudians think also of the sibling relationship of Dorothy and William Wordsworth: Dorothy's journals as William's poetic resource and William's poetic assertion that Dorothy had given him eyes and ears.) This notion of fusion or assimilation is extended throughout English Romanticism to appropriation also of maternal characteristics and functions. In the novel *Frankenstein* by Mary Shelley, Victor Frankenstein seizes the maternal role through rationality and science (and against nature) to create a child as monster.

The idea of androgyny illuminates other Romantic obsessions, such as the cult of youth and the return to nature in the quest for ultimate wholeness. Literary examples include Wordsworth's pantheism and fascination with memory's mystical powers ("emotion recollected in tranquility" in *The Prelude, Tintern Abbey*, and the elegaic Lucy poems; Coleridge's narcotic dream of utopian Xanadu and his sense of art as "the mediatress between, and reconciler of, nature and man"; Keats's self-destructiveness and "consciousness of genius" in his odes; Shelley's idealism and Promethean sublimities; and Byron's *Don Juan* as a wickedly androgynous physicality).

Similarly, androgyny permeates the English Romantic visual arts: George Stubbs's natural violence; Constable's "pure appreciation of natural effect," Turner's visionary landscapes, and Fuseli's Gothic sensibility; John Martin's grandeur; and Blake's prophetic "inner-eye" images. The myth of the bisexual androgyne as a feminine male was central to the Romantic paradigm of artistic genius.

Anne T. Ciecko

Works Consulted

Abrams, M.H. *Natural Supernaturalism*. New York: Norton, 1971.

Alexander, Meena. *Women in Romanticism*. Savage, MD: Barnes, 1989.

Battersby, Christine. *Gender and Genius*. London: Women's, 1989.

Ellison, Julie. *Delicate Subjects: Romanticism, Gender, and the Ethics of Understanding*. Ithaca: Cornell UP, 1990.

Fletcher, Ian, ed. *Romantic Mythologies*. New York: Barnes, 1967.

Heilbrun, Carolyn. *Toward a Recognition of Androgyny*. New York: Norton, 1973.

Mellor, Anne K. *Romanticism and Feminism*. Bloomington: Indiana UP, 1988.

Quennell, Peter. *Romantic England: Writing and Painting*. New York: Macmillan, 1970.

Weil, Kari. "Romantic Androgyny and Its Discontents: The Case of *Mlle. De Maupin*." *Studies in Romanticism* 78 (1987): 348–58.

Antiquarianism

Despite Blake's injunction in *The Marriage of Heaven and Hell* to "Drive your cart and your plow over the bones of the dead," the Romantics were at least as fascinated as their Neoclassical predecessors with the distant past. The Hellenic Revival, fostered by several decades of archaeological discovery and by the contemporary struggle for Greek independence, prolonged, with some change in emphasis, the 18th-century interest in the classical world. At the same time, two centuries of antiquarian exploration of Britain's Celtic, Anglo-Saxon, and medieval-Christian past, plus the collection of living remnants of the past preserved in folk literature, provided the Romantics with a rich source of material very much in keeping with Rousseauistic primitivism and imaginative, antirationalist spontaneity. Romantic Hellenism was an important expression of the spirit of the age, particularly its love of beauty and freedom, but without antiquarianism, the character and content of that age might have developed radically differently. (*See also* Classicism, Decorative Arts, Elgin Marbles, Hellenism, Rosetta Stone.)

Antiquarianism existed at least from the time of Henry VIII, when John Leland, as official government antiquary, gathered documents vital to preserving the British cultural heritage. That task was continued by public and private collectors during the Age of Elizabeth and beyond and was encouraged by the growing scholarly interest at Cambridge and Oxford in the language, literature, and history of the Old and Middle English periods. Not even the political turmoil of the 17th century, including the iconoclastic excesses of Cromwellian Puritanism, could entirely extinguish Britain's interest in the pre-Reformation past. Indeed, in 1655, during the Protectorate itself, William Dugdale began publication of his *Monasticon Anglicanum*, a work that became important to 18th-century imitators of medieval design. Following Cromwell's death, and perhaps in reaction to his iconoclasm, the antiquarian desire to retrieve and preserve the native past fully reasserted itself through intense study of such subjects as ancient architecture, genealogy, and local history. By 1707, the reestablishment of the London Society of Antiquaries led to a proliferation of such groups throughout the kingdom.

Antiquarian study remained a popular avocation throughout the 18th century, but its influence began expanding from the realm of pure scholarship to the realm of pure imagination. This phenomenon is frequently illustrated through discussions of the impact of Gothic architecture and interior design on Horace Walpole's creation of the first Gothic novel, *The Castle of Otranto* (1764). (*See also* Gothicism.) Even before Gothic Revivalist elements came to dominate British architecture, Inigo Jones, John Vanbrugh, and Christopher Wren occasionally designed structures in the Gothic mode; Gothic ruins became fashionable additions to English gardens; and Batty Langley published in 1742 and 1747, two works compendiously illustrating Gothic architectural style. Beginning in the late 1740s, Walpole, in an eccentric manifesta-

tion of this burgeoning medievalism, gothicized his mansion, Strawberry Hill, and, during his second decade of immersion in this Gothic world of his own creation, had a bizarre dream in which he saw a giant armored hand at the top of a staircase. In a fever of composition following this dream, he produced the novelistic progenitor of the works of such writers as Lewis, Maturin, Radcliffe, and Mary Shelley. Underscoring the antiquarian associations of *The Castle of Otranto* is the claim by Walpole's invented translator that the book "was found in the library of an ancient Catholic family in the north of England." A similar claim of discovery, and thus of authenticity, was made by other 18th-century creators of imitation antiquities.

Walpole's fascination with the sublimity of the Middle Ages, clearly anticipating the similar fascination of the Romantics, is echoed by, among others, Richard Hurd in *Letters on Chivalry and Romance* (1762) and Thomas Warton in *The History of English Poetry* (1774–81), both of whom were steeped in antiquarian knowledge. Antiquarianism also produced the interest in a largely misperceived Druidism, which was later to pervade Romantic prose and poetry, particularly the works of Blake. In *Stonehenge, A Temple Restored to the British Druids* (1740), William Stukely, who had been a central figure in reestablishing the Society of Antiquaries, argued that the Druids were lineal descendants of Abraham and that their poetry echoed the religious truths of the patriarchs, an assumption that would evolve into the Romantic association of the powers of the Druidic bards with the powers of the Old Testament prophets. Thomas Gray's *The Bard*, printed in 1757 by Walpole's Strawberry Hill Press, is a pre-Romantic example of such a poetry of prophetic utterance. Further ennobling the Druids and encouraging their use in literature were *The Origin of Language and Nations* (1764) by Rowland Jones and *The Way to Things by Words* (1766) by John Cleland; both traced the beginnings of human language to Druidical Celtic.

This discussion of Celtic and Medievalist antiquarianism would not be complete without mentioning the two most famous literary frauds of the 18th century: Macpherson's Ossianic poems and the Rowley poems of Chatterton. In *Fragments of Ancient Poetry, Collected in the Highlands of Scotland . . .* (1760), Macpherson presented a refreshingly impassioned collection of works purportedly by the blind third-century poet Ossian. When the volume produced a sensation, Macpherson followed up his triumph with *Fingal* in 1762 and *Temora* in 1763. Despite a justified scholarly skepticism about the authenticity of the Ossianic poems, Macpherson's efforts captured the imagination of a reading public grown weary of the rational and the orderly in literature and helped to establish, through the persona of Ossian, the theory of natural genius espoused in William Duff's *Essay on Original Genius* (1767) and elsewhere.

This theory gave impetus to the careers of Burns, Clare, and many less worthy "primitives" and became an article of faith among the Romantics. It had as a corollary that great minds are too often cruelly neglected, an assertion illustrated by the life of Chatterton. An extraordinary linguistic prodigy, Chatterton capitalized on contemporary antiquarian interests and on his own antiquarian knowledge to produce, at a very youthful age, a set of forged medievalesque poems attributed to the cleric Thomas Rowley. Unfortunately, following the Macpherson controversy, publishers were more resistant to the acceptance of "authentic" antiquities, Chatterton's various attempts to earn his

way as a writer failed, and he committed suicide in 1770 while still in his teens. As a result, painters and poets of the next several decades used him as a symbol of victimized genius.

Received oppositely from the Rowley poems was Thomas Percy's *Reliques of Ancient English Poetry* (1765). It was neither the first nor the most scholarly of ballad collections but certainly the most influential of all antiquarian publications. Volumes of collected ballads had been appearing at least since the first quarter of the 18th century, and before century's end, Joseph Ritson and others would introduce a scholarly rigor into the collecting process far superior to Percy's own. Nevertheless, it was Percy whose volume was read and frequently reprinted, who helped to inspire the Continental collecting and theorizing efforts of Johann Gottfried Herder and folk ballad imitations of Gottfried August Bürger, and who most directly prepared the way for the *Lyrical Ballads* of Wordsworth and Coleridge.

Despite the pervasive Romantic debt to the antiquarian movement, benefiting most from Percy in particular and from antiquarianism in general, was Scott, the greatest of all antiquarian Romantics. Scott's career as a poet began in 1796 with the publication of *William and Helen* and *The Wild Huntsman*, both translations of ballads by Bürger. Scott's contributions to Matthew Gregory Lewis's *Tales of Wonder* (1801), a work inspired by Percy-influenced Germanic balladry, sustained his literary ambitions, and his own ballad collection, *The Minstrelsy of the Scottish Border* (1803), confirmed him as a significant man of letters. There then followed the learned and heavily footnoted poems and novels which manifested the full literary power of antiquarianism and thereby made Scott the most popular British writer before Charles Dickens.

Robert O'Connor

Works Consulted

Chandler, Alice. *A Dream of Order: The Medieval Ideal in Nineteenth-Century English Literature.* Lincoln: U of Nebraska P, 1970.

Gaull, Marilyn. *English Romanticism: The Human Context.* New York: Norton, 1988.

Pierce, Frederick E. *Currents and Eddies in the English Romantic Generation.* New Haven: Yale UP, 1918.

Prickett, Stephen, ed. *The Context of English Literature: The Romantics.* New York: Holmes, 1981.

Renwick, W.L. *English Literature, 1789–1815.* Oxford: Clarendon, 1963.

Walpole, Horace. *The Castle of Otranto.* Ed. W.S. Lewis. London: Oxford UP, 1964.

Architecture

The early 18th century was marked by the rise of Neoclassicism, which was adopted as the "proper" architectural style all over Europe. It corresponded to the development of rationalism in philosophy, regularity in music and poetry, the elevation of the Greek and Latin classics as models in literature, and the general tendency toward clear rules and principles in all arts. Classical architecture was the most rational and the most clearly defined of all styles. Later, however, as individualism and pastoralism crept into classical designs, new, more clearly English styles emerged. One architect who marked this transition was Robert Adam (1728–92). He had a long list of country houses to his credit, including Syon House, Middlesex (1761–69), and Saltram House, Devon (1768–69). Unlike his predecessors, he did not have rigid, doctrinaire principles but rather a strong desire to please with designs that created spatial drama and complexity and expressed movement, variety, and gaiety.

The effects that had been achieved in compositional techniques in the country by Adam and others were transported to an urban setting in London through the Regency style. Its great achievement was not so much in the sphere of individual buildings as in a new concept of town planning; its greatest exponent was Nash, who laid out a great complex of parks, streets, terraces, squares, and churches in London's West End, from Regent's Park to St. James's Park. The whole Nash scheme combined a classical elegance with a Romantic quality: formal architecture in an informal setting. Both parks had informal glades, sloping lawns, and rich foliage patterns around a winding lake, reminiscent of the great landscape architect Lancelot ("Capability") Brown (1715–83) in such settings as Blenheim Palace.

Another influential English architect of this time was Sir John Soane (1753–1837), designer of the Bank of England (1788–1808). His Hellenic Romanticism was extremely individualistic as well as delicate and austere. He founded no school, but was influential with succeeding generations because he adopted a position between Classical and Gothic, jostling fragments of both in his house and museum in Lincoln's Inn Fields (1812–13).

By 1830, Hellenic purity—crystallized in the design by Robert Smirke (1780–1867) for the British Museum (begun in 1823)—gave way to Gothic elaboration, an expression of the Romantic style that was coming to pervade the arts and literature. Classical and Gothic architecture share a nostalgia for antiquity, but through the influence of the English Enlightenment and the French Revolution, the sense of dream was heightened. Good design (e.g., proportion, scale, symmetry, and harmony) was no longer enough. Charm, novelty, and escape were what was required. Early examples of such fancy include Walpole's Gothic mansion at Strawberry Hill (remodeled in 1750) and James Wyatt's Fonthill Abbey (begun in 1796). The reasons for their existence were literary rather than architectural—an evocation of the *jeu d'esprit* of an age in which humanity acquired a new perspective on society and itself. (*See also* Decorative Arts.)

The Gothic style is the clearest representation of Romanticism's contribution to architecture. Adam, Nash, and Soane all produced Gothic buildings when circumstances warranted (Nash had a Gothic "department" in his office and even built himself a castle in the Isle of Wight). These early structures were expressions of folly and eccentricity—two qualities easy to come by if the patron was rich and extravagant. By the beginning of the 19th century, however, the choice of architectural style acquired more serious overtones; behind the fantasy of the Gothic imagination there lay a profound dissatisfaction with the state of society, following the outbreak of war and collapse of revolutionary fervor. The result, in artistic terms, was an attitude of longing, antagonism, and a desire to escape. The architectural reaction was the Gothic Revival. (*See also* Gothicism.)

For the architects already mentioned, styles were inextricably linked to fashion and class taste. The general appeal of the Gothic, however, clearly reflected changing sentiments within English society as a whole. Along with the escapist tendency, brought about by pessimism, came extravagance and conspicuous waste, founded on a new prosperity and a rising middle class. The increased wealth of 19th-century Britain allowed and encouraged the building not only of Gothic fantasy houses and churches but also of Gothic railway stations, town halls, and even sewage works. If it may be suggested that architecture is a more communal art than literature or painting (i.e., depending on a relationship between the user and creator that is much closer than in other arts), then the extent of Gothicism in all levels of society points to the mood of English society at the time.

The Revival was almost wholly an English phenomenon. It carried such weight that in 1834, when most of the Palace of Westminster was destroyed by fire, it was decreed that it should be rebuilt in a "national style," which at that time was perceived as either Elizabethan or Gothic. The adoption of a Gothic design, the brain child of Sir Charles Barry (1795–1860) and Augustus Pugin (1812–52), marked this style's preeminence in the public mind.

Pugin, because of his extraordinary genius, energy, and vision, may be called the orchestrator of the Gothic Revival. A convert to Roman Catholicism, he took his work very seriously and held up Gothic as an exemplar of true Christian faith. His work on the Houses of Parliament (begun in 1836), which extended to designing such minutiae as Gothic inkwells and coat hooks, influenced not only style, but also materials and color. Although fanciful, his work was also solid and durable. He always bore in mind not only the decoration of the building but also its functionality and (almost without exception) its cost. His abandonment of the 18th-century Neoclassical principles of proportion and symmetry in favor of structural expression affected the whole nature of architecture and design. Pugin's receptivity to technological advances and his use of new materials (e.g., iron and encaustic tiling) influenced the creations of his ecclesiastical and secular successors and, literally, changed the face of England. (*See also* Domestic Architecture; Revett, Nicholas.)

Leon B. Litvack

Works Consulted

Clark, Kenneth. *Civilisation: A Personal View.* London: Murray, 1969.

———. *The Gothic Revival, An Essay in the History of Taste*. London: Constable, 1928.

Dixon, Roger, and Stefan Muthesius. *Victorian Architecture*. London: Thames, 1978.

Jordan, Robert Furneaux. *Victorian Architecture*. Harmondsworth: Penguin, 1966.

———. *Western Architecture: A Concise History*. London: Thames, 1969.

Pevsner, Nikolaus. *An Outline of European Architecture*. Harmondsworth: Penguin, 1968.

Trappes-Lomax, Michael. *Pugin: A Mediaeval Victorian*. London: Sheed, 1932.

Watkin, David J. *English Architecture: A Concise History*. London: Thames, 1979.

———. *Morality and Architecture*. Chicago: U of Chicago P, 1984.

Associationism

While the notion of the association of ideas goes back at least to Aristotle (e.g., *De Anima* and *De Memoria*), British associationism or associational psychology received its chief impetus in the early 18th century. John Locke coined the phrase "association of ideas" in an interpolated chapter of the *Essay Concerning Human Understanding* (1700). It was from the physician-theologian David Hartley (1705–59), however, that associationism received its fullest and most systematic treatment. In the influential *Observations on Man* (1749), Hartley proposed to account for all mental phenomena by reducing them to an association of basic units of sensation. In doing this, he hoped to explain not only the workings of the mind, but also the genesis of moral sentiments, thereby showing the agreement between natural and revealed religion. The theological dimension of Hartley's project was central, though sometimes forgotten by later commentators. In 1775, the chemist Priestley published a condensed version of *Observations* as *Hartley's Theory of the Human Mind*, deleting the discussion of moral and religious knowledge. It was especially these moral and religious implications that profoundly influenced the early Romantics, including Wordsworth, Hazlitt, and Coleridge, who mentioned Hartley twice in his poem *Religious Musings* (1794) and even named his first son David Hartley in honor of the philosopher.

Hartley started with the Lockean model of the mind, a blank slate to be filled by sensations (see Empiricism). Each sensation produces a simple idea, and what one recognizes as thoughts are complexes of simple ideas. Unlike Locke, however, Hartley was more fully cognizant of the mind's relation to human physiology and thus was a pioneer in psychophysiology. Thereby borrowing Newton's theory that repeated vibrations deposit minute vibrations in an object, Hartley argued that each mental impression generates both a simple idea in the mind and deposits a parallel trace vibration along the nerves of the brain. Further, impressions that occur in frequent or intense conjunction with each other form complex ideas. Sensation A is associated with sensation B, forming the complex idea (A^*B) with a parallel set of vibrations. If the association (A^*B) is strong enough, a subsequent sensation A will, through the action of the deposited trace vibrations (A^*B), raise the associated sensation B, even though the object or quality that originally produced B is absent.

To some degree, Hartley's philosophical psychology anticipated the theory of conditioned reflexes in Pavlov's physiological psychology. Indeed, experimental psychology on the Continent was an outgrowth of associationism. Hartley, however, insisted on the distinction between mind and brain function, preferring a spiritual conception of mind. Further, he saw the mind playing an active role in the arrangement of complex ideas to raise associated ideas and sensations. By this mechanism, Hartley proposed to demonstrate how the production of ideas could produce physical effects, thereby accounting for all mental/physical phenomena, including understanding, affection, memory, and imagination as well as voluntary and involuntary actions.

Later associationists simplified Hartley's model, anticipating a more strictly physiological conception of mind. Hartley had distinguished two types of association: (1) "contiguous" or "simultaneous," in which ideas occurring together are associated; and (2) "successive," in which ideas that follow each other are associated. By contrast, the Utilitarian James Mill (1773–1836) argued that all association could be reduced to contiguity alone. Further, in the *Analysis of the Phenomena of the Human Mind* (1829), Mill reduced Hartley's conception of mind to a passive mechanical process in which the mind exercised no creative function.

Associationist concepts in aesthetics can be found as early as Joseph Addison. Several concepts of Hartley's associationism, however, had especially important ramifications for the Romantics. If all ideas can be resolved into their hierarchy of associated components, all knowledge can be shown to have a common ground. That being the case, Hartley contended, there is a fundamental harmony deriving from the common basis for all knowledge between knowledge based on revelation and knowledge based on experience. The divine order in the world can be established empirically. Moreover, each unique individual experience can be coordinated by association into an integrated whole. Both notions support Wordsworth's conception of the poet and poetic knowledge, suggesting the mechanism for the intimations of immortality. This is evident not only in the *Prelude* and related poems, but in the 1800 preface to *Lyrical Ballads*.

Hartley's model also suggested how an aesthetic fiction created by a poet has the power to evoke real sensations in its audience. There is some resemblance to Coleridge's "esemplastic power," though Hartley had criticized the suggestion of the Earl of Shaftesbury and Mark Akenside that human creativity was an imitation of divine creation. Human creativity, Hartley suggested, is necessarily limited and imperfect next to God's perfection. He conceived of art as strictly imitation and not the product of creativity, per se, but rather the reorganization of associated ideas into complex thoughts, a notion closer to Coleridge's conception of fancy than imagination. While Coleridge eventually became disenchanted with associationism, especially in its mechanical psychology, he never entirely rejected it, devoting the fifth and sixth chapters of the *Biographia Literaria* (1817) to it.

While later associationists focused on the physical implications of Hartley's theory of mind, which provided a groundwork for experimental psychology, Hartley and the Romantics who were influenced by him looked to the moral and theological dimensions. For them, associationism was not merely a theory of mind that showed the relationship between body and brain but a bridge between the limited and subjective realm of individual experience and a universal divine order. It validated the intimations of an immanent God. Moreover, for the Romantics, memory was a crucial element in the functioning of the mind and in its creative expressions. Memory was seen as both personal and collective, and associationism validated memory as a creative faculty.

Thomas L. Cooksey

Works Consulted

Bate, Walter Jackson. *From Classic to Romantic: Premises of Taste in Eighteenth-Century England.* Cambridge: Harvard UP, 1946.

Christensen, Jerome. *Coleridge's Blessed Machine of Language*. Ithaca: Cornell UP, 1981.

Cohen, Ralph. "Association of Idea and Poetic Unity." *Philological Quarterly*, 36 (1957): 465–73.

Engell, James. *Forming the Critical Mind: Dryden to Coleridge*. Harvard: Harvard UP, 1989.

Hartley, David. *Observation on Man, His Frame, His Duty, and His Expectations*. 2 vols. 1749. New York: Garland, 1971.

Haven, Richard. "Coleridge, Hartley, and the Mystics." *Journal of the History of Ideas*, 20 (1959): 477–94.

Kallich, Martin. *The Association of Ideas and Critical Theory in Eighteenth Century England*. Hague: Mouton, 1970.

Marsh, Robert. *Four Dialectical Theories of Poetry: An Aspect of English Neoclassical Criticism*. Chicago: U of Chicago P, 1965.

Oberg, Barbara Bowen. "David Hartley and the Association of Ideas." *Journal of the History of Ideas*, 37 (1976): 441–54.

Ong, Walter J. "Psyche and the Geometers: Associationist Critical Theory." *Rhetoric, Romance and Technology: Studies in the Interaction of Expression and Culture*. Ithaca: Cornell UP, 1971: 213–36.

Watson, Robert I. *The Great Psychologists from Aristotle to Freud*. Philadelphia: Lippincott, 1963.

Austen, Jane

(1775–1817)

Jane Austen is the Romantic era's greatest novelist. The six novels produced by the unmarried daughter of a country clergyman have been widely read and critically acclaimed since their publication. Austen situates fiction within the familiar world of the drawing room and the ballroom of the rural gentry of the late 18th and early 19th centuries, wherein society was orthodox and manners and morals were highly conventional. Austen's wit and satire are directed against the artificial, the ostentatious, and the mean-spirited members of this society. The customary plots of the novels arise from the subject of court-

ship and marriage, in which the mercenary, the proud, and the unprudent are most often the objects of ridicule. Early in her career, Austen was fond of burlesque, ridiculing the unrealistic characters and exaggerated plots of the sentimental and Gothic novels of the period. Her later novels are marked by realistic detail and psychological depth with highly individualized and memorable characters. She is renowned for the simplicity, precision, and grace of her writing style.

The six major novels that secured her literary reputation since the mid-19th century are *Sense and Sensibility, Pride and Prejudice, Mansfield Park, Emma, Northanger Abbey*, and *Persuasion*. In addition, a collection of *Juvenilia* (1787–93), unfinished works and fragments of novels—*Lady Susan* (1793–94), *The Watsons* (1804–05), and *Sanditon* (1817)—the *Plan of a Novel* (1816), opinions of *Mansfield Park* and *Emma* (1815–16), verses, and prayers were collected and published as *Minor Works* in 1954.

Austen was born on 16 December 1775 to the Rev. George Austen, rector of Steventon parsonage, and Cassandra Leigh Austen. She was the seventh child in a family of eight children, six of whom were brothers. The Rev. Austen educated his young children at home and took in pupils to supplement his church income. Considered a fine scholar, he was educated at Oxford, although his family was of the lower levels of rural English society. Cassandra Leigh was from a more eminent family than her husband's. She was reputed to be witty and generally good-humored, although subject to hypochondria. Austen's brothers James (1765–1819) and Henry (1771–1850) were educated at home and at Oxford, and much of her education must have come from them. James would take orders and inherit his father's position at Steventon rectory, while Henry worked in banking in London, married his widowed cousin Eliza de Feuillide, and eventually took orders in the church as well. Francis (1774–1865) and Charles (1779–1852) went into the Navy and rose to the rank of Admiral. The second son George (1766–1838) was mentally ill and lived away from the family. Edward (1767–1852), the third born, was adopted by childless cousin Thomas Knight and inherited his Godmersham estate in Kent, taking the name Knight. Austen's only sister, Cassandra (1773–1845), was her lifelong companion and neither sister ever married.

Besides learning from their father and brothers, Jane and Cassandra had some formal training outside the home: a one-year tutorial, about 1782, with Mrs. Cawley at Oxford and Southampton, and several years at the Abbey School at Reading. After 1785, both she and Cassandra returned home to read in the family's extensive library under the guidance of their father and brothers. Jane read extensively in Shakespeare and the 18th-century novelists, Sterne, Smollett, and Goldsmith and especially her favorites, Richardson and Fielding. She was well acquainted with the works of Johnson and the late 18th-century poets Cowper and Crabbe. She avidly attended the theater when visiting her brother Henry in London, and the family was known to produce amateur theatricals at the parsonage. Austen was well read in English history and very knowledgeable of current events of the day. She subscribed to a lending library that supplied current fiction.

Austen's writing career began in the late 1780s and can be divided into three periods. The first is the Steventon period from 1775 to 1801. During this time, she composed what is collected as *juvenilia*, mostly satirical parodies, including *The History of England from the reign of Henry the 4th to the death of Charles the 1st* (1791), *Love and Freindship* [sic] (1790), *Catherine* (1792), and *Lesley Castle* (1792). These were collected in three manuscript notebooks, containing 27 items, which afforded much amusement for the Austen family. The *juvenilia* provides early evidence of Austen's wit and her keen sense of artistic judgment in the burlesque of sentimental and Gothic fiction. She composed *Lady Susan* around 1794, using the epistolary form that would be her mode of discourse for *Elinor and Marianne* (1795) and, it is believed, *First Impressions* (1796–97). The latter was offered for publication in 1797 but was rejected. *Susan* was written in the same year and was later revised into *Northanger Abbey*.

The second phase of Austen's writing career is from 1801 to 1809. During this time, which is characterized by the lack of original works, Austen prepared *Susan* for publication and wrote the fragment *The Watsons* (1803–04). Because of her father's illness, the family moved to Bath in 1801, where she felt uprooted and unhappy. Her father died in 1805, and since James Austen had succeeded him at Steventon rectory, the sisters Jane and Cassandra and their mother were left without a home. Their residence in Southampton from 1806 to 1809 was crowded and noisy, provided little solitude or opportunity for writing. Not surprisingly, Austen would depict Bath and the naval seaport of Portsmouth unfavorably in her novels.

The final period is Chawton, 1809 to 1817, which was Austen's most productive. Her brother Edward Knight had succeeded his benefactor to the estate at Godmersham, and upon the death of Edward's wife, he offered a cottage in his possession in the village of Chawton to his mother and sisters. The return to the rural countryside renewed Austen's writing and publication. She successfully retrieved the manuscript of *Susan*, which had been retained by publisher Richard Crosby since 1803. She transformed the epistolary *Elinor and Marianne* into the direct narrative of *Sense and Sensibility*, which was published anonymously in 1811. The novel, through its two protagonists, points out the dangers of "sensibility," of excessive emotion and fervor.

Also during this period, *First Impressions* was "lop't and crop't," as Austen would describe it, and transformed into *Pride and Prejudice*, which was published in 1813. Considered her most popular novel, *Pride and Prejudice* is the story of Elizabeth Bennet, one of five daughters, who prides herself on her discernment but who is blinded by prejudice. She receives a second offer of marriage from the handsome and wealthy Mr. Darcy after she learns to understand herself and to value good judgment. The novel is characterized by its wit, gaiety, and light tone.

While revisions of *Pride and Prejudice* were under way, the composition of *Mansfield Park* was begun. Unlike the "light, bright, and sparkling" tone of *Pride and Prejudice*, this novel is marked by an emphasis on order, restraint, and conservatism. The sole *bildungsroman* in Austen's canon, *Mansfield Park*, is the Cinderella story of Fanny Price, who grows up in the home of her rich and privileged cousins, only to win the heart of the second son through her moral virtue. The novel was published in 1814.

With a heroine Austen believed "no one but myself would much like," *Emma* appeared in 1815. This novel, with its lively and witty heroine, is less serious than the novel that precedes it. Emma has fortune, cleverness, and beauty but suffers from her interference in the lives of those less fortunate. Stylistically, it is considered Austen's masterpiece for complexity and effect. *Emma* was favorably noted by Scott, and its author received an invitation from the Prince Regent to tour his library and the permission to dedicate the novel to him.

The writing of her last completed novel, *Persuasion*, which would appear in 1818, was undertaken while Austen was becoming seriously ill. This work, marked by an autumnal tone, returns to the story of a marriage proposal rejected, but here the heroine, Anne Elliot, receives no second offer until eight years later. The mature heroine speaks about loss and endurance in a way not found in the earlier novels.

During this time, perhaps because she was aware of the limited time left to her, Austen wrote a preface to *Catherine* (or *Susan*), which would be published after her death as *Northanger Abbey*. In 1817, she began *Sanditon*. Set in a seaside resort, this unfinished fragment reflects a new direction in Austen's writing. Highly satirical, like much of the *juvenilia*, it shows Austen's understanding of the new Romantic literature of the period. Likewise, *Sanditon* reflects the poor state of Austen's health with its preoccupation with hypochondria and sickness.

Austen gave up work on *Sanditon* when she became too ill to write. Her last days were spent under a doctor's care in Winchester, where she died on July 18, 1817. Her death has been attributed to Addison's disease. She was buried in Winchester Cathedral. Her brother Henry published *Northanger Abbey* and *Persuasion* in 1818, revealing in a "Biographical Notice" the identity of the novelist.

Although she lived and wrote in the same period as the great Romantic poets, aspects of Austen's work seem closer to the late 18th century writers. Her valuing of restraint, propriety, order, and tradition is regarded as a Neoclassical virtue that marks her affinity with Richardson, Fielding, and Johnson.

Stylistically, a feature of her novels that can be considered "Romantic" is her individuation of character, an effort to understand human nature in its variety and richness, not as an abstraction or as a universal. Her characters exhibit a depth of feeling and imagination uncharacteristic of the writings of the earlier century. Finally, her depiction of the transforming quality of time is an inherent feature of Romantic poetry. Her novels make sophisticated use of varied modes of speech and thought presentation, indicating an awareness of how varied perceptions are the means to knowing one's self and one's world.

A recent critical concern has been with her feminism. Writing in a time of intense interest in feminist thought, Austen could hardly have failed to understand the relevant issues of the controversy. The problem of female education is raised as early as *Northanger Abbey*, in which the young Catherine is faulted for her dependence on Gothic novels for her vision of reality. Property laws and marriage rights figure prominently in Austen's works, such as in *Pride and Prejudice*, in which Elizabeth and her friend debate the differences between prudent and mercenary marriages. Austen must have understood fully the predicament of the young woman without property or marriage protection. More essentially, Austen argues in her fiction for the education of women in moral values and reasoning ability, placing her in the tradition of rational feminism. While separating herself publicly from the feminist movement of the time, Austen in her writings gives ample evidence of her concern for the fate of the ordinary woman, not the idealized or highly privileged one in her society.

The issue of Austen's conservative politics has also recently surfaced. While early critics thought of Austen as politically neutral or unaware, at least as revealed by her novels, later studies have branded her a Tory conservative, the object of propaganda for reactionary ideas, and even a propagandist herself for the same ideas. More recent scholarship has focused on her awareness of political issues of the time and on the originality of her works and ideas, even calling her "subversive" of the values of her society. She is now being seen as a spokeswoman for the range of classes within society, instead of as a bonded member of the gentry class and the upper realms of the ruling society. By claiming that the "personal is the political," current scholars have found in her fiction the basis for their contention that Austen was actively aware of the political ideas and movements of her time, and that her response to them was progressive and innovative.

The standard text of the novels, including minor works, fragments, and *juvenilia*, is the R.W. Chapman edition in six volumes, published from 1923 to 1954. (*See also* Novel.)

Louise Flavin

Works Consulted

Butler, Marilyn. *Jane Austen and the War of Ideas*. Oxford: Clarendon, 1975.

Cecil, Lord David. *A Portrait of Jane Austen*. New York: Hill, 1979.

Duckworth, Alistair M. *The Improvement of the Estate*. Baltimore: Johns Hopkins UP, 1971.

Honan, Park. *Jane Austen: Her Life*. London: Weidenfeld, 1987.

The Jane Austen Companion. Ed. J. David Grey. New York: Macmillan, 1986.

Jane Austen's Letters to Her Sister Cassandra and Others. Ed. R.W. Chapman. New York: Oxford UP, 1979.

Johnson, Claudia L. *Jane Austen: Women, Politics, and the Novel*. Chicago: U of Chicago P, 1988.

Kirkham, Margaret. *Jane Austen, Feminism and Fiction*. Totowa, NJ: Barnes, 1983.

Litz, A. Walton. *Jane Austen: A Study of Her Artistic Development*. London: Chatto, 1965.

Morgan, Susan. *In the Meantime: Character and Perception in Jane Austen's Fiction*. Chicago: U of Chicago P, 1980.

Poovey, Mary. *The Proper Lady and the Woman Writer: Ideology as Style in the Works of Mary Wollstonecraft, Mary Shelley, and Jane Austen*. Chicago: U of Chicago P, 1984.

Tave, Stuart M. *Some Words of Jane Austen*. Chicago: U of Chicago P, 1973.

Autobiography and Confession

While the popularity of biographical and autobiographical writings was established in the 18th century, the forms these biographical texts assumed was elaborated during the Romantic period. James Boswell's *Life of Samuel Johnson* (1791) and Johnson's *Prefaces Biographical and Critical, to the Works of the English Poets* (1779–81), popularly known as the "Lives of the English Poets," announce an increasing interest in the individual self, and the creative self in particular. The Romantic writers' preoccupation with themselves as individuals, and as artists in particular, yields an enormous amount of autobiographical and confessional writing. In 1804, Coleridge referred to Wordsworth's *Prelude* as a "divine self-biography," and the OED even attributes the first use of the word "autobiography" in 1805 to the Romantic writer Southey.

Many generic definitions associate autobiography with prose, a categorization that becomes a problem in the Romantic period in which much poetry can be considered autobiographical. The prominence of the author's self and the consciousness of relating this reflective self to the surroundings are touchstones for Romantic autobiographical writing.

From the mid-18th century, the emphasis in English literature falls on the individual, the private self as opposed to the public self. The ideas of Locke, Hume, and Kant contributed to the late 18th-century idea of the self. The presentation of the Romantic self, with its emphasis on memory and imagination, is largely defined by the importance of empirical experience, the perception of consciousness as function rather than substance, and the necessity for a moral self that is subjectively contingent. Within the text, the evocation of the processes of memory and imagination triggers the presentation of a selection of events that the author perceives to be meaningful in the portrayal of his or her life. The events are often considered turning points in the author's development, such as Wordsworth's "spots of time" in his verse autobiography, *The Prelude, or Growth of a Poet's Mind* (1805, 1850). Childhood figures prominently in Romantic autobiographies, and the quest that Romantic autobiographies portray often focuses on the attempts to recapture innocence in artistic maturity.

"Autobiography" proper can be distinguished from autobiographical writings. Autobiography can be defined as a text that the author consciously presents to an audience as a version of her or his life story. Autobiography is retrospective; it imposes an order on a selection of elements from the author's life. Autobiographies are inevitably influenced by the author's position in and perception of her or his life at the moment of writing, and by the author's stand toward the audience, and they are often self-fulfilling prophecies, highlighting events that are favorable for the author's reputation. Autobiographies are usually continuous and continually being tinkered with. Unlike biographies, they are "unfinished" by not covering the death of the subject so that they are then published posthumously.

"Autobiographical" writings differ from autobiographies proper in that they do not necessarily have a public audience in mind at the time of writing. Diaries (intimate day-by-day accounts), journals (less intimate, more selective than diaries), letters, memoirs, essays, travel literature, and poems can all be considered autobiographical. Much autobiographical writing in the Romantic period is confessional, focusing on the probing, mind-searching, and often self-justifying activity of the subject itself. The tradition of confessional writing in Europe goes back to Augustine's *Confessions* (fifth century) in which Augustine confesses his sins (*confessio peccati*) to a God in whom he has complete faith (*confessio laudis*). The Romantic confession is secularized and in many ways a justification of individual behavior to an unsympathetic audience; Rousseau's *Confessions* (1764–70) is a famous example. Many English Romantic poems are confessional; they present an often unconventional poetic speaker in thinly disguised autobiographical frame.

While not many male Romantic authors wrote prose autobiographies, many women produced autobiographies to justify their actions in a male-dominated world. Their narrative accounts can be related to the development of the novel after 1750. Examples include Ann Sheldon's *Authentic and Interesting Memoirs* (1787); Elizabeth Sarah Gooch's *Life* (1792); Mary E. Bowes Strathmore's *The Confessions of the Countess of Strathmore* (1793); Margaret Leeson's *Memoirs* (1797); Arabella Euston's *Lover's Looking Glass* (1800?); Maria "Perdita" Darby Robinson's *Memoirs* (1801); *The Life, Voyages, and Surprising Adventures of Mary Jane Meadows* (1802); Phebe Phillips's (alias Maria Maitland's) *The Woman of the Town* (1810); and Eliza Bradley's *An Authentic Narrative* (1820).

In the widest sense, all writing can be seen as autobiographical, but the following list gives a taste of what was going on in the Romantic period: Wordsworth's *The Prelude* (probably the most famous example in poetry); Byron's *Childe Harold* (1809–17) and *Don Juan* (1818–22); Coleridge's conversation poems: *The Eolian Harp* (1795), *This Lime-Tree Bower My Prison* (1797), *Frost at Midnight* (1798), *The Nightingale: A Conversation Poem* (1798), *Dejection* (1802), and *To William Wordsworth* (1807); Wordsworth's *Tintern Abbey* (1798) and the *Intimations Ode* (1802–04).

Among the diary and autobiography writers are Frances Burney's *Diary and Letters* (1842–46); Benjamin Robert Haydon, who produced *Autobiography* (1853) and 26 diary volumes; and Hunt (*Autobiography*, 1850). Many Romantics were indefatigable letter writers. Keats's letters, in which he situates himself among the English poets, are among the most instructive. Byron's letters and journals, the correspondence of Montagu, Coleridge, Dorothy and William Wordsworth, Hazlitt, Charles Lamb, all provide autobiographical glances.

Many women celebrate the men in their environment by deprecating their own talents. Their journals, however, indirectly portray strong and artistic personalities. Examples include Hester Lynch Thrale Piozzi's *Autobiography, Letters, and Literary Remains* (1861); Dorothy Wordsworth's *Alfoxden Journal* (1798) and *Grasmere Journals* (1800–03); Mary Wollstonecraft Shelley's *Journals* (1814–44); and Mary Russell Mitford's *Recollections of a Literary Life* (1852).

Among the confessions are Hazlitt's dark *Liber Amoris* (1823) and De Quincey's *Confessions of an English Opium Eater* (1822) and *Autobiographic Sketches* (1853). Hogg's *The Private Memoirs and Confessions of a Justified Sinner* (1824) can be classified among Gothic fiction. The increasingly popular periodical press also attracted autobiographical writing: Hazlitt's *Table Talk* essays (1821–22) and Charles Lamb's *Essays of Elia* (1823, 1833) first appeared in *London Magazine*. Among the literary criticism of the period, Coleridge's *Biographia Literaria* (1817), although sparse in its personal revelations, unfolds the growth of a critic's mind.

Heidi van de Veire

Works Consulted

Altick, Richard D. *Lives and Letters: A History of Literary Biography in England and America.* New York: Knopf, 1965.

Benstock, Shari, ed. *The Private Self: Theory and Practice of Women's Autobiographical Writings.* Chapel Hill: U of North Carolina P, 1988.

De Man, Paul. "Autobiography As De-Facement." *The Rhetoric of Romanticism.* New York: Columbia UP, 1984: 67–81.

Jellinek, Estelle C. *The Tradition of Women's Autobiography: From Antiquity to the Present.* Boston: Twayne, 1986.

Morris, John N. *Versions of the Self: Studies in English Autobiography from John Bunyan to John Stuart Mill.* New York: Basic, 1966.

Olney, James, ed. *Autobiography: Essays Theoretical and Critical.* Princeton: Princeton UP, 1980.

Pascal, Roy. *Design and Truth in Autobiography.* Cambridge: Harvard UP, 1960.

Shumaker, Wayne. *English Autobiography.* Berkeley: U of California P, 1954.

Smith, Sidonie. *A Poetics of Women's Autobiography: Marginality and the Fictions of Self-Representation.* Bloomington: Indiana UP, 1987.

Spengemann, William C. *The Forms of Autobiography.* New Haven: Yale UP, 1980.

Baillie, Joanna
(1762–1851)

In 1798, when Joanna Baillie anonymously published the first volume of a series of dramas—later titled *Plays on the Passions*—she inspired a revival of poetic drama in England that would stretch into the Victorian era. In over 25 plays, Baillie conveys her intense preoccupation with the psychological crises that occur in her characters' private lives, a focus not unlike Wordsworth's in the *Lyrical Ballads*, published the same year as Baillie's first group of dramas. Her concern with her protagonists' domestic, or "closeted," experiences and her practice of publishing plays prior to their production established the pattern for much of Romantic verse drama. With the exception of critic Jeffrey (until his 1811 review), the major Romantic writers praised Baillie as an innovative and moving poet, and in the first half of the 19th century, a stream of artists honored her achievement with visits to her residence in Hampstead Heath. From the time of their first meeting in 1806, Scott was Baillie's most ardent reader and friend.

Baillie was born a premature twin (the sibling died) in Bothwell, Scotland. Athletics consumed her energies as a young girl until she was sent to a Glasgow boarding school in 1772, where she excelled in mathematics, acting, and music. Six years later, her minister father died, leaving his wife and three children dependent for survival on the generosity of male relations. The famous anatomist William Hunter (Baillie's maternal uncle) provided for the family; at his death in 1783 he left Baillie's brother, Matthew, a physician, money, the use of his London house, the school of anatomy he founded, and a museum. This is how Baillie became an urban resident, living in London or its outskirts until her death in 1851, with brief excursions to Edinburgh, Wales, and Switzerland. Throughout her life she shared a home with her mother (who died in 1806) and her sister (who lived to be 100).

Although in the prefaces to her plays she follows the convention of apologizing for her limited education and lack of literary sophistication, Baillie had in fact a serious commitment to scholarship and creative writing. Her unmarried status, her supportive family, and the intellectual climate of her Hampstead home suggest a dedication to literary criticism and dramatic writing that resulted in Baillie's steady outpouring of publishable work for 50 years.

In 1790, Baillie published a volume of poems, *Fugitive Verses*, and her first play, *Arnold*, which does not survive. In 1798, she published the first volume of the plays on the passions with a lengthy introductory essay explaining her dramatic concerns. In this essay, Baillie proposes to have written dramas that chart the emotional and physical manifestations of such "passions" as love, hate, anger, and envy. She claims to be less interested in the public behavior of men and women—on battlefields, in the street, in political forums—than in those moments of intense feeling visible only to one intimate with a hero's or heroine's domestic life. Because of her concentration on character psychology and her blank verse format, Baillie was often compared to Shakespeare by contemporary reviewers.

Baillie's second and third collections of plays on the passions appeared in 1802 and 1812, with a volume called *Miscellaneous Plays* published in 1804. The drama, *The Family Legend*, with a prologue and epilogue by Scott and Henry Mackenzie, was published in 1810 and, through Scott's influence, performed at the Edinburgh Theatre.

In 1821, Baillie published a book celebrating in rhymed couplets the lives of famous persons in whom she had an abiding interest, among them William Wallace and Lady Griselda Baillie (*Metrical Legends of Exalted Characters*). Two years later, she edited a volume of poems whose contributors are testimony to her literary reputation. Besides Scott's political drama, *Mac Duff's Cross*, the volume contains sonnets by Wordsworth and poems by Campbell, Hemans, Catherine Fanshawe, and Barbauld and Southey's *The Cataract of Lodore*. The impressive list of subscribers to

the volume (included in the text) also attests to Baillie's literary popularity.

Two plays, *The Martyr* and *The Bride*, appeared in 1826, and 10 years later Baillie had enough new material to issue three more volumes of drama. Numerous Scottish songs and a religious essay, "A View of the General Tenor of the New Testament Regarding the Nature and Dignity of Jesus Christ," comprise her complete works, which were collected and published shortly before her death.

During Baillie's lifetime, at least five of her plays were produced, some of them several times at different theaters: *De Montfort; Constantine Paleologus* (performed as the melodrama *Constantine and Valeria* at the Surrey Theatre); *The Family Legend; The Separation*; and *Henriquez*. And while initially meeting with an indifferent reception for the most part, Baillie's plays were rewarded with first-rate productions at theaters such as Drury Lane and Covent Garden and acted by the greatest actors of the period, Sarah Siddons, John Philip Kemble, and Edmund Kean. At the instigation of the Chief Justice of Ceylon, both *The Bride* and *The Martyr* were translated into Cingalese.

Baillie's writing, especially her theory of theater, influenced Romantic critics, playwrights, and other writers, such as Scott, Coleridge, Wordsworth, and Maria Edgeworth. (*See also* Mental Theater, Theater.)

Catherine Burroughs

Works Consulted

Carhart, Margaret. *The Life and Work of Joanna Baillie*. New Haven: Yale UP, 1923.

Carswell, Donald. "Joanna Baillie." *Sir Walter: A Four-Part Study in Biography*. London: Murray, 1930.

Pieszczek, R.C. *Joanna Baillie*. Berlin: Schade, 1910.

Rowton, Frederic. *The Female Poets of Great Britain*. (1853). Ed. Marilyn L. Williamson. Detroit: Wayne State UP, 1981.

Tytler, Sarah [Henrietta Kiddie], and J.L. Watson. Vol. 2 of *The Songstresses of Scotland*. London: Strahan, 1871.

Ballad

The ballad is a narrative or dramatic poem composed in quatrains and often accompanied by music. The most common ballad stanza contains unrhymed iambic tetrameter in lines one and three and rhymed iambic trimeter in lines two and four, but the pattern is highly variable. The ballad emphasizes action over setting and characterization, and concentrates on the climactic moments of an event, often of a sensational or emotionally potent nature, rather than on the gradual development of plot. Despite its frequent sensationalism, the ballad usually creates an impression of terse, almost incantatory impersonality. Its capacity to deal, in unadorned simplicity, with the most powerful moments of human life, both real and wondrously imaginary, strongly appealed to the Romantic poets, who imitated the form in many of their most important works.

The ballad originated in preliterate cultures as oral folk poetry. This origin helps to explain some of the form's characteristics, particularly its prosodic regularity and its use of repetitive lines and phrases, devices that evolved, in part, to assist the memory of the ballad's oral performer. The existence of multiple versions of most folk ballads is another result of their oral, and thus communal, composition; a single individual must have been responsible for the introduction of a particular story into ballad lore, but without the authority of print to fix the form of the tale, it inevitably altered with each creative retelling, until particular performances were finally collected and published, sometimes with additional "improvements," by amateur antiquaries or professional folklorists. Even a cursory examination of Francis James Child's standard British ballad collection, *The English and Scottish Popular Ballads*, amply suggests how diversely the same ballad tale could be rendered. The ballad referred to in the opening lines of Coleridge's *Dejection: An Ode, Sir Patrick Spens*, for example, is given in 18 full or fragmentary variants.

Folk ballads were sometimes inspired by events of great historical importance and sometimes by the Christian and chivalric traditions. More often, however, they reflected the primitive superstitions, regional legendry, and dramatic local events (e.g., murders, family betrayals, and sexual infidelities) that shaped so much of the imaginative life of the common people. Thus a continuing tradition of folk-ballad performance, supplemented by the popularity of the printed broadside ballad, maintained a literary repository of wonder and passion, from the tender to the tempestuous, in a world given over more and more, publicly at least, to empirical reason. If anything, the broadside ballad, originating in the 16th century and flourishing well into the 19th, intensified the nonrational element in the ballad's popular appeal. Sometimes based on traditional communal ballad material but often composed by single authors to fit the tastes of the purchasing public, these ballads were frequently as topical as modern newspaper stories and as sensational as contemporary scandal sheets, with elements of the supernatural frequently included.

In addition to the living traditions of folk-ballad recitation and broadside-ballad publication, antiquarians and collectors published anthologies containing ballads and other folk poetry. These encouraged the fascination with the ballad form, present to some extent during the 17th century and increasingly evident during the 18th. Samuel Pepys, adding to the collection of

John Selden, gathered approximately 1,800 broadside ballads, now among the holdings of Cambridge University, and a series of collectors beginning with Robert Harley accumulated the 1,300 or so broadside ballads of the British Museum's Roxburghe Collection. *A Collection of Old Ballads* (1723–25) and Allan Ramsay's *The Tea-Table Miscellany* (1723–37) and *The Ever Green* (1724) contain important ballad materials and reflect the taste for the ballad's simplicity and purity of expression enunciated by Joseph Addison in 1711 in "The 'Chevy Chase' Papers."

Interest in the ballad intensified during the 18th century's final decades and continued unabated into the first decades of the 19th. David Herd's *The Ancient and Modern Scottish Songs and Ballads* appeared in 1769, with a second edition in 1776, and other products of Herd's collecting efforts circulated in manuscript. James Johnson's *The Scots Musical Museum*, completed with extensive editorial assistance from Burns, was published in six volumes from 1787 to 1803. Joseph Ritson produced several volumes in the century's last decade, which helped to introduce greater scholarly rigor into ballad collecting and publishing. Toward century's end, too, Mrs. Brown of Falkland worked with several collectors, including William Tytler, Alexander Fraser Tytler, and Robert Jamieson, to preserve both the words and the music of the many ballads she had mastered. Finally, during the Romantic period north-country collections were published: Scott's *Minstrelsy of the Scottish Border* (1802–03), Jamieson's *Popular Ballads and Songs from Tradition* (1806), and George R. Kinloch's *Ancient Scottish Ballads* (1827).

Initiating this period of intense interest in the ballad and certainly the single most important event in the ballad revival was the appearance in 1765 of Percy's *Reliques of Ancient English Poetry: Consisting of Old Heroic Ballads, Songs, and Other Pieces of our Earlier Poets (Chiefly of the Lyric Kind), Together with Some Few of a Later Date.* Despite the somewhat miscellaneous nature of his collection, a characteristic of a number of the anthologies, and despite his frequent lack of scholarly fidelity to his sources, Percy captured the imagination of the reading public as no previous compiler of ballads had, and much of the later influence of the ballad is attributable, directly or indirectly, to the *Reliques*. In addition to encouraging the ongoing collecting and publishing efforts, the *Reliques* draw Continental, particularly German, attention to the ballad, with certain odd consequences for British literature.

Inspired at least in part by Percy, the *Sturm und Drang* theorist Johann Gottfried von Herder called for a renewal and purification of the German folk tradition, one outcome of which was the writing of several ballads by Gottfried August Bürger. The most important of these, *Lenore*, appeared in the *Göttinger Musenalmanach* for *1774* and was an immediate success. It told the story of a young woman who curses God when her lover fails to return from the wars and who is then carried off to her grave in punishment by the lover's risen corpse. The ballad is a lengthened and intensified offshoot of the supernatural folk ballad, more specifically the revenant ballad, which had long existed both in Britain and on the Continent. The fact that it was a contemporary poem rather than collected from folk sources contributed to the development of the art and Gothic ballad.

The earliest known English translation of *Lenore* was completed by William Taylor of Norwich by 1790 but was circulated only in manuscript for the next several years. Among the first to see it — and certainly the first to be influenced by it — was

John Aikin, later the editor of the *Monthly Magazine*, whose poem *Arthur and Matilda* is loosely based on the Taylor translation. Aikin's sister and Taylor's former teacher, Anna Barbauld, was also shown Taylor's translation at an early date, and an often repeated story concerns her spirited reading of the poem before a group of Edinburgh intellectuals at the home of Dugald Stewart during the summer of 1794. After hearing one of Stewart's guests quote two particularly striking lines of the translation, Scott, who had recently begun studying German, obtained a copy of Bürger's works and undertook his own translation. That poem, along with his translation of another of Bürger's horror ballads, *Der Wilde Jäger*, became his first publication when it appeared in the fall of 1796.

The success of *Lenore* inspired many young British writers, particularly Southey, Lewis, and Scott. In emulation of Bürger, Southey produced several horror ballads between 1796 and the turn of the century, including *Mary, the Maid of the Inn*, *Donica*, *Rudiger*, *Lord William*, *Jaspar*, *St. Patrick's Purgatory*, *Bishop Bruno*, *The Pious Painter*, *Cornelius Agrippa*, *The Old Woman of Berkeley*, and *God's Judgment on a Wicked Bishop*. Eight of Southey's ballads appear in Lewis's anthology of Gothic poetry, *Tales of Wonder* (1801), as do approximately a score of Lewis's own, among them *Alonzo the Brave* and a series of elementary spirit ballads translated from or written in imitation of Continental originals. The last poems, including *The Erl-King*, *The Erl-King's Daughter*, *The Water-King*, and *The Cloud-King*, are an early manifestation of that invasion of lamias, vampires, and other bogies which so strongly influenced the literature of the next several decades. Another elementary spirit ballad, *The Fire-King*, was written by Scott at Lewis's request. In addition, *Tales of Wonder* contains Scott's *Glenfinlas*, *The*

Eve of St. John, *Frederick and Alice*, and *The Wild Huntsman*, making him the third most represented of the collection's many contributors.

An artistically more important manifestation than *Tales of Wonder* is Coleridge's *The Rime of the Ancient Mariner*. It was originally intended, not coincidentally, for publication in Aikin's *Monthly Magazine*, where Taylor's translation of *Lenore* first appeared. Its appearance instead in Wordsworth and Coleridge's *Lyrical Ballads* achieved one of the important purposes of that epoch-making volume: to explore the poetic power of the supernatural. That power, obvious to both poets not only from immediately contemporary ballads but perhaps even more importantly from many of the poems of Percy's *Reliques*, was one of the reasons for the two poets' attraction to the ballad form. Finally, the ballad's unadorned artlessness, so unlike the artificiality and linguistic contrivance of much of 18th-century verse, provided a model for renovating poetic style and affirmed Wordsworth's theories about poetic diction.

During the Romantic period, then, the ballad supplied forms and subjects for imitation and lessons in plain style. The ballad form could be expanded into the almost epic power of *The Ancient Mariner* and, more faithfully imitated, could produce quieter masterworks like Scott's *Proud Maisie* and Keats's *La Belle Dame Sans Merci*. Indirectly, its strains of superstition and wonder, even when the ballad form was not used, contributed much to that sense of the marvelous pervading such poems as Coleridge's *Christabel* and *Kubla Khan* and Keats's *Lamia* and *The Eve of St. Agnes*. On the other hand, its fascination with the passion and agony of mundane human existence encouraged such works as Wordsworth's *The Thorn*, *Ruth*, and *The Ruined Cottage*. Finally, its simplicity registered a shift in literary sensibility from an admiration of elaborate artifice to a quest for the natural. (*See also* Poetry.)

Robert O'Connor

Works Consulted

Abrams, M.H. *A Glossary of Literary Terms.* New York: Holt, 1981.

Child, Francis James, ed. *The English and Scottish Popular Ballads.* 5 vols. 1882–98. New York: Dover, 1965.

Emerson, Oliver Farrar. "The Earliest Known Translations of Bürger's Lenore: A Study in English and German Romanticism." *Western Reserve Studies* 1.1 (1915): 3–120.

Fowler, David C. *A Literary History of the Popular Ballad.* Durham: Duke UP, 1968.

Gaull, Marilyn. *English Romanticism: The Human Context.* New York: Norton, 1988.

Greenbie, Marjorie L. Barstow. *Wordsworth's Theory of Poetic Diction: A Study of the Historical and Personal Background of the Lyrical Ballads.* New York: Russell, 1966.

Johnson, Edgar. *Sir Walter Scott: The Great Unknown.* 2 vols. New York: Macmillan, 1970.

Leach, MacEdward, ed. *The Ballad Book.* New York: Harper, 1955.

Little, William A. *Gottfried August Bürger.* New York: Twayne, 1974.

Noyes, Russell. *William Wordsworth.* New York: Twayne, 1971.

Shepard, Leslie. *The Broadside Ballad: A Study in Origins and Meaning.* Hatboro, PA: Legacy, 1978.

Ballantyne, James

(1772–1833)

James Ballantyne was one of Scott's closest friends and the printer of nearly all of his voluminous works. The finances of his Ballantyne Press were tied up with Scott's own resources and the connection contributed to Scott's bankruptcy in 1826. The degree to which Ballantyne was to blame has long been debated.

Ballantyne and Scott became friends in 1783, when both were children at the Kelso grammar school. According to an often repeated anecdote, Scott would finish his lessons and whisper, "Come, slink over beside me, Jamie, and I'll tell you a story." Ballantyne's delight in his friend's tales lasted throughout his life. In young adulthood, the two drifted apart. Ballantyne studied law and set up practice in Edinburgh, with little success. He moved back to his hometown of Kelso in 1795. Never fully committed to a career in law, Ballantyne soon drifted into other jobs on the side, including selling insurance. In 1796, he became editor of a weekly newspaper, *The Kelso Mail*, the political stance of which was conservative and antidemocratic. In the course of his work with the paper, he became expert in printing techniques.

In 1799, Scott visited Kelso, and the old friends met again. Scott casually mentioned that Ballantyne ought to seek out printing work from publishers during the periods between issues of the newspaper. Proud of his abilities and anxious to show them off to his friend, Ballantyne printed a dozen copies of some short ballads of Scott's under the title *An Apology for Tales of Terror.* Delighted with the quality of the printing, Scott engaged Ballantyne in 1802 to print what was to be an epochal work, his *Minstrelsy of the Scottish Border.* From then on, the relationship of author and printer was never interrupted, and Ballantyne soon moved to Edinburgh and set up a greatly expanded printing office.

This relationship became more complicated when Scott became a partner in the Ballantyne business (which by 1805 included Ballantyne's brother John). Scott's motives in the partnership remain unclear. Although helping out his childhood friend and having more control over the printing of his own work were likely motives, Scott was a silent partner who used his enormous literary prestige to drum up business for the Ballantyne Press, without letting it be known that it was his business also.

The amount of business—and the amount of profit—was huge; in fact, the Waverley novels alone could easily have made a printer's fortune. But Ballantyne was not a careful businessman; his brother John was even less so; and Scott himself was so wrapped up in purchasing land and glamorously outfitting his estate of Abbotsford that he frequently used the firm as a sort of bank, acquiring cash by taking out notes against the printing business. Constable, Scott's publisher, was likewise consumed by debt, some of it owing to, some of it owing from, Ballantyne and Company. The irresponsibility could not go on forever, and, as part of the general financial crises of the period, Constable's bankruptcy in 1826 brought down Scott and Ballantyne too. (Publishing houses across Britain were also failing.)

When Lockhart, Scott's son-in-law, published his extensive biography of Scott in 1837–38, he placed most of the blame for the ruin on Ballantyne. Ballantyne's son and the trustees of his estate printed a pamphlet defending the printer; Lockhart responded with his own pamphlet, and the Ballantynes issued an angry reply. This conflict was fought out in public in 1838 to 1839, five years after Scott and Ballantyne, who had remained friends until the end, were dead.

Ballantyne's importance to Scott went beyond friendship; he often criticized early drafts of Scott's novels. Many of his suggestions were adopted; even Lockhart credits Ballantyne for fine descriptive touches in some of Scott's novels. Ballantyne was among the few from whom Scott would take such criticism, which in itself is one measure of their closeness. His dubious bookkeeping skills no doubt contributed

to his financial ruin and to that of his friend, but his intelligence, fervor, and pride in the work that came from his press make him one of 19th-century Edinburgh's most interesting and likeable figures. (*See also* Publishing.)

Raymond N. Mackenzie

Works Consulted

Ballantyne and Company. *The Ballantyne Press and Its Founders, 1796–1908*. Edinburgh: Ballantyne, 1909.

The Ballantyne-Lockhart Controversy, 1838–1839. New York: Garland, 1974.

Buchan, John. *Sir Walter Scott*. New York: Coward, 1932.

Lockhart, John Gibson. *Narrative of the Life of Sir Walter Scott, Bart., Begun by Himself and Continued by J.G. Lockhart*. New York: Dutton, 1906.

Barbauld, Anna Laetitia
(1743–1825)

Anna Barbauld, unlike many of her contemporary female poets, has never been entirely forgotten. Her lasting reputation is partly due to her famous and talented acquaintances. They included Priestley (a frequent subject of her verse), Wordsworth, Coleridge (who directed his publisher to send Barbauld a prepublication copy of the just-printed *Lyrical Ballads*), and Scott, as well as her brother John Aikin (with whom she wrote in 1792 to 1795 the six volumes of *Evenings at Home* for children) and such important literary women as Hannah More, Joanna Baillie, and Elizabeth Montagu. Partly, her lasting fame is the result of her work as an editor: she published a six-volume *Correspondence of Samuel Richardson* (1804) and a 50-volume *Edition, with Essay and Lives, of the British Novelists* (1810), among others. Finally, she has been remembered for her most famous book, *Hymns in Prose for Children* (1781), which may have been either a target of satire or an object of admiring emulation of Blake's *Songs of Innocence and Experience*. The great popularity of these hymns, the hybrid form of which is particularly interesting in light of the subsequent popularity of similar experiments in prose poetry, led the book to be translated into French, German, and Italian.

Her education was unusual for a girl of the time. Her father, the Nonconformist minister John Aikin, taught her English literature, French, Italian, and, then, with reported reluctance, Latin and Greek. She became an outstanding educator in her turn. She married a Dissenting minister named Rochemont Barbauld in 1774, and together they established a boys' school in Palgrave, Suffolk, which they ran successfully for 11 years. Though she edited a selection of English literature specifically for girls— *The Female Speaker* (1811)—she held that girls should be educated with a view to their becoming wives and mothers. This conservative view of education is not characteristic of her overall politics: she wrote in support of the principles of the French Revolution in such works as *Civic Sermons to the People* (1792) and *Sins of the Government, Sins of the Nation* (1793), and, again, promoting the abolition of slavery in *Epistle to William Wilberforce* (1791). Her belief in activism is apparent in her poem *The First Fire*, in which she varied the form of the greater Romantic lyric by using the ending of the poem to call the reader to direct social action. Her most controversial political work was a desponding prediction of the collapse of British civilization. This poem, published as a pamphlet and titled *Eighteen Hundred and Eleven*, was so harshly criticized that Barbauld published nothing more during her lifetime. Her niece, the poet Lucy Aikin, edited her *Works* in two volumes in 1825, the year of Barbauld's

death, adding a posthumous third volume in the following year.

John Anderson

Works Consulted

Blain, Virginia, Isobel Grundy, and Patricia Clements, eds. *The Feminist Companion to Literature in English*. London: Batsford, 1990.

Griggs, Earl Leslie, ed. *Collected Letters of Samuel Taylor Coleridge*. Oxford: Clarendon, 1932.

Lonsdale, Roger, ed. *Eighteenth-Century Women Poets*. New York: Oxford UP, 1990.

Todd, Janet, ed. *British Women Writers*. New York: Bedrick, 1989.

— — —. *Dictionary of British and American Women Writers, 1660–1800*. Totowa, NJ: Rowman, 1985.

Beaumont, Sir George Howland
(1753–1827)

Sir George Howland Beaumont is best known for founding the National Gallery of Art and for his generous patronage of poets and artists. He was born in 1753 at Great Dunmow, Essex, into a family that belonged to one of the oldest branches of the British nobility. Following the death of his father in 1762, he became Viscount Beaumont. At age 11, Sir George entered Eton, where he was apparently happy despite the harsh conditions that existed in public schools. Inclined to corpulence as a child, he became a swimmer, spending hours in the water in the belief that it would reduce his weight. Though the classical curriculum of Eton had changed little since the time of Henry VIII, Beaumont was expected to learn Shakespeare and Milton as well as Addison and Pope—all writers for whom he developed a lasting enthusiasm. His taste for art was aroused by his tutor, Alexander Cozens, a gifted drawing teacher who was famous for his studies of clouds. At Oxford, Beaumont continued to pursue his interest in painting, taking lessons to perfect his talents. After leaving the university, he married Margaret Willes, an aristocratic young woman who shared his love of literature and art. He took his bride on a honeymoon tour of the Lake District largely because of the Cumberland's reputation as "painter's country." From 1784 to 1787 he and his wife journeyed across Europe, visiting the galleries of Paris and Rome to view the works of his idols, Claude and Raphael.

In time, Beaumont became a respectable amateur landscape painter, but following the expectations of those of his class he decided to enter politics and bought a seat in parliament after his return to England. Neither his temperament nor his talent prepared him for the role of statesman, however, and his Tory prejudices were out of step with the reform tendencies of the time. Therefore, he left political life for good in 1798 and returned to the old family manor at Coleorton Hall, which he had refinished and landscaped by George Dance, a fashionable architect. He spent the next 10 years involved in rebuilding this country house, which would contain his growing collection of works by some of Europe's Old Masters as well as pictures by himself and contemporary artists like Gilpin, Hearne, Girtin, and Wilson. Although his own artistic taste first tended toward the Neoclassic—he knew Dr. Johnson and Sir Joshua Reynolds personally—it is his enthusiasm for the work of Romantic poets and painters for which he is recognized. Though Beaumont was not as progressive in his thinking about art as about literature, he encouraged the young John Constable and Wilkie; even the petulant Haydon was for a time a protegé until quarreling with Beaumont over the gigantic scale of Haydon's pictures.

Among the poets who enjoyed the patronage of Beaumont were Coleridge and Wordsworth. Both were ardent republicans at the time they received the support and friendship of this wealthy Tory who abhorred their revolutionary politics but admired their nature poetry and recognized the genius of both. Beaumont provided Coleridge a house in Keswick so he could profit from close contact with Wordsworth. During this time a warm friendship developed between Lady Beaumont and Dorothy Wordsworth that is revealed in their correspondence. Moreover, it was one of Sir George's paintings, "Peele Castle in a Storm," a typically Gothic painting of a ruined tower on a crag against a dark sky with a small boat in a heavy sea in the distance, that inspired one of Wordsworth's finest poems, *Elegaic Stanzas*. All the details were chosen to arouse the sense of the sublime through a fearful scene. Its subject had a personal meaning to Wordsworth, who had lost his brother John in a shipwreck off the coast of Weymouth in 1805.

The crowning achievement of Beaumont's life, however, was the founding of the National Gallery in 1826, which would house his own fine art collection and any future collections acquired by the nation. He died in 1827, having been a generous patron during his lifetime to poets and painters, and through his charitable behest, he provided a gift to lovers of the arts for posterity.

Hallman B. Bryant

Works Consulted

Greaves, Margaret. *Regency Patron: Sir George Beaumont*. London: Methuen, 1966.

Owen, Felicity. *Sir George Beaumont, Artist and Patron*. 1969.

Whitley, W.T. *Artists and Their Friends in England*. London: The Medici Society, 1928.

Beckford, William

(1760–1844)

Now best known as the author of the Oriental tale *Vathek*, in his lifetime, William Beckford was notorious in England for reasons unconnected to literary achievement. Beckford's father was a successful businessman and twice Lord Mayor of London; his mother was of noble descent. Raised in such a prominent family, Beckford was intended, by his overindulgent yet autocratic parents, to become influential in British politics and empire building. Despite the best private education money could buy—at various times the eight-year-old Wolfgang Amadeus Mozart was Beckford's piano teacher and Sir William Chambers, architect to the King, his drawing and architecture instructor—he was destined to disappoint his family.

Beckford spent much of his life repudiating the mores and sensibilities of the privileged class into which he had been born, often doing so with an ostentation that was publicly offensive. From his youth, he indulged a deep fascination with Oriental (i.e., Middle Eastern) culture and literature, perhaps as much for the imaginative release and escape from an overwhelming maternal presence as for intrinsic aesthetic attractions. The result of this lifelong interest was his popular short novel *Vathek*. Beckford's considerable (and, later in his life, much reduced) wealth enabled him to travel extensively, which led to further literary publication in *Italy; with Sketches of Spain and Portugal* (1834) and *Recollections of an Excursion to the Monasteries of Alcobaça and Batalha* (1835). Well-known as a collector of fine art, he built one of the most famous private houses in England, the neo-Gothic mansion Fonthill Abbey, where he could display his collection. Designed by the prominent architect James Wyatt and unfinished after 26 years of sporadic construction, Fonthill Abbey was popularized by some of the most respected literary and visual artists of the period. They were attracted by the mansion's great central tower, which repeatedly collapsed; the elaborately landscaped grounds (designed by Beckford); and the luxurious but often artificial appointments.

Behind this deserved recognition, however, lies Beckford's scandalous notoriety as a pederast. His bisexuality was recognized by Beckford's family when he was age 19, shortly after his encounter with the 11-year-old William ("Kitty") Courtenay (later ninth Earl of Devon), with whom Beckford remained fascinated, even obsessed, for years. To divert public attention, Beckford was married to Lady Margaret Gordon in 1783; they had two daughters before her death three years later. But only a year after the marriage, Beckford was publicly accused of sodomy by Courtenay's uncle, Baron Loughbor-ough, a Chief Justice and long-time political nemesis of the Beckfords. Formal charges were never brought, and much of the evidence suggests that Loughborough maliciously fabricated the episode, but the infamy attached to Beckford as a result, rendered him virtually *persona non grata* in the circles of Britain's elite for the rest of his life.

This notoriety, however, cannot eclipse Beckford's contribution to English literature. In addition to the works already mentioned, Beckford authored obscure works, the most important of which are a satire on contemporary artistic practice (*Biographical Memoirs of Extraordinary Painters* [1790]), two satires on novel writing (*Modern Novel Writing* [1796] and *Azemia* [1797]), and the early travel book *Dreams, Waking Thoughts, and Incidents*, published in 1783 but withheld from distribution, perhaps because of a subjectivity and sentimentality that Beckford's family found inappropriate. Of greatest consequence is *Vathek* (and three associated tales, unpublished by Beckford, collectively known as *The Episodes of Vathek*). Begun in 1782, *Vathek* was composed in French; Beckford shortly thereafter commissioned his friend Samuel Henley to translate the work into English and add explanatory notes. Impatient with Beckford's delays, Henley published an unauthorized and anonymous translation in 1786; outraged, Beckford rushed a French edition into print in 1787, following it with a more polished revision the next year.

The fantastic tale of a sybaritic Oriental potentate who pursues a Faustian pact with the devil, *Vathek* is the culmination of an Oriental tradition in English letters that goes back through Johnson's *Rasselas* (1759) to the translation into English of *The Thousand and One Nights* (1707–12). Beckford's work crowns this tradition because it rises above the imitative didacticism of most Neoclassical "Oriental" tales to capture a sense of wonder and of the exotic that approach more nearly than any of its predecessors a recognizably Oriental atmosphere. *Vathek* offers a world of demons and angels, grotesque characters, beautiful maidens, and outrageous evil and powerful magic. Renouncing Mohammed in favor of the satanic Eblis, Vathek, encouraged by his wicked mother, commits sundry crimes and atrocities on his journey to the Hall of Eblis. He there expects to acquire wisdom and the treasure of the pre-Adamite sultans but finds instead that he and his beloved Nouronihar are condemned to eternal despair.

Like its author, *Vathek* bridges two literary periods. In its moralistic ending, the work constitutes a fairly conventional warning against hubris, and this, along with

Beckford's concrete sense of imagery, aligns the work with Neoclassical sensibilities. But *Vathek* also influenced the Romantic writers. Vathek himself is both a murderous tyrant and a buffoon; the resulting tension produces a moral ambiguity that, in conjunction with the work's self-conscious irony and powerful emotionalism, foreshadows such writers as Byron (an avowed admirer of *Vathek*). While not achieving the Promethean heights of Romantic introspection (which some of Beckford's other works approached), the novel does trace an individual's quest to fulfill an unquenchable desire against a background of shifting moral landmarks. Perhaps these proto-modern elements, as much as any historical value, account for the continued life of this curious and fascinating work. (*See also* Gothicism, Novel, Satire.)

Jack G. Voller

Works Consulted

Alexander, Boyd. *England's Wealthiest Son: A Study of William Beckford*. London: Centaur, 1962.

Brockman, H.A.N. *The Caliph of Fonthill*. London: Werner Laurie, 1956.

Chapman, Guy. *Beckford*. London: Hart, 1952.

Fothergill, Brian. *Beckford of Fonthill*. London: Faber, 1979.

Gemmet, Robert James. *William Beckford*. Boston: Twayne, 1977.

Lees-Milne, James. *William Beckford*. Tisbury, England: Compton Russell, 1976; Montclair, NJ: Allanheld, 1979.

Mahmoud, Fatma Moussa, ed. *William Beckford of Fonthill, 1760–1844. Bicentenary Essays*. Cairo: Tsoumas, 1960. Port Washington, NY: Kennikat, 1972.

Oliver, John. *The Life of William Beckford*. London: Oxford UP, 1932.

Redding, Cyrus. *Memoirs of William Beckford of Fonthill*. 2 vols. London: Charles Skeet, 1859.

Beddoes, Thomas Lovell
(1803–49)

Thomas Lovell Beddoes was one of the most gifted poets active in the two decades between Shelley's death and the rise of Tennyson as a major poet. Born into a family with serious intellectual, scientific, and literary preoccupations, he took a precocious interest in literature as a student at Charterhouse School, reading widely in Elizabethan literature and writing *Scaroni, or The Mysterious Cave*, a short Gothic romance.

After distinguishing himself at Charterhouse, Beddoes left to attend Oxford in 1820. At Oxford, Beddoes continued to immerse himself in Elizabethan poetry and drama, and in 1821, at age 18, he published a volume of poetry entitled *The Improvisatore*. This volume contains, along with several experimental short poems, three Gothic stories in verse dealing with madness, demon lovers, horrid death, and ghostly murderers. Despite the extravagant and conventional Gothicism of this work, it shows the youthful Beddoes already in command of a facile and occasionally striking power of poetic expression.

In the following year, 1822, Beddoes published a work of much greater significance, his pseudo-Jacobean drama, *The Brides' Tragedy*. Writing out of his deep study of Webster, Tourneur, and Beaumont and Fletcher, Beddoes produced, if not a great theatrical play, at least a poetic drama of considerable interest. The plot of *The Brides' Tragedy* revolves around the love, murder, emotional conflict, and revenge typical of revenge tragedy, but Beddoes' dramatic blank verse and the psychological insight of his best scenes represent a significant advance over *The Improvisatore*. Moreover, in the lyrics of *The Brides' Tragedy*, Beddoes achieves some of the concentration, prosodic brilliance, and metaphoric originality that later characterize the great lyrics in his masterpiece, *Death's Jest-Book*. *The Brides' Tragedy* was a critical success, gaining favorable reviews from Darley, Wilson, and B.W. Procter ("Barry Cornwall").

Between 1822 and 1825, Beddoes became friends with Thomas F. Kelsall, who would later be his devoted literary executor; made several literary acquaintances in London, including Mary Shelley; and continued to devote himself to poetic composition. From this period his most important poems are *Lines Written in a Blank leaf of the Prometheus Bound*, a splendid tribute to Shelley; *Pygmalion*, a Keatsian narrative poem concerning artistic creation; and a fragmentary but haunting poem, *Lines Written at Geneva*. Also during this period Beddoes's fascination with Elizabethan drama continued, and he attempted to write at least four more plays in Renaissance style: *The Last Man* (1823), *Love's Arrow Poisoned* (1823), *The Second Brother* (1824), and *Torrismond* (1824). Although only fragments, they are at their best powerful. The extraordinary single act of *Torrismond* looks forward to *Death's Jest-Book* and contains one of Beddoes's finest lyrics, "How Many Times Do I Love Thee, Dear."

In 1825, Beddoes left England to study medicine at Göttingen. This began a wandering career during which he studied medicine at Würzburg, became involved in radical German politics, was deported for his political activities, escaped to Strasbourg, and settled in Switzerland, returning only infrequently to England. He committed suicide at age 45 in 1849.

Although Beddoes published nothing of literary importance between 1825 and 1849, he was throughout these years working on his one great work, *Death's Jest-Book*, which was finally published by Kelsall in 1850. This remarkable play is a sprawling, 4,000-

line extravaganza in which Beddoes's knowledge of Jacobean tragedy, his intense preoccupation with death, his lyric genius, his verbal virtuosity, and his apocalyptic but crepuscular Romanticism all find intense expression. In dramatic structure and plot, Beddoes's work is hopelessly flawed, while his characters, with the notable exception of Isbrand (villain, jester, and revenger), are totally unconvincing. The blank verse, the dramatic prose, and, especially, the lyrics of the play, however, attain a metaphoric power and a sheer verbal vitality that raise this strange work to greatness.

It is finally the lyrics of *Death's Jest-Book* that are Beddoes's best work. These lyrics display a delicacy of form, a voluptuous horror, an imagistic compactness and suggestiveness, and, occasionally, a grotesque comic power that are absolutely unique. Among the best of the individual lyrics are the ghostly "Sibylla's Dirge"; the subtle "The Swallow Leaves Her Nest" (which deals with Beddoes's favorite theme of the intrusion of the dead upon the living); "If Thou Wilt Ease Thine Heart" (a delicate lyric of sadness and regret); and "A Cypress Bough and a Rose-Wreath Sweet" (which combines deathly horror and sensuous expectation in Beddoes's best manner). Among Beddoes's lyrics in the grotesque and comic style, Isbrand's songs, including "The Oviparous Tailor," are important, especially by demonstrating that Beddoes's essentially lyric gift can contribute to dramatic effect. Despite his narrow range and macabre obsessions, Beddoes is an important Romantic poet. Few figures between 1820 and 1840 so clearly suggest the fortunes and the adversities of the late Romantic imagination.

Phillip B. Anderson

Works Consulted

Bloom, Harold. *The Visionary Company*. Ithaca: Cornell, 1971.

Donner, Henry W. *Thomas Lovell Beddoes: The Making of a Poet*. Oxford: Blackwell, 1935.

Donner, Henry W., ed. *The Works of Thomas Lovell Beddoes*. Oxford: Blackwell, 1935.

Heath-Stubbs, John. *The Darkling Plain*. London: Eyre, 1950.

Reeves, James, ed. *Five Late Romantic Poets*. London: Barnes, 1974.

Snow, Royall H. *Thomas Lovell Beddoes: Eccentric and Poet*. New York: Covici, 1928.

Thompson, James R. *Thomas Lovell Beddoes*. Boston: Twayne, 1985.

Bell, Andrew

(1753–1832)

A Scottish cleric and educator, Andrew Bell devised the Madras system of mutual instruction among students. In 1811, he helped to form the Society for Promoting the Education of the Poor in the Principles of the Established Church and served as its first superintendent.

Bell was born in St. Andrews into a family of modest means but some education. Sent to school at age 4, he apparently suffered under the discipline of a rigid master. Later, having studied mathematics and natural philosophy at St. Andrews University, he traveled to the United States, where he tutored the children of a Virginia planter. Through private trading in tobacco, he also began to acquire wealth.

After returning to England in 1781, Bell was ordained in the Anglican church. His first church assignment was in Leith, but in 1787 he went to India and soon acquired several simultaneous appointments to army chaplainships. Since these positions paid well but carried with them few responsibilities, he was able also to become superintendent of the Madras Male Orphan Asylum. This institution had been established by the East India Company to provide education for the sons of military men, but its poorly paid teachers displayed little dedication, and most students made slow progress. Faced with such problems, Bell assigned an able student the task of teaching the alphabet to other boys. This 8-year-old tutor assisted his fellow students in drawing letters in the sand. From this simple beginning, Bell's scheme of mutual instruction soon expanded to include most other subjects. Also, Bell disapproved of corporal punishments and stressed the need to teach reading and writing together. His plan for such simultaneous instruction was later termed ILTO, a name composed of what were thought the simplest letters of the alphabet and thus intended to sum up the idea that instruction should always proceed from basic to more complex matters.

In 1796, poor health motivated Bell to return to England. The following year he published an account of his work in India entitled *An Experiment in Education Made at the Male Asylum of Madras; Suggesting a System by Which a School or Family May Teach Itself under the Superintendence of the Master or Parent*. Bell's innovations received relatively little attention until 1803 when Lancaster, a Quaker teacher in Southwark, published a description of his own successful use of student tutors. At first Bell commended Lancaster for his original contributions to the system of mutual instruction, but soon the two became embroiled in a religious controversy. Supporters of the Church of England were suspicious of Lancaster and sided with Bell. On the other hand, many who wished to make education nonsectarian backed Lancaster. In a popular caricature of the day, the two combatants were labeled "Bel and the Dragon."

Stimulated by this controversy over whether the established church should control education, Bell worked to organize schools throughout England under the general supervision of parish clergy. When efforts to pass a national education bill failed, Bell was instrumental in forming the private Society for Promoting the Education of the Poor. Bell was encouraged by many prominent literary figures, including Coleridge, Wordsworth, and Southey (who, along with his son Charles, wrote a detailed account of Bell's life). In 1816, Bell traveled on the Continent to promote his views on education, but his impact abroad was minimal.

In his later years, Bell received numerous church appointments. He became master of Sherburn Hospital in Durham (1809), canon of Hereford Cathedral (1818), and prebend of Westminster (1819). He continued to write extensively on education, but these later works added little to his ideas stated originally in *Experiment*. Bell hoped that his friends Southey and Wordsworth would collect and edit his works, but they did not. On his death in 1832 Bell left large bequests to St. Andrews University and several other institutions for use in promoting his educational theories. (*See also* Education.)

Albert E. Wilhelm

Works Consulted

Meiklejohn, John Miller Dow. *An Old Educational Reformer, Dr. Andrew Bell*. Edinburgh: Blackwood, 1881.

Salmon, David, ed. *The Practical Parts of Lancaster's Improvements and Bell's Experiment*. Cambridge: Cambridge UP, 1932.

Southey, Robert, and Charles Cuthbert Southey. *Life of the Rev. Andrew Bell*. 3 vols. London: Murray, 1844.

Bennett, Agnes Maria
(1750?–1808)

The novelist Agnes Maria Bennett was one of the more colorful literary figures of the Romantic period. Though immensely popular in her own day, she is now one of the most obscure of her time. During the 20-year span of her literary career, she produced eight known novels, including *Anna, or the Memoirs of a Welch Heiress, Interspersed with Anecdotes of a Nabob* (1785), *Juvenile Indiscretions* (1786), *Agnes de Courci, A Domestic Tale* (1789), *Ellen, Countess of Castel Howel* (1794), *The Beggar Girl and her Benefactors* (1797), *De Valcourt* (1800), *Vicissitudes Abroad, or The Ghost of My Father* (1806), and *Faith and Fiction, or Shining Lights in a Dark Generation* (published posthumously in 1816). These works are now available only in the collections of major libraries.

Little is known of Bennett's early life. Her name is listed by the Minerva Press as "Anna," but other contemporary sources and the Library of Congress call her "Agnes." She was probably born in 1750 in Merthyr Thydfil, Glamorganshire, and she grew up in Bristol. Her father, David Evans, was a Custom House officer. Married young and widowed by the early 1780s, she supported her young family by working as a slop-seller, in a chandlery, as a workhouse superintendent, and, later, as housekeeper to Admiral Sir Thomas Pye at his Tooting, Surrey, estate. After he died in 1785, Bennett inherited his townhouse on Suffolk Street and her son Thomas Pye Bennett, married Pye's daughter, Mary, in 1787.

Bennett began writing, while supplementing her literary income by training her daughter, Harriet Esten, for the stage, and managing her career. But in 1793, a legal struggle with John Jackson and Stephen Kemble over the managership of the Edinburgh Theatre Royal ended their stage careers. Bennett's claim was supported by the Duke of Hamilton, who held the patent, but her case was weakened by a suit brought by James Esten against the Duke for "criminal intercourse" with his wife. Bennett and Harriet fled to London. Bennett's huge financial investment in the theater was not recovered by Kemble's settlement of a 200-pound annuity, and not until Hamilton died in 1799, leaving his personal property and pictures to Harriet in trust for her daughter by him, did their financial difficulties end. In the interim, Bennett returned to writing. *Ellen* appeared in 1794, with a preface describing its author's poor health and spirits resulting from the Kemble affair.

Bennett's later novels maintained her popularity, and her literary celebrity continued unabated until her death at Brighton in 1808. The arrival of her funeral procession at The Horns, Kennington Common, London, was met by a large crowd of friend, relatives, and admirers of her fiction.

During her life, Bennett was one of the most popular writers associated with William Lane's Minerva Press, and in addition to enormous sales, her works were widely distributed through its circulating library. However, the Press was far from being perceived as a fountainhead of great literature, a fact to which Bennett makes ironic reference in several of her novels. Although such critics as Coleridge praised her, she wrote her books to please the public taste, and she wrote at length to increase their price. Moreover, her style is marred by occasional slips in grammar and in her use of French and by inconsistencies in the naming of characters.

On the other hand, she had read Swift and Rabelais with evident enjoyment, and her novels are highly comic. Her style is loose and paratactically linked, giving her prose fluidity and a fast pace. She uses traditional plot motifs (Cinderella in *Anna* and *The Beggar Girl*; Patient Griselda in *Ellen*) and engages in such 18th-century artifices as mistaken identities, genteel foundlings, and type names. In this sense, her works are reminiscent of Fielding, to whom her obituarist compared her. But the ironic tone of her narration and her epigrammatic dismissal of evil or foolish characters prefigure Austen, while her democratic sentiments and mingling of moneyed and impoverished, rural and urban characters provide antecedents for the early Dickens. Though neither outstandingly powerful nor strikingly original, her work remains highly readable. Her novels may be valued as a bridge between the comic romance of the 18th century and the novel of manners and social novel of the 19th.

Miranda J. Burgess

Works Consulted

Allsop, Thomas, ed. *Letters, Conversations and Recollections of S.T. Coleridge.* New York: Harper, 1836.

Baker, Ernest. *The History of the English Novel.* Vol. 5. London: Witherby, 1929.

La Biographie portative et universelle des contemporains. Vol. 1. 1836.

Dictionary of National Biography, s.v. "Bennett, Agnes Maria."

Farington, Joseph. *The Diary of Joseph Farington.* Eds. Kenneth Garlick and Angus Macintyre. New Haven: Yale UP, 1984.

Fuller, J.F. *Omniana: The Autobiography of an Irish Octogenarian.* New York: Dutton, 1916.

Lewes, Charles Lee. *The Memoirs of Charles Lee Lewes.* London: Phillips, 1805.

[Smith,] Dorothy Blakey. *The Minerva Press 1790–1820.* London: Oxford UP, 1939.

The Thespian Dictionary; or, Dramatic Biography of the Present Age. 2nd ed. London: Cundee, 1805.

Tompkins, J.M.S. *The Popular Novel in England 1770–1800.* Lincoln: U of Nebraska P, 1961.

Bentham, Jeremy

(1748–1832)

An odd man with numerous personal quirks, Jeremy Bentham nonetheless influenced his age and after. He ranked among the two dozen men whom Hazlitt selected to represent the spirit of the age, and John Stuart Mill named Bentham and Coleridge the "two great seminal minds of England." Certainly Bentham's philosophy of utilitarianism was a touchstone for Romanticism and a wellspring for Victorianism.

Born in 1748 to a family whose prosperity had been achieved in trade, Bentham spent a solitary, sober, and studious childhood in London, under the tutelage of his father, who was determined to shape the child into a miniature adult. Jeremiah Bentham sought to dictate every aspect of his son's education and development in his determination to groom his son to be not only a pillar of successful Anglican and establishment authority but also Lord Chancellor. The elder Bentham sent his firstborn son, at age 12, to Oxford, where he earned his M.A. three years later, succeeded by training at the bar.

While outwardly conforming and industriously applying himself, young Bentham was tacitly and secretly building resistance. An independent income allowed him to abandon his legal career after his first case and devote himself to his own reflections and studies, aiming at not the acme of English law, but its complete overhaul. Never married, Bentham turned his back on and cast off his grim upbringing, becoming increasingly independent and radical, even youthful and eccentric with age. He gave amusing personal names to his walking stick, his teapot, and the rooms of his house. On his cat, in deference to its advanced and settled age, he bestowed the title the Reverend Sir John Langborn.

But beyond exemplifying stereotypical Romantic idiosyncrasy, Bentham's gifts lay in philosophy. He was determined to prove through his voluminous works—many of which were published outside of England first and not available in his homeland until after his death—that improving the human condition could not be realized without first accepting that humanity was driven by two precepts: pleasure and pain. He abandoned the impersonal and intangible ethics of his father's catholic Anglicanism for a much more pragmatic and personal approach. Any object or idea must be judged by its "utility," by which he meant how much pleasure it would cause or how much pain it would prevent. (*See also* Utilitarianism.) In his moral scheme, pleasure was a virtue; pain, a vice. He postulated that an individual will do whatever is necessary to increase pleasure and decrease pain, both of which, he believed, were measurable in a calculus of hedonism. Bentham went to great lengths to quantify pain and pleasure, which he labeled as either simple or complex. A complex motive included both pain and pleasure. He codified 12 areas of simple pleasure and 12 of simple pain. From these concepts, government, he said, was necessary to ensure that the most good was brought to the most people. It would be able to accomplish this by a series of rewards and punishments, which he set forth in *Principles of Morals and Legislation* (1789), the major document of his beliefs published during his lifetime. He was determined to establish that the punishment must fit the crime, a revolutionary idea in an age when the law administered hanging as the cost of many relatively minor offenses.

In *Panopticon* (1791), Bentham laid out his designs for the ideal prison, a model adopted by Quakers in Philadelphia in the early 1800s (and later one of the two places in America Dickens most wanted to visit): it would resemble a cartwheel of cells with spokes radiating from a central observation tower. Bentham advocated this prototype for schools and hospitals, as well, and

devoted 20 years and much capital to constructing it, although his efforts failed.

Besides penal reform, his utilitarianism had numerous other positive contributions to reform and to the efforts of humanitarianism. (*See also* Humanitarianism.) He championed the rights of children, animals, the insane, religious minorities, and slaves and argued that the problems of unwed mothers, failed suicides, and homosexuals were personal and not matters for prosecution. Although many of his goals were enacted in the first Reform Bill of 1832, Bentham died the night before its passage.

Skeptical of symbols, incredulous of an afterlife, he died into a symbolic eternity: he gave his body to science, to the University College of London he had helped to found; it now permanently displays his fully dressed skeleton—the "auto-icon"—set off by his signature straw hat and Dapple, the walking stick. Although a stuffed head is in place, his skull lies at his feet.

Jo Ann Ferguson

Works Consulted

Albee, Ernest. *A History of English Utilitarianism.* New York: Collier, 1962.

Bentham, Jeremy. *The Utilitarians: An Introduction to the Principles of Morals and Legislation.* Garden City: Doubleday, 1961.

Bryant, Arthur. *The Age of Elegance. 1812–1822.* London: Collins, 1950.

Capaldi, Nicholas. *Bentham, Mill, and the Utilitarians.* New York: Monarch, 1965.

Costigan, Giovanni. *Makers of Modern England. The Force of Individual Genius in History.* New York: Macmillan, 1967.

Gaull, Marilyn. *English Romanticism: The Human Context.* New York: Norton, 1988.

Mack, Mary P. *Jeremy Bentham: An Odyssey of Ideas.* New York: Columbia UP, 1963.

Priestley, J.B. *The Prince of Pleasure and His Regency.* New York: Harper, 1969.

Ryan, Alan. *J.S. Mill.* Boston: Routledge, 1974.

Thomson, David. *England in the Nineteenth Century.* London: Cape, 1950.

Berkeley's Idealism

The idealism, or more properly "immaterialism," of Bishop George Berkeley (1685–1763), signifies the denial of the existence of material substance. Positing that "Existence is *percipi* or *percipere*," Berkeley believed that existence can be validated only through the act of perceiving or being perceived.

As an 18th-century British philosopher, Berkeley wrote in response to both rationalism and Lockean empiricism. Establishing the foundation for immaterialism in his first major treatise, *An Essay Towards a New Theory of Vision* (1709), Berkeley rejected the rationalist belief in abstract shape and dimension, asserting, instead, that objects of perception exist in the mind and that humans derive their ideas of magnitude and distance through the association of the different senses. Then, in his next major works, *A Treatise Concerning the Principles of Human Knowledge* (Part I, 1710) and *Three Dialogues Between Hylas and Philonous* (1713), Berkeley developed his argument for immaterialism, primarily a response to Locke's *Essay Concerning Understanding* (1690). According to Locke, knowledge results from the perception not of things themselves but of the ideas of things which mediate between external reality and the mind. Accepting Locke's position, then, according to Berkeley, means there can be no actual knowledge of material reality: one can know only the ideas but have no means of verifying the existence of those objects they are supposed to represent.

In the *Principles*, Berkeley delineates his philosophy of immaterialism by first refuting Locke's belief in abstract ideas. Identifying language as the source of the error, Berkeley directs the reader to look beyond the words to discover the truth of falsity of concepts. He then develops his essential belief that "existence is to perceive or to be perceived." Asserting three sources of knowledge — (1) ideas imprinted on the senses; (2) ideas perceived through the emotions or reason; and (3) ideas formed through the operation of memory and imagination — he concludes that external bodies are not necessary for producing ideas.

Having refuted the existence of matter, Berkeley then defends his theory against possible objections by positing the existence of God. To the question of whether something exists if no one is present to perceive it, he responds that the omnipresent God perceives all. (*See also* Commonsense Philosophy; German Idealism, Influence of.)

Sheila A. Spector

Works Consulted

Berkeley, George. *A Treatise Concerning the Principles of Human Knowledge*. Ed. Colin Murray Turbayne. Indianapolis: Bobbs, 1970.

———. *A Treatise Concerning the Principles of Human Knowledge*. Ed. Kenneth Winkler. Indianapolis: Hackett, 1982.

———. *The Works of George Berkeley, Bishop of Cloyne*. Eds. A.A. Luce and T.E. Jessop. 9 vols. London: Nelson, 1948–57.

Flage, Daniel. *Berkeley's Doctrine of Notions: A Reconstruction Based on his Theory of Meaning*. London: Croom, 1987.

Foster, John, and Howard Robinson, eds. *Essays on Berkeley: A Tercentennial Celebration*. Oxford: Clarendon, 1985.

Moked, Gabriel. *Particles and Ideas: Bishop Berkeley's Corpuscularian Philosophy*. Oxford: Clarendon, 1988.

Winkler, Kenneth P. *Berkeley: An Interpretation*. New York: Oxford UP, 1989.

Betham, Mary Matilda
(1776–1852)

Mary Matilda Betham, a talented poet and portrait artist, published four books of poetry and a biographical dictionary of women. She was one of 14 children of Mary Damant and the Rev. William Betham, headmaster at Stonham Aspel, Suffolk, and author of *The Baronetage of England*. The family encouraged Betham to develop her literary and artistic abilities, and her close friend Lady Charlotte Bedingfield gave her constant support and advice.

Like many clergymen's daughters, Betham depended for her education on her father's library. Her first book, *Elegies* (1797), opens with the Druidic ballad "Arthur & Albina," and includes several short poems translated from Italian, which Betham studied in Cambridge in 1796 under the tutelage of Agostino Isola. This early work brought her accolades from Coleridge, who wrote *To Matilda Betham from a Stranger* (1802).

In 1804, after six years of research, Betham published the 774-page *Biographical Dictionary of the Celebrated Women of Every Age and Country*, a more concise reference work than Mary Hays's six-volume *Female Biography* (1803). Both writers intended their books for young women, but only Hays states a definite feminist aim. Among Betham's wide-ranging choice of subjects are Bowanny from East India, Cleopatra, Mrs. Godwin, the Arabian heroine Khaula, Mary Magdalene, and Madame Roland.

As a poet, Betham was a gifted metrist and excelled in psychological realism. Her strongest collection, *Poems* (1808), contains several convincing characterizations. In *The Daughter*, she describes not only a young wife mourning her dead father, but also the reaction of the husband. Her frequent use of a poem within a poem adds dramatic interest. In *Fragment*, for example, a pilgrim visits the home of a tyrannical chief and overhears the chief's abused wife sing to her child. The singsong effect of the triplets accentuates the wife's pathetic struggle for survival, and Betham skillfully and poignantly gives a voice to the victim of abuse.

Betham's book-length *The Lay of Marie* (1816), written in couplets, is an imaginative story about the medieval minstrel Marie de France, which illuminates the hardships and success of a woman who pursued a poetic vocation. Betham had found a poetic foremother, and she capitalized on recent interest in English editions of Marie de France's work. She added a scholarly appendix, as Southey advised, increasing the antiquarian value of the work.

Occasional pieces for friends dominate her final collection, *Vignettes: In Verse* (1818), which closes with a moving elegy for her brother Edward, who died in an East Indiaman shipwreck. Betham's poetry is carefully composed and written with Neoclassical decorum rather than with the sentimental excess of many of her contemporaries. Her chief forms are lyrics (often melancholic in tone), ballads, and historical narratives. In the 1820s, illness and financial constraints impeded her career, but by 1830 Betham again became active in London literary circles and regularly studied in the British Museum.

She continued painting, having previously exhibited at the Royal Academy and earlier made miniature portraits of the Coleridges and Southeys. A lifelong friend of Charles and Mary Lamb and George Dyer, she wrote bridal verses for Lamb's adopted daughter Emma Isola, who married Edward Moxon in 1833, and read regularly to Dyer from the onset of his blindness to his death in 1841. She was an energetic correspondent with her young niece and future biographer Matilda Barbara Betham-Edwards (1837–1919), and in 1848, when she was age 72, she wrote verses celebrating old age.

Deborah Kennedy

Works Consulted

Betham, Ernest, ed. *A House of Letters*. London: Jarrold, 1905.

Betham-Edwards, M. *Six Life Studies of Famous Women*. London: Griffith, 1880.

Burgess, Glyn S. *Marie de France: An Analytical Bibliography*. London: Grant, 1977.

Dictionary of National Biography, s.v. "Betham, Mary Matilda;" "Betham, William;" "Betham, Sir William."

Betty, William Henry West

(1791–1874)

As "the Young Roscius," William Henry West Betty enjoyed a brief but phenomenal success on the late Georgian stage. Before that he had spent his childhood in Ireland, where his mother taught him declamation after he showed early promise in the dramatic set pieces of the time; he also developed a remarkable memory for blank verse lines.

Betty first entered a theater at Belfast in 1801, when he saw Mrs. Siddons play Elvira. He then declared that he must be an actor or die. Two years later, at age 11, he triumphed in Aaron Hill's *Zara* in Belfast, went on to a succession of other roles (including Romeo) and then took Dublin by storm, playing his first Hamlet at the Crow Street theater. In 1804, he appeared in Glasgow and Edinburgh: in the latter city several critics claimed that he outshone Kemble, the then reigning monarch of tragedy. An engagement in Birmingham led him toward London, and in December 1804, when barely age 13, he created a furor at Covent Garden. Moving on to Drury Lane, he caused scenes of mass hysteria with Home's *Douglas* and other stock plays of the time. Pitt adjourned the House of Commons so that members could witness his Hamlet. In London and the provinces during 1805, Betty earned a fortune which was to keep him in comfort for the rest of his long life.

Betty's vogue passed quickly, and his last appearance as a boy actor was at Bath in 1808. In later years, he returned to the stage several times, but with only moderate success at best, and in 1824 he retired completely. He was an agreeable man, and modest, having no illusions about the shallowness of the mistaken cult of infant prodigies and ideas about the child as a channel for natural genius, which had carried him to what might now be called star status for a couple of years in his boyhood. (*See also* Theater.)

William Ruddick

Works Consulted

Booth, M.R., ed. *The Revels History of Drama in English. 1750–1880*. New York: Harper, 1975.

Clinton-Baddeley, V.C. *All Right on the Night*. London: Putnam, 1954.

Playfair, G. *The Prodigy*. London: Secker, 1967.

Bewick, Thomas

(1753–1828)

Preeminent among wood engravers and illustrators, Thomas Bewick worked most of his life in Newcastle upon Tyne and established a school of engraving there. Attracted by birds and beasts, Bewick was a naturalist from boyhood and through his own observations became acquainted with the character of domestic and wild animals. He drew from nature, often making engravings from his own watercolors.

His celebrity as both illustrator and engraver rests essentially on the detailed accuracy of two natural history books. The first, *A General History of Quadrupeds* (1790), introduced the most distinctive feature of his work—tiny scenes of rural life and miniatures of animals usually set in precisely drawn backgrounds suggestive of their habitats. These "little whimsies," or "tale-pieces," as he punningly called them, depict both the animals' and birds' temperaments as well as their physical appearances. In addition, his work is marked by energy, an unsentimental view of nature, a love of the small and exquisite, and a wry, sometimes scatological, humor. The two-volume *A History of British Birds* (*Land Birds* and *Water Birds*) was published in 1797 and 1804. In these books' vignettes, particularly in the backgrounds, his technical mastery and artistry reach their peak. Among his other important works are *The Select Fables* (1784) and *The Chillingham Bull* (1798).

Bewick was born at Cherryburn, Northumberland. Although lacking formal artistic training, in 1777, he entered into a partnership with Ralph Beilby (1744–1817), to whom he had been apprenticed at age 14. Beilby was a general engraver; Bewick took over the wood-engraving side of the business. His delicate cutting skills exploited wood's expressive possibilities and raised its use as an engraving medium from the level of a cheap, popular reproductive art to one that could compete with copper. Wood seemed appropriate for conveying his own affection for nature; by both designing and engraving on wood, his very handling of the medium expressed himself.

Bewick refined the white-line method, which involves working the end grain, as distinct from wood planed along the grain, with such metal engraver's tools as a graver or burin instead of knives. He adapted his technical skill to demonstrate a remarkable tonal range of textures and foliage. This was done not through cross hatching but through varying the width of parallel lines and by lowering parts of the block to receive less pressure and print grey (e.g., the breast of a bird). Bewick termed this distinctive quality "color"; this combination

of tone and texture, together with his fine sense of design and keen eye, has made him outstanding among English graphic artists.

Though with less artistic talent, a number of pupils and followers continued Bewick's white-line technique. Among these were his younger brother John Bewick, first an apprentice and then a member of the partnership with Beilby; his son Robert Eliot Bewick, also part of the firm; Robert Johnson, a draftsman and accomplished watercolorist; and Luke Clennell. For the rest of his life Bewick replaced old cuts and added tailpieces to *British Birds*. Audubon, the American bird artist, gives an account in *Ornithological Biography* (1831) of his working on one in 1827. The *Memoir*, begun in 1822 though not published until 34 years after his death, communicates Bewick's minute observations and sociable, down–to–earth character.

D.C. Woodcox

Works Consulted

Bain, Ian, ed. *Thomas Bewick: Vignettes*. London: Scholar, 1978.

Bewick, Thomas. *A Memoir of Thomas Bewick Written by Himself*. London: Lane, 1924.

Marsack, Robyn, ed. *Selected Work*. Manchester: Fyfield, 1989.

Stone, Reynolds. *Wood Engravings of Thomas Bewick*. London: Hart, 1953.

Weekley, Montague. *Thomas Bewick*. New York: Oxford UP, 1953.

Bible, The, and Biblical Criticism

Perhaps the greatest literary influence, besides Milton, on the writers and the writings of the Romantic period is the Bible. Wordsworth called the biblical writings "the grand store-house of the imagination" while Blake referred to the Scriptures as "the Great Code of Art."

Two forces operated in the Romantic period to elevate the Bible to such a place of veneration. First, by the early to mid-19th century, especially in England, the access of the lower and middle classes to novels and other popular writings created a new reading class, thus enabling "common readers," for the first time, to read and to interpret the Bible for themselves. In such a context, the Bible became a revolutionary and a political document, expressing in a kind of universal language the freedom of individuals in a divinely created natural order. Second, the consequence of the Romantic reaction against the language and the stylistic devices—derived largely from Greek epic and lyric poetry—of Neoclassical poetry was an emphasis on ordinary diction and natural style, both of which were infused, especially in the eyes of Wordsworth, Coleridge, and Blake, with the style and structure of biblical language.

In addition to the feeling among Romantic poets that the language of the Scriptures was universal and could be used to express the feelings of the New Jerusalem—a paradigmatic poetic design of human history.

Henry L. Carrington, Jr.

Blackwood's Edinburgh Magazine

Blackwood's Edinburgh Magazine ran from 1817 through 1967—the kind of long and prestigious life that makes a periodical an institution. But during the Romantic era, *Blackwood's* was known primarily for its free-swinging criticism, controversy, and satire; few then would have predicted such a long and respectable future for the magazine.

It was founded in 1817 by William Blackwood (1776–1834). He had apprenticed with printers and publishers in Edinburgh and London, and in 1804 set up his own bookselling business. In 1808, he began publishing; his first project was a bibliographic catalogue of the books in his shop, a catalogue so well done that it still is sometimes cited as a bibliographic standard. The catalogue caught the attention of the rising London publisher, Murray, and Murray made Blackwood his Edinburgh agent in 1811. The connection lasted for only eight years, but it greatly helped Blackwood establish himself in the highly competitive world of Scottish publishing. Since Murray was the publisher of the Tory *Quarterly Review*, his alliance with Blackwood set Blackwood up firmly in opposition to Constable, the great Edinburgh Whig publisher. Writers who could not abide Constable's politics began to gather around Blackwood's establishment. (*See also* Journalism.)

No doubt the presence and daily conversation with the best and brightest of Edinburgh's young conservative intellectuals gave Blackwood the idea that there was material here for a periodical—a periodical more current and more dynamic than the *Quarterly*, one that would provide a proper forum for the kinds of views he heard daily from his young visitors. He was also convinced that the tone of such a periodical need not be solemn or pedantic, as the *Quarterly*'s so often was. Finally, in April 1817, he brought out the first issue, then titled *The Edinburgh Monthly Magazine*.

Blackwood engaged James Pringle and Thomas Cleghorn as editors, but after the first issue he began to see that he had made a mistake. Pringle and Cleghorn, naturally enough, insisted on control of the magazine independent from the publisher, but they used their independence to produce a timid publication that made almost no impression on the reading public. Worse yet, in ensuing issues, they began to print articles with distinctly Whig overtones.

Blackwood became increasingly unhappy and shared his dissatisfaction with Wilson and Lockhart, two young men who began in 1817 to frequent his office. They in turn gave their opinions about how a magazine ought to be run. Blackwood fired Cleghorn and Pringle and turned the reins over to Wilson and Lockhart.

Their first issue—renamed *Blackwood's Edinburgh Magazine*—appeared in October 1817. It gave Blackwood all the dynamism he could have hoped for and then some. The chief piece in that issue was a scandalous satire called "Translation from an Ancient Chaldee Manuscript." James Hogg had concocted the idea, and he, Wilson, and Lockhart jointly wrote it. Purporting to be a recently discovered manuscript from biblical times, the piece satirized contemporary Edinburgh figures under only thinly veiled disguises; everyone from Constable and Scott to the young authors themselves figured in the plot. Many were outraged, some threatened lawsuits, but nearly everyone in Edinburgh read it.

The lead article in that first issue also caused a great stir. Titled "The Cockney School of Poetry," the article (unsigned but primarily written by Lockhart) heaped abuse on what it saw as immoral tendencies in some contemporary writers, chief among them Hunt and Keats. Hunt in particular was outraged, and began legal proceedings against the magazine several times over the next few years, though none ever came to trial. The article, abusive and unfair as it was, nonetheless immediately established *Blackwood's* as an entity to be reckoned with on the literary scene. Blackwood himself could not have been happier with his choice of Wilson and Lockhart. Those two, with Hogg, loosely shared editorial control of the new magazine, with

Blackwood himself having veto power (though he rarely exercised it).

The magazine was, then, a collective enterprise though it bore one man's name. It acquired the nickname "Maga," which was sometimes also used as a synonym for the group of authors and editors: to be admitted to Maga was like being a member of a select club. But not a small club, for Blackwood himself was indefatigable in seeking out new writers for his periodical. He was remarkably persuasive, managing to talk Coleridge into submitting a number of articles beginning in 1819, even though Coleridge had been vilified in *Blackwood's* a number of times. Blackwood also managed to maintain good relations with Wordsworth although the magazine had mauled his work on occasion, and Wordsworth contributed a number of sonnets to the magazine. Blackwood also encouraged the young De Quincey, and many of his finest essays first appeared in *Blackwood's*. The roster of writers who contributed to Maga, during the Romantic era and after, is long and distinguished.

One of the most important features in the magazine, and certainly one of the most popular, was a column entitled "Noctes Ambrosianae" (i.e., nights at Ambrose's tavern). Originally a collectively written piece, it soon evolved into Wilson's alone; his pen name for the column was Christopher North. The Noctes were set up as loose, rambling dialogues among the semifictional denizens at Ambrose's. One of the chief characters was the Ettrick Shepherd—based on Hogg, but soon taking on a life of its own, turning Hogg into a nearly mythical figure. (Neither Hogg or his wife always liked what Wilson was doing and frequently complained about it.) The column became one of Blackwood's most beloved features, and it was later reprinted in four volumes by Wilson's son.

The tone of the Noctes could vary dramatically, and so the column served as a kind of pressure release; as Maga became more established, the rough-and-tumble tone of its first issues became smoother; but off-the-cuff jests, attacks, and satires could always find a place in the Noctes. However, the main body of the magazine was soon devoted to more serious (and more conventional) criticism and essays. In 1822, Hogg, never fully a member of the inner circle of Maga even though the Ettrick Shepherd was virtually synonymous with it, submitted a rough satire, and Blackwood turned it down on the grounds of seriousness and sobriety, which it now celebrated. *Blackwood's* was well on its way to becoming a Scottish institution. Over the next century, it published many important writers, such as Galt, Landor, George Henry Lewes, Margaret Oliphant, George Eliot, Anthony Trollope, and Joseph Conrad (*Lord Jim* first appeared in *Blackwood's*). But its origins were in the rough world of Scottish reviewing during the Romantic era, and during those years Maga had its greatest historical importance.

Raymond N. Mackenzie

Works Consulted

Lochhead, Marion. *John Gibson Lockhart*. London: Murray, 1954.

Olipant, Mrs. [Margaret]. *Annals of a Publishing House: William Blackwood and His Sons, Their Magazine and Friends*. 3 vols. Edinburgh: Blackwood, 1897.

Blake, William

(1757–1827)

A self-styled poet-prophet for whom the Bible was "the Great Code of Art," William Blake was largely ignored until after his death; during his lifetime, he was known primarily as an engraver and painter. Blake never achieved more than moderate fame in these vocations: his personal eccentricity, political and theological radicalism, and refusal to exhaust his talent on popular commissions such as miniature painting kept his art relatively obscure. But obscurity could not suppress Blake's visionary genius. He wrote, and frequently illuminated, an assortment of poetic forms, from simple lyrics to a prophetic epic designed to rival Milton's *Paradise Lost*. Among his major poetic works are *The Book of Thel* (1789); *The Marriage of Heaven and Hell* (1790–93); *America, a Prophecy* (1793); *Europe, a Prophecy* (1794); *Songs of Innocence and Experience* (1789–94); *The Book of Urizen* (1794); *The Four Zoas* (1797–1805); *Milton* (1804–08); and *Jerusalem* (1804–20). Like the poetry of Wordsworth and Shelley, these works celebrate the power of the transforming imagination. But they finally frustrate a clear association with any literary period, shaping a myth that is uniquely Blake's.

Blake was one of seven children born to a London hosier and his wife, and though (at his own request) he was never formally educated, his parents did what they could to nurture his creativity, although James Blake, an Anglican (though perhaps a Dissenting one), held his son's visions in contempt, almost beating the boy on one occasion when he claimed to have seen angels in the treetops on Peckham Rye. But the father recognized William's artistic potential and sent him, at age 10, to Henry Pars's drawing school in the Strand. At age 14, Blake was apprenticed to James Basire, engraver to London's Society of Antiquaries. As part of his apprenticeship, Blake made drawings of the Gothic statuary in Westminster Abbey, developing a tenacious affection for Gothic form that weathered his growing disillusionment with orthodox Christianity.

When Blake left Basire in 1779 as a journeyman engraver, he enrolled briefly in the Royal Academy of Art, where he hoped to master the techniques of painting. He soon discovered that the Academy's emphasis on life drawing and admiration for the masters of chiaroscuro were at odds with his linear and stylized method of drawing. Although several of his history paintings were included in the Academy's 1780 exhibition, Blake abandoned his Aca-demy training and returned to engraving, taking commissions from friends, such as the sculptor Flaxman. In 1782, he married Catherine Boucher, the illiterate daughter of a Battersea market-gardener, and briefly shared the ownership of a printshop with his friend James Parker. By 1785, he had left the partnership and launched his career as an engraver in earnest.

His apprenticeship as a poet, however, had just begun: between 1783 and 1795, Blake experimented with a variety of verse forms, searching for a poetic medium that would sustain and nourish a dissident imagination. Initially he turned to pastoral, celebrating the visionary power of innocence to transform a world corrupted by hypocrisy and self-interest. (Such innocence was incarnated, for Blake, in his younger brother Robert, who died in 1787 but continued a visionary dialogue with Blake until his death.) As he began to appreciate better the problematic nature of human experience, Blake assumed the voice of a prophet, inspired to wrestle with the enigma of evil in works as disparate as *Songs of Experience* and the Lambeth prophecies. By 1795, he had discovered the prophetic epic, a form that would accommodate his apocalyptic vision in his longest and most formidable poems: *The Four Zoas*, *Milton*, and *Jerusalem*.

Blake's earliest poetic attempts, begun when he was only age 11, were published in 1783 as *Poetical Sketches*. Although the lyrics in this collection are the most conventional of Blake's works, they reflect his radical humanism. Four of the poems, for instance, personify the seasons of the year— a pastoral convention accordant with 18th-century canons of taste. But Blake's personifications are not abstract or didactic; they interact freely with the "piper," Blake's persona, as if to suggest that nature is humanized by poetic perception.

The French Revolution intensified Blake's radicalism and infused his art with the themes of liberty and enslavement; 1789 was one of his most prolific years as a poet. In that year, although it was never printed, Blake completed the text and illustrations of his first prophetic book *Tiriel*, whose title character anticipates Blake's most famous mythical oppressor, Urizen. He may also have begun his unengraved poem *The French Revolution*, which transformed the historical events in revolutionary Paris between 17 June and 15 July 1789 into a visionary apocalypse. (Blake's employer, the publisher Johnson, prepared a page-proof of the first book of *The French Revolution* in 1791, but either Blake or he withdrew the poem before it could be published, fearing, perhaps, reprisals from the English government.) Most significantly, Blake wrote and illuminated *Songs of Innocence*; composed several of the *Songs of Experience* he was to publish in conjunction with *Songs of Innocence* in 1794; and began to compose and etch plates for his first illuminated poetic narrative, *The Book of Thel*.

Although the *Songs of Innocence* appears to have been written for children, it avoids the naive dogmatism so common to 18th-century children's literature. The volume's title, in fact, belies the poetry's preoccupation with "Experience" as well as "Innocence." In Blake's evolving myth, these are two stages or "states" of life through which all must pass if they are to undergo inner apocalypse, or liberation, from the internal and external forces that blunt the imagination. Innocence without Experience eventually becomes a state of pure illusion, just as Experience, without vision, deteriorates into cynical despair. To remain fixed benightedly in either stage is to deny the fullness of one's humanity and is for Blake the greatest anathema.

The "Introduction" to *Songs of Innocence* suggests that Innocence and Experience should be engaged in a creative dialectic. The poem is an invocation to the narrator's unorthodox muse—a child who paradoxically weeps for joy. Like his counterpart in *The Lamb*, who is Christ-like without looking beyond himself for divinity, the child-muse demonstrates the vision later called "organized" innocence—a spontaneity and freshness of perception armed with a self-knowledge only Experience can teach. In two of the collection's most famous poems, *The Chimney Sweeper* and *Holy Thursday*, the limitations of "unorganized" Innocence become apparent in the protagonists' passive acceptance of physical and spiritual oppression. Blake celebrates the formidable visionary power of chimney sweeps and charity-school children, but he also implies that submission to the status quo (here, to Britain's rigid class system) limits the imagination's capacity to liberate the individual, or society as a whole, from dehumanization.

This theme becomes more pronounced in *Songs of Experience*. These lyrics were not engraved until 1794, but Blake had them bound with the *Songs of Innocence*, intending the two volumes to be read together. Written when the revolution in France was deteriorating into the Reign of Terror, many of the *Songs of Experience* depict a world stripped of illusion, yet unredeemed by a higher Innocence, a fallen world in which even children must confront and struggle with the darker aspects of life. In *The Chimney Sweeper* and *Holy Thursday* of this volume, the urban landscape is a wasteland where Blake's innocents, deprived of vision, succumb to hopelessness. And in *London*, the city is the nadir of Experience, its underclass made miserable by both an oppressive state power (abetted by the Church of England) and the "mind-forg'd manacles" that discourage victims of injustice from rebellion.

But Blake was no nihilist: several poems in *Songs of Experience* argue that oppression, though never justified, can be an agent in the recovery of Innocence. The poetic narrator of the volume's "Introduction" anticipates this theme by assuming the stance of a Bard, a figure who combines the skill of a poet with the apocalyptic fervor of a prophet. Blake's Bard asks his readers to look squarely at the nature of human Experience, abandoning fear for understanding and action. As if to illustrate this prophetic injunction, the narrator of *The Tyger* challenges conventional responses to the omnipotence of God, responses Blake felt were prompted by fear, self-degradation, and a blind commitment to religious dualism. And Lyca, the 7-year-old protagonist of *The Little Girl Lost* and *The Little Girl Found*, challenges parental authority, exercising self-reliance and transforming the desert wilderness in which she is lost (a biblical but also Blakean symbol of Experience) into an Edenic garden.

The first of Blake's mythical narratives to be illuminated places the states of Innocence and Experience in what some critics see as a Neoplatonic framework. Blake's Thel, who resembles Lyca in her untried Innocence, descends into the state of Experience, here defined as the cycle of birth, growth, dissolution, and death that characterizes the natural world. But instead of immersing herself in nature (and thereby embracing sexual and imaginative freedom), she retreats from it. In the dominant critical view, Thel's obstinacy, like the "Selfhood" that will later afflict his prophetic characters, is self-destructive, an insidious form of repression, but according to some recent feminist interpretations, her resistance is admirable.

In 1790, Blake's determination to be a prophet of imaginative liberation deepened. He and Catherine moved to the borough of Lambeth in London, where they lived until 1800. Although Blake's Lambeth years were among his happiest and most productive as an artist, they were also to inflame his social conscience. Near his home were three symbols of Britain's inflexible social hierarchy—a charity school, an asylum for female orphans, and the London residence of the Archbishop of Canterbury, Lambeth palace. Blake's experiences in Lambeth also challenged his already precarious faith in institutional religion. It was here that he severed his intellectual bond with Emanuel Swedenborg, a Swedish scientist and theologian whose theories regarding androgyny, mystical communion with the dead, and the natural equilibrium of contraries had convinced the Blakes to join the Church of the New Jerusalem in 1789. (*See also* Swedenborgianism.) When Blake learned that Swedenborg's *Divine Providence* argued the merits of predestination, his admiration turned to contempt. He began to see strong parallels between the political ideology of the English ruling class and all systematic theologies, from orthodox Christianity to Deism. The result was his most famous visionary satire, *The Marriage of Heaven and Hell*, composed between 1790 and 1793. (*See also* Satanism.)

Blake's *Marriage* is a miscellany of literary forms, from proverbs to parables, all intended to subvert their models. The "marriage" of the title reflects the common thread running through the satire, Blake's conviction that human experience should be a dynamic interplay of "Contraries," of harmony and discord, not a denial of ambivalence or a cautious progression toward a static ideal. On the basis of this conviction, Blake attenuates the terms "Good" and "Evil" and "Heaven" and "Hell," which in his estimation promote dualistic thinking and privilege those in positions of political or ecclesiastical power. For Blake, one man's good may be another man's evil; heaven and hell are states of mind which can be governed by creative genius, but are too often interpreted literally, as static symbols of reward and punishment. Blake prefers to celebrate the opposition of "Energy" and "Reason," or "Desire" and "Restraint," and roundly declares society's "Reprobates" to be of better character than the self-righteous "Elect," subverting Calvin's relentless classifications. In the course of the *Marriage*, Blake's prophetic persona convinces even Swedenborg's Angels, who reek of orthodoxy, to join "the Devil's party" (the "party" of Milton's Satan, a Blakean Reprobate) and embrace the complex life of the imagination—the highest form of religion. The various religious systems Blake had come to distrust are painted, in turn, as decayed forms of poetry.

By 1793, Blake was so thoroughly immersed in his prophetic role that he wrote and engraved *America: A Prophecy*, followed, in 1794, by *Europe: A Prophecy*. Like the Book of Daniel and the Book of Revelation, *America* and *Europe* use vision as a vehicle for spiritual truths. Blake extends the chronology of biblical history to accommodate contemporary events, but he is no millenarian. He portrays the American Revolution and the war between England

and France that erupted in 1793 as harbingers of apocalyptic change, in both political and spiritual contexts, not as literal manifestations of Armageddon.

The spirit of revolutionary energy in *America* is Orc, a mythical figure who resembles both Christ and Prometheus and is a composite symbol of the colonial patriots. Enlisting the aid of various revolutionary heroes—Washington, Franklin, and Paine among them—Orc hastens the downfall of "the Guardian Prince of Albion," George III, and "Albion's Angels," the British Redcoats. What follows transcends political allegory, however, and lays the groundwork for Blake's mature myth: Orc's struggle with Albion's Prince becomes a struggle with Urizen, the sometimes overzealous limiter of Energy who can corrupt the individual psyche as surely as he can the body politic. Accordingly, Orc's triumph inspires liberation on all fronts, political, religious, intellectual, emotional, and sexual, as Blake gradually redefines the nature of apocalypse.

In *Europe*, political allegory becomes even more peripheral to Blake's mythopoeic world: the war between Britain and France, which had such millenarian implications for many of Blake's contemporaries, is subsumed by the conflict between Los and Enitharmon, Orc's parents. Los is Blake's symbol of the creative imagination, the source of revolutionary energy; Enitharmon is his consort, or "Emanation," and as such represents the spiritual insight that shapes mere random musings into visionary perception. (*See also* Androgyny.) But at the beginning of *Europe* Enitharmon rebels, declaring her independence from Los—a husband as uxorious, it seems, as Milton's Adam. By thus giving dominion to the "Female Will," Enitharmon and Los fragment the human spirit and, ironically, initiate the cycle of human history, with its dull

round of ineffectual wars and revolutions. Again, Urizen steps forward as the embodiment of tyranny, and Orc assumes the role of savior, emerging from the vineyards of France to fill Los with apocalyptic energy. But the "strife of blood" to which Orc calls his father is apparently not a literal conflict, or not exclusively, at least—its primary battleground is the psyche.

America and *Europe* were followed, in 1794 and 1795, by *The First Book of Urizen*, *The Song of Los*, *The Book of Ahania*, and *The Book of Los*, all of which extend and enrich the myth that began taking shape in the first of Blake's Lambeth prophecies. In these prophetic poems, Blake concentrates on various psychological manifestations of the biblical Fall, which he depicts, in its essence, as psychic chaos. That chaos is precipitated by the divisive struggle between Los and Urizen, who demonstrate what happens to imaginative energy when it has no rational direction and to reason when it ceases to nurture creativity and faith. Like the Yahwistic god of the Old Testament (as Blake read it), the fallen Urizen creates "Thou shalt nots," distorting even the human body into a sensual prison. And Los, a cerebral blacksmith whose task is to hammer thought into creative form, mistakenly generates the fallen world of natural existence.

None of the minor prophecies fully resolves the conflict between Los and Urizen, a challenge Blake reserved for *Vala*, the epic psychodrama that would become *The Four Zoas*. Blake began *Vala* in 1797, but never finished it; by 1804, his energies were fully absorbed by *Milton* and *Jerusalem*. The poem is important, nevertheless, as a primer for Blake's completed epics, for it introduces almost every element of his mature myth.

The Four Zoas is the first of Blake's prophetic poems in which Albion, Blake's symbol of psychic wholeness, is given center stage. Not to be confused with "Albion's Prince" of *Europe*, the Albion of the later prophecies is descended from Adam Kadmon, the Universal Man of the Cabbala, and his loss of equanimity is as cataclysmic an event in Blake's psychomachia as is the fall of Adam and Eve in biblical history. As Blake's minor prophecies anticipate, Albion's weakness is his painful susceptibility to the destructive whims of his sons, Los, Urizen, Tharmas, and Luvah. These "Zoas" (a Greek term Blake gleaned from the first chapter of Ezekiel and the fourth chapter of Revelation) personify the most fundamental aspects of the human personality: imagination, reason, instinct, and sexuality (or desire); their fragile interdependency is crucial to Albion's well-being.

The nightmare universe of *The Four Zoas*, originally subtitled "A DREAM of Nine Nights," is one in which the fourfold unity of the Zoas has been dissolved. The resulting confusion affects even the poem's narrative line, which is a conundrum. There is, nevertheless, a rough structure to *The Four Zoas*: the first three Nights describe Albion's fall and subsequent slumber; the next three, the warfare among the Zoas and the horrors of the fallen psyche; and the last three, Albion's resurrection.

In *The Four Zoas*, Albion's troubles begin not with the struggle between Los and Urizen, but with a quarrel between Tharmas and his Emanation Enion, who subsequently fall into a state Blake calls "Generation" and give birth to Los and Enitharmon. A familiar pattern emerges here. Since Tharmas, in his unfallen state, is the instinctive, untested Innocence that obstructed Thel, his fall is synonymous with entering the state of Experience. He becomes, in other words, the archetypal adolescent, a living paradox for whom self-

division and a burgeoning of creative energy go hand in hand. Before Experience can yield wisdom, however, both Tharmas and Los—instinct and imagination—become subject to Urizen, the Lawgiver (obsessive rationalism), driving Albion into a death-like sleep on the Rock of Ages. Urizen subsequently subdues Luvah, harnessing the libido to an inflexible code of morality, and builds the "Mundane Shell," the purely phenomenological world which for Blake, as for Wordsworth, could obfuscate the human imagination. After a power struggle of epic proportions, in which Urizen himself is driven to suicide, Jesus intervenes to set limits to the destruction the Zoas have wrought, and the poem moves toward an apocalyptic harvest that reinforces one of Blake's most salient (and Miltonic) themes: redemption is the liberation of the imagination through the creative strife of contraries.

Three years after beginning *The Four Zoas*, the Blakes moved to a cottage in Felpham, a small seaside village on the eastern coast of England, where Blake cast his fortunes with a new patron, Hayley. A critic, playwright, and poet in his own right, Hayley fiercely supported the artists in his acquaintance (including the sculptor Flaxman and the painter George Romney), and he offered Blake a generous series of commissions, the majority of which reflected the conservative tastes of Hayley's aristocratic circle. Initially, Blake thrived under Hayley's patronage, but as his zeal to work on his own singular creations increased, his enthusiasm for portrait and miniature painting waned. In 1803, the Blakes returned to London—and to a life of genteel poverty, for between 1803 and 1818, Blake either lost or alienated many of his previous patrons and gained a firm reputation as an eccentric.

However disenchanted Blake may have

felt when he left Felpham, he had found there the inspiration for his "Sublime Allegory" *Milton*, the most accessible of his prophetic epics. Blake's reverence for Milton rivaled his veneration of Jesus and the biblical prophets; next to the Bible, Milton's poetry and prose were Blake's greatest sources of inspiration. But Blake felt that his predecessor's art had been sabotaged by an immoderate reliance on reason as the highest human faculty. *Milton* is Blake's attempt to purify Milton's vision; it is also a kind of *Bildungsroman* in which Blake describes his difficult journey toward prophetic maturity, adapting the plots of both *Paradise Lost* and *Paradise Regained* to the fall and resurrection of his own spirit. In fact, Blake injects himself—not his persona—into this mythic psychodrama, joining Milton in a self-redeeming struggle to restore unity among the divisive forces of the spirit.

In that struggle, Albion emerges as Blake's (and later Milton's) fragmented psyche. Again, Albion's sons, Los and Urizen, initiate the prophet's intellectual warfare, but their struggle is overshadowed by the dissonance among Los and Enitharmon's sons: Rintrah, Palamabron, and Satan. Rintrah, "Reprobate," symbolizes the just prophetic rage that inspired prophets like Isaiah and Jesus. The "Redeemed" Palamabron manifests the gentler, more vulnerable characteristics of a prophet such as Jeremiah. And Satan, the "Elect," epitomizes all forces (internal and external) responsible for imaginative repression. In an allegory that has biographical resonance in Blake's quarrel with Hayley, Satan gains control of the harrow, Blake's symbol of creative inspiration, from his brother Palamabron, driving Albion into a death-like sleep.

Ultimately, Milton takes on the burden of Albion's redemption: he acknowledges his own Satanic portion, which is revealed as Urizen, and is transfigured into a Blakean Christ. Blake then internalizes Milton's redeemed vision (his "Eternal Form") and unites with Los, confirming a new confidence in his own role as prophet and poet. Albion awakes; both Milton and Blake reunite with their Emanations (Blake on the garden path in front of his cottage at Felpham); and Blake, in preparation for his epic masterpiece, *Jerusalem*, poises Los and his plowshare before an apocalyptic landscape.

Jerusalem is a fitting sequel to *Milton*, for it is Blake's testimony to self-inspired prophecy and creative biblical exegesis: using many of the narrative patterns first introduced in *The Four Zoas*, Blake literally recasts the Book of Ezekiel and the Book of Revelation, drawing contemporary historical events (like the Napoleonic wars), into the familiar framework of his prophetic theodicy. The poem's title character is both the Bride of Christ and Albion's Emanation, a type of the imaginative Paradise within every visionary's reach; in a broader sense, she symbolizes Christian liberty.

Albion's fall into "Moral Virtue," the event that opens *Jerusalem*, is precipitated by his Urizenic denunciation of Jerusalem. With Albion's fall, Satan's rise to power (with Vala, or delusory Nature, as his consort) is recapitulated, and the ubiquitous Los, Blake's persona, again finds himself divided from his Spectre (his rational powers) and his Emanation (his inspiration). But with a vigor not seen in Blake's earlier prophecies, Los resists despair and sets himself the task of limiting Albion's Error and restoring his equanimity by building Golgonooza, the "City of Art," a type of St. John's New Jerusalem (without its transcendence). Initially, Albion, whose intellectual despotism rivals that of Blake's demonic trinity (Bacon, Newton, and Locke), descends into Ulro, a state of blind and destructive complacency. Los persists, however, in hammering out "eternal Forgiveness" and in turning the strife of Contraries toward progression. With the humanism so characteristic of Blake, Jesus, inspired by Los, appears and convinces Albion to undergo a "Last Judgement" of the spirit, casting off his "Selfhood" and rejoining Jerusalem in a paean to *inner* apocalypse.

Blake wrote *Jerusalem* over a period of 16 years; the tensions in the poem reflect, in part, the professional disappointment and humiliation he experienced after he returned to London in 1803. His professional misfortunes culminated in his exhibition of 16 tempera and watercolor drawings, including "The Canterbury Pilgrims," at his brother James's house on Broad Street in 1809. Few came to the exhibition, but among those who did was Robert Hunt of *The Examiner*, who ruthlessly attacked the exhibition and its catalog in his review. Failing to secure public recognition, Blake found his reputation as an eccentric enhanced, and between 1810 and 1818 his art was ignored by all but his most intimate patrons, such as Thomas Butts.

In 1818, however, Blake's fortunes changed. Although he was to produce no more poetic masterpieces, his artistic career was revitalized when he was introduced to two artists, Linnell and Linnell's former drawing master, John Varley, who became Blake's devotees. Linnell was also an enthusiastic patron, who commissioned some of Blake's finest designs, including the *Illustrations of the Book of Job* and a set of both the *Paradise Lost* and *Paradise Regained* watercolors. He also introduced Blake to Palmer, a young art student. Palmer and his friends George Richmond and Frederick Tatham became Blake's most fervent artistic disciples. Blake's final years were invigorated by the publication, in 1826, of his engraved *Illustrations of the Book of Job*, with their extraordinary marginal commentary, and by his absorption in a series of designs illustrating Dante's *Divine Comedy*. He died August 12, 1827. (*See also* Ancients and Visionary Landscape Painting.)

Patricia Elizabeth Davis

Works Consulted

Bentley, Gerald E. *Blake Records*. Oxford: Clarendon, 1969.

Bloom, Harold. *Blake's Apocalypse: A Study in Poetic Argument*. Ithaca: Cornell UP, 1963.

Curran, Stuart, and Joseph Anthony Wittreich, Jr., eds. *Blake's Sublime Allegory: Essays on The Four Zoas, Milton, and Jerusalem*. Madison: U of Wisconsin P, 1973.

Erdman, David. *Prophet Against Empire*. 1954. Rev. ed. Garden City: Anchor, 1969.

Frye, Northrop. *Fearful Symmetry: A Study of William Blake*. 3rd ed. Princeton: Princeton UP, 1969.

Gallant, Christine. *Blake and the Assimilation of Chaos*. Princeton: Princeton UP, 1978.

Gilchrist, Alexander. *Life of William Blake*. Cambridge: Macmillan, 1963.

Glen, Heather. *Vision and Disenchantment: Blake's Songs and Wordsworth's Lyrical Ballads*. Cambridge: Cambridge UP, 1983.

Howard, John. *Infernal Poetics: Poetic Structures in Blake's Lambeth Prophecies*. Rutherford, NJ: Fairleigh Dickinson UP, 1984.

Miller, Dan. *Critical Paths: Blake and the Argument of Method*. Durham: Duke UP, 1987.

Paley, Morton. *Energy and Imagination: A Study of the Development of Blake's Thought*. Oxford: Clarendon, 1970.

Wagenknecht, David. *Blake's Night: William Blake and the Idea of Pastoral*. Cambridge: Harvard UP, 1973.

Wilson, Mona. *The Life of William Blake*. 3rd ed. Ed. Geoffrey Keynes. London: Oxford UP, 1971.

Blake, William (as engraver)

Although William Blake is perhaps best known for his imaginative works in poetry and prose, he worked to support himself during his entire lifetime as an engraver. In addition to the engraved designs he produced to accompany his own works, Blake produced over 1,200 commercial illustrations, including 800 separate designs on copperplate. Despite the sheer volume of Blake's work as an engraver, his talents as a book illustrator have been less attended to due to the critical reputation of the authors of the texts he illustrated and the misguided assumption that Blake's commercial designs are mere visual accompaniments to some rather mundane texts.

This is particularly true of Blake's work in intaglio engraving composed in the early years of his career while still under the influence of his master, James Basire. The intaglio method limits Blake stylistically, as it does any engraver, in that it is a method more suited for reproducing, in exacting detail, a copy derived from an original illustration than for imaginatively rendering original compositions. It has been frequently noted by Blake scholars that many of his intaglio engravings, particularly his commercial work, lack the imaginative energy found in his "illuminated books," although Blake used the intaglio method throughout his career. Scholars suggest the existence of the two distinct and separate styles: his visionary style, which was reserved for his own imaginative texts and those of major canonical literary figures, and his commercial style, which reflected the tedious and unimaginative workings of the reproductive engraver. However, this arbitrary division of styles fails to account for the fact that the dots, lozenges, and cross-hatching typical of commercial intaglio engravings are apparent even in some of his most famous series of original designs in illuminated printing such as *America, a Prophecy* (1793), *Europe, a Prophecy* (1794), and the title page to *Milton* (1804). In addition, his 22 designs to the book of Job reveal his mastery of the intaglio technique in what remains today his most admired series of engravings. Had Blake been commissioned to engrave more of his many illustrations drawn from the Bible, from *Paradise Lost*, and to *The Grave*, his reputation as an engraver would perhaps be as great as his stature as a poet.

Despite Blake's rather limited success as a commercial illustrator, he received commissions to illustrate some extremely popular texts, including Wollstonecraft's *Original Stories from Real Life* (1791) and Edward Young's *Night Thoughts* (1797), though the *Night Thoughts* publisher ran out of money before the series could be completed. Blake's designs also appeared in various serial publications, such as *The Monthly Magazine* and *The Novelists' Magazine* during the years 1782 to 1797. A testimony to Blake's enduring obscurity as a commercial engraver is the fact that he reached his largest audience with the publication of his unsigned engravings in a commercial catalogue. In 1816 he was paid £16 for the 18 plates of 189 figures of pottery which were published in the Wedgwood catalogue. Blake's designs were included in this catalogue for the next 27 years until the last design was finally replaced in 1843, 16 years after his death. Financial success as an engraver also eluded Blake. In 1783, only four years after the completion of his apprenticeship to a trade he would practice for another 44 years, he received his most lucrative commission, the sum of £80 for *The Fall of Rosamund*.

Blake's training as an artist began at age 10, when he attended the drawing school of Henry Pars. Here he learned drawing by copying prints in drawing books and casts from the antique. On 4 August 1772, Blake was apprenticed for seven years to the famous antiquarian engraver, James Basire. From Basire he learned the intaglio engraving technique and developed an enthusiasm for the aesthetic qualities of medieval and Gothic art and architecture, in opposition to the popular rococo Gothic of artists such as Walpole. Some of Blake's earliest engravings reflecting medieval and Gothic interests were published (with Basire's signature) in Richard Gough's *Sepulchral Monuments in Great Britain* (1786) and *Vetusta Monumenta* (1789). In addition to attempting to restore the lost art of the Greeks, as he intended to do in his eight engravings for George Cumberland's *Thoughts on Outline* (designed 1794–95), Blake's early engravings reflect a profound interest in historical subjects. For example, *The Penance of Jane Shore* and *The Ordeal of Queen Emma* are both drawn from historical subjects and reflect a highly gothicized setting.

During his apprenticeship to Basire, Blake engraved a few designs from some prints he had collected. The only surviving engraving is derived from a print, probably by Beatrizet, from a figure in Michelangelo's *Crucifixion of St. Peter*, in the Pauline Chapel (1773). Blake reengraved this print, added a background of rocks and sea, and entitled the design *Joseph of Arimathea among the Rocks of Albion*.

During the 1780s, Blake began earning his living as a commercial engraver, and by 1785 he had designed as many as 33 commercial plates after the illustrations of Thomas Stodhard. It is from Stodhard that Blake borrowed the technique of portraying figures in dance-like postures, often in pastoral settings, clad in various combinations of costume and traditional dress. Some

of Blake's commercial engravings after Stodhard appear in Joseph Ritson's *A Select Collection of English Songs* (1783), *The Poetical Works of Geoffrey Chaucer* (1782), *The Protestant's Family Bible* (1780–81), and Thomas Commins's *An Elegy Set To Music* (1786).

Blake is best known for his designs in illuminated printing. Borrowing techniques derived from woodcuts, intaglio prints, and the popular illustrated books of his day, Blake developed a technique for engraving and printing his own designs to accompany his poetry. This method of relief etching, first employed by Blake some time after 1788, is essentially a reversal of the traditional intaglio engraving process. In intaglio engraving, the copper plate is completely covered with a ground, and then the lines representing the design are carved into the surface of the copper plate. In Blake's method of relief etching, he applied a ground only to the areas of the copper plate where the actual lines of the design would emerge from the surface of the plate. Text and design are painted on the plate using a solution impervious to acid. When the plate is then bitten in an acid solution, the area of the design to be inked is raised rather than recessed. Blake improved upon this process by 1793 and described his method in a memorandum found in his notebook (Rossetti manuscript). Blake's method for "woodcutting" on pewter or on copper, as he characterizes it, is different from more traditional methods in that he used a burin instead of a knife and often created a white-on-black, rather than black-on-white, design. Blake's first use of this technique appears to be in the designs for *America, a Prophecy*. In this series, the white line is used extensively to break up masses of black in each plate.

Blake's greatest achievements in illuminated printing are *Songs of Innocence* and

Songs of Experience, designed between 1789 and 1794. Drawing from sources and images from contemporary children's books, Blake's designs range from traditional illustrations of scenes drawn directly from the text to extremely complex visual-verbal relationships that have been the subject of scholarly commentary since the turn of the century.

From 1795 to 1804, Blake produced nothing more in illuminated printing. During this nine-year period he was involved in producing designs for Young's *Night Thoughts* and in writing *The Four Zoas*. It was not until *Milton*, composed between 1804 and 1808, that Blake etched his own designs and text in relief. Of the 42 pages of text in *Milton*, Blake left room on each plate for only small marginal designs of simple relief outline. The title page and three of the full-page illustrations are all executed in white line. To the imagery of the poem, Blake's designs add contraries by using graphic techniques to convey symbolic value. The text of the poem and the graphic structures of the plates themselves are of equal importance in understanding the iconographic significance of any of the individual plates.

It is in Blake's 22 engraved designs to the book of *Job* that he achieves his greatest success as an intaglio engraver. Each of the 22 plates consists of an engraved central design surrounded by a border containing a supplementary design, which is accompanied by text. The central focus of Blake's response to the book of *Job* is that the eternal drama of the Fall and Redemption is acted out in the mind of Job. The actual events of the narrative, the destruction of Job's crops and of his children, reflect a mental process that ultimately leads to Job's recognition of the falseness of his obedience to Jehovah. Of interest in these plates is that although they reflect Blake's mastery of the intaglio technique, he departs from the traditional methods of reproductive engraving by abandoning the practice of preliminary etching on the copper plate. Here, Blake worked directly on the plate itself without the aid of preliminary etching to guide the strokes of his burin. The first lines appear to be etched with a stipple burin, and afterward the short heavy lines were added that would have ordinarily been done by the preliminary etching process. It is in the *Job* engravings that the influence of Albrecht Dürer's closely cut lines and flick and stipple work is most evident. It is important to note that in the *Job* engravings Blake most completely achieves his goal of freeing himself from the bondage of reproductive engraving techniques and of restoring his craft to its original function of creative invention.

The engravings to the book of *Job* are the last series of designs Blake completed before his death in 1827. In the summer of 1824, Linnell had commissioned Blake to illustrate a series of designs to the works of Dante, but Blake was able to compose little more than 100 watercolors and to engrave seven plates to Dante's *Inferno*. Close examination of these plates suggests the extensive use of drypoint for preliminary etching, a technique that creates a much freer style than the effects of the stipple burin Blake employed in the *Job* designs. In Blake's engravings to the *Inferno*, the heavy lines and cross-hatching typical of reproductive engraving are, with few exceptions, virtually abandoned. Had Blake completed his designs to the works of Dante, they might well have rivaled the magnificence of his engravings to the book of *Job*.

Jeffrey D. Parker

Works Consulted

Bentley, G.E., Jr. *Blake Books*. Rev. ed. Oxford: Clarendon, 1977.

Bindman, David. *Blake as an Artist*. Oxford: Phaidon, 1977.

Binyon, Lawrence. *The Engraved Designs of William Blake*. New York: Da Capo, 1967.

Essick, Robert N. *William Blake: Printmaker*. Princeton: Princeton UP, 1980.

Keynes, Geoffrey, and Edwin Wolf, II. *William Blake's Illuminated Books: A Census*. New York: Grolier, 1953.

Bligh, William

(1754–1817)

Chiefly remembered for the mutiny on board his ship, the HMS *Bounty*, an event that inspired Byron's late narrative poem *The Island*, Bligh was a navigator of great skill and harsh temperament who eventually rose to the rank of vice admiral.

Having joined the Royal Navy in 1770, Bligh took part in the second and third Pacific voyages of Cook (1772–75 and 1776–80). It was during the earlier of these that breadfruit was discovered in Tahiti, then Otaheiti, in the Society Islands. In 1787, "Bread-fruit Bligh," as he became known, was dispatched in command of the *Bounty* with the task of taking the fruit from Tahiti to the West Indies for commercial replanting. Arriving in late October 1788, the ship's company spent five months on the island—since then, renowned for the beauty of its landscape and its people—gathering trees and engaging in seemingly unlimited sexual intercourse with the natives.

Opinions vary as to whether it was this experience that was responsible, but scarcely three weeks had elapsed on the westward trip to the Caribbean when, on April 28, some of the crew mutinied under the leadership of Fletcher Christian, the master's mate. Bligh was bound and cast adrift on a 23-foot open boat with 18 men supposedly loyal to him. Owing to his remarkable expertise and courage, Bligh succeeded in navigating the launch some 3,600 miles to the Indonesian island of Timor, where he obtained passage on a schooner in which he and 12 survivors reached England in March 1790.

The *Bounty* returned to Tahiti, where 16 of her crew chose to stay, and then proceeded under Christian (now with six Tahitian men and 12 women) eastward to Pitcairn Island, where a settlement was founded. Composing *The Island* in 1823, however, Byron appears to have been fairly unfamiliar with the post-mutiny progress of the *Bounty*, despite the publication of certain reports; rather, he draws chiefly on Bligh's *Narrative of the Mutiny* (1790) for the first canto and upon William Mariner's *Account of the Natives of the Tonga Islands* (1817) and his own imagination for the remaining three cantos. Bligh's relation of events to the British government saw the dispatch of the *Pandora* to fetch the mutineers back for trial and that frigate's arrival at Tahiti in March 1791, the precedent for the close of Byron's tale.

Bligh, meanwhile, resumed his tree-ferrying mission and later distinguished himself in action at Camperdown (1797) and under Nelson at Copenhagen (1801). In 1805, he was appointed governor of New South Wales. In that post his dictatorial manner brought about another mutiny; this time he was imprisoned for two years by Major George Johnston, who was eventually dismissed in disgrace. On his release, Bligh returned to England, and there received promotion to rear admiral (1811) and vice admiral (1814). (*See also* Orientalism/Exoticism.)

Andrew Paxman

Works Consulted
Blackstone, Bernard. *The Lost Travellers*. London: Longmans, 1962.

Bligh, William. *An Account of the Mutiny on H.M.S. Bounty.* Ed. Robert Bowman. 1981. Gloucester: Sutton, 1989.

Kennedy, Gavin. *Bligh.* London: Duckworth, 1978.

— — —. *Captain Bligh: The Man and his Mutinies.* London: Duckworth, 1989.

Bonington, Richard Parkes
(1802–28)

A native of Nottingham, watercolorist, lithographer, and painter, Richard Parkes Bonington moved to Calais with his family as an adolescent. After having briefly studied watercolor there with another Englishman, at age 17, he moved to Paris and for two years studied painting with Antoine-Jean Gros, a leading figure in the development of Romanticism in French art. While a student of Gros's, Bonington became acquainted with the great French Romantic artist Eugene Delacroix, who admired and was influenced by Bonington's light style.

Bonington achieved some note when he began exhibiting his bright watercolors in Paris at age 21, but he established a solid reputation with his landscapes. At the famous Salon of 1824, which featured both his works and those of Constable, he won a gold medal.

In 1825, Bonington and Delacroix encountered each other again in England where they studied Constable's and Turner's works and where Bonington was influenced by the English taste for paintings that depicted historical scenes or exotic scenes from distant travels. The British fascination with foreign scenes was created by the paintings of an artist who had accompanied Captain Cook on one of his voyages. (*See also* Orientalism/Exoticism.) Later, when the two shared working space in Paris, Delacroix studied Bonington's technique and wrote admiringly of it.

Lithography was still a young technique in Bonington's time, and it was one he picked up eagerly. He produced lithographs to illustrate Goethe's *Faust*, as well as works by Scott and Byron. Byron's Gothic imagination excited Bonington's artistic sensibilities, and he produced excellent illustrations for the writer's work.

Later, Bonington lived and studied in Venice, where his historical pictures were influenced by the prevailing school. He produced some of his finest works there, but he also overtaxed himself, his health suffered, and he contracted consumption. Returning to England, he died shortly before his 26th birthday.

Although his life was short, he was remarkably influential both in England and in France. He is responsible for evolving new technical feats in art, one being the *pochade*, a quickly produced oil sketch capturing a scene or a fleeting moment, which he, Constable, and Turner established.

Linda Jordan Tucker

Works Consulted

Chilvers, Ian, ed. *The Concise Oxford Dictionary of Art and Artists.* New York: Oxford UP, 1990.

Holt, Elizabeth Gilmore, ed. *From the Classicists to the Impressionists: Art and Architecture in the Nineteenth Century.* Vol. 3 of *A Documentary History of Art.* Garden City, NY: Doubleday, 1966.

Murray, Peter and Linda. *A Dictionary of Art and Artists.* Baltimore: Penguin, 1965.

Vaughan, William. *Romantic Art.* New York: Thames, 1985.

Bowles, William Lisle
(1762–1850)

The Rev. William Lisle Bowles, a prolific poet, published *The Battle of the Nile* (1799), *The Sea of Discovery* (1805), *The Missionary* (1822), *The Grave of the Last Saxon* (1823), and *St. John in Patmos* (1832), among others. His fame, however, rests on his *Sonnets* (1789), a collection admired by Southey, Wordsworth, and especially Coleridge. His life was marked by esthetic controversy. Editing an edition of Alexander Pope, his comments on the limits of Pope's genius provoked a debate with Byron and others on the merits of Pope and the nature of genius and the sublime. In both his poetry and aesthetic writings, Bowles advocated a natural poetry, taking its subject from nature and expressing itself in a simple and direct diction and syntax. Anticipating the experiments in the *Lyrical Ballads*, he stands at a transition between Neoclassicism and Romanticism.

Born at Kings Sutton, Northamptonshire, the son and grandson of clergymen, Bowles received his early education at Winchester as a pupil of Joseph Warton, the poet and author of *Essay on the Genius and Writings of Pope* (1756). Bowles entered Trinity College, Oxford, in 1781, completing his degree in 1792.

Disappointed in love, he toured northern England, Scotland, and parts of the Continent for consolation. Always interested in poetry related to the picturesque, his experiences became the basis of a cycle of sonnets published in 1789 as *Fourteen Sonnets written chiefly on Picturesque Spots during a Journey*. The work proved very successful, going through eight editions by 1805. Bowles's sonnets were marked by a subdued melancholy and sentiment in the spirit of William Cowper, Oliver Goldsmith, and Warton. His fluency with the form and the simplicity of his language contributed to a revival of interest in the sonnet and were influential on Coleridge and Wordsworth.

He married in 1797, and in 1804 became vicar of Bremhill, Wiltshire, his chief residence for the rest of his life. Near Landsdowne Mansion, and not far from Sloperton Grange, the retreat of the poet Moore, Bowles enjoyed a cultured society. Moore's *Journals* offer a series of portraits of Bowles as a congenial if somewhat eccentric poet and parson. In 1818, Bowles became chaplain to the Prince Regent, and later he became a canon of Salisbury.

In 1806, Bowles published a 10-volume edition of the works of Pope. In the preface, he questioned the merits attributed to Pope's genius. This brought a reaction from Campbell, leading to a dispute that raged for years. Bowles responded in *The Invariable Principles of Poetry* (1819), which was followed by an exchange of letters and pamphlets with Byron and William Roscoe. Bowles asserted that imagery drawn from nature was more sublime than that drawn from art, that nature poetry was therefore inherently greater than poetry of "manners," based on artificial objects. Byron responded that by association some artificial objects may produce more powerful effects than natural ones.

Bowles continued to publish poetry throughout his life, though none received the attention or fame of *Sonnets*. He died in 1850, and was buried in Salisbury Cathedral, having outlived most of his admirers.

Thomas L. Cooksey

Works Consulted

Fairbanks, A. Harris. "'Dear Native Brook': Coleridge, Bowles, and Thomas Warton, the Younger." *The Wordsworth Circle*, 6 (1975): 313–15.

Fayen, George S., Jr. "The Pencil and the Harp of William Lisle Bowles." *Modern Language Quarterly* 21 (1960): 301–14.

Gilfillan, George, ed. *The Poetical Works of William Lisle Bowles with Memoirs, Critical Dissertation, and Explanatory Notes*. 2 vols. Edinburgh: Nimo, 1868.

Greever, Garland, ed. *A Wiltshire Parson and His Friends: The Correspondence of William Bowles*. Boston: Houghton, 1926.

Van Rennes, Jacob Johan. *Bowles, Byron and the Pope-Controversy*. New York: Haskell, 1966.

Bray, Anna Elizabeth
(1790–1883)

Anna Elizabeth Bray made her literary reputation as a novelist. She was born in 1790 to John and Ann (Arrow) Kempe and married Charles Alfred Stothard in 1818. Stothard, who devoted his life illustrating the historical monuments of Great Britain, died in 1822 from a fall while working on an illustration in Beer Ferrers church. His work, "The Monumental Effigies of Great Britain," was completed by his widow and her brother Alfred John Kempe and published in 1832. Ann Stothard published his memoir the year following his death.

She began novel writing during her marriage to the Rev. Edward Atkyns Bray, vicar of Tavistock. Between 1826 and 1874, she published at least 12 novels, but was best known for her historical romances of the most prominent families in the counties of Devon and Cornwall. Her popularity can be measured by Longmans's issuance in 1845 to 1846 of a 10-volume set of her writings. In 1884, her works were reprinted by Chapman and Hall. Other works dealt with foreign travel, such as *The Talba, or the Moor of Portugal*, a work that began her acquaintance with Southey. One of her best-known and most entertaining works is *The Borders of the Tamar and the Tavy*, which was published in 1836 in three volumes. Written as a collection of letters to Southey, *The Borders* describes the superstitions and legends associated with the city of Tavistock. After being reviewed by Southey in the *Quarterly Review*, the collection was reissued in 1838, and a new edition in two volumes was published in 1879.

Bray's *Autobiography* details her observations of Southey, taken from his correspondence and visits to the Bray home; in addition, it contains letters from Southey critiquing her works. Together Bray and Southey encouraged the publication of fables and verses by the natural poet, Mary Colling. Other prominent works by Bray include *A Peep at the Pixies, or Legends of the West* (1854), a collection for young people of stories on the legends of Dartmoor and North Cornwall. In 1870, she fictionalized in French history with publication of *The Good St. Louis and His Times, The Revolt of the Protestants of the Cevennes*, and *Joan of Arc*.

In addition to fiction writing, Bray edited her second husband's poems and sermons following his death in 1857. She had been accused in 1846 of having stolen a piece of tapestry while visiting in Bayeux, France, but she was subsequently cleared of the charges and her reputation restored. She died in London in 1883. Her nephew, John A Kempe, published her autobiography in 1884.

Louise Flavin

Works Consulted
Bray, Anna Eliza. *Autobiography of Anna Eliza Bray*. Ed. John A. Kempe. London: Chapman, 1884.

Brothers, Richard
(1757–1824)

Richard Brothers, religious enthusiast and fanatic, was born on December 25, 1757, in Placentia, Newfoundland, the son of a gunner. Although his brothers and sister remained in Newfoundland, Brothers went to England as a youth. Following some education at Woolwich, he entered the Royal Navy as a midshipman at age 14. Between 1771 and 1783 (when he was discharged at half-pay), he served primarily in the West Indies, finally earning the rank of lieutenant. After his discharge, he traveled in France, Spain, and Italy, before marrying Elizabeth Hassall in 1786. The relationship appears to have been doomed from the church door. One account reports that Brothers left his wife immediately after the ceremony but was shocked to find her the mother of children when he returned a few years later. By September 1787, Brothers was in London, living on a vegetarian diet and worshiping in nonconformist chapels.

For the rest of his life, Brothers placed himself in conflict with governmental officials. Objecting to the oath that was required as a qualification for receiving his half-pay, he addressed a letter (to the Admiralty) which appeared in the *Public Adventurer*. Brothers's attack on the word "voluntarily" in a compulsory oath led Pitt to change the form, but Brothers was not exempted, as he had requested, from taking the oath. Without financial support, Brothers lived briefly in the open country and then took lodgings for which he could not pay. Testifying before the board of governors for the poor, Brothers asserted that he had resigned his commission because a military life was incompatible with Christianity. Although he was receiving shelter in the workhouse, Brothers left this arrangement in early 1792, convinced that God was calling him to a special work.

On May 12, 1792, he wrote to the King, the ministry, and the Speaker, claiming that God had commanded him to inform the House of Commons that the time had come for the fulfillment of Chapter Seven of the book of Daniel. This prophecy was followed by a series of predictions, some of which came to pass (e.g., the violent deaths of the king of Sweden and Louis XVI), some of which did not (e.g., his prediction that a devastating earthquake would level London). After more difficulties with the government and continuous financial problems, Brothers resolved to "leave England forever; with a firm resolution also never

to have anything to do with prophesying." Unable to follow through on this resolution, by 1793, he was describing himself as "nephew of the Almighty, and prince of the Hebrews, appointed to lead them to the land of Canaan." One of his followers, Nathaniel Brassey Halhead, M.P. for Lymington and an Orientalist, explained later that Brothers was descended from one of Christ's siblings.

By the end of 1784, Brothers began to publish his interpretations of prophecy, his first book being *A Revealed Knowledge of the Prophecies and Times* (1794). Central to his prophecies was the problem of the Diaspora. According to Brothers, the Jews of the dispersion were hidden among the nations of Europe. In fact, some believers in the Anglo-Israel theory of the Diaspora regard Brothers as the first writer championing their cause. Believing that he was a descendant of King David, that he was to be revealed as prince of the Hebrews and ruler of the world on November 19, 1795, and that the rebuilding of Jerusalem was to begin in 1798, he prophesied the death of the King and the end of the monarchy. On March 2, 1795, he was arrested for treason and confined as a criminal lunatic.

In May 1795, he was moved to a private asylum where he wrote pamphlets that gained him many believers, including William Sharp, the engraver. When November 1795 passed without his being "revealed" as prince of the Hebrews and ruler of the world (as he had predicted), popular enthusiasm for his cause dissipated. Brothers continued to publish pamphlets at intervals. Through the efforts of his most faithful disciple, John Finlayson, Brothers was released in 1806 but not before he fell in love with a fellow inmate, Frances Cott. Shortly after her release, it was revealed to Brothers that she was to be his queen, but she married someone else. From 1815 until his death in 1824, Brothers lived in the home of Finlayson, occupying himself with astronomical dreams. He died in 1824.

In addition to his *A Revealed Knowledge of the Prophecies and Times*, Brothers published a series of pamphlets and letters concerning his views on a variety of topics. His topics included the doctrine of the Trinity, etymology, Cott's descent from King David, the New Jerusalem, the palace of Solomon, and an account of the Saxon invasion of England, which repeats his assertion that the descendants of the Ten Tribes of Israel migrated to England.

James E. Barcus

Works Consulted

Allibone, S. Austin, ed. *A Critical Dictionary of English Literature and British and American Authors*. Philadelphia: Lippincott, 1898.

A Biographical Dictionary of the Living Authors of Great Britain and Ireland. London: Colburn, 1816.

Brougham, Henry

(1778–1868)

Born in Edinburgh and proficient in mathematics and science, Henry Brougham was a reviewer and journalist before settling in England and becoming a controversial Whig reformer in Parliament and then Lord Chancellor. Not only was he ambitious, he was well-educated and well-read, and he contributed substantially to society, politics, law, and education, being influenced by Bentham, Malthus, and Owen. Scholars have found over 50,000 papers that he wrote, attesting to his wide-ranging knowledge and his prodigious, often manic energy.

Although he later claimed descent from venerable English aristocrats, Brougham's family line did not become ennobled until he was elevated to the peerage. Nonetheless, his family had enough resources to provide a sound education for him. He attended the scientifically based and renowned university in Edinburgh, where he wrote his first scientific papers and studied for the bar. And he maintained his interest in science until his death. At the same time, he developed his debating expertise, which became a keystone of his political career. Despite his legal training, he only briefly practiced law before helping to launch the *Edinburgh Review* in 1802, for which he remained an indefatigable writer and reviewer for decades. (So closely associated with the *Edinburgh Review* was he, in fact, that its blatant partisanship toward him was frequently criticized by other journals.) Brougham also became a proponent of the antislavery movement, a cause to which he would continue to devote much effort.

Three years later, Brougham settled in London. He soon became friendly with Lord Holland, Wilberforce, and the Whigs and reform in general. He read English law and achieved prominence through various public activities. Lord Holland and others secured a seat in Parliament for him in 1810. From this position he championed many liberal causes, including mercantile policy, antislavery, popular and technical education, freedom of the press, and franchise and common-law reform. (*See also* Parliament.)

Brougham was the epitome of liberalism. When Keats visited the Lake District, he mourned Wordsworth's support of the Tory Lowther candidacy against Brougham, who sought a seat there. In speaking ardently for his causes, Brougham developed a reputation for theatrical oratory.

Brougham became embroiled in the coronation negotiations of the feuding Prince Regent and his wife, Princess Caroline, at times advising her and at times conspicuously but fruitlessly mediating; some historians have judged that the only person who may have benefited from these efforts was Brougham. He was Caroline's advocate at her notorious trial for adultery, a charge brought when the King, himself an adulterer, tried to discard her. Caroline was very popular with the English people, who considered her most ill-used by the Hanovers, so that her trial was very much a cause *célèbre*, and the government was forced to drop its charges. (*See also* Royal Family.)

In 1821, Brougham married Mary Ann Eden Spalding. They had two daughters; one died in infancy, the other died at age 18. The deaths of his children caused Brougham great sorrow.

As a result of his political involvements, when the Whigs came to power, Brougham was named Lord Chancellor in 1830 (for which he became a peer), dedicating himself to legal reform. Peacock wrote a satire on the occasion, "The Fate of a Broom," anticipating that this elevation would effectively neutralize the clean-sweeping reformer. Nonetheless, Brougham continued to promote many reforms. He was instrumental in the founding of London University. And, he became famous, as well, for driving around London in a small, specially made carriage that became the model for the vehicles of Rolls Royce named for him.

Once again, as Lord Chancellor, Brougham found himself enmeshed in controversy as a result of an inflammatory speech. Although his sentiments were liberal, by attempting to support the claims of the middle class against the "mob" of the poor, he was seen as an emblem of aristocratic disdain. Nonetheless, the middle classes were his true constituency for whom his many efforts were directed.

Brougham lost his post in 1835, follow-ing political differences with powerful interests, but he remained active through the early years of Victoria's rule. He spent his remaining years writing, speaking, and traveling. He died in his chateau in Cannes in 1868.

Laura Dabundo

Works Consulted

Briggs, Asa. *The Making of Modern England, 1783–1867: The Age of Improvement.* 1959. New York: Harper, 1965.

Crowther, J.G. *Statesmen of Science.* Chester Springs, PA: Dufour, 1966.

Dictionary of National Biography. s.v. "Brougham, Henry."

Himmelfarb, Gertrude. *The Idea of Poverty: England in the Early Industrial Age.* 1983. New York: Vintage, 1985.

Trevelyan, George Macaulay. *British History in the 19th Century and After. 1782–1919.* 1922. New York: Harper, 1966.

Brummell, George Bryan "Beau"
(1778–1840)

The notorious dandy Beau Brummell was born in 1778 and christened George Bryan Brummell. He was the second son and third child of William and Ann Richardson Brummell of Westminster. William Brummell worked diligently at his clerkship in the Treasury and established a comfortable life for his family, whom he moved to Berkshire when the future Beau was age 4. In 1786, when Brummell was 8 and his brother, William, was 9, the two boys entered Eton. Before he left Eton in 1793, George Bryan had become known as "Buck" Brummell and had achieved a reputation for the splendor of his dress.

Among Brummell's father's fashionable friends were Charles James Fox, former Lord of the Admiralty, and Richard Brinsley Sheridan, the playwright. The young Brummell amused these two men of the world sufficiently that they presented him to the Prince of Wales, the future George IV, and the Prince obligingly gazetted Brummell to the Tenth Hussars in May 1794, the year Brummell's father died. In the same month, Buck entered Oriel College, Oxford, but he quit the school six months later.

Brummell stayed with the Hussars until 1798, a tenure that tided him over until he came into his inheritance of £30,000 in 1799. With this advantage in life, the 21-year-old Brummell took quarters on Chesterfield Street, rapidly established himself as something of the Prince's fool, and became well known as "Beau" Brummell for his fashions and affectations. Brummell cultivated women of high rank—he was especially close to Georgiana, Duchess of Chesterfield—and spent a great deal of time and money at fashionable clubs like Watier's. He was profligate in his spending and decisive in his cuts and snubs. He was friendly with Moore and Byron, but sneered at Madame de Stael and treated Monk Lewis with contempt. Brummell's closest companions in the club world were Lord Alvanley, Sir Henry Mildmay, and Henry Pierrepont; Byron referred to these four and their followers as the "Dandy Club."

But despite his intimacy with the Prince Regent, Brummell presumed too much and found himself cut off from royal patronage. His error lay in ridiculing too openly one of the Regent's most favored mistresses, Maria Fitzherbert. One of Brummell's jests was inspired by the hall porter at Carlton House, known as Big Ben for his corpulence. Aware of the Regent's sensitivity to this own fatness and to Mrs. Fitzherbert's surpassing stoutness, Brummell named them "Ben and Benina." This was a good but costly joke, and by 1813 Brummell and his Prince were completely estranged.

By 1814, Brummell's wasteful habits had impoverished him, and he soon was in such desperate straits with his creditors that he was forced to sneak out of the country on May 16, 1816. Safely across the Channel, Brummell put up at Calais in quarters owned by a bookseller, M. Leleux, and ingratiated himself with M. Jacques Leveux, a banker. The inadequacy of these expediencies eventually forced Brummell to wangle a consulship at Caen in 1830, while leaving behind debts of 24,000 francs in Calais. This sinecure lasted but two years, and the last eight years of Brummell's life witnessed his painful decline into bad health and constant torment from creditors. He spent several months of 1835 in debtor's prison in Caen, a misery finally relieved by the kindness of old friends. A series of small paralytic strokes debilitated him, and by the late 1830s he was sunk in squalor and decrepitude of both mind and body. In his last years, he hosted mock parties at which he would welcome his long-dead Duchess of Devonshire and others to his whist table. By 1839, he was incontinent and incapable of taking care of himself. In May of that year he was admitted to Bon Sauveur, an asylum run by 75 nuns of the Sisters of Charity in the countryside near Caen. In this comfortable setting, well attended, Brummell died in 1840. He was buried in the Protestant Cemetery in Caen, sped on his way in a ceremony largely unattended. (*See also* D'Orsay, Count Alfred.)

Frank Day

Works Consulted

Connely, Willard. *The Reign of Beau Brummell.* New York: Greystone, 1940.

Franzero, Charles Marie. *The Life and Times of Beau Brummell.* New York: Day, 1958.

Moers, Ellen. *The Dandy, Brummell to Beerbohm.* New York: Viking, 1960.

Tenenbaum, Samuel. *The Incredible Beau Brummell.* South Brunswick, NJ: Barnes, 1967.

Brunton, Mary

(1778–1818)

Mary Brunton, the author of three novels, was a contemporary of and an influence on Austen, especially evident in Austen's *Emma* (1815).

Popular in her lifetime, although virtually ignored since, Brunton has been rediscovered as an important contributor to the development of the 19th-century British novel. Her novels, each more accomplished than the previous, are *Self Control* (1810), *Discipline* (1815), and *Emmeline* (1819). Brunton proposed "to delight and to teach," and a moral didacticism, earnestly and charmingly pursued, infuses each novel. The charges of improbability leveled against her stories probably troubled Brunton but little; the elevating element in her art was her primary concern, and her novels are gracefully written.

During the time of Brunton's career, novel reading, not to mention writing, was considered frivolous or even immoral. The piety exhibited in her novels enabled her to practice her art without condemnation from the critics. The salient features of her novels are illustrated in *Discipline*, in which the heroine, Ellen, is led through a series of incidents beginning with a "fortunate fall" and ending with her salvation through the attainment of discipline. Lest the reader miss the point of Ellen's sometimes glamorous and selfish pursuits, Brunton ends most chapters with a sermonette admonishing the "dear reader" to search her soul for any hint of Ellen's weaknesses. Ellen's extreme trials after the loss of her family and fortune prompt the penance necessary to justify her restoration to love and riches in the end. *Discipline* is a delightful moral fairy tale.

Brunton led a life of piety and rectitude and applied herself diligently to achieving the discipline promoted in her novels. Her craft improved with each effort, and her early death at age 40 while giving birth to her first child seems a compounded tragedy.

Len McCall

Works Consulted

Spender, Dale. "Mary Brunton: premature death and a rich bequest." *Mothers of the Novel*. New York: Pandora, 1986: 325–38.

Weldon, Fay. Introduction. *Discipline*. By Mary Brunton. 1986.

Burke, Edmund

(1729–97)

A politician, philosopher, and man of letters, Edmund Burke embodied many apparent contradictions. Burke was born in Dublin, Ireland, to an Irish Protestant father and a Roman Catholic mother, educated at a Quaker school; later at Trinity College, Dublin; and then at the Middle Temple, London. Burke advocated the rights of Irish Catholics, American colonists, and the native inhabitants of British India. At the same time, he was a vigorous opponent of the French Revolution, appealing to the authority of tradition and the British Constitution. An opponent of the power of the King, Burke was the intellectual father of British conservatism.

While Burke was trained in the law, he was never called to the bar, preferring a literary career that he initiated with the publication of his first books, *A Vindication of Natural Society* (1756) and *A Philosophical Enquiry into the Origins of our Ideas of the Sublime and the Beautiful* (1757). (*See also* Picturesque, Sublime.) The former was a parody of the political theorizing of the philosopher Bolingbroke and reveals

Burke's lifelong antipathy to rational systems based on empty abstractions. The latter was an attempt to account for the aesthetic categories of the sublime and the beautiful in terms of an association of ideas with the sensations of pain and pleasure. What one associates with the sublime, Burke argued, has a mental link with pain, while what one recognizes as beautiful has a link with pleasure. Burke's treatment was widely read and deeply admired by thinkers as diverse as Samuel Johnson, Gotthold Ephraim Lessing, and Immanuel Kant. In 1758, Burke also became the editor of *The Annual Register*, holding this position for 32 years. A man of deep learning, diverse interests, and incisive wit, Burke earned the respect of Johnson, becoming one of the founding members of "The Club" in 1764.

In 1765, Burke entered politics as the secretary of the Marquis of Rockingham, who brought him into parliament, beginning a governmental career that lasted until 1794. Burke soon became a leading member of the "constitutionalist" opposition group, known as the Rockingham Whigs, who opposed the encroachment of royal prerogative in George III's so-called personal government and upheld the authority of the British Constitution that had emerged from the Glorious Revolution of 1688. In this capacity, Burke advocated the rights of both Irish Catholics and the American colonists. In the *Speech on American Taxation* (1774) and *On Conciliation with the Colonies* (1775), he contended that the King had usurped the traditional rights and liberties of Englishmen. (*See also* Fox, James Charles.)

Burke was also concerned with the problem of British India. The collapse of the Moghul empire had placed the rule of India into the hands of the East India Company. In his *Speech on Mr. Fox's East India Bill* (1784) and *Speech on the Nabob of Arcot's Debts* (1785), Burke argued that the East India Company exploited the natives and that the British government should take control. The matter reached a crisis over the apparent financial improprieties of Warren Hastings, the Governor General of the Bengal. Burke led the attack, composing the *Articles Against Warren Hastings* (1786) and conducting the impeachment trial. Hastings was eventually acquitted in 1795.

The outbreak of the French Revolution in 1789 led to a split between Burke and the Rockingham Whigs who supported it. Burke contended that the French Revolution was predicated on questionable abstract rights and had broken with tradition, arguing his position in his *Reflections on the Revolution in France* (1790). The work was first begun as a letter of Charles Depont, a young French friend, and later expanded in reaction to a sermon favorable to the Revolution by the Dissenting preacher, Richard Price. The work sold 19,000 copies within six months and earned many responses, the most famous being Tom Paine's *Rights of Man* (1791–92) and Wollstonecraft's *A Vindication of the Rights of Men* (1790), followed by her more famous *Vindication of the Rights of Woman* (1792).

Since Burke's opposition to the French Revolution alienated him from the Whigs, he became politically isolated. He spent the last part of his career trying to justify his position and his political principles in works such as *Appeal from the New to the Old Whigs* (1791) and later *Letters on a Regicide Peace* (1796) and *Letter to a Noble Lord* (1796).

Thomas L. Cooksey

Works Consulted

Ayling, Stanley. *Edmund Burke: His Life and Opinions*. New York: St. Martin's, 1988.

Boulton, J.T. Introduction. *A Philosophical Enquiry into the Origin of our Ideas of the Sublime and the Beautiful*. By Edmund Burke. New York: Columbia UP, 1958. xv–cxxvii.

Canavan, Francis P. *The Political Reason of Edmund Burke*. Durham: Duke UP, 1960.

Cobban, Alfred. *Edmund Burke and the Revolt Against the Eighteenth Century: A Study of the Political and Social Thinking of Burke, Wordsworth, Coleridge, and Southey*. New York: Barnes, 1961.

Cone, Carl B. *Burke and the Nature of Politics*. 2 vols. Lexington: U of Kentucky P, 1957–64.

Copeland, Thomas W., ed. *The Correspondence of Edmund Burke*. 10 vols. Cambridge: Cambridge UP, 1958–70.

Courtney, C.P. *Montesquieu and Burke*. Oxford: Blackwell, 1963.

Fussell, Paul. *The Rhetorical World of Augustan Humanism: Ethics and Imagery from Swift to Burke*. Oxford: Clarendon, 1965.

Kramnick, Isaac. *The Rage of Edmund Burke: Portrait of an Ambivalent Conservative*. New York: Basic, 1977.

Oliver, Barbara C. "Edmund Burke's 'Enquiry' and the Baroque Theory of the Passions." *Studies in Burke and His Times* 12 (1970): 1661–76.

Parkin, Charles W. *The Moral Basis of Burke's Political Thought*. New York: Russell, 1968.

Reid, Christopher. *Edmund Burke and the Practice of Political Writing*. New York: St. Martin's, 1985.

Stanlis, Peter J. *Edmund Burke and the Natural Law*. Ann Arbor: U of Michigan P, 1958.

Burnet, Thomas

(?1635–1715)

A scholarly cleric and sometime candidate for Archbishop of Canterbury, Thomas Burnet is important in the history of science and literature for his *Telluris Theoria Sacra* (1681), which he translated as *The Sacred Theory of the Earth* in 1684. Burnet was to spend much of his life revising and readjusting this book to meet charges from scientists and orthodox theologians alike. Already suspect among the orthodox for his early association with the Cambridge Platonists, Burnet effectively lost any chance for the primacy because of his attempt, in the *Archaeologiae Philosophicae* (1692), to reconcile his *Sacred Theory* with Genesis by reading the biblical account allegorically.

In the *Sacred Theory*, Burnet divides world history into three segments defined by four events. Of interest for historical geology are the first two segments and events; the third segment and last two events are eschatological and pertain to God's future burning of the earth and the Millennium. Between the Creation and the Deluge, the earth was perfectly smooth, without mountains, valleys, or seas; the water that was to become the ocean existed in "the abyss," as the liquid of an egg exists inside its shell. With humankind's sinfulness, the smooth shell burst, releasing the traditional flood and forming the mountains from the shell's cracked pieces.

The importance of this vision, fanciful even for the geology of the time, was twofold. First, it inspired the Catastrophist view that informed the Neptunism of Abraham Gottlob Werner and his international followers. Second, it led to the uneasy combination of increased geological observation and biblical literalism that was to dominate earth science until James Hutton.

Burnet's literary effect was great. To the present, he remains noted as one of the finest stylists of his time. Joseph Addison addressed a Latin ode to him in 1689, and in *Spectator* 146 Richard Steele greeted the *Sacred Theory* approvingly, as did Joseph Warton in 1806. Added to the book's literary quality, Burnet's description of the Alps—recorded firsthand from trips starting in 1671—delivered the right degree of sublimity to inspire Wordsworth and Coleridge. Burnet was caught between deploring mountains because of their departure from pre-fallen, geometrical smoothness, and standing in awe of them as a sign of God's historical design. Wordsworth copied passages from Burnet to publish as notes with *The Excursion*, and in addition to frequent references in his notebooks, Coleridge proposed rendering Burnet's *Sacred History* in verse. He quoted from Burnet in the revealing epigraph to *The Rime of the Ancient Mariner.*

Burnet's other writings include "Remarks" against Locke's sensationalism and an unorthodox account of damnation and resurrection (*De statu mortuorum et resurgentium*), privately printed and published only posthumously starting in 1720. A copy with marginalia appears in Coleridge's library. (*See also* Geological Sciences, Vulcanism.)

William Crisman

Works Consulted

Alkon, Paul. "Thomas Burnet's *Sacred Theory of the Earth* and the Aesthetics of Extrapolation." *Hard Science Fiction*. Ed. George E. Slusser, et al. Carbondale: Southern Illinois UP, 1986: 99–120.

Nicolson, Marjorie Hope. *Mountain Gloom and Mountain Glory: The Development of the Aesthetics of the Infinite*. New York: Norton, 1959.

Willey, Basil. *The Eighteenth Century Background: Studies on the Idea of Nature in the Thought of the Period*. New York: Columbia UP, 1940.

Burns, Robert

(1759–96)

Robert Burns died during the same year that Wordsworth began to draft *The Ruined Cottage* and just two years before the publication of *Lyrical Ballads*. His closest affinity with Wordsworth and later Romantic poets is in theme: in his emphasis on human liberation (*A Man's a Man For a' That*), on the revolutionary force of the individual "voice" (*Love and Liberty: A Cantata*), and on the link between poetic vision and transgression (*The Vision*). In such works as *John Anderson My Jo* and *The Auld Farmer's New-year-morning Salutation*, Burns seems

to have suggested to Wordsworth the symbolic resonance of peasant speakers; and the Scottish poet also seems recalled in the revolutionary incantations of Shelley and the mock-epic wit of Byron.

Burns was born in 1759, the first child of Agnes Broun and William Burnes. Burnes (or "Burness," as Robert signed an early letter—the poet later shortened his surname) had been a gardener but upon his marriage set up as a tenant farmer. A careful parent who wrote a brief *Manual of Religious Belief* for the use of his family, Burnes rejected the harsh "Auld Licht" Calvinism favored in his parish and encouraged his seven children to practice tolerance and kindness. Burnes also departed from local custom in refusing to hire his children out as day-laborers on nearby farms. As Burns's father advanced in age—he had been nearly 40 when he married—the poet, as eldest child, became chief laborer on the farm.

Burns, who suffered throughout his adult life from poor health, survived rheumatic fever during his early teens but seems to have sustained heart damage, worsened by the stress of hard labor and severe financial difficulties. The poet's father died in February 1784, less than a month after winning an appeal that averted bankruptcy proceedings, leaving Burns at the head of a large family. Creatively, it was the most prolific two years of Burns's life. This childhood experience as eldest boy and then surrogate father in a warmly attached but somewhat brooding family, oppressed with a sense of unmerited hardship and injured worth, left its mark on the poet, who grew up resentful of privilege and keenly attuned to issues of power (and powerlessness).

Burns had less than two years of formal schooling, and that was owing to his extraordinary father, who—finding that the parish had no school—had arranged with several other local tenants to share a private tutor. This schoolmaster, John Murdoch, taught the Burnes children according to his own interests, which included the poetry of Pope, the familiar letters of "the wits of Queen Anne's reign," and the works of Milton and Shakespeare. Burns also, by age 23, had committed to memory his favorite works of fiction: Henry Mackenzie's sentimental best-seller *The Man of Feeling* and the first two volumes of *Tristram Shandy*. Sentimental themes pervade Burns's early poetry, and a Shandean tendency toward an almost burlesque self-representation is particularly marked in the poet's vernacular epistles and early letters.

By 1786, the poet had completed a book-length manuscript but had decided to emigrate to Jamaica as the only way out of his "chearless" life as a farmer. His plans were interrupted by the surprising success of this book, *Poems Chiefly in the Scottish Dialect* (1786), which sold out in less than a month and launched Burns on an ambiguous and ultimately frustrating career as literary celebrity and patronage-seeker in Edinburgh. After two years in the capital, Burns took the only two offers he had received—a lease on a farm at Ellisland and a part-time appointment with the Excise as a riding officer. But he soon gave up the farm, where he was a ploughman, and from 1791, he lived in the town of Dumfries, busy with Excise work and the revision of Scottish song.

Burns's poetry, like his life, breaks down into pre- and post-Edinburgh phases. The first edition of his poems was almost exclusively narrative in focus, including many that still rank among his most popular: *To a Mouse*, *To a Louse*, *The Cotter's Saturday Night*, and the vernacular epistles to John Lapraik. The 1787 Edinburgh edition of the same title was an expanded version, adding 22 poems (including *Address to the Unco Guid*, *To a Haggis*, and *Death and Dr. Hornbook*). But his only major narrative poem written after 1787 was the mock-epic *Tam o'Shanter* (1790). Otherwise, Burns focused during the last decade of his life almost exclusively on the revision and creation of Scottish song. Between 1786 and 1796, there was a gradual conversion to purely lyric statement.

Burns's songs (over 300) were published in successive volumes of James Johnson's *Scots Musical Museum* (1787–1803) and George Thomson's *Select Collection of Original Scottish Airs* (1793–1826), songbook series in which Burns's contributions were not always properly credited. Thus, Burns's career also shows a movement away from a stance as a self-conscious, frequently satiric, celebrity-poet (Burns was much feted during his two years in Edinburgh, though little patronage ever materialized) to near-anonymous national bard. It is entirely typical of Burns's later "bardic" stance that he attempted to conceal his authorship of *Auld Lang Syne* (1788).

The last ten years of Burns's rather short life (he died at age 37) were complicated by his frequently voiced sympathy for the French Revolution. Sometimes his sentiments were covertly expressed, as in *Scots Wha Hae* (1793), which displaces back to the 13th century the poet's cry for national liberation.

Often, however, Burns's distaste for the Hanoverians and enthusiasm for the revolution in France were openly expressed. In 1792, as a gesture of solidarity, Burns shipped to the French Convention four "carronades" (i.e., ships' cannons) purchased at an Excise auction (he had also participated in the raid on the ship, the smuggler *Rosamond*). According to Scott, who later traced the shipment, the ordnance was seized by Customs at Dover.

The Scottish were especially sensitive to political disaffection—particularly in a "national bard"—because of Scotland's history of support for the Stuarts' dynastic claims. The political climate in Dumfries during Burns's final years was actively hostile even to free assembly and free speech—the Prime Minister, Pitt, had supported measures outlawing both as an emergency counter-revolutionary measure. It is not then surprising that Burns's by turns Jacobite and Jacobin sympathies got him into frequent trouble. Under pressure by his superiors, Burns did join the Dumfries militia; but one of his final requests—ignored—was that he not be given a military funeral.

The break in Burns's career between narrative poet and lyric national bard has been problematic for subsequent criticism, which has tended to devalue the songs and to label the final decade of Burns's life a period of "decline." The later songs, however, constitute Burns's chief link with Romanticism, because it is as a writer of songs that Burns shows most powerfully the evocative force of a simplified diction.

In narrative poetry, particularly such longer works as *Tam o'Shanter*, Burns retains many of the mock-epic conventions of Neoclassical poetry, particularly the work of Pope and also from the Scottish vernacular tradition itself: Burns's chief predecessors, Allan Ramsay and Robert Fergusson, were also attentive readers of Pope, Prior, Gay, and such minor figures as Thomas D'Urfey and Ambrose Philips.

Burns's searching critique of "man's inhumanity to man"—the phrase occurs in Burns's *Man Was Made To Mourn* (1784–85) and is recast by Wordsworth in *Lines Written in Early Spring* (1798)—strongly impressed the later Romantics. Keats and Wordsworth both made pilgrimages to Burns's grave, and "The Banks o' Doon"

was Byron's favorite song. Indeed, Byron's *She Walks In Beauty* recalls, in its lyric depth and simplicity of diction, such songs by Burns as "Ae Fond Kiss." Yet Burns's natural affinities with Romanticism—especially in his later songs—were downplayed in the generation following his death, when Burns was invoked as a counter-Romantic by Jeffreys in the sustained attack on Wordsworth conducted by *The Edinburgh Review*

Carol McGuirk

Works Consulted

Bentman, Raymond. *Robert Burns*. Boston: Twayne, 1987.

Crawford, Thomas. *Burns: A Study of the Poems and Songs*. Stanford: Stanford UP, 1960.

Daiches, David. *The Paradox of Scottish Culture: The Eighteenth Century Experience*. New York: Oxford UP, 1964.

— — —. *Robert Burns*. New York: Macmillan, 1964.

Jack, R.D.S., and Andrew Noble, eds. *The Art of Robert Burns*. Totowa, NJ: Barnes, 1982.

Low, Donald, ed. *Critical Essays on Robert Burns*. London: Routledge, 1975.

— — —. *Robert Burns*. Edinburgh: Scottish, 1986.

— — —, ed. *Robert Burns: The Critical Heritage*. London: Routledge, 1974.

McGuirk, Carol. *Robert Burns and the Sentimental Era*. Athens: U of Georgia P, 1985.

Simpson, Kenneth. *The Protean Scot: The Crisis of Identity in Eighteenth Century Scottish Literature*. Aberdeen: Aberdeen UP, 1988.

Byron, George Gordon; Lord Byron
(1788–1824)

George Gordon, Lord Byron, a figure central to European as well as to English Romanticism, was born in London, the son of Catherine Gordon of Gight and Captain John ("Mad Jack") Byron. Byron was born with a deformed right foot. Mrs. Byron, deserted by her irresponsible husband and impoverished by his reckless spending, took her very young son to her native Scotland. There, Byron lived with his mother in an atmosphere marked by financial difficulty and her emotional instability. During these early years, Byron developed a love of wild Scottish scenery, had his first romantic involvement (with his cousin, Mary Duff), and began his education.

In 1798, Byron succeeded to the title of the Byron barony and became the sixth Lord Byron. Shortly after, he was brought to England, and in 1801 placed at Harrow School, where he was an intelligent but undisciplined student who showed a talent for making close friends and a gift for athletics. In 1803, while on vacation from school, Byron became involved with another cousin, Mary Chaworth, who inspired one of his early lyrics.

In 1805, Byron entered Cambridge, where he lived lavishly and went into debt. At Cambridge, as at Harrow, he was a careless student, but he made lasting friendships with John Cam Hobhouse, Davies, C.S. Matthews, and John Edleston. In 1806, Byron gathered his first collection of juvenile verse, *Fugitive Pieces*, but on the advice of a friend, it was suppressed. In January 1807, Byron privately printed a second version of his juvenilia under the title *Poems on Various Occasions*. In the summer of 1807, Byron published yet a third version of his early poetry, *Hours of Idleness*, which elicited, in 1808, severe criticism from the *Edinburgh Review*. During the next year and a half, Byron took his M.A. at Oxford, assumed control of his estate at Newstead, acceded to his seat in the House of Lords, and, most important, published his vigorous satire *English Bards and Scotch Reviewers* (1809). This work attacked such contemporary poets as Wordsworth, Coleridge, Southey, and Scott and offered

Byron's response to the Scottish review of his early poetry. *English Bards and Scotch Reviewers* shows a sharpness and strength that could not have been predicted from his sentimental *Hours of Idleness* and reveals Byron's affinity for the Neoclassical idiom of Dryden and Pope. The satire was a popular and critical success.

In 1809, with the help of a large loan, Byron left England with Hobhouse to tour Portugal, Spain, Gibraltar, Malta, Albania, and Greece. During his travels, Byron met the Ali Pasha, Turkish despot of Albania and western Greece, swam the Hellespont, saved the life of a Turkish girl condemned to be drowned for sexual misconduct, and met in Greece the young girl whom he celebrated poetically as the "Maid of Athens." Characteristically, all of these experiences found expression in his poetry, for while on his tour, Byron worked on a number of poems, the most important of which was an autobiographical "romaunt" in Spenserian stanzas that was to tell of *Childe Burun*.

In July 1811, Byron returned to England. His "romaunt," retitled *Childe Harold's Pilgrimage* (Cantos I and II), was published by Murray in 1812, and Byron became immediately famous. His exotic poem with his brooding hero became the talk of London. Welcomed into the fashionable society of the Melbourne House circle, Byron engaged in a series of affairs with Lady Caroline Lamb, Lady Oxford, and a number of women, including an alleged incestuous relationship with his half-sister Augusta.

During this period of social and personal tumult, Byron began a series of Oriental narrative poems that confirmed his position as the most popular and successful of English poets. *The Giaour* and *The Bride of Abydos* were published in 1813 and *The Corsair* and *Lara* in 1814. These poems were written quickly and often carelessly, but their facile narration, exoticism, and dark, brooding, and fascinating heroes made them immensely popular.

In September 1814, Byron, perhaps seeking a refuge from scandal and emotional confusion, became betrothed to Annabella Millbanke, and married on 2 January 1815. Byron and Annabella were poorly matched, and their marriage was a tragic mistake from the beginning. In late 1815, their daughter, Augusta Ada, was born, but on 15 January 1816, Lady Byron left Byron, never to return. During this period of marriage and separation, Byron continued to write, producing *Hebrew Melodies* in 1815 and *The Siege of Corinth* and *Parisina* in early 1816.

Following his separation from Lady Byron, Byron was ostracized in London, and, on 25 April 1816, left England forever. In Europe, Byron began a tour that took him to Bruges, Antwerp, Brussels, and Waterloo. He continued up the Rhine to Geneva, where he met Shelley, who was with Mary Godwin and Claire Clairmont, whom he had met before he left England. For a brief period in Geneva, Byron, his physician Polidori, Shelley, Godwin, and Clairmont formed a circle that produced both literature and scandal.

Inspired during this period by Switzerland, by Shelley, by the indirect influence of Wordsworth through Shelley, and by his own increasing creative powers, Byron wrote some of his most impressive poetry. In *Childe Harold*, Canto III, Byron gave expression to a power of self-dramatization, natural description, and poetic intensity which was a great advance over Cantos I and II. Furthermore, the emotional depths and Prometheanism of Canto III were echoed in *Prometheus, The Dream, Darkness,* and *The Prisoner of Chillon.* A little later, this period of Byron's life produced his most important poetic drama, *Manfred,* published in 1817. In *Manfred,* Byron created perhaps his most compelling and psychologically convincing version of the hero to be named for him.

In late 1816, Byron left Switzerland and traveled to Venice. Among his most important liaisons during this period were his affairs with Marianna Segati and Margarita Cogni. Byron's life in and around Venice in 1817 and 1818 inspired two very different literary productions. The first of these, Canto IV of *Childe Harold* (1818), is an eloquent and richly melancholy meditation on the fading glories and ruinous beauty of Italy. Byron's other important Venice-inspired poem of this period is *Beppo* (1818). After reading J.H. Frere's *Whistlecraft* (1817), the versification of which is based on Pulci's *ottava rima,* Byron was inspired to employ the *ottava rima* stanza to tell a comic story of loose Venetian morals and Italian domestic life. This poem—in its versification, digressions, colloquial tone, and cynical humor—marks a crucial development in Byron's maturation as a poet. With *Beppo,* Byron found the prosody, tone, diction, and narrative devices that would allow him to express most fully his genius as a poet and to achieve his two greatest masterpieces, *Don Juan* and *The Vision of Judgment.*

In 1819, Byron published a lively Cossack tale called *Mazeppa,* but the great accomplishment of that year was the publication of Cantos I and II of *Don Juan.* Although neither his publisher nor the reading public was very receptive to *Don Juan,* Byron was convinced of its quality and importance. Also in 1819, Byron formed the last significant emotional attachment of his life when he became the lover of Teresa Guiccioli, the young wife of an elderly count. This relationship lasted until Byron left Italy in 1823.

In 1820, Byron moved to Ravenna to be with Teresa, became interested in Italian politics, joined the Carbonari against Austrian domination, and began a series of poetic dramas, several of which were based on political and historical themes. Of these, *Marino Faliero* was published in 1821, and *The Two Foscari, Sardanapalus*, and *Cain* were published in 1821. Of this group *Cain* is perhaps the most important. It does not deal with the political and historical concerns of the other plays, but rather with psychological, moral, and metaphysical issues closer to *Manfred* and Byron's later *Heaven and Earth* (1823).

Meanwhile, Byron was continuing *Don Juan*, publishing Cantos III to V in 1822 and Cantos VI to VIII in early 1823. Also, in late 1821, Byron moved to Pisa to be near Shelley. At Pisa, Byron came to know Edward John Trelawney and Shelley's cousin, Thomas Medwin, both of whom would later write unreliable, if colorful, accounts of Byron. In 1822, Hunt joined Byron and Shelley with the idea, encouraged by Shelley, that the three of them would produce a new literary journal. Tragically, Shelley drowned shortly after Hunt's arrival. Without Shelley's mediating presence, the relationship between Byron and Hunt quickly deteriorated. Despite this, in 1822 and 1823, four numbers of their periodical, *The Liberal*, were published. The first contained Byron's brilliant satire on Southey, *The Vision of Judgment* (1822). In this work, Byron achieves a unity of structure and a concision of expression that are unique in his canon. Furthermore, his combination of wit, farce, and parody here are sparklingly effective.

By 1823, Byron had settled down to a quietly stable relationship with Teresa, and in April and May of that year he received a pleasant visit from the Earl and Countess Blessington and Count D'Orsay. This encounter resulted in Lady Blessington's *Conversations of Lord Byron* and a fine sketch of Byron by D'Orsay. In July 1823, Byron left Teresa and Italy to go to Greece in order to join the fight for Greek independence from Turkey. During this period, Byron continued to work on *Don Juan*, publishing Cantos IX to XVI between August 1823 and March 1824.

Arriving in Greece at Missolonghi, Byron found the Greek forces divided and in disarray. He gave his support to the moderate leader Mavrokordatos and showed considerable skill and courage in his attempts to bring order and efficiency to the Greek effort. Despite this, he was constantly plagued by Greek dissension, miserable weather, undisciplined soldiers, and tactical mishaps. On April 9, 1824, he was caught in a heavy rain while riding and became ill. His pain and fever grew worse over the next few days, and, on April 19, weakened by his physicians' repeated recourse to bleeding, he died.

Byron was unquestionably the most popular and widely influential poet of his day. Throughout Europe, his influence on writers, composers, painters, and general culture was immense. As a poet, his glamorous travelogues of the East and Europe, his Oriental romances, his ability to write effectively for a large audience, his memorable if sometimes unsubtle lyricism, his power of melodramatic self-dramatization, his creation of the "Byronic hero," and his genius for satire and ebullient comedy in verse made him and continue to make him a commanding figure. (*See also* Androgyny; Bligh, William; Bonnington, Richard Parkes; Byronic Hero; Classicism; Davies, Scrope Berdmore; D'Orsay, Count Alfred; Hamilton, John; Incest; [the] Luddites; Mental Theater; Poetry; Reynolds, John Hamilton; Satanism; Satire.)

Phillip B. Anderson

Works Consulted

Cook, M.G. *The Blind Man Traces the Circle: On the Patterns and Philosophy of Byron's Poetry.* Princeton: Princeton UP, 1969.

Foot, Michael. *The Politics of Paradise: A Vindication of Byron.* London: Collins, 1988.

Gleckner, Robert F. *Byron and the Ruins of Paradise.* Baltimore: Johns Hopkins, 1967.

Jump, John D. *Byron.* Boston: Routledge, 1972.

———, ed. *Byron: A Symposium.* New York: Barnes, 1975.

Langford, Elizabeth. *The Life of Byron.* Boston: Little, 1976.

McGann, Jerome J. *Fiery Dust: Byron's Poetic Development.* Chicago: U of Chicago P, 1968.

Manning, Peter J. *Byron and His Fictions.* Detroit: Wayne State UP, 1978.

Marchand, Leslie A. *Byron: A Biography.* 3 vols. New York: Knopf, 1957.

———. *Byron: A Portrait.* New York: Knopf, 1970.

———. *Byron's Poetry: A Critical Introduction.* Boston: Houghton, 1965.

Martin, Philip W. *Byron: A Poet Before His Public.* New York: Cambridge UP, 1982.

Moore, Doris Langley. *The Late Lord Byron.* Philadelphia: Lippincott, 1961.

Robinson, Charles E. *Shelley and Byron: The Snake and Eagle Wreathed in Fight.* Baltimore: Johns Hopkins UP, 1976.

Storey, Mark. *Byron and the Eye of Appetite.* New York: St. Martin's, 1986.

Byronic Hero

"I want a hero," Byron says in Canto I of *Don Juan* (1819), describing a character-type who figures prominently in his poetry and drama and who has appeared throughout Western literature. Descended from Prometheus, the Wandering Jew, Milton's Satan, and Goethe's Faust, the Byronic hero is derived from the Romantics' fascination with the nature of sin, the fallen world, rebellion, and the world of sensibility.

Many diverse sources exist for the Byronic hero, from the *Sturm und Drang* movement of the late 18-century to the Gothic novel, culminating in Byron's own protagonists in *Childe Harold's Pilgrimage* (1812–18), *Manfred* (1817), and *Cain* (1821). Later uses of the Byronic personality are Herman Melville's Captain Ahab from *Moby-Dick* (1851) and Emily Brontë's Heathcliff from *Wuthering Heights* (1847), as well as many other characters from 19th-century literature.

The Byronic hero has been variously described, through studies of Byron's poetic drama and his influence on Victorian and modern literature, as both cruel and courteous, sympathetic and sadistic. There can be no doubt that the heroes of Byron's works invariably are linked with the personality and legend of Byron himself. Though he tried, unsuccessfully, to separate himself from the hero who many thought was an extension of his life and loves, Byron could not be surprised when the public saw his personality in Cain, Manfred, Don Juan, and Childe Harold.

Other characteristics of the Byronic hero are an energetic spirit, a rebellious individualism, and a vast capacity for feeling and suffering; he is an exile or outcast whose tormented life is a search for meaning in a meaningless world. He is often guilty of a crime or a sin, but his quest for a meaning in life elicits sympathy from the reader. His suffering inspires awe, and his eloquent ability to defy conventional morality and social codes raises him above the average mortal.

A telling characteristic of the Byronic hero is a self-analytic, self-critical stance that Byron's protagonists often assume, which is at the heart of the Romantic tradition of sensitivity, feeling, and world-weariness. The antisocial stance of a Childe Harold or the humanistic complexity of a Don Juan is linked to what has been called the "Zeluco theme," after a novel by John

Moore in 1789. (Byron himself, in an 1813 letter, linked his name with Zeluco.) This theme exemplifies the remorseful individual or the social misfit who rejects society, but who is himself also rejected.

Another literary tradition behind the Byronic hero and much of the Romantic movement's sense of heroism, disillusionment, and desire for transcendence is typified by Goethe's *Faust* (Part I, 1808) and *The Sorrows of Young Werther*, translated into English in 1779. The thirst for knowledge and the lust for experience of Faust or Werther are evident in Byron's life and the personalities that are romantic extensions of that life. The self-tortured temperament and guilt-laden sensibility are certainly characteristics Byron saw in himself, and his heroes merely project what he viewed as his role in defying society.

Whether he is classified as the "Child of Nature," the "Man of Feeling," the "Gloomy Egoist," the "Gothic Villain," or the "Noble Outlaw"—Peter Thorslev's terms—the Byronic hero is a rebel who is proudly defiant in his attitude toward conventional mores and religious beliefs. He stands apart, suffering from a moral or spiritual sin, yearning to purge himself of whatever demons pursue him. His strong sense of honor, love of music or poetry, and metaphysical rebellion classify him as a typical Romantic figure. While Byron created the type in the nineteenth century, he still best exemplifies it. Byron saw himself as the embodiment of Everyman, a hero whose aspirations and descents are incarnate in a handful of memorable characters and whose work defined a generation looking inward for meaning. (*See also* Prometheanism, Satan, Vampire.)

Gary Kerley

Works Consulted

Beckson, Karl, and Arthur Ganz. *Literary Terms: A Dictionary*. New York: Farrar, 1975.

Bloom, Harold, ed. *George Gordon, Lord Byron: Modern Critical Views*. New York: Chelsea, 1986.

———, ed. *Lord Byron's Don Juan: Modern Critical Interpretations*. New York: Chelsea, 1987.

Lovell, Ernest J., Jr. *Byron: The Record of a Quest*. Hamden: Archon, 1966.

Praz, Mario. *The Romantic Agony*. Trans. Angus Davidson. 2nd ed. New York: Meridian, 1957.

Rutherford, Andrew, compiler. *Byron: The Critical Heritage*. New York: Barnes, 1970.

Thorslev, Peter L. *The Byronic Hero: Types and Prototypes*. Minneapolis: U of Minnesota P, 1962.

Camelion Poet

The Camelion Poet (Keatsian orthography) is a category of poets with whom Keats aligned himself in a letter to Richard Woodhouse (1818). The Camelion Poet loses his identity in the objects of his interest—"The Sun, the Moon, the Sea and Men and Women." Keats illustrates this ability by writing that when he enters a room his speculations so fill his mind that others press in on him to annihilate his own identity. The Camelion Poet is as interested in the dark side of men and women as in the light, in death as life, in evil as good. He lives with intensity (a term Keats later favors over the word "gusto" that he uses in this letter) "be it foul or fair, high or low, rich or poor, mean or elevated."

Keats contrasts the poetic character of the Camelion Poet with that of the Wordsworthian or egotistical sublime. Poets of the second category interpret all experience by and through their own egos, whereas, for Keats, the opposite type of poet identifies himself with his object, in order that, like the chameleon, he could so take on the feelings and characteristics of the object that he would merge with it.

Woodhouse in a letter to John Taylor (1818) interprets Keats's meaning: "The highest order of poet . . . will be able to throw his own soul into any object he sees or imagines, so as to see feel be sensible of, & express, all that the object itself would see feel be sensible of or express—& he will speak out of that object—so that his own self will with the Exception of the Mechanical part be 'annihilated.'" Woodhouse continues by writing that when Keats speaks of the poet having no identity, he is speaking of the poet at the time when the poetic "fit" is upon him. When the poet through his imagination creates "ideal personages substances & Powers, . . . he lives for a time in their souls or Essences or ideas."

Earlier in a letter to George and Tom Keats (1817), Keats identified Shakespeare as the ideal poet and called the ability to identify with the object "negative capability." A poet with negative capability is able to be in "uncertainties, Mysteries, doubts, without any irritable reaching after fact and reason." In developing the concept of a Camelion Poet who possesses to extraordinary degree negative capability, Keats was greatly influenced by Hazlitt, particularly by his essay "Of Gusto" (1816) and his lecture "On Shakespeare and Milton" (1818). Keats's emphasis on dramatic objectivity and the ability to enter into the thoughts and actions of characters in the Camelion Poet echoes Hazlitt's views in On Shakespeare and Milton: "The poet may be said, for the time, to identify himself with the characters he wishes to represent, and to pass from one to another, like the soul successively animating different bodies." In the same lecture, Hazlitt speaks of Shakespeare: "He was the least of an egotist that it was possible to be. . . . He had only to think of any thing in order to become that thing, with all the circumstances belonging to it." (*See also* Negative Capability.)

The Camelion Poet, because of his ability to enter into the sensations of his objects, can perhaps be best seen in his imagery. In Keats's poetry, Keats participates in the objects through images of synaesthesia, kinesthesia, and tactility. Such imagery gives greater depth to the development of his characters and ideas. Indeed, although Keats sees Shakespeare as his mentor and as exemplar of the Camelion Poet, he himself is not just aligned with that ideal but exemplifies it in his own writing. (*See also* Synaesthesia.)

Martha Watson Bargo

Works Consulted

Abrams, M.H. *Natural Supernaturalism: Tradition and Revolution in Romantic Literature.* New York: Norton, 1971.

— — —. *The Mirror and the Lamp: Romantic Theory and the Critical Tradition.* New York: Oxford UP, 1953.

Bate, Walter Jackson. *John Keats.* Cambridge: Belknap, 1963.

Bush, Douglas. "Keats and His Ideas." *The Major English Romantic Poets: A Symposium in Reappraisal.* Eds. Clarence D. Thorpe, Carlos Baker, and Bennett Weaver. Carbondale: Southern Illinois UP, 1957: 231–45. Rpt. in *English Romantic Poets: Modern Essays in Criticism.* Ed. M.H. Abrams. New York: Oxford UP, 1960: 326–39.

Stillinger, Jack. "Wordsworth and Keats." *The Age of William Wordsworth: Critical Essays on the Romantic Tradition.* Eds. Kenneth R. Johnston and Gene W. Ruoff. New Brunswick, NJ: Rutgers UP, 1987: 173–95.

Campbell, Thomas

(1777–1844)

Thomas Campbell, well known at the peak of his career, holds only secondary status among 19th-century British poets, although many of his lines have survived as proverbs. Campbell was a transitional figure who influenced his better-known contemporaries, such as Byron, Shelley, Crabbe, Tennyson, and the Brownings.

Born in Glasgow in 1777, Campbell was the youngest of 11 children. The collapse of his father's tobacco shipping business during the American Revolution affected Campbell financially all his life. His fondness for the classics influenced the poetry he began writing at age 10, and he entered Glasgow University at age 14 to study and translate the Latin and Greek writers.

Campbell's university stay was difficult. He worked as a tutor to supplement his family's finances, but he could not complete a degree and therefore lacked the formal requirements to enter a profession. In 1797, he clerked in a Glasgow law firm, where he met Robert Anderson, author of *Lives of the British Poets,* who became his advocate and friend. Campbell's financial insecurity forced him to write for an income, and his first commission, through Anderson, was an abridgment of Bryan Edwards's *West Indies.*

Seeking better prospects, Campbell moved to Edinburgh, attended lectures at the university, and resumed tutoring. He also worked on *The Pleasures of Hope,* a poetry collection published in 1799 and dedicated to Anderson. He was then dedicated to earning his living as a professional writer. The popular reception of *The Pleasures of Hope*, which was praised for its morality, patriotism, and evocation of the national spirit, hailed him as the successor to Burns. Campbell's influential acquaintances grew with his fame, and his career as a poet was auspiciously launched.

Campbell decided to travel to the Continent, particularly to Germany, to broaden his education. A major, if paradoxical, influence in Germany came from the military pomp and circumstance and the horror of war, which he witnessed at the French capture of Ratisbon. The carnage there inspired many of his most memorable poems, such as *Hohenlinden*. Although suffering homesickness, financial problems, and illness (which became chronic), Campbell wrote many of his best poems in Germany.

The political unrest on the Continent forced Campbell to flee to London in 1801. His father's death soon took him to Edinburgh, where he assumed the lifelong burden of his family's financial problems.

After two years in Edinburgh without prospect of financial gain, Campbell returned to London. The profits from *The Pleasures of Hope* enabled him in 1803 to marry Matilda Sinclair, his second cousin. They had two sons, Thomas Telford (1804) and Alison (1805). These added responsibilities forced Campbell to focus his creative efforts on areas of assured financial reward. He wrote periodical and encyclopedia articles and worked for *The Star* newspaper and *The Philosophical Magazine* while continuing to write poetry. His progress was slowed by ill health and alcohol. Then he was stricken by grief when his son Alison died of scarlet fever in 1810 and his mother died in 1812.

Public lectures at the Royal Institution and a bequest of £5,000 in 1815 from a Scottish cousin eased Campbell's financial difficulties. *Specimens of the British Poets* appeared in 1819, and after a trip to Germany with his family, Campbell became editor of the *New Monthly Magazine*, which published his lectures. While editor, he promoted his idea—conceived in Germany—of a major university without religious requirements open to all, and he began a subscription campaign to raise funds. His success led to the founding of University College, London, which with King's College became the University of London in 1836. Campbell was elected Lord Rector of Glasgow University in 1826.

Tiring of his editorial work, Campbell resigned from the magazine in 1830. His wife had died in 1828, and his mentally ill son had to be put in an asylum. Evidence suggests that Campbell's ill health, his wife's death, and his son's insanity were all results of Campbell's long-term syphilis.

After leaving the *New Monthly Magazine*, Campbell in 1831 became editor of the *Metropolitan*, a new periodical, mainly to repay debts incurred during his previous position. He soon left and devoted many of his remaining productive years to writing the biography of Sir Thomas Lawrence, a famous painter who had befriended Campbell and painted his portrait. When he abandoned this project, in 1834 he completed a biography of Sarah Kemble Siddons, the famous tragic actress.

Campbell, next went to Paris to collect materials for a book on ancient geography, but switched his interest to a book on Algiers. His subsequent travels in Algiers made him a popular dinner guest when he returned to London in 1835. In 1836, he went home to Scotland to collect material for a poem on *The Pilgrim of Glencoe*, published in 1842 to unfavorable critical response. Unable to earn money from his poetry, Campbell endorsed several moneymaking literary projects in his last years and completed the editing of *Life of Plutarch*, published in 1841.

With his health and funds declining, Campbell decided to sell his house in London and move to Boulogne, France, where he could enjoy the sea air and live more cheaply. Accompanied by his niece, Mary, he moved in the summer of 1843 and died in Boulogne in 1844. He was buried in Westminster Abbey in the middle of Poets' Corner.

Critical judgment of Campbell varies widely, but his message of hope, his social concern, his philanthropic endeavors, and his historical significance represent both Neoclassical and Romantic styles.

Len McCall

Works Consulted

Beattie, William, ed. *Life and Letters of Thomas Campbell*. 3 vols. 1849, New York: AMSP, 1973.

Miller, Mary Ruth. *Thomas Campbell*. Boston: Twayne, 1978.

Carlyle, Thomas

(1795–1881)

Thomas Carlyle, considered the prophet of Victorian England for his critique of its social and political conditions, influenced generations of British writers and thinkers. He acquired the skills for his role from a long and important period as an essayist, translator, critic, and author and produced two masterpieces: *Sartor Resartus* (1833), which approaches a novel but defies classification, and his history, *French Revolution* (1837). In addition, he helped introduce German literature to the British public.

Carlyle was born in Ecclefechan, Scotland, and spent his formative years there. His family, headed by his stonemason-farmer father James and his pious mother Margaret, was large and close. From his parents he inherited strong-mindedness and enormous conversational powers. He attended village schools and then Annan Academy, where he was miserable, as he portrays in the semiautobiographical *Sartor Resartus*.

At age 13 Carlyle entered Edinburgh University, at which his parents hoped he would study for the ministry. However, he became more interested in mathematics and lost his stable childhood religious faith. He was lonely and unhappy at Edinburgh and found solace in reading extensively in the university library. After a year of divinity school, he determined not to become a minister and worked as a schoolmaster at his old school Annan and at Kirkcaldy.

In school he had learned French, Latin, and Greek, but in 1819 he persuaded an old schoolfellow Robert Jardine to teach him German in exchange for French lessons. After a year he was publishing a review of a German book on magnetism. He was especially impressed by the writings of Goethe, Schiller, and Richter: to his own uncertainties about religion and a career, they seemed vitally creative in their use of instinct, emotion, tradition, history, and the concept of nation to challenge the Enlightenment values of reason, skepticism, and objectivity.

Carlyle drew inspiration from the writings of German Romantics rather than his English contemporaries such as Wordsworth, Coleridge, and Shelley. But Carlyle was not poetic in nature, and Wordsworth and Coleridge seemed too sublime or picturesque for his taste. When he did meet Coleridge, he was disappointed that the poet was unhelpful in answering his questions about German metaphysics.

Though Carlyle read extensively in German, he did not always understand what he read and sometimes distorted German ideas by taking them out of context. In reading about Schiller, for example, in order to write a biographical sketch of him for *London Magazine*, Carlyle seemed to be reading about himself. The Schiller of whom he read had loving, pious parents; studied and rejected the practice of law; chose history over fiction; and suffered throughout his life from severe illness.

Carlyle's philosophy amalgamated Puritan, Enlightenment, and German Romantic ideas. He believed strongly in a transcendent spiritual order underlying the materialistic world, an order that gives the world reality. From Immanuel Kant he drew his distinction between understanding, which handles the quantifiable world, and reason, which gives profound insight into the real nature of things. From Johann Fichte he drew inspiration for his idea of the literary man as prophet of the transcendent order (Johann Goethe became his supreme example of this).

As a young man, Carlyle suffered because of stomach disorders and nerves, and mental and spiritual agony because of his loss of faith. In August 1822, however, he began his recovery with a mystical experience at Leith Walk in which he felt he came to what he believed. As a free man, he could deny both doubt and logic, indeed anything that demeaned life an destroyed spirit. As a sentimentalist, he could trust his own feelings and instincts.

Carlyle continued his German studies and began to publish, first an essay on *Faust* in 1822, then a series of articles on Schiller (later expanded into a book), and finally a translation of the first part of *Wilhelm Meister*. Between 1822 and 1832 he published some 20 major essays on German literature and helped to shape the attitude of the educated British audience to German literature.

In 1826, he married Jane Baillie Welsh, an intelligent woman who also had literary aspirations. In the first months of their marriage, he worked on *Wotton Reinfred*, a semiautobiographical novelette obviously influenced by Goethe's *Wilhelm Meister*. The hero Wotton, troubled in body and spirit, is burdened by memories of disappointed romance and work. To seek relief from his world-weariness, he travels.

Carlyle never finished *Wotton Reinfred*, but seven years later he published *Sartor Resartus* in installments in *Fraser's Magazine*. Not really a novel, it satirizes fashionable religion and intellectual, philosophical, and fictional excesses. In it, Carlyle first proclaims the "natural supernaturalism" which he found in German Idealism. He discusses the "Philosophy of Clothes," his metaphorical representation of the idea that the material world, limited by the illusions of time and space, "body forth," or project, the spiritual, eternal realities.

The main voice of *Sartor Resartus* is that of the Editor, who is presenting the ideas of an eccentric German philosopher, Diogenes Teufelsdröckh (God-created Devil's Dung). Teufelsdröckh's work appears in quotations and paraphrases intermixed with the sometimes dubious, sometimes admiring, commentary by the Editor. Halfway through the work, the Editor tries again to clarify Teufelsdröckh's ideas by writing a biography of him. The source of his information is a mass of fragmentary jottings sent to him by a friend in Weissnichtwo (Don't Know Where). Carlyle clearly bases this most famous and commonly anthologized section of the book on his own mental struggles. He entitles these chapters the "Everlasting NO," "Centre of Indifference," and "Everlasting YEA."

The style of *Sartor Resartus* is extraordinary. It includes Germanisms, such as capitals at the beginnings of words and regular use of the second-person singular. Carlyle also regularly employs metaphor in juxtaposing two or more seemingly very different objects or situations to force the reader to recognize their similarity. The utterances of Teufelsdröckh in particular are rhapsodical and hyperbolic. Whatever the supposed predecessors of this style may be, it is unique—an extreme nonconforming self-expression.

Carlyle was also interested in history, but history based on the imagination through which one can recover and revivify the past. Unlike the typical Britisher who feared the mob and despised the French Revolution, Carlyle saw the event as the most important movement of modern history: the workings of divine justice on corrupt 18th-century society and the sign of hope for a new era. The *French Revolution* (1837), on which he worked for three years, demonstrates high historic and imaginative art and combines accurate, objective history with Romantic self-expression. In some ways it can be seen as a projection of its author in his choices of which scenes vividly to recreate and which merely to summarize. Carlyle clearly believed large areas of history were best forgotten. He also effectively employs symbols, such as in Book II where he uses paper in the form of money, reform schemes, warehouses, and balloons to symbolize the weakness, pomposity, and emptiness of French society in the 1780s. He emphasizes the importance of instinct over reason and sees the mob as a creative force, though blind and frightening. Indeed, both the style and content of the work were revolutionary.

After *French Revolution*, Carlyle became more interested in contemporary British social problems and less interested in German Romanticism. In 1837, he described himself as "far parted now" from Goethe and rarely referred to German literature in his books and correspondence (though he gave six lectures on German Romanticism in May of that year). He never renounced Romanticism, continued to admire all things German, and was forever indebted to German Idealism which, combined with Old Testament morality, formed his own new faith which so appealed to a generation of British society disillusioned by traditional Christianity.

Ann W. Engar

Works Consulted

Campbell, Ian. *Thomas Carlyle*. New York: Scribner, 1974.

Harrold, Charles Frederick. *Carlyle and German Thought: 1819–1834*. New Haven: Yale UP, 1934.

Kaplan, Fred. *Thomas Carlyle: A Biography*. Ithaca: Cornell UP, 1983.

LeQuesne, A.L. *Carlyle*. Oxford: Oxford UP, 1982.

Castlereagh, Viscount Robert Stewart
(1769–1822)

Viscount Robert Stewart Castlereagh was British foreign secretary from 1812 to 1822; he helped guide the alliance against Napoleon and participated in the Congress of Vienna, which defined the boundaries of Europe after Napoleon's defeat in 1815. At the same time he was involved in foreign affairs, Castlereagh served under Liverpool as Leader of the House of Commons. During this period, he became identified with the repressive policies of the years 1815 to 1819, such as the temporary suspension of habeas corpus and the Six Acts of 1819.

Castlereagh was Irish chief secretary during the suppression of the rebellion of 1798 and the union with Great Britain. In Henry Addington's ministry, Castlereagh was appointed president of the Board of Control responsible for Indian affairs (July

1802). He became secretary of state for war (July 1805) when Pitt returned as Prime Minister (May 1804) and strengthened the recruitment practices of local militia.

During his tenure as British war minister under the Duke of Portland (1807–09), Castlereagh was responsible for the achievements of the Peninsular Army against Napoleon. He overhauled military administration and improved recruitment, selecting Sir Arthur Wellesley (later Duke of Wellington) to command the British Army in 1809.

As foreign secretary under Perceval and Liverpool, Castlereagh advocated the use of a congressional system in order to maintain a balance of power in Europe. In the Treaty of Chatillon (1814) and the Treaty of Chaumont (1814), he committed allies to carry on the war until Napoleon's defeat. The Vienna Congress Settlement of 1815 achieved Castlereagh's foreign policy objectives of curbing further French aggression but not imposing punitive peace terms. Preparing to attend the Congress of Verona before his death in 1822, he outlined Britain's policy of nonintervention in the internal affairs of other states. (*See also* Napoleonic Wars, Parliament, Satire.)

Jonathan Gross

Works Consulted

Derry, John W. *Castlereagh*. New York: St. Martin's Press, 1976.

Hinde, Wendy, *Castlereagh*. London: Collins, 1981.

Kissinger, H. *A World Restored; Metternich, Castlereagh and the problems of peace, 1812–1822*. Boston: Houghton, 1957.

Catastrophism

Catastrophism is the name of the traditional reading of geology in vogue during the early 19th century. Influenced by the discoveries of fossils at different strata, Catastrophists believed that the earth had been rocked by a succession of geological catastrophes, each one of which had exterminated the species of animals living at that time. Among the advocates of Catastrophism were religiously minded individuals who believed that this geological theory confirmed the account of the great flood in the Bible and political radicals like the publisher Richard Carlile, who argued that this theory called into question religious beliefs and would ultimately turn humanity away from religion and toward reason and science. Of the Romantic poets, Shelley and Byron were particularly influenced by Catastrophism.

Before writing *Queen Mab* (1813), Shelley read James Parkinson's *Organic Remains of a Former World* (1811), in which Parkinson argued that the world had been created in stages and life on its surface had been destroyed at each stage by floods. The large animals later found as fossils were seen as victims of these natural catastrophes. In one of the notes to *Queen Mab*, Shelley uses the notion of drastic geological change to justify his hope that a future improvement in the earth's climate might usher in an era of universal health and happiness, and in his *Prometheus Unbound* (1820), Shelley has his character Panthea describe the wrecks of civilizations destroyed by a prehistorical deluge and buried deep beneath the earth's surface. But while geological change does not seem to have affected Shelley's optimistic futurism, in Byron's works Catastrophism is seen from a much darker perspective. Byron's poem *Darkness* (1817) was probably inspired by the theories of Georges Buffon, who believed that the earth would become increasingly cool and ultimately freeze, just as in *Darkness* the world becomes a lifeless lump. *Darkness*, in turn, influenced Mary Shelley's apocalyptic novel *The Last Man* (1826). The theories of the great French Catastrophist, Georges Cuvier, formed a scientific basis for Byron's "Mystery" dramas, *Cain* and *Heaven and Earth*. Byron notes his debt to Cuvier in his preface to *Cain*, particularly his interest in the idea that the earth has been destroyed not once but many times. In *Cain*, however, Byron goes beyond Cuvier's ideas and has his character Lucifer speculate that these successive catastrophes destroyed races of intelligent beings who were actually superior to man. Byron's less heterodox *Heaven and Earth* deals with the death and devastation caused by the biblical deluge as seen through the despairing eyes of one of Noah's sons. In essence, Byron used Cuvier's theories to draw a rather grim picture of the earth's past and future. Catastrophism also influenced the painter John Martin and helped inspire such works as *Sedak in Search of the Waters of Oblivion* (1812) and *The Deluge* (1826). Martin succeeded in giving visual expression to his age's fascination with apocalyptic destruction. (*See also* Geological Sciences.)

William D. Brewer

Works Consulted

Gaull, Marilyn. *English Romanticism: The Human Context*. New York: Norton, 1988.

Grabo, Carl. *A Newton Among Poets: Shelley's Use of Science in Prometheus Unbound*. Chapel Hill: U of North Carolina P, 1930.

McGann, Jerome J., ed. *Byron*. The Oxford Authors. New York: Oxford UP, 1986.

Rudwick, M.J.S. *The Meaning of Fossils: Episodes in the History of Paleontology*. London: MacDonald, 1972.

Censorship

The Romantic period was distinguished, paradoxically, both by its free press and by the government's aggressive policy of press prosecutions. From a strictly legal standpoint, England had had a free press since 1695, when Parliament allowed the Licensing Act to expire. In practice, however, this meant only that writers were free to publish without the prior approval of a government censor. It did not mean that they were immune from legal sanctions if the government deemed that the publication demonstrated a "tendency to cause a breach of the peace" — a phrase sometimes interpreted so broadly as to include anything that might disturb the King's peace of mind. Writers and publishers thus had to be cautious about the works they produced lest they find themselves in court answering charges of libel. In the contentious political climate following the French Revolution, the Tory government turned increasingly to the law of libel to snuff out the inflammatory productions of the radical press, and this draconian policy had a powerful influence on the character of Romantic public discourse.

There were four types of libel with which a writer of the Romantic period could be charged: (1) personal libels slandered individuals; (2) obscene libels dealt rather too warmly with sexual matters; (3) blasphemous libels questioned the tenets of the English church; and (4) seditious libels tended to encourage a lack of respect for the monarchy, the Parliament, or the judiciary. A conviction on any one of these counts often led to a substantial fine and a prison sentence of several months or even years.

More important than these official sanctions, however, were the incidental penalties incurred by the defendant during the prosecution. It was common for a writer or publisher, after being arrested, to wait several months in prison before the prosecutor either brought the case to court or simply dropped the charges without explanation or restitution. And, since prosecutions were initiated by an indictment from the Society for the Suppression of Vice or by an *ex officio* information from the attorney general, these authorities in effect had the power to imprison without due process. If the case did come to trial, the accused was not guaranteed anything like an impartial hearing. The special juries appointed to decide libel cases (after the passage of Fox's Libel Act in 1792) were typically packed with men that the prosecutor knew would be sympathetic to the government's cause. Indeed, because jurors were paid one guinea apiece for each case they heard, some invariably decided in favor of the prosecution so as to ensure that they would be called again for jury duty. In spite of all these obstacles, many defendants were acquitted, but they were nevertheless expected to pay court costs, which sometimes ran into the hundreds of pounds and constituted a *de facto* fine upon a supposedly innocent writer.

The law of libel thus offered the government an effective weapon in its struggle to maintain control over an increasingly powerful and rebellious media and therefore over the political attitudes of readers as well. It was the radical opposition writers who felt most directly the stings of the libel laws. Cobbett's experience was fairly typical. In 1809, Cobbett was incensed by a report of the flogging of five English soldiers, and he published a vivid, highly critical account of the event in his *Political Register* (by far the most popular and influential of all the radical newspapers). In the government's view, the article was seditious because it encouraged disrespect for the due actions of people of rank. The case came to trial in June 1810; Cobbett was found guilty, fined £1,000, and sentenced to two years in Newgate, from which he continued to publish the *Register*.

The real blow to Cobbett's influence came, however, in 1816 to 1817 when his political pamphlets—the infamous *Twopenny Trash* of the Regency period—were at the forefront of the reform movement. Parliament voted to suspend habeas corpus in March 1817, and Cobbett, knowing that he would soon be imprisoned once again, fled to America. The move enraged many leading radicals; they saw it as an act of cowardice and labeled Cobbett as a defector from the political struggle. Though he continued to publish the *Register* from America and again in England after his return in 1819, Cobbett was never able to command the influence he had held over the public consciousness in the years before his flight.

Cobbett's experience illustrates both the direct and indirect power of the government's libel prosecutions to stifle public criticism, and Cobbett was by no means the only writer to labor under the threat of prosecution. In 1811, for example, Leigh and John Hunt, the publishers of the *Examiner*, who had already been the targets of two abortive prosecutions, were tried for printing an article that criticized the harshness of military discipline. The government's case was built chiefly on the Cobbett precedent, but, largely due to the expert defense of Brougham, their attorney and friend, the Hunts were acquitted. The victory was short-lived—in December 1812, the Hunts were once again in the docket, charged with a seditious libel against the new Prince Regent. This time the brothers were sentenced to two years in separate jails and fined £500 each.

Dozens of other writers and publishers faced a similar fate in the years between 1808, when Parliament confirmed the attorney general's right to issue *ex officio* informations, and 1817, when habeas corpus was suspended. Despite the 26 prosecutions pursued in 1817, the government's grip on the press seemed to loosen when Thomas Wooler successfully challenged the procedure for selecting special juries and when William Hone earned "not guilty" verdicts on three separate charges of blasphemous libel. By 1820, however, after the "Peterloo" massacre and the passage of the highly repressive "Six Acts," the government redoubled its prosecution campaign. At year's end, most of the prominent radical critics were in prison—including Wooler, Richard Carlile, Francis Burdett, and many others.

The major writers were for the most part able to avoid direct libel prosecutions; similarly, although Godwin's *Political Justice* advocated anarchy, it was so obscure no one could understand it and so expensive no one could buy it. Poetry tended to attract a highly literate, well-educated audience, and the government's concern was always with texts that, in its view, might inspire the lower orders of society to acts of insurrection. Nevertheless, in their function as intermediary between writer and audience, the libel laws undoubtedly exerted an influence on literature. Shelley and Byron frequently altered questionable lines prior to publication, though it is rarely certain whether they did so for fear of prosecution or out of a more general concern for "taste." It is certain, however, that Shelley's most pointedly political works— *The Mask of Anarchy* and *Oedipus Tyrannus*— were suppressed before they could reach a popular reading audience, and the libel laws may even have contributed to Shelley's use of oblique allegorical and mythological forms for his commentaries on politics. At any rate, *Queen Mab* (1813) achieved its midcentury popularity largely through a series of pirated editions initiated in 1821 by William Clark, who was immediately prosecuted and imprisoned. Similarly, the

1822 publication of Byron's *Vision of Judgment* resulted in John Hunt's conviction for a libel "against the memory of George III."

Kyle Grimes

Works Consulted

Halevy, Elie. *A History of the English People in 1815.* 1924. London: Ark, 1987.

———. *The Liberal Awakening.* 1926. London: Ark, 1987.

Howell, T.B. *A Complete Collection of State Trials.* 34 vols. London: Longman, 1823.

Klancher, Jon. *The Making of English Reading Audiences, 1790–1832.* Madison: U of Wisconsin P, 1987.

Thomas, Donald. "Press Prosecutions of the Eighteenth and Nineteenth Centuries: The Evidence of King's Bench Indictments." *The Library* 5th ser. 33 (1977): 315–32.

Thompson, E.P. *The Making of the English Working Class.* 1963. New York: Vintage, 1966.

Wickwar, William. *The Struggle for the Freedom of the Press, 1819–1832.* London: Allen, 1928.

Chatterton, Thomas

(1752–70)

Thomas Chatterton was born in 1752, in Bristol, the city where he spent all except the last four months of his life. His father having died three months before he was born, Chatterton lived with his mother and sister in the neighborhood of the medieval church of St. Mary Redcliffe. The dreamy, contemplative boy spent hours alone in this church reading, until age 8 when he was sent to Colston's School, a strict Church of England institution run by a charitable foundation and dedicated to educating boys for careers in commerce. Feeling he was destined for something higher than the life of a tradesman, Chatterton rebelled against this education and later against his apprenticeship as scrivener to an attorney. He spent the ample free time this position left him, as well as a good part of his schooldays, writing satirical verses and reading esoteric books on religion, history, biography, and heraldry from circulating libraries and in the local booksellers' shops.

During his apprenticeship, Chatterton was involved with a group of teen-aged literati who exchanged satirical verses and "oddities" in *Felix Farley's Bristol Journal*. When he was 15, he began to produce and offer publication several medieval manuscripts, in both prose and verse, which he claimed were written by a 15th-century monk named Thomas Rowley and found by Chatterton's father in an old chest in St. Mary Redcliffe. Finding that local antiquaries were interested in these "antiques," Chatterton began searching further afield for a more prestigious patron. Among the many he corresponded with was politician and writer Walpole, whose *Castle of Otranto* had also contributed to the revival of interest in Gothic subjects in the 1760s.

The mass of "Rowley" material, all of which was produced between the summer of 1768 and the spring of 1769, included historical and biographical chronicles, lyrics, and dramas. Much of it is heroic in nature and centers on William Canynge, the mayor of Bristol, who was Rowley's friend and patron and the man responsible for the restoration of St. Mary Redcliffe. The most successful of the Rowleian works is a tragedy in verse, *Aella*, a drama of weddings, war, betrayal, and death set in Saxon England and composed, like all the Rowley poems, in a version of medieval English.

Though Chatterton maintained the authenticity of the Rowley manuscripts throughout his life, some of his acquaintances were immediately suspicious. Chatterton had, in fact, invented his own imagined world, developed his own form of medieval diction and spelling, and artificially aged the "parchments." Based on the relative success of the Rowley adventure, though, Chatterton resolved to pursue a career as a writer. He contrived to obtain a dismissal from his apprenticeship by leaving a false suicide note and a satirical "will" on his employer's desk, and set off for London in April 1770. During the next four months he produced a great volume and range of material, including elegies, prose essays, love and political letters, libretti for musicals, and long satires and met with some success among editors and booksellers (though not as much as he claimed in boastful letters to his mother and sister in Bristol). Yet ambition, pride, egotism, and a conviction of his own merits had always been hallmarks of Chatterton's personality, and he was downcast by rejections and delays in publishing his work. Irregular payments for work that was accepted obliged him to live in a garret in a seedy area of Holborn and eventually brought him near starvation. On August 25, he was found dead in his room surrounded by scraps of paper; he had drunk arsenic. Suicide was probable and was accepted as the cause of death as far as his contemporaries were concerned, though it has since been conjectured that he died accidentally while trying to administer a remedy for severe gonorrhea.

Chatterton produced some admirable works, including *Aella*, *The Parlyamente of Sprytes*, the *African Eclogues*, and *An Excelente Balade of Charitie*, but his significance in English literary history lies more in the way later poets regarded him and his writing. First, Chatterton's Rowley manuscripts, along with James Macpherson's Ossian poems (which also appeared in the 1760s and likely influenced Chatterton), are the great literary forgeries of the 18th century. Both contributed to the revival of interest in a heroic and medieval past. Chatterton, in particular, celebrated a world in which ideal relationships between poet and patron could exist. Some have interpreted this as a reaction against his position in virtual servitude in a city dedicated to commerce or as a search for the father he never had. Though the spurious nature of the Rowley poems was established by scholars like Thomas Tyrwhitt and Thomas Warton soon after Chatterton's death, a controversy nonetheless erupted over Chatterton, making him the dominant topic of conversation in literary circles, particularly in 1781 and 1782. While it was difficult to believe the Rowley manuscripts were genuine, it seemed equally incredible that a 15-year-old could have invented and composed the entire body of work.

Second, Chatterton's significance lies in the myth that grew up around him in the Romantic period that followed. By the 1780s, he was considered the paradigm of a genius poet, ruined by the indifference and neglect of a philistine society. Virtually all of the major and minor Romantic poets allude to him with either praise or regret. He appears in Coleridge's *Monody on the Death of Chatterton* and in Shelley's *Adonais*; Wordsworth refers to him in *Resolution and Independence* as "the marvellous boy," and the epithet has stuck. Keats, who was of all the Romantic poets closest to Chatterton in his love of medieval romance and in his tragically short life, dedicated *Endymion* to Chatterton and insisted he was "the purest writer in the English Language." For both generations of Romantic writers, Chatterton symbolized the rebel against 18th-century rationalism and the neglected genius who had tried to revive medieval romance. (*See also* Primitivism.)

Angela Esterhammer

Works Consulted

Holmes, Richard. "Thomas Chatterton: The Case Re-opened." *Cornhill Magazine* 178 (1970): 203–51.

Meyerstein, E.H. W. *A Life of Thomas Chatterton.* New York: Scribner's, 1930.

Taylor, Donald S. *Thomas Chatterton's Art: Experiments in Imagined History.* Princeton: Princeton UP, 1978.

Children's Literature

The poetry of Blake and Wordsworth ushered in a new vocabulary of childhood, one informed by a belief in the visionary, spiritual power of joy and imagination. Blake's *Songs of Innocence* (1789) and Wordsworth's *Lyrical Ballads* (1798) remain key documents in an emerging mythology of childhood that glorified the spontaneous, unconscious knowledge inherent in early childhood that was lost with maturity and acculturation. Childhood, these poets insisted, is a state closest to God and to nature. Wordsworth, in particular, articulated a "creed of childhood" in the Great Ode that bestows upon the adult a lasting blessing. He exalted "this infant sensibility,/Great birth-right of our being" in *The Prelude* and proclaimed the enthronement of childhood and its supreme authority.

An interest in childhood developed through the 18th century, fueled by the writings of Locke and Rousseau. But poets and writers in the 19th century, including Lamb, Coleridge, Clare, and Hazlitt, created a new vision of the child: a creature not born as a blank slate, but empowered by a link with the otherworldly. These writers repeatedly returned to childhood memories, to states of early joy and transcendence, in order to seek nurturance from what Wordsworth called this splendid vision.

Thus one of the hallmarks of the Romantic age was its great interest in children. Ironically, this Romantic ideology of childhood affected children's literature only later in the 19th century. Indeed, literature for children written between 1790 and 1830 broke little new ground (although *The Three Bears* was written then), and the one work now associated with radically shifting the present understanding of childhood, Blake's *Songs of Innocence*, was an obscure, little-read volume in its day. The prominent writers for children during the Romantic age, Trimmer, More, Sherwood, Richard and Maria Edgeworth, all continued the moral, rational, and utilitarian underpinnings thought necessary for children's writing since Locke published his groundbreaking *Some Thoughts Concerning Education* (1693). The philosophies informing children's writings were complex during this age, but most writers accepted the emphasis on instruction rather than on delight. Certainly the French Revolution and its aftermath influenced children's writers, who were concerned that their literature not inflame untoward ambition in lower class readers nor undercut the social hierarchy thought necessary for stability. The lengthy Napoleonic Wars, which ended in 1815, further restrained literature written for children; diversion and fancy were too trifling and imagination too subversive in an age unsettled by war and uncertain of its future.

Writers for children were sensitive to their roles as educators who must inculcate love of country, a sense of duty, and an unshaken faith. Evangelical writers, headed by Trimmer and More, turned their attention principally to original sin and the threat of eternal damnation if children were not spiritually prepared. The revolutionary belief that a child could be father of the man countered such evangelical writers' firm faith in an authoritarian God in heaven paralleled by authoritarian parents on earth. A writer like Trimmer held that reason inevitably brought one back to God and to acceptance of things as they are. She is now remembered as the originator of *Guardian of Education* (1802–05), a publication that provided anxious parents with a guide to appropriate and moral literature (i.e., literature that promoted subordination to God and His created social order). In particular, Trimmer hoped to counter what she considered the subversive pleasures of street literature, the inexpensive chapbooks that reprinted medieval romances, folktales, ribald ballads, and exotica.

One of the leaders of the Sunday School movement, More also hoped to provide a substitute for the "immoral" influence of chapbooks. Her *Cheap Repository Tracts* (1795–98) was enormously popular and paved the way for the Religious Tract Society (established 1799) and its prodigious outpouring of evangelical children's literature in the 19th century. *The Children's Companion* (1824–1930), a religious magazine, attests to the power and influence evangelical writers for children accrued for nearly 150 years. Indeed, in the early 19th century, religious literature for children headed the lists of children's book publishers, verifying the importance of such literature to parents, who were faced with high infant-mortality rates and must have felt deeply the need to prepare children for unpredictable death.

Trimmer and More carried an earlier, 18th-century evangelism, with its twin mission of conversion and reform, into the Romantic age. Sherwood infused the goals of earlier evangelicals with a sentimentality peculiar to her time. Her fiction stressed religious feeling and emotional states, as well as concern for the individual; thus works like *History of Little Henry and His Bearer* (1814) or *The Little Woodman and His Dog Caesar* (1818) presented children's lives realistically, with detail and psychological insight. However, Sherwood is now remembered for her nightmarish tale of a family's religious quickening. Her infamous *The Fairchild Family* (1818) vividly presented the wages of sin and the eternity of damnation children would suffer if not adequately prepared for God's kingdom. Throughout this book, the author graphically described death, putrefaction, and the horror of hellfire in order to press urgently into the minds of the young the need for piety and obedience. Hers is an unrelenting Calvinist vision of innate depravity. That Sherwood's novel was enormously popular underscores how divided children's writers were during the Romantic age. To many, childhood was not a time of innocence and joy, but a time of intense moral scrutiny and spiritual purging, in preparation for a purer afterlife. Repentance and self-abasement, an emphasis on a vital, active Christianity, as well as a profound belief in the world's wickedness, marked the evangelical children's books.

Not all writers for children were so vigorously Puritan as the evangelical writers. But even those rationalists, like the Edgeworths, who downplayed religion, emphasized the necessary role of adults in shaping children's development and in restraining the imagination. The three main virtues of rationalist writers—reason, morality, and usefulness—have strong roots in 18th-century orthodoxy, and the rationalists' distrust of folklore and adventure and Gothic fiction was shared by evangelical authors. From Locke and Rousseau, the rationalists emphasized writings that matched children's "natural" development and that held their interest. In this way, rationalist writers for children, in their

scrutiny of maturation and of parenting practices, as well as in their concession that sometimes children do know what is best for them, were less rigid writers for children than were those driven by, to use More's phrase, "the absolute claims of religion." They were no less conservative in their goals—obedience, moderation, industry, respectability—but their writings are often entertaining despite their didacticism. Their fictive protagonists, for the first time in children's literature, approximated Wordsworth's "race of *real* children; not too wise/Too learned, or too good," as noted in Book V of *The Prelude*.

Richard and Maria Edgeworth reigned as the champions of rationalism. Though initially drawn to Rousseau and his emphasis on the essential goodness of children, a lack of social restraint, and a delayed education, as expressed in the enormously influential *Emile*, Richard revised his ideas on childhood late in the 18th century. His voice, clearly sounding through the writings of his daughter, Maria, returned to Lockean themes: tolerance, hard work, moderation, and education through the senses and carefully chosen writings. Their output was prolific, and among the works that most influenced children's literature of the Romantic age were *Parent's Assistant* (1795, 1796, 1800); *Practical Education* (1798); *Early Lessons and Moral Tales* (1801); and *Popular Tales* (1804). Maria's fictive tales, epitomized by her *The Purple Jar*, were well-crafted (she was a gifted storyteller), realistic, fundamentally moral, and dismissive of the imagination. Invariably, her young protagonists' feet remain squarely on the ground. Three years before his death, Richard published *Continuations of Early Lessons* (1814), reiterating once more his ideas on the art of educating children. Books, he declared, should supplement what children observe and discuss in life. The best books for children, moreover, are those that entertain while instructing. It is important to stress that the Edgeworths can in no way be called writers of imaginative children's literature. The fanciful, adventurous, romantic, and Gothic received harsh words from them. Children, according to their agenda, were to learn their place in the social order and ascend the throne of reason.

Maria continued writing until her death in 1849, projecting her father's synthesis of Locke and Rousseau into the nurseries of Victoria's subjects. Thus the rationalist agenda, so instrumental in shaping children's books during the Romantic age, like the evangelical agenda, enjoyed a long life.

Much of the literature written for children during this age, then, bore the heavy hand of dutiful adult creators. Improved printing methods, efficient distribution of books, and numerous eager parents wealthy enough to purchase children's literature assured the proliferation of moral and religious titles. Moreover, a well-financed, highly motivated evangelical movement published millions of inexpensive volumes and made sure the poor of the nation received instruction, too. A large number of volumes were devoted to improving young minds: geographies, grammars, ABCs, natural histories, conduct guides, Bibles, guides to knowledge, moral fables (including the ever-popular Aesop), didactic juvenile novels, religious and devotional books, atlases, and histories crowded the shelves in the "juvenile libraries" of bookstores. The many writers for children between 1790 and 1820 filled the spectrum between evangelism and rationalism. Aikin (1781–1864), Maria Elizabeth Budden (?1780–1832), Lucy Cameron (1781–1858), Mary Belson Elliot (?1794–1870), Barbara Hofland (1770–1844), Mary

Robson Hughes (fl. 1820), Alicia Catherine Mant (?1788–1869), Mary Pilkington (1766–1839), and Ann (1787–1830) and Jane Taylor (1783–1824) were among the more popular moral authors then writing for children.

Though reform-minded adults controlled much of the publishing industry, they could not stifle the production of popular forms: fairytales, folklore, ballads, and romances. Chapbooks and broadsides reached their heydey in the years before 1820, providing children with an alternative to overt didacticism and wan realities. Even serious writers, like Ann and Jane Taylor, whose *Original Poems* (Part 1, 1804; Part 2, 1805) presented comic poems, imaginative lyrics, and homely scenes, as well as the usual moral fare, occasionally embraced the joys of fantasy. The most effective countervail to the moralists came from business-minded publishers. Poets cultivated a new interest in the imagination, the primitive, and the exotic. Their readers also desired literature that examined the extremities of history and of the human mind: moments of heightened passion, sublimity, or terror. Most assuredly, readers wanted to be entertained and delighted. Some publishers, led by John Harris, Vernor and Hood, and J. Walker, eagerly supplied volumes for this new audience. Reprints from the 18th century—Clara Reeve's *Old English Baron* (1777), John Marshall's *Primrose Pretty-face* (c. 1785), Robert Patlock's *Peter Wilkins* (1788), among them—reintroduced stories found unfit by Trimmer. Charles Perrault's (1628–1703) *Mother Goose Tales* (1697) and Countess d'Aulnoy's (1650–1705) *Diverting Works* (1707) enjoyed a revival, as did numerous traditional English tales.

The years following 1803 proved a watershed in the return of fanciful, Gothic, and balladic works that excited the imagination, inflamed the sentiments, or provoked comic, at times bawdy, humor. Tongue-twisters, poetry games, and limericks became fashionable, and witty, fanciful pieces like William Roscoe's (1753–1831) *Butterfly's Ball and the Grasshopper's Feast* (1806) endorsed a poetry that was nonsensical and fun. In their preface to *Tales from Shakespear* (1807), Charles and Mary Lamb extolled delight, beauty, and the enrichment of fancy, virtues found everywhere in Shakespeare and argued that an expanded imagination was a primary benefit of reading the plays to children.

The publishers Benjamin Tabart (fl. 1801–18) and Godwin were pivotal figures in popularizing fairytales, despite the opposition of evangelists and rationalists alike. Godwin proclaimed in 1802 that imagination, not knowledge, must be the foundation of children's literature. The many fairytales, romances, and adventures, like the English translation of J.D.R.Wyss's *Swiss Family Robinson* (1814), that rolled off Godwin's presses helped change the destiny of children's literature. By 1820, just three years before M.M. Grimm's translated *German Popular Stories* (1823–26) began to appear in booksellers' stalls, fairytales enjoyed an exalted status, no longer condemned as amoral trifles. In the next decades, Victorian writers would reinvent the fairytale and take it to new highs—as well as new lows.

Another factor in the growing enjoyment of children's literature was the advent of hand-tinted steel engravings, lithography, and improved wood-block illustration. Eighteenth-century children's books were adorned with primitive-looking prints. New technology, however, allowed greater subtlety and individual craftsmanship. The artwork of William Mulready (1786–1863), Stothard, Flaxman, and Cruikshank altered forever the role of illustration in children's literature. The new artwork, interpretive in nature, complemented the texts. A gifted artist could exploit moments of humor, sentiment, or psychological complexity, providing the reader an added visual level of understanding. The pleasure gained by illustrated texts helped loosen the grip Puritanism had secured around English children's literature since its beginnings in the 17th century. The art of book illustration, emanating from the Romantic age, gained in stature and rose to brilliant achievement during the 19th century—evidence of the developing interest in imaginative form and aesthetic delight.

While the early decades of the 19th century have long been associated with an idealization of childhood, in truth a cult of childhood did not emerge until the middle of Victoria's reign. Prevailing attitudes toward children between 1790 and 1830 were strongly reflected in the moralistic literature published for them. Such literature exalted the moral authority of adults; promoted obedient, subservient children; and praised traditional virtues: modesty, duty, forbearance, and faith. However, a thriving subculture of "lowly" literary forms— folktales and fairytales, romances, ballads— resisted the moralists' ideologies and provided needed outlets for adventure, fantasy, imagination, and humor. By the 1820s, this subculture was on the rise, empowered by advocates of childhood. Thus, Romantic attitudes toward children arrived late in juvenile libraries. Not until the 1830s was a mythos of innocence, joy, and imagination generally accepted by both writers and consumers of children's literature. Even then, evangelical literature remained an effective counterforce in the lives of children.

Susan Naramore Maher

Works Consulted

Cutt, Margaret Nancy. *Ministering Angels: A Study of Nineteenth-Century Evangelical Writing for Children.* Wormley: Five Owls, 1979.

Harvey Darton, F.J. *Children's Books in England: Five Centuries of Social Life.* New York: Cambridge UP, 1982.

Jackson, Mary V. *Engines of Instruction, Mischief, and Magic: Children's Literature in England from Its Beginnings to 1839.* Lincoln: U of Nebraska P, 1989.

Meigs, Cornelia Lynde. *A Critical History of Children's Literature.* New York: Macmillan, 1969.

Summerfield, Geoffrey. *Fantasy and Reason: Children's Literature in the Eighteenth Century.* Athens: U of Georgia P, 1984.

Children, View of

Children in the imaginations of Blake, Coleridge, Wordsworth, and Southey are treated idealistically as innocents and divines; they are creatures of instinctive goodness sparkling with spiritual insights beyond the confines of the natural world. If uncorrupted by society, children exemplify the innate nobility of Rousseau's noble savage (*Emile*, 1762; *Confessions*, 1781). Pure and innocent in thought and body, most children depicted by Romantic writers romp joyfully through nature, with which they share a spiritual affinity. Affected by Rousseau's idealization of the primitive state of humanity, the Romantic poets created a belief in the natural goodness of simple people and used children—with their simplicity, spontaneity, instinctive benevolence, and uninhibited free expression—as the medium to demonstrate this purity. (*See also* Coleridge, Hartley.)

Children embody the essential ingredients of the Romantic spirit: curiosity, love of beauty, free-flowing imagination, and innate goodness. Communion with nature allows the child to partake of the sublime. Blessed with natural piety, children have transcendental powers to commune with nature from whose educative force they learn simplicity, beauty, and goodness.

Such sensitivities are reserved to children and available only through childhood memory to the poet. To the Romantic writers, childhood is the origin of the imagination and divinity in humanity, the seat of inspiration for the soul and the poet; hence, children are visionary. These writers revered childhood as the source of the poet's creative imagination and energies. Containing the seeds of all virtues and strengths, the child serves as a model for the adult and the source, from the child's sensuous joy, of the perception of beauty. It is through the writer's youthful memories that the adult can identify with the aesthetics of childish appreciation.

In addition to their virtues and because of their innocence, children are sometimes victims of the forces of evil, either real or imagined. Children can be terrorized by their own imaginations or seduced for evil purposes by adults. Some Romantic poets, such as Blake and Coleridge most often portray children as lost, motherless, orphaned, and susceptible to self-indulgence and corruption.

In essence, however, children in the early poets' works embody their longing for the past or a prenatal stage of innocence of the human soul. The Romantic element of striving—the desiring to fulfill; the grasping for perfection, yet never achieving it—is best represented in youth, itself an emerging process.

These children possess divine insights because their perceptions go beyond that of adults to a higher reality. Blake uses children symbolically to suggest the creative impulse, such as an incorporeal child on a cloud inspiring pipers and poets. Exemplifying innocence, children in Blake's poems often represent the mystical union of humanity of child with God. In *The Lamb* from *Songs of Innocence* (1789) for example, the creator of this innocent creature blends with the child and the creation itself.

In other poems, Blake treats children sentimentally, indicating their pathetic state in a decadent world. Blake also shows how the child must succumb to the fallen world through maturity and experience, and in his *Songs of Experience* (1794) children become victims and must balance their pure spirits with reality, their visionary innocence with a fallen world. To Blake the child stays innocent as a result of his imagination, until he grows up. As in his "lost child" poems and "nurse" poems, Blake laments the descent of innocence of youth into the world with a contingent loss of its ideality. Experience destroys the child, and his innocence can exist only in his imagination.

It is Wordsworth who, above all, articulates the Romantic conception of childhood. Influenced by Rousseau's view of the sainted child and by Plato's philosophy of preexistence and immortality, Wordsworth also uses the notion of childhood as ideal state. For him, in the poem *My heart leaps up when I behold* (1804), "The Child is the father of the Man" in that childhood purity fosters the quest for further spirituality, the Romantic drive for perfection that paradoxically once was had.

Ode: Intimations of Immortality from Recollections of Early Childhood (1807) contains Wordsworth's finest statements about children. From childhood comes the springs of inspiration for the poet. As in *Tintern Abbey* (1798), the poet evokes a sense of loss of the awe inherent in a child, invoking in the poem the loss of childhood as a loss of glory. The youth for Wordsworth is a priest of nature. In Book I of *The Prelude* (1850), Wordsworth deals with the "Childhood and Schooltime" of his boyhood in the Lake District, where he becomes attuned to the beauty and mystery of nature. The child's power comes from his feelings, usually suppressed by adulthood. The role of the child is to help develop perception of the soul's heritage. In children, the first-generation poet sees the self and the self's own possibility of creative imagination. Wordsworth, for one, depicts himself as a child deeply affected by nature. His nostalgic, sentimental view of childhood is predominantly that of a blissful, harmonious existence.

Later writers depict childhood as a stage of innocence that is soon lost by the changes brought on by time, experience, and maturity. In later writings, not only are children victims of the adult real world, but, susceptible to sin and guilt, they become corrupted. The naturally sainted child and the child of nature lose their innocence and exuberance and often become demonized.

Norma W. Goldstein

Works Consulted

Auerbach, Nina. *Romantic Imprisonment; Women and Other Glorified Outcasts*. New York: Columbia UP, 1985.

Fairchild, Hoxie Neale. *The Romantic Quest*. New York: Columbia UP, 1931.

Gleckner, Robert F., and Gerald E. Enscoe. *Romanticism, Points of View*. Englewood Cliffs: Prentice, 1962.

Hough, Graham. *The Romantic Poets*. Ed. Basil Willey. New York: Norton, 1964.

Pattison, Robert. *The Child Figure in English Literature*. Athens: U of Georgia P, 1978.

Schapiro, Barbara A. *The Romantic Mother: Narcissistic Patterns in Romantic Poetry*. Baltimore: Johns Hopkins UP, 1983.

Church of England

Traditionally, during the 18th and early 19th centuries, the Established Church in England was characterized by conservative attitudes, a "high" conception of itself, and a fervent hatred of what was perceived as "enthusiasm" (i.e., fanaticism or religious hysteria). It was a time when church and state seemed inseparable, and the privileges enjoyed, especially in the upper echelons of the Anglican hierarchy, were jealously guarded. Given poor organization throughout the country, the Church seemed disinterested in its flock and impervious to change. Out of this stagnation emerged the Evangelical Revival, a movement that was to have a lasting effect on the Anglican communion. (*See also* Religion.)

Evangelicalism was steadfastly opposed to the High Church, though the parties were never monolithic. Evangelicals preached the cross, the depravity of humanity, and justification by faith alone. They pondered long and daily over the Bible, and displayed a friendliness toward nonconformists, to which High Churchmen were not easily reconciled. Evangelicals placed much less emphasis on the institutional Church than did the High Churchmen, who stressed the visible church, the ministry, and the sacraments. Instead, the Evangelicals attached great importance to itinerant and field-preaching, sometimes by laity, as well as the consolidation of converts into small societies in that they could relate their spiritual experience. These techniques in particular led to the success of a revival that its beneficiaries saw as the providential effusion of the Holy Spirit in national life.

Evangelicals were so called because they placed great emphasis on their zeal in spreading the Evangel or Gospel. The Evangelical idea of sin was that since the Fall, it was endemic in human nature and prevented obedience to God's law. Accordingly, the only way to escape eternal punishment was to lay hold of the prom-

ises made in the Gospel. This process, which demanded divine inspiration, resulted in a conversion, an intense religious experience—such as that of John Wesley (1703–91), the leading spirit in Methodism, on 24 May 1738—leading to assurance, the certainty of personal salvation.

The attention that Methodism in general, and Wesley's conversion in particular, have received has obscured the origins of the Evangelical Revival. There were indications early in the 18th century that a revival—retrospectively labeled "Methodist"—was well under way. Its distinguishing characteristics, the experience of personal salvation and the preaching of a "New Birth" were firmly established by the time George Whitefield (1714–70) and Wesley began their outdoor oratory to the Kingswood miners (February 1739). It is therefore difficult to attribute the Evangelical Revival to a single source. Its history, like that of Romanticism, shows how those faced by similar intellectual or spiritual crises can, in isolation from each other, pass through a strikingly similar odyssey toward similar conclusions. The rapid consolidation of the Revival in its early phases was due not only to field-preaching to the disinherited poor, but also to successful recruitment from the High Church, which claimed among its ranks many members of the Anglican religious societies. These groups did much to propagate knowledge of the movement, for in addition to calls for regular church attendance, members were enjoined to take part in semiliturgical devotions, often on a Sunday evening, in a vestry or hired room, and there discussed spiritual problems. The ethos of these societies and the mentality of the members were readily appreciated by the preachers who sought to win them. Also, their structure was congenial to evangelistic techniques—particularly those of Wesley's

"Connexion," wherein the lower echelons, adherents were fused together into societies, bands, and classes. Thus, from the Anglican religious societies, the Revival drew a dedicated and disciplined following, who helped to organize and educate those converts won by field-preaching to the poor. This formidable synthesis helped to give shape and substance to the growing movement.

Anglican Evangelicalism and Methodism shared not only doctrinal sympathies but also a common spiritual heritage. Many of the early Evangelicals sympathized with the aims of Methodism, and accepted the blanket title of "Methodist." But with the licensing of Methodist preaching houses in 1760 and the ordination of the first Methodist minister by Wesley in 1784, it became clear to all who considered themselves Anglicans that there was a fundamental conflict between Methodists and Evangelicals concerning the parochial system and Church discipline. When after Wesley's death, the Methodist "Connexion" became the Methodist Church (numbering 72,000, although four times that number attended their services), the final separation was effected. The intensity of fellowship among Methodists became a substitute for, rather than an auxiliary to, the services of the Church, which seemed cold by comparison. By 1800, "Evangelical" had become a party epithet within the Established Church, but markedly distinct from the High Church.

The majority of Anglican Evangelicals had, by the turn of the century, become moderate Calvinists, due to the influence of their leaders, which included John Fletcher (1729–85), Henry Venn (1725–95), and John Newton (1725–1807). They claimed to be Anglicans first and foremost, drawing their doctrine not from Calvin's *Institutes* but from the Scriptures as interpreted by the Reforming divines of the 16th century in the prayer book, articles, and homilies. Their preaching emphasized the practical piety that was evidence of humanity conversion. The party began to carry influence in the universities, largely through the efforts of the magnetic Cambridge preacher Charles Simeon (1759–1836). Their piety and humanity won them a large following in the 19th century, and they played a major role in missionary work and social reform.

The rising stature that Evangelicalism enjoyed did not, however, sound the death knell for the High Church. At Oxford there were those who wished to redefine the "high" conception of the Anglican Church by recalling its adherents to an appreciation of its Catholic (i.e., universal) character. Their goals were to deemphasize the Erastian nature of their Church, and also to show that it was the historic Catholic Church of the land. This they did by appealing to the 17th-century Caroline divines and through them to the early Church Fathers and the undivided Church of the first 11 centuries. They held fast to the Bible, the historic creeds, the sacraments (including baptismal regeneration), and the apostolic ministry. The leaders of this group—including John Henry Newman (1801–90), Richard Hurrell Froude (1803–36), John Keble (1792–1866), and Edward Bouverie Pusey (1800–82)—founded the Oxford Movement (1833) and helped to foster what came to be known as the Anglo-Catholic Revival. Through the efforts of Froude in particular, many of these arguments were bolstered by an appeal to the Middle Ages. The interest in this period expressed by Romantic writers, artists, and architects, led to fanciful innovations in architecture, hymnody, liturgy, vestments, and church furnishings. The work of John Mason Neale (1818–66) and others in enhancing these visible aids to faith injected new interest into Anglican worship and ensured the survival of the Anglican High Church.

Leon B. Litvack

Works Consulted

Carus, William, ed. *Memoirs of the Life of the Rev. Charles Simeon, M.A., with a Selection from His Writings and Correspondence.* London: Hatchard, 1847.

Cragg, Gerald R. *The Church and the Age of Reason, 1648–1789.* The Pelican History of the Church 4. Harmondsworth: Penguin, 1960.

Davies, Rupert E. *Methodism.* Harmondsworth: Penguin, 1963.

Jay, Elisabeth, ed. *The Evangelical and Oxford Movements.* Cambridge English Prose Texts. Cambridge: Cambridge UP, 1983.

Norman, Edward. *Church and Society in England, 1770–1970.* Oxford: Clarendon, 1976.

Rowell, Geoffrey. *The Vision Glorious: Themes and Personalities of the Catholic Revival in Anglicanism.* Oxford: Oxford UP, 1983.

Rupp, E. Gordon. *Religion in England, 1688–1791.* Oxford History of the Christian Church. Oxford: Oxford UP, 1986.

— — —, et al., eds. *History of the Methodist Church in Great Britain.* 4 vols. London: Epworth, 1978–88.

Vidler, Alec R. *The Church in an Age of Revolution, 1789 to the Present Day.* The Pelican History of the Church 5. Harmondsworth: Penguin, 1974.

Walsh, John D. "Origins of the Evangelical Revival." *Essays in Modern Church History, in Memory of Norman Sykes.* Eds. G.V. Bennett and J.D. Walsh. London: Adam, 1966: 132–62.

Clairmont, Mary Jane (Claire)
1798–1879)

Mary Jane Clairmont, better known after 1814 as Claire Clairmont, was a prominent member of the circles around Godwin and Shelley. She was the daughter of Godwin's second wife, the widow Jane Clairmont, from her first marriage (if there was indeed a first marriage); Clairmont was hence stepsister to Mary Wollstonecraft Shelley (*née* Godwin). She joined Mary and Percy on their elopement from Godwin's house in July 1814, and accompanied Mary Shelley throughout most of the eight years of her relationship to Percy, until his death in 1822. Her ambivalent status and mixed welcome in the Shelley household, and above all her rivalry with Mary, feature prominently in the journals she kept at this time, which are now a major source of biographical material concerning the Shelley circle.

Vivacious and ambitious, Clairmont in early 1816 determinedly set about the seduction of Lord Byron while both were still in England. Her relationship with Byron formed an initial bridge between the two poets in Switzerland, but a daughter born of this very one-sided affair, Allegra (1817–22), became the center of a great deal of friction between the two households, with Percy Shelley often acting as go-between in negotiations as to rights over the child.

After the double catastrophe of the deaths of Percy Shelley and Allegra (of typhus), Clairmont moved in with her brother Charles in Vienna and thence to Russia and a career of governessing. She lived subsequently in Italy and Paris. A legacy of £12,000 from Shelley, not received until 1844 after the death of Timothy Shelley, was lost mainly in reckless investments. She eventually settled down to a life of pinched independence with her niece Pauline in Florence, dying there in 1879. Attempts by a young scholar named Edward Silsbee to obtain from Clairmont some supposed love letters from Percy Shelley prompted Henry James's story *The Aspern Papers* (1888).

Timothy J.A. Clark

Works Consulted

Clairmont, Clara Mary Jane. *The Journals of Claire Clairmont*. Ed. Marion Kingston Stocking. Cambridge: Harvard UP, 1968.

Dictionary of National Biography, *s.v.* "Clairmont, Mary Jane."

Holmes, Richard. *Shelley: The Pursuit*. New York: Dutton, 1975.

St. Clair, William. *The Godwins and the Shelleys: The Biography of a Family*. New York: Norton, 1989.

Clare, John

(1793–1864)

The poet John Clare was born in 1793 in the small village of Helpston, the son of a thresher, Parker Clare, who was himself the illegitimate son of an itinerant Scottish schoolmaster. Although Clare's parents were under constant financial pressure, they were able to send him to school for at least three months a year until he was about age 12. An avid reader, he devoured such sixpenny-chapbook romances as *Cinderella* and *Jack and the Bean Stalk* and also benefited from his father's wide knowledge of folk ballads. At school he met Mary Joyce, some four years his junior, who was his girlfriend until their relationship was suddenly broken off at about the time Mary's father died. Many years later, after he had been committed to an asylum, Clare was to suffer under the delusion that Mary Joyce was his wife, and she became the subject of many of his later poems.

After his school days ended, Clare worked at a number of menial agricultural jobs, unable to settle on a profession. But one day he read part of James Thomson's *Seasons* and discovered his true vocation. From that day on he wrote verse on any scrap of paper that he could find and was not discouraged by the fact that his illiterate mother used much of his early poetry to kindle fires.

In 1817, encouraged by a local bookseller, he circulated a proposal for publishing a volume of his verse by subscription. By happy chance, this proposal was noticed by Edward Drury, a Stamford businessman, who sent some of Clare's verse to his cousin, the publisher John Taylor. Taylor was already an enthusiastic promoter of new talent—he was Keats's publisher—and Clare's first book of verse, *Poems Descriptive of Rural Life and Scenery*, was published in 1820. Advertised by Taylor as the work of a young, day-laboring peasant, the volume was an immediate popular and critical success and went into four editions. Soon after the success of his first book, Clare married Martha "Patty" Turner, a loyal and supportive wife who was to bear him eight children.

During his brief years of celebrity, Clare visited London on four occasions, and he met such luminaries as Lamb, Hazlitt, De Quincey, Coleridge, and J.H. Reynolds. But despite the success of his first volume and a subscription fund started on his behalf, Clare was still forced to work as an agricultural laborer, and his popularity faded. Taylor became increasingly critical in his editing of Clare's poems, reducing *The Shepherd's Calendar* from 3,382 lines to 1,761, and Clare's literary output was hampered by illness and chronic depression. While 3,616 copies of *Poems Descriptive* were sold, by 1829 *The Village Minstrel* (1821) had sold a disappointing 1,250 copies and only 425 volumes of *The Shepherd's Calendar* (1827) had been purchased. And although *The Rural Muse* (1835) was well-reviewed, few copies of it were sold. When Clare insisted on an accounting of his profits from book sales in 1829, he was informed that his publications had actually put him £140 in debt.

In 1831, Clare sought to better his financial position by moving to a cottage and small-holding in Northborough to set himself up as an independent farmer. Although only three miles from Clare's native Helpston, Northborough seemed an alien place to him. His days there were not happy, and he declined both physically and mentally, becoming convinced that he had two wives, both his actual wife Patty and the sweetheart of his youth, Mary Joyce. Finally, in June 1837, Taylor had Clare conveyed to an asylum for the mentally ill at High Beach, from which Clare escaped in 1841, walking home to his family in Northborough.

Although he suffered from many delusions during this period of his life—most prominently the belief that he was a number of famous people, including Byron, Shakespeare, and Nelson—his poetic career was not over. In fact, two long poems, *Child Harold* and *Don Juan*, date from his asylum years. After his escape from High Beach, Clare was admitted to Northborough Asylum in December 1841, and remained there until his death in 1864.

As a careful observer of nature and its phenomena, Clare was able to present the natural world accurately and clearly. In *The Nightingales Nest*, for example, Clare describes the shy brown bird as he had actually seen it in the woodlands. And Clare's presentations of rural life have a special importance because he lived and worked with peasants—he was in a position to see the effects of enclosure directly. Clare's poetry is characterized by a lack of punctuation, a general disregard for grammar, and a frequent use of dialect. While his nature poetry may well constitute his greatest achievement, he is also important as a writer of ballads, love poetry, poems against enclosure, satires, and, in his later years, visionary poems that sometimes recall Blake.

William D. Brewer

Works Consulted

Grainger, Margaret, ed. *The Natural History Prose Writings of John Clare*. Oxford: Oxford UP, 1983.

Robinson, Eric, ed. *John Clare's Autobiographical Writings*. Oxford: Oxford UP, 1983.

Robinson, Eric, and David Powell, eds. *John Clare*. New York: Oxford UP, 1984.

Storey, Edward. *A Right to Song: The Life of John Clare*. London: Methuen, 1982.

Storey, Mark, compiler. *Clare: The Critical Heritage*. London: Routledge, 1973.

Classicism

The influence of Greek and Roman models on Romantic writers and artists was paradoxical. Classicism was linked to the heavy hand of 18th-century prescriptivism; its appeal to absolute, rational judgment and its claims to the universal and the permanent were antithetical to Romantic relativism and intuition. Yet, at the same time, the purity of its forms served as the perfect backdrop for Romantic investigations of impure, unpredictable human emotion. Thus, even as they rejected the spirit of Classicism, the Romantics embraced its incarnation. (*See also* Antiquarianism, Decorative Arts, and Hellenism.)

The clearest example of this ambivalence can be found in the work of Jacques-Louis David. During the last years of the Bourbon monarchy, David could safely comment on current political controversies only by disguising them in classical clothing; best known are *The Oath of the Horatii* (1785) and *The Lictors bringing back to Brutus the bodies of his sons* (1789), in which the architecture, clothing, and even the poses have specific Roman models, but the message is totally contemporary. Such works impress a moral or political lesson on the spectator, since Neoclassicism dictated at the same time that they express the artist's and spectator's deep emotional ferment. After David became one of the leaders of the Revolution, his best paintings—*Marat Dead* (1794) and *Napoleon Crossing the Alps* (1800)—needed no classical allusions. But he continued to draw upon either Greek or Roman models for lesser works, such as *The Sabine women enforcing peace* (1799) and *Leonidas at Thermoplylae* (1815). Throughout his career, the discipline of a classical setting enabled David to incorporate a great depth of emotion, and a relative freedom of technique, without descending into sentimentality or illegibility; in contrast, when Eugene Delacroix painted *The Massacre at Chios* in 1824 there was no hint of Classicism in setting or style, although the subject in actuality *was* Greek.

The Greek and Roman models, in fact, symbolized quite distinct paradigms for Romantic painters and writers. Greece, as defined by Johann Winckelmann in *Reflections on the Imitation of Greek Art* (1755), symbolized purity and tranquility, an ideal Arcadian state of existence which had been lost to successive occupations; its simplicity was typified by the Doric order. Rome, on the other hand, was experienced through reports from excavations at such late-Roman towns as Baalbek and Palmyra, the meditations of Comte de Volney's *Les Ruines* (1791), and parallels between its long decline and that of the Roman Catholic Church; thus it came to symbolize a continuing struggle between republican virtue and imperial aggrandizement, youthful energy and incipient decay. Republican Rome served as the primary model for the French and the Americans; but it was Periclean Athens that fired the imaginations of the Germans and the English.

For Shelley, as for David, the revival of pre-Christian mythologies allowed him to develop new non-Christian myths that would speak to contemporary England.

Shelley was passionately committed to political action; unfortunately, England's heroes in this post-Napoleonic period were Nelson and Wellington, not Alastor and Prometheus, his own first heroes. Therefore, the Greek models were used mainly for travesty rather than aggrandizement, as in *Oedipus Tyrannus; or, Swellfoot the Tyrant* (1819). When Shelley used Greek models without ulterior political ambitions, as in the *Hymns to Apollo and Pan* (1820) and *Epipsychidion* (1821), the result was some of his most beautiful poetry, fusing lyricism and intensity.

Even more steeped in Greek models than Shelley was Keats, whose death provided Shelley with a subject for yet another pseudo-Greek poem, *Adonais*. In *Ode On a Grecian Urn* (1820), Keats meditates on the permanence of art, but at the same time he questions whether a life devoted to art can achieve emotional fulfillment. It remains to this day unclear whether it is Keats, or only the urn, proclaiming "Truth is Beauty, Beauty Truth." Keats also develops his epistemological question in works addressed "To Psyche," "To Apollo," and reworkings of the stories of Endymion and Hyperion.

The Romantic artists' and writers' identification with Greek models and their preference for ruins ultimately converged with their belief in the need for political reformation during the Greek struggle for independence of the early 1820s. The fact that it was a forlorn struggle only heightened the attraction. Byron remained at Missilonghi long after it had become clear there was nothing to gain, seemingly waiting for the miasma of the place to kill him. Delacroix, painting *The Massacre at Chios*, made the death of thousands almost invitingly languorous. The spirit of Classicism inspired the struggle for the universal values of liberty and equality.

Perhaps the finest symbol of Romantic dealings with the classical world, and one of the most disturbing, is the Elgin Marbles. Lord Elgin, British ambassador to Turkey, decided in 1799 to have casts made of the Greek monuments so that Western students of art could learn from them. Their embodiment of time's depredations would be as inspiring as the perfection of their form. In 1801, however, at the urging of Dr. Philip Hunt, Elgin dictated an agreement with the Turks allowing him to remove, not just copy, any pieces of marble that were not necessary for the defense of the citadel. Over the next two years Elgin's men not only "cleared" the bulk of the stones that had been blown clear of the Parthenon when it exploded during a 1687 war between the Venetians and the Turks, they pried off entire sections that were firmly attached. He shipped them to England, where they were eventually installed in the newly formed British Museum and helped inspire the poems of Keats and the paintings of John Martin. (*See also* Elgin Marbles; Nash, John.)

Hartley S. Spatt

Works consulted

Bruno, Vincent J., ed. *The Parthenon*. New York: Norton, 1974.

Clark, Kenneth. *The Romantic Rebellion*. New York: Harper, 1973.

Gaull, Marilyn. *English Romanticism: The Human Context*. New York: Norton, 1988.

Cobbett, William

(1763–1835)

William Cobbett, a very influential journalist of the Romantic period, was born in Farnham, Surrey. The son of a prosperous small farmer, Cobbett spent his first 20 years engaged in agricultural tasks and living an energetic outdoor life in the productive countryside that, throughout his career, would stand as the cherished symbol of England's agrarian strength. (*See also* Censorship.)

After an impulsive move to London in 1782, Cobbett worked for a few gloomy months as a law clerk and then joined the army. From 1784 to 1791 he served in New Brunswick as the clerk to his regiment, eventually achieving the rank of sergeant-major. Shortly after his return to England, Cobbett married Ann Reid, whom he had met in New Brunswick, and he filed charges of peculation against his former officers. The charges aroused suspicion only against Cobbett, and he fled first to France and then to America where he settled near Philadelphia and, using the pseudonym "Peter Porcupine," began his career as a political writer and satirist. Cobbett's British sympathies did not sit well with the American Democrats, and he often found himself fighting what he considered the "tyranny of the mob." His autobiographical *Life and Adventures of Peter Porcupine* (1796), in fact, is a highly polemical defense of his political opinions provoked by some ill-informed personal jabs from his American critics.

When Cobbett returned to England in 1800, the Tory government welcomed him and even offered him the editorship of a pro-government newspaper. He declined the offer, but in 1802 he established the *Political Register*, which continued its weekly political commentaries for the next 33 years. While writing about English politics and society at first hand—rather than as an English visitor writing to an American audience—Cobbett's political attitudes began to shift. He could now see for himself the corruption of the "Pitt-system" of public finance; he could see the devastating effects of the burgeoning industrial economy on the growing underclass of factory workers and of the enclosures and the Speenhamland system on the traditional peasantry; and he could see that Parliament, as it was then constituted, was incompetent to address such problems. Because Cobbett spoke out strongly against these social wrongs, he soon fell out of favor with the government. In 1809, he was convicted on a charge of seditious libel for publishing an article critical of the brutality of military discipline. He spent the next two years in Newgate, from which he continued to direct the management of his farm near Botley (purchased in 1805) and to publish the *Political Register*. The *Register* itself flourished—reaching a weekly circulation of well over 50,000 copies, many of which were handed around among friends or read aloud in taverns and coffeehouses, thus making the actual readership many times that figure.

In 1817, Cobbett was near the zenith of his popular influence, when the government—in response to an increasingly rebellious press and to violent anti-government uprisings—voted to suspend habeas corpus. Rather than endure another stint in Newgate (the likely result of the government's action), Cobbett fled once again to America where he established a small farm on Long Island. He returned two years later only to see his campaign of popular opposition severely restricted by the Six Acts of 1819. Despite his bankruptcy in 1820, Cobbett continued his attacks on England's political and economic structure and his staunch advocacy of Parliamentary reform. He also began taking annual excursions on horseback "to see the *country*; to see the farmers at *home*, and to see the labourers *in the fields*." The record of these excursions, originally published in the *Register*, was finally combined into what is now Cobbett's most famous work, *Rural Rides* (1830). In 1832, Cobbett was elected to the first reformed Parliament as M.P.

for Oldham, a seat he held until his death.

Cobbett's politics are usually described as "radical," but the term is somewhat misleading. While his support of reform and his vigorous attacks on the government aligned him with the radical community, he eschewed the numerous societies—the Hampden Club, for instance—organized to promote social change, and he was always skeptical of the ideals of the French Revolution. "We want nothing new" is a common refrain in his political writing. His aim was not to bring forth a new, egalitarian social order but rather to bring back "old England," an idealized past symbolized for him by the benign and generous stewardship of the landowners and by the neat cottages of an industrious, prosperous, and happy peasantry. In short, Cobbett's social ideal had its roots in the 18th century of his boyhood, not in the new politics of France or of America.

Cobbett's politics were grounded in his economic thinking, and his economic thinking, in turn, was grounded in the concrete. His aim was always to fill the bellies of the workers, and he had little time for abstract arguments based on political conceptions of national strength or on religious notions of the virtue of patient suffering. It was Cobbett's materialism that led him to advocate Parliamentary reform: this body had to be restructured in such a way that its policies would satisfy the material needs of the general population rather than protect the profits and life-styles of an aristocratic or industrial elite. Cobbett's materialism also underlies his attitude toward the fledgling industrial economy. He was not against the mechanization of industry or the technological advancement of agriculture—he spoke out against the framebreaking of the Luddites, for instance—but he saw more clearly than most the social consequences of the new modes of production, and he objected to the tendency of industrial capitalism to consolidate wealth in the hands of the "Lords of the Loom" while simultaneously condemning ordinary laborers to lives of destitution and despair.

If Cobbett saw a solution to the political and economic troubles of the early 19th century, it was that the working classes had to look out for their own welfare and not simply rely on their political and economic superiors to care for them. Practically speaking, this meant that the working classes had to know how to read and write, and Cobbett produced his epistolary *Grammar of the English Language* (1818) to help people teach themselves the rudiments of practical literacy. Likewise, it meant that people had to be aware of various ways to supplement their shrinking wages by adopting the techniques of small-scale, independent cottage industry, the central topic of *Cottage Economy* (1822).

Cobbett's prose style—emphatic, exuberant, sometimes comic, always personal—is remarkable for its descriptive concreteness. A penchant for agricultural metaphors enabled Cobbett more than any other political writer to communicate both with farm laborers themselves and with the many recently dispossessed peasants who were huddling into the new industrial centers. His power as a political writer rests ultimately on his ability to link the realities of his readers' daily lives to his own critiques of public policy and policymakers. In Cobbett's hands, distinctions of social class are obliterated; issues of politics and economics become personal conflicts between individual politicians or landowners and individual laborers.

Kyle Grimes

Works Consulted

Cole, G.D.H. *The Life of William Cobbett*. 1924. New York: Russell, 1971.

Osborne, John W. *William Cobbett*. New Brunswick, NJ: Rutgers UP, 1966.

Sambrook, James. *William Cobbett*. New York: Routledge, 1973.

Spater, G. *William Cobbett: The Poor Man's Friend*. 2 vols. New York: Cambridge UP, 1982.

Williams, Raymond. *Cobbett*. New York: Oxford UP, 1983.

Colburn, Henry

(?–1857)

An extremely successful, often unpopular publisher of the Regency period, Henry Colburn is remembered for his conservatism and his publishing firm's sponsorship of the society, or silver-spoon, novel. Colburn's extreme Tory sympathies found a welcome audience in an England still wary of the lesson of the Revolution across the channel: suspicions of radicalism lingered because of the Reign of Terror and Napoleon's campaign. He founded his conservative journal, the *New Monthly Magazine*, in 1814, a year before the victory at Waterloo. It took its title from the older *Monthly Magazine*, and answered that journal's radical views with conventional arguments drawn from Burke, who urged the House of Commons to beware the Revolution. Colburn avoided the political arena in his second journal, the *Literary Gazette*, which emphasized a bantering, light style and appeared weekly, competing successfully with the somber monthlies and quarterlies.

His magazines provided capital to support his book publishing house. It flourished, unlike such older houses as Constable and Ballantine (which once held the copyrights to Scott's work, the Encyclopedia Britannica, and the *Edinburgh Review*), bankrupted. His firm published the vast majority of Regency novels. Many of these books were aimed at the lowest common denominator in the readership, emphasizing gossip, the latest styles in furniture and clothing, and the manners of the ballroom and opera house. The objects of these satires were amused and read them avidly.

Much of Colburn's success, however, lay with his luck in publishing books that appealed to every stratum of English society at a time when almost everyone had access to them. Novels were still extremely expensive, often costing up to a half guinea a volume, (i.e., the equivalent of US $100 today), but the increasing literacy rate and the rise of the lending libraries provided a new readership eager for a literature that taught the manners of social superiors while confirming suspicions about their morals.

Colburn was often reviled. His novels were called trivial and seem more so today in the shadow of the Victorian novel of social responsibility. Some of his writers, however, such as Disraeli, Bulwer-Lytton, and Gore, sometimes surpassed the genre to create substantial characters. Moreover, although it is impossible to make great claims for any of the authors, the tendency of the novels to dwell on the specifics of social life was shared by more than one 19th-century author. Austen and Dickens, among many, had an interest in social verisimilitude and the protocols of social mobility. Possibly the genre's greatest limitation was in the narrow social focus of its satire, a limitation not shared by the time's major novelists.

Although Colburn could be considered the father of contemporary advertising techniques, his methods would be thought mild today. He used his magazines to puff his books, but his reviewers usually stopped after a brief, if tantalizingly vague, description of the latest book's contents. Regardless, his competitors charged him with unsavory business practices, and his methods were the subject of much talk.

His unpopularity did not extend to his authors, whom he paid extremely well. As a result, Colburn attracted a large number of people from a wide variety of backgrounds to the profession of novel writing, perhaps encouraging a still broader readership and opening new corridors for social advancement. Because he disliked serial publication, which tied up funds for long periods of time, he also encouraged the production of what could be called the well-made novel and therefore helped reduce the popularity of the novel of lengthy adventures.

Colburn may be more deservedly well-known for his misjudgments. Thackery disdained the type of novels advertised in the *Literary Gazette*, but in *Vanity Fair* created the best example of the type. Colburn rejected the early manuscript of one volume, and Thackery did not let him see any of the completed volumes. Colburn also rejected *Wuthering Heights*, not understanding why he had been bothered with a book so unlike any he had published. (*See also* Publishing.)

Gregg Johnson

Works Consulted

Rosa, Matthew Whiting. *The Silver Fork School.* New York: Columbia UP, 1964.

Stevenson, Lionel. *The English Novel.* Boston: Houghton, 1960.

Sutherford, J.A. *Victorian Novelists and Publishers.* Chicago: U of Chicago P, 1976.

Coleridge, Hartley
(1796–1849)

For Blake, Wordsworth, Coleridge, and the other Romantics, the myth of the child as natural genius was an important philosophical and psychological construction, with implications that reverberate throughout their poetry. (*See also* Children, View of.)

The life of the minor lyric poet Hartley Coleridge, first son of Samuel Taylor Coleridge and Sara (Fricker) Coleridge, provides the reader of Romantic poetry with a laboratory for the study of this conflict between life and art. A careful reading of the text of Hartley's life, especially his childhood, will certainly lead to a clearer understanding of both Romantic poetry and Romantic pedagogy, for the way in which the poets of early Romanticism treated the figure of the child reveals their beliefs concerning psychology, education, and epistemology. Certainly, the distance between figuration and fact had a continuing disruptive effect on the life and poetry of Hartley Coleridge.

Before the late 18th century, neither creative writers nor philosophers had considered children worthy of special attention, nor were they recognized as possessors of special attributes, abilities, or powers. The Romantic poets came to believe in the perceptual and moral superiority of the young. Childhood had begun to emerge as a philosophical concept and social construction.

While Wordsworth was still a child, Blake had already identified childhood with spiritual and philosophical innocence, a theme that would be developed by several subsequent generations of British poets. Blake's project was to show how every person could recreate for him- or herself a mythical golden age or visionary outlook; significantly, to proceed with this undertaking, he realized that he had to begin by recreating childhood. By elevating imagination to a supreme position in his philosophy, Blake hoped to preserve the flexible perceptual categories of childhood within the reasoning adult personality.

Blake composed the *Songs of Innocence* within the emerging genres of children's literature, influenced in particular by Barbauld and Wollstonecraft. The *Songs* were intended to be read to and by children, as well as by adults who aspired to the innocent condition they represented in Blake's imaginative vision. The *Songs* represent children as morally and perceptually finer than adults, who for the most part live in the world of Experience, locked in the prison of ordinary perception and language. A similar pedagogical intent is evident in Wordsworth's early pair of poems, *Expostulation and Reply* and *The Tables Turned*, in which characters named Matthew and William (Coleridge or Hazlitt; and Wordsworth), argue the competing virtues of books and nature, one could almost say, of schoolmaster and child. These two poems are related to Blake's *Songs* in both tone and versification, each poet's work owing much to both the ballad and nursery rhyme traditions, though Wordsworth's language possesses a satirical undertone that Blake would only come to in the *Songs of Experience*.

When Wordsworth writes in the *Immortality Ode* (a poem composed at least in part as a result of his friendship with the young Hartley) that "Shades of the prison house begin to close about the growing boy," he is extending a line of thought begun by Blake in *The Marriage of Heaven and Hell*: "How do you know but ev'ry Bird that cuts the airy way/Is an immense world of delight closed by your senses five?" For both poets, children's moral innocence allows them to sense the divinity behind "the light of common day." Both Blake and Wordsworth were attracted by Neoplatonism, and their elevation of children into creatures of myth attempted to respond to the Allegory of the Cave, with all its epistemological implications. Children, for Blake and Wordsworth, have, in addition to the normal human senses, a sense of the divine that allows them to perceive the natural world in its fullness and glory.

And yet there was at least one child of flesh and blood coming of age among these philosophical notions and religious musings. Hartley was born in 1796, in the midst of the *annus mirabilis* leading to the publication of *Lyrical Ballads*. In retrospect, Hartley's upbringing looks like a casual experiment in education and child psychology undertaken by his father, with the help of Southey and Wordsworth.

In *Frost at Midnight*, addressed to the infant Hartley asleep in his cradle, Coleridge, himself "reared/In the great city, pent mid cloisters dim," proposes a pedagogy based on the myth of the natural child, vowing that his infant son will "Wander like a breeze/By lakes and sandy shores, beneath the crags/Of ancient mountains…" And the elder Coleridge concludes the second part of *Christabel* with a direct reference to his son: "A fairy thing with red round cheeks/That always finds and never seeks… [.]" Wordsworth, in another poem, suggests that "a wise passiveness" before the beauteous forms of nature is the proper attitude for a child to adopt. Blake's connection between childhood and perception is reiterated here—"so shalt thou *see and hear* / The lovely shapes and sounds," as it is a few years later in Wordsworth's *Immortality Ode* when he conjures the scene, "Apparelled in celestial light,/The glory and the freshness of a dream." The word "glory," repeated in this and other poems, denoted a specific optical effect for both Wordsworth and Coleridge; specifically, it was used to indicate either that haze of light around an object with the sun behind

it or the halo signifying divine inspiration around a saint's head in medieval religious paintings, a sense now lost.

For poets like Wordsworth and Coleridge, the process of maturation deprived the adult of the ability to perceive such "glory." That is, growing into the world of Experience, as Blake called it, was a progressive process of loss, and the great problem for Blake and Wordsworth especially, though it concerned other writers as well, was how to recover some sense, however limited, of the paradisal condition of childhood existence. For Coleridge and Wordsworth, with their profound interest in epistemology, the figure of the child represents an authentic and unalienated relationship to nature.

Hartley's early education was irregular and eccentric. Later, it would become somewhat more formal, though still informed by Romantic ideology. Left to wander and dream, he learned to read rather later than most children. In a letter to Matthew Coates when Hartley was age 5, his father wrote that his son was considered a genius by Wordsworth and Southey, but that he was slow learning to read and write. Coleridge theorized that since he himself loved books, Hartley would come along in time, as indeed he did. In his maturity, Hartley would look back on this idyllic childhood with a tone of misgiving. In a sonnet dedicated to his father opening the one book of poems he would publish in his father's lifetime, in 1833, he wrote:

> The prayer was heard: I
>   "wander'd like a breeze,"
> By mountain brooks and
>   solitary meres,
> And gathered there the shapes
>   and phantasies,
> Which, mixed with passions
>   of my sadder years,
> Compose this book. If good

therein there be,
That good, my sire, I dedicate
to thee.

As a boy, Hartley was by all accounts precocious, with the sort of highly developed imagination valued by the Romantics as evidence of genius. On hearing a history of the royal families of England, he invented a history of the kings who were yet to be. Asked how this could be, he responded that since they were in his mind, such monarchs must surely exist. Even earlier, after not enjoying a ride in a wheelbarrow as much as he had expected, he told his father, "the pity is, I'se always thinking of my thoughts." Many children have imaginary playmates, but Hartley created an imaginary kingdom, Ejuxria, and kept track of its history, politics, and citizens.

In his poem, *To H.C. Six Years Old*, Wordsworth worries over the fate of such an unusual child, perhaps sensing some of the dangers inherent in a "poetic" childhood such as Hartley's. Wordsworth, with his almost obsessive interest in his own childhood, was an acute observer of Hartley's and his fears proved prophetic.

During Hartley's later childhood, he was profoundly troubled by his father's extended absence in Malta, a journey undertaken partly for health (opium addiction) and partly as an escape from the unhappy marriage. Though Sara Coleridge and her children lived at Greta Hall with Southey and his family during this period, it is no accident that Wordsworth, the great poet of childhood, should have served as Hartley's surrogate father and poetic mentor. He grew into an odd young man, short of stature, with large eyes and an excitable manner. Sara wrote in a letter about this time that Hartley was often to be found "flying about in the open air, and uttering his poetic fancies aloud: this he does constantly, when the fit is on him, whether it rain or shine, whether it be dark or light, and when we are sitting in the Parlour with the curtains drawn, between the whisperings of the wind, we hear him whizzing by, and sometimes his uncle [Southey] calls out to him 'whither so fast Endymion?'"

Hartley's adult life was almost entirely uneventful; it was marked by one incident, however, that in retrospect came to seem emblematic of his entire life—his failure to establish himself as a fellow of Oriel College, Oxford. As an undergraduate at Oxford, Hartley had begun to write poems that were recognizably his own, though he was bitterly disappointed at not winning the Newdigate Prize for *The Horses of Lysippus*, writing in his notebook that "[i]t was almost the only time in my life wherein I was keenly disappointed; for it was the only one upon which I felt any confident hope." Neither of his subsequent attempts to win the prize proved any more successful than the first.

After taking a second-class degree, Hartley was elected a probationary fellow at Oriel College. An academic life seemed assured. But the combination of his constitution and his unusual childhood left him unprepared to enter the world of experience represented by life as an Oxford don. As an undergraduate, he had already begun to show signs of the alcoholism that would later in life lead him "to pot-house wanderings," in Wordsworth's memorable phrase. It was said he sometimes came home drunk, thus endangering the College with his wobbling candle. Hartley came to the common room, when he came at all, unshaven and ill-dressed, and at times absented himself from the company of the Oriel Fellows for a week at a time, preferring the company of undergraduates. It was also rumored that he had fallen in love with a shopkeeper's daughter, and since fellows were expected to remain celibate, this was cause for grave concern among the senior fellows.

Hartley was not reappointed to a second probationary year, and it was suggested he resign. Both Hartley and his family were shattered by this disgrace. Though Coleridge, already famous as a poet and critic, tried to intervene on his son's behalf, the Oriel stood firm in its rejection of the troubled young man who had shown such promise. After this failure, Hartley tried to make a living as a literary journalist in London; within two years, however, he was back in the Lake District, having reluctantly accepted a job as a schoolteacher arranged for him by his father. He was still composing verse, his poems showing increasing sophistication of technique as well as delicacy of manner, and his life began at this time to settle into a pattern that would only rarely be broken in the coming years.

During his years as a schoolmaster, Hartley matured into an effective, though minor, lyric poet. *The Anemone* is typical of his mature style, characteristically linking smallness and frailty with beauty. He associates weakness and slightness with fear and shame, which is also characteristic of his poetry generally—and of his own view of his life. In this poem, he finds a metaphor in the out-of-season flower for his own life, which he already considered a failure. The line "bearing thy weakness in thy name," though literally true of the anemone, seems also an unconscious reference to the "infirmity of will" Hartley's friends and family, as well as his subsequent biographers, believed he inherited from his father.

Nearly all of Hartley's best poems look back on his childhood in an attempt to explain the complex forces that seemed always to push him toward irresolution, failure, and disappointment. Another poem from the period explores the poet's inability to adapt to adult patterns of life. The stately and dignified Shakespearian diction of the poem's conclusion, combined with its lamentlike tone, demonstrates that the poet is not unconscious of the predicament in which his romantic childhood has left him.

With the exception of a brief stint as a literary biographer in Leeds in 1832, Hartley's adult life had assumed its final pattern. Though still a lively conversationalist, often entertaining visiting student "wine parties" from Oxford, and though he continued to write poems until just before his death, Hartley, like a child, was unable to concentrate for sustained creative effort. Contracted, in his later years, to write a *Life* of his famous father, all he produced was the dedicatory sonnet. (The sonnet came to be his preferred poetic form—he loved the play of rhyme, and the briefness of the form fitted his attention span.) Hartley died in 1849. "Let him lie by us, he would have wished it," said Wordsworth, who was so distraught at his death that he could not view the body, bedecked with the flowers the younger man had loved, even in his "pot-house wanderings." The poet was buried in Grasmere churchyard, where, the following spring, the Sage of Rydal would join him.

It is difficult to say whether Hartley Coleridge was a victim of a misguided pedagogy or of his genetic inheritance or some combination of the two. The difficulties of his day-to-day life, however, certainly suggest a conflict born of those Romantic notions of childhood instilled in him virtually from the day of his birth. Hartley's life reenacts the drama of loss constructed by the discourse of Romanticism; more precisely, Hartley's inability to grow up dramatizes the Romantics own epistemological quandary: how to live in an increasingly urban, industrial, and capitalist society while maintaining the perceptual innocence of a mythic imaginative childhood.

Joseph Duemer

Works Consulted

Adams, Hazard, ed. Introduction. *William Blake: Jerusalem, Selected Poems and Prose.* New York: Holt, 1970.

van den Berg, J.H. *The Changing Nature of Man.* New York: Dell (Delta), 1975.

Davis, Michael. *William Blake: A New Kind of Man.* Berkeley: U of California P, 1977.

Griggs, Earl Leslie. *Hartley Coleridge: His Life and Work.* London: U of London P, 1929.

Griggs, Grace Evelyn, and Earl Leslie Griggs, eds. *Letters of Hartley Coleridge.* New York: Oxford UP, 1941.

Hartman, Herbert. *Hartley Coleridge, Poet's Son and Poet.* Oxford: Oxford UP, 1931.

Reed, Arden. *Romanticism and Language.* Ithaca: Cornell UP, 1984.

Stephens, Fran Carlock. *The Hartley Coleridge Letters: A Calendar and Index.* Austin, TX: Humanities Research Center, 1978.

Coleridge, Samuel Taylor

(1772–1834)

Born in 1772, Samuel Taylor Coleridge was the tenth and last child of John and Ann (Bowden) Coleridge. The vicar at Ottery St. Mary and master of the grammar school, Coleridge's father had been a reputable scholar of Latin and Greek at Cambridge. Coleridge was only age 8 when his father died, but his life-long philosophical, literary, and religious interests had already been nurtured under his father's solicitous care. In his autobiographical letters to Poole (1797), he fondly recalls how his father encouraged his readings and aroused his fascination with the mysteries of the universe.

After his father's death, Coleridge was sent to Christ's Hospital, where his propensities in philosophy and language were guided by the schoolmaster James Bowyer. Although some critics have doubted his precocious mastery of Greek philosophy, several accounts corroborate Lamb's portrait, in *Christ's Hospital Five and Thirty Years Ago*, of Coleridge holding forth on Jamblichus and Plotinus, and reciting Homer and Pindar in Greek. His habits of voracious reading already well established, he began an extensive exploration of the philosophers and was especially stimulated by Boehme and Spinoza.

He was age 19 when he entered Jesus College, Cambridge, in 1791. The French Revolution excited much discussion, and Coleridge read during his Cambridge years Thomas Paine's *Rights of Man* (1791–92) and Godwin's *Political Justice* (1793). His religious thinking, too, began to show the same leftward list as his politics. The Unitarian challenge to the Established Church, as promoted by Hartley and Priestley, seemed to have won a convert in the young Coleridge. Certainly it required long deliberation before he began to oppose Hartley's argument in *Observations of Man* (1749) that all mental processes, including divine revelation, could be explained in terms of physical laws.

Associationist psychology, Unitarianism, and republicanism merged in the radicalism espoused by Frend, a Fellow at Jesus College, who was put on trial and banished from Cambridge in 1793. Coleridge, more from enthusiasm than from abiding intellectual commitment, allied himself with Frend's supporters. In the midst of this turbulence at Jesus College, Coleridge suddenly vanished. Distraught over unpaid debts, perhaps over unrequited love as well (he was infatuated with Mary Evans, whom he had met on school vacations with her brother Tom), he ran off to London in December and, giving his name as Silas Tomkyn Comberbache, enlisted in the King's Light Dragoons. George Coleridge, who succeeded their father as chaplain at Ottery St. Mary, obtained a discharge by claiming that his younger brother suffered insanity.

Although he returned to Cambridge in April 1794, Coleridge was soon beset with new distractions. In June, he met Southey, and the two hatched a plan to establish a utopian commune on the banks of the Susquehanna. As founding families of this "Pantisocracy," as Coleridge dubbed it, they required wives. Southey solved the problem. In Bristol, Coleridge was introduced to the Fricker sisters: Edith (Southey's betrothed) and Sara (Coleridge's designated bride). Back at Cambridge for the autumn term, Coleridge was preoccupied with pantisocracy, Southey, and Sara Fricker. He may not have devoted much time to academic studies, but he wrote a number of poems, including the *Monody on the Death of Thomas Chatterton*, and 12 *Sonnets on Eminent Characters*.

Without taking a degree, Coleridge left the university in December 1794. In a flurry of political activism, he wrote a series of lectures and pamphlets during the following months at Bristol. The planned pantisocracy was abandoned. He quarreled with Southey, but he kept his word to Sara Fricker. They were wed, 4 October 1795, and settled in a cottage at Clevedon. During this period, he gives his poetry dramatic new dimension by introducing Sara as assumed auditor. In the verse epistle, *Lines Written at Shurton Bars*, he anticipates the moment when "with a husband's care,/I press you to my heart." *The Eolian Harp* is a conversation in their

cottage bower, and *Reflections on Having Left a Place of Retirement* uses the same conversational setting.

The happiness of these early months was soon troubled by financial difficulties. *The Watchman*, a weekly organ for Coleridge's political and religious views, brought him no profit and was dropped after 10 issues from March to May. The first of his four children, David Hartley, was born in 1796. Desperate for some means to support his family, he projected a variety of schemes: he might open a private school or become a Unitarian minister or publish a series of German translations. Temporary relief was provided by Poole, who offered him a cottage in Nether Stowey and found subscribers to support him in his scholarly work.

In spring 1797, Coleridge met Wordsworth, who was living with his sister Dorothy in Racedown, Dorset. Coleridge persuaded them to join him in Stowey, where they rented nearby Alfoxden House. Wordsworth was in the midst of a play, *The Borderers*, and Coleridge decided to join him as a playwright with *Osorio* (1797). With their collaboration on the *Lyrical Ballads*, the two poets began experiments in adapting the ballad form and combining the commonplace with the strange. Coleridge's major contribution was *The Rime of the Ancient Mariner*. (*See also* Burnet, Thomas.) His other supernatural ballads, *The Three Graves* and *The Dark Ladie*, remained fragments, as did the haunting poem of demonic seduction, *Christabel*. To escape the small cottage, where Hartley was now a toddler and Sara again pregnant, Coleridge retreated to a vacant farmhouse near Culbone Church where he could medically treat himself with opium without alarming Sara. There, probably toward the end of 1797, he began work on a version of *Kubla Khan*.

His second son, Berkeley, was born in 1798. Coleridge continued to write his conversation poems: *This Lime-Tree Bower My Prison* (1797); *Frost at Midnight, France: An Ode, Fears in Solitude*, and *The Nightingale* (1798). Leaving Sara and the children with Poole and the manuscript of *Lyrical Ballads* with the publisher Cottle, Coleridge embarked with the Wordsworths on 15 September 1798 for what was to be a two-month trip to Germany. The Wordsworths wintered in Goslar, and Coleridge engrossed himself in philosophical lectures at Göttingen. In spite of complaints from Sara, the two months became 10. The infant Berkeley became ill and died in February 1799. The death notice did not reach Coleridge until April, but still he would not return. In May, he ascended the Brocken to see its famed apparitions. When he came back to Sara at the end of July, he could not heal the emotional injury caused by his long neglect.

He chose to escape her anger. He did mend his relationship with Southey, and the two went on a walking tour during September and October. While in Bristol, Coleridge visited Dr. Thomas Beddoes's Pneumatic Institute, where Davy was engaged in experiments with nitrous oxide. As volunteer subject, Coleridge provided Davy with an account of his experience while under the gas. Since their return from Germany, the Wordsworths had been staying with the Hutchinsons in Sockburn, Durham. Cottle accompanied Coleridge on a visit to Wordsworth in October to discuss a second edition of *Lyrical Ballads*. Coleridge was immediately attracted to Sara Hutchinson, unaware of Wordsworth's affection for Mary Hutchinson. He spent the rest of October and November on a walking tour with Wordsworth through the Lake District. On November 24, he stopped once more at the Hutchinson

farm. Years later, he would note that day as the anniversary of his passionate and hopeless love for Sara Hutchinson. In December, Dorothy and William relocated to Dove Cottage in Grasmere.

The Coleridge family left Nether Stowey, although Poole supported Sara Coleridge in protesting the move. They stayed briefly in London, then went to Keswick in the Lake District in July 1800—not far from the Wordsworths, nor from the Hutchinsons. Coleridge had been writing at great speed, translating Friedrich Schillers's *Wallenstein* and completing within the year some 50 articles for the *Morning Post*. After settling into Greta Hall, Keswick, he gradually acquiesced to the demands of opium addiction. (*See also* Opium and Laudanum.) (Meanwhile, born in 1800, his son Derwent was apparently a colicky infant [Dorothy mentions his convulsion fits].) Coleridge wrote through the sleepless nights and finished Part II of *Christabel*, introducing the visionary minstrel, Bard Bracy, and adding Geraldine's seduction of Sir Leoline. He read the poem to William and Dorothy on his wedding anniversary. In spite of his delight with the poem, William thought it unsuited to the *Lyrical Ballads*. Coleridge seemed to concur but was disappointed that little of his own poetry was included.

A rift with Wordsworth was growing, and Coleridge was losing his self-confidence. His "Asra" poems—*The Keepsake* (1800); *On Revisiting the Seashore, Ode to Tranquillity, To Asra* (1801); *A Day-Dream, The Picture* (1802)—record his secret love for Sara Hutchinson, whom he visited during July and August of 1801. That Christmas he stayed with Poole, who accompanied him to London. When he returned to Greta Hall, he tried to calm domestic strife. Mrs. Coleridge became once again pregnant. But his love for Sara

Hutchinson made him all the more discontented at home. Revised from his verse letter to Sara Hutchinson (April 1802), *Dejection: An Ode* was published on his wedding anniversary, the same day as Wordsworth's marriage to Mary Hutchinson. He now denied the passive inspiration of which he had sung in *The Eolian Harp* and claimed instead, "O Lady! we receive but what we give,/And in our life alone does Nature live;/Ours is her wedding garment, ours her shroud!"

The Coleridges' last child, daughter Sara, was born in 1802. The *Morning Post* ran his series on "The Men and the Times" in July and August. Accompanied by William and Dorothy for the first two weeks of a tour through Scotland, he continued on alone for another two weeks. Back at Greta Hall in mid-September, he worked sporadically on an autobiography intended to trace his metaphysical inquiries. He left Keswick for London in January 1804, spent a few months writing for the *Courier*, then departed for Malta in April. Recording his hallucinations in his Malta notebooks, he expressed fears that opium was destroying his sanity. During a visit to Rome in 1806, he met Ludwig Tieck and translated excerpts from his works. Two years and four months elapsed before his return to England in August 1806. Determined on separation from his wife, he could manage only a troubled relationship with Sara Hutchinson. With her and Wordsworth, he visited Sir George and Lady Beaumont at Coleorton. Stopping at the Queen's Head, 27 December 1806, Coleridge in a jealous hallucination thought Wordsworth shared his bed that night with his sister-in-law.

At Coleorton he heard Wordsworth read *The Prelude*, and he penned his *Lines to William Wordsworth* in response. Although Southey, who had been supporting

Coleridge's family, objected that no adequate income would be earned, Coleridge proceeded with arrangements for a series of lectures on the "Principles of Poetry" to commence in January 1808. He gave the first two and then was incapacitated by opium. Wordsworth made the trip from Grasmere to London to help his friend, even assisting him with notes for the lectures. At the end of March, after an interruption of eight weeks, he was able to resume his lectures, which continued until June. He managed to write a review on abolition of the slave trade in July, but his productivity was at a low ebb. In September, he moved into a room at the Wordsworths' new home at Allan Bank. With Sara Hutchinson taking notes and transcribing, he began publication of *The Friend*, which ran through 27 numbers from June 1809, to March 1810. Just before the last issue was out, Sara left for Wales.

Hospitality at Allan Bank had no doubt been strained by Coleridge's 17-month visit. Thus, when Basil Montagu proposed that Coleridge stay with him in London so that he could seek medical assistance, Dorothy advised Montagu to arrange lodgings rather than keep Coleridge in his home, and William warned of the severity of the opium addiction. In repeating the account to Coleridge, Montagu used such phrases as "absolute nuisance" and "rotten drunkard." In his notebooks, Coleridge had castigated himself in worse terms, but he could not bear that his closest friend had condemned him. Not until April 1812, was Wordsworth able to mend the relationship.

In the meantime, Coleridge stayed in Hammersmith, London, with John Morgan, his wife Mary, and her sister Charlotte Brent. With their loyal support, he struggled against his debilitating addiction. He continued writing for the *Courier*, reissued *The Friend*, and turned once more to lecturing. His 17 lectures on Shakespeare and Milton (November through January of 1811) began with meager attendance, but soon audiences packed the Great Room of the London Philosophical Society. From Schlegel's *Vorlesungen über dramatische Kunst und Literatur* (1809–11), Coleridge took the distinctions between mechanical and organic form, sculpturesque Greek drama and picturesque Shakespearean drama. He also adapted Schlegel's account of an imaginative participation in illusion to his own concern with the decisive act of will: illusion depends not only on the volitional acceptance of the spectator; the artist must also have the necessary volitional control over his own creative genius. He elaborated his distinction between the copy as a replica of the real and the imitation as the imaginatively created ideal. A copy reflects only the accidents of the moment. An imitation reveals the informing presence of the mind, which imposes a difference that never allows a willing acceptance of the "truth" of art to lapse into a mistaken belief that it is real. A copy is the result of strict observation; an imitation requires the interest of meditation.

Coleridge's subsequent series "Lectures on the Drama" (May and June 1812) related dramatic illusion to the visual referentiality of language. A "bookish" language is inappropriate to drama because it fails to conjure up visual images. Coleridge distinguished between a language of nature and a language of symbols. The former refers to objects; the latter appropriates the former but shifts the referenced to feelings or ideas. The language of symbols derives its power of visual evocation from the language of nature, but acquires a wide-ranging freedom. The visual power that words possess through virtual identity with the thing represented is liberated in symbols that become "self-manifestations" of

that visual power. During the 12 "Lectures on Belles Lettres" (November 1812 to January 1813), Coleridge was preoccupied with the preparations for the production of *Remorse*, which opened at Drury Lane in January, just before the final lecture.

Remorse, a revision of *Osorio*, put his critical concerns into practice by thematizing illusion in plot, character, and dialogue. Those in the audience who had been attending the lectures at the Surrey Institute would recognize the efforts of Alvar and Teresa to discriminate between illusion and delusion. The production was a popular and financial success. It was produced again at Bristol in 1814; at Calne, Wiltshire, in 1815, while Coleridge was visiting the Morgans; and it was revived at Drury Lane in 1817. His effort to repeat the success with *Zapolya* was disappointing. When it was rejected at Convent Garden, he sent a copy to Lord Byron, April 1816, for consideration at Drury Lane. Douglas Kinnaird, Byron's friend, promised to produce the play during the Christmas season, but negotiations were broken off. *Zapolya* was published in 1817.

In the Shakespeare lectures delivered at Bristol (October and November 1813), Coleridge repeated earlier arguments, but went on to analyze how a character creates, or falls prey to, illusion in terms of psychological process. Coleridge observed how Macbeth indulged the "sophistry of self-delusion," which he belatedly recognized as phantoms of his own jealous delirium. In discussing Hamlet, too, he explored the problems of self-wrought illusions and delusions. Reasserting his conception of Shakespeare's judgment as observation, meditation, and self-projection, he asserted that in the character of Hamlet Shakespeare had demonstrated how this very process of judgment may go awry.

An exhibit of Washington Allston's paintings in Bristol motivated Coleridge's essays "On the Principles of Genial Criticism" (August and September 1814). From Schelling's "Über das Verhältnis der bildenden Künste zu der Natur" (1807) he borrowed several ideas that he was to use again in his lecture "On Poesy and Art" (1818). Echoing Schelling's account of "Poesie" as the active principle informing all art, Coleridge began the second of the three essays with the statement that poetry is "the regulative idea of all the Fine Arts." Schelling referred to the wisdom in nature and art as a link between form and idea or body and soul. Taste, for Coleridge, is the enabling faculty that connects intellect and sensations, ideas and images. Beauty, as *multeity in unity*, realizes a harmony of nature and mind. In appropriating Schelling's account of the reconciliation of the conscious and the unconscious, Coleridge altered the notion that freedom and vitality in art are simply an expression of spontaneity and productivity prompted by the confrontation between the ideal and the real. He insisted upon the act of will. (*See also* Reconciliation of Opposites.)

Although no notes survive, the prospectus advertising his six lectures on Milton and Cervantes (April 1814) delineates his intention to examine poetic taste in relation to *Paradise Lost* and to provide a philosophical analysis of *Don Quixote*. At the end of April he attempted to lecture on the French Revolution and Napoleon. The first lecture terminated early; the second was postponed, then cancelled. His mind and body wracked by opium, he submitted to medical care. After a year of lethargy and depression, he was stirred to action by the arrival of Wordsworth's *Poems* (1815).

He immediately set to work on a preface to his own poetry. The collection of poems would be entitled *Sibylline Leaves*;

the preface became *Biographia Literaria*. He devoted two years to the project, but even then it would not have been possible without the diligent assistance of John Morgan and the care of Dr. James Gillman, into whose home he was accepted as a live-in patient in April 1816. Coleridge could muster astounding reserves of energy. During the months following, he published *Christabel*, with *Kubla Khan*, and *The Pains of Sleep* (May 1816) and *The Statesman's Manual* (December 1816). He also composed *The Theory of Life* (posthumously published, 1848). The second *Lay Sermon* appeared in April 1817. Finally, after printing complications and delays, *Sibylline Leaves* and *Biographia Literaria* were published in July 1817. (*See also* Willing Suspension of Disbelief.)

The will had come to mean much to Coleridge, personally as well as critically. He thus gave particular emphasis to the will in *Biographia Literaria*: he granted that "[t]he medium, by which spirits understand each other is . . . the *freedom* which they possess in common," but that freedom must be brought into consciousness by discipline: "the inner sense has its direction determined for the greater part only by an act of freedom" (Ch. 12); the secondary imagination may be an echo of the primary imagination but it functions only through "co-existing with the conscious will" (Ch. 13).

Recalling the collaboration on the *Lyrical Ballads*, he described the mutual experiment in terms markedly different from those Wordsworth had presented in the Preface. The "two cardinal points of poetry," *novelty* and *familiarity*, were to be neglected by neither poet: Wordsworth was to enhance the ordinary with a sense of strangeness; Coleridge was to lend to the supernatural "a semblance of truth" which would make the strange seem familiar. Coleridge's poetry thus encourages the imagination and a "willing suspension of disbelief" (Ch. 14). If these had been the guiding concerns, *Christabel* would not have been excluded as unsuited to *Lyrical Ballads*. Coleridge also criticized the claim in the Preface that the goal had been to imitate rustic language. Wordsworth had mistaken copy for imitation. Imitation is the result of meditation, copy requires only observation. He listed among the defects of Wordsworth's poetry a failure to blend observation and meditation. As a result, unwanted particularization disrupts the illusion of verisimilitude. In calling for poetic judgment to balance opposites in art, he elaborated his definition of poetry as "the balance and reconciliation of opposite or discordant qualities" (Ch. 14).

Coleridge's "Treatise on Method" appeared as introduction to the *Encyclopedia Metropolitana* (January 1818). At the same time, he commenced a series of 14 lectures on the principles of judgment (January to March 1818). In the lecture "On Poesy and Art," Coleridge cited Joshua Reynolds's affirmation of mimesis and proposed that the doctrine need only be corrected so that art is understood properly to imitate the mind's apprehension of nature rather than nature itself. He thus paraphrased Schelling, who had cited Winckelmann to the same purposes. From Schelling, too, he described imitation as the infusion of difference into sameness. Although presented within an attractive philosophical exposition of the dynamic interaction and primal identity of mind and nature, Schelling's ideas provided Coleridge with nothing to correspond to his own concern with the act of will. Art had its freedom, for Schelling, through a paradoxical determinism in which powers of nature are said to be manifest as the power in the work. Coleridge shifted the emphasis from the work to the willing participation of the responding individual.

With major revision, Coleridge's *The Friend* was published in a three-volume edition in November 1818. He delivered six lectures on Shakespeare (1818 and 1819) and, immediately following, seven lectures on Shakespeare, Milton, Dante, Spenser, Ariosto, and Cervantes (1819), which were given on alternate evenings along with the series of 14 philosophical lectures (1818 and 1819). He was not yet content with the theory of illusion that he had been evolving for 10 years. When he reworked his notes on the dialectics of judgment, he introduced the concept of play: not free play, but the structured play of game. If humanity is to entertain improbability, he wrote, "there must be Rules respecting it." Copy and imitation, real and ideal, observation and mediation remain, as before, the essential attributes of that art which elicits the voluntary engagements of illusion. He went on in the lecture series of 1818 and 1819 to naturalize genius as the revelation of judgment.

In the final decade of his life, Coleridge began to reap modest recognition for his years of labor. Distinguished visitors came to meet and listen to the Sage of Highgate: Irving, Carlyle, Rossetti, Chalmers, Sterling, Mill, Emerson. Among the visitors were even his wife and daughter (November 1822, to February 1823). The *Table Talk*, assembled by his nephew Henry Nelson Coleridge and his daughter Sara, documents his power to captivate his auditors. But Coleridge had not become a mere talker. He continued to refine his philosophy of religion, in *Aids to Reflection* (1825; 2nd ed. 1831), and religious polity, in *On the Constitution of Church and State* (1829; 2nd ed. 1830). His Rhine tour with Wordsworth and Wordsworth daughter Dora (21 June to 7 August 1828) marked a warm reconciliation of old friends. They came together for the last time in 1831. Coleridge's three-volume edition of his *Poetical Works* (1828) met with greater success than he had anticipated. A second edition was prepared for the following year, 1829, and he had just received the proofs for a third edition when he died, at Highgate on 25 July 1834. (*See also* Androgyny; Ballad; Conversation Poems; Frend, William; Irving, Edward; Lake School; Lyrical Ballads; Mathias, Thomas James; Mental Theater; Poetry.)

Frederick Burwick

Works Consulted

Barth, J. Robert, S.J. *Coleridge and Christian Doctrine.* Cambridge, MA: Harvard UP, 1969.

Bate, Walter Jackson. *Coleridge.* New York: Macmillan, 1968.

Beer, John. *Coleridge The Visionary.* New York, Chatto, 1959.

———. *Coleridge's Poetic Intelligence.* London: Macmillan, 1977.

Gravel, Richard, and Molly Lefebure, eds. *The Coleridge Connection.* London: Macmillan, 1990.

Harding, Anthony John. *Coleridge and the Inspired Word.* Montreal: McGill-Queen's UP, 1985.

Holmes, Richard. *Coleridge.* Oxford: Oxford UP 1982.

Lefebure, Molly. *Samuel Taylor Coleridge: A Bondage of Opium.* New York: Stein, 1974.

McFarland, Thomas. *Coleridge and the Pantheist Tradition.* Oxford: Clarendon, 1969.

Willey, Basil. *Samuel Taylor Coleridge.* London: Chatto, 1972.

Coleridge, Sara

(1802–52)

In her time, Sara Coleridge was acclaimed for her beauty, intellect, and high moral character. With scrupulous concern for truth, generosity of spirit, and complete devotion, she edited the works of her father, Samuel Taylor Coleridge. Southey, Wordsworth, and De Quincey admired her learning and scholarship and praised her modest character. After the death of her husband, when Sara Coleridge became the sole editor of her father's works, her literary circle grew to include Carlyle, Elizabeth Barrett Browning, and Henry Crabb Robinson, as well as Aubrey de Vere, an Irish poet and theologian. Sara knew all the English classics and was familiar with the writers of her time—Arnold, Carlyle, and Tennyson, as well as Edgeworth, Martineau, and Austen; she also admired Mme. de Staël. Yet her knowledge and interest also ranged outside of literature. She corresponded with F.D. Maurice, an important English theologian, on religious philosophy. Thomas Macaulay's *The History of England* she criticized for important omissions of fact and misleading analysis of character, while she admired the scientific works of Erasmus Darwin who, like Macaulay, was also a personal friend.

When Sara Coleridge was born at Greta Hall, Keswick, 1802, her father registered his surprise and disappointment at a female child. It was typical of Coleridge to frequently absent himself from his family, and he left for Malta only two years after Sara's birth. Even after his return in 1806, only on rare occasions during her childhood did Sara spend extended time with him. In 1808, Coleridge, pleased with his daughter's appearance and intelligence, invited her to accompany him to Allan Bank, the current residence of the Wordsworths. After she came, he indicated his displeasure with her for not demonstrating sufficient affection for him. In 1810, when Sara was age 7, Coleridge instructed her in Latin for several months; and in 1812, he expressed astonishment at her ability to read both French and Italian and took pleasure in her appealing moral character. While Coleridge saw his sons on many occasions during school vacations, he did not see Sara again until she and her mother visited him in London, in January 1823.

Except for brief excursions to Rydal Mount, where the Wordsworths lived after 1812, Sara remained with her mother at Greta Hall, the residence of the Southeys, her aunt's family, with Sara later contributing to her and her mother's upkeep by teaching the Southey children at the home where she had been educated by her uncle and her mother. From childhood, she listened to discussions on contemporary issues and literary matters, with such visitors as Scott, Jeffrey, and Wilberforce. Always an avid reader, Sara by age 20 mastered five languages; her interests, even at a young age, extended from literature to botany, theology, and politics. In 1822, Sara's three-volume *An Account of the Abipones, and Equestrian People of Paraguay*, translated from the Jesuit Latin of Martin Dobrizhoffer, was published anonymously by John Murray. For this work Sara was paid £125. It was a project she had initially begun at age 17 in order to contribute money toward her brother Derwent's Cambridge education.

Also during 1822, Sara journeyed away from Greta Hall to visit her father at Highgate, London, and to have her first fling in London society, where for her ethereal beauty, she was called the "sylph of Ullswater." Later, Sara visited her brother Derwent at Cambridge and her father's family, the "Ottery Coleridges" in the west of England. One of the Ottery Coleridges, a cousin, Henry Nelson Coleridge, she had met at Highgate. He was a devoted admirer of her father's writings and an exponent of his ideas; he became her husband in 1829.

In 1823, secretly engaged, Sara Coleridge experienced nervous strain. This tension was partly alleviated by beginning work on a translation from the French of the 16th-century memoirs of Chevalier Bayard. Research for the translation required that she define obscure military terms and become familiar with remote events in Italian history. The translation appeared anonymously in 1825.

The three years before her marriage were distressful for Coleridge and her mother. While she proved useful to the Southey family as teacher to the Southey children and as cataloger of Southey's approximately 6,000 volumes, she and her mother were nevertheless financially dependent on the Southeys. During these years Mrs. Southey's mental disease, exacerbated by her daughter Isabel's death, led her repeatedly to threaten to evict her poor relatives. At last, on 3 September 1829, with James Coleridge's approval, Sara and Henry were married in Keswick. Later they established a brief residence in London, moving to Hampstead during the summer of 1830, where Mrs. Coleridge joined them.

Coleridge's first child, Herbert, was born in 1830; her daughter Edith, in 1832. After Edith's birth, Coleridge, always frail and high-strung, suffered a nervous collapse, in part induced by puerperal poisoning. Her nervous illness, frequently accompanied by hysterical fits, considerably worsened when in 1834 she gave birth to twins, who lived only a few days. Between 1836 and 1839 she suffered three miscarriages and in 1840 bore a daughter who lived just over a week. She remained chronically ill with nervous ailments until 1837, having already become by 1834 addicted to opium—as her father had been for most of his life.

Though Coleridge's illness at the end of 1832 had prevented her from seeing her father regularly, the two often visited at

Hampstead and at the poet's home at Highgate. After her father died in 1834, Coleridge became absorbed in reading and analyzing reviews of her father's works and essays which discussed his character and his relationship with his family. Immediately after his death, she transcribed all her father's notes, later to be issued by her husband Henry as *Literary Remains* (1836). Both she and Henry sought to popularize Coleridge's works as well as to establish his fame. In 1835, *Table Talk* was published, edited by Henry Nelson Coleridge with two entries contributed by Coleridge in the first volume and the materials in the second volume selected and arranged by her. Her name however, does not appear on either volume, nor is her support acknowledge for either volume. In fact, until Henry's death in 1843, Sara Coleridge, who had shared with her husband the task of transcribing and editing her father's works, received no recognition for her efforts.

Coleridge was particularly aroused by reviews that alleged plagiarism in her father's works and by articles that subjected his personal character to dogged condemnation; thus she was incited not only to protect his professional status but to defend his intellectual and private morality.

Henry Taylor Coleridge, with his wife's assistance, continued to edit S.T. Coleridge's works. In 1837 the third edition of *The Friend* was published; in 1838 a new edition of *On the Constitution of the Church and State*, and in 1840, *Confessions of an Inquiring Mind*. Sara Coleridge made her only trip outside of England in 1841 when she toured Belgium with her husband. In 1842, Henry, a victim of spinal disease, was already an invalid. Early in 1843, he died and was buried near his father-in-law in Highgate.

After her husband's death, Coleridge resumed the task of editing her father's works, in the process revealing not only her usual scholarly discipline, erudition, and critical discernment, but also an independence of thought and expressive writing style. In this effort, she also seems to have found herself. More and more through her experience in editing S.T. Coleridge's works, she discovered similarities between her father and herself—in their styles of writing, ways of thinking, and personalities. Reading her father's diaries and unpublished notebooks gave her a sympathetic understanding of her father's weaknesses.

Coleridge became both advocate and apologist. The fragmentary nature of her father's writings she judged the result of his desiring a profundity that was too wordless to grasp.

In 1843, the fifth edition of the *Aids to Reflection* was published in two volumes, with Sara Coleridge's "Essay on Rationalism" appearing as an appendix in the second volume together with some of her original views on theology. As she continued to edit her father's works—some projects compelling the close scrutiny of many other works, the meticulous and detailed research into sources for quotations and philosophical doctrines, the identification and translation of difficult materials—she was, all the while, concerned with providing for her children's education. After her husband's death, she faced difficulties in securing money from her father's publishers and had to depend on familial assistance to acquire funds for Herbert's education at Eton and Cambridge and for Edith's private instruction.

Briefly in 1848 to 1849 Coleridge became a reviewer for *Quarterly Review*, writing articles on Tennyson's "The Princess" and Dyce's edition of *Beaumont and Fletcher*, both published anonymously. Originally undertaken for monetary benefit, her brief journalistic career ended when she discovered that the editorial policy was dictated by party politics and that the editor made changes in manuscripts without first consulting the writers. Even as she proceeded in her life work, Coleridge commented on the lack of compensation, either in financial gain or in intellectual recognition.

Her editions continued: *Notes and Lectures on Shakespeare* (1849) and *Essays on His Own Times* (1850), together with the *Biographia Literaria* (1847), regarded as her major scholarly contributions. *Essays on His Own Times* was a particularly grueling project during which she had to read hundreds of essays in order to identify her father's articles. For this work she was able to rescue many of her father's writings and, by interpretation and extrapolation, to clarify many of the formerly misconstrued political ideas. In addition to these three major editions, in 1849 she published the second edition of *Confessions of an Inquiring Mind* and published her father's *Treatise on Method*, used as introduction to *Encyclopedia Metropolitan*. During the last eight months of her life, while afflicted with cancer, Coleridge directed the editing of a new edition of *The Poems of Samuel Taylor Coleridge*. Before she died in 1852, she had made plans for an edition of *Lay Sermons and Church and State* to be published in separate volumes. While *The Poems*, which appeared weeks after her death, listed Sara and Derwent Coleridge as co-editors of the volume, Derwent publicly admitted that his sister had written the preface and most of the notes; that it was she who was also responsible for the selection and arrangement of the poems.

Marilyn Jurich

Works Consulted

Coleridge, Sara. Note. *Confessions of an Inquiring Spirit* by Samuel Taylor Coleridge. Rpt. from 3rd ed., 1853. Ed. H. St. J. Hart. London: Adam, 1956.

Griggs, Earl Leslie. *Coleridge Fille: A Biography of Sara Coleridge*. New York: Oxford UP, 1940.

Lefebure, Molly. *The Bondage of Love, A Life of Mrs. Samuel Taylor Coleridge*. New York: Norton, 1987.

Memoir and Letters of Sara Coleridge Edited by Her Daughter. Ed. Edith Coleridge. Rpt. from 1874 ed. New York: AMS, 1973.

Minnow among Tritons: Mrs. S.T. Coleridge's Letters to Thomas Poole, 1799–1834. Ed. Stephen Potter. Bloomsbury: Nonesuch, 1934.

Mudge, Bradford. *Sara Coleridge, A Victorian Daughter: Her Life and Essays*. New Haven: Yale UP, 1989.

Sara Coleridge and Henry Reed: Reed's Memoir of Sara Coleridge, Her Letters to Reed, Including Her Comment on His Memoir of Gray, Her Marginalia in Henry Crabb Robinson's Copy of Wordsworth's Memoirs. Ed. Leslie Nathan Broughton. London: Oxford UP, 1937.

Colman, George, the Younger
(1762–1836)

A popular and versatile playwright and theater manager in the early 1800s, George Colman the Younger was born into a theatrical family. His father, a dramatist and owner of the Haymarket Theatre, was associated with such leading lights as Garrick, Foote, and Sheridan. Colman the Elder sent his son to Westminster and Oxford for a classical education, but the younger Colman's proclivity for womanizing necessitated a move to King's College, Aberdeen University. It was there he began writing plays and comic operas. His first great success was *Inkle and Yarico*, which opened at the Haymarket Theatre on August 11, 1787. A sentimental comic opera, the play deals with the theme of the inconstancy of the male sex (for a change), in a plot centering around the West Indian slave trade. Also successful was Colman's most serious work, *The Iron Chest*, a dramatic adaptation of Godwin's *Caleb Williams* which, in its 1796 production, proved an excellent vehicle for the well-known actor Edward Kean. Colman's best-known comedies are *The Heir at Law* (1797) and *John Bull* (1803). Because his plays were sentimental, used stock characters, and often involved music, he may be seen as an early experimenter of melodrama.

In 1789, Colman the Elder succumbed to the aftereffects of a paralytic stroke and was committed to an asylum. His son was suddenly called upon to take over the management of the theater. The transition was orderly and uneventful, and Colman the Younger proved a successful manager.

Colman was an amusing versifier, and his collections of light and satirical poems, *Broad Grins and Eccentricities for Edinburgh*, were well received. A man of considerable wit and charm, Colman was a frequent companion of Byron, who compared the company of Colman with that of Sheridan by saying "Sheridan was a company of life-guards, but Colman a whole regiment — of *light infantry*, to be sure, but still a regiment."

There are two other noteworthy facts about Colman. First, he invented the phrase "not to be sneezed at." Second, in 1824 he was appointed Examiner of Plays for the Lord Chamberlain's office, from which, in a remarkable about-face from his own racy life and writings, he took his responsibilities as censor seriously, ushering in a new era of prudery on the Victorian stage. He died in 1836. (*See also* Theater.)

Andrea Rowland

Works Consulted

Bagster-Collins. *George Colman the Younger*. New York: King's Crown, 1946.

Colman, George the Younger. *Broad Grins and Eccentricities for Edinburgh*. Ed. Donald Reiman. New York: Garland, 19773

Tasch, Peter A., ed. *The Plays of George Colman the Younger*. New York: Garland, 1981.

Colquhoun, Lady Janet
(1781–1846)

Lady Janet Colquhoun, daughter of the Right Honorable Sir John Sinclair of Ulster, bart., by his first wife, Sarah, was born in London in 1781. Her life and her literary work reflect the religious zeal of a committed believer dedicated to propagating the Christian faith, especially in its more evangelical form, and to bettering the lives of the less fortunate.

With her older sister Hannah, Lady Janet spent her childhood with her grandmother, Lady Janet Sinclair, daughter of William, Lord Strothnaven, at Thurso Castle. Later, their grandmother took the sisters to live in Edinburgh before they completed their education at Stoke Newington. After being introduced to Edinburgh society at about age 15, Janet married Major James Colquhoun, eldest son of Sir James Colquhoun of Luss, bart., in June 1799. When her husband succeeded to the family title in 1805, the couple made Rossdhu on Loch Lomond their home.

For the rest of her life, Colquhoun was keenly interested in religious issues and conflicts, as well as charitable causes. For example, the Luss and Arrochar Bible Society was one of her favorite philanthropies. After 1820, when she suffered serious physical illness, she turned her attention from active participation in religious and worthy projects to the composition of religious works, which were published anonymously.

Although her religious enthusiasm does not compensate for her lack of literary merit, her books received considerable attention during her lifetime. Her biographer, James Hamilton, apologizes for her ineptitude, but argues that grace and truthfulness compensate for her defects.

Her first volume, *Despair and Hope* (1822) was followed by *Thoughts on the Religious Profession* (1823) and *Impressions of the Heart* (1825). According to the reviewer for the *Scottish Guardian*, her work is "pervaded throughout by a tone of the most evangelical devotion."

The Kingdom of God was published in 1836 and *The World's Religion as Contrasted with Genuine Christianity* in 1839. The reviewer for the *London Watchman*, perhaps tongue-in-cheek, apparently praised her books by comparing them to those by Hannah More: "The pious and gifted writer treats her subjects under the evident influence of great spirituality of feeling, very clearly, and very impressively."

When the Scotch church experienced controversy and division in 1843, Colquhoun was active in the issues, supporting the Free church side ardently. She died at Helensburgh in 1846.

James E. Barcus

Works Consulted

Allibone, S. Austin, ed. *Allibone's Dictionary of English Literature and British and American Authors*. Philadelphia: Lippincott, 1897.

Colquhoun, Janet, Lady. *The Collected Works of Lady Colquhoun, of Rossdhu*. London, 1852.

Dictionary of National Biography. s.v. "Colquhoun, Janet."

Hamilton, James. *A Memoir of Lady Colquhoun*. London: Nisbet, 1849.

Combination Acts

The Combination Acts, passed by Parliament in 1799 and 1800, prohibited workers from organizing ("combining") for the purpose of obtaining higher wages and better working conditions. The legislation, reflecting anxieties about Revolutionary France and the possibility of imported unrest, was also one of the earliest British attempts to control workers' reactions to the conditions of industrial wage labor. The ancient system of guilds had broken down in the late 18th century, as masters and journeymen fought over the latter group's powerlessness to improve its situation. As ever greater numbers of journeymen went on strike, masters of various guilds lobbied Parliament to prevent such disruptions; their efforts bore fruit with the passage of the Acts, which in addition to other restrictions on combinations, also specifically forbade striking.

Although viewed by some historians as exceptionally repressive, the new laws were in fact less severe than other operative labor laws from earlier centuries. The initial 1799 Act approved summary trial of offenders by local magistrates and allowed for up to three months' imprisonment for combination activities regarding wages and hours. The revised 1800 version of the law modified the severity of these strictures; it mandated mediation of labor disputes by justices not associated with the trade in question and increased by two the number of magistrates hearing cases against individuals. Furthermore, the Combination Acts were extended to masters as well, prohibiting collusion among employers, but that provision was rarely enforced.

Actually, the law as a whole was notably inefficient. It did not stop workers from organizing. In fact, there was some degree of public sympathy for combinations. But unions nevertheless had to conduct themselves with caution and secrecy. The Combination Acts were repealed in 1824, largely through the efforts of breech-maker and political activist Francis Place. The repeal occasioned an upswing in strike activity, however, and a modified Combination Act was passed in 1825, prohibiting breach of contract and use of intimidation tactics toward employers.

Sue Petit Starke

Works Consulted

Brown, Kenneth D. *The English Labour Movement 1700–1951*. New York: St. Martin's, 1982.

Cole, G.D.H. *A Short History of the British Working-Class Movement 1789–1947*. Rev. ed. London: Allen, 1960.

Dobson, C.R. *Masters and Journeymen: A Prehistory of Industrial Relations 1717–1800*. London: Croom, 1980.

Musson, A.E. *British Trade Unions, 1800–1875*. London: Macmillan, 1972.

Pelling, Henry. *A History of British Trade Unionism*. 3rd ed. London: Macmillan, 1976.

Commonsense Philosophy

Dr. Johnson's kicking a stone is usually cited as the prime example of commonsense philosophy, his appeal to everyday reason, or common sense, being used to refute apparently nonsensical philosophical assertions. Developed as a response to the idealism of Berkeley and the skepticism of Hume (both of which had been paralyzed by such impossible questions as whether the external world existed and if it did, how would one know it), commonsense philosophy revolves around the cluster of beliefs generally accepted as true by the majority of people.

In the 18th century, most commonsense philosophy emerged from the "Scottish School," revolving around Thomas Reid (1710–96), James Beattie (1735–1803), and Douglas Stewart (1753–1828), though George Campbell and James Oswald are sometimes included as well. As the central figure in the group, Reid intended to refute philosophical paradox and skepticism

with the appeal to common sense. In his *Inquiry into the Human Mind on the Principles of Common Sense* (1764), Reid maintained that while common sense cannot be demonstrated deductively, its truth emerges through the absurdities of its contrary, specifically, Hume's theories of perception, thought, and memory. The primary objection to Reid's philosophy is that he canonized "the judgment of the crowd." While he felt that his theory was predicated on philosophical principle, he failed to demonstrate how common sense validated his theories of metaphysics.

Reid's colleague, Beattie argued against Berkeley and Hume in his *Essay on the Nature and Immutability of Truth, in Opposition to Sophistry and Skepticism* (1770). Asserting that common sense enables humanity to perceive truth instantaneously and instinctively, independently of an act of will, Beattie felt that this faculty could be used to demonstrate Berkeley's and Hume's lack of truth.

Stewart, the third major figure, was Reid's student. Considering his work to be in the tradition of Baconian reformation of the philosophy of mind, Stewart disapproved of the term "common sense," believing it implied an appeal to the masses as opposed to the learned; and in his *Elements of the Philosophy of the Mind* (1792), *Philosophical Essays* (1810), and *Philosophy of the Active and Moral Powers of Man* (1828), Stewart used observation and experimentation to discover the science of nature, asserting that reason, not common sense, is the faculty that will yield the truths to which Reid appealed. (*See also* Berkeley's Idealism, Human Skepticism.)

Sheila A. Spector

Works Consulted

Barker, S.F., and T.L. Beauchamp, eds. *Thomas Reid: Critical Interpretations*. Philadelphia: University City Science Center, 1976.

Grave, S.A. *The Scottish Philosophy of Common Sense*. Oxford: Clarendon, 1960.

Jones, Peter, ed. *The "Science of Man" in the Scottish Enlightenment: Hume, Reid and their Contemporaries*. Edinburgh: Edinburgh UP, 1989.

Rendall, J. *The Origins of the Scottish Enlightenment 1707–1776*. London: Macmillan, 1978.

Constable, Archibald

(1774–1827)

Archibald Constable is one of the great figures of early 19th-century publishing, occupying a place in the emergence of Edinburgh as an important center for the book trade and undertaking the encouragement of original talent comparable to that of John Murray in London.

Constable was humbly born and not well educated, but having become apprenticed to Peter Hill, an Edinburgh bookseller, he rapidly acquired an understanding of both new and antiquarian publications. He set up his own shop in 1795, specializing in rare books. But he soon began to sponsor new publications and in 1801 became proprietor of the long-established *Scots Magazine*.

Constable's great period began in 1802, when he became the publisher of the *Edinburgh Review*. He paid its editor, Francis Jeffrey, and the other contributors well, thereby attracting writers of genuine ability. Among these was Scott, then making his name as an editor of folk poetry. Quickly recognizing Scott's gifts as an original poet and later as a novelist, Constable laid the foundations for Scott's productivity and financial success—and ultimately for the financial failure of both Scott and his own firm.

Constable published vigorously and variously, playing a major part in the renaissance of Scottish letters in the first quarter of the 19th century. In 1812, he purchased the copyright of the *Encyclopaedia Britannica*; his *Supplement* incorporates articles of lasting merit by some of the most notable specialists of the day. Over the years he had various partners in his business: by the early 1820s the last of these, his son-in-law, Robert Cadell, was warning him of the dangerous extent to which the firm (which was seriously under-capitalized) was relying on anticipated profits and an elaborate system of promissory notes exchanged with their London agents, Hurst Robinson, and the printing firm of Ballantyne, which was virtually owned by Scott.

Constable's health was deteriorating in these years, but he remained fertile in literary projects: Scott's *Life of Napoleon* and *Constable's Miscellany* originated with him. But in 1826 the slump in the book trade carried Robinson, the Ballantyne Press, Constable, and Scott before it. Scott assumed responsibility for the entire debt of over £120,000 and shortened his life by overwork, trying to pay it. Constable never recovered and died in 1827. Only Cadell, a cautious and determined man, succeeded in retrieving anything lasting from the ruin: by concentrating largely on publishing and reprinting Scott's works he died a rich man.

William Ruddick

Works Consulted

Constable, T. *Archibald Constable and his Literary Correspondents*. Edinburgh: Edmonston, 1873.

Grierson, H.J.C. *Sir Walter Scott: A New Life*. London: Constable, 1938.

Lockhart, J.G. *Peter's Letters to His Kinsfolk*. Edinburgh: Blackwood, 1819.

Constable, John

(1776–1837)

John Constable, best known for his seemingly comfortable landscapes of the British countryside, created an iconography of Romanticism at the same time that he used painting to illustrate his view of nature. Perhaps his best known work, *The Hay Wain* (1821), illustrates his view of nature, in which humanity works in harmony with nature but is nonetheless dominated by it. One of his later works, *Hadleigh Castle* (1829), exhibits a typical Romantic scene by integrating a ruined castle by the sea into the landscape. Constable created images that are now taken as typically Romantic, and his variety of subject matter and style is testament to the changing quality of his art throughout his life. (*See also* Landscape Painting.)

The second son of a wealthy miller, Constable was not at first thought to be talented enough to become an artist. His father actively discouraged his son's pursuit of art as a career, thinking Constable would perhaps be more successful in the family business. As a result of this attitude and of having to work for a time in his father's mill, Constable did not become a student at the Royal Academy until 1800, at age 23, which was considered quite late to take up artistic training.

In 1806, Constable's uncle provided him with three years' financing for the purpose of painting landscapes of the Lake District. Upon completion of this series, he abandoned the picturesque in favor of a looser, more Romantic style. Most of the pictures in this style were oil sketches of his native scenery. He spent several of these early years, though, painting portraits in order to support himself. In 1816, the year of his marriage, Constable began painting his six-foot exhibition paintings.

Many critics feel that Constable had difficulty bringing the immediacy of his preliminary sketches to the finished pictures. This is particularly evident in *The Hay Wain*, one of the six-foot paintings. Otherwise, it is noted for its dominant sky painted in impressionistic, Romantic strokes rather than having the smooth, glassy surface of a classical landscape. This particular sky deeply influenced many French Romantic painters and Gericault and Isabey arranged for the work to be exhibited at the Paris Salon of 1824. It was there that Delacroix viewed it and was led to repaint the entire background of his *Massacre of Chios* in a style similar to Constable's. (*See also* Bonington, Richard Parkes.)

The Hay Wain, generally considered one of Constable's more poetic paintings, appears to offer an impersonal point of view. It might illustrate a Wordsworthian "spot of time" in that the scene depicted, a man at work, is a frozen moment. Yet, the particularity of the scene belies its universality, for it is a familiar moment, easily recognizable and therefore appealing. It has none of the negative or violent aspects that appear in the work of Turner and the French Romantic artists.

Hadleigh Castle is perhaps the most Romantic of Constable's paintings. It was painted after his wife's death, which plunged Constable into a severe depression. Taking as its subject a ruined castle by the sea—a romantic symbol *par excellence*—the work has an immediately obvious painterly quality. It also displays more completely than any of Constable's other painting the technique of chiaroscuro (i.e., using extremes of dark and light). In fact, the dark is in active conflict with the light, creating a sense of tension rare in Constable's work. It is, however, a natural tension, rather than the kind of artificial humanity-versus-nature tension characteristic of much Romantic art.

It is significant that *Hadleigh Castle* was Constable's exhibition painting for the Academy in 1829, which was the year he was finally elected to full membership of the Royal Academy. His most overtly Romantic work, illustrating some of the despair and isolation he felt at that time, signals the attainment, at last, of Constable's professional goal.

Constable spent the last years of his life lecturing on landscape painting. His final lecture series was delivered in 1836, one year before his death. This series consisted of four lectures, presented in London between May 26 and June 16, covering the history of landscape painting, from its Italian and German beginnings in the 15th century to the present. In these lectures, Constable relied heavily on his audience's knowledge of varied works of art, making it very clear that any artist, to be effective, must be thoroughly familiar with the artistic past. Constable's last public presentation, a lecture on 25 July 1836, before the Literary and Scientific Institution at Hampstead, offered a general discussion of landscape and its importance in painting.

Also in 1836, Constable painted what is perhaps his most unusual picture, *The Cenotaph to Sir Joshua Reynolds at Coleorton*. While most of his works are landscapes illustrating spring or summer, this is Constable's first (and only) winter scene. The openness of the landscape apparent in Constable's other works is missing in this composition; here, the landscape is enclosed, with very little of the trademark Constable sky which so influenced other artists. The scene is stark, and the artificiality of the cenotaph and the opposing busts of Raphael and Michelangelo, which face each other, contrast with and appear to trap the stag in the foreground. There is far more conflict here between humanity and nature than anywhere else in Constable's art. This conflict appeared only in the final version of the painting, for his preliminary drawing depicted only the cenotaph and the tree from Sir George Beaumont's park, the stag, and the attendant busts.

Within a year of painting this remarkable elegiac homage to a fellow painter, Constable was dead. His ground-breaking work in style, technique, and subject matter influenced both painter and writer alike.

Linda A. Archer

Works Consulted

Clark, Kenneth. *The Romantic Rebellion: Romantic versus Classical Art*. New York: Harper, 1973.

Kroeber, Karl. *Romantic Landscape Vision: Constable and Wordsworth*. Madison: U of Wisconsin P, 1975.

Leslie, C.R. *Memoirs of the Life of John Constable*. Ed. Jonathan Magore. Ithaca: Cornell UP, 1980.

Paulson, Ronald. *Literary Landscape: Turner and Constable*. New Haven: Yale UP, 1982.

Conversation Poems

Conversation poems are chiefly associated with the poetry of Coleridge, who gave the name "conversational poem" to his poem *The Nightingale*, which was published in *Lyrical Ballads* (1798). Beginning with G.M. Harper in 1928, the term has been applied to five other major poems by Coleridge, all written between 1795 and 1798: *Reflections on Having Left a Place of Retirement*, *The Eolian Harp*, *This Lime-Tree Bower My Prison*, *Frost at Midnight*, and *Fears in Solitude*. Some scholars have extended the list to include *Dejection: An Ode*, and *To William Wordsworth*.

Coleridge's conversation poems share common elements of style, structure, and theme. They feature a solitary persona speaking in a relaxed and informal tone, who at some point in the poem addresses an absent or silent auditor (a friend, wife, or child). Each poem is written in paragraphs of blank verse of varying lengths and possesses a three-part, circular structure. The poem begins by evoking a physical setting in some detail. The scene is usually quiet and tranquil, which sets the tone for the meditation that follows. The poem then moves inward, to the speaker's thoughts and feelings. He may reflect on an event in childhood (as in *Frost at Midnight*) or in the recent past (*Reflections on Having Left a Place of Retirement*), or on the current political situation (*Fears in Solitude*). As the contemplation proceeds, the speaker may gain an insight into his own situation or he may come to some realization about the nature of the universe (as in *The Eolian Harp*). The poem then rounds back on itself, to end where it began, but with enriched understanding.

The form of the conversation poem was a perfect vehicle for Coleridge's metaphysical beliefs. It dissolved the rigid boundaries between subject and object by showing the human mind in creative interaction with the external world. It also developed Coleridge's intuition that objects in nature are symbols for something that exists within human consciousness. And the circular form of the poem reflects Coleridge's belief that a poem should embody the circular structure of reality.

The conversation poem has its origins, first, in the 18th-century "local" poem, which consisted of a description of a landscape and some thoughts suggested by the scene. Sir John Denham's *Cooper's Hill*, was the first of the genre; Thomas Gray's *Ode on a Distant Prospect of Eton College* is another example. But the immediate stimulus for Coleridge was the sonnets of Bowles.

These sonnets begin with a description of a landscape, followed by the melancholy personal emotions and memories that are stimulated by it. Coleridge writes in the first chapter of *Biographia Literaria* of the impact Bowles's sonnets made on him. In Coleridge's hands, however, the form developed into a more profound meditation, enriched by Coleridge's idealist and mystic philosophy.

M.H. Abrams has pointed out that the conversation poem, which he calls the "greater Romantic lyric," was used by all major English Romantic poets, with the exception of Byron. Wordsworth's *Tintern Abbey*, and *Ode: Intimations of Immortality* are examples of the genre, as are Shelley's *Stanzas Written in Dejection* and, with variations, his *Ode to the West Wind*. (*See also* Coleridge, Samuel Taylor; Mental Theater.)

Bryan Aubrey

Works Consulted

Abrams, M.H. "Structure and Style in the Greater Romantic Lyric." *From Sensibility to Romanticism: Essays Presented to Frederick A. Pottle*. Eds. Frederick W. Hilles & Harold Bloom. New York: Oxford UP, 1965.

Gérard, A. "The Systolic Rhythm: The Structure of Coleridge's Conversation Poems." *Coleridge: A Collection of Critical Essays*. Ed. Kathleen Coburn. Englewood Cliffs: Prentice, 1967.

Harper, G.M. "Coleridge's Conversation Poems." *English Romantic Poets: Modern Essays in Criticism*. Ed. M.H. Abrams. 1960. 2d ed. New York: Oxford UP, 1975.

Cook, James

(1728–99)

Along with Captain James Cook's undeniable contributions to navigation, science, and imperialism, his impact on the popular imagination was immediate, widespread, and durable. And, as with many popular heroes, Cook's sensational death, to be hammered down and dismembered by angry natives in the Sandwich Islands (modern-day Hawaii), lent additional luster to his brow. Cook's death was commemorated in numerous hangings on the walls of English homes at least through the time of Dickens, as shown in *Bleak House, Great Expectations*, and *Little Dorrit*.

In 1847, the American sailor-novelist Herman Melville was linked to Captain Cook by a review of *Mardi* in *The Morning Chronicle*, while in *Moby-Dick*, Melville mentions John Ledyard, an American who had traveled with the final Cook expedition, from 1776 to 1780. Cook's characteristic plainspokenness in voice and writing elevated him in the opinion of the common person as well as such elite subjects as the members of the Royal Society, who praised the style he employed. A mythic fascination with the man and his work has persisted even to the late 20th century. In 1989, TNT cable television broadcast a miniseries, starring Keith Mitchell as the explorer who broke class ranks to become a commissioned Royal commander from the lowliest of backgrounds. But Cook's posthumous reputation has suffered under modern anticolonialist ideologies. For instance, Bernard Smith serves a left-handed compliment to the mariner's accommodation with island natives as a means of imperialist conquest.

The second child of James and Grace Cook, James Cook was born in 1728, at Marton village, Cleveland (near Middlesbrough) Yorkshire. His father was an agricultural worker and later a farm manager for Thomas Skottowe, of Airyholme. By 1745, at age 17, James was working for William Sanderson, dealing in groceries and haberdashery. He does not appear to have liked being a shopkeeper. Later, in 1746, with Sanderson handling

the legal arrangements, Cook was apprenticed to the Quaker John Walker, an owner and master of ships, who encouraged him to learn both the theory and the practice of sailing. Under Walker's auspices, James made his first voyage, aboard the *Freelove*, in 1747. During 1748 to 1749, he worked on another Walker vessel, the much larger *Three Brothers*, gaining valuable experience in the shipping trade as well as staying close to the physical details of ship construction and operation.

Demonstrating great faith in his ability and trust in the young man's 11 years of experience, Walker offered Cook his own command. But, having already spent a decade in the North Sea and the Baltic region and running coal between Newcastle and London, Cook was ready for wider seas. In June 1755, he joined the Royal Navy. (Inasmuch as the work was hard and volunteers rare, even for patriotic reasons, some scholars have suggested that Cook's enlistment may have been precipitated by imminent smuggling charges.) By month's end, he was a Master's Mate on *Eagle*; by age 19, he had gained a Master's warrant. It was aboard the *Eagle* that Cook first engaged the hostile French and became well acquainted with Sir Hugh Palliser, who sponsored his rapidly rising career. In June 1757, Cook became master of the *Solebay*, under Captain Robert Craig, patrolling Scotland and guarding against the French and the Dutch. His next appointment was to the *Pembroke*, a much larger ship of the line, under Captain John Simcoe.

In 1759, Cook distinguished himself as a hydrographic surveyor when the British needed to enter the St. Lawrence River after the French had removed nautical guides and signals from the treacherous channel. In September of that year, shortly after the deaths of Wolfe and Montcalm at

Quebec, Cook was reassigned to the *Northumberland*, on which he remained until 1762. At year's end, he married Elizabeth Batts, of Barking, Essex.

Cook returned to Newfoundland as master surveyor in 1763, remaining until 1767, meticulously mapping that important trading coast, while in 1764 his mentor Palliser had become governor of that province. From him, Cook received his first command, the *Grenville*, extending his exemplary charting abilities to encompass Labrador and Nova Scotia, publishing those nautical papers around 1768. His abilities as mathematician and astronomer were being noted, especially with regard to the solar eclipse on August 5, 1766.

In 1768, Cook's accomplishments led to his being sent on a Pacific voyage for both the Royal Navy and the Royal Society. The immediate impetus was twofold. In June 1767, Captain Samuel Wallis had rediscovered Tahiti and revived some beliefs in a great southern continent, "Terra Australis Incognita," purported to be of a mass to balance Eurasia at the other end of the globe; and in 1769, the planet Venus was scheduled to pass dramatically between earth and the sun. Cook's masterful style of observation and reportage would serve both purposes well from a vantage in the Pacific.

Commissioned to lead a group of sailors and scientists, including Sir Joseph Banks, he set sail August 25, 1768, in the *Endeavour*, a sturdy, capacious vessel of 370 tons. On April 13, he came to Tahiti, later surveying the Society Islands. He charted the coastline of New Zealand, including the channel ("Cook Strait") that separates the two main islands, north and south. Foreshadowing his fatal encounter at Hawaii, Cook's men were met with hostility by the natives and prevented from meaningful land exploration. The voyage solidified British

claims upon these major islands of the Pacific, as Cook's careful mapping of the eastern shore of Australia did for that continent.

Following a course back around the Cape of Good Hope, Cook returned to England in the summer of 1771; and, being promoted to commander in August, he was commissioned to pursue yet again the elusive southern continent. Aboard the *Resolution*, accompanied by the *Adventure*, Cook departed on July 13, 1772. He sailed to the Cape of Good Hope, the dangerously icy Antarctic Circle, and back to New Zealand. He charted accurately the location of Easter Island. Sailing widely, back and forth, in relentless support of his mission of refutation, Cook managed to present a survey of the positions and coastlines of the Marquesas, the Friendly Islands, the New Hebrides, the whole Pacific basin from Australia to the Cape of Good Hope. Equally impressive as the range and recording of this voyage was the preservation of the health of the crew from scurvy and the fact that there was only one fatality.

The *Resolution* reached home almost exactly three years after its departure. On August 9, 1775, Cook was appointed captain in the Greenwich hospital, and unanimously elected to the Royal Society, which bestowed a gold medal on him for the best experimental paper.

With his experience in the Pacific, it was not unreasonable for Cook to try to discover a way "over" the North American continent to the Atlantic while others tried to find their way through to the Pacific. After passing the Cape of Good Hope, he revisited Tahiti, Tasmania, and New Zealand; and he discovered more islands not touched on his previous voyages. In particular, early in 1778 he came upon the Hawaiian, or Sandwich, Islands. He proceeded to the North American coast, which he charted as far as the Bering Straits. He gave names to several locations in what is now Alaska, as well as the Russian-Asian side of the straits, and his observations of the people there are studiously recorded.

When Cook made his way back to the Sandwich Islands—Maui and Hawaii, in particular—he anchored in Kealakekua Bay, from which station he led a landing party bent on retribution for a boat stolen from the *Discovery*. Using one of his favorite techniques of coercion, Cook captured King Kalani'opu'u as hostage for the stolen boat. As a result of the people's outrage, Cook and four of his men were killed on February 14, 1779. On the 16th, with the recovery of portions of his body, Cook's crew retaliated with shot and cannon, killing a few islanders and piking their heads.

In his three Pacific voyages, Cook circumnavigated and prepared maps of New Zealand, charted the eastern coast of Australia, rediscovered Hawaii (which likely had been visited by the Spaniard Gaetano in 1555), and skirted the great northwest coast of America. His work produced the most complete picture of the Pacific Ocean boundaries that the world had ever known. His naturalistic and astronomical observations, his exercise of the navigational arts, his success in dealing with medical problems such as scurvy on long voyages, and his startling, charismatic blend of romance and reason set him apart as one of the world's greatest explorers.

Robert W. Hill

Works Consulted

Banks, Joseph. *The "Endeavour" Journal of Joseph Banks 1768–1771*. Ed. J.C. Beaglehole. 2 vols. Sydney: 1962.

Beaglehole, J.C. *The Life of Captain James Cook*. Stanford: Stanford UP, 1974.

Cameron, Ian. *Lost Paradise: The Exploration of the Pacific*. Topsfield, MA: Salem, 1987.

Cameron, Roderick. *The Golden Haze: With Captain Cook in the South Pacific*. Cleveland: World, 1964.

Conner, Daniel, and Lorraine Miller. *Master Mariner: Capt. James Cook and the Peoples of the Pacific*. Vancouver: Douglas, 1978.

Fisher, Robin, and Hugh Johnston, eds. *Captain James Cook and His Times*. Seattle: U of Washington P, 1979.

Hough, Richard. *The Last Voyage of Captain James Cook*. New York: Morrow, 1979.

Mackay, David. *In the Wake of Cook: Exploration, Science & Empire, 1780–1801*. New York: St. Martin's, 1985.

Moorehead, Alan. *The Fatal Impact: An Account of the Invasion of the South Pacific 1767–1840*. New York: Harper, 1966.

Rickman, John. *Journal of Captain Cook's Last Voyage to the Pacific Ocean, on Discovery; Performed in the Years 1776, 1777, 1778, 1779, Illustrated with Cuts, and a Chart, Shewing the Tracts of the Ships Employed in this Expedition*. 1781. Ann Arbor: University Microfilms, 1966.

Robertson, George. *The Discovery of Tahiti: A Journal of the Second Voyage of H.M.S. "Dolphin" Round the World by George Robertson*. Ed. Hugh Carrington. London: 1948.

Smith, Bernard. "Cook's Posthumous Reputation." Fisher 159–85.

Withey, Lynne. *Voyages of Discovery: Captain Cook and the Exploration of the Pacific*. New York: Morrow, 1987.

Corn Laws

Controlling the importation and exportation of corn, that is, all types of grain, seems to have a long history in England. The original purpose was to provide protection for the citizens. Due to the nature of early transportation, it was often easier to sell on the Continent than to transport grain to the more remote regions of the country. The first formal Corn Law was enacted in 1536 during the reign of Henry VI. It provided that when the price fell below a certain amount, grain exports without government permission were allowed; the purpose was to increase profits for the landowner.

The period of warfare in the second half of the 18th century and a growing population pushed the price of grain up because supplies of foreign grain were reduced while the demand for bread increased. Burke's law of 1773 is a good example of the Corn-Law theory. Forty-eight shillings a quarter (i.e., eight bushels) was the top price at which home farmers could expect protection. Above that, foreign corn was allowed in at the small charge of six pence. One result of the law was hardship among the lower classes, particularly the laboring poor. But there is no doubt the laws encouraged the landowners to increase production.

The question of protectionism assumed crisis proportions toward the end of the Napoleonic Wars. Until 1814, the price of grain remained high, but the defeat of the French and an excellent harvest in 1813 caused a rapid drop. The new Corn Law of 1815 for the first time prohibited foreign grain when the price fell below 80 schillings a quarter, but prices continued to fall. Parliament established a sliding scale instead of the choice of total prohibition or total freedom in importing foreign grain. When prices rose in 1823, renewed agitation against price controls began.

A period of speculation led to a shattering economic crisis in 1826, a crisis that was made worse by bad harvests. A new sliding scale was established when the price reached 73 shillings a quarter. During the early 1830s, harvests were good, and the price remained relatively low.

Renewed agitation for repeal followed a series of bad harvests and an industrial depression in 1836. Anti-Corn-Law leagues appeared and proved to be some of the most effective pressure groups and worst poets in English history (the anti-Corn-Law rhymes were terrible). By the early 1840s, conditions improved again, but a new economic philosophy was making itself felt.

In 1841, the Tory Sir Robert Peel (1788–1850) became Prime Minister. He was influenced by growing support for what was popularly called free trade, an outgrowth of classical economics. Peel seems to have become a believer even before he learned of the failure of the potato crop in Ireland during 1845. After five months and despite strong opposition from the protectionists, Peel successfully reduced the duty on wheat, oats, and barley. The bill passed on 25 June 1846. (*See also* Parliament.)

Peel had split his party, ended his career, and shaped the political structure of England for the next 20 years. The agitation for repeal had proved far more important than the economic results. It did not alleviate the famine in Ireland, and, while it did lower the price of grain, the reduction was not large. In the last part of the century, the problem came from outside: improvements in transportation led to much greater competition—the wheat fields of North America and Australia.

K. Gird Romer

Works Consulted

Arnstein, Walter. *Britain Yesterday and Today: 1830 to the Present.* 5th ed. Lexington: Heath, 1988.

Gash, Norman. *Politics in the Age of Peel: A Study in the Technique of Parliamentary Representation 1830–1850.* New York: Longmans, 1953.

Gregg, Pauline. *Modern Britain: A Social and Economic History Since 1760.* 5th ed. rev. New York: Pegasus, 1965.

Moore, David Cresap. *The Politics of Deference: A Study of the Mid-Nineteenth Century English Political System.* New York: Barnes, 1976.

Watson, J. Steven. *The Reign of George III, 1760–1815.* Oxford: Clarendon, 1960.

Willcox, William B., and Walter L. Arnstein. *The Age of Aristocracy 1688–1830*. 5th ed. Lexington: Heath, 1988.

Woodward, Sir Llewellyn. *The Age of Reform 1815–1870*. 2nd ed. Oxford: Clarendon, 1962.

Cosway, Richard

(1742–1821)

Richard Cosway was the most prominent and successful painter of miniature portraits in late 18th-century England, but at the height of his career he and his wife Maria, also an artist, were known as much for their flamboyance and extravagant social lives as for their talent as painters.

The son of a Tiverton schoolmaster, Cosway studied under Thomas Hudson and later in Shipley's school. He won several important prizes before age 20, working in various media and genres. At first, he aspired to conventional portraiture, and many of his exhibition works were on canvas. But when he was elected to the Royal Academy in 1771, it must have been on the strength of his miniature paintings on ivory, which are much more impressive. In 1781, he married Maria Hadfield, whose father had owned an inn in Florence that was popular with English travelers. Because he was very short and something of a dandy, Cosway's appearance was widely ridiculed, and Maria's beauty, talent, and exoticism brought attention as well. In 1784, they moved to Pall Mall and became famous for their parties, which attracted the height of Whig society, including the Prince of Wales.

Maria exhibited a number of pictures, mostly of literary subjects, at the Royal Academy and in general deserved the frequent comparisons of her talent to that of Angelica Kauffmann, her former mentor.

Even when living together, the Cosways were reputed to be countenancing mutual infidelities, and after 1789, they drifted apart. Maria was said to have had affairs with both the Prince and Thomas Jefferson, among others, and in the late 1790s Cosway traveled and lived openly with Mary Moser, the "Lady Academician." Maria stayed mostly on the Continent until she died in 1838, though she returned briefly before the death of their daughter in 1795 and was in England when Cosway died in 1821. While abroad, she founded a college in Italy, which she later converted to a convent.

After 1795, Cosway became increasingly eccentric: late in life he painted from visions, claimed to have conversed with historical figures, and was at various times a passionate advocate of the French Revolution, Swedenborgianism, and evangelical Christianity. He was also a student of animal magnetism and various mystical sciences, interests he shared with Blake and several other artists of the time. But these enthusiasms are not apparent in his work. Aside from some drawings and very few historical and literary subjects, almost all of Cosway's oeuvre is miniature portraiture.

His mature miniature style (1785–1800) is distinguished by delicate transparent washes on the ivory, relatively large ovals (about three inches rather than two or less), elaborate but subtle modeling of the cheeks and chin, sparing calligraphic strokes for the hair, elongated necks, and enlarged eyes. His portraits of the Prince of Wales are typical. Most of these works are essentially confections, albeit immensely successful ones—the mode did not encourage even the polite intellection that characterizes the period's more ambitious portraits. After the turn of the century, Cosway's miniatures darkened, becoming less colorful and dwelling less on sweet circularities and lines of beauty in faces and hair. Though still far from melancholy, his sitters appear more thoughtful, as in his *Princess Amelia* (1802) or his *Arthur Wellesley, Duke of Wellington* (1808).

In his last years, Cosway suffered from paralytic fits, and in 1821, he died during a therapeutic carriage ride. Maria commissioned a monument in St. Marylebone Church by Richard Westmacott, with verses by William Coombe ("Dr. Syntax"), Cosway's brother-in-law.

Alexander S. Gourlay

Works Consulted

Reynolds, Graham. *English Portrait Miniatures*. Rev. ed. Cambridge: Cambridge UP, 1988.

Williamson, George C. *Richard Cosway, R.A.* London: Bell, 1905.

Cotman, John Sell

(1782–1842)

John Sell Cotman was born in Norwich in 1782 and is remembered today as a watercolorist and etcher. The majority of his paintings are rather stylized landscapes, typically revealing the use of a flat, broad wash, in which he attempted to evoke passionate emotions roused by things seen. Unlike the painters of the Norwich School of which he was a part, Cotman altered the landscapes he painted to suit his esthetic purpose. His use of color and his mastery of both form and silhouette lend an almost surreal quality to his work.

In his first year as a member of the Norwich Society of Artists in 1807, he exhibited 20 drawings; in 1808, he submitted 67. In addition to landscapes, Cotman drew from architectural and antiquarian subject matter. During his lifetime, he engraved a number of copperplate etchings that reveal a moderate degree of accomplishment.

In 1798, Cotman came to London, where he exhibited between 1800 and 1806. He lived in Norwich until 1812, when he moved to Yarmouth. It was in Yarmouth that Cotman painted the majority of his seascapes, along with a number of wash-and-line drawings. Perhaps the most important trips for Cotman, in terms of his development as an artist, occurred during the years 1817, 1818, and 1820, when he visited Normandy. His visits to Normandy not only provided him with additional subject matter for his watercolors and etchings, the change in scenery resulted in a much more liberal use of color, adding a greater vitality to his work.

In 1825, Cotman's skill as a watercolorist was recognized in the form of an appointment as Associate of the Society of Painters in Water-Colours. His first contributions as Associate were *Dieppe* and *Mont St. Michel, showing the Phenomenon of the Mirage*. In 1833, with the help of friends, Cotman secured the position of Drawing Master at King's College School, London. During this period, Cotman executed figure paintings and imaginary landscapes, but none was very successful. In 1841, he painted 20 black-and-white studies of autumn; the most interesting is *The World Afloat*.

Cotman was also a prolific etcher. His early attempts on copperplate were collected and eventually published in a series entitled *Liber Studiorum* (1838). Of the 48 plates in this collection, 39 were of landscapes. In 1811, Boydell and Co. published *Etchings by John Sell Cotman*, a collection of 24 plates, 23 of which are of architectural antiquities. Cotman's other collections include *Norman and Gothic Architecture in Norfolk* (1817), containing 50 plates, and *Architectural Antiquities of Norfolk* (1818), a series of 60 plates with each plate dedicated to a patron. In 1819,

Cotman published *Sepulchral Brasses of Norfolk* and *Antiquities of St Mary's Chapel at Stourbridge, near Cambridge*. Probably the most important series is *Architectural Antiquities of Normandy* composed of 100 etchings, each one containing descriptions by Dawson Turner.

Jeffrey D. Parker

Works Consulted

Baker, C.H. Collins. *British Painting*. London: Medici Society, 1933.

Holme, Geoffrey. *The Norwich School*. London: The Studio, 1920.

Cottle, Joseph

(1770–1853)

The life of Joseph Cottle, bookseller, author, and Unitarian, is of interest largely because of his early association with Coleridge, Southey, and Wordsworth. The brother of Amos Cottle, the antiquarian, Cottle showed a love of reading early in life, and his schoolmaster, John Henderson, encouraged him to become a bookseller. Cottle set up business in Bristol in 1791, and in 1794 the poet Robert Lovell introduced him to Coleridge and Southey. The two young poets were preparing to emigrate to America, and Cottle helped to arrange lectures on the proposed scheme of pantisocracy. Having some poems of his own in the press, Cottle was also sympathetic to the poetic efforts of Southey and Coleridge, and he offered them 30 guineas each for the copyright to their poems. Both readily accepted, since this was far more than they had been offered elsewhere. Cottle also offered Southey 50 guineas for his epic poem, *Joan of Arc*, which he published in quarto in 1796. He also promised Coleridge a guinea and a half for every hundred lines of his future poetry.

Cottle next published Coleridge's periodical *The Watchman* (1796), bearing much of the expense himself. Coleridge introduced him to Wordsworth, and the result was the publication of *Lyrical Ballads* (1798). The following year Cottle retired from business and began to produce several volumes of his own poetry, including *Malvern Hills* (1798); *John the Baptist, a Poem* (1801); *Alfred, an Epic Poem* (1801); *The Fall of Cambria* (1809); and *Messiah* (1815). His efforts were enough to attract the sarcasm of Byron in *English Bards and Scotch Reviewers* (although Byron confused Cottle with his brother Amos). Cottle kept up his acquaintance with Coleridge, remonstrating with him about his opium addiction in letters in 1814 and 1815. Coleridge described Cottle in *Biographia Literaria* as "a friend from whom I never received any advice that was not wise, or a remonstrance that was not gentle and affectionate."

Ignoring the advice of his friends, Cottle published *Early Recollections, chiefly relating to the late Samuel Taylor Coleridge* (1837), which included the sorry details of Coleridge's opium addiction and the correspondence on the matter between the two men. The book has many inaccuracies, including incorrect dates and garbled quotations, and Southey complained that it was confused. Nonetheless, it contains valuable information about the early careers of Coleridge and Southey. A second edition, with additions and revisions, was published in 1847 as *Reminiscences of Coleridge and Southey*. Cottle died in Bristol in 1853. (*See also* Journalism, Publishing.)

Bryan Aubrey

Works Consulted

Cottle, Joseph. *Early Recollections, chiefly relating to Samuel Taylor Coleridge*. London, 1837. 2d ed. *Reminiscences of Coleridge and Southey*. London: Houston, 1847.

Haller, William. *The Early Life of William Southey*. New York: Columbia UP, 1917.

Southey, Charles Cuthbert, ed. *The Life and Correspondence of Robert Southey*. Vol. 1. New York: Harper, 1849.

Cowper, William

(1731–1800)

Cowper was an influential poet in England during the youth and early manhood of Wordsworth and Coleridge and during the time of Blake's composition of *Songs of Innocence and of Experience*. Of chief importance are the Olney Hymns (1779), the lyrics and moral satires published in *Poems*, the extraordinarily popular comic ballad *John Gilpin*, and *The Task*, a popular long poem published in the last quarter of the 18th century. Cowper's best poetry is distinguished by its grace and clarity and by its religious conviction, psychological penetration, and (especially in *The Task*), feeling for natural beauty. These qualities are evident in his letters, which are regarded as among the best in the language.

Cowper was born in 1731 at his father's rectory, Great Berkhampstead. The death of his mother in 1737 was devastating to the 6-year-old boy. A shy and delicate child, Cowper nevertheless thrived academically and socially at Westminster (1741–48), excelling in his studies of Greek and Roman authors and writing English and Latin verse. After leaving Westminster, Cowper was articled to a solicitor, but neglected his studies, preferring instead the company of Edward Thurlow (later Lord Chancellor) and the three daughters of his uncle Ashley Cowper. He was in residence at the Middle Temple from 1752 to 1758 (called to the bar in 1754). He became a member of the Nonsense Club, contributed essays to the *Connoisseur* and other London publications, and had a brief love affair with his cousin Theadora.

Named Commissioner of Bankrupts in 1759, Cowper moved to the Inner Temple. In 1763, he was offered the position of clerk of the journals of the House of Lords, but suffered a mental collapse in anticipation of the requisite public examination. Cowper's madness—the first of several attacks that plagued him throughout his life—involved an intense conviction of his own impending damnation, and he attempted suicide. He was placed under the care of Dr. Nathaniel Cotton at St. Albans. *Lines Written During a Period of Insanity* (1763) provides a terrifying self-portrait of Cowper during this time.

As a consequence of this breakdown, Cowper in 1765 severed all ties to the law and to London and began the life of rural retirement that would later become both source and subject of his best poetry. From late 1765 until late 1767, he resided at Huntingdon with the Rev. Morley Unwin, his wife Mary, and their children. Among the Unwins, Cowper says, he achieved a renewed sense of God's love for him. Biographers have noted that he also found a surrogate mother in Mary Unwin, with whom he lived at Olney and Weston, from the death of her husband in 1767 until her death in 1796.

At Olney, where Cowper and Mary moved in 1768, he came under the influence of the Evangelical curate John Newton, with whom he composed the enormously popular Olney Hymns (published 1779), several of which are generally recognized as among the finest English hymns. In January 1773, a second bout of insanity began with a dream that Cowper said destroyed all hope of consolation for him. He was moved into Newton's house, where he remained for a year. Again he attempted suicide, and again he came under the care of Dr. Cotton. During his recovery, he began to keep, for therapeutic purposes, the pet hares he writes about with gentle affection and good humor in verse and prose.

Cowper always considered poetry an amusement rather than a vocation, saying that he had as much right to be called a poet as a man who builds a mousetrap has to be called an engineer. And until 1780, he had produced little beyond his short pieces. In the winter of 1780, he began to engage in more substantial work and between then and 1785 composed most of the poetry upon which his reputation rests. In 1782, Joseph Johnson, who had already published the Olney Hymns and Cowper's mildly successful satire against polygamy, *Anti-Thelyphtora* (1781), published his *Poems*. This volume contained, in addition to 34 lyrics (most written before 1781), eight moral satires in decasyllabic couplets: *The Progress of Error, Truth, Table Talk, Expostulation, Hope, Charity, Conversation*, and *Retirement*. A preface by Newton discussing Cowper's retreat from London society in search of God's grace and emphasizing the religious purpose behind the poems was printed but suppressed. Even without Newton's preface, the volume is clearly Evangelical in tone and intention. In the moral satires, Cowper adopts a specifically religious point of view, setting himself apart from his satirist predecessors—particularly from Pope—in ways that would become important in the development of Romantic poetry. Cowper's tendency to oppose the clear, simple, and inspiring truth of religious faith to the enervating influences of worldly intrigue and sophistication leads him naturally to emphasize the insufficiency or delusory character of social convention and literary artifice. This emphasis in turn leads him to regard with suspicion the stylistic urbanity of Pope and his school. In *Table Talk*, he launches a famous attack on the "mere mechanic art" of Pope (in comparison with the unruly energy of Churchill) in terms anticipating various Romantic formulations, from Blake to Keats, of expressive aesthetic doctrines. *Table Talk* also contains a passage on the true poet as a person of comprehensive moral vision, the substance of which would be echoed many times in the Romantic period.

It has often been noted that Cowper is at his best when his subject is himself. But with the exception of *Retirement* (the last of the moral satires to be composed) and some of the lyrics, Cowper's focus in *Poems* was too broad and his purpose too specifically didactic to accommodate the reflective and discursive personal voice that would eventually emerge in his most important and enduring poem—*The Task*. Lady Austen, whom Cowper had met in 1781, and who in 1782 had told him the story on which he based *John Gilpin*, suggested to Cowper in 1783 that he write a blank verse poem. When he protested that he had no subject, Lady Austen set him to his task: to write upon the sofa. The poem, which begins in mock-Miltonic style with a history of chairs, eventually grew to six books, and was published, along with *John Gilpin* and other poems, in 1785. The plan of *The Task* was to have no regular plan. The resulting poem proceeds at an easy pace, organized solely according to the speaker's habits of association and held together by Cowper's moral reflections—most on country-versus-city themes—and by periodic lyric celebrations of the natural world or the joys of walking, gardening, and conversation. Cowper's celebration of the retired life, his views concerning the sanctity and interconnectedness of all living things, and his creation of a flexible, conversational blank verse medium appropriate to his wandering and wide-ranging observations and speculations all served to make *The Task* extraordinarily popular, as well as an important influence on the emerging new generation of writers. In 1786, a second edition of the 1785 volume, together with *Poems* (1782), was called for, and Cowper's reputation as the leading poet of his day was secure. The late 1770s and early 1780s also marked a gradual change in Cowper's choice of companions, as he began to reconnect himself with the world outside Olney. In 1785, he resumed his correspondence with his cousin Lady Hesketh, with whom he had lost touch during the years of his most intense devotional exercises. During this period, too, Cowper's letters attain their singular vivacity and candor, after a period in which their language had been colored by Evangelical formulae.

In 1786, Cowper moved from Olney to Weston. His last years were devoted to translating and editing, work that helped provide relief from two recurrences of insanity (in 1787 and 1794). He translated Homer (published by subscription in 1791), continuing, through his choice of blank verse over couplets, his lifelong, uneasy rivalry with Pope. In 1791, he undertook editorship of what was planned by Johnson to be a sumptuous edition of Milton, illustrated by Fuseli, and began to translate Milton's Latin and Italian poems. This work brought him into friendly contact with William Hayley, later Blake's patron, who was also planning an edition of Milton. A few original poems belong to these last years, most notably his homage to Mary Unwin in *To Mary* (composed 1793) and his summation of his excruciating sense of alienation from God, *The Castaway* (1799). Cowper died in 1800 at East Dereham.

Cowper's strong influence on Wordsworth, Blake, and Coleridge is indisputable. Wordsworth, who read *The Task* shortly after it was published, ranked Cowper with Burns and Percy's *Reliques* as among the most salutary poetic influences of the later 18th century. Southey published a *Life* with his edition of Cowper's works in 1835 to 1837. The importance of Cowper's blank verse style for Wordsworth, Southey, and especially Coleridge in the conversation poems has often been noted. Convincing arguments have been made for the influence of *The Task* on *The Prelude* and for the genesis in Cowper's poem of imagery in *Kubla Khan* and *Adonais*, while *John Gilpin* played a part in the resurgence of interest in the popular ballad.

Brennan O'Donnell

Works Consulted

King, James. *William Cowper: A Biography*. Durham: Duke UP, 1986.

Newey, Vincent. *Cowper's Poetry: A Critical Study and Reassessment*. Totowa, NJ: Barnes, 1982.

Priestman, Martin. *Cowper's Task, Structure and Influence*. Cambridge: Cambridge UP, 1983.

Crabbe, George
(1754–1832)

George Crabbe had two literary lives. From 1780, when he went to London to make his fortune, until 1785, he wrote poems that eventually earned him the respect and assistance of such men as Burke, Fox, Joshua Reynolds, and Samuel Johnson. He published nothing in the 22 years between *The Newspaper* (1785) and *Poems* (1807). Then came *The Borough* (1810), *Tales* (1812), and *Tales of the Hall* (1819). These latter volumes brought him considerable popularity and income, the critical acclaim of Jeffrey and Byron, and the friendship of Scott, Rogers, Moore, Campbell, and others.

Crabbe's 20th-century critical reputation is as Janus-faced as was his career. A self-professed literary realist whose often bleak vision was couched in the rhythmically familiar heroic couplets of the previous age, Crabbe has been claimed both as a belated 18th-century satirist in the mold of Pope and as a forward-looking observer of the often sordid details of the everyday, in whose narrative poems the sad music of humanity is frequently more harsh and grating than in the work of his more overtly imaginative and Romantic contemporaries.

Crabbe was born at Aldeburgh, the Suffolk fishing village that later furnished the setting for many of his tales. His father was a collector of salt duties known for his fondness for alcohol and his violent temper. Crabbe had little formal schooling and spent some of his youth working, much to his disgust, in a warehouse on the quay at Slaughden. Apprenticed to a village doctor in 1768, transferred in 1771 to a surgeon at Woodbridge, and sent in 1775 to London to study surgery, he set up practice in Aldeburgh from 1775 to 1780. By his own admission, he was a failure as a surgeon. Having fallen in love with a woman who refused to marry imprudently and having previously dabbled in poetry (his *Inebriety*, published anonymously in 1774, is an imitation of and homage to Pope), Crabbe determined in 1780 to escape through his writing from the life to which his mean birth and upbringing had condemned him. He set out for London with £3 in cash, some surgical instruments, and his manuscripts.

The Candidate (1780), addressed to the editors of the *Monthly Magazine*, was slightly noticed. By 1781, with his arrest for debt pending, Crabbe was desperate enough to appeal to Burke in a letter that told his history and his difficulties. Crabbe was a stranger to Burke, but Burke read his poems in manuscript, selected *The Library* as the most likely to succeed, and persuaded Dodsley to publish it. Burke welcomed Crabbe to Beaconsfield and introduced him to Fox, Reynolds, Johnson, and their circle.

With Burke's encouragement and support, Crabbe took deacon's orders in December 1781, and returned as curate to Aldeburgh. In 1782, he went to Belvoir as chaplain to the Duke of Rutland. His treatment at Belvoir seems to have been gracious on the whole, but various statements in the prose and verse of his later life concerning the indignities attending literary patronage suggest that the homely mannered Crabbe was not entirely at ease among the great. At Belvoir, he completed *The Village*, a poem that attempts to undercut the idealized depiction of rural people and occupations so common in the pastoral tradition (as in Goldsmith's *The Deserted Village*), which foreshadows much of Crabbe's later work. The vigor and antipastoral sentiment of the poem pleased Johnson, who made suggestions for its final revision and predicted its success. It was published in 1783.

Thurlow presented Crabbe small clerical appointments at Frome St. Quentin and Evershot, Dorsetshire, and the Archbishop of Canterbury conferred upon him the degree of LL.B. In 1785, he accepted the curacy of Stathern, and, having married in December 1783, moved into the village parsonage. After publishing a brief memoir of Rutland's brother, Lord Robert Manners (1784), and *The Newspaper* (1785), Crabbe ceased publication and devoted himself to a clerical career that took him from Stathern to Muston, Parham, Great Glenham, back to Muston, and, finally, to Trowbridge, Wiltshire. During this period, Crabbe indulged his passionate interests in botany. He also wrote a great deal but destroyed most of this work in periodic outdoor "incremations" in which the entire family would assist. According to his son, this lost work included three novels and a complete *Essay on Botany*.

As a clergyman, Crabbe was notable for his vocal resistance to enthusiasts of all kinds and for his vigorous opposition to dissent. In the 1790s, his generally Whiggish views and his criticism of the origins of the war earned him the reputation among the locals at Parham as a Jacobin. His son denies the charge, explaining in his *Life* of Crabbe that his father was one of many who greeted the revolution with hope and condemned its subsequent developments. Crabbe's domestic life during these years was saddened by the death of five of seven children and the consequent nervous disorders of his wife. He also began, in 1790, to take opium under a doctor's care and began to experience strange dreams, the imagery of which would later find its way into some of his poems.

Crabbe had been working on the tales that make up *The Parish Register* since 1798, and this work, along with other poems, including *Sir Eustace Grey*, was ready for publication in 1806. Although important continuities exist between *The Village* and *The Parish Register* (especially in what might be called their anti-idealizing strain), these new poems also exhibit a new focus and voice for Crabbe. Most significant, these are individual narratives, whereas the earlier work had been generally more unified according to a didactic plan. The new poems also exhibit to a much greater degree that attention to minute—and frequently unlovely—detail that is both admired and reviled in criticism of Crabbe's later poetry. The volume was favorably received. Jeffrey approved, taking the opportunity to compare Crabbe's successful treatment

of characters from the middle and lower orders of society with Wordsworth's simplistic failures. This review in 1808 begins a long history in the commentary of what Arthur Pollard calls using Crabbe as a stick to beat Wordsworth. Many, including Scott, responded with joy that the writer of *The Village* had emerged from obscurity. Scott's long letter to Crabbe in response to *Poems* began a friendship that would eventually draw Crabbe to Scotland in 1822.

During the next 12 years, Crabbe's output was prolific; he produced three more volumes of tales in the manner of *The Parish Register*: *The Borough*, *Tales in Verse*, and *Tales of the Hall*. These volumes helped to fuel intense debate in the reviews concerning the nature of poetry. Criticized as graceless and unimaginative ("Pope in worsted stockings," in Horace Smith's famous formulation), a mere versifier whose matter-of-fact tales were better written in prose, Crabbe responded in his Preface to *Tales in Verse* by identifying two kinds of poetry. One is the imaginative, which gives to airy nothings a local habitation and a name (and which he took to be in the ascendent at that time). The second, exemplified by Chaucer, Dryden, and Pope, Crabbe associates, recalling the *ut pictura poesis* tradition, with the use of words to paint people, manners, and society as they really are. Byron's well-known praise of Crabbe, "Though nature's sternest painter, yet the best," acknowledges this painterly aspect of Crabbe's work. Crabbe claims that his critics may regard him as a mere versifier, rather than as a poet, only according to a narrow and historically indefensible definition of poetry. Admirers from Austen to Byron, from Edward Fitzgerald to Ezra Pound and Benjamin Britten (whose *Peter Grimes* is based on a tale in *The Borough*), have agreed with Crabbe's claims.

Beginning in 1817, Crabbe was popular with London literary society. His popularity was such that in 1819 Murray paid him £3,000 pounds for rights to *Tales of the Hall* and the earlier works, and brought out a seven-volume collective edition in 1820. A five-volume edition followed in 1823; the eight-volume *Poetical Works*, which included a *Life* by the poet's son, appeared in 1834. The *Life* portrays Crabbe as an engaging combination of pastoral firmness, intense intellectual activity, and considerable benevolence, qualities that appear in his best work in a rare mixture of satire and pathos. (*See also* Smith, James and Horace.)

Brennan O'Donnell

Works Consulted

Blunden, Edmund. Introduction. *The Life of George Crabbe*. By George Crabbe, Jr. London: Cresset, 1947.

Dalrymple-Champneys, Norma, and Arthur Pollard, eds. *George Crabbe: The Complete Poetical Works*. 3 vols. Oxford: Clarendon, 1988.

Edwards, Gavin. *George Crabbe's Poetry on Border Land*. Lewiston, NY: Mellen, 1990.

Pollard, Arthur, ed. *Crabbe: The Critical Heritage*. Boston: Routledge, 1972.

Sigworth, Oliver F. *Nature's Sternest Painter: Five Essays on the Poetry of Crabbe*. Tucson: U of Arizona P, 1965.

Criminality

Crime, particularly in London, ran rampant through England in the years before the passage of the Metropolitan Police Act in 1829, which created the force called "peelers" or "bobbies." Crime became more organized during the fifty years before passage of the Act.

Nightwatchmen, called Charleys because their position was instituted during the reign of Charles II, were incapable of maintaining peace on London streets. They carried only staves and lanterns during their nightly patrols. Private citizens and some institutions, such as banks, hired men first made available by Henry Fielding and his brother John at their headquarters on Bow Street. The Bow Street Runners, as they came to be known, were renowned for their spectacular exploits as "thief-takers".

The 18th century idea of dealing with crime was much like the Queen's in "Alice in Wonderland". By the late part of the century, more than 200 offenses were punished by hanging. These crimes could be as trivial as picking a pocket or setting fire to a pile of hay. Fury and fear turned the streets into a war zone. Few from the upper and middle classes went out, even in the middle of the day, without protection.

Fascination with the criminal element possessed the English, much to the horror of visitors from the Continent. A hanging at Tyburn, especially of a well-known criminal, was a festive event. Crowds lined the street to watch the condemned ride in his own coffin to his hanging. Women were not spared from the gallows, unless they were pregnant.

The number of robberies increased dramatically in the late 18th century, disproving the idea of hangings as a deterrent to crime. Rich and poor lived side-by-side in London, providing an opportunity for frustration to grow. In some neighborhoods, the main source of employment was crime.

The Gordon Riots of 1780, which were ostensibly sparked by anti-Catholicism but became an excuse for robbery and destruction, turned the streets of London into a battlefield, and this was not an isolated incident. During the 18th century, dozens of riots ripped through England's cities. The oppressive laws established to benefit the upper classes forced many in the lowest classes into crime to pay for food and shelter, while few in the lower classes had any experience or much use for politics, which was viewed as the realm of the privileged.

In the wake of the riots, several bills were introduced to create a single police force for London. In 1785, Sir Archibald MacDonald's bill was defeated by the city fathers of London who were more concerned about losing control than with the effects of rioting. Many people feared that the police would be spies for the government instead of trying to keep the peace.

As the 19th century dawned, the criminal underworld was well established with its own customs, hierarchy, and language. Contemporary estimates cite that over 100,000 residents of London were involved in criminal activity. This included the thieves, prostitutes, beggars, and a rough element among the gypsy population. With the arrival of the Regency and the hedonistic tendencies of the aristocracy, gambling, and frequenting the bawdy houses became sport. It was the middle classes during the flurry of reform in the 19th century that demanded a police force that would wrestle the city streets from the criminals.

Jo Ann Ferguson

In December 1811, at the same time Coleridge was lecturing on Shakespeare and the Regent assumed authority from his mad father, London was gripped in terror as a result of a series of murders whose horror was not exceeded until Jack the Ripper's Reign of Terror at the end of the century. In "On the Knocking at the Gate in *Macbeth*," De Quincey observed that "All other murders look pale by the deep crimson of [accused John Williams's actions]."

Seven people, including an infant, were viciously beaten to death in attacks at two households near Ratcliffe Highway, a dangerous neighborhood both sustained and ravaged by the trade surrounding the Thames waterfront and its sea-faring clientele. It is the haunt of Bill Sykes, Dickens's murderous outlaw in a novel set during the Romantic era. The Ratcliffe Highway crimes highlighted the ineptitude and inadequacy of London law enforcement at the time. Although only a few days elapsed before the arrest on circumstantial evidence of a nomadic sailor, John Williams, his subsequent suspicious suicide while incarcerated gave prosecutors a convenient and silent scapegoat who would never protest his innocence. The case was closed. Meanwhile, London newspapers experienced the thrills and sales of sensational journalism and the populace, the need for vastly improved police.

However, 20th-century investigators suggest that Williams was also a victim of the murderer, likely another sailor, home on furlough long enough to have exhausted his pay, who systematically killed two families and their servants for easy pocket money. But the identity of the culprit, like that of Jack the Ripper, remains uncertain.

LD

Works Consulted

Erickson, Carrolly. *Our Tempestuous Day*. New York: Morrow, 1986.

James, P.D., and T.A. Critchley. *The Maul and the Pear Tree: The Ratcliffe Highway Murders 1811*. New York: Mysterious, 1971.

Low, Donald A. *Thieves' Kitchen*. London: Deut, 1982.

Priestley, J.B. *The Prince of Pleasure and His Regency*. New York: Harper, 1969.

Thomson, David. *England in the Nineteenth Century*. London: Cape, 1950.

Waugh, Mary. *Smuggling in Kent and Sussex 1700–1840*. Newbury: Countryside, 1985.

White, R.J. *Life in Regency England*. New York: Putnam, 1970.

Williams, E. Neville. *Life in Georgian England*. New York: Putnam, 1970.

Croker, John Wilson
(1780–1857)

Born in Galway, Ireland, and educated at Dublin's Trinity College and London's Lincoln Inn, John Wilson Croker was a prominent Tory member of Parliament, first Secretary of the Admiralty (from 1810), and co-founder and regular contributor to the *Quarterly Review* (beginning in 1811). He is remembered for his notorious criticism of Keats's *Endymion* (1818) and Tennyson's *Poems* (1832). Both Shelley (see Preface to *Adonais*) and Byron ("Who killed John Keats?") contributed to the opinion that Croker's review hastened the death of Keats. Yet Croker's comments on *Endymion* were more moderate than Lockhart's harsh treatment in *Blackwood's Magazine*.

Croker was nonetheless opposed to most of the younger writers of his time. His critical position was the result of his regard for classicism and his Toryism. He greatly admired the classical decorum and polished satire of Pope (as a boy Croker memorized Pope's translation of Homer). Later he prepared material for an edition of Pope, which he never completed, although the material was subsequently used by Elwin. As might be expected, he was opposed to any innovation in versification or poetic diction. Croker, with many of his contemporaries, stressed the importance of feeling tempered by religion and morality; he also valued the didactic and realistic in the novel, realism, that is, tempered by moral considerations. His reviews are characterized by a liberal use of extracts, hearkening to the style of review begun in the late 18th century. Periodically, Croker's search for errors in the work under review led to such a deluge of detail that the sense of his argument was lost.

Croker's contacts and understanding of the political world made him invaluable to the *Quarterly*. From 1807 until 1830, he held a seat in Parliament for a number of constituencies. His maiden speech and subsequent pamphlet on the state of Ireland, *A sketch of Ireland past and present*, led to close relationships with Canning, Percival, and Wellesley. He later became a confidant of Peel, though Croker's objection to the repeal of the Corn Laws ended their relationship. For 22 years he served as secretary of the Admiralty and earned a reputation for honesty and efficiency. He also established himself as a first-rank debater; an exchange in Commons in which Croker got the better of Thomas Macaulay led to enmity and to Macaulay's attack on Croker's edition of Boswell's *Life of Johnson*.

Croker was an expert on 18th-century Britain as well as contemporary France; his interest in France led to his assembling an extensive collection of contemporary French pamphlets, now in the British Museum. He is also credited with first employing the appellation "Conservative" in the January 1830 *Quarterly*.

Croker's most important writings appear in the *Quarterly*, to which he contributed approximately 270 articles. His other works include *An Intercepted Letter from Canton* (1804), an edition of Boswell's *Life of Johnson* (1831), *Military Events of the French Revolution of 1830*, and *Essays on the Early Period of the French Revolution* (1857). (*See also* Journalism, Publishing, Satire.)

Martin P. McNamee

Works Consulted

Brightfield, Myron F. *John Wilson Croker*. Berkeley: U of California P, 1940.

Morgan, Peter F. *Literary Critics and Reviewers in Early 19th-Century Britain*. London: Croom-Helm, 1983.

Reiman, Donald. Introduction. *Familiar Epistles to Frederick Jones, Esq., The Amazoniad, Histrionic Epistles, The Battles of Talavera.* By John Wilson Croker. New York: Garland, 1979.

Shattock, Joanne. *Politics and Reviewers: The* Edinburgh *and The* Quarterly *in the Early Victorian Age.* New York: Leicester UP, 1989.

Crome, John

(1768–1821)

Born in Norwich in 1768, John Crome exhibited some 307 paintings, etched 33 designs on copperplate which were never published, and founded Britain's first provincial art society (The Norwich Society) in 1803. Today, Crome is considered one of the foremost representative painters of the Norwich School of painting, which includes Cotman, James Stark, George Vincent, Robert Ladbrooke, John Thirtle, and other painters living in and around Norwich.

Crome was apprenticed at age 15 to Francis Whistler, a coach and sign painter, from whom he learned the basics of perspective, developed a skill at detail work, and learned the process of grinding and mixing paints. From 1796 to 1798, Crome was an art student of the amateur painter Thomas Harvey, of Catton. It was from Catton that Crome inherited an admiration for the works of Gainsborough and Richard Wilson by studying and copying prints in Catton's collection. Although Crome executed his first sketch in oils perhaps as early as 1790 when he was age 22, he spent the vast majority of his 53 years as a drawing master and picture restorer. Overall, Crome's paintings are drawn from topographical views of Wales, scenes from the Lake District, and various landscapes in and around Norwich. His few watercolors bear little if any relationship to his paintings, and, since they were executed for the instruction of his pupils, they provide few indicators of Crome's development as an artist.

In his paintings between 1805 and 1813, his work manifests certain qualities of Gainsborough, particularly in the rather sparse use of heavy brush work and the technique of thinly applying paint, which enables Crome to achieve clarity of distance and a sense of spatial recession. *Moonrise on the Yare* and *View on the Yare* reveal the influence of Gainsborough and Richard Wilson along with a slight degree of independent experimentation. Although the influence of Gainsborough is important, Crome soon became interested in the realism of such Dutch landscape painters as Meindert Hobbema and Jacob van Ruisdael, and from their example he began more serious experimentation with the tonal complexities of natural light and shade. From the fusing of his own personal emotions and perception with the example of the Dutch landscape painters, Crome transforms the earlier Hobbema/Ruisdael tradition into a new expressiveness, which is found in his *Mousehold Heath Norwich*, (1818-20) and *Porlingland Oak* (1818).

Crome received little financial success as an artist, and, as late as 1816, he continued to paint, retouch, and gild signs. Although his development as an artist was rather sporadic and his innovations are generally of a technical nature, his painting *Slate Quarries* (1805) demonstrates a high degree of innovation; here Crome is able to create a wider field of vision by using successive diagonal planes of composition, which suggest that space and atmosphere are part of the pictorial reality.

Jeffrey D. Parker

Works Consulted
Baker, C.H. Collins. *British Painters.* London: Medici Society, 1933.

Clifford, Derek, and Timothy Clifford. *John Crome.* Greenwich, CT: New York Graphic Society, 1968.

Holme, Geoffrey, ed. *The Norwich School.* London: The Studio, 1920.

Cruikshank, George

(1792–1878)

Perhaps the most colorful and important English caricaturist and book illustrator of the early 19th century, George Cruikshank was the son the artist Isaac Cruikshank, also a well-known etcher and wood engraver.

The younger Cruikshank was famous for his political, social, and theatrical caricatures, producing over 5,000 etchings, lithographs, and wood engravings. In fact, before age 18, he was a full-time caricaturist working in several London print shops and notably capturing the misfortunes of Napoleon and the immoral conduct of the Prince Regent (George IV). Other favorite subject matter included The Prince Regent's friends and relatives, especially his brother the Duke of York. Some of the more outstanding satirical works of Cruikshank's early period, the teens of the 19th century, include *Interior View of the House of God* (a satire on the pulpit and dissenting ministers), *The Examination of a Young Surgeon* (a spoof of the medical profession), *Little Boney Gone to Pot* (an 1814 piece ridiculing Napoleon), and *The Blessings of Peace, or the Curse of the Corn Bill* (an 1815 work mocking the passage of the unpopular Corn Laws). Also, in 1826, appeared a series of well-known illustrations to *Grimm's Fairy-Tales,* published as *German Popular Stories.* Here, humor is mixed with a love of fairy lore, fantastical grotesques and fiends, and devils.

Cruikshank's artistic middle period was one in which his true sense of humor and genial public spirit appeared. Between 1833 and 1836, he published *My Sketch Book* in nine parts. A famous comical chapter, for instance, is "A Chapter on Noses," in which he vehemently satirizes his publisher William Kidd and all the other printsellers, publishers at whose mercy he had been for almost 30 years. As a genuine caricaturist, he sets up a "shared joke" or *double entendre,* by means of a grotesque figure, whose tap on the nose and leery wink suggest that "nose" may be read as "penis." Furthermore, the array of 33 noses in the cartoon demonstrates not only versatility and imagination (the artist Cruikshank's nose became a standard of judgment for other noses) but "game-plays" on *the correct* taste established by previous drawing masters. Also, Cruikshank comically suggests a liaison between types of noses and personalities.

Also appearing during this middle period was Cruikshank's *Comic Almanack* (1835–52), a yearly publication consisting of an etched plate for each month of the year and smaller decorations and woodcuts. Notable, too, are the illustrations that Cruikshank drew for approximately 863 books, among them Dickens's *Sketches by Boz* (1836–37) and *Oliver Twist* (1838). A feud developed, unfortunately, between these two independent artistic types and freethinkers in the late 1830s, ending an earlier strong Dickens-Cruikshank relationship. Cruikshank also illustrated *Don Quixote* and *Robinson Crusoe.* It was not until the 19th century that artists began to sign their children's illustrations — Cruikshank being among the first to do so with his first edition of *Grimm's Fairy-Tales* and *Rumplestiltskin.*

In Cruikshank's later life he became involved with the temperance issue, creating such memorable works as the woodcuts *The Bottle* (1847) and *The Drunkard's*

Children (1848). However, his monumental work entitled *Worship of Bacchus* (13'4" by 7'8")—although a masterpiece of social consciousness—was not considered a successful oil painting (1862).

Cruikshank has been remembered for this historical accuracy in depicting the details of his subjects: for his illustrations' faithfulness in referring to the language (more than to the direct scenes or objects that the language imitates), and for the profound sense of humor that penetrates his etchings and book illustrations. (*See also* Satire.)

Constance Pedoto

Works Consulted

Chesson, W.H. *George Cruikshank*. New York: Dutton, 1908.

Everitt, Graham. *English Caricaturists and Graphic Humourists of the Nineteenth Century*. Freeport, NY: Books for Libraries, 1972.

Feaver, William. *Masters of Caricature (from Hogarth and Gillray to Scarfe and Levine)*. New York: Knopf, 1981.

Mullins, Edwin, ed. *The Arts of Britain*. Oxford: Phaidon, 1983.

Osborne, Harold, ed. *The Oxford Companion to Art*. Oxford: Clarendon, 1970.

Cunningham, Allan

(1784–1842)

Allan Cunningham was born in the parish of Keir, Dumfriesshire, in 1784. The fourth son of a family of nine children, Cunningham was apprenticed as a stonemason before discovering his literary talents.

An avid reader as a youth, Cunningham began writing poetry in his teens. In 1809, he met the London publisher R.H. Cromek, to whom he showed some of his poems. Cromek was unimpressed, but when Cunningham resubmitted them disguised as old songs, Cromek, although probably aware of the ruse, accepted them and encouraged Cunningham to come to London to pursue literature as his trade. Cunningham went to London in 1810 and wrote more poetry as well as essays for *Blackwood's* and, later, *The London Magazine*.

Cromek introduced Cunningham to the sculptor Sir Francis Chantrey, a prominent member of the Royal Academy. In 1814, he was engaged by Chantrey as secretary and superintendent of the works, a position he held until Chantrey's death in 1841. He also continued writing for magazines and, in 1820, submitted a drama entitled *Sir Marmaduke Maxwell* to Scott. Scott praised the poetry but felt the drama unsuited for production. In 1822, two volumes of *Traditional Tales of the English and Scottish Peasantry* and, in 1825, four volumes of *The Songs of Scotland, Ancient and Modern*, with a lengthy introduction including history and critical commentary, were published. In both 1829 and 1830, he brought out an "anniversary," the fashion of the day, with contributions from Southey, Lockhart, Hogg, Procter, and others. The texts included engravings by Turner, Gainsborough, and Lawrence and were dedicated to the Royal Academy. These anniversaries contained more Cunningham's verse than that of any other author.

Cunningham's most famous work, *Lives of the Most Eminent British Painters, Sculptors, and Architects*, was published in 1836. The selections range from the Tudors to the 19th century, excluding living artists. Fashioned after Johnson's *Lives of the Poets*, Cunningham's *Lives* focuses more on biographical elements than on critical approaches, although Cunningham does make some comments that show his familiarity with the critical theories of his age. The *Lives* was well received and sold well. An eight-volume edition of Burns was Cunningham's last important work.

Cunningham had an enduring and happy marriage with Jean Walker, with whom he had five sons and a daughter. He was an honest and kind man who was respected by this contemporaries and befriended by them. Carlyle gave a testimonial speech on Cunningham's behalf at a dinner in 1831. Chantrey left Cunningham an annuity upon his death, with a reversion to Mrs. Cunningham.

Cunningham died in 1842.

Len McCall

Works Consulted

Dictionary of National Biography, s.v. "Cunningham, Allan."

Currency Question

Throughout the 1700s, everyday monetary transactions were increasingly carried out using paper money, or notes, issued by banks. These were exchangeable on demand of the bearer for legal tender: government-issued gold or silver coin. Though this practice had been previously considered a safe, even beneficial, economic development, it grew during the Romantic age into a controversy called the "currency question." When what was to have been a brief, emergency wartime suspension of "cash payments" (i.e., the exchangeability of notes for gold or silver coin) dragged on for more than 20 years, the nation was forced to reconsider the potential benefits and drawbacks of a fiduciary currency and to what extent government should control the economy.

The outbreak of war with France in 1792 precipitated an economic crisis in England. Since international trade was conducted exclusively in unminted gold, or "bullion," expenditures for the Continental army, subsidies to the allies, and a series of poor harvests—which necessitated large-scale grain importation—combined to drain the Bank of England's bullion reserves. Bankruptcies of several Scottish banks and important London lending institutions in 1796 undermined confidence in paper money, prompting widespread redemption of notes for "safer" gold coin. The landing of 1,200 French soldiers in Wales in February 1797, began a run on banks, so depleting bullion reserves that on May 3, Parliament passed the Bank Restriction Act, which suspended cash payments until June 24.

The next 20 years saw continual extension of the Act, as well as months of parliamentary debate and scores of pamphlets on the currency question. Bullionists, so named for their opposition to the Act, accused banks of issuing notes in amounts exceeding their gold reserves, artificially augmenting and therefore depreciating the nation's money supply. This "imaginary wealth" had, they argued, produced the era's steady rise in the prices of consumer goods. Antibullionists, usually aligned with banking interests, denied that note issues exceeded reserves, and held that paper money, by replacing an expensive instrument of exchange with a cheap one, freed up more gold bullion for investment and international trade. In 1810, after extensive hearings, Parliament's "Bullion Committee" found that banks had overissued notes and recommended an immediate return to cash payments. But antibullionists persuaded the government that taking this step during wartime would result in economic recession. When prices continued to rise after Waterloo, however, the bullionist position seemed substantiated, and cash payments were resumed on July 2, 1819.

Though the monetary system before and after the suspension looked essentially similar (i.e., a mix of paper and precious metal coins), the currency question inaugurated significant governmental controls of what previously had been a largely unregulated economy. To a small extent, the suspension was an expression of the particularly Romantic faith in the power of representation, translated from aesthetic to economic terms: "imaginary" was just as good as "real" money, so long as people believed in it. The subsequent rejection of a fiduciary currency at the close of the era thus mirrors the general turn from Romantic idealism to Victorian realism. (*See also* Napoleonic Wars, Parliament.)

Matthew T. Schneider

Works Consulted

Cannan, Edwin, ed. *The Paper Pound of 1797–1821*. London: King, 1919.

Fetter, Frank Whitson. *The Development of British Monetary Orthodoxy 1797–1875*. Fairfield: Kelley, 1978.

Maclaren, James. *A Sketch of the History of the Currency*. London: Groombridge, 1858.

Peacock, Thomas Love. "Paper Money Lyrics." *Poems and Plays. Works*. v. 7. London: Constable, 1931.

Dallas, Robert Charles
(1754–1824)

A prolific writer during the first two decades of the 19th century, Robert Charles Dallas is now remembered primarily because of his associations with Byron. Dallas's sister married George Anson Byron, Byron's uncle, and through this indirect connection Dallas became acquainted with the poet.

Dallas's father was a physician who emigrated from Scotland to Kingston, Jamaica. Dallas was born there in 1754 but was educated primarily in Kensington at the school of James Elphinston, a friend of Johnson's who is mentioned prominently in Boswell's *Life*. For a short time, Dallas studied law at the Inner Temple but soon returned to Jamaica to claim the family estates he had inherited. After his marriage to Sarah Harding of Nelmes, Essex, Dallas discovered that the Jamaican climate was harmful to his wife's health. The couple then moved to Europe where they remained until the outbreak of the French Revolution forced them to emigrate to the United States. Dallas's brother, Alexander James, also emigrated and eventually became a prominent lawyer in Pennsylvania and Secretary of the Treasury of the United States. (Alexander's son, George Mifflin Dallas, served as vice president of the United States from 1845 till 1849, and Dallas, Texas, is named for him.) Robert, however, was not happy in the United States and soon returned to England.

In January 1808, Dallas introduced himself to Byron in a fawning letter of praise for the recently published *Hours of Idleness*. In the following year, after reading the manuscript of *English Bards and Scotch Reviewers*, Dallas suggested omissions and offered two dozen of his own lines for inclusion (an offer Byron promptly declined). Dallas arranged for the publication of Byron's satire and was with Byron frequently until the poet left England on 2 July 1809.

Upon Byron's return in 1811, Dallas read manuscripts of *Hints from Horace* (which did not please him) and the first two cantos of *Childe Harold's Pilgrimage*. Dallas praised *Childe Harold* but encouraged Byron to delete several stanzas, expressing religious and political skepticism. Ultimately, Byron agreed to certain omissions, assigned the copyright to Dallas, and allowed him to arrange for publication by Murray.

By 1813, Dallas's relations with Byron had begun to cool, but he also received the copyright for *The Corsair*. In the meantime, Dallas prepared an unauthorized account of Byron's life between 1808 and 1814 based on letters Byron sent to his mother during his travels in the East. After Byron's death in 1824, Dallas attempted to publish this account, but he was prohibited from doing so by an injunction obtained by Hobhouse and Hanson, the poet's executors. (The book was eventually edited and published by Dallas's son and contains an account of this legal dispute.)

Dallas's own literary efforts were quite varied. He published history, moral essays, poetry, several novels, and at least three plays. In addition, he translated several works from French. Standard reference books cite *Ode to the Duke of Wellington* as one of Dallas's works, but recent scholarship suggests that this poem was written by a younger poet with the same name. Dallas died in 1824 in Ste.-Adresse, Normandy, and was buried at Havre.

Albert E. Wilhelm

Works Consulted

Allibone, S. Austin. *Critical Dictionary of English Literature*. Philadelphia: Lippincott, 1870.

Dallas, Robert Charles. *Recollections of the Life of Lord Byron*. London: C. Knight, 1824.

Marchand, Leslie A. *Byron: A Biography*. 3 vols. New York: Knopf, 1957.

Reiman, Donald H. Introduction. *Adrastus*. By Robert Charles Dallas. Garland Romantic Context Reprint Ser. 44. New York: Garland, 1977.

Dalton, John

(1766–1844)

John Dalton, chemist and natural philosopher, was born in 1766, at Eaglesfield in Cumbria to Quaker parents. His father, a weaver and the owner of small farm property, had married Mary Greenup, a determined woman from a family with growing social connections.

Dalton displayed an enthusiasm for learning early in his life and is said to have copied scientific entries from the *Ladies Diary*. He attended a Quaker school until, when he was age 12, the schoolmaster left; Dalton then took over as teacher, though with limited success. After a brief stint as a field worker, Dalton joined his brother Jonathan, who was an assistant in a Quaker boarding school at Kendal, which was run by a distant cousin. The brothers, who took over in 1785, were strict schoolmasters, a practice that may have lost them some patronage. Nevertheless, because the school was well-equipped and Kendal was a frequent stopping point for itinerant natural philosophers, this period was important in Dalton's life. He read assiduously during the 12 years he spent at Kendal and became good friends with John Gough (1757–1825), the blind scientist and mathematician. Gough, the model for Wordsworth's scientist in *The Excursion* and a tutor to William Whewell, instructed Dalton in languages and mathematics. Dalton was developing a modest reputation from his public lectures and from his successful responses to prize problems in the *Gentlemen's* and *Ladies Diaries*. His work became more focused as, under Gough's tutelage, he began to apply himself to a systematic study of meteorology and to the study of local trees and plants.

In 1793, Dalton moved to Manchester, where he was made a professor of mathematics and natural philosophy at New College, which was recently established by local Dissenters. In the same year, he published his *Meteorological Observations and Essays*, which evinced an early interest in the mixture of gases and fluids; the book was also significant in establishing meteorology as an independent discipline. In 1794, Dalton was elected a member of the Manchester Literary and Philosophical Society (which was established in 1781); not only did Dalton become a central figure in the society, as lecturer, secretary, vice president (1807–17), and president (1817–44), but the society also housed his laboratory. Shortly after his election to the society, Dalton lectured on color vision. Dalton, who was colorblind, was the first to describe that condition (frequently referred to as "Daltonism"). Perhaps unhappy with his salary or his colleagues, Dalton left New College in 1800 to open his own academy of mathematics and natural philosophy.

Dalton gave a series of lectures in 1801 dealing with the effects of pressure and temperature on fluids and gases. Although ostensibly lectures in meteorology, they dealt with the chemical and physical concepts implicated in the proportions of gases in the atmosphere. It was clear to Dalton that air, which was widely believed to be a kind of chemical solvent, is a mixture of independent gases that exert their own pressures. Developing the law of partial pressures, of Dalton's law, Dalton felt confident enough in his findings to send them to Nicholson's *Journal of Natural Philosophy, Chemistry and the Arts*. Dalton was particularly interested in the absorption of gases in both air and water and assumed that the solubility of materials was the result of differing atomic weights. He believed that all elements are composed of fundamental units, or "atoms," that are specific to that element. When his friend, William Henry, determined that water will always take up the same volume of a gas in a given temperature (Henry's law), Dalton applied the findings to his own work. "Why," he wondered, "does water not admit its bulk of every kind of gas alike?" By observing the proportion of combination with a specific quantity of water, he realized that he could determine not only their combining proportions, but their weight. He developed a list of 21 atomic weights with hydrogen, still the lightest element, as the base.

Dalton's work came to the attention of important scientists, including Thomas Thomson and William Hyde Wollaston. Dalton's *A New System of Chemical Philosophy*, which was published in two parts (1808; 1810), explained his theories and presented a method of notation that he called "ideographs." The *System* advanced the term "atom" to describe the units or "particles" so basic that they cannot be divided. Dalton's atoms, though able to form compounds with other atoms, cannot themselves be changed or, following Lavoisier's law of conservation of matter, destroyed. Nevertheless, Dalton's view did not distinguish between molecules and atoms of elements. The initial critics of his work included Davy, who gradually shifted from the belief that the fundamental units of all elements are actually identical and simply arranged differently. He later came to accept Dalton's system of individually different atoms with fixed weights.

Although elected to the Royal Society in 1822, Dalton did not appear there until 1834. This was perhaps one of the few societies in which he was not actively engaged. In addition to his connection at Manchester's Literary and Philosophical Society, Dalton lectured frequently at the Royal Institution and was a founding member of the British Association for the Advancement of Science (which was established in 1831). Dalton, for many scientists, was emblematic of a new kind of scientist; not only was he, as a Dissenter, outside of the Anglican tradition, but he was also from humble social origins. Though very much of an autodidact, the extent of his self-education and simplicity has often been exaggerated; he was a quiet and practical man who had achieved fame on the basis of scientific merit and persistence.

Awarded a government pension in 1833, Dalton's last years were comfortable. Both Oxford and Edinburgh awarded him honorary degrees, and the city of Manchester commissioned a sculpture of him. Dalton suffered a series of strokes in 1837, which restricted his very active schedule and disabled him until his death. Dalton had become one of Manchester's most famous residents, and his funeral was a significant event for the city. Tens of thousands viewed the casket, and the funeral procession is said to have been close to a mile long. (*See also* Elective Affinity.)

Alan Rauch

Works Consulted

Hartley, Harold. *Studies in the History of Chemistry*. Oxford: Oxford UP, 1971.

Holton, Gerald, and Stephen G. Brush. *Introduction to Concepts and Theories in Physical Science*. 2nd ed. Princeton: Princeton UP, 1985.

Knight, David M. *The Age of Science: The Scientific World-view in the Nineteenth Century*. Oxford: Blackwell, 1986.

———. *Atoms and Elements: A Study of Theories of Matter in the Nineteenth Century*. London: Hutchinson, 1967.

Patterson, Elizabeth. *John Dalton and the Atomic Theory*. Garden City, NY: Doubleday, 1970.

Rocke, Alan J. *Chemical Atomism in the Nineteenth Century: From Dalton to Cannizzaro*. Columbus: Ohio State UP, 1984.

Thackray, Arnold. *Atoms and Powers*. Cambridge, Harvard UP, 1970.

———. *John Dalton: Critical Assessments of His Life and Science*. Cambridge: Harvard UP, 1972.

Darley, George
(1795–1846)

George Darley, born in London in 1795, was the youngest of Arthur and Mary Darley's seven children. Darley was a lonely child who was left in the care of his grandfather for several years while his parents went to America.

Darley went to Trinity College, earning a degree in mathematics and classics in 1820. After graduating, he moved to London, hoping to earn a living as a writer. Although *The Errors of Ecstasie: A Dramatic Poem with Other Pieces* (1822) received little popular notice, Darley met such literary figures as Lamb, Carlyle, Beddoes, and Clare. However, Darley avoided company, possibly because of his shame about the severe stammer he had had since childhood, which Beddoes described in 1824 as a "stammering to a most provoking degree, so much so as to be almost inconversible." Darley himself thought it "a hideous mask upon my mind which not only disfigures, but nearly suffocates it."

Darley worked as a drama critic for *London Magazine* from 1822 to 1825. Under the name "John Lacy," he wrote six letters to the dramatists of his period, chastising them for confusing poetry with drama. This criticism is ironic, since in the best parts of his own plays lyrics are interspersed throughout.

The mid-1820s were Darley's most active as a writer. He wrote a series of stories, *The Labours of Idleness*, in 1826 under the name "Guy Penseval." The best of these is *Lilian of the Vale*, which contains the once popular song, *I've been Roaming*. He also wrote several mathematics textbooks, including *A System of Popular Geometry* (1826) and *The Geometrical Companion* (1828), which went into several editions, unlike any of his literary efforts. Darley published *Sylvia, or the May Queen*, a comedy, in 1827, and although the work had such distinguished admirers as Coleridge and Elizabeth Barrett Browning, it was not a popular success.

Disappointed over the poor reception of *Sylvia*, Darley confined himself for the next 10 years to writing textbooks and contributing to periodicals. Many of his poems, including his six *Syren Songs*, were published in magazines. His most famous lyric, *It is Not Beauty I Demand*, first appeared anonymously in the *Literary Gazette* in 1828. This poem was attributed to a 17th-century poet in Palgrave's *Golden Treasury* in 1861.

Darley was bitter about his lack of popularity as a poet, feeling that he would rather be a "piping bullfinch." He seemed, however, to will such a condition upon himself, publishing much of his work under pseudonyms or privately, seen only by a few friends.

Nepenthe, usually considered his best work, was privately, but carelessly and poorly published. Darley endeavored in its first canto to counter discontentedness, while in its second to depict complacency. Canto III, supposed to reconcile the opposing forces demonstrated in the first two cantos, was never completed. Possibly Darley never intended to finish it.

As in his other work, Darley's choice of diction in *Nepenthe* is often obscure, yet it has flashes of genius. But Darley never again achieved the level of *Nepenthe*. He edited the works of Beaumont and Fletcher in 1840 and wrote two closet dramas, *Thomas a Becket* (1840) and *Ethelstan* (1841), which were not well received by critics. He wrote literary and art reviews for the *Aethenium* (1834–46) in which he criticized all the major writers of his day despite the influence of Keats and Shelley in his own work. However, his usual independent

spirit is evident in a review praising early Italian painters long before the Pre-Raphaelites embraced them.

Darley led a solitary life. He never married, but his letters speak of unrequited love and the absence of family life. He died in 1846, probably from consumption, and was buried in a grave whose eventual overgrowth a poem of his had once predicted.

Louis J. Parascandola

Works Consulted

Abbott, Claude Colleer. *The Life and Letters of George Darley: Poet and Critic*. 1928. Oxford: Clarendon, 1967.

Brisman, Leslie. "George Darley: Buoyant as Young Time." *Romantic Origins*. Ithaca: Cornell UP, 1978: 183–223.

Heath-Stubbs, John. "The Defeat of Romanticism." *The Darkling Plain: A Study of the Later Fortunes of Romanticism in English Poetry from George Darley to W.B. Yeats*. London: Eyre, 1950: 21–61.

Darwin, Erasmus
(1731–1802)

Erasmus Darwin, the grandfather of Charles Darwin and one of the leading intellectuals of his day, exerted a powerful influence on the Romantic poets even though his poetic techniques more closely resemble those of the earlier Neoclassicists and were ridiculed by poets and critics like Coleridge and Byron.

Born near Nottingham in 1731, Darwin was educated at Cambridge and Edinburgh and began practicing medicine in 1756. He possessed expertise in aesthetics, botany, chemistry, geology, philosophy, physics, and zoology.

In 1751, he began writing occasional verse—much of it witty and humorous—in a variety of poetic forms. Nothing in this clever but minor work predicted the success of his first two long poems, *The Loves of the Plants* (1789) and *The Economy of*

Vegetation (1791), which together form *The Botanic Garden* (1791). *The Loves of the Plants*, although published first, is the second part of the completed *Botanic Garden* and explains Linnaeus's sexual classification of plants in graceful and fluid heroic couplets. The combination of skillful versification, wit, and originality made the poem a popular success and temporarily established Darwin as a major poet. The heroic couplets of *The Economy of Vegetation* are more labored than those of *The Loves*; *The Economy* is ponderous, eclectic, and somewhat reminiscent of Thomson's hodgepodge *The Seasons*. Like Thomson's work, the poem's organization is associative rather than syllogistic, subverting any possible overall design.

After the 1798 publication of the *Lyrical Ballads* gave poetry a new direction, Darwin's poetic stock rapidly fell. Whereas he had been extravagantly praised by such literary figures as Walpole, he became an object of derision to new wave figures like Coleridge and Byron. When *The Temple of Nature* was published posthumously in 1803, it met with critical disdain, although today some find it the best of Darwin's three major poems. This poem, also written in heroic couplets, is an eclectic compendium of Darwin's scientific knowledge and theory, expressing his views of the problem of good and evil, psychology, reproductive systems, and the origins of life. He contributed to the scientific understanding of evolution, photosynthesis, and fossils.

Today, Darwin's verse is of interest only to specialists, most of whom read him to determine his influence on the Romantic poets. Certainly his interest in nature would have been influential, and specific verbal echoes are discernible even in poets who most disliked Darwin's work. The organicism of the Romantics seems based,

in part, on Darwin's views of nature, and Coleridge's "willing suspension of disbelief" has affinities with his work as well. Shelley's ideas on necessity and his Neoplatonism owe much to Darwin. Some of Keats's image patterns seem to be derived from Darwin's medical, animal, and plant imagery.

In 1801, one of Darwin's patients gave him a cold, which escalated into a serious illness and lingered for a year. He never recovered and died peacefully in 1802.

John A. Stoler

Works Consulted

Hassler, Donald M. *The Comedian as the Letter D: Erasmus Darwin's Comic Materialism*. The Hague: Nijhoff, 1973.

———. *Erasmus Darwin*. New York: Twayne, 1973.

King-Hele, Desmond. *Erasmus Darwin*. New York: St. Martin's, 1963.

Logan, James V. *The Poetry and Aesthetics of Erasmus Darwin*. Princeton: Princeton UP, 1936.

Schofield, Robert E. *The Lunar Society of Birmingham*. Oxford: Clarendon, 1963.

Sewell, Elizabeth. *The Orphic Voice: Poetry and Natural History*. New Haven: Yale UP, 1960.

Davies, Scrope Berdmore
(1782–1852)

Scrope Berdmore Davies was, in his time, known as a wit, gambler, dandy, and Fellow of King's College, Cambridge. He is best remembered as one of Byron's closest and most trusted friends.

Byron and Davies became friends at Cambridge in 1807. From that time on, Davies's intelligence, urbanity, and charm made him one of Byron's favorite companions. During the many years of their friendship, Davies served Byron as an advisor in literary matters, guarantor of loans during Byron's financial difficulties, supporter following the poet's separation from Lady

Byron, and literary courier to the publisher Murray during Byron's exile from England. Byron dedicated *Parisina* to Davies and spoke of him fondly before his death at Missolonghi.

Apart from his relationship with Byron, Davies's career as a Regency dandy and London man-about-town was colorful and varied. He knew Beau Brummell well and was a central figure in the Regency sporting scene and, somewhat incongruously, an effective and active figure in Reform politics. His knowledge of the Regency boxing world was such that he could advise Moore on the slang of "the fancy" for *Tom Crib's Memorial to Congress* (1819).

In 1820, Davies's career as a London gambler came to an end when he fled to the Continent to escape his creditors. The rest of his life was spent in obscure and wandering exile. In 1976, a trunk he had left at a London bank in the hurry of his 1820 departure from England was discovered and opened. It contained letters from Byron and important manuscripts of poems by Byron and Shelley.

Phillip B. Anderson

Works Consulted

Burnett, T.A.J. *The Rise and Fall of a Regency Dandy: The Life and Times of Scrope Berdmore Davies.* Boston: Little, 1981.

Marchand, Leslie. *Byron: A Biography.* 3 vols. New York: Knopf, 1957.

Moore, Doris Langley. *The Late Lord Byron.* London: Murray, 1961.

Davy, Humphry

(1778–1829)

A chemist, self-taught from Lavoisier's *Traité élémentaire de chimie* — which he would spend much of his career refuting — Humphry Davy became an inspiration to modern chemistry through his insistence on proportioned chemical reactions among discrete, detectable elements. Davy was not a theorist; he repeatedly denounced theoretical systems as speculation and in his final work extolled the earliest youth of science at its ideal moment before the advent of theory. Also, while he remains noted as an inventive experimentalist, he did not rigorously pursue experimental precision, leaving both experimental and theoretical perfectionism to other contemporaries, like Count Rumford, William Wollaston, Jöns Berzelius, and Dalton. His one intentionally scholarly work on chemical theory, *Elements of Chemical Philosophy* (1812), was projected for two volumes but reached only one and never went into a second edition. Davy's vogue among the audiences of the popular Bakerian Lectures (1806–26) came from his not fully systematized intuitions about unusual or controversial experimental events, an intuitional approach fully in keeping with his code of appropriate science.

Davy's first experimental project and publication, *An Essay on Heat, Light, and the Combinations of Light* (1799), was an important step in the centuries-long debate over combustion. Earlier phlogistonist chemists had thought burning resulted from the decomposition of an elemental phlogiston, detectable only through the weight loss of most objects burned. This misbelief came from inattention to the chemistry of gases, or "pneumatic chemistry" as the Romantics called it. Davy's chemical work began as scientists were starting to see burning as a chemical process in which the gases produced equaled the net loss of weight in a burned solid. Davy's interpretation of this reaction was that oxygen combines with light, which Davy considered a barely ponderable element of its own. Davy retained this belief in light as an element throughout his life, and he maintained an almost Plotinian conviction in light as a psychological and metaphysical, as well as physical, force.

Of particular interest to the history of science is Davy's emphasis on the attractive and repulsive forces in different states of matter, with solids representing maximum attractive and light representing maximum repulsive motion. This vision of dynamism among elements of conserved mass prefigures Davy's most significant work, with voltaic cells. After long wrestling within the debate between those who saw battery current as a product of contact between metals and those who saw it as a chemical reaction, Davy decided for chemical reaction. By extrapolation, electricity could be seen as a force in binding and repelling elementary particles. Such an emphasis on elements variously bound produced later papers. In one, *Some Experiments on the Combustion of the Diamond and Other Carbonaceous Substances* (1814), Davy demonstrated the kinship of diamonds and coal, understanding that the crude, or crystalline, outer properties of bodies do not reveal their inner electrical and elemental composition.

Davy's work in various sciences and technologies was wide ranging. His *Elements of Agricultural Chemistry* (1813) was the first treatise in its field. He also delivered what he proclaimed to be the first popular lectures in geology (1805). In the debate between Vulcanists and Neptunists, he tried always to chart a middle course, finding the Vulcanists scientifically preferable but disliking their uniformitarian emphasis on a steady state without progress. Technologically, he invented the "Davy lamp" (1815) to help avoid methane explosions in coal mines. He is perhaps best known for his experiments with nitrous oxide, which he undertook in the Pneumatic Institute from 1799 to 1800. His experiments with breathing gases as a

source of disease control led to the 1800 publication of *Researches Chemical and Philosophical Chiefly Concerning Nitrous Oxide*. Its rapturous descriptions produced a national vogue for sniffing the new "laughing gas."

Davy's main influence on his literary contemporaries came through his friendship with Coleridge, who, with Southey, participated in the Pneumatic Institute gas-sniffing experiments. Coleridge was attracted to Davy's thoughts about light in relation to matter and consciousness and saw in the doctrine one of a world spirit, which appears in Davy's work from 1799 to the posthumously published *Consolations in Travel* (1830). Coleridge registered shock that Davy might have accepted Dalton's material atomism, of which Davy was actually suspicious, but evidently Coleridge was mistaken. Davy repeatedly discovered new elements and, like Dalton, insisted on elemental discreteness and proportion; however, Davy also insisted on the chemically irreducible principle of spiritual vitality, to which Coleridge also subscribed. (*See also* Elective Affinity.)

An international celebrity in his time and president of the Royal Society from 1820 to 1827, Davy died from stroke complications at age 50.

William Crisman

Works Consulted

Hartley, Harold. *Humphry Davy.* 1966.

Haven, Richard. *Patterns of Consciousness: An Essay on Coleridge.* 1969.

Knight, David M. "The Scientist as Sage." *Studies in Romanticism* 6 (1967): 65–88.

Russell, Colin A. "The Electrochemical Theory of Sir Humphry Davy." *Annals of Science* 15 (1959): 1–25; 19 (1963): 255–71.

Siegried, Robert, et al., eds. *Humphry Davy on Geology: The 1805 Lectures for the General Audience.* 1980.

Siegried, Robert. "Sir Humphry Davy on the Nature of the Diamond." *Isis* 57 (1966): 325–35.

Deacon, William Frederick

(1799–1845)

William Frederick Deacon, a minor critic and writer of fiction, had a fine sense of the comic and was a gifted parodist of his contemporaries in the Romantic movement. His most popular book, *Warreniana* (1824), deserves to rank with the Smith brothers' *Rejected Addresses*, and his other comic writings possess some of the vivacity and invention that characterize Dickens's early work.

Born the son of a wealthy London merchant, Deacon attended Reading School, where Thomas Noon Talfourd was a senior schoolfellow, and headmaster. Dr. Valpy instilled in Deacon a love of literature. After leaving Cambridge University without a degree, Deacon contemplated taking Holy Orders. Instead, he embarked on a desultory literary career, having already made a promising debut in 1817, when Hone published *Hacho, or the Spell of St Wilten*, an epic poem influenced by Scott. A £100 annuity and the security of his parents' home made Deacon's choice of profession relatively safe, although his father was unhappy with his decision.

Following the simultaneous launch in January 1820, of two London magazines, Deacon soon became involved in the lesser known *London Magazine, and Monthly Critical and Dramatic Review*, published by Gold and Northhouse and dubbed *Gold's* to distinguish it from its illustrious rival *Baldwin's*, which John Scott edited for Baldwin, Cradock, and Joy. Deacon appeared to regard the pages of *Gold's* as his personal launching pad into the literary firmament. From at least March 1820, until April of the following year, he contributed a steady stream of literary criticism, verse, drama, Romantic fiction, comic sketches, and parody—all of which were doubtless wel-

comed by the publishers of a magazine thin on quality and whose rival could boast the work of Hazlitt, Wainewright, Clare, Barry Cornwall, and Lamb. The precocious Deacon saw himself as their equal and in his comic contributions seldom lost an opportunity to promote himself and *Gold's* at the expense of *Baldwin's*.

Much of Deacon's serious writing is of marginal interest and too often bears the mark of someone (as Talfourd suggests in a biographical sketch of his schoolfellow) steeped from an early age in three-decker novels and romances. The best of the seriocomic sketches are autobiographical and show the writer drawing on his schooldays at Reading (e.g., *Black Monday* and *Breaking Up*). It is interesting to note that *A Day at the Mill*, which describes a stay at Three Mile Cross, appeared in *Gold's* at about the time that Mitford, who knew both Valpy and Talfourd, was beginning to immortalize her tiny community as "Our Village." Was Mitford inspired by Deacon's sketch? There is evidence that Deacon read Mitford but none that Mitford was familiar with *Gold's* or that the two writers ever met.

Deacon's comic sketches appeared in a regular feature, "The Alchymist." Their influences, Washington Irving among them, seldom obtrude, and although the comic invention and sheer exuberance of the writing are peculiar to Deacon, they nonetheless are frequently reminiscent of early Dickens. But unlike the radical Dickens, Deacon's literary prejudices were strongly with the Tory Blackwood's men in their campaign, against the Cockneys led by Hunt. Hunt and his Hampstead set were always good for a cheap laugh in *Gold's*, and in one sketch, *On Authors*, Hunt, John Hamilton Reynolds, and other usurpers, including the whole Baldwin's Crew, are dismissed as worthless in comparison with Irving and Scott. Moreover, in the serial

"Immortality in Embryo," Wordsworth and Coleridge are ridiculed and the latter singled out for special treatment in a brilliant parody of *Christabel*.

In October 1820, Deacon launched a twopenny-literary miscellany—*The Déjeuné. or Companion for the Breakfast Table*—probably modeled on Hunt's *Indicator*. Deacon contributed most, if not all, of the material, some of which was reprinted from *Gold's*, which itself featured *Déjeuné* pieces and published a most favorable review of the magazine. But by now the strain of work on Deacon was beginning to tell. The new venture folded after just three months. Soon after, *Gold's* merged with the *Theatrical Inquisitor*, the past editors of which had included the notorious George Soane, to whom Deacon acknowledged an editorial debt of gratitude. Deacon's final fling in *Gold's* was as the irrepressible Paul Clutterbuck, whose principal delight was to gloat over the plight of *Baldwin's* and its editor John Scott, then enmeshed in literary controversy with *Blackwood's*. By early 1821, Deacon had probably assumed the editorship of *Gold's*, but Clutterbuck disappeared from the scene in April, and evidently by June a serious illness had forced Deacon to retire from his duties. *Gold's* struggled on for another month, printing a mass of Deacon material in its final issue in July, when Taylor and Hessey, owners of *Baldwin's* since April, bought out Joyce Gold and closed down his magazine.

Meanwhile Deacon, convalescing in a cottage near Llangadock, South Wales, wrote to his hero Scott requesting advice on whether to pursue literature as a career despite his father's opposition. Scott stressed the advantages of a steady profession over the perils of authorship, but Deacon ignored this advice. A first collection of prose pieces—*Dons and Duns*—had been advertised in 1820 but failed to appear. Deacon was more successful with *The Inn Keeper's Album* (1823), a volume of sketches and tales inspired by his sojourn at Llangadock. *Warreniana* (1824), a series of parodies purporting to be puffs for Warren's shoe blacking, was well received and became a best seller. The core of the book is revised versions of parodies from *Gold's*, and Deacon's victims include Hunt, Wordsworth and Coleridge (who are brilliantly captured), Southey, Byron, Scott, and Irving. Another collection of tales, *November Nights* (1826), reflected the author's interest in romance; it was followed by a comic novel, *The Exile of Erin*, in 1835. By this time, Deacon was editing the *Sun* newspaper. Later in the 1830s, he wrote seriocomic sketches for *Blackwood's*, which were collected and published posthumously as *The Picture Gallery* (1858).

Deacon died at age 46 at his home in Islington, North London. His posthumous novel *Annette* (1852) contains a valuable memoir by old schoolfellow Talfourd.

R.M. Healey

Works Consulted

Curling, Jonathan. *Janus Weathercock*. London: Nelson, 1938.

Deacon, William Frederick. *Annette*. London: Colburn, 1852.

Dobell, Bertram. *Sidelights on Charles Lamb*. London, 1903.

Healey, R.M. "The Other London Magazine: Gold's and Its Contributors," *Charles Lamb Bulletin* 61 (1988): 155–64.

Decorative Arts

Decorative Arts, also known as applied arts, underwent distinctive changes during the 19th-century.

The first half of the century saw the continuation and development of the imitation of antique or classical styles. (*See also* Antiquarianism, Classicism.) Highly influenced by French and Italian artists, English decorative arts became a triumph of elegant decadence. Gilt was much in favor, as were such rich materials as silk, velvet, and brocade. Exposed wood was painted, for example, with scenes depicting Greek myths. If not painted, wood was carved with such ornamentation , so deeply incised, as to make it impossible to lean back in a chair. Carved moldings and plaster reliefs were common elements of interior design; the more the better. Marble, onyx, malachite, and pearl were the most common choices for inlays in furnishings and were often used as tile, while porcelain, enamel, and stained glass were used in everything from furniture to windows.

Zealous ornamentation and the reappearance of gargoyles and chimera might have spread unchecked except for dramatic changes occurring in the art world. During the mid-19th century, British artists reacted to increasing industrialization with the Arts and Crafts Movement. The machine, it was felt, deprived craftspeople of the pleasure of work. Quality and beauty were set aside in favor of mass production and profits. Moreover, the restrictions of creating within an accepted, limited framework contributed to the frustrations of artists who were already seeing their livelihood destroyed by industrialization.

Additionally, decorative artists hoped to produce integrated designs. Each room of a house was furnished and decorated with careful attention to line, form, proportion, and detail. Any object not originally planned in the design would disrupt the entire room. This "holistic" design is a hallmark of the decorative-arts movements of the latter half of the 19th century.

Decorative-arts movements of the 19th century were not merely artistic, they were also political. They were anti-aristocratic.

This meant excessive ornamentation was eliminated because it was considered a sign of status and vulgar wealth. Liberalism was important to all aspects of the decorative-arts movements. The Victoria and Albert Museum, established in 1832, has the stated aim of elevating the taste of the general public. The Victoria and Albert was the first large national museum to be devoted to the decorative arts.

With honesty and sincerity as the ideals, artists left evidence of the way objects were made. Wood and joints were left exposed and undecorated; metal rivets might be made part of a decoration — utility coupled with design.

These movements all shared the belief that art was an element of design and combined utility with beauty. The lines and forms are simpler, ranging from the merely clean lines of the Arts and Crafts Movement, to the austere, stylized designs of Art Nouveau at the end of the century. These movements served to elevate temporarily the position of decorative arts in relation to the fine arts, but eventually the decorative arts were relegated to a lower position, where they remain today.

The elements of these movements— simple decoration, integrated design, and careful proportion—were succeeded by a return to excessive ornamentation and the eclectic, unintegrated furnishings of high Victoriana.

Jennifer Lawler

Works Consulted

Aslin, Elizabeth. *E. W. Godwin: Furniture and Interior Decoration*. London: Murray, 1986.

Brandt, Frederick. *Late Nineteenth and Early Twentieth Century Decorative Arts: The Sidney and Frances Lewis Collection in the Virginia Museum of Fine Arts*. Seattle: Washington UP, 1985.

de Groer, Leon. *Decorative Arts in Europe 1790–1850*. Trans. Office du Livre, S.A., Fribourg, Switzerland. New York: Rizzoli, 1986.

Frangiamore, Roy. *A Thing of Beauty: Art Nouveau, Art Deco, Arts and Crafts Movement and Aesthetic Movement Objects in Atlanta Collections.* Atlanta: The Museum, 1980.

Morris, Barbara. *Inspiration for Design: The Influence of the Victoria and Albert Museum.* Surrey: South Leigh, 1986.

Read, Sir Herbert. *A Concise History of Modern Painting.* New ed. New York: Oxford UP, 1974.

Roth, Linda Horwitz, ed. *J. Pierpont Morgan, Collector: European Decorative Arts from the Wadsworth Atheneum.* London: Balding, 1986.

Deism and Natural Supernaturalism in the 18th Century

Two of the most significant philosophical influences on Romantic thought were deism and natural supernaturalism. Each can be defined as a set of metaphysical and epistemological assertions that celebrate the power of the human mind and the spiritual authority of Nature. Yet they are radically opposed in their theories of knowledge and in their understanding of the human relationship to Nature. In fact, the concept that natural supernaturalism connotes was embraced by Romantic theory as, in part, a reaction against "natural religion," the hallmark of deism.

As controversies fueled by deism in the 17th and 18th centuries suggest, the term had a variety of meanings, adapting itself to theological positions as disparate as those of Voltaire and the English philosopher John Toland. Nevertheless, all varieties of deism share several generic principles. For the deist, reason is a universal human faculty, whose operations lead to conclusions that are universally acceptable; only through reason can humankind know God or shape a coherent set of theological beliefs. Indeed, only beliefs derived through reason are normative (or accessible to the whole human community). Since unaided reason is competent as a means to truth, for the deist it supersedes both tradition and the authority of dogma. But its truth is not subjective: deism shuns both particular revelation and its secular counterpart, original, or poetic, genius, as sources of enlightenment.

It is not surprising, then, that even general revelation was subject to the scrutiny of reason. For many deists, the Bible was at best an eloquent statement of moral law, at worst an uneven text obscure in origin, marred by historical inaccuracies, and reliant on unverifiable supernatural occurrences to justify its theology. For these reasons, the "text" to which most deists turned for theological insight was Nature itself, the prototype and working model of providential design. With characteristic objectivity, however, a majority of deists denied God's immanence in Nature, contending that the deity's primary role was that of a creator who, having devised the natural laws operating throughout the universe, had retired, like the proverbial watchmaker, to observe his masterpiece.

Since the most essential characteristic of deism was its reliance on human reason to discover truth, deistic thought can be traced back through the history of Western philosophy to Socrates. But in the 17th century, it became a distinct set of beliefs that aroused controversy but appealed to a wide variety of intellectuals, particularly those of a scientific bent and those distrustful of religious enthusiasm. Deism made great strides during the scientific revolution, for science provided those uncomfortable with Christianity's reliance on revelation with a natural and rational means of discovering the will of God. Among orthodox Englishmen (even those nominally opposed to "natural religion"), a growing distaste for the zeal of many religious sectarians gave deism added impetus. And its principles gained intellectual respectability through the efforts of Anthony Ashley Cooper, third Earl of Shaftesbury, who celebrated deism as a trademark of good breeding, good taste, and gentlemanly refinement.

It was the epistemology and empirical methodology of Locke, however, that validated deism most forcefully. Locke's most famous foray into theology, *The Reasonableness of Christianity as Delivered in the Scriptures* (1695), questioned both prophecy and miracles as the means of anticipating the coming of the Messiah or revealing his divinity. Locke praised instead the plain, direct language with which Christ is announced in the Bible. Locke also touted the power of the new physics to reveal God's design in Nature and to justify a natural religion informed by empirical observation, not intuition or faith. Toland, Locke's famous disciple, made logical persuasion and observation the most significant bases of religious conviction in *Christianity Not Mysterious* (1696), a controversial book that popularized Locke's approach to religion and epistemology. At the instigation of such deists as Toland, Anthony Collins, and Matthew Tindal, deism began to lead some of the most orthodox of Anglicans to disavow a Christianity based exclusively on abstruse mysteries.

Ironically, the gradual assimilation of certain aspects of deism by orthodoxy led to its decline as a religious position; by 1800, deism was, again, an informal philosophy, a sensibility that would both repel and attract artists and philosophers of the Romantic period, indirectly nourishing the philosophy known as "natural supernaturalism."

Natural supernaturalism, deriving from Germanic *naturphilosophie* and related to later American transcendentalism, raises Nature to the level of the supernatural, recognizing the divinity and spiritual vitality of the natural world. It can be used as another name for the philosophy that displaced formal religion for many Romantic artists and philosophers, and, like deism, it reflects a preoccupation with human experience and the power of the human mind. But the Romantics were not as concerned as their deistic predecessors with Nature's orderly design or consonance with reason. For the Romantics, Nature's regenerative powers and organic cycles gave it a spiritual character, which for deists it distinctly lacked, linking it to the creative process and animating it with divine energy.

The term natural supernaturalism was not introduced into literary history until the serialization of Carlyle's *Sartor Resartus* in *Fraser's Magazine* in 1833 and 1834. In *Sartor Resartus*, natural supernaturalism provides Teufelsdröckh with a triumphant, life-affirming response to the "Everlasting No." The concept had nevertheless been central to Romanticism from its beginnings in 18th-century philosophy. Lessing, Schiller, and Fichte all anticipated natural supernaturalism by secularizing and adapting the organic plot of the biblical narrative (with its recurring imagery of fall and redemption) to the theodicy of the human spirit seeking reunification with itself and outer Nature. Other prominent Romantic philosophers, such as Hegel, also valued the dynamic process by which Nature evolved and found in that process a correlative for systematic thought and, ultimately, for history itself. And Schelling, whose philosophical writings influenced both Coleridge and Goethe, devised a *naturphilosophie* that argued the immanence of God in Nature. But Rousseau surpassed his German contemporaries by making a religion of Nature. His Romantic primitivism, as well as his conviction that the emotions and the most subjective of human faculties, the conscience, were springs of religious truth, played a significant role in discrediting the natural religion of the deists, inspiring a new attitude toward Nature and its antecedent, the human imagination.

In the literary arena, natural supernaturalism finds its most forceful expression in the poetry of Wordsworth, Coleridge, and Shelley. Each wrote lyrics in which a determinate speaker (usually the poet himself, who, as Wordsworth explained in the Preface to the 1800 edition of *Lyrical Ballads*, has an "organic" imagination) engages in a sustained colloquy with Nature and is so nurtured by its regenerative powers that he experiences an abrupt creative illumination analogous to the biblical apocalypse. A sense of imaginative and spiritual rejuvenation follows; as a result of the interplay between mind and Nature (symbolized for all three poets by what Wordsworth called a "correspondent" or "intellectual" breeze), the poet-perceiver understands with new fervor what it means to be fully human. The perceptual process that produces this inner apocalypse can occur only in Nature, for only Nature can dissolve the barriers between the subjectivity of the poet and the objectivity of the external world.

The principle is clearest in Wordsworth's *Prelude*, a paradigm for the spiritual autobiography in which Nature, priest-like, inspires spiritual and intellectual change in the poet; in Coleridge's *Frost at Midnight*, his most triumphant—and, some would argue, his most beautiful—expression of Nature's power to redeem the solipsistic poet alienated from all that is "other" than he (an experience analogous to the biblical fall); and in Shelley's *Mont Blanc*, in which the controlling image is, perhaps, the most complex symbol of the organic relationship between Nature and the transcendent

imagination in Romantic poetry. (*See also* Natural Supernaturalism and Twentieth-Century Critics.)

Patricia Elizabeth Davis

Works Consulted

Abrams, Meyer Howard. *Natural Supernaturalism: Tradition and Revolution in Romantic Literature.* New York: Norton, 1971.

Brantley, Richard. *Locke, Wesley, and the Method of English Romanticism.* Gainesville: U of Florida P, 1984.

Butler, Marilyn. *Romantics, Rebels, and Reactionaries: English Literature and its Background 1760–1830.* Oxford: Oxford UP, 1981.

Sullivan, Robert E. *John Toland and the Deist Controversy: A Study in Adaptations.* Cambridge: Harvard UP, 1982.

De Quincey, Thomas
(1785–1859)

Thomas De Quincey was born in 1785 in Manchester, in the north of England. He was the fifth child of a prosperous linen merchant. Years later, De Quincey would describe his relatively pleasant rural upbringing in a series "Autobiographic Sketches" in Tait's *Edinburgh Magazine*. Most of his first six years were passed on a family farm near Manchester, with plenty of books to read, several brothers and sisters, and a pious, strict mother. The deaths of two beloved sisters in 1790 and 1792 were traumatic experiences to which De Quincey often later referred. His father died in 1793, and the family moved to Bath in 1796.

Young Thomas's experiences at a grammar school, from age 11, were generally unhappy, and in 1802, he ran away from school. For several months, he wandered through the countryside of Wales, camping at night in a tiny tent he had constructed. In November, he arrived in London, where he lived some time in the disreputable area of Soho. Many years later, De Quincey wrote of his friendship in 1802 and 1803 with Ann, a 16-year-old London prostitute, whom he claimed had saved his life. De Quincey emphasized her essential innocence, the betrayals and poverty that had reduced her to accept a degrading profession, and the harshness of her existence.

With funds running low, and after losing contact with Ann, the 17-year-old De Quincey returned to his mother's home in the spring of 1803. In May of that year, he wrote a reverential letter to Wordsworth. He received a kind reply and an invitation to visit Westmorland.

De Quincey entered Oxford University in December 1803. There, he led a quiet existence, applying himself to classical studies, private reading, and keeping aloof from the other students. In later years, De Quincey claimed that he profited little from formal education. On his own initiative, he began to study German language and literature in earnest. In 1808, after completing the first day of his final examinations, he suddenly quit Oxford. He never returned and never graduated.

De Quincey first took opium during a stay in London in 1804, as a cure for rheumatic pains. According to his account, he was an occasional user for a number of years afterward.

After leaving Oxford, at age 23, De Quincey moved to Grasmere, in the Lake District. For the first time, he met his idols Wordsworth and Coleridge, and other local writers, including Southey and John Wilson. He moved into Dove Cottage, formerly occupied by the Wordsworths. In 1809, De Quincey briefly resided in London to assist in the publication of Wordsworth's pamphlet *The Convention of Cintra*. De Quincey soon became a trusted friend of William, Dorothy, and Mary Wordsworth. Meanwhile, his dependence on opium increased, and by 1813 he was firmly addicted to the drug. The following year, De Quincey traveled to Edinburgh and, through his friend John Wilson, met several Scottish literary figures, including Hogg, Lockhart, and the philosopher Sir William Hamilton.

De Quincey's first child was born in 1816. In early 1818, he married the boy's mother, Margaret. With a second child born in the same year, De Quincey watched his remaining finances dwindle almost to nothing. In July 1818, with the help of a testimonial from Wordsworth, he became the editor of the local weekly newspaper, *Westmorland Gazette*. For the next 16 months, he regaled subscribers with a characteristic melange of articles on politics, economics, crime, executions, crocodiles, poetry, and German philosophy. His personal habits, however, were unsuitable for the role of a newspaper editor, and he was fired in November 1821.

In many ways, De Quincey's early manhood was a series of failures and false starts, especially marked by his appalling struggles to escape enslavement to opium. (*See also* Opium.) Badly in need of cash, he turned to London in 1821, with another testimonial from Wordsworth. At the offices of the new *London Magazine*, he met the editor, John Scott, and many new London writers, such as Lamb and Hazlitt, and the poets Hood, Clare, and Cunningham. At this time, he wrote his most famous work, *The Confessions of an English Opium-Eater: Being an Extract from the Life of a Scholar*. After it first appeared in the *London Magazine* in 1821, the *Confessions* was re-issued as a book in 1822. De Quincey found himself an overnight celebrity. His rhapsodic *Confessions* is Romantic in its stress on emotional heights and depths, as well as in its extreme emphasis on the quality of personal experience. With very little explicit attention to morality, it recounts the steps by which De Quincey gradually became enslaved to opium. The work fluctuates wildly between reciting the miseries of addiction and dwelling on the dreams and visions that opium brought him. Like Wordsworth's *Prelude* or Coleridge's *Biographia Literaria*, De Quincey's *Confessions* tells of the growth of the writer's mind from childhood to early maturity.

De Quincey's meetings with Lamb, Hazlitt, and the other writers for the *London Magazine* were among the most productive experiences of his creative life. In 1823, De Quincey published his impressionistic essay "On the Knocking on the Gate in Macbeth." This experiment in psychological literary criticism was a landmark in the Romantic reassessment of Shakespeare. It considers the dark sense of solitude, inferiority, and alienation from society, which Macbeth experiences as a result of his crimes. (The subject of murder, with its potential for solitude and personal inwardness, continued to fascinate De Quincey for many years; his famous essay "On Murder considered as One of the Fine Arts" appeared in two parts in 1827 and 1839.)

Unfortunately, De Quincey also published in the *London Magazine* an ill-considered attack on the young Carlyle's translation of Goethe's *William Meister's Apprenticeship*, which greatly embarrassed its author in later years. The piece was omitted from all the collected editions of his essays and has never been reprinted in full.

Meanwhile, De Quincey's friend Wilson became the editor of *Blackwood's Edinburgh Magazine*, a popular journal that paid its contributors higher fees than its southern rival. As the *London Magazine*

became less interested in his work, De Quincey returned to Westmorland to concentrate his energies on the Edinburgh market. His first main essay in *Blackwood's* was a lively, humorous, opinionated review of Robert Gillies's translation of *German Stories*, published in *Blackwood's*; this article, too, has never been reprinted since its first appearance in 1826.

One of De Quincey's minor masterpieces was the long essay "The Last Days of Immanuel Kant," which appeared in *Blackwood's* in 1827. Like the *Confessions*, this work cultivates an engaging and fertile ambivalence toward its subject. It foreshadows De Quincey's later essays on Wordsworth, Coleridge, and Southey in its combination of respect for Kant's intellectual vision, on the one hand, and its very amusing retailing of Kant's personal failings and stubbornness on the other. The delicate, complex, and Romantic ambiguity of De Quincey's fond portrait of the philosopher is a little like Austen's ambivalent portraits of Emma Woodhouse or Fanny Price. Like many of De Quincey's essays, the work on Kant was loosely based on a popular book of the day, from which De Quincey derived the basic facts of Kant's life.

Desperate for money, De Quincey undertook to write anonymously for the *Edinburgh Saturday Post* newspaper. Here he published long reviews of *Blackwood's*, the *Edinburgh Review*, the *Quarterly Review*, and *Foreign Quarterly Review*, as well as essays on politics and emigration, on the Danish poet Klopstock and the English essayist Junius, and on other subjects. The *Post*, mainly written and edited by three Presbyterian clergymen, was chiefly concerned with Scottish affairs and religious disputes; it was an unlikely harbor for an Englishman—let alone an "English opium-eater." Nevertheless, De Quincey became friends with some of the *Post* writers, including its editor the Rev. Crichton and David Moir. At this time in Edinburgh, De Quincey also became a friend of Carlyle, despite some initial awkwardness because of De Quincey's scathing review of Carlyle in the 1823 *London Magazine*. Several of De Quincey's columns for the Edinburgh *Post* were highly polemical—he gave rein to his extremely reactionary views on politics and the Irish question. In subsequent years, he learned to be more moderate in expressing his political opinions.

De Quincey continued to write for the *Post* newspaper after it became the *Edinburgh Evening Post* in 1828. In 1829 he wrote for, and briefly became a co-editor of, the *Edinburgh Literary Gazette*, a companion-journal to the *Post*. After short trips to his home in Westmorland, De Quincey finally brought his family to Scotland in 1830. Throughout the 1830s, he was often obliged to seek refuge in the debtor's sanctuary for long periods. His wife Margaret, by whom he had eight children, died in 1837. He remained in Scotland, living in Edinburgh, Glasgow, and Lasswade, until his own death in 1859.

Of De Quincey's magazine pieces, the most relevant to the Romantic age were probably the reminiscences of Wordsworth, Coleridge, Southey, Wilson, and other friends, which he supplied for Tait's *Edinburgh Magazine* from 1834 to 1851. In these essays, he displays a discriminating interest in the spirit of Romantic poetry, together with a mature awareness that the individuals often failed to live up to the ideals of their poetry. He tells, for example, of his gradual estrangement from Wordsworth, whom he found sometimes to be cold or overbearing. In the end, De Quincey says that he found Wordsworth incapable of equal friendship. It is important to realize that these reservations do not detract from De Quincey's deep enjoyment of Wordsworth's poetry. On the contrary, the essays on Wordsworth, like De Quincey's earlier work on Kant, establish an engaging ambivalence which comprehends both the "inner" Romantic vision and aspiration and the personal foibles which are perhaps inevitable in day-to-day relationships. De Quincey applied the German term "einseitig" to describe Wordsworth.

De Quincey similarly traces the same quality of "onesidedness" in his pieces on the other Lake Poets. He describes, for instance, Coleridge's personal failings and his plagiarisms, while stoutly defending the quality of Coleridge's poems and philosophical writings. His analysis, as in most of his best work, is personal, ambivalent, and Romantic rather than "objective" or reductive in its judgments. Nonetheless, his articles on Wordsworth, Coleridge, and Southey caused grave offense in Westmorland, where they were perceived as impolite intrusions into the private lives of respectable authors.

The same willingness to see different and conflicting sides of a single personality is very evident in De Quincey's autobiographical writings. From his *Confessions* to his "Autobiographic Sketches" of the 1830s, and in many other essays as well, De Quincey is frank in conceding many of his own failings. In 1845, he returned to autobiography with a series of articles entitled *Suspiria de Profundis; Being a Sequel to the Confessions of an English Opium-Eater*. (The main title, from the Latin translation of the Bible, means "Sighs from the Depths.") This work stresses the importance of childhood experiences, as well as solitude, suffering, faith, and dreams in the development of a mature individual. In one central passage, he compares the human mind to a medieval palimpsest (i.e., a scroll for writing), which has been written upon by a series of authors through several centuries. An individual mind, in other words, has a succession of layers representing various experiences through the different stages of life. On this palimpsest, the most recent experiences are inscribed clearly, while earlier experiences survive in the form of faint, underlying traces. The symbol of the palimpsest expresses De Quincey's conviction that childhood experiences survive unconsciously or semiconsciously in the adult mind. In De Quincey's view, those lingering childhood memories often determine crucial aspects of an adult personality.

De Quincey was primarily a journalist. Virtually all of his writings first appeared in Edinburgh magazines or newspapers. He probably owes much of his literary reputation to James Fields, an enterprising American publisher who first proposed a collected edition of his work. Fields published the first volume of De Quincey's *Writings*, containing the *Confessions of an English Opium-Eater* and *Suspiria de Profundis*, in Boston in 1851. Although De Quincey had not given his permission for the edition, he was pleased when it appeared and pleased to receive a share of the profits. (*See also* Essay, Lake School.)

David Groves

Works Consulted

De Luca, V.A. *Thomas De Quincey; The Prose of Vision*. Toronto: U of Toronto P, 1980.

Devlin, D.D. *De Quincey, Wordsworth and the Art of Prose*. New York: St. Martin's, 1983.

Eaton, Horace A., ed. *A Diary of Thomas De Quincey*. London: Douglas, 1927.

Goldmann. *The Mine and the Mint; Sources for the Writings of Thomas De Quincey*. Carbondale: Southern Illinois UP, 1965.

Groves, David. "De Quincey's 'Daughter of Lebanon' and the Execution of Mary McKinnon." *The Wordsworth Circle* 19 (1988): 105–07.

Jordan, John E. *De Quincey to Wordsworth; A Biography of a Relationship*. Berkeley: U of California P, 1962.

Lindop, Grevel. *The Opium-Eater; A Life of Thomas De Quincey*. New York: Taplinger, 1981.

Snyder, Robert Lance, ed., *Thomas De Quincey; Bicentenary Studies*. Norman: U of Oklahoma P, 1985.

Tave, Stuart M., ed. *New Essays by De Quincey: His Contributions to the Edinburgh Saturday Post and the Edinburgh Evening Post 1827–1828*. Princeton: Princeton UP, 1966.

Whale, John C. *Thomas De Quincey's Reluctant Autobiography*. Totowa, NJ: Barnes, 1984.

Dibdin, Charles
(1745–1814)

Dibdin, Charles Isaac Mungo
(1768–1833)

Dibdin, Thomas John
(1771–1841)

During the Romantic era, the Dibdins occupied a central position in the world of popular theater. In relation to the canonical Romantic writers, however, this family of authors-actors-managers-singers-composers now stand on a very slim margin of literary history.

Charles Dibdin was the father of two illegitimate sons, Charles, Jr., and Thomas, whose mother, Harriet Davenet, was a chorus singer at Covent Garden. Born in the midst of the flourishing theatrical world of the late 18th century, the young Dibdins quite readily accepted their destinies as performers, authors, and managers. David Garrick, friend and colleague of the elder Dibdin, cheerfully assumed an avuncular role. Moreover, one of the children made his stage debut thanks to him. The senior Dibdin was prominently involved in

Garrick's spectacular Stratford Jubilee celebrating the 200th anniversary of Shakespeare's birth, which should have taken place in 1764 but actually occurred in 1769. For the occasion, Dibdin performed his *Warwickshire* ballad. The event in Stratford also included Boswell, the music and conducting of Thomas Arne, and Garrick's own *Ode to Shakespeare*. Dibdin's account, sometimes hostile, of the Shakespeare Jubilee appears in *The Professional Life of Mr. Dibdin Written by Himself* (1803). Three years after the Stratford festivities, 4-year-old Tom Dibdin appeared at Drury Lane as Cupid in a Garrick revival of the Shakespeare Jubilee, which featured William Siddons as Macbeth and his wife Sarah Kemble Siddons as Venus.

In addition to *Professional Life*, the elder Dibdin wrote *Complete History of the English Stage* (1800), in which, expectedly, Shakespeare looms large. In time, the sheer bulk of the combined theatrical output of the Dibdins came to loom monstrously large. After his earlier successes—entertainments such as *The Cobler* (1759), *Rose and Colin* (1764), and *The Wives Revenged* (1775), all derived from 18th-century French originals—Charles Dibdin continued writing and performing well into the first decade of the 19th century. When in 1809 he expanded his *Professional Life* to six volumes, he included 600 songs. Among them were his popular sea songs: *The Lass that Loved a Sailor* and *Tom Bowling*, this last inspired by the naval career of his brother Thomas, who died in 1780 at Cape Town and for whom Thomas J. Dibdin was named. As an actor, songwriter, and composer of operas and entertainments, Charles Dibdin energetically catered to the popular tastes of the Romantic era.

The English theater of the late 18th and early 19th centuries offered its audiences an overwhelming number of frothy musicals; melodramas; mangled versions of Shakespeare as well as relatively acceptable adaptations of Shakespeare; operas; burlettas; and extravaganzas using the most sophisticated visual effects of the day. One of Charles Dibdin's pieces, *The Deserter* (1769), featured a talented dog called Moustache and 13 other similarly gifted canines acting as soldiers storming a fort. This swashbuckling stage show (a precursor of the Rin-Tin-Tin and Lassie adventures) ends up with one of the dogs having to face a firing squad as the deserter of the play's title. Other spectaculars featured sea battles, the use of horses onstage, or such epics as the storming of the Bastille. These overt kinds of drama were well attended, as were the less technologically ambitious melodramas and musical entertainments.

Although Shakespeare's comedies enjoyed a revival during this period, frequently only fragments from his work were used to bolster the thin texture of much of the dramatic material. Playwrights also sought plots, characters, and literary substance from novels. Fielding and Smollett were popular sources. So were such novelists as Scott and Mary Shelley, whose *Frankenstein* (1818) was adapted several times for the stage. During the Dibdin era, Gothic novels generally did well on the stage. In the hands of "Monk" Lewis, Walpole's *Castle of Otranto* (1765) became the popular and much-revived melodrama of *The Castle Spectre* (1797), whose verse prologue celebrates the enchantress Romance, she who thrives, writes Lewis, on moonlight and solitude.

Other examples of Gothic Romanticism created for the stage at this time were William Siddons's *The Sicilian Romance* (1794), taken from Ann Radcliffe's 1790 novel of the same name, and James Boaden's *The Italian Monk* (1797), based on Radcliffe's *The Italian* (1797). Suggestive (at least in part) of this popular tradition are Thomas John Dibdin's *Alonzo and Imogene; or, The Bridal Spectre* (1801); *The Invisible Witness; or, The Chapel in the Wood* (1818); *The Bride of Lammermoor; or, The Spectre at the Fountain* (1819), adapted from the Scott novel; and *Orsino; or, The Vaulted Cavern* (1820). These melodramas are among the 200 or more stage pieces of various kinds that T. J. Dibdin composed. Among the many farces, extravaganzas, burlesques, and comedies, one finds adaptations of Scott's novels (other than *The Bride of Lammermoor*), of Goldsmith's *Vicar of Wakefield* (staged in 1817), and of Smollett's *Humphrey Clinker* (1818). T. J. Dibdin also fashioned a melodrama drawn from Coleridge's *Zapolya: A Christmas Tale* (1817), a blank verse play that modestly imitates Shakespeare's *Winter's Tale* as it invokes Shakespeare's *Twelfth Night* by setting the opening part in Illyria. Adding a "t" to the Queen of Illyria's name, Dibdin calls his play *Zapolyta: The War Wolf* (1818). Another T. J. Dibdin adaptation, that of Henry Hart Milman's *Fazio* (1815), which he called *The Italian Wife* (1816), made popular a play that otherwise might never have appeared (in its original form with its original title) at Covent Garden in 1818 with Eliza O'Neill as Milman's heroine Bianca. Seen by Shelley and Peacock, according to Mary Shelley, she was ever in Shelley's thoughts as he created the role of Beatrice in *The Cenci* (1819).

Thomas Dibdin refers favorably to the Milman play in his autobiography *The Reminiscences of Thomas Dibdin*. This is a witty account of the author's career and the theatrical scene during the Romantic period. Much reference is made to Byron, an acquaintance, and to such luminaries as Garrick, Mrs. Siddon, and the Kembles. Evaluations of productions and performances abound. At one point, Dibdin even criticizes himself for attempting to mount a production of *Hamlet*. Shakespeare, in fact, becomes a vital subtext in *The Reminiscences*. Dibdin refers to him and frequently quotes from the plays. Dibdin's main concern, however, is the world of the Romantic theater and his reactions to that world. His work is conveniently enumerated at one point to demonstrate the variety of his offerings: comedies, melodramas, three-act operas, comic pantomimes, musical afterpieces, farces, and burlettas. And the theaters at which his works were performed would make any playwright tingle with envy: Covent Garden, Drury Lane, The Haymarket, Surrey, Astley's, The Olympic, The Lyceum Circus, and Sadler's Wells.

In 1772, Charles Dibdin, Sr., began writing for Sadler's Wells, and, in 1794 23-year-old Thomas began working for the same theater. By 1796, the younger Dibdin was stage manager. Thomas's older brother, Charles, Jr. (age 31), started his tenure at Sadler's Wells in 1799 and proceeded to fill the boards with his dramatic compositions. Although older than Thomas, Charles was not as experienced in theatrical matters. In time, however, he enjoyed the success of the others. Sadler's Wells featured aqua-dramas, using the abundant water supply of the wells nearby, the comic genius of Joe Grimaldi, and spectaculars that included Charles, Jr.'s specialty: transformation scenes. Among his melodramas were *An Bratach; or, The Water Spectre* (1805); *The Invisible Ring; or, The Water Monster and Fire Spectre* (1806); *The Ocean Fiend; or, The Infant's Peril* (1807); *The Spectre Knight* (1810), based on Scott's *Marmion*; and *The Weird Sisters; or, The Thane and the Throne* (1819), based on *Macbeth*. The Romantic theater was soaring to adventurous heights and literally plunging to watery depths in these sometimes broadly dramatized stage pieces, which combined highly visual drama with either magical transformations or Gothic effects. (*See also* Theater.)

Vincent F. Petronella

Works Consulted

Arundell, Dennis. *The Story of Sadler's Wells: 1683–1964*. London: Hamilton, 1965.

Cave, Richard Allen, ed. *The Romantic Theatre: An International Symposium*. Totowa, NJ: Barnes, 1986.

Clunes, Alec. *The British Theatre*. New York: Barnes, 1964.

Dibdin, Thomas. *The Reminiscences of Thomas Dibdin* (1827). 2 vols. New York: Harper, 1828.

Nicoll, Allardyce. *Late Eighteenth-Century Drama: 1750–1800*. 1927 Cambridge: Cambridge UP, 1952.

– – –. *Early Nineteenth-Century Drama: 1800–1850*. 1927 Cambridge: Cambridge UP, 1952.

Schoenbaum, S. *Shakespeare's Lives*. Oxford: Clarendon, 1970.

Thomas, Dwight, and David K. Jackson, eds. *The Poe Log: A Documentary Life of Edgar Allan Poe, 1809-1849*. Boston: Hall, 1987.

Thorndike, Ashley H. *English Comedy*. New York: Cooper Square, 1965.

Watson, Ernest Bradlee. *Sheridan to Robertson: A Study of the Nineteenth-Century London Stage*. Cambridge: Cambridge UP, 1926.

Wickham, Glynne. *A History of the Theatre*. New York: Cambridge Up, 1985.

[The London] Diorama

The London Diorama, which likely opened in 1823 in Regent's Park, was modeled on the commercially successful Paris Diorama founded the previous year by Louis-Jacques-Mandé Daguerre (1787–1851) and Charles-Marie Bouton (1781–1853). Within a building designed by Augustus Charles Pugin (1762–1832) and James Morgan, up to 200 customers sat in an amphitheater darkened to eliminate any sense of space or distance and peered down a tunnel at Bouton's *Interior of Trinity Chapel, Canterbury Cathedral*, a picture about 70 by 50 feet in size painted on transparent cloth. After 15 minutes, the manually operated amphitheater rotated, and a landscape by Daguerre, *The Valley of Sarnen in Canton Unterwalden, Switzerland*, came into view. Representative of the images exhibited throughout the 28 years of the London Diorama's existence, these topographical paintings enthralled audiences and critics alike with their faithful reproductions of reality and with theatrical changes in mood and atmosphere created by an illusion of depth and the mechanical manipulation of natural lighting effects. Pictorial realism and melodramatic effects, when coupled with the belief that the pictures' content possessed educational value, made the London Diorama an immediate success, and it welcomed an estimated 2,000 paying visitors on Easter Monday of 1824.

The diorama was but one of numerous commercial entertainments in which the public could sate an ever-growing craving for images during the first half of the 19th century. Contemporary writers traced its ancestry to the Eidophusikon, opened in the early 1780s by Philippe-Jacques de Loutherbourg. However, of more immediate importance was the panorama, patented by Robert Barker in 1787, and its numerous progeny, for they still drew London crowds to Drury Lane, Covent Garden, or the Colosseum during the 1820s to view topical as well as topographical scenes, and its Parisian counterpart operated by Pierre Prévost had earlier provided training for both Daguerre and Bouton. Demand for images that edified as they entertained encouraged a host of similar ventures, but as the panoramas and other forms of visual entertainment multiplied, the expectations of the public grew in sophistication, and the diorama responded, providing the expected realistic images while adding sensational effects, first of light and then of sound.

From its opening until 1832, the London Diorama showed views already successful in Paris, and 17 original pictures, nine by Daguerre and eight by Bouton, were presented in pairs. Most popular of the pictures exhibited in both cities was Daguerre's *Ruins of Holyrood Chapel, Edinburgh, by Moonlight*, which opened in London in March of 1825. Its loss, like that of all the dioramas, makes difficult any comprehension of the sensation they created, but a painting by Daguerre of Holyrood Chapel conveys some sense of the original. Daguerre and Bouton sought from the outset to identify their pictures with established traditions in the visual arts, so they decorated the ceiling of the diorama with portraits by Old Masters, such as Rembrandt, and with works by modern artists, such as Reynolds and Gainsbor-ough. To a degree, this effort succeeded, for new diorama pictures were reviewed as works of art in the periodical press. Most critics, like the reviewer in the *Mirror of Literature* (1827) of one of Daguerre's images of Gothic ruins in a mist, rhapsodized over their extraordinary verisimilitude, calling attention to the perfection of illusion and to the magical quality of the dramatic lighting effects. In 1830, *The Spectator* found his Mount St. Gotthard so true to life that it excited a sublime response equivalent to that produced by Nature itself. The best dioramas were accordingly the most lifelike, and viewers debated such topics as whether a cobweb in Bouton's diorama of Chartres was real or painted. On the rare occasions the critics found a diorama wanting, the causes often were details that destroyed the illusion of reality.

Beginning in 1830, Bouton moved to London to manage the diorama, while Daguerre remained in Paris, where he soon undertook the experiments that would lead to the invention of the daguerreotype. After 1831, no new dioramas by Daguerre were sent to London, but his innovations in Paris remained influential. To satisfy audiences' craving for ever greater novelty, Daguerre introduced the "double-effect diorama" in 1834, with views of Ghent and a midnight mass at Saint-Etienne-du-Mont. Unlike the earlier dioramas, where the picture seen by the viewer was simply modified through the use of lighting effects, the double-effect diorama permitted a complete and dramatic transformation, turning day into night or a building into a ruin. Bouton followed Daguerre's lead, introducing the double-effect pictures in 1835 with *The Interior of the Church of Santa Croce, Florence*, which also featured the Kyrie from a Haydn Mass played on an organ. Others followed, such as the *Village of Alagna in Piedmont*, melodramatic depiction of an avalanche, and the *Basilica of St. Paul-Without-the-Walls, Rome* (1837), which illustrated the destruction wrought by the fire of 16 July 1823. In all, eight new dioramas by Bouton are known between 1834 and 1839, the last being *The Coronation of Queen Victoria*, the sole topical diorama.

Following Bouton's return to Paris in 1840, new artists were recruited for the London Diorama, and it continued to exhibit double-effect pictures, again with the occasional addition of novel effects. The *Exterior View of Notre Dame, Paris, in Evening Light* (1843) by Charles Caius Rénoux (1795–1846) won praise, as did his *The Shrine of the Nativity, Bethlehem* (1840) based on a drawing by David Roberts. Following Rénoux's death, pictures were executed by Diosse, one of Daguerre's students, and his *Interior of St. Marks's, Venice* (1847), was accompanied by the Kyrie from a Mozart mass, while his *Mount Etna* (1848) depicted the mountain transformed from calm to nocturnal eruption. Despite the sale of the London Diorama to Sir Thomas [Samuel?] Morton Peto in 1848, exhibitions continued until 1851, with the last two pictures being *The Castle of Stolzenfels* by Nicholas Meister of Cologne and Diosse's *Mount Etna*. When the London Diorama finally closed, the public's thirst for dioramic images had yet to be slaked, for there were still five rival dioramas open in London as well as a host of imitators, both in London and other British cities. Indeed, so popular had this type of picture become, the word "diorama" was applied indiscriminately to a variety of visual media. And, outside of London and Paris, dioramas operated in Breslau, Berlin, Cologne, and Stockholm, and pictures sent from London even reached the United States.

The diorama's success can be attributed to various factors. The taste of the 19th-century public for topographical images enhanced by melodramatic effects grew rather than declined with the appearance of new media and such establishments as the diorama, perhaps because the subject matter of the dioramas provided an inexpensive, comfortable, and vicarious form of the grand tour. The dioramas also aspired to instruct, and there are explanatory guidebooks for the Holyrood Chapel and the Chartres Cathedral paintings that describe their history and architecture. Richard Altick suggests, in this regard, that the diorama appealed to the religious who were forbidden to attend plays, and the frequency of religious scenes exhibited in London during 1830s and 1840s supports this view. Whatever the reasons underlying the diorama's attraction for the public, by mid-century the term had en-

tered the common vocabulary, and George Eliot uses it in *Middlemarch* to suggest the operations of the memory.

The popularity of the dioramas generated a debate over whether their pictures were art. The press discussed them as "exhibitions of art." But if the dioramas were art, it was a mundane art, and it rarely elevated the viewer's taste. Indeed, if contemporary reactions are to be believed, the highest artistic achievement the diorama could attain was providing an entertaining substitute for reality. These pleasant but uncomplicated images required little or no preparation or serious thought, certainly not of the sort required to view the then fashionable paintings based on literary or historical themes. They offered instead an effortless way to learn a few smidgens of geography or architectural history. In doing so, the diorama may have broadened slightly the outlook of its audience, but it remained a commercial venture that fed the public demand for novelty, and the end of its popularity coincided not surprisingly with the spread of photography.

Robert W. Brown

Works Consulted

Altick, Richard D. *The Shows of London*. Cambridge: Belknap, 1978.

Daguerre, Louis-Jacques-Mandé. *An Historical and Descriptive Account of the Various Processes of the Daguerréotype and the Diorama*. London: McLean, 1839.

Gernsheim, Helmut and Alison. *L.J.M. Daguerre. The History of the Diorama and the Daguerreotype*. Rev. ed. New York: Dover, 1968.

Gill, Arthur T. "The London Diorama." *History of Photography* 1 (1977): 31–36.

P.,I.B., and Britton, J. "An Account of the Diorama." *Illustrations of the Public Buildings of London: With Historical and Descriptive Accounts of Each Edifice*. Comp. J. Britton and A. Pugin. 2 vols. London: Taylor, Britton, and Pugin, 1825–1828. I: 66–71.

Disinterestedness

Disinterestedness is an important theme in Romantic theory, advanced and developed most fully by Hazlitt although anticipated by Kant in Germany, the Third Earl of Shaftesbury, and other Anglo-Scottish moralist-critic-aestheticians in 18th-century England.

The theme seemingly stands against the familiar Romantic emphasis on the subjective, Wordsworth's conception on poetry as the spontaneous expression of strong feeling, or Shelley's image of poets as inspired prophets and legislators of the world. Yet Hazlitt is clearly an advocate of a poetry of intense emotion, of what he calls gusto in art. What is different is his insistence that strong feeling be rooted in something beyond the self, outside the mind, in some worthy object, situation, or character. The vital power in this process is the sympathetic imagination, which identifies with its object, captures its essential characteristics vividly, and expresses those characteristics concretely.

Kant in his *Critique of Judgment* (1790) had preceded Hazlitt, arguing that the judgment of taste is aesthetic and disinterested, treating its objects in themselves, without reference to some larger and external purpose. Hazlitt's idea finds its earliest expression in his *Essay on the Principles of Human Action* (1805), opposing theorists like Hobbes, Condillac, and Helvetius and their view of human nature as essentially selfish and contending that greatness in art, as in moral action, involves losing one's sense of self in something greater and dearer. The theme of disinterestedness pervades not only his theoretical writing but also his practical criticism. Shakespeare, unlike the more self-centered Wordsworth or Rousseau, is his hero, greater than Chaucer or Milton. He is "the least of an egotist that it was possible to be," the chameleon-dramatist who could be now Hamlet, now Claudius, now Cordelia, now Goneril and Regan. His idea of gusto is ultimately rooted in this power of disinterestedness. Gusto is the power of passion informing its object, the imagination's intense involvement in and realization of something beyond the ego.

Keats in several of his memorable letters dramatizes the impact of Hazlitt's thought. For Keats, disinterestedness is "negative capability." The poet has no identity, no fixed bias. He is capable of living with uncertainty and with mystery without demanding some ultimate resolution or reason. The intensity of *King Lear* is one of his favorite examples of Shakespeare's ability to enter imaginatively into another being, another consciousness.

Arnold's emphasis, especially in the Preface to the 1853 edition of his poems, on excellent human actions rather than on mere feeling, on the poet seeing things as they are, carries the tradition forward. In the 20th century, Eliot echoes the idea in his 1917 essay "Tradition and the Individual Talent," emphasizing that the true poet expresses not a personality, but a medium that combines a variety of experiences in a special way. His "objective correlative," a striking example of disinterestedness, was a major addition to the critical vocabulary of the time. And the American New Critics of the 1930s and 1940s — Ranson, Brooks, Tate, Warren, and others — are a still later development with their emphasis on the poem itself (rather than on the author) and on a close reading and analysis of the workings of its language and imagery. (*See also* German Idealism, Influence of.)

John L. Mahoney

Works Consulted

Albrecht, William. *Hazlitt and the Creative Imagination*. Lawrence: U of Kansas P, 1965.

Bate, Walter Jackson. *Criticism: The Major Texts*. New York: Harcourt, 1970.

Mahoney, John L. *The Logic of Passion: The Literary Criticism of William Hazlitt*. New York: Fordham UP, 1981.

Park, Roy. *Hazlitt and the Spirit of the Age: Abstraction and Critical Theory*. Oxford: Clarendon, 1971.

Schneider, Elizabeth. *The Aesthetics of William Hazlitt*. New York: Octagon, 1969.

Wellek, René. *A History of Modern Criticism, 1750–1950*. 6 vols. New Haven: Yale UP, 1955–1986. Vols. 1, 2.

Domestic Architecture

Residential building was significantly transformed between 1780 and 1832. Housing styles and locations shifted dramatically for most social classes. These changes were particularly striking for the rapidly expanding and often affluent middle classes and the numerous displaced rural workers. Architectural books, official documents, and diaries from the period provide particularly valuable evidence of social, political, economic, and aesthetic transformations.

Many upper- and middle-class urban dwellers lived in what later came to be called the "Georgian" terraced house, the most common housing type in this period, often built on speculation. The number of attached houses in a unit varied, as did the shape of the unit that contained them: a row, a crescent, even a circle. Typically three or four stories with a basement, town houses varied in size. A large London house in fashionable Belgravia might have 20 rooms, excluding smaller rooms for servants. Large terraces in Brighton and the near western suburbs of London might have 15 rooms. All of these structures relegated the wine and coal cellars, kitchen, pantry, and housekeeper's and servants'

rooms to the basement and the servants' sleeping quarters to the garret, virtually invisible from the street. By the end of this period, the cook might have a gas stove. The family enjoyed the more important public rooms—parlor or drawing room, dining room, library, and breakfast room—on the ground level. The dining room, as large as 26 feet by 17 feet, was particularly important for entertaining, which indicated a family's social status. The private rooms—lady's drawing room, dressing rooms, and family sleeping chambers—were on the next levels. Most town houses included water closets by the end of the 18th century.

More novel and prestigious were detached suburban dwellings, including the popular villa or ornamented cottage, for the expanding, affluent middle classes. Increased wealth and improved transportation systems enabled industrialists and professionals like attorneys and physicians to find domestic retreat in picturesque settings on the outskirts of the city after daily commercial activities. An increased separation of women's and men's spheres accompanied this change, since women no longer assisted men in their places of business.

In 1833, John Loudon described the villa as the quintessence of English residential architecture in his popular *Encyclopedia of Cottage, Farm, and Villa Architecture*. Loudon included a design for a grand two-story villa with seven large principal rooms, service areas, and servants' quarters on the ground floor. Styles varied, although Old English, Italian, and Gothic were particularly popular. Ideally, villas and the slightly smaller ornamented cottages were situated in beautifully landscaped terrain that afforded fine views.

In country mansions, more prestigious than the villa, the upper and upper-middle classes reacted against the rigid symmetry of classical mansions by building asymmetrical structures in picturesque settings. Many houses, including Luscombe Castle, Devon, designed by Nash, were built in the Gothic style. Public living rooms were moved from the first floor to the ground floor so the residence opened into Nature. The vast public rooms of the sprawling Ashridge Park included a drawing room, dining room, conservatory, and library. Country houses were set up for extensive, informal house parties of several days or weeks rather than formal balls, as in the previous generation. Dozens of ornamented cottages were being built at seaside resorts as well as in the traditional country location of English aristocracy and gentry.

Elaborate entertaining extended to tenants, laborers, and local residents. Hundreds of locals attended lavish banquets sponsored by upper-class landlords who sought, perhaps, to recreate the stability of feudal relationships and discourage peasant unrest that had exploded into revolution in France.

Increasingly, agricultural and industrial changes resulted in the relocation and rehousing of workers and laborers. Many workers were victims of the Enclosure Acts and the shift of spinning and weaving from the cottage to factories. Numerous publications of the period urged combining philanthropy and sound business sense through land reform and rebuilding of workers' lodgings. Industrial villages grew up around water-powered rural spinning mills, including a 1795 project by Lancaster cotton manufacturers to build cheap brick houses in long rows to attract workers to that rural area. Reformers Owen and William Allen proposed communitarian villages with central buildings for cooking and infant care. Most rural workers, however, lived in small, thatched-roofed cottages with dirt floors and poor outdoor sanitation that had been in existence for decades or longer. Laborers who moved to cities like Manchester or London often lived in decayed and subdivided houses once owned by commercial and professional classes in the centers or in small, cramped terraces just outside the centers. Upwardly mobile skilled or semiskilled workers moved from lodgings of one or two rooms to quarters of three or four. By 1832, the problems of overcrowding, disease, poor sanitation, poverty, and vice caused reformers to propose numerous plans to reclaim and improve the cities, including suggestions to build low-rise urban cottages. Multistoried tenement blocks, however, proved more economical. Whether discussing rural or urban poor, reformers thought to improve manners, morality, and productivity along with housing.

Clearly, as this period progressed, an increased separation between classes, as well as between work and home, accompanied the move of the middle classes from cities to the suburbs. Because of their improved earning power, advances in transportation, and improved technology for domestic comforts, the middle classes were able to achieve more spacious housing with modern conveniences in a country setting. The challenge of providing adequate housing and sanitation for the lower-class urban dwellers had just begun. (*See also* Architecture.)

Carol Shiner Wilson

Works Consulted

Archer, John. *The Literature of British Domestic Architecture, 1715–1842.* Cambridge: MIT P, 1985.

Barley, Maurice. *Houses and History.* Boston: Faber, 1986.

Burnett, John. *A Social History of Housing, 1815–1970.* Newton Abbot: David, 1978.

Gauldie, Enid. *Cruel Habitations: A History of Working-Class Housing, 1780–1918.* London: Allen, 1974.

Girouard, Mark. *Life in the English Country House: A Social and Architectural History.* New Haven: Yale UP, 1978.

Quiney, Anthony. *House and Home: A History of the Small English House.* London: British Broadcasting, 1986.

Simpson, M.A., and T.H. Lloyd, eds. *Middle-class Housing in Britain.* Newton Abbot: David, 1977.

d'Orsay, Count Alfred

(1801–52)

The son of one of Napoleon's generals, Alfred, Count d'Orsay, was born in Paris, but his family took him to London in 1815. In 1821, d'Orsay formally and brilliantly entered English society. He was almost immediately accepted as a central figure in the world of fashion and as a dandy without peer. During this period, he was taken up by Lord and Lady Blessington, one of the leading couples in Regency society, and for the rest of his life he was closely associated with the circle of Lady Blessington.

In 1822, d'Orsay accompanied the Blessingtons to Italy where, in 1823, they encountered Byron in Genoa. Out of this meeting came Lady Blessington's *Conversations of Lord Byron* and d'Orsay's remarkable sketch of the poet. For his part, Byron was taken with d'Orsay's physical beauty and his manners. Further, Byron read d'Orsay's journal and was much impressed by the young dandy's understanding of English society.

In 1829, d'Orsay returned to England with Lady Blessington and over the next two decades, he became a legendary figure in London society. As a dandy and arbiter of fashionable elegance, he was Beau Brummell's only real successor. Despite d'Orsay's seemingly frivolous and somewhat scandalous career, he was a man of genuine talent. He and Lady Blessington eventually became the center of early Victorian literary society. He drew admiring responses from Thackeray, Dickens, Carlyle, and Tennyson. Disraeli and Bulwer-Lytton both created fictional characters based on him.

In 1849, d'Orsay's extravagant life caught up with him, and he fled from England to France to avoid his creditors. In 1852, Napoleon III appointed him Director of Fine Arts for the Second Empire, but within a few months he was dead at age 51. He was buried by the side of Lady Blessington.

Phillip B. Anderson

Works Consulted

Connely, Willard. *Count D'Orsay: The Dandy of Dandies.* London: Cassell, 1952.

Marchand, Leslie. *Byron: A Biography.* 3 vols. New York: Knopf, 1957.

Moers, Ellen. *The Dandy: Brummell to Beerbohm.* London: Secker, 1960.

Sadleir, Michael. *Blessington-d'Orsay: A Masquerade.* London: Constable, 1947.

Economic Conditions

The late 18th and early 19th centuries were a period of economic upheaval for England. Industry's rapid transformation from predominantly domestic manufacturing to a factory system, coupled with wartime scarcities and difficulties in international trade, presented hitherto unimagined economic problems.

Since the Middle Ages, England's consumer goods were largely produced by individual tradespeople working in their homes. Each community had its weavers and shoemakers, who provided life's necessities to their neighbors. The application of mid- to late-18th-century advances in science and technology (such as the steam engine) to manufacturing, however, quickly rendered such cottage industries obsolete. Mechanization and division of labor in large factories greatly increased and cheapened production. In the cotton textile industry, for example, inventions like the spinning jenny and the power loom automated what had previously been laborious by-hand processes, in turn making English cloths the cheapest in the world—despite the added cost of having to import all the raw cotton.

Though this "Industrial Revolution" drastically altered the nation's demographics and contributed to an unprecedented increase in population (from 6.5 million in 1750 to over 9 million in 1801), life for the new industrial wage-earner was not much better than it had been for his predecessor, the agricultural laborer. The concentration of capital in the hands of factory owners produced a steady inflation in prices that nullified the buying power of higher wages. In addition, vastly increased production of goods made the national economy more market sensitive, introducing new industrial costs (e.g., advertising), the development of a distribution infrastructure, and the search for new markets. These factors tended to destabilize the economy, replacing what had been comparatively steady economic expansion that matched slow population increase with periods of "boom and bust." With the industries more interdependent than ever before, disruptions in any one sector often resulted in a nationwide economic downturn. (*See also* Industrial Revolution.)

The era's greatest economic disruption was the war with France, which occurred between 1793 and 1815. Hostilities brought not only the immediate cessation of trade with France, but also French interference with the overseas commerce on which the highly productive English economy increasingly relied. France's 1793 declaration that any foreign nationals living in any French possession would be arrested and have their property confiscated was countered by an English blockage of many of the largest French ports. France responded with a series of increasingly stern measures prohibiting the import of English goods, culminating in Napoleon's 1806 declaration of a complete blockade of the British Isles. England countered this threat by forcing all neutral trade with France to pass first through an English port, where heavy duties were levied. Duty-free English goods were then smuggled into French-controlled continental markets, displacing other imports. Though this measure accomplished the English purpose of securing for itself continental markets, it especially angered the United States; these economic tensions eventually erupted into the War of 1812. (*See also* Napoleonic Wars.)

The war also disrupted England's domestic economy. Hoarding and speculative timidity precipitated banking failures and financial panics in the 1790s, ultimately resulting in the Bank of England suspending cash payments for its notes in February 1797. While the mining and weapons industries experienced a wartime boom, the textile industry, cut off from many overseas markets, slumped; and when a series of bad harvest spurred rising food prices, workers vented their frustration in sporadic outbursts of machine-breaking. The worst of these riots occurred in 1811 to 1812, when after nearly two years of rising foods prices the Luddites destroyed machinery and burned textile factories in the midlands and north of England. Though the Luddites were harshly suppressed, their

activities brought to the attention of the government the special problems faced by the industrial laborer, particularly after 1815, when peace plunged the nation into yet another severe depression. (*See also* Luddites.)

Though pauperism in England had risen steadily throughout the war, massive unemployment of industrial workers in the immediate postwar period burdened the nation's outmoded system of poverty relief almost to the breaking point. Existing welfare laws were unable to cope with the exploding population of the periodically unemployed. Most efforts to remedy these new problems did not come until the Victorian age. Both the Romantic and Victorian eras, however, found that while an industrial economy presented unprecedented opportunities for increasing national wealth, it also created the urgent social problem of how the state should be organized to provide life's necessities to an increasingly specialized and therefore market-reliant workforce.

Matthew T. Schneider

Works Consulted

Caddick, David W. *The Outline of British Trade*. London: Harrap, 1924.

Henderson, W.O. *Industrial Britain During the Regency. 1814–18*. New York: Kelley, 1968.

Levi, Leone. *History of British Commerce and of the Economic Progress of the British Nation*. London: Murray, 1880.

Redford, Arthur. *The Economic History of England, 1760–1860*. London: Longmans, 1960.

Edgeworth, Maria
(1767–1849)

During the first two decades of the 19th century, Maria Edgeworth was one of the most acclaimed authors writing in English. Well-known for her children's stories and educational works, Edgeworth became a successful novelist with the publication of *Castle Rackrent* (1800). This work, now recognized as the first Anglo-Irish novel, inspired Scott to write about Scotland as Edgeworth had written about Ireland. Like her contemporary Austen, Edgeworth is often called anti-Romantic, and her early reviewers noted the realism in her novels, particularly her accurate reporting of Irish speech and customs. After *Castle Rackrent*, Edgeworth wrote and published 12 other novels and tales, earning unprecedented sums for her work.

Born at Black Bourton, Oxfordshire, in 1767, Edgeworth was the third child and first daughter of Anna Maria Elers and Richard Lovell Edgeworth. Her mother died in 1773, and Edgeworth also lost two stepmothers, Honora Sneyd (d. 1780) and Elizabeth Sneyd (d. 1797), before Richard Edgeworth married his fourth and last wife, Frances Anne Beaufort, in 1798. These four marriages produced 21 additional children, and Edgeworth, along with her father and stepmothers, was actively engaged in educating most of them. Her children's stories found their first audience here, an early collection appearing in 1796 as *The Parent's Assistant*, and she co-authored with her father *Practical Education* (1798), a treatise on education which began as observations on the learning processes of the Edgeworth children.

During her childhood, Edgeworth spent a number of years at girls' schools in England, but in 1782 she moved permanently with her family to Ireland to an estate her father had inherited in county Longford. This estate had been in the Edgeworth family for several generations; it was granted to Francis Edgeworth in 1619 as part of James I's decision to locate Protestants of English descent in Ireland, on land confiscated from Irish Catholics. The Edgeworths were thus members of the colonizing Anglo-Irish class, but unlike many landowning Protestants in Ireland, they were early supporters of Catholic Emancipation. This ambiguous political position exposed them to considerable danger during the Irish Rebellion of 1798 when they faced attacks by both Irish Catholic rebels and Protestant Orangemen.

Edgeworth composed *Castle Rackrent* during the period leading up to the Irish Rebellion. She adopted the voice of an Irish Catholic servant to tell her story at a time when, quite literally, Irish Catholic peasants were preparing for open revolt. The choice was a bold one: even though the narrator, Thady, presents himself in the novel as the loyal Rackrent steward, the tale he narrates is of the Rackrent family's ruin and the purchase of their landed estate by Thady's own son. *Castle Rackrent* could thus be read by anxious Anglo-Irish landowners as confirmation of their worst fears—the loss of their Irish property to the Irish Catholics. Edgeworth's family and friends feared the novel's implications in the face of an Irish Catholic rebellion and persuaded her to add a lengthy glossary to her novel just before it was published. By supplying an editorial voice in the glossary that acquiesced to stereotypes of the Irish as drunken, lazy, and irrational, Edgeworth disrupted Thady's tale of the rising fortunes of his son Jason and distanced herself from the radical implications of her narrative. However, she also included an advertisement in *Castle Rackrent*, preserved in later editions, as a disclaimer to the glossary that made clear that it had been added only at the insistence of others.

Edgeworth went on to write three more novels set in Ireland—*Ennui* (1809), *The Absentee* (1812), and *Ormond* (1817)—and in them she took up another theme begun in *Castle Rackrent*: the ruin of Irish tenants and Irish estates under absentee landlords. She was, along with her father, appalled by Protestant landowners residing in England who left the management of their Irish estates to oppressive middlemen. Responsible only for providing the highest sums for employers and themselves, middlemen engaged in rack-renting by subletting land to tenants at outrageous prices. Edgeworth urged Anglo-Irish landlords to follow the example of her fictional characters who, like Lord Colambre in *The Absentee*, learn that their responsibility as landowners requires them to reside in Ireland and manage their estates.

Edgeworth's personal context was unusual on two counts. First, she belonged to an Anglo-Irish family that resided and invested its energy in its Irish estate rather than the more usual practice of draining the estate of rents. Second, her status within her family was uncommon for the time: as a young woman she assisted her father in managing the estate and became thoroughly acquainted with the nature of the improvements he sought to make as well as the Irish Catholic tenantry. These experiences, along with her extensive reading in Irish history and politics, gave her a broad basis for interpreting and recording Irish life. Besides her Irish novels, Edgeworth also wrote a study of Irish humor, *Essay on Irish Bulls* (1802), in which she corrected the attitudes of English readers prone to ridicule the Irish, especially Irish speech. Arguing that there is nothing particularly Irish about verbal blunders, Edgeworth in this work maintains that those who amuse themselves at the expense of the Irish are vulgar and bad-mannered themselves.

The relationship between Edgeworth and her father has been much debated. A progressive intellectual, inventor, and member of the famous Lunar Society, Richard Edgeworth read and contributed to much

of his daughter's work. Although some have faulted him for interfering with her writing projects, Maria valued their literary partnership and invited collaboration from other members of her family as well. Moreover, no evidence suggests that she slavishly submitted to his intellectual and literary will. Rather, by providing her with intellectual training and support for her literary talents in a period when few women, even in England, had access to education, Richard Edgeworth provided his daughter with an environment crucial to her development as a writer and an intellectual. She finished and published her father's *Memoirs* after his death in 1817.

Edgeworth experienced the prejudice against female authors early in her writing career. In 1782, shortly after her arrival in Ireland, she began a translation of Mme. de Genlis's *Adèle et Théodore*. When the first volume of *Adelaide and Theodore* was sent to the printer in London, Edgeworth learned that a rival volume had appeared; though she finished her translation, the novel was never published. Rejoicing in the failure of this effort, a close family friend, Thomas Day, took the opportunity to express his strong disapproval of women writers to Richard Edgeworth and to urge him against allowing his daughter to continue writing for a public audience. A response to this criticism, Edgeworth's first published work, *Letters for Literary Ladies* (1795), attempted to reconcile the literary activity of writing with the rules of propriety which constituted a lady. In this conduct book for women, Edgeworth argues for the importance of female education and maintains, as Wollstonecraft had done before her, that improving the status of women would ultimately improve the domestic realm for men. (*See also* Education.)

Besides her Irish novels, Edgeworth published English society novels. The first,

Belinda (1801), is a female *Bildungsroman* and probably influenced Austen's *Northanger Abbey* and *Sense and Sensibility*. This novel drew fire from critics of the day who disliked Edgeworth's rational heroine: when Belinda finds her unspoken affection for an English aristocrat apparently unreturned, she sets about redirecting her feelings toward a man who seems a more reasonable choice. However, Belinda's second attachment, to the West Indian Creole, Mr. Vincent, did not meet with her critics' approval. Edgeworth was persuaded to revise, and in the 1810 edition of *Belinda* the romantic relationships between English women and West Indian men were effectively censored. Edgeworth's other English society novels include *Leonora* (1806), an epistolary novel which some say is based on Edgeworth's only serious romance; *Patronage* (1813), Edgeworth's longest and least popular novel; and *Helen* (1834).

In the years after her father's death, Edgeworth again turned to writing children's stories. Though her brother Lovell inherited the Edgeworth estate, he encumbered it with debt, and Edgeworth took over the family finances. After weathering this financial crisis, she continued as agent of Edgeworthtown until she was 71. Although she remained a supporter of Catholic Emancipation, with O'Connell's campaigns and the country again in turmoil, she no longer felt able to speak for or about the Irish in fiction. During the Irish famine of 1846, she worked, at the age of 80, to distribute food to the poor.

Later in the 19th century, Edgeworth's children's stories continued to be read after her adult fiction was forgotten. Today, however, thanks to the efforts of feminist scholars, many of her novels are again in print. (*See also* Children's Literature.)

Kathryn Kirkpatrick

Works Consulted

Butler, Marilyn. *Maria Edgeworth: A Literary Biography*. Oxford: Clarendon, 1972.

Canny, Nicholas. *Kingdom and Colony: Ireland in the Atlantic World, 1560–1800*. Baltimore: Johns Hopkins UP, 1988.

Deane, Seamus. *A Short History of Irish Literature*. London: Hutchinson, 1986.

Hurst, Michael. *Maria Edgeworth and the Public Scene*. London: Macmillan, 1969.

McCormack, W.J. *Ascendancy and Tradition in Anglo-Irish Literary History from 1789 to 1939*. Oxford: Clarendon, 1985.

Owens, Coilin. *Family Chronicles: Maria Edgeworth's Castle Rackrent*. Dublin: B&N Imports, 1987.

Edgeworth, Richard Lovell
(1744–1817)

An Anglo-Irish inventor and educational theorist, Richard Lovell Edgeworth was the father of the novelist Maria Edgeworth, with whom he collaborated on several works. Their most significant joint effort was *Practical Education* (1798), a collection of essays influenced strongly by Rousseau's *Émile*.

Edgeworth was born in County Longford into an English family resident in Ireland since 1583. Although he eventually became a notable educational reformer, his education had several false starts. As a schoolboy, he excelled more in sports than in scholarship, and his first university term (at Trinity College, Dublin) was wasted. After transferring in 1761 to Corpus College, Oxford, he became a more serious student, but his formal education ended two years later when he eloped to Scotland with Anna Maria Elers.

After a brief residence in Ireland, Edgeworth's continuing interest in science drew him back to England, where he worked with a brother of the painter Gainsborough and became acquainted with Darwin. After settling at Hare Hatch, he also met Thomas Day, the author of *Sandford and Merton*. Day shared Edgeworth's reverence for Rousseau and supported his interest in educational reform. Edgeworth proceeded to rear his eldest child, Richard, according to Rousseau's principles, and, on a trip to Paris in 1771, he presented the boy to Rousseau as an embodiment of the fictional Émile.

Seeing that this educational experiment was nonetheless not entirely successful, Edgeworth, with the help of his second wife Honora Sneyd and his daughter Maria, set out to refine Rousseau's theories. Edgeworth disapproved of learning by rote, favored rewards over punishment, suggested that many valuable lessons could be learned through play, and emphasized the need for toys that would stimulate productive activity. His comments about giving the student a strong motive to learn and about matching the task to a child's age and ability may seem commonplace today, but his writings on education have been called the most important since Locke.

After inheriting the family estates near Edgeworthstown, Edgeworth devoted much of his energies to scientific experiments. His schemes for reclaiming bogs and constructing better roads considerably improved conditions for his tenants. His interest in mechanics also led to experiments with telegraphing (possibly the first) and to the invention of sailing carriages, a one-wheeled chaise, a prize-winning machine for measuring land, and an improved turnip-cutter.

Edgeworth spent most of his later years in Ireland; between 1806 and 1811, he served on a board investigating Irish education. In addition to *Practical Education*, he published *Professional Education*, in 1808. Several of Maria's early stories for children were intended to illustrate the Edgeworth theories of education as set forth in these works, and of those stories *Harry and Lucy* was apparently written largely by Richard and Honora. Edgeworth continued to exert a strong influence on the writings of Maria until his death in 1817, an influence, according to some scholars, that was not always favorable.

Albert E. Wilhelm

Works Consulted

Clarke, Desmond. *The Ingenious Mr. Edgeworth*. London: Oldbourne, 1965.

Memoirs of Richard Lovell Edgeworth, Esq., Begun by Himself and Concluded by His Daughter, Maria Edgeworth. 2 vols. London: Hunter, 1820.

Paterson, Alice. *The Edgeworths: A Study of Later Eighteenth Century Education*. London: Clive, 1914.

Edinburgh Literary Gazette

The weekly *Edinburgh Literary Gazette* of 1829 to 1830 was one of the most ambitious and important literary periodicals of its time. (It is not to be confused with another journal of similar title, which flourished in 1823.) The *Gazette* has been unjustly neglected since 1830, possibly as a result of its policy of publishing all articles, reviews, stories, and poems anonymously.

The most frequent contributor was David Moir (known to readers of *Blackwood's Magazine* as the poet "Delta"). Moir later recalled, in his "Life of Dr. Macnish," how he and De Quincey became the two literary co-editors with the first issue of 16 May 1829.

All of Moir's and De Quincey's articles in the *Gazette* were anonymous. An important three-part essay, "Sketch of Professor Wilson (In a Letter to an American Gentleman)," is known to be De Quincey's, but was never published under his name until 1889, when its first part was included in De Quincey's *Collected Writings*. The

"Sketch" recalls De Quincey's long friendship with John Wilson, first in the Lake District (where both writers were associates of Wordsworth and the other Lake Poets) and then in Edinburgh (where Wilson edited *Blackwood's Magazine*). It contains revealing reminiscences about Wordsworth, Coleridge, Southey, and the Lake District in general. Some other articles in the *Gazette* also seem to be De Quincey's, but in most cases definite proof is lacking. De Quincey corresponded with David Blackie, who owned both the *Gazette* and the *Edinburgh Post* newspaper (for which De Quincey also wrote) until at least June 1830.

Two other contributors were Hood, De Quincey's London friend, and Moir's friend Galt. Hood contributed amusing weekly letters in his usual punning style, describing recent events in English literary and theatrical circles. The novelist Galt, living in North America in 1829, regularly sent news about his activities, travels, and writings. When Galt returned to London in 1830, he sent his supernatural tale "The Black Ferry" to the *Gazette*. It is one of the few stories by Galt to adopt a deliberately fantastical and Romantic style.

Another frequent contributor, and a friend of both De Quincey and Moir, was the London poet Allan Cunningham, who had been an acquaintance of Blake. This connection probably led the *Gazette* to publish in February 1830 an enthusiastic essay of Blake via a review of Cunningham's *Lives of the Most Eminent British Painters, Sculptors, and Architects*. The review (one of the very few favorable notices of Blake published outside England during the period) praises Blake's painting and poetry as "wildly impressive."

De Quincey and Moir directed the *Gazette* toward Romantic attitudes and emphasis. Each issue contained reviews and other notices of Romantic writers, such as Coleridge, Southey, Byron, Mary Shelley, and James Hogg, and the German theorist Friedrich Schlegel. Most issues also began with a general essay about one writer of the age, with the most attention being paid to Wordsworth and Scott. In one fairly typical leading article, a critic argued against Jeffrey and the *Edinburgh Review* in order to present the Romantic argument that "Poetry deals only with the shadowy, the vague, and the undefined; in other words, with those objects on which imagination may be exerted."

The Gazette helped, in a modest way, to spread Romantic concepts and theories across national boundaries. It made a point of following recent developments in English and continental literature and literary theories. A long review of Goethe's edition of *The Poetical Works of Alessandro Manzoni*, in the first issue of the *Gazette*, discussed Goethe's views on contemporary literature, and contrasted Goethe and Manzoni with Byron. A few of the other areas of sustained interest in the *Gazette* included Danish writing, Italian opera, recent scientific discoveries, drama, foreign literature of all kinds (including classical, Arabic, and American), contemporary painting, and sculpture.

The owner of the *Gazette* became bankrupt in July 1830, and his journal expired without notice. Shortly afterward, his sudden death from cholera prevented the fulfillment of his promise to provide an index identifying the author of each article, story, and poem. But during its 14 months of existence, the *Gazette* presented readers with a fertile mixture of English, Scottish, German, and American literature and literary theory. (*See also* Journalism, Publishing.)

David Groves

Works Consulted

The Collected Writings of Thomas De Quincey. Ed. David Masson. 14 vols. Edinburgh: Black, 1889–90.

Cunningham, Allan. *Lives of the Most Eminent British Painters, Sculptors, and Architects*, 6 vols. London: Murray, 1829–33.

The Edinburgh Literary Gazette; Devoted Exclusively to Literature, Criticism, Science, and the Arts. Edinburgh: Ritchie, 1829–30.

Groves, David, "John Galt, the *Edinburgh Literary Gazette*, and 'The Black Ferry.'" *Scotia; American-Canadian Journal of Scottish Studies 12* (1988): 44–54.

———. "Thomas De Quincey, the *Edinburgh Literary Gazette*, and 'The Affinity of Languages.'" *ELN 26* (1989): 55–69.

Moir, David M. "Life of Dr. Macnish," *The Modern Pythagorean; A Series of Tales, Essays and Sketches, by the Late Robert Macnish*. 2 vols. Edinburgh: Blackwood, 1838.

Tave, Stuart, ed. *New Essays by De Quincey; His Contributions to the Edinburgh Saturday Post and Edinburgh Evening Post 1827–1828*. Princeton: Princeton UP, 1966.

Edinburgh Review

(1802–1929)

Launched in 1802 as a quarterly periodical, the *Edinburgh Review* was established by Sidney Smith, Francis Jeffrey, Francis Horner, and Henry Brougham and published by Archibald Constable of Edinburgh and Thomas Longman of London. For the first number, Smith served as editor, but he was soon replaced by Jeffrey, who held the position until 1829 when he was succeeded by his son-in-law, Macvey Napier. The *Edinburgh* quickly became the review in which authors wished to be reviewed and for which most reviewers wished to write.

The *Edinburgh Review* established several precedents. It was not connected with booksellers, a major criticism of the older reviews. Rather than tout any single firm's list, the *Edinburgh*'s policy was to review only the most significant books; as a result, the Review promptly achieved intellectual authority. It was published quarterly rather than monthly, which allowed for a greater variety of selection. Another precedent was the anonymity of the contributors. Articles were unsigned; the *Edinburgh*'s was a collective voice with responsibility ultimately resting with the editor. This also offered some protection to those who did not wish it known that they were writing for a periodical. Since the editor and all contributors were paid at a high rate, there was no opportunity for class division among contributors.

Moreover, the *Edinburgh* was partisan in its politics; it was generally associated with Whiggism. However, it was not begun as a party organ. During the first decade of the century, Whiggism was not so much a party as a loose affiliation of groups competing for the favor of the monarch. The reviewers of the *Edinburgh* may be said to have created Whiggism as much as popularized it in that the review served as the forum in which the new ideology was defined. Moreover, the Whigs were never entirely secure from criticism by the *Edinburgh*. Its willingness to dissent from the party on paramount issues is evident in its promise that no consideration of party would influence its opinion in discussing the Catholic question. Its championship of Catholic emancipation and refusal to consider compromise opposed the position of Lord Grey and many Foxites, who called for royal veto power over the appointment of bishops as a condition for Irish Catholic claims.

The *Edinburgh* took what it considered the liberal, or reform, view on virtually every major public issue, including opposition to the sale of army commissions, flogging in the British Navy and Army, the Test and Corporation Acts, and the American war, as well as support for legal and prison reform, accommodation with Napoleon, and a European balance of power.

The *Edinburgh* is often considered Whiggish in literary criticism as well as politics. Yet despite its opposition to the Tory government and its own liberal politics, the *Edinburgh* was cautious and preferred a more gradual change in literature and the general cultural life. Jeffrey believed that the fundamental principles of literature were determined long ago and held contemporaries to those established forms and conventions. His rigidly classical literary taste led him to denigrate Wordsworth, Coleridge, and Southey as the "Lake School" (a term originated in the October 1807 number). Still he praised both Scott's poetry and *Waverley*, wrote with insight on Crabbe, realized the genius of Keats, and acclaimed *Childe Harold's Pilgrimage* despite being attacked in *English Bards and Scotch Reviewers* (1809), which was itself provoked by Brougham's criticism of *Hours of Idleness*. Moreover, under Jeffrey's editorship the Edinburgh became a forum for more discerning and profound critics and raised the quality of the profession.

From its inception, the *Edinburgh* was influential, providing significant and thoughtful commentary on the literature and life of the time. It provided a medium for established writers and served as an entry for such young writers as Macaulay, Carlyle, and Empson. Its successful formula inspired two notable competitors: the *Quarterly Review*, founded by Scott in 1809, and the *Westminster Review*, founded by James Mill and Bentham in 1824. (*See also* Journalism, Publishing.)

Martin P. McNamee

Works Consulted

Clive, John. *Scotch Reviewers: The Edinburgh Review, 1802–1815*. London: Faber, 1957.

Fontana, Biancamaria. *Rethinking the Politics of Commercial Society: The Edinburgh Review 1802–1832*. New York: Cambridge UP, 1985.

Morgan, Peter F. *Literary Critics and Reviewers in Early 19th-Century Britain*. London: Croom-Helm, 1983.

Shattock, Joanne. *Politics and Reviewers: The Edinburgh and The Quarterly*. New York: Leicester UP, 1989.

Education

Unlike Scotland, which had long provided nearly universal education through its parochial school system, and other European nations, England had no centralized educational system until well into the 19th century and did not enact major educational legislation until 1870. Nonetheless, education was one of the most vital and widely debated social issues in the early decades of the 19th century, which saw numerous and profound changes in educational theory, methods, and institutions. Many of the current notions concerning education (and the closely related phenomenon of childhood) were either popularized or formed during the Romantic period, in theoretical, literary, or polemical modes of discourse.

Theories on education in the Romantic era were broadly shaped by Locke's *Some Thoughts Concerning Education* (1693) and Rousseau's *Emile* (1762). Locke, working from the associationist principles developed in his *Essay Concerning Human Understanding* (1690), compared the infant's mind to a "sheet of white paper," open to inscription by sense experience, with education thus empowered significantly to direct (if not determine) later development. *Some Thoughts* details a pedagogy designed to guide the child toward rational autonomy informed by carefully instilled principles of moral behavior.

In *Emile*, Rousseau developed an organic conception of the child's mind (likened to a "young plant") and a pedagogical and social agenda more thoroughly reformist than that of Locke. Rousseau follows Locke, however, in advocating a carefully supervised education within an environment (however "natural") scrupulously controlled by the tutor, leading toward rationality, independent judgment, and principled behavior. Both thinkers advise gaining the child's trust and affection over engaging in corporal discipline, and both caution against exposing children to such "irrational" influences as imaginative fiction and the example of servants.

The most important educational treatise of the Romantic period in Britain was *Practical Education* (1798) by Richard Edgeworth and his daughter Maria. It drew on both Locke and (with reservations) Rousseau. The Edgeworths claimed to base their educational theory on "experimental" (empiricist) grounds: their observation of the growth and education of the children in their own household. In its associationist principles, emphasis on the child's active participation in the learning process, recommendation of an affectionate pedagogical style, and advocacy of useful over fashionable knowledge and skills, *Practical Education* shares much common ground with the educational thought of both Wordsworth and Coleridge. Yet Wordsworth's critique of modern education in Book V of *The Prelude* may well be directed against the Edgeworths, who (following Locke and Rousseau) caution against fairytales and other forms of imaginative literature and valorize reason and scientific knowledge. They prescribe an

environment and educative process so thoroughly controlled by the parent-teacher that little room is left for spontaneous discovery, the unmotivated appreciation of nature, the boisterous games and intensely joyful (or fearful) bodily experiences described to such effect in the early books of *The Prelude*, or those moments (greatly valued by Wordsworth and Coleridge) when the child forgets himself.

Although Locke, Rousseau, and the Edgeworths recommend a domestic education guided by parent or tutor, schools proliferated during the Romantic period, varying markedly in their aims and methods. A parliamentary survey in 1819 counted (roughly) 4,000 endowed or "public" schools (including 700 traditional grammar schools); 14,000 unendowed, or "private venture," schools; and 5,000 Sunday schools; together, these schools probably taught half of England's children. Many children (especially those of the lower classes) attended school only for a year or two; on the other hand, much basic instruction (at all social levels) took place at home.

While some grammar schools (i.e., endowed schools designed to teach Latin and Greek, many dating from the 16th century) languished during the period, others (e.g., Wordsworth's Hawkeshead) thrived and were modernized by adding subjects like mathematics and science to their curricula. The select great public schools (e.g., Eton and Harrow) increasingly lost sight of their initially charitable mission and became elitist institutions; and the late 1820s saw the beginnings of the modern public school in Thomas Arnold's Rugby.

Endowed schools also included the charity schools, which were designed to provide elementary instruction to poor children. Many, however, had taken on the character of work schools ("schools of industry") by the end of the 18th century. Both the charity schools and Sunday Schools (also designed for poor children) stressed obedience, acceptance of the social order, and "habits of industry," with the Bible and catechism at the heart of their curriculum. As the 19th century progressed, however, some Sunday Schools became community-based, working-class institutions.

The "private venture" schools included everything from dame schools, which took children off their parents' hands and (often) provided elementary literacy for a few pennies a week, to the great Dissenting academies, which educated middle- and upper-class Dissenters whom the Test Acts kept from Oxford and Cambridge; the best academies, such as Warrington (where Priestley taught) provided courses in the physical and theoretical sciences far in advance of anything taught in the two universities, both in decline throughout this period. Other private academies specialized in preparation for commercial and professional life; some were abysmal, proto-Dickensian prisons; others (like Keats's Enfield), quite good. Many led the way in providing training in the vernacular and in subjects like history and modern languages. Between 1819 and 1833 the number of children attending unendowed schools more than doubled, from 450,000 to over a million.

English education was remarkably decentralized and unregulated during this period. However, the beginnings of systematization can be seen in the Society for Promoting Christian Knowledge's network of charity schools, the Sunday Schools run by various denominational (or interdenominational) groups, and the rival "monitorial" or "mutual" systems designed by Bell and Lancaster to provide mechanistic instruction to poor children at low cost.

Lancaster's efforts, along with the Scottish system of parish schools, helped inspire Samuel Whitbread's parochial schools bill in 1807, which failed after heated debate in Parliament. Brougham's similar education bill failed in 1820, as had Pitt's earlier proposal (1796) to legislate a system of work schools throughout England.

Many called for increased educational provisions during this period, from a wide variety of motives. Radicals, such as Godwin, saw education as the key to reforming society and easing class distinctions, but feared the potential for social domination in a national schools system. Others, like Malthus, saw nationalized education as a way to impart orderly habits and middle-class values to a newly mobile (and potentially rebellious) working class. Some conservatives opposed altogether schools for the lower orders, viewing them as hotbeds of radicalism and freethinking; others supported them as a means for imparting lessons in social complacency and Christian submission along with elementary reading skills.

Debates on women's education were similarly widespread and equally lively. Most girls' schools at this time offered little in the way of a sound education, concentrating instead on decorum and accomplishments (e.g., needlework, dancing, and music), although decent instruction in English, French, and Italian and simple accounting were sometimes available. Early feminists (e.g., Catherine Macaulay and Wollstonecraft) saw educational reform as central to redressing social inequality between men and women; both called for educating boys and girls together without distinction. Darwin, Maria Edgeworth, and other liberals felt instead that female education, particularly in the sciences, could be vastly improved without upsetting the social order: educated women would better perceive the justice of the existing scheme of things. Conservatives like More and West agreed that female education should be reformed, but as a means of buttressing rather than challenging the status quo; improved education would make women more content within their separate (private or domestic) sphere and render them better able to exert an indirect moral influence on society.

The growing importance of education and the spread of educational opportunities were reflected in new kinds of reading material. Graded readers, beginning with easy words of one or two syllables, were for the first time produced by children's writers like Eleanor Fenn and Trimmer in the 1780s. Similar primers—like John Parson's *First Book for English Schools* and Trimmer's *Charity School Spelling Book*— were published for use in schools. Maria Edgeworth wrote an elaborate and influential series of children's books based on her and her father's educational theory, designed to impart rational habits of thought, moral principles of behavior, and practical knowledge. A new kind of self-help literature, designed (like the Mechanics' Institutes) to facilitate the self-education of skilled laborers, was pioneered by the Society for the Diffusion of Useful Knowledge. Women writers, including Wollstonecraft, Edgeworth, More, and West, made the issue of female education central to the domestic novel; Austen's novels constitute a particularly subtle response to this tradition. Male novels of development, such as Holcroft's *Hugh Trevor* and Scott's *Waverley*, began to proliferate as well, and the age's two most important epic-length poems— Wordsworth's *Prelude* and Byron's *Don Juan*—are concerned with depicting their hero's education in the broadest sense.

Blake satirized the increasingly disciplinary charity schools in his *Holy Thursday* poems and contended, as did Cobbett, that he was fortunate in not having had a regular education. The careers of Blake, Burns, and Clare all attest to the importance of self-education in the Romantic period and the related cult of the "uneducated" poet. Wordsworth attacked rationalist education schemes in the "Immortality" ode as well as in *The Prelude* and, with Coleridge and Southey, was an active supporter of Bell's version of the monitorial system. Although neither Wordsworth nor Coleridge wrote systematically on education, their scattered remarks became quite influential for later 19th century educational thought. Campbell was instrumental in the founding of the London University (open to Dissenters) in the late 1820s. By the end of the Romantic period, English literature had emerged as an academic subject, pioneered in private venture schools in England and English-language schools in India and made an integral part of the London University curriculum. (*See also* Bell, Andrew; Sunday School Movement.)

Alan Richardson

Works Consulted

Chandler, James K. *Wordsworth's Second Nature: A Study of the Poetry and Politics*. Chicago: U of Chicago P, 1984.

Ferguson, Frances. "Reading Morals: Locke and Rousseau on Education and Inequality." *Representations* 6 (1984): 66–84.

Foucault, Michel. *Discipline and Punish: The Birth of the Prison*. Translated from French by Alan Sheridan. New York: Vintage Books, 1979.

Laqueur, Thomas Walter. *Religion and Respectability: Sunday Schools and Working Class Culture 1780–1850*. New Haven: Yale UP, 1976.

Lawson, John and Harold Silver. *A Social History of Education in England*. New York: Barnes, 1973.

Pinchbeck, Ivy and Margaret Hewitt. *Children in English Society.* 2 vols. London: Routledge, 1969–73.

Richardson, Alan. "The Politics of Childhood: Wordsworth, Blake, and Catechistic Method." *ELH* 56 (1989): 853–68.

Simon, Brian. *Studies in the History of Education 1780–1870.* London: Lawrence, 1960.

Stone, Lawrence. *The Family, Sex and Marriage in England 1500–1800.* London: Weidenfeld, 1977.

Viswanathan, Guari. *Masks of Conquest: Literary Study and British Rule in India.* New York: Columbia UP, 1989.

Egotistical, or Wordsworthian, Sublime

In a letter to Richard Woodhouse (1818), Keats reveals to his friend the culmination of his thoughts on the nature of the "poetic character." In his discussion, he rejects the "wordsworthian or egotistical sublime." In other letters and conversations about Wordsworth's works, Keats had expressed appreciation for the sublime that Wordsworth found in nature, ordinary people, vast landscapes, the mysterious, the transcendent, the infinite. Keats particularly praises Wordsworth for his insight into the human heart.

In a letter to Reynolds (1818), he emphasizes the "fine imaginative or domestic passages" in Wordsworth's work. But in the same letter he reacts against the egotist (Wordsworth) who would bully a reader into agreeing with a certain philosophy and writes that he "will have no more of Wordsworth." He further suggests in this letter that the egotist "brood[s] and peacock[s] over [his speculation] till he makes a false coinage and deceives himself." Later in the letter he illustrates his contention by writing that when Wordsworth sees an old man on an evening walk and talks to him about little or nothing, he feels compelled to "stamp it down

in black and white" and make the encounter "henceforth sacred."

In both letters Keats is reacting to what he conceives as Wordsworth's self-absorption. In Keats's thinking, Wordsworth saw objects not as an opportunity to enter the beauty and sublimity of the object but as an excuse to explore his own thoughts. In other words, Keats believed Wordsworth had become solipsistic.

Keats includes Milton in his rejection of Wordsworth and his approach to experience. Keats's desire was to enter so completely into the objects and persons that his own identity, at least in the role of a poet, was obliterated. He sought to go beyond Wordsworth and Milton in understanding the nature of good and evil and the extent that suffering has on the development of the human soul. To gain a sense of identity, Keats believed that "the heart must feel and suffer in a thousand and diverse ways" and "thus does God make individual beings, souls, Identical Souls of the spark of his own essense" (1819). Keats writes in this letter to George and Georgiana Keats that "a man's life of any worth is a continual allegory."

While acknowledging Wordsworth as a "great poet," Keats also recognized the egotism in the personality of the poet. In an earlier letter to his brothers, George and Thomas Keats, he commented that Wordsworth had "left a bad impression" during his visit to London with his personal "egotism, vanity, and bigotry" (1818). In rejecting the egotistical sublime, Keats was also rejecting Wordsworth's and Milton's style and choices of form. Although the influence of Wordsworth and Milton is pervasive in Keats's writing, he was seeking in 1818 to find his own voice, to be his own self as a poet. His experiments in metrics, his condensation of imagery (particularly his use of synaesthesia), his adaptation of the sonnet to his own ode form, his mastery of assonance, all culminate in the individual style of his great odes in May 1819. (*See also* Synaesthesia.)

Keats is contrasting the egotistical poet with the ideal poet who so loses himself in the object he contemplates that he subsumes his personality to the point that he has no identity. In an 1817 letter to George and Thomas Keats, Keats calls this quality in a poet "Negative Capability." A poet who possesses negative capability, he writes, is "capable of being in uncertainties, mysteries, doubts, without any irritable reaching after fact & reason." Perhaps Hazlitt, who had a tremendous influence on Keats during this crucial year, best summarizes the concept of the wordsworthian, or egotistical, sublime in his attack on the Lake Poet whom Wordsworth symbolized: This poet "does not even like to share his reputation with his subject; he would have all proceed from his own power and originality of mind. . . . He tolerates only that which he creates; . . . He sees nothing but himself and the universe."

Martha Watson Bargo

Works Consulted

Abrams, M.H. *Natural Supernaturalism: Tradition and Revolution in Romantic Literature.* New York: Norton, 1971.

———. *The Mirror and the Lamp: Romantic Theory and the Critical Tradition.* New York: Oxford UP, 1953.

Bate, Walter Jackson. *John Keats.* Cambridge, MS: Belknap, 1963.

Ende, Stuart A. *Keats and the Sublime.* New Haven: Yale UP, 1976.

Stillinger, Jack. "Wordsworth and Keats." *The Age of William Wordsworth: Critical Essays on the Romantic Tradition.* Eds. Kenneth R. Johnston and Gene W. Ruoff. New Brunswick: Rutgers UP, 1987: 173–95.

Wlecke, Albert O. *Wordsworth and the Sublime.* Berkeley: U of California P, 1973.

Egremont, Lord [George O'Brien Wyndham] *(1751–1837)*

Sir George O'Brien Wyndham, Third Earl of Egremont, was one of England's richest men, an important patron of the arts, and an agricultural innovator and experimenter; he acquired a reputation as an eccentric by going his own way on a relatively large scale and caring little when others disapproved. His huge estate, Petworth, was often crowded beyond the possibility of formality with guests of all kinds and classes; it housed one of the country's finest art collections (still largely intact), including works by Renaissance and Baroque masters and contemporary Englishmen, notably Barry, Blake, the Daniells, Flaxman, Fuseli, Gainsborough, Hoppner, Northcote, Romney, Turner, and many others.

Egremont succeeded to the peerage at age 12, but never showed substantial interest in national politics. After attending Westminster School, he toured Europe twice, mostly in the north. As a young man he was prominent in London society. One woman wrote in 1774, "He is a pretty man, has a vast fortune, and is very generous, and not addicted to the vices of the times." But projected society matches fell through; he kept mistresses and from the 1780s to 1803 lived with Elizabeth Ayliffe (or Iliffe), who bore him several illegitimate children and was known as Mrs. Wyndham as well as the Countess of Egremont. He married her in 1801, legitimizing their offspring but losing the title; they lived apart from 1803 until her death in 1822.

Egremont became interested in Turner very early in the painter's career, buying *Ships Bearing up for Anchorage* ("The Egremont Seapiece"), exhibited at the

Royal Academy at 1802, and many other works, mostly from Turner's London gallery. After 1820, Turner was regularly in residence at Petworth until the 1830s, recording its daily life in lively sketches, studying works in Egremont's collection, and executing commissions from him. Other artists visiting or taking refuge at Petworth included Haydon, Charles Leslie, Richard Collins, Constable, and the sculptors Edward Carew and Francis Chantrey, from most of whom Egremont also bought or commissioned works.

Egremont was perhaps the most important patron for both Turner and Carew, though his taste was rather conservative. Flaxman's *St. Michael Overcoming Satan* and *Pastoral Apollo* at Petworth are among the sculptor's most successful freestanding works. Blake's only important aristocratic commissions came from Petworth House, perhaps through Hayley: *A Vision of the Last Judgment* and a version of *Satan Calling up His Legions* were commissioned by the Countess, and Lord Egremont purchased *The Characters of Spenser's "Faerie Queen"* from Blake's widow.

Alexander S. Gourlay

Works Consulted

Butlin, Martin, Mollie Luther, and Ian Warrell. *Turner at Petworth: Painter and Patron*. London: Tate Gallery, 1989.

Dictionary of National Biography, s.v. "Wyndham, Sir George O'Brien."

Elective Affinity

The concept of elective affinity originated in 18th-century scientific theories explaining the attraction of particles of matter in the making of compounds. The term, probably first used by William Cullen in 1748, denoted the selectivity of chemical combination (e.g., the inability of a given substance to combine with more than a certain amount of another). Scientists believed that substances such as metals have specific and measurable attractions to other materials; when put in a solution together, some combine and others do not. Substances sharing a strong affinity bind together even if they were originally part of another compound. The word "elective" in this context means "determinative"; in Newtonian Enlightenment chemistry, elective affinity was seen as an absolute force, but around 1800 Claude-Louis Berthollet discovered the role of other physical factors, such as concentration, solubility, and precipitation, in the formation of compounds.

The Newtonian tradition sought to identify and measure short-term affinities between substances rather than examine the physical nature of the substances themselves. By contrast, British chemists Dalton, who attempted to identify atomic weights, and Davy, who attributed attraction between substances to their respective electrical properties, focused on the specific physical characteristics of matter. They elaborated on basic theories of affinity, but their work greatly surpassed in sophistication earlier deterministic explanations of chemical combination.

Eighteenth-century scientists explored chemical mechanisms as a way of arriving at a law of attraction common to all matter, whereas 19th-century efforts increasingly concentrated on the individual units of matter and the resultant structure of compounds. This latter approach to chemistry reflects a preference for organic models based on Romanticism's exaltation of individualism. The old notion of elective affinity nevertheless implied a unity of natural forces that appealed to Romantic writers, who sought to unite the human and scientific realms. Goethe, for example, employed the term as a metaphorical model for human relationships in his 1809 novel of adultery, *Elective Affinities*.

Sue Petitt Starke

Works Consulted

Bynum, W.F., E.J. Browne, and Roy Porter, eds. *Dictionary of the History of Science*. Princeton: Princeton UP, 1981.

Cunningham, Andrew, and Nicholas Jardine, eds. *Romanticism and the Sciences*. Cambridge: Cambridge UP, 1990.

McCann, H. Gilman. *Chemistry Transformed*. Norwood, NJ: Ablex, 1978.

Rocke, Alan J. *Chemical Atomism in the Nineteenth Century From Dalton to Cannizzaro*. Columbus: Ohio State UP, 1984.

Thackray, Arnold. *Atoms and Powers*. Cambridge: Harvard UP, 1970.

Elgin Marbles

The temple on the Acropolis known as the Parthenon was built in the third quarter of the fifth century B.C.E. when Pericles was leader in Athens. It was dedicated to the goddess Athena, but before it was completed, the Persians invaded Greece and burnt the temple. For a generation, the area lay desolate, but in the middle of the fifth century Pericles appointed architects and a sculptor to create a new temple and statue of Athena. The Parthenon was finished in 432 B.C.E. For the next nine centuries, it continued to be the temple of Athena. It then became a Christian Church for approximately a thousand years, from about 450 to 1458 (C.E.) until Athens was taken over by the Turks and the temple converted into an Islamic mosque. In 1674, the Marquis de Nointel, French Ambassador to Turkey, visited Athens, accompanied by a draughtsman, Jacques Carrey of Troyes, who made drawings of the architectural and sculptural remains. His drawings form an invaluable record, for in 1687 the Parthenon was once again destroyed by the Turks. From this time onward, the temple was a ruin. But for the intervention of Lord Elgin in 1800, it is probable that many of the sculptures would have perished or been damaged beyond recognition. (*See also* Sculpture.)

Thomas Bruce, Seventh Earl of Elgin, was born in 1766. Educated at Harrow and Westminster, he entered the diplomatic service in 1790. He served as envoy in Brussels, envoy extraordinary in Berlin, and, in 1799, ambassador in Constantinople. Elgin resolved that his term in Constantinople should be of service to the arts and proposed to the government that he make drawings and casts of the monuments of Athens at public expense. His proposal was denied, so he determined to carry out his project at his own cost. With the aid of his private secretary, William Richard Hamilton, Elgin secured the services of a distinguished Neapolitan topographical painter, Giovanni Battista Lusieri, as well as a Tartar painter, Feodor Ivanovitch, architects Vincenzo Balestra and Sebastian Ittar, and molders Bernardino Ledus and Vincenzo Rosati.

The artists reached Athens in July 1800. To enter the Acropolis, they were required to pay a fee of five guineas a day and were allowed to do no more than make drawings. Lusieri visited Constantinople in 1801 to report to Elgin and impress on him the necessity of a *firman*, or authority, from the Turkish government for their operations. Elgin secured the document and had it despatched to Athens, but it never reached its destination. In May 1801, Philip Hunt, embassy chaplain at Constantinople, came to the aid of Elgin and encouraged him not only to secure another *firman*, but to change his plans. Beyond the drawing, measuring, and molding of the sculptures undertaken, he recommended the sculptures be removed to preserve them for posterity. Elgin was able to negotiate successfully with the authorities, and from this point on, his men worked in the Acropolis without hindrance. Their work lasted from July 1801, until 1804.

Elgin himself visited Greece for the first time between 1 April and 25 June 1802. In 1803, he left Constantinople at the conclusion of his embassy, leaving Lusieri behind to continue collecting the sculptures and packing them for shipment. Unfortunately, Elgin was in France when war was declared against England on 18 May 1803; he was arrested and remained in France as a prisoner of war until 1806.

As a result of the English declaration of war on Turkey in February 1807, it took nearly 12 years for the entire shipment of sculptures to reach England. When Elgin himself arrived back in England in 1806, he arranged to have the sculptures that had already arrived placed in a shed on the grounds of a house he had leased at the corner of Park Lane and Piccadilly. Beginning in the summer of 1807, permission was given to selected visitors, including the artists Flaxman, Wilkie, Haydon, Fuseli, West, and Lawrence, to view the marbles. All were deeply impressed by what they saw, especially Haydon, who declared: "I felt as if divine truth had blazed inwardly upon my mind, and I knew that they would at last rouse the art of Europe from its slumber of darkness."

The shed was never intended by Elgin as more than a temporary storage place for the marbles, but the difficulty of providing permanent accommodations out of his own resources prompted him to discuss the possibility of a sale with Joseph Planta, principal librarian of the British Museum, and the speaker of the House of Commons. Elgin offered his collection to the nation for £62,440, a sum comprising his actual expenses and 14 years' interest. No formal reply was made to Elgin's request,

but it was intimated that the government was willing to pay only £30,000. Elgin next approached the Duke of Devonshire to request another temporary storage place for the sculptures at Burlington House. His request was granted, and visitors continued to view the sculptures there. Among them was Ennio Visconti, the most celebrated archaeologist of the day. In 1815, Elgin learned that Burlington House had been sold. A decision on the future of the marbles was now urgent. Elgin once again opened negotiations with the British Museum, this time offering to allow a special committee to set a price on the sculptures. After a series of negotiations, an act of Parliament was passed to transfer ownership of the Elgin Marbles to the nation for £35,000.

The marbles were transferred from Burlington House to the British Museum in 1816, and a temporary gallery was constructed to receive them. In 1835, the entire collection of marbles was moved to a permanent gallery, the "Elgin Salon," where they remained until 1869. From 1869 to 1939, the Parthenon sculptures were exhibited in the Elgin Room. The museum's guiding principle was to present the sculptures of the Parthenon in as complete a form as possible. (*See also* Fragment.) Although this was a valuable arrangement for the archaeologist, it tended to confuse many visitors. In 1928, criticisms were expressed in a public report of the Royal Commission on National Museums and Galleries. The report elicited a generous offer from Lord Duveen to build a new gallery for the sculptures at his own expense. In 1930, John Russell Pope, an American architect, drew up plans for the new Duveen Gallery, which was completed in 1938. However, in expectation of immediate air-raids, the sculptures were moved to stronger parts of the museum. The

Duveen Gallery was severely damaged by the bombing in 1940, and the room was not completely restored until 1961. Since the 1962 opening exhibition, the Elgin Marbles have been housed in Duveen Gallery. (*See also* Antiquarianism, Classicism, Hellenism.)

Mary Susan Johnston

Works Consulted

Ashmole, Bernard. *Architect and Sculptor in Classical Greece*. London: Phaidon, 1972.

Boardman, John. "The Parthenon Frieze—Another View." *Festschrift für Frank Brommer*. Mainz/Rhein: von Zabern, 1977.

Brommer, Frank. *The Sculptures of the Parthenon*. London: Thames, 1979.

Carpenter, R. *The Architects of the Parthenon*. Harmondsworth: Penguin, 1970.

Cook, B.F. *The Elgin Marbles*. Cambridge: Harvard UP, 1984.

Gialoures, Nikolaos. *Classical Greece; The Elgin Marbles of the Parthenon*. Greenwich: New York Graphic Soc., 1960.

Robertson, Martin. *A History of Greek Art*. London: Cambridge UP, 1975.

Robertson, Martin, and Alison Frantz. *The Parthenon Frieze*. New York: Oxford UP, 1975.

St. Clair, William. *Lord Elgin and the Marbles*. New York: Oxford UP, 1983.

Traulos, Iōannēs. *Pictorial Dictionary of Classical Athens*. London: Thames, 1971.

Emotion Recollected in Tranquility

In the Preface to the second edition of the *Lyrical Ballads* (1800), Wordsworth declares that poetry is the "spontaneous overflow of powerful feelings," the phrase that most students quote as his definition of poetry. Yet it is the second part of his statement that provides a key to both his vision and the vision of Romanticism in general about the origin of the creative act of writing poetry. When Wordsworth writes that "poetry takes its origin from emotion recollected in tranquility," he acknowledges that although Nature in her awe and terror inspires the poet and elicits the powerful feelings that spontaneously overflow, it is the "contemplation" of the feelings that act as the creative forge to form the poem. (*See also* Literary Criticism and Literary Theory; Spontaneous Overflow of Powerful Feelings.)

The act of contemplating, however, is but the interim stage in this process. The emotion is contemplated "till, by a species of re-action, the tranquility gradually disappears." At that point, the feelings that so spontaneously overflowed become transmuted (by the contemplative action of the mind) to an emotion like the original emotion, or in Wordsworth's thinking, the emotion that the poetic mind knows after the period of tranquility is "kindred to that which was before the subject of contemplation." The transmuted form, then, is produced gradually and "does itself actually exist in the mind." It is at this point in the process, in this "mood," that "successful composition generally begins." The keynote at this stage is pleasure, and the mind will, in general, be in a state of enjoyment as the poet describes any passions.

The pleasurable state of the poet's mind produced by his tranquil recollection teaches the poet that the art created should, in turn, communicate to readers a similar pleasure, or even, an "overbalance of pleasure." And since powerful descriptions of the deeper passions touch upon painful feelings, these painful feelings need tempering. This is accomplished by the poet's "music of harmonious metrical language" and by the readers' previous association of pleasurable feelings with reading poetry.

The power of the poetic mind to record, assimilate, and transmute these deeper passions and their accompanying pain into pleasurable feelings is the power that draws the human mind and heart to read and contemplate a poem time and time again when a passage of prose may not bear even a rereading. Hence, the poet, by cultivating a contemplative habit of mind to meditate upon feelings, experiences, and images, opens the mind to moments of revelation, to epiphanies that present themselves in concrete images, and in that presentation invite the tranquil and contemplative mind to discern philosophical verities. The senses partly perceive and partly create. The beneficent powers of nature nurture the transcendental powers of the human mind, and as Wordsworth perceived a "Presence" in nature, he believed this consciousness or being or spirit disciplined the mind to transmute the powerful feelings into emotions that have the power to humanize the soul.

Nature "ministers" to the human heart by inspiring the spontaneous overflow of powerful feelings. The transcendental powers of the human mind allow the mind to recollect these feelings in tranquility. Thus, the spiritual affirmation, the gratitude and tenderness inspired and affirmed by poetry, serves as compensation for the loss of celestial light.

Paula P. Yow

Empiricism

The word "empiricism" derives from the Greek noun *empeiria*, meaning experience, and denotes a range of theories that share the basic premise that experience rather than reason is the ultimate source of knowledge. The theories differ according to what is meant by experience and the nature of knowledge. In broad terms, according to rationalism knowledge is predicated on certain primary axioms that exist independent of experience. By contrast, according to empiricism knowledge is based on fundamental elements that compose the structure of experience. The origins of empiricism stretch beyond the horizon of ancient philosophy. There are elements of it in Aristotle, and the Greek atomist Epicurus offers the earliest extant version of a radical empiricism, asserting that the senses are the ultimate source of knowledge. Perhaps the most important contributions came from the so-called British empiricists of the 17th and 18th centuries, developing the Baconean proposition that all science must start from careful observation.

The physician and philosopher Locke, an older contemporary of Newton, launched British empiricism. His *Essay Concerning Human Understanding* (1690), the first empirical science of the mind, became the primary text for philosophical instruction in British universities, especially Cambridge, until the start of the 20th century. In addition, through the enthusiastic advocacy of Voltaire and others, it became one of the philosophical cornerstones of the Enlightenment.

Locke's starting point was an attack on the theory of innate knowledge found in the doctrine of the Cambridge Platonists, and ultimately, Descartes. Adapting Aristotle's notion that the mind begins as a *tabula rasa* (a blank slate), Locke argued that ideas that furnish the mind are produced by experience rather than being innately present. He distinguished two types of experience: sensation, the mind's perception of the world, and reflection, the mind's perception of its own operations. These acts of perception generate ideas. For Locke, the idea is not an abstraction but a basic unit of perception that represents the object of experience. The idea of a snowball, for instance, is a complex cluster of simple ideas, such as shape, color, texture, temperature, and so forth that represent corresponding qualities in the object.

Locke defined a quality as an object's power to give rise to an idea. He identified two kinds: primary qualities, such as shape and extension, which persist from one observer to the next, and secondary qualities, such as color and taste, which vary from one observer to the next. In this way, he proposed to account for the subjectivity of individual experience (secondary qualities), while preserving the possibility of some objective experience (primary qualities).

Because the ideas that furnish the mind correspond to qualities, they are representations of the world rather than direct manifestations. One can have no knowledge of anything that lacks qualities or has qualities that lack the power to produce ideas. Thus Locke was cognizant of an unbridgeable gap between the world and what the mind is capable of knowing about it. Certain things may fall outside the realm of the knowable. Strictly speaking, then, knowledge about things is a probable opinion rather than an actuality.

While Locke did not deny the existence of a spiritual substance, his model of the mind favored a materialist metaphysics. George Berkeley, the Anglo-Irish cleric and philosopher, while accepting Locke's theory of perception, attacked the materialist elements. Specifically, he questioned the distinction between primary and secondary qualities, contending that both are contingent on the mind. That being the case, there is no reality independent of the mind. The world exists only insofar as it is perceived—*esse est percipi*.

Unlike Berkeley, the physician David Hartley wished to provide a material account of the mind and especially of moral sentiments. In his influential *Observations on Man* (1749), he accepts Locke's premise

that the mind is initially devoid of content to be filled by sensation. These ideas, he argues, are associated with sensations (see Associationism). Through the process of association, the complex mental life of human beings is built out of simple sensations. In this way, Hartley proposed to account for the genesis of moral and religious feelings.

David Hume is arguably the most profound of the British empiricists. In the *Treatise of Human Nature* (1739–40), Hume takes Lockean theory to its logical extreme. The implications of this are most clear in his discussion of the problems of causation and identity. According to Hume, knowledge of a causal connection between events is limited to the similarity and contiguity of the events. One cannot, however, show a causal connection between events from sense impressions. Psychologically, Hume contends, the association of the two events leads one to suppose that there is a necessary connection, but this association does not prove an actual connection. One's knowledge of causation is a matter of habit or custom, not logical certainty. Concomitantly, one's knowledge of the world, even with the physical sciences, is at best a probability or highly determined belief. It was to circumvent these problems that the German philosopher, Kant addressed his *Critique of Pure Reason* (1781). (*See also* German Idealism.)

In examining the identity of the self from one time to the next, Hume asks what impression gives rise to the idea of the self. Locke had equated personal identity with consciousness, the content of that consciousness being ideas. Since the Lockean idea was understood as a unit of perception that corresponds to a quality, there can be no simple fixed idea of self, since self is the awareness of ideas. Rather, what one calls the self, Hume concludes, is a constantly changing "bundle of sensations," with no permanent center of identity.

Hume's contribution to empiricism has largely shaped the subsequent debate in the 19th and 20th centuries. Philosophers have either acquiesced to the implications of Hume, especially in Anglo-American philosophical circles, exploring its limits in science, ethics, and language, or struggled to get around them, especially in continental philosophy from Kant onward.

Thomas L. Cooksey

Works Consulted

Aune, B. *Rationalism, Empiricism, and Pragmatism*. New York: Random, 1970.

Bennett, Jonathan. *Locke, Berkeley, Hume: Central Themes*. Oxford: Clarendon, 1971.

Copleston, Frederick Charles. *A History of Philosophy*. Vol. 5. Garden City: Image Books-Doubleday, 1962.

Feyerabend, Paul K. "Classical Empiricism." *The Methodological Heritage of Newton*. Eds. Robert E. Butts and John W. Davis. Toronto: U of Toronto P, 1970. 150–70.

Flew, Anthony. *David Hume: Philosopher of Moral Science*. New York: Blackwell, 1986.

Harris, Wendell V. *The Omnipresent Debate: Empiricism and Transcendentalism in Nineteenth-Century English Prose*. DeKalb: Northern Illinois UP, 1981.

Richetti, John J. *Philosophical Writing: Locke, Berkeley, Hume*. Cambridge: Harvard UP, 1983.

Yolton, John W. *Locke: An Introduction*. New York: Blackwell, 1985.

Epic

Eighteenth-century British critics increasingly rejected the rigorous criteria for epic established by French Neoclassicism, and in his 1755 *Dictionary*, Johnson defines epic simply as a narrative that often contains heroic action. The Romantic emphasis on the uniqueness of each poetic expression further blurred any serious genre distinction, and Romantic epic tends

to be simply a long poem, the style of narration and content of which are as individual as the writers themselves. The idea of the genre, however, held a special allure for many of the poets. Such compositions offered expansive opportunity for moral, social, and political critique. Long poems also presented a challenge: success in epic composition was often perceived by the Romantic poets as a crucial test of artistic merit. (*See also* Poetry.)

As Blake's ideas progressed, he developed an entire personal mythology and cosmology, and his writing moved away from the relatively concrete themes often addressed in his earlier poems. The works of Blake's later years are often lengthy, highly idiosyncratic rewritings of traditional religious texts. *The Marriage of Heaven and Hell* (1790), his first long poem, combines elements of shorter genres, such as the aphorism, with the more grandiose and allegorical style that dominate later mystical epics, such as *Vala, or The Four Zoas* (1804), *Milton* (1815), and *Jerusalem* (1820).

Wordsworth spent much of his life trying to write an epic he originally planned in the 1790s with the aid of Coleridge. The proposed work, *The Recluse*, was to be the great philosophical poem of the age and to have three sections. The epic would concern the ideas of a poet living in rural seclusion, but the exact subjects to be treated were perpetually in flux. At Wordsworth's death, only two portions of the poem were complete.

The only portion of *The Recluse* published during the poet's lifetime was *The Excursion* (1814). It included a prospectus explaining *The Excursion*'s status as the second part of a three-part epic. *The Excursion* received hostile reviews from many prominent critics, although Keats was among its admirers. The other completed portion of *The Recluse*, *The Prelude*, was published posthumously in 1850. *The Prelude, or The Growth of a Poet's Mind* is a detailed, brilliant autobiography in verse, but in the poet's mind it was only an introduction to the three-part poem proper. Since Wordsworth's death, scholars have discovered many fragments, including "Home at Grasmere" and "The Tuft of Primroses," which were intended for *The Recluse.*

Coleridge's poetic ambitions largely faded after 1800 as his health worsened and his personal life became increasingly unhappy. He never attempted an epic himself, but his ideas were crucial in Wordsworth's plans; when Wordsworth completed the second major draft of *The Prelude* in 1805, it was imperative to Wordsworth that Coleridge appraise the poem's worth.

During his brief life, Keats was obsessed with the completion of a long poem. His letters make it clear that, for him, composing an epic was a test of poetic talent. Keats realized his ambition with the publication of *Endymion* (1818), very loosely based on the Greek myth of a shepherd who falls in love with the moon goddess. Many of the reviews of *Endymion* were scathing. One critic was so vituperative that Shelley, among others, believed the review hastened Keats's tuberculosis and early death.

Keats tried again. He began *Hyperion*, another myth-based epic that chronicles the fall of the Greek deities, such as Saturn and Hyperion, and was stylistically influenced by Milton. He was unable to complete the project, partially because it was interrupted by his brother's death. It was published as a fragment and the last offering in Keats's 1820 *Poems.* He began a third epic, *The Fall of Hyperion*, which incorporates some of the original *Hyperion* material, but failing health prevented Keats from completing the work before his death at age 25.

Byron's first long poem, *English Bards and Scotch Reviewers*, was in the satirical tradition of Pope, mercilessly criticizing both the reviewing establishment and the authors it examined. Subsequently, Byron wrote epics primarily in installments, unapologetic (unlike Wordsworth) for their serial appearance. *Childe Harold's Pilgrimage*, presenting the wanderings of a Regency wastrel widely identified with Byron himself, was published in three sections over six years. The publication of the first two cantos in 1812 resulted in instant fame, with the result that virtually anything Byron wrote sold well. His masterpiece *Don Juan* follows the exploits of the title character from his youth in Spain to a diplomatic position representing Catherine the Great at the British court. Left incomplete at Byron's abrupt death, *Don Juan* was published in installments from 1819 to 1824. While it is similar in tone to *English Bards*, its wide-ranging attacks on social customs and marriage, war, and politics during and after the time of Napoleon are more embittered than in the earlier poem.

Like Coleridge, Shelley evinced little apparent interest in personally composing an epic. He promoted democratic ideals and denigrated tyranny primarily through lyrics. His longest compositions were dramas, among them *Prometheus Unbound* and *The Cenci*, which attack both despotism and the violence often used to combat it. Shelley left *The Triumph of Life* uncompleted at his death; it is unclear whether he intended the poem as an epic.

Toby Benis

Works Consulted

Abrams, M.H. *Natural Supernaturalism: Tradition and Revolution in Romantic Literature.* New York: Norton, 1971.

Gaull, Marilyn. *English Romanticism: The Human Context*. New York: Norton, 1988.

Gleckner, Robert F., and Gerald E. Enscoe, eds. *Romanticism: Points of View*. Detroit: Wayne State UP, 1975.

Epipsyche

Epipsyche, derived from the title of Shelley's poem *Epipsychidion*, has been used to refer to Shelley's concept of "a soul within our soul," an idea that he develops in his essay "On Love." This smaller soul is a miniature replica of one's self, except that it reflects only what is most pure and beautiful in human nature. According to Shelley, humans are compulsively attracted to this inner soul and continually search for its external embodiment (what he calls its "antitype"), but this idealized object toward which love strives remains forever unattainable. The dynamics of this attraction to an image of inner perfection and the subsequent failure to possess it in an external form constitute the "epipsyche" theme, which appears first and most starkly in Shelley's *Alastor* and later, with variations, in *The Revolt of Islam*, *Prometheus Unbound*, *Adonais*, and *The Triumph of Life*.

In *Epipsychidion*, Emilia Viviani, to whom the poem is addressed, functions as the epipsyche to Shelley's persona, who calls her "this soul out of my soul." Shelley urges her to elope with him to an island, but in the last lines he envisions their final union leading to mutual annihilation.

Some critics have questioned the legitimacy of the term and its etymological derivation from *Epipsychidion*. The title was initially analyzed into two parts, the diminutive *idion* and *epipsyche*, a term that, critics speculated, Shelley coined on the basis of its analogy to "epicycle" (just as the word "epicycle" suggest a wheel within a wheel, "epipsyche" would seemingly sug-gest a soul within a soul). But since "epipsyche" is not a Greek word and Shelley himself never uses it elsewhere, other interpretations of the title have been offered that do not require the term. One approach has been to analyze the title in stricter accordance with Greek grammar and lexical conventions, breaking it down into the Greek preposition *epi*, meaning "on" or "about," and the Greek noun *psychidion*, meaning "little soul" (from *psyche*, "soul," and the diminutive *idion*, "little"). Taken together, these components pro-duce a title that reads "On the Little Soul" or "About the Little Soul." Another ap-proach has been to interpret the title in a manner similar to other Greek terms for poetic songs, such as *epinicion* or *epithalamium* (a song in honor of a victory or in celebration of a marriage). In this context *Epipsychidion* would mean a song in celebration of the little soul, or more sim-ply, a soul-song.

Paul M. Wiebe

Works Consulted

Baker, Carlos. *Shelley's Major Poetry: The Fabric of a Vision*. Princeton: Princeton UP, 1948.

Cameron, Kenneth Neill. *Shelley: The Golden Years*. Cambridge: Harvard UP, 1974.

Hogle, Jerrold E. *Shelley's Process: Radical Trans-ference and the Development of His Major Works*. New York: Oxford UP, 1988.

King-Hele, Desmond. *Shelley: His Thought and Work*. 3rd ed. London: Macmillan, 1984.

Locock, C.D., ed. *The Poems of Percy Bysshe Shelley*. Vol. 2. London: Methuen, 1911.

Notopoulos, James A. *The Platonism of Shelley: A Study of Platonism and the Poetic Mind*. Durham: Duke UP, 1949.

Rogers, Neville. *Shelley at Work: A Critical Inquiry*. 2nd ed. Oxford: Clarendon, 1967.

Wasserman, Earl R. *Shelley: A Critical Reading*. Baltimore: John Hopkins UP, 1971.

Essay

The Romantic authors most often celebrated for their essays are Hazlitt, Hunt, Landor, De Quincey, and Lamb. When describing the essay of the period, many critics rightly point to Hazlitt's assertion that the essays of Montaigne were his primary models. In general, Montaigne's essays would be characterized by the initial presence of an organizing thought that leads into a discussion, sometimes quite lengthy, or experiences, often supplemented by anecdotes and quotations based on Montaigne's memories of them. Quoting from memory, because of its obvious convenience, was widespread among Romantic essayists, and eventually Montaigne's familiar essay was popularized by periodical essayists in magazines such as *The Examiner* (1823), which featured essays under such titles as "The Indicator," "Table Talk," "Imaginary Conversations," and "Conversations With the Dead." As these titles suggest, the Romantic essay was both critical and fictional, functional and imaginary, guided by the presumption of polite conversation among learned readers who shared the interests of the essayist. Thus, a resemblance between the letters of Keats, for instance, which are at once personal and critical, and the essays of Hazlitt, which convey an intelligent appreciation of his subjects in a familiar tone, can be seen. The Romantic combined the adage, the conversation, and the lecture with the scientific document and the reference book. (*See also* Journalism.)

The average length of the Romantic topical essay, as distinct from the review essay, was between 2,000 and 3,000 words or between eight and 12 paragraphs. Subjects for periodical essays ranged from the personal (e.g., reading at home) to an account of a public event (e.g., Hazlitt's "The Fight"). Wordsworth and Coleridge in *The Friend* employed a style comparable to that of a public lecture wherein a thesis or assertion was presented and supported by references to authorities, often with direct quotations from sources such as Shakespeare. For example, in the fourth essay of *The Friend*, Coleridge illustrates the differences between the educated and the ignorant man by quoting large representative dialogues from both *Hamlet* and *Henry IV, Part I*. Wordsworth, in his essay on epitaphs for the same periodical, cites the poets Simonides, John Edwards, and Milton to exemplify his theory that epitaphs should praise the deceased within the proper boundaries of temperance and restraint. A similar model is directly followed in the book reviews that writers such as Scott and Southey contributed to periodicals like *The Quarterly Review*, in which the reviews were used to argue for literary standards and good taste.

The instructional voices of *The Friend* essays are different from those of Hunt's *Indicator*, which in essay number 78 begins, "Sitting last winter among my books . . . I began to consider how I loved the authors of those books . . . ." Hunt then proceeds to give the reader a tour of his favorite works, culminating in a reflection on how much Shelley enjoyed reading the same authors. Here, the speaker adopts a voice of apparent indifference to anything but his own pleasure in sitting in his library while simultaneously making personal points about the proper taste a gentleman should possess in literature and expressing grief over Shelley's death. Yet, he is restrained and speaks in a generalizing mode which engages the reader in silent, mental conversation with the carefully constructed persona.

In his essay of 26 May 1816, Hazlitt writes for the *Examiner* on the quality of "gusto" which he sees as necessary to artistic composition and central to his own essays of art and literary criticism. Hazlitt's essays reveal his keen eye and strong descriptive and taxonomical powers. He writes in a clear style and employs both precise diction and vivid images to promote whatever he thought was noteworthy, valuable, or new, showing some courage, for instance, in his assertions about Shakespeare's personality in "On Shakespeare and Milton" (1818).

Whereas Hazlitt couches his expressions of taste in assertions, Lamb, who used the pseudonym Elia to contribute to *The Reflector*, the *Examiner*, and *The Indicator*, wrote essays that synthesized his personal experiences with his literary interests and his observations about human nature. For instance, Lamb's 1811 essay "On the Tragedies of Shakespeare" focuses on his "opinion that the plays of Shakespeare are less calculated for performance on a stage than those of almost any other dramatist whatever." He then goes on to stress the individual reader's need privately to experience the pain the tragedies such as *King Lear* evoke and how much of Lear's character cannot be accurately depicted on the stage. The personal nature of Lamb's essays, which keeps them close in spirit to letters, was warmly praised by De Quincey in his 1848 essay "The Prose of Hazlitt and Lamb" in which he salutes Lamb's honest genius and criticizes Hazlitt's faulty quotations, among other things.

De Quincey and Landor were men of letters who conveyed their ideas with humor, irony, and imagination. For Landor, the "Imaginary Conversations" created a medium to discuss such topics as the moment of action, the soul approaching death, the beauty of nature, the meaning of art, and the destructive power of tyranny. Following his own dicta that prose compositions should be based on the fluid connection of ideas expressed in sentences that build upon and modify each other, De Quincey reinforced the century's debt to Montaigne in the numerous pieces he contributed to *The London Magazine*, the *Examiner*, *Blackwood's Magazine*, and, later, *Tait's Magazine*. (*See also* Publishing.)

Beverly Schneller

Works Consulted

Fowler, Alastair. *Kinds of Literature. An Introduction to the Theory of Genres and Modes*. Cambridge: Harvard UP, 1982.

Good, Graham. *The Observing Self. Rediscovering the Essay*. London: Routledge, 1988.

Ferrier, Susan Edmonstone
(1782–1854)

Susan Edmonstone Ferrier is best known as the author of three Scottish novels of manners: *Marriage* (1818), *The Inheritance* (1824), and *Destiny* (1831). The first two novels are particularly refreshing, witty portraits of Scottish society, and the last, the most perfect architecturally, is more overtly moral and sober. Ferrier published her works anonymously, the first two with Blackwood, permitting her name to appear at last, when her identity was an open secret, in an 1841 edition of her works. Although her novels were popular, *Destiny*, dedicated to Scott, was the most rewarding financially. Scott, Ferrier's friend, negotiated with Cadell publishers for £1,700 over the far lesser sums Blackwood had paid for her other works.

Ferrier, born in Edinburgh, was the tenth and last child of James Ferrier, a lawyer, and Helen Courts Ferrier, who died when Susan was age 15. As older brothers and sisters died or moved away from home, Ferrier became devoted housekeeper and later nurse to her father until his death in 1829. She never married.

Ferrier became close friends with Charlotte Clavering, who was related to the Duke of Argyll, one of James Ferrier's most important clients. Although in 1809 the friends first planned to write a novel together, Ferrier's superior skills as writer over Clavering's as critic prevailed, and *Marriage* appeared as Ferrier's production nine years later. Argyll's Inverary Castle, with its rugged highlands landscape and active social life, was a model for many scenes in Ferrier's works.

Marriage tells the story of Lady Juliana, a silly and spoiled young Englishwoman. She marries for love, against her father's wishes, only to discover that her romantic notions cannot tolerate life with little money and social interaction with her Scottish husband's dull and unfashionable relatives. The brilliance of this work is the vitality of satiric descriptions, including that of Lady Juliana's first visit to her Scottish relatives, her noisy menagerie in tow, as she recoils from her husband's five awkward sisters, a bellowing bagpipe, and a greasy Scotch broth of leeks and greens. Ferrier implicitly criticizes the uselessness of the education of most young women of good birth. Her criticism and biting satire extend to bluestockings, members of Mrs.

Bluemits's literary circle in the novel, whose learning is shallow and showy.

The Inheritance recounts the tale of Gertrude, supposedly the daughter of the widowed Mrs. St. Clair, who falls in love with Edward Lyndsay, of whom Gertrude's tyrannical and wealthy uncle, Lord Rossville, disapproves. Discovering that she is the daughter of a serving maid, Gertrude becomes a pauper and is befriended by another uncle, the eccentric Uncle Adam. By the end of the novel, she marries Edward, who inherits the Rossville estate, and is restored to the family. The interest of the narrative lies in the conflict between mother and daughter, the portrait of Uncle Adam, a complex character modeled on Ferrier's father, and the character of Miss Bessie Duguid, a spinster constantly in service of family members who assume that since she has no husband and children, she has nothing valuable to do with her time.

Destiny is less spontaneous than Ferrier's first novels, reflecting in part the deaths of her family members, concerns about the poor health of Scott and her father, her own declining eyesight and health, and her increasing reliance on religion as solace. Particularly vivid is Ferrier's portrait of Glenroy, the disagreeable and petty laird whose sole concern is property. In a carefully constructed plot, Ferrier recounts the crisscrossings of love relationships, finally rewarding Glenroy's neglected and penniless daughter, and his poor relation, with marriage and rightful estate.

Throughout her works, Ferrier pen is unfailing. Whether sprightly or serious, her novels successfully capture individual characters and family dynamics, especially the role of women and domineering father figures, within the context of a society full of material and moral traps for young women who must, like Austen's heroines,

learn to balance emotions and good sense.

Carol Shiner Wilson

Works Consulted

Cullinan, Mary. *Susan Ferrier*. Boston: Twayne, 1984.

Grant, Aline. *Susan Ferrier of Edinburgh, A Biography*. Denver: Swallow, 1957.

Parker, W.M. *Susan Ferrier and John Galt*. London: Longmans, 1965.

Flaxman, John

(1755–1826)

Art historians generally categorize John Flaxman as a sculptor, although his work is not limited to sculpture. His line drawings on classical subjects were quite well known and influenced several Romantic artists. These drawings were also contemporary with interest in the Elgin Marbles. Flaxman is generally considered more of a Neoclassicist than a Romantic, but works like his sketch *Thomas Chatterton Taking the Bowl of Poison from the Spirit of Despair* are distinctly Romantic.

Flaxman was born in York but was taken to London at the age of six months by his father, a plaster model and cast merchant. Encouraged by his father, he was an artistic prodigy who began sending drawings to the Free Society of Artists at age 12. He was admitted as a student to the Royal Academy at 15.

In 1775, Wedgwood hired the 20-year-old Flaxman to design friezes for vases, plaques, and similar objects, much along the line of the Wedgwood designs of today. While supervisor for the Wedgwood workers in Rome, Flaxman spent seven years in Italy, from 1787 to 1794, with his wife Ann Denman. This experience furthered his education in the classical style.

On Flaxman's return from Rome, he became well established as a sculptor. He was made an associate of the Royal Academy in 1797 and a full member in 1800. The government commissioned him to execute public monuments for Joshua Reynolds (1807) and Lord Nelson (1808).

Art was important in Flaxman's personal, as well as professional, life. His friends included Romney and Blake; in fact, it was through Romney, at salons of a Mrs. Mathews, that Flaxman met Blake. He and Blake had much in common, including their interest in the teachings of Swedenborg, and the friendship lasted until Flaxman's death. There is some indication of Flaxman's influence in some of Blake's earlier work, but this influence is not evident in his later drawings. (*See also* Sculpture.)

Flaxman's *Thomas Chatterton* sketch reflects a Romantic spirit that does not come through in his other two-dimensional work, primarily line drawings based on the *Iliad*, the *Odyssey*, and Aeschylus and the final 1817 series on Hesiod. There is a life in this work, a pathos, that is missing from the Neoclassical line drawings. There is also an element of Blakean influence in the figure of Chatterton. Chatterton's expression is strongly reminiscent of Blake's *Ghost of a Flea* and other figures.

Despite the sterility of Flaxman's classically based works, they inspired several major artist of the Romantic period, most notably David, Blake, Géricault, and Ingres. Specifically, these drawings influenced David's *Sabine Women* and Ingres's *Jupiter and Thetis*. Sarah Symmons pointed out distinct similarities in the Ugolino figures of Flaxman and Géricault, which carry through to the father figure in Géricault's *Raft of the Medusa*.

A chair of sculpture was specially created for Flaxman at the Royal Academy in 1810. His lectures dealt primarily with the ideals of the Neoclassical style, which is the enduring hallmark of his art in both two-dimensional and three-dimensional forms.

Linda A. Archer

Works Consulted

Brion, Marcel. *Art of the Romantic Era.* New York: Praeger, 1966.

Cummings, Frederick J. *Romantic Art in Britain: Paintings and Drawings 1760–1860.* Philadelphia: Philadelphia Museum of Art, 1968.

Holt, Elizabeth Gilmore, ed. *From the Classicists to the Impressionists: A Documentary History of Art and Architecture in the Nineteenth Century.* New York: New York UP, 1966.

Symmons, Sarah. "Géricault, Flaxman and 'Ugolino.'" *Burlington Magazine* (Oct. 1973): 672.

Food and Culinary Habits

Eating and drinking in England at the turn of the 19th century were often precarious pleasures. Scarce, costly provisions caused hardship and periodic hunger riots. Regardless of social class, consumers were at risk from adulteration of food and drink.

Meal hours among the well-to-do shifted considerably during this period. By 1800, the dinner hour had moved from midday to 7 or 8 p.m. Grand social affairs, dinners lasted four or five hours and were sizable meals. Varieties of beef, veal, mutton, fish, fowl, game, pies, pastries, and other sweet dishes loaded the tables of the king to those of minor members of the gentry. The light 10 a.m. breakfast of bread and toast with tea, coffee, or chocolate gave way to an earlier, more substantial hot breakfast that might include eggs, meat, and fish. The gap between an early breakfast and late dinner was filled by a hot luncheon and a light late-afternoon "tea" of cakes and, eventually replacing wine, the increasingly popular tea. Despite the advent of tea, alcohol consumption continued to be high among the wealthy, who preferred cognac, brandy, and wine. Amid this abundance of food and drink was an increasing abhorrence of corpulence, once valued as a sign of prosperity. Numerous women and men of fashion followed dangerously slimming diets. Byron, for example, damaged his health by dining only on biscuits and soda water for weeks at a time.

Working people, whether rural or urban, had always breakfasted earlier than the upper classes. Their midday meal remained the most substantial, and their "tea" was the meal at night. The diet of rural laborers varied from North to South, with the more numerous Southerners faring worse after Enclosure. Northerners used the potato daily and relied on oatmeal rather than on wheat bread. They were more likely to be able to keep livestock on lands as yet unenclosed. Workers in the South preferred white bread and would not eat potatoes, popular among the upper classes in cities at the time. Residents of both regions regularly took cheese, butter, bacon, sugar, and tea. Fresh meat, eaten perhaps twice or three times a week, was usually boiled. High alcohol consumption among the poor was as common as among the rich, although their spirits were often cheap and illegally produced gin and beer.

For workers and the unemployed, getting enough to eat was an intense struggle. Harvests were especially poor in 1794 and 1795; food prices were usually high during the Napoleonic wars; and in 1815, the Corn Laws prevented importation of foreign grain until domestic prices on limited supplies rose to 10 shillings per bushel. Frustrated and angry after years of struggle, many hungry poor, whose wages could not keep up with spiraling food costs, rioted in protest.

By the beginning of the 19th century, the systematic adulteration of food and drink put all social classes at risk. Bakers routinely added alum to bread, which whitened poor-grade flour and increased the size of loaves. Chalk and bone ash were other popular additives. Frequently, false vinegar was made from oil of vitriol (concentrated sulfuric acid), and products were often pickled in copper pots, which turned the victual green. Vitriol also provided an even color in tea, which might have been mixed with dust or dry leaves. In response to increased competition from tea, dishonest brewers bolstered their profits by watering beer and adding the potentially paralytic Coculus India Berry. Despite efforts like those of Fredrick Accum, whose *Treatise on the Adulterations of Food and Culinary Poisons* (1820) shocked the public, significant official concern was not apparent until the Analytical and Sanitary Commission was appointed in 1850 and the Food, Drink and Drugs Act was passed in 1872.

Adulteration was not the concern of the numerous cookbooks of the period. Most of these were written for women of the upper-middle ranks who did not cook themselves but supervised servants who did. Still immensely popular were Hannah Glasse's *The Art of Cookery Made Plain and Easy* (1747) and Elizabeth Raffald's *The Experienced English Housekeeper* (1769), both of which had gone into dozens of authorized and pirated editions by 1810. Recipes were often long, with vague measurements and extensive commentary. Frequently, cookery books also included instructions for preparing medicinal herbs (taken from the reader's garden) and tips on supervision of servants, discipline of children, and general household economy. Authors routinely condemned elaborately prepared and sauced French dishes, equated with excess and flawed morality, compared with the plain roasts and pies of virtuous, unpretentious England. Although Glasse included some French recipes, she was careful to explain that she did so only because the dishes were already known by their French names.

In 1817, Dr. William Kitchiner published *The Cook's Oracle*. Kitchiner included exact quantities in weight and measure of ingredients, suggesting as much the increased value society placed on scientific precision as concern for the cook. Also prominent were cookbooks by chefs in London taverns, now fashionable dining sites for gentlemen. Three of particular note are John Farley's *The London Art of Cookery* (1783), Richard Brigg's *The English Art of Cookery* (1788), and *The Universal Cook* (1792) by Francis Collingwood and John Woollams. As the first two titles indicate, culinary accomplishments by male chefs were often considered art, and those chefs, artists.

Food consumption was clearly a powerful political and social issue. Despite shortages for all during the Napoleonic wars, the poor suffered the most and continued to struggle as Parliament imposed legislation that drove food prices even higher. Although some products, like tea and white bread, ostensibly linked all social classes, most dishes marked the significant disadvantage of the working classes. Such differences provided crucial material for reformers' debates in the Victorian era.

Carol Shiner Wilson

Works Consulted

Burnett, John. *Plenty and Want: A Social History of Diet in England from 1815 to the Present Day*. 2nd ed. London: Scolar, 1979.

Burton, Elizabeth. *Georgians at Home, 1715–1830*. London: Longmans, 1968.

Drummond, John C., and Anne Wilbraham. *The Englishman's Food: A History of Five Centuries of English Diet*. 2nd ed. London: Cape, 1958.

Mennell, Stephen. *All Manner of Food: Eating and Taste in England and France from the Middle Ages to the Present*. New York: Blackwell, 1985.

Palmer, Arnold. *Moveable Feasts, a Reconnaissance of the Origins and Consequences of Fluctuations in Meal-Times, With Special Attention to the Introduction of Luncheon and Afternoon Tea*. New York: Oxford, 1952.

Read, Jan, and Maite Manjon. *The Great British Breakfast*. London: Joseph, 1981.

Wilson, C. Anne. *Food and Drink in Britain from the Stone Age to Recent Times*. London: Constable, 1975.

Fox, James Charles
(1749–1806)

During his long, iconoclastic career, James Charles Fox was best known for his opposition to the war against the American colonies, his support of the French Revolution, and the many antagonisms these views provoked. Outspoken from the time he entered Parliament at age 20, Fox alienated both friend and foe by speaking his mind, often without regard for those who disagreed with him and what consequences would follow. He made enemies of George III with an early speech before the House of Commons, a mistake from which he never fully recovered, for the king effectively kept Fox from higher office for most of his life.

Fox entered Parliament as a Tory, but after George III pressed Lord North to dismiss him from the Treasury Commission, he joined the opposition on the back bench. As he led the Whigs' attack on British participation in the colonial wars, praised the fall of the Bastille, and urged the abolition of the slave trade, he helped define the two-party system. (*See also* Parliament, Slavery.)

During his early years in Parliament, his contemporaries had reason to consider him personally reckless. A gambler who borrowed heavily to cover his losses (in 1773, his debts totaled £140,000), Fox often spent his nights at the gaming tables.

However, he became a diligent MP who fought to maintain the independence of Parliament. In addition, his casual, forceful oratorical style, which contrasted effectively with the more ornate eloquence of opponents like Burke, won him admirers even among the Tories. Burke called Fox one of the greatest men England had ever produced, and his reputation as one of the ablest speakers to stand before Parliament remains intact.

One must be careful not to simplify Fox. Although he took political positions consonant with those of most English liberals of the time, he was not always a liberal in the modern sense. He opposed restrictions against the American colonies, but not because he agreed with Jefferson. He viewed the colonies as bound by British law and the colonists as subjects of the Crown but saw that refusing to repeal the Stamp Act and install a less objectionable way to raise revenues would force the colonies into open revolt. He feared a long and distant war that would strain resources and become tactically difficult. When Burke suggested a compromise position that maintained Parliament's right to tax the colonies but left that right unexercised, Fox urged his fellow Whigs to cross party lines to support it.

Fox's reputation as a firebrand was well deserved. In 1780, he took the reins of the radical Westminster association, which urged the reform of the House of Commons and a curb on the influence of the Crown. One speech before Parliament saw him arguing against the divine right of kings and on another occasion, after his reference to "Our Sovereign the People," Pitt considered sending him to the Tower.

His debates with Burke began early in his career but reached their height in his attacks on *Observations on the Late Revolution in France*. Although most of his countrymen supported assistance to the revolutionaries, his argument emphasized reason and patience, perhaps to avoid further offending George III, who was not eager to see any blow against absolutism succeed. Privately, Fox called the storming of the Bastille the "greatest event in the history of the world" and continued to support the cause even as the aftermath of the Revolution became known and popular opinion shifted toward Burke. However, Fox should not be seen as a homebound Thomas Paine. A career politician descended from the Bourbons on his mother's side and the grandson of a Lord Commissioner of the Treasury, Fox was shocked by Paine's proposals for a democracy and refused to even finish reading *The Rights of Man*. Accused of Republicanism, Fox was more concerned with limiting the influence of kings, whether British or French. He also shared the popular view that internal trouble across the Channel would shift the balance of power toward England.

In the last year of his life, Fox fulfilled his ambitions for higher office when he was appointed Secretary for Foreign Affairs in the All Talents Cabinet. He was unable to persuade Napoleon to make peace, despite what some saw as extreme conciliatory measures (after learning of a plot to assassinate Napoleon, Fox sent an envoy to warn him), but he successfully lobbied for an end to the slave trade. His book, the *History of the Early Part of the Reign of James II*, was published two years after his death. He was buried in Westminster Cathedral. His statue in Bloomsbury Square holds a copy of the Magna Carta.

Gregg Johnson

Works Consulted

Derry, John W. *Charles James Fox*. New York: St. Martin's, 1972.

Lascelles, Edward. *The Life of Charles James Fox*. London: Oxford UP, 1937.

Reid, Loren Charles. *James Fox: A Man for the People*. Columbia: U of Missouri P, 1969.

Trevelyn, George Otto. *The Early History of Charles James Fox*. New York: Harper, 1900.

Fragment

The Romantic fragment is an aesthetic and cultural category that encompasses a wide variety of artifacts (e.g., literary, sculptural, architectural, and visual). The concept of the fragment, and of the value of the fragmentary, derives from Romantic ideas about a fall from original unity—cosmic, natural, or psychic—into divisive multiplicity. Attention to the fragmentary is a consequence of seeing the world as divided and diverse but also of emphasizing the power of fragments to reveal a potential for eventual reunification. Romantic aesthetics describes art as one way of compensating for a pervasive post-Enlightenment sense of the fragmentary.

Emphasis on fragments also arises when an artist's conception, or the natural world, is seen as so expansive that it cannot be contained within a single, unified vision. This leads to emphasis on artistic spontaneity, a sense that an inspired work should be abandoned rather than labored over, and to a belief in the revelatory power of the isolated object or moment. The Romantic shift from a mimetic to an expressivist aesthetic implies that an artist's partial conceptions should produce expressions that are also incomplete. In addition, aesthetic fragments question classical notions about the definition of unified form and the value of closure and completion.

The Elgin Marbles offer a sculptural prototype for this view of the fragmentary. Though existing only as shattered bits of a vastly more comprehensive work, they were seen to contain immeasurable artistic energy. This emphasis was also conditioned by the recognition that the sculptures were part of an ancient and functional structure. Keats's Grecian urn extends this idea to the fragmentary quality of all art by representing fragments of a story that is not known but must be assembled from residual traces. The appeal of architectural ruins—classical temples, Gothic towers, ruined battlements—derives from a similar sense of a formerly unified grandeur that exists only in pieces. (*See also* Elgin Marbles.) Shelley's *Ozymandias* uses sculptural fragments to emphasize the transitory nature of the material world and the destructive power of human history. Fragmentation also becomes a way of suggesting the limits of human perception, as in Blake's mythic works.

The Romantic fragment as a poetic form becomes particularly important in the early 19th century. Intentional fragments and "remains" were produced before this time, but by 1800 the fragment had become a significant literary form. Schlegel defined the work of his contemporaries as "fragments at their inception." Coleridge and Wordsworth included four titled or implied fragments in *Lyrical Ballads* (1798). Hazlitt noted that the only way to write an autobiography was by gathering fragmentary recollections from the past. Byron claimed that his own mind was a fragment. Major works by the English Romantics include various forms of identified or implied fragments: Coleridge's *Kubla Khan* and *Christabel*, Wordsworth's *Recluse*, Byron's *Don Juan*, Keats's Hyperion poems, Shelley's *The Triumph of Life*. Shelley's *Julian and Maddalo* presents the fragmentary speech of a maniac within a story that declares itself to be incomplete. Blake's *Four Zoas* exists only as an unrevised manuscript, extending the definition of the fragment to include edited and published works that were incomplete or unrevised by their authors. Shelley said that Keats should have published fragments from *Endymion* rather than the whole poem. Tennyson considered *Fragments of an Elegy* as a possible title for the linked lyrics that became *In Memoriam*. Goethe, Novalis, and Schiller all produced poems or criticism that addressed the fragment as having literary significance.

In other arts, the fragment also becomes a self-consciously Romantic form: the sketch, the architectural detail, torso statuary, the unfinished score, the detached overture. Visual works by Turner, Constable, Blake, Friedrich, Goya, and Delacroix, like musical compositions by Mozart, Schubert, and Beethoven, raise questions about the aesthetics of the incomplete and the value of the initial conception. For the Romantic sensibility, however broadly it is defined, the fragment becomes a way of making art and a way of looking at the world.

Ashton Nichols

Works Consulted

Bostetter, Edward. *The Romantic Ventriloquists*. Seattle: U of Washington P, 1963.

Levinson, Marjorie. *The Romantic Fragment Poem*. Chapel Hill: U of North Carolina P, 1986.

Kritzman, L., and J. Plottel, eds. *Fragments: Incompletion and Discontinuity*. New York: New York Literary Forum, 1981.

McFarland, Thomas. *Romanticism and the Forms of Ruin*. Princeton: Princeton UP, 1981.

Rajan, Balachandra. *The Form of the Unfinished: English Poetics From Spenser to Pound*. Princeton: Princeton UP, 1985.

Frame Narrative

A distinctive narrative structure, the frame narrative finds expression in many genres of the Romantic period, including the narrative poem — *The Rime of the Ancient Mariner*, and *Alastor*; the novel — *Frankenstein* and *Wuthering Heights*; the ballad — *La Belle Dame sans Merci*; the autobiographical essay — *Sartor Resartus*; and even Carlyle's early short story, *Cruthers and Jonson*. The frame narrative is commonly defined as a story within a story or as a narrative told within the framework of another setting and situation; put more precisely, the frame narrative is a narrative inscribed or embedded in the instance of its own utterance.

Critics distinguish two types of frame narratives. The so-called book-end, or framed, narrative begins with an initial, short narrative and setting; tells a single, longer story embedded within the exterior frame; and concludes by returning to the incipient setting and dramatic situation. Coleridge's *The Ancient Mariner* exemplifies this type of narrative frame, as does Joseph Conrad's later *Heart of Darkness*. The "Chinese-box," or embedded, narrative consists of a series of narratives enfolded within narratives, like boxes within boxes. Shelley's *Frankenstein* and Emily Brontë's *Wuthering Heights* employ this kind of frame narrative. The remarkably Byzantine framing structure of Maturin's *Melmoth the Wanderer* includes an opening and concluding book-end frame told by John Melmoth the Younger, several interpolated stories about Melmoth the Wanderer, and a series of Chinese-box stories within stories within stories retold predominantly by Alonzo de Monçada.

Despite this general distinction in classification, most frame narratives share the following structural characteristics: the exterior frame presents a normative, even conventional world view; a character/witness recounts extraordinary experiences told to an explicit audience, ostensibly for their instruction; the enframed narrative is transmitted either orally, in epistolary fashion, or through a mixture of both modes; other characters contribute to the telling of the narrative, which often becomes increasingly "interior"; and the narrative concludes with a return to the outermost setting and offers an overt moral, itself rendered problematic by the events occurring within the enframed narrative.

How such a distinctive but relatively obscure narrative form became prominent during the Romantic era is intriguing. Critics once posited that the frame narrative highlighted the writer's closing off of the exterior world in order to concentrate better on the private, interior world. The Romantic preoccupation with and emerging understanding of the self and its relation to the Other may have prompted writers to incorporate multivocal, dialogic strategies within a single narrative. From this perspective, the frame narrative's shifting speakers decenter the authorizing "self" of the narrative as but one voice among voices and, yet, still privilege the Romantic notion of identity. Thus, frame narratives as diverse as *The Ancient Mariner* and *Frankenstein* can be read as giving coherent expression to the incoherent, unspeakable, and often terrifying voices competing within the self, and at the same time, contextualizing (or restraining) these explorations by enframing them within normative, everyday social settings.

In a different vein, novelists especially were conscious of the increasing upper-middle-class reading audience with its moral conservatism, fascination with the Romantic hero, and fondness for exotic or antiquarian settings. Since some frame narratives depict subject matter deemed controversial, even amoral, yet appealing to the public readership, an oblique narrative strategy insulated the author and provided the reader with a needed distance. For example, Lewis's sensational, even calculated, explorations of sexuality and sadomasochism in *The Monk* both attracted

and repelled the popular readership. For Mary Shelley—writing about monsters, science, and parricide—the oblique quality of the frame narrative afforded a judicious mechanism from which to approach these subjects. Scott's use of the frame narrative in *The Heart of Midlothian* positions his audience within the dual settings of a contemporary world and a romanticized past. In sum, the frame facilitates voicing conflicting aspects of a single personality, distancing the author from potential charges of libel or scandal, and situating the reader in the tantalizing, yet safely distanced, position of the voyeur witnessing exotic, mysterious settings.

The frame narrative's method of narrative transmission has been characterized as ornate, effaced, and indirect. Such a method calls attention to the epistemological disjunction between speakers and listeners during the act of communication: who is speaking becomes problematic. This decentering of the narrative disrupts commonplace notions of identity and communication in frame narratives such as *Wuthering Heights*, wherein Ellen (Nelly) Dean, Lockwood, Isabella, and Heathcliff all compete for the power of narrative enunciation. As a result of this oscillation, the relationship between narrators and characters is destabilized, since characters narrate and narrators usurp the characters' power to speak for themselves. One consequence of this shifting position between narrators and characters is that the listener/reader becomes situated as a character within the text itself and is invited to conclude his or her own telling of the tale.

Although the frame narrative is not unique to the Romantic period, it can be contextualized within a Romantic aesthetic. The frame narrative shares common characteristics with the ballad: both employ a book-end frame structure; emphasize a spoken and oblique method of narrative transmission; and often treat controversial, violent subject matter. To varying degrees, Wordsworth, Coleridge, Keats, Scott, and Emily Brontë employ elements of the ballad-frame narrative structure. The method of embedding several tales within tales may have its roots in Romantic Orientalism, specifically the popular *1001 Arabian Nights*, a book known to have influenced *The Rime, Wuthering Heights*, and *Melmoth*. Chaucer's *Canterbury Tales* offered a more canonical example of embedded, multivocal tales. Also, the Romantic fascination with ruined castles and abbeys provided a ready-made structure—the fractured, partially exposed construction— upon which to model narratives that foreground the teller of the tale. Considered within a more traditional Romantic aesthetic, the circular nature of the frame narrative, with its emphasis on the speaker's self before and after an extraordinary experience, resembles the structure of the greater Romantic lyric.

A framing device employed in Romantic literature and often associated with the frame narrative postulates an editor of a found document who organizes the text, as does the editor of Diogenes Teufelsdröckh's manuscripts in *Sartor Resartus* or as does Jedediah Cleishbotham of Peter Pattieson's record of tales told at the Wallace Inn of Gandercleugh in Scott's *Tales of My Landlord* series. Maria Edgeworth's *Castle Rackrent* employs a preface, an elaborate glossary, and an editor who writes down Thady Quirk's tale of the Rackrents.

To a degree, the frame narrative as constructed in the Romantic era has been supplanted by or has evolved into new forms that call attention to narratology and audience reception. These innovations can be seen in the Victorian multiplot novels of Dickens, in multivocal narratives such as Wilkie Collins's *The Woman in White* and Browning's *The Ring and the Book*, and in so-called unreliable narratives, such as James's *The Turn of the Screw*.

Once devalued as stylistically awkward, frame narratives are now viewed as particularly apt illustrations of literary problems regarding narrative voice, the relationship between tellers and listeners, the boundary of the text, and the self-reflexive nature of literature.

David W. Ullrich

Works Consulted

Ali, Muhsin Jassim. *Scheherazade in England: A Study of Nineteenth-Century English Criticism of the Arabian Nights*. Washington: Three Continents, 1981.

Caws, Mary Ann. *Reading Frames in Modern Fiction*. Princeton: Princeton UP, 1985.

Chatman, Seymour. *Story and Discourse: Narrative Structure in Fiction and Film*. Ithaca: Cornell UP, 1978.

Derrida, Jacques. "The Parergon." Trans. Craig Owens. *October* 9 (1979): 3–41.

Haggerty, George, E. *Gothic Fiction/Gothic Form*. University Park: Pennsylvania State UP, 1989.

Kiely, Robert. *The Romantic Novel in England*. Cambridge: Harvard UP, 1972.

Kramer, Dale. *Charles Robert Maturin*. Twayne's English Authors Series. New York: Twayne, 1973.

Macovski, Michael S. "*Wuthering Heights* and the Rhetoric of Interpretation." *ELH* 54 (1987): 363–84.

Matthews, John T. "Framing in *Wuthering Heights*." *Texas Studies in Literature and Language* 27 (1985): 25–61.

Newman, Beth. "Narratives of Seduction and the Seductions of Narrative: The Frame Structure of *Frankenstein*." *ELH* 53 (1986): 141–63.

———. "'The Situation of the Looker-on': Gender, Narration, and Gaze in *Wuthering Heights*." *PMLA* 105 (1990): 1029–41.

Poovey, Mary. "My Hideous Progeny: Mary Shelley and the Feminization of Romanticism." *PMLA* 95 (1980): 332–47.

Tennyson, G.B. *Sartor Called Resartus: The Genesis, Structure, and Style of Thomas Carlyle's First Major Work*. Princeton: Princeton UP, 1965.

Wasserman, Earl, R. *Shelley: A Critical Reading*. Baltimore: Johns Hopkins UP, 1971.

French Revolution

The French Revolution—born of the desire to destroy a repressive order and to build a new social system based on liberty, equality, and fraternity—was an important historical event for the Romantics. The faith in human nature and democratic principles on which it was based appealed to most Romantic writers at some time in their lives. The complicated history of the French Revolution, however, ultimately affected the beliefs of Romantic poets in different ways. (*See also* Nationalism.)

At the fall of the Bastille in July 1789, hopes for the revolution ran high. The ideals of the Revolution were first endangered when several European nations declared war on France shortly after the execution of King Louis XVI in 1793. The situation became even more ominous when an internal power struggle resulted in Robespierre's rise to power and the executions of the "Reign of Terror." The fall of Robespierre in July 1794, seen by many as a hopeful sign of a new liberation, did not prove to be so, for France embarked on an imperialistic venture, marked by the rise of Napoleon, who became First Consul of France in 1799 and Emperor in 1804. (*See also* Napoleon.)

For the first generation of Romantics, old enough to experience the progress of events firsthand, the Revolution initially seemed an apocalyptic event, bound to usher in a new era in Europe. Wordsworth, for instance, who traveled through France in the early days of the Revolution, described the feeling of many young idealists in *The Prelude*. Looking back on this time in his life, he recalled the enthusiasm and optimism many of his contemporaries felt:

"Bliss was it in that dawn to be alive,/But to be young was very heaven!" However, the Terror and subsequent events, such as the invasion of Switzerland, caused Wordsworth to reexamine his political beliefs and to abandon the idea that political changes could produce lasting human happiness.

Coleridge, too, initially saw great promise in the Revolution but lost faith when violence and chaos followed. In *France: An Ode* he concludes that freedom cannot be achieved by governments but only by individuals sensitive to God in Nature. Disillusionment with the French Revolution led him, like Wordsworth, to join the ranks of the conservatives.

Many of Blake's works of this period, including *The Marriage of Heaven and Hell*, *America*, and *The Songs of Innocence and Experience*, echo the spirit of revolt and optimism surrounding the French Revolution. He deals with its early days specifically in *The French Revolution* (1791), praising defiance of a repressive old regime and the fraternity that supplants it. Years later, Blake criticized Bonapartism and saw limitations in the revolutions in America and France, which, he felt, had overcome monarchic restraint but had not resulted in genuine freedom.

Two poets of the second generation of Romantic writers, Byron and Shelley, although too young to experience the horrors of Robespierre and Napoleon, maintained the spirit of the French Revolution throughout their careers. Beginning to write mature verse when Wordsworth and Coleridge had long been disillusioned with the French Revolution, they both used poetry to support political revolt, remaining throughout their lives sympathetic to those struggling against repression.

Susan Meisenhelder

Works Consulted

Brinton, Crane. *The Political Ideas of the English Romanticists*. New York: Russell, 1962.

Chandler, James K. *Wordsworth's Second Nature: A Study of the Poetry and Politics*. Chicago: U of Chicago P, 1984.

Dawson, P.M.S. *The Unacknowledged Legislator: Shelley and Politics*. Oxford: Clarendon, 1980.

Deane, Seamus. *The French Revolution and Enlightenment in England, 1789–1832*. Cambridge: Harvard UP, 1988.

Erdman, David V. *Blake, Prophet Against Empire: A Poet's Interpretation of the History of His Own Times*. Princeton: Princeton UP, 1969.

Everest, Kelvin. *Coleridge's Secret Ministry: The Context of the Conversation Poems 1795–1798*. New York: Barnes, 1979.

Friedman, Barton R. *Fabricating History: English Writers on the French Revolution*. Princeton: Princeton UP, 1988.

Hancock, Albert Elmer. *The French Revolution and The English Poets: A Study in Historical Criticism*. New York: Holt, 1899.

Todd, F.M. *Politics and the Poet: A Study of Wordsworth*. London: Methuen, 1957.

Watson, J.R. *English Poetry of the Romantic Period 1789–1830*. New York: Longmans, 1985.

Williams, John. *Wordsworth: Romantic Poetry and Revolution*. New York: Manchester UP, 1989.

Woodring, Carl. *Politics in English Romantic Poetry*. Cambridge: Harvard UP, 1970.

French Romanticism

Nineteenth-century Romanticism was one of the most fertile periods of French intellectual, artistic, and literary life. Its first phase included the work of Chateaubriand, Constant, and Senancour and lasted to about 1817. A second phase, 1818 to 1830, excited more public interest and brought into prominence painters like Géricault and Delacroix and writers such as Vigny, Lamartine, Hugo, and Musset. During this time, the movement defined its doctrines and general goals. The third phase began roughly in 1830 with the inauguration of the new government of Louis-Philippe and the advent of a new set of official policies governing economics, religion, and personal liberties. These years also witnessed the spread of the Industrial Revolution and its attendant problems of urban poverty, slums, unemployment, child labor, and the misery of the factory system. Convinced that their art must have a purpose and that it should not be isolated from the world, the now mature writers of the second period recognized and were attentive to these problems. Yet, at the same time, there emerged in the years after 1830 a position that condemned any social or political involvement on the part of the artist and, instead, extolled a belief in "art for art's sake." Anything useful was by definition ugly and excluded from literary or artistic activity. The 1840s saw the decline of Romanticism as a distinct movement.

In general, the Romantics saw themselves as moderns, creating a literature and a style in art for their own age and society and becoming the spokesmen and women for this new society. The Romantic possessed not only a gift for literature but also a gift for politics and the military. The artist thus had a responsibility to influence society and to shape public opinion as well as to interpret its ideas, values, or preoccupations. Society, philosophy, religion, and even history all entered into the Romantic vision which, far from rejecting reason, combined it with imagination and sensibility to produce a more complete individual than the merely rational man of the 18th century. The Romantics used the drama, the novel, prose nonfiction, and poetry to express their thoughts and feelings. But for Lamartine, poetry in particular offered everything to its readers: ideas for the mind, feelings for the soul, pictures for the imagination, and music for the ears. In the first part of the century, the artist had not broken his ties to his public; he still had hopes of being heard, of perhaps identifying with his reader or even of raising the public to a higher level. According to Henri Peyre, only later, after the repeated failure of attempts at social and political reform, did alienation take over as the dominant artistic attitude toward the world.

Yet, despite their attachment to the world and their conviction that their art served a social purpose, the Romantics simultaneously extolled the virtues of solitude and introspection. They maintained that their superiority to ordinary men was due to their very isolation from them. They suffered from the *"mal du siècle,"* expressed by Musset as the disillusionment of a generation born too early and too late, nostalgic for the lost glory of the First Empire and disgusted by the mediocrity of the Bourbon Restoration. Thus, in their solitude they suffered from melancholy; they were tempted by suicide and obsessed with death; they were prey to madness and nervous breakdowns; they despaired of ever reconciling their ideal, their dreams, with the reality of the materialistic and authoritarian industrial society that surrounded them. They deplored the laissez-faire economic individualism of their age, and espoused a different individualism that proposed to use the personal and autobiographical to express more general, even universal, themes. This was especially true for Hugo. The personal element was permissible in his work solely because it might reflect general or universal concerns; when he wrote about himself, he was convinced that he was also writing about his reader. The ultimate goal of the artist, however, was always to be the pursuit of truth, whether in literature, history, philosophy, religion, society, fine arts, or life in general.

The tensions in French society that were mirrored in the work of the Romantics stemmed in large part from a struggle in French society, a legacy of the Revolution and the First Empire. The struggle once again polarized much of French society between royalists and republicans: those who wanted to restore the old regime and those who advocated a complete transformation of French society in order to complete the political, social, and economic reforms begun after 1789. These tensions were also present within the literary community. But, no matter what their original opinions, most of the Romantics ultimately rejected any kind of authoritarianism and embraced more liberal, even democratic, ideas in both politics and religion.

In religion, the conflict arose between orthodox religious faith and unbelief. Among the early Romantics, Chateaubriand wrote the apology for Catholicism with *Le génie du Christianisme*, while Senancour represented a more skeptical position. The second generation of Romantics (Hugo, Musset, Vigny, Lamartine to mention the best known), began as Catholics and later abandoned religious orthodoxy, although not religion and ethics.

In political and social thought, the Romantics distinguished themselves by their concern for individual liberties. They were well aware of the government's tendencies toward authoritarian rule, the plight of the worker, and other social ills. Hugo, Vigny, and Lamartine all involved themselves in politics. However, they were not revolutionaries but rather advocates of gradual reform. Partisans of neither the right nor the left, they were often condemned by their more ideological and passionate compatriots. Their revolution, if any, was confined to their art.

Finally, in the realm of prose nonfiction, the writing of history—particularly the history of the French Revolution—became an important activity for the 19th century. One can even speak of Michelet, Tocqueville, Guizot, and others as the Romantic historians. Although they did not suffer as acutely as their more literary brethren from the *mal du siècle* many of them, notably Michelet, did bring a Romantic sensibility to their work. They were all influenced by their personal experience of the Revolution and Empire. They were convinced of the importance of working with documents and other primary sources and determined that history should be didactic. It should explain why things happened and it should also tell a story, the story of France and of the French people, not just of kings and princes. Thus began the practice of writing national histories. Here again, as in poetry and prose fiction, the individual approach is apparent. Historians as greatly at variance in their interpretations as Michelet and Tocqueville proposed to discover the "soul of France." Thus, according to François Furet, what is important is not that Tocqueville's *L'Ancien Régime et la Révolution* is farther to the right than that of Michelet in its interpretation of events, but that it is a *different* history. Both are highly individual works; both have a theme to communicate; and both are reflections of the society that produced them.

The Romantics thus penetrated every aspect of French society prior to 1840. Some, like Hugo, lived well into the second half of the century and continued to be productive. They were an eclectic group, a study in contradictions, convinced of their modernity and their uniqueness. Yet, despite their popular image as introspective misfits unable and unwilling to participate in the world, most of the French Romantics were acutely aware of the world around them, hence their *mal du siècle*.

Elaine McAllister

Works Consulted

Barzun, Jacques. *Romanticism and the Modern Ego*. Boston: Little, 1947.

Charlton, D.G. *The French Romantics*, 2 vols. New York: Cambridge UP, 1984.

Furet, François. *Penser la Révolution française*. Paris: Gallimard, 1978.

Milner, M. *Le Romantisme, I: 1820–43*. Paris: Arthaud, 1973.

Peyre, Henri. *Qu'est-ce que le Romantisme?* Paris: Presses Universitaires de France, 1971.

Frend, William
(1757–1841)

Mathematician, linguist, economist, Cambridge don, radical pamphleteer and journalist, Unitarian activist—all describe William Frend, the son of a wealthy Canterbury wine merchant. After graduating in 1775 from King's School, Canterbury, Frend attempted to enter his father's business, crossing the ocean to learn the wine trade in Quebec, where he joined the British Army to combat the American revolutionaries. His military stint was brief, for Frend soon returned to England, was accepted at Jesus College, and went up to Cambridge in 1776. It was there, under Paley's tutelage, that Frend read and excelled in mathematics and began the academic career which occupied him for the next 17 years.

At the end of three years, Frend took his degree (and somewhat later, Holy Orders) and became both Tutor and Fellow of Jesus College. During his subsequent time at Cambridge, he became increasingly critical of the Church of England's hierarchy and dogma and especially of its exclusion of Dissenters from the university. Under the influence of Theophilus

Lindsey, who seceded from the Established Church in 1774 to found Unitarianism, Frend resigned his position in the church in 1787 to embrace Lindsey's cause. At this point, Frend began to write pamphlets, penning *Thoughts on Subscription to Religious Tests* (1788), an argument against barring from Cambridge students whose religious beliefs did not conform to the Thirty-Nine Articles. In September 1787, he wrote a Unitarian tract "exhorting [the inhabitants of Cambridge] to turn from the false worship of Three Persons to the Worship of the One True God." At Cambridge, the tract was construed as heresy, and Frend was dismissed from the Office of Tutor (the privilege of teaching) at Jesus, where he remained Fellow until 1793.

Frend vacationed on the Continent in the summer of 1789, but experienced little of Europe's growing unrest. Nevertheless, he was affected by the revolutionary spirit that spread across the Channel and became active in democratic organizations in England, including the Constitutional Society, Benjamin Flower's radical newspaper *The Intelligencer*, and the London Corresponding Society. (In the same period, Frend collaborated with Priestley on a translation of the Bible. The manuscript, however, perished in a fire at Priestley's Birmingham home on July 14, 1791.)

The source of Frend's contemporary notoriety dates from the winter to spring of 1792 and 1793, when he began a pamphlet recommending parliamentary reform, expanded religious toleration, and England's abstention from war with France. The rest of the pamphlet, published with an appendix as *Peace and Union* (1793), was only moderately critical, by contemporary standards. But it was the appendix to *Peace and Union*, Frend's badly timed response to the January regicide and England's involvement in foreign war,

that left quite another impression. After Louis XVI's execution and the Convention's declaration of war against Britain in February, Frend's likening of prosecution of the French king to the banishment of James II in 1688—a parallel highly charged since Burke's *Reflections*— was extraordinarily provocative. Equally inflammatory were Frend's concluding objections to the war tax (3p. on each shilling earned) and its catastrophic burden on the poor. To a "Church and King" readership, then, the appendix appeared the work of a would-be regicide and a rabble-rousing Jacobin.

Cambridge responded to Frend's pamphlet with uncharacteristic severity. In May 1793, an inquiry held at Jesus College accused him of violating an obscure, never enforced "grace" (college statute) with his "scandalous book." At this well-attended inquiry (the undergraduate Coleridge was in the audience to cheer the radical Fellow), Frend defended himself eloquently but unsuccessfully and, refusing to retract his appendix, was "banished" from the university. After an abortive appeal of this verdict, Frend left Cambridge and academia in the summer of 1793.

The exiled Cantabrigian spent the remaining years of the century in London, surviving on income from contributions to Flower's *Intelligencer* and from occasional lessons in mathematics. He was also involved in raising funds for the legal defense of victims of Pitt's increasingly repressive treason and sedition laws, among them the famed three of the 1794 show trials, Thelwall, Horne Tooke, and William Tooke. During the same years, Frend produced nonpopular writing, *Principles of Algebra* (1795 and 1799), and pamphlets on economics, theology, and astronomy. He also associated with London's literati, including Godwin, Wollstonecraft, Lamb,

George Dyer, and Crabb Robinson. (*See also* Hays, Mary.)

In the final 40 years of his life, Frend remained faithful to democratic causes. As a journalist for the Unitarian W.J. Fox's *Monthly Repository* (1806–37), Frend turned against French imperialism following the Peace of Amiens in 1802, but refused to support the Peninsular War (1808–14) and Britain's alliance with the reactionary Bourbon monarchy in Spain. Just before his marriage in 1808, Frend was appointed actuary to the Rock Life Assurance Company. (After Dr. Richard Price's interest in it, life insurance remained a working person's cause.) At roughly the same time, he became a friend of Francis Burdett, radical parliamentarian and, for a time, a collaborator of Cobbett.

Old age and increasingly poor health did not curb Frend's political dedication. In the 1820s, he helped to establish London University and to organize George Birbeck's Mechanic's Institute and even crusaded for the first Reform Bill in 1832. Suffering two strokes in the late 1830s, Frend began to decline and succumbed in 1841, after a long confinement.

John F. McElroy

Works Consulted

Hone, J. Ann. *For the Cause of Truth: Radicalism in London 1796–1821*. Oxford: Clarendon, 1982.

Knight, Frida. *University Rebel: The Life of William Frend, 1757–1841*. London: Gollancz, 1971.

Thompson, E.P. *The Making of the English Working Class*. London: Gollancz, 1963.

Frere, John Hookham

(1768–1846)

John Hookham Frere went to Eton, where he became a friend of Canning and helped run a magazine. At Cambridge, he pursued writing, and on entering Parliament in 1796 he was soon drawn into Canning's group of Tory wits who wrote for the short-lived but brilliant magazine *The Anti-Jacobin*. Frere wrote most of *The Loves of the Triangles*, a devastatingly funny parody of Darwin's *The Loves of the Plants*, and collaborated with Canning on the send-up of Southey, "The Friend of Humanity and the Knifegrinder." Frere, Canning, and Ellis also produced *The Rovers, or the Double Engagement*, a superb burlesque of a German tragedy. Their efforts are among the finest examples of parody in English.

Frere had a busy career as a diplomat until he inherited money and retired in the 1810s. He devoted himself to literary work thereafter, translating Aristophanes and other classic writers with great skill. But his most important literary work was the relatively short *Prospectus and Specimen of an intended National Work, by William and Robert Whistlecraft of Stowmarket in Sussex, Harness and Collar Makers. Intended to comprise the most interesting particulars relating to King Arthur and his Round Table*. This mock-epic narrative, the first two cantos of which appeared in 1817 and a further several in 1818, is a poem of genuine quality. It represents an early instance of the revival of interest in Arthurian legend and tells its stories with wit and narrative skill. Frere adopted the octave stanza of Pulci, Berni, and Casti for his storytelling (the poem was retitled, in direct reference to its subject matter, *The Monks and the Giants* from 1818 onward). Among the writers who imitated its style and manner of narration was Byron, who acknowledged his direct obligation to Frere in writing *Beppo* and *Don Juan*.

William Ruddick

Works Consulted

Elton, Oliver. *A Survey of English Literature, 1780–1830*. Vol. 2. London: Arnold, 1912.

Festing, G.J.H. *Frere and His Friends*. London: Nisbet, 1899.

Walker, Hugh. *English Satire and Satirists*. New York: Dutton, 1925.

Fuseli, Henry

(1741–1825)

An artist noted for bizarre and original works, Henry Fuseli was born Johann Heinrich Füssli in Zurich, Switzerland, where he grew up in a stimulating intellectual milieu. As a young man, his ideas were shaped by reading Rousseau, Lavater, and Heinrich Hess. He was especially stimulated by Johann Bodmer, whose aesthetic theories laid the groundwork for the *Sturm und Drang* movement. Despite his developing interests in art and literature, Fuseli was compelled by his parents to study theology and was ordained a Zwinglian minister in 1761. He followed this vocation for only a year before fleeing his native country because of political intrigues. Fuseli sought refuge in Berlin in 1763 where he came in contact with artists, poets, and philosophers whose bohemian ways appealed to him more than the clerical life. He also absorbed the liberal political views expressed during the early stage of German Romanticism and grew to distrust all sources of authority. In 1764, he went to England because of its reputation for giving sanctuary to continental dissidents and because it was also the country of Shakespeare, whose works obsessed him.

Intending to make his living in London as a writer, Fuseli's first literary work was ironically a translation of Winckelmann's *Reflections on the Paintings and Sculptures of the Greeks*. Its critical doctrines of restraint and moderation were the antithesis of Fuseli's belief in the creative value of unleashing the emotions. In 1767, on the advice of Reynolds, he abandoned his writing career and devoted himself to art. Accompanied by John Armstrong, the physi-cian-poet, he went to Rome in 1800 and remained there for the next eight years, learning to draw from copying classical statues and immersing himself in the study of Michelangelo, whose works embodied the expression of the then-current conception of the sublime, especially fear. The terrorized sinners and horrible devils in Michelangelo's *Last Judgment* seemed to confirm what Burke had argued in his treatise, *An Inquiry Into the Origins of the Sublime* (1756): scenes of pain, danger, and violence can excite agreeable sensations of awe and wonder.

In his choice of subject, Fuseli shows a passion for the strange, the dreamlike, and the fantastic. His imagination was given impetus by English poetry, especially the highly dramatic episodes from Shakespeare and Milton, which he rendered in the distorted style of the Neomannerist and with the pictorial language of Michelangelo. Some of Fuseli's most famous paintings focus on the irrational side of Shakespeare's dramas—such as the moments of terror from *Macbeth* and the enchantment scene from *A Midsummer Night's Dream*. An imaginative artist, he attempted to depict elemental worlds of witches, fairies, and elves. Like Blake, he was impatient with art that was a mere realistic rendering of nature. "Hang nature," he exclaimed, "she puts me out"; thus, he favored the worlds beyond nature where images emanated from the mind rather than the eye. For this reason, Fuseli's pictures have been more interesting from a literary and psychological perspective than as paintings per se.

The Freudian significance of a work like *The Nightmare* (1782) is unmistakable. It depicts in surrealistic terms Fuseli's preoccupation with two major components of the human psyche—fear and sex. The dream world, he shows, prior to Freud, is the seat of deepest neurosis. A sleeping woman seems to writhe on a bed in either agony or ecstasy under the influence of a disturbing dream; the substance of her dream is symbolized by a sinister-looking horse's head (the "nightmare") and a grotesque goblin that squats menacingly on her voluptuous form. Although Fuseli was known for his erotica in the 18th century, the sexual aspect here is symbolized by phallic images rather than given concrete form. The detached and leering heads are projections of woman's sexual anxiety and tensions pent up during waking hours but released in dreams.

Though Fuseli's pictures were shocking to Neoclassical canons of taste, and his personal behavior, often outrageously profane and belligerent, he became a Professor of Drawing and finally the Keeper of the Royal Academy of Art before his death in 1825. Although not a great artist, being too much an illustrator, his works are an important portent of Romanticism. And though he is quite different from Blake, especially in his lack on concern for right and wrong, he created the Expressionist style that became the hallmark of Blake's visual art.

Hallman B. Bryant

Works Consulted

Antal, Frederick. *Fuseli Studies*. London: Routledge, 1956.

Clark, Kenneth. *The Romantic Rebellion*. New York: Harper, 1973.

Gaull, Marilyn. *English Romanticism; The Human Context*. New York: Norton, 1988.

Jaloux, E. *Johann-Heinrich Füssli*. Montreaux: Editions de l'Aigle, 1942.

Knowles, John. *The Life and Writings of Henry Fuseli*. London: Colburn, 1831.

Mason, E.C. *The Mind of Henry Fuseli*. London: Routledge, 1951.

Todd, Ruthven. *Tracks in the Snow; Studies in English Science and Art*. New York: Scribner's, 1947.

Galt, John
(1779–1839)

The Scottish novelist John Galt was born in Ayrshire; its small-town life, people, and speech became integral to the quality of his best novels. While a clerk at Greenock, Galt began to write poetry. Before long, he was sent to investigate trading opportunities in Gibraltar, Malta (where he met Byron), Athens (where they met again), and Asia Minor. On his return, he published his *Voyages and Travels* (1812) and then settled into a life of literary journalism and editing, without, however, losing contact with the commercial world.

Galt began to publish novels with *The Majolo* in 1816, but his great decade as a Scottish regional novelist opens in 1820 with *The Ayrshire Legatees*. *The Annals of the Parish* (1821) is perhaps his masterpiece: it presents the autobiography of a country minister through 50 years of accelerating change and development, from 1760 to 1810, with unfaltering historical accuracy and a perfect ear for vernacular speech.

Galt's successes of the 1820s include *The Provost* (1822) and *The Entail* (1823), this last, the richest, most emotionally charged, and most firmly structured of his longer books. In the mid-1820s, he visited Canada to develop schemes for settlement, founding the town of Guelph in what is now Ontario and playing an important part in the development of the province. His novel *Lawrie Todd* (1830) draws on his Canadian experiences.

The last decade of Galt's life is a sad story of ill health and money difficulties. But during these years he produced notable short stories and the diffuse but interesting volumes of his *Autobiography* (1833) and *Literary Life and Miscellanies* (1834). His best novels are true originals. Writing in the age of Scott (who appreciated his excellence), he developed his own line of contemporary Scottish regional fiction; usually comic, dry, pawky, and observant, with an ear for vernacular speech which is equaled only by Scott's in the literature of their period.

William Ruddick

Works Consulted

Aberdein, J.W. *John Galt*. London: Oxford UP, 1936.

Gordon, I.A. *John Galt: The Life of a Writer*. Edinburgh: Oliver, 1972.

Gordon, R.K. *John Galt*. Toronto: Oxford, 1920.

Pritchett, V.S. *The Living Novel*. New York: Reynal, 1946.

Geological Sciences

During the Romantic era, geology, in many ways, came of age. Initially motivated by questions borne of natural theology—a search for the design of the creator in physical surroundings—it evolved in fits and starts into a distinct discipline focused on unraveling the earth's history. (*See also* Burnet, Thomas.) Two factors contributed to this evolution. First, for some geologists (Hutton and Jameson and their followers), the rocks consistently provided the wrong answers, challenging, not confirming, biblical accounts. In addition, understanding geologic history proved stimulating, provocative, and satisfying enough to stand apart from understanding the relationship among humanity, the cosmos, and the creator.

The development of geologic ideas of the time was complex, involving British, German, French, Russian, Swiss, and Italian naturalists and geologists, each with a unique focus, different geologic resources to learn from, and distinct scientific traditions. This led to vigorous debate—debate that focused on the relation of the past to the present, the length of geologic time, and the history of life. Most important, geologists of the 1830s recognized that fossils provided a relative time scale and could be used to correlate distant rock bodies and to develop global geologic history. The resolution of these debates and the ability to build a geologic time scale formed the initial foundation of modern geology. For this reason, historians of science have labeled the period 1780 to 1830 the "Golden Age" of geologic investigation. (*See also* Catastrophism.)

One of the formative debates of the period, the relationship between the earth's past and its present, can be understood by considering three principal schools of thought: the Neptunists, led by the German, Abraham Gottlob Werner; the Vulcanists, championed by the Frenchman, Nicholas Desmarest; and the Plutonists, formulated by the Scotsman, James Hutton.

Werner (1749–1817), internationally known mineralogist at the Mining Academy in Freiberg, Saxony, published *Kurze Klassification* (1787) in an attempt to chronicle the earth's history, which he divided into a five-tiered universal succession. His "short classification" put forth a more detailed stratigraphic succession than had previously been worked out. The oldest rocks he named *urgebirge*, or primitive rocks (granites, gneisses, schists); *uerbergangsgebirge*, or transitional rocks, comprised his second tier (limestones, basalts, graywackes). The third unit contained *floetzgebirge*, or sedimentary rocks, followed by a fourth unit, the *aufgeschwemmtegebirge*, or unconsolidated deposits. *vulkanische gesteine*, or volcanic rocks, Werner considered recent, local, and on the whole unimportant in his scheme.

Werner went beyond mere classification, however, and proposed a mechanism for the creation of these universal rock units. From an ancient ocean, whose composition remained a mystery, chemical precipitates built up successive deposits, forming the earth's crust. As this ancient, universal ocean continued to evolve and slowly subside, rocks were precipitated and mechanically deposited by the erosion of primitive rocks, creating the universal transitional unit. Fossils occasionally were found in these strata, but the ocean was too turbulent to support much life. The ocean dropped further, thus explaining the predominance of deposited sediments in the rock record. Life forms began to proliferate, possibly because the ocean was now calmer, resulting in an increased fossil record. Alluvial deposits, formed by the eroding older formations and only locally distributed, completed the rock record. Where underlying layers of coal caught fire, volcanic rocks could form, but Werner discounted the importance of such events. Indeed, his emphasis on the formative role of the ocean led others to dub his model "Neptunist." Werner's simple, elegant theory greatly appealed to his contemporaries and students, among whom were such eminent naturalists as Leopold von Buch (1774–1853), J.F. d'Aubuisson (1796–1841), Robert Jameson (1774–1854), John Murray (d. 1820), and Alexander von Humboldt (1769–1859).

According to the Neptunists, ancient geologic events had little relation to present geologic processes. Since rock type was unique to a given geologic episode, those that formed early in the earth's history had no counterpart in younger rock units. The violence of the past, with turbulent seas shaping steep mountains and deep valleys plastered by unusual precipitates, could in no way shed light on present quiescent times. Werner was not a religious man, but his theory appealed greatly to biblical scholars, who also stressed a decoupling between antediluvial and postdiluvial times. The past witnessed creative forces of considerable power; recent geologic processes, in Werner's view, chronicled a mostly static earth undergoing erosion and decay.

The first significant challenge to Werner's Neptunism came from the Vulcanists; the focus was on the formation of basalt, and the key was the district of Auvergne in France. (*See also* Vulcanism.) Based on detailed field observations, Desmarest, a fanatical investigator of rocks, demonstrated that basalt in Auvergne was found in close association with prehistoric but well-preserved volcanic land forms as part of a solidified old lava stream. Basalt was therefore volcanic, igneous in origin, not a sedimentary precipitate. A visit by Desmarest to Italy, the site of historic vulcanism, helped to confirm his arguments. Curiously, Desmarest did not recognize the significance of his discovery; he remained a supporter of Werner and later never accepted Hutton's arguments for igneous intrusions. Still, the Vulcanist school grew as others accumulated evidence in the scientific literature for the igneous origins of basalt. In 1816, Pierre Louis Cordier (1777–1861) proved conclusively the composition of modern and older basalts were the same.

Vulcanists' work might have been a serious blow to Werner's scheme, since the basalts of Auvergne and of Italy were obviously quite young and not *floetz* in age. Rock type was not a guide to geologic age—the same rock type had formed in different periods in the earth's history. The geologic past therefore had in common, at least, basalt and vulcanism with the geologic present. However, the response by many was to accommodate vulcanism into the Wernerian scheme as a minor exception to the sedimentary character of most rocks. Without an alternative global geologic history, the Vulcanists could not see the significance of their observations.

In Edinburgh, Hutton (1726–97) was pondering the processes that continually created and broke down land forms. He agreed with Vulcanists that volcanic activity held essential clues to the earth's workings. But Hutton's observations of granitic formations convinced him that heat within the earth both forced up intrusive rocks and deformed contact rocks; a process of metamorphism, effected by heat, was central to Hutton's geology. Intuiting the principal role of subsurface heat, Hutton searched the Scottish countryside for igneous formations, finding them in the Salisbury Crags, the Grampion Highlands, and Galloway and Arran.

Because Hutton believed (correctly) granites and other intrusive igneous rocks crystallized within, not outside, the earth's crust, he and his followers were called Plutonists. In 1795, his volume *Theory of the Earth* appeared, proposing a cyclic, steady, infinite-time model of the earth, built on the premise that the present is the key to the past. Hutton obviously was not interested in an historical system or in articulating a definitive history of the strata he studied. In fact, he envisioned an infinite time scale in which geologic phenomena played out their roles. Hutton's continuous cycle of deposition, erosion, and uplift, all working their changes slowly, opposed Werner's insistence on a predominantly static present decoupled from past events. Hutton's theory made clear that present processes have been at work changing the earth for an infinitely long time.

When John Playfair (1748–1818) popularized Hutton's model in *Illustrations of the Huttonian Theory of the Earth* (1802), he began a 20-year debate between Neptunists and Plutonists. Murray, in *A Comparative View of the Huttonian and Neptunian Systems of Geology* (1802), answered Playfair's challenge. Summarizing both models, Murray dismissed Hutton's emphasis on the formative role of heat, claiming that heat had dissipated from the earth ages ago. Without such heat, Murray insisted, rocks could not solidify nor layers of strata rise up dramatically from the sea floor. The rocks themselves and not the processes currently at work on earth explain the past, Murray argued.

One of the most vehement attacks against Hutton was from Richard Kirwan (1733–1812), president of the Royal Irish Academy. One of Kirwan's most strident criticisms was that Hutton's views conflicted with Genesis. Kirwan and many other naturalists of the time (e.g., Jean de Luc, 1727–1817), especially in Great Britain, had modified the Neptunian scheme in an attempt to reconcile it with the biblical creation. They argued that *floetz* strata were post- or syndiluvial (after the biblical flood), while the underlying, older formations were all antediluvial. Through rigorous biblical scholarship, Bishop Ussher, in the 16th century, had computed that the earth had been created 26 October 4004 B.C. Many subsequent naturalists, who could not forsake religion, used his computation as a general guide. William Buckland (1784–1856), author of *Relics of the Flood* (1823) and renowned scholar at Oxford, was a major proponent of this offshoot Neptunist school, a group labeled Diluvialists. To Buckland's followers, fossils documented a former Golden Age populated by giants but now supplanted by a diminished present, an Iron Age of postdiluvial degeneration. Buckland pointed to fossils high in the Andes and Himalayas as proof that the biblical flood once covered the earth. Other evidence he cited for the deluge included gravel deposits, gorges, and ravines, as well as erratic boulders scattered on hills; mere erosion and deposition, weak forces of a degenerate age, he reasoned, could not have fostered these various phenomena. After careful search in supposed deluge sediments reclaimed no relics of pre-Noachian humanity, Buckland, altering biblical chronology, postulated that the deluge must have been before humankind's creation. As continued geologic investigations encountered increasing complexities, an uneasy compromise between geological and biblical history had to be made.

Count Georges Buffon (1707–88), author of *Epoques de la Nature* (1778), reported experiments using heated cannon-balls (he owned a foundry) to approximate the time it took for the earth to cool from an original incandescent state to its present temperature. His estimate for the earth's age (115,000 years) was an early and radical departure from the thousands of years permitted by literal interpretation of the Bible. While his estimate bore little fruit in the Romantic period, his general perspective of a cooling earth fueled debates among Victorian scientists trying to quantify the earth's age. With the exception of Buffon, few in the Romantic era tried to provide dates for the earth history they were developing, nor could they agree on a means of doing so. Biblical chronology continued to constrain investigators. At the other end of the spectrum, Hutton, a deist, assumed the earth was of practical (in terms of determination) if not actual infinite age. Others chose not to address the question. The tool necessary for providing the means of temporally correlating distant rock bodies and thereby producing a global geologic history (but one without numbers) was only to develop late in the Romantic era.

On the continent, two Frenchmen, Georges Cuvier (1769–1832) and Alexander Brongniart (1770–1847) studied, in detail and with a new approach, strata in the Paris Basin; their *Essai sur la geographie mineralogique des environs de Paris* (1808) and Cuvier's *Recherches sur les ossemens fossiles de quadrupedes* (1812) considered fossils the essential character for definition and temporal correlation of stratigraphic units. Their work marked a notable departure from both Werner's and Hutton's approach, where mineralogy and rock texture were essential characteristics, and fossils, considered accidental.

Independently, William Smith (1769–1839), a self-educated canal and mining engineer, also realized the significance of fossils, publishing *Stratigraphical system of organized fossils* (1817). He also produced one of the first detailed geologic maps of England. Through publications and contact with his contemporaries, Smith became a key figure in the development of fossil correlation (biostratigraphy) in England. In recognition of his contributions, the newly formed (1807) Geological Society of London presented him with the first Wollaston Medal, then and now its highest honor. Fossil correlation, which met with great success, was one of the most important geologic developments of the Romantic period. Without it there was no defendable geologic history.

Cuvier interpreted the succession of fossil species in the geologic record as a series of creations and extinctions associated with catastrophic events. Catastrophists influenced by Cuvier grew in number in the 1820s, blending elements of Neptunism with Huttonian Plutonism and its cycles of mountain building. Catastrophists still argued for a decoupling of the present from the past and still built into the geologic histories the biblical deluge, although it occupied an increasingly minor portion of that history. Most of the Catastrophists were thus what today would be labeled "creationists." J.B. de Lamarck (1744–1829) and Darwin, in the minority, dabbled with the thought of evolution and the "great tree of life." Smith, it should be noted, was also a Catastrophist.

During the 1820s, Charles Lyell (1797–1875), lawyer turned geologist, pursued his science in Great Britain and on the Continent. He met Cuvier, Brongniart, and von Humboldt in Paris in 1824; with the French geologist Constant Prevost he studied Tertiary strata in the Paris Basin. Cuvier and Brongniart, in their study of the Paris Basin, saw no connection between modern and ancient freshwater sediments; Lyell could not agree. Ancient freshwater deposits, both Scottish and French, preserved fossil representatives of still extant species and contained similar textures to modern sediments. On the Massif Central in 1828, with Roderick Murchison (1792–1871), he noted uplift and deformation of sedimentary strata above the volcanic center. Where others had argued for rapid, catastrophic uplift, Lyell perceived instead evidence for the slow, steady, cumulative work of many small movements associated with earthquakes. The Auvergne formations convinced Lyell that current, gradual processes held the key to the geologic past, an approach now labeled gradualism.

Studying recent vulcanism in Italy, Lyell continued to accumulate data that suggested gradual uplift. Again he saw uplifted strata containing fossil remains of species similar to those still living. Indeed, the fossil-containing strata he had analyzed throughout Europe provided Lyell with necessary data for classifying the Tertiary. By studying the proportion of fossil shells in strata belonging to extant species, Lyell was able to break the Tertiary into three long periods: the oldest, or *Eocene*; the middle, or *Miocene*; and the *Pliocene*, or youngest. From the *Pliocene* to the *Eocene*, Lyell saw a consistent decrease in the proportion of fossils that still had living representatives. As he peered back in time, the fossils became less familiar, but gradually so and with links of continuity.

Drawing on a decade's field experience in Great Britain and on the Continent, Lyell published in 1830 the first volume of what became an enormously popular geologic text, *Principles of Geology*, and forcefully countered the Catastrophists. With the help of biostratigraphy and careful, meticulous fieldwork, Lyell was able to confirm Hutton's conviction that great spans of time were needed to build and rebuild the earth. He saw no reason to

invoke catastrophism when the steady forces of erosion and sedimentation, the periodic rises and declines in sea level, as well as the gradual work of earthquakes and vulcanism, could explain many of the perplexities in the rock record. Lyell also put Werner's stratigraphic history to rest.

The conditions under which rocks formed, not their age, determined their characteristics. Additionally, these conditions were recurrent, not unique; thus, if geology were to develop as a science, Lyell argued, present processes had to be thoroughly studied. Finally, Lyell's *Principles* championed Hutton's theory of cyclical, nonprogressive geologic processes within an infinite time scale. Once again, the notion of "deep time" entered into geologic discussion. Adding his own signature to Hutton's original idea (i.e., the present is the key to the past), Lyell theorized that the energy that builds mountains, shifts and deforms land, and recycles sediments has always been uniform. His contemporaries termed his model "uniformitarianism." Lyell insisted that natural laws of the past and present were essentially the same. Indeed, he could see no reason to accept the theory that the earth was cooling; rather, the long history of European vulcanism suggested a steady source of heat-propelled uplift. It took 35 years before Hutton's theory of the earth, rearticulated by Lyell, gained acceptance among geologists.

In his second and third volumes, Lyell considered the question of species extinction (he was, at this time, an anti-evolutionist) and proposed a comprehensive classification of Tertiary strata. *Principles* proved so successful that it went through 12 editions by 1876. In fact, the young Charles Darwin in 1831 carried Lyell's two volumes on board the *H.M.S. Beagle*. Lyell represented a culmination of the best

Romantic geology: the meticulous strati-graphic work of the Wernerians, the care-ful correlation of fossils perfected by Smith and Cuvier, plus the theoretical vision of Hutton. By combining all these approaches, Lyell was able to decipher the Tertiary rock record and propose principles that helped establish geology as a science di-vorced from cosmology and biblical specu-lation. Lyell, moreover, helped shape geo-logic debate for the remainder of the century. For instance, he touched on the questions of climate and sea-level change, internal heat, polar magnetism, and rock compaction, although he offered no solu-tions. This work was left to the next gen-eration of earth scientists.

During the Romantic age, then, geol-ogy informed scientific, theological, and literary thought. Mountains, such sublime reminders of the earth's power, and caves, believed to hold the secrets of the earth's— and humanity's—origins, took on almost totemic power in the emerging *naturphilosophie*. The great Goethe himself, an enthusiastic collector of fossils; the nov-elist Novalis, a student of Werner; and the English Romantic poets, particularly Coleridge, Wordsworth, and Shelley, ac-quainted with geologists both German and British, all turned to the earth's formations for literary inspiration. More important, geologic discovery, in contravening reli-gious orthodoxy, began a debate, still rag-ing, that shook the very foundations of Christian faith. When Charles Darwin, aided by his *Principles of Geology*, embarked in 1831 on a scientific voyage around the globe, the geology of the Romantic period had already discomfited religious circles. Importantly, the geology emerging at the end of the Romantic period countered Romantic thought. Lyell's steady-state, nonprogressive model of geologic pro-cesses, rather than conforming to the Ro-mantic ideology of a paradoxical degen-eration and progression, introduced un-certainty into the character of history, both geologic and human.

Harmon Droge Maher
Susan Naramore Maher

Works Consulted

Albritton, Claude C. *The Abyss of Time: Changing Conceptions of the Earth's Antiquity after the Six-teenth Century*. San Francisco: Freeman, 1980.

Cunningham, Andrew, and Jardine, Nicholas. *Romanticism and the Sciences*. New York: Cam-bridge UP, 1990.

Gauil, Marilyn. *English Romanticism: The Human Context*. New York: Norton, 1988.

Greene, Mott T. *Geology of the Nineteenth Century: Changing Views of a Changing World*. Ithaca: Cornell UP, 1982.

Hallam, A. *Great Geological Controversies*. Oxford: Oxford UP, 1983.

Laudan, Rachel. *From Mineralogy to Geology: The Foundations of a Science, 1650–1830*. Chicago: U of Chicago P, 1987.

Porter, Roy. *The Making of Geology: Earth Science in Britain 1660–1815*. Cambridge: Cambridge UP, 1977.

Thompson, Susan J. *A Chronology of Geological Thinking from Antiquity to 1899*. Metuchen: Scare-crow, 1988.

German Fairytales

The German *Kunstmärchen*, or literary (also referred to as original or poetic) fairytale, differs from the *Volksmärchen* (folktale) in several respects. A folktale derives from popular oral tradition and has been preserved by word of mouth. Its style and contents are shaped and molded by the individuality of the person relating the tale, who may shorten, lengthen, or change it at will. The literary fairytale is an original invention of its author, and its style and contents normally reflect the author's particular artistic concerns. While being related to the folktale and being influenced by it, the literary fairytale can incorporate influences completely foreign to the *Volksmärchen*. The *Kunstmärchen* can also reflect and be subject to the prevailing literary trends. (*See also* German Romanticism.)

Literary fairytales by the German Romantics create their own myths and mythology, taking over motifs and narrative style from the folktale and fashioning them with deliberate artistry and a more ambitious narrative technique. Fairytales were the purest form of poetry for the German Romantics, and Novalis even called the fairytale the canon of poetry. The German Romantics deliberately mixed realistic with supernatural elements, and realistic and fantastic planes exist side by side in the world of their fairytales. In contrast with the hero of the folktale, the more modern hero of the *Kunstmärchen*, product of the Enlightenment, is surprised when the miraculous discloses itself to him or her. Expressions like *wundersam, wunderlich, wundervoll* which describe these wondrous and strange happenings, indicate the transition into the magical world. The German Romantic literary fairytale takes its point of departure as the inner, emotional life of its heroes, another contrast to the folktale hero. The heroes of the *Kunstmärchen* are driven by a melancholy yearning to leave their homes, and although they may offer a variety of reasons for their decision, they are really searching subconsciously for a higher truth. Yet when they have reached their goal, they are often too unsettled and unsteady to find lasting peace, as in the *Kunstmärchen* of Ludwig Tieck. Love is of great importance for the literary fairytale hero—this is not the case for the folktale hero—for whom the beloved becomes the embodiment of all wisdom and truth. Many literary fairytale heroes achieve a kind of permanent right of domicile in the world of the wondrous through union with the beloved.

Early German Romanticism was inspired not so much by the folktale as by Goethe's *Märchen*, published as the final story of his *Unterhaltungen deutscher Ausgewanderten* in 1795. This cryptic narrative concerning rivers, green serpents, and temples makes use of Oriental and romance motifs in a symbolical and allegorical manner. Novalis takes over the form of Goethe's fairytale to couch the *Atlantis* tale from his *Heinrich von Ofterdingen* in the form of an allegory, and Book One of Novalis's novel is concluded by another fairytale, this time told by Klingsohr. In the literary fairytales of Tieck (*Der blonde Eckbert, Der Runenberg*) the Romantic hero wants to fathom the ultimate wonders of nature but is destroyed by Nature in the process. The demonic side of Nature characterizes Tieck's tales and determines their outcome. The unfathomable side of Nature proves to be the hero's undoing, along with the conflicting feelings and impulses within his own soul. In Tieck's *Der Liebeszauber* and *Der Pokal*, miraculous and realistic elements are blended, and fairies determine the action and outcome of *Die Freunde* and *Die Feen*. Friedrich de la Motte Fouqué's *Undine*, in which a water sprite marries a mortal, mixes the genres of fairytale, Novelle, and short story (it is called an *Erzählung*, or "tale").

The late German Romantic E.T.A. Hoffmann followed Tieck's lead in blending wondrous, demonic, and realistic elements. His heroes live right in the middle of the world of the philistines, and the wondrous is revealed to them in the midst of the everyday world (e.g., the allegorical fairytale *Der goldene Topf*). Hoffmann was also very successful at deploying topoi from folk literature and poetry. His realistic literary fairytales (e.g., *Meister Floh*) influenced Adalbert von Chamisso, whose *Peter*

Schlemihls wundersame Geschichte places reality and the marvelous side by side (the hero's shadow is bought by a man in grey in return for the inexhaustible purse of Fortunatus). In contrast with *Peter Schlemihl*, Chamisso's allegorical literary fairytale *Adelberts Fabel* reveals the influence of Novalis.

Another representative of late Romanticism, Clemens Brentano, published two cyclical collections of literary fairytales, the *Italienische Märchen* and the *Rheinmärchen*. The former collection includes the tale *Gockel, Hinkel, und Gackeleia*, with Gackeleia's description of a fantastical city of mice. Brentano's literary fairytales can be linked to the folktale through the similarity in motifs and themes and through their obvious pleasure in constructing outrageous story lines, whereas his intellectual attitude connects him to the early German Romantic literary fairytale. Brentano's tales are characterized by a strong musicality in their language and by cheerfulness, merriment, and an almost childlike belief in magic and miracles.

In the literary fairytales of Joseph von Eichendorff, all the elements of the German Romantic fairytale are modified. The beginnings of a transition to the conservative homely realism of the *Biedermeier* period of German literature can be clearly seen. The literary fairytales of this period reflect its general artistic trends (i.e., a love of the small and insignificant, a need to lavish care and attention, a joy in collecting things, and a deep respect for the workings of God as reflected in everyday reality). The heroes in the tales of Wilhelm Hauff (*Das kalte Herz, Zwerg Nase*) and Eduard Mörike (*Der Schatz,* "Märchen von sichern Mann," written in classical hexameters) come mostly from a middle-class background, and after wondrous events have paved the way to modest happiness, they return to the reality of their somewhat bourgeois lives.

German Romantic *Kunstmärchen* are very much the creations of the individuality of their authors. The German Romantics were attracted to the *Volksmärchen* by their mythical and archetypal elements and their stock of independent, self-contained motifs that can be easily transferred to and taken over by another genre. The *Kunstmärchen* of the German Romantics influenced Washington Irving's Americanized versions of folktales (*Rip Van Winkle* and *The Legend of Sleepy Hollow*). Other writers of literary fairytales outside of Germany were Hans Christian Andersen from Denmark, and Lewis Carroll (*Alice in Wonderland*), John Ruskin, Oscar Wilde (*The Happy Prince, The Fisherman and His Soul*), and Rudyard Kipling from England. (*See also* Grimm Brothers.)

Paul Davies

Works Consulted

Apel, F. *Die Zaubergärten der Phantasie: Zur Theorie und Geschichte der Kunstmärchen.* Heidelberg: Winter, 1979.

Birrell, G. *The Boundless Present: Space and Time in the Literary Fairy Tales of Novalis and Tieck.* Chapel Hill: U of North Carolina P, 1979.

Franz, M.L. v. *An Introduction to the Interpretation of Fairy Tales.* New York: Spring, 1970.

Klotz, B. *Das europäische Kunstmärchen.* Stuttgart: Metzler, 1985.

Ranke, K., ed. *Enzyklopädie des Märchens.* New York: deGruyter, 1977.

Schumacher, H. *Narziß an der Quelle. Das romantische Kunstmärchen: Geschichte und Interpretation.* Wiesbaden: Athenaion, 1977.

Tismar, J. *Kunstmärchen.* 2nd ed. Stuttgart: Metzler, 1983.

Zipes, J. *Breaking the Magic Spell: Radical Themes of Folk and Fairy Tales.* Austin: U of Texas P, 1979.

German Idealism, Influence of

It is in the *Biographia Literaria* and the lectures of Coleridge that German Idealism seems to have exerted its most profound influence on English Romanticism, but many other writers of the period— including Henry Crabb Robinson, De Quincey, and Beddoes—were attracted by the ideas of Kant, Fichte, and Schelling. As Coleridge explained the mighty attraction, Kant had explored more thoroughly than any previous philosopher the *a priori* capacities of the mind to order thought and interpret perception.

Describing the mind as a passive recipient of external data—a *tabula rasa* upon which the senses recorded their information, or a *camera obscura* which received and retained sensory images—Locke could declare that nothing existed in the mind but the empirical impressions mediated through the senses. Before empirical impressions came rushing in, according to Kant, nothing existed in the mind but the mind itself. Affirming an active agency rather than a passive receptivity of mind, Kant distinguished in his *Critique of Pure Reason* (1781) between the intuitive reason and the discursive understanding. With the empiricists, Kant agreed that all knowledge begins in experience. Temporally, experience must precede knowledge. But this does not mean that knowledge derives exclusively from experience. Perhaps experience itself is shaped and organized by certain dynamic processes of the mind.

By analyzing how sensory data is organized, Kant identifies "categories" that exist in the mind prior to experience. His "transcendental aesthetic" studies sensory response and the relation between subject and object. His "transcendental logic" explains how perceptions are structured into conceptions upon which judgment may be predicated. Knowledge is constructed from phenomena; the mind never has immediate access to the noumenon, the thing-in-itself. Kant's "transcendental dialectic" demonstrates how the reason, making use of a methodology kindred to the rigorous analytics applied to the phenomenological dialectic of subject and object, may pursue ultimate questions beyond the scope of objective experience. It was this speculative endeavor that prompted Schelling, and Coleridge too, to seek more in Kant's noumenon than was immediately apparent.

Kant's followers sought to reconcile the phenomenological and transcendental dialectic, to bridge the gap between phenomenon and noumenon. The one thing-in-itself to which the mind does have immediate access, Fichte argued, is its own noumenal identity. He thus posited the self as his philosophical ground. As both object and subject, the self is the coincidence of thing and idea. Because that coincidence is never static, the Fichtean self is defined as acting: always reflecting on its own being as well as participating in the exterior world of things. To the extent that the self actively engages and comprehends the world of things, it succeeds in making the strange familiar. In terms of its experience as a self actively encountering and appropriating other, the I generates in its own consciousness a Not-I. For the I to act intellectually and morally, it needs the challenge of the Not-I. The Not-I establishes the limits that the I must confront, the barriers against which it may struggle, the opposition it may strive to overcome.

The attempt to claim the I as the one accessible thing-in-itself had not been unanticipated by Kant. According to Kant, even self-consciousness or self-awareness is phenomenal rather than noumenal. The mind can observe only the effects and consequences, not the origins, of its own operations. It can ascertain "the: I think" as phenomenon but cannot witness the noumenal processes from which conscious awareness arises. If Kant was right in asserting the phenomenal nature of apperception, then it was only a self-delusion that Fichte's introspective thought-experiments enabled him to explore the noumenal mind. Instead of claiming that the noumenon could be consciously experienced, Schelling said that it could nevertheless be demonstrated by the philosopher and realized by the artist.

Adapting from contemporary science in his *Naturphilosophie*, Schelling asserted that all material reality was a construct of pervasive energy. The whole of the visible universe is bound together by electricity, magnetism, and gravity. The energy of mind and the energy of physical nature are essentially identical: one is capable of self-reflection, the other is not, but both owe their phenomenal presence to the energy that informs their noumenal identity. While the philosopher can offer nothing more than a demonstration of identity of the noumenal and phenomenal, the artist, by imposing the dynamic energies of the creative imagination upon the inert matter of his artistic medium, bridges the gap between subject and object. Matter is transformed so that it reveals the image of the mind.

Coleridge, in his lecture "On Poesy or Art" (1818), drew from Schelling the argument that "in every work of *Art* the Conscious is so impressed on the Unconscious, as to appear *in* it." Long before Coleridge, Crabb Robinson was intimately familiar with Schelling's account of the presence of mind in matter. Attending Schelling's lectures on the philosophy of art at Jena, Robinson had kept thorough notes. In spite of Coleridge's endeavor to convince him that he had not learned from Schelling's notions, Robinson immediately recognized the passages from Schelling in *Biographia Literaria*.

As a student at Göttingen (1825–29) and Würzburg (1829–32), Beddoes, too, acquired extensive knowledge of German philosophy. In *Death's Jest Book*, a sprawling but unfinished poetical drama on which he wrote throughout his years in Germany and Switzerland, Beddoes thematizes the inaccessibility of the noumenon by sending his characters in a morbid quest for essence. As in Schlegel's formulations of Romantic irony, the irreconcilable division of ideal and real engenders a "transcendental buffoonery." Because Isbrand, Beddoes's Iago-like villain, is disguised as a court fool, he appears now in deadly intrigue against Duke Melveric, now in grotesque banter with the zany Homunculus Mandrake. Although most of the characters die, the morbid jest is that even in the realm of spirit there is no union with essence. The dead, like the living, remain caught in the web of mere phenomena.

In his several essays on Kant (written in 1824, 1830, and 1833), De Quincey's comprehension of transcendental idealism, as René Wellek has argued, seems superficial. Where Coleridge endeavored to elaborate the intuitive ground of German Idealism, De Quincey wanted intuition to inform and direct the emotions. Thus he remains opposed to the aesthetic "disinterestedness" advocated in Kant's *Critique of Judgment* (1790). Although he attributes "the Literature of Knowledge and the Literature of Power," respectively, to the discursive understanding and the intuitive reason, he engages the latter not in a Kantian dialectic with the senses but in aesthetic play with the passions.

Coleridge turned to German Idealism

firm the capacity of imagination to participate in the "Infinite I AM." This was problematic for Kant had been accused of undermining traditional theology, and Schelling, who posited a "World-Soul" and an "Absolute Identity," refused to locate it in God. Schelling's idealism consequently reverts to pantheism. As Thomas McFarland has shown, Coleridge sought the "I AM," but Schelling led him into the externality of "it is." In the *Logos* of the Johannine Gospel, Coleridge declared that division between phenomenon and noumenon is bridged. In interpreting "the Word made flesh," he states that the noumenon becomes directly accessible through the phenomenon. But adhering to the strictures of Kant's "transcendental dialectic," he admits that the intuitive reason cannot reach beyond mere speculation into the mystery of God incarnate.

By giving primacy to spiritual inspiration over intellectual inquiry, De Quincey inverts the Kantian postulate in his essay on "Protestantism." After summarizing how Kant successfully collapsed the physicotheological proof, the cosmological proof, and the ontological proof "to demonstrate the indemonstrability of God," De Quincey observes that with the "same *apodeixis*, which he had thus inexorably torn from reason under one manifestation, Kant himself restored to the reason in another (the *praktische vernunft*)." For Kant, reason is the given, from which follows a subjective need, and therefore a moral duty, to assume the existence of God. For De Quincey, a "sympathy with the invisible" is the given, from which follows the injunction to explore the unknown as far as reason will allow.

Inspiration means much more to De Quincey than scriptural revelation. Inspiration intrudes upon consciousness as an irrational or suprarational presence. It may itself resist rational scrutiny, but it arouses the rational faculties, stimulating an activity of mind, like Wordsworth's "correspondent breeze," "vexing its own creation." In their reciprocity, inspiration and development bring about revelation, and revelation promulgates continuing interaction.

Because subject-object dialectics are pervasive in English Romanticism, it is easy to read the abundant images of perceptual liminality as if they were wrought with conscious awareness of Kant, Fichte, or Schelling. Wordsworth's "transports" in feeling "the sentiment of Being spread/ O'er all that moves," as E.D. Hirsch has noted, aptly express Schelling's idea of transcendental perception. Hirsch denies direct influence and argues, instead, the unity and coherence of Romanticism as an international movement that found its expression in literature, music, and art, as well as in philosophy. Whether one is willing to place Urizen and Vala within Kantian *Verstand*, Los and Enitharmon within *Vernunft*, or talk about the competing demands of inward and outward consciousness in "Crystal Cabinet" as if they were instances of the dire separation of phenomenon and noumenon, it remains evident that Blake, too, struggled against the threatening solipsism that had arisen with the new individualism of the age. Byron's regret that "this clay will sink/Its spark immortal," or Keats's complaint that "the fancy cannot cheat so well/As she is fam'd to do," add to the evidence that the poets found much the same difficulty in urging the primacy of mind and imagination as did the philosophers. (*See also* Berkeley's Idealism, Disinterestedness, Kant and Theories of German Idealism.)

Frederick Burwick

Works Consulted

Abrams, M.H. *The Mirror and the Lamp*. New York: Oxford UP, 1953.

———. *Natural Supernaturalism: Tradition and Revolution in Romantic Literature*. New York: Norton, 1971.

Ashton, Rosemary. *The German Idea: Four English Writers and the Reception of German Thought 1800–1860*. New York: Cambridge UP, 1980.

Coleridge, Samuel Taylor. *Biographia Literaria*, 2 vols., Ed. James Engell and Walter Jackson Bate. *The Collected Works of Samuel Taylor Coleridge*, 7. Princeton: Princeton UP, 1983.

———. *Lectures 1808–1819: On Literature*, 2 vols., Ed. Reginald Foakes. *The Collected Works of Samuel Taylor Coleridge*, 5. Princeton: Princeton UP, 1987.

De Quincey, Thomas. "Protestantism." *The Collected Writings of Thomas De Quincey*. Ed. David Masson. Vol. 8. Edinburgh: Black, 1889–90: 244–309. 14 vols.

Engell, James. *The Creative Imagination. Enlightenment to Romanticism*. Cambridge: Harvard UP, 1981.

Hirsch, E.D., Jr. *Wordsworth and Schelling. A Typological Study of Romanticism*. New Haven: Yale UP, 1960.

McFarland, Thomas. *Coleridge and the Pantheist Tradition*. Oxford: Clarendon, 1969.

Orsini, Gian. *Coleridge and German Idealism*. Carbondale: Southern Illinois UP, 1969.

Wellek, René. *Immanuel Kant in England, 1793–1838*. Princeton: Princeton UP, 1931.

German Romanticism

Nearly all major English Romantic writers had contact with German literature: Coleridge, Shelley, Byron, Scott, Hazlitt, De Quincey, and Carlyle. German Romantic writers include not only the established members of the school (e.g., Friedrich and August Wilhelm Schlegel, Tieck, Wackenroder, Novalis, Arnim, Brentano, E.T.A. Hoffmann, Eichendorff) but also those whose writings betrayed more than the occasional Romantic trait (e.g., Jean Paul and Heinrich von Kleist). The German *Sturm und Drang*, which preceded Romanticism, shared with Romanticism the emphasis on the primacy of feelings, cult of the individual, and cultivation

of the irrational. Gottfried Bürger's *Lenore* (1773) can also be considered Romantic for its uncanny, ghostly atmosphere and its rejection of Enlightenment Rationalism. Even the works of Goethe and Schiller possess Romantic features, and the early works of their *Sturm und Drang* period in particular are Romantic in their evocation of nature and emphasis on the individual genius.

Two decisive impulses for the dissemination of German literature in England in the late 18th and early 19th centuries were Madame de Staël's *De l'Allemagne* and the literary circles in Edinburgh, Bristol, and Norwich. In Edinburgh, Henry Mackenzie's *Account of the German Theatre*, delivered as a lecture before the Royal Society of Edinburgh in 1788, was of seminal importance in spreading information of the German *Sturm und Drang* and early Classicism throughout Britain. Robert Pearse Gillies made the dissemination of German literature in Britain his life's work and wrote numerous articles on German writers for *Blackwood's Magazine*. During the last decade of the 18th century, Bristol became a center for German studies under the guidance of Beddoes, and the Norwich circle was dominated by William Taylor, who was well versed in contemporary literature and a skilled translator. Also, Henry Crabb Robinson dedicated himself to the task of encouraging understanding and empathy among the Romantic poets of Germany and England.

The efforts of such mediators received support from Staël's *De l'Allemagne*, which appeared in England in 1813 in its French original, followed immediately by an English translation. Part two of her book deals with German literature and art in the form of reviews of the leading figures of German literature, including the Romantics Zacharias Werner, Novalis, the

Schlegel brothers, Tieck, and Jean Paul. *De l'Allemagne* is one of the cornerstones on which 19th-century England based its romanticized image of Germany as a land of poets and thinkers.

Wordsworth and Coleridge visited Germany from September 1798 to July 1799. Coleridge used his stay in Göttingen in 1799 to study German literature, language, and philosophy. He subsequently produced translations of Schiller's *Wallenstein* and *Die Piccolomini*; Tieck's "Herbstlied," which he then incorporated into his drama *Zapolya* as "Glycine's Song"; poems by Goethe and Schiller; and adaptations and free paraphrases of folksongs, such as "Wenn ich ein Vöglein wär" ("Something Childish but very Natural").

The first work of German literature Coleridge read was Schiller's *Die Räuber* at Cambridge in 1794, and his enthusiasm was expressed in *The Sonnet to the Author of the Robbers*, first published in 1796. The effect that this drama and Schiller's *Der Geisterseher* had on Coleridge manifest itself in his dramas *Osorio* and *Remorse*, a recasting of *Osorio* written in 1797. The first three acts of *Remorse* are taken with some modifications from the Sicilian's story of Jeronymo and Lorenzo in Schiller's *Geisterseher*.

Coleridge was the only English Romantic to make a genuine effort at systematically formulating his own theory of art in a manner similar to the methods of the German Romantic philosophers. He acknowledged Schelling's originality and considered him the founder of the philosophy of Nature. Coleridge's theory of beauty as developed in the *Essay on the Fine Arts* (1815) revolves around the concept of "multeity in unity," which in turn is indebted to Schelling's definition of artistic beauty as an *Ineinsbildung des Mannigfaltigen*. Long passages in chapters 12 and 13 of

Biographia Literaria (1817) drawing a distinction between Fancy and Imagination could have their origin either in Schelling or in Jean Paul, who attempted to draw a line between *Einbildungskraft* and *Bildungskraft* in the first book of his *Vorschule der Ästhetik* (1808).

Coleridge also took up the ideas of A.W. Schlegel, becoming acquainted with his Vienna lectures on the history of drama (*Vorlesungen über dramatische Kunst und Literatur*, 1809) in December 1811, during Coleridge's second course of Shakespeare lectures. Coleridge felt that what Schlegel had to say about Shakespeare confirmed his own views, and when he repeated his Shakespeare interpretations in 1813 and 1814, they converged to a great extent with Schlegel's. The translation of Schlegel's lectures by John Black (1815) contributed enormously to the dissemination of German culture in England and decisively molded English interpretation of Shakespeare. In *Progress of the Drama* (1811), Coleridge borrowed Schlegel's polar terms "Classical" and "Romantic" in order to distinguish between the literature of the ancient world and that of the Middle Ages and Shakespeare's times, respectively.

Coleridge met A.W. Schlegel in Godesberg in 1828, and Tieck visited Coleridge in the summer of 1817. Coleridge made no secret of his feeling that he and Tieck were kindred spirits. In a letter to the publisher Murray (1814), he called Tieck and Schlegel the leading lights of contemporary German literature, and after Tieck's visit he read in quick succession Tieck's *William Lovell*, *Franz Sternbald*, and the *Phantasien über die Kunst* of Wackenroder/Tieck.

Coleridge almost certainly introduced Wordsworth to the basics of German Transcendentalist philosophy. There are spiritual affinities between the *Lyrical Ballads*

(1798) and Schelling's *Ideen zu einer Philosophie der Natur* (1797–1801), indicating that Wordsworth and Schelling simultaneously developed a broadly similar world view. Wordsworth believed the Germans to be the best critics in Europe, and he admired them for praising Shakespeare. Schiller's exhortation, "aus der sanfteren und fernenden Erinnerung mag er dichten" ("May the poet compose from gentle and faraway recollection") from his review of Bürger (1791), is a probable source for Wordsworth's definition of poetry as "emotion recollected in tranquillity," Wordsworth's attention having been drawn to Schiller's review by one of Coleridge's letters from Göttingen.

Shelley first studied German during his final year at Eton, from 1809 to 1810, and after 1815 his interest in German literature increased. He read Wieland, Goethe, and Schiller and was impressed by Goethe's *Werther* and *Faust I* and by Schiller's *Räuber*. His prose fiction, *Zastrozzi* and *St. Irvyne*, was influenced by the German Gothic novel, hardly surprising in view of the meeting that took place at the Villa Diodati on Lake Geneva in 1816, where the Shelleys and Byron read German ghost stories in French translation. Shelley was fascinated by Bürger's *Lenore*, echoes of which may be perceived in the ballad "Sister Rosa" in *St. Irvyne*. An earlier poem of Shelley's, *Ghasta or, The Avenging Demon* (1801), was prefaced with an acknowledgment that the idea came from German stories.

In 1815, Shelley translated the *Erdgeistszene*, *Osterspaziergang*, *Prolog im Himmel*, and *Walpurgisnacht* from Goethe's *Faust I*, and the influence of Goethe's drama can be seen in Shelley's *Hellas* and *Alastor*. The structure of the fragmentary prologue to *Hellas*, with Satan, Christ, Mahomet, and a chorus of angels, is similar to that in *Faust I*, and in *Alastor*, written in the autumn of 1815 (the year Shelley first read *Faust I*), the youth's thirst for knowledge resembles that of Goethe's Faust. The poem's Preface and Invocation also strike a Faustian tone.

Byron's interest in German literature was kindled by Schiller's *Geisterseher* and *Räuber*. He first came into contact with Goethe's *Faust* at Lake Geneva in 1816, where his guest "Monk" Lewis read to him impromptu translations from Goethe's drama. Byron described his own *The Deformed Transformed* as a Faustian type of play, and the first scenes of both plays have a Devil appearing out of a vapor without being summoned. Like Faust, Byron's Arnold intends to see the world with the Devil as guide. The meter to the song "Shadows of beauty," sung by the Stranger near the end of Scene One, could have been inspired by the chorus "Christ ist erstanden" in Goethe's *Faust I*. The Stranger himself certainly has some Mephistophelian traits, as does Lucifer in Byron's *Cain*, especially Mephisto's cynical humor. The title hero of Byron's *Manfred* reminded Goethe of his own Faust (in a review in *Kunst und Alterthum*), and the first scene of *Manfred* (in the Gothic Gallery at Midnight) is made up of a monologue and the conjuring up of an earth spirit, as in the first scene of Goethe's *Faust I*.

Scott had an impressive collection of over 300 volumes of German books, including more than 30 volumes of the German Romantic Friedrich de la Motte-Fouqué; Bürger's collected works in two volumes; the *Hausmärchen*, *Altdeutsche Wälder*, and *Deutsche Heldensagen* of the Grimm Brothers; two volumes of Tieck's poems along with three of his *Volksmärchen*; his novelle *Der Geheimnisvolle*; and his drama *Kaiser Octavianus*. The other German Romantics represented in his library were Brentano, Arnim, the Schlegel brothers, and Hoffmann, each with two or three volumes.

Scott developed an early enthusiasm for *Lenore*, translating it in 1794 and 1795, thereby contributing to the ballad's popularity in England at that time. According to Scott's own accounts in *Imitations of the Ancient Ballad*, he also translated Bürger's *Wilde Jäger* and a couple of his other poems, which resulted in "The Chase, and William and Helen: two ballads from the German." Scott adapted many themes and characters from Goethe's *Götz von Berlichingen*, particularly the elements of medieval knightly life and custom, in such works as *House of Aspen* (1800), *Anne of Geierstein* (1829), *Ivanhoe* (1819), and in the Romantic narrative poems *Lay of the Last Minstrel* (1805) and *Marmion* (1808). He translated *Götz* in 1799, and followed this with some translations of minor ballads as well as Goethe's "Erlköning" ("The Erl-King").

Scott had an especial admiration for la Motte-Fouqué's *Undine*, and the White Lady of Avenel in *The Monastery* (1820) is by his own admission in the introduction of the work an adaptation of la Motte-Fouqué's tale. Finally, Scott wrote an essay on Hoffmann entitled *On the Supernatural in Fictitious Composition* (1827), which was to draw Poe's attention to the German Romantic author. In general terms, it could be claimed that Scott's Romantic feeling for the past in his medieval romances was enhanced by his reading of German literature.

Carlyle can at least be associated with Romanticism early in his career because of his antirationalism, his idealism, his dislike of rules, and his support for the creative artist. He started to publish a *Life of Schiller* in the *London Magazine* (1823–24), and in 1824 he translated the first part of Goethe's *Wilhelm Meister*. Among his many articles for the *Edinburgh Review* were "Jean Paul Richter" (1827) and "The Present State of German Literature" (1828). In the *Foreign Review*, he had eight essays published on German literature, such as "Goethe," "Goethe's Helene," and an essay on Novalis with sample translations (1829). He became interested in Transcendental philosophy through reading Fichte's critique of 18th-century rationalism, and from 1858 to 1865 he composed the epic six-volume *History of Friedrich II of Prussia, called Frederick the Great.*

Carlyle's four-volume edition of translations entitled *German Romance* (1827) contains works by Musäus, Tieck, la Motte-Fouqué, Hoffmann, and Jean Paul and Goethe's *Wilhelm Meister*. As part of the Jean Paul section, Carlyle translated *Qintus Fixlein* and the *Reise nach Flätz*. Carlyle's interest in Jean Paul is further supported by the articles "Jean Paul Richter" (1827 and 1830, the latter for the *Foreign Review*) and an article on Jean Paul's critique of Staël's *De l'Allemagne* (1837). In fact, *Sartor Resartus (The Life and Opinions of Herr Teufelsdröckh)*, which was published in 1836, is modeled on the structure of a typical Jean Paul novel as well as serving as a perfect example on Carlyle's infamous contorted Germanic style. Jean Paul even appears in person in the first book of Chapter Four of *Sartor Resartus*, and Diogenes Teufelsdröckh has both a Jean Paulian name and character. Otherwise there are numerous verbal loans in Carlyle's works, such as his concept of "self-annihilation," a translation of Novalis's *Selbsttötung*.

Hazlitt published the most well-informed review that Schlegel's Vienna lectures received in England in the *Edinburgh Review* in 1816. Hazlitt also believed, like

Coleridge, that Schlegel's views on Shakespeare closely reflected his own. In his book *On the Characters of Shakespeare's Plays* (1817), Hazlitt praised the merits of Schlegel's lectures; Schlegel is quoted in great detail; and Hazlitt adopts Schlegel's outline of the history of the drama, his general distinction between Romantic and Classical, and the description of the different types of drama.

De Quincey was one of the main channels through which knowledge of German philosophy reached England. He had an intense interest in German literature and studied the works of Fichte and Schelling at Oxford. He most probably did some translations of German writings, and an article on Jean Paul appeared in the *London Magazine* in 1821. He launched a series of articles in *Blackwood's* called "A Gallery of the German Prose Classics," and a chapter on "German Studies" appears in his *Autobiographical Sketches*. De Quincey's short story *The Love Charm* is a translation from Tieck, and the short stories *The King of Hayti* and *Mr. Snackenberger* are free adaptations of German originals.

In spite of these contacts and influences among German and English Romantics, the two movements differed. The German Romantics were nearly all Roman Catholics or converts to Catholicism, whereas the English Romantics were Protestants and did not share their German counterparts' Catholicized view of the world, of literature, and of history. German Romanticism developed a program for literature and culture that aimed at all fields of art, science, and society, while English Romanticism remained a predominantly literary movement, more empirical and less philosophical than was the case in Germany. The German Romantic conception of music as the most important and Ro-

mantic of the arts was not shared by the English Romantics, who were equally disinterested in the German Romantic desire to break down the barriers between art forms. The literary genres were of a different character: in England there was the reflective, meditative lyric poem, in Germany *Gemütserregungskunst*, or poetry of the cultivation of the soul; in England the historical novel (Scott) and the novel of manners, in Germany, the novel of development or education patterned on Goethe's *Wilhelm Meister*. In addition, English Romanticism did not really develop a counterpart to the Romantic irony of the German Romantics, in which artistic illusion is deliberately destroyed by having characters comment on the work or manipulate the conventions of the novel or play.

The similarities between the two movements lie in their common Germanic heritage, the same spiritual roots in the Age of Sentimentalism (Rousseau, Goethe's *Werther*), and a similar experience of the French Revolution (initial euphoria followed by gradual disillusionment). Both movements had a tendency toward the Gothic and satanic, and the Gothic tradition can be found in Tieck, Arnim, Brentano, and Hoffmann as well as in Coleridge, Shelley, and Scott. Both movements share a common background in the Neoplatonic tradition, in varieties of pietism, and in mysticism (e.g., that of Jakob Böhme). Last, but not least, both German and English Romanticism brought forth talented and underrated women writers: in England, Dorothy Wordsworth, Charlotte Smith, Mary Lamb, Jane Austen, Maria Edgeworth, Mary Wollstonecraft, Mary Shelley, and the Brontë sisters; in Germany, Sophie Mereau, Dorothea Tieck, Karoline von Günderrode, Bettina von Arnim, and Caroline Schlegel. (*See also*

German Fairytales; German Idealism, Influence of; Grimm Brothers; Incest; Munchhausen, Karl Friedrich Hieronymus, Freiherr von.)

Paul Davies

Works Consulted

Hoffmeister, Gerhart. *Deutsche und europäische Romantik*. Stuttgart: Metzler, 1978.

Mason, Eudo C. *Deutsche und englische Romantik: Eine Gegenüberstellung*. Göttingen: Vandenhoeck and Ruprecht, 1966.

Oppel, Horst. *Englisch-deutsche Literaturbeziehungen*. Vol. 2: *Von der Romantik bis zur Gegenwart*. Berlin: Schmidt, 1971.

Schirmer, W.F. *Der Einfluß der deutschen Literatur auf die englische im 19. Jahrhundert*. Halle/Saale: Niemeyer, 1947.

Stokoe, F.W. *German Influence in the English Romantic Period 1788–1818: With Special Reference to Scott, Coleridge, Shelley, and Byron*. New York: Russell, 1963.

Gifford, William

(1756–1826)

William Gifford is remembered now as a rather shadowy celebrity who was a satirist, an editor of Jacobean drama, and the first editor of the *Quarterly Review*. He came from good stock, but his father was a wholly irresponsible, drunken spendthrift whose death left his family in utter distress. Gifford received some education at Ashburton in Devon and even practiced as a pupil teacher there for a while, but an unsympathetic guardian took him from school and apprenticed him to a shoemaker, from which plight he was saved only by the benevolence of local people.

Gifford was physically small and badly crippled, but he inspired affection and was helped by his friends. Those at Ashburton contrived to send him to Oxford, where he gained the patronage of Lord Grosvenor, who sent him on the Grand Tour as tutor-companion to his son. Gifford had begun translating Juvenal at Oxford, and his literary reputation was made in the mid-1790s by two works of contemporary satire, his poems the *Baviad* (1791) and the *Maeviad* (1795). These attacked the florid extravagances of style and emotionalism of the "Della Cruscan" group of versifiers and enjoyed a considerable success as late but vigorous examples of the school of literary satire which had been energized by Pope's *Dunciad*.

Gifford was chosen to be the editor of the pro-government satirical paper the *Anti-Jacobin* during its brief but meteoric existence in 1797 and 1798. The friends he had made in that group (including George Canning) thought of him when, with the help of the great publisher Murray, they set up the Tory *Quarterly Review* in direct competition with the *Edinburgh Review* in 1809. Gifford's own reviews were of literature, and his standpoint was rigidly traditional. Frequently vituperative, he did nothing to check the political extremism or literary savagery of his collaborators: Hazlitt and the other radical writers of the day detested him and his journal alike. But Gifford kept a distinguished team around him, including Scott, Southey, Croker, and Barrow. In spite of their political differences, Byron thought highly of Gifford's critical judgment and was keen to have his views on each new work, as his letters to Murray show. Gifford edited the *Quarterly Review* until 1824.

Gifford's translation of Juvenal appeared in 1802, and he wrote other lesser translations and satires. But his most enduring work is to be found in his editions of the old dramatists, of Massinger (1805), Jonson (1816), and Ford (1827). These have stood the test of time and provide a firm basis for standard modern editions. (*See also* Wolcott, John.)

William Ruddick

Works Consulted

Clark, Roy B. *William Gifford: Tory Satirist, Critic and Editor*. New York: Columbia UP, 1930.

Elton, Oliver. *A Survey of English Literature 1780–1830*, Vol.1. London: Arnold, 1912.

Hazlitt, William. *The Spirit of the Age*. London: Colburn, 1825.

Gillray, James

(1756–1815)

The leading caricaturist of the Georgian period and perhaps the foremost graphic satirist Britain has produced, James Gillray brought to his art a fineness of execution, an inventiveness of imagery, and a ferocity of attack that have rarely been equaled. He raised personal caricature to stinging precision; he transformed emblematic satire into an art of topical reference and metaphor; and, in his most elaborate designs, he turned the heroic and the sublime against themselves in travesty and burlesque. (*See also* Satire.)

Gillray's father was a Scotsman who had enlisted in the British Army and lost an arm at the Battle of Fontenoy. He was admitted to Chelsea Hospital and there joined the Moravian Church, in which he became a sexton. His son James, born in 1756, was the only one of five children to survive infancy. Gillray's early schooling under the Moravians provided a sound education and a religious training that stressed the worthlessness of human life and the inherent corruption of humankind. In early adolescence, Gillray was apprenticed to a leading writing engraver in London. By his 20s he was producing caricatures. In 1778, he was admitted as an engraver to the Royal Academy (where he was a contemporary of Blake).

Throughout the 1780s, Gillray alternated between the lucrative profession of engraving and the more temperamentally satisfying work of graphic satire. He soon became the best caricaturist of his day. He worked for a variety of printsellers, but in 1791 he committed himself almost exclusively to Hannah Humphrey. Their association, operating latterly out of Humphrey's famous shop at 27 St. James's Street, dominated the upper end of the caricature market for the subsequent 20 years.

In a total output of a some 1,000 plates, Gillray divided his attention between social and political satire, the latter producing the richer and more complex work. His designs were etched, often carefully hand colored, and usually measured about 8 inches by 14 inches. He perfected the art of the individual satiric portrait, to be used again and again, and left vivid versions of the leading politicians of the day—Pitt, Fox, Sheridan, Addington, Canning, and many others. He also turned his wit onto the royal family: *A Voluptuary under the horrors of Digestion* (1792) gave an image of the debauched Prince of Wales from which the Prince's reputation never recovered. So inclusive was Gillray's satiric vision that many of his more complex political plates are finally ambiguous in their judgments, especially when he imitates the grand academic manner of historical, mythological, or religious painting. In such prints as *Sin, Death, and the Devil* (1792), *Light Expelling Darkness* (1795), *Presages of the Millenium* (1795), *The Death of the Great Wolf* (1795), *Confederated-Coalition* (1804), and *Phaeton alarm'd* (1808), all the participants are caught up in a comprehensive mockery that extends to the artistic origins and conventions of the designs themselves.

Nominally, however, Gillray's political sympathies were with the Tories. These were consolidated as the French Revolution began to threaten the country and when he developed a close relationship with George Canning and his circle. Many of his works were based on ideas or sketches supplied by this circle, and in 1797 Canning arranged for Gillray to receive a government pension of £200 per year. Gillray's reaction to the French Revolution and its aftermath is most celebrated in his Napoleonic caricatures. In some 40 plates, with unending variation and scorn, he established the English view of their adversary—"little Boney," an undersized, overdressed toy general, who raves and postures, and glowers like a spoiled child.

In 1807, Gillray's mind began to fail, apparently suffering from manic-depression. By 1810, he had become insane. He was cared for by Humphrey and died in 1815, 16 days before the defeat of Napoleon at Waterloo. Although other caricaturists took up where Gillray had left off, in particular Cruikshank, no one in the 19th century matches the fury of his vision, the brutal energy of his line, or his sardonic exposure of human pretension and behavior.

Jonathan E. Hill

Works Consulted

Hill, Draper. *Mr. Gillray: The Caricaturist*. London: Phaidon, 1965.

— — —, ed. *The Satirical Etchings of James Gillray*. New York: Dover, 1976.

Paulson, Ronald. *Representations of Revolution (1789–1820)*. New Haven: Yale UP, 1983.

Stephens, Frederic George, and Mary Dorothy George, eds. *Catalogue of Prints and Drawings in the British Museum. Division I. Political and Personal Satires*. London: Trustees of the British Museum, 1870–1954.

Girtin, Thomas

(1775–1802)

A landscape watercolorist, Thomas Girtin was a bold technical innovator. His influence on other artists rivaled and par-alleled that of his friend Turner, who is said to have remarked, "If Tom Girtin had lived, I should have starved." Girtin's distinctive style was not universally admired at the time of his early death—one critic dismissed his "loose, free manner, with more effect than truth"—but his strong colors and innovations in applying them changed the way most watercolorists worked, marking the transition between 18th- and 19th-century landscape watercolors in England.

Girtin's background, like Turner's, was lower middle class. His father was a Southwark brush and rope maker who died when Girtin was age 3; his mother took over the business and later married a pattern draftsman and designer. Girtin was apprenticed at age 13 to Edward Dayes, an accomplished topographical watercolorist. Much of Girtin's early work reflects the mechanical nature of his topographical training—the genre concentrated on relatively objective representations of English architecture and landscapes, modestly employing picturesque formulae, and its technical features were largely determined by the needs of reproductive engravers, who required clear outlines and weak tints. Although English landscape watercolorists before Girtin worked in many ways, for most the medium was still essentially tinted drawing rather than painting with colors.

Girtin began exhibiting at the Royal Academy in 1794, at first showing expert but conventional watercolors, some of them based on drawings by Dayes and others. In the next five years, he began to experiment, especially with more open, longitudinal compositions, freer brush techniques, shorthand dotted rendering of details, and deeper, more opaque colors, all of which were essential to his later style. In some paintings, he introduced Piranesian sublime perspectives on architectural subjects, as in one view of Peterborough Cathedral in which the tower shoots off the paper. He departed from other picturesque conventions, often minimizing the conventional human figures and masses of busily rendered foliage. In another important innovation, he began to use regularly a coarse, highly absorbent, buff-colored cartridge paper, becoming one of the first watercolorists to employ the texture of the paper as an effect in itself.

Girtin's most distinctive works were executed in the last four years of his life. In 1800, he painted *White House at Chelsea*, a sunset river scene that stunned Turner and other contemporaries and continues to impress viewers for whom its most influential features are no longer novel. The picture, about 12 inches high and 20 inches wide, is immediately striking: the upper half is a subtle, hazy sky; the foreground is a deep expanse of peaceful river; and the remainder, an elegant sliver of riverine landscape in complex perspective. At left center, the side of an ordinary white house gleams brilliantly, illuminated by the last rays of the sun, its reflection towering upon the water. The extraordinary overall effect, which combines exceptional formal control and Romantic intensity, corresponds to the delicate but free brush-and-wash techniques that are here used most effectively and are Girtin's most influential legacy.

The White House is often treated as a counterpart to Girtin's most unusual work, the lost *Eidometropolis*, an 18- by 108-foot panorama in oils, exhibited in the round, depicting the city of London from a high point near Blackfriars Bridge. The painting, executed around 1800, was finished and exhibited in 1802, and later sent to Russia, where it disappeared.

Girtin married in 1800, exhibited his first oil (and last painting) at the Royal Academy in 1801, and died in 1802 after, a long illness. His influence, which had been strong in his lifetime (especially through his part in semiformal sketching clubs), continued to grow for several decades. Various aspects of his style can be seen in the work of Cotman, Francia, Cox, Bonington, and De Wint, as well as Turner, Constable, Linnell, Varley, and several important amateurs.

Alexander S. Gourlay

Works Consulted

Girtin, Thomas, and David Loshak. *The Art of Thomas Girtin*. London: Black, 1954.

Hardie, Martin. *Watercolour Painting in Britain 2: The Romantic Period*. London: Batsford, 1967.

Hawcroft, Francis W. *Watercolours by Thomas Girtin*. London: Whitworth Art Gallery, 1975.

Morris, Susan. *Thomas Girtin: 1775–1802*. New Haven: Yale Center for British Art, 1986.

Gleig, George Robert
(1796–1888)

George Robert Gleig, clergyman, novelist, and military historian, was born in Stirling, Scotland. His father was a clergyman who eventually became Bishop of Brechin. Gleig was first educated by his father at home but later attended grammar school at Stirling. In spite of his delicate health, he mastered his lessons easily. At age 10, he was sent to Leith, where he finished school at age 13 and then went to Glasgow University. He entered Oxford in 1811 but left shortly thereafter for a commission in the army. The army, along with the church, was instrumental in shaping his life.

Gleig traveled widely in the army. After serving as an ensign in Ireland for two years, he was transferred to the Peninsula in Spain where he served in 1813 and 1814 as a lieutenant and where he was wounded three times. When he was not on duty, he would entertain his comrades with songs and jokes. He was also in the war in America, where he was wounded three more times, near the end of the War of 1812. Gleig was present at battles in Baltimore, New Orleans, and Washington, D.C. After fighting in America, he returned to Europe where he participated in the Napoleonic Wars. After the Battle of Waterloo, Gleig was put on half-pay, as were most officers. He returned to Oxford in 1816 to finish his education. He was awarded his B.A. from Magdalen College in 1818 and his M.A. in 1821.

In 1819, Gleig married a ward of his father, the daughter of Captain Cameron. In 1820, he was ordained, having devoted a year to studying for Holy Orders, and spent the rest of his life affiliated with the church. He served as curate and rector of three separate churches in Kent for the next two years. He attempted to supplement his income by taking in students, but he found this occupation intolerable and gave it up. In 1826, Gleig sold his half-pay pension. From 1830 on, he worked very hard because he had a large parish and a large family. In 1834, he was appointed chaplain of Chelsea Hospital, the history of which he later wrote. The success of his first novel, *The Subaltern*, established him as a successful writer.

In 1844, Gleig was appointed chaplain-general of the army and suggested a plan that would provide for the education of soldiers and their children. Probably no post could have made him happier than that of chaplain-general for it combined the religious and the military, the two most important aspects of his life. He retained this post for the next three decades. A flag he had captured at Bladensburg was always displayed at his pulpit in the hospital.

In 1846, he also became inspector general of military schools.

Though Gleig was strongly conservative in politics, he took little part in public affairs except to attack the Reform Bill of 1832. He resigned the post of inspector general of military schools in 1857, and he gave up the post of chaplain general in 1875. He died in 1888, after his health had begun to fail earlier in the year. At the time of his death, he was the last officer left alive who had served under the Duke of Wellington, one of the important influences on his life.

Shirley Laird

Works Consulted

Kunitz, Stanley J., and Howard Haycraft. *British Authors of the Nineteenth Century*. New York: Wilson, 1936.

Dictionary of National Biography, s.v. "Gleig, George Robert."

Sutherland, John. *The Stanford Companion to Victorian Fiction*. Stanford: Stanford UP, 1989.

Godwin, William

(1756–1836)

William Godwin was minister, schoolteacher, political philosopher, pamphleteer, novelist, dramatist, historian, biographer, literary critic, and author of children's books. He was the husband of Mary Wollstonecraft, father of Mary Shelley, and inspired an entire generation of writers, especially Wordsworth and Percy Shelley. Although his trials of love and disappointment modified his views on the importance of feelings in right action, Godwin's main principle of behavior, the right to private judgment, consistently shaped his writings.

Godwin was born in 1756 in Cambridgeshire, one of 13 children of an impoverished Dissenting minister, who was the son of one, and his wife of propertied gentry in Durham. Young William was reared through a very sickly childhood by a cousin of his father's. Her more liberal tendencies moderated some of his father's extremist religious influence, although she could not prevail against his parents' religion, which forbade vaccination, when he contracted smallpox.

Twice when William was very small, his father's dour Calvinism fell out of favor with his flock, and the family relocated. Godwin's father was an active minister but not a bookish man, and only the Bible, which William knew quite well from very young, and other religious texts were permitted in their household. William mastered reading by age 5, when he declared his ambition to follow in his father's and grandfather's footsteps, but he did not learn to write until he was age 10 and in country day school. The next year he went off to board for three years with a violently puritanical Dissenting minister, who frequently beat him. Godwin's father died in 1772, and the boy was enrolled at a Dissenting academy in London for five years (the universities were open only to members of the Church of England).

At age 22, Godwin assumed the first of a series of clerical appointments, but like his father, he had difficulties with his congregation over his independent stances. As he meditated upon his conflicts, he encountered the French *philosophes*, whose Enlightenment rationality proved nearly intoxicating to him. Although he called himself "the Rev. William Godwin" for several years, he abandoned his calling, moved to London, and became a journalist. He produced novels, reviews, and articles to support himself, becoming increasingly politically aware and radically active.

He had served as a Dissenting minister but his religious faith was so weakened by 1792 that he became an atheist, and he wrote *An Enquiry concerning the Principles of Political Justice, and Its Influence on General Virtue and Happiness*. Published in 1793, it surveyed "The Powers of Man Considered in His Social Capacity" and analyzed "Property" as the basis of errors and prejudices interfering with the perfectibility of humankind. Godwin's book argued that property leads to government as the obstacle to happiness because it encourages vice and discourages faith in perfectibility. The basic right of humankind is individual judgment based on reason, and political justice is possible as reason increases with the development of the mind. The book concludes that individuals must be freed from government restraints, including marriage laws derived from laws of ownership. (*See also* Censorship.) Malthus, in 1798, reacted with a thesis that suffering is caused by overpopulation, not government, while Percy Shelley, in 1811, read Godwin's book as a call to political action and began his campaign to emancipate the Irish from British tyranny.

Godwin explored the complicated relationships of individual rights and political justice as he experienced love and suffered loss in the trials of his own family troubles. In 1794, he published *Caleb Williams*, a precursor of the modern psychological detective novel. The criminal Falkland persecutes the innocent Williams, though both are innocents before the corrupting influence of society. By the time Godwin reached his late 30s and early 40s, he had achieved a solid and respected position as a writer and a measure of social success among the literati and theatrical and Whig cliques. He was liked and admired, although his amatory adventures were ill-starred for a time.

He had met Mary Wollstonecraft in 1792, after the publication of her *Vindication of the Rights of Woman* but before she had gone to France. He resumed his acquaintance with her when she returned to England, illegitimate child in tow, even though she was widely reputed to be a wicked influence on wayward husbands. (*See also* Hayes, Mary.) Soon, their friendship led to romance, intimacy, and prospective parenthood, so that the two adversaries of marriage wed in 1797.

Mary died in childbirth six months after the wedding, and when William recovered from his grief, he undertook to rear her daughter, Fanny, and theirs, Mary. He continued to edit and write prolifically to support them. *St. Leon* (1799) shows the effects of his loss in 1797 of his wife. In it, the Count of St. Leon becomes an alchemist after the death of his wife. He barely escapes execution by the Inquisition, grows younger, becomes involved in the politics of Austria and Hungary, and is rescued from prison by his son Charles, older than his father.

In 1800, Godwin wrote *Antonio*, a drama in which Antonio kills his sister, who betrayed their dying father when she married someone other than Antonio's best friend. These themes of marriage, betrayal, and revenge reflect the private concerns of the author, who, in 1801, married Mrs. Clairmont, supposedly a widow. In spite of the honorific and her two children, she had never been married. Like his first wife, his second was well-traveled and highly educated, and like his first marriage, this one was necessitated by pregnancy. Their affection seems, for the most part, to have lasted the 30-odd years of their marriage, although Clairmont was volatile and would periodically decamp, annoyed at their low station and relentless financial concerns. As Godwin's biographers love to remark, from a singular solitude, in less than six years he had advanced to at least joint responsibility for

five children less than eight years old, no two of whom had the same set of parents. At about the same time, for the next six or seven years, Godwin suffered from neurotic episodes for which he turned to vegetarianism for cure.

Fleetwood (1805) reflects, like *St. Leon*, Godwin's own widower's experience of marriage and death. Casimir Fleetwood wanders Europe in disillusionment until he learns to revive his social feelings. Fleetwood marries, suffers, acknowledges errors, and is more fully humanized. In 1805, Godwin began publishing under the pseudonym, Edward Baldwin, first, *Fables, Ancient and Modern*, to entertain children and point morals of individuality. Then, in 1806, he wrote *The History of England*, also for children. In 1807, his *Faulkner, a Tragedy in Prose* played with Sarah Siddons in a leading role at Drury Lane Theatre for several nights. Captain Faulkner, like Caleb Williams, is determined to uncover a secret, which leads to violence. Godwin returned as "Edward Baldwin, Esq." in 1809 with *The History of Rome* and in 1811 with *The History of Greece* (a celebration of struggles for independence), both for the Juvenile Library.

In 1814, Mary Godwin and Jane ("Claire") Clairmont fled with Shelley to Calais. In 1816, Fanny Godwin committed suicide. Later Harriet Shelley drowned herself, and Percy married Mary Godwin. Confronting all that, in 1817, Godwin came out with *Mandeville*, which again reflects his personal suffering. After a childhood exposed to brutalizing trials, Mandeville spends his adult life hurting his innocent sister through persecution of her husband, and he carries a scar on his face which symbolizes the scar on his maddened soul. Between 1824 and 1828, Godwin's *History of the Commonwealth of England* was published with a concluding focus on the complicated, even tragic, character of Oliver Cromwell as a person with principles and causes like Godwin's own. In 1830, he published *Cloudesley*, a novel about a cynical servant who has suffered from unjust imprisonment. Cloudesley learns to love mankind through his service in the cause of the wrongly persecuted Julian.

In 1833, *Deloraine* appeared. The widower in this novel kills the lover of his young second wife. Margaret's servant pursues Deloraine for vengeance, but in the end Deloraine's daughter Catherine, revealing the influence of Mary Godwin Shelley's writing, persuades the avenger to end his pursuit by showing him that he has turned into an inhuman monster. In 1834, Godwin published *The Lives of the Necromancers*, written to show how easily human beings can be deluded if they relax the vigilance of reason. Godwin died in 1836, still championing reason and individual liberty against the perverting laws and customs of society. (*See also* Frend, William.)

Richard D. McGhee

Works Consulted

Clark, John P. *The Philosophical Anarchism of William Godwin*. Princeton: Princeton UP, 1977.

Locke, Don. *A Fantasy of Reason: The Life and Thought of William Godwin*. Boston: Routledge, 1979.

Philip, Mark. *Godwin's Political Justice*. London: Duckworth, 1986.

Smith, Elton Edward, and Smith, Esther Greenwell. *William Godwin*. New York: Twayne, 1965.

St. Clair, William. *The Godwins and the Shelleys: The Biography of a Family*. New York: Norton, 1989.

Tysdahl, B.J. *William Godwin as Novelist*. London: Athlone, 1981.

Gordon Riots

The London uprising called the "Gordon Riots" took place on 2 June 1780, and lasted nearly a week, until June 6. It began as an anti-Catholic demonstration but quickly spread far beyond the original goals of its organizers. Its name derives from Lord George Gordon, younger son of the Duke of Gordon, a largely disregarded member of Parliament during the North Ministry who seized upon the always popular cause of anti-Catholicism to satisfy his yearning for notoriety and importance. Parliament at the same time sought to recruit more troops for the defense of its imperiled colonies in America. A statute of William III made it necessary for anyone enlisting in the Army to swear he was Protestant. Those who refused such an oath, such as Roman Catholics, could not enlist, and North's advisers thought that an untapped pool of the population would become available for enlistment if the regulation barring Catholics from the Army was relaxed. The Catholic Relief Bill of 1778 that resulted from consultations with powerful English Catholics repealed the act of William III but still imposed an Oath of Allegiance. Moreover, many of the severe liabilities imposed on Catholics remained in effect, especially disenfranchisement and exclusion from public office. Thus, the bill passed quietly and easily.

Meanwhile, with the entry of the traditional and Catholic enemies of England—France and Spain—into the American wars on the side of the rebelling colonies, the always excitable Protestant associations found new cause for alarm and anti-Catholic agitation. Pamphlets and broadsides proliferated, followed by a burgeoning series of mass meetings. Riots broke out in Edinburgh and Glasgow, in which Roman Catholic churches were burned and the houses of Catholics attacked. Lord George Gordon made himself popular with anti-Catholic speeches in the House, widely reported in Scotland. A speaking tour in the north confirmed his popularity, and he became president of the London Protestant Association. This association sponsored a petition for the repeal of the Catholic Relief Act and, to drum up more signatures, held a mass meeting at St. George's Fields at which Lord George Gordon was the featured speaker. The crowd of more than 50,000 quickly grew out of control as it marched on the Houses of Parliament to present its petition.

Members of Parliament on their way to the House were jeered and attacked. Lord George Gordon spoke on behalf of the gathered mob and moved for the repeal of the bill. The outraged House voted down his measure, which was supported by only seven other members. The Foot and Horse Guards were called out, but their efforts seemed only to incite the growing crowd, which refused to disperse. The days and nights that followed were filled with unremitting riots. Catholic chapels, such as those attached to the Sardinian and Bavarian Embassies, were attacked and burned. After this foray into the fashionable quarters, the mob turned its attention to the Irish slums of Moorfield. Irish laborers were hated for undercutting the wages of English workers, and this fact may have stimulated the ferocity of the anti-Catholic mob's assault. The attempts of the magistracy and the Army to restore order were useless, although a few rioters were arrested and confined in Newgate prison.

Newgate became the next focus of the mob's rancor; the crowd laid siege to this enormous symbol of oppression, freed the convicts, and torched the prison. More fashionable houses were then attacked, and other prisons in London, such as Bridewell

and New Prison, forced open and burned. What began as an anti-Catholic uprising became directed not only at the Irish or at Catholics but at anyone of power and authority. The mob assaulted Downing Street and the Bank of England and burned down the houses of whatever rich families attracted its attention. This incoherent, quasi-revolutionary rampage finally subsided on June 6. By this time, arrest had been made, and on June 9, Lord George Gordon was arrested and charged with high treason. He was subsequently acquitted, but 21 rioters were later hanged. Approximately 850 people were killed in the uprising.

Kenneth Watson

Works Consulted

De Castro, J. Paul. *The Gordon Riots*. London: Oxford UP, 1926.

Hibbert, Christopher. *King Mob: The Story of Lord George Gordon and the London Riots of 1780.* Cleveland: World, 1958.

Gothicism

Used originally to deride anything barbaric or uncouth, Gothicism is now applied to a particular literary form first codified by Walpole in *The Castle of Otranto* (second edition subtitled "A Gothic Story") in 1764. Gothicism arose in a time of revolution and changing intellectual attitudes, characterized by the shift from the early 18th century's reliance on the enlightened rationality of humanity to the questioning of the self and acknowledgment of the unconscious and darker side of the human psyche late in the century.

That the Gothic is firmly rooted in the psychology of the self, especially the unconscious, is supported by the number of Gothic writers who attribute their inspiration to dreams. For example, Walpole claims that he began writing *The Castle of Otranto* the evening after he dreamed of a gigantic armored hand on the banister of a castle's staircase. Similarly, Shelley began *Frankenstein* (1818) the day after she dreamed of a phantasm animated by a student of the black arts. Just as Robert Louis Stevenson found the image and the transforming power of Hyde within two successive dreams, so did Bram Stoker dream of Dracula rising from his grave, after, Stoker says, a crab dinner.

But the Gothic was more than an expression of the writer's unconscious. The sociopolitical conditions of the late 18th century were important influences on the early development of the genre. Not only the French and American Revolutions politically but also the Industrial Revolution sociologically shattered irrevocably the emphasis on the link between rationality and moral action conceived by Dryden, Johnson, Pope, and Fielding. Indeed, the Gothic highlights how tenuous is humanity's hold on rationality by plunging the reader through trapdoors into subterranean passages analogous to the twisting labyrinth of the mind.

The attributes of Gothic fiction are numerous, but the primary characteristic, present in all variations, is concern for the workings of the mind manifest through the supernatural, which can be presented as real within the context of the fiction or as contrived by one or more characters (usually the villain). Although the supernatural is integral to the structure of Gothic form and essential to the genre, other ingredients include natural phenomena, such as lightening and storms, to reinforce the supernatural; ominous atmosphere that threatens the central characters and builds suspense; remote setting temporally and/ or spatially; light-dark imagery to reinforce the reader's comprehension of evil; and unresolved paradoxes that emphasize epistemology. In fact, the importance of setting cannot be overstated. Enclosures, such as castles, ancestral estates, and crumbling manses, reflect the decay of the old order, closely associated with the villain; in marked contrast, the new order (represented by the ingenue, hero, heroine, or both) struggles against the allure and entrapment of the past. Frequent use of first-person narration, editors of ancient documents, and plots nested within plots calls into question the narrative reliability and heightens the ominous atmosphere of many Gothic novels. The reader must constantly weigh evidence and draw conclusions about characters' motives and about the believability of the supernatural. The plots are frequently convoluted but pivot on the need to understand the self as a unique entity as well as part of a family and of society, hence the emphasis on inheritance, lost wills, usurpation, familial lines, and incest, especially in the flood of Gothic novels immediately following Walpole.

The Castle of Otranto established the pattern of the Gothic novel with the villain Manfred, who usurps Otranto from its rightful heirs and persecutes not only the helpless maiden Isabella under his protection but also kills his daughter Matilda, whom he mistakes for Isabella in the dark. The young hero Theodore is identified as the rightful heir to the kingdom when his "strawberry birthmark" (first in a long series of birthmarks that disclose Gothic heroes) is discovered and the gigantic specter of his ancestor Alfonso the Good rises in the midst of the castle, which crumbles around Manfred. An animated portrait, a gigantic helmet, and huge armored hands and feet haunt Manfred's castle and reflect his mental state and lack of self-awareness. Meanwhile, the persecuted Isabella frantically hastens through subterranean vaults and passages from which Theodore must rescue her. Hence the characteristic setting, characters, and atmosphere of the genre are clearly established by Walpole's novel.

Although Walpole can be seen as the progenitor of Gothicism, the form was actually shaped by Radcliffe, whose *Mysteries of Udolpho* (1794) is the seminal Gothic work. Here the orphaned Emily St. Aubert falls under the control of the villainous Montoni, in whose ancient and threatening castle she succumbs to fears induced by apparent specters that are later explained as natural, although odd, phenomenon. Suspense is emphasized as the reader, along with Emily, wonders what lies beyond the black veil and whose disembodied voices have been heard in the castle. Characteristically, Radcliffe uses Walpole's basic setting of a remote castle, but she expands the significance of the setting so that the architectural and natural surroundings are integral to the character delineation. Further, she shifts emphasis away from the relationship of hero and heroine to the relationship of heroine and villain, which becomes the mainstay of Gothic fiction. Although the supernatural manifestations are all explained (as opposed to Walpole's supernatural devices which are all accepted as genuine), Radcliffe maintains a suitably frightening atmosphere in which the heroine can be menaced.

Early in the evolution of Gothic form two distinct types emerged. First are those that emphasize ancestry and inheritance, such as Clara Reeve's *The Champion of Virtue* (1777), republished and retitled *The Old English Baron* (1778), the less successful variant. Second are those that stress and exaggerate the supernatural and the darker side of humanity, such as Beckford's *Vathek* (1786), Lewis's *The Monk* (1796), Maturin's *Melmoth the Wanderer* (1820), and other, later novelists who pursued Lewis's excavation into perversity.

In *Vathek* the sadistic title character, after excesses of flesh and spirit, journeys to an underworld of eternal fire where he is condemned to perpetual wandering in the labyrinth of his own unfulfilled longings. The novel focuses on Vathek himself, not on his ancestors or heirs. Lewis's protagonist and villain, Ambrosio, may rape his sister and kill his mother, but the danger of suppressing drives, especially lust, is stressed over familial bonds. Although the monk's excesses are punished by a literal fall from the talons of Lucifer, the novel emphasizes the psychology of evil and the destructive power unleashed suppressing the human darker side.

The psychology of the darker side within a familial and societal context is the focus of Shelley's *Frankenstein* (1818), which blends the two emphases. The monster's tale is the core of the novel as well as the psychological center. In his obsession with the creation of life, Victor isolates himself from his family as he retreats into a solitary room to create a monstrous form, which can be seen as the embodiment of Victor's own failure to recognize his familial role. As Victor's double, the monster is responsible for the deaths of Victor's brother, father, and wife. Yet the monster's guilt is mitigated by the abuse society inflicts because of his grotesque appearance (the result of Victor's inability to perceive the perversity of the monster's conception). The complexity of the psychology in *Frankenstein* demonstrates the evolution of the genre in half a century. The ominous atmosphere of the castle is still present in Victor's makeshift laboratory, but the emphasis on the mind, only slightly noted in *The Castle of Otranto*, is by the early 19th century central to the genre and ready to be fully exploited by Maturin.

Melmoth the Wanderer continues the Gothic's focus on the psychology of the mind with an exploration of eternal life, monomania, and the role of evil in the life of the Übermensch. Over many decades Melmoth searches for someone willing to sell his soul to free himself from the immortality acquired in his own quest for forbidden knowledge. During the search for a victim, Melmoth encounters individuals who must work out their identities and come to knowledge in order to escape Melmoth's temptations.

The assumption of some critics that the Gothic novel essentially ended in 1820 with Maturin's *Melmoth the Wanderer* overlooks Gothic characteristics in Charlotte Brontë's *Jane Eyre* (1847), Emily Brontë's *Wuthering Heights* (1847), Joseph Sheridan LeFanu's *Uncle Silas* (1865), Robert Louis Stevenson's *The Strange Case of Dr. Jekyll and Mr. Hyde* (1886), Bram Stoker's *Dracula* (1897), to name a few prominent examples.

Yet another proof of the strength of Gothicism as well as its popularity comes from the number of parodies of the form that arose in the early 1800s. For example, Austen's *Northanger Abbey* (1818) exaggerates the persecuted heroine in showing Catherine Morland, who believes evil lurks behind every pillar of the abbey she is visiting. At one point, she finds a mysterious document that proves to be a misplaced laundry list. Likewise Peacock's *Nightmare Abbey* (1818) illustrates the folly of viewing life through the Gothic prism by gathering eccentric intellectuals at the ancestral estate of the Glowrys. Here Peacock mocks Percy Shelley in the character of Sythrop Glowry, Byron in Mr. Cypress, and Coleridge in Mr. Flosky. These parodies assume the reader has a thorough understanding of Gothic conventions and recognizes the excesses of the characters' reactions.

The lasting interest in the Gothic form has been attributed to causes as various as an innate fascination with violence, to the need to escape the real horrors of living, to the desire to relieve the fear of the unknown in an incomprehensible universe. By vicariously experiencing the perils and terrors that threaten to overwhelm the denizens of Gothic vaults and caverns, readers can confront the grounds or groundlessness of their own fears and better understand their own identities. (*See also* Antiquarianism, Hellenism, Incest, Negative Romanticism, Novel, Supernaturalism.)

Karen McGuire

Works Consulted

Bayer-Berenbaum, Linda. *The Gothic Imagination: Expansion in Gothic Literature and Art.* Rutherford, NJ: Fairleigh Dickinson UP, 1982.

Carroll, Noel. *The Philosophy of Horror or Paradoxes of the Heart.* New York: Routledge, 1990.

Carter, Margaret L. *Specter or Delusion? The Supernatural in Gothic Fiction.* Ann Arbor, MI: UMI Research, 1987.

Day, William Patrick. *In the Circles of Fear and Desire.* Chicago: U of Chicago P, 1985.

DeLamotte, Eugenia C. *Perils of the Night: A Feminist Study of Nineteenth-century Gothic.* New York: Oxford UP, 1990.

Ellis, Kate Ferguson. *The Contested Castle: Gothic Novels and the Subversion of Domestic Ideology.* Urbana: U of Illinois P, 1989.

Fleenor, Juliann E., ed. *The Female Gothic.* Montreal: Eden, 1983.

Graham, Kenneth W., ed. *Gothic Fictions: Prohibition/Transgression.* New York: AMS, 1989.

Grixti, Joseph. *Terrors of Uncertainty: The Cultural Contexts of Horror Fiction.* New York: Routledge, 1989.

Haggerty, George E. *Gothic Fiction/Gothic Form.* University Park: Pennsylvania State UP, 1989.

Heller, Terry. *The Delights of Terror: An Aesthetics of the Tale of Terror.* Chicago: U of Illinois P, 1987.

Lovecraft, Howard Phillips. *Supernatural Horror in Literature.* 1945. New York: Dover, 1973.

MacAndrew, Elizabeth. *The Gothic Tradition in Fiction.* New York: Columbia UP, 1979.

Napier, Elizabeth R. *The Failure of the Gothic: Problems of Disjunction in an Eighteenth-century Literary Form.* New York: Oxford UP, 1987.

Praz. *The Romantic Agony.* 1933. Trans. Angus Davidson. New York: Oxford UP, 1970.

Punter, David. *The Literature of Terror: A History of Gothic Fictions from 1765 to the Present Day.* New York: Longman, 1980.

Sedgwick, Eve Kosofsky. *The Coherence of Gothic Conventions.* New York: Methuen, 1986.

Todorov, Tzvetan. *The Fantastic: A Structural Approach to a Literary Genre.* 1970 Trans. Richard Howard. Cleveland: P of Case Western Reserve U, 1973.

Tracy, Ann B. *The Gothic Novel 1790–1830.* Lexington: UP of Kentucky, 1981.

Tymn, Marshall B., ed. *Horror Literature: A Core Collection and Reference Guide.* New York: Bowker, 1981.

Varma, Devendra P. *The Gothic Flame.* 1957, rpt. Metuchen, NJ: Scarecrow, 1987.

Varnado, S.L. *Haunted Presence: The Numinous in Gothic Fiction.* Tuscaloosa: U of Alabama P, 1987.

Grant, Anne (MacVicar)

(1755–1838)

Anne (MacVicar) Grant was the author of popular early 19th-century nonfictional and fictional works. These include *Letters from the Mountains* (1803), *Memoirs of an American Lady: Sketches of Manners and Scenery in America as They Existed Previous to the Revolution* (1808), and *Essays on the Superstitions of the Highlands* (1811).

Grant was born of Scottish parents. Her father, an officer in the British Army, was posted to America in 1757, and the following year his family joined him. They eventually moved to Albany and from there to Oswego. During her stay in America, Grant was exposed to influences that became the basis for *Memoirs of an American Lady.*

As an adult, Grant lived in England, and from 1810 on, she lived in Edinburgh, with her husband, the minister of Laggan, Iverness-shire. There she was admitted to the highest literary circles. Her work was

so well regarded that one Scottish literary society provided her with a pension. Her writing had such a great emotional power and influence that during her life, and for sometime thereafter, people named their children after her.

Her best-known work, *Memoirs of an American Lady*, was also the one most popular. It details the life and relationships of her Aunt Schuyler, who lived near Grant's family in Albany. All of Grant's work is based on lives and relationships she observed from a detached perspective. Her accounts, while tending toward the objective and factual, are fictionalized to a greater or lesser degree, depending on her aim. Like many Scottish and American writers of the period, she was interested in examining and comparing provincialism with European sophistication and drawing moral conclusions.

The genteel or aristocratic amateurism that characterized American literature of the time is evident in Grant's work. This lent her writing a credibility and honesty that were well regarded at the time. As writers and writing grew more professional, amateurs such as Grant were considered inferior, and their works fell into disfavor.

Jennifer Lawler

Works Consulted

Coultrap-McQuin, Susan. *Doing Literary Business: American Women Writers in the Nineteenth Century.* Chapel Hill: North Carolina UP, 1990.

Dictionary of National Biography. s.v. "Grant, Anne."

Manning, Susan. *The Puritan-Provincial Vision: Scottish and American Literature in the Nineteenth Century.* Cambridge: Cambridge UP, 1990.

Grimm Brothers

Jacob (1785–1863) and Wilhelm (1786–1859) Grimm are famous primarily for their collections of folksongs and folktales. They are also credited with having established the scholarly study of German language and literature.

The Brothers Grimm had their interest in folk poetry awakened by the German Romantic Clemens Brentano while they were studying law at the University of Marburg (1802–06). At the instigation of Brentano and Achim von Arnim, who had themselves collaborated on the influential collection of folksongs *Des Knaben Wunderhorn* in 1805, the Grimms published the *Kinder- und Hausmärchen* (generally known as *Grimm's Fairy Tales*) in two volumes from 1812 to 1814, along with the *Deutsche Sagen* in two volumes from 1816 to 1818. With their numerous notes and comments, these two collection founded the study of folklore as an academic discipline. In deliberate contrast to the literary fairytales of German Romanticism school, the 200 stories in the *Kinder- und Hausmärchen* were mostly taken from original oral sources. The *Deutsche Sagen* is a collection of historical and local German legends which influenced the study of the folk narrative. The Grimm Brothers also edited the periodical *Altdeutsche Wälder* (1813–16), which, among other material, published Jacob's studies on old German language and literature.

Jacob went on to write the *Deutsche Grammatik* (1819–37), which established the systematic study of Germanic philology from a comparative historical perspective. His *Deutsche Rechtsaltertümer* (1828) is a study of ancient law practices and beliefs, and his *Deutsche Mythologie* (1835) traces the pre-Christian faith and superstitions of the German people from poetry, fairytales, and folklore. It made an important contribution to the Germanic theory of folklore. His last completed work, the two-volume *Geschichte der deutschen Sprache* (1848), deals in particular with those Germanic languages of which no written records have remained. The work marked a new epoch by applying comparative philology to old Germanic history and ethology. Jacob's most ambitious project was the *Deutsches Wörterbuch*, the German equivalent of the *Oxford English Dictionary*. It started to appear in 1852, but did not go beyond the fourth volume in Grimm's lifetime. It was eventually completed in 1860.

Wilhelm assisted his brother with the *Deutsches Wörterbuch* and collaborated in the *Deutsche Sagen* and the *Altdeutsche Wälder*. His talent for storytelling and his mastery of prose and poetical description ensured that the *Kinder- und Hausmärchen* became a popular success. In 1829, he wrote *Die deutsche Heldensage*. This collection of names and themes from heroic legends in art and literature from the sixth to the 16th centuries also includes essays on the art of the German heroic tale or saga. In addition, Wilhelm's many editions of medieval German texts are of lasting value because they simultaneously looked into questions of language and literary history. (*See also* German Fairytales; German Idealism, Influence of; German Romanticism.)

Paul Davies

Works Consulted

Denecke, L. *Jacob Grimm und sein Brüder Wilhelm*. Stuttgart: Metzler, 1971.

Denecke, L., and K. Schulte Kemminghausen. *Die Brüder Grimm in Bildern ihrer Zeit*. Kassel: E. Roth, 1963.

Gerstner, H. ed. *Die Brüder Grimm: Ihr Leben und Werk in Selbstzeugnissen, Briefen und Aufzeichnungen*. Ebenhausen: W. Langewiesche-Brandt, 1952.

Hammond, M.E. *Jacob and Wilhelm Grimm: The Fairy-Tale Brothers*. London: Dobson, 1968.

Michaelis-Jena, R. *The Brothers Grimm*. New York: Praeger, 1970.

Peppard, M.B. *Path Through the Forest: A Biography of the Brothers Grimm*. New York: Holt, 1971.

Hamilton, Elizabeth

(1755–1816)

Born in Belfast in 1755 or 1758, Elizabeth Hamilton, a moral, social, and religious writer, was the second daughter and last child of Charles and Katharine Mackey Hamilton. Her father died the year she was born and her mother died in 1767, leaving her to the care of her paternal aunt, Mrs. Marshall, and her farmer husband on their property in Stirlingshire.

Hamilton's interest in writing began early. She wrote to her brother during his tour of duty in India and kept a journal. In 1785, she published prose and poetry in the *Lounger*. In 1792, she met Dr. George Gregory, whose literary, religious, and political views undoubtedly provided a strong and encouraging influence on her.

Hamilton's work provides a clear picture of the energy her interests produced. In 1796, she published *Letters of a Hindoo Raja*, a satiric view of English manners. In 1800, her *Memoirs of Modern Philosophers* appeared and was a best-seller. This time the satire was directed against certain English radicals. *Letters on Education* (1801) and *Memoirs of the Life of Agrippina, Wife of Germanius* (1802) came next, followed by *Letters on the Formation of the Religious and the Moral Principle to the Daughter of a Nobleman* (1806). *The Cottagers of Glenburnie: A Tale for the Farmer's Ingle-nook* (1808) is one of her most popular novels and presents the harsh life of the tenant farmer. Hamilton often wrote about the less fortunate, believing that both prose and fiction could awaken the consciousness of society; a book like *Exercises in Religious Knowledge* (1809), for example, portrayed the lives of young inmates of the Female House of Industry in Edinburgh, a house that Hamilton helped found.

Although Austen praised Hamilton in particular for her ability to explore ways in which women were useful to society, it is more accurate to see Hamilton as a humanist who believed that knowledge brings freedom—for man or woman. Her *Popular Essays on the Elementary Principles of the Human Mind* (1812) and her final *Hints Addressed to the Patrons and Directors of Public Schools* (1815) before her death in 1816 show an inquisitive mind that had evidently found that freedom and used it to expand and explore the world, making it, perhaps, as much her own as the world described in the song she wrote, "My Ain Fireside."

Jo-Anne Cappeluti

Works Consulted

Luria, Gina. Introduction. *The Cottagers of Glenburnie: A Tale for the Farmer's Ingle-nook.* By Elizabeth Hamilton. New York: Garland, 1974.

Stapleton, Michael, ed. *The Cambridge Guide to English Literature.* New York: Cambridge UP, 1983.

Hamilton, Emma

(1765–1815)

The child baptized Emy Lyon on May 12, 1765, was the daughter of an illiterate blacksmith who died before she was one year old. Brought up by her grandmother, the sweet and generous child was a nursemaid by age 13. At age 16 she was mistress to Sir Harry Fetherstonhaugh, who repudiated her and "Little Emma," their child born in 1780 or 1782.

Brought to London by the Honorable Charles Greville as his mistress, Hamilton stayed with him for four years. Known as Emma Hart, she became a singer and amateur actress. She was high-spirited and known for her captivating beauty. When Greville's 54-year-old uncle Sir William Hamilton came to England in 1784, he was enchanted with her. Sir William, a widower for two years, was ambassador to Naples; Emma and her mother followed him there in 1786. It has been assumed that she was Sir William's mistress.

Returning to England in 1791, she and Sir William married on September 6. As Lady Hamilton, she became a leader of society, where her beauty and her artistic enacting of Attitudes (a kind of pantomime) made her an admired celebrity. Goethe called her figure "perfect," and Romney produced numerous portraits and sketches of her, at least 14 paintings in one year alone.

Hamilton's lasting fame undoubtedly rests with her passionate romance with Lord Horatio Nelson, the English admiral whose defeat of Napoleon's fleet at the Battle of Trafalgar in 1805 made him a national hero. Lord Nelson and Lady Hamilton met in September 1793, when he was 35, she was 28, and Sir William was 63 and in failing health. Though Lord Nelson and Lady Hamilton pretended even to friends that their relationship was innocent, they were passionately in love. Nelson was often seen in the company of the Hamiltons, accompanying them on a tour of the Continent and living with them in London.

Lady Hamilton gave birth in 1801 to Horatia, presumed to be hers and Nelson's. Nelson had married Fanny Nesbit, but by the time he returned to England in June 1801—six months after Horatia was born—he and his wife were separated; they eventually divorced. Sir William died in 1804, but it was Nelson's death in 1806 from a spinal wound received at Trafalgar that devastated Hamilton.

After Nelson's death, Hamilton suffered physically and financially. She drank too much to escape her grief, and at age 40 she was plump, self-indulgent, and in failing health. Desperate for money—she and her daughter were in the King's Bench prison for debt—she sold reminiscences of and her letters from Nelson to hack writer James Harrison, who published in 1806 the *Life of Nelson*. (Nelson had destroyed all of her letters to him.)

Hamilton spent the last few years of her life in Calais, France, where she rarely left her bed, had bouts of drunkenness, and suffered from dropsy and jaundice. She died in 1815.

Gary Kerley

Works Consulted

Bowen, Marjorie [pseud.]. *Patriotic Lady: A Study of Emma, Lady Hamilton and the Neopolitan Revolution of 1799*. London: Lane, 1935.

Fraser, Flora. *Emma, Lady Hamilton*. New York: Knopf, 1986.

Gamlin, Hilda. *Emma, Lady Hamilton, An Old Story Re-told*. Liverpool: Howell, 1891.

Hardwick, Mollie. *Emma, Lady Hamilton*. London: Cassell, 1969.

Jeaffreson, John Cordy. *Lady Hamilton and Lord Nelson*. London: Hurst, 1888.

Lofts, Norah. *Emma Hamilton*. New York: Coward, 1978.

Moorhouse, E. Hallam. *Nelson's Lady Hamilton*. London: Methuen, 1906.

Sichel, Walter. *Emma, Lady Hamilton*. London: Constable, 1905.

Simpson, Colin. *Emma: The Life of Lady Hamilton*. London: Bodley Head, 1983.

Solmi, Angelo. *Lady Hamilton*. Milano: Rusconi, 1982.

Tours, Hugh. *The Life and Letters of Emma Hamilton*. London: Gollancz, 1963.

Hastings, Warren

(1732–1818)

Warren Hastings had unusual beginnings for a person who would be one of the most capable British representatives to hold power in India. He was born in the small village of Churchill in Oxfordshire. His mother died shortly after his birth, and his father, who later died in the West Indies, deserted him. Hastings received a limited education at the village charity school until he was age 8. At that time, Howard Hastings, his uncle, took responsibility for him. In 1749, his uncle died, and although Hastings had been an excellent student, it was decided that his future was with the East India Company.

At the time, India was ruled by the Mogul dynasty; however, central power was collapsing, and local rulers were assuming more authority. India was also part of the imperial conflict between England and France, which was decided in England's favor at the Treaty of Paris in 1763. Robert Clive (1725–74), who was becoming the foremost British military figure, would have much to do with the growing British control of India.

After a voyage that lasted from six to 18 months, the future leaders of British India usually arrived in the country when they were young. Although they started their careers with the boring job of "writer" (letter copier and cargo checker), authority came quickly if they survived the first few months.

Hastings landed in Bengal at the city of Calcutta in 1750 and spent the next 14 years in Bengal. He served as resident in the court of Mir Jafar (1691?–1765), the ruler of Bengal, a position many considered the second most important post in Bengal. Hastings then became a member of the Council in Calcutta, which was the East India Company governing body in the region.

Due to disputes, Hastings resigned and returned to England in 1764. British activities between 1760 and 1765 were among the most scandalous in imperial history, but Hastings was not part of them.

Hastings, who returned to India in 1769 as second in the Madras Council, became governor of Bengal in 1772. He attempted to carry out financial- and judicial-appeal reforms with some success.

The government of the Prime Minister, Lord North, had become convinced that a joint-stock company ruling a country was an anomaly. The Regulating Act of 1773 was passed; its purpose was to relieve the East India Company of some of its governmental powers. The act subordinated the ruling authorities in Madras and Bombay to that of Bengal, created a four-member council appointed by Parliament, and provided for a weak governor-general. In 1774, Hastings was appointed the first governor-general, but the new structure had little chance of working because three of the four council members were Hastings's enemies. The most important of these was Philip Francis (1740–1818), who strongly disliked Hastings. Amid charges and countercharges the two fought a duel in 1780; Francis was wounded and returned home to carry on the feud.

Until 1784, Hastings was fully occupied with local conflicts, French attempts to regain its position in India, and financial problems. There is little doubt that his adroit handling of these helped preserve the British hold on India. But in 1784, Pitt, the young Prime Minister, passed the India Bill. It gave political control of India to the British government, while allowing the East India Company to retain economic control. Hastings was not reappointed and returned to England in 1785.

Francis had done his work. Hastings was impeached in 1788 and charged with corruption and cruelty during his administration in India. The East India Company had many enemies; Hastings had become the scapegoat for its ills, both real and imagined. Finally in 1795, after a sensational trial, the House of Lords found him not guilty.

The trial had almost bankrupted Hastings. To its credit the East India Company provided an annuity in recognition of his services. He died in 1818 at age 86.

Hastings was one of the most able British representatives to serve in India. Unlike many of his associates, he had a deep respect for the Indian people and was sincerely interested in preventing the exploitation of them; his attitudes were usually returned. He is credited with developing civil administration and judicial techniques. His diplomacy helped preserve the empire in India during a very difficult period. The final statement on the greatness of Hastings was made by the House of Commons in 1813 after the old man had testified at an inquiry: the members stood with their heads uncovered in respect while Hastings left the chamber. (*See also* Tipu Sultan.)

K. Gird Romer

Works Consulted

Marshall, P.J. *The Impeachment of Warren Hastings*. London: Oxford UP, 1965.

Mason, Philip. *The Men Who Ruled India*. New York: Norton, 1985.

Moon, Penderel. *Warren Hastings and the Making of British India*. New York: Macmillan, 1949.

Williamson, James A. *A Short History of British Expansion: The Old Colonial Empire*. London: Macmillan, 1930.

Haydon, Benjamin Robert
(1786–1846)

Benjamin Robert Haydon was a historical painter, prolific reader and writer, art educator, and champion of the Elgin Marbles at a time when their authenticity was still questioned. As a painter, Haydon is largely forgotten now; *Christ's Triumphant Entry into Jerusalem* (which depicts Keats, Wordsworth, Hazlitt, Newton, and Voltaire among the onlookers) and *Wordsworth on Helvellyn* are probably more remembered as illustrations of the figures they present than as artistic achievements. Haydon's writings, however, provide a fascinating, panoramic view of the state of the arts and the position of the artist in the late 18th and early 19th centuries. Haydon's literary friends included Hazlitt, Keats, Lamb, Leigh and John Hunt, Wordsworth, Elizabeth Barrett Browning, and Mitford. Keats, Wordsworth, and Leigh Hunt dedicated sonnets to him.

Haydon's debut under the protection of Beaumont and Mulgrave had been promising, but he lost patronage because of his inflexible ideas about art. He was fiercely dedicated to historical painting in an age of portrait painting and inimical to the dictates of the Royal Academy, which he associated with a thwarting of the individual artist and a decline in art on a large scale. The flamboyant Haydon fought a lonely battle for state patronage and an educational vision based on a communal, guild-like Renaissance model. In both 1826 and 1827, he applied for Royal Academy membership; in neither year did he receive a single vote. His frustrated attempts to reform English art into his vision of grandiose, state-sponsored historical painting ended with his suicide in 1846. During the last 15 years of his life, his megalomania found expression in about 40 paintings of Napoleon.

If his painting has to be considered largely a failure, Haydon's writing can be classified among the most clear and entertaining of his age. Both his public and private writing support his vision of historical art in a national, English context. His public writing consists of numerous articles in Leigh Hunt's radical *Examiner*, the *Annals of the Fine Arts*, the *Lectures on Painting and Design* (1846), and the posthumously published *Autobiography*. His private writings consist of enthusiastic letters and an impressive collection of 26 diary volumes. The diaries in particular testify to the changing perspectives on patronage in the Romantic period, the role of art and the Royal Academy in the state, and Haydon's personal frustrations as artist *par excellence*. They movingly trace his personal calling for historical art, his urge to identify and place himself in a tradition, his religious need for confession, and his

resolution as a moral artist. (*See also* Sculpture.)

Heidi van de Veire

Works Consulted

Cummings, Frederick. "B.R. Haydon and His School." *Warburg and Courtauld Institutes Journal* 25 (1962): 367–80.

George, Eric. *The Life and Death of Benjamin Robert Haydon 1786–1846*. London: Oxford UP, 1948.

Haydon, B.R. *The Autobiography and Memoirs of Benjamin Robert Haydon*. Edited from his journals by Tom Taylor. A New Edition with an Introduction by Aldous Huxley. New York: Harcourt, 1926.

———. *The Autobiography and Memoirs of Benjamin Robert Haydon*. Ed. Alexander P.D. Penrose. London: Bell, 1927.

———. *The Diary of Benjamin Robert Haydon*. Ed. Willard Bissell Pope. Cambridge: Harvard UP, 1960.

———. *Sentiment des Connoisseurs sur les Ouvrages de l'Art, comparé avec celui des Artistes; et plus particulièrement sur les Marbres de Lord Elgin*. London: Schulze, 1818.

Kearney, Colbert. "B.R. Haydon and the *Examiner*." *Keats-Shelley Journal* 27 (1978): 108–32.

Lang, Varley. "Benjamin Robert Haydon." *Philological Quarterly* 26 (1947): 235–47.

Olney, Clarke. *Benjamin Robert Haydon: Historical Painter*. Athens: U of Georgia P, 1952.

Parry, Graham. "The Grand Delusions of Benjamin Haydon." *Keats-Shelley Memorial Bulletin* 31 (1980): 10–21.

Paston, George. *B.R. Haydon and His Friends*. London: Nisbet, 1905.

Stoddard, Richard Henry. *The Life, Letters and Table Talk of Benjamin Robert Haydon*. New York: Scribner, 1876.

Hayley, William
(1745–1820)

In his lifetime, William Hayley was a popular and prolific poet, a biographer, a translator, and a friend to Blake, Anna Seward, George Romney, Flaxman, Edward Gibbon, Cowper, Joseph Wright of Derby, Emma Hamilton, and others. Hayley was an energetic patron and supporter for many of these friends, but some, most famously Blake, found his well-meant attentions exasperating; furthermore, Hayley's elegantly periphrastic verse and prose have been widely condemned by subsequent generations as feeble, insincere, and pompous.

Hayley's father, a provincial clergyman's son who had become rich by his first marriage, died when Hayley was age 3. Because of childhood disease, much of Hayley's early education fell to his mother, who read poetry to him, and to Greek and Latin tutors. At age 12, he went to Eton, then to Cambridge, adding French, Spanish, and Italian to his languages and painting to his accomplishments (at some point he also learned German and Portuguese). In 1769, he married his first wife, Eliza, and began unsuccessfully to write plays and poems and, more successfully, to cultivate the acquaintance of eminent persons. Among these were Wright and, after the family moved to the estate at Eartham, the fashionable portrait painter Romney, who stayed regularly at Hayley's house over the next 20 years. Hayley's *An Epistle on Painting, Addressed to George Romney* (1778) exhorted the artist to move from the "lucrative drudgery" of portraiture to the more exalted field of history painting; it was the substantial first drop in what became an unremittent stream of occasional, didactic, and panegyric verse from Hayley's pen, most of it whiggishly advanced in politics and aesthetics. In 1780, he began *The Triumphs of Temper* (1781), his greatest commercial success, which argued that a young woman's chief asset in marriage is a good disposition. It went through more than two dozen distinguishable editions, but his own marriage was already a failure: in

1780 he also had a son by a housemaid, the daughter of his childhood nurse. The boy was raised as an adoptee, and Hayley and Eliza were increasingly alienated until her death in 1797.

Upon discovering in 1792 that he and Cowper were both working on biographies of Milton, Hayley wrote the older poet to assure him that the projects would not compete, thus beginning a warm friendship. Although a famous and popular (but impoverished) writer, Cowper was then subject to fits of terrified despair. Hayley tried to cheer him and secured a government pension for him, but it was granted only after Cowper had suffered a complete breakdown, and it was rarely paid.

In 1800, both Cowper and Hayley's beloved son Thomas died in a single week; Romney, ill and melancholic, had recently gone north to die. Hayley distracted himself by working on Cowper's biography, engaging Flaxman's friend Blake to engrave the illustrations to this and other books. Hayley also persuaded Blake to rent a cottage near his newly built marine villa at Felpham and commissioned (and solicited commissions for) dozens of works, including the decoration of his library, illustration of his *Ballads*, portrait miniatures of his friends, and engravings after Maria Flaxman for the 12th edition of *The Triumphs of Temper* (1803). Although Blake benefited from some of Hayley's efforts, he apparently resented such pragmatic encouragement, and by 1802, Blake had resolved to return to London. Shortly before his lease at Felpham ran out, Blake was charged by a soldier with sedition and assault. Hayley engaged his friend Samuel Rose to defend Blake and testified on his behalf; Blake was acquitted. Meanwhile Hayley's *Life of Cowper* (1803) was a huge success, and he began work on a *Life of Romney* (1807), which was not.

In 1809, Hayley remarried, but this wife departed after only three years. He remained in retirement at Felpham, publishing nothing after 1811, but continuing to write poems for friends and epitaphs for anyone lately deceased. In 1820 he died, having provided for himself a more substantial memorial: his two-volume *Memoirs* (1823), 1,200 pages written in the third person.

Hayley was not long influential as a poet, unless perhaps as the discreditor of one insipid strain of Neoclassicism. As a friend and patron, he directly inspired mostly minor work from Cowper, Romney, Flaxman, and Blake. On the other hand, his social introductions were crucial to some major commissions for Flaxman and Blake; he further extended Cowper's reputation; he surely helped all four to live more comfortably; and he gave them and others access to cultures that they would not otherwise have known. Perhaps his greatest contribution was as a promoter of literature in Italian, Spanish, and Portuguese. This was the role in which Southey cast him in a generous review of the *Memoirs*; Hayley may even have helped to inspire Blake's deathbed project of illustrating Dante.

Alexander S. Gourlay

Works Consulted

Bishop, Morchard [Oliver Stoner]. *Blake's Hayley: The Life, Works, and Friendships of William Hayley*. London: Gollancz, 1951.

Hayley, William. *Memoirs of the Life and Writings of William Hayley, Esq.* 2 vols. London: Colburn, 1823.

Southey, Robert. [Review of Hayley's *Memoirs*.] *Quarterly Review* 31 (1825): 263–311.

Hays, Mary
(1760–1843)

Born into a family of Rational Dissenters, Mary Hays was encouraged by her widowed mother to take advantage of an education not generally available to late-18th-century girls. Although her childhood activities remain obscured, she apparently studied French, mathematics, and religious literature in lieu of the usual music and drawing.

In 1777 or 1778, Hays fell in love with John Eccles, from whom she fervently hoped to learn theology, philosophy, science, and especially Latin, but their union was strongly discouraged by their parents. Nevertheless, Hays continued the relationship secretly, writing—and receiving—copious love letters and meeting Eccles clandestinely. Finally, the lovers were granted permission to marry, but weeks before the wedding, Eccles died of a mysterious fever.

In her grief at Eccles's death and to overcome the prostration she later described as culturally dictated, Hays began a decade of intensive reading, writing, and attending lectures at the Dissenting Academy at Hackney. Here she became acquainted with Dr. Robert Robinson, and through him was introduced to Priestley, Theophilus Lindsey, and John Disney. In 1790, a member of the academy, Gilbert Wakefield, published a stinging criticism of Dissenting styles of worship. This occasioned Hays's first published piece of writing, a sharp and well-received rebuttal of Wakefield, *Cursory Remarks on an Enquiry into the Expediency and Propriety of Public or Social Worship*. Published under the pen name "Eusebia," it soon went into a second printing.

Hays's most prolific period as a writer was during the radical 1790s. She became a member of publisher Joseph Johnson's revolutionary circle, which included George Dyer, Blake, Ann Batten Cristall, Barbauld, Godwin, and Wollstonecraft, and continued to mature and refine her opinions on education and the position of women in her society. Dyer furnished Hays with a copy of *A Vindication of the Rights of Woman* in 1792, and her great admiration for the piece led to a breakfast meeting with Wollstonecraft and an agreement that Wollstonecraft would edit and comment on Hays's drafted *Letters and Essays, Moral and Miscellaneous*. The two formed a close reciprocal friendship. In 1793, Hays published *Letters*; Wollstonecraft's most well-known advice was the suggestion that Hays refrain from pleading female weakness in the Preface. Instead, Hays's only apology consists of an acknowledgment of societal restrictions on women, accompanied by a trenchant reference to Wollstonecraft's *Vindication*. The volume is a mixture of personal letters, sketches, anecdotes, and poetry containing strong and well-argued condemnations of the corruptions and abuses that she saw as characteristic of contemporary English government as well as the social tyranny men held over women.

In 1794, Hays initiated a friendship with Godwin when she wrote to him asking for a copy of *Political Justice*. At this time, she was deeply embroiled in her unrequited love for Frend (who seems to have encouraged her at the outset). Depending on Godwin's guidance in the affair, she wrote him voluminous letters, often 20 or more closely written pages, to which he would respond in person at teas and suppers. It appears to have been Godwin who suggested she attempt to work through her feelings for Frend by fictionalizing them. Consequently, in 1796, Hays's first novel,

The Memoirs of Emma Courtney, was published to almost immediate scandalized outcry. Although she was careful in her Preface to dissociate herself from any approval of her protagonist, the public persisted in believing she advocated Emma's forthright pursuance of her beloved Augustus Harley. The book is remarkable not only for its undeniable insistence on the validity of a woman's emotions and her right, even moral obligation, to express them, but also it openly and unashamedly drew upon Hays's personal life, making use of private letters and feelings (Godwin appears as the philosopher Mr. Francis, while Frend is Harley) in an intensely public and political way. Emma recognizes her "moral martyrdom" in the face of societal repression, yet persists, just as Hays worked against the conventions of the times to create a thoroughly human woman, intelligent, caring, yet self-pitying and heroic.

Whether or not it helped resolve her feelings for Frend, *Emma Courtney* created a reputation for Hays. She continued to write, contributing book reviews to the *Analytical Review* during 1796 at Wollstonecraft's request, and philosophical essays on feminism and environmentalism to the *Monthly Magazine* during 1796 and 1797. Also in 1796, she reintroduced Wollstonecraft and Godwin, which led to their friendship and marriage. She was one of the few told of this marriage and nursed Wollstonecraft through her childbirth and death in 1797; her eulogies for Wollstonecraft appeared in the *Monthly Magazine* in 1797 and in *Annual Necrology, 1797–1798* in 1800. Her first strictly feminist work came out in 1798, published by Johnson, entitled *An Appeal to the Men of Great Britain in Behalf of Women*. Although anonymous, her authorship was implied by details in the Preface and was widely assumed. For declaring such convictions as the heaven-designed and -sanctioned equality of women and men and for challenging standard masculine readings of Scripture and philosophy, she was decried as "Wollstonecraftian" and part of a "blasphemous band" by the Rev. Richard Polwhele's *The Unsex'd Females* (1798), mocked in Charles Lloyd's *Edmund Oliver* (1798), and satirized as Bridgetina Botherim in Hamilton's *Memoirs of Modern Philosophers* (1800).

Her second novel appeared under her name in 1799, again published by Johnson. Entitled *The Victim of Prejudice*, it details the life of Mary, whose mother was seduced, abandoned, driven to prostitution, and finally hanged for her involvement in a tavern killing. Mary's illegitimacy is used as an excuse to deny her marriage to the man she loves and leaves her open to be pursued and raped by a baronet. Echoing her mother's accusation that society allows no way back for the "ruined" woman, Mary dies amid the poverty, disease, and decay of debtors' prison. In its review, the *Monthly Magazine* praised Hays's "strong natural powers." In 1803, *Female Biography, or Memoirs of Illustrious and Celebrated Women of all Ages and Countries* (six volumes) was published, delineating the lives and accomplishments of nearly 300 notable women of the past.

During the 19th century, Hays grew more obscure, although she remained friends with Crabb Robinson until her death. She was admired by Southey but excoriated by Coleridge, who found her unattractive and therefore unworthy of "exsyllogizing." Her final publications were chiefly moral tales for the poor: *Historical Dialogues for Young Persons* (1806–08), *The Brothers, or, Consequences* (1815), and *Family Annals, or, The Sisters* (1817), the last two of which were patterned after the

works of More and Maria Edgeworth. *Harry Clinton, or A Tale of Youth* (1804) stressed the value of a good education, while *Memoirs of Queens* (1821) mostly reworked *Biographies*.

Jacqueline Labbe

Works Consulted

Adams, M. Ray. "Mary Hays, Disciple of William Godwin." *MLA*, 55 (1940): 472–83.

Luria, Gina M. Introduction. *An Appeal to the Men of Great Britain in Behalf of Women*. By Mary Hays. New York: Garland, 1974: 5–15.

— — —. "Mary Hays's Letters and Manuscripts." *Signs* 3 (1977): 524–30.

Pollin, Burton R. "Mary Hays on Women's Rights in the *Monthly Magazine*." *Etudes Anglaises* 24 (1971): 271–82.

Spencer, Jane. "Mary Hays." *Dictionary of British Women Writers*. Ed. Janet Todd. London: Routledge, 1989: 320–21.

— — —. *The Rise of the Woman Novelist*. Oxford: Blackwell, 1986: 129–32.

Spender, Dale. *Mothers of the Novel*. London: Pandora, 1986: 263–68.

Todd, Janet. "Mary Hays." *A Dictionary of British and American Women Writers, 1660–1800*. Ed. Janet Todd. Totowa, NJ: Rowman, 1985: 156–57.

Hazlitt, William

(1778–1830)

William Hazlitt, a major prose writer of the Romantic period, began his career as a philosopher and painter; he eventually became a literary critic of extraordinary intelligence and range and an essayist of brilliant and highly individual achievement. He also made significant contributions to the art, theatrical, and political criticisms of his age.

Hazlitt was born in 1778 in Maidstone, Kent. His family eventually settled in Wem, Shropshire, where his early education was supervised by his father, a Dissenting minister. In 1793, Hazlitt was sent to the New

College at Hackney near London to study for the ministry. At Hackney, Hazlitt read widely in philosophy from Locke to Godwin, came under the powerful influence of 1790s radicalism, and gave up his plans to become a clergyman in favor of philosophy.

In 1798, Hazlitt encountered Coleridge and Wordsworth. This meeting was crucial to his development as both a personality and writer and formed the subject of one of his finest essays, "My First Acquaintance with Poets."

In 1799, Hazlitt came under a new and important influence when, at the Orleans Collection in London, he saw for the first time original paintings of the Italian Renaissance. Inspired by this experience, he began to study painting, and between 1802 and 1804 he pursued a rather unsuccessful career as a portrait painter. Although Hazlitt failed to achieve eminence as an artist, his study and practical experience of art laid the foundation for his later achievements in art criticism.

During this period as a painter, Hazlitt was continuing work on philosophy, and in 1805 his *An Essay on the Principles of Human Action* was published. Although of very minor philosophical significance, this work's critique of empiricist philosophy, its assertion of man's natural "disinterestedness," and its central emphasis on the imagination had important implications for Hazlitt's later writing. The years between 1804 and 1812 are otherwise notable for Hazlitt's developing friendship with Lamb, his marriage to Sarah Stoddart in 1808, and his struggling efforts as a miscellaneous writer and philosophical lecturer. In 1812, Hazlitt was hired by the *Morning Chronicle*, thus beginning a long association with journalism out of which came much of his most characteristic work. Over the next several years, he contributed numerous articles to the *Champion, Edinburgh Magazine, London Magazine,* and Leigh and John Hunt's *Examiner.*

Hazlitt's first successes as a journalist were as a theater critic, and the reviews in which he championed the Romantic acting style of Kean constitute perhaps his first great contribution to the culture of his time. Hazlitt's mounting reputation as a journalist of literature, art, theater, and politics led him in 1815 to join the prestigious *Edinburgh Review* and to publish in 1817 *The Round Table* and *Characters of Shakespeare's Plays.* The *Round Table* contains some of Hazlitt's best early essays, including "On Gusto." The *Characters of Shakespeare,* in its vigorous style, psychological insight, and combination of analysis and impressionism, is his first major achievement in literary criticism. Moreover, Hazlitt's vivid responsiveness to Shakespearean characterization, his ability to capture the essence of a play through a discussion of its central characters, and his imaginative exuberance in discussing Shakespeare's creative art mark him as a central Romantic interpreter of the greatest English dramatist. These works initiate Hazlitt's richest and most productive period, during which he became an admired lecturer on English literature, a feared political satirist and essayist, and the author of *A View of the English Stage* (1818), *Political Essays* (1819), and *Lectures on the Dramatic Literature of the Age of Elizabeth* (1820).

Even more important, Hazlitt published during this period two critical works and one collection of personal essays upon which rests much of his lasting reputation. Of these, *Lectures on the English Poets* (1818) is notable for its great opening essay "On Poetry in General"; its sensitive explorations of Chaucer, Shakespeare, Spenser, and Milton; its Romantic but incisive treatment of Dryden and Pope; and its telling accounts of Wordsworth, Coleridge, Scott, and Byron. This work was followed by *Lectures on the English Comic Writers* (1819), in which Hazlitt extends the range of his criticism to Jonsonian comedy, Restoration comedy, the 18th-century periodical essay, and sentimental comedy. Hazlitt also becomes in this work the first serious critic of the modern novel, with striking discussions of Henry Fielding, Tobias Smollett, Samuel Richardson, Laurence Sterne, and Scott. The last work of what might be called Hazlitt's middle period was his *Table-Talk*, editions of which appeared between 1821 and 1825. This work contains such famous essays as "On Familiar Style," "On the Fear of Death," "The Indian Jugglers," and "The Fight." In *Table-Talk* Hazlitt achieves a vigor of style, an insight into human character, a power of imagination, and an honesty of self-revelation that place him in the first rank of English essayists.

It is perhaps ironic that as Hazlitt was developing and achieving success as a writer, his personal and psychological life was increasingly troubled and strained. His steadfast allegiance to liberal political hopes led to his disillusionment with Coleridge and Wordsworth and to his being vilified in the Tory press. He was nearly crushed by Napoleon's defeat at Waterloo, and the return of legitimacy in post-Napoleonic Europe tormented and embittered him. Furthermore, his marriage failed and, in 1820, he began an obsessive and tragically ludicrous affair with Sarah Walker, the daughter of his London innkeeper. This affair was the subject of his indiscreetly autobiographical *Liber Amoris* (1823). The last years of Hazlitt's life were marked by another failed marriage, increasingly poor health, financial difficulties, and one masterpiece, *The Spirit of the Age* (1825). In this remarkable book,

Hazlitt emerges as a major cultural critic. In his most mature style, he writes short essays on what he sees as the crucial thinkers, politicians, and writers of his age. In these accounts, he combines a deep sense of his age as one who generally failed to realize its potential with sensitive and often generous insights into individual achievement. In Bentham, Godwin, and Coleridge he sees both the philosophical limitations and attainments of the period. He sees Wordsworth as both a flawed egotist and a great poet. Byron is a poet of genuine intensity and force but with all the flaws of his aristocratic background. Scott is both a singularly magical novelist and a prejudiced conservative. It is only when Hazlitt turns to the Tory politicians and writers of his period that his disappointment with his age grows bitter and angry. Canning, Lord Eldon, Malthus, and Gifford are treated with brilliant sarcasm and disdain.

After 1825, Hazlitt's publications are less important, though several are of some significance. *Notes on a Journey Through France and Italy* (1826) deals interestingly with his last trip abroad and is especially notable for its passages on art. *The Plain Speaker* (1826) is a collection of lively familiar essays, and its general equality, though not so fine as *Table-Talk*, is nevertheless quite high. In his *Conversations of James Northcote* (1830), he creates out of his discussions with an old painter and friend experimental essays in dialogue form. Despite these late successes, Hazlitt failed in what he hoped would be his masterpiece, a huge, four-volume *Life of Napoleon* (1828–30). This work is a derivative and incoherent disaster, more a record of Hazlitt's political frustration than of his genius. He died in 1830, poor and, with the exception of the faithful Lamb, virtually alone at age 52.

The final evidence for Hazlitt's greatness is in his works, which reveal him to be a uniquely gifted prose stylist, a literary critic of incisive power and judgment, a major spokesman for Romantic esthetics, England's greatest art critic before Ruskin, a crucial influence on Keats, and a thinker especially sensitive to literature as a social institution. In this last regard, he offers an important alternative to Coleridge's transcendentalism, and modern scholarship is beginning to reveal a figure whose status must be measured, not with Lamb and Hunt, but rather in company with Keats, Wordsworth, and Coleridge. (*See also* Disinterestedness.)

Phillip B. Anderson

Works Consulted

Baker, Herschel. *William Hazlitt*. Cambridge: Belknap, 1962.

Bromwich, David. *Hazlitt: The Mind of a Critic*. New York: Oxford UP, 1983.

Jones, Stanley. *Hazlitt: A Life*. New York: Oxford UP, 1989.

Kinnaird, John. *William Hazlitt: Critic of Power*. New York: Columbia UP, 1978.

Wardle, Ralph M. *Hazlitt*. Lincoln: U of Nebraska P, 1971.

Hellenism

The Renaissance in the West began with the recovery of Greek learning, first in Latin translation and then in the original. The Greek Revival may be regarded as another Renaissance, as archaeologists and architects, poets and translators introduced Greek culture into everyday life to the enrichment of all the arts.

Writers and artists in the 1740s and 1750s abandoned as sources of inspiration Roman models for those of the Middle Ages and Greece. Gothicism and Hellenism may be viewed as antithetical—faith versus reason, passion versus logic, spontaneity versus order. Yet both represented simplicity, purity, primitivism, and liberty in contrast with the restraint and sophistication of the prevailing Neoclassical mode. Hence both tendencies could appeal to the same people. Richard Payne Knight, who built a medieval castle at his estate, Downton, designed the Greek chlamys that in 1790 replaced the Roman toga as the official attire of the president of the Society of Dilettanti. Uvedale Price, champion of the picturesque and an admirer of Gothic architecture, translated Pausanias' *Description of Greece* (1780), and J.B. Rebecca combined Gothic and Greek elements at Castle Goring, Sussex (1791–1825). Bretforton Hall, Worcestershire (1830), exhibits a similar eclecticism, as does Sir John Soane's museum in Lincoln Inn Fields.

Influential in the rise of Hellenism in England was the Society of Dilettanti. Between 1734 and 1852, it spent some £30,000 financing expeditions to Greece and publishing their findings. Among the most significant of these undertakings was Stuart and Nicholas Revett's journey in 1751. They remained in Greece almost four years, and in 1762 these two architects issued the first volume of *Antiquities of Athens*, a model for admirers of Greek taste. In 1758 to 1759, Stuart initiated the Greek Revival in architecture with his Doric temple at Hagley Park, Worcestershire. Revett soon contributed to the new taste with a Grecian portico at Standlynch, Wiltshire (1766). About the same time, Robert and James Adams, who had not gone to Greece, rejected the older Palladian style for one that incorporated Greek elements.

While English and French archaeologists were recovering the artifacts of ancient Greece and architects were translating these into modern buildings, Johann

Joachim Winckelmann's *Gedanken über die Nachahmung der griechischen Werke* (1755; *Reflections on the Painting and Sculpture of the Greeks*, 1765) captured and diffused the Hellenic spirit, declaring, "Good taste was first formed under Greek skies." Sir William Hamilton, British envoy to Naples from 1764 to 1800, also fired the British imagination with his collections of Greek vases and the volumes illustrating them. They inspired Josiah Wedgewood and Flaxman, his designer. In turn, Flaxman's depictions of scenes from Homer, Hesiod, and Aeschylus influenced Ingres and David. For Emma Hart, later Lady Hamilton, the envoy ordered Greek costumes, in which she enchanted Goethe and such painters as George Romney and Johann Heinrich Wilhelm Tischbein. The arrival of the first of the Elgin Marbles in England in 1803 furthered the love of things Greek. Upon seeing them, the Swiss-born Fuseli exclaimed, "De Greeks were godes! de Greeks were godes!"

Indicative of the triumph of the new aesthetic was the success of the architect William Wilkins. In 1804, he defeated James Wyatt, Surveyor General, in the competition for the design of Downing College, Cambridge, and the next year he triumphed over Holland for the East India College, Haileybury, Hertfordshire. In both cases, Greek designs were chosen over Roman (in part because Napoleon was identified with the Roman). Sir Robert Smirke's Covent Garden Theatre, London (1809), with its portico patterned after the Parthenon, confirmed the victory. By 1836, W.R. Hamilton could compile a long list of public buildings reflecting the age's philohellenism; among these were the National Gallery, the Mint, the British Museum, and the Post Office in London, custom houses in Liverpool and Dublin; and town halls in Manchester and Birming-

ham. Augustus Pugin, no friend of the Grecians, sardonically complained that though he was in the heart of England, "I am sitting in a Grecian coffee room in the Grecian Hotel with a Grecian mahogany table close to a Grecian marble chimney piece, surmounted by a Grecian scroll pier glass, and to increase my horror the waiter has brought in breakfast on a Grecian sort of tray with a pat of butter stamped with the infernal Greek scroll." He might have mentioned, too, the women wearing their hair *à la grèque* and all the tourists had just returned from Hellas.

Yet Pugin would have the last word. The decision to rebuild Westminster Hall (1840–67) in Gothic rather than in Neoclassical style; Ruskin's attack on the Greek mode as without life, honor, merit, or goodness; and the defeat of Alexander Thomson's Greek designs for the Albert Memorial (1861) and the Natural History Museum, Kensington (c. 1863) signal the end of the Greek Revival in architecture.

In literature, also, the 1740s witnessed the new interest in Greece; Mark Akenside in *Pleasures of Imagination* (1744) promised to "tune to Attic themes the British lyre." Warton, Collins, and Gray followed Grecian models rather than Horace or Juvenal while the first English translation of Plato's *Republic* appeared in 1763, of Aeschylus in 1777. As Greek buildings arose across Britain, Wordsworth wrote on Greek themes in *Laodamia* and *Ode to Lycoris*; Blake studied Greek under Hayley and wrote to John Trusler that he sought "to renew the lost art of the Greeks"; Keats adapted Greek myths in *Endymion* and *Hyperion*; and finally Shelley declared in the Preface to *Hellas*, "We are all Greeks." Certainly he was. He translated Plato's *Symposium* for his second wife, Mary; mourned the death of Keats in *Adonais*, which draws on the pastoral elegies of Bion and Moschus (both of which Shelley also translated) as well as the myth of Adonis; and created his own version of Aeschylus's lost *Prometheus Unbound*. Byron's *Childe Harold's Pilgrimage* both reflected and stimulated the current fascination with Greece: while Byron was visiting the country in 1810 he commented on the large number of his countrymen in Athens.

Though Hellenism in the Victorian era ceased to be the dominant literary force it had been in the early decades of the 19th century, it remained influential. Like the Romantic movement itself that Hellenism so much affected, the rediscovery of Greece remained a powerful force long after the death of its most prominent exponents. (*See also* Antiquarianism, Classicism, Elgin Marbles.)

Joseph Rosenblum

Works Consulted

Buxton, John. *The Grecian Taste: Literature in the Age of Neo-Classicism*. New York: Barnes, 1978.

Crook, J. Mordaunt. *The Greek Revival: Neo-Classical Attitudes in British Architecture 1760–1870*. London: Murray, 1972.

Larrabee, S.A. *English Bards and Grecian Marbles*. New York: Columbia UP, 1943.

Hemans, Felicia

(1793–1835)

Felicia Hemans was one of the most well-known poets during the early 19th century. Throughout the 19th century, her collected works were regularly reprinted in England, and individual poems, familiar to many Victorians, were used in giftbooks and school texts. Numerous editions of her poetry were published in the United States, where she also achieved popularity.

Felicia Dorothea Browne was born in Liverpool in 1793. Her father, George Browne, was a wealthy Irish merchant, and her mother, Felicity Wagner, was the daughter of the Tuscan consul at Liverpool. In 1800, the family moved to a seaside mansion in Abergele, North Wales. Felicia was educated by her mother, who had the resources of an extensive library. The young girl demonstrated a precocious intelligence and remarkable memory, and her adolescent verses showed enough promise that she published her first book in 1808. One of her early poems, *England and Spain*, inspired by her brother's involvement in the Spanish campaign, demonstrates her characteristic celebration of martial glory.

The family moved to the nearby St. Asaph area in 1809, and Hemans continued her private studies. A talented musician, she played the harp and piano, and years later many of her lyrics set to music became popular Victorian songs. As her translations and epigraphs attest, she learned to read six languages: French, Italian, German, Spanish, Portuguese, and Latin. Later she read German, including books by Novalis, Tieck, and Korner, though her favorites were Schiller's *Wallenstein* and Coleridge's translation of it.

In 1812, she married Captain Alfred Hemans and moved to his base in Daventry, but they soon settled in Wales and her maternal home. Hemans had five sons in quick succession, and then in 1818 her husband left to reside in Rome. Though they corresponded, they never met again, and she raised her sons with the help of her mother and sister.

Hemans made European culture and history the subject of many of her poems, for example, *The Restoration of the Works of Art to Italy* (1816), *Modern Greece* (1817), and *Tales and Historic Scenes* (1819). *Tales* contains her acclaimed "The Abencerrage," a patriotic romance about the Castilian annexation of the Moorish kingdom of Granada. Her voracious reading and her love of national airs led to several collections, including *Welsh Melodies* (1822). In the early 1820s, she began contributing to the *Edinburgh Monthly Magazine* and *New Monthly Magazine* and won literary prizes.

Hemans's work met with critical favor and sold well in England and the United States, where her editor was Professor Andrews Norton. Her fame overshadowed that of such writers as Lydia Sigourney, known as "The American Mrs. Hemans." Nevertheless, reviewers often showed an awkwardness about how to deal with such a talented *woman* poet. The *Monthly Review* called her delineation of certain scenes "masterly," but then asked in a footnote, "May we use this word with application to a female?" The *Quarterly Review* praised her for showing the proper delicacy of an English lady, not the ill behavior often attributed to women of talent and learning. *The Edinburgh Review* claimed that she wrote the best occasional verse in England but that she should leave to men the longer poems which she was unsuited to write.

On the other hand, Bishop Reginald Heber, her friend and literary adviser, encouraged Hemans to overcome her feminine reserve and have her tragedy, *The Vespers of Palermo*, produced. The performance at Covent Gardens in December 1823, received poor reviews, but the play was successful the following year in Edinburgh. Hemans continued her historical research to produce her next book, *Lays of Many Lands* (1826), a collection of 21 poems commemorating international events. In the same year, one of her best-known works appeared. *The Forest Sanctuary* (1826), written in a skillful variation of the Spenserian stanza, is a long historical romance about a 16th century Protestant who takes refuge from the Spanish Inqui-

sition in the North American forest with his son. It is a gripping story of love, fortitude, and religious trial.

The death of her mother in 1827 left a void in Hemans's life, and her own health began to deteriorate. But she was fortunate to be able to correspond with other women writers. She counted among her friends Maria Jewsbury, who was one of the few people with whom Hemans felt she "fully unsealed" herself, and Baillie, to whom she dedicated her *Records of Woman* (1828). The 19 poems in *Records of Woman* paint passionate but depressing pictures of woman's lot. In each poem except *The Switzer's Wife*, the long-suffering heroine is in a state of acute emotional anguish, and her death or that of a loved one gives the story its morbid end.

In 1828, by now a famous poet, Hemans moved to Wavertree near Liverpool, where she "felt the want of hills" and privacy. Though she found her celebrity wearying, she could still joke about the visitors who expected sparks of fire to come out of her mouth, and the young women who leveled their albums at her like pocket-pistols. In 1829, she enjoyed a trip to Scotland and a visit with Scott, and the next year she traveled to the Lake District where she happily met one of her favorite poets, Wordsworth. Wordsworth's letters show that he considered Hemans's work pleasing.

In 1831, Hemans moved to Ireland to live near her brother George. Despite her weakening health, she continued to write and to supervise her sons' education. Her later work demonstrates her preoccupation with devotional poetry, especially her last publication, *Scenes and Hymns of Life* (1834). Contracting tuberculosis, Hemans died in Dublin in 1835. (*See also* Mental Theater.)

Deborah Kennedy

Works Consulted

Chorley, Henry F. *Memorials of Mrs. Hemans*. New York: Saunders, 1836.

Hughes, Harriet M.B. Owen. *Memoir of the Life and Writings of Mrs. Hemans. By Her Sister*. Vol. 1 of *The Works of Mrs. Hemans*. 6 vols. London: Cadell, 1839.

Ross, Marlon B. *The Contours of Masculine Desire: Romanticism and the Rise of Women's Poetry*. Oxford: Oxford UP, 1989.

Wordsworth, William. *The Letters of William and Dorothy Wordsworth: The Later Years*. Vol 5. Ed. Alan G. Hill. Oxford: Clarendon, 1979.

Herschel, William

(1738–1822)

The astronomer William Herschel achieved popular success and professional advantage from his discovery of Uranus, the first "new" planet of historic times. Among historians of science, he is considered a ground-breaking figure—sometimes called the "Darwin of astronomy"—for his theory that stars and nebulae form and develop over time. Experimental astronomers still revere him as the premier telescopist of his age for pioneering lens and mirror techniques, still known as "Herschelian," that allowed many measurements, little different from those of the late 20th century.

Born Friedrich Wilhelm Herschel in Hannover, Germany, Herschel initially followed his father into a music career. Expatriating to England during the Seven Years War, Herschel pursued a successful career as teacher, performer, and aspiring composer from 1757 to 1782. A marked transition from musical to astronomical interest dates from 1772. The temptation to see this development synthetically as a unity of sciences is great. Herschel's sister Caroline, his lifelong assistant and herself a noted observer of comets, later recalled a connection between the very young

William's discussions of music and of Euler and Newton; moreover, the often-cited watershed event leading to astronomy is Herschel's 1760 discovery of Robert Smith's *Compleat System of Opticks* through an initial musical interest in Smith's *Harmonics*. Since the avowed shift to astronomy occurred some 12 years later, however, both Herschel and his biographers tend to take that more as a break than as a continuity.

Herschel's freedom from his musical vocation came from his discovery of Uranus in March 1781. This discovery, coupled with the concession from the Royal Observatory that he had produced the best available telescopes, won him fellowship in the Royal Society and an annual pension from the King. The discovery also marks his greatest influence on Romantic literature. Keats's sonnet *On First Looking Into Chapman's Homer* derives its image of the "new planet" from John Bonnycastle's *Introduction to Astronomy*, which Keats received as a prize at Enfield Academy in 1811. Bonnycastle's exuberant account positions Herschel's discovery of the planet as a culmination of imaginative cosmological "discoveries," including Milton's.

Herschel's abiding contribution to cosmology, the major model of stellar evolution deriving from his work from 1783 to 1802 in cataloging nebulae, had no appreciable effect on his literary contemporaries. Nonetheless, pinpointing stars with his advanced telescopes, Herschel at first seemed to put an end to the debate about whether nebulae were composed of individual stars or of a "nebulous" fluid. The evolutionary model developed from his 1790 observation of NGC 1514, which indeed exhibits "true nebulosity" by being a star surrounded by nonstellar light. Herschel's 1791 paper "On Nebulous Stars, properly so called" proposes that the "nebulous" material is in the process of condensing into stars. This model of change over time augments his long-standing work with binary stars, which Herschel came to understand as bound by gravity. With this, gravitation received a cosmic theoretical and observational generality it had lacked before.

In addition to considerable work with the planets and their moons (including proposing the word "asteroid" in 1802), Herschel posited in 1800 the existence of infrared radiation. In keeping with Romantic speculation, he devoted great publication effort to analogical accounts of life on other heavenly bodies (including, in 1795, the sun); he also devoted lifelong experimental effort to mapping the distribution of the stars. While providing 20th-century scientists with crucial inspiration in statistical methods, his enterprise in this latter project remains an example of historical error. Herschel doggedly felt the luminous magnitudes of the stars differed not intrinsically but only according to distance.

William Crisman

Works Consulted

Armitage, Angus. *William Herschel*. Garden City: Doubleday, 1963.

Hoskin, Michael. *William Herschel and the Construction of the Heavens*. London: Oldbourne, 1963.

———. *William Herschel: Pioneer of Sidereal Astronomy*. New York: Sheed, 1959.

Sidgwick, J.B. *William Herschel: Explorer of the Heavens*. London: Faber, 1953.

Hodson, Margaret Wrench Holford

(1778–1852)

Margaret Wrench Holford Hodson published under her maiden name Holford. She married Septimus Hodson of Sharow House near Ripon and corresponded regularly with Southey. Her translation of Quintana's lives of Balboa and Pizarro is dedicated to Southey.

Holford's 1799 comedy *Neither's the Man* was acted by the Chester company of the Theatre-Royal, but never made it to London. The reviews were tepid: the play was deemed interesting but not novel. Other works by Holford include *Fanny*, *Sclima*, and *Gresford Vale*.

Her correspondence with Southey is marked by its political discussions, concern for Southey's financial welfare, and occasional touches of wry humor. Hodson and Southey agreed that they both disliked and distrusted any person who called himself a professor.

Kit Ayars

Works Consulted

Curry, Kenneth, ed. *New Letters of Robert Southey*. New York: Columbia UP, 1965.

Holford, Margaret. *Neither's the Man* (1799). *Three Centuries of Drama: English*. New York: Larpent Collection, 1954. (Microprint.)

Jones, Stephen. *Biographica Dramatica; or a Companion to the Playhouse*. London: Longman, 1812.

Southey, Rev. Charles Cuthbert, ed. *The Life and Correspondence of Robert Southey: Volume VI*. London: Longman, 1850.

Hogg, James

(1770–1835)

The Scottish novelist and poet James Hogg worked as a shepherd from age 7 until his mid-30s. At age 15, he purchased a fiddle and taught himself to play; at 20, he was singing and playing the fiddle at local fairs and weddings. Although the young shepherd had less than six months of formal education, he taught himself to read and write in order to set down the lyrics of songs he was composing. During the 1790s he joined a circulating library and read works by Shakespeare, Spenser, Milton, Fielding, Smollett, Goldsmith, Dryden, and Pope, as well as the memoirs of Captain Cook and other explorers. He began to use his pseudonym of "the Ettrick Shepherd" in 1804.

In 1802, Hogg began a lifelong friendship with Scott. For one year beginning in 1810, he ran a weekly magazine called *The Spy*, which failed because of the indelicacy of some of his stories. His poem *The Queen's Wake* (1813) was his first major success; it contains 12 ballads in a fictional framework set at the court of Mary Queen of Scots in 1561. Three of the ballads, "Kilmeny," the comic "Witch of Fife," and "The Abbot McKinnon" were widely acclaimed and won approval from Wordsworth, Byron, Jeffrey, and Washington Irving.

Hogg met Wordsworth in Edinburgh in 1814. He was then entertained in Westmorland for some weeks by the Wordsworths, the Southeys, De Quincey, and Wilson. Although deeply impressed by Wordsworth's poetry, Hogg did not have a high opinion of *The Excursion*. He composed three parodies of it, and other amusing parodies of Coleridge, Southey, Wilson, Byron, and Scott, for his satirical volume *The Poetic Mirror*, published anonymously in 1816.

Hogg's most ambitious and complex poetic work was *Midsummer Night Dreams*. Because a friend convinced him to publish the main section of this tripartite work, *The Pilgrims of the Sun*, as a single poem in 1815, the *Dreams* was never published as a whole during his lifetime. *Pilgrims of the Sun* tells of a visionary journey through the universe, during which the heroine Mary Lee gradually abandons her former sense of identity and prejudices and experiences a mystical union with nature. The other main part of the *Midsummer Night Dreams*, a comic poem called *Connel of Dee*, describes a nightmare in which a man imagines himself pursued by his murderous wife until he drowns himself and is somehow painfully consumed by eels.

Both poems enact a temporary loss of personal identity: Mary Lee experiences loss of self in a joyous and spiritual sense; Connel undergoes disintegration in a painful, physical sense. The *Pilgrims* and *Connel of Dee* are precisely complementary in many ways: the first describes a young woman on her expansive, conscious, daytime journey upwards through the heavens, while the second describes a young man on a harrowing dream-journey downward into the element of water. Like Coleridge's *Rime of the Ancient Mariner* and some other long poems of the Romantic age, Hogg's *Pilgrims of the Sun* and *Connel of Dee* tell of proud or self-sufficient protagonists who gradually learn to accept the relativity and fragility of the self, and finally discover a deeper personal integrity based on community, nature, and love. Finally, Hogg's *Dreams* ends with the ironically titled *Superstition*, an account of the poet's opposition to modern rationalism and gentility.

With the founding of *Blackwood's Magazine* in 1817, Hogg found a ready market for his stories and poems. However, *Blackwood's* severely misrepresented Hogg by signing his name to some works he did not write, and by mimicking his Scots language and lower-class origins in its series *Noctes Ambrosianae* (1822–35). These attacks, combined with Hogg's depiction of lower-class life and reputation for satirizing or ignoring genteel ideals, greatly eroded his contemporary reputation.

Hogg's *Winter Evening Tales* (1820) contains many of his best stories, including the novella *Basil Lee*, an antiheroic tale of a Scot who fights in the American War of Independence and falls in love with a woman who had been a prostitute. A comic novella in the same collection, *Love Adventures of Mr. George Cochrane*, tells of the amorous misfortunes of a young ne'er-do-well.

Hogg's *Three Perils of Woman* is an experimental novel satirizing genteel norms in life and fiction. Of its three interconnected stories, the first concerns two women and their vastly different experiences of love, and the second, their cousin, a man who forgives his wife after discovering her adultery. The third part, set at the time of the Jacobite Rebellion of 1745, ends with the heroine committing suicide, with her baby, on the grave of her husband and her reputed former lover. A few allusions to Edinburgh prostitutes, and to an unnamed illness which some readers probably suspected to be venereal, led critics to condemn the *Perils of Woman* unanimously.

Hogg returned to many of these themes in *Private Memoirs and Confessions of a Justified Sinner* (1824). This, his greatest novel, divides into two parts. One half is the narrative of the so-called editor in 1823, as he recounts and tries to understand the life of the protagonist Robert Wringhim a century earlier. The other half is Wringhim's autobiography, ending with his suicide in 1712. Both narrators are proud, intolerant, deceitful, and blinded by preconceptions. Wringhim, fanatically religious, believes he is predestined for eternal salvation despite his acts of deceit and murder. The editor, although much more modern, rational, and commonsensical, slowly reveals his underlying affinity with Wringhim. Just as Wringhim is led astray by his fascination for a mysterious, demonic figure named Gil-Martin, so the editor is led on a parallel descent into confusion through his fascination for the mysterious figure of Robert Wringhim.

Near the end of their respective accounts, the two narrators leave their private studies to embark on an almost identical journey from Edinburgh down to Ettrick Forest near the border with England. Wringhim, fleeing from the law in 1712, begins to lose his cherished religious certainties, until he kills himself in despair. The editor, searching for Wringhim's grave in 1823, similarly begins to lose his rationalistic certainties, until he, too, implicitly admits the fundamental importance of uncertainty in human life. The failings of the editor are less obvious, and much less disastrous, than those of Robert Wringhim, but Hogg uses the parallel structure of the novel to develop affinities between two opposite character types and to suggest underlying parallels between narrow religion and shallow rationalism. The two halves of the novel are as complementary as the two main parts of the *Midsummer Night Dreams*.

Confessions was universally condemned by the critics of 1824. Its satire of extreme religion and its honest, sympathetic descriptions of Edinburgh prostitutes (particularly in contrast with its ironic portraits of pious, intellectual, or well-to-do persons) did not enhance Hogg's reputation. The novel received no serious attention until an appreciative essay by André Gide in 1947. From 1815, Hogg was also a sheep farmer in his native Ettrick Forest. His outdoor activities included fishing, archery, curling, and organizing the annual St. Ronan's Games, a local athletic festival. His wife Margaret, whom he married in 1820, bore five children. During his last decade he became alienated from *Blackwood's* and suffered increasing poverty. Most of his belongings were sold to pay creditors at a forced auction in 1830. A journey to London, where he stayed three months in 1832, briefly revived his prospects. Among his later works were the *New*

Poetic Mirror (containing parodies of Wordsworth, Moore, Crabbe, Campbell, and Montgomery), his autobiographical *Memoir of the Author's Life* (1832), and *Series of Lay Sermons* (18340. Numerous shorter pieces appeared in *Fraser's Magazine*, the *Edinburgh Literary Journal*, and various Chirstmas annuals.

Hogg disliked revising his work. Many of his poems, and some of the stories, suffer from hasty composition. Yet few writers of the Romantic age were more varied in achievement. The ironies and breadth and power of Hogg's best novels and poems were obscured for many years by the puritanical and snobbish reactions of reviewers and by savagely bowdlerized Victorian editions. His *Lay Sermons*, the one work in which he discusses his literary intentions, has never been reprinted and has been generally ignored by critics. Hogg's firsthand knowledge of rural working life and his generous use of satire, parody, folklore, dreams, and the supernatural bring to his writing a striking diversity and full-bloodedness.

David Groves

Works Consulted

Crawford, Thomas. "James Hogg: The Play of Region and Nation." *The Nineteenth Century*, Ed. Douglas Gifford Vol. 3. *The History of Scottish Literature*. Gen ed. Cains Craig. Aberdeen: Aberdeen UP, 1988: 89–106.

Gide, André. Introduction. *The Private Memoirs and Confessions of a Justified Sinner*. By James Hogg. London: Cresset, 1947.

Groves, David. *James Hogg and the St. Ronan's Border Club*. Dollar: Mack, 1987.

———. *James Hogg: The Growth of a Writer*. Edinburgh: Scottish Academic P, 1988. Papers Given and the Second Conference of the James Hogg Society. Ed. Gillian H. Hughes. Edinburgh: Scottish Academic, 1987.

Hogg, Thomas Jefferson
(1792–1862)

Born at Stockton-on-Tees, County Durham, and educated at Durham grammar school, Thomas Jefferson Hogg was a close friend of Shelley's during the early period of the poet's life and an intermittent correspondent during Shelley's residence in Italy (1818–22). As fellow undergraduate at University College, Oxford, Hogg and Shelley formed a close and idealistic friendship. Hogg's introduction to Shelley of many radical and skeptical texts culminated in their joint composition of *The Necessity of Atheism* (1811), the first published defense of atheism in the language. Refusal to acknowledge authorship of the pamphlet led to their joint expulsion from the university in late March 1811.

Another literary product of these years was Hogg's novel *The Memoirs of Prince Alexy Haimatoff* (1813). Shelley reviewed it in the *Critical Review* for December 1818, criticizing the sexual promiscuity depicted in it, its formlessness, and a certain political cynicism in the actions of Haimatoff, who seems otherwise to be based partly on Shelley.

After his expulsion, Hogg resumed his legal studies, eventually being called to the bar in 1817. Although Shelley and Hogg were estranged for a time by Hogg's infatuation with Harriet Westbrook Shelley (the poet's first wife) in late 1811, Hogg on various occasions stayed with Shelley until the poet left for Italy. Hogg, Mary Godwin, and Claire Clairmont were members of the radical commune of friends that Shelley briefly established in London in the winter of 1814 to 1815.

In 1823, after Shelley's death, Hogg met Jane Williams, widow of Edward Williams, who had drowned with Shelley. She eventually became Hogg's *de facto* wife.

His legal career in the north of England was interrupted by an attempt to gain a professorship in civil law at the newly created University of London, but the post was never established. Hogg continued to publish various minor literary works, notably the reminiscences of Shelley at Oxford, which appeared in the *New Monthly Magazine* in 1832. In 1858, he published two volumes of his *Life of Percy Bysshe Shelley*. Hogg's surrender to the values of the establishment is apparent in the way these memoirs, for all their humor and vividness, misrepresent Shelley's radicalism by depicting the poet as an idealistic eccentric. At times, Hogg even deliberately tampers with the texts of Shelley's letters. The remaining volumes never appeared, because Hogg was refused access by Shelley's heirs to the necessary material on the grounds that he might render both Percy and Mary Shelley objects of ridicule.

Timothy J.A. Clark

Works Consulted

Dictionary of National Biography, s.v. "Hogg, Thomas Jefferson."

Hogg, Thomas Jefferson. *The Life of Percy Bysshe Shelley*. Ed. Humbert Wolfe. New York: Dutton, 1933.

Holmes, Richard. *Shelley: The Pursuit*. New York: Dutton, 1974.

Holcroft, Thomas

(1745–1809)

Born in London, the son of a shoemaker and peddler, Thomas Holcroft received little formal education. His early life reads like a picaresque tale, with episodes as shoemaker, stable boy, and strolling player. Yet Godwin later described Holcroft as one of his "four principal oral instructors"; he became one of the leading radical intellectuals of his time; and his prominence in the London Corresponding Society and the Society for Constitutional Information was such that he was charged with high treason in 1794.

Holcroft's reputation—as popular dramatist and operatic collaborator, celebrated radical, novelist, and "acquitted felon"—testifies to the volatility of public opinion in English society in the last two decades of the 18th century. After nearly starving as a strolling player in the country, Holcroft presented himself to the manager of Drury Lane. He was refused employment. In desperation, he wrote the aptly named farce *The Crisis, or Love and Famine*, contrived to have it read by the manager's wife, and, on the basis of the farce and his musical abilities, was engaged at a small salary. His advance as an actor being blocked, he persisted in his literary endeavors, producing *Alwyn* (1780), a modestly successful novel; an account of the Gordon Riots; a promising comedy, *Duplicity* (1781); and several operas performed at Covent Garden. Success came in 1784, when he and a friend pirated Beaumarchais' *Mariage de Figaro*, currently running in Paris, and adapted it for an English audience. A series of successful plays followed which brought Holcroft financial success and fame as a popular dramatist. His *Tale of Mystery* (1802) introduced melodrama to the English stage and allowed the popular theater to develop because, with musical accompaniment, any play could overcome the Licensing Act.

Meanwhile Holcroft had imbibed many of the radical principles current in the revolutionary atmosphere of the late 1780s. He took up the general line of Enlightenment doctrine: commitment to rationality, circulation of reason through education, socialism, decline of governments and patriotism, brotherhood, and weakening of exclusivity of family unit, as well as faith in progress and general optimism. Holcroft's politics was purely speculative; he had no real plan for change. Trusting to the force of reason and argument over time, he never advocated violence. His novel *Anna St. Ives* (1792) is a kind of monument to his beliefs. Like many other novels published during the early 1790s, *Anna* is a part of the debate over the French Revolution, the terms of which were largely set by Paine's *Rights of Man* and Burke's *Reflections*.

Hazlitt's assessment of *Anna* is remarkably durable. He observes that the chief characters in the novel are not so much distinct individuals as they are the means of expressing ideas in particular contexts. Overall, Holcroft fares better than most novelists in the endeavor to represent goodness. Although his virtuous characters seem preachy, pedantic, and cold—much like Sir Charles Grandison, the fictional predecessor acknowledged by Holcroft— Holcroft was well aware of the difficulties of writing a novel along these lines. *The Monthly Review* contains a series of reviews by Holcroft (1792–96) that, taken together, provide both a useful account of the Jacobin view of fiction and a fairly intricate meditation on the technical difficulties faced by novelists of a radical stamp.

Holcroft was caught up in the government's campaign of harassment and innuendo against prominent radicals in 1794. The government attempted to discredit radicals by placing reports in ministerial papers about forthcoming warrants. Holcroft, angered at the manipulation of his reputation, appeared before the Chief Justice to demand that he be taken into custody and apprised of the charges against him. The Chief Justice had no information about the warrant, and the ministerial party was unprepared for Holcroft's forthright demand. Possibly to save face, a warrant

was later issued, and Holcroft was confined to Newgate for almost eight weeks. The charges were general, the case (with 208 prosecution witnesses) impossible to prepare against, and the outlook for the radicals dim. Yet Horne Tooke and Thomas Hardy were acquitted, and a swift acquittal followed for Holcroft. In the general anti-Jacobin fervor, however, Holcroft, like many other radicals, became the object of much distrust and hatred.

Godwin and Holcroft met in 1786. The two make an interesting pair of collaborators, since one received perhaps the finest formal education possible at the time and the other was an autodidact. Along with Charlotte Smith, Robert Bage, and Elizabeth Inchbald, they set the tone of the Jacobin novel in England.

Mark Parker

Works Consulted

Baine, R.M. *Thomas Holcroft and the Revolutionary Novel.* Athens: U of Georgia P, 1965.

Boulton, James. *The Language of Politics in the Age of Wilkes and Burke.* London: Routledge, 1963.

Kelly, Gary. *English Fiction of the Romantic Period: 1789–1830.* New York: Longman, 1989.

———. *The English Jacobin Novel, 1780–1805.* Oxford: Clarendon, 1976.

Hazlitt, William. *Memoirs of the late Thomas Holcroft.* In Vol. 3 of *The Complete Works of William Hazlitt.* Ed. P.P. Howe. London: Dent, 1932.

Hone, William
(1780–1842)

Born into a sternly religious Anglican family, William Hone received his early education largely through his father's tutoring, his own love of reading, and occasional stints at neighborhood schools. In the 1790s, Hone began to doubt the conservative religious precepts that dominated his childhood, and he became involved in the radical politics of the London Corresponding Society. After his marriage in 1800, he began the rather haphazard career in writing, publishing, and bookselling that would make him a prominent critic of the Regency government and a powerful champion of the freedom of the press. (*See also* Satire.)

Hone found himself at the forefront of the radical movement in December 1817, when he was tried before the King's Court on three *ex officio* informations charging him with blasphemous libel. As writer and publisher of the *Reformist's Register* (1816–17), Hone had become a popular and influential critic of the government, but the offending publications, produced in February 1817, were parodies based on the catechism, the litany, and the creed of the *Book of Common Prayer*. Though the parodies are clearly political in character, it was much easier at this time to "prove" blasphemous libel than seditious libel; the government apparently saw an opportunity to secure a guilty verdict and thereby silence one of its most outspoken critics. Hone's supporters saw the trials as little more than government persecution of an innocent, freethinking journalist.

The trials, widely publicized and attended by as many as 10,000 spectators, were remarkable for the contrast between the exasperation of the presiding justices and the steady persistence of Hone, who defended himself and amused the gallery by citing parodies on religious texts. In each case, when the jury returned its verdict of "not guilty," the courtroom erupted in cheers of support for both defendant and jury. Shortly after the last trial, a group calling itself the Friends of the Liberty of the Press and Trial by Jury met at a London tavern to celebrate Hone's acquittal and to take up a subscription for his financial support—among the many hundreds of contributors were Sir Francis Burdett, Lord Cochrane, Shelley, Leigh and John Hunt, Thomas Wooler, and Major Cartwright.

The successful defense was a humiliating blow to the government, and it effectively earned for Hone an immunity from further libel prosecutions. Consequently, Hone redoubled his literary efforts, producing a popular edition of *The Three Trials of William Hone* (1818) and such antigovernment satires as *The Political House That Jack Built* (1819), *The Queen's Matrimonial Ladder* (1820), *The Political Showman—At Home* (1821), and *A Slap at Slop* (1822). Many of these latter works were illustrated by Cruikshank, Hone's friend and frequent collaborator.

During the 1820s, Hone gradually retreated from the contentious arena of political criticism. Ill health and financial difficulties forced him to abandon plans for his magnum opus, a long-advertised *History of Parody*, and, beginning in 1825, he was chiefly occupied in writing and compiling those "literary kaleidoscopes," *The Every-Day Book*, *The Table Book*, and *The Year Book*. He died in 1842, having befriended Lamb and the young novelist Charles Dickens and having once again embraced the English Church.

Kyle Grimes

Works Consulted

Hackwood, Frederick. *William Hone: His Life and Times*. London: Unwin, 1912.

Hone, William. *The Late John Wilkes's Catechism, The Political Litany, and The Sinecurist's Creed or Belief*. 1817. Newcastle upon Tyne: Graham, 1970.

———. *The Three Trials of William Hone*. London: Hone, 1818.

Thompson, E.P. *The Making of the English Working Class*. 1963. New York: Vintage, 1966.

Hood, Thomas

(1799–1845)

Thomas Hood was a comic poet with a love of the grotesque and macabre. He influenced other poets, such as Poe, and his humor is precursor to the modern *comédie noire*. Hood also wrote serious verse, such as *The Plea of the Midsummer Fairies*. Had *Midsummer Fairies* succeeded with the public, Hood may have turned away from the comic world in which he excelled.

Hood was born a true Cockney in the Poultry, London, the son of the partner of the leading publishing firm Vernor and Hood. At school in London, Hood mastered French and Latin and read voraciously but left at about age 14 to enter a counting house. He was apprenticed to an engraver, but illness necessitated a protracted convalescence at Dundee, where he occupied himself reading, sketching, and writing verse. He returned south around 1817 to take up engraving again and found a niche with the celebrated Le Keux. In mid-1821, he was spotted by John Taylor, editor of the *London Magazine*, who made him a subeditor. Before long, Taylor entrusted him with writing the replies to the correspondents feature known as the "Lion's Head." Hood's new role allowed him to exercise his passion for punning and brought him into contact with the *London* regulars: Reynolds, whose sister he later married; Lamb, who took the fledgling writer under his wing; and Wainewright. Hood's own contributions to the *London*, the last of which appeared in June 1823, were verse and tended to follow the styles of, first, Byron; then, Shelley; and, finally, Keats. By his early 20s Hood had hit upon the main subjects he later employed regularly. His colleagues on the magazine were impressed. Wainewright hailed him as a new Ovid—proof of how close were the founts of laughter and tears. Lamb, whose prose style influenced Hood, dubbed him "that half-Hogarth."

Hood's first book, *Odes and Addresses to Great People* (1825), was published anonymously with Reynolds. Modeled on the Smith brothers's *Rejected Addresses*, the volume was Hood's idea, and he contributed most of its 15 poems, which were in praise of such worthies as the gastronome Dr. Kitchiner, the explorer Captain Parry, and the prison reformer Elizabeth Fry. Coleridge was convinced that this dazzling *tour de force* of outrageous puns, epigrams, and comic analogies was the work of Lamb. Soon afterward came Hood's solo debut— *Whims and Oddities* (1826)—a collection characterized by Hood's obsession with the comic potential of death, disease, mutilation, and other morbid themes. Of the many extraordinary poems in this remarkable book *The Last Man*, an apocalyptic vision of the future, stands out and prefigures modern angst of the atomic age. A second series, arguably more pathologically morbid than the first, came out in 1827, which also saw *National Tales* and, more significantly, *the Plea of the Midsummer Fairies*—Hood's only collection of wholly serious verse.

With *Midsummer Fairies*, Hood was attempting to win a name as a poet of substance. The title poem was dedicated to Lamb; a companion piece, *Hero and Leander*, was dedicated to Coleridge; and the book's entire contents show Hood as a sensitive young writer susceptible to the influences of Coleridge, Wordsworth, and most noticeably, Keats. The third of the triumvirate of long poems, *Lycus the Centaur*, was inspired by Book III of Keats's *Endymion*, and all three pieces are consciously literary. Hood also adopted a Keatsian language for *Ode: Autumn*, which borrows lines from the poet; *Ruth*; and *Ode to Melancholy*, among others. Most of these poems are exercises in imitation and succeed only on that level. The intellectual structure that underpinned Keats's originals is entirely missing from Hood's versions. Hood had no instinctive sympathy with Keats's type of poetry; he had no deep appreciation of the mythological world and no serious conception of the artist as creator. He was mainly concerned with exploiting the rich trappings of the Keatsian style to point out a moral, for unlike Keats, Hood had a strong core of moral concern—a trait that sets him apart from the true Romantics. Nevertheless, some of the sonnets in *Midsummer Fairies* triumph over their influences and show Hood to have been one of the more gifted writers of the little lyric in English. *Silence*, for instance, is a skillfully wrought evocation that deserves to rank with Keats and Shelley and was imitated by Poe.

Critical reaction to *Midsummer Fairies* was mixed, and the book sold badly. The disappointed Hood bought up the remainder of the edition and never again issued a volume of straight verse. He continued to compose the occasional Romantic poem, but for the rest of his creative life most of his published verse was comic in tone, and with the enormous success of his *Comic Annuals* he became identified to the reading public as a comic writer and inveterate punster.

The annuals began in 1829. A year before, Hood had become editor of the *Gem* and attracted distinguished contributors, such as Lamb, Hartley, Coleridge, and Scott. Among his own poems published in the *Gem* was *Dream of Eugene Aram*, a tale of sin and remorse based on a real 18th-century case and told in a narrative style based on *the Rime of the Ancient Mariner*. The poem caught the imagination of Poe. Hood had an almost pathological fear of being

taken at face value. Like the Byron of *Don Juan*, Hood cannot resist undercutting a moment of genuine suspense with a comic twist, and his use of the pun in such serious poems appears perverse—the manifestation of an incurable nervous tic. Hood reveals that all has been a dream or, in the case of *The Demon Ship*, an illusion. This particular handling of Romantic irony is peculiar to Hood and, in a way, appealing to the English.

Hood's first novel, the three-volume *Tylney Hall*, appeared late in 1834 and was favorably received by critics and public alike. They found its characteristic mixture of high comedy, pathos, and good humor adequate compensation for a lack of plot and poor characterization. By early 1835, however, the collapse of his finances coupled with his own bad health and the grave illness of his wife had brought Hood close to a nervous breakdown. In March 1835, he left England for a more economical life in Coblenz, Germany, from where, after over two years, he moved northward to Ostend. Abroad, he continued to conduct his annual while writing *Hood's Own* (1839) and a second novel, *Up the Rhine* (1840). This largely autobiographical work shows Hood still experimenting with the techniques of Romantic irony and features the author disguised as a disgruntled exile, Markham. Also while abroad Hood demonstrated a heightened interest in the social and political issues of England, producing such poems as *Agricultural Distress*, *The Doves and the Crows*, and *A Plain Direction*, that revealed a passionate radical outlook. And when a wealthy Evangelical Scot attacked him for a relaxed attitude toward church attendance and alcohol, Hood hit back with a new vehemence in an *Ode to Rae Wilson Esquire* (1837). By now Hood had become the master *par excellence* at sugaring the moral pill with brilliant comic invention, and soon after his return to England in mid-1840 he completed his most celebrated comic morality poem—*Miss Kilmansegg and her Precious Leg*. In it, the sickening commercialism of his time is symbolized by a golden leg that eventually kills its owner.

Other poems of social protest followed *Miss Kilmansegg*, most notably *A Drop of Gin*, *The Pauper's Christmas Carol*, *The Song of the Shirt*, *The Workhouse Clock*, and *The Bridge of Sighs*. Of these, *The Song of the Shirt*, which appeared in the Christmas 1843 issue of *Punch*, and trebled its circulation almost overnight, is arguably the best-known protest poem written in English. Within a week of its publication the first issue of a new venture, *Hood's Monthly Magazine*, included *The Haunted House*, a poem that stylistically recalled Hood's Keatsian phase of 20 years before. *Miss Kilmansegg* also contains echoes of Keats, whose influence Hood seemed reluctant or unable to throw off. It has been argued that the crisis of early 1835 that reactivated Hood's social conscience also heightened his awareness of the pain of existence, to which Keats, an invalid like Hood, was unusually sensitive. Perhaps Hood came to identify himself with Keats.

Hood's final year of life was fraught with domestic tension, mounting debts, and collapsing health. Nevertheless, his magazine was kept afloat largely through the generosity of such contributors as Browning and Landor, who offered free material. In November 1844, Peel bestowed a pension on Hood's wife. Hood's final poem, *Farewell, Life. My senses swim*, appeared in the February 1845 issue of *Hood's Magazine* and shows the poet resigned to his fate. After lingering on for three further months, exhausted and racked by pain, Hood died in 1845—victim of the chronic heart condition that had plagued

him since childhood. (*See also* Reynolds, John Hamilton; Satire.)

R.M. Healey

Works Consulted

Broderip, Frances Freeling, ed. *Memorials of Thomas Hood*. Boston: Ticknor, 1860.

Chilcott, Tim. *A Publisher and his Circle*. Boston: Routledge, 1972.

Clubbe, John. *Victorian Forerunner: The Later Career of Thomas Hood*. Durham: Duke UP, 1968.

— — —, ed. *Selected Poems of Thomas Hood*. Cambridge: Harvard UP, 1970.

Curling, Jonathan. *Janus Weathercock*. New York: Nelson, 1938.

Jerrold, Walter, ed. *Complete Poetical Works of Thomas Hood*. New York: Frowder, 1911.

Reid, J.C. *Thomas Hood*. London: Routledge, 1963.

Humanitarianism

At the same time that Romanticism was developing into a full-fledged literary movement, public concern over social problems was increasing. These concerns developed into a social philosophy and reform movement known as humanitarianism.

As a social philosophy, humanitarianism arose out of the religious awakening that began in England early in the 18th century under the leadership of John and Charles Wesley and their colleague George Whitefield. These Evangelicals took their message to the working people on the streets of industrial towns and in the alleys of London's poor districts, preaching a message of hope and salvation. Emphasizing the value of each person, the importance of fellowship, and the awakening of sympathy for others, these social concerns soon carried over into practical programs to aid the masses.

First in importance of the humanitarian reforms was the ending of slave trade. Since the Treaty of Utrecht in 1713, the English had a world monopoly on this lucrative business. Humanitarian criticism of slavery as it existed in the British Empire first appeared in England after the middle of the 18th century. The Quakers were the first to oppose slavery, and Wesley's *Thoughts Upon Slavery* (1774) furthered the cause. Other voices of protest were heard from Johnson, Bentham, Adam Smith, Burke, Paine, and Pitt. But it was Wilberforce who led the crusade that finally ended the slave trade when Parliament passed the abolition bill of 1807. A gifted orator, Wilberforce opened up the question of the slave trade before the House of Commons in 1789. In his first great speech made before the House on the abolition of the slave trade, he received enthusiastic applause and the support of Burke and Pitt, but victory was nearly 20 years in the future. Three readings of his bill were brought before the House of Commons and in the House of Lords before the English finally passed a bill that abolished the slave trade. (*See also* Fox, James Charles; Slavery.)

Another humanitarian reform movement involved prisons. The movement for prison reform had its greatest advocate in John Howard, whose famous *State of Prisons* (1777) led to improved conditions in the country's prisons by 1800. Various other reform movements were also launched about this time. In 1819, a child-labor law limited children to 11 working hours a day, and in 1833, Shaftesbury steered through Parliament another law to further limit working hours. Homes and hospitals for deserted children were founded, and in 1758, a home for unwed mothers. The first Sunday Schools were established in 1780 by Robert Raikes, whose primary aim was to reach the country's poor and neglected children. In 1783, Mary Wollstonecraft brought out her treatise *A Vindication of the Rights of Women*, a founding classic of the feminist movement. The English police system and criminal code were humanely revised, and moral and social ills due to excesses of drinking were struck at in temperance drives under the leadership of Christian groups. Thus, the humanitarian concerns that developed out of the spirit of religious revival and a desire for democracy soon became a way of life in England after 1750.

Mary Susan Johnston

Works Consulted

Briggs, Asa. *The Making of Modern England, 1783–1867: The Age of Improvement.* New York: Harper, 1959.

Halevy, Elie. *A History of the English People in the Nineteenth Century: England in 1815.* Vol. 1. Trans. E.I. Watkin and D.A. Barker. 1924. New York: Barnes, 1961.

Harris, Ronald W. *Romanticism and the Social Order, 1780–1830.* New York: Barnes, 1969.

Klingberg, Frank. *The Anti-slavery Movement in England: A Study of English Humanitarianism.* Hamden, CT: Archon, 1926.

McCullach, Samuel Clyde, ed. *British Humanitarianism: Essays Honoring Frank Klingberg.* Philadelphia: Church Historical Society, 1950.

Somervell, D.C. *English Thought in the Nineteenth Century.* London: Methuen, 1947.

Trevelyan, G.M. *British History of the Nineteenth Century.* New York: Longmans, 1937.

— — —. *English Social History.* New York: Longmans, 1942.

Hunt, Leigh
(1784–1859)

Leigh Hunt was a writer and literary figure of varied and significant accomplishment. As editor, journalist, critic, essayist, and poet, he made important contributions to 19th-century English literature across six decades. He was also a central figure in the social history of English Romanticism, playing a crucial role in the development of such figures as Keats,

Shelley, Hazlitt, and Lamb. (*See also* Essay, Journalism, [The] *Liberal*.)

Born in Southgate, Middlesex, to American Loyalist parents who had immigrated to England, Hunt was sent in 1791 to Christ's Hospital School. There, following in the footsteps of Coleridge and Lamb, he studied the Classics and became fluent in composing English prose and verse.

Hunt left Christ's Hospital in 1799. Between 1801 and 1805, he published *Juvenilia* (1801), a collection of poetry, and wrote essays and theatrical criticism for a variety of periodicals, including his brother John's *News*. *Juvenilia*, consisting largely of imitations of Spenser, Thomson, Gray, and others, enjoyed a remarkable success, going through four editions in England and one in America.

In 1808, Hunt published *Critical Essays on the Performers of the London Theatres*, a volume of his collected theatrical criticism. In its perceptiveness, independence, and lively concreteness, it had a major impact on the development of dramatic criticism during the period.

Also in 1808, Hunt and his brother John began the *Examiner*, a weekly radical newspaper which became immediately popular. Over its long history, the *Examiner* was perhaps the liveliest and most intelligent of Romantic periodicals. Although it was more moderate in tone and style than such radical papers as Cobbett's *Political Register*, the paper's open and often witty attacks on government corruption, foreign and military affairs, and parliamentary ineptitude led to a series of governmental legal actions against the journal between 1808 and 1811.

Initially, these governmental actions were unsuccessful; the *Examiner* flourished, and in 1810 and 1811 the energetic Hunt established a quarterly magazine, the *Reflector*, which offered him a more purely literary outlet than did the *Examiner*. In this short-lived but significant journal, Hunt published several important pieces, including "Atys the Enthusiast" (a fine translation from Catullus); "A Day by the Fire" (a familiar essay in his best manner); and his satiric poem *The Feast of the Poets*. The *Reflector* is also notable for its publication of several of Lamb's best early works.

In 1813, government's legal actions against the *Examiner* finally took effect when both Leigh and John Hunt were found guilty of seditious libel against the Prince Regent and were fined and sentenced to two years in prison. Leigh Hunt's two years in Horsemonger Lane Gaol quickly became and have remained one of the most durable legends of English Romanticism. Having decorated his prison rooms with bookcases, paper rose trellises, and plaster busts, Hunt and his family received visits from the Lambs, Hazlitt, Moore, Byron, and others.

Following his release from prison in 1815, Hunt vigorously resumed his literary career and began his most productive period as a poet. His longest and perhaps most significant poem, *The Story of Rimini*, was published in 1816 with a dedication to Byron. *Rimini*, based on Dante's account of Francesca and Paolo in Canto V of the *Divine Comedy*, is remarkable for its experiments with colloquial diction, its loosening of the Neoclassical couplet, and its demonstration of Hunt's abiding interest in Italian romance. The poem enjoyed considerable success and had a major influence on Keats's development as a poet.

Rimini was followed in 1818 by the collection of *Foliage* and in 1819 by two poems on mythological subjects, *Hero and Leander* and *Bacchus and Ariadne*. *Foliage* contains one of Hunt's best poems, the mythological and sensuously descriptive *The Nymphs*. Although Hunt was preoccupied with Classical myth during this period, his handling of mythic themes usually lacks the originality and reinterpretive power that Keats and Shelley deployed toward similar subjects.

Perhaps Hunt's most significant contribution to English literature between 1815 and 1821 was his emergence as a mentor and critical defender of what has come to be called the rising second generation of Romantic writers. Throughout this period, Hunt's house in the "Vale of Health" in Hampstead was the center for a circle of writers that included Shelley, Keats, Lamb, Hazlitt, and John H. Reynolds. Hunt became close friends with Shelley following the suicide of Harriet Shelley in 1816 and advised the young poet on the publication of his *Laon and Cythna*. To Keats, he was a constant encourager and friend and, during the difficult period of Keats's final illness, he was a generous if not always effective comforter.

As editor and critic, Hunt was a brilliantly prescient and courageously determined advocate of the best among the younger Romantics. During 1816 and 1817, Hunt, in the *Examiner*, published the first six poems of Keats to appear in print; published Shelley's *Hymn to Intellectual Beauty*; reviewed Keats's *Poems* (1817) with discriminating enthusiasm; and, in December 1816, presented Keats, Shelley, and J.H. Reynolds to the world as the "young poets" of the future. Hunt's campaign on behalf of Keats and Shelley, thus begun, continued tirelessly throughout the remainder of his life.

Hunt's other significant achievement during the period between his release from prison and his move to Italy in 1822 was his weekly called the *Indicator*, published between 1819 and 1821. In this journal, Hunt published some of the best of his familiar essays, such as "Getting Up on Cold Mornings," "Coaches and their Horses," and "A 'Now' Description of a Hot Day." In these, he reveals the charm, the chatty ease, and the quiet wit that form his distinctive contribution to the Romantic personal essay.

In 1821, Shelley, living in Italy, began to encourage Hunt to come and join him, with the idea that he, Hunt, and Byron might collaborate on a new literary journal. After various false starts and delaying storms at sea, Hunt and his family arrived in Italy in June 1822. Shortly after Hunt's arrival, Shelley was drowned, and his death led to difficult relations between Hunt and Byron. Without Shelley's mediating influence, the two would-be collaborators became increasingly disaffected with one another. Despite worsening relations throughout the next few months, Hunt and Byron issued four numbers of the *Liberal* during 1822 and 1823. The *Liberal* published some important works, including Byron's *The Vision of Judgment* and Hazlitt's "My First Acquaintance with Poets," but its somewhat erratic quality, its controversial character, and, most of all, the troubled and unstable relationship between its editors led to its premature demise.

With the end of the *Liberal*, Byron left Italy for Greece, leaving an embittered and poor Hunt to shift for himself in Genoa. For the next two years Hunt remained in Italy, coming to know Landor and receiving a visit in 1825 from Hazlitt. Perhaps Hunt's most important literary work during this period is his vigorous translation of Francesco Redi's dithyrambic *Bacchus in Tuscany* (1825). Otherwise, Hunt's two years in Italy were notable mainly for his increasingly difficult financial situation and for what was the beginning of a long and bitter dispute with his brother John over proprietorship of the *Examiner*.

In October 1825, aided by an advance from the publisher Colburn, Hunt returned to England. Unfortunately, his finances were still precarious and, driven by debt and resentment toward Byron, he published *Lord Byron and Some of His Contemporaries* in 1828. This unflattering account of Byron was both a considerable success and a disaster for Hunt. On the one hand, its easy style, lively portraiture, and scandalous revelations about Byron made the book popular, even sensational. On the other hand, the overwhelming impression left by the volume was that Hunt had revealed himself as low-bred, spiteful, tasteless, and shameless in his attack on a great poet whose recent death had enshrined him as a hero in the public mind.

In the years following the publication of *Lord Byron*, Hunt's reputation slowly rebounded. Despite poverty and personal difficulties, his ceaseless efforts in literature and journalism and his survival as one of the last of the Romantic giants eventually conferred upon him the status of a virtual literary and public institution. His later significance, however, was far from merely historical or honorific. He remained a shrewd critic and was one of the first to recognize Tennyson's greatness. He was respected by such a stern judge as Carlyle, and he continued to write occasionally with great energy and insight. Two of his later works stand out. One is *Imagination and Fancy* (1844), with its important essay on "What Is Poetry?" and its keen appreciation of Coleridge, Keats, and Shelley. Second is his vivid and unflaggingly entertaining *Autobiography* (1850); certainly, its memorable accounts of Christ's Hospital, Hunt's imprisonment, his literary warfare with the Tories, his love of Shelley, and his ill-fated trip to Italy are indispensable Romantic documents.

Despite the dark cloud cast by Dickens's portrait of him as Harold Skimpole in *Bleak House* (1852–53), Hunt's later years were productive and generally happy. He received a Civil List pension in 1847 and, writing to the last, died at Putney in his 75th year.

Phillip B. Anderson

Works Consulted

Blainey, Ann. *Immortal Boy: A Portrait of Leigh Hunt*. New York: St. Martin's, 1985.

Blunden, Edmund. *Leigh Hunt*. London: Cobden-Sanderson, 1930.

Houtchens, L.H., and C.W. *Leigh Hunt's Literary Criticism*. New York: Columbia UP, 1956.

Kendall, Kenneth E. *Leigh Hunt's Reflector*. Paris: Mouton, 1971.

Landre, Louis. *Leigh Hunt (1784–1859): Contribution à l'histoire du Romantisme anglais*. 2 vols. Paris: Société d'édition "Les Belles-lettres," 1935–36.

Marshall, William H. *Byron, Shelley, Hunt, and the Liberal*. Philadelphia: U of Pennsylvania P, 1960.

Thompson, James R. *Leigh Hunt*. Boston: Twayne, 1977.

Hymnody

English hymnody emerged as legitimate and respectable literature when early 19th-century hymnodists determined to loosen themselves from the homiletical dominance of their 18th-century predecessors. The psalm paraphrases and hymns of Isaac Watts, Samuel Davies, and Charles Wesley arose directly from the sound and the sense of the sermon; such pieces had to edify and to suggest specific moral conclusions.

Some writing during the Romantic movement, on the other hand, demonstrated that English congregations might be persuaded to sense the light from spiritual idealism and holy imagination. For English congregational song, Romanticism led to opportunities wherein true poetry might arouse dull feelings and reproduce, within the context of the worship service, conditions relative to those experienced by the poet during composition. Then followed the development of the literary hymn, the highest level at which English hymnodists have ever soared. Within the limits and under the inspiration of contemporary poetry, English hymnody assumed both literary quality and religious enthusiasm, a poetic grace and ornamentation that had never existed within the framework of that genre.

Romantic hymnody began with Reginald Heber (1783–1826), Bishop of Calcutta. A year following his death *Hymns Written and Adopted to the Weekly Service of the Year* appeared. Heber had written 57 of its 98 hymns, including such classic pieces as "God, Who madest earth and heaven"; "The Son of God goes forth to war"; "Virgin-born, we bow before Thee"; "Creator of the rolling flood"; "Holy, Holy, Holy! Lord God Almighty!"; "Hosanna to the living Lord"; "From Greenland's icy mountains"; and "There was joy in heav'n."

As early as October 1811, Heber had lamented in *The Christian Observer* "the fulsome, indecorous or erotic language found in popular collections of sacred poetry," maintaining that his work stood upon the page free from such "profanities." Other than problems of language, he sensed a strong bond between his verse and the principal Romantic strains of the times. Thus, in 1816, he projected a hymn collection with literary emphasis, a collection of sacred verse for public worship. Initially, he bowed to writers of previous ages: Drummond, Ken, Dryden, Addison, Pope, Cowper, Watts, the Wesleys; yet he also cast his hand toward his contemporary Romantics: Scott, Byron, Moore, Campbell, Southey, Henry Hunt Milman, and certainly himself.

Heber submitted an abbreviated draft of his hymnal to the Bishop of London, who refused to authorize its publication, claiming that the Church was not ready to adopt an authorized collection. Heber then carried his manuscript to India, hoping to publish it there. His death precluded that possibility, and his wife, upon returning to England, presented it to Murray. The London publisher produced the work not as a hymnal, but as a collection of religious verse. Nonetheless, Heber had created a new standard for English hymnody, carefully applying the notes of restrained devotion to accommodate the Church year with the rhythm, grace, and ornamentation of legitimate poetry.

Essentially, Heber illustrated the degree to which Romanticism influenced English hymnody. In "From Greenland's icy mountain" (1819), for example, he stepped out of Scriptures to capture the essence of the missionary's vision: ideally, the Church labors amid the highly imaginative environs of coral, sunshine, golden sand, and spicy breezes. Heber draws a clear line between such pleasant prospects and the vile heathen residing upon and within it. Clearly, he embraced the Western notion of a person committing the soul to God, of a human being existing and functioning as an enlightened being who must carry the Word until "each remotest nation/Has learn'd Messiah's name." Thus, he focused on an individualistic and imaginative milieu that, until then, had not found expression in English congregational song.

The difference between Heber and the secular poets who influence his work concerns purpose and audience. The poets of English Romanticism stood apart from English Romantic hymnody. For example, Coleridge's "Ere on my bed my limbs I lay" (1803, 1816) has strong hymnodic qualities in its rhythm and prayerful tone, but neither directs itself toward God nor resides within the substantive context of the Christian Church. Instead, the poet looks to love (or its absence), writing in the pain, anguish, and even horror it engenders. Three years later, however, Coleridge produced a true hymnodic variant of "The Pains of Sleep," reducing the original's 52 lines to 20 and retitling it "A Child's Evening Prayer" (1806).

James Martineau inserted that hymnodic prayer into his *Hymns of the Christian Church and Home* (1840) and *Hymns of Praise and Prayer* (1873), retaining Coleridge's title. It was never accepted by English or American congregations (Unitarian or otherwise). Coleridge's other hymnlike pieces fared no better, principally because he never intended them to be sung in churches. His "Anthem for the Children of Christ's Hospital" (1789), beginning "Seraphs! around th' Eternal's seat who throng," limits itself in context and prevents a clear connection to general congregational needs and interests.

One of Wordsworth's three hymnodic pieces, "The Labourer's Noon-Day Hymn" (1835), begins "Up to the throne of God is borne." It gained acceptance among worshipers. According to the poet, he sought to fill a void between the morning and evening hymns of Bishop Thomas Ken (1695). Although never gaining favor from congregational singers, two other Wordsworth "hymns" are worthy representatives of Romantic hymnody: the fifth and final section of the 1820 "Inscriptions Supposed To Be Found in and near a Hermit's Cell" ("Not seldom, clad in radiant vest") and, also 1820, the "Hymn for the Boatmen, As They Approach the Rapids under the Castle of Heidelberg" ("Jesu! bless our slender Boat"). Both pieces underscore the forces of active Nature and the fragility of the spiritual and physical

states of humans when pitted against them. Unfortunately, for the purposes of traditional religious institutions, the poet is not concerned with the role of the Church within that context.

The contributions of Scott, Moore, and Byron influenced the tone and language of the Romantic hymn. Scott tried to condense *Dies Irae* with "That day of wrath, that dreadful day," as found at the close of *The Lay of the Last Minstrel* and entitled "Hymn for the Dead." "Rebecca's Hymn" ("When Israel of the Lord beloved") from *Ivanhoe* caught some congregational attention because of its context: the imaginary trial of Rebecca the Jewess by a court of the Order of the Templars on the charge of sorcery. But the poet carefully merged his Romantic surroundings with the thesis of Psalm 105, thus its acceptance by worshipers during the remainder of the 19th century.

In terms of quantity, Thomas Moore may well rank primary among those poets who drifted, occasionally, upon the tide of hymnody. Of the 32 poems in the first edition of his *Sacred Songs* (1816), 12 found places in English and American hymnals and at least eight continue to be sung by worshipers. "Come ye disconsolate, where'er you languish"; "O Thou Who driest the mourner's tear"; and "Thou art, O God, the Life and Light" remain the most popular. Given the poet's instinct for music and song, his emotion more than compensated for his lack of religious consistency, and he proved most astute in pairing his verse with the proper musical air.

Finally, Byron associated himself with hymnody through three pieces from the *Hebrew Melodies* (1815): "The wild gazelle on Judah's hills," "The King was on his throne" ("Vision of Belshazzar"), and "The Assyrian came down like the wolf on the fold" ("The Destruction of Sennacherib"). Although current versions suffer somewhat from hymnal editors' revisions, they continue to appeal. Certainly the poet made little or no personal claim to religion, but he recognized the fundamentals of Christian morality and piety of others. The lyrics of *Hebrew Melodies* allowed him, at least, to assume the existence of God; to the hymnal editors fell the task of recasting those assumptions into the practice and the praise (by others) of institutional religion.

While Wordsworth, Coleridge, Scott, Moore, and Byron had neither interests nor aims toward English congregational song, they impressed upon their hymnodic colleagues the notion that poetry could help the worshiper establish a relationship with God. The poets also weakened, in hymnodists' eyes, the Johnsonian dictate (set down in his lives of Waller and Watts)

that communication of the soul and God could not be (nor should it be) through poetry. Heber, James Montgomery, and Thomas Kelly (the last in Ireland), elevated the poetic standard of the English hymn and defined and refined hymnodic tastes of English Protestants (both within and without the Established Church). Without realizing what they had done, the major poets of English Romanticism planted the literary seeds that would produce, in 1861, the most bountiful harvest within English hymnody, *Hymns Ancient and Modern*. (*See also* Music.)

Samuel J. Rogal

Works Consulted

Benson, Louis F. *The English Hymn. Its Development in Use and Worship*. New York: Doran, 1915.

Hymns Ancient and Modern. For Use in the Services of the Church. London: Clowes, 1909.

Julian, John, ed. *A Dictionary of Hymnology*. 2 vols. 2nd ed., rev. 1907. New York: Dover, 1957.

Imagination

The concept most closely associated with English Romantic poetry is that of the imagination. Intellectual explorations of the concept peaked at the end of the 18th century and were followed by poetic pronouncements on the efficacious power of the imagination in Blake, Wordsworth, and Coleridge, with these pronouncements expanded in the second generation, by Keats and Shelley in particular. Yet the celebration of the imagination in the works of these poets can be seen as a culmination rather than an innovation. At the end of the 17th century, influential English writers, embracing Neoclassical and empirical systems, assigned imagination (and its synonym "fancy") two mental roles: the passive function of image formation as "a mode of memory" and the active function of linking "sensations" to generate something new. As late as the 1757 publication of Burke's *A Philosophical Enquiry into the Origins of our Ideas of the Sublime and Beautiful,* the imagination is represented as being dependent on volition, on consciousness.

The dual functions initially assigned to the imagination, in fact, provide the framework for the imagination's expansion. Thus, in diverse fields of endeavor in England and across the continent, as James Engell has demonstrated, a dialectic that vibrated between the outer and inner worlds, between nature and the self, between object and subject was discovered. This dialectical strain of thought is particularly influential in Germany, making its most profound impact in Kant's philosophic system, and a considerable impact of Kantian and other German thought can be seen in Coleridge's *Biographia Literaria* and in Burke's *Enquiry.* Yet in its very title the *Biographia* equally points to attempts to map mentality through personal reflection, an orientation shared with Blake's *Four Zoas* and Wordsworth's *Prelude.*

Blake and Wordsworth poetically pursue the poles of the dialectic of spirit and nature in their anatomizations of mental function and their valorizations of the imagination as primary psychic element. Blake claims "The Eternal Body of Man Is the Imagination;" Wordsworth, in Book XIII of *The Prelude,* announces "Imagination [has] been our theme." Nowhere is the primary status accorded the imagination by Romantic writers better articulated than in Mary Shelley's Introduction to *Frankenstein:* "My imagination, unbidden, possessed and guided me, gifting the succession of images that arose in my mind with a vividness far beyond the usual bounds of reverie." The dual elements that had configured the imagination in the English philosophical tradition, as imagistic memory and as image combination in creativity, are both present in Shelley's introductory remarks. Yet her remarks also promote the imagination as the privileged psychological attribute for engaging what might be equally termed the supernatural or the unconscious.

The imagination supplies the means through which to tap the elements of mentality that escape conscious control, to direct mental energy toward what Geoffrey H. Hartman terms antiselfconsciousness. For Wordsworth, his epiphany of antiselfconsciousness occurs in his crossing of the Simplon Pass as recorded in *The Prelude*, where "Imagination" is "that Power" which halts the mind, which usurps rational thought processes to reveal "the invisible world." With increasing emphasis placed on the imagination as one defining aspect of Romanticism came two essential distinctions by Coleridge between primary and secondary imagination, with both defined independent of fancy.

Thought concerning the role imagination plays in image formation inevitably tied the concept to theories of language, and by extension to poetic processes. Percy Bysshe Shelley articulates this position in *A Defence of Poetry*, which describes the "imperial faculty" of imagination as the portal into "the invisible nature of man," with the well-spring of imagination pointing to "the nature itself of language." For Shelley, then, "Imagination is the poetic faculty." A similar view of imagination as the physical embodiment of unglimpsed realms of psychic truth is put forth in one of Keats's letters: "The Imagination may

be compared to Adam's dream—he awoke and found it truth. . . . Imagination and its empyreal reflection is the same as human Life and its Spiritual repetition." For Shelley and Keats, the imagination's embodiment in language is the highest aspiration for poetic production, binding the poets of the first and second generations to analogous views of the efficacious elements of the imagination as the primary mental faculty.

One salient feature of the imagination was an introspective turn that followed the external expansion of the imagination in relation to nature. Harold Bloom has described this turn as the "internalization of quest-romance," in which poets sought a paradise within. And, as other critics have argued, the imagination was also the vehicle through which to apprehend the living nature of the universe. Repeatedly during the period, in the poetry of Wordsworth, Coleridge, Keats, and Shelley, the imagination assumes a redemptive function in relation to nature, then returns back into itself; in M.H. Abrams's reading of Wordsworth, the imagination becomes a secularized savior in the grand Miltonic story. It is through the imagination that Romantic poets and writers perceive and interpret what Berkeley called, in a slightly different context, the "universal language of the Author of nature." Such a reading perhaps points to Shelley's *Mont Blanc*, in which the poet's imagination seeks conversation with what has been termed in postmodern theories "otherness": "And what were thou, and earth, and stars, and sea,/If to the human mind's imaginings/ Silence and solitude were vacancy?" Through the agency of the imagination, the human mind enters a discourse with a universe that remains mute without the infusion of the imagination. This is perhaps Blake's point when, in *The Marriage of*

Heaven and Hell, he claims, "Where man is not, nature is barren." As Blake realized earlier in the period, and as Keats and Shelley came to know early in their lives, nature can entrap the mind. However, the redemptive qualities of the imagination, as Shelley goes on to argue, extend to others as well as to nature itself, since the sympathetic faculty of the imagination enables one to imagine being another.

The enthrallment of the imagination with the erotic otherness of exotic cultures is exemplified in Byron's popular Oriental poems. As the sale of 10,000 copies of *The Corsair* prior to publication indicates, Byron evoked a fictive poetic world capable of tapping English cultural curiosity for alterity, a curiosity perhaps fueled by English colonialism. Other poems, like Southey's *Thalaba the Destroyer* and Shelley's *The Revolt of Islam*—also drew upon what Edward Said has termed "orientalism" as an imaginative stimulation of this cultural desire. But Byron, more than any other poet, addressed the imagination to society's fascination with such otherness.

The valorization of the imagination provides a unifying force that binds the first and second generations of Romantic poets, but the differences among the poets usually associated with the Romantic endeavor must be clarified. Certainly, the most impassioned, and perhaps eccentric, belief in the transformational powers of the imagination is voiced by Blake. For Blake, the imagination provides the necessary vortex of mental energy that allows the individual to unify the extra- and intramental, and when the activities of the imagination are stymied, civilization is endangered: "Art Degraded Imagination Denied War Governed the Nations." For Wordsworth, in *Sonnet on Imagination*, "Imagination is that sacred power" capable of elevating "the more-than-reasoning Mind" and illuminat-

ing "life's dark cloud." Both poets heavily emphasize the transforming power of the imagination; it is the imagery of their expressions that marks their difference. Because of Wordsworth's insistent emphasis on self as subject, the later Romantics revolted against what Keats termed "the wordsworthian, or egotistical, sublime." For Keats, the egotistical sublime leads to a privileging of identity, which his poetry, *Endymion* for example, seeks to overcome. Shelley too pursues an eclipse of identity in poems like *The Triumph of Life.* Keats, Shelley, and Blake find imaginative communication with nature more problematic than either Wordsworth or Coleridge, and, like Blake, they both found the dream or the unconscious a more trustworthy guide in mapping the mind's engagement with phenomena. In spite of these differences, the poets now associated with English Romanticism, through their exploration and exploitation of the imagination, uncover a fundamental foundation of being: that identity and life itself belong to the province of the imaginative. (*See also* Camelion Poet; Egotistical, or Wordsworthian, Sublime; Reconciliation of Opposites; Spots of Time.)

Mark Lussier

Works Consulted

Abrams, M.H. *The Mirror and the Lamp: Romantic Theory and the Critical Tradition.* New York: Norton, 1958.

———. *Natural Supernaturalism: Tradition and Revolution in Romantic Literature.* New York: Norton, 1971.

Berkeley, George. *Principles, Dialogues, and Philosophical Correspondence.* Ed. Colin Murray Turbayne. Indianapolis: Bobbs, 1965.

Bloom, Harold. "The Internalization of Quest-Romance." Ed. Bloom. *Romanticism and Consciousness: Essays in Criticism.* New York: Norton, 1970: 3–24.

Burke, Edmund. *A Philosophical Enquiry into our Ideas of the Sublime and Beautiful.* Ed. James Boulton. Oxford: Blackwell, 1987.

Engell, James. *The Creative Imagination: Enlightenment to Romanticism.* Cambridge: Harvard UP, 1981.

Hartman, Geoffrey H. "Romanticism and 'Anti-Self-Consciousness.'" Ed. Harold Bloom. *Romanticism and Consciousness.* New York: Norton, 1970: 46–56.

Hill, John Spencer, ed. *The Romantic Imagination: A Casebook.* London: Macmillan, 1962.

Piper, H.W. *The Active Universe: Pantheism and the Concept of Imagination in the English Romantic Poets.* London: Athlone, 1962.

Reed, Arden, ed. *Romanticism and Language.* Ithaca: Cornell UP, 1984.

Said, Edward. *Orientalism.* New York: Pantheon, 1978.

Weiskel, Thomas. *The Romantic Sublime: Studies in the Structure and Psychology of Transcendence.* Baltimore: Johns Hopkins UP, 1976.

Incest

Despite strong societal taboos against incest, many Romantics assimilated the concept into their imaginative lives, either consciously or subconsciously, to varying degrees and purposes. Furthermore, their personal lives often were the subject of rumor and speculation concerning possible incestuous brother-sister relationships.

Byron's relationship with his half-sister Augusta Byron Leigh seems the most credible of the theorized improprieties. No doubt exists about the strength of Byron's feelings for Augusta; their mutual affection is readily apparent in their letters, in poems by Byron, and from firsthand accounts of their love for and dependence on each other. Indeed, rumors and charges of incest and homosexuality surrounded Byron's separation from his wife, Lady Anna Isabella Milbanke Byron.

The topic of incest or allusions to it occur frequently in Byron's work. His original intentions for *The Bride of Abydos* included a brother-sister involvement, but

more important is the role of incest in *Manfred*, where the hero's blighted life revolves around his secret crime and obsession with his dead sister Astarte, for whom he has a forbidden love. Other hints of dark, unlawful passions occur in *Childe Harold I and II.* Byron's turbulent life, affairs, and poetry suggest a man determined to defy society—sexually and otherwise—a man who felt doomed in a fallen world where complete love is all but impossible.

Shelley was perhaps led to an idealized view of incest because of his vigorous support of women's rights. In his work, incest is a metaphor for true equality between the sexes and for the ideal sympathetic relationship between a man and a woman. Such a relationship he thought possible only if the couple is like twins or mirror images of each other, so that they come to represent the harmonious reunion of an individual's psyche with its exact sentimental mate. Only by sharing upbringing, interests, purpose, education, and opportunities can man and woman find this true equality and thus become the embodiment of ideal union—like finding like, brother finding sister. In the suppressed version of *Laon and Cythna* (*The Revolt of Islam*), the protagonists are siblings who have this bond and equality and so naturally become lovers as well. They lead a revolt to overthrow the tyrant and recreate society free of tyranny of all kinds—sexual, political, and religious. Although they are ultimately martyred for their beliefs, they remain spiritually joined. In *The Cenci,* Beatrice's forced incest with her father is a tragedy because it is an act of violation and malice, not love. Indeed, Shelley seems to have regarded incest as principally a socially condemned act, not a perversion of human nature. In *Epipsychidion,* Shelley wishes he and Emilia Vivani had been born of one mother and makes her fictionally his wife's sister—consequently, his sister and his metaphorically incestuous ideal love.

Presumably, no literal incest occurred in Shelley's life, although numerous rumors circulated that his relationships with Mary Godwin and Claire Clairmont at Lake Geneva were incestuous, since Claire was mistakenly thought to be Mary's half-sister, instead of her stepsister. Later rumors of a relationship between Shelley and his sister Elizabeth seem perhaps the result of garbled alterations of some of Shelley's correspondence with an admirer of Elizabeth. Nevertheless, Freudian critics have made much of the Oedipal undertones in Shelley's relationship with his mother and father.

Wordsworth's extraordinarily close relationship with his sister Dorothy occasioned comments, but there seems little reason to suspect a sexual relationship existed. In *Tintern Abbey*, Dorothy does appear to the poet as a sort of spiritual twin who completely shares his sympathies and pleasures.

Byron, Shelley, and Wordsworth were not the only writers of the period associated with literal or literary incest. In 19th-century American literature, Edgar Allan Poe's *The Fall of the House of Usher*, Nathaniel Hawthorne's use of the Cenci legend in *The Marble Faun*, and Hawthorne's somewhat unusual relationship with his mother and sister are three examples. But why the Romantics were drawn to this subject and why they often elevated it to an ideal invite speculation. Although the ancient Greeks discussed incest, and other non-European societies had permitted it, the Romantics may have seized on the topic as part of their social rebellion. Perhaps its attraction was part of the Romantic desire for new experiences, new sexual boundaries,

and new norms to match the Romantic world view and art; perhaps, it came from a seeking after one's own kind or self, a kind of Romantic narcissism or artistic elitism in which the "gods" must marry their sisters to ensure "divine" purity; perhaps it was an archetypal impulse to wholeness or, in some cases, just good Romantic Gothicism. But undoubtedly, incest permeated and tinted the fabric of the Romantic period. (*See also* Gothicism.)

Dorothy H. Graham

Works Consulted

Brown, Nathaniel. *Sexuality and Feminism in Shelley*. Cambridge: Harvard UP, 1979.

Gleckner, Robert F. *Byron and the Ruins of Paradise*. Baltimore: Johns Hopkins UP, 1967.

Gunn, Peter. *My Dearest Augusta: A Biography of Augusta Leigh, Lord Byron's Half-Sister*. New York: Atheneum, 1968.

Paglia, Camille. *Sexual Personae: Art and Decadence from Nefertiti to Emily Dickinson*. New Haven: Yale UP, 1990.

Inchbald, Elizabeth
(1753–1821)

Elizabeth Simpson Inchbald was an actress, playwright, novelist, and editor of drama anthologies. She left her family in Suffolk at age 18 to become an actress in London only to find that a theatrical career was difficult for a young woman on her own. After she married Joseph Inchbald, a painter and touring actor with two children, she was cast opposite Joseph in female leads (e.g., Cordelia, Desdemona, Cleopatra) in provincial productions. While touring, she met Siddons and Kemble; the three remained friends for the rest of their careers.

After her husband died in 1779, and her first novel, *A Simple Story*, was rejected for publication, Inchbald went to London, where she was cast in secondary roles.

Eventually, she returned to the provincial theaters to play lead parts, only performing in London during the patent-theater off-season.

To achieve financial security, Inchbald began to write for the theater. Although she had no formal education, she had read widely in dramatic literature, biography, history, and political works and had taught herself French and German. Her first play (*A Mogul Tale*) was performed at the Little Theatre, Haymarket in 1784, with Inchbald in the cast though not listed as the author. Over the next 21 years, she wrote at least as many plays, primarily comedies and farces based on relations between the sexes and between the classes. Her best—*Such Things Are* (1787); *Wives as They Were and Maids as They Are* (1797); *Lover's Vows* (1798), an adaptation of A.F. von Kotzbue's *Child of Love*; and *To Marry, or Not to Marry* (1805)—address controversial social issues (e.g., prison reform, women, and the value of marriage) in the idiom of popular sentimental comedy.

As a professional writer, Inchbald became friends with Holcroft and Godwin. Using Godwin's suggestions on prose style, she reworked and published *A Simple Story* in 1791, reminiscent of Rousseau, about the education of an inexperienced Roman Catholic girl. Although set in 17th-century France, Inchbald's play *The Massacre* (1792) addressed contemporary political events in France; it was never performed or published during her lifetime. Her second novel, *Nature and Art* (1796), explicitly presents her ideas on educational reform and her criticism of English economic injustice.

In 1806, Inchbald began writing prefaces to *The British Theatre* (1806–09), a 25-volume series of plays. These introductions for a general readership reflect her theatrical practicality and moral judgment.

She selected plays for two other anthologies—*Collection of Farces and Afterpieces* (1809) and *The Modern Theatre* (1811). Though these projects brought her limited income, they kept her from completing her memoirs, which were destroyed when she died in 1821. (*See also* Theater.)

Thomas C. Crochunis

Works Consulted

Boaden, James. *Memoirs of Mrs. Inchbald*. London: Bentley, 1833.

Inchbald, Elizabeth. *A Simple Story*. Ed. and intro. by J.M.S. Tompkins. London: Oxford UP, 1967.

Manvell, Roger. *Elizabeth Inchbald: A Biographical Study*. New York: UP of America, 1987.

———. Introduction. *Selected Comedies*. By Elizabeth Inchbald. New York: UP of America, 1987.

Industrial Revolution

The Industrial Revolution was actually a gradual evolution. Over the course of a century, England's basic manufacturing industries were transformed from water-powered piecework establishments to steam-powered factories. In the process, the English countryside and the demands on the English worker were changed forever. Although some Romantic writers and artists refused to acknowledge these changes, their impact on others was tremendous; the Industrial Revolution changed their life-styles, their economic prospects, and sometimes their entire esthetics. (*See also* MacAdam, John Loudon; Telford, Thomas.)

The Industrial Revolution was based on three major accomplishments: (1) the development of reliable, efficient steam power; (2) the manufacture of increasingly complex machines run by that power; and (3) the production of cast and wrought iron in sufficient quantity to build prime movers and machines. These three developments can be traced back to the first decade of the 1700s.

In about 1705, Thomas Newcomen built an engine powered by the pressure resulting from the difference between condensing steam and the outside atmosphere. His engine ran quite slowly and consumed inordinate amounts of fuel. It was uneconomical, except for pumping water out of coal mines. But over the next 50 years, it was refined to the point that by the 1760s it was producing more power than it consumed. Watt added the three refinements that transformed Newcomen's engine from an accessory into the prime mover of the next century: a separate condenser, which allowed the engine's speed to be increased tenfold; a parallel linkage, which further doubled the number of power strokes; and a speed governor, which allowed the engine's rate of operation to be controlled by the operator. The one further necessary refinement was high-pressure operation, which was achieved by Oliver Evans and Richard Trevithick in the early 1800s. The era of locomotives, steamships, steam hammers, and all the other productive forces that make up the "New Industrial State" was at hand.

Watt's achievements would have been impossible without the ingenious men who are sometimes called the first engineers. Joseph Harrison, in the early decades of the century, set a standard for precision when he constructed the first reliable chronometer, accurate to less than one second per day. Henry Cort, in the 1780s, took out a series of patents for smelting and rolling iron, which eventually led to the mass production of rolled stock, from sheet metal to rails.

Henry Maudsley developed a slide rest in 1794. When combined with a continuously turning lathe and steel tools, it allowed unheard-of precision in manufacture—tolerances of as little as 1/10,000 of an inch. Thirty years before, "the thickness of an old shilling" was deemed sufficient; 15 years later, Maudsley produced the first true factory, a combination of 43 different machines which produced blocks for the Portsmouth naval shipyard. Maudsley also trained men whose names have become synonymous with 19th-century British craftsmanship: Bryan Donkin, perfecter of the Fourdrinier paper-making machine; James Nasmyth, inventor of the steam hammer; and Joseph Whitworth, who standardized screw threads and gauges.

Finally, the production of usable cast iron was essential to the wide application of both steam power and precision machinery. Abraham Darby succeeded in smelting cast iron in 1709, using the specially selected iron ore and coke he had produced at Coalbrookdale. In 1779 Darby's grandson, Abraham, built a bridge entirely of cast iron. The sight of the smoke and flames issuing from tall coking ovens and smelting furnaces, working day and night, inspired paintings by such artists as Joseph Wright of Derby and Philip James de Loutherbourg.

The effect of these changes was felt gradually at first, but became exponential. John Kay in 1733 invented a "flying shuttle." It reduced by one-half the manpower needed to produce a given piece of goods and speeded up its production. In 1785, Edmund Cartwright applied power to such looms, vastly increasing their speed. In 1822, Richard Roberts built a power loom of a type still in use today. Unfortunately, however, violence greeted each new innovation; the basic conservatism of craftsmen and merchants alike slowed acceptance of each new machine. Cartwright's first large cotton factory was burned by rioters in 1791; in 1813, only 2,400 power looms were in use throughout England. But, over the next two decades, the textile industry finally accepted industrialization. By 1833, there were 100,000 power looms in use, and their operators earned 30 per cent more than their hand-loom counterparts. (*See also* Luddites, The.)

The impact of these developments on society was enormous. A wide range of consumer goods and opportunities appeared, from indoor plumbing and inoculation to steam radiators and railroads. But each innovation was associated with a cost in terms of social upheaval and environmental impact, which workers and capitalists alike were not eager to pay. Inadequate workers' housing remained a primary source of city dwellers' illnesses and social privations throughout the 19th century. Industrial by-products fouled the air, the streams, and the landscape, once cursed as the landlords' domain but now dreamed of as an escape from the warrens of dingy streets and courtyards. Children no longer died of pneumonia caught while working in the fields; they now died of tuberculosis caught in the factory or in the tenement. But many more lived; population growth, which had been minimal throughout the 1700s, soared in the next century.

Some artists saw these changes as blessings—others as cursed. Blake dreamed of supernatural visitations that might restore England's natural beauty; Wordsworth, apostrophized relics of pre-Industrial society. Others, particularly if they were scientifically oriented, recognized that the permanent virtues of the land and its people were not threatened by recent material changes: Keats (training to be a doctor), Thoreau (a land surveyor), and Turner (a student of optics) all found pleasure in at least some products of the Industrial Revo-

lution. Perhaps the clearest statement of ambivalence is in *Frankenstein*. Its hero loses everything because of his desire to take technology to its extremes, but its creative impulse is ultimately affirmative: "Oh! be men, or be more than men. . . . [The world] is mutable, and cannot withstand you, if you say that it shall not." In this desire to be "more than men," to outdo nature, lies the seeds of the Industrial Revolution, as well as its consequences.

Hartley S. Spatt

Works Consulted

Briggs, Asa. *Iron Bridge to Crystal Palace*. London: Thames, 1979.

Klingender, F.J. *Art and the Industrial Revolution*. London: Carrington, 1947.

Kranzberg and Pursell, eds. *Technology in Western Civilization*. New York: Oxford, 1967.

Influence, Anxiety of

The concept of "the anxiety of influence" is associated with Harold Bloom's 1973 book with that title. It is the genesis of Bloom's system worked out in terms of poets during and following the Romantic period. Initially, for purposes of establishing an interpretive foundation, such anxiety can be seen as assuming two forms: weak and strong poets confronting the influence of either a strong antecedent poet or a strong contemporary poet. For the Romantics, the major poet of the prior age is Milton, as Joseph A. Wittreich has argued. But, as Jonathan Bate has recently argued, Shakespeare also exerts such an influence on the Romantic poets. Yet, as the relationship of Coleridge and Wordsworth or Shelley and Byrōn shows, the influence exerted by one poet upon another is not necessarily that of a dead poet upon living ones.

The most obvious anxiety of influence is at the level of epic desires, with every

Romantic poet seeking at some point to construct an epic or large poem on the scale of Milton's *Paradise Lost*. This influence can be most clearly read in Blake, whose illuminated books of prophecy directly engage Milton. It can be seen relatively early in Blake's canon, in *The Marriage of Heaven and Hell*, where Blake literally offers a reading of the Miltonic epics. But Blake was not satisfied with merely "reading" Miltonic epic; in his penultimate epic prophecy *Milton*, Blake deconstructs Milton so that from a Bloomean point of view this work provides a model for the overcoming of influence as Milton literally enters Blake to confront and correct his own errors.

No writer in the period suffered more from the anxiety of immediate influence than Coleridge. His long, troubled relationship with Wordsworth created such immense anxiety as to stymie creative production. Certainly, Wordsworth was not immune from the problems of influence, with the Simplon passage of *The Prelude* establishing imagination as the final safeguard of the poetic identity against Miltonic influence. If one is to believe Hazlitt, Wordsworth can function as the poetic plumbline by which to measure "the spirit of the age," but Coleridge, while embracing and revering Wordsworth, also suffered greatly from his close proximity to the last poet laureate of Romanticism. In Bloom's words, Coleridge is a student of Wordsworth, and Bloom then wonders whether Coleridge gave more than he received in the relationship. However, Coleridge, perhaps more than any other Romantic poet, also sheds light on the genesis of Bloom's theory of poetry, since Coleridge seems to anticipate Bloom in his understanding of the tensions within the English tradition: Shakespeare became what he created while what Milton created took on his character.

Within the second generation, the relationship between Byron and Shelley mirrors that between Coleridge and Wordsworth with regard to influence. For Byron and Shelley, as well as Keats, lived under the growing influence of Wordsworth. Yet neither Byron nor Shelley, unlike their first-generation counterparts, were creatively paralyzed by such close relations, although the relationship was not without its dark undertones, as recorded in Shelley's poetic dialogue *Julian and Maddalo*. Both poets are strong in Bloom's sense, but each pursues an individualized vision; Byron pursues an exterior otherness, as his satirical sojourn poems (*Childe Harold's Pilgrimage* and *Don Juan*) and Oriental tales (*The Island*, *The Giaour*, and *The Corsair*) indicate. The influence of Miltonic epic on Byron has received considerable critical commentary, with the Byronic hero (actually an antihero in relation to social and cultural expectation) shaped in relation to Milton's powerful characterization of fallen Satan. The strength of works like *Childe Harold* and *Don Juan* is precisely their ability to situate themselves as the repressed Other to cultural normalcy, a stance that can be traced back to the reception of Satan in *Paradise Lost*. Yet with Byron, against the rather mundane daily existence of Blake, the poet embodies the repressed and exerts a "demonic" influence on close associations, like Shelley, as well as more distant audiences, like a British reading public hungry for the forbidden that Byron's life represented.

Shelley, against Byron's external questing, pursues interior otherness in various forms, as Bloom argues in his chapter on Shelley in *The Visionary Company*. His early quest-romance *Alastor, or The Spirit of Solitude* is a turning away from the world, and Shelley's response to the changed, later

Wordsworth. The same thrust, a movement toward interiority, is established in the *Hymn to Intellectual Beauty* and *Mont Blanc*, where nature is an elusive shadow that reflects, that returns the gaze of the poet, back to the perceiving mind. Although the later *Epipsychidion*, which takes as its thematic center the effort to love, confronts the promise of establishing contact with an exterior object of desire, it shares with the earlier poem a tendency to rebound back onto the poet.

The types of influence discussed above — that of absent poetic "fathers" upon their progeny and that of contemporary poets on their present companion poets — also vary in degree. For example, one of Keats's earliest poems is an imitation of a Spenserian sonnet, an obvious case of a former poet exerting influence. Still at the beginning of his career, Keats comes to idolize and imitate the unbridled energy of Leigh Hunt's poetry, in which the anxiety of influence functions in relation to a contemporary poet, but as most critics agree, within two years of their first meeting, Keats surpasses Hunt in poetic power and production. This situation of contemporary influence occurs again in 1817, when Keats, although not fully open to a relationship with Shelley, could record his anxiety over the influence that Shelley's poetry might have exerted upon *Endymion*.

Bloom's concept of poetic anxiety has developed into a more encompassing theory of poetry based on misprision and revision, with this theory still intersecting major Romantic poets but also pushing beyond them into the current century. Certainly, Bloom's critical canon continues to meet the challenges of its (mis)readers, from feminists literary critics who see in Bloom's patriarchal model a reflection of the western literary patriarchy to this author's reduced "reading" of Bloom's theories of poetic anxiety in relation to the Romantic poets he has read in such length and depth. The resilience of Bloom's "anxiety of influence" construct testifies to its ability to illuminate crucial aspects of Romantic poetry, re-visioning poetic relations in such a way as to facilitate a deeper understanding of individual poets and the processes through which poetry is produced.

Mark Lussier

Works Consulted

Bate, Jonathan. *Shakespeare and the English Romantic Imagination*. Oxford: Clarendon, 1986.

Bloom, Harold. *Agon: Towards a Theory of Revisionism*. New York: Oxford UP, 1982.

———. *The Anxiety of Influence: A Theory of Poetry*. New York: Oxford UP, 1973.

———. "The Anxiety of Influence." *New Perspectives on Coleridge and Wordsworth*. Ed. Geoffrey H. Hartman. New York: Columbia UP, 1972: 247–67.

———. *Poetry and Repression: Revisionism from Blake to Stevens*. New Haven: Yale UP, 1976.

Jacobus, Mary. *Romanticism Writing and Sexual Difference*. Oxford: Clarendon, 1989.

Ross, Marlon B. "Romantic Quest and Conquest: Troping Masculine Power in the Crisis of Poetic Identity." *Romanticism and Feminism*. Ed. Anne K. Mellor. Bloomington: Indiana UP, 1988: 26–51.

Weiskel, Thomas. *The Romantic Sublime: Studies in the Structure and Psychology of Transcendence*. Baltimore: Johns Hopkins UP, 1976.

Wittreich, Joseph Anthony, Jr. *Milton and the Line of Vision*. Madison: U of Wisconsin P, 1975.

———. *Visionary Poetics: Milton's Tradition and His Legacy*. San Marino: Huntington Library, 1979.

Insanity and Eccentric Genius

Substantial changes took place at the beginning of the 19th century in the way English society regarded, defined, and treated mental disorder. Some of these changes can be linked to the fascination that Romantic poets and artists had for the concept of genius and their attempt to redefine the born genius as qualitatively different from ordinary human beings.

On the one hand, the connection between madness and poetic genius has a long history in the Western imagination; it is alluded to in Plato's *Ion* and *Phaedrus* and Shakespeare's *A Midsummer Night's Dream*. Yet when 18th-century writers analyzed the workings of genius they tended to stress attributes like judgment, taste, and memory, rational qualities that adequately balanced any irrational components. During the same period, insanity was regarded as a little-understood affliction that turned human beings into wild beasts. The two main types of mental disorder, melancholia and mania, were both conceived of in terms of an irrational but unshakable attachment to mistaken ideas. Treatment of the insane involved attempts to rid the body physically of whatever substance was causing these erroneous notions. Victims of mental illness were to be tamed and terrified into submission. Moreover, 18th-century madhouses doubled as a form of entertainment, charging admission to visitors of the human menagerie.

It was not until the late 18th century and the early 19th century that theories about genius and theories about insanity began to draw more closely together. Poets cultivated the association among insanity, eccentricity, and genius in their lifestyles and their work to distinguish themselves from the philistine public and from writers of lesser talent. Blake exploited rumors about his madness in order to insist on the importance of mental reality and of an individual imaginative perspective. Byron practiced bizarre, extravagant behavior by traveling about Europe with such a menagerie of strange animals and people that he earned the reputation of being "mad, bad, and dangerous to know."

Genuine mental illness afflicted several Romantic writers, including Clare, who wrote his best verse in an asylum, and the German writers Heinrich von Kleist and Friedrich Hölderlin, the latter of whom spent the last 36 years of his life suffering from schizophrenia. Among the English Romantic figures, Dorothy Wordsworth, Williams's sister and a gifted writer herself, and Mary Lamb, the sister of Charles Lamb, spent significant portions of their lives in states of potentially violent insanity. Finally, the insanity of King George III was a factor to be dealt with in English politics throughout the period, since the king suffered the first of many mental breakdowns in 1765 yet continued as reigning monarch until 1820.

Two general reasons for the prevalence of genuine and feigned madness in this period were the increased acceptability of public displays of emotion and the cult of the genius poet. The generation before Romanticism, sometimes called the Age of Sensibility for its obsessive indulgence in emotionalism and hyperbole, produced a number of talented but insane writers. William Collins, Cowper, and Christopher Smart all spent much of their lives in asylums. Chatterton, the adolescent prodigy who had the greatest influence on the popular conception of the genius poet, may not have been clinically insane but certainly underwent some kind of breakdown, which resulted in his suicide. Compounded with these was the fictional example of Werther, the young, artistically gifted, but unstable and suicidal hero of Goethe's wildly popular novel of 1774. These true and fictional examples generated a feeling that the inspired poet set himself or herself apart from the opinions of ordinary people and the conventions of society, to the point of acting or being destructively insane. The term "genius" acquired a negative connotation in some cases, since it came to refer to a haughty, Wertherian young man whose bizarre behavior flouted the rules of good society.

Romantic artists also gravitated toward madness as a subject for their poetry and painting. Wordsworth writes of the madness brought on by social injustice and intolerance in some of the *Lyrical Ballads*, particularly *The Thorn* and *Her Eyes Are Wild*; Coleridge portrays the poet as a frightening, abnormal figure in *Kubla Khan*. Shelley, despite his conviction that the poet has a role to play in guiding society, describes the poet-hero of *Alastor* and *Hymn to Intellectual Beauty* as a young man driven to distraction, and perhaps destruction, by a vision of ideal beauty. In *The Fall of Hyperion*, Keats compares poets with fanatics, dreamers, and visionaries. Romantic artists in other countries displayed an even more explicit fascination with madness and genius. The Spanish painter Goya and the German writer Hoffmann visited asylums to observe the behavior and treatment of lunatics, and the influence of such experiences is evident in a painting like Goya's *The Madhouse* or Hoffmann's stories "Mademoiselle de Scudery" and "The Sandman."

Supported by both the behavior and the productions of Romantic artists, the association between insanity and genius became so widespread that it entered contemporary psychiatry and medical literature. By the mid-19th century, the alienating and extravagant behavior of the Romantics tended to be regarded in pathological terms, and physicians throughout Europe were speculating on how to categorize genius according to the known types of mental disorder. French physicians began the debate in the 1830s, though the most vehement supporter of the insanity of genius was the Italian doctor Cesare Lombroso (1835–1909). The controversy over the clinical madness of genius continued well into the 20th century.

Yet actual insanity remained markedly different from and more tragic than some poets' pretentions to eccentric genius or the poignant madness of those they wrote about, and at least one Romantic writer tried to disprove the connection between insanity and genius. Lamb, who witnessed genuine mental illness during the years he spent caring for his murderously insane sister, published in 1826 a rebuttal of the popular fallacy that great poetic ability goes hand-in-hand with madness. The work of minor poets, Lamb argues, might display the disconnectedness and inconsistency that signals a disordered mind, but great art is always subject to the artist's control and waking judgment. Lamb uses the principle that poets depict what is probable or believable, ultimately derived from Aristotle, to prove that true artists must possess sanity, balance, and a sense of what can reasonably be believed.

The sympathy that some Romantic artists demonstrated for the insane and their often romanticized depictions of madmen and madwomen paralleled society's increasing awareness of the injustice and cruelty of traditional methods of treating mental illness. Eighteenth-century remedies, such as bloodletting, purging, or induced vomiting, were based on the idea that madness could be physically eliminated from the sufferer's body, and potentially violent or offensive lunatics were subjected to severe physical restraint, as well as to beatings and humiliation. Beginning in the 1790s, however, there was a move toward more humane asylums and methods of treatment. The founding of the York Retreat by the Quaker brothers William and Samuel Tuke in 1796 testified to a new interest in moral rather than medical or physical treatment of insanity, as did a famous decision by the French physician Philippe Pinel to unchain the lunatics at the Bicêtre in Paris. Instilling a sense of authority and guilt in victims of mental illness without using physical violence became the accepted method of controlling violent or outrageous behavior, and patients were even released, at times, to the care of relatives and friends. This gentler treatment may be interpreted partly as a cause, partly as a consequence, of the Romantics' interest in alienation, originality, and imaginative genius.

Angela Esterhammer

Works Consulted

Becker, George. *The Mad Genius Controversy: A Study in the Sociology of Deviance.* Beverly Hills: Sage, 1978.

Bynum, William F., Jr. "Rationales for Therapy in British Psychiatry, 1780–1835." *Madhouses, Mad-Doctors, and Madmen: The Social History of Psychiatry in the Victorian Era.* Ed. Andrew Scull. Philadelphia: U of Pennsylvania P, 1981: 35–57.

Christiansen, Rupert. *Romantic Affinities: Portraits from an Age, 1780–1830.* New York: Putnam, 1988.

Foucault, Michel. *Madness and Civilization: A History of Insanity in the Age of Reason.* Trans. Richard Howard. New York: Pantheon, 1965.

Kessel, Neil. "Genius and Mental Disorder: A History of Ideas Concerning Their Conjunction." *Genius: The History of an Idea.* Ed. Penelope Murray. Oxford: Blackwell, 1989: 196–212.

Porter, Roy. *Mind-Forg'd Manacles: A History of Madness in England from the Restoration to the Regency.* Cambridge: Harvard UP, 1987.

— — —. *A Social History of Madness: Stories of the Insane.* London: Weidenfeld, 1987.

Scull, Andrew. *Social Order/Mental Disorder: Anglo-American Psychiatry in Historical Perspective.* Berkeley: U of California P, 1989.

Irony

Irony is a rhetorical figure and theatrical device for Romantic writers. Irony develops plots for Gothic drama, such as *The Borderers* (1796) and *The Cenci* (1819), as well as for Gothic fiction, such as *The Mysteries of Udolpho* (1794) and *The Monk* (1796). Ironic perspective governs the satire of novels by Austen and Peacock and the essays of Lamb and Hazlitt. However, unique traits of Romantic irony are mainly found in the poetry. Romantic irony is a tendency of mind from which figures and narratives emerge. Refusal to make commitments to absolutes presents the Romantic with a predicament of uncertainty, relativity, and unbounded process. Ironic stances and tropes of irony in paradoxical forms communicate this predicament: uncertainty employs irony of speculative interrogation; relativity produces a dialectic of contraries; and unbounded process requires versatility and experimentation.

Wordsworth and Keats are masters of the speculative interrogative. When desire to be satisfied by natural experience is disappointed, energies of uncertainty are contained by language of questioning in a subjunctive mood. *Tintern Abbey* (1798) originates in a gap between experience and understanding, while *Ode to a Nightingale* (1819) terminates in a separation of identity from being. These poems illustrate irony in the Romanticism of uncertainty. When the speaker of *Tintern Abbey* cannot account for phenomena, he does not assert a confidence in a noumenon to calm intellectual doubts and emotional anxieties; instead, he subjects uncertainties to doubt until they dissipate beneath the pressure of his determined presence. Ironically, then, *Tintern Abbey* achieves a tone of confidence from a profound dislocation of mind from being, sight from sound, memory from observation. *Ode to a Nightingale* descends from ecstasy of union to dismayed confusion of vision with sensation, from joy of synaesthesia to dejection of anesthesia. The ironic adventure of the speaker in *Ode to a Nightingale* is a process of imaginative dissolution in a poem of organic wholeness.

Blake and Shelley are artists of irony as a dialectic of contraries. Their writings alternate binary oppositions, setting off circuits of electric charge in fields of expanding visionary energy. In *Milton* (1804–08) and *Prometheus Unbound* (1818–19), differences in meaning are functions of differences in points of view, while resolutions of conflicts are reached by an enlargement of vision without the elimination of opposition. Movement occurs because forces conflict at points where irony is intense and tolerance extends. When Milton ascends from Ulro, Los despairs. When Ololon descends from Eden to meet the regenerate Milton in Blake's garden at Felpham, the Daughters of Beulah lament Ololon's apparent fall. But the poet's spirit is lifted to heights of hope by Ololon's descent. The end of ignorance and intolerance is a painful bursting of Satanic pride, a joyful birth of virginal wisdom and trust. Irony saves the smug spirit of Milton from an eternity of self-delusion.

On the other hand, Jupiter's fall from supreme confidence in *Prometheus Unbound* is an ironic reflection of Prometheus's rise from self-delusion. As forces move up to bring down tyranny, move down to bring up freedom, Shelley's poem thrives on ironic differences of direction as well as on ironic similarities of circumstances. Shelley's poem of cosmic optimism grows out of psychological despair, and Blake's poem of apocalyptic energy bursts through puritanic restraint. Both disturb symme-

tries, reverse entropy, and exploit the literality of relativity.

Coleridge and Byron exemplify the ironic plight of searching for an adequate style and genre to express the inadequacy of conventions: their lives are barely separable from their writings as unbounded developments of versatile styles. Both found the story of Cain a convenient narrative to express ironic predicaments: to know the best requires suffering through the worst, to recognize home requires alienation. Guides to wandering exiles are not sufficient for *The Rime of the Ancient Mariner* (1797–98) or *Childe Harold's Pilgrimage* (1812, 1816, 1818), in which process is a paradox of permanence: the Mariner must always tell his story; Harold is satisfied with insatiability. Neither life nor art can be complete in an incomplete world, and the styles of Coleridge and Byron express their improvisational answers to provisional existence. Their ironies are instances of experiment to test the limits of convention and adequacy. Byron surrendered his fictional pose as "Childe" Harold and damned himself to an unending trial of wandering as Don Juan. Ironic openness to experience led Coleridge on a search for a solution to the ultimate paradox of the Trinity, continuously reexamining every detail of experience to find its place in the cosmic unity. For Byron, openness to irony meant the end of contentment, but it also meant content of becoming as endless means. All Romantic writers, in prose or in poetry, are determined by refusal to be contained by terminals of convention: they bring chaos out of order to make clear the essential irony of sincerity in human existence.

Richard D. McGhee

Works Consulted

Mellor, Anne K. *English Romantic Irony.* Cambridge: Harvard UP, 1980.

Simpson, David. *Irony and Authority in Romantic Poetry*. Totowa, NJ: Rowan, 1979.

Irving, Edward

(1792–1834)

Edward Irving was born in Annan, Scotland in 1792. He attended a nonconforming congregation at Ecclefechan, the birthplace of Carlyle. Matriculating at Edinburgh University at age 13, he left at 19 to teach school in Kirkcaldy, Scotland. In Kirkcaldy, he became a close friend of Carlyle, who was teaching at a rival school in the same town. Carlyle later wrote about him in his *Reminiscences*. Irving also became acquainted with the young Jane Welsh, who was his own pupil.

A powerful preacher and a pious, ambitious man, Irving grew bored with schoolteaching and left Kirkcaldy to assist Thomas Chambers, minister of St. John's Church, Glasgow, in 1818. Chambers was one of the most well-known preachers of his day. In 1822, Irving accepted a post at the tiny and impoverished Caledonian Chapel in London. He was technically unqualified for the position, since he knew no Gaelic, but his impressive preaching overrode any objection to his appointment. The fame of that preaching soon spread, and attendance at the Caledonian Chapel rose rapidly. His sermons were for a brief period attended by the titled and powerful. Hazlitt, in his *Spirit of the Age*, determined that Irving's success was not merely due to his talents as a preacher but to his physical beauty, made all the more intriguing by his substantial height and slight, not unattractive squint. Irving gained some friends in literary circles, among them Lamb and Coleridge.

In 1822, Irving began to publish theological works. He married Isabella Martin in 1823. Though fashionable attendance fell off at his chapel, Irving's influence remained considerable. In 1827, Irving moved his congregation—its size and wealth appreciably augmented—to a new edifice in Regent Square. Irving became an increasingly controversial preacher. His sermons grew more literal in their eschatology, interpreting recent historical events as signs of the coming apocalypse. His Christology, too, developed. In his *Six Sermons on the Incarnation*, Irving seemed to say that Christ's flesh was sinful, although he also maintained that Christ himself was sinless. In December 1830, the London Presbytery brought him to trial for heresy over the doctrine of "Christ's sinful flesh" and found him guilty. Irving avoided its strictures by walking out before the verdict was delivered.

The activities of his parishioners were also problematic. Mary Campbell, who had begun speaking in tongues in 1830, joined the congregation in 1831, and soon a sizable portion of the congregation followed her lead. Irving never spoke in tongues himself, but did believe that the occurrence of glossolalia in his congregation was the work of the Holy Spirit.

The addition of glossolalia to the theological controversies surrounding Irving finally destroyed his work. Traditional Presbyterians left the Regent Square Church, and in 1832, Irving was removed from its pulpit. With 800 followers, he reestablished his congregation at a picture gallery on Newman Street. This remnant was to become the Catholic Apostolic Church. In March 1833, the Presbytery of Annan deprived Irving of the status of a clergyman of the Church of Scotland, again over the issue of Christ's sinful flesh. His own congregation suspended and reinstated him; it was controlled by members who spoke in tongues and who regarded Irving as below them spiritually because he did not. Shortly afterward, missioning independently in Wales and Scotland, symptoms of the tuberculosis that was to kill him became apparent. Irving died in 1834.

James Najarian

Works Consulted

Christenson, Larry. "Pentecostalism's Forgotten Forerunner." *Aspects of Pentecostal-Charismatic Origins*. Ed. Vinson Synan. Plainfield: Logos, 1975.

Dallimore, Arnold. *Forerunner of the Charismatic Movement*. Chicago: Moody, 1983.

Merricks, William S. *Edward Irving: The Forgotten Giant*. East Peoria: Scribe's Chamber, 1983.

Jeffrey, Francis
(1773–1850)

Co-founder and editor of *The Edinburgh Review*, one of the 19th century's foremost quarterly periodicals, Francis Jeffrey helped establish the distinctive form of the lengthy review essay in which the text under consideration, while being closely scrutinized, also serves as the occasion for a broad-ranging, general discussion of the topics and questions it raises. This achievement, however, has been overshadowed by the use to which he put the form in his own literary criticism: he wrote notorious attacks on Wordsworth, Coleridge, and Southey in particular and failed conspicuously to appreciate the radical effect their work was having on literary theory and practice. (*See also* Essay, Journalism, Literary Criticism and Literary Theory.)

Jeffrey was born in 1773. His father, a deputy clerk in the Edinburgh law courts, was a high Tory who throughout his son's education attempted, without success, to prevent him from coming under the influence of Whiggish teachers. Jeffrey attended high school in Edinburgh and then Glasgow University. He also went to Oxford, but left after a year, disappointed in the quality of his fellow students. His Scottish education was broad, encompassing all of the humanities. He had early determined to become a writer, and he read widely. But he trained as a lawyer and in 1794 was admitted to the Scottish bar. By then he had become a Whig, and since all branches of Scottish government and administration, including the law courts, were dominated by Tories, for many years, despite his gifts, he achieved professional advancement only very slowly.

His literary talents and his sociability brought him into contact with other promising young intellectuals in Edinburgh. With a small group of these, including Sydney Smith and Brougham, he founded *The Edinburgh Review* in 1802. He became its first editor and held the post until 1829. The periodical swiftly achieved wide sales and established a powerful influence over educated public opinion. Jeffrey proved a first-class editor. Primarily Whig in outlook, *The Edinburgh Review* was politically liberal, but Jeffrey attempted to ensure a balance of views and tone. One mark of its success was the other periodicals that sprang up to compete with it, in particular the Tory *Quarterly Review* (1807) and the utilitarian *Westminster Review* (1824).

The essays Jeffrey wrote for *The Edinburgh Review* (first collected in four volumes in 1844) were mainly on literary subjects, and in them Jeffrey established a reputation as a harsh if principled reviewer. His political liberalism included a deep fear of popular radicalism, and this, in addition to traditional Neoclassical views on the nature and function of poetry, left him thoroughly hostile to the challenging innovations he found in the poetry of Wordsworth and those Jeffrey associated with Wordsworth. Jeffrey objected to their egocentric self-absorption, resentful discontent with the shape of society, touches of German mysticism and, most of all, disregard of artistic decorum in language and subject matter.

Jeffrey's essays represent early 19th-century conservative literary criticism at its most characteristic: he evokes general and common standards of excellence, which he finds best represented in the literature of the past; he reiterates these standards with clarity, assurance, but no originality; and then he turns scorn and mockery upon writers who fail to measure up, especially if they exhibit evident genius. His indignant dogmatism achieved its most wounding outburst in the opening sentence to his review of Wordsworth's *The Excursion*: "This will never do!" (1814). And yet when he is not sweepingly judgmental, Jeffrey is an acute critic, and his reception of contemporary literature is often warm and appreciative: in differing ways Scott, Burns, Crabbe, Byron, Keats, and Hemans all received his praise.

Jeffrey's editorial and writing duties were always incidental to his legal career which, when the Whigs came to power in 1830, progressed rapidly. In 1832, he was elected to Parliament; in 1834, he was made a judge and became Lord Jeffrey. His contacts with the world of letters re-mained wide, and with his second wife (his first died after only four years of marriage) he entertained liberally. He befriended the young Carlyle; he became a paternal confidant and ardent admirer of Dickens, in particular the Dickens of pathos and sentiment; and he was financially generous to writers in need. He died in 1850. In his day, Jeffrey was universally liked and admired, even by those who had felt the sting of his criticism.

Jonathan E. Hill

Works Consulted

Cockburn, Henry. *The Life of Francis Jeffrey*. 2 vols. Edinburgh: Black, 1874.

Greig, James A. *Francis Jeffrey of the* Edinburgh Review. Edinburgh: Oliver, 1948.

Houghton, Walter E., ed. *The Wellesley Index to Victorian Periodicals 1824–1900*. Vol 1. London: U of Toronto P, and Routledge, 1966.

Morgan, Peter F., ed. *Jeffrey's Criticism*. Edinburgh: Scottish Academic, 1983.

Johnson, Joseph

(1738–1809)

Until his trial and conviction for sedition, Joseph Johnson contributed significantly to the dissemination of radical ideas in late 18th-century England. Responding to the demands of an inquisitive audience, Johnson published books that opposed the status quo and questioned the validity of many contemporary attitudes. (*See also* Publishing.)

Born in Liverpool in 1738, Johnson likely attended grammar school there before being apprenticed to London publisher George Keith until 1761, when he established his own business. Through contacts with the liberal academy at Warrington and through his lifelong friendships with Fuseli and Priestley, Johnson was exposed to the kind of unorthodox thought that influenced his publishing business for the rest of his life. Thus early in his career, Johnson published books on theology and religion, including English editions of works by the American Jonathan Edwards.

From the early 1770s on, Johnson's shop became a center for liberal writers whose treatises advocated Unitarianism, repeal of the Corporation and Test Acts, new medical and scientific advances, and social and political reform—notably, women's rights and abolition of the slave trade. In 1779, Johnson published essays by Benjamin Franklin and Cowper's *Olney Hymns*. Among his friends were Wollstonecraft, Gilbert Wakefield, Horne Tooke, Thomas Christie, Erasmus Darwin, Blake, Joel Barlow, Godwin, and Paine. His publications included Wollstonecraft's *Thoughts on the Education of Daughters* (1787), Barbauld's *Lessons for Children from Two to Three Years Old* and *Lessons for Children Three Years Old* (1788), and John Howard's *State of Prisons in England and Wales* (1777). Also, in 1788, Johnson established the *Analytical Review*, a radical intellectual magazine that contained anonymous articles attacking the government's political and social conservatism, while suggesting alternatives so popular that they threatened the overthrow of the government.

At the same time that conservatism swept through England in response to the war with France, Johnson's circle began to diminish. Priestley moved to America, Barlow to France; Paine was in exile; and Christie, Wollstonecraft, and Enfield had all died. Although he was not directly involved, Johnson's association with the publication of Paine's *Rights of Man*, along with his support of Unitarianism and the *Analytical Review*, led to his 1798 trial and subsequent six-month sentence for sedition. After his release from prison, Johnson continued publishing the same kinds

of books, but advanced age and physical frailty, along with changing times, forced him to curtail his productivity. He died in 1809.

Sheila A. Spector

Works Consulted

Tyson, Gerald P. *Joseph Johnson: A Liberal Publisher*. Iowa City: U of Iowa P, 1979.

Jones, Sir William
(1746–94)

Nearly every major text of historical linguistics attributes the discovery of similarities between Sanskrit and classical languages to Sir William Jones, but he aspired toward and accomplished much more. Born a commoner in Anglesey in Wales, his upbringing was nonetheless exceptional. His father, also William, although descended from a yeoman family, possessed such a talent for mathematics that he was appointed to the Royal Society in 1712. After her husband's death, Jones's mother left Wales to return to London, her place of origin, where she managed her husband's inheritance and raised her children on Locke, Newton, and the English poets.

After initial health problems, Jones excelled in school, especially at languages. By the time he went to Oxford in 1764 as a commoner of University College, he was so advanced in his study of languages that he pursued extra courses, learning Persian and Arabic from a Syrian friend. Elected a fellow of University College in 1766, he received the B.A. in 1768 and took the M.A. in 1773. While keeping his terms at Oxford, Jones was appointed private tutor to Lord Althorp, the only son of Earl Spenser. Traveling with this family provided Jones not only the livelihood that he needed but also some useful exposure, which served to advertise, as it were, his linguistic skills.

These skills were first put to a test in 1768 when Christian VII of Denmark had Jones translate a Persian text, a life of Nadir Shah, into French. Jones published it in 1770. During the subsequent four years, he continued his Oriental studies while pursuing legal studies at Middle Temple. Following the biography of Nadir, he published the *Traité sur la Poésie Orientale*. The next year, Jones brought out a *Dissertation sur la littérature* and *Grammar of the Persian Language*. In 1772, he published *Poems, consisting chiefly of translation from the Asiatick Languages, with two Essays on the Poetry of the Eastern Nations, and on the Arts called Imitative*; and in 1774, he issued *Poeseos Asiaticæ Commentariorum Libri Sex*. The reputation of Jones's activity was established. In 1772, he was elected a fellow to the Royal Society and was also admitted to the exclusive Literary Club led by none other than Dr. Johnson.

Although successful in his literary endeavors, Jones was not satisfied with his situation. Therefore, he set aside his poetry and was called to the bar at Middle Temple in 1774. He pursued this career with the same energy that he exhibited earlier, publishing several important essays on the law. His *Essay on the Law of Bailments* was very highly regarded and, even long after his death, has been hailed as a classic. Still ambitious, in 1780 he sought a seat in Parliament. His liberal views, however, particularly his opposition to the American War, were too unpopular, and his quest for political office was unsuccessful. Undaunted, Jones applied for a post in Bengal, which he thought would satisfy both his legal and Oriental interests, but he was put off. During this delay, he published *The Moallakat, or Seven Arabian Poems, which were suspended on the Temple at Mecca, with a Translation and Arguments* (1783); it attracted some attention in Europe, notably Goethe's.

Finally, Jones received, in March 1783, an appointment as judge to the high court in Calcutta. Knighted in March of that year, he set sail in April with his new bride, Anna Maria, for India. Although Jones claimed he would return to England, India would be his life. Certain that cultural contexts were fundamental to understanding any subject, he set out to learn India—its customs, music, religion, laws, and language. One year after his arrival, he established the Bengal Asiatic Society (modeled on The Royal Society) to which he delivered 11 anniversary essays as president. During his work with the society, he wrote about Indian history and botany, Hindu mythology, religion, music, as well as continued his famous studies of languages. The publications of the society, *The Asiatic Researches*, had a significant following in Europe. In 1789, Jones translated Calidas's play *Sakontala*, the German translation of which influenced German Romanticism.

In linguistics, Jones is famous for discovering the relationship between Sanskrit and European languages, and this discovery is generally supported by a quotation from Jones's third "Anniversary Discourse," "On the Hindus," delivered February 2, 1786. It has recently been argued that the connection between Sanskrit and other languages had been made earlier and that the actual basis of modern philology was laid by Friedreich Schlegel, who moved philology into modern science by rejecting fanciful etymologizing, focusing on the historical over philosophical study of language, and attending to structural, syntactical, rather than lexical, comparisons between languages. However, Hans Aarsleff has ably demonstrated that all of these advances were taken by Schlegel from Jones's 11 discourses to the Asiatic Society.

Jones's study of Sanskrit was motivated by his desire to understand the law first-hand, rather than relying on others' descriptions, translations, or commentary. The long-range goal of his personal reading of Indian law was to compile a complete digest of Hindu and Muslim law as recognized in India. He did not achieve his goal before his death, but he did publish the *Institutes of Hindu Law, or the Ordinances of Manu* (1794). The work was perhaps too much for him. After his wife left Calcutta because of ill health in December 1793, he sank into depression. His own health was also poor, and he died in 1794 and was buried in India. Jones's work in India, perhaps his greatest legacy, is considered an important force in the development of what would become the Indian Renaissance.

Lisa Plummer Crafton
John Micheal Crafton

Works Consulted

Aarsleff, Hans. *The Study of Language in England, 1780–1860*. 2nd ed. Minneapolis: U of Minnesota P, 1983.

Jones, Sir William. *The Works of Sir William Jones* 13 vols. London: J. Stockdale, 1807.

———. *The Letters of Sir William Jones*. Ed. Garland Cannon. Oxford: Clarendon, 1970.

Mukherjee, S.N. *Sir William Jones: A Study in Eighteenth-Century British Attitudes to India*. London: Cambridge UP, 1968.

Jordan, Dorothy

(1761–1816)

Dorothy [Dorothea] Jordan, an English actress, remains best known for her performances in broad comedy as the spirited romp or hoyden. Although authorities disagree on the exact date and place of her birth, most accounts conclude that she was born near Waterford, Ireland, in 1761. She was the daughter of Grace Phillips, a Dublin actress and oldest child of a Welsh clergyman, and Francis Bland, a gentleman whose family had the marriage annulled.

Taking her father's given name, Jordan first appeared as Miss Francis, in 1779, at Thomas Ryder's theater in Crow Street in the role of Lucy in *The Virgin Unmasked*. She was first billed in *The Governess*, on May 20, 1780, her first breeches part. In this same play, Ryder allowed Jordan to introduce a song into the dialogue, a practice that was to become one of her hallmarks, usually bringing an ovation from her audiences despite her lack of formal voice training. It is reported that later as Ophelia, she interrupted a performance with a song taken from the Shakespearean forgery, *Vortigern and Rowena*.

Jordan left Crow Street and joined the rival Smock Alley Theatre, a step up for her career, where she appeared with Kemble. Fleeing a financial and personal entanglement with the unscrupulous manager of Smock Alley, Richard Daly, Jordan arrived in England in 1782. Destitute, she auditioned in Leeds before Tate Wilkinson, an actor and manager of the York company who was possibly responsible for the change of name to Mrs. Jordan. Tate hired her; on July 11, 1782, she appeared at Leeds as Calista in *The Fair Penitent*. Jordan continued on the circuit after the birth of her first child (Daly's) and was enthusiastically received by the crowd assembled at York for the race week.

Jordan initiated an important change in her repertoire for her debut at London's Drury Lane Theatre where she was scheduled to play in *Philaster*. Sensing that her talents were best suited for comedy rather than the tragic roles she had been performing, Jordan persuaded Sheridan's stage manager to substitute Garrick's bawdy play *The Country Girl*, in which she took the role of Peggy for her debut on the night of October 18, 1785. Her portrayal in this and other comic roles—such as Priscilla Tomboy in *The Romp*, Miss Hoyden in *A Trip to Scarborough*, Sir Harry Wildair in *The Constant Couple*, and Miss Prue in *Love for Love*—established her as a favorite among London audiences.

During the rebuilding of Drury Lane, Jordan performed in Haymarket Theatre and was admired by the Duke of Clarence, later King William IV. From 1790 to 1811, she was the "affectionate companion" and mistress to the Duke of Clarence, continuing her acting career in London and on tour while bearing ten children, all of whom were later ennobled.

In April 1814, Jordan made her final appearance in London at Covent Garden, where she played in *Debtor and Creditor*. Her final appearance on the stage was at Margate in August 1815. There are varied reports regarding Jordan's final years, especially in regard to her uncertain financial status resulting from dealings with Edward Marsh, a son-in-law, yet there is evidence that she lived on a diminished income in France until her death in St. Cloud.

Jordan relied on her personal magnetism, an infectious laugh, and a natural style of acting, deftly avoiding a mechanical delivery. It was said that she charmed audiences not as an actress but as herself. Coleridge remembered her voice, and Byron praised her talent in acting the spirited youth. Despite a varied career with some scandal attached and intermittent public criticism for her unconventional life, her reputation as an accomplished actress as the comic romp stands.

Susan Taylor Baltimore

Works Consulted

Aspinal, A. *Mrs. Jordan and Her Family*. London: Barker, 1951.

Banham, Martin, ed. *The Cambridge Guide to World Theatre*. Cambridge: Cambridge UP, 1988.

Boaden, James. *Mrs. Jordan; Including Original Private Correspondence, and Numerous Anecdotes of Her Contemporaries*. Vol. 1. London: Bull, 1831.

Fothergill, Brian. *Mrs. Jordan: Portrait of an Actress*. London: Faber, 1965.

Hartnoll, Phyllis. *The Oxford Companion to the Theatre*. 3rd ed. London: Oxford UP, 1967.

Journalism

The period between the French Revolution and the first Reform Bill was a tumultuous and fertile era for British journalism. During these decades the press was subject to governmental repression, technological innovation, immense expansions in readership, vitriolic literary and political debate, and some superlative writing.

The French Revolution was a tremendous impetus for London daily newspapers, but it also spurred governmental control. The three leading London dailies, *The Morning Chronicle*, *The Morning Post*, and *The Times*, increased their circulations modestly over the period, held in check by heavy taxation and aggressive governmental prosecution. Until late in this period, circulation for all three papers hovered between 3,000 and 4,500.

The government used three methods to muzzle the press. The stamp tax imposed on each sheet of newsprint (the only way papers could be sent through the post) inched up, peaking at four pence after 1819. There were other "taxes on knowledge" (Leigh Hunt's phrase) as well: a tax on advertisements, an excise duty on paper, and a small assessment on pamphlets.

Many newspapers were also directly subsidized by the government. Mainline

Whigs had their organ in James Perry's *Morning Chronicle*, while Tories found some support in John Walter's *Times*, though the papers did not consistently toe the party line. The government spent £12,000 in 1811 alone for subsidies and grants to the press.

The stick was used as well as the carrot. Even Walter faced prosecution for libel in *The Times*. Effectively muzzling the non-Establishment press with the Libel Act of 1792 and the Newspaper Act of 1798, the government's campaign proved increasingly ineffective after 1800. Between 1808 and 1811, 42 libel charges were filed. By 1830, working-class defiance of the law became widespread.

While the high cost of newspapers (seven pence in 1819) limited buyers to the wealthy, there were alternatives. Coffeehouses, clubs, corresponding societies, subscription libraries, and neighbors and families passed issues through many hands; one author estimates that 20 people read each issue. The success of many illicit radical publications depended on just such sharing.

Governmental policy was, ironically, especially stimulating for the weekly press, which jumped from one London paper in 1777 to 34 in 1813. The most famous of these must be John and Leigh Hunt's *Examiner*, first published in 1808. The *Examiner* espoused a policy of independence in criticism and political commentary and refused bribes from theater owners as well as government agents. It cost the Hunts financially and personally. In 1813, they were fined £1,500 and jailed for two years after running Leigh Hunt's famous "fat Adonis" portrait of the Prince Regent.

Coleridge wrote extensively for *The Morning Post*, as well as starting two periodicals of his own. *The Morning Chronicle* and *The Times* also regularly ran poems, commentaries, and criticism by major and minor writers. Indeed, the extent to which Romantic literature was shaped by the press and "the form and pressure of the times," as Hazlitt said, is probably undervalued by modern critics. For the first time, writers could earn a living with their pens.

They also wrote for the great *Reviews*: the *Edinburgh Review*, established in 1802, and the *Quarterly* (1809) and the *Westminster* (1824). Initially, part of the impetus behind the reviews was political: under Jeffrey, the *Edinburgh* was predominantly Whig, while the *Quarterly*, led by Scott, was a Tory response. The *Westminster*, edited by James Mill, was the Utilitarian entry, and the Nonconformists offered the short-lived *Annual Review* (1803–08). The practice of unsigned reviews led to vicious attacks on books and authors, and fostered puffing, where the publisher of a journal promoted his own books and damned those of his competitors.

The scurrility of the press reached new depths in 1817 with the publication of *Blackwood's Edinburgh Magazine*. "Maga" — supported by writers like Scott, Coleridge, Henry Mackenzie, De Quincey, Gifford, Lockhart, and Croker Wilson — published the infamous "Chaldee Manuscript," a satirical slander on thinly veiled public figures. With this issue, circulation jumped from 3,500 to 10,000, and peaked, in the early 1820s, at 17,000. Its radical counterpart, the *London* (1820–29), had a top circulation of 3,000 to 4,000. The most famous literary magazine of the era, *The Liberal*, supported by Byron and the Hunt brothers, lasted only four issues, but printed pieces by Byron, Hunt, Hazlitt, and Shelley. *A Vision of Judgment* appeared in its first number.

The convention of anonymity may obscure the contributions of many women.

In the 1790s, William's letters from revolutionary France were widely reprinted in the newspapers, and just before her death in 1800 Robinson contributed extensively to *The Morning Post* under many pseudonyms. Barbauld and her niece Aiken wrote for the *Annual Review*; Martineau contributed to the *Monthly Repository* (1806–37); Mitford wrote for the *Literary Gazette* (founded in 1817), as well as the *London*, to which Mary Shelley also contributed. Several journals were written by women, such as *The Lady's Monthly Museum*, established in 1798; and many aimed at women's intellectual and religious education, not entertainment, such as *The Lady's Magazine* (1770-1847), *La Belle Assemblée* (1806), and *The Female Preceptor* (1813), the last dedicated to More. But as Cynthia White notes, after 1820 women's magazines began to emphasize fashion, illustrations, and "light reading."

Women were probably also engaged in the burgeoning religious press. The number of religious periodicals quadrupled between 1790 and 1825, and these monthly magazines had, in 1807, circulations 6,000 higher than the two great *Reviews*. Wesley's *Methodist Magazine* is still published. The religious press also had its reviews, especially the High Church *British Critic* (1823–43), and, more significantly, the Nonconformist *Eclectic Review* (1805–68). Though clearly exempted from libel law, the religious press still suffered from taxation.

With the revolution of 1830 and the clamor for reform, radical journalism revived. Inventive publishers issued their papers as pamphlets, printed legal and illegal editions, and circumvented the postal system with their own distribution network. The circulations were astounding. Cobbett's *Political Register* printed 40,000 copies in 1816, the highest total for the Regency, but even by the 1830s radical papers were selling up to 16,000 copies in the "War of the Unstamped." A mass audience, a "luxuriant misgrowth," as Coleridge called it, had been born.

The unstamped papers thrived partly because they were based mainly in the provinces. The provincial press, like the press generally, mushroomed between 1789 and 1832. Scottish journals jumped from 13 in 1795 to 31 in 1820; in 1783, there were three Irish papers and, by 1820, 56.

The decades between revolution and reform witnessed remarkable growth in the British press, a fact epitomized by *The Times*'s introduction of steam-powered presses in 1814. A national journalism hounded by prosecution, burdened by taxation, catalyzed by political turmoil, patronized by a widening readership, and blessed with remarkable writers truly became "literature in a hurry."

Joel Haefner

Works Consulted

Altholz, Josef L. *The Religious Press in Britain, 1760–1900*. New York: Greenwood, 1989.

Altick, Richard. *The English Common Reader: A Social History of the Mass Reading Public, 1800–1900*. Chicago: U of Chicago P, 1957.

Fox Bourne, H.R. *English Newspapers: Chapters in the History of Journalism*. 2 vols. 1887. New York: Russell, 1966.

Graham, Walter. *English Literary Periodicals*. New York: Nelson, 1930.

Koss, Stephen. *The Rise and Fall of the Political Press in Britain*. 2 vols. Chapel Hill: U of North Carolina P, 1981.

Madden, Lionel, and Diana Dixon. *The Nineteenth Century Periodical Press in Britain: A Bibliography of Modern Studies 1901–1971*. New York: Garland, 1976.

White, Cynthia. *Women's Magazine, 1693–1968*. London: Joseph, 1970.

Wiener, Joel H. *The War of the Unstamped: The Movement to Repeal the British Newspaper Tax, 1830–1836*. Ithaca: Cornell UP, 1969.

Kant and Theories of German Idealism

During the period of English Romanticism, German philosophy was undergoing what Kant termed a "Copernican revolution." Beginning with Kant and continuing in the work of his disciples Fichte, Schelling, and Hegel, German philosophy sought to explore the relationship of the mind to the world by focusing on the human subject as knower, rather than on objects of knowledge as earlier philosophy had done. The resulting philosophical systems seemed to emphasize the mind's role in the creation of the external world, the active rather than the passive quality of perception, the freedom of the human subject, and the harmony of mind and nature—all themes that are central to Romanticism as a literary and cultural movement. (*See also* German Romanticism.)

Kant's epistemological system in particular has been called the basis of Romantic thought. In the first of his three major "critiques," the *Critique of Pure Reason* (1781), Kant sought to reconcile two opposing trends in 17th- and 18th-century philosophy. These were empiricism, the idea that all knowledge is acquired from the external world through the senses, and rationalism, the idea that knowledge depends on innate or *a priori* concepts in the mind. Though he was often misunderstood as veering toward one of these two extremes, Kant sought a middle ground by proposing that all knowledge comes from experience, but does not arise out of experience, since cognition depends on certain *a priori* or "transcendental" structures in the mind which are triggered by stimuli from the external world. Among the concepts that Kant referred to as transcendental are space and time. He identified these as forms by which to understand experience, rather than as absolutes inherent in experience. Since external things can be understood only according to concepts present in the mind, Kant went on to postulate that all objects of cognition must have a dual nature. He distinguished between the pure object or "thing-in-itself," which is unknowable, and the representation of the object, which *is* available to knowledge. The realm of pure objects, which also includes such "transcendent" concepts as freedom, eternity, and God, is an illegitimate object of reasoning because it is beyond human cognition: a philosophy of nature and of human action must be based on the practical reason that deals with representations.

Kant's contemporaries were attracted by the creative role he assigned to the mind in shaping the world that humans understand and by the way his concept of space and time seemed to offer freedom from necessity or arbitrariness. Yet Kant insisted that things-in-themselves exist objectively and independently of human awareness, even though language can say nothing about them. His followers went a step further, concluding that the pure object is irrelevant and that reality is, in effect, created by the mind.

Fichte began as a disciple of Kant but soon altered Kant's teaching by ignoring things-in-themselves and assigning even more responsibility for cognition to the human mind; that is to say, he distorted Kantianism by emphasizing individuality and subjectivity in a way that would appeal to Romantic poets in Germany and, eventually, in England. Fichte's system rests on a single absolute principle, the "I." Because the I requires opposition and struggle in order to progress, it posits as an opposite for itself, the "Not-I," or everything else in the world, and posits also the relationship between them.

Schelling began as a disciple and explicator of Fichte but eventually modified Fichte's system. While retaining the opposition or dialectic and the notion of action or "becoming" that was central to Fichte's thought, Schelling reinterpreted the opposed terms of I and Not-I as spirit and nature. The apparent disjunction of these two terms, however, proves to be a delusion caused by human reflection. In reality, nature and spirit interconstitute one another; nature is visible spirit, and spirit is invisible nature. On the grounds of this identity, Schelling develops his system of thought as a *naturphilosophie*, or "philosophy of nature." In contrast to experimental science or physics, it involves a conception of nature as organic and teleological, as the self-unfolding of the absolute. The other significant development in Schelling's philosophy over that of Fichte concerns aesthetics, which now takes precedence over ethics. For Schelling, the creation and contemplation of art is the ultimate expression of human freedom, since it constitutes the realization of the identity of spirit and nature.

The work of Hegel was, for the most part, inaccessible to the major Romantics, but it should be mentioned as the most complex systemization of 19th-century idealism. Building on the principle of dialectic and synthesis that was at least latent in all these systems and presenting his philosophy in the form of the human spirit's journey toward knowledge, Hegel united epistemology, aesthetics, and ethics into one grand system which was tremendously influential in the later 19th century.

It was Schelling who, because of his inclusion of nature as a fundamental principle and his emphasis on the imagination and on a dynamic world view, was particularly attractive to an English Romantic thinker like Coleridge. Coleridge's writing was the initial channel by which German ideas made their way to a contemporary English readership. Coleridge's earlier enthusiasm for Kant's transcendental philosophy as a solution to the dilemma of 18th-century thought and for Fichte as the originator of "dynamic" philosophy is also reflected in his writing.

From 1800 to 1805, Crabb Robinson studied at Jena, the university at which all the idealist philosophers held lectures at various periods. In 1802, he began to publish a series of letters in London's *Monthly*

Register, which provided one of the earliest explications of Kant's system for an English readership. The letters were not widely read and soon petered out, but Robinson remained a significant figure for the transmission of German thought because he collected and lent books to others, including Coleridge, who were interested in the subject.

During the early decades of the 19th century, the English reading public generally remained ignorant of and even hostile toward the fundamental changes that were taking place in German philosophy. The satirical novels of Peacock, in which Coleridge is lampooned as a "transcendental philosopher," provide a testimony to the still skeptical English reaction. Carlyle, writing in the 1830s, eventually did the most to prepare the English public for the large-scale introduction of German ideas that occurred later in the 19th century. During the Romantic period itself, German idealism essentially developed independently of, yet parallel to, English literary culture, both of them moving in the direction of individuality, subjectivity, imagination, and feeling. (*See also* German Idealism, Influence of.)

Angela Esterhammer

Works Consulted

Ashton, Rosemary. *The German Idea: Four English Writers and the Reception of German Thought, 1800–1860.* Cambridge: Cambridge UP, 1980.

Copleston, Frederick. *Wolff to Kant* and *Fichte to Nietzsche*, Vols. 6 and 7 of *A History of Philosophy*. Ed. Edmund F. Sutcliffe. Westminster, MD: Newman, 1961, 1965.

Engell, James. *The Creative Imagination: Enlightenment to Romanticism.* Cambridge: Harvard UP, 1981.

Kaufmann, Walter. *Goethe, Kant, and Hegel*. Vol. 2 of *Discovering the Mind*. New York: McGraw, 1980.

Kippermann, Mark. *Beyond Enchantment: German Idealism and English Romantic Poetry.* Philadelphia: U of Pennsylvania P, 1986.

Orsini, G.N.G. *Coleridge and German Idealism: A Study in the History of Philosophy with Unpublished Materials from Coleridge's Manuscripts.* Carbondale: Southern Illinois UP, 1969.

Roubiczek, Paul. "Some Aspects of German Philosophy in the Romantic Period." *The Romantic Period in Germany: Essays by Members of the London University Institute of Germanic Studies.* Ed. Siegbert Prawer. New York: Schocken, 1970.

Kean, Edmund
(1787?–1833)

That a life so sketchy and so marked by contradicting information, rumor, and myth could give rise to four full-scale biographies and countless articles is a testimonial to Edmund Kean's genius at captivating audiences. His childhood, like much of his early career, remains a mystery. Shrouded by his own misrepresentations, Kean's birth date is still disputed. Although most scholars list 4 November 1787, others including his latest biography (1983), suggest 17 March 1789.

Born out of wedlock to Anne (Nance) Carey, hawker and itinerant performer, and Edmund Kean, one of three brothers of Irish descent, Edmund Kean (the younger) became one of Britain's greatest tragedians of the 19th century. Abandoned by his mother at age 2, Kean came to live with his aunt and his father's two brothers, Aaron and Moses. At age 4, Moses Kean put Kean in the care of his mistress Charlotte Tidswell, who was then pursuing an acting career at Drury Lane Theatre.

Scholars agree that Kean's debut on the stage took place at an early age. One apocryphal story told by singer and performer Michael Kelly portrays Kean as an eager, elf-like child, whose large black eyes won him the role as Cupid in Drury Lane's lavish production of *Cymon*, opening in 1791. More likely, it was through Tidswell's connection with the theater that Kean was first cast in child roles and gradually developed his talent for performing.

Eyewitness accounts by such noted literary figures as Hazlitt, Douglas Jerrold, and Coleridge attest to the distinguished tragic style and poignantly moving performances of Kean's later career. All three declared him London's leading tragedian without peer, even among actors from preceding decades. In 1865, English actor and historian Henry Irving credited Kean with originating a new convention of acting, which popularized spontaneity and passionate acting. Kean also stretched the former limits of realism in the theater. For example he was reported to have waited an entire night to view a public execution in order to portray death realistically on the stage the following day. Among actors, Kean's influence proved far-reaching. His blend of what Irving called the romantic and the real inspired not only Kean's leading competitor William Charles Macready but an ensuing generation of actors, including George Vandenhoff, Samuel Phelp, and Kean's son Charles, as well as an American school led by Junius Brutus Booth, Edwin Forrest, and Abthorpe Cooper.

Alcohol indulgence troubled Kean's career, but his career also suffered from the cultural malaise of undefined distinctions among the performing arts. He rose to fame in a time when the theater suffered from the stigma attached to other areas of the performing arts. Actors often shared the stage and their reputation with tumblers, equestrians, and circus entertainers. Subsequent generations of actors benefited under Queen Victoria's royal support, which reinvigorated the theater and gave it a new social credibility, such support having lapsed under previous monarchs. Drury Lane, originally redesigned by Sir Christopher Wren in the late 17th century

and refashioned by David Garrick in the mid-18th century, had declined in stature. With the secession of the Kembles and Kean's first starring role as Shylock in 1814, Drury Lane regained its preeminence among London theaters.

The opening night of Shakespeare's *Merchant of Venice* marked Kean's return to Drury Lane after years away, and it singularly propelled him into fame. Hired by the stage manager to play Shylock, Kean faced skeptics in every corner. Recovering from the death of his eldest son Howard, Kean resisted the Drury Lane committee's insistence that he play a lesser role. The audience, wary of newcomers and partly aware of Kean's reputation as troublemaker, remained dubious. The management regretted the unfortunate engagement. But Hazlitt's review the following day in the *Morning Chronicle* hailed Kean for his rich performance; his natural acuity of character, both his subtlety and bravado; and his overwhelming sense of tragedy; Hazlitt summed up the audience's reaction to the revelation of a star.

Only about five feet four inches in height, Kean projected a physicality on stage that surpassed even Kemble's monumental grace and dwarfed Macready's large stature. No feature of his acting, however, received more praise and evoked more awe than his voice. Even in Drury Lane, a theater built to seat 2,000 people, Kean's use of subtle intonations, his strident tones ranging from a gruff baritone to a hollow soprano scream, and his rich conversational melody were proverbial. Vandenhoff described Kean's rendering of Othello's farewell speech, often cited as one of his best moments, as the music of a broken heart.

Three additional Shakespearean roles became the hallmarks of Kean's theatrical career in the 1820s. Critics acclaimed his role as King Lear in Drury Lane's production opening in 1820, a masterpiece of histrionic art. The production, still using much of Nahum Tate's revision, replaced the original ending for the first time in nearly a century. Kean broke from the traditional mold of Iago as the dark, embittered and ironic, consummate villain. Hazlitt depicted Kean's Iago as a cheerful, lighthearted monster. Richard III was Kean's favorite role, which he played more than any other. Often he used the role to open the London theater season and most special engagements in England and also the United States during his tours in 1820 and 1825.

In 1833, during his performance as Othello, Kean faltered and, hardly breaking character, called out, "I am dying; speak to them for me," as he collapsed into the arms of his son Charles, who played Iago. Kean died almost two months later and is buried in the Richmond churchyard. His life, however, persists in dramatic form through the play written about him by Alexandre Dumas *père* and revised by Sartre in 1954. It received a London production in 1990.

Gregory S. Jackson

Works Consulted

Agate, James. *These Were Actors*. New York: Blom, 1969.

Archer, William, and Robert W. Lowe, eds. *Hazlitt on Theatre*. New York: Hill, 1957.

FitzSimons, Raymund. *Edmund Kean: Fire from Heaven*. London: Hamilton, 1976.

Irving, Henry. *English Actors, Their Characteristics and Their Methods*. London, 1886.

Lewes, George Henry. *On Actors and the Art of Acting*. New York: Grove, 1957.

Playfair, Giles. *The Flash of Lightning: A Portrait of Edmund Kean*. London: Kimber, 1983.

Keats, John
(1795–1821)

Introduction

John Keats, the youngest of the traditionally major English Romantic poets, created poetry that reworked, restored, and ultimately transcended classical mythology. While his early works focus primarily on the idyllic and the natural world, Keats's middle and late poetry explores the relationships between the poet and art, the ideal and the real, myth and humanity. (*See also* Androgyny, Classicism, Poetry.)

Keats's poetry is highly speculative. The changes his poetry undergoes reveal a poet who did not attempt a dogmatic reconciliation of antitheses. The odes of spring (1819) are, for example, a series of different perspectives on the questions Keats poses and the resolutions he seeks. He is known for simultaneously exploiting contrary stances within his poetry as a way of coming to terms with the problems he attempted to resolve. Partly because of this, Keats's poetry includes a large number of oxymora to allow for his paradoxical view of the poems' subjects. While answers may not ultimately exist, Keats believed an increase in awareness and wisdom is necessary to humankind.

Some of Keats's questions about the purpose of poetry serve as exemplar of his own increasingly tragic vision. In the early poetry, Keats questioned whether poetry should offer an imaginative escape through a network of idealized visions that delineate a world beyond. In the later poetry, the questions concentrated on the lives and sorrows of this world.

Several of Keats's theories regarding the imagination and creation of poetry can be found in the letters to his friends and family. Perhaps the most famous of his theories is that which he called "negative capability." (*See also* Negative Capability.) Similar to what is termed "esthetic distance" today, negative capability implies a wholly objective stance toward one's own creation and the ability to recognize and respond to different avenues of thought without regard for the "true" one. Another well-known theory of Keats, that of the "poetical character," contends that the imagination is, by its very nature, chameleon-like and changes to accommodate itself to the spectrum of poetic subjects. (*See also* Camelian Poet; Egotistical, or Wordsworthian, Sublime.)

Life and Work

Keats was born in 1795, the oldest of five children (four of whom survived infancy). His parents managed the prosperous livery stables of Frances Jennings Keats's father in the north of London, so that the family was well on its way toward security.

Keats discovered his love for poetry at the Clarke School at Enfield, which he attended from 1803 to 1811. In 1804, the security started to disintegrate when his father died after falling from a horse, followed in 1810 by his mother's death from consumption. (Her illness and death had such an impact on the young Keats, who had nursed his mother in her final days, that he decided to devote his life to medicine.)

While yet a student at Enfield, Keats was introduced to literature by Charles Cowden Clarke, the headmaster's son. Having read *The Fairie Queene*, Keats became enthralled with Spenser's use of metaphor, writing his first poem in 1814, a testimony to the beauty and power of the imagination, *Imitation of Spenser*. His first poems were published in 1817. While it is

obvious the young Keats was not a prodigy, the initial volume contains the rudiments of his mature poetry. Many of the early works explore the tenuous relationship between the poet and the imagination that later supersede all other themes in Keats's poetry.

The poems of the 1817 volume convey the literary path the poet sets up for himself. The early poems are often primarily literary catalogues of the pastoral landscape, creating the appropriate fictive settings to represent the qualities that serve as subjects for the poems, copying neo-Spencerian parts of sensibility. Keats realized early that he must abandon the pastoral as subject in order to create the type of poetry on which he would eventually concentrate—that which explores and empathizes with humanity.

After their parents' deaths, the Keats children were cared for by their maternal grandmother, who was five years widowed. She appointed Richard Abbey, from her home village, as trustee and guardian along with a merchant acquaintance. Abbey, however, was a successful London businessman, and he took the dominant role. Reports concerning the size of the estate conflict, but Abbey was a most penurious overseer and determined that the two elder boys, John and George, would train to support themselves. George was put in Abbey's counting house, while John found himself, in 1811, apprenticed to Thomas Hammond, a surgeon and apothecary.

But Keats was also an apprentice poet and maintained his friendship with Cowden Clarke. Nonetheless, Abbey's authority was absolute so that when their grandmother died in 1814, the Keats children were completely at his mercy. Tom, the third son, went to work with George, and Fanny, the youngest, went to live with Abbey's family. The three younger children were now in London, so because of that as well as because of some dissatisfactions with Hammond, Abbey terminated John Keats's five-year apprenticeship by one year and had him registered at Guy's Hospital to study surgery. Keats was nearly 20. After completing the course nine months later, he examined and licensed as a surgeon and apothecary. But rather than pursuing this professional career, Keats devoted himself to his poetic craft and met three influential figures: Leigh Hunt, whose poetry he was emulating; Haydon the artist; and John Hamilton Reynolds, who would lead Keats toward other friends. When Keats renounced his medical career, Abbey was infuriated, but Keats resolutely applied himself to poetry. Through Hunt, he met Shelley and produced *Endymion*.

Endymion: A Poetic Romance (1817), following the germinal volume, is generally considered a response to Shelley's *Alastor*. It is Keats's first extended work. A reworking of the myth of the shepherd with whom the moon goddess falls in love, the poem is the first to pair an immortal (the goddess Cynthia) with a mortal (Endymion), a practice that continues throughout Keats's career.

Endymion sets up one of the great themes of Keats's poetry: the discomforting marriage between the limitations of mortality and the ideal of art, and it continues the quest for Keats's own poetic identity begun in the volume of shorter poems. It is a quest that dominates Keats's poetic career, especially after several of the contemporary journals—including *Blackwood's Edinburgh Magazine*, the *British Critic*, and the *Quarterly Review*—viciously panned the first volume and *Endymion* with what became known as the "Cockney School attacks."

This period of Keats's life was the last time he and his brothers were together, because Tom died of consumption, and George married and emigrated to America. After this, Keats was on his own.

Keats's next major poem, *Isabella* (1818), is a romance narrative that reworks Boccaccio's myth; Keats had planned, but never executed, a series of narrative poems based on Boccaccio. A morbid tale of murder and madness, the poem may be read as an *anti*romance in actuality, which exploits (and often condemns) the conventions of romance. *Isabella* pits the beauty of the romance of the lovers against the horror of the poem's literal events and creates an oxymoronic duality that serves as symbol of the real world and theme of the later poems. The theme of perceived duality, or contraries, recalls Blake earlier. With *Isabella*, it becomes repeatedly characteristic of Keats's poetry.

In the early months of 1819, Keats worked on the first *Hyperion*—an elevated poem that recounts the mythic battle between the Titans (deities of the earth) and their opponents and successors, the Olympians (deities of heaven). The poem ends with the birth of the Olympian sun god Apollo—no doubt a symbol of the superiority of the kind of poetry to which Keats aspired. It is widely believed, however, that Keats felt more empathy with the fallen Titans, whose identities had been usurped by the Olympians. This may explain why the poem remains fragmentary.

Another reason that Keats could not finish *Hyperion* is that on 1 December, 1818, while working on the poem, his brother Tom, whom the poet had been nursing, died of consumption at age 19. It was an event that greatly affected both Keats's life and his poetry. In February 1819, he wrote *The Eve of St. Agnes*, the second in the trilogy of what may be termed "antiromances" (*Lamia* is the third). This extended narrative, written in Spenserian stanzas, has a lushness of imagery reminiscent of *The Fairie Queene* and a sense of tactility within the images which became characteristic of all of Keats's poetry. Keatsian imagery at its best views as sensuous the way the world sees and feels and incorporates thought and imagination with actuality. The images are the result of layers of concrete details that become suggestive of the level of intensity to which he aspires. *The Eve of St. Agnes* is not only an example of the richness of Keatsian imagery, but it also produces the first of Keats's several internal arguments over the merits of dreaming in order to reach the ideal.

The act of dreaming as an escape from reality is a recurrent theme in Keats's poetry. In the early *Imitation of Spenser* (1817), the poet speaks of a place that can be reached only through the dream-like visions of imagination. The dream vision *The Eve of St. Agnes* becomes an ironic reality rather than an escape, thus undermining the concepts of romance and illusion.

Keats's belief in escape through the imagination is further shattered by the poems to follow: *La Belle Dame sans Merci*, (1819), the odes of spring (1819), *Lamia*, (1819–20), *The Fall of Hyperion* (1819), and *To Autumn* (1819).

In *La Belle Dame sans Merci*, the odes of spring, and *Lamia*, the imagination that had once transported the speaker into a mythology of the ideal now deceives and eludes. As his vision becomes more tragic, caused in part by the death of Tom, his relationship with Fanny Brawne whom he was courting from next door in Hampstead Heath, and the prolonged separation from George, who had by now emigrated to America, and his sister Fanny the mature Keats no longer views the imagination as easily accessible and salutary.

In the spring of 1819, Keats wrote what many critics believe to be not only his greatest works, but the greatest single series of poems as well: the odes to Psyche, to a Nightingale, on a Grecian Urn, and on Melancholy. Each of the odes attempts to offer a solution to the conflicts Keats encountered with the process of imagination. Through the mythical symbols of the goddesses Psyche and Melancholy, the natural symbol of the nightingale, and the manmade art of the urn, Keats ponders and sustains his questions regarding the conditions that allow creativity, the different forms that creativity can take, the relationship between art and nature, and the relationship between art as immortal and its mortal creator.

Keats's greatest works are those that can be called "dramatic"; that is, they explore all aspects of an experience. Understanding and awareness occur intrinsically and simultaneously with the event itself. This is the type of dramatic character found in the odes. Each presents a narrative debate between speaker and symbol and manifests a continuing self-criticism as well, begun as the quest for poetic identity in the earliest poems, and elevated now to mythological dimensions. The quest for the means of controlling and sustaining a recalcitrant imagination becomes in the odes an extended and intrinsic process of deliberate symbolization, with the apotheosis occurring in the final great ode, *To Autumn*.

Each ode contemplates and meditates on the questions intrinsic to Keats's finest poetry, and each is united to the others not only by conceptual and stylistic similarities, but also through the empathic relationship the speaker creates with the symbols. These symbols are delineated as feminine because Keats, more than any other Romantic poet, conceived of both the imagination and the resultant poetry as female. The relationship between poet and imagination becomes, then, metaphorically sexual and procreative as well as creative.

The final use of the sexual metaphor and the final pairing of a mortal with an immortal occur in Keats's last extended narrative, *Lamia*, written in 1819 and revised in 1820. The poem reworks Robert Burton's original tale from his *Anatomy of Melancholy* (1621) into an extended Drydenesque narrative of two parts. Lamia is a serpent who becomes a woman in order to love the mortal Lycius. The results of the relationship are disastrous: Lycius dies and Lamia vanishes.

The poem has long been controversial; some readers find that Keats's sympathies lie with the serpent Lamia, who exchanged her immortality for Lycius's love. Others see the poem's outcome as Keats's final admonishment and abandonment of an imagination that denies the earth by seeking the ideal of immortality through illusion.

More recent readings of the poem note an ambivalence on Keats's part toward the theme and the characters. The thesis contrasts the rational with the sensuous, the conceptual with the empirical, but offers no solution. The denouement provokes divided sympathies among readers, thus disallowing an uncomplicated and forthright judgment of Keats's intentions. The complications derive in part from the fact that none of the characters is flawless at the end; each contributes to the poem's tragic ending and lack of resolution. *Lamia* emerged at a time during which Keats was preoccupied with questions regarding his own psychological and intellectual growth as an artist—the same types of questions that precipitated the odes.

The development of identity takes on even greater significance in Keats's final major poems, when the speaker confronts the most powerful of the poetry's females, and the works emerge as the most autobiographical.

The speaker of *The Fall of Hyperion* (1819), ironically known as "The Dreamer," seeks identity through the wisdom of the goddess Moneta. He is chastised by her for his inability to confront the miseries of the world, for his desire to escape through dreaming. Intended as a continuation of the earlier *Hyperion*, *The Fall of Hyperion*, like its predecessor, ends as a fragment. The primary differences between the two poems are the autobiographical element of the later and the growth revealed within Keats as a poet. Moneta's face and the wisdom it reveals offer no answers but beautifully document the powerful mystery of human suffering that Keats was incapable of understanding in the earlier poem.

In a Dantesque dream vision, *The Fall of Hyperion* tests the same values that had been tentatively brought forth in *Hyperion*. This time, however, alienation is embodied within the speaker himself rather than within an entire race. The problem has become internalized into a personal rather than racial mythology. In *To Autumn*, written in September of 1819, an external richness, once again of the landscape, becomes internalized. The final ode differs from the odes of spring because it endorses rather than questions the process of creativity. With its idealization of the earth, *To Autumn* is the product of an ironic and hard-won acceptance on Keats's part toward the questions that had haunted his poetic career.

Keats died of consumption at the age of 25 years, four months, in 1821. He died in Rome, where he and his friend, the artist Joseph Severn, had traveled for Keats's health. Keats is buried in the Protestant

Cemetery there. His epitaph, "Here lies one whose name was writ in water," was at Keats's request, a legend that makes clear he did not believe he had achieved immortality.

Karla Alwes

Works Consulted

Baker, Jeffrey. *John Keats and Symbolism.* New York: St. Martin's, 1986.

Bates, W. Jackson. *John Keats.* Cambridge: Belknap, 1963.

Butler, Marilyn. *Romantics, Rebels and Reactionaries: English Literature and its Background.* New York: Oxford UP, 1981.

Curran, Stuart. *Poetic Form and British Romanticism.* Oxford: Oxford UP, 1986.

Levinson, Marjorie. *Keats's Life of Allegory: The Origins of a Style.* Oxford: Blackwell, 1988.

Perkins, David. *English Romantic Writers.* New York: Harcourt, 1967.

Vendler, Helen. *The Odes of John Keats.* Cambridge: Belknap, 1983.

Waldoff, Leon. *Keats and the Silent Work of Imagination.* Urbana: U of Illinois P, 1985.

Ward, Aileen. *John Keats: The Making of a Poet.* New York: Viking, 1963.

Kemble, John Philip

(1757–1823)

Manager of the Drury Lane Theatre from 1788 to 1802 and the Covent Garden Theatre from 1803 to 1817, John Philip Kemble was considered the leading Shakespearean actor and director of his day, taking up the mantle from Garrick, and, eventually, surrendering it to Kean. Like so many actors, he began life as a humble and impoverished strolling player. He was aided in his London debut in 1783, however, by the fact that his sister Sarah, known as Mrs. Siddons, was already popular with London playgoers. (*See also* Theater.)

As an actor and manager, Kemble mainly contributed what might be termed a new decorum of style to productions of Shakespeare. This decorum called for acting of great dignity and polish, coupled with a relatively accurate reproduction, in properties and costumes, of the periods in which the plays were set. This innovation was perhaps Kemble's most noted achievement, although his approach has since been criticized as concentrating too much on "trappings" and not enough on texts.

Kemble rose to prominence in the theatrical world quite swiftly, but his career was plagued with catastrophes and near catastrophes. As Drury Lane's manager, he had to deal with the difficult and profligate Richard Sheridan, who was patentee of the theater. When relations between the two soured irrevocably in 1803, Kemble became manager of Covent Garden Theatre. Unfortunately that great theater burned to the ground six years later. Although the generosity of the public and swiftness with which funds were raised to build a new Covent Garden theater testifies to Kemble's popularity at the time, the new theater brought this popularity to a new low when the public discovered he had devoted the entire third circle of the theater to expensive private boxes and had raised the price of tickets a shilling for the boxes and sixpence for the pit. Some were angered by what they viewed as elitism—an impression to which Kemble's habitual hauteur contributed—and some by the aristocratic depravity and vice which they felt (no doubt correctly) private boxes fostered. Whatever the cause, Kemble and his theater were subjected to many weeks of abuse. Audiences drowned out every performance, and vandalism and fighting in the theater became the norm, in what came to be known as the O.P. ("old price") riots, until Kemble finally capitulated, agreeing to lower ticket prices and reduce the number of private boxes.

In spite of the vicissitudes of his career, Kemble's energy, perseverance, and talent allowed him to dominate the London stage for over 30 years. Although his detractors called him "Black Jack," his admirers, among them Byron, felt that he brought an elevating sense of dignity and grandeur to the British theater. He retired in 1817, with much pomp and feasting, and died of a stroke in 1823 at age 66.

Andrea Rowland

Works Consulted

Baker, Herschel. *John Philip Kemble*. New York: Greenwood, 1969.

Fitzgerald, Percy. *The Kembles*. New York: Bloom, 1969.

Watson, Ernest Bradlee. *Sheridan to Robertson: A Study of the Nineteenth-Century London Stage*. Cambridge: Harvard UP, 1926.

Kitchiner, William

(c.1775–1827)

William Kitchiner, an odd-looking man of eccentric habits and eclectic tastes, was famed for his salons. Invitations to his dinners and *conversazione* were sought after by both the eminent and the obscure.

Born in London, Kitchiner was educated at Eton and took his medical degree at Glasgow. His independent income enabled him to forego practicing medicine and freed him to indulge his varied interests, among them gastronomy, optics, and music. He was extremely tall, bony, and gangly, a man of conservative dress and personal habits who generously entertained his friends, but asked them, especially the women, to eschew finery in their dress for his parties.

Kitchiner's conviction that good health depended on, among other things, the proper preparation of foods led him to conduct ceaseless culinary experiments. His book *The Cook's Oracle* was a best seller and contained 600 of his personal recipes. His other volumes extolling health and thrift were *The Art of Invigorating and Prolonging Life by Food, Clothes, Air, Exercise, Wine, [and] Sleep* (1822) and *The Housekeeper's Ledger: a Plan of Keeping Accounts of the Expenses of Housekeeping* (1825).

He shared his epicurean talents with his friends at small, intimate luncheons and the large, famous Tuesday evening *soirées* which, by his decree, began promptly at 7 p.m. and ended exactly at 11 p.m. Latecomers were not admitted, and he held up dinner for no one. All were willing to obey his rules, for an invitation to his home meant introductions to distinguished, learned fellow guests: wealthy businessmen and celebrated figures from the worlds of art, literature, and music. Accounts of his salons appear in several memoirs of the time, and an essay by Mrs. Walker entitled "An Evening at Dr. Kitchiner's" was published in *Friendship's Offering*, a popular literary miscellany. Editor and poet Watts was an admirer of Kitchiner and recalled in later years that the doctor usually shared his wisdom in epigrammatic speech. As late as 1870, Kitchiner's famed sauces were still remembered; in *The Mystery of Edwin Drood*, Dickens used their zest as a metaphor.

Music was often part of a Tuesday evening with Kitchiner because he fancied himself a musician and wrote music as well as being the collector of a considerable library of manuscripts and printed music. His collections provided selections for *Loyal, National, and Sea Songs of England* (1822).

Kitchiner's optical studies and his passion for the telescope led to his writing *A Companion to the Telescope* (1811) and *Prac-

tical Observations on Telescopes, Opera-glasses, and Spectacles (1815).

Though Kitchiner married a Miss Oram at age 24, the union produced no children, and the couple separated. Kitchiner's only heir was an illegitimate son who inherited his father's estate.

After dining with a friend one evening, Kitchiner returned home and suffered an apparent heart attack; he died in 1827, mourned by many who had relished both his delicious dishes and his quirky company.

Linda Jordan Tucker

Works Consulted

Bennett, Betty T. *Mary Diana Dods, A Gentleman and a Scholar*. New York: Morrow, 1991.

Dictionary of National Biography. *s.v.*, "Kitchiner, William, M.D."

Watts, Alaric Alfred. *Alaric Watts: A Narrative of His Life*. 2 vols. London: Bentley, 1884.

The Lake School

The "Lake School," "Lake Poets," or the "Lakers" were terms used by early 19th-century literary critics to refer to Wordsworth, Coleridge, and Southey. All three poets at one time lived in the Lake District in Northwest England and were all acquainted with each other. It was generally assumed that they had common ideas about poetic theory and practice.

The first critic to use the term in print appears to have been Jeffrey in a review of Coleridge's *Biographia Literaria* in the August 1817 *Edinburgh Review*. However, on several earlier occasions in the *Edinburgh Review*, Jeffrey had identified the three poets as forming a distinct school of modern poetry. In October 1807, for example, in a review of Wordsworth's *Poems in Two Volumes*, he referred to a "brotherhood of poets, who have haunted for some years about the Lakes of Cumberland."

The idea of a unified school of Lakers soon gained currency among poets and critics. One reviewer of Coleridge's *Sibylline Leaves* wrote that where the poet lived and with whom he consorted were easily to be determined from his verse. The term was often used in a derogatory sense, and there were regular satirical jibes about "Lakish Ditties" and "Pond Poets." Leigh Hunt, reviewing Wordsworth's *Peter Bell* in *The Examiner* (1819), safely assumed that his readers were familiar with the label and that he could have fun with it: he suggested that Peter Bell "has rambled about the country, and been as willful, after his fashion, as any Lake poet." The best known jibe is Byron's reference to Southey in the Dedication to *Don Juan*: "And now, my Epic Renegade! what are ye at?/With all the Lakers, in and out of place?"

Jeffrey launched the most serious attacks on the Lake School. Beginning as early as October 1802, in a review of Southey's epic poem *Thalaba the Destroyer*, Jeffrey identified a "sect of poets" that prided itself on the originality of its theories and practice. But according to Jeffrey, the ideas of the Lake Poets, far from being original, were derived from several sources, including the social doctrines of Rousseau; the simplicity of the German poets Kotzebue and Schiller; and the language of poets as various as Cowper, Quarles, and Donne. In subsequent reviews, Jeffrey attacked the diction and subject matter of poetry of the new school. Hazlitt also attacked the Lake School in his essay, "On the Living Poets."

However, no distinct Lake School of poetry existed. It was for the most part a journalistic invention, like the so-called Satanic School of Shelley and Byron, and the Cockney School of Keats and Leigh Hunt. (It is interesting that Southey, a Laker, was in part responsible, because of his attacks on Byron, for popularizing the term Satanic School.) Most often when the Lake School was discussed, Wordsworth alone was the target. For his part, Coleridge refers, in *Biographia Literaria* to the "fiction of a new school" of poetry. And as his most recent biographer points out, Coleridge might more properly be called the poet of the Quantocks rather than the Lakes, since most of his best poetry dates from his stay at Nether Stowey in Somerset and was inspired by his wanderings in the nearby Quantock Hills.

Southey's links to the Lake School have best been discussed by De Quincey, in his reminiscences of Coleridge written in 1834. De Quincey argued that Wordsworth and Southey had never had a single principle in common, and he reports that in 1812 Southey had told him that he disapproved of Wordsworth's theories and practice. De Quincey also denied that there had ever been a distinct Lake School of poetry. He described the circumstances through which each poet came to live in the Lake District, and then mocked the critics who erroneously believed that the poets had gathered there because of their common views about poetry. Compounding their mistake, critics then proceeded to discover in the poetry the common themes they were looking for. Ironically, however, the term Lake School still had enough credence at the time for De Quincey to entitle his several essays on the poets, published in *Tait's Magazine* in 1839, "The Lake Poets."

Bryan Aubrey

Work Consulted

Hayden, John O., ed. *Romantic Bards and British Reviewers*. Lincoln: U of Nebraska P, 1971.

Lamb, Lady Caroline
(1785–1828)

Caroline Ponsonby, known in childhood as "Caro," was the only daughter among four children born to Frederick Ponsonby, third Earl of Bessborough, and the former Lady Henrietta Frances Spencer. A typical product of Whig aristocracy, Caroline's family moved to Italy for three years when she was age 3. Caroline had no formal education, growing up largely in her own imagination and knowing little of the outside world.

Caroline Ponsonby has been described as precocious, spoiled, and rebellious. Often dressing like a boy, she had tomboyish attitudes and a stubborn disposition. Romantic and sensitive, she became a vain, well-read young woman who made her society debut in 1803. She kept diaries, commonplace books, and wrote letters; she read and liked the works of Coleridge.

In 1805, aged 19, Caroline married William Lamb, ten years her elder; Lamb later became Lord Melbourne, Queen Victoria's Prime Minister and adviser. Caroline Lamb was moody and lived in a world of fantasy. Intelligent, though with a childlike attitude about herself, she suffered two miscarriages; she often pretended she had engaged in numerous affairs and kept bad company. Perhaps these and other reasons prepared her for her infatuation with Byron; their subsequent affair shocked and entertained English society and made Caroline Lamb famous.

Caroline Lamb met Byron in 1812, shortly after his success with *Childe Harold*. She recorded in her journal that he was "mad, bad, and dangerous to know." She was infatuated with not only Byron physically, but also with his image — "That beautiful face is my fate." At that time, she was 27; he 24. Their affair ended in the autumn of 1812, leaving Caroline Lamb frustrated and precipitating her neurosis. Three years later, Byron married Anne Isabella Milbanke, who gave birth to their daughter in December of that year. Life for the Lambs became unbearable. She was restless, hysterical, and believed she was going mad. (They eventually separated in 1825, the year after Caroline Lamb accidentally met Byron's funeral procession on the way to Newstead.)

Byron's family tried to have Caroline Lamb declared insane. Her affair with Byron, his marriage, and problems with his family led her to pills, brandy, and laudanum to cover up her broken heart. She had several clandestine affairs, one with a young Bulwer Lytton who was half her age.

Caroline Lamb also had a literary career; she was a poet, letter writer, and novelist. Her literary reputation rests mostly on her first novel *Glenarvon* (1816) which was reprinted in 1865 as *The Fatal Passion*. A thinly disguised *roman à clef* about her relationship with Byron, the novel caricatures Byron and attempts to show, through the title character, the characteristics of an ideal hero. Gossipy and badly written, it made enemies of the women she parodied; nonetheless it allowed its author to ridicule the foibles of society.

Her second novel, *Graham Hamilton* (1820), was, like all her works, published anonymously, though most everyone knew that she was the author. Inspired by exotic Eastern tales, her third novel, *Ada Reis*

(1823), was her favorite. Caroline Lamb also published poetry in *A New Canto* (1819), and in 1829, I. Nathan edited *Fugitive Pieces and Reminiscences of Lord Byron with Some Original Poetry*.

Caroline Lamb spent her last years with her father-in-law and only surviving child, George, who was mentally retarded and lived to be only 29. She died of dropsy at Whitehall at age 42 and is buried at Hatfield.

Gary Kerley

Works Consulted

Blyth, Henry. *Caro: The Fatal Passion: The Life of Lady Caroline Lamb*. New York: Coward, 1973.

Cecil, David. *The Young Melbourne and the Story of His Marriage with Caroline Lamb*. 1939. New York: Readers Club, 1943.

Dictionary of National Biography, s.v. "Lamb, Lady Caroline."

Jenkins, Elizabeth. *Lady Caroline Lamb*. Boston: Little, 1932.

Joyce, Elizabeth. *British Women Writers: A Critical Reference Guide*. Ed. Janet Todd. New York: Continuum, 1989.

Mayne, Ethel. *A Regency Chapter: Lady Bessborough and Her Friends*. London: Macmillan, 1939.

Paul, C. Kegan. *William Godwin: His Friends and Contemporaries*. Boston: Roberts, 1876.

Stickland, Margot. *The Byron Women*. New York: St. Martin's, 1974.

Lamb, Charles

(1775–1834)

Known as the author of Elia's essays, Charles Lamb was also a charming letter writer, astute critic, creator of enduring works for children, poet, dramatist, and novelist. His productivity is astonishing considering he worked for 33 years at least nine hours a day, six days a week, for the East India House (1792–1825). In addition, the fact that he quotes from over 130 authors is impressive, since he left school at age 14.

Introspective, he might have echoed Montaigne by saying, "It is myself that I portray," for though he thinly disguised his experiences, virtually everything he wrote derives from and remains close to autobiography. Even the fabulous "A Dissertation Upon Roast Pig" reflects a personal love for this dish and incorporates an episode from his childhood. The white melancholy that pervades his productions reflects the numerous disappointments in his life, his frequent humorous sallies serving, in Emily Dickinson's words, as "the mail of anguish." (*See also* Essay.)

The son of John and Elizabeth (Field) Lamb, Charles was born in 1775, at the Inner Temple, London. One of his finest essays recalls the Inner Temple, where he spent the first seven years of his life. He owed what he regarded as this good fortune to Samuel Salt, whom the elder John Lamb (Charles's brother was named for their father) served as "clerk, his good servant, his dresser, his friend, his 'flapper,' his guide, stop-watch, auditor, treasurer" ("The Old Benchers"). Salt provided lodging for the Lambs and secured for the junior John Lamb his post with the South Sea Company (of which Salt was a director) and for Charles his admission to Christ's Hospital and later his job at the East India House. Salt also allowed Charles and his sister Mary free range of his library, where the young Lamb first found many of his lifelong enthusiasms, such as Walton's *The Compleat Angler*.

Lamb often spent his vacations at Blakesware, Hertfordshire, a mostly deserted country house cared for by his grandmother, Mary Field. These visits supplied the material for Elia's essays, "Mackery End, in Hertfordshire" and "Blakesmoor in H—shire," and during one of these occasions he met Ann Simmons. She was his first great love, and his fit of madness

at the end of 1795 may have resulted from the realization that they would never marry. She became the eponymous heroine of Lamb's 1798 novel, *A Tale of Rosamund Gray*, in which Lamb, in the guise of Allan Claire, is her lover. She was the subject of some of his sonnets, and she appears as Alice W—n in the essays "New Year's Eve," "A Chapter on Ears," and "Dream Children."

This romance probably dates from 1791, since his grandmother's death the following year ended his regular visits to Hertfordshire. By this time, Lamb had completed his formal schooling at Christ's Hospital (1782–89), where he acquired an excellent grounding in the classics and composition. Here, too, he met people who were important later in his life, most notably Coleridge, whose death in 1834 probably hastened Lamb's own.

A fine student, Lamb might have gone to Oxford had he not been afflicted with a stutter that made a career in the church impossible and put a scholarship out of reach. In "Oxford in the Vacation," he speaks of having "been defrauded in his young years of the sweet food of academic institution." Instead of following Coleridge to Oxford, Lamb entered the commercial world. Henceforth, books, the theater, and conversation were his university.

In 1796, Lamb suffered a blow greater than the loss of Oxford, greater than the loss of Simmons. His father had grown feeble, his mother and aunt were constantly bickering, and money was scarce. Under the strain, Mary, in the first and most violent of several bouts of madness, killed her mother. To save his sister from lifelong confinement, Lamb agreed to care for her; she moved in with him after their father's death in 1799, and they remained inseparable, except during her periods of insanity, until he died.

Five days after his mother died, Lamb wrote to Coleridge, "Mention nothing of poetry. I have destroyed every vestige of past vanities of that kind." In December, he added, "I burned all my own verses; all my book of extracts from Beaumont and Fletcher and a thousand sources; I burned a little journal of my foolish passion which I had a long time kept." Soon, however, he recovered. His sonnets appeared in the 1796 and 1797 editions of Coleridge's poems, and in 1798 he published *Blank Verse* with Charles Lloyd, whom he met through Coleridge. The collection includes one of Lamb's best-loved pieces, *The Old Familiar Faces*, the meter deriving from that of the 17th-century's Massinger. Lamb's novel appeared that year, and he began working on the five-act tragedy *John Woodvil*; its Elizabethan language and Restoration setting again demonstrating his admiration for these periods. Although he was an excellent theatrical critic and a lifelong lover of the stage, Lamb had little skill as a playwright. Never produced, *John Woodvil* was published, at Lamb's expense, in 1802.

After 1800, Lamb attempted journalism to supplement his income. Though he earned enough to supply his needs, he may have worried about his sister's relapses; and he certainly enjoyed haunting the London bookstalls. After contributing to the short-lived *Albion* (1801), he became joke writer and occasional columnist for *The Morning Post*. Among the pieces he wrote for this newspaper is "Londoner" (1802), one of his many paeans to his native city. Lamb was not "romance-bit about *Nature*," as he wrote to Thomas Manning in 1800. He concluded this letter with a list of London's charms; "for these may Keswick [Coleridge's rural retreat] and her giant brood go hang."

Through Coleridge, Lamb met Godwin, for whose Juvenile Library he wrote sev-

eral works between 1805 and 1811. Notable among these are the two books he composed with his sister, *Tales from Shakespeare* (1807) and *Mrs. Leicester's School* (1809). He also provided the epilogue to Godwin's *Antonio* (1800) and the prologue to his *Faulkener* (1807). In this period, Lamb again attempted to write a play: the farce *Mr. H—* opened and closed on December 10, 1806, at Drury Lane. More successful was his *Specimens of English Dramatic Poets Contemporary with Shakespeare* (1808), which established his reputation as a critic. In his "Autobiographical Sketch" Lamb claims to have initiated public interest in past dramatists. Though the claim is exaggerated, the anthology and his notes contributed much to the Romantic interest in these authors.

Over the next decade Lamb produced occasional pieces. The best appeared in Leigh Hunt's *Reflector*. "On the Genius and Character of Hogarth" argues convincingly that Hogarth is not merely a caricaturist but a brilliant satirist with a tragic sense, comparable in skill to Reynolds. More controversial is Lamb's assertion in his essay "On the Tragedies of Shakespeare" that Shakespeare's tragedies do not translate well to the stage because performance limits their power.

In 1818, when Lamb's *Works* appeared, he had created a respectable body of poetry, criticism, and occasional essays. Yet his best work lay ahead. When John Scott started the *London Magazine* in 1820, he invited Lamb to contribute. Soon Lamb was the highest paid essayist on the staff, and his writing earned him an invitation to dine with the Lord Mayor of London. Ranging widely, Lamb, under the pen name of Elia, revealed life's humor and pathos. Over his experiences, he cast a nostalgia, with titles that proclaim this love of the past, and a wistful longing for childhood.

As he wrote of himself in the Preface to *The Last Essays of Elia* (1833), "The *toga virilis* never sate gracefully on his shoulders. The impressions of infancy were burnt into him, and he resented the impertinence of manhood." Good company himself, his essays, too, are most companionable.

After 1825, Lamb never wrote so well again. The best of his late pieces were his "Popular Fallacies." Modeled on Browne's 17th-century exploration of "vulgar errors," it appeared in the *New Monthly Magazine* in 1826. For his friend and future son-in-law Edward Moxton (who married Charles and Mary Lambs' adopted daughter), he assembled *Album-Verses* (1830). Still trying his hand at drama, he wrote *The Wife's Trial* and *The Pawnbroker's Daughter*; neither was produced.

Lamb died in 1834, and is buried at Edmonton; Mary died in 1847 and was interred with him. Henry Crabb Robinson, one of Lamb's closest friends, wrote after Mary's funeral, "We all talked with warm affection of dear Mary Lamb, and that most delightful of creatures, her dear brother Charles—of all the men of genius I ever knew, the one the most intensely and universally to be loved." (*See also* Frend, William; Irving, Edward.)

Joseph Rosenblum

Works Consulted

Barnett, George L. *Charles Lamb*. Boston: Twayne, 1976.

———. *Charles Lamb: The Evolution of Elia*. Bloomington: Indiana UP, 1964. Haskell House, 1973.

Blunden, Edmund. *Charles Lamb and His Contemporaries*. Cambridge: Cambridge UP, 1933.

Courtney, Winifred F. *Young Charles Lamb 1775–1802*. New York: New York UP, 1982.

Lucas, Edward V. *The Life of Charles Lamb*. London: Methuen, 1905.

Lamb, Mary
(1764–1847)

Mary Lamb was the sister of critic Charles Lamb. She collaborated with him in writing children's books, including the popular *Tales from Shakespeare*. Eleven years his senior, she was his devoted surrogate mother and lifelong companion. Cursed by reoccurring bouts of insanity, a legacy of their high-strung family, Mary lived two distinct lives: one of good sense and kindness, the other of frightening madness. The sane Mary, quiet and plain, loved home and literature and devoted herself to her brother's happiness and sympathized with his joys and sorrows. The insane Mary erupted into a frenzy of loquacity and restlessness that sometimes resulted in violence.

John and Mary Lamb of Inner Temple, London, saw three of four children survive infancy: John, Mary, and Charles. John Lamb, the elder, was employed by an ex-member of Parliament and was too occupied to devote time to his children. As mother, Mary loved her children, but she was a distant, unaffectionate parent who made her first son, John, her favorite. Little Mary lacked the warm approval that her delicate, nervous disposition craved. When Charles was born, Mary turned her entire capacity for affection and love to Charles, the skinny, delicate, stuttering, but charming child that her brother was. In turn, Charles adored Mary. They had an affinity of spirit that was reflected in similar interests: the theater, literature, long walks, stimulating conversation (Mary liked to listen; Charles liked to talk), and convivial friends.

Though Charles wanted to write, he worked as a clerk with the East India Company to earn a living; Mary worked as a dressmaker to earn extra income for the family. She also cared for her increasingly senile father, invalid mother, and elderly aunt. In one of her earliest attacks of madness, at age 32, Mary's delicate constitution succumbed to the stress and fatigue of her responsibilities. Irrational and violent, she assaulted her father and fatally stabbed her mother.

For the remainder of her life, Mary was in and out of mental asylums. Charles, in the most profound decision he ever confronted, rejected his older brother's advice to commit his sister for life. He promised the medical authorities that he would take lifelong responsibility for her. He sacrificed the chance for marriage, accepted that his writing would take second place to a permanent job as a clerk, and made her care the most important object of his life. And this he did without regret or blame.

Mary survived the anguish of her insanity and the horror of her actions by separating her insane self from her sane self. Finding serenity in the knowledge that she was not to blame for what she had done in her madness, she even trusted that the affliction was visited on her by God's divine will for some mysterious purpose. Furthermore, she believed the spirit of her mother was aware of this and forgave her.

After their father died in 1799, Mary left a private asylum and came to live with Charles. When she was well, they entertained friends in each of the shabby dwellings they occupied. Their wide circle of friends and acquaintances included some of the most famous and infamous persons of the day: Coleridge, Wordsworth, Hazlitt, Southey, Godwin, Mary Shelley, Keats, Moore, Carlyle, and others. They never had a permanent home after their parents' deaths for neighbors shunned them once Mary's madness and her notorious past became known. Anxious to keep his sister calm, Charles moved them periodically. Between 1799 and 1823, they moved eight times.

Insanity descended on her about once a year for the remainder of her adult life. Toward the end of her life, the attacks grew more frequent, though less violent. The Lambs always knew when she was about to become ill; and they would pack her bag, including her straitjacket, and would walk, arm-in-arm, both in tears, to the asylum where she would be committed until the dreadful attack passed and she returned once again to her senses.

Between the attacks, the Lambs learned to seize happiness where and when they could and shut their eyes to anything beyond the immediate future. They read, studied, wrote, took long walks, and welcomed friends with whist, conversation, and modest refreshments. These evenings were the high points in their lives, and their friends reported that such evenings were often uncommonly brilliant, since Charles had a unique gift for good-humored, whimsical, often eloquent conversation.

The Lambs tasted the joys of parenthood when in 1823 they adopted 11-year-old Emma Isola, a long-time little friend whose father had died. They took responsibility for her education, and later she married the publisher Edward Moxton.

In 1833, Mary's illness was recurring at increasingly frequent intervals, and Charles decided to put her in a home for mental patients. So that she would not feel deserted, Charles also made his home there. He reported to friends that when she was not violent, her rambling chatter was better to him than the sense and sanity of the world. He was the devoted brother to the end. He died of an infection following a fall in 1834. Mary lived calmly but semi-insanely, until 1847.

Kathryn Young

Works Consulted

Barnett, George L. *Charles Lamb*. Boston: Twayne, 1976.

Cecil, Lord David. *A Portrait of Charles Lamb*. London: Constable, 1983.

Courtney, Winnifred F. *Young Charles Lamb*. New York: New York UP, 1982.

Howe, William D. *Charles Lamb and His Friends*. New York: Bobbs, 1944.

Marrs, Edwin W., Jr. ed. *The Letters of Charles and Mary Anne Lamb*. Ithaca: Cornell UP, 1975.

Lancaster, Joseph

(1778–1838)

Joseph Lancaster, influential educator and writer on pedagogy, was and remains a controversial figure in 19th-century social history. Born in Southwark, London, he left home at age 14 and attempted (unsuccessfully) to reach Jamaica to "teach the poor blacks the word of God." After a short period as a naval volunteer, he returned to Southwark in 1798 to begin a different educational mission: teaching the children of the poor the elements of literacy at minimal cost.

Initially, Lancaster had no funds for hiring assistants, so he developed what later became famous as the "monitorial" system. Under this system, the pupils become instructors, or "monitors," for those immediately below them in the school's elaborate system of ranks and forms. The monitorial system was marked by an unusual amount of cooperation and productive activity among the students. It also put disciplinary considerations ahead of educational ones. The Lancasterian school was quasi-military in its hierarchical structure and rules of order. Its emphasis on continual work and relentless supervision was drawn from the contemporary vision of the factory as exemplary disciplinary institution.

In 1803, Lancaster published the educational treatise *Improvements in Education*, detailing the success of his school in the Borough Road. His efforts to spread his system throughout England gained the attention of several members of the royal family, and in 1805, George III promised Lancaster his patronage. The proliferation of schools on the Lancasterian plan, however, was met with envy from and anxiety by the Church of England establishment: Lancaster (a Quaker) taught a nondenominational version of Christian doctrine, which was perceived as fomenting dissent and undermining the church's standing among the lower classes. Trimmer, the conservative educationalist and children's author, attacked Lancaster in *A Comparative View* (1805) and encouraged the Anglican cleric Bell, who had independently developed his own version of the monitorial method (the "Madras" system) in India, to develop a rival network of schools for poor children sponsored by the Established Church. Trimmer was seconded by Coleridge, who promoted Bell and assailed Lancaster in a lecture on education given at the Royal Institution in 1808, and by Southey, who took Bell's part and attacked Lancaster at much greater length in a *Quarterly Review* article (1811), later expanded into the pamphlet *The Origin, Nature and Object of the New System of Education* (1812).

Lancaster's supporters, in what came to be known as the "Bell-Lancaster controversy," included Sydney Smith and Brougham, both writing in the *Edinburgh Review* (1806, 1810); the Quaker Joseph Fox, who wrote a *Comparative View* of his own; and James Mill, who defended Lancaster's nondenominational approach to education in an anonymous pamphlet entitled *Schools for All in Preference to Schools for Churchmen Only* (1812).

The differences between the rival systems of Lancaster and Bell—apart from the religious question—should not be over-estimated. The monitorial and Madras systems were equally mechanistic and disciplinary, with a good deal more emphasis on constant surveillance and instilling orderly behavior than on teaching students anything beyond the rudiments of education. Lancaster's approach, however, was marked by bizarre punishments (based on shame rather than on physical pain) lacking in Bell's: refractory students might be labeled with humiliating signs, placed in wooden shackles, or hung in baskets from the classroom ceiling. On the other hand, Lancaster claimed that only financial constraints kept him from providing his students with a more liberal education, while Bell wrote that teaching poor children anything beyond reading and church catechism—even to write and cipher—might constitute a threat to the social order.

Lancaster was a disastrous financial manager and by 1808 had ceded control of his schools in England to the Royal Lancasterian Society, led by Fox and another Quaker, William Allen. The society was reconstituted in 1810 as the British and Foreign School Society. Leaving England in 1818, Lancaster realized his youthful dream of promoting education in the New World and established schools in such far-flung cities as Baltimore, Caracas (with the patronage of Simon Bolivar), and Montreal. He died in New York in 1838.

Under the aegis of the British and Foreign School Society, the Lancasterian method was spread throughout the world. In addition to the efforts of Lancaster and others in the Americas, monitorial schools were instituted in France, Spain, Russia, Greece, Denmark, and Sweden. The society gave special attention to British colonies, establishing schools in Jamaica, the Bahamas, Malta, Ceylon, India, Australia,

Sierra Leone, and the Cape of Good Hope. This attention to the British colonies suggests links between Lancaster's enterprise of training lower-class children in elementary literacy, uniform behavior, and industrious habits and the larger enterprise of British colonialism: both were concerned with bringing subject populations into line with an industrialized economy and increasingly regimented social order. Although a pioneer in the area of teacher training and obviously committed to the lower-class children he educated, Lancaster's emphasis on hierarchy, orderliness, and work habits attests to how pervasively popular education was linked, in the Romantic period, with questions of social discipline. (*See also* Education.)

Alan Richardson

Works Consulted

Dickson, Mora. *Teacher Extraordinary: Joseph Lancaster, 1778–1838.* Sussex: Book Guild, 1986.

Foakes, R.A. "'Thriving Prisoners': Coleridge, Wordsworth and the Child at School." *Studies in Romanticism* 28 (1989): 187–206.

Johnson, Richard. "Notes on the Schooling of the English Working Class 1780–1850." *Schooling and Capitalism: A Sociological Reader.* Ed. Roger Dale et al. 1976. 44–54.

Kaestle, Carl F., ed. *Joseph Lancaster and the Monitorial School Movement: A Documentary History.* New York: Teacher's College P, 1973.

Landon, Letitia Elizabeth (L.E.L.)

(1802–38)

After Letitia Elizabeth Landon's death in 1838, Edgar Allan Poe commented that one of the two greatest women poets of England had just died. His assessment of her reputation was based on a large body of published works; in only 20 years, she had produced seven collections of poetry: *The Fate of Adelaide* (1821), *The Improvisatrice*

(1824), *The Troubadour* (1825), *The Golden Violet* (1827), *The Venetian Bracelet* (1829), *The Vow of the Peacock* (1835), and *The Zenana* (1839) and four works of fiction (*Romance and Reality* (1831), *Francesca Carrara* (1834), *Traits and Trials of Early Life* (1836), and *Ethel Churchill* (1837). She also wrote critical reviews for the influential *Literary Gazette*, contributed approximately 150 works of poetry and prose to popular periodicals and annuals, and wrote the entire *Drawing Room Scrap Book* (1832–38), *Book of Beauty* (1833), and *Flowers of Loveliness* (1837).

Landon began her prolific literary career in an attempt to improve her family's finances. Born in Chelsea in 1802 to John and Catherine Bishop Landon, people of "gentle condition" and moderate income, Landon had a pleasant, normal childhood. When she was age 13, her father's investments and the army-agency business with which he was associated failed, and the consequent reduced circumstances forced the family into seclusion.

Eventually, Landon began to consider the writing with which she had always entertained her family as a possible source of income. With the help of William Jerdan, a neighbor and editor of the *Literary Gazette*, several of her poems were published. Jerdan's continued encouragement and editorial help also aided Landon in writing her first long poem, *The Fate of Adelaide*. Because of the failure of the publishing company, the poet received no money for the volume; however, from 1821 to 1824, a series of "Poetical Sketches" for the *Gazette*, signed with her initials L.E.L., captured the public's fancy, established her poetic reputation, and made subsequent publications financially rewarding. In fact, after her father's death in 1824, Landon's writing became the support for three households—her mother's, her brother's, and her own.

Because much of the motivation for her writing was financial, Landon—like many women writers of the time—became a master of gauging and responding to public taste. Her poetry, in particular, struck a sympathetic chord with the mass readership of the day. Borrowing superficial traits from Byron, Scott, Leigh Hunt, and Moore—exotic scenes and settings; tragic episodes; a melancholy, self-pitying tone; an extemporizing style; and an idealization of a poet-hero—Landon produced verses that toned down the intensity of the best Romantic poetry to a ladylike pathos. But she gave her readers enough thought and originality that they could feel elevated by what was essentially escapist poetry. In short, her work had the facile sensuality, extreme seriousness, and conformity to prevailing tastes associated with best sellers of any age.

Landon's career as a popular literary figure was closely linked to the annuals—gift-book anthologies of art work illustrated by original prose and poetry—that were a fashionable and financially successful publishing phenomenon of the time. Her reputation as a well-known poet, her ability to improvise, and her constant need for money combined to make this genre a natural and lucrative outlet for her talents. In some of her prose published in the annuals, Landon shows competence in several types of stories and a refreshing (and unusual for the annuals) use of humor and satire; however, her poetry in them is of indifferent quality. In fact, the intrinsic limitations of the popular genre were detrimental to the development of her poetic art.

Landon's shift in the 1830s to writing novels indicates her recognition of a general shift from Romanticism to Victorianism and of a gradual change occurring in the public's reading tastes—a change reflected in the emergence of the novel as the popular literary genre. Her characteristic poetic work was not particularly suited to the format of the three-volume novel, and her first attempts show only rudimentary skill in developing character and plot. But her last novel, *Ethel Churchill*, although marred with a sentimentality and lack of unity typical of all her prose, is the most realistic of her work and is vastly improved in novelistic technique and in grasp of character. Despite its deficiencies, Landon's prose is instructive to the modern reader: it gives insight into her development as a popular writer responding to her public, and it reveals much about Landon's age because it reinforces then-current concerns and interests, as all popular fiction must.

By the early 1830s, when Landon approached the zenith of her fame, she had produced a substantial body of poetry and prose from which she had derived considerable financial rewards. But she was far from content in her personal life. Criticism of her as a woman living without masculine "protection" and working in the male-dominated field of publishing had already, in the 1820s, led to malicious rumors suggesting improprieties in her relationships with two well-known literary figures. In 1834, these slanders were revived, and, as a result, her engagement to John Forster, the future biographer of Dickens, was broken. The next two years reached a low ebb in Landon's mental and physical health, but her personal crisis seemed to be resolved when, in 1836, she met George Maclean, home on leave from the Gold Coast and his duties as governor of the Cape Coast colony there.

Friends of Landon and Maclean considered them incompatible, but their engagement was announced soon after they met. Although Maclean apparently attempted to get out of the agreement, they were eventually married in 1838 and sailed for Africa. At the end of the year, Landon's letters to friends and relatives arrived in England—along with the announcement of her sudden death. The British press was filled with rumors of murder alternating with accounts of suicide, and her family and friends went to great lengths to discover the truth. However, no evidence was found to dispute the official verdict that she had died from accidentally poisoning herself by taking too much of a medicine prescribed for spasms. But the facts are conflicting, and, even now, her death remains a mystery.

Brenda H. Hutchingson

Works Consulted

Ashton, Helen. *Letty Landon*. New York: Dodd, 1951.

Blanchard, Samuel Laman. *Life and Literary Remains of Letitia Elizabeth Landon*. London: Colburn, 1841.

Courtney, Janet E. "Alphabetical Graces." *London Mercury*, 26 (1932): 326–38.

Enfield, D.E. *Letitia Elizabeth Landon: A Mystery of the Thirties*. London: Hogarth, 1928.

Metcalf, B.E. *Maclean of the Gold Coast*. London: Oxford UP, 1962.

Stevenson, Lionel. "Miss Landon, 'The Milk-and-Watery Moon of Our Darkness,' 1824–30." *Modern Language Quarterly*, 8 (1947): 355–63.

Thrall, Miriam M.H. *Rebellious Fraser's: Nol Yorke's Magazine in the Days of Maginn, Thackeray and Carlyle*. New York: Columbia UP, 1934.

Whiting, Mary B. "Letitia Elizabeth Landon—A Century-Old Tragedy." *Congregational Quarterly*, 13 (1935): 335–45.

Landor, Walter Savage
(1775–1864)

Best remembered as the author of *Imaginary Conversations* and a handful of memorable lyrics, Walter Savage Landor was born in Warwick, in 1775, the eldest son of a physician who gave up his profession on succeeding to the family inheritance. From his parents, Landor inherited wealth and estates that left him financially independent all his life.

Landor went to Rugby School, where he displayed a remarkable facility in the classics and began to write Latin verses. He also displayed what became the dominant feature of his personality—a volatile and furious temper, which later led to endless strife and litigation. He was compelled to leave Rugby after an argument with the headmaster. In 1793, he went to Trinity College, Oxford, where another outburst caused him to be rusticated, and he never returned.

There followed years of living at home and traveling and the beginnings of his literary career. His early work, the poetic romance *Gebir* (1798), attracted the enthusiastic attention of Southey, Coleridge, and later Shelley. A radical and republican, he went to Spain in 1808 to support the Spanish rising against the French. On his return to England, he became embroiled in the management and improvement of a huge estate he had purchased in Monmouthshire. In 1811, he married Julia Thuillier, a woman of Swiss descent much younger than he. They had three sons and a daughter, but the marriage was troubled, and they spent much time apart. Financial problems with his estate and acrimonious relations with his neighbors compelled Landor to leave England in 1814, first for Jersey, then France, and finally Italy. In 1821, he settled in Florence, where he spent the remainder of his life, save for occasional stays in England.

His experiences in Spain led him to write the dramatic tragedy *Count Julian* (1812). Later he wrote a trilogy of historical dramas: *Andrea of Hungary* (1839), *Giovanna of Naples* (1839), and *Fra Rupert*

(1840). None are performable; their plots are confused and they lack dramatic structuring. Landor's distinctive gift was in less structured, free-flowing dialogue, and in his *Imaginary Conversations* he found his vehicle. He published five volumes of these in the 1820s—the first two in 1824, the third in 1828, the fourth and fifth in 1829. By the end of his life, he had written some 160 of them. The majority take the form of dialogues, with speakers drawn from classical antiquity up to Landor's own day, and most are celebrated artists, philosophers, statesmen, or sovereigns. The conversations display Landor's remarkable range of reading and knowledge. Sometimes his elevation of the language and sentiments of his speakers results in a style that is stilted and obscure and characters who turn into rhetorical mouthpieces. But at its best, especially when treating loss and death, his prose can suddenly sound with poignant and harmonious grandeur, as when his Sidney says, "We are motes in the midst of generations." Landor put the form to further use in *Pericles and Aspasia* (1836), this time in letters written by several correspondents in ancient Greece, and in *The Pantameron* (1837), a series of dialogues between Petrarch and Boccaccio.

Landor's lyric poetry reflects his classical learning and temperament in its epigrammatic and polished incisiveness. Much of his best verse is addressed to women he knew, and, as with his prose, it achieves its most intense pathos in recording the effects of time and loss: thus his lyric beginning "Past ruined Ilion Helen lives," celebrating the beauty of "Ianthe" (Joan Sophia Swift), and his most famous poem, written in memory of Rose Aylmer, "Ah, what avails the sceptered race." In his writing, what is so often labored and overstrained can yield unforgettable moments of consoling and elegant gravity. Landor's work was as prolific, unpredictable, and idiosyncratic as his personality. His moods of anger and belligerence could be followed by acts of impulsive and noble generosity.

Landor had an appreciative following among his fellow writers, but beyond that he was quite indifferent to popular fame. His irascible personality left him almost alone toward the end of his long life. He lived apart from his family in his final years in Florence, but he was aided by Browning among others. One of his last contacts with the world of letters was a visit in 1864 from the young Swinburne, who dedicated *Atalanta in Calydon* (1865) to him. He died that same year.

Jonathan E. Hill

Works Consulted

Dilworth, Ernest. *Walter Savage Landor*. New York: Twayne, 1971.

Pinsky, Robert. *Landor's Poetry*. Chicago: U of Chicago P, 1968.

Super, R.H. *Walter Savage Landor: A Biography*. New York: New York UP, 1954.

The Wordsworth Circle. 7.2 (1976). (Special Landor number).

Landscape Painting

Between the 1780s and the 1830s, landscape painting emerged as an important and independent art form in Great Britain. It was represented not just by the oils and watercolors of its two greatest practitioners, Constable and Turner, but also by the works of Girtin, Crome, Cotman, and Bonington.

Prior to the middle of the 18th century, few British artists painted English landscapes, and landscape painting was largely associated with French, Italian, and Dutch painters, especially Poussin, Gaspard Dughet, called Poussin, Lorraine, and Salvator Rosa. Likewise popular were landscapes and the *vedute* of Venetian painters like Canaletto and landscapes by the 17th century Dutch masters, especially van Ruisdael and Cuyp. By mid-century, however, English landscape painters had become more common, but many, like Richard Wilson (1713–82), still composed in an Italianate style and under the influence of foreign masters, and few painted the native English countryside. Only Thomas Gainsborough (1727–88) may be an exception, though his landscapes were often picturesque evocations of a pastoral utopia replete with idealized peasants.

In the decades immediately before and after 1800, the nature and status of landscape painting changed quite abruptly in Great Britain. Not only did landscape painting became valued in and of itself, but British artists also cast off foreign influences and borrowed models, turning for inspiration and subject matter from the idealized landscape to their own countryside. Important, too, was a more positive attitude toward nature, especially toward the beauty and particularities of the natural setting. This attitude was expressed in verse and prose long before it appeared on paper or canvas, an appreciation in part esthetic (picturesque and sublime) and in part scientific (geology, botany, and meteorology all shaped Turner's and Constable's values in the landscape). Credit, too, must be given to the contemporary taste for the sublime and the picturesque, for both privileged the natural scene, and to the Rev. William Gilpin, author of *Three Essays: On Picturesque Beauty; On Picturesque Travel; and On Sketching Landscape* (1792), who also wrote and illustrated guidebooks to the English countryside, such as *Observations on the River The Wye* (1782). The difficulty of travel on the European continent during the wars of the French Revolution and Napoleonic years may have equally inclined the English to discover their own country, especially Wales, Yorkshire, and the Lake District, and some no doubt felt its value enhanced by threats of foreign invasion. Interest in poignant medieval ruins, especially those overgrown with vines and seeming to blend in with nature, was similarly important.

In recent years, scholars have noted the coincidence in time of the emergence of landscape painting and the transformation of the English countryside by the Enclosure Movement of the 18th century, as well as by the encroachments of the Industrial Revolution and the increasing urbanization of Great Britain during the first half of the 19th century. Although industrial landscapes—such as Philippe Jacques de Loutherbourg's *Coalbrookdale by Night* (1801) or Paul Sandby Munn's *Bedlam Furnace* (1802)—exist, they are rare, and the predominant rural landscapes possibly appealed to those nostalgic for the traditional countryside and for a vanishing political, social, and economic order. Whatever the causes, the public's appreciation for landscapes significantly expanded the market for this genre during the first half of the 19th century.

To a great extent, Constable shaped the image of the English landscape, not only for his own day but also for succeeding generations. He spent much of his life painting Stour Valley scenes long familiar to him and for which he had an abiding affection; he also painted important views of Salisbury and its cathedral and of Hampstead Heath. Although he knew well the work of earlier landscape painters, such as Lorraine, Ruisdael, or Richard Wilson, he said that when sketching from nature he tried to forget having seen pictures by others. His landscapes accordingly appear natural, not sublime or melodramatic, like many of those by his great

contemporary Turner. Constable's landscapes depict an unexceptional and commonplace world of trees, fields, and rivers, a nature worked by humans but not radically transformed or abused by them and where a serene harmony between humanity and nature appears to exist. In his genuine affection for nature, Constable, as scholars have repeatedly noted, has much in common with the Wordsworth of the *Lyrical Ballads*. Both believed the divine present in every aspect of nature and that from the intense contemplation of nature, insight and moral benefits accrue; both were attracted to the essential simplicity of rustic life; and both drew inspiration from recollected scenes of their childhood, Constable apparently much longer than Wordsworth.

Constable's profound reverence for the particularity of nature notwithstanding, his best known paintings—like *The White Horse* (1819), *The Hay Wain* (1821), and *The View of the Stour Near Dedham* (1822)—were not direct imitations of nature but finished canvases worked up in the studio from sketches and full-size studies. Their serene character no less than their meditative qualities led Karl Kroeber to liken such six-footers as *The Hay Wain* to Wordsworth's "spots of time" passages in *The Prelude*. What gives these canvases, and indeed all of Constable's best paintings, their special quality is his ability to capture the effects of light and the weather on nature, whether with flecks of light that convey a sense of freshness or with dramatic and emotional uses of light and shade, as in *Dedham Vale* (1828).

Turner was recognized throughout his life and is known today for his extraordinary use of color and as a painter of drama, light, and atmosphere. He began as a topographical watercolorist, with, for example, picturesque evocations of Tintern Abbey

(1794) and Lincoln Cathedral (1795), and ended up as the painter of the almost abstract *Rain, Steam, and Speed—the Great Western Railway* (1844) and the *Snowstorm—Steamboat off a Harbour* (1844). In between, the enigmatic Turner painted an extraordinary range of watercolors and oils in an equally wide range of styles, making an artistic career that defies easy summation.

For landscape pictures, many of which resulted from numerous trips to the Continent, Turner favored the sublime and dramatic, painting towering mountains and plunging valleys in the midst of violent storms. *His Snowstorm: Hannibal and His Army Crossing the Alps* (1812) portrays men and animals rendered insignificant within a swirling vortex created by the forces of nature. Unlike Constable, Turner drew on literature and history for inspiration, even though he occasionally painted lyrical landscapes, like *Frosty Morning* (1813) and the once popular *Crossing the Brook* (1815). Later in his career, particularly after visits to Italy released his sense of color, he became the painter of firelight, sunsets, and sunrises. In the works of the 1830s and the 1840s, such as *Norham Castle*, form and content almost completely dissolve into light and atmosphere.

Constable and Turner so dominate modern ideas of English landscape painting during the first half of the 19th century that other talented landscapists have been unjustly obscured. Girtin, for example, began as a topographical draftsman, but about 1794 he broke not only with this tradition but also with the the concept of the formulaic landscape. He painted in watercolor such scenes as the hauntingly evocative *Kirkstall Abbey* (1802), where the ruins almost disappear into an infinite countryside. In Norwich, Crome painted luxuriant and tranquil landscapes and founded the Norwich Society of Artists (1803), a group of local landscape painters which included Cotman. Cotman's watercolors of landscapes and ruins, for example *Croyland Abbey* (1802), many painted during trips to Wales and Yorkshire, have a detached quality, as is evident in his series of scenes along the River Greta in Yorkshire. Bonington, who worked mainly in France but within the English landscape tradition, painted, in addition to such superb landscapes as *Stormy Landscape with a Waggon Descending a Hill* (1827), French coastal scenes and picturesque townscapes. (*See also* Painting.)

Robert W. Brown

Works Consulted

Barrell, John. *The Dark Side of the Landscape. The Rural Poor in English Painting, 1730–1840.* New York: Cambridge UP, 1980.

Bermingham, Ann. *Landscape and Ideology. The English Rustic Tradition, 1740–1850.* Berkeley: U of California P, 1986.

Clark, Kenneth. *Landscape into Art.* 1949. New York: Harper, 1976.

Cormack, Malcolm. *Bonington.* New York: Cambridge UP, 1989.

———. *Constable.* Oxford: Phaidon, 1986.

Gage, John. *J.M.W. Turner: "A Wonderful Range of Mind".* New Haven: Yale UP, 1987.

Hawes, Louis. *Presences of Nature: British Landscape, 1780–1830.* New Haven: Yale Center for British Art, 1982.

Kroeber, Karl. *Romantic Landscape Vision: Constable and Wordsworth.* Madison: U of Wisconsin P, 1975.

Lister, Raymond. *British Romantic Painting.* New York: Cambridge UP, 1989.

Paulson, Ronald. *Literary Landscape: Turner and Constable.* New Haven: Yale UP, 1982.

Rajnai, Miklos, ed. *John Sell Cotman, 1782–1842.* Ithaca: Cornell UP, 1982.

Rosenthal, Michael. *British Landscape Painting.* Ithaca: Cornell UP, 1982.

———. *Constable. The Painter and His Landscape.* New Haven: Yale UP, 1983.

Wilton, Andrew. *Turner and the Sublime.* Chicago: U of Chicago P, 1980.

Landseer, Edwin

1802–73

A child prodigy who exhibited his first picture at the Royal Academy when age 13, Edwin Landseer became a popular English artist of the 19th century. He is primarily famous as a painter of dogs and other animals, especially in hunting and sporting scenes, light anthropomorphic studies, and sentimental subjects. He also excelled in other modes, including portraits, landscapes, sculpture, and book illustration. His father, the engraver John Landseer, was a fierce advocate of the dignity of his craft, but trained several of his children, including his youngest son Edwin, in other branches of art.

Edwin also studied briefly with Haydon, who encouraged him to learn from the old masters, the Elgin Marbles, and Haydon's own pictures of the dissection of a lion. Landseer's works evince both anatomical and art-historical awareness, as well as profound attention to the movements (if not always the behavior) of living wild and domestic animals. Much of this knowledge was acquired in the menageries of London, which he frequented all his life. He also had an unfailing grasp of the taste of his audiences, and from his earliest to his last works, he consistently pleased critics, aristocratic patrons, and the public, many of whom knew his pictures from prints executed by other members of his family.

Although notoriously childish even as an adult, Landseer was charming in person and moved easily in the highest society. From age 21 onward, he particularly pleased the Duchess of Bedford and is credited with fathering her last two children. The Duchess and her offspring appear regularly in his works, sometimes but not always as themselves. Landseer was also a friend of Scott, introducing the au-

thor, his animals, and his estate into several pictures and adopting Scotland as the home of his particular brand of nature, romanticizing both the sublime and humble aspects of the country and countryside.

Landseer's interests changed little over his career, and although enthusiasms and commissions sometimes led him to explore new ways of working, his crowd-pleasing formulae remained the same. His most popular animals are never quite animals, however naturalistic, but rather furry human beings, often yet not always sentimentalized. Correspondingly, Landseer's popular portraits with or without animals often suggest some doggy virtue in the sitters. *The Cat's Paw*, exhibited at the British Institution in 1824, exemplifies less saccharine Landseerian themes. Set in the laundry room of a prosperous household, it depicts a sadistic monkey using a cat's paw to flip hot chestnuts from the top of an ironing stove. As a study in cruelty, *The Cat's Paw* is in a realm entirely different from that of Hogarth's *First Stage of Cruelty*, which defines cruelty as radically human; by contrast, one Landseerian animal uses another in a peculiarly human way. This focus on pain is a recurrent motif in Landseer's work, which often depicts animals at the moment of violent death. The emphasis falls somewhere between, on one hand, the celebration of animal vitality in such works as the Elgin Marbles, Gericault's horses, or even Rubens's hunting scenes and, on the other, the sumptuous glorifications of dead flesh in Dutch genre painting.

Other famous Landseerian works invite the audience to regard the animals as possessing more exalted human characteristics, especially loyalty, as in *The Old Shepherd's Chief Mourner* (a solitary dog leans its chin upon its master's coffin), or dignity, as in *The Monarch of the Glen* (a highland stag sniffs the air heroically). The titles of some pictures impose a chivalric perspective upon the animals, as in *The Challenge* (a stag bellows at a rival) or *None But the Brave Deserve the Fair* (a crowd of hinds observes two stags at rut). The anthropomorphism, sexual tension, and accessible but ambiguous allegories of class in Landseer's best-known works are barely subordinated to an unprecedented naturalism; together all these contributed to the extraordinary popularity of these works and make them particularly susceptible to political and psychosocial analyses that have as yet barely begun.

In addition to the kind of work that made him famous, Landseer painted surprising landscapes, some of them devoid of both beasts and children, as well as several fine and undoggy portraits (especially *John Gibson, R.A.*); in the 1860s he sculpted those self-conscious emblems of empire, the huge lions in Trafalgar Square. A member of the Royal Academy since 1831, he was offered but declined the presidency of the institution in 1865. Following a long illness, he died in 1873.

Alexander S. Gourlay

Works Consulted

Lennie, Campbell. *Landseer: The Victorian Paragon*. London: Hamilton, 1976.

Manson, James A. *Sir Edwin Landseer, R.A.* New York: Scribner's, 1902.

Ormond, Richard. *Sir Edwin Landseer*. London: Thames, 1981.

Stephens, Frederic G. *Sir Edwin Landseer*. London: Low, 1883.

Lewis, Matthew Gregory

(1775–1818)

Known primarily as the author of *The Monk*, Matthew Gregory "Monk" Lewis also was a prolific translator, a popular playwright, a skilled poet, and a sensitive journal writer. He is an important literary figure because *The Monk* added a new dimension to Gothic fiction and because his translations introduced German Romanticism into the English literature.

The oldest of four children, Lewis was born in London of parents who separated when he was age 6. Throughout his life he maintained a forthright but loving correspondence with his mother, although it was she who had deserted the family, but his relationship with his father was turbulent until the two reconciled just prior to his father's death in 1812. Lewis had begun writing seriously by the time he was age 16, having written a farce, two volumes of an uncompleted novel, a partial translation of a French opera, and possibly, versions of two plays—*The East Indian* and *Village Virtues*—which were produced later. In 1796, he published *The Monk*, the only novel he wrote but the publication that established his literary reputation.

The Monk is a remarkable achievement, especially for one so young because it altered the course of Gothic fiction which until then had been characterized by the Radcliffean sentimental tale of terror. Lewis adds horror—that is, fear accompanied by a feeling of disgust or revulsion—to the genre, shocking his audience with a tale of sorcery, mob violence, rape, incest, and murder, including matricide. Many literary critics blasted the book as blasphemous and tasteless pornography, but this sensationalized reception only served to whet the reading public's appetite for the novel, which went through five editions in four years. It continues to appeal to the Gothic taste today, although modern readers, while perhaps finding parts of it vulgar, are unlikely to find it shocking. Because of the enormous publicity surrounding the book's appearance, its author was forever branded "Monk" Lewis, a nickname that he came to prefer to his given name. In spite of the success of *The Monk*, Lewis never returned to novel writing, preferring to pen verse and to write or translate for the theater, although he published three books of translated fiction: *The Bravo of Venice* (1805), *Feudal Tyrants* (1806), and *Romantic Tales* (1808).

Lewis's first love was the theater, and he published or had performed 17 dramatic pieces, three of them revisions of earlier works, during his lifetime. He wrote tragedies and Gothic dramas, and he translated and adapted plays from the German and French. His works were designed to satisfy the tastes of his age for spectacle and elaborate stage effects, and thus they have little modern appeal except for historians of the theater and students of Romanticism.

A little more than a year after the publication of *The Monk*, Lewis burst upon the theatrical scene with the production of his popular Gothic play *The Castle Spectre*, which ran for 48 nights at the Drury Lane Theatre beginning in 1797. Contemporary critics generally hated the play, but the audiences greeted it with unbridled enthusiasm, and it continued to be produced in England and America until 1834. Its popularity stemmed from its Gothic devices (a ghost, secret passages, a totally villainous villain, etc.), an elaborate setting and stage effects, and sentimental and melodramatic scenes. After the success of *The Castle Spectre*, Lewis turned to comedy with *The East Indian* (1799) and to farce with *The Twins* (1799); both were failures—*The Twins* had but one performance—but Lewis revised *The East Indian* in 1812 as a comic opera, *Rich and Poor*, also unsuccessful. Because of these dramatic failures, Lewis went back to his strength, the Gothic, with *Adelman, the Outlaw* (1801), but it, too, was unsuccessful.

Lewis next tried his hand at blank-verse tragedy, but *Alfonso, King of Castile* (1802) is not as tragic as it is melodramatic; it is undermined as effective tragedy by its emphasis on sensational devices and wooden characterization. But many critics admired it—possibly because of the dearth of contemporary tragedies at the time—and it found some success with audiences and readers, remaining relatively popular for a decade. This modest success was followed by an experimental monodrama, *The Captive* (1803), which was so vividly presented that during its initial performance many in the audience became hysterical; so extreme a reaction prevented the piece from being staged again. In the same year, *The Harper's Daughter* was produced successfully. It is an abridged version of *The Minister*, Lewis's 1797 translation of Schiller's *Kabale und Liebe*. Lewis's next theatrical effort was the highly successful *Rugatino, the Bravo of Venice* (1805), a dramatized version of his prose translation of J.H.D. Zschokke's *Aballino, der grosse Bandit*. This highly melodramatic play ran for 30 nights and played in the United States until 1826.

After these successful productions, Lewis brought out his most spectacular play yet, *The Wood Daemon* (1807), which was expanded in 1811 and retitled *One O'Clock*. The play combines virtually all of the day's Gothic conventions with a Faustian story, fairy lore, music, and pageantry. The play was performed 30 times in London and was well received in New York. Also in 1807, Lewis's tragedy, *Adelgitha; or, The Fruits of a Single Error*—four editions of which had been published in 1806—was staged eight times. It continued to be performed sporadically until 1835. In 1808, Lewis adapted a French Play, de Monvel's *Victimes cloîtrées*, as *Vernoni; or, The Monk of St. Marks*, which was at first unsuccessful but which when revised, ran for 18 performances early in 1809. His last play—outside of the revisions that appeared as *One O'Clock* and *Rich and Poor*—was *Timour the Tartan* (1811), which is more spectacle than drama with live horses, a waterfall, elaborate costumes, colorful pageantry, and a Gothic/Oriental setting. It was highly successful, running 44 nights in London and more than 50 in New York after its 1812 opening there.

Although his contemporary fame was based on *The Monk* and his plays, Lewis was also considered an accomplished poet. Scott, Shelley, and Coleridge, among others, admired some of his verse, much of which was originally published in *The Monk* and in his plays. In 1801, he issued *Tales of Wonder*, an anthology containing eight of his original poems and several of his poetic translations. In 1812 *Poems*, a collection of the work he considered his best, was published. His best poems, as is true with his plays, have a Gothic strain. His strength was not in his originality or profundity, but rather in his mechanical skills: he wrote smoothly in a wide variety of verse forms, but he left no poetry of lasting value.

Perhaps Lewis's finest work, although known today by only a handful of literary specialists, is his *Journal of a West India Proprietor*, published posthumously in 1834. The journal is a record of his two trips to Jamaica in 1815 and 1817 to supervise the two plantations he had inherited from his father. The stilted diction of *The Monk* and the declamatory style of the plays are not present here, but rather a direct and natural style laced with warmth and humor. The journal reflects Lewis's humanitarian views—which were well ahead of his time—concerning the welfare of the slaves on his plantations, and it is a vehicle for his recording of several Nancy stories (native folktales) still of great interest to folklorists.

Lewis was stricken with yellow fever on his second trip to Jamaica; he died of it on his way back to England in 1818, and was buried at sea. His burial was a fitting end for one who loved spectacle and melodrama; the weights on his coffin broke loose and the coffin resurfaced, the wind and current carrying it out of sight in the direction of Jamaica. (*See also* Antiquarianism, Gothicism, Novel.)

John A. Stoler

Works Consulted

Evans, Bertrand. *Gothic Drama from Walpole to Shelley*. Berkeley: U of California P, 1947.

Irwin, Joseph J. *M.G. "Monk" Lewis*. Boston: Twayne, 1976.

Parreaux, Andre. *The Publication of "The Monk": A Literary Event, 1796–1798*. Paris: Didier, 1960.

Peck, Louis F. *A Life of Matthew G. Lewis*. Cambridge: Harvard UP, 1961.

The *Liberal*

The *Liberal*, a journal of literary and political opinion edited by Byron, Leigh Hunt, and Shelley, helped define the political views of the younger generation of Romantic poets. In letters to Hunt in 1820, Shelley discussed Byron's desire to collaborate on a journal to be written for an English audience but to be edited in Pisa.

Shortly after Hunt's arrival in Italy to collaborate on this journal, Shelley drowned. Soon the journal was the cause of acrimonious feelings between Byron and Hunt, since Byron was compelled to support Hunt and his family single-handedly. Despite disagreements about money and divergent views on poetry, the four issues of the *Liberal* that appeared from October 1822, to July 1823, contain works of high literary merit and include, in addition to the work of its editors, contributions from

Mary Shelley, Hazlitt, Hogg, Charles Armitage Brown, and Horace Smith.

As Hunt and Byron prepared their periodical in 1822, revolutions had already occurred in Spain, Naples, and Portugal, and revolutionary sentiments existed among soldiers in France, Russia, and Prussia. In 1820, King Ferdinand of Spain attempted to suppress the revolt of his colonies in South America, but his army rebelled and demanded that he restore the constitution of 1812. A constitutional revolution occurred in Naples, and in August of that year, the Portuguese army rebelled and forced their monarch, then residing in Brazil, to adopt the Spanish constitution in a slightly altered form. With the exception of the German Empire, the entire south of Europe had become Jacobin.

The editors of the *Liberal* signaled their support for revolutionary changes brewing in Southern Europe in their subtitle, "Verse and Prose from the South." In choosing to call the journal, the *Liberal*, moreover, Byron may have been influenced by the Spanish party known as "the liberales," which had sought to impose a constitution on King Ferdinand in 1812. As early as 1816, the word "liberal" was used by Tory critics in England, first in its Spanish and then in its English form, to characterize the more radical members of the Whig opposition. When Byron joined the Carbonari in 1820 to liberate Italy from Austrian rule, he referred to his comrades as "liberals."

Despite its title, the *Liberal* was not conceived of by either Hunt or Byron as a political magazine. In fact, the *Liberal*, and Hunt in particular, objected to the mean, partisan spirit of politics. To nurture the liberal values of tolerance and sympathy, Hunt declared the journal's intention to publish poetry, essays, tales, and translations, emphasizing the works of Italian writers, like Alfieri and Ariosto, but also French and German translations as well. The *Liberal* was to be cosmopolitan in its literary tastes, fighting parochialism and blind partisanship wherever they appeared.

Even before its first issue arrived in England, however, the *Liberal* was attacked as the sworn enemy of religion, morals, and legitimacy. *Blackwood's Edinburgh Magazine* and *John Bull*, Scottish and English periodicals, respectively, decried the editorial union of a lord with a cockney, while *The Courier* attacked Shelley as a writer of infidel poetry. Hunt answered these charges in his preface to the first number of the *Liberal*. He defended Shelley, arguing that Shelley's very differences with religion proved his religious sensibility. Shelley and the editors of the *Liberal* defined morality more broadly than their critics, as a sense of justice and beneficence and not as a blind adherence to religious dogma. Lastly, Hunt questioned the meaning of legitimacy, criticizing those who propped up despotic regimes by making specious appeals to such a doctrine.

As Hunt had promised, the first number of the *Liberal* (October 15, 1822) was characterized by a mixture of politics and literature. Byron's *The Vision of Judgment* was a satire of Southey's *Vision of Judgment*, in which Southey praised King George III and depicted his triumphal entry into heaven. Byron portrayed the king as the enemy of liberty movements in America and France. No less controversial was the poet's squib on Castlereagh's suicide, which described the foreign secretary as the man who had slit his country's throat.

Hunt's contributions exposed the dangers of political partisanship. In *The Florentine Lovers*, based on Mario Lastris's *L'Osservatore Florentino*, he tells how the youthful love of Ippolito and Dionas enables them to transcend the ancient political rivalry of their parents' families. Hunt's translations from Alfieri, Politian, and Ariosto were meant to broaden the taste of his readers. Shelley's sole entry was his translation of "May Night" from Goethe's *Faust*.

Though Byron's *Heaven and Earth* opened the second number of the *Liberal* (January 1, 1823), the most overtly political entry was Hunt's *The Dogs*, a verse satire on the Duke of Wellington.

In their advertisement to the third number (April 25, 1823), the editors of the *Liberal* praised the Spanish liberals for resisting King Ferdinand and welcomed George Canning as a more liberal foreign secretary than Lord Castlereagh, the man he replaced. As early as its first issue, the *Liberal* criticized Foreign Secretary Castlereagh for a system of congressional diplomacy that involved England too closely in the affairs of Eastern autocrats, like Austria's Metternich. Although Canning continued Castlereagh's policy, he won the support of the Whig opposition by recognizing the independence of Spain's South American colonies (1824), using British force to defend constitutional government in Portugal (1824), and supporting the cause of Greek independence (1826).

With the exception of the advertisement, the third volume treated only political topics through the medium of literature. The volume opened with Byron's "The Blues, A Literary Eclogue," a satire of aristocratic women who attend literary functions in Regency England.

By the time the fourth issue of the *Liberal* was published (July 30, 1823), Byron had been persuaded by critics and friends like Moore and John Cab Hobhouse to abandon the publication.

Reaction to the *Liberal* ranged from indifference to outrage. Whig and Radical papers, such as Richard Carlile's *Republican* and Cobbett's *Political Register*, did not rally to support the *Liberal* because they were more interested in politics than in literature. Conservative papers like the *Morning Post* and the *New Times*, on the other hand, kept silent for fear of increasing the sales of such a seditious work. Typical of the more vocal opponents of the *Liberal* was the *Literary Chronicle and Weekly Review*, which faulted the editors for failing to live up to the title of their periodical. Byron's *Epigrams on Lord Castlereagh* was cited as a particularly illiberal treatment of the foreign secretary. While praising Shelley's translation of "May Night" and Byron's *Heaven and Earth*, *Blackwood's Edinburgh Review* commented on the unequal partnership of Byron and Hunt, a recurrent theme in other reviews as well.

Influenced by negative reviews and poor sales of the *Liberal*, as well as by his own desire to set out for Greece in July 1823, Byron withdrew from the journal, claiming that his contributions had done more to hurt the publication than to promote it. Not surprised by Byron's withdrawal, Leigh Hunt had already invested his energies elsewhere, working on the first issue of the *Literary Examiner*, which appeared in 1823. He published his own version of his collaboration with Byron on the *Liberal* five years later in *Lord Byron and Some of His Contemporaries* (1828). The remainder of the Pisan circle returned to England to face a country more conservative than the editors of the *Liberal* would have liked. (*See also* Journalism.)

Jonathan Gross

Works Consulted

Blunden, Edmund. *Leigh Hunt and His Circle*. New York: Harper, 1930.

Byron and Leigh Hunt: The Liberal, Verse and Prose From the South. Vols. 1–4. Salzburg: U of Salzburg P, 1978.

Cline, C.L. *Byron, Shelley and Their Pisan Circle.* New York: Russell, 1969.

Halévy, Elié. *A History of the English People in the Nineteenth Century.* 2 vols. Trans. E.I. Watkin. New York: Smith, 1949.

Houtchens, Lawrence and Carolyn. *Leigh Hunt's Political and Occasional Essays.* New York: Columbia UP, 1962.

Marshall, William. *Byron, Shelley, Hunt, and the Liberal.* Philadelphia: U of Pennsylvania P, 1960.

Woodring, Carl. *Politics in English Romantic Poetry.* Cambridge: Harvard UP, 1970.

Linnell, John

(1792–1882)

John Linnell was a popular landscape painter in Britain after the death of Turner in 1851. Although Linnell was known best for "poetic landscapes"—a hybrid of the picturesque and a religiously inspired love of nature—he also produced portraits, miniatures, drawings, biblical illustrations, etchings, and engravings. His detailed landscapes include such oil paintings as *The River Kennet near Newbury*, *The Kensington Gravel Pits*, and *Noah: The Eve of the Deluge*. Linnell's theories of nature, beauty and art were at odds with those of Reynolds, Fuseli, Flaxman and the 19th-century English art establishment, which believed that close observation and recording of nature were not, in themselves, art.

At age 13, Linnell was apprenticed to John Varley. During this time, he encountered the picturesque—undulating, gnarled forms and a delight in rugged ruin—and nature, by working in oil colors out of doors. Although belief in individuality and the equality of all later caused him to abandon organized religion in favor of a personal interpretation of the Scriptures, his conversion to the Baptist faith in 1811 proved a powerful influence on his depiction of nature. Linnell understood nature's design as direct proof of God's existence.

Truth to nature formed an artistic witness; therefore, accurate, enlightened description constituted a moral obligation. But while "visionary," his was not an innocent eye; it was conditioned by his Royal Academy training and, in his early work, a commitment to location. Unlike Blake, he never relied on an imaginary landscape; his works show an empirical observation of material fact.

Linnell was intimately connected with Palmer and Blake, whom he met in 1818. He helped and encouraged Blake by commissioning 21 watercolors (1821) and 22 engravings (1823) illustrating Job, as well as the Dante plates (1824). Despite their differences in favored genres and mediums for composition, the friendship between Blake and Linnell led to their collaboration on a projected annual publication with plates by both artists. Linnell also introduced many younger artists to Blake's circle, including Varley, Palmer, and Calvert. In fact, Palmer married Linnell's daughter Hannah (1818–93), who was also an artist. (*See also* the Ancients.)

Until about 1845, Linnell painted and engraved portraits, chiefly for economic reasons. Thereafter, he devoted himself to portraying landscapes and historical landscapes with religious subjects (e.g., *The Journey to Emmaus* and *The Halt by the Jordan*). Although Ruskin considered its fidelity to nature scrupulous but almost too refined, Linnell's *Noah: The Eve of the Deluge* (1848) made his reputation. His works were admired and sought after but not officially sanctioned. He submitted his name for associateship to the Royal Academy for 21 successive years, only to be excluded each time. Linnell then refused every suggestion that he reapply; by the 1860s, that an artist of such repute was not a member caused some embarrassment for the Royal Academy.

Linnell's injunction to study nature and learn from the exactness of Dürer's engravings recommended him to the Pre-Raphaelites, whom he defended at the Royal Academy exhibition of 1851. His later style consisted of quick, impressionistic brushstrokes and an attempt to erase all reference to particular places, thereby freeing his landscapes from topographical connotation. He referred to his later pictures as "aspects of nature." By the end of his career, his vision of landscape had developed into a dramatic, apocalyptic view of nature in which specific features were less significant than total effect. The purely visual quality of his early work gave way to a literal symbolism: his sheep, harvests, and storms made ideal religious icons for mid-Victorian England. Nonetheless his artistic beliefs and constant love of nature allowed him to be one of the few landscape artists of his time to offer awe in place of pastoral sentimentality. (*See also* Landscape Painting; Visionary Landscape Painting.)

D.C. Woodcox

Works Consulted

Crouan, Katherine. *John Linnell: A Centennial Exhibition*. 1982.

Essick, Robert N. "John Linnell, William Blake, and the Printmaker's Craft." *Huntington Library Quarterly*. (1983).

Firestone, Evan Richard. "John Linnell, English Artist: Works, Patrons and Dealers." Diss. U of Wisconsin, 1971.

Story, Alfred T. *The Life of John Linnell*. 2 vols. London: Bentley, 1892.

Vaughan, William. *Romantic Art*. London: Thames, 1978.

Literacy

Literacy is notoriously difficult to measure before the mid-19th century, since literacy figures as such were not kept. But contemporary comment, as well as statistical evidence gleaned from existing records, suggests that literacy expanded gradually but significantly during the Romantic period in England.

Literacy was widely perceived as a potent force—for good or ill—in British society. Methodists distributed religious literature and confined their instruction to reading only because they saw the rise in literacy among the lower orders as a profoundly destabilizing force, threatening the very basis of the social order. Others heralded the spread of basic literacy (particularly if managed by the church, the state, or the professional classes) as a means to control or contain an increasingly mobile and restive populace, whether through imparting "habits of subordination" along with the rudiments of letters or through educating the lower classes to consider their interests congruent with those of the dominant group. Others (though surprisingly few) welcomed the growth of literacy as a leveling or democratizing force—the common view today.

The only reliable means of gauging literacy rates during this period is to extrapolate from changing percentages of those able to sign their names in parish marriage registers. (The number of those able to read at some level was probably significantly higher than the number of those able to sign.) Studies of literacy—suggestive rather than definitive—based on marriage registers have been made by Lawrence Stone and R.S. Schofield.

Stone, organizing his data by social class, maintains that literacy rates for the upper classes (i.e., landed gentry, clergy, and professionals) remained at near 100 percent between 1640 and 1900; that rates rose from 75 to 95 percent for the rural middle classes (i.e., yeomen and husbandmen) and from 85 to 95 percent for the urban middle classes (i.e., artisans and shopkeepers) between 1780 and 1840; and that literacy rates for laborers, after remaining stable throughout the 18th century, rose from 40 to 60 percent in the early 19th century.

Schofield, organizing his data by gender, concludes that the percentage of women able to sign their names rose from 35 to 40 percent in 1750 to better than 50 percent in 1840, with a turning point in the mid-1780s; the percentage for men rose (with some variation) from 60 percent in 1795 to about 75 percent by 1840, with noticeable improvement occurring between 1805 and 1815.

The slow pace of change these studies suggest, particularly when contrasted with the rapid growth of literacy in the later 19th century, does not invalidate the notion of a literacy "crisis" or "problem," beginning in the 1790s, posed by earlier social historians like Richard D. Altick and Robert Kiefer Webb. That many during this period considered the unforeseen emergence of a reading public a critical issue cannot be denied; but the sense of crisis probably stemmed from the belated recognition, beginning in the 1790s, of a phenomenon slowly building over the course of a century or more. The unprecedented sales of Paine's *Rights of Man*— 50,000 copies of the first part (1791) and from 200,000 to 500,000 of the inexpensive second part (1793)—caused widespread unease among the established interests. Radical tracts were prohibited in 1795 and 1798, and legislation facilitating censorship was again passed in 1817 and 1819; the stamp duty was raised to limit the circulation of antiestablishment newspapers in 1797 and in 1815. Groups like the Society for Promoting Christian Knowledge and the Religious Tract Society took up the mission of counteracting "seditious" pamphlets with pious tracts designed for popular consumption. Some two million of More's *Cheap Repository Tracts*—modeled on popular chapbooks and charged with political and social conservatism—were distributed in the late 1790s. The British and Foreign Bible Society issued 2.5 million copies of the Bible between 1804 and 1819.

Educational institutions catering to poor children, such as the Sunday Schools and Bell's "Madras" schools, imparted habits of obedience and social complacency along with basic reading skills. Like Bell and others in the period, More (active in the Sunday School movement) held that reading, but not writing, should be taught to poor children, since knowing how to write might make them discontented with their station. Other conservatives argued that schools for the poor should be discouraged altogether. Liberals like Maria Edgeworth believed instead that literacy could be a means of teaching the lower classes their true interests. Edgeworth's *Popular Tales* (1804) built on the earlier efforts of More and Trimmer, who aimed her *Family Magazine* (1788–89) at "cottagers and servants," by helping to establish a new, moralized popular literature to counteract both radical pamphlets and the uncensored and unregulated chapbooks. Trimmer and Edgeworth were also key figures in the reformation of children's literature, which had become a lucrative trade only in the mid-18th century. Beginning in the 1780s, children's fiction became a major growth industry, providing middle-class parents with graded, sanitized, and didactic readings with which to teach their children.

Not only children's and popular literature were affected by the spread and growing importance of literacy during the Romantic period. A new array of journals and newspapers emerged at this time in response to—while helping to shape the reading habits of—new audiences. The growing number of literate middle-class women with leisure time to read undoubtedly facilitated the increased popularity of the novel—particularly the Gothic and domestic genres—during the late 18th and early 19th centuries. The same group provided a readership for popular women poets, like Hemans and Landon. It is likely, though perhaps impossible to prove, that a poetics such as that of the early Wordsworth—grounded in "language really used by men," concerned with "common" experience, and addressed to the general rather than specialized reader—is related to the emergence (or perceived emergence) in this period of a more widely based readership. In his later years, however, Wordsworth came to share the anxiety regarding a large "Reading Public," which Coleridge expresses in *The Statesman's Manual* (1816). This attitude was parodied by Peacock in *Nightmare Abbey* (1818) and attacked by Hazlitt in his essay "What is the People?" (1818).

If the extent and effects of the spread of literacy in the Romantic period are harder to judge than the reactions of contemporary observers suggest, its causes are difficult to determine as well. Certainly provisions for education, especially among the middle and lower classes, grew significantly throughout the period. But more schools do not always correlate with higher literacy rates, and many in the period—from all social classes—received their most basic instruction at home.

Historians no longer believe that industrialization is directly related to increased literacy; in fact, literacy rates often fell in highly industrialized areas (due mainly to the prevalence of child labor). Cultural factors—such as the stress on Bible reading among Methodists, Evangelicals, and other Protestant groups and the promi-

nent role of reading and writing in working-class political life—may be equally or more directly important than economic factors. Educational and polemical writings of the period frequently cite the need to impose order on a populace shaken loose from its traditional moorings in church and local community as a primary reason for encouraging (passive if not active) literacy. (*See also* Children's Literature, Education, Lower Classes.)

Alan Richardson

Works Consulted

Altick, Richard D. *The English Common Reader: A Social History of the Mass Reading Public, 1800–1900*. Chicago: U of Chicago P, 1957.

Klancher, Jon P. *The Making of English Reading Audiences, 1790–1832*. Madison: U of Wisconsin P, 1987.

Laqueur, Thomas W. "Toward a Cultural Ecology of Literacy in England, 1600–1850." *Literacy in Historical Perspective*. Ed. Daniel P. Resnick. 1983: 43–57.

Schofield, R.S. "Dimensions of Illiteracy, 1750–1850." *Explorations in Economic History* 10 (1973): 437–54.

Smith, Olivia. *The Politics of Language, 1791–1819*. Oxford: Clarendon, 1984.

Stone, Lawrence. *Literacy and Education in England, 1640–1900. Past and Present*. Boston: Routledge, 1981.

Webb, Robert Kiefer. *The British Working Class Reader, 1790–1848: Literacy and Social Tension*. London: Allen, 1955.

Literary Criticism and Literary Theory

During the Romantic period, literary critics explored with originality and insight issues that remain significant two centuries later. Drawing inspiration from late-18th-century German philosophy and British psychology and criticism, as well as from contemporary innovations in poetry and fiction, critics revolutionized literary theory and criticism. The Romantics placed feeling, rather than reason and skill, at the center of creativity and literary influence, and they redefined such significant critical terms as nature, imagination, symbol, and sympathy. They also introduced new standards, values, and critical practices and revised the canon of literary classics in favor of Dante, Spenser, Shakespeare, and Milton.

The Romantic writers, like earlier generations of Western critics, used the term "poetry" for all imaginative literature written in verse, yet they reversed earlier priorities by treating lyric poetry as the central genre and by occasionally extending the term "poetry" to all creative efforts concerned with human emotions rather than facts.

Responsible for most of this period's lasting contributions to literary theory are a few major poet critics whose insights are widely scattered among their prose writings and poems. Among them, only Coleridge, in *Biographia Literaria* (1817) and elsewhere, produced a significant body of literary theory and put it to effective use in criticism of works by Shakespeare and by his friend Wordsworth. Wordsworth and Shelley wrote critical manifestos—the Preface to the 1800 edition of *Lyrical Ballads* and *A Defence of Poetry* (written in 1821)—and incorporated ideas into major poems, as Wordsworth did in *The Prelude* (written 1805). Less immediately influential were the views of other major poets, expressed by Keats in poems and letters to his family, by Byron in poems and letters to his friends, and by Blake in poems, witty epigrams for *The Marriage of Heaven and Hell*, and angry annotations to Reynolds's Neoclassical classic, *Discourses on Art*.

Romantic contemporaries recognized in Romantic poems and in Wordsworth's Preface only a limited range of innova-tions: personal feelings, common-life subjects, ordinary diction, and reduced emphasis on metrics. They had little wider knowledge of critical theory, finding Coleridge's theoretical writings unintelligible and knowing other major figures only as poets. Since 1830, however, each generation of English-speaking literary theorists and historians has reinterpreted and reevaluated Romantic theory and literary practice. When such Victorian critics as Arnold, Carlyle, and Pater adapted Romantic ideas to their own purposes, they drew attention to Wordsworth's interest in the poet's emotions, Coleridge's theory that poetic symbols mediate between reality and the human mind, and the Romantic movement's broader appeal to the universally human trait of curiosity.

But some Victorian generalizations about Romantic criticism and poetry suggest that Romanticism was immature: emotional at the expense of intellect and education, subjective rather than attentive to reality, self-cultivating instead of socially and morally committed. T.S. Eliot argued that the fusion of intellect and emotion which he admired in poetry was destroyed in the 18th century and only revived in late-19th-century France; Irving Babbitt (1919) deplored Rousseau's influence, emotionalism at the expense of moral and aesthetic standards; T.E. Hulme called Romanticism a "spilt religion" (1924) that sacrificed precision to yearning after the infinite; and Mario Praz (1933) deplored its nihilism and decadence.

In the mid-20th century, Herbert Read (1936) affirmed the Romantics' interest in the imagination and the unconscious; Marxists, like Christopher Caudwell (1936), deplored their bourgeois individualism, while Jacques Barzum (1943) defended their constructive and creative response to revolutionary changes.

Two influential mid-century studies, each an inspiration for later commentary, gave modern scholars parameters for generalizing about Romanticism and Romantic criticism. The first, Rene Wellek's "The Concept of Romanticism" (1949), identifies three common elements in European Romanticism: "imagination for the view of poetry, nature for the view of the world, and symbol and myth for poetic style." The second, M.H. Abrams's *The Mirror and the Lamp* (1953), isolates a single unifying characteristic of Romantic criticism: its focus on the poet as central to literary creation. For his historical survey of literary theories, Abrams describes four coordinates of literary creation, any one of which can become central to a literary theory: reality, the reader or the audience, the poet, and the text itself. Abrams argues that Romantic critical theory overturns two older positions—the reality-based mimetic notion that poetry is a mirror of experience and the pragmatic concern with how literature affects readers—and replaces them with an expressive poet-centered belief that poetry is the product of a writer's unique perceptions, a lamp that transforms experience. This theory was overturned by modern formalist emphasis on the poetic text itself.

Abrams's coordinates may help to suggest a multifaceted unity. The major Romantic critics are similar, first, in their way of understanding reality, which they associated with nature as life force and dynamic process. Modifying the associationist psychology of Hartley and drawing at times on German philosophers Kant and Schlegel, Romantic critics sought to know reality or truth, to bridge the separation of perceiving subject from perceived object, through feelings and imagination. These allow the human mind to take an active role and apprehend aspects of reality not accessible to the intellect alone, or to the senses, or to the passive recall that Coleridge terms the fancy. (*See also* German Idealism, Influence of; Kant and Theories of German Idealism.) All humans participate in this higher process, a creative activity that Coleridge, in *Biographia Literaria*, calls the "primary imagination" and describes as "the living Power and prime Agent of all human perception, . . . a repetition in the finite mind of the eternal act of creation in the infinite I AM."

But the process of apprehension and the reality apprehended are variously understood. For Wordsworth, reality is always present in nature but comes to the surface of human awareness only gradually, by an ongoing dialectic interaction with an egotistical mind, an interaction whose emblem is the vision of Mount Snowdon's peak through mist at the climax of the *Prelude*. For Coleridge, the apprehending mind must become one with a transcendent reality; for Blake, reality is transcendent yet encompasses the world of the senses; while for Keats, who wrote "what the imagination seizes as Beauty must be truth," reality is a dimension of the sensual world absorbed into the self.

When describing the poet, Romantic critics built on their psychology of knowledge and singled out the poet for heightened resources of imagination, feeling, and insight, for exceptional memory, creativity, and communication, and even for prophetic powers. The Romantic notion of the poet as hero and mythmaker has roots in 18th-century criticism, but the Romantics also insisted on common ties of feeling and experience that poets share with all humans. Thus, for Wordsworth in the 1800 Preface, poetic creation begins with "the spontaneous overflow of powerful feelings," which are nourished by thought and understanding and revived in the act of creation as "emotion recollected in tranquility"; in an 1802 appendix, he describes the poet as "a man speaking to men . . . embued with more lively sensibility, . . . who has a greater knowledge of human nature, and a more comprehensive soul" than the average person. (*See also* Emotion Recollected in Tranquility, Real Language of Men, Spontaneous Overflow of Powerful Feelings.) Coleridge calls the poet's gift the "secondary imagination," which "dissolves, diffuses, dissipates, in order to recreate . . . [or] struggles to idealize and to unify"; Shelley and Blake ascribed to the poet exceptional sources of inspiration. In Shelley's *Defence of Poetry*, the "mind in creation is as a fading coal" that lights up with inspiration and gains direct insight into the order and beauty of the universe; Blake, in *The Marriage of Heaven and Hell*, credits Milton with unconscious awareness that life is dynamic and composed of contraries. Even Byron, Neoclassical in defending poetic craftsman Pope, associated his own creative work with periods of intense feeling, even madness. By assigning a prominent role to imagination and emotions, the Romantics made the poet's private experience central to poetic creation, whereas 18th-century poets had spoken as public figures.

The reader, therefore, experiences poetry first as pleasure but also feels a psychological and moral impact that not only strengthens the imagination and molds sympathies in individuals but also as a potential for reforming society. Wordsworth in the 1800 Preface, after comments about enlightening his reader and improving the reader's affections, concludes with the hope that poetic pleasures may have lasting moral influence. Coleridge shows concern with readers when describing the genesis of *Lyrical Ballads:* the two poets, believing that a poem might combine "the power of exciting the sympathy" that derives from "truth of nature" with "the interest of novelty" that requires "modifying colours of the imagination," decided that Coleridge would make the supernatural seem real enough to produce a "willing suspension of disbelief" and Wordsworth would "give the charm of novelty to things of every day" to produce "a feeling analogous to the supernatural." (*See also* Willing Suspension of Disbelief.) The former would cultivate the imagination; the latter, "[awaken] the mind's attention from the lethargy of custom" and "selfish solicitude" by which "we have eyes, yet see not, ears that hear not, and hearts that neither feel nor understand."

Blake's provocative assertions about history and literature in *The Marriage of Heaven and Hell* challenge readers to question traditional standards, both aesthetic and moral. And when Shelley declares, in *The Defence of Poetry*, that "poets are the unacknowledged legislators of the world," he makes strong claims for the power of literature, as it gives pleasure, to influence the political and social order by morally improving its readers. Since "the great secret of morals is Love," a good person must "put himself in the place of another and of many others; the pains and pleasures of his species must become his own. The great instrument of moral good is the imagination; and poetry administers to the effect by acting on the cause."

When the Romantic poet critics described the poem or literary text and suggested suitable subjects and standards of excellence, they took over 18th-century questions about the nature of poetry. But they overturned earlier answers, favoring particularities as well as general truths of human nature, subject matter from both enduring myths and living persons from all walks of life, vocabulary also suited to prose, imagery, and symbols from nature, and poetic form that instead of following rules takes shape organically and brings harmony to contrasts. The classic document is Wordsworth's Preface of 1800: if poetry is to provide direct experience of a reality apprehended by feeling, unmediated by artifices of language and culture, it should draw on lower-class lives not only for its subject matter but also for its language, while retaining metrical verse for pleasurable effects. Coleridge, recognizing that Wordsworth's language is hardly that of the common person, contributes to Romantic poetics the definition of beauty as "multeity in unity" and a preference for the symbol, which "partakes of the Reality which it renders intelligible" and mediates between reality and language, over allegory, which separates.

The Romantic age was rich as well in critical writing and reviewing, mostly anonymous, by other poets and novelists, by lawyers and church dignitaries, and by professional men of letters, attracted to criticism by the value their age placed on literature as well as by significant increases in fees. During the 18th century, improvements in literacy, education, leisure time, and incomes had helped shape a substantial middle-class reading public that spurred growth of literary and critical writing. Though books and periodicals were expensive, serial publication, reprint series, and lending libraries made reading material accessible. Vehicles for criticism included not only literary biographies and histories, book prefaces, poems, and venerable monthly reviews, but also, especially after 1800, the *Edinburgh* and *Quarterly* reviews, new weekly and monthly magazines, daily newspapers, and lecture series. Literature was not yet an academic discipline, so criticism was journalism; no journal or critic focused exclusively on

imaginative literature. For their expanded public, poets like Hunt and Southey wrote essays and reviews, and novelist Scott, prefaces and articles. Among men of letters, Hazlitt produced the most significant critical writings; essayists De Quincey and Lamb also left their marks, as did reviewers Jeffrey of the *Edinburgh* and Lockhart of the *Quarterly*. (*See also* Journalism.)

The best of the lesser critics stated principles that resemble those of the major poets but offered new perspectives as well. Thus, Hazlitt, in "On Poetry in General" (1818), asserted that poetry expresses emotions but also appeals to the intellect and morality, yet later defined poetic genius, in contrast to the high seriousness of Wordsworth, as self-forgetful and spontaneous. De Quincey in 1823 stated his belief, later elaborated in his essay "Literature of Knowledge and Literature of Power" (1848), that the "power" of poetry derives from awakening and giving shape to human emotions. Other critics preserved 18th-century values, notably Jeffrey, who insisted on refined language and subject matter.

Romantic practical criticism—anonymous, rich in quotation, and impressionistic rather than based on systematic application of theory—includes much insightful appreciation and analysis. It is a modern commonplace to speak of Romantic reviewing as partisan and contentious, but much evinces widespread fair-mindedness and a serious critical purpose of offering guidance to writers. Though Jeffrey's 1814 rebuke to Wordsworth's *Excursion*, "This will never do," remains a widely quoted instance of the reception of poets and though reviewers seized on the minor flaws in what became the lasting poetic works of the age, critical responses to Romantic poetry were largely favorable. Each poet found fit critics—Wordsworth in Coleridge and John Wilson ("Christopher North"), Shelley and Keats in Hunt, Byron in Lockhart — and a few writers inspired classics of literary biography, such as Lockhart's *Life of Scott* (1838) and Moore's *Life of Byron* (1830).

More influential than analyses of contemporary poets were the Romantics' revaluations of earlier British writers. The plays of Shakespeare, for instance, inspired many lecture series, essays, and books. From Hazlitt's *Characters of Shakespeare's Plays* (1817), Coleridge's lectures of Shakespeare (1811–14), Lamb's "On the Tragedies of Shakespeare Reconsidered" (1811), and De Quincey's "On the Knocking at the Gate in Macbeth" (1823) emerged both the strengths and the limitations of the 19th-century image of the Bard. Reading the plays as novels in verse, critics slighted dramatic and theatrical elements, preferring to analyze style, poetic imagery, and above all the psychology of characters ranging from Hamlet to Iago. Other Renaissance and Jacobean playwrights were appreciated for their emotional impact on readers by Lamb in *Specimens of English Dramatic Poets* (1808) and by Hazlitt in *Dramatic Literature of the Age of Elizabeth* (1820).

The Romantics also contributed the earliest serious British criticism of the novel, a genre which, though not widely recognized as poetry or art, would dominate the Victorian literary scene. Scott, the most popular novelist, wrote appreciative criticism of his own writings and of works by fellow novelists from Defoe and Fielding to Austen and Edgeworth. Hazlitt's *Lectures on the English Comic Writers* (1819) called attention to a comic tradition established by English and Continental novelists and to dramatists of the two preceding centuries. Romantic reviewers of contemporary fiction, concerned about the novel's wide audience, valued truthful portrayal of character and paid special attention to moral influence. In prose fiction, realistic portrayals of contemporary life and of history, which would flourish among the Victorians, were preferred to supernatural fictions and to philosophical tales like those of Godwin.

Toward the end of the Romantic period, expectations from imaginative literature became increasingly diversified. Valuing literature for psychological, spiritual, or aesthetic effects were writers ranging from the utilitarian Mill to religious leaders Keble and Newman, as well as poet critics like Arthur Henry Hallam and Richard Hengist Horne. Other critics expressed what would become mid-Victorian concerns, expecting literature to be a vehicle for teaching facts, or questioning the value of poetry in a practical age, as did satirist Peacock in fictional caricatures and in "The Four Ages of Poetry" (1818), the inspiration for Shelley's "Defence," or Thomas Bibington Macaulay in "Milton" (1825), where poetry is called a "magic lantern" whose light was fading. Meanwhile Carlyle, in "Characteristics" (1831), *Sartor Resartus* (1833–34), and *On Heroes and Hero Worship* (1840), was articulating what would become a central theme of Victorian criticism, feeding reservations about the Romantics: literature sustains modern humanity in its spiritual, moral, and emotional nature, while shaping each nation's culture.

Monika Brown

Works Consulted

Abrams, M.H. *The Mirror and the Lamp: Romantic Theory and the Critical Tradition.* New York: Oxford UP, 1953.

Bate, Walter Jackson. *From Classic to Romantic: Premises of Taste in Eighteenth Century England.* 1946. New York: Harper, 1961.

Engell, James. *Forming the Critical Mind: Dryden to Coleridge*. Cambridge: Harvard UP, 1989.

Gleckner, Robert F., and Gerald E. Enscoe, eds. *Romanticism: Points of View*. 2nd ed. Englewood Cliffs: Prentice, 1970.

Hayden, John O. *The Romantic Reviewers, 1802–1824*. Chicago: U of Chicago P, 1968.

Kroeber, Karl. *British Romantic Art*. Berkeley: U of California P, 1986.

McGann, Jerome J. *The Romantic Ideology: A Critical Investigation*. Chicago: U of Chicago P, 1983.

Mahoney, John L. *The Whole Internal Universe: Imitation and the New Defense of Poetry in British Criticism, 1660–1830*. New York: Fordham UP, 1985.

Parrinder, Patrick. *Authors and Authority: A Study of English Literary Criticism and Its Relation to Culture, 1750–1900*. Boston: Routledge, 1977.

Prickett, Stephen. ed. *The Romantics*. New York: Holmes, 1981.

Wellek, Rene. *Concepts of Criticism*. Ed. Stephen G. Nichols. New Haven: Yale UP, 1963.

———. *The Romantic Age*. 1955. Cambridge: Cambridge UP, 1981. Vol. 2 of *A History of Modern Criticism, 1750–1950*. 5 vols. 1955– .

Lockhart, John Gibson

(1794–1854)

John Gibson Lockhart was one of Scotland's most prominent men of letters in the early 19th century. Today, he is most remembered as a critic and biographer, but he was also a journalist, editor, poet, and novelist. (*See also* Essay, Journalism, Literary Criticism and Literary Theory.)

Lockhart attended the University of Glasgow before he went to Oxford on a fellowship, graduating in 1813. He studied law in Edinburgh and became a lawyer, but his interests were always in literature. In 1817, these interests found an outlet in the new *Blackwood's Edinburgh Magazine*. *Blackwood's* outlook was Tory, and its owner was looking for more lively material than that in the chief Tory organ, the *Quarterly*

Review. Lockhart, together with Wilson and Hogg, began writing for the magazine, sometimes in collaboration and sometimes individually. Their most notorious joint effort was the "Chaldee Manuscript" (October 1817), a highly irreverent satire on contemporary Edinburgh literary society. The piece became a scandal, greatly boosting *Blackwood's* circulation and encouraging Lockhart in even more free-swinging satire. This impulse spilled over into his literary criticism also, and he became known as "the Scorpion" (a nickname he invented) because of his vicious reviews of writers he considered inept or immoral.

Keats, Leigh Hunt, and Coleridge were among Lockhart's early targets. Lockhart invented the abusive term "the Cockney school of poetry" and consigned Hunt and Keats to it. His attack on Keats's *Endymion* (1818) was widely rumored to have hurt the poet so badly that his death was hastened (the rumor figures in Shelley's *Adonais*). Lockhart's review is cruel, even by the rough-and-tumble standards of the age, and it certainly angered Keats, but to say it caused his death is exaggeration. Even Byron found it hard to believe, as he put it in *Don Juan*, that Keats's soul, "that fiery particle," could have been extinguished by "an article."

Another harsh review caused Lockhart personal trouble. In 1821, John Scott, the editor of the *London*, challenged Lockhart to a duel over some *Blackwood's* pieces (not all of which were Lockhart's). Lockhart went to London to meet Scott, who then backed down from the challenge. After Lockhart left, Scott became angry again, now forcing a fight with Lockhart's friend and second, Jonathan Christie. In the ensuing duel, Christie shot and killed Scott. The sad affair sobered Lockhart greatly, and he began to temper the intellectual arrogance behind his biting reviews.

His recent marriage to the daughter of Walter Scott was also helping to tame his arrogance and make him more thoughtful and tolerant. Scott had enormous influence over his new son-in-law, which led Lockhart to distance himself from *Blackwood's*, with its rough reputation, and to look into other literary pursuits. One of his last forays into the harsh world of literary warfare was his anonymously published pamphlet, *John Bull's Letter to Lord Byron* (1821). The tone of the letter is extremely insolent, though its content is surprising: Lockhart praises *Don Juan* highly and describes most of Byron's earlier work as "humbug"—he was one of the few critics to see the genuine value in *Don Juan* at the time. Because of the tone and the many snide remarks about other authors, such as Wordsworth, the pamphlet caused a stir. Lockhart was anxious that Scott not find out that he had been the author, knowing that it would lower Scott's opinion of him. And Scott's opinion clearly was of more merit to him now than was his reputation as the Scorpion. Between 1820 and 1824 he wrote four novels. None were successful in their time or since. However, the best of them, *Adam Blair*, is worthy of modern reader's attention: a tragic tale of adultery and repentance, it powerfully integrates the brooding Scottish scenery with the characters and their fates.

In 1825, Lockhart accepted the offer of the editorship of the *Quarterly Review*—an even more respectable publication than *Blackwood's*. He moved to London to take up the post, which he held until 1853. He handled the job admirably and proved to be an indefatigable and highly effective writer and editor. One of his chief contributors was Croker, who in some ways played the role of scorpion for the *Quarterly*, reviewing Tennyson in 1833 with the same kind of cruel contempt that Lockhart had used with Keats. By this time, however, Lockhart had largely mellowed.

During this period, Lockhart began to write biography, producing a life of Burns in 1829 and beginning a life of Napoleon the same year. Both were successful, and both are worth reading today. But the death in 1831 of Scott, his deeply loved father-in-law, spurred him to write his masterpiece, the massive seven-volume *Life of Sir Walter Scott* (1837–38). The book was an enormous success and continued to be so long after Lockhart's death; even today, some critics feel that after Boswell's *Life of Johnson*, Lockhart's biography of Scott is the greatest in the language.

Lockhart's stated intention in the book is to present Scott as much as he can through Scott's own words, using letters and journals wherever possible. And in fact, about one-half of the *Life* consists of material from such sources. But this should not minimize Lockhart's contributions to the book. His narrative is well-constructed and often his scenes powerful (e.g., his long section untangling the financial arrangements that led to Scott's ruin and, in the final volume, his description of Scott's sad final months). Later critics have charged that family loyalties caused Lockhart to leave out much that was negative about Scott; to some degree this is true, but most of his omissions can be justified. Perhaps the most striking aspect of the *Life* is the image it gives of Lockhart: in the place of the Scorpion is a critic who combines discrimination with generosity. In a letter in 1838 he wrote: "I now think with deep sadness of the pain my jibes and jokes inflicted on better men than myself, and I can say that I have omitted in my mature years no opportunity of trying to make reparation where I really had been the offender."

After the death of his wife Sophia in 1837, he continued as the *Quarterly* editor and devoted himself to his children. His daughter Charlotte was a great friend and solace to him in his later years, but his son Walter got into several scrapes, eventually leading to a complete estrangement from his father. This poisoned Lockhart's later years, and his son's early death in 1853 was a blow from which he never recovered. He died in 1854 at Scott's estate of Abbotsford.

Raymond N. Mackenzie

Works Consulted

Hart, Francis R. *Lockhart as Romantic Biographer*. Edinburgh: Edinburgh UP, 1971.

Hildyard, M. Clive, ed. *Lockhart's Literary Criticism*. Oxford: Blackwell, 1931.

Lochhead, Marion. *John Gibson Lockhart*. London: Murray, 1954.

Strout, Alan Lang, ed. *John Bull's Letter to Lord Byron*. Norman: U of Oklahoma P, 1947.

London Magazine

One of Britain's premier literary magazines, the *London Magazine* was published between 1820 and 1829, although the title has been used by other periodicals. During its heyday, between 1820 and 1824, the *London* featured prose by De Quincey, Lamb, Landor, and Hazlitt and poetry by Keats and Clare, to name a few of the contributors. Until a change in ownership in 1825, the *London* consistently championed the cause of the Cockney school and offered some of the liveliest prose and most perceptive art, drama, and literary criticism of the period. (*See also* Journalism, Publishing.)

John Scott, the first editor and an experienced journalist, proposed a journal that afforded "the best panoramic view" of what was occurring in European arts, sciences, and politics. He meant for his magazine to reflect the energy and shape of the English capital. In contrast to the great *Reviews*, the *London* balanced criticism with original, creative prose and poetry: De Quincey wrote in an 1821 draft advertisement that the *London* would unite critical with creative works. Scott indicated that social philosophy as well as art criticism would be found in the magazine, and indeed the spirit of inquiry in the best *London* articles is speculative, broad, and profound. While there was a liberal Whig, sometimes radical, bent to the magazine, it was unusually independent and politically nonpartisan, which may account for its poor circulation.

Another goal of the magazine was to correct the misconceptions promulgated by the *Reviews*. *Blackwood's Magazine* was the model and nemesis for Scott's venture, and that rivalry—political, national, literary, and ultimately personal—eventually resulted in Scott's death.

Scott carefully cultivated his contributors and was by all accounts an excellent editor. The inaugural volume of the *London* includes criticism by Hazlitt and Cunningham, the Elia essays by Lamb, art criticism by Wainewright and Haydon, and verse by Leigh Hunt and P.G. Patmore. The September 1821, number (issued after Scott's death) is one of the most memorable magazines in British literary history: included are pieces by Hood, Mitford, Clare, Cunningham, J.H. Reynolds, Wainewright, and two gems: "The Old Benchers of the Inner Temple" by Lamb and the first part of De Quincey's *Confessions of an English Opium-Eater*.

By the end of 1820, Scott attacked *Blackwood's*, "the Mohock Magazine," as he dubbed it, for its *ad hominem* style of criticism and its assault on Keats, Hazlitt, and the Cockney school. On February 16, 1821, Scott was mortally wounded in a duel with Lockhart's second. Taylor and Hessey, a house that had published Keats's poetry, bought the magazine from its first publisher, Robert Baldwin, and John Taylor took over the editorship of the magazine. Taylor estimated that the circulation was only 1,600 when he bought it in July 1821; at the same time, both *Blackwood's* and the *Edinburgh Review* were printing around 14,000 copies per issue. Taylor held on to most of the earlier contributors and added De Quincey; he cemented the spirit of bonhomie that gave the magazine its identity by hosting monthly dinners, which often served as inebriated brainstorming sessions for essays, verse, ribald songs, and puns. But Taylor was a heavy-handed editor, and by the end of 1823, some contributors, notably Hazlitt, rebelled against his editorial intrusions. Although Hood helped maintain a whimsical ambience, the magazine lost its unifying spirit. Hazlitt referred to it as an unboiled, rich plum pudding.

With circulation slipping from a high of perhaps 2,250, Taylor sold the magazine to Henry Southern, a Utilitarian. By imposing a clear ideology and failing to pay contributors, Southern quickly lost the few mainstays (including Lamb), and filled the pages with long book reviews. By March 1828, Southern sold out to Charles Knight and Barry St. Leger; a year later the *London* was absorbed by one of its chief rivals, the *New Monthly Magazine*. "Arrah, honey, why did you die?" eulogized Hood. "Had you not an editor, and elegant prose writers, and beautiful poets, and broths of boys for criticism and classics, and wits and humorists?" And indeed the *London* afforded a forum to some of the finest writers of the period.

Joel Haefner

Works Consulted
Bauer, Josephine. *The London Magazine, 1820–29.* Copenhagen: Rosenkilde, 1953.

Chilcott, Tim. *A Publisher and His Circle: The Life and Work of John Taylor, Keats's Publisher.* London: Routledge, 1972.

Graham, Walter. *English Literary Periodicals.* New York: Nelson, 1930.

Prance, Claude A. "The London Magazine." *Charles Lamb Society Bulletin* 101 (1951): 3–5.

Riga, Frank P., and Claude A. Prance. *Index to the London Magazine.* New York: Garland, 1978.

Zeitlin, Jacob. "The Editor of the London Magazine." *JEGP* 20 (1921): 328–54.

Lower Classes

At the end of the 18th century, the terms "common people" or "lower orders" were replaced by the 19th-century term "lower classes." Both referred to those dependent on others for their livelihood, both urban or rural, who were kept in their place by tradition and lack of opportunity.

The Industrial Revolution brought many changes to the lower classes. It created a new labor force that worked regular if long hours and was more strictly disciplined than farm hands or skilled artisans. Many factory workers believed they were part of an upwardly mobile group, not a permanent mudsill, and rejected the deferential role expected of their class. Despite their optimism, they found factory work hard and dangerous, bending workers of all ages to the pace of the machine. Even if conditions in a factory were adequate, the long work week, as much as 74 hours, often shattered family relationships. Economic depression had also reduced traditional job opportunities in the country, bringing hardship to farm laborers and their families. Many were increasingly dependent on paternalistic poor relief from their local parish or were forced to move.

The lower classes often resorted to drunkenness to ease their misery. They consumed an incredible amount of beer and gin. Stiff excise taxes on imported gin reduced its consumption somewhat, but drunkenness remained a problem along with the poverty, brutality, and violence it encouraged.

The lower classes also flocked to public amusements whenever possible. They loved violent entertainments, such as prize fights; bear, badger, and bull baiting; and cockfights. Also popular were fairs, freak shows, waxworks, and the new circuses that were built all over England in the 1780s.

Most of the middle and upper classes agreed that the poor were impoverished and undernourished not by low wages and long hours but by an excess of drunkenness, gambling, and sexual abuse. The establishment developed the workhouse, a form of charity so unpleasant that only the most desperately poor fell prey to it. The upper classes also believed that educating the lower classes was wasteful and dangerous; thus a vast majority of the poor were illiterate. However, charity schools, private schools with fees paid by benevolent local residents, sprang up in urban areas after 1780. There poor children were taught to read and write, but the emphasis was on Bible reading, discipline, and contentment with their station in life. But Sunday Schools provided the rudiments of education and religious training, on their only day off, for most of the poor children and adults who worked in the factories or mines. (*See also* Education.)

After the Napoleonic Wars, reduced wages and rising food costs increased the misery of the poor and led to the appalling conditions criticized by Dickens. The workers' reaction in the industrial North and Midlands was the Luddite movement. The Luddites, a secret society of workers and technicians, smashed the machinery of employers that exploited their workers.

Although the government and manufacturers used troops, spies, and agents against them, few of the Luddites were caught. (*See also* Luddites.)

Conditions in rural England were also depressed, due in part to the unfeeling attitude of the gentry. Farm laborers rioted all over England after 1815 to protest low wages and the increasing use of machinery. This was their only recourse, since they had no vote. The rise of the Chartist movement in the 1830s was the first step toward universal manhood suffrage in England and gradual improvement of conditions for the lower classes. (*See also* Poor Law of 1834.)

Elsa A. Nystrom

Works Consulted

Briggs, Asa. *The Age of Improvement, 1785–1867*. New York: Longmans, 1959.

Halevy, Elie. *England in 1815*. New York: Barnes, 1960.

Hibbert, Christopher. *The English: A Social History, 1066–1945*. New York: Norton, 1987.

Langford, Paul. *A Polite and Commercial People, England, 1727–1783*. New York: Oxford UP, 1989.

Perrot, Michelle, ed. *A History of Private Life: From the Fires of Revolution to the Great War*. Cambridge, Belknap, 1990.

[The] Luddites

In 1811, an organized band of textiles workers began a series of raids (which lasted through 1816), attacking and smashing textile machinery in Nottingham, some because they believed the machinery to be costing them jobs, some for other labor-related grievances. Their mythical leader was General, or King, "Ned Ludd," whose threatening letters to employers preceded the attacks. Lacking effective bargaining power at a time when legislation opposed labor unions, the workers could strike an effective blow against employers in the hosiery, lace, and woolen industries by destroying equipment. The Luddites carried out their numerous widespread attacks, at night and in disguise, when they felt that other means of resolving their grievances had been exhausted. Though begun in Nottingham, the movement spread through nearby counties and even into Scotland, the most intense activity occurring in December 1811 and January 1812.

The Luddites did not originate the idea of smashing machinery; such attacks had occurred sporadically in other occupations, such as mining, since the late 17th century. However, the term "Luddite" has come to mean anyone opposed to progress, especially through mechanization. But many Luddites did not oppose machinery per se; instead they used it as a handy target to protest certain employment practices and to demonstrate their demands. It is true that the introduction of machinery upset the traditional roles of the workers; a seven-year apprenticeship was no longer called for when a worker could learn to operate the equipment in a matter of months or a year, but the Luddites were willing to work with the manufacturers when they felt that labor practices were fair. In an early attack, employees destroyed equipment because a factory had hired unapprenticed workers to operate the frames, compromising production standards and taking jobs away from properly trained workers.

On principle, the Luddites shunned violence against people, but occasionally they attacked private property as well as industrial equipment. For the most part, they enjoyed public support; in 1816, Byron wrote a poem entitled *Song for the Luddites* in which he endorsed their cause in the line "down with all Kings but King Ludd!" Nonetheless, many in the ruling class feared them, and those less sympathetic to their cause lumped other criminal activity with theirs and blamed them for a general unrest and outbreak of crime. A newspaper in Leeds, for instance, acknowledged openly that it saw no difference between the Luddites and any others who committed crimes or otherwise disturbed the peace of a respectable society. There is evidence that many thieves, robbers, and even food rioters seized on Luddism as a cover; so, while some citizens did not see the movement as criminal in itself, they believed it incited the widespread illegal activity that paralleled the time frame of the Luddite movement. Some newspapers, in reporting crimes, were careful to distinguish between ordinary lawbreakers and the authentic Luddites. Others claimed that the Luddites were motivated by a desire for political revolution and great political power. Rumors and misinformation, some of it deliberate, abounded. Thus, historians have sometimes had difficulty separating the many allegations about the goals and activities of the Luddites from the reality. Understandably, the workers themselves did not keep written records of their activities.

Ultimately, the victimized manufacturers and the law united against them. Frame-smashing was made a capital offense, though Byron successfully introduced into Parliament the bill that changed the crime from a felony to a misdemeanor. As the authorities began rounding up, prosecuting, and executing Luddite leaders, they dealt a crippling blow to the movement. Although uprisings occurred after the Napoleonic Wars, Luddism was coming to an end, not only because of governmental repression and the loss of vital leaders, but also because a stronger economy alleviated many of the conditions that had provoked the Luddites' grievances.

Historians disagree about the efficacy of the movement. Some argue that the workers succeeded only in venting their personal frustrations to no larger end; others believe that the reforms that came a couple of decades after the movement subsided can be traced back to its efforts. In any case, reform finally came, and collective bargaining replaced machine-smashing. (*See also* Economic Conditions, Lower Classes; Industrial Revolution.)

Linda Jordan Tucker

Works Consulted

Halévy, Élie. *A History of the English People in 1815.* Trans. E.I. Watkin and D.A. Barker. New York: Harcourt, 1924.

Thomis, Malcolm I. *The Luddites: Machine-Breaking in Regency England.* Library of Textile History. Hamden, CT: Archon, 1970.

Lyric

The Romantic poets sought repeatedly to write in the epic and dramatic genres, but it was the lyric at which they were perceived to excel. Such lyrics as Coleridge's *Frost at Midnight*, Wordsworth's *Immortality Ode*, Keats's *Ode to a Nightingale*, and Shelley's *Ode to the West Wind* are central to the revolution in poetic style achieved during the period. (*See also* Poetry.)

In the new lyric mode, poetic structure was determined from within by a focus on the individual consciousness, usually that of the poet. This mode was so successful, in fact, that by the early 20th century the lyric was seen by authorities such as Croce to be the essence of poetry: what was not lyric was not poetry. Beginning with the Romantic poets, therefore, the term "lyric" shows a tendency to subsume all poetry. Even where a poet writes in a different genre, such as the epic of Wordsworth's *Prelude* or *Excursion* or the drama of Shelley's *Prometheus Unbound* (subtitled *A Lyrical Drama*), central passages remain in the lyric mode and clearly build on the technical achievements of the shorter lyric poems that preceded them. Coleridge, in *Biographia Literaria* (1817), points to the elevated status now bestowed on the lyric mode. "Poetry" in this comment is synonymous with "lyric."

The resulting indeterminant boundaries of the lyric make modern attempts to define the term perhaps not entirely fruitful. While in ancient Greece the term "lyric" certainly meant a song, accompanied by a lyre, the Romantic lyric moved well beyond any literal allegiance to music. More productive have been attempts to see the Romantic lyric as part of an historical evolution, during which the consciousness of the poet has moved to the center of the poetic stage. Romantic poetry shows certain continuities here with 17th-century meditative verse, such as those of Herbert and Vaughan, which dramatized the experience and feelings of the religious consciousness. This new seriousness of theme signals the elevation of the lyric mode. In the same period the *Pindaric ode*, recreated by Cowley in the 1650s, became enormously popular for its sublimity and for the freedom from strict form it appeared to confer; many examples were produced, the most successful by Dryden and Gray. Earlier generations had accepted the Greek division of poetry into epic, dramatic, and lyric, which placed lyric at the lower end in the scale of values. But the intensity and passion of the new form led Dennis, in 1704, to group together "Epick, Tragick, and the greater Lyrick Poetry." Anne Williams has shown that as the 18th century progressed, both the epic and dramatic genres were levied for contributions to the lyric, enriching its thematic and stylistic range. By the end of the century, it was also no longer necessary for a sublime poem to be a long poem: even very short poems, such as the sonnet (which was being written in quantity again from the 1780s onward), could contain the passion or terror of the sublime. Thus, by the Romantic period, all the elements of the new lyric mode were present: a freedom from strict form together with the elements of both dramatic style and a potentially epic range of reference.

While no one characteristic is defining, the main features of the Romantic lyric derive from the question of consciousness. In this respect, the Romantic lyric shows a distinct turn away from the 18th-century model, which was generally public and apostrophic. The Romantic lyric is, by contrast, a meditative, usually first-person, utterance (although third-person lyrics also occur, such as Wordsworth's *There was a Boy* or *Poor Susan* in the *Lyrical Ballads*). Second, the lyric meditation is often initiated by reflection on a discord or problem presented to consciousness, which subsequent reflection in the poem may resolve. In Coleridge's *This Lime-Tree Bower my Prison*, for example, by the end of the poem the speaker has ceased to regard his garden bower as a prison. Third, the speaker may attempt to widen or dissolve the boundaries of consciousness—such boundaries present part of the initial problem—by reaching out to encompass some wider scene beyond the speaker; this enables the speaker to participate in a timeless or transcendent realm beyond the narrow confines of the self, and such progress invariably requires a development in the speaker's faculty of imagination. Fourth, a prerequisite to elevation may be a descent beneath consciousness, to gather resources from the memory or the subconscious. For example, Wordsworth typically developed a "double consciousness" in his lyrics, as he came to call it in *The Prelude* (1850),

deploying the insights that came from comparing the earlier self of memory with his self now (*Tintern Abbey*; *Immortality Ode*). Keats, by contrast, may begin with a state of sleep or reverie, such as the "drowsy numbness" that initiates *Ode to a Nightingale*. Fifth, the elevation is often followed by a return to the scene with which the poem started, which may now be seen in a renovated light.

A sixth characteristic, more notable of the founding poems in this mode by Coleridge and Wordsworth, is the unassuming, conversational tone that such poems appear to adopt. "Well, they are gone, and here must I remain," says Coleridge informally at the opening of *This Lime-Tree Bower*. But the poetic voice contains within it many subtleties of diction, and it is capable of modulating to high points of rhetorical splendor. This flexibility in diction is perhaps one of the more remarkable technical achievements of the genre and one that has proved most attractive to subsequent poets. Later lyrics by Keats and Shelley tend to adopt the apostrophic mode (Keats addresses his nightingale; Shelley speaks to the west wind), placing them beyond the illusion of private meditations or intimate conversations.

Finally, the form of the lyric is governed by an emotional logic rather than by any other structuring principle. As Wordsworth put the matter in the Preface to the *Lyrical Ballads* (1800), reversing the order of priorities traditional to the ballad, "the feeling . . . developed gives importance to the action and situation and not the action and situation to the feeling." Although several lyrics are presented in stanza form, sometimes following this strictly (as in Shelley's *Ode to the West Wind*), the stanzas are often irregular in order to embody the successive emotional developments underlying the poem.

The first major lyrics of the period are Blake's *Songs of Innocence* (1789) and *Songs of Experience* (1794). But these were little noticed in Blake's time; thus the inaugural collection is undoubtedly the *Lyrical Ballads* (1798) of Wordsworth and Coleridge. It contains poems in a variety of styles, including one of the "greater lyrics" of the period (to adopt the term of M.H. Abrams), *Tintern Abbey*, as well as a variety of shorter, dramatic pieces. As the title suggests, the narrative vehicle of the ballad is deployed to lyric purpose, shifting the focus of the poem away from the tale onto the consciousness of the speaker, whether the consciousness is that of an actor (*The Thorn*, *The Rime of the Ancient Mariner*) or of the poet (*The Nightingale*, *The Tables Turned*). Wordsworth went on to write many other short lyrics: among these the "Lucy" poems, which are perhaps the best known, still adopt the ballad meter. His longer lyrics include both an ode (*Immortality Ode*) and an elegy (*Elegiac Stanzas Suggested by a Picture of Peele Castle*).

The characteristics of the Romantic lyric are also apparent in important poems by Keats and Shelley, including Keats's great odes and such poems of Shelley as *Mont Blanc* and *Stanzas: Written in Dejection*. While Byron wrote no poems that fall within this mode, he excelled at shorter, songlike lyrics, such as *Stanzas for Music* and *So We'll Go No More A-Roving*. Many other lesser poets of the period, from Bowles and Robinson to Moore, also produced poems in the lyrical mode which were very popular in their time.

Modern discussion of the Romantic lyric is indebted to a seminal essay of M.H. Abrams (first published in 1965), in which he coined the term "greater Romantic lyric." Recent accounts of the lyric have tended to attack the notion, attributed to the New Critics, of the lyric as a separate, autonomous work speaking in a monologic voice. More attention has been paid to relationships between successive poems, in which issues raised in one poem are taken up again in another, as in Paul Magnuson's account of Coleridge and Wordsworth. Other critics, such as Tilottama Rajan, have emphasized the multiple voices often present in the lyric or the intertextual references to previous poems, undermining in this way the notion of the solitary, spontaneous voice that tended to dominate earlier accounts of the lyric. Far-reaching discussions of the function of the image and of the symbol in Romantic poetry by Paul de Man have also had a major influence on recent understanding of the metaphysical aims of the greater Romantic lyric.

David S. Miall

Works Consulted

Abrams, M.H. "Structure and Style in the Greater Romantic Lyric." *The Correspondent Breeze: Essays on English Romanticism*. Ed. Jack Stillinger. New York: Norton, 1984: 76–108.

Culler, Jonathan. "Apostrophe." *The Pursuit of Signs: Semiotics, Literature, Deconstruction*. London: Routledge, 1981: 135–54.

de Man, Paul. "The Rhetoric of Temporality." *Blindness and Insight: Essays in the Rhetoric of Contemporary Criticism*. 2nd ed. London: Methuen, 1983: 187–228.

MacLean, Norman. "From Action to Image: Theories of the Lyric in the Eighteenth Century." *Critics and Criticism: Ancient and Modern*. Ed. R.S. Crane. Chicago: Chicago UP, 1952: 408–460.

Magnuson, Paul. *Coleridge & Wordsworth: A Lyrical Dialogue*. Princeton: Princeton UP, 1988.

Rajan, Tilottama. "Romanticism and the Death of Lyric Consciousness." *Lyric Poetry: Beyond New Criticism*. Eds. Chaviva Hosek and Patricia Parker. Ithaca: Cornell UP, 1985: 194–207.

Stillinger, Jack. "Imagination and Reality in the Odes." *The Hoodwinking of Madeline and Other Essays on Keats's Poems*. Urbana: U of Illinois P, 1971: 99–119.

Williams, Anne. *Prophetic Strain: The Greater Lyric in the Eighteenth Century*. Chicago: Chicago UP, 1984.

Lyrical Ballads

Lyrical Ballads is traditionally considered a literary landmark, a convenient place to mark the beginning of Romanticism in England. *Lyrical Ballads* announces the Romantic writers' interest in psychology and explorations of the self; the supernatural and revelatory powers of nature; democratic principles; and the motif of the outcast as hero. Poems within this collection introduce many of the literary genres that achieved prominence during the Romantic era, including the conversational poem, the literary ballad, the ode, and the fragment. For these and other reasons, this slim volume of poetry has often been designated as the founding document of the Romantic movement.

Lyrical Ballads, With a Few Other Poems is the complete title of the volume of poetry written by Wordsworth and Coleridge and published anonymously in 1798. These poems represent the collaborative efforts of the creative and stimulating relationship Wordsworth and Coleridge enjoyed between July 1797 and June 1798. During this time, William and Dorothy, his sister, resided at Alfoxden, and Coleridge lived nearby at Nether Stowey. The idea for a joint project grew out of the two poets' almost daily discussions and their initial collaboration on *The Rime of the Ancient Mariner*. Coleridge continued *The Ancient Mariner*, completing it by the end of March, and eventually contributed *The Foster-Mother's Tale*, *The Nightingale*, and *The Dungeon* to the collection. For his part, Wordsworth furnished 19 poems, which can be divided into two groups. One group, including *The Thorn*, *The Idiot Boy*, *Goody Blake and Harry Gill*, and *We Are Seven*, was written between early March and mid-May, when Wordsworth had the idea of *Lyrical Ballads* in mind. Together with *The*

Ancient Mariner, these poems illustrate the more experimental aspects of *Lyrical Ballads*. The "few other poems" mentioned in the title, and not part of the "plan" of *Lyrical Ballads*, include, most notably, Wordsworth's *Tintern Abbey*, the last poem to go into the first edition (1798) of the volume. The collection was printed for publication in early September, but not published until October 4, 1798, due to difficulties with the publisher. The contemporary critical response was modestly favorable; however, Southey's infamous review scorned *The Ancient Mariner* as "a Dutch attempt at German sublimity."

In January 1801, *Lyrical Ballads* was republished under Wordsworth's name alone and in a very different format. The so-called 1800, or second, edition was published in two volumes, retained Coleridge's contributions, introduced several new poems by Wordsworth, and included his important Preface, which is still thought to be the best critical introduction to the volume. *Lyrical Ballads* sold modestly well, totaling four British and one American edition over the next seven years.

The hybrid term "lyrical ballad" suggests that these poems combine the ballad's properties of narrative action, dramatic incident, and metrical charm with the lyric's capacity for sustained expression of feeling. These experiments were the product of Wordsworth's and Coleridge's interests in several areas, including the ballad revival inspired by Percy's *Reliques of Ancient English Poetry* (1765); the English translations of Bürger's ballads in 1796; the lyric poets Mark Akenside, Bowles, Burns, and Cowper; and a mutual fascination with the psychology of guilt and the curse motif.

Literary scholars refer to *Lyrical Ballads* as a poetic manifesto. It represents a revolt against an 18th-century poetics that privileged conventionally heroic characters and classes and that valued an ornamental poetic diction, governed by traditional rules of decorum. In his Advertisement to the 1798 edition and his Preface to the 1800 edition, Wordsworth distinguishes his poetry from both this artificial poetic diction and the "gaudiness and inane phraseology" of the popular German tragedies. He separates *Lyrical Ballads* from these other works for three reasons. First, the more experimental poems of *Lyrical Ballads* depict rustics, vagrants, and even the mentally impaired as appropriate subjects for serious poetry because these people speak an unrefined language and are emotionally honest. For example, *The Idiot Boy* illustrates a simple yet powerful example of human selflessness and love. Second, Wordsworth felt that the diction and metrics used in *Lyrical Ballads* were more appropriate than those of his predecessors because they approximated or intensified credible psychological states of mental excitement. For example, in *The Thorn* the loquacious sea captain's speech pattern is represented in rapid meter and compulsively repetitious language in order to reveal his superstitious, powerful fixation on Martha Ray and her purportedly tragic history. Last, Wordsworth felt that *Lyrical Ballads* differed from the poems of his day in that "the feeling gives importance to the action and situation and not the action and situation to the feeling." In other words, the poems are designed to reveal the psychological associations of the mind at particularly intense moments brought about by distress or crisis in order to disclose the "essential passions of the heart." In this context, *Goody Blake and Harry Gill* can be read as a psychological study of Harry Gill's greed, guilt, and hysteria.

Although no rigorous distinction applies, many of Wordsworth's contributions to the volume render common people and everyday incidents as extraordinary, and some of Coleridge's poems render supernatural incidents, agents, and characters as psychologically plausible. Thus, in *The Ancient Mariner* Coleridge dramatizes and makes credible the excruciating suffering of the Mariner by placing him in situations where he supposes himself to be under supernatural agency. With these general tenets in mind, the joint program of *Lyrical Ballads* can be seen to represent common men and women in states of intense psychological excitement in response to natural events that seem uncanny or supernatural.

In later years, Wordsworth and Coleridge each attempted to clarify their respective intentions and claims to *Lyrical Ballads*. Their dialogue can be traced in three sources: Wordsworth's *Preface* to the *Lyrical Ballads* of 1800 and subsequent revisions of this document; Wordsworth's appended *Notes* to *The Thorn* and *We Are Seven*; and Coleridge's *Biographia Literaria* (1817), especially Chapter 14, and to a lesser extent, Chapters 4, 17 to 20, and 22. However, Wordsworth and Coleridge became embroiled in a feud for many years, and this unhappy fact casts some doubt on the accuracy of their competing claims, which were sometimes reconstructed years later.

In a letter to Cottle (28, May 1798), Coleridge likened *Lyrical Ballads* to an ode, stating that the various poems of the volume were as stanzas in a single poem. This Romantic metaphor can show how the various experiments in diction and ballad metrics, the appeals for democratic and humanitarian principles, and the testaments to the revelatory power of nature all combine in *Lyrical Ballads*. (*See also* Ballad, Poetry.)

David W. Ullrich

Works Consulted

Bialostosky, Don H. *Making Tales: The Poetics of Wordsworth's Narrative Experiments*. Chicago: U of Chicago P, 1984.

Danby, John F. *The Simple Wordsworth: Studies in the Poems 1797–1807*. 1960. London: Routledge, 1971.

Hayden, John O., ed. *Romantic Bards and British Reviewers: A Selected Edition of the Reviews of the Works of Wordsworth, Coleridge, Byron, Keats, and Shelley*. Lincoln: U of Nebraska P, 1971.

Jacobus, Mary. *Tradition and Experiment in Wordsworth's Lyrical Ballads (1798)*. Oxford: Oxford UP, 1976.

Jordan, John E. *Why the Lyrical Ballads? The Background, Writing, and Character of Wordsworth's 1798 Lyrical Ballads*. Berkeley: U of California P, 1976.

Page, Judith W. "The Preface in Relation to the *Lyrical Ballads*." *Approaches to Teaching Wordsworth's Poetry*. Ed. Spencer Hall with Jonathan Ramsey. New York: MLA, 1986: 75–78.

Parrish, Steven Maxfield. *The Art of the Lyrical Ballads*. Cambridge: Harvard UP, 1973.

Reed, Mark L. *Wordsworth, The Chronology of the Early Years: 1770–1799*. Cambridge: Harvard UP, 1967.

Watson, John Richard, *English Poetry of the Romantic Period, 1789–1830*. Longman Literature in English Series. New York: Longmans, 1985.

MacAdam, John Loudon
(1756–1836)

John Loudon MacAdam was born in 1756 in Ayre, Scotland. As a young man, he gained fame as an engineer. Named surveyor-general to the London turnpike system, MacAdam became the first great transport administrator. One of the first of his generation to recognize that dry soil better supports the weight of traffic than does soggy earth and that paving soil aids in keeping it dryer, he developed a paving substance known as "Macadam pavement." Macadam pavement, which is still in use today, consists essentially of crushed rock packed into thin layers and applied one on top of the other.

Before MacAdam's time, England's main roads consisted of earth piled up higher than the surrounding ground, hence the name "highways." Highways were protected by Kings' men and were open to all travelers. Private roads then were known as "byways." The roads in England at that time were described by most as deplorable. Arthur Young in his well-known *Tour*, remarks on the "excreable muddy road from Bury to Sudbury in Suffolk." He found the method of mending ridiculous in as much as it was repaired with simple loam with some stones in it, no more solid than soil. In 1755, Parliament passed an act compelling districts to construct turnpike roads and to charge a set toll accordingly. Between 1760 and 1764, Parliament passed more than 450 acts concerning the formation of new roads and the repair and alteration of old highways throughout the country. These acts sought to regulate activities such as the weight of a load carried over a road, the number of horses to a wagon, and the breadth of a wagon or a carriage-wheel's rims. All these policies had one goal in common—making traffic conform to the roads.

But it was not until the beginning of the 19th century that self-taught engineers, such as MacAdam and Telford—whose ideas placed a greater emphasis on a solid foundation as a means to achieve a more durable road—developed ways of constructing roads that were more suitably adapted to the use for which roads were originally intended—traffic. (*See also* Industrial Revolution.)

Marilyn Jean Clay

Works Consulted
Ashton, T.S. *The Industrial Revolution, 1760–1830.* New York: Oxford UP, 1948.

Mitton, G.E. *Jane Austen and Her Times*. 1905. New York: Kennikat, 1970.

Thomson, David. *England in the Nineteenth Century*. London: Caber, 1950.

Mackintosh, Sir James

(1765–1832)

A Scottish writer, philosopher, and Whig politician, James Mackintosh was educated as a physician and took his medical degree at Edinburgh in 1787. But he was ambivalent about pursuing a medical career, and after marrying Catherine Stuart, sister of the future editor of the *Morning Post*, he moved to London and began writing for newspapers such as the *Oracle*.

His emerging interest in politics culminated in the 1791 publication of *Vindiciae Gallicae*; along with Paine's *Rights of Man*, it was the only liberal defense of the French Revolution in the face of Burke's *Reflections on the Revolution in France*. At this point, Mackintosh resolved to pursue a career in law and politics; by 1795, he had joined the bar.

As the decade progressed, Mackintosh showed new respect for Burke's principles and eventually adopted his view of the French Revolution. After the death of his first wife in 1797, he married Catherine Allen, sister-in-law to the Wedgwood brothers. He met Coleridge at John Wedgwood's house in the winter of 1797 to 1798, and on the strength of Mackintosh's introduction, Coleridge became a contributor to the *Morning Post*.

Mackintosh became an established reasoner and political figure with his lectures on the law of nature and nations, presented in 1799 and again in 1800. In these lectures, he attacked the progressive, humanistic ideas of Godwin and what he viewed as his own early radicalism.

Coleridge disliked the five lectures he attended; generally, he considered Mackintosh unoriginal and parochial in his thinking. Another contemporary, Hazlitt, viewed Mackintosh as a thorough, learned reasoner but also as a dry orator who had betrayed the liberal principles he championed in the early 1790s.

The lectures, however, secured approval for Mackintosh from such politicians as Pitt and Canning, and he prospered professionally and socially: his dining club was frequented by Lord Holland, economist Ricardo, and literary reviewer Jeffrey. In 1803, he was knighted when he accepted a recordership in Bombay; he did so in part to pursue literary schemes he felt were incompatible with an active professional career. But Mackintosh soon found life in India socially isolated and intellectually limited, and his health declined as a result of the climate. In 1811, he returned to Britain and received a Whig seat in Parliament in 1813 for the county of Nairn; his maiden speech in the Commons protested allied interference in Holland and Switzerland. At this time, he also began writing a history of England from 1688 to the French Revolution.

Forced by his health into a three-year absence from London life and politics, Mackintosh returned to Parliament in 1819, this time representing Knaresborough. He opposed repressive measures following the end of the Napoleonic Wars, such as the Seditious Meetings Bill of 1817, and supported reducing the number of capital offenses. In 1827, he was named Privy Councillor in Canning's administration, but his influence was nominal because he was not considered practical politically and because he was in poor health. At the formation of the next Whig government in 1830, he was given a perfunctory post. He supported the Reform Bill in 1831, but died suddenly from complications after swallowing a chicken bone. His *History of the Revolution in England* was published after his death.

Toby Benis

Works Consulted

Coleridge, Samuel Taylor. *Biographia Literaria*. Eds. James Engell and W. Jackson Bate. Princeton: Princeton UP, 1983.

Dictionary of National Biography, *s.v.* "Mackintosh, Sir James."

Hazlitt, William. *The Spirit of the Age*. Garden City: Doubleday, 1960.

Macpherson, James

(1736–96)

James Macpherson's name has been synonymous with fraudulence ever since the "Ossianic Controversy" in 1761. The obsessive ambition of this impassioned literary debate was to discover the extent to which Macpherson's ostensible translations of ancient Celtic poetry were, in fact, his own imaginative work. When the dust kicked up by the debate finally settled in the early 19th century, it was demonstrated to the satisfaction of most that Macpherson had indeed adorned his source material imaginatively and substantially. His talent and his contribution to the work of major poets who followed him has consequently been underassessed. (*See also* Primitivism.)

Born in rural Inverness-shire in the Scottish Highlands, Macpherson was raised in a traditional culture rich in the oral poetry and legends of Celtic heroism. Despite a university education in metropolitan Aberdeen and Edinburgh, the strains and images of his native Gaelic culture haunted him with an intensity undiluted even by his later residence in London. In 1758, he published *The Highlander*, a poetic narrative that fused ancient Scottish heroic themes and motifs with English

Neoclassical sensibility. Encouraged by Alexander Carlyle and Hugh Blair, Professor of Rhetoric at Edinburgh University, Macpherson published, in 1760, *Fragments of Ancient Poetry, Collected in the Highlands of Scotland, and Translated from the Galic or Erse Language*. Ostensibly, these were translations of Gaelic poetic manuscripts in his possession, but they were formed, in reality, more by the imposition of his own idealizing esthetic.

Public interest in this volume persuaded Macpherson to accept in 1760, a commission to collect from oral informants and old manuscripts any remains of a national epic that would achieve for ancient Scotland what Homer's had achieved for Greece. In 1761, he published *Fingal, An Ancient Epic Poem, In Six Books: Together with several other Poems, composed by Ossian the Son of Fingal* to a rhapsodic reception at home and abroad. *Fingal* and its sequel, *Temora* (1763), captivated readers in countless thousands; many, however, were incredulous that such poetry could have survived thus intact for 1,500 years. Notable among the skeptics was Dr. Johnson, whose suspicions about the poems' authenticity were, for him, confirmed by Macpherson's refusal to submit his original manuscripts to public scrutiny. The main protagonist on Macpherson's behalf, meanwhile, was his benefactor Hugh Blair whose "Critical Dissertation" prefaced the collected edition of *The Poems of Ossian* (1763). Macpherson stayed largely aloof, allowing the truth to emerge gradually that his method had been to streamline, unify, and embellish his source materials in a way that happened to accord with contemporary Neoclassical poetry and Enlightenment philosophy.

Despite the controversy, the song of Ossian rang through Europe and the world, in close harmony with the work of

Rousseau, Goethe, and Herder and promoted by a chorus of superlatives from Napoleon and Jefferson. At home, Ossian's influence joined with that of Percy's *Reliques of Ancient English Poetry* to shape the main contours of early Romanticism. Blake's debt to Macpherson's mythologizing of the ancient past is as clear as is that of *Lyrical Ballads* to the innovative poetic diction and sublime landscapes. In Scotland, Macpherson's synthesis of oral tradition and literary sensibility prefigured the more rigorous, enduring successes of Burns and Scott, whose names have since become synonymous with the authentic voice of Scottish culture.

Jack Truten

Works Consulted

Bysveen, Josef. *Epic Tradition and Innovation in James Macpherson's Fingal*. Stockholm: Almqvist, 1982.

de Gategno, Paul J. *James Macpherson*. Boston: Twayne, 1989.

Nutt, Alfred. *Ossian and the Ossianic Literature*. London: Nutt, 1899.

Rubel, Margaret Mary. *Savage and Barbarian: Historical Attitudes in the Criticism of Homer and Ossian in Britain, 1760–1800*. New York: North-Holland, 1978.

Saunders, Thomas Bailey. *The Life and Letters of James Macpherson*. New York: Macmillan, 1894.

Smart, J.S. *James Macpherson: An Episode in Literature*. London: Nutt, 1905.

Stafford, Fiona. *The Sublime Savage: James Macpherson and the Poems of Ossian*. Edinburgh: Edinburgh UP, 1988.

Thomson, Derick. *The Gaelic Sources of Macpherson's Ossian*. Edinburgh: Oliver, 1952.

Mail and Mail Coaches

Rapid and widespread industrialization in the late 18th and early 19th centuries created the demand for a swift and reliable means of nationwide communication. The Romantic era met this demand by developing a network of fast, horse-drawn coaches that conveyed both mail and passengers throughout the British Isles with unprecedented speed and regularity.

As late as the 1780s travel in Britain was slow, difficult, and irregular. The once fine system of Roman roads had been largely allowed to deteriorate into a rambling collection of dirt wagon-tracks, which were often impassable in rain and snow. His Majesty's mail was carried on horseback, and choice of public transport was limited to hired horses or lumbering stagecoaches that rarely exceeded three miles per hour: in 1770, the 176-mile trip from London to Exeter took at least two days. Consequently, news traveled slowly; remote areas might remain ignorant of important national and international events for months.

All this changed in 1784, when Bath theater proprietor John Palmer proposed that the Post Office contract for mail delivery only with operators of fast coaches. Palmer argued that if horse teams were changed every 10 instead of every 20 miles and strict limitations were placed on the number of passengers and weight of cargo carried, average speed could be increased to at least 10 miles per hour. With the backing of Prime Minister Pitt, Palmer proved the feasibility of his scheme by completing a trip from London to Bristol in 15 hours. Palmer's success was immediately and widely imitated, and by the turn of the century fast coaches were the national norm. The system's popularity and efficiency in turn spurred extensive road building and improvement, which allowed more numerous and even faster coaches. By 1830, England, Scotland, and Wales were crisscrossed by more than 25 mailcoach lines as well as dozens of fast stagecoach lines, and Exeter could be reached from London in only 16 hours.

Even more beguiling to Romantic Britain than the speed and efficiency of mail coaches was their charm. Drawn by four spirited horses, the highly varnished, scarlet and black "mails" were an impressive sight. Drivers, renowned for their earthy wit, daring, and inveterate drunkenness, captured the public imagination as emblems of Regency society's sense of its Byronic recklessness. The coachmen dearest to the age, however, were the guards, Post Office employees assigned to each coach and entrusted with the safe and punctual delivery of the mail. In addition to a mail bag and official timepiece, guards were supplied with a cutlass, a brace of pistols, and a blunderbuss to protect passengers and cargo from the robbers and highwaymen that plagued the open road. The guards also carried what many regarded as the symbol of coaching life: a horn. Many guards achieved local and sometimes national celebrity for their proficiency on this instrument, particularly when the key bugle, imported from Germany shortly after 1800, replaced the original curved horn used to announce arrivals and departures. The era's most famous guard, John Goodwin, reputedly could imitate any animal on his key bugle.

Romantic artists and essayists were especially captivated by the mail coach's combination of quaintness and modern efficiency. Painter James Pollard's scenes of coaching life were widely reproduced throughout the 19th century. In his essay "The Letter Bell" (1831), Hazlitt wrote that London offered fewer sights more sublime than that of mail coaches pouring out of Piccadilly. The most extensive Romantic appreciation of the mail-coach system, however, occurs in De Quincey's *The English Mail Coach* (1849). De Quincey combines detailed reminiscences of the golden age of coaching—roughly between 1800 and 1830—with an impassioned, visionary paean to the mail coach as an embodiment of the galloping progress of British unity and empire. The coach's headlong rush, he wrote, symbolized England's early 19th-century career to the forefront of the world's nations.

The mail-coach system united Britain as it had not been perhaps since Roman times. By the mid-1830s, however, the Industrial Revolution was beginning to outstrip the limitations of horse-drawn transport; by the end of the decade, railroads had replaced the mail-coach system as the nation's primary mode of mail conveyance and long-distance travel. The heyday of the mail coach therefore closely corresponds to the era of Romanticism. Through the remainder of the 19th century this quaint mode of transport and communication continued to be associated with an age gone by, though fondly remembered.

Matthew T. Schneider

Works Consulted

Anderson, R.C., and J.M. *Quicksilver: A Hundred Years of Coaching, 1750–1850*. Newton Abbot: David, 1973.

Hanson, Harry. *The Coaching Life*. Dover: Manchester UP, 1983.

Robinson, Howard. *The British Post Office: A History*. Westport, CT: Greenwood, 1948.

Malthus, Thomas Robert
(1766–1834)

One of the originators of modern economic theory, Thomas Robert Malthus was a priest of the Church of England and a college professor whose ideas dominated Romantic thought. Drawing from Locke, Smith, and the Scottish philosophers and taking issue with Godwin and Ricardo, among others, Malthus influenced

Bentham, the Mills, Marx and Engels, and Darwin, who derived the idea of natural selection from Malthusian demographic pressures. Moreover, English politics and society, most immediately in the shape of 1830s reform legislation, reflect Malthus's work. And, Malthus's influence is still detectable, although the contraceptive efforts of "Malthusian" and "Neo-Malthusian" leagues stand in marked contrast to the beliefs of this married father of three. For his contemporaries, the age was more Malthusian than Romantic.

The man who came to occupy such a central position in his times and beyond lived a modest life. Born at "The Rookery" in Surrey, Malthus was the second son in a family of seven children. He suffered throughout his life from a congenital cleft palate, which interfered with his speech to differing degrees according to different accounts. As an enlightened member of the gentry, Daniel Malthus gave his family comfortable and cultured circumstances. He was a friend and disciple of Rousseau and arranged for fairly radical thinkers to tutor Robert.

In 1784, young Malthus entered Cambridge, under the tutelage of the extremist Frend. He had an exemplary collegiate career, excelling principally in mathematics, although he read extensively in French and English literature. In 1788, he took Holy Orders, received his M.A. in 1791, and became a fellow of his college in 1793, the same year that he accepted a curacy near his family home.

The first tract that Malthus intended for publication, *The Crisis*, was written in 1796. It was an attack on Pitt's government and failed to find a publisher. No copy of it survives.

In 1798, the year the *Lyrical Ballads* focused poetic interest on impoverished conditions, Malthus published anony-

mously the first edition of *An Essay on the Principle of Population*, provoked most directly, perhaps, by recent essays of Godwin that developed ideas of the interrelatedness of human rationality, morality, and justice. Additionally, at the time of publication, large families among the laboring classes and a subsequently increasing population were seen by Pitt and many others as one of England's greatest strengths. In contrast, Malthus's principle found that population tends to increase geometrically while sustenance increases arithmetically. Accordingly, a balance can be maintained only at the price of the exigency and corruption of the masses. In short, conditions in England were bad and worsening. Although in two years Pitt had converted to Malthus's thinking, the book aroused much opposition on economic and even heretical grounds—that is, many saw it as an attack against divine beneficence.

Inspired by the controversy, Malthus revised the book and dedicated himself to the study of population. Besides reading, in 1799, he began traveling, first to Scandinavia, then to Russia, and finally throughout the Continent. Although ultimately Malthus's opus went through seven editions (all but the last during his lifetime), the second edition, of 1803, represented his most extensive reworking of the problem of population and its exposition.

In the second edition, which he signed, Malthus enlarged his argument from the polemical to the scholarly. He discussed what he saw of population control in his travels; objected to Owen's economic utopianism; considered the Corn Laws, which he saw as necessary protectionism; and proposed ways to deal with poverty, which, paradoxically, the Corn Laws exacerbated. He proposed elimination of the Poor Laws, the rudimentary welfare system of the 18th century, by morally obligated personal charity, although he endorsed family relief.

However, the crux of his position remained his principle that population was doubling every 25 years where there were no wars or natural catastrophes to shortchange it. In the first version, Malthus saw the only possible solutions to the ravages of unregulated population growth as birth control, abortion, and infanticide, respectively unreliable, dangerous, and immoral, so that his text ends lugubriously. Upon revision, he held out an imperative to postpone marriage until children could be supported, in other words, moral restraint. This both lightened the grimness of the first edition and also, significantly, admitted the possibility of human will and control into his erstwhile exclusively arbitrary equations. Thus, while Malthus's theories are frequently characterized as rigidly numerical and systematic, he makes room for the individual, liberty, and hope, a subtle return to the optimism of Rousseau in which he had been bred, the perfectibility of Godwinian thought he had opposed, and the centrality of self that Wordsworth and Coleridge were simultaneously entertaining.

Malthus married his cousin Harriet Eckerstall in 1804, for which he was obliged to surrender his fellowship. However, he was at the same time appointed to one of the first professorships of history and political economy at the brand-new East India College, which was charged with education for the civil service in India. Malthus held this position for the remainder of his life, sometimes also serving as chaplain (delivering admired sermons with evidently small hindrance from his speech defect), and meanwhile garnering public honor after honor, testimony to the respect with which his influence and contributions were held. He died following a heart attack in 1834 and was buried in Bath Abbey.

Laura Dabundo

Works Consulted

Albrecht, William P. *William Hazlitt and the Malthusian Controversy*. 1950. Port Washington, NY: Kennikat, 1969.

Appleman, Philip, ed. *An Essay on the Principle of Population. Text, Sources, and Background*. New York: Norton, 1976.

McCleary, G.F. *The Malthusian Population Theory*. London: Faber, 1953.

Petersen, William. *Malthus*. Cambridge: Harvard UP, 1979.

Martin, John
(1789–1854)

Probably the most popular artist of the 1820s and 1830s, John Martin produced biblical pictures which in their original form or as steel engravings strongly affected the imaginations of figures as distinctive as the Brontë sisters and Cecil B. De Mille.

Martin's training was gained in Newcastle upon Tyne, first as a coach painter and then as a painter of china: the love of finical details and hard, bright colors, which this gave him, lasted all his life. Moving to London in 1806, he soon began to attract notice as a painter of Old Testament and exotic scenes, scoring a great success with *Joshua Commanding the Sun to Stand Still* in 1817. *Belshazzar's Feast*, finished in 1821, was a sensation. It was exhibited in various parts of the country and gained even greater popularity as a steel engraving (Martin often worked on the plates of his engravings himself, and they are remarkably detailed). From this point until about the end of the 1830s, Martin commanded popular success with his vast canvases, full of chiaroscuro effects, architectural panoramas, reeling humanity, and elemental convulsion of sky, earthquake, and ocean, generally finding their origin in one of the more melodramatic episodes of the Old Testament. But Martin could also operate on a smaller scale: some of his illustrations to an edition of *Paradise Lost* have genuine merit, even if his imagination was (perhaps inevitably) more fired by the murk of Pandemonium than the light vistas of Eden or the sublimities of the Plains of Heaven.

Martin exhibited in France, where his natural successor was Gustave Doré and was patronized by the Belgian government. The Brontës knew his engravings from childhood and were profoundly influenced by them. His imagination was powerful, but luridly theatrical in the main. Yet he caught the eyes and expressed the psychological neuroses of the Evangelical decades in which his popularity was at its height with a remarkable acuteness and accuracy. He is probably the artist who benefited most fully from the technological improvements in illustration in the early part of the 19th century. Steel engravings multiplied his images of catastrophe almost limitlessly, and better communications sent them the length and breadth of the land.

William Ruddick

Works Consulted

Feaver, W. *The Art of John Martin*. Oxford: Clarendon, 1975.

Klingender, F.D. *Art and the Industrial Revolution*. London: Carrington, 1947.

Mathias, Thomas James
(1754?–1835)

At the end of the 18th century and the beginning of the 19th few recent volume-length English poems were more widely discussed and praised than Thomas James Mathias's *The Pursuits of Literature*. A satire, with notes, on the state of contemporary writing, this work was published anonymously in four parts, or "dialogues," from 1794 to 1797. Its appeal might elude a reader to whom its concerns are no longer immediate, and indeed a generation later it was almost forgotten.

Born to a family that had occupied posts at the English court, Mathias attended Trinity College, Cambridge, where he became a Fellow in 1776 and where he apparently was at one point tutor to Spencer Perceval, the future Prime Minister. In 1782, he was appointed subtreasurer to Queen Charlotte, later becoming her treasurer, then librarian at Buckingham Palace.

A reclusive man of letters, he began publishing satirical poems, none of them under his own name. Besides *The Pursuits of Literature*, they include *An Heroic Epistle to the Rev. R. Watson, D.D.* (1780); *The Imperial Epistle from Kien Long, Emperor of China, to George the Third, King of Great Britain* (1795?); *An Epistle in Verse to the Rev. Dr. Randolph* (1796); *An Equestrian Epistle in Verse, to the R. Hon. the Earl of Jersey* (1796); and *The Shade of Alexander Pope on the Banks of the Thames* (1799). A prominent scholar of Italian literature, Mathias translated Milton, Spenser, Thomson, and other poets into Italian and edited several Italian authors. In 1817, reasons of health led him to move to Italy, where he continued with his literary and scholarly endeavors. He died at Naples in 1835.

The first dialogue of *The Pursuits of Literature* (all of them are between the "Author" and his friend "Octavius") was published in 1794, the second and third in 1796, and the fourth, by far the longest, in 1797. Seeing Jacobin import in much modern writing, Mathias aimed to demonstrate how "Government and Literature are now more than ever intimately connected." He won readers with his condemnations of such writers as Godwin, Lewis, and Wollstonecraft and with his Tory antipathy toward things French, Roman Catholic, democratic, or decadent. The work had many advocates, although opinion often divided on party lines. Cobbett, then of conservative sympathies, termed it "matchless," and Richard Polwhele wrote in a note to his antifeminist poem *The Unsex'd Females* (1798) that "many in this country, whose politics and even religion have been long wavering, are now fixed in their principles by 'the Pursuits of Literature.'" The work went through 16 editions by 1812; in some, the many quotations from Latin, Greek, French, and Italian in the notes were translated so that they could reach a wider audience. Some of the numerous published responses to *The Pursuits* identified Mathias as the poet, but he kept asserting, in added prefatory material, that anonymity was essential to satire, and he publicly disowned its authorship until after he moved to Italy.

Many readers of *The Pursuits* have agreed with Coleridge's observation in *The Friend* that the author's "patch-work Notes" possess only "the comparative merit of being more poetical than the Text." Lacking the wit and imagery found with a Pope or a Byron, Mathias's verse often serves merely as an excuse for his long discursive footnotes, which are overburdened with redundant quotations in foreign languages (indeed, with the notes and prefaces this poem of only 1,500 lines occupies a volume of over 300 pages). Less a satire than a critical essay, *The Pursuits of Literature* is valuable today primarily as a document of literary history and as evidence of what sympathies moved a significant portion of the reading public. (*See also* Satire.)

Gary R. Dyer

Works Consulted

Coleridge, Samuel Taylor. *The Friend*. Ed. Barbara Rooke. Princeton: Princeton UP, 1969.

Dictionary of National Biography, *s.v.* "Mathias, Thomas James."

Hopkins, Kenneth. *Portraits in Satire*. London: Barrie, 1958.

Lockwood, Thomas. *Post-Augustan Satire: Charles Churchill and Satirical Poetry, 1750–1800*. Seattle: U of Washington P, 1979.

[Mathias, Thomas James.] "An Introductory Letter to a Friend." *Pursuits of Literature: A Satirical Poem in Four Dialogues, with Notes*. 1794–97. Philadelphia: Dickens, 1800.

[Polwhele, Richard.] *The Unsex'd Females: A Poem Addressed to the Author of The Pursuits of Literature*. 1798. 2nd ed. New York: Cobbett, 1800.

Maturin, Charles Robert
(1780–1824)

The creator of *Melmoth the Wanderer*, the single work by which Charles Robert Maturin is known today, was born into a middle-class family in Dublin, Ireland, in 1780. Although often denounced for its sprawling plot and dark view of humanity, *Melmoth the Wanderer* (1820) is now recognized as the high-water mark of the Gothic genre's early years. But *Melmoth* was only one of Maturin's novels and plays, many with Gothic settings and motifs, published in his lifetime.

Until 1809, Maturin lived with his wife, Henrietta Kingsberry, and their children in Dublin, where he was curate of St. Peter's after his graduation from Trinity College in 1800. However, in 1809, his father was dismissed from his government post on charges of fraud. The financial difficulties resulting, no doubt, from his father's dismissal contributed to Maturin's drive to publish; his salary as curate was meager even though the church itself was in affluent surroundings, and his position in the Anglican church brought social prestige. Indeed, Maturin had to live in his father's home even after marrying in 1804. In 1807, under the pseudonym Dennis Jasper Murphy, Maturin published *The Family of Montorio* (renamed *Fatal Revenge* by his publisher, much to Maturin's annoyance) and in 1808, *The Wild Irish Boy*. Both were published at Maturin's expense, a luxury hardly possible after his financial difficulties, which were compounded by a relative who defaulted on the loan for which Maturin stood as security. As one supplement, he took in students from the College of Dublin as boarders and protégés. Well-read in the classics as well as in contemporary fiction, Maturin was a knowledgeable tutor but found teaching difficult and eventually abandoned it.

Maturin's financial difficulties were further complicated by his personality, which indulged in self-pity. His letters, even those written to publishers and business acquaintances, consistently lamented his circumstances. During this period of dire financial difficulties, Maturin published *The Milesian Chief* (1812), his first novel to turn a profit (£80 for the copyright—about the same as a curate's yearly salary).

Maturin considered himself a serious writer, but his primary occupation as well as source of income in his early years was within the Anglican church. In spite of his popularity as a preacher, he had no hope for preferment in the church because of the unorthodox subjects in his novels—especially in his next work, *Bertram*, a play which included adultery as well as murder. His chances for advancement in the church were further dimmed by his outspoken espousal of Calvinism, which was not appreciated by his Anglican superiors. Maturin could hope only that literature would offer financial reward in a time when few could earn a living by writing.

In 1816, Maturin had turned from novels to drama with the successful presentation of *Bertram*, first performed at Drury Lane Theatre on May 9 to enormous popular acclaim. Praised and encouraged by Byron and especially by Scott, who had become a mentor to Maturin after receiving letters in 1812, Maturin was overwhelmed by his success, including £350 for the copyright to *Bertram* and a healthy share of the theater receipts. Unfortunately, he began living beyond his means with elaborate dress, parties, and home furnishings so that he was financially little better off than in his earlier years. *Bertram* was successful not only in England but also in the United States and France, where it was translated and produced in 1822.

His next play, *Manuel* (1817), failed after only five nights at Drury Lane, and *Fredolfo* (1819) was even less successful at Covent Garden. In fact, audiences laughed and walked out on the performance. Accordingly, Maturin returned to fiction with *Women: or Pour et Contre* (1818), which relieved his immediate financial needs. But needing money for his growing family just to survive, Maturin published a collection of his sermons. Although his financial situation was never stable, an advance of £500 for *Melmoth the Wanderer* in 1819 allowed him to devote much time and effort to his work. Sadly, during the time he was composing *Melmoth*, his wife became ill and his youngest child died; nonetheless Maturin committed himself to his novel, which was published in the spring of 1820.

Melmoth the Wanderer is a watershed of Gothicism, with traces of Satan, Faust, and the Wandering Jew embodied in the novel's central (although little-seen) character Melmoth. The plot concerns Melmoth's unsuccessful attempt, over many decades, to find someone willing to sell his soul to free Melmoth from immortality acquired through his own quest for forbidden knowledge, but the narrative is structured in convoluted tales within tales unified around Melmoth and his descendant of the same name, who is the auditor of the novel. The appropriately Gothic setting includes dark nights during tumultuous storms, gloomy monasteries, prisons of the Inquisition, madhouses, and ancestral homes where family portraits seem to move and candles dim for no discernible reason. Maturin must have found the Gothic mode an ideal vessel for his hatred of institutionalized religion, specifically Roman Catholicism, since the Gothic novel was traditionally anti-Catholic (especially in Lewis's *The Monk* published in 1796). Maturin may have planned a sequel to *Melmoth the Wanderer* to which other tales could have been added, but he did not live to complete such a project.

Little is known of the last years of Maturin's life, for he lived in seclusion and poverty, alienated from his church because of his persistent attacks on organized religion as well as because of the fascination with the diabolical and occult shown in his novels and plays, for which he, as an Anglican clergyman, was particularly condemned. Rumors of his dismissal from St. Peter's were circulated in 1816, although he retained his position until his death in 1824. Prior to his death, Maturin published his last novel, *The Albigenses*, an historical romance patterned after *Waverly*.

Maturin's sometimes flamboyant and often eccentric behavior (including extremes of dress from rags to eloquent styles) gave rise to a rumor that he had precipitated his own death through a mix-up of his medications. But his most recent biographer, Robert E. Lougy, says such rumors were unfounded. However, the suggestion of something sinister surrounding Maturin's death seems appropriate for someone who spawned Melmoth and had a lifelong fascination with the macabre. No doubt overwork contributed more to his death than medications; he was survived by his wife and four children. Although Scott proposed reprinting Maturin's novels with a biographical sketch, the project fell with the collapse of Scott's Ballantyne bookselling house. So a Maturin revival was not forthcoming. (*See also* Gothicism, Novel.)

Karen McGuire

Works Consulted

Kramer, Dale. *Charles Robert Maturin*. New York: Twayne, 1973.

Lougy, Robert E. *Charles Robert Maturin*. Lewisburg: Bucknell UP, 1975.

Mavrokordatos, Alexandros
(1791–1865)

One of the leading political and military figures of the Greek Revolution, Alexandros Mavrokordatos was a friend of the Shelleys at Pisa and enlisted the personal support of Byron at Missolonghi. He became Prime Minister three times under Otto, first king of Greece, and held various diplomatic and governmental posts.

Born into a family of distinguished Phanariots (i.e., Greeks of Turkish Constantinople), Mavrokordatos served as Secretary of State of Wallachia under his uncle Ioannis Karadja, thereby earning the title of "prince." Forced with Karadja into exile in 1818, he settled in Pisa, where he had earlier studied law, medicine, and military strategy and where he now italianized his name to Mavrocordato. In December 1820, he was introduced to the Shelleys, developing a close relationship with Mary, whom he taught Greek in exchange for lessons in English, and a less certain relationship with her husband. Though initially attracted to the romantic exile, Shelley (possibly jealous of Mary's closeness to him) later confessed regret at not finding his "turbaned friend" more to his liking. However, in November 1821, five months after the prince's departure for Greece (where revolution had begun that March), Shelley dedicated his lyrical drama *Hellas* to him; Mavrokordatos's insights into Turkish instability had certainly influenced its composition.

Established at Missolonghi as provisional governor of Western Greece, Mavrokordatos oversaw the drafting of a constitution by the National Assembly at Epidaurus and in January 1822, was elected its president—Greece's first native ruler since Byzantium fell to the Turks in 1453. Factional antagonism rendered the government virtually impotent and so he returned to Missolonghi, where he resisted a siege the following winter with 500 soldiers against 20,000 Turks. His heroic stand made him famous throughout Europe, and a correspondence with Byron ensued. After military infighting caused Mavrokordatos to flee to the island of Hydra, Byron made a loan of £4,000 with which to reactivate his fleet and in January 1824, joined him at Missolonghi, bringing a large quantity of medical supplies and his considerable financial wealth. Over the four months prior to Byron's death, the relationship between the two men was not close and was characterized chiefly by requests for "loans," with which Byron complied with increasing caution. The prince's plans for Byron to lead an attack on Lepanto and for them both to attend an interfaction congress at Salona were confounded by disorganization and the bad weather that led to Byron's death.

In 1825, Mavrokordatos entered into negotiations with Britain—facilitated by Byron's earlier dispatches to the Greek Committee in London—and successfully brought about talks between the three protective powers (Britain, France, and Russia) and the Turkish government. After the allied destruction of the Turkish and Egyptian fleets at Navarino in 1827 and further Russian victories, these talks resumed and culminated in a multilateral recognition of the independence of Greece in 1830. By this time, Mavrokordatos was leader of the opposition in the ever more dictatorial government of Ioannis Kapodistrias, and his subsequent years of service, divided between foreign embassies and ministerial positions, frequently saw conflict between his reformist beliefs and the autocratic methods of King Otto. He resigned from his third brief premiership in 1855.

Mavrokordatos has been variously described as an honest, unselfish patriot and a deceitful and indecisive soldier-pretend. Shelley and Byron were both ambivalent about him, and his triumphant defense of Missolonghi has to be set beside the disastrous defeat at Peta that preceded it—though the extent of his blame for this has been debated. There is, however, strong consensus as to his intelligence, courage, and dedication to an independent, democratic Greece.

Andrew Paxman

Works Consulted

Huscher, Herbert. "Alexander Mavrocordato, Friend of the Shelleys." *Keats-Shelley Memorial Bulletin*, 14 (1965): 29–38.

Marchand, Leslie A., ed. *For Freedom's Battle*, 1823–1824. Vol. 11 of *Byron's Letters and Journals*. London: Murray, 1981.

Mavrocordato, Prince Alexander. "Rendez-vous at Missolonghi." *Byron Journal* 4 (1976): 44–57.

St. Clair, William. *That Greece Might Still be Free*. London: Oxford UP, 1972.

Medievalism

In his *Account of Architects and Architecture* (1664), John Evelyn expressed the prevailing view of his age when he wrote, "the Goths and Vandals, having demolished the Greek and Roman architecture, introduced in its stead a certain fantastical and licentious manner of building which we have since called modern or Gothic." One hundred eighty years later, *Weale's Quarterly Papers on Architecture* (1844) complained of an apparent 11th commandment, "Thou shalt not worship the grandeur of Egypt, nor the beauty of Greece, nor the grandeur of Rome . . . —but thou shalt worship only GOTHICISM!" This shift in taste constitutes the Gothic Revival, the fascination with things medieval that so pervades Romanticism that Kenneth Clark virtually equated the two movements.

Interest in the Middle Ages had never completely vanished from the culture. Spenser's *Faerie Queene* (1590–96) used pseudomedieval English to recount its allegorical tales of chivalric knights, and the greatest Elizabethan dramatists wrote plays about Edward II, John, Richard II, and the Wars of the Roses. Malory's *Morte d'Arthur* was reprinted until 1634; Addison and Steele praised the medieval ballad "Chevy Chase" and the archaic Spenser; *A Collection of Old Ballads* was published in 1723, and Allan Ramsay's *The Evergreen*, an anthology of ancient Scottish songs, the following year, while Gothic churches continued to be built occasionally throughout the 18th century.

But in the 1740s and 1750s, this trickle of medievalism became a flood. Batty Langley's *Gothic Architecture Improved* (1742), based on two decades of research, sought to encourage understanding and appreciation of the form. Four years later, Sanderson Miller began a vogue for Gothic

ruins when he erected one at Edgehill; he produced another at Hagley in 1747. Around 1750 Walpole started Gothicizing his villa, Strawberry Hill, at Twickenham, and Richard Payne Knight's Downton Castle (1774–78) established a craze for castellated country houses. One Charles Lamb (not the essayist) went so far as to order a set of battlemented hutches for his guinea pigs. Supporting the comment in *Weale's Quarterly Papers* is the statistic that of 214 churches constructed as a result of the Church Building Act (1818), 174 were Gothic. After the Old Palace at Westminster burned in 1834, it was rebuilt in Gothic style.

This same fascination with the medieval is evident in the literature of the age. Percy's *Reliques of Ancient Poetry* and Walpole's *The Castle of Otranto*, the first Gothic novel, were both published in 1765. Three years earlier, Richard Hurd had declared in his *Letters on Chivalry and Romance* that Gothicism was a better source of inspiration "than the simple and uncontrolled barbarity of the Grecian." Macpherson's Ossianic forgeries that so beguiled Napoleon and Chatterton's pseudomedieval Rowley poems that fooled Walpole would have been pointless a few decades before; in the age of Pope few would have cared for such "primitive" literature. Although Austen in *Northanger Abbey* (1818) mocked the popularity of Gothic novels, they enjoyed immense appeal: Radcliffe, Lewis, and Maturin delighted audiences with pleasurable frissons, and Scott capitalized on this taste for monks, knights and castles in his poetry (*The Lay of the Last Minstrel, Marmion, The Lady of the Lake*, and *The Lord of the Isles*) and fiction (*Ivanhoe, The Abbot*, and *The Monastery*). In fact, few writers of the Romantic era were untouched by this trend. Keats's *La Belle Dame Sans Merci* and *The Eve of St. Agnes*; Southey's translations of

Amadis of Gaul, Palmerin of England, and *Chronicles of the Cid*—medieval romances all—as well as his 1816 edition of Malory's legends of King Arthur, the first to appear since 1634; Coleridge's *Christabel*; the first English translation of Dante all reflect the age's obsession with the Middle Ages.

Old armor was removed from attics where Neoclassical taste had consigned it, dusted off, and displayed in Gothicized country homes. Those lacking metallic paraphernalia could purchase these new symbols of status; in 1789, Christie's responded to the tide of taste by holding its first recorded armor auction. Not only did people alter their houses to appear more medieval, they also changed their names: Charles Tennyson (uncle of the laureate) became Charles Tennyson d'Eyncourt, Ambrose Lisle Phillipps became Ambrose Phillipps de Lisle. In 1787, Benjamin West began a series of seven panels on the life of Edward III for the King's Audience Chamber at Windsor Castle; over the next century countless medieval knights appeared on canvas and in stained glass. Occasionally, as at the 1839 Eglinton Tournament, they showed up in person.

As Hurd suggested, the Gothic Revival in part reflected the search for new sources of literary and artistic inspiration to substitute for the heavily used Roman models of the Neoclassical age. Nationalism, too, played a role, as artists sought native subjects. In a world where "roads and newspapers lay everything open" (*Northanger Abbey*), the misty Middle Ages enchanted many. Conservatives confronting revolution and republicanism admired the stable hierarchy of a bygone age, while reformers associated Gothicism with freedom, Magna Carta, and Christian socialism.

Like so many other facets of Romanticism, medievalism did not end in 1832 or in 1837. The Oxford Movement, Tennyson's *Idylls of the King* (1859–74), William Morris's work, and Kelmscott Press attest to the Victorian fascination with the Gothic. The revival had its silly, even tragic side—England and Germany may have willed World War I as a purifying chivalric contest—but it also encouraged scholarly research and promoted a code of behavior that at its best sought just treatment for all and protected the weak against exploitation. If the Gothic Revival created Olde English Tea Shoppes and fake ruins, its greater legacy enriched English art, architecture, and literature with enduring monuments of the creative spirit.

Joseph Rosenblum

Works Consulted

Clark, Kenneth. *The Gothic Revival: An Essay in the History of Taste.* London: Constable, 1928.

Girouard, Mark. *The Return to Camelot: Chivalry and the English Gentleman.* New Haven: Yale UP, 1981.

Meeke, Mary

(?–1818)

Of the writers of Gothic fiction for Minerva Press, Mary Meeke was one of the most popular and prolific. For over 20 years, she produced one or two novels per year, sometimes under the pseudonym Gabrielli. She also translated French and German works and wrote stories for children.

Not much is known about her life. She was probably the wife of Francis Meeke, a minister in Staffordshire who wrote poetry. Other than this information, the record of her work is the only record of her life.

Meeke's first work, *Count St. Blancard, or the Prejudiced Judge* (1795), is the only one in modern reprint. It is the story of a young doctor who falls in love with a young noblewoman but is prevented from courting her because of the difference in their social standings. After grave illnesses, attempted rape, and imprisonments in a dungeon and a convent, the two are happily married when it is revealed that the doctor is really the son of a high government official. The novel was well received as a piece of light entertainment by the critics.

Over 30 works followed. Imitating Radcliffe, Meeke added supernatural elements to her work but had little understanding of or feeling for the irrational world. Her world is solidly middle class, with emphasis on love and merit in choice of a marriage partner and on money and position in society. Her novels vary only slightly. Well-plotted but with little description, they follow a formula of genealogical puzzles leading to revelation of the hero or heroine's noble birth. Her later works, written when Gothic fiction was diminishing in popularity, center more on domestic life with only a few Gothic elements intermingled.

Meeke, in the Introduction to *Midnight Weddings* (1802), revealed that commercial, not great artistic, success was her goal. And she reached it. Her novels were widely read: Macaulay and Mitford were among her devoted readers. Today, they are rarely read and then mostly for evidence of popular taste in the early 19th century. (*See also* Gothicism.)

Ann W. Engar

Works Consulted

Blakey, Dorothy. *The Minerva Press, 1790–1820.* London: Printed for the Bibliographical Society at the UP, Oxford, 1939.

Dictionary of National Biography, s.v. "Meeke, Mary."

Frank, Frederick S. *The First Gothics: A Critical Guide to the English Gothic Novel.* New York: Garland, 1987.

Varma, Devendra. Foreword. *Count St. Blancard, or The Prejudiced Judge.* By Mary Meeke. New York: Arno, 1977.

Melancholy

The roots of melancholy extend at least as far back as the Middle Ages, but it is later that melancholy becomes a pleasurable and enjoyable experience. The Romantics and Pre-Romantics are probably the most famous for their love of melancholy.

Melancholy is general depression, usually without basis. It results in pensive and introspective contemplation, which leads to perceptive conclusions by the poet. It is much absorbed in personal feeling and the examination and expression of these feelings. Romantic poets love elegies, deaths, and graveyards, all of which cause them to inspect and revere simple lives that have come to nothing in terms of fame and fortune. More important, however, these lives have remained uncorrupted by the sophisticated ideas and associations of urban life.

Probably the best example of poetic melancholy is Thomas Gray's *Elegy Written in a Country Churchyard*. In this poem, the poet is sitting at twilight in a small country churchyard. Sitting alone near the simple cemetery as others go home, the poet is left alone in the darkness. Looking at the tombs, he thinks of those lying buried, uneducated and unknown, and of missed opportunities that might have led them to be great military generals, poets, or musicians. But if obscurity denies them those rewards, it also saves them from corruption. They died simple and virtuous, qualities that are more important than fame possibly based on crime. Pensive and introspective, Gray contemplates these dead unknowns.

Though *Elegy Written in a Country Churchyard* may be one of the purest examples of lyric melancholy, it is by no means alone. Coleridge's *Dejection: An Ode*, Keats's *Ode on Melancholy*, and Shelley's *Stanzas: Written in Dejection* all testify to the poetic riches despair bequeaths. Wordsworth refers to the time in *Lines Written in Early Spring* when he reclined in a grove and sad thoughts intrude upon his pleasant mood. In *Resolution and Independence*, one fine morning, the poet's good mood plummets to despair. Meeting the leech gatherer while he is in this mood teaches him to count his blessings. An examination of the poet's place in life results in a philosophical readjustment to it.

Though elegies are often primarily pastoral, it is the sober and thoughtful look at death that causes a thoughtful reflection on the contribution of the subject of the elegy. In *Adonais*, for example, grief and subsequent examination of his own feelings lead Shelley to praise Keats. It is important to have an appropriate epitaph for a life well and productively lived, and this is what Shelley provides for Keats in his poem.

The Romantics, paradoxically, loved to be depressed because it was through this depression and subsequent introspection that they realized the important truths. A melancholy contemplation of what is and what was often leads to a philosophic realization that what matters in life are excellence of character and a love and respect for others.

Shirley Laird

Work Consulted

Reed, Amy Louise. *The Background of Gray's Elegy.* New York: Russell, 1962.

Mental Theater

The term mental theater was coined in the 19th century by Byron in a letter to John Murray (23 August 1821). Similar language, however, was used as early as 1765 by Johnson and as late as 1903 by Hardy (in his Preface to *The Dynasts*). In each case, these writers are describing the experience of reading poetic dramatic texts in order to experience them imaginatively. In the Romantic period, mental theater became important to dramatic critics, who, characteristic of their age, preferred reading plays to viewing them on the stage, and to playwrights who had little concern for stage presentation.

The dramatic critics of the Romantic period, responding to both the conditions of the stage and their own interest in character psychology, pointed out the incompatibility of material presentation and imaginative understanding of character. Lamb, Hazlitt, and Coleridge all questioned the suitability of Shakespeare's plays for the stage, arguing that Shakespeare emphasized development of character and not action. Hazlitt's *Characters of Shakespeare's Plays* (1817) reflects this focus on characters and on readers' imaginative identifications with them. According to these critics, any performance, and perhaps particularly the performances of the early 19th century, interrupted the intimate experience of character that readers experience. Lamb's "On the Tragedies of Shakespeare . . ." (1811) articulates the general argument against performance by drawing attention to the various traits of Shakespearean characters (e.g., Othello's race, Lear's age) that in performance block audience identification. *Hamlet* became a touchstone of Romantic Shakespearean criticism because it allowed a critic like Coleridge to view Hamlet's psychological dilemma as the exclusive focus of the play.

But it was not only the critics who imagined dramatic form distinct from theatrical performance. The *Plays of the Passions* of Baillie (first volume published in 1798) represents one of the earliest sustained attempts by a playwright to investigate a series of characters' inner lives through verse drama. Although some of Baillie's plays were performed, albeit unsuccessfully, her introduction to their first edition describes the internality of character that made their staging infrequent. Both Wordsworth's *The Borderers* (1797, not published until 1842) and Coleridge's *Osorio* (1797; revised and performed as *Remorse* in 1813) used dramatic forms drawn from German *Sturm und Drang* to present similarly complex internal conflict. Byron criticized the 19th-century public's taste for spectacle and structured his experimental verse dramas—*Manfred* (1816–17) and *Cain* (1821)—around the ethical and psychological struggles of tortured central figures. However, his only staged play, *Marino Faliero* (1821), resembled the popular historical dramas of the time. Shelley presented the consciousness of his characters, both by experimenting with a wide variety of poetic and dramatic forms in *Prometheus Unbound* (1819) and by adopting verse and plot structure closer to Shakespearean models in *The Cenci* (also 1819). Byron's and Shelley's attempts to explore character subjectivity by going beyond the limits of the stage anticipate later expressionist theatrical forms.

Dramas written as mental theater influenced the poetic drama of Tennyson, Browning, and other Victorian poets, but perhaps the early dramatic monologues—like Coleridge's conversation poems, Wordsworth's *The Thorn*, and the poems of Hemans—were the most directly influential form of mental theater to emerge. By developing these Romantic forms, both the Brownings and Tennyson demonstrated that the psychological action of character speech reveals a dramatic situation.

The "theater of the mind" in the early 19th century influenced subsequent developments in dramatic and poetic form.

Numerous reasons have been advanced to explain the growth of nontheatrical drama, including (1) the growth of a psychology of interiority; (2) the consequent importance of character, rather than action, in Romantic drama; (3) the influence of Goethe's *Faust*; (4) the "deteriorating" state of the stage—from the style of performance to the system of theatrical management; (5) the censorship of plays in England and the related restriction of the theatrical marketplace; and (6) the iconoclastic distaste of some writers for the theater public.

While each explanation deserves consideration, their combination suggests that mental theater, or closet drama (as it is disparagingly called), emerges from complex historical, economic, and intellectual developments that highlight the relationship between popular and literary culture in England during the Romantic period. (*See also* Theater.)

Thomas C. Crochunis

Works Consulted

Donahue, Joseph W., Jr. *Dramatic Character in the English Romantic Age*. Princeton: Princeton UP, 1970.

Langbaum, Robert. *The Poetry of Experience: The Dramatic Monologue in Modern Literary Tradition*. New York: Norton, 1963.

Otten, Terry. *The Deserted Stage: The Search for Dramatic Form in Nineteenth-Century England*. Athens: Ohio UP, 1972.

Richardson, Alan. *A Mental Theater: Poetic Drama and Consciousness in the Romantic Age*. University Park: Pennsylvania State UP, 1988.

Wang, Shou-ren. *The Theatre of the Mind; A Study of Unacted Drama in Nineteenth-Century England*. New York: St. Martin's, 1990.

Metrical Theory and Versification

Hazlitt's proclamation that the poets of the 1790s had banished regular meter along with regular government is an important, if hyperbolic, reminder that the Romantic period in England was a time of extraordinary changes in the theory and practice of versification. The relative uniformity in metrical theory and practice that had dominated English poetry from the Restoration through the mid-18th century increasingly gave way to diversity of opinion in the 1770s and after; by the 1790s much of English verse was being composed on principles that Pope and his contemporaries would not have allowed. (*See also* Poetry.)

Among the most significant developments in the metrical theory that underpins Romantic practice is the gradual rejection of syllabic prosody in favor of various systems that take account of the accentual nature of English rhythms. Edward Bysshe's handbook of poetic craft *The Art of Poetry* (1702; nine editions by 1762) provides the clearest and most influential statement of the strict syllabic system. Superimposing French rules on English verse (the prosodic section of Bysshe's work is in fact a virtual translation from the French of Claude Lancelot), Bysshe defines English verse solely in terms of the number of syllables per line, assigning only minor importance to accent.

The English heroic line is decasyllabic, not five-stress, or pentameter. As long as the poet observes proper syllable count and follows certain other rules governing the proper placement of pauses in the line, he is composing metrically. Supernumerary syllables are treated as faults, unless they are subject to one or more of the rules governing pronunciation in verse: for example, contraction ("ta'en" for "taken"); syncope of the penultimate vowel before intervocalic "r," "l," "n," or "m" ("past'ral" or "trav'ling"); synaeresis ("volupt-yus" for "voluptuous"); or apocope ("th' east" for "the east"). The art of poetry, then, involves fitting the disorderly phonetic material of English words into the confines of a ten-, eight-, or six-syllable verse. Paul Fussell has argued that an 18th-century reader would have found such regularizing of irregular phonetic material a chief source of poetic pleasure. Johnson's discussion of prosody in the "Grammar" prefixed to his *Dictionary* (1755) provides a convenient summary of syllabist principles, as well as evidence of the currency of Bysshe's ideas among the leading writers at mid-century.

The two most influential responses to syllabism in the Romantic period come from "foot verse" theorists and proponents of the music-verse analogy. Both focus on the treatment of what Bysshe would consider extrametrical syllables, and both frequently use Milton's blank verse as the chief source for their examples of legitimate heroic lines of more than ten syllables.

For foot-verse prosodists, the occasional use of supernumerary syllables has ample precedent both in classical and in pre-Restoration English verse. Once the line is defined not as a fixed number of syllables but as a collection of smaller "feet" dependent on the strong stresses of the verse, certain "substitutions," well known to students of classical foot-based prosody, are allowed. The most common substitution sanctioned by these prosodists is the occasional use of a three-syllable foot in an otherwise disyllabic meter (anapests in iambic meters; dactyls in trochaic meters). Theories that sanction such substitution obviate the need for the elaborate systems of poetic contractions set forth by Bysshe and others. So long as the extra syllables form an allowable substitution, one need not drop the offending syllable from pronunciation: "Of Man's First Disobedience and the Fruit" need not be read with "disobedience" as a four-syllable word ("dis-o-bed-*yence*"), as it had to be for syllabic readers. It may be read as foot verse: "Of Man's/First Dis/o-bed/*i-ence and*/the Fruit," with "i-ence and" considered a trisyllabic substitution. Milton's line is for these new readers no longer decasyllabic; it is pentameter.

Proponents of the music-verse analogy also justify the use of varying numbers of unstressed syllables. But for these theorists, the English line is best understood not as a series of feet, but as a sequence of time units equivalent to the musical bar. Just as each measure of music in a composition may contain varying numbers of notes and still be performed in an amount of time equal to all other measures, so the line of verse may be thought of as a sequence of equal units of time in which varying numbers of syllables may be pronounced. Many of these writers also introduce into metrical theory the concept of the musical "rest" to describe apparent irregularities in syllable count and alternation of stress. The most innovative and influential of these theorists is Joshua Steele, whose *Prosodia Rationalis* was published in 1779. Among Steele's disciples in the Romantic period was John Thelwall, who published a treatise on meter in 1812.

Stemming from both of these theoretical emphases is a more general loosening of strictures on a number of metrical elements. Topics of discussion among foot-verse theorists include, for example, the use of trochaic substitution in iambic lines (generally eschewed by earlier writers, except in the first position in a line) and the legitimacy of unrhymed verse for a wide range of types of poetry. For many of these writers, advocacy of accentual prosody has nationalist implications, since it involves throwing off superimposed French rules in favor of descriptive ac-

counts based on native qualities of the language. In general, these arguments tend to sanction, either as expressive or as productive of pleasing variety, many types of metrical freedom that to the earlier 18th century would be regarded as simply incorrect. These theories also tend to emphasize natural pronunciation as the chief guide to the proper reading of verse; that is, whereas the rules of syllabic prosody as advocated in the earlier 18th century emphasize fitting words to the demands of meter, most late-18th century and Romantic writers emphasize the need for a metric that respects qualities of English as it is actually spoken.

Arguably the most important development in accentualist theory and practice in the Romantic period is Coleridge's *Christabel* (Part I composed probably 1797). Coleridge's note claims that he had founded the meter on a new principle—counting only the accents in each line, not the syllables. Thomas Omond argues that Coleridge actually may have been influenced, perhaps through Thelwall, by Steele and the music-verse theorists. George Saintsbury sees the meter as perfectly standard foot verse with liberal allowance for weakly stressed syllables and suggests that the same principle was already at work in *The Ancient Mariner* and in other late-18th-century lyrics and ballads (e.g., Blake's *Poetical Sketches* and *Songs*). Whatever the genesis of the meter, there is no doubting its influence in bringing about a break between 18th-century prosody and the various innovations, from sprung rhythm to free verse, which were to follow in the later 19th and earlier 20th centuries.

Two key elements of the meter and of Coleridge's description of it should be noted: (1) its virtually unlimited flexibility in the use of weakly stressed syllables (Coleridge's lines range in length from four to 12 syllables) and (2) the justification of such variation on the ground that it corresponds with transitions in imagery or in the passion of the speaker. In short, the metrical character of the line itself is subordinate to, and determined by, the demands of expression. The relationship between these views and the Coleridgean preoccupation with "organic" versus "mechanic" form is sufficiently obvious; the theoretical distance between this view and the rationalizing tendencies of the syllabists is vast.

Christabel meter is the most celebrated of many innovations in metrical practice during a period distinguished by a profusion of various kinds of verse. Between 1660 and 1750, metrical theory and practice had been dominated, despite notable exceptions, by the heroic couplet. The couplet remained an important form in the Romantic period—from Wordsworth's *An Evening Walk*, to Crabbe's tales, and Keats's *Lamia*—but by the last quarter of the 18th century, the search was on for new ways of proceeding. Some innovations represent direct challenges to conventional meter and rhyme, as in the poetic prose of Macpherson's "Ossian" work or in the long lines of Blake's prophesies; some are more or less original inventions, or at least rediscoveries, of metrical rules and schemes, as are *Christabel* meter and Southey's experiments in unrhymed verse other than pentameters (*Thalaba* influenced the verse of Shelley's *Queen Mab*); some represent direct borrowing from other literatures (e.g., Southey's accentual hexameters in *The Vision of Judgment*; Byron's *ottava rima* in *Beppo* and *Don Juan*; Shelley's *terza rima* in *Ode to the West Wind* and *The Triumph of Life*).

By far the richest metrical innovations are reprisals or revisions of pre-Restoration kinds of English lines and stanza forms.

Just as the theorists had awakened to the peculiarly mixed heritage of English verse—with its Germanic, Romance, and classical influences—so poets in the mid- to late-18th century began increasingly to regard their predecessors from Chaucer to the Metaphysicals and the Jacobean lyricists not as incompetent writers of syllabic verse but as energetic and varied writers of accentual-syllabic verse. Editions of the elder poets that had been appearing throughout the later 18th century—Tyrwhitt's Chaucer (1775), the several 18th-century editions of Shakespeare, Henry Headley's *Select Beauties of Ancient English Poetry* (1787), the first four volumes of Anderson's *British Poets* (1793), and especially Percy's inestimably influential *Reliques of Ancient English Poetry* (1765)—gave poets and readers access to an extraordinary mixed body of verse, which exemplified in practice the various prosodic traditions that had influenced English poetry. Imitations of Chaucer and Chaucerian verse forms (including variations on rhyme royal and the enjambed couplets of Hunt and the earlier Keats), of the Spenserian stanza and the various stanzas of the *Shepheardes Calender*, of Shakespearean and Jacobean lyric, and especially of various traditional stanzas associated with music—from hymns to drinking songs, from ballads to nursery rhymes—begin to appear in profusion in the work of Chatterton, Burns, Blake, Southey, Coleridge, Wordsworth, Moore, Shelley, Byron, Beddoes, and others.

Except for minor exceptions, the sonnet had fallen into virtual oblivion in the 18th century; but it was reborn during the period. Charlotte Smith's *Elegiac Sonnets* (1784) claimed the form for the literature of sensibility; Coleridge, Charles Lloyd, and Lamb composed sonnets in the 1790s, partly in imitation of Bowles's *Fourteen*

Sonnets (1789). But it was Wordsworth, who, under the direct influence of Milton's sonnets, began in 1802 to give new life to the form. More than 500 sonnets appear in the final lifetime edition of Wordsworth's *Poetical Works*, including five sonnet sequences. Several of Shelley's sonnets, most notably *Ozymandias* and *England in 1816*, are important in the history of the form. Keats's struggle with the sonnet (e.g., "If by dull rhymes our English must be chained"), besides producing some brilliant poems, also helped him to develop the stanzas that he used in his most famous odes.

Romantic nondramatic blank verse also benefits from the confluence of various traditions. Milton is of chief importance in the development of the blank verse poetry in the period. But of interest, too, is the influence of Cowper's less elevated, more conversational blank verse in the widely popular *The Task* (1785). This work affected Romantic innovations in the poetry of simplicity and reflection, exemplified by Coleridge's conversation poems (e.g., *The Eolian Harp* and *Frost a Midnight*) and in the later poems that these to varying degrees influence, from Wordsworth's *Tintern Abbey* to Shelley's *Alastor* to sections of Keats's *The Fall of Hyperion*.

Although none of the major poets wrote a systematic description or defense of his own metrical theory and practice, several important and suggestive statements bearing on the study of meter appear in the midst of other concerns in the prefaces, letters, and recorded conversations of these poets. Among the most significant of these statements are Blake's remarks "To the Public" on the meter of *Jerusalem*; Wordsworth's Preface to *Lyrical Ballads* (especially in its 1802 form); and Coleridge's *Biographia Literaria* (especially Chapter 18). Southey's Prefaces (especially

those to the fourth edition of *Thalaba* and to *The Vision of Judgment*) and letters contain many careful and perceptive remarks about the relationship of meter to meaning. The *Defence of Poetry* includes tantalizing hints about Shelley's views on poetic rhythm and harmony.

Brennan O'Donnell

Works Consulted

Bate, W. Jackson. *The Stylistic Development of Keats*. New York: MLA, 1945.

Brogan, T.V.F. *English Versification, 1570–1980*. Baltimore: Johns Hopkins UP, 1981.

Culler, A. Dwight. "Edward Bysshe and the Poet's Handbook." *PMLA* 63 (1948): 858–85.

Curran, Stuart. *Poetic Form and British Romanticism*. New York: Oxford, 1986.

Fussell, Paul. *Theory of Prosody in Eighteenth-Century England*. New London: Connecticut College Monographs, 1954. Hamden: Archon, 1966.

O'Donnell, Brennan. *Numerous Verse: A Guide to the Stanzas and Metrical Structures of Wordsworth's Poetry*. Studies in Philology 86, (Texts and Studies Series, 1989).

Omond, Thomas. *English Metrists*. Oxford: Clarendon, 1921.

Ostriker, Alicia. *Vision and Verse in William Blake*. Madison: U of Wisconsin P, 1965.

Saintsbury, George. *A History of English Prosody*. 3 vols. London: Macmillan, 1910. New York: Russell, 1961.

Wesling, Donald. *The New Poetries: Poetic Form since Wordsworth and Coleridge*. Lewisburg: Bucknell UP, 1985.

Middle Classes

"Middle classes" replaced the earlier "middling sort" used to describe the social group immediately below the English aristocracy in power and influence. Contemporaries described the middle class as both industrious and moral, but it was unclear who belonged to this group. It undoubtedly included a variety of occupations and incomes. The lower fringe might include anyone who could claim a measure of respectability, owned property, or hired employees. In addition, England's open society virtually allowed anyone who dressed like a gentleman to be accepted as one.

In the 18th century, a gentleman received his income from land ownership, but the Industrial Revolution brought "new men" to prominence and power, some from very humble origins. They included industrialists, managers, engineers, architects, and the doctors, lawyers, and clerks who served them and their betters. Although they were not truly gentlemen, they were not part of the lower classes either. Respectability was their goal, and they studiously copied the dress and manners of the upper class. The most successful bought country estates and married their children into the aristocracy. The middle class also included shopkeepers, teachers, skilled artisans, poor parsons, and lesser professionals of all types. Inclusion in the middle class was determined by ability to be self-sufficient as well as by respectability.

By 1830, the middle class had grown so influential that its values began to dominate English society. Most considered the aristocracy indolent and licentious and the poor, lazy. The middle class had a commitment to establish a new way of life, with the home as its spiritual, emotional, and material core. Expanding industrial opportunities demanded a man's presence in an amoral marketplace, but a woman's place was in the home. There she presided over a genteel safe haven of domestic virtue and provided her husband shelter from the pressures of the material world. Respectability, duty, responsibility, and morality were the keystones of the middle-class creed. The middle class attempted to impose its values on the working poor and was encouraged in doing so by the Evan-

gelical movement of the late 18th and early 19th centuries. Evangelicals preached obedience to authority and contentment. These ideals were popular with employers as well as conservative politicians.

The middle class also popularized new male and female roles. It rejected the 18-century gentleman's preoccupation with outdoor sports, drink, and food. The man took seriously economic and family responsibilities, rejecting the sexual dissipation and indulgence of the aristocracy. The new woman was concerned with her family, church, and charity, rather than social amusements. Middle-class men were educated outside the home, articled, or apprenticed. Middle-class women were educated at home, learning about domestic management and perhaps something of the family business.

Middle-class influence kept pace with its growing wealth. In 1800, it was usual for a middle-class family to live on or near its place of business. A merchant might have a family apartment above his shop, while lawyers often had offices in their homes. Even industrialists built houses next to their factories, and only the wealthiest could afford a separate residence. By 1830, many were contemplating a move to the new suburban developments or buying land in the country. The middle class had little respect for King George IV because of his immoral and self-centered way of life. It eagerly supported Victoria when she became Queen and was rewarded by her support of middle-class standards, giving her name to the decades of its greatest power and influence.

Elsa A. Nystrom

Works Consulted

Briggs, Asa. *The Age of Improvement, 1764–1867*. New York: Longmans, 1959.

Halevy, Elie. *England in 1815*. New York: Barnes, 1961.

Hibbert, Christopher. *The English, A Social History, 1066–1945*. New York: Norton, 1987.

Langford, Paul. *A Polite and Commercial People, England, 1727–1783*. New York: Oxford UP, 1989.

Perrot, Michelle, ed. *A History of Private Life; From the Fires of Revolution to the Great War*. Cambridge: Belknap, 1990.

White, R.J. *Life in Regency England*. New York: Putnam, 1963.

Milton

While one might castigate the Romantics for their Satanist position—their assertion that Milton's Satan, a magnificent poetical creation, is worthy of admiration and sympathy—Romantic criticism of Milton has been undervalued, dismissed as having no relevance to the modern critical enterprise. But Romantic criticism can be considered the basis for modern approaches to Milton.

While the Romantics have been erroneously portrayed as fragmenting the three interrelated aspects of Milton—the man, the thinker, and the poet—their criticism balances out his nature, for they believed the greatness of the man to have been determined by the expansiveness of the mind that produced the poetry. In their criticism, the Romantics expanded the restrictive view of Johnson, whose Milton was unlikable—uncongenial and cantankerous, politically rigid, and literarily conventional. In contrast, the Romantics enlarged the perspective, focusing on Milton's dignity, sublimity, learning, and art to portray his individuality, spirituality, and originality, until he became the apotheosis of most Romantic ideals: a rebel, a republican, an iconoclast, a thinker, and most important, a poet.

Not only did the Romantics comment on Milton, but they were influenced by him as well. Two major Romantic concepts, the shift of attention from the audience to the poet and the view of poetry as an "overflow," find antecedents in Milton. Like Milton, at various times Blake, Wordsworth, and Coleridge all complained about the reading public and expressed the hope that they could educate their audiences, morally and literarily. Also, while descriptions of poetic creation in terms of birth, spilling over, and, ultimately, God and Creation and references to the poet as a shepherd, prophet, and priest are associated with Romantic criticism, they can all be found in *Paradise Lost*, as well as in other of Milton's works. In addition, Romantic interest in the intuitive and spontaneous, the belief that language should be immediate and authentic, and the emphasis on learning all derive from Miltonic attitudes.

As critics, the Romantics fall into two categories: those who reflect the more popular reading public (Lamb, Landor, Hazlitt, Hunt, and Byron) and the revolutionaries (Blake, Wordsworth, Coleridge, Shelley, Keats, and De Quincey). Concerned with bridging the gap between creation and criticism, the Romantic critics posited the imagination as the faculty that enabled poets to create and critics to analyze that which the poet created. For the Romantics, Milton does more than provide the basis for a literary theory; he taught them how to be revolutionary artists.

Sheila A. Spector

Work Consulted

Wittreich, Joseph Anthony, Jr., ed. *The Romantics on Milton: Formal Essays and Critical Asides*. Cleveland: Case Western Reserve UP, 1970.

Mitford, Mary Russell

(1787–1855)

Mary Russell Mitford is best known for *Our Village*, a series of sketches of country life that first appeared in the *Ladies' Magazine*, beginning in 1819, and later in a series of five volumes published between 1824 and 1832. Her first published work was a collection of *Miscellaneous Poems* (1810), followed by the longer poems *Christina, or the Maid of the South Sea* (1811), *Blanch of Castile* (1812), and *Poems on the Female Character* (1813). Her poetry was received with some acclaim, encouraging her to write professionally to support her family, which was impoverished by her father's financial irresponsibility. In addition to writing poetry, *Our Village*, and the novel, *Belford Regis* (1835), she wrote several tragic dramas that were performed on the London stage in the 1820s and 1830s: *Julian* (1823) at Covent Garden; *Foscari* (1826), again at Covent Garden; *Rienzi* (1828), generally regarded as her best dramatic work, at Drury Lane; and *Charles I* (1834), which had to be produced on the Surrey side of the Thames because the Lord Chamberlain's office refused to license it for production in London. Mitford's tragedies were moderately successful with the public, and she believed her greatest literary abilities were dramatic. Later readers and critics, however, have found more to value in *Our Village* and in her lively and witty letters, several volumes of which were collected and published after her death.

Mitford was born in the small town of Alresford, Hampshire, in 1787, the daughter of Dr. George Mitford (from an old Northumberland family) and Mary Russell Mitford of Alresford. Dr. Mitford was a charming but extravagant, self-centered, and dissipated man, whose love of sports, gambling, and financial speculation ruined him; he had already gone through his inherited fortune when he married Mary Russell, an heiress ten years his senior, and promptly lost hers as well. By 1797, when daughter Mary was age 10, the impoverished Mitford family was living in London, Dr. Mitford a debtor under the rules of the King's Bench. Late in 1797 or early in 1798, Dr. Mitford took Mary to select a lottery ticket, which paid the substantial prize of £20,000. Dr. Mitford used his daughter's winnings to settle his debts and to build a large country house at Grasely, near Reading, where the family lived until 1820.

Although Mitford spent five years (1798–1802) at a fashionable boarding school at Hans Place, London, run by a French emigré, her real education came largely through wide reading. In addition to Homer and Greek drama in translation, she discusses in her letters English writers from Chaucer and Shakespeare to Dryden and Pope, Swift and Johnson, and the novelists Fielding, Richardson, and Smollett, as well as Fanny Burney, Charlotte Smith, and Edgeworth, Scott, and Austen. Two favorite books were White's *Natural History of Selborne* and Walton's *Compleat Angler*, which perhaps influenced her best work, the meditative-descriptive prose pastorals in *Our Village*. She also read French fluently and comments on such French writers as Madame de Sévigné, Rousseau, Molière, Balzac, Sand, and Hugo. Later, she also became familiar with American writers, such as Irving, Cooper, Channing, Emerson, and Hawthorne.

Family connections and her father's wide acquaintances in political and literary circles enabled Mitford to move easily into the social life of London after she left school. She rapidly met many of the important literary figures of the day who encouraged her early literary efforts; for example, Coleridge, a family friend, reviewed the manuscript of "Blanch of Castile" before its publication. In later life, in spite of poverty, ill-health, the requirements of authorship, and her father's increasingly autocratic demands on her time as he got older, Mitford maintained and extended her friendships through an active correspondence and occasional visits to London. Among her acquaintances were such figures as Samuel Rogers, Wordsworth, the painter Haydon, and John Kenyon, who introduced her in 1836 to Elizabeth Barrett, beginning a friendship that continued even after Barrett's marriage to Browning. Later, Ruskin was an admiring and affectionate correspondent.

Mitford's social and literary successes were darkened, however, by her father's extravagance. He was constantly in debt, and, by 1820, his financial difficulties resulted in the sale of his house and property; that year, the Mitfords moved into a small cottage at Three Mile Cross, a few miles from their old home, where Mitford lived until 1850. From this cottage, she struggled to support, first, both her parents, then after her mother's death in 1830, her father, by her writing. To provide money, Mitford not only composed for the stage, but also contributed to the *London Magazine*, other periodicals, and many annuals of the day; edited *Stories of American Life* (1830) and *American Stories for Children* (1832); and edited the popular annual *Finden's Tableaux* from 1838 to 1841. She published *Recollections of a Literary Life* in 1852 and her last book, *Atherton and Other Tales*, in 1854.

In 1837, Mitford's friends successfully petitioned the Prime Minister to award her a Civil List pension of £100, thereby providing her with some security; in 1842, at her father's death, friends raised a subscription to pay his final debts. In 1850, Mitford moved from the cottage at Three Mile Cross to another in the nearby village of Swallowfield, six miles from Reading, where she lived until her death in 1855.

Gail B. Walker

Works Consulted

Chorley, Henry, ed. *The Letters of Mary Russell Mitford*. 2nd Series. London: Bentley, 1872.

Horn, Pamela. "Alresford and Mary Russell Mitford." *Hatcher Review* 3 (1986): 86–94.

Hunter, Shelagh. *Victorian Idyllic Fiction: Pastoral Strategies*. Atlantic Highlands, NJ: Humanities, 1984.

Idol, John L., Jr. "Mary Russell Mitford: Champion of American Literature." *Studies in the American Renaissance: 1983*. Ed. Joel Myerson. Charlottesville: UP of Virginia, 1983.

L'Estrange, A.G.K., Rev. *The Life of Mary Russell Mitford, Told by Herself in Letters to Her Friends*. 2 vols. New York: Harper, 1870.

———. *The Friendships of Mary Russell Mitford, As Recorded in Letters from Her Literary Correspondents*. New York: Harper, 1882.

Pigrome, Stella. "Mary Russell Mitford." *Charles Lamb Bulletin* 66 (1989): 53–62.

Watson, Vera. *Mary Russell Mitford*. London: Evans Brothers, 1949.

Montagu, Lady Mary Wortley
(1689–1762)

Born in London as the Honorable Mary Pierrepont, Mary Montagu was the daughter of Evelyn Pierrepont, a wealthy Whig peer who became Duke of Kingston, and the Honorable Mary Fielding, daughter of the Earl of Denbigh. Fielding died when Montagu was age 5.

As a child, Mary Pierrepont and her friend Anne Montagu began a correspondence that, after Anne's death in 1709, was continued by her brother Edward Wortley Montagu. He and Pierrepont subsequently eloped in 1712, married, and had two children.

Wortley Mantagu was elected to Parliament in 1716 and then named ambassador to Turkey. While in Turkey, Mary Montagu learned Turkish and brought back to England the new practice of inoculation. After the couple separated by mutual consent in 1739, Montagu never saw her husband again, although they corresponded. After the separation, Montagu lived on the Continent, mostly in Italy, and did not return to London until after her husband's death in 1761. She died of breast cancer six months after her return to England.

Montagu, who had educated herself in her father's vast library, showed early promise, and her wit and beauty were displayed to her father's literary friends, who included Addison, Steele, and Congreve. She wrote imitations of Pope by age 12 and carefully kept her juvenilia. Her immersion into London cultural society began with her father's influence and continued most of her life. Best known for her letters—some 900 exist—she also wrote verse satires, a fairytale, eclogues, translations, and essays. A leader in London society, Montagu was first befriended and later attacked by Pope; she wrote verse attacks on Pope and Swift, and she also became bitter enemies with Walpole.

Besides her letters, Montagu also published, with Pope and John Gay, *Court Eclogues* (1715). These so-called court poems are satirical vignettes on contemporary morals and manners. She also wrote an essay for *The Spectator* in 1714 and published nine issues of a periodical *The Nonsense of Common-Sense* (1737–38), one number of which was a feminist essay, influenced by her childhood friend Mary Astell.

It is with her letters, however, that Montagu's reputation and fame rest. Her best known work is the *Embassy Letters*, which were based on her experiences while her husband was ambassador to Turkey and published in 1763, a year after her death. They are known for their easy style and faculty for description. Written mostly to her sister Lady Mar, they are entertaining and witty and show an empathy for the people with whom Montagu visited. Her descriptions of her journeys and adventures in Turkey and on the Continent show a wit and learning rarely surpassed.

Montagu's literary fame is largely posthumous because she discouraged printing her works in her lifetime. That preference for privacy, however, did not keep her works from circulating in manuscript and demonstrating to London social and literary circles a woman of wit, candor, and common sense. A feminist and a moralist, her whimsical sketches of London social life satirize the irregularities and gossip of polite society in the 18th century.

Gary Kerley

Works Consulted

Barry, Iris. *Portrait of Lady Mary Montagu.* Indianapolis: Bobbs, 1928.

Dictionary of National Biography, s.v. "Montagu, Lady Mary Wortley."

Kunitz, Stanley, and Howard Heycraft, eds. *British Authors Before 1800: A Biographical Dictionary.* New York: Wilson, 1952.

Melville, Lewis. *Lady Mary Wortley Montagu: Her Life and Letters.* London: Hutchinson, 1925.

Paston, George. *Lady Mary Wortley Montagu & Her Times.* London: Methuen, 1907.

Rogers, Katherine, ed. *Before Their Time.* New York: Ungar, 1979.

Todd, Janet, ed. *British Women Writers: A Critical Reference Guide.* New York: Continuum, 1989.

The Monthly Magazine; and British Register

The Monthly Magazine; and British Register was an essay periodical published between

1796 and 1843; it comprised 95 volumes. Founded by Richard Phillips (1767–1840), the magazine had four editors and three name changes in its 47-year history. From 1796 to 1806, John Aiken was the editor, and the magazine was named *The Monthly Magazine; and British Register*; from 1806 to 1826, George Gregory replaced Aiken; and from 1826 to 1835, the magazine was known as *The Monthly Magazine; and British Register of Literature, Science and Belleslettres* under the editorship of John A. Heraud. In 1826, *The Monthly* absorbed *The European Magazine and London Review*. In its final years, *The Monthly* was edited by Benson E. Hill. (*See also* Journalism.)

The Monthly contained essays, poetry, book reviews, correspondence, and public notices. Editing what was described as a Jacobinist periodical, Aiken announced two purposes in his "Argument" appearing in the first issue: (1) to entertain and (2) "to lend aid to the propagation of those liberal principles respecting some of the most important concerns of mankind, which have been either deserted or virulently opposed by other periodical miscellanies; and upon the manly and rational support of which the Fame and Fate of the age must ultimately depend." Here, Phillips and Aiken directly attack their rivals, *The Gentleman's Magazine* and *The London Magazine*.

The Monthly was distinguished by its erudite essays on such topics as politics, commerce, technology, industry, and peoples of the world. A review of the highlights of the magazine's first full year's publication illustrates the typical contents of this periodical as well as its commitment to liberal politics. The first issue opened with a review of the weather in 1795; that was followed by "Ought Freedom of Inquiry be Restricted?"—the first of William Enfield's "Enquirer" columns. Topical correspondence addressed the debt's relation to population growth; the formation of the Literary Fund; and two essays on the history of the Jews in England and John Ireland's discovery of a "Shakespeare manuscript," later proved a forgery. There were also original verses by George Dyer and Erasmus Darwin, and columns on agriculture, foreign and domestic news culled from the daily papers, and "A Retrospective of the Drama," on the productions at Drury Lane and Covent Garden in 1795.

Some additional features of the first 12 numbers illustrate the tone and tenure of the periodical, which attracted the attention of many of the leading writers of the 19th century. In April, the biographical series contained the first of several extended entries on eminent persons connected with the French Revolution, and, inspired by the publication of Wollstonecraft's *A Vindication of the Rights of Women*, the "Enquirer" asked "Are Literary and Scientific Pursuits suited to the Female Character?" The June edition carried a "Table for Reducing Dates of the New French Calendar to the Dates of the Georgian Calendar" and a economic chart pointing out the inflated prices of household goods in 1796. In July, *The Monthly* published Lamb's sonnet, *We are two pretty Babes*, in an issue that also featured "Songs of the Negro of Madagascar" translated into English from a 1787 French text. There was also a discussion of the state of poetry in Spain and Portugal with reflections by the "Enquirer" on the importance of verse in poetry. By August, much correspondence were being published in response to remarks by the "Enquirer" on women, which led in November to an announcement that a "woman" would be given the last word on the subject and all further correspondence must cease. The September issue carried an announcement that the relief efforts for Burns's widow and children were successful, and Coleridge's poem *On a late Connubial Rupture in High Life* was published. In October, another Coleridge poem, *Reflections on Entering the Active Life* was featured.

For 47 years *The Monthly* upheld its commitment to looking beyond Britain for literary, political, and cultural events, and it continued to deal with issues pertaining to oppression, freedom, and gender.

Beverly Schneller

Works Consulted

Mumby, Frank, and Ian Norrie. *Publishing and Bookselling*. London: Cape, 1954.

Sherbo, Arthur. "From *The Monthly Magazine and British Register*: Notes on Milton, Pope, Boyce, Johnson, Sterne, Hawkesworth, and Prior." *Studies in Bibliography* 43 (1990): 190–97.

Moore, Thomas

(1779–1852)

Thomas Moore was an Irishman, born in Dublin in 1779. His father, John Moore, owned a grocery store where the family lived; and his mother, Anastasia Codd Moore, came from English Protestants who converted to Roman Catholicism after settling in County Kerry. Thomas had two younger sisters.

Moore was a good student. He attended a private school for one year and won a medal for history before being enrolled at age 7 in the English Grammar School. He soon rose to the top of his class, excelling in Greek and Latin. The headmaster, Samuel Whyte, stressed poetry, music, and the stage, and Moore loved all three; he published his first poem at age 14. After a year of preparation at Dr. Carr's Latin School, Moore entered Trinity College in 1795. His religion disqualified him for the scholarship that his examination marks justified.

At Trinity, Moore was soon involved in translating Anacreon and flirting with revolutionary politics. He was close to Robert Emmet and Edward Hudson, two students who cast their lot with the United Irishmen radicals aligned under Wolfe Tone. The upshot of their activities was a brutal suppression of the radicals' rebellion in 1798. Tone died in prison, Hudson was exiled, and Emmet escaped, only to be hanged five years later in a subsequent insurrection.

In the aftermath, the university interrogated students suspected of complicity, Moore included. But Moore refused to testify about anyone but himself, and his performance was so cool and principled that he was allowed to graduate in 1799. With this episode behind him, he went to London to finish the *Odes of Anacreon*, returning to Dublin before the *Odes* were published in London in 1800. The popularity of the *Odes* led to Moore's being called "Anacreon Moore." The trivial juvenilia he published anonymously in 1801 as *Poetical Works of Thomas Little, Esq.*, added to his reputation as a versifier.

Back in Dublin, poised for a literary career, Moore found a much-needed patron in the Earl of Moira, later the Marquis of Hastings. Moira and Captain Joseph Atkinson, a Dublin supporter of the arts, contrived to invent for Moore an Irish Laureateship, an honor that Moore quickly spurned. The next-best post Moira could offer was a sinecure as registrar of the admiralty prize court in Bermuda. Sailing to Norfolk in late 1803, Moore finally took up his sparse duties in Bermuda in January 1804.

A petty bureaucrat's life in a far-off colony was not Moore's preference, and after three months he turned the job over to a deputy and left Bermuda to travel for six months in the United States and

Canada. He did not like America, finding its wide-open ways crude and offensive.

Back in the congenial literary milieu of England, Moore flourished among the greats; Wordsworth, Coleridge, Southey, and Lamb were among his acquaintances. His facetious *Epistles, Odes, and Other Poems* shocked the pious in 1806, prompting an outburst of self-righteous condemnation from Jeffrey in the *Edinburgh Review*. Moore challenged Jeffrey to a duel, but at the last moment the police arrived to stop the fiasco. The two antagonists became close friends, and Moore wrote for the *Edinburgh Review*. The whole absurd drama was repeated with Byron in Jeffrey's role, yielding the same result.

Moore's reputation prompted the Power brothers—James was a London publisher; William, a Dublin publisher—to encourage Moore to supply words for the many Irish folk tunes recently transcribed at a convocation of country harpists. Accordingly, the first two volumes of *Irish Melodies* appeared in Dublin and London in 1808. The success of Moore's melodies was enormous, and the collection swelled to 10 volumes by 1834. Moore survives on the popularity of these melodies, many of them enduring popular songs.

In 1811, Moore married Elizabeth Dyke, an English actress whom Moore met while performing in amateur theatricals in Kilkenny. They married in an Anglican church in London and settled in that city. The marriage was apparently happy, and it produced three daughters and two sons.

Moore published the satirical *Intercepted Letters, or the Two-Penny Postbag* in 1813 and began writing for the *Edinburgh Review* in 1814. In 1816, he published the first volume of *Sacred Songs*, a hymn collection. His major effort in these years was the immensely successful *Lalla Rookh* (1817), four narrative poems catering to a middlebrow audience's appetite for an exotic tale dressed up in a bogus Oriental setting.

The triumph of *Lalla Rookh* was overshadowed by the death of his first child, in a fall. The next year, 1818, Moore moved to Wiltshire, where he spent the rest of his life. Later that year his satirical *Fudge Family in Paris* by "Thomas Brown the Younger" was well received.

Trouble struck Moore in 1819. Sheddon, the deputy whom Moore had appointed in his place in Bermuda, absconded with £6,000, for which Moore was responsible. Faced with the possibility of debtor's prison, Moore left to settle in Paris. He traveled in France, Switzerland, and Italy with Lord John Russell, Bertrand Russell's grandfather, and in Venice had a final meeting with Byron, who gave Moore his manuscript memoirs to publish after Byron's death. Moore's wife, Bessy, joined him in Paris, where they lived until November 1822, when they were able to return to Sloperton Cottage in Wiltshire after various sources, including a relative of Sheddon's, had helped pay off Moore's debt.

Hard up for money, Moore produced another popular work in 1823: *The Loves of the Angels*, a series of three poems telling the stories of three seraphs who fell in love with mortal women. Orthodox Christians, not surprisingly, expressed shock at this theme, and so Moore accommodated the pious by changing the angels to Muslims in the fifth edition. *Fables for the Holy Alliance*, another satire by "Thomas Brown the Younger," also appeared in 1823.

Moore presented a different work to the public in 1824: the "memoirs" in prose of Captain Rock, a durable hero in Irish folklore for his Robin Hood depredations against the callous landlords. But the popular success—in Ireland if not in England where the landlords lived—of *Captain Rock* was overshadowed in 1824 by a dispute over the memoirs Byron had left Moore. The result of the tangled claims on these papers was that they were burned unread in the publisher John Murray's fireplace. Since Murray had gotten the memoirs in the first place as surety for a loan to Moore, their destruction meant that Moore had to pay off the loan of £2,000 from the biography of Byron that he published in 1830 as *Letters and Journals of Lord Byron, With Notices of His Life.*

Before the Byron biography, however, Moore published various other works, notably a biography of Richard Brinsley Sheridan (1825) and the satirical *Odes upon Cash, Corn, Catholics, and Other Matters* (1828). In 1831, Moore completed a biography of Lord Edward Fitzgerald, his old rebel friend from Trinity College, and the Catholic Emancipation Bill (1829) led to *Travels of an Irish Gentleman in Search of a Religion*, published in 1833.

Moore's only remaining daughter died in 1829, his mother in 1832, and a sister in 1834. After the lukewarm reception in 1835 to *The Fudge Family in England*, Moore began to write an exhausting four-volume *History of Ireland*, finally published in 1846. Old and revered by this time, Moore was awarded a pension of £300 a year in 1835 and was mysteriously elected to the British Association for the Advancement of Science in the same year. Moore paid his last visit to Ireland in 1838.

The crowning work of Moore's last years was the ten-volume *The Poetical Works of Thomas Moore, Collected by Himself*, published in London in 1841. The satisfaction of receiving the order of merit from Frederick the Great of Prussia in 1842 was overridden by the death of a son later that year. When his only remaining child died in 1846, followed soon after by a sister, Moore and Bessy were left by themselves. Moore

became senile in 1849, but lived on until 1852. He was buried in Bronham Churchyard, near his long-time home at Sloperton Cottage, where Bessy lived until her death in 1865.

Frank Day

Works Consulted

De Ford, Miriam Allen. *Thomas Moore.* New York: Twayne, 1967.

Gwynn, Stephen. *Thomas Moore.* London: Macmillan, 1905.

Jones, Howard Mumford. *The Harp That Once: A Chronicle of the Life of Thomas Moore.* New York: Holt, 1937.

Strong, Leonard Alfred George. *The Minstrel Boy: A Portrait of Tom Moore.* New York: Knopf, 1937.

More, Hannah

(1745–1833)

Hannah More is perhaps best remembered as a friend to and correspondent with some of the late 19th century's foremost figures, including Walpole, Garrick, Johnson, Sheridan, Burke, Wilberforce, and many aristocrats, politicians, and high church officials. What gave her access to them and why they desired acquaintance with her were her popular and varied writings: verses, plays, didactic and pedagogic essays, morality stories, religious tracts, and a novel. (*See also* Children's Literature.)

More's father was the master of a grammar school on the outskirts of Bristol. She was the fourth of five sisters, but because of her intelligence and frailty, she was the family favorite. In 1757, the sisters, all of whom remained unmarried, established a school for girls in Bristol; it soon became one of the most successful and respected in southern England. By 1767, they had their own school built in one of the best areas of the city. Through increased contact with

London society in the early 1770s, More became close to the Garricks, especially Mrs. Garrick after the death of her husband in 1779. More also became involved with the Bluestockings, conversation parties of well-to-do ladies often with an invited *littérateur*.

In 1789, the More sisters retired from their school to live at Bath, and More in particular became interested in abolition, establishing Sunday Schools for the poor, and philanthropic work. She was also successful in producing for the poor and uneducated readings that were designed to reinforce their lot in life by comforting them with the virtues of evangelical Anglicanism and British righteousness. But her schools, writings, and acts of good will were not without critics and questionable consequences. For example, between 1800 and 1803, she was at the center of a well-publicized and bitter controversy involving the charge that her schools (and the Blagdon school in particular) were run on Methodist lines. She was also accused of having a conflict of interest in controlling the finances of Ann Yearsley, the milkwoman poet she discovered and tutored. More outlived all of her sisters, and despite her continued involvement with schools, writing, and charities, as well as being overwhelmed with visitors, she spent her last years somewhat out of touch with her times. She died at age 88.

More's writing career began with providing material for the students of her school. While in her teens, she wrote versified dramatic tales appropriate for teaching her students Christian morality, including *Sacred Dramas* (published 1782) and *The Search After Happiness* (1773). Within 15 years, the latter had sold more than 10,000 copes. Her interest in drama continued, and in Bath in 1774, her first produced play, *The Inflexible Captive*, was

well received. With Garrick's production assistance, her next play, *Percy*, was performed at Covent Garden in the winter of 1777 to 1778. An extraordinary success, it was staged numerous times over the next decade, both in Britain and on the Continent. But her next play was her last. *The Fatal Falsehood* (1779) was also performed at Covent Garden but played only three nights. The tragedy of Garrick's death surrounded it before its staging, and another playwright publicly charged plagiarism. All of More's plays were directed at moral issues and especially the conflict between duty and love.

More also wrote and published many poems during her long life. Some of these are ballads, such as *Sir Eldred of the Bower and the Bleeding Rock: Two Legendary Tales* (1776), but she was best known for her poem on the Bluestockings, *The Bas Bleu; or, Conversation* (1786), which was widely circulated before its publication. George III asked her to make a personal copy for him.

The French Revolution motivated More to write political pamphlets warning of the Jacobin overthrow of the status quo in Britain. Paine's *Rights of Man* (1791–92) was the enemy. *Village Politics* (1792), published anonymously but soon discovered to be the work of More, attempted to demonstrate that law and the existing order needed to prevail in the face of revolution. The following year, she wrote an open letter, *Remarks on the Speech of M. Dupont*, condemning the subversive atheism she believed Dupont to be promoting. Again, she was successful and praised openly in high places.

More's educational and didactic writings on manners and appropriate behavior had similar influence and immediate popularity. For example, her *Thoughts on the Importance of the Manners of the Great to Gen-*

eral Society (1788) urged the middle and upper classes to set standards for those below them. More also wrote to instruct this same audience not merely to pay lip service to Christianity but strictly to observe its rules in, for example, *Estimate of the Religion of the Fashionable World* (1790). Likewise and because of her profession, More was very much interested in curriculum. Her *Strictures on the Modern System of Female Education* (1799) once more promoted Christian values as the way by which women could fulfil their family and social duties. Education was seen as the correction for corrupt human nature. Her reputation as an educationalist was such that in 1805 she was asked to produce an educational guide for the granddaughter of George III. This *Hints Towards Forming the Character of a Young Princess* was another success. She continued to publish books on Christian morality and conduct, and with *Practical Piety; or the Influence of the Religion of the Heart on the Conduct of Life* (1811) her reputation reached a high point.

Perhaps More's most ambitious plan involved supplying inexpensive reading material designed to enlighten and improve the working classes. With their newly gained literacy and the development of circulating libraries, the working classes had a seemingly endless desire for popular literature. More's aim was not to make money, but to counter the seditious broadsides, vulgar chapbooks, and Painite propaganda that were widely sold. Thus, the *Cheap Repository Tracts* were established in 1794 and 1795 to supply edifying reading material (mostly colorful stories and ballads) promoting patriotism and the Anglican virtues of industry, servility, humility, honesty, and self-reliance. Within a year, the sales in England alone were over two million, and of the approximately 115 tracts published while More was in charge of the project (until 1798), it is estimated that at least 50 were written by her.

More's only novel, *Coelebs in Search of a Wife* (1808), was a reaction to the popular novels the growing literate public were reading in vast numbers. *Coelebs*, the story of an idealized middle-class young man in search of perfect women, lacks plot and character; most of the novel concerns promoting modesty and virtue as exclusively feminine virtues. Nonetheless, *Coelebs* outsold all of her other single works (15 editions by 1818) and certainly influenced aspects of the 19th-century novel of manners. Similarly, the marketing strategies used by More to produce *Coelebs* and the *Tracts* significantly changed the business of publishing popular literature in Britain.

G. Kim Blank

Works Consulted

Hopkins, Mary Alden. *Hannah More and Her Circle*. New York: Longmans, 1947.

Jones, M.G. *Hannah More*. Cambridge: Cambridge UP, 1952.

Meakin, Annette M.B. *Hannah More: A Biographical Study*. London: Smith, 1911.

Pederson, Susan. "Hannah More Meets Simple Simon: Tracts, Chapbooks, and Popular Culture in Late Eighteenth-Century England." *Journal of British Studies* 25 (1986): 84–113.

Roberts, William, ed. *Memoirs of the Life and Correspondence of Mrs. Hannah More*. New York: Harper, 1836.

Morier, James Justinian

(1780–1849)

James Justinian Morier, diplomat and author, was born in Smyrna and educated at Harrow. He was the second son of Isaac Morier, the Consul General of the Levant Company, in Constantinople. Some time before 1807, he joined his father in Constantinople; in 1807, he entered the diplomatic service, where he spent ten years.

Morier's first posting was to Persia as the private secretary of Sir Hartford Jones. After arriving in Tehran, in 1809, he was promoted to secretary of the legation; but he remained in Tehran only about three months before he was ordered home. On his way home, he traveled through such countries as Turkey, which he later wrote about with wit and skill. He published a book recording this journey, which became an important travel guide and authority in England for the little-known country of Persia. It was even translated into French and into German. In 1810, he became secretary to Sir Gore Ouseley, ambassador extraordinary to Tehran. He continued with the Embassy to Tabriz where he took part in negotiations attempting to obtain Persian support against the Russo-French alliance. Morier describes in *A Second Journey Through Persia* his work on the treaty, which was eventually signed in 1812. When Sir Ouseley returned to England in 1814, Morier was left in charge of the embassy in Tehran, but he was recalled in 1815. In 1817, after receiving a pension from the government, he returned to England, where he lived in London. Several years later, his diplomatic skills resulted in his appointment as special commissioner to Mexico (from 1824 to 1826). He was among the dignitaries who signed the treaty with Mexico in 1826.

After the expiration of his commission, Morier was able to devote himself to literature. In 1824, his best novel, *The Adventures of Hajji Baba of Ispahan* was published. It is a skillful satire about a well-read Persian barber who cheats his patrons as he shaves them, all the while soothing them with poetic quotations. The book was quite popular and was translated into several languages, and Morier became quite famous as a fine novelist, a reputation his later books did not live up to.

Morier wrote several other novels. Two, *Zohrab the Hostage* and *Ayesha, the Maid of Kars*, each give accurate pictures of Persian life. Most of his romances, however, are of little merit, though several were translated into other languages.

Shirley Laird

Works Consulted

Day, Martin S. *History of English Literature, 1660–1837*. Garden City: Doubleday, 1963.

Dictionary of National Biography, s.v. "Morier, James Justinian."

Kunitz, Stanley J., and Howard Haycraft. *British Authors of the Nineteenth Century*. New York: Wilson, 1936.

Sutherland, John. *The Stanford Companion to Victorian Literature*. Stanford: Stanford UP, 1989.

Morland, George
(1763–1804)

George Morland was a prolific, popular, and profligate English artist who specialized in depictions of domestic and rural life. A child prodigy as a draughtsman, Morland received instruction from his artist father and exhibited at the Royal Academy by age 16. He soon rebelled against his father's strict domination and began aborted efforts to set himself up as a portrait painter in Margate and in France. Returning to London, Morland quickly found his forte—genre scenes with an emphasis on country folk and barnyard animals (particularly horses and pigs). His pictures became well known through mezzotints and engravings produced by a large number of craftsmen, including William Ward (Morland's brother-in-law), J.R. Smith, and Blake, who executed in stipple two companion plates *The Idle Laundress* and *The Industrious Cottager*. Five hundred sets of prints of Morland's *Dancing Dogs* and *Selling Guinea Pigs* were sold within a few weeks of their publication.

As Morland's fame spread, he became prey to sharp picture dealers who employed hirelings to copy his designs. Always in need of money, Morland rapidly turned out thousands of drawings, watercolors, and oil paintings. As his production increased, so did his consumption of gin and brandy. He was caught in a self-destructive cycle of incessant labor, liquor, lucre, and the demands of avaricious dealers. Morland was never accepted into respectable society and indeed preferred low companions and vulgar pleasures. By the early 1790s, he was burdened with debts and by the end of the decade was briefly imprisoned. Drink and worry led to an early death at age 41, his wife following to her own grave a few days later. Shortly before his demise, Morland composed his own unvarnished epitaph: "Here lies a drunken dog."

Morland was one of the first British artists to work without direct patronage or commissions and instead had to sell his paintings to clients through dealers or other intermediaries. In spite of this independence, his art followed popular taste for the rustic and picturesque and rarely attempted the sublime. In his own day he was considered a skilled realist, always truthful to nature and without stylistic affectations. The considerable interest in his work in the early 1800s is signaled by the publication of four biographies within a few years of his death. An active trade in his paintings and in the over 400 engravings based on his works continued through the 19th century. But his reputation among critics and connoisseurs of British art declined precipitously in this century. He is now generally thought of as a minor figure in the Romantic period and of more significance as a chapter in the history of taste than as an artist of lasting merit. Very recently, there has been a slight revival of interest in Morland based on a consideration of the informal disposition of figures in his pictures as an indication of his egalitarian social attitudes.

Jenijoy LaBelle

Works Consulted

Barrell, John. *The Dark Side of the Landscape*. Cambridge: Cambridge UP, 1980.

Cunningham, Allan. *The Lives of the Most Eminent British Painters and Sculptors*. Ed. Mrs. Charles Heaton. Rev. ed. 3 vols. London: Bell, 1879.

Hassell, J. *Memoirs of the Life of the Late George Morland*. London: Cundee, 1806.

Redgrave, Richard and Samuel. *A Century of British Painters*. New ed. New York: Oxford UP, 1947.

Thomas, David. *George Morland: An Exhibition of Paintings and Drawings*. N.p.: Arts Council of Great Britain, 1954.

The *Morning Post*

The *Morning Post*'s first issue was published on November 2, 1772, and subtitled *Daily Advertising Pamphlet*. Its format as a pamphlet, although its contents were those of a newspaper, was an apparent attempt to evade the newspaper tax. But the proprietors must have been quickly called to account, for by November 17, the *Post* assumed a new format, forthrightly that of a newspaper, and a new subtitle, *Cheap Daily Advertiser*; by February 12, 1773, it finally rested in the title *Morning Post, and Daily Advertiser*. The founding conductor, the Rev. Henry Bate, was a colorful character who would stop at almost nothing to gain publicity for his business venture, up to and including engaging in fisticuffs and duels with swords or pistols. This procedure became Bate's hallmark, and during his editorship he repeatedly used his paper to insult someone until a challenge was issued and a duel resulted, all of which would then be zestfully written up to the evident pleasure of the *Post*'s readership, for circulation continued to increase.

Such methods of publicity point out that the *Post* was a new kind of newspaper. It contained only as much information as might be found entertaining, such as selected summaries of Parliamentary debates, from a political position generally in support of the North Government. When the paper's popularity demonstrated the value of its procedures, the North Government paid the paper a handsome subsidy for its continued support. Sporting and theatrical news received central emphasis along with criminal trials, especially if they involved prominent people. These emphases provided ample opportunity for what were the *Post*'s most important stocks in trade: scandal, gossip, innuendo, and insult, sometimes witty and sometimes not; failing duels, suits for libel were a frequent feature of its early history. These occasionally resulted in fines and even prison sentences for some of the staff, and the proprietors evidently regarded such consequences as part of the cost of operation. The *Post*, in its early guise as a scandal sheet, was the first of its kind, and is the ancestor of 20th-century supermarket tabloids. Its mounting popularity in London's West End taught a lesson.

Eventually, Bate's antics were too much even for the *Post*. He was forced to sell his shares in the paper in 1780, at a considerable profit, because of an affair involving protracted abuse of the Duke of Richmond. The new conductors were not notably more scrupulous or ethical and followed Bate's lead by abandoning the North Ministry when its fortunes fell with the British defeat in America and putting the paper in the pay of the King's Friends. The King's Friends—identifiable if not coextensive with the Shelburne Whigs—were chiefly devoted to keeping Fox out of office. By 1783, after a complicated political battle in which the *Post* was bought out from under the King by Sheridan and then recovered by the King's party, and during which Fox briefly held office in an unstable coalition government, the Shelburne Whig's candidate Pitt the younger became Prime Minister. Sheridan's countercampaign involved the suborning of every newspaper for which he could outbid the Pitt ministry, and he soon regained control of the *Post*, only to be outbid again when Pitt made George Rose the Secretary of Treasury, and the paper again became ministerial. From 1784 on, Rose and Sheridan bid against each other for control of the London daily press. The proprietors of the *Post* became skilled at intrigue and counterintrigue, manipulating any source of subsidy in order to increase their profits.

Generally, the government was in a better position to subsidize newspapers (or even buy them outright) than the Sheridan-Fox opposition (then called the Rockingham Whigs). Despite the considerable but sometimes unreliable resources of Carleton House and the Prince of Wales at the disposal of the Rockingham Whigs, the Pitt Government could better afford the valuable services of scandalmongering that the *Post* provided, and thus—with the aid of many other propaganda instruments, huge sums in bribes, and "secret influence"—maintain a decisive Parliamentary majority. Nonetheless, and no doubt to its profit, the *Post* eventually became known as a paper of the Opposition, though with a few notable lapses.

In the early 1780s, Daniel Stuart arrived from Edinburgh to join his brothers Charles and Peter in London, and they rapidly established themselves in the newspaper business. Throughout the political intrigues and society scandals of this decade, the Stuarts played an increasing role in the conduct of the *Post* and of many other papers, as printers, publishers, proprietors, editors, writers, and reporters. Daniel Stuart edited the paper briefly in the mid-1780s but because of some backstairs maneuvers surrounding the Prince of Wales's clandestine marriage to the Catholic Mrs. Fitzherbert and the prospect of a regency as a result of the King's insanity—prime subjects for gossip and scandal—the paper was sold out from under him.

He regained control with a vengeance in 1795, buying the entire paper and all its apparatus. By then, the popularity and political importance of the paper were in steep decline. Stuart worked hard to recover lost ground and to acquire a reputation for sagacity and probity. Still, it is likely that Stuart used the paper to enrich himself in ways typical of the earlier proprietors. Personalities, anecdotage, and political and social intrigue and scandal remained the paper's prominent features under his editorship, but somewhat moderated, and with the addition of more or less solid political reporting and commentary, and information and controversy surrounding the conduct of the Napoleonic Wars. Stuart and his successors who had the good sense or good luck to enlist an excellent staff of occasional contributors, including at one time or another Lamb, Mackintosh, Southey, and Arthur Young, and contributions of poetry from Moore and Wordsworth, among many others. As a result, the paper's circulation increased and its importance returned.

Stuart's most famous contributor during his editorship, which lasted until 1803, was Coleridge. His sustained and frequent contributions provide a major resource for tracing the development of his political and social thought from the early post-

Cambridge days of utopian schemes, the English Jacobinism of his Bristol lectures and the radicalism of the *Watchman*, through to the next major statement of his political thinking as embodied in the *Friend*. When Stuart left the *Post* for the *Courier*, Coleridge's contributions followed him, continuing until 1818. Stuart provided Coleridge with much needed income and considerable leeway for what and when to contribute; Coleridge provided Stuart with an able controversialist and leader writer.

Mackintosh, Stuart's brother-in-law, first approached Coleridge with an offer from Stuart. By 1798, when Coleridge's first contributions appear, his political thinking was very much in harmony with the line the paper had already begun to advance. By all testimony, his contributions were of great value to Stuart. His essays on the newly proclaimed French constitution, published during December 1799, struck just the right note. Subsequently, Coleridge provided leaders and commentary that alternated between stringent criticism of the Pitt Ministry's policies at home and abroad and attack's on the French government. For instance, he wrote pieces comparing and contrasting Pitt and Napoleon, and while Pitt comes off the worse, Napoleon did not escape his measure of harsh censure. Coleridge also worked as an occasional reporter of Parliamentary debates, and the results compare favorably with the efforts of other reporters.

Mackintosh was probably largely responsible for the initial political position of Stuart's editorship. The author of a well-known reply to Burke, the *Vindiciae Gallicae*, and an important member of the Society of Friends of the People, a quasi-Jacobin club which Stuart also joined, Mackintosh encouraged Stuart's collaboration on attacks on Pitt and the War Ministry and mild agitation for parliamentary electoral reform. Mackintosh's opinions had moderated with the unfolding of events. In any case, an unabashed Jacobinical paper probably would not have been tolerated by the government, but Stuart surely never wanted to put this to the test. His paper could deplore the excesses of Robespierre, the Directory, and the subsequent Napoleonic regime at the same time that it attacked Pitt's policies for exacerbating those excesses. Support for the British troops, exaltation of their victories, and lamentations for their sufferings made good copy when combined with sympathy for the people, whether English or French. The cause of liberty could be upheld and the government's repressive measures at home and the war abroad opposed as long as these efforts were judiciously combined with rhetoric about the glorious safeguards of the English Constitution "rightly understood," so that the results seem very much of a piece with full-fledged membership in His Majesty's Loyal Opposition.

Stuart sold the *Post* in 1803, after his work and that of his contributors had made it highly profitable. Nicholas Byrne became its next conductor, and the complexion of the paper changed again. The Prince Regent received its most fervent support, and from being an unpredictable organ of the Opposition, the *Post* became a stalwart supporter of the Establishment while society gossip and scandal continued to absorb many of its pages. For a limited reactionary view of England under the Prince Regent and George IV, the paper is not without interest, even if most of its contributors lack the distinction that the Stuart editorship had fostered. Byrne's editorship concluded sensationally when he was murdered while working alone at night in the *Post*'s offices in 1833. His murderer was never apprehended, and the reasons for his assassination remain obscure. The *Post* continued in operation, with a variety of ups and downs, until 1937, when it merged with the *Daily Telegraph*. (*See also* Fox, James Charles; Napoleonic Wars; Pitt, William; Regency.)

Kenneth Watson

Works Consulted

Colmer, John. *Coleridge: Critic of Society*. Oxford: Clarendon, 1959.

Hindle, Wilfred. *The Morning Post, 1772–1937: Portrait of a Newspaper* London: Routledge, 1937.

Werkmeister, Lucyle. *The London Daily Press, 1772–1792*. Lincoln: U of Nebraska P, 1963.

Münchhausen, Karl Friedrich Hieronymus, Freiherr von

(1720–97)

Born on his family's estate at Bodenwerder, Hanover, Karl Friedrich Hieronymus Münchhausen served as a cavalry officer in the Russian army and took part in the Turkish campaigns of 1740 and 1741. He retired to his estate in 1760 and became a raconteur of extraordinary and unbelievable stories, regaling his guests and friends with tales of his alleged experiences as a soldier, hunter, adventurer, and sportsman. (*See also* German Romanticism.)

Seventeen of the stories attributed to Baron Münchhausen were published in the eighth and ninth part of the *Vademecum für lustige Leute* between 1781 and 1783 under the headings *M-h-s-nsche- Geschichten* and *Noch zwey M— — — —Lügen*. The German professor and librarian Rodolf Erich Raspe (1737–94), who fled to England in 1775, reworked and expanded this collection and then published it anonymously at Oxford under the title *Baron Münchhausen's Narrative of his Marvellous Travels and Campaigns in Russia*. The German poet Gottfried

Bürger translated the stories back into German from the second English edition and added 13 more tales. They were first published in London in 1786 as *Wunderbare Reisen zu Wasser und zu Lande, Feldzüge und lustige Abenteuer des Freyherrn von Münchhausen.*

Bürger's version, much more so than Raspe's, takes up motifs and characteristics from the older tradition of *Lügendichtung* (mendacious stories) in European literature: in Germany, Christian Reuter, whose *Schelmuffsky* (1694) is a forerunner of Bürger's own braggart romance, the comical tales of Hans Sachs, and the stories of the *Schildbürger* (the German equivalent of the English Gothamites) and of the *Schlaraffenland* (Cockaigne); in France, Rabelais's *Pantagruel* (1532) and *Gargantua* (1534); and in England, Jonathan Swift's *Gulliver's Travels* (1726). In fact, most of the stories from Bürger's collection can be traced back to an earlier source, such as the Baron climbing up to the moon on a beanstalk, which shares similarities with the English fairytale *Jack and the Beanstalk.*

Bürger's highly popular version did the most to contribute to Münchhausen's reputation as "der Lügenbaron" ("the lying Baron"), and he endowed the tales with humor, local color, an appropriate contemporary atmosphere, and a unified style.

Paul Davies

Works Consulted

"Münchhausen." *Brockhaus Enzyklopädie.* 1971 ed.
Rose, William. *Men, Myths, and Movements in German Literature.* London: Allen, 1931.

John Murray, Publishers

The publishing firm of John Murray was founded in 1768 by John MacMurray, who dropped the Scottish prefix to his family name and sold his commission in the Royal Marines to purchase the book trade of the London businessman William Sandby. Murray was moderately successful, largely due to the patronage of his former fellow officers. In 1795, two years after Murray's death, Murray's son John (born in 1778), dissolved the partnership his father had with Samuel Highley and, in 1802, set out on his own. From 1803 until his death in 1843, Murray was among the leaders in book and periodical publishing. His son, also John Murray (1808–92), succeeded at his father's death. He published the celebrated travelers' handbooks in their red bindings.

In 1951, John Murray became a limited company; it celebrated its 200th anniversary in 1968. Since the 1830s John Murray has been located at 50 Albermarle Street, and it is among the few family-owned publishing houses still extant. (*See also* Publishing.)

Between 1780 and 1830, John Murray was well-known for its fiction, nonfiction, and poetical publications. From 1779 to 1781 Murray and Longman issued Johnson's *Lives of the Poets*, and in 1821, John Murray was among the many British publishers to engage in the edition of Shakespeare's works edited by Edmund Malone. Of the many authors whose works were published by John Murray and his son, the best-known are Austen, Byron, Walpole, Disraeli, Isaac D'Israeli, Henry Hallam, Hemans, John Cam Hobhouse, James Hogg, Washington Irving, Sir John Malcolm, Moore, Mungo Park, Scott, Southey, Sharon Turner, and Helen Maria Williams. John Murray's books were always characterized by their high-quality printing and excellent bindings.

At the instigation of Scott, the politicians George Canning, George Ellis, and John Croker joined with John Murray to create the *Quarterly Review*, which premiered in 1809, to compete with the *Edinburgh Review*. (*See also* The *Quarterly Review*.)

Beverly Schneller

Works Consulted

Knight, Charles. *Shadows of the Old Booksellers*. London: Bell, 1865.

Morgan, Peter F. *Literary Critics and Reviewers in Early Nineteenth-Century Britain*. London: Croom, 1983.

Mumby, Frank, and Ian Norrie. *Mumby's Publishing and Bookselling*. London: Cape, 1974.

Smiles, Samuel. *A Publisher and His Friends. Memoir and Correspondence of the late John Murray*. 2 vols. London: Murray, 1891.

Music

Composers and writers during the Pre-Romantic and Romantic periods both in England and on the Continent were interested in the relationship of music and poetry. Reflecting this 18th-century phenomenon, Anselm Bayly, in 1789, published *The Alliance of Musick, Poetry, and Oratory*, a work that refers to music, poetry, and oratory as sister arts joined by nature with delight, utility, pleasure, and innocence.

By the late 18th century, a prospering English populace frequented the opera, attended concerts, and supported musical organizations of their choice. Foreign composers and musicians, especially the Italians, were lured to England, while English composers and musicians traveled to Europe to study. Young women in particular were encouraged to receive some formal musical instruction, often on the pianoforte. Because of the increasing interest in music and of the influence of Johann Heinrich Pestalozzi (1746–1827) in education, music education spread to the schools.

During the 1790s, amateur interest in music increased. Local communities organized orchestras and bands, held concerts, and sent selected singers to regional oratorio festivals at Manchester, Liverpool, York, Chester, Birmingham, and elsewhere. By 1825, the beginnings of the English brass band were evident in such villages as Long Martin, Stanhope, and Garrigill. Amateur orchestras were founded in Salisbury, Canterbury, and Chichester by John March (1752–1828). People who could afford instruments purchased pianos, guitars, violins, violoncellos, serpents, dulcimers, or flutes, making these instruments popular in both concert halls and homes.

Songs and folk music were popular in rural areas, while attending the opera became fashionable not necessarily because of good performances but because of social prestige. Throughout the 18th century, the English venerated the works of Handel, whose influence dictated their musical tastes well into the 19th century. Eventually, the interest in music shifted from the Italian to the German, resulting in a revival of the music of Bach. The music of Haydn and Mozart also received acclaim in England, while some were very receptive to the works of Beethoven. In 1823, Rossini came to England with his wife, Isabella Colbran, a famous singer, and delighted his audience, which included George IV. The following year, the 13-year-old Liszt visited England and played private concerts, amazing people with his virtuosity and improvisations. In 1829, Mendelssohn appeared in London through the Philharmonic.

Impressed by the exoticism of foreign tongues, the British enjoyed Italian, German, and French operas in addition to the works of earlier composers, such as Locke, Leveridge, and Purcell. From 1810 to 1825, most Londoners preferred light and frivolous opera in the form of pantomimes, musical plays, sentimental comedies, and farces. The operas lacked refinement and severely declined in England by 1830.

Vocal musicians attained great status, and people attended concerts and operas to hear renditions of singers who competed for audience favoritism. At the turn of the century, James Bartleman (1769–1821) held the supreme position among the English bass singers, while Samuel Harrison (1760–1812), who sang Handel's airs very well and had participated in the Handel Commemoration of 1784, was a typical tenor of the age. In contrast with modern practice, two males, Charles Knyvett (1712–1822) and his son William (1779–1856), were leading alto singers. Prominent sopranos included Eliza Salmon (1787–1849); Catherine Stephens (1794–1882), who played Mandane in Thomas Arne's opera *Artaxerxes*; Mary Anne Paton (1802–64); and Elizabeth Billington (?1765–1818). Two foreigners who appeared in England were Gertrud Mara (1749–1833) and the popular and egotistical Angelica Catalini (1780–1849).

Introduced into England by Handel, the oratorio became popular with the British middle-class public. Used vaguely, the term *oratorio* eventually included almost any choral work produced in a concert room or theater. Because of its popularity, many composers produced oratorios, and the works became repetitious. But no composer, including the admired William Crotch (1775–1847), could compete with the famed Handel.

Church anthems were also popular. Composers included Thomas Attwood (1765–1838), a Chorister at the Royal Chapel and organist at St. Paul's for 30 years, and Samuel Arnold (1740–1802). The greatest church composer was Samuel Wesley (1766-1838). Differing from his contemporaries in that he wrote no oratorios after age 11, he wrote several masses reflecting the Italian influence, numerous anthems, choral works, glees, and songs. His motets and antiphons for choral voices are considered among his greatest works. Wesley's third son, Samuel Sebastian (1810–76), also became prominent, producing 23 anthems and two full church services, among other works.

The glee, a native vocal music form generally written entirely for male voices, was common in England from 1780 to 1860. Set to the lyrics of writers such as Shakespeare, Jonson, Sidney, John Lily, Nicholas Breton, Dryden, William Shenstone, and Burns, the glee depended on an expressive delivery of its words for successful presentation. Samuel Webbe (1740–1816), a popular and typical glee composer, wrote about 300 glees and published nine volumes of them. Some authorities believe that the glee reached perfection in beauty and originality in his works. Although a number of extremely fine glees were written, many were mediocre, and the form declined in importance.

Ballads treating such recreations as racing, poaching, boxing, and fox hunting, as well as the pastimes of the common people, appeared. They were also composed to satirize the repressors of amusement—the temperance promoters, politicians, and constables—and to comment on what the singers considered unjust acts of Parliament. Because of the popularity of ballads, broadsides were printed for use by the common people. (*See also* Ballads.)

William Shield (1748–1829), Charles Dibdin (1745–1814), Charles Horn (1786–1849), Attwood, and Henry Bishop (1786–1855) wrote popular songs and folk-type songs. An earlier writer, Thomas Arne (1710–78), whose genius was essentially lyrical, composed songs that continued in popularity well into the 19th century.

One of the few bright spots in instrumental music production was in piano, where Clementi, Dussek, and Cramer produced works of some merit. Without a doubt, the most influential pianist was Muzio Clementi (1752–1832), Italian by birth, who came to England as a boy. Called "the Father of the Piano," he exerted great influence both as a performer and teacher and headed a very successful publishing and manufacturing business. A prolific composer, he wrote about 60 sonatas for the piano. Interested in music education, he produced *Gradus ad Parnassum*, a series of studies of 100 pieces, including brilliant technical studies, fugues, canons, movements to sonata form, capriccios, scherzos, and a few impressionistic pieces. The contents of his three-volume series foreshadow the later pianistic styles of such composers as Schumann, Chopin, Liszt, Brahms, and Debussy. Through his publishing business, Clementi introduced some of Beethoven's large-scale works to the British public. He also performed in Europe, competing against Mozart, with whom he became antagonistic. But some of Clementi's sonatas influenced Beethoven, whom Clementi met in 1807.

Also influencing Beethoven was Dussek, a Bohemian who came to London in 1790 at age 29. Remaining in London for 10 years as a successful pianist, teacher, and composer, he wrote sonatas that compete with those of Clementi in richness and variety and in anticipating the stylistic techniques of later composers, such as Brahms and Schumann. Like Clementi's works, Dussek's tend to be relegated into educational channels and so have fallen into oblivion.

The most able piano student of Clementi was John Baptist Cramer (1771–1858), the son of a Mannheim violinist. An important virtuoso and composer, he was famous for his piano studies and also founded the pianoforte and music-publishing house of J. B. Cramer and Company. Authorities indicate he was the only contemporary British pianist noted by Beethoven.

Another celebrated student of Clementi was John Field (1782–1837), an Irishman by birth who became an apprentice to Clementi at an early age and was eventually held in high esteem as a performer, composer, and teacher, especially in Russia, where he lived from 1804 to 1832. He composed seven piano concertos but is remembered primarily for his nocturnes, which introduced a new pianoforte style, one later developed more fully by Chopin.

A prominent inventor, John Broadwood (1732–1812), contributed to the development of the pianoforte. He produced the first grand piano in 1781; three years later, he patented the damper and piano pedals; then in 1788, he improved the harpsichord principle by abolishing the continuous long bridge and introducing a separate bridge to carry the bass strings.

Outstanding instrumental soloists emerged during the period. Flute playing was popular, and England produced good performers, the leading flutist during the 1820s and 1830s being Charles Nicholson (1795–1837), who succeeded Andrew Ashe (1759–1841) in this position. Several London publishers worked to improve flute music and such journals as the *Fluticon* emerged. Other instrumentalists excelled in playing the oboe, bassoon, horn, clarinet, trumpet, and drums.

Musical societies were formed to encourage the composition of vocal music. From 1787 to 1858, the Glee Club worked zealously to promote glee writing. The Vocal Concerts (1792–1821) advanced musical knowledge, especially from 1800 to 1815. Other societies included the Coventry Union Choral Society, founded in

1813, and the Blackburn Choral Society, established in 1829.

In 1813, a group of professional musicians, recognizing that instrumental music in England had seriously deteriorated, organized the Philharmonic Society of London for the purpose of promoting the best orchestral music. The founders of the organization included veteran violinist William Dance (1755-1840), Cramer, Philip Anthony Corri (?1784–1832), and Vincent Novello (1781–1861). The first concert was presented on March 8, 1813, at the Argyll Rooms on Regent Street, with Johann Salomon (1745–1815) as leading violinist and Clementi presiding at the piano. The Society popularized the works of Beethoven, Haydn, and Mozart, while diminishing the popularity of Handel.

By 1823, regular reviews of new music were featured in *Gentleman's Magazine*. Its critics considered Beethoven the greatest living composer. In 1826, the publishers indicated that music was a great rage and all young ladies must learn to play the pianoforte or the more expensive harp. The *Examiner*, in a section titled "Theatrical Examiner," occasionally carried commentary on music production with the criticisms primarily focused on the vocalists and instrumentalists and their performances.

Several music publications appeared during the Romantic era. From 1797 to 1802, James Harrison printed the *Piano-Forte Magazine*, while from 1818 to 1829 the *Quarterly Musical Review*, founded by Richard Mackenzie Bacon, was published. From 1823 to 1833, the *Harmonican* was edited by W. Ayrton, a son-in-law of composer Samuel Arnold (1740–1802).

During the 18th century, the music publishing firm of T. Boosey and Company, controlled by Thomas Boosey, had been founded. Another publishing firm headed by Samuel Chappell started in 1810. Chappell, with his partners, Cramer and Francis Tatton Latour, was primarily interested in publishing contemporary music.

An important 19th-century figure who assisted in uniting the musical and literary worlds was Novello, a close friend of the musicians Cramer and Attwood, as well as of the writers Coleridge, Leigh Hunt, Keats, and Shelley. The group assembled in Novello's dining room to discuss drama, literature, watercolor painting, and music. Receiving his music instruction from Webbe, Novello became organist of the Portuguese Embassy Chapel in 1797. When Mendelssohn and Liszt visited in England, Novello acted as host. He published a number of musical works, his great editorial achievement being the five-volume *The Fitzwilliam Music* (1825). His interest in music publishing led to the founding of the Novello Publishing Company by his son Joseph Alfred in 1829.

Although music permeated British life during the Romantic era, the greatest composers and musicians of the age lived on the Continent. (*See also* Hymnody; Thomson, George.)

Doris A. Clatanoff

Works Consulted

Bayly, Anselm. *The Alliance of Musick, Poetry and Oratory: Under the Head of Poetry Is Considered the Alliance and Nature of the Epic and Dramatic Poem as It Exists in the Iliad, Aeneid, and Paradise Lost.* London: Stockdale, 1789.

Blom, Eric. *Music in England.* New York: Penguin, 1942.

Crowest, Frederick J., ed. English Music 1604–1904. 2nd ed. New York: Scribner's, 1906.

Dale, Kathleen. *Nineteenth-Century Piano Music: A Handbook for Pianists.* London: Oxford UP, 1954.

Davey, Henry. *History of English Music.* 1921. New York: Da Capo, 1969.

Fuller-Maitland, J.A. *Music in the Nineteenth Century.* 1902. Wolfeboro, NH: Longwood, 1976.

Haweis, H.R. *Music and Morals*. New York: Harper, 1904.

Hunt, Leigh. *Musical Evenings: Or Selections, Vocal and Instrumental*. Ed. David R. Cheney. Columbia: U of Missouri P, 1964.

Mackerness, E.D. *A Social History of English Music*. London: Routledge, 1964.

Nettel, Reginald. *The Orchestra in England: A Social History*. London: Cape, 1956.

Sadie, Stanley, ed. *The New Grove Dictionary of Music and Musicians*. 20 vols. London: Macmillan, 1980.

Walker, Ernest. *A History of Music in England*. Oxford: Clarendon, 1907.

Young, Percy M. *A History of British Music*. New York: Norton, 1967.

Napoleon (Bonaparte)

(1769–1821)

The narrative of Napoleon Bonaparte's life is a drama of famous battles—Marengo, Austerlitz, Jena, Borodino, among others, and the crushing denouement at Waterloo. The early battles proved his genius, made him famous, and swept him to power. The later battles revealed his overreaching megalomania, disillusioned his supporters, and led to his slow death in isolation on an island in the South Atlantic. (*See also* Nationalism.)

Napoleon was born in 1769, in Ajaccio, Corsica, a large Mediterranean island ceded by Genoa to France only the year before. Napoleon was the second of eight children born to the lawyer Carlo Maria Buonaparte and his wife, Letizia. Napoleon dropped the "u" from his name in 1796.

At age 10, Napoleon entered the military school at Brienne in northern France, where he felt alienated by his accent and his relatively humble social origins. His excellent performance at Brienne earned him admission at age 15 to the École Militaire in Paris. His social insecurity continued, but his truculence did not cripple him in school, and in 1785, he was commissioned as a second lieutenant of artillery.

Napoleon was posted to an artillery regiment at Valence. After an extended furlough necessitated by his mother's death, he distinguished himself as a strategist in artillery attack. During the historic events of the Revolution, Napoleon spent much of his time on leave in Corsica and was charged with desertion in 1792. He responded by returning to Paris and pleading his case so successfully that he was made a captain just 11 days before the King was imprisoned in 1792. He was soon back in Corsica, where Corsican revolutionaries were rising up against France. Napoleon sided with the loyalists and removed the Buonaparte family to France in April 1793. From this point on, Napoleon identified with France.

Four months later, Napoleon stopped over at the naval base of Toulon in southern France, where the revolutionary government was besieging Royalist forces holding the city with support from the British Navy. (King Louis XVI had been beheaded in January, and the foreign powers were maneuvering for advantage over France.) While Napoleon was in Toulon, the commander of the rebels' artillery was wounded, and Napoleon agreed to take charge. This was the beginning of his career. Napoleon reorganized the attacking artillery and eventually drove the British out and took the city. He was promoted successively to major, adjutant general, and brigadier general by December 1793.

Following this triumph and fast rise, Napoleon was assigned to the Army of Italy in 1794. During this Italian period, Napoleon met Desiree Clary, whose wealthy parents rejected the unpromising young general. At this time, Napoleon came under the patronage of the notorious Maximilien Robespierre, mastermind of the Reign of Terror that sent so many of his political enemies to the guillotine. This association proved almost fatal to Napoleon, for Robespierre was judged guilty of excess and executed by his own favored instrument. Napoleon was subsequently arrested, and although he was cleared of all charges, he was denied a command of any consequence for a while.

Rejecting a posting to fight Royalist farmers in western France, Napoleon stayed in Paris and involved himself with Marie Josephe Rose de Beauharnais, widow of the recently executed Viscount Alexandre de Beauharnais. Then, in 1795, the National Convention created the Directory, a group of five men appointed to run the country. The Royalists immediately marched in arms on the Convention, and General Paul Barras, who had orchestrated Robespierre's overthrow, appointed Napoleon to put down the rebels. Napoleon's success with what he called "a whiff of grapeshot" saved the new constitution and the Directory, and when Barras resigned to become one of the five new Directors, he made Napoleon commander in chief of the Army of Italy. Soon afterward, Napoleon, age 26, married Josephine de Beauharnais, age 33, in 1796.

Napoleon inherited a difficult assignment in Italy, which was a jumble of separate states controlled by various political entities. Venice and Genoa, for instance, were independent republics, but Milan, Mantua, Tuscany, and Modena were ruled by the powerful Austrian empire. One of Napoleon's motives in Italy—besides claiming spoils for France—was to force Austria into recognizing a recent Franco-Prussian treaty that ceded to France the territories on the left bank of the Rhine River.

Napoleon's accomplishment with his 27,000 hungry, ill-clothed troops was miraculous: he immediately foraged food, raised their morale, and led them to four victories in northern Italy. By early 1797, he had whipped the Austrians and was moving on Vienna and had forced Austria to sign the Treaty of Leoben.

Back in Paris, the Directors were astonished by Napoleon's successes, intimidated by his growing power, and annoyed by his independent diplomatic maneuvering. They were also at odds with each other, as well as threatened by Royalist advances in the recent elections in the Council of Elders and the Council of Five Hundred, the two houses of the French Parliament. Rather than return to Paris—and possibly be on the losing side—Napoleon sent General Augereau, who subdued the Royalists by early September. With the Directory strong and Napoleon triumphant, Austria quickly signed the Treaty of Campo-Formio in October 1797, giving France the Low Countries, parts of Italy, and a promise to surrender claim to the left bank of the Rhine. Napoleon shaped the treaty independently, and when he returned to Paris in December, the nervous Directors feigned delight but quickly sent him off as commander of the Army of England.

Rejecting any idea of invading England,

Napoleon sailed for Egypt with a large military force and a contingent of scientists and artists. His adventures in the Middle East were a failure, culminating in defeats at Aleppo in Syria and at the Mediterranean fortress of Acre. The archeological research that Napoleon sponsored, however, was important, most notably for unearthing the Rosetta Stone with its hieroglyphic inscriptions that Champollion deciphered in 1821. (*See also* Rosetta Stone.) With the Royalists on a rampage again back home and the Directory in disarray, Napoleon returned to France in August 1799. With the connivance of one of the Directors, Emmanuel Sieyès, Napoleon lured the Parliament to a meeting outside of Paris, where, in a series of confused events, the frightened legislators dissolved the Directory and replaced it with a Consulate made up of Sieyès, Napoleon, and Roger Ducos. Napoleon solidified his grip on France by a risky march on the Austrians in Italy, winning a decisive victory on June 14, 1800, at Marengo.

Napoleon's next moves were to sign the Concordat of 1801 with Pius VII and to transform the tattered French legal system into the Napoleonic code. But the benign and civilizing aspects of Napoleon's reforms as First Consul were marred by his oppressive responses to the several attempts made on his life, and his ambition overtook him fatally in his decision to crown himself Emperor in December 1804.

Despite the defeat of his fleet by Admiral Nelson at Trafalgar (a battle that cost the British Admiral his life) in October 1805, the new Emperor destroyed the Russians and Austrians at Austerlitz two months later. In October 1806, Napoleon thrashed the resurgent Prussians at Jena, leaving only the British and the Russians still defiant. To subdue Britain, Napoleon instituted his Continental System, an un-successful attempt to stop other nations from trading with Britain.

As for the stubborn Russians, Napoleon took his troops to Poland and won a bloody battle at Eylau in February 1807, forcing the Treaty of Tilsit in which Prussia ceded much territory and Russia considerably less. At this time, Napoleon's empire was at its greatest, but his fortunes took a turn for the worse after Tilsit, partly because his foreign minister, Talleyrand, was scheming behind his back.

Having had illegitimate children by two women in Poland, Napoleon divorced Josephine in 1809 for giving him no heir. He then married the Archduchess Marie Louise of Austria, by whom he had a son, François-Charles-Joseph, in 1811. But the years 1810 to 1812 were troublesome. Napoleon had gone adventuring in Spain, only to face a rebellion supported by the British, and his relatives were not pleasing him in their numerous appointments throughout the Empire.

In June 1812, Napoleon made a reckless move, leading a huge army into Russia. He won a narrow victory at Borodino in September 1812, but when he marched into Moscow, he found the city deserted and in flames. In their retreat, the Russians had destroyed everything a victorious army could survive on, and Napoleon found himself in bitterly cold Russia with no supplies. His retreating army—reduced to 26,000 from 500,000—was practically annihilated by Cossacks at the Beresina River in November 1812, and Napoleon barely escaped with his life to Paris.

A year later, the British, the Austrians, the Swedes, and the Prussians ganged up on their old tormentor and whipped him at Leipzig, and in March 1814, they drove him from Paris. Thus, on April 6, 1814, the French were once again ruled by Bourbons.

Exiled to the small island of Elba, near his native Corsica, Napoleon escaped in February 1815, taking 1,000 volunteers with him. Although Napoleon assembled an army of 128,000 after his return to Paris, the British and the Prussians opposed him on the north and the Austrians and Russians on the east. The historic showdown came at Waterloo on June 15, 1815, with Napoleon's defeat by the army of the Duke of Wellington. Trying to escape to America a week later, Napoleon was seized by the British and sent into hopeless exile on the tiny South Atlantic island of St. Helen's.

Napoleon died on St. Helen's in 1821, at age 51. Evidence indicates that he was slowly poisoned by arsenic, probably by Bourbon supporters who feared his return to France. When his remains were returned to France for burial in 1840, the coffin revealed a perfectly preserved body even though it had never been embalmed—presumably due to the preservative effect of the arsenic.

Napoleon remains a complicated and controversial historic personage. A man of great talents and indisputable accomplishments, he was a victim of his own ambition. The thousands who lined up to follow him attest to his power over human emotions; the thousands who died are a testimony to his folly.

Frank Day

Works Consulted

Barnett, Corelli. *Bonaparte*. 1978.

Butterfield, Herbert. *Napoleon*. New York: Collier, 1962.

Castelot, Andre. *Napoleon*. New York: Harper, 1971.

McGuire, Leslie. *Napoleon*. New York: Chelsea, 1986.

Napoleonic Wars

The initial English response to the French Revolution was one of approval. However, the execution of Louis XIV in January 1793, and the September massacres planted doubts in the minds of many reformers, and conservatives feared that Jacobin ideas might spread to England. British intervention in French affairs ultimately resulted from the perception of danger to British security as well as turning popular opinion. Britain's first official response to French expansion took place in 1793 when Prime Minister Pitt sent troops to France and to the West Indies. Both British forces met defeat, and only the strength of British naval victories saved prestige and prevented the immediate invasion of England by the French Directory. The subsequent uneasy peace was broken when British Admiral Nelson blockaded Egypt and destroyed Napoleon's dream of an Eastern empire at the Battle of the Nile in 1798.

Next the British pursued a European coalition that included Austria and Prussia against France in 1799, but King George III rejected Napoleon's offers of peace until after Napoleon became First Consul, and the coalition fell apart. England and France signed the Peace of Amiens in 1802, but it was shattered 14 months later because of British opposition to Napoleon's unbridled ambition. Napoleon refused to be satisfied with the territory he had already gained, but Britain also resented his interference in the liberty of free European states, such as Italy, Holland, and Switzerland. The resulting war lasted until the French defeat at Waterloo and Napoleon's final exile on St. Helena.

In the first stage of the war, Napoleon defeated the Austrians at Ulm and Austerlitz and the Prussians at Jena. After defeating the Russians several times, he signed a peace treaty with Tsar Alexander in 1807. Only Britain still opposed Napoleon, due to the strength of the British Navy and Nelson's victory at Trafalgar in 1805. However, by 1807, both Pitt and Nelson were dead. Through the confusion and delay that attended the formation of a new government and policy, the British Navy continued to harass the French, but the army had few successes. The tide of fortune finally in Britain's favor turned due more to Napoleon's mistake than British strategy.

Napoleon hoped to weaken the British through economic control of the Continent. The conquest of Spain was necessary for the plan's success. While it was fairly easy for him to take over the weak Spanish government, the Spanish people resented the French conquerors and resisted fiercely. The native guerrilla forces in Spain and Portugal were ably supported by British troops under the command of Wellington. Yet despite some success, General Sir John Moore was killed in a major defeat at Corunna in 1809, probably the darkest period of the war for Britain. Though further changes in the government took place, Britain continued to support Wellington's forces in the Peninsular War. Wellington defeated the French forces at Ciudad Rodrigo and Badajoz (1812) and Vittoria (1813). The French were forced back over the Pyrenees in 1814. Napoleon's disastrous Russian campaign in 1812 had also revitalized continental opposition. For the first time since 1807, Napoleon was faced with an army of four major powers—Austria, Prussia, Russia, and Britain—united by their desire to defeat him. Despite much political disagreement, their armies defeated Napoleon's forces and entered Paris in March 1814. Napoleon abdicated in April and was exiled with military honor to the island of Elba off the Italian coast. The allies met at the Congress of Vienna to restore the Bourbon dynasty, settle political differences, and arrange a lasting peace for Europe. However, the war was not yet over.

Napoleon escaped from Elba and returned to France. The decisive battle of the war was fought on the Belgian border. Wellington commanded a mixed force of allied troops against the best that Napoleon had left. Despite some initial errors, the final victory went to Wellington in the closely fought and bloody battle of Waterloo. Napoleon abdicated again and was sent to the remote island of St. Helena in the South Atlantic, where he died in 1821.

Napoleon rode a wave of nationalism that aided him in his plan to control Europe and eliminate the enemies of France, but his ambition and the opposition of Britain caused his defeat. (*See also* Castlereagh, Viscount Robert Stewart; Currency Question; Economic Conditions.)

Elsa A. Nystrom

Works Consulted

Briggs, Asa. *The Age of Improvement, 1784-1867.* New York: Longmans, 1959.

Chalfont, Lord. *Waterloo.* New York: Knopf, 1980.

Durant, William and Ariel. *The Age of Napoleon.* New York: Simon, 1975.

Longford, Elizabeth. *Wellington, The Years of the Sword.* New York: Harper, 1969

Riehn, Richard K. *1812: Napoleon's Russian Campaign.* New York: McGraw, 1990.

Nash, John

(1752–1835)

John Nash, an architect of the late 18th and early 19th centuries, was known for his original eclecticism and use of the picturesque style. He gained distinction for his numerous country cottages and estates in Wales and Ireland and the major architectural structures in London and England (e.g., Blaise Hamlet Cottages, All-Souls' Church, the Harmonic Institution, Caerhays Castle, the Royal Pavilion, and Marylebon Park). His repertoire also included bridges, jails, municipal improvements, and garden-city parks.

Nash's working associations with King George IV and landscape-gardener Humphrey Repton gave him his initial access to the world of architecture. Born in London in 1752 to engineer and millwright William Nash, who died when the boy was age 8, and his wife, Nash grew up in Wales. From 1767 to 1778, Nash served as clerk and apprentice to architect Robert Taylor. During this time, he lived in the town of Lambeth with his first wife Jane, who died sometime around 1795. Nash remarried in 1798 to 25-year-old Mary Anne Bradley.

Nash then began his career as a builder and carpenter. Financial problems and even bankruptcy during the 1780s prevented him from successfully establishing himself until he entered into partnership with Repton in 1797. The partnership lasted until 1802 when an irreconcilable rift developed. Nash, while still gaining clients from the association with Repton, set out on his own.

One of the most intriguing architects of his time, Nash had both controversial personality and architectural style. His participation in the architectural world was competitive and full of conflicts. It is said that some of his eclecticism also drew on some "ghost" designers (e.g., John Adey), in addition to the specific echoes of fellow architects' styles (e.g., Henry Holland's use of Ionic columns). Furthermore, credit for Nash's work on some 103 estates was never acknowledged in Repton's published works, specifically his *Observations on the*

Theory and Practice of Landscape Gardening (1803), which followed the work *Sketches and Hints on Landscape Gardening* (1794). Nash did not produce theoretical works as Repton did but rather became famous for his numerous architectural structures.

Nash's architectural style for country cottages employed the picturesque quality reminiscent of the Romantic world of rural landscape and cottage folk portrayed in Wordsworth and Coleridge's *Lyrical Ballads*. Yet, some of Nash's works were built for the socially prominent. He preserved a rural Classicism, blending Norman, Gothic, and early English influence. His style boldly included verandas, octagons, ellipses, and silhouettes.

In line with his interest in rural environs and parks, Nash became Surveyor of the Office of Woods and Parks in 1806. During a time when artists revolted against traditional Classicism, Nash's eclectic use of Neoclassical style embraced even the Oriental decorativeness characteristic of the Romantic interest in exotic influences from the East. In the Royal Pavilion, Nash created a curiosity in architecture that also demonstrated his universalism. In a controversial takeover in 1815 of the drawings of Repton commissioned for King George IV, Nash finished the project in 1818. Although known for its Indian and Islamic influences, the Royal Pavilion also incorporated an interior Chinese decor and influence. Considered by many the predominant figure of the picturesque style in the 19th century, Nash retired to East Cowes Castle in 1831 and died in 1835.

Donna Ferrantello

Works Consulted

Davis, Terence. *John Nash—Prince Regents' Architect*. London: Country Life, 1966.

Gardner, Helen. *Art Through The Ages*. Rev. by Horst de la Croix and Richard G. Tansey. New York: Harcourt, 1975.

Summerson, John. *John Nash—Architect to King George IV*. London: Allen, 1935.

— — —. *Architecture in Britain, 1530–1830*. Harmondsworth: Penguin, 1970.

— — —. *The Life and Work of John Nash, Architect*. Cambridge: MIT P, 1980.

Temple, Nigel. *John Nash and The Village Picturesque—with special reference to the Reptons and Nash at the Blaise Castle Estate*. Gloucester: Sutton, 1979.

Nationalism

A multifaceted concept that defies precise definition, nationalism may be described as a consciousness of identity with those who inhabit a definable territory, who speak, most often, a common language in which are encoded the stories and ideals of the people, whose societal structure is based on one political system, and whose inspiration, beliefs, and moral codes may, in some cases, be founded in a common religion that is embraced by the majority of those who compose the nation.

Nationalism, in essence, may be traced to ancient Egypt, Mesopotamia, and Phoenicia; modern nationalism in the West, however, arose after the decline of the Holy Roman Empire and the collapse of feudalism. As the 16th-century monarchs of Europe developed absolute power, king and nation came to be identified. This identification was reinforced by such writers as Machiavelli; but during the 17th century, the intellectual and political revolutions in England and, in particular, the ideas expressed by philosophers, political theorists, and such literary giants as Locke and Milton directed attention toward the rights of the individual.

The concern for freedom and individual rights was carried forward during the Enlightenment by the writings of Voltaire and Rousseau, whose works provided inspiration for the French Revolution.

Rousseau's *Social Contract* (*Le Contrat Social*) (1762) has been considered a founding document of modern nationalism and a major influence on movements toward democracy. With his forceful rhetoric about nature, the natural man, and humans' right to freedom, Rousseau helped bring about both the Romantic movement and the intense democratic and national sentiments of the 19th century, sentiments that pervade much European literature of the century.

Just as the development of vernacular languages and literature advanced national consciousness during the Middle Ages and the Renaissance, during the 19th century when national feelings were strong in England, on the Continent, and in Ireland, many poets expressed the national mood. Among English poets, Southey lashed out against the dictator Napoleon, who distorted the aims of the French Revolution and carried a militant nationalism abroad to further his own imperialist goals. Scott portrayed the history of Scotland and of England in his novels where, even with his Scottish nationalism, he acknowledged, particularly in *Rob Roy* (1818), the necessity and advantages of the 1707 union with England. Overtly expressing his deep love of country, Wordsworth dedicated a series of lyric poems and odes to national independence and liberty. Composed between 1802 and 1816, several, being occasional poems, relate directly to national and international events. In his more famous poem written in Germany, *I Travelled among Unknown Men*, Wordsworth conveys how his experience abroad made him more conscious of his deep love of England.

In many other works of the English Romantic period, nationalism or identification with the nation may be implicit, while emphasis is given to the individual and to natural elements of the English countryside. Even so, this poetry too helped to intensify national consciousness and national pride among the English and the Scots of the 19th century.

Mary D. Zoghby

Works Consulted

Babbitt, Irving. *Rousseau and Romanticism*. 1919. Cleveland: World, 1968.

Cobban, Alfred. *Rousseau and the Modern State*. 2nd ed. Hamdem: Archon, 1964.

Carr, Edward Hallett. *Nationalism and After*. London: Macmillan, 1945.

Kohn, Hans. *Nationalism: Its Meaning and History*. Rev. ed. New York: Van Nostrand, 1965.

Rousseau, Jean-Jacques. *Rousseau: Political Writings*. Ed. and trans. Frederick Watkins. New York: Nelson, 1953.

Snyder, Louis L. *Varieties of Nationalism: A Comparative Study*. New York: Holt, 1976.

———. *The Meaning of Nationalism*. New Jersey: Rutgers, 1954. New York: Greenwood, 1968.

Natural Supernaturalism and 20th-Century Critics

As a dominant theme in Romantic poetry and philosophy, "natural supernaturalism" was made famous by M.H. Abrams. In *Natural Supernaturalism: Tradition and Revolution in Romantic Literature* (1971), Abrams argues that what unifies the writers of the late 18th and early 19th centuries—what constitutes Romanticism, in fact—is a tendency to reinterpret traditional Judeo-Christian patterns of thought—fall, redemption, and the restoration of paradise—in a secular context, of both history and philosophy and their own lives. Romantic writers, catalyzed by the French Revolution, according to Abrams, thought of themselves as seers or poet-prophets, and what they prophesy is the renewal of the world by a "sacred marriage," such as that described by St. John in the Book of Revelation. A spiral-shaped pattern emerges in which an initial period of innocence is followed by a fall into conflict and disruption, but a return to a higher innocence or integration of contraries is possible in the end.

Abrams's argument centers on Wordsworth, and particularly on Wordsworth's "Prospectus" to *The Recluse*, which Abrams regards as a manifesto of natural supernaturalism. This poem envisions a marriage between mind and nature, a goal that is pursued in Wordsworth's *Prelude* as well as in the work of other English Romantic poets and German philosophers. Abrams traces the structure of Romantic thought back to writers of religious autobiography like St. Augustine, who analyzed the journey of the human soul through conflict to a higher unity. The same enterprise is pursued in the popular Romantic genres of confession, *Bildungsroman* (the story of the soul's education), and *Universalgeschichte* (the story of humanity's education or progress).

Abrams not only regards Romantic literature as a coherent whole but also feels that one of its major unifying factors is the drive toward unity in individual works— unity, that is, between mind and nature, ego and nonego, or subject and object. In the decade after *Natural Supernaturalism* was published, other critics responded with counterarguments about the concept of Romanticism. Many have felt that Abrams's formulation is too coherent and far-reaching and that it necessarily excludes phenomena that do not fit its specific definition of Romantic. Anne K. Mellor, for instance, attempts to extend Abrams's definition to include forms of writing that do not necessarily work toward reintegration but instead exalt skepticism, social turbulence, fragmentation, paradox, and the limitations of human knowledge. Tilottama Rajan suggests that Abrams and other traditional critics who concentrate on the positive elements of imagination and romance fail to notice that Romantic works are constantly questioning the assumptions of their own language. Jerome J. McGann, in a series of books beginning with *The Romantic Ideology: A Critical Investigation* (1983), has launched the most extensive challenge to Abrams's interpretation. He uses Abrams's work to demonstrate that traditional readings of Romantic literature are unacknowledged ideologies that deliberately exclude certain phenomena, like social and political realities, as well as individual writers, like Byron and Keats.

To return to *Natural Supernaturalism*, the passage from which Abrams has taken his title may provide a further indication of the importance of the concept to Romantic literature. The term "natural supernaturalism" was originally used by Carlyle in *Sartor Resartus* (1834). Carlyle is describing the natural world as a phenomenon that embodies the miraculous and the infinite; humans can experience it in this way, he believes, if they make an effort to transcend the bounds of custom, space, and time, which dull their perceptions. Before Carlyle's time, let alone Abrams's, Romantic poets announced they were striving for a renewed vision of this kind. When Wordsworth and Coleridge collaborated on *Lyrical Ballads*, according to Coleridge, they agreed that Wordsworth would write about ordinary nature so as to make it appear defamiliarized and, in a sense, supernatural, while Coleridge would write about supernatural characters in such a way as to awaken interest on a human level. This marriage of naturalism and supernaturalism, involving a renewal of the self that allows looking at the surroundings in a new way, informs many of the key texts of English Romanticism, including Wordsworth's *Tintern Abbey*, Coleridge's

Rime of the Ancient Mariner, Blake's *Songs of Innocence and of Experience*, Shelley's *Prometheus Unbound*, and Keats's *Fall of Hyperion*.

Since it draws elements of supernaturalism from the Bible, medieval romance, Milton, folklore, and other sources and combines them with a renewed interest in natural surroundings, Romantic poetry necessarily relates the divine, the human mind, and nature in ways that might be characterized as "natural supernaturalism." By choosing the term as title for a book, which is now considered a landmark of Romantic scholarship, Abrams added a new dimension of meaning to it, using it to define Romanticism as a coherent, humanistic revolution with Judeo-Christian tradition. Whether other critics agree or disagree with his theory, it has come to be central to the question of how Romanticism may be defined. (*See also* Deism and Natural Supernaturalism in the 18th Century.)

Angela Esterhammer

Works Consulted

Abrams, M.H. *Natural Supernaturalism: Tradition and Revolution in Romantic Literature.* New York: Norton, 1971.

Lawrence Lipking, ed. *High Romantic Argument: Essays for M.H. Abrams.* Ithaca: Cornell UP, 1981.

McGann, Jerome J. *The Romantic Ideology: A Critical Investigation.* Chicago: U of Chicago P, 1983.

Mellor, Anne K. *English Romantic Irony.* Cambridge: Harvard UP, 1980.

Rajan, Tilottama. *Dark Interpreter: The Discourse of Romanticism.* Ithaca: Cornell UP, 1980.

Necessity, Doctrine of

The "doctrine of necessity" is often used to refer to a philosophical position held by Shelley during his early youth. It is quoted from one of Shelley's polemical notes to

Queen Mab (1812). This note, along with *Queen Mab* and the rest of the notes (really miniature political and philosophical essays), forms part of Shelley's general effort to revive philosophical doctrines inseparable from the radical republicanism of the early 1790s in the less propitious atmosphere of the early Regency. Heavily indebted to Godwin's *An Enquiry concerning Political Justice and its Influence on Morals and Happiness* (1793), especially the chapter "Of Free Will and Necessity," Shelley's essay expounds a necessitarian and deterministic theory of causality. According to this, any action or event in either the natural or the human world must be understood as an inevitable and necessary effect of the total chain of events in the universe that preceded it.

Shelley, following Godwin, attempts to rid this doctrine of its seemingly forbidding nature by observing that an assumed and changeless regularity in the relation of cause to effect is the basis of a day-to-day sense of order and that without it the transactions of normal life and indeed the idea of physical science would be inconceivable. A corollary of the doctrine of necessity is that notions of freedom of the will are delusory and incoherent, for it is self-evident that the will acts in accordance with the force of the motives acting on it and that the notion of a freedom of the will is as absurd a supposition as that of a cause without an effect. This argument bolsters Godwin's and Shelley's radical positions in politics in three ways. First, it tends to introduce "a great change into the established notions of morality" by making nonsense of the notion of someone *deserving* punishment, for the action at issue could not have been other than it was. Government punitive systems are thus irrational, as unjust as concepts of revenge. Second, the doctrine of necessity therefore

demands an attitude of rational and compassionate detachment upon human affairs. Finally, the doctrine tends "utterly to destroy religion" by rendering absurd the anthropomorphic conceptions of freedom of will and desire to reward or to punish that are often predicated of some supreme supernatural being.

Both Godwin and Shelley rest heavily on Hume's work on necessity, in particular on section VII ("Of the Idea of Necessary Connexion") of *Enquiries concerning Human Understanding and concerning the Principles of Morals* (1777). They miss totally the subtlety of Hume's argument, especially in relation to the skepticism latent in the heart of it. Hume had argued that the idea of the necessary connection of cause and effect is derived from mere customary transition or inference—the fact that every observation of *A* is followed by an observation of *B* leads one to posit a relation of causal necessity between them, whereas in fact there is no absolute justification for the idea of necessity. The young Shelley, while quoting Hume's argument that one knows "nothing more of causation than the constant conjunction of objects and the consequent inference of one from the other," mistakenly ascribes necessity to phenomena themselves rather than recognizing it as a law of the human mind in the understanding of phenomena.

There is still some dispute as to how far Shelley retained aspects of this notion of necessity in later life. It is undeniable, however, that by the time of the fragment entitled "How the analysis should be carried on" (probably 1815–16), he had come to a Humean view that man's "own mind is his law; his own mind is all things to him." In *A Defence of Poetry* (1821), imagination, not necessity, is described as the principle of synthesis among ideas.

Aspects of a similar doctrine of necessity, again relating to Godwin, but more especially to the associationism of Hartley's *Observations on Man: His Frame: his Duty and his Expectations* (1749) had a large formative influence on Coleridge in the 1790s, though by the early 1800s Coleridge came to reject mechanistic concepts of necessity. A retrospective account of the philosophical issues involved appears in *Biographia Literaria* (1817).

Timothy J.A. Clark

Works Consulted

Beauchamp, Tom L., and Rosenberg, Alexander. *Hume and the Problem of Causation*. New York: Oxford UP, 1981.

Cameron, Kenneth Neill. *The Young Shelley: Genesis of a Radical*. London: Golancz, 1951.

Evans, F.B. "Shelley, Godwin, Hume and the Doctrine of Necessity." *Studies in Philology* 37 (1940): 632–40.

Jenkins, Patricia Mavis. *Coleridge's Literary Theory: The Chronology of Its Development*. Fairfield: Fairfield UP, 1984.

Sperry, Stuart B. "Necessity and the Role of the Hero in Shelley's *Prometheus Unbound*." *PMLA* 96 (1981): 242–254.

Negative Capability

The term "negative capability" is used by Keats to describe the quality that forms great poets. In a letter (1817) to his brothers, Keats states that negative capability refers to the poet's ability to encounter and endure "uncertainties, Mysteries, doubts, without any irritable reaching after fact & reason." For Keats, Shakespeare is the preeminent poet of negative capability; Coleridge, on the other hand, lacks this quality, since he is not content with an artful metaphor or simile but must strive for a more complete understanding than is hinted at by the figure. Keats notes that if the implications of this concept were pursued further, they would lead to the idea that a poet's sense of beauty should outweigh any other concerns.

Keats does not mention "negative capability" again in his writings, but in several of his later letters he returns to the issues raised in the negative-capability letter. In a letter to J.H. Reynolds (1818), Keats reproaches Wordsworth and his contemporaries, much as he did Coleridge earlier, for egotistically forcing their philosophical positions on their readers. These poets, Keats contends, concern themselves too much with their speculations, when they should have the confidence to present their initial experiences, their necessarily incomplete "halfseeing," without philosophical embellishment. Poetry should be unobtrusive and engage the reader with its subject matter, not its philosophy. In this letter, more strongly than in the negative-capability letter, Keats creates a distinction between egotistical, or subjective, poetry (which is interested in the personal reactions and philosophical deductions of the poet) and objective poetry (which concerns itself solely with its subject matter). These ideas are developed further in a letter to Richard Woodhouse (1818), in which Keats discusses the poetical character and how it should be distinguished from the "wordsworthian or egotistical sublime." The poet opposed to the Wordsworthian type is a chameleon who enters into whatever objects or characters excite his imagination, whether they be appealing or disgusting, virtuous or evil. He loses his identity or self in order to live through his poetic creations.

Taken as a whole, Keats's scattered comments on the themes raised in the negative-capability letter outline a theory of poetry with philosophical, psychological, and aesthetic components. Great poets should be willing to suspend their desire for philosophical explanation and closure;

they should suppress their egos and allow themselves to flow into the objects of their creation; and they should always give their sense of beauty priority over other considerations.

Paul M. Wiebe

Works Consulted

Bate, Walter Jackson. *John Keats*. Cambridge: Belknap-Harvard UP, 1963.

Fitzpatrick, Margaret Ann. "The Problem of 'Identity' in Keats's 'Negative Capability.'" *Dalhousie Review* 61 (1981): 39–51.

Keats, John. *The Letters of John Keats: 1814–1821*. Ed. Hyder Edward Rollins. 2 vols. Cambridge: Harvard UP, 1958.

Sperry, Stuart M. *Keats the Poet*. Princeton: Princeton UP, 1973.

Negative Romanticism

Based on the notion of the dynamic organicism of Romanticism, Negative Romanticism is the state of mind and being of the defiant Romantic rebel in the throes of a soul-struggle with the 18th century's static, purely rational view of the world. It is a stage whereby the profoundly discontented Romantic individual is marked by doubt, despair, isolation, and dissatisfaction.

In his own period of *sturm und drang* (storm and stress) against the view of the universe as a steam engine, the Negative Romantic can neither reconcile personal belief and being nor arrive at gnosis or faith in any other meaningful view of existence. The theory was developed from the 1770s revolt against Classicism and Carlyle's "Everlasting No" from *Sartor Resartus* (1820s), which pictures spiritual crisis in a purposeless, indifferent universe. Negative Romanticism is a first and necessary stage of the Romantic's ultimate development of thought and art into an organic sense of unity or Positive Romanticism (Carlyle's "Everlasting Yea").

"Negative Romanticism" is a term originally proposed by literary scholar Morse Peckham in 1951 to suggest the despairing condition of the defiant Romantic hero who rejects the Enlightenment's mechanistic view of the world and yet finds no subsequent value or meaning. Peckham uses the term to describe the unsettled stage of the individual who is disassociated from existential meaning. While Peckham believes the Romantic figure can eventually progress to faith in organicism or Positive Romanticism, the Negative Romantic is trapped for the time being in his profound discontent, failing to develop faith or value (what Peckham calls "secular conversion").

Striving against the prevailing social forces, the Negative Romantic is a brooder, an outcast, a nonbeliever dissatisfied with the limitations of human knowledge. In the struggle to explore the outer reaches of human knowledge, the Negative Romantic is willing, not unlike Faust, to engage the powers of evil.

Negative Romanticism was theoretically developed by Peckham to account for Byron (and individuals like him) and Byron's creation of the archetypal Byronic hero. (*See also* Byronic Hero). Like Byron himself, Negative Romantics are cut off from nature, restless, and wandering, as demonstrated in Byron's *Childe Harold*, (begun in 1809 and depicting the first Byronic hero), *Manfred* (1817), and *Don Juan* (first installment published 1819).

According to Peckham, Act III, Scene 1 of *Manfred*, for example, illustrates the failure of traditional Christianity and most of the themes of Negative Romanticism: anger, fear, guilt, alienation, isolation, loss of values, and loss of identity. In his confrontation with the abbot of St. Maurice in Manfred's castle in the Alps, the Faustian figure of Manfred shows no desire to reconcile his tormented soul with heaven; he suffers the alienation and isolation that is Negative Romanticism.

Such cosmic negation and defiance mark Negative Romanticism. It is the impulse behind Coleridge's *The Rime of the Ancient Mariner* (1798), Wordsworth's Solitary character in *The Excursion* (1814), Shelley's *Alastor, or the Spirit of Solitude* (1816), Byron's *Cain: A Mystery* (1821), Maturin's *Melmouth, the Wanderer* (1820), Mary Shelley's *Frankenstein, or the Modern Prometheus* (1818), Lewis's *The Monk* (1796), and Melville's *Moby-Dick* (1851), works that all share the theme of rejecting an orderly notion of the world. In these novels and poems, Negative Romantics despair and defy their positions as outcasts, ultimately embracing nothing but their own insatiable quests.

Other literary critics have argued about the term, Rene Welleck calling Negative Romanticism synonymous to familiar states of mind, such as *Weltschmerz, mal du siecle*, and pessimism.

Elaborating on the Peckham-Welleck hypotheses and on his own considerations of Dark Romantic and Gothic writing, critic Robert D. Hume sorts out three types of Negative Romanticism between 1780 and 1830: (1) "exuberant gloom," as in Beckford's *Vathek: An Arabian Tale* (1782); (2) "existential agony," as in the *Ancient Mariner, Cain, Childe Harold*, and *Frankenstein;* and (3) "heroic despair," as in *Melmouth* and *Manfred*. Hume speculates that each of these forms of Negative Romanticism is based on the central Faustian myth and results when the Romantic lacks the otherwise typically Romantic optimism of understanding one's place and becomes trapped in a determination to achieve a more-than-ordinary human view of the world. This search for understanding often leads toward the powers of darkness.

According to Hume, *Vathek* reworks the Faustian legend but in a burlesque fashion developed from Beckford's exuberant energy and comic tone. *Cain* and *Frankenstein* demonstrate the pain and damnation patterns of existential agony, while the works of heroic despair glorify the Faustian archetype into a superhuman figure suffering from a grandeur of pain and displacement.

In addition to Byron, Peckham admits the notion was based on autobiographical accounts of Wordsworth, Coleridge, Shelley, and Carlyle. Historically, Peckham finds in the notion of Negative Romanticism an explanation of the personal and artistic development of the Positive Romantic's discovery of self and the creation of self as a central myth in the 19th and 20th centuries. (*See also* Gothicism.)

Norma W. Goldstein

Works Consulted

Hume, Robert D. "Exuberant Gloom, Existential Agony, and Heroic Despair: Three Varieties of Negative Romanticism." *The Gothic Imagination, Essays in Dark Romanticism*. Ed. G.R. Thompson. Pullman: Washington State UP, 1974.

Peckham, Morse. *Romanticism and Behavior, Collected Essays II*. Columbia: U of South Carolina P, 1976.

— — —, ed. *Romanticism: The Culture of the Nineteenth Century*. New York: Braziller, 1965.

— — —. *The Triumph of Romanticism* Columbia: U of South Carolina P, 1970.

Welleck, Rene. *Concepts of Criticism*. New Haven: Yale UP, 1963.

Nelson, Horatio (Viscount Nelson)

(1758–1805)

Horatio Nelson was born in 1758 in the small village of Burnham Thorpe, in Norfolk, where his father, Edmund Nelson, was vicar. His mother, Catherine Suckling, a distant relative of Sir Robert Walpole, died in 1767, leaving the vicar with eight children.

Nelson was educated at the Royal Grammar School in Norwich and the Paston School in North Walsham. His obvious ability encouraged his uncle Captain Maurice Suckling of the Royal Navy to take an interest in him. In 1770, Suckling had Nelson accepted as a midshipman and in 1771, Nelson joined his first ship, the H.M.S. *Raisonnable,* but was soon transferred to H.M.S. *Triumph* under his uncle's command.

Over the next few years, Nelson gathered experience. He served in the West Indies, the Baltic, and off the coast of New York during the American Revolution. His first combat came in a disastrous expedition to Nicaragua in 1780, and his second exposure came in 1783 during an attempt to retake Turk Island in the Bahamas from the French.

Between the American and French Revolutions, Nelson had several important experiences. For a time, he commanded the frigate *Boreas;* in 1786 and early 1787, he served as aide-de-camp for Prince William Henry, the future William IV (1765–1837); in 1787, he married the widow Francis Nesbitt, and they departed for England when Nelson was placed on half pay.

In 1793, England was at war with France; Nelson was given command of H.M.S. *Agamemnon.* It was also in 1793 that Nelson first met Sir William Hamilton, British minister to Naples and his wife Emma Hamilton. This was the quiet beginning of one of the more famous love affairs in history.

For the next seven years, he was engaged in almost continuous combat. His major campaigns included Corsica, where in the conflict at Calvi he lost his right eye;

the Battle of St. Vincent, after which he was promoted to rear admiral; and, finally, in 1797, the failed attack on Santa Cruz, Tenerife, in the Canaries. There, he was wounded in the right arm and the arm had to be amputated. The operation was poorly performed with the result that Nelson had to spend several months in England.

In 1798, Nelson was at sea again. It was clear that the French had a major operation planned because of fleet activities at Toulon, France. Nelson was given command of the naval forces assembled to interrupt the French plan—it proved to be Napoleon's invasion of Egypt. Ultimately, Nelson discovered the French fleet at Aboukir Bay (Alexandria) and, in one of the finest battles of his career, destroyed it on 1 August 1798 in the Battle of the Nile.

The year 1801 was particularly busy. Nelson was made vice admiral; the growing affair with Emma Hamilton resulted in a child; and Nelson was made second in command to Sir Hyde Parker in an expedition designed to weaken an alliance of northern powers guided by Tsar Paul of Russia. At Copenhagen, Nelson disregarded Parker's order to retire (he put the telescope to his blind eye and said he could not see the signal), and the resulting Battle of Copenhagen eliminated any possible Danish naval interference for months.

During the short Peace of Amiens (1802–03), Nelson lived with the Hamiltons, and when Sir William died in 1803, the admiral and Emma continued their relationship publicly. War resumed, and Nelson was recalled and given command of the Mediterranean fleet. He flew his flag on the 100-gun H.M.S. *Victory.*

From 1803 until his death in 1805, Nelson's consuming passion was the French fleet. He chased it from one side of the Atlantic to the other. On 21 October 1805, he caught the combined French-

Spanish fleet off Cape Trafalgar, and the battle he had so desired took place. The result was one of the most momentous sea battles in history. When it was over, the combined fleet was largely destroyed and with it any thought Napoleon may have had of invading England, but Nelson was dead, his spine shattered by a musket ball from the French ship *Redoubtable*. England celebrated and grieved at the same time.

Nelson's body was returned to England, where it lay in state at the Royal Hospital in Greenwich. In 1806, Nelson was buried at St. Paul's in London.

It was called the "Nelson touch." Nelson believed in winning because he was convinced England was right, and his men believed in him. He was one of the few commanders who took his captains into his confidence; they knew what was expected of them. Nelson could be a terrible egoist, and he loved adulation, but he had the ability to inspire his men. He took risks, and he used revolutionary tactics; however, he fought and won decisive battles. His masterpiece was Trafalgar, and he helped give England a century of naval supremacy.

K. Gird Romer

Works Consulted

Keegan, John. *The Price of Admiralty*. London: Hutchinson, 1988.

Mahan, Alfred Thayer. *The Life of Nelson*. Boston: Little, 1897.

Marcus, G.J. *The Age of Nelson: The Royal Navy in the Age of Its Greatest Power and Glory, 1793–1815*. New York: Viking, 1971.

Pocock, Tom. *Horatio Nelson*. New York: Knopf, 1988.

Walder, David. *Nelson*. London: Hamilton, 1978.

Neoplatonism

For Plotinus (205–70 A.D.), and Neoplatonists generally, mystical union with the highest principle (the One or the Absolute) occurs through ecstasy, the soul's out-of-body experience. That the One transcends being removes it from the status of Supreme Being of the Judeo-Christian tradition. In this way, secular-minded Romantics interested in transcendental truth need not be theists in any conventional, sectarian way. In fact, as Thomas Taylor (1758–1835) explains, Neoplatonists may be seen as polytheists, that is, as believers in the existence of divine natures, the progeny of the One with which those natures are ultimately linked. Renaissance Neoplatonism accepted these divinities as media for planetary influences and hence as intermediaries between earth and the heavens. By the time of Taylor and the Romantic era, such demons/daimons were summoned as metaphors or necessary fictions. Coleridge's *Rime of the Ancient Mariner* (1798) and Shelley's *Prometheus Unbound* (1820), Blake's Los, and Edgar Allan Poe's Demon in "Silence—A Fable" (1838) exemplify different uses of the minor deities, the demons/daimons of Neoplatonism.

Spiritual quest in Neoplatonism—tracing a circular path of emanation from the source, rapture in contemplating the source successfully, and eventual return to the source—is easily taken up and modified by the Romantic writer to enrich a relatively linear quest toward at least a momentary glimpse of the realm of forms and ideas, those archetypal entities separated from the knowing mind. Such a glimpse may blossom into Neoplatonist or Romantic ecstasy and the concomitant awareness that between subject and object all distinction is lost, that the perceiving self and the observed external world coalesce in unity.

In Wordsworth's *Tintern Abbey* (1798), at least two features of Neoplatonism occur: the optimistic view of the universe embedded in the assertion that a loved nature will not betray humanity and the ecstatic moment in which the breath/soul is suspended above the body so that the subjective self becomes all-soul and hence coalesces with the perceived world. Despite Wordsworth's denial elsewhere that he does not follow the Platonists, his well-known definition of poetry as an overflowing in the 1800 Preface to the *Lyrical Ballads* is a microcosmic equivalent to the Neoplatonic doctrine of emanations descending from the level of the One into the world of mutable things where the soul is immured in the human body. Moreover, in Chapter 12 of the *Biographia Literaria* (1817), Coleridge quotes from Wordsworth's *Excursion* in the context of discussing Plotinus. This occurs just after Coleridge develops an extended metaphor distinguishing the lofty land of pure philosophy (i.e., the transcendental) from the range of hills surrounding the valley of ordinary human life (i.e., the merely transcendent). Following Kant, Coleridge speaks Neoplatonically of the visionary powers of intuitive knowledge.

It is the realm of pure philosophy, says Coleridge, where ecstatic union with the Absolute is possible, where the distinction between subject and object disappears to effect transcendental unity. It is the same realm that Emerson speaks of in *Nature* (1836): the transcendental place where egotism vanishes and becomes ecstatically a medium through which the divine is perceived. Briefly Shelley had glimpsed that realm in his *Hymn to Intellectual Beauty* (1817), seeing it from a terrestrial valley of tears. And in Keats's *Ode to a Nightingale* (1819), Shelley's valley of tears is the death-ridden world of the Here that contrasts painfully with the nightingale's song that celebrates an eternal, transcendental There. Keats's ode centers on a failed quest; the Neoplatonic vision is but a dream, at once fleeting and puzzling. Keats's questions

create open-endedness, indeterminacy, and the result is a Romantic irony that subverts the natural supernaturalism of the secularized Neoplatonism implicit and explicit in the poem.

This skeptical or ironic reading of Neoplatonic values is vividly demonstrated in Poe's story *Morella* (1835) with its epigraph from Plato's *Symposium* and its deconstructively grim satire of Neoplatonic metempsychosis and love-theory. Similarly in Poe's *Berenice* (1835), transmigratory horrors are dramatized through a narrator who perceives his world as an emotionally disturbed Neoplatonist: for him everyday life is visionary, but dream-visions have materiality. Like Marsilio Ficino (1433–1499), Poe considers a Platonic text and offers his own literary commentary on the philosophical issues raised.

For the Romantics, then, Neoplatonism serves as a source of rich and beautiful thoughts. These are transformed into a myriad of applications, sometimes to bolster a particular Romantic article of faith, other times to assess such an article with irony. (*See also* Androgyny, Hellenism.)

Vincent F. Petronella

Works Consulted

Abrams, M.H. *Natural Supernaturalism: Tradition and Revolution in Romantic Literature.* New York: Norton, 1971.

Ficino, Marsilio. *Commentary on Plato's Symposium on Love.* Trans. and ed. Sears Jayne. Dallas, Spring, 1985.

Harper, George Mills. *The Neoplatonism of William Blake.* Chapel Hill: U of North Carolina P, 1961.

Mellor, Anne K. *English Romantic Irony.* Cambridge: Harvard UP, 1980.

Notopoulos, James. *The Platonism of Shelley: A Study of Platonism and the Poetic Mind.* Durham: Duke UP, 1949.

Pistorius, P.V. *Plotinus and Neoplatonism.* Cambridge: Bowes, 1952.

Raine, Kathleen, and George Mills Harper. Eds. *Thomas Taylor the Platonist: Selected Writings.* Princeton: Princeton UP, 1969.

Thompson, G.R. *Poe's Fiction: Romantic Irony in the Gothic Tales.* Madison: U of Wisconsin P, 1973.

Wallis, R.T. *Neoplatonism.* New York: Scribner's, 1972.

Novel

The novels of the Romantic period have not always been appreciated, being overshadowed by such 18th-century works as *Tom Jones* and *Clarissa* and the Victorian masterpieces of Dickens and Eliot. In many studies of the novel, only the works of Austen and Scott are mentioned; in others, no novels of the period appear. The Romantic period was a time of experimentation and stretching for the novel, yet some of the experimentation and stretching became exaggeration and excess. Romantic ideas have, however, influenced, several fine novels and culminate in a great novel, *Wuthering Heights.*

The Romantic novel began as a reaction against the verisimilitude of the 18th-century novel, with its squires, drawing rooms, Anglican churches, country inns, and relatively peaceful countryside. Such characters and settings did not provide fertile ground for the imagination to set out on flights of fantasy, nor did they provide an easy setting-off place for a journey into the inner psyche and emotions. The novels of Fielding and Richardson, Romantic writers contended, were not truly epic: they were not written in lofty and elevated language and lacked marvelous and mysterious deeds. In short, they were plain and familiar rather than grand and wild. As Walpole, the leader of the Romantic revolution in the English novel, wrote, "the great resources of fancy have been dammed up by a strict adherence to common life."

Romantic novelists claimed inspiration from Dante, Shakespeare, Marlowe, and the *Arabian Nights* rather than from Richardson or Fielding. It is interesting that they claimed inheritance not from novelists but from playwrights and poets. This claim gave them freedom to expand the expected boundaries of the novel. From drama, they took grand and exaggerated gestures and emotional intensity. From poetry, they gained inspiration for experimentation with rhythmic and metaphoric prose. Scott even incorporated ballads in his novels, while the prose of *Wuthering Heights* transforms at times almost into a lyric.

One of the great achievements of the 18th-century was the rediscovery of the past, especially the Middle Ages. Thomas Gray and Bishop Percy undertook serious study of medieval literature, Icelandic sagas, and ballads. This historical impulse also manifests itself in the novel, for example, in Scott's portrayal of characters as part of social forces and historic processes (though he perhaps takes historical authenticity too far with his prefaces, digressions, footnotes, and appendices). The historical impulse also freed novelists from representations of contemporary settings and characters so that, instead of foxhunting squires and benevolent ministers in country towns, they could picture ruined abbeys and labyrinthine castles peopled by monks, knights, and caliphs. The freedom gained, however, did not result in increased quality of plot and characterization: the flamboyant, luxurious, and grotesque accumulated into sensational and silly details without unity.

Along with the change in settings and characters came a change in the emotional and intellectual worlds of the novel. Romantic authors longed to reveal a world of private vision and darker emotions, to discuss feelings, dreams, and the imagination rather than an ordered world of reason bulwarked by the family, parish, and society. In so doing, they ran into problems of tone and of the limitations of language. Before Freud, there was a paucity of words to describe many of the emotions Romantic novelists wanted to convey. At its best, their language became suggestive and evocative; at its worst, it was almost hysterical with exclamation marks.

As with the problems of language and tone, the choice of point of view presented problems to the Romantic novelist. Romantic novelists wanted intimacy with their readers while at the same time reaching for sublime heights. The omniscient narrator, however, would not work: in using this point of view, the voice of the novel became detached from its content and even ironic. Instead, Romantic novelists settled on using the first person, which helped in creating a personal world but lost the multiplicity of views presented in earlier novels like *Clarissa*.

The first novel to try to break with the conventions of Fielding and Richardson was Walpole's *Castle of Otranto* (1764), which began the cult of the Gothic novel. (*See also* Gothicism.) Walpole claimed the inspiration for the story came from a dream. Set in a medieval Catholic atmosphere, the novel explores fear rather than love and presents madness, death, and riot. Unfortunately, Walpole was not skilled in characterization: his characters' behaviors are determined by external conditions rather than by their individual personalities and internal motivations. Rather than revealing the soul, mind, and heart of his characters, Walpole portrays frantic cartoon figures, and the dominant tone of the novel mixes boredom with humor and mystery. The plot, too, seems more an imposition or architectural construct.

Walpole looked to Shakespeare as a model to liberate his story from the conventions of his time. But his three drops of blood falling from the nose of Alfonso's statue are far from Shakespeare's carefully evocative use of the supernatural with Hamlet's ghost or the witches in *Macbeth*. Walpole also tried to imitate Shakespeare's intermingling of tragedy and comedy, the sublime world of heroes contrasted with the naive and often clumsy world of the servants. Though this intermingling of high and low life has been one of the strengths of the English novel, in Walpole's hands it failed: his talkative servants who chatter emptily frustrate rather than amuse. Yet, for all its faults, *The Castle of Otranto* is enormously important for what it tried to do and for the novels that followed its lead.

The second work to break from the mold of the 18th-century novel is Beckford's *Vathek*, which was written in French between 1781 and 1782 and translated into English without his permission two years later. Vathek is a caliph who, like Faust, sells himself to the powers of evil while pursuing knowledge and power. Unlike Faust, however, Vathek has no conscience, intelligence, or moral dimension.

Vathek is important for its use of an Eastern setting and in its Romantic emphasis on the self. Beckford drew inspiration for his fantasy from *Persian Tales, Mogul Tales*, and *The Adventures of Abdalla*. Unlike earlier writers (such as Johnson in *Rasselas*) who used Eastern settings to comment on life in England, Beckford uses his Eastern setting to create an imaginary world of self. He disliked literary realism and instead envisioned a nonstatic, nonrational, subjective world. The storyline of *Vathek* does not proceed sequentially; actions are not always completed; and the reader is often as much manipulated as the characters are. Everything revolves around the central character: other characters exist only as sources of his pleasure and pain, and nature exists to illuminate his ego. *Vathek* was shockingly original in its egocentricity and lack of morality: all is subsumed in the search for sensual gratification, whether it be appreciation of beauty or indulgence in debauchery. *Vathek* influenced Byron's *The Giaour* (1813), and its psychological images and style can be linked to Lewis's.

The Gothic novel came to full bloom in the works of Radcliffe, with her ruined castles on rocky cliffs, dungeons, forests, bandits, villains, monks and nuns, fainting heroines, and explainable ghosts. Her most famous work, *The Mysteries of Udolpho* (1794), is set in 1584 in Catholic France and Italy. Radcliffe is most original in her presentation of environment and its relationship to the characters. The environments in her novels permeate the characters and are inseparable from them. The castle in *The Mysteries of Udolpho* forms the central image and stands in symbolic relation to the characters. Through Emily, the main character, the readers feel wonder, awe, and terror at the supernatural but also sadness and melancholy at mutability and the inability to feel. Radcliffe explores the irrational and portrays the tension of human behavior at odds with moral principles. In *The Italian* (1791), she dramatizes a world where even the most self-controlled and moral must fear the malignant, wild forces surrounding them. In the character of Schedoni, she creates a heroic-demonic Romantic individual: he is solitary, passionate, even tormented, yet strangely powerful. Radcliffe's work influenced many writers, including Lewis, Maturin, Byron, Scott, Dickens, Poe, Faulkner, and succeeding writers of both thriller and psychological works.

Other important novelists of the period include Lewis, Maturin, Mary Shelley, and James Hogg. Lewis's *The Monk* (1796) has a dream atmosphere and structure with a quintessential Gothic villain Ambrosio, whose great nature has been deformed by his upbringing and who is left torn between rigid self-discipline and deviant eroticism. Influenced by German drama, Lewis, in turn, was influential in his example of probing the subconscious. Maturin's *Melmoth the Wanderer* (1820) is ingeniously constructed with contrasting stories set within one another. It gives some of the darkest views of human nature in all of English literature. Shelley's *Frankenstein* (1818) has as its central figure a Romantic quester whose monstrous creation, originally innocent, is perverted by human neglect. Hogg's *The Private Memoirs and Confessions of a Justified Sinner* (1824) mingles the supernatural with criticism of religious fanaticism. All four works set violent passions against the restrictions of civilization, a theme that culminates powerfully in Brontë's *Wuthering Heights*.

Austen and Scott, the premier novelists of the period, are more toward the realistic tradition of the 18th-century novel than the extravagant emotions and fantasy of Romanticism. Yet their novels display tendencies of the age. Austen mocks the excesses of Romanticism in *Northanger Abbey* (1798–99) yet, like a Romantic, criticizes commonplace morality and the social values of the unthinking middle class. Scott's novels, such as *The Bride of Lammermoor* (1819), contain supernaturalism. Scott is most Romantic in his nationalism and Wordsworthian presentation of lower-class figures.

Whatever their faults, what the Romantic writers achieved was recognition that the novel, for all its greatness in 18th-century realism, could expand to be much more.

Ann W. Engar

Works Consulted

Allen, Walter. *The English Novel: A Short Critical History*. London: Phoenix, 1954.

Kiely, Robert. *The Romantic Novel in England*. Cambridge: Harvard UP, 1972.

Priestley, J.B. *The English Novel*. London: Benn, 1927.

Skilton, David. *The English Novel: Defoe to the Victorians*. New York: Barnes, 1977.

Van Ghent, Dorothy. *The English Novel: Form and Function*. New York: Rinehart, 1959.

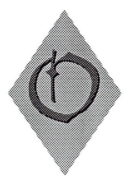

Oliphant, Carolina, Baroness of Nairne

(1766–1845)

Poet and songwriter, Carolina Oliphant's ambiguity in literary history has ranged from being described as Scotland's greatest woman poet to being lumped with distinctly minor poets.

Oliphant's father and grandfather had served the Jacobite cause; both had been exiled for 17 years for their participation in the Rebellion of 1745. Her mother's family, the Robertsons, were also devoted Jacobites, some remaining in French exile until Oliphant was in her late teens. From her early years, Oliphant, named for "Bonny Prince Charlie," heard, and was later influenced by, tales of gallantry and pursuit. In addition to these influences was the landscape she observed every day until her marriage. Strathearn, the region where she was born and in which she grew up, was near historic battlefields and castle strongholds. Thus, Oliphant's many political songs (e.g., "Charlie's Landing," "Who'll be King but Charlie," "The Hundred Pipers," and "The White Rose o' June") derive from this early and considerable Jacobite background.

Oliphant was born in 1766, to an aristocratic family—her father, Lawrence Oliphant, the laird of Gask in Perkshire, and her mother, Margaret Robertson of Strowan, daughter to the chief of the Donnochy clan. She enjoyed a privileged childhood; along with her two sisters and two brothers, she was educated by a governess and learned to play several musical instruments. As a young woman fond of dancing and social gatherings, Oliphant—vivacious, tall, graceful, with large, compelling eyes—was "the flower of Strathearn." After her father's death, she continued to live in the family house at Gask with her brother, Lawrence, successor to the lairdship, and his wife.

In 1806, Oliphant married her second cousin, Major William Murray Nairne, who was restored to his barony in 1824. The couple settled at Duddington, a suburb of Edinburgh. Two years later, their son, William Murray, was born.

Before her marriage, Oliphant had been inspired by Burns's work. She wrote several songs, including some Jacobite lays and celebrations of rural life. Her best known song, sometimes attributed to Burns, is "The Land O' the Leal." It is a poignant expression of grief and religious faith. Like Burns, Oliphant sought new lyrics for old tunes; unlike him, she was specifically concerned with improving the moral tone of traditional lyrics.

Oliphant contributed to the national minstrelsy in 1821. In that year, she became an influential member on an Edinburgh committee of women formed to prepare a collection of national airs to be published by Robert Purdie. The project, under the editorship of Robert Archibald Smith, took three years to complete, and both songs and melodies were included. Oliphant sent many anonymous songs for this publication, with the initials SM (Scottish Minstrel), BB (Mrs. Bogan of Bogan), or others. Neither the editor, the publisher, her friends, nor her husband knew the songwriter's identity. During interviews with Purdie, Oliphant dressed as an old gentlewoman and repeatedly enjoined Purdie and Smith to preserve the anonymity even of the gender, for she feared that a work by a woman writer would be undervalued. *The Scottish Minstrelsy* was published in six volumes in 1824, the same year Oliphant assumed the title Baroness Nairne.

After the death of her husband in 1830, Oliphant moved to Ireland with her son, the new Lord Nairne; the warmer climate, she hoped, would restore his health. Settling in Wicklow, at Enniskerry, she composed songs sympathetic to the Irish peasants. Their afflictions, she felt, were caused by an avaricious priesthood. "Wake Irishman, Wake" is a rousing call to the Irish to reclaim their freedom.

Many of the songs Oliphant composed are precisely dated only when there is evidence of a performance (e.g., "The Pleughman" was played for her brother and his tenants in 1792); documentary proof (e.g., "Land of the Leal" accompanied a letter of condolence in 1798); an

allusion to a contemporary literary work (e.g., "Jeanie Deans" is based on a character in *The Heart of Midlothian*, published in 1818); or an autobiographical incident is reflected (e.g., "Farewell Edinburgh" records Oliphant's removal from her home there in 1831).

"Would You Be Young Again" was composed in 1842, when Oliphant was age 76. It is uncertain, however, how many songs she wrote after her son's death in 1837, when she resumed the travels on the Continent that they had taken in 1834 to improve his failing health. Only in 1843 did she return to Gask, where she settled with her nephew James Blair Oliphant and his wife. There, she devoted her time to anonymously supporting public charities and religious schools. After her arrival in Gask, she allowed her songs to be published in a separate volume—with the stipulation that she remain anonymous. But because she died (in 1845) while publication of the songs was still being planned, her sister, Margaret Keith, believed that her name should be disclosed. Keith approved the title as it appeared in 1846: *Lays from Strathearn by Carolina, Baroness Nairne, Arranged with symphonies and accompaniments for the pianoforte by Finlay Dun*; 70 songs were in that volume.

Oliphant's songs reveal humor ("John Tod"), religious devotion ("Gud Nicht, an' Joy"), respect for ordinary folk ("Caller Herrin"), nostalgia for the manor house ("Castell Gloom"), and domestic concerns ("Cradle Song," "The Country Meeting"). Her best songs celebrate the landscape ("O Mountain Wild"), realistically portray how young women respond to courtship and marriage ("Jamie The Laird"), and historically depict the violence attending Scottish loyalties ("Lament of the Covenanter's Widow"). The verses are appealing for comic effects ("The Heiress"), for philosophical awareness ("The Regalia"), for lyrical charm—and their melodies often lift and transform what would otherwise be somewhat ordinary.

As poems, rather than songs, the pieces may be deficient for their conventional description, ineffective repetition, and too abundant rhymes and for expressing what is sentimental or trite. Oliphant's best poems are admirable for the transforming melody that attaches to the song aspect and for inventive diction and dialect, a spirited tone, and a simplicity of statement.

Marilyn Jurich

Works Consulted

British Women Writers. Ed. Janet Todd. New York: Continuum, 1988.

Masson, David. *Edinburgh Sketches and Memories.* Edinburgh: Adam, 1892.

Rogers, Rev. Charles. *Life and Songs of the Baroness Nairne with a Memoir and Poems of Carolina Oliphant The Younger.* Edinburgh: Grant, 1896.

———. *The Scottish Minstrel: The Songs of Scotland Subsequent to Burns with Memoirs of the Poets.* Edinburgh: Nimo, 1870.

Sampson, George. *The Concise Cambridge History of English Literature,* 3rd ed. London: Cambridge UP, 1970.

Watson, Roderick. *The Literature of Scotland.* New York: Schocken, 1985.

Ollier, Charles

(1788–1859)

Charles Ollier, with his brother James, was publisher to several significant Romantic writers. Among the works he published were *Keats's Poems* (1817), *Hazlitt's Characters of Shakespeare's Plays* (1817), *Hunt's Foliage* (1818), *Lamb's Works, Medwin's Sketches in Hindoostan* (1821), and most of Shelley's works. He also published *The Literary Pocket Book* for 1819 through 1823 and a *Literary Miscellany* (1820), which included Peacock's *Four Ages of Poetry.*

Ollier was born in Bath to Charles Ollier and Sarah Tuttle. By 1802 he had settled in London where he was employed as a junior bank clerk; in 1810, he joined the firm of Coutts' bank and apparently remained in banking as late as 1816. In 1810 he also became acquainted with Leigh Hunt, and with Charles Cowden Clarke by 1812. He met Shelley and Keats in the winter of 1816 to 1817. In February 1817, he and his brother James embarked on a career as publishers, booksellers, and proprietors of a circulating library. During the next six years, the Olliers published over 50 works. In early 1823, the business failed, due most likely to a lack of capital; the brothers chose a more propitious occupation, possibly as stationers. Subsequently, Ollier returned to the business of publishing; from autumn 1825, until November 1839, he served as literary adviser and reader for publisher Henry Colburn and later for publisher Richard Bentley. In this capacity, he solicited, read, edited, and at times rewrote or completed the works of other writers.

In 1845, Ollier embarked on a second career as a publisher; this time at Southampton Street, Strand. During the next three years, he issued close to 20 titles; his list included such authors as Charlton Carew, the Rev. John Hobart Cauter, Harriet Kearney, Mary Molesworth, and John Reade. This second endeavor failed in 1849; from 1850 until his death in 1859 Ollier served as G.P.R. James's agent, edited family papers, revised or completed novels by other writers, and lectured.

Ollier also was an author; among his works are *Altham and His Wife* (1818), *Inesilla* (1824), and *Ferrers* (1842). In addition, he published articles in several publications, including *Blackwood's Magazine, Leigh Hunt's Examiner, Bentley's Miscellany,*

Ainsworth's Magazine, and the *Literary Souvenir*. (*See also* Publishing.)

Martin P. McNamee

Works Consulted

Chilcott, Tim. *A Publisher and His Circle: The Life and Work of John Taylor, Keats's Publisher*. Boston: Routledge, 1972.

Ollier, Edmund. "A Literary Publisher." *Temple Bar: A London Magazine for Town and Country Readers*. 58 (1880): 243–52.

Plant, Majorie. *The English Book Trade*. 3rd ed. London: Allen, 1974.

Robinson, Charles E. "Percy Bysshe Shelley, Charles Ollier, and William Blackwood: the Contexts of Nineteenth-Century Publishing." *Shelley Revalued: Essays from the Gregynog Conference*. Ed. Kelvin Everest. Leicester: Leicester UP, 1983.

Opie, Amelia Alderson

(1769–1853)

The author of unabashedly sentimental novels, poems, moral tales, and stories for children, Amelia Alderson Opie was born in Norwich, England, in 1769. She was the only child of James Alderson and Amelia Briggs Alderson. Her father was a prominent physician, a radical in politics, and a Unitarian. Her mother, a member of an established Norfolk family, saw to it that Amelia Alderson received the "appropriate" training for a girl of her class: tutoring in French and music and dancing lessons. After her mother died in 1784, she became her father's hostess and was introduced to society at age 15.

Attractive, animated, and intelligent, Alderson wrote poems, plays, and stories and entertained guests with songs she had written since childhood. Although she showed an interest in the stage (Sarah Siddons and Elizabeth Inchbald were family friends), her first professional effort was a novel, *The Dangers of Coquetry*, published anonymously in 1790. Prince Hoare

considered dramatizing it, and *The Critical Review* approved its moral, if not its style or plot; but overall it was ignored. In 1791, Alderson completed a play, *Adelaide*, and her father permitted her to mount two performances of it at a private theater, casting herself in the title role. The drama was set in Paris and concerned the relationship of a father and son estranged by the son's marriage to a woman of low birth. Godwin, a family friend and for a time one of Alderson's suitors, read some of her early dramatic efforts and offered his encouragement; but her first popular success came in 1801 with her second novel, *Father and Daughter*.

During a visit to London in 1797, she met the painter John Opie. He was immediately smitten with her and pressed his suit despite her initial lack of interest. The son of a carpenter, Opie was divorced; his speech revealed his native Cornwall; and his appearance and manners were rough. Neither Alderson's father nor her friends considered him appropriate for her. However, Opie was a successful painter, had been elected to the Royal Academy in 1787, and—though largely self-educated—was widely read. They married in 1798. During their marriage, John Opie painted 10 portraits of his wife. After her husband died in 1807 from a mysterious illness involving inflammation of the brain, Opie endeavored to have him buried in St. Paul's, as he wished, near a vault housing the remains of Sir Joshua Renolds. In 1809 Opie prepared and published a volume of her husband's lectures on art; it included a memorial tribute to him.

Early in her marriage, Opie published the works that made her reputation as an author. The plot of her first publicly acknowledged novel, *Father and Daughter*, is similar to that of *Clarissa*: a young woman is seduced, betrayed, and dies of shame.

Befitting the taste of the time, the work is replete with pathetic scenes, and the style is excessively sentimental. Opie had once confessed to a friend that she found it most enjoyable to make people cry over her stories, and they apparently liked to do so. When Scott met her, he said *Father and Daughter* had made him weep, and Prince Hoare declared that reading it made him too upset to sleep. Fannie Kemble borrowed from its plot for her play *Smiles and Tears,* and Paer based his opera *Agnese* on it. *Father and Daughter* went through at least 10 editions in the next four decades and, during Opie's lifetime, remained the most widely read of her works.

In 1802, Opie published a volume of poetry that included two of her most enduringly popular poems, *The Orphan Boy* and *The Felon's Address to his Child.* Several influential reviews offered restrained praise and commended its moral purpose and pathos; the public was more enthusiastic. *Poems* went through six editions between 1802 and 1811 and, with *Father and Daughter,* helped to assure Opie's social success. Soon she became part of the preeminent London Bluestockings, which included the Countess of Cork, Lady Lamb, and Lady Bessborough.

Opie's liveliest and most skillfully written novel was *Adeline Mowbray, or The Mother and Daughter,* published in 1804. Loosely based on the life of her close friend Wollstonecraft, the work was probably meant to be an indictment of Godwin's theoretical opposition to marriage; it can also be read as an indictment of marriage. Early chapters of the novel portray Adeline's mother, a woman of intellectual pretension, with sharpness and wit. Mowbray devotes herself ostentatiously to avant-garde social ideas until she is horrified to find her daughter plans to adopt those ideas by living with her lover. In later chapters, pathos reigns, and the quality of writing declines. Although the critics gave *Adeline Mowbray* less notice than *Father and Daughter,* the public generally approved it, and modern audiences usually find it her work of most enduring interest.

In 1806, Opie issued the four-volume *Simple Tales.* It was followed by *The Warrior's Return and Other Poems,* published in 1808. Both received mixed reviews. After her husband's death, Opie had returned to her father's household in Norwich and had become a close friend of Joseph John Gurney, a well-known Quaker who offered her spiritual advice. Between 1812 and 1823, she published works of strongly moral intent, including *Temper* (1812), *Tales of Real Life* (1813), *Valentine's Eve* (1816), *Tales of The Heart* (1820), *Madeline* (1822), and *Self-Delusion, or Adelaide D'Hauteroch* (published anonymously in 1823). She remained a popular author, but neither critics nor friends approved the increasingly didactic turn of her work, and—although *Tales of Real Life* sold well, and Southey liked *Madeline,* an epistolary love story—most readers preferred her earlier volumes.

In 1823, having attended Friends' meetings for nearly a decade, Opie stopped writing the novel *The Painter and His Wife* because, she declared, she had decided to become a Quaker. She never wrote another novel. She continued, however, to publish moral essays and stories, including *Illustrations of Lying* (1825), *Tales of the Pemberton Family, for the Use of Children* (1825), *The Black Man's Lament, or How to Make Sugar* (1826), and *Detraction Displayed* (1828); while she lost some of her English readership, these didactic works attracted a large audience in America. Opie traded her brightly colored silk gowns for the browns and grays the Society approved and employed the "thees and thous" it favored in conversation. But despite the preachments of John Gurney and others in the Society, she was never able completely to give up the social whirl. Her visits to Friends' meetings, the sick, the poor, and the imprisoned were always interspersed with visits to friends in London society.

In 1829, she returned to Paris, where she had once traveled with her husband. Between visits to hospitals and prisons, she met Lafayette and other members of the fashionable world and agreed to sit for a medallion by the sculptor David d'Angers. She attended the 1840 Anti-Slavery convention in London as a delegate for Norwich, and she was one of those portrayed in Haydon's well-known picture of the meeting. At age 82, infirm but spirited, she attended the Great Exhibition in a wheelchair and challenged an old acquaintance, similarly ensconced, to a race. She died in 1853, and she was buried in the Friends' cemetery at Norwich with her father.

Gayla S. McGlamery

Works Consulted

Macgregor, Margaret Eliot. *Amelia Alderson Opie: Worldling and Friend* 14. Northhampton, MA: Smith College Studies in Modern Languages.

Smith, C. Dale Spender. *Mothers of the Novel: 100 Good Women Writers Before Jane Austen*. London: Pandora, 1986.

Stevenson, Lionel. *The English Novel: A Panorama*. London: Constable, 1960.

Opium and Laudanum

In the 18th and early 19th centuries in England, the use of opium and laudanum, the alcoholic tincture of opium, was widespread and without stigma. Physicians treated painful complaints—gout, rheumatism, dysentery—with these drugs. Overall, people at the time were also unaware of opium's addictive dangers, failing perhaps to recognize the cause of symptoms of withdrawal if they became addicted. By mid-century, however, opium use had become disgraceful but exotic, condemned but glamorized, especially among the intelligensia. This paradoxical view of its use as depraved and destroying, but illuminating and inspiring, has several sources. Influenced by German Romanticism and travel accounts of the Orient and Arabic lands, including pleasant drug experiences, people began to desire new experiences and sensations and to take a romanticized view of opium use. (*See also* Orientalism.) However, an increasing recognition of the damage it could cause also resulted in condemnation of its use. From a literary standpoint, Coleridge and De Quincey are perhaps most closely associated with these views regarding opium abuse.

Coleridge was addicted to opium perhaps as early as 1801, and its subsequent effect on his life and career is both recorded and debated. Coleridge's poems and literary philosophy are full of the language of dreams, visions, illusions, and reveries. His 1816 Preface to *Kubla Khan* describes its composition as the result of a dream, induced by "an anodyne," from which, upon awakening, he recalled and recorded the exact words and images of the dream poem, until he was interrupted by the celebrated man from Porlock and later could remember no more. The inference is that opium made possible a unique vision and creation that could have resulted only in a creative mind under magical influence. Other such assertions by Coleridge and the publication of De Quincey's *Confessions of an English Opium Eater* (1822) helped to popularize a belief in opium as the creator of beautiful hallucinations, heightened sensation, and extraordinary creative powers, despite other frightening descriptions of its effects by both authors. By mid-century, Coleridge and De Quincey were both cited as examples of the damage caused by opium abuse.

Debate about the role opium played in Coleridge's life centers on why he became an opium-addicted procrastinator, liar, debtor, and, apparently, plagiarist who abandoned his family and was unable to complete the endeavors he began; but controversy also surrounds the contention that opium creatively inspired and aided him.

One theory posits that Coleridge's original nature was a contradictory combination of sloth and self-doubt, coupled with an egotistical desire to be unique and superior in his accomplishments. Here, opium is the symptom, not the source, of his basic inadequacies, which caused his personal problems. These psychological problems also either caused him to prefer leaving works unfinished to avoid negative final judgment or often left him unable to bring his creative genius to fruition. His attendant desire to be thought remarkable can then be understood as the cause of a fabricated 1816 *Kubla Khan* Preface as well as other such pronouncements regarding opium inspiration, designed by him to create a favorable public view of his opium use and to rationalize to himself his continued reliance on it.

On the other hand, Coleridge's addiction has been theorized as a result from treatment for an early physical malady, a response to his basic inability to deal with harsh realities, and easy access to the drug through associates who were abusers. While conceding opium's creative and physical damage to Coleridge, as well as the damage to his perception of the truth, this argument maintains that Coleridge recognized his terrible predicament, wished to end it rather than justify or enjoy it, and sought help by placing himself under a physician's constant supervision for, what

became, the last 18 years of his life. During this time, he lived with a medically supervised and controlled habit that allowed him to experience somewhat of a creative and intellectual renaissance. Unfortunately, despite his rehabilitation, the public had come to see him as a couch-reclining, irresponsible drug addict and failed poet.

Both theories, however, reach the same conclusion: Coleridge's reputation and career were ruined—his great intellectual and creative powers lost.

Dorothy H. Graham

Works Consulted

Lefebure, Molly. *Samuel Taylor Coleridge: A Bondage of Opium*. New York: Stein, 1974.

Schneider, Elisabeth. *Coleridge, Opium and Kubla Khan*. New York: Octagon, 1966.

Organic Form

Organic form is a concept associated with Romanticism from its 18th- and 19th-century beginnings to its full flowering in the critical theory of Coleridge and in the poetry of Wordsworth, Coleridge, and others. "Organic"—suggesting living, growing, and developing; involving associations with living organisms; and connoting something, at the root, basic and fundamental—was a word that served its originators well concerned as they were with criticizing earlier and more classical and Neoclassical ideas. One of those ideas was of mechanical form, advanced especially by Enlightenment critics. It offered an image of a static order, of something fixed, determined, already completed, wherein parts play their determined and appropriate roles as contributors to an overall unity in a fixed chain of being and characters have a specific, unchanging form. Pope's description of nature as "One clear, unchang'd, and universal light" in the *Essay on Criticism* and of humans as dwelling on the "isthmus of a middle state" in the *Essay on Man* catch some of that mechanical concept of form, against which German and English Romantics reacted.

Romantics like Coleridge were greatly influenced by German philosophy and aesthetics, especially those of Schelling and Schlegel. (*See also* German Idealism.) Schelling's *On the Relation of the Plastic Arts to Nature,* for example, wonders how to "spiritually melt this apparently rigid form, so that the pure energy of things may flow together with the force of our spirit and both become one united mold?" And Schlegel, in his *Lecture on Dramatic Art and Literature,* speaks of the progress of feeling in Shakespeare's characters, of how each play "is like a world of its own, moving in its own sphere." What emerges, and how often the plant is used as a model, is an idea of form as evolving from primitive origin to mature flower. An inner life generates this vitality; parts become not mere building blocks but unique and vital participants in an overall unity.

It is not the power of sensation or reason or even fancy that creates organic form. Rather, it is the magical power of imagination—with its sympathetic power to enter into, shape, and organize the materials of experience into images and symbols—that creates organic form. Coleridge uses this concept of form in both his theoretical and practical criticism. In his essay "On Poesy or Art," he discusses the imitation of the beautiful in nature, describing beauty "in the concrete" as the "union of the shapely (formosum) with the vital." The artist, far from merely copying nature, imitates what is within the object, "that which is active through form and figure." A poem, he notes in the *Biographia Literaria,* offers "such delight from the whole, as is compatible with each component part." Distinguishing mechanical regularity from organic form in his essay "Shakespeare's Judgement Equal to His Genius," he sees the organic as "innate, as shaping as it develops from within."

Coleridge has little patience with the Neoclassical tradition of Shakespearean criticism that praised the dramatist only as a rough-hewn genius who caught truth in a flash and brought no artistry to the shaping of his materials. On the contrary, Coleridge argues, Shakespeare's judgment was equal to his genius, and the source is not in qualities he shares with the ancients, but in the differences, in "symbols of living power as contrasted with the lifeless mechanism." In a most suggestive sentence, he characterizes the organic form that characterizes Shakespeare's work: "Such as the life is, such is the form." Likewise, in the Wordsworthian sections of his *Biographia Literaria,* he praises the poet's immortality ode for its power to engage those special readers accustomed to observing the ebb and flow of the inner life, that living being that can be expressed adequately only through symbols.

Coleridge's concept of organic form has been noted by most historians of criticism as having deeply influenced the New Criticism in England and America with its emphasis on the object, on the living quality of the work of art. (*See also* Shakespeare.)

John L. Mahoney

Works Consulted

Appleyard, J.A. *Coleridge's Philosophy of Literature.* Cambridge: Harvard UP, 1965.

Barfield, Owen. *What Coleridge Thought.* Middletown, Conn.: Wesleyan UP, 1971.

Barth, J. Robert. *The Symbolic Imagination: Coleridge and the Romantic Tradition.* Princeton UP, 1977.

Bate, Walter Jackson. *Criticism: The Major Texts.* New York: Harcourt, 1970.

Wellek, Rene. *A History of Modern Criticism, 1750–1950.* Vols. 1–2. New Haven: Yale UP, 1955–86.

Orientalism/Exoticism

During the second half of the 18th century, the European powers found themselves owning the entire globe. That undisputed possession did not last; in 1783, the United States broke away from England, and, by 1825, nearly all of South America was free of its former rulers. But those successful rebellions in the New World helped to focus more attention on European relationships with the Old Worlds — Islam, India, and East Asia. And as the thrill of conquest faded, a new excitement took its place: the joy of discovering new cultures, new forms of thought and behavior, and new arts and sports, all of which gave new illumination to Europe's old ways and means.

For the Romantics, the Islamic world was probably a most compelling lure. As Hugo put it regarding his poem *Les Orientales* (1829): "Au siècle de Louis XIV on était helléniste, maintenant on est orientaliste" ("In the era of Louis XIV everyone was a Hellenist; now everyone is an Orientalist"). Perhaps the best known example of the Romantic fascination with Islamic life is Napoleon, who invaded Egypt in 1798 accompanied by a scholarly team whose sole purpose was to record Egyptian culture, geography, and religion. The result, the 23-volume *Description de l'Égypte,* published between 1809 and 1828, remains one of the great monuments of Romantic Orientalism. Less well known, but more influential, was the work of Silvestre de Sacy, France's leading Orientalist scholar from 1769 to 1832. Through his masterwork, the anthology of poetry and prose known as the *Chrestomathie arabe* (1806–27), and through the generations of students he trained, Sacy laid the foundations for scientific study of Islam and its milieu.

Many writers and artists were fascinated with the Islamic world. In England, those included Beckford (*Vathek,* 1782) and Scott (*The Talisman,* 1825) to Byron, who gained fame with such Orientalizing works as *Childe Harold's Pilgrimage* (1811) and continued to develop Mideastern subjects with *The Giaour* (1813) and *The Dream* (1816). For all these authors, exotic settings allowed them to focus on passions and forms of behavior that would be unthinkable in a contemporary English setting. Romantic painters, too (especially the French), were attracted to the intricate patterns, intense light, and exotic costumes of Islamic subjects. Delacroix was early drawn to such subjects as depicted in *The Death of Sardanapalus* (1827), while many later masterpieces, such as *Woman of Algiers* (1834) and *The Sultan of Morocco* (1845), were based on his 1832 journey to Morocco. It was not even necessary to visit the East, as Ingres proved with three great pictures of Turkish harem women, or "Odalisques," painted in 1814, 1839, and 1863; Ingres traveled no further south than Rome. On the other hand, J.F. Lewis spent a dozen years in Spain, Turkey, and Cairo, making some 600 paintings and drawings, which inspired his work for 25 years after his return to London in 1850; *An Intercepted Correspondence* (1869) captures both the jewel-like interior of a sultan's drawing room and the gemlike flame of illicit passions lurking just below that surface.

India was almost exclusively an English obsession, but its greatest effects on art and literature were not felt until the Victorian period. In fact, Europeans first learned of India's beauties in 1795, when Thomas and William Daniell began to publish their *Oriental Scenery,* not completed until 1808. Its six volumes transformed English standards of the picturesque and inspired a

series of "Indian Gothic" buildings, the
greatest of which was the Royal Pavilion
at Brighton, designed by Nash and built
between 1815 and 1822 for King George
IV. Sir William Jones, studying Sanskrit
philology in connection with the legal studies that had drawn him to India in 1783,
discovered a linguistic kinship with both
the Germanic and Latinate families of languages that later inspired thinkers from
Schlegel to Ernest Renan.

China was also mainly an English concern during this period. From 1792 to
1794, Lord Macartney made the first official and serious attempt to establish normal relations with China. Though the effort failed — Macartney was sent home after
only one ceremonial audience with the
Emperor — the overall result of the expedition was invaluable. The artist William
Alexander made nearly a thousand sketches
of the Chinese landscape and people; Sir
George Staunton, Macartney's aide, published two volumes about the expedition;
his son, the only member of the Embassy
to learn Chinese during the expedition,
eventually helped found the Royal Asiatic
Society; and Dr. James Dinwiddie, one of
the Embassy's scientists, had samples of
Chinese tea plants transplanted in India,
where they ultimately flourished.

Finally, Captain Cook's voyages of 1768
to 1771, 1772 to 1775, and 1776 to 1777
widened English horizons, as Count
Bougainville's voyage in 1766 to 1769 had
for the French; after a series of expeditions, colonization of Australia was begun
in 1788. By 1840, however, when transportation to New South Wales ended,
Australia had lost much of its exoticism,
being perceived by emigrants as a "green
and pleasant land" that had been spared
the ravages of industrial England. The
contradictions between the lure of the exotic and the tyranny of convention are

epitomized in the career of Captain Bligh.
While leading an expedition to Tahiti in
1789, Bligh's overbearing manner led his
crew to mutiny; after an epic 1000-mile
voyage to safety in an open boat with very
little food and water, and the lengthy trials
of the mutineers, he was rewarded for his
actions by being appointed governor of
New South Wales in 1806. Once again, his
actions led the populace to rebel and imprison him. Released in 1810, he returned
to England; a figure of colonial pride rather
than condemnation, he was promoted to
admiral. (*See also* Incest, Rosetta Stone.)

Hartley S. Spatt

Works Consulted

Said, Edward. *Orientalism*. New York: Pantheon,
1978.

Scwab, Raymond. *Oriental Renaissance: Europe's
Rediscovery of India and the East, 1680–1880*. New
York: Columbia UP, 1984.

Sweetman, John. *The Oriental Obsession*. Cambridge: Cambridge UP, 1988.

Owenson, Sydney (Lady Morgan)

(1778?–1859)

Sydney Owenson may have been the
first woman to support herself entirely by
her pen, producing over 70 volumes of
fiction, verse, and prose and an opera. She
was the first woman to be granted a pension for service to literature, an award of
£300 per annum presented by Lord
Melbourne in 1837. Attractive, witty, and
outspoken, she became a darling of Dublin
society after the success of her third novel,
The Wild Irish Girl (1806), an epistolary
work treating the romance between a young
English gentleman traveling incognito and
an Irish beauty whose ancestors were impoverished by those of the gentleman.
Writing at a time when the English government had suspended the right of *habeas*

corpus and Irish nationalist views were being summarily suppressed, Owenson boldly mingled politics with romance in the novel, expounding upon Irish history, defending Irish culture, and appealing to the English and the Irish, Catholics, and Protestants to abandon their prejudices.

Her staunch advocacy of Catholic emancipation, lifelong criticism of landlord absenteeism, and support of Republican governments frequently occasioned virulent literary and personal attacks from Tory reviewers, especially Gifford and Croker. Well-researched, but hastily composed, her novels are an uneven mixture of eloquence, sentimentality, and polemic. All include copious footnotes, numerous Shakespearean quotations, and passages in French, Italian, and Latin—perhaps defensive attempts to assert intellectual authority—and the heroines of each bear an uncanny resemblance to Owenson.

Owenson was born on Christmas Day during a voyage from England to Ireland, either on the Irish Sea midway between the two countries, as legend has it, or in port shortly after the ship had docked. Her father was Robert MacOwen, a popular Irish comic actor and singer, a distant cousin and friend of Oliver Goldsmith, who anglicized his name at the prompting of a well-to-do patron. Her mother, Jane Hill, the daughter of a prosperous English tradesman and a staunch Methodist, died when Owenson and her sister Olivia were young. After her mother's death, Owenson attended a Huguenot school near Dublin. When the family's fortunes waned, she labored briefly as a governess, then—noting the financial success of Fanny Burney—tried her hand as an author.

Her first effort, *Poems, Dedicated by Permission to the Countess of Moira* (1801), imitates the poetry of Thomas Gray, Cowper, and Oliver Goldsmith with some versatil-

ity and feeling; it is marred, however, by irregular syntax, poor diction, and the author's over-appreciation of her merits. Owenson's first novel, *St. Claire* (1803), echoes Goethe's *Werther* and Rousseau's *Nouvelle Héloïse*, but without much skill. The work takes most of its charm from its vivacious heroine, Olivia, named after Owenson's younger sister. In *The Novice of St. Dominick* (1805), Owenson experimented with historical fiction, placing the action of the novel in France at the end of the 16th century and anticipating the form Scott later perfected and made popular. From the proceeds of *The Novice*, Owenson bought the famous Irish harp she used in accompanying herself on social occasions when she sang the Irish songs of her youth. Moore studied her translations of some of these traditional songs, distributed under the title *Twelve Original Hibernian Melodies* (1805), before he composed his Irish airs.

By the end of the decade, Owenson had written *Patriotic Sketches* (1807) and *Woman, Ida of Athens* (1809) and had become a celebrated author and coveted guest in the dining rooms and salons of Dublin. Under the patronage of the Marquis and Marchioness of Abercorn, she was welcomed by the *haut ton* of London society. Through the Abercorns, she also met Charles Morgan, a scholarly physician and freethinker, whom she reluctantly married in 1812, after a protracted correspondence and Morgan's receipt of a knighthood, at the prompting of Lady Abercorn. Despite its unprepossessing beginning, the marriage appears to have been happy, and the two collaborated on several projects.

In 1814, Owenson published *O'Donnel,* her most incendiary work. In it, she supports the Irish patriots and defends the political novel. *O'Donnel* was a bestseller, witty and satirical, more realistic and better written than earlier works. Scott enjoyed it, as did Maria Edgeworth, but it earned Owenson implacable enemies in Ireland. Lord Manners burned his copy and refused to speak to her for the rest of his life.

After a tour of France, during which Sir Charles and Owenson visited Lafayette and mingled with the lions of French society, Owenson published *France* (1818), a compendium of historical material, cultural observation, lively anecdotes, and epigrammatic commentary. Although she was harshly criticized for its Republican views, the book was so popular that Colburn, her publisher, offered £2,000 for her to write a book on Italy in the same style. Owenson completed *Italy* in 1821 after a tour of the country, and while it was equally successful, some of the Italian friends she complimented in the book were jailed for their liberal opinions, and the book was banned by papal and Austrian authorities. Byron, though ill-disposed toward Owenson beforehand, read *Italy* and praised it highly.

Owenson's other works include *Florence McCarthy* (1818), a satiric novel in which she takes her revenge on the critic Croker by caricaturing him as Counsellor Conway Crawley, a bilious egotist; *The Life and Times of Salvator Rosa* (1824), a biography Hazlitt damned with faint praise; a three-part article on *Absenteeism* (1825), which was widely read and issued in volume form; and *The O'Briens and the O'Flahertys* (1827) a patriotic novel darker and more disillusioned than her earlier Irish works.

Once the battle for Catholic emancipation had been won, Owenson found herself less in the center of affairs. Sales of her works suffered in the 1830s after she quarreled with her enterprising publisher. When she took her business to another firm, Colburn undermined sales of *France in 1829–30* (1830) by selling her other works at half

price. Neither *Dramatic Scenes from Real Life* (1833) nor *The Princess, or the Beguine* (1835) were widely noticed.

In 1840, amity was restored, and Colburn issued Owenson's *Women and Her Master*. It is a feminist reading of history benefiting from comparison to Harriet Martineau's more strident writings and generally well received, even by her nemeses, the critics of the *Quarterly Review*. In 1843, Sir Charles died, and while Owenson continued to enjoy the pleasures of London society, younger authors had begun to take her place as the focus of attention. Her only notable contributions after her husband's death were an 1851 pamphlet addressed to Cardinal Wiseman—who had been responsible for *Italy*'s having been placed on the *Index Expurgatorius*—and *Passages from My Autobiography* (1859). The pamphlet ran to five editions, and *Punch* made the argument between the Cardinal and her the subject of numerous jokes.

In 1859, Owenson died peacefully at home, her age still a mystery even to her closest friends. By means of personal economy in her old age, she accumulated a fortune of between £15,000 and £16,000 to leave to her nieces. Among her bequests were £100 for a tablet in St. Patrick's Cathedral to the Irish bard Carolan, £100 to the Theatrical Fund for actors, and £200 to the Governesses' Benevolent Association. (*See also* Satire.)

Gayla S. McGlamery

Works Consulted

Spender, Dale. *Mothers of the Novel: 100 Good Women Writers Before Jane Austen*. London: Pandora, 1986.

Stevenson, Lionel. *The Wild Irish Girl: The Life of Sydney Owenson, Lady Morgan (1776–1859)*. London: Chapman, 1936.

Wilson, Mona. *These Were Muses*. London: Sidgwick, 1924.

Paine, Thomas

(1737–1809)

Thomas Paine occupies the singular position of having agitated for revolution in three countries in the 18th century. He was truly a man of the hour, and although his native land spurned his revolt, he participated actively in the successful overthrow of the tyrants holding America and France captive. Though he died in ignominy, his is still a name to suggest revolution, and he was certainly one of the more controversial figures of the early Romantic period in England.

Born in Norfolk in 1737, Thomas Pain (who added the final "e" in his name years later) was the only son and older child of Joseph Pain, a Quaker shopkeeper and women's corsetmaker, and Frances Cooke, 11 years his elder, who was the daughter of a local Anglican attorney. Although the boy was baptized and later confirmed, he was for the most part reared as a Quaker. The Society of Friends seems to have made a deep impression on young Paine, who, lifelong, preserved at some level its principles of nonconformity: a tendency toward pacifism, sanctity of all life, and austerity of dress. From a supplemental farm,

Joseph Pain secured enough income to send his son to a grammar school for eight years, where Paine studied history, mathematics, and science, for the last of which he had great facility. He did not study Latin, as would have been typical of the day, since the Quakers disapproved of Latin culture.

Following his schooling, for three years Paine was apprenticed to his father. At age 16, probably inspired by the tales of one of his schoolmasters who had served on a man-of-war, he ran away to the coast to sail off on the *Terrible*, whose senior officer was appropriately named Death. His alarmed father retrieved him before he could set sail, and he continued three more years of apprenticeship. When hostilities broke out between France and England in 1756, however, young Paine temporarily suspended his Quaker beliefs and enlisted with the privateer *King of Prussia*.

After a year at sea, Paine turned landward for employment with corset makers in London and Dover before opening his own shop in Sandwich. In 1759, he married Mary Lambert, who was a maid and the daughter of a customs officer. These early efforts to establish a life were blighted when his business failed and Mary died a year later. Resourceless, Paine returned to his parents' home to prepare himself to follow the career of his father-in-law.

In 1762, he was appointed to the position of examining brewers' casks, from which he was promoted to smuggler patrol of the Lincolnshire coast. In 1765, the typically overworked officer was dismissed for the not uncommon practice of having approved a shipment he had not actually inspected. Consequently, Paine was forced back to the evidently loathsome corsetmaking, though he wrote the requisite abject apology for reinstatement with customs. His appeal was accepted, but no vacancy materialized for 18 months or so, and meanwhile Paine turned to yet a new field: teaching English in London.

In 1768, he became a customs official near the Sussex coast, boarding with a tobacconist and local constable named Ollive, who died in 1769. Thereupon, Paine and Ollive's widow expanded the business to include groceries. Paine boarded elsewhere for a short time, returning in 1771 upon marriage to Mrs. Ollive's daughter Elizabeth, who was 22.

Once again, Paine's business failed, and Paine faced bankruptcy. In response, he printed, at mostly his own expense, his first polemical pamphlet, *Case of the Officers of Excise*, bewailing the inadequately recompensed responsibilities of customs officers. He spent much of the winter of 1772 to 1773 in London trying to sell the 4,000 copies of the tract to MPs and other potential benefactors. Nonetheless, Parliament showed little interest, and, in fact, Paine lost his job again, ostensibly for shirking his duties. The next year he and his wife legally separated. As a result of a separation rather than a divorce, neither was able ever to remarry, and Paine only intermittently, and then anonymously, provided any money for his wife, who ulti-

mately moved in with a brother and rarely, if ever, heard from or of him again. Biographers seem agreed that after the separation Paine remained celibate.

In London again, a mutual friend introduced Paine to Benjamin Franklin, who was serving as an agent for the colonies. Franklin was favorably impressed with Paine, urged him to emigrate, and wrote him a letter of introduction to Franklin's son-in-law in Philadelphia. Crossing the Atlantic, Paine nearly died of scurvy, but once recovered, was assisted by Franklin's son-in-law into posts as tutor, from which he segued into journalism. He contributed pieces to the new monthly *Pennsylvania Magazine*, of which he became an editor and, for the first time in his professional life, discovered success, increasing its circulation over two and a half times. He also wrote for many other periodicals in Pennsylvania, on subjects ranging from humanitarian to more quotidian interest.

In January 1776, *Common Sense* appeared, an anonymous pamphlet that personally unified Paine's heretofore scattershot life as disgruntled agent of the Crown, developing writer, and quintessential outsider, while publicly unifying the British colonies in America against the Crown for the first time. It was the initial popular declaration of independence, condemning monarch, monarchy, and empire and calling for a constitutional republic. The document was wildly successful, with 150,000 copies sold by the end of the year. Its greatest triumph was that it aroused the sentiments of the common people who had not yet been involved in the revolutionary operations of the political leaders of the colonies and created a consolidated front. When war intensified, even Paine enlisted in a Middle-Atlantic militia, where he served as secretary, eventually to George Washington.

Though Paine represented himself as a warrior, throughout his life his veracity was not his strong suit, and his larger contribution in any case was a series of military dispatches for the newspapers. *The Crisis* served to inform its audience and inspirit the troops, the first one memorably opening, "These are the times that try men's souls."

Paine became the clerk of the Pennsylvania Assembly in 1779, writing, it is thought, Pennsylvania's statement abolishing slavery, which made it the first state to do so, and evidently for his troubles being awarded an M.A. from the University of Pennsylvania, his only academic honor. Paine involved himself in numerous affairs of the states, expressing his opinions on various political and social issues and making many enemies. He was constantly in desperate financial straits, although in 1784, the Assembly of New York bestowed on him a farm in New Rochelle confiscated from a Loyalist.

Having retained his childhood interest in science, Paine began to meditate upon a scheme to erect one of the first single-arch iron bridges. His attempts to secure backing took him to England, where he met and conferred with Burke, as well as visiting his parents (following the death of his father, he endeavored to assist his mother) and also to Paris in 1787 where he involved his friends Jefferson and Lafayette in his plans. However, Paris had more use for political engineers, and Paine was quickly caught up in the turmoil of Revolutionary France.

In 1790, Paine's acquaintance Burke published *Reflections on the Revolution in France*, the musings of which were essentially hostile. In a directly engaged response, Paine published what is considered his masterpiece, *The Rights of Man*. In two parts dedicated to Washington and to Lafayette, it was published in England in 1791 and 1792. Paine argued for natural rights, arising out of a rational social contract rather than from Burke's more sentimental assertion of tradition. Paine declared the French Revolution a success and in the second part called for an English revolution and an English republic. The work had tremendous impact in both America, where it made the French cause popular, and England, where Paine was indicted on charges of subversion. So Paine fled to France, which had named him an honorary citizen, a title he had previously been given in America. Meanwhile, riots broke out in England against Paine, and he was tried and convicted in absentia and banished from his native land forever.

However, France proved only a short-term refuge. Once the Reign of Terror and Paine's penchant for making enemies overtook him, he was arrested. He was known to have opposed the regicide, but in retrospect, it appears that his intricate politicking among Americans and the French collided in the suspicious and sanguinary Parisian air. He languished in Luxembourg Prison for ten months, where he was very ill and by his report avoided execution only by an oversight. He was finally released in recognition of his American citizenship.

Concomitant with Paine's arrest was publication of his next major work, *The Age of Reason*. In this work, he embraces deism or natural religion against the competing claims, he asserts, of atheism, though his argument leads him into a brutal repudiation of Christianity as noxious and superstitious mythology. Although less attended to in England than his previous work, this one prompted many rebuttals and landed one bookseller in jail for blasphemy.

Paine remained in France under Napoleon, growing increasingly skeptical of him, until it seemed wise, in 1802, to return to America. He continued his public campaigns from his home in New Rochelle, actively commenting on all affairs of the new republic, but he was little heeded. He died quietly in 1809 of a recurrence of the fever he had had in prison. He had requested to be buried in a Quaker cemetery, but this was denied, and the whereabouts of his remains are unknown.

Laura Dabundo

Works Consulted

Aldridge, Alfred Owen. *Man of Reason: The Life of Thomas Paine*. Philadelphia: Lippincott, 1959.

Ayer, A.J. *Thomas Paine*. New York: Atheneum, 1988.

Williamson, Audrey. *Thomas Paine: His Life, Work, and Times*. London: Allen, 1973.

Painting

Romantic painting in England represented a shift away from the predominant Neoclassical forms of the 18th century. It took subjects and ideas that had previously been unacceptable for artistic representation and made them not only acceptable, but interesting and dynamic studies as well. This was a natural progression in artistic development, which led, in the later part of the 19th century, to realism. Romanticism developed, however, as the result of the rejection of the rational and moral basis of Neoclassical art and the emphasis on the freedom of passion and nature. Romantic painting also rejects the frivolity of some 18th-century painters, particularly the frivolity espoused by Fragonard and Watteau. Freedom of imagination and freedom from artificial constraints are the hallmarks of the Romantic period and Romantic painting. (*See also* Landscape Painting, Visionary Landscape Painting.)

English Romantic painting encompasses all fields of visual art—from landscape to visionary to Gothic revival to history paintings—and includes such disparate artists as George Stubbs, Blake, Constable, and Turner. Five types of painting highlight this period: literary, historical, animal, visionary/psychological, and landscape, each with at least one famous artist and a number of followers.

Many artists derived inspiration from the literature of this period. The most commonly used authors in this context were Shakespeare and Milton. Fuseli, enamored of Shakespeare, produced canvases depicting scenes from *Macbeth* and *A Midsummer Night's Dream*; he also did several paintings dealing with Milton's Satan, a favorite topic for the Romantic poets. Even Sir Thomas Lawrence (1769–1830), normally specializing in portraiture, produced *Satan as a Fallen Angel with Beelzebub* (1797). Bonington, a friend of Delacroix, painted literary pictures also, using primarily the works of Scott as inspiration. Byron was also a source of inspiration from the literary world, though his works influenced more French painters than British. These French artists were also influenced by the animal genre of English painting.

Animal themes were dominant in the work of George Stubbs (1724–1806). Horses are most often depicted in his work, making him influential with the great French Romantics, Géricault and Delacroix. For Géricault, Stubbs provided anatomical knowledge, which is evident in all of Géricault's horse paintings. For Delacroix, Stubbs's influence was in subject matter (e.g., Stubbs provided the basic idea and compositional form for Delacroix's *Lion Hunt*). Much of Stubbs's anatomical knowledge came from dissections, which was unusual for the Romantic artist. Beyond the animal theme, Stubbs explored another major area of English Romantic painting—the psychological study. His *Labourers* (1767) represents a common day's work, with expressions of toil and strain emphasizing station in life and attitudes of hopelessness and resignation.

John Singleton Copley, a transplanted American, also painted interesting psychological studies, particularly *Watson and the Shark* (1782). The facial expressions of the people in the boat trying to kill the shark evince horror and rage, and fear is strongly evident on the face of the man whom the shark is attacking. This painting—and others of its type—would have been unacceptable for the Neoclassicists, since it neither points out a moral nor shows any frivolity; instead it illustrates a struggle between humanity and nature, which humanity is not guaranteed to win.

Fuseli took the realm of psychological studies to its extreme. *The Nightmare* (1782), his most well-known painting, moves into the realm of the visionary, a province he shared with Blake. Fuseli was Swiss by birth, but he emigrated to London, where he remained. He received much encouragement from Reynolds, which seems unusual considering *The Nightmare*. This painting, unlike Reynolds's traditional, conservative work, is full of sexual imagery, revealing a psychological expression of repression.

Repression also characterized much of Blake's work, since Blake nearly always deals with the repression of energy—political, social, and sexual. (*See also* Blake, William (as engraver).) Blake is predominantly known as a poet, but his poems (all illustrated and hand-lettered and colored) are themselves works of art. *The Songs of Innocence and Experience* take on social and religious institutions with the colors used in the illustrations enhancing the meanings of the poems. Blake's art followed a more linear style than Fuseli's, but the visionary

aspect was congruent. Blake's linear drawings and prints speak of a definite world view, an idea of unblocking all energy to the benefit of both soul and psyche. Blake's visionary ideas had a natural basis, though. He abhorred the unnatural strictures of society and based his poetry and painting on what he considered the natural spheres of human existence—nature and imagination. Even though his work was not well known to the general public, Blake influenced artists he knew, such as Fuseli and Flaxman. Blake's unique landscapes which appear in the background of his poetic illustrations are generally full of vegetable images, twining vines, and enveloping trees. His landscapes are generally atypical of the traditional Romantic landscape.

The landscape in English Romantic art was central to this movement, with watercolor as the original medium for this type of art. Girtin was well known as a landscape watercolorist of great talent. Blake used watercolor, and Turner, too, throughout his career, though more sporadically. It was Constable, though, who made a breakthrough in English landscape art by effectively using oil as his medium. Constable's oil skies influenced Delacroix, who, upon viewing *The Hay Wain*, promptly repainted the sky of *The Massacre of Chios*.

What made English landscape painting unique at this time was the realistic local scenes as subject matter. Previously, landscapes had been idealized representations or purely imaginary. The Romantic landscape was a clear, recognizable painting of an identifiable English scene. The two primary motivations for this change of painting were the works of Lorrain, which influenced many landscape artists, and the peculiar nature of the English countryside itself, with its mists and varied colors and the changeable play of light and shadow.

When Turner, beyond his landscapes and later experimental work, did several drawings and paintings of local ruins, he created another hallmark of English Romantic art, the Gothic revival. (*See also* Turner, Joseph Mallord William.) The Gothic revival appeared in English painting primarily in landscape form, with the Gothic monuments and ruins (often decorative ruins) appearing as perhaps the focal point, or even the only structure in the painting. (*See also* Gothicism.) Beckford hired Turner to immortalize his Fonthill Abbey, which, like Walpole's Strawberry Hill, was structurally unsound and already beginning to crumble. These pseudo-Gothic structures had been appearing everywhere, but generally in the form of "ruins" to decorate gardens. Girtin painted Kirkhill Abbey, which, unlike Beckford's Fonthill, was an actual abbey and was, through the ravages of time rather than poor building materials, crumbling.

This fascination with ruins provides an interesting comparison with another major aspect of English Romantic art. History has always been a popular subject for art, particularly painting, but during the Romantic era, it took a different turn. The Romantic artists began painting history pictures using contemporary figures and events as subjects; thus they were recording history, rather than illustrating what had happened in the distant past. These paintings were far more successful with the general public than the others had been, because they were so identifiable. Although his early works were nearly all biblical, Haydon was one of the primary history painters. Two of his more well-known works in this genre are *Wellington Musing on the Field of Waterloo* (1838–39) and its companion work, *George IV and the Duke of Wellington on the Field of Waterloo* (1842–45). Copley also did history paint-ings, as did Angelica Kauffman (1741–1807).

History painting lasted through Napoleon's reign as propaganda for both Napoleon and for the English in representing the scenes of their glorious victory at Waterloo. This style of painting did not survive into the age of realism, and it was totally gone by the time Impressionism arrived. English art began to lose its Romantic aspects around 1840, moving into a realism out of which the Victorian pre-Raphaelite style arose and became dominant in the world view of art and literature.

Linda A. Archer

Works Consulted

Brion, Marcel. *Art of the Romantic Era*. New York: Praeger, 1969.

Cummings, Frederick. "Romanticism in Britain, 1760–1860." *Romantic Art in Britain: Paintings and Drawings, 1760–1860*. U.S.A.: Falcon, 1968: 17–24.

Gaunt, William. *A Concise History of English Painting*. New York: Praeger, 1964.

Staley, Allen. "British Landscape Painting, 1760–1860." *Romantic Art in Britain: Paintings and Drawings 1760–1860*. U.S.A.: Falcon, 1968: 25–30.

Vaughan, William. *Romantic Art*. London: Thames, 1978.

Paley, William
(1743–1805)

While the Rev. William Paley was not original in his contributions to philosophy or theology, his books and sermons are noteworthy for their clarity and confident vigor. Writing in opposition to deists and to such skeptics as Hume, Paley's major works, *Principles of Moral and Political Philosophy* (1785), *A View of the Evidence of Christianity* (1794), and *Natural Theology* (1802), were widely read and represent one of the clearest statements of the orthodox synthesis of natural science and theology in the 18th century. They remained standard works well into the 19th century when Darwin and the theory of evolution offered a different account of unity and diversity in nature.

The son of a clergyman-schoolmaster, Paley was born in Peterborough and raised in the English north country. He was admitted to Christ College, Cambridge, in 1759. There, he excelled in mathematics, taking top honors. In 1772, he was elected a fellow and tutor at Christ College, where he lectured on metaphysics, ethics, and the Greek Testament. His lectures derived from Locke's metaphysics and were based on the *Essay Concerning Human Understanding*. (*See also* Empiricism.) Although he was a popular and effective teacher, Paley left Cambridge in 1776 to become a clergyman in the diocese of Carlisle, where he enjoyed the friendship of the dean, Thomas Percy, editor of the *Reliques of Ancient English Poetry* (1765).

Encouraged by his friends, especially his former colleague John Law, Paley worked his Cambridge lectures into his first book, *Moral and Political Philosophy*. It articulated a sort of Christian utilitarianism in which acts are judged according to an expectation of divine reward or retribution.

His next book, *The Evidences of Christianity*, attacked the skepticism of Hume's *Enquiry* (1752). Accepting Bishop Butler's contention in *The Analogy of Religion* (1732) that natural and revealed truth are equivalently predicated on probabilities, a view congruent with Locke's theory of knowledge, Paley argued that there is as much reason to accept the probability of a miracle as not, if it can be shown that the witness had no reason to give a false report and was willing to suffer for it. This book proved successful. In 1795, he received a Doctor of Divinity from Cambridge. He was also made rector of the parish of Bishop Wearmouth, where he spent the rest of his life.

Natural Theology was Paley's most important and influential work. All natural theologies are based on the assumption that religious truth may be deduced from nature. Paley offered an important version of the teleological argument, or argument from design, for the existence of God, that is, that the existence of design, or deliberate order, in the world predicates the existence of a designer, God. While most versions of the teleological argument focused on astronomical examples, Paley chose biological ones. In a favorite analogy, he suggested that as the lenses of a telescope indicate a maker, so the adaptations of the lenses of an eye also point to a maker other than chance. Paley's views held sway until Darwin's theory of evolution offered an alternative account for natural adaptation.

Thomas L. Cooksey

Works Consulted

Barker, Ernest. "Paley and His Political Philosophy." *Traditions of Civility: Eight Essays*. Cambridge: Cambridge UP, 1948: 193–262.

Clarke, M.L. *Paley: Evidences for the Man*. London: SPCK, 1974.

Copleston, Frederick. *Modern Philosophy: The British Philosophers: Part I: Hobbes to Paley*. Vol. 5 of *A History of Philosophy*. Garden City: Doubleday, 1964.

Hurlbutt, R.H. *Hume, Newton, and the Design Argument*. Lincoln: U of Nebraska P, 1985.

LeMahieu, D.L. *The Mind of William Paley: A Philosopher and His Age*. Lincoln: U of Nebraska P, 1976.

McPherson, T. *Arguments from Design*. London: Macmillan, 1972.

Paley, William. *Natural Theology; Selections*. Ed. Frederick Ferré. Indianapolis, 1964.

———. *The Works of William Paley, D.D.* 6 vols. London, 1830.

Stephen, Leslie. *English Thought in the 18th Century*. Vol. 1. 3rd ed. 1902. New York: Harcourt, 1962.

Palmer, Samuel

(1805–81)

Samuel Palmer, one of the greatest exponents in English painting of pastoral Romanticism, was born in London in 1805; his father, also named Samuel, was a bookseller. From his earliest years young Palmer was an omnivorous reader, devouring books from his father's stock, ranging from the poetry of Spenser and Cowley, to the Bible, *The Pilgrim's Progress*, and John Ray's *English Proverbs*.

Love of poetry was instilled early by his nurse Mary Ward. When he was age 4, she pointed at the moon rising behind a group of elms casting their shadows on the floor, while she quoted from Edward Young's *Paraphrase of Job*: "Fond man! the vision of a moment made!/Dream of a dream! and shadow of a shade." Palmer always remembered those moony shadows and Young's lines, and they inspired paintings of moonlit landscapes throughout his life.

Palmer received formal education for only the short time he attended Merchant Taylor's School. There, the roughness of school life made him thoroughly unhappy—he thought the older boys resembled baboons—and he was allowed to leave.

At this time, Palmer and his father took long walks together, during which his father did all he could by way of conversation and discussion to improve his son's mind. A favorite walk on Sundays took them beyond Greenwich Park to Dulwich, which Palmer later called "the gate into the world of vision," imagining a world of pastoral abundance and innocence in the countryside beyond.

During his adolescence, Palmer became passionately enthralled with the Anglican church and its architectural, musical, and artistic manifestations. These interests were reflected in his crayon and watercolor studies of imaginary ministers, cathedrals, and abbeys, which his parents interpreted as signs of artistic promise and hired an obscure watercolorist, William Wate (d. 1832), for instruction. Wate probably used David Cox's *A Treatise on Landscape Painting in Watercolours* (1813) as a textbook, for several of Palmer's early watercolors (e.g., the 1821 *Study of Old Buildings*) seem to indicate that he used Cox's methods.

Palmer's early watercolors are competent conventional landscapes. He had some success with them when he was only 14, selling his first drawing, a landscape now untraced, at an exhibition at the British Institution. In 1821, three of his works were exhibited at the Royal Academy, but what was more important for the development of his art, he saw and was moved by Turner's *Entrance to the Meuse: Orange Merchant on the Bar*. From this time, and throughout his career, his work was much influenced by the great landscapist. Striking examples of work so influenced are *At Hailsham Sussex: Storm approaching* (1821), *Tintagel Castle, approaching Rain* (1848), and *Morning or The Dripping Eaves* (1869?).

Even more potent influences were at hand, for in 1824 Palmer met the artist Linnell, who not only changed the direction of his art, but also became his father-in-law. The change wrought by Linnell in Palmer's work is demonstrated in one of his two surviving sketchbooks, that begun in 1824. In it, on page after page, the English landscape is transformed into an earthly paradise, its figures transmuted into protagonists in visual georgics and eclogues. This change in direction, indeed of inspiration, was reinforced by Blake, to whom Palmer was introduced by Linnell in 1824, and who Palmer saw as one who "did not accept greatness, but confer it" and who "ennobled poverty." Of Blake's work, Palmer was especially impressed by his tiny wood-engravings to the First Eclogue in Robert John Thornton's school edition of *The Eclogues of Virgil* (1821), which were visionary interpretations of country life and landscapes.

Palmer's highly poetic—almost hallucinatory—early landscapes, often realized in monochrome (e.g., the 1825 *Valley thick with Corn*) but sometimes in vivid colors (e.g., the 1830 *Magic Apple Tree*) depict the world in a golden age, often drenched in moonlight, but sometimes under magnificent diurnal skies with enormous clouds. This spiritual vision became intensified for a few years, from 1826 to 1835, when Palmer lived intermittently, often in the company of other young artists (the "Ancients"), at Shoreham in Kent, near enough to London to allow visits when necessary, yet affording a beautiful and inspiring pastoral and agrarian world of little hills and valleys.

In many ways, Palmer's imagination was reluctant to discard the Romantic yearnings of his adolescence. But towards the end of this period, in the mid-1830s, when he became engaged to Linnell's daughter Hannah, the realization that he would need to paint salable works in order to support her turned him toward more straightforward and "realistic" landscape painting, which nonetheless almost always retained traces of his more imaginative work.

In search of new subjects, Palmer visited North Wales several times during the 1830s. He made excellent watercolors and oil paintings of Welsh mountains and waterfalls, among them *Snowdon from Moel Siabod* (1835 or 1836), *Pistyll Mawddach* (1835), and *View from the Bridge near Capel Curig* (1835 or 1836); some of these works stand comparison with work by Turner.

In 1837, Palmer married Hannah Linnell, and the couple immediately set off to visit Italy with Mr. and Mrs. George Richmond (Richmond was one of the Ancients). Palmer was enthralled with Italy and Italian art, and for a time his work deteriorated as he tried unsuccessfully to emulate the grandeur of Italian art. Until this time, Palmer's art had been intimate: even his Welsh mountain studies were conceived in a minor key. When he tried to overstep the limits of his art, to portray subjects like *Rome from the Borghese Gardens* (1837), he lost his perspective. On the other hand, *The Forum, Rome*, an intimate study painted at about the same time, was successful. Late during the Italian visit, he produced more convincing panoramas, such as *Rome and the Vatican from the Western Hills* (1838 or later) and *View from the Villa d'Este, Tivoli* (1839).

The Palmers returned home in 1839. It was an unhappy homecoming, for there were religious and political differences between Linnell and Palmer, which had given rise to acrimonious correspondence during the Italian visit. Added to this were the tensions and responsibilities of married life, for which Palmer was ill equipped. Further, although Linnell bore three children, she had many miscarriages and was otherwise often ill. At the death of his elder son at age 19, Palmer was prostrate with grief and never fully recovered.

It is surprising that despite all his troubles most of Palmer's work is consistently good and sometimes even retained some of its earlier visionary quality: such are the watercolors *Evening in Italy: the deserted Villa* (1845), *The Sleeping Shepherd* (c. 1857), and *A Mountain Stream and a Ancient Fortress* (1879).

Most of Palmer's notable later work falls into three main categories: (1) 27 studies and watercolors made between 1856 and 1877, based on subjects from the poems of Milton; (2) 24 illustrations made between 1874 and 1880, for his own translation of Virgil's *Eclogues* (published posthumously in 1883); and (3) brilliant etchings, 13 of which he completed himself between 1850 and 1880; and four others commenced by himself and completed posthumously by his son, A.H. Palmer.

In these three groups of works, Palmer combined recollections of his earlier visionary studies and work of Italian and English landscape with quotations from the work of the greatest landscape artists, especially Lorrain. They embrace much of his best work and sum up all that was best in his artistic credo. An example is *A Towered City or The Haunted Stream* from Milton's *L'Allegro* (1868?), the composition of which is based on plates in Lorrain's *Liber Veritatis*. The Virgil designs are preliminary etchings, most of which were never even begun. Yet they have an appeal, recalling in several places landscapes by Lorrain and Blake's Virgil engravings. Above all they evoke a mood of happy bucolic youth. The etchings especially contain much that is supreme in Palmer's later creations. He recaptured in them, in more tranquil mood, some of the spellbinding qualities of his finest early work, imbued with much that he had assimilated later, as is amply demonstrated in such plates as *Christmas or Folding the Last Sheep* (1850), *The Bellman* (1879), and *The Lonely Tower* (1879), the last two being etched versions of two of his Milton watercolors. (*See also* The Ancients, Visionary Landscape.)

Raymond Lister

Works Consulted

Abley, Mark, ed. *Samuel Palmer: The Parting Light*. New York: Carcanet, 1985.

Cecil, David. *Visionary and Dreamer: Two Poetic Painters: Samuel Palmer and Edward Burne-Jones*. Princeton: Princeton UP, 1970.

Lister, Raymond. *Catalogue Raisonné of the Works of Samuel Palmer*. Cambridge: Cambridge UP, 1988.

———. *The Paintings of Samuel Lister*. Cambridge: Cambridge UP, 1985.

———. *Samuel Palmer—His Life and Art*. Cambridge: Cambridge UP, 1987.

———. *Samuel Palmer's Italian Honeymoon*. New York: Oxford UP, 1968.

Panorama

The panorama, a popular 19th-century form of pictorial art, existed in two major varieties: stationary and moving. The original version of the panorama was a large stationary painting consisting of a broad scene depicted on a cylindrical canvas such that the entire circle of the horizon was presented from an elevated vantage point.

Irishman Robert Barker, with the help of his 12-year-old son Henry Aston Barker, painted the first panorama in 1788 from drawings created by placing a square frame on top of Calton Hill in Edinburgh and then rotating it so that he could sequentially capture a 360-degree view. Barker further devised a system of curved lines that would correct the distortion encountered when horizontal lines were hung in a circle. In 1787, he obtained a patent for a large circular display building for panoramas. To view the painting, one ascended to a platform where lighting was admitted only from above, and no doors or windows interrupted the continuity of the scene. This gave the illusion that the viewer was at the locale depicted. After first exhibiting his view of Edinburgh in London in 1789, Barker opened his circular building in Leicester Square, London's popular entertainment center, in 1794. This building contained a lower circle in which he hung his panorama of the grand fleet at Spithead and an upper circle in which he placed another panorama, *London from the Roof of Albion Mills*.

The idea of the panorama caught on immediately, although most of the so-called panoramas created in the early years of the 19th century were not actually panoramas, since they did not form complete circles.

Furthermore, the word "panorama" (Greek for "all-sight") was also applied retrospectively to designate past paintings and engravings that merely represented wide topographical areas, thus replacing the older term "prospect." In fact, the name "panorama" came to have a wide variety of applications, meaning virtually whatever the exhibitor wanted it to mean—from large pictures to ordinary-sized pictures in a series. Sometimes it even functioned as a generic term for all pictorial shows (the root "orama" was added to a multitude of prefixes to create further variations). These name discrepancies—together with the fact that no English, and only a few American, panoramas from before the 1860s have survived—complicate panorama research. Many were destroyed by fires; others were cut up or painted over, their value being that of temporary show material rather than high art.

The Barkers regularly replaced their paintings with others, and the Leicester Square establishment became the leading panorama display center in London. After Robert Barker's death in 1806, Henry Aston, assisted by John Burford, took over the business; Burford's son Robert became the sole proprietor in 1826. Various painters assisted with the creation of the panoramas, most notably Henry Courtney Selous, who worked on nearly every one at Burford's after 1844.

One major subject for the panoramas was the portrayal of events and places associated with the Napoleonic Wars. Not only did panoramas serve this newsreel-like function, but they also stimulated and answered the public's curiosity for foreign lands. Viewing a panorama of another country was an alternative for those who could not afford the Grand Tour. Other panorama subjects included scenes from the Bible and sites from antiquity. Thus, the panorama served as a useful educational tool for learning history and geography. London was a popular subject for panorama painters. The most notable panorama of the city was permanently installed in the Colosseum, an enormous structure built between 1824 and 1832 in Regent's Park. This painting was created from 2,000 sketches made by the artist Thomas Hornor from the top of St. Paul's Cathedral, where he took advantage of temporary repair scaffolding to make his drawings. Painter Edmund Thomas Parris and various assistants transferred the sketches to the Colosseum's canvas, reputedly creating more than an acre of painting. Visitors ascended the building in London's first passenger elevator to view the city depicted 20 miles in all directions.

As interest in panoramas spread throughout Western Europe and North America, many of the pictures portrayed the cities where they were exhibited. This suggests that the public was fascinated by the detailed depiction of actual sites. In fact, the vast majority of panorama criticism was concerned with the panorama's ability to realistically represent; intrinsic beauty was not a consideration of the critics. Yet frequently panoramas had picturesque or sublime sceneries as their subjects. This characteristic, together with the large size of the paintings, linked panoramas with Romantic art of the time.

The spread of the panorama from England to France was the work of American inventor Robert Fulton, who obtained a French patent for Barker's invention in 1799, slightly modifying the idea by providing a detailed method by which the artist would view and record the scene. In France, one of the leading panorama painters was Pierre Prévost, whose assistant Louis-Jacques-Mandé Daguerre later developed the diorama and daguerreotype. (*See also* Diorama.) Frenchman Colonel Jean-Charles Langlois was famous for his battle panoramas, and his work influenced that of Anton von Werner, the German painter who in 1883 displayed the most well-known panorama of the era of the new German Kaiserdom: *The Battle of Sedan.*

In 1848, American John Banvard was responsible for popularizing the moving panorama in London with his *Geographical Panorama of the Mississippi River*, though the art form had actually originated in London as early as 1820. Moving panoramas offered more variety than stationary ones by providing the viewer with a rapid succession of pictures. A canvas was drawn from one cylinder to another via a hand-operated crank, which turned a pulley attached to the cloth. Stage props and music enhanced the performance, while a lecturer described the scenery and entertained the audience. In contrast, stationary panoramas were silent entertainments with only souvenir pamphlets to describe the scenes.

Albert Smith's narrated pictorial show *The Ascent of Mont Blanc*, which included a vertically moving panorama depicting the ascent of the mountain, opened in 1852 to become one of the biggest hits of the Victorian era. But the downfall of the panorama was under way. The last major event to be depicted by the panorama was the Sepoy Mutiny of 1857. The reasons for the decline included the increasing competition from other forms of entertainment in London, including improved playhouses and new music halls and public museums, as well as new technological advances in photography, slide shows, and newspaper engravings. In 1863, the Leicester Square establishment closed; the great appeal of

the panorama was over for London, though its popularity in other areas of the world continued till the end of the century.

Elizabeth Mihaly

Works Consulted

Altick, Richard D. *The Shows of London.* Cambridge: Belknap, 1978.

Avery, Kevin. "Whaling Voyage Round the World: Russell and Purrington's Moving Panorama and Herman Melville's 'Mighty Book.'" *The American Art Journal* 22.1 (1990): 50–78.

Needham, Gerald. *19th-Century Realist Art.* New York: Harper, 1988.

Philip, Cynthia Owen. *Robert Fulton: A Biography.* New York: Watts, 1985.

Sternberger, Dolf. *Panorama of the Nineteenth Century.* Trans. Erich Heller. New York: Urizen, 1977.

Pantheism

Among the more vexing questions of English Romanticism are whether, or to what degree, Wordsworth and Coleridge, in the early years of their association, were pantheists, and if so which was first and so influenced the other in that direction. Pantheism was indeed present in many early 19th-century writings. It was woven into many of the philosophies that appealed to the Romantic poets and other thinkers of the time, as well; for instance, Blake encountered pantheism through Swedenborg; Coleridge and Godwin found it in Unitarianism.

Pantheism came to the Romantic period through a branch of German philosophy originally codified by Spinoza. For Spinoza, the relationship of the creator to his creation is not one of an immanent or transcendent maker but rather of a God who not only is within and of his creation but who is actually at one with it. Thus, Wordsworth's lines in *Tintern Abbey* (1798): "And I have felt/A presence that disturbs me with the joy/Of Elevated thoughts: a sense sublime/Of something far more deeply interfused, . . ./A Motion and a spirit, that impels/All thinking things, all objects of all thought,/And rolls through all things." Here Wordsworth appears to attest to a pantheistic unity of animated nature.

Coleridge likewise does the same when he discusses the One Life in *The Eolian Harp* (1795): "O! the one life within us and abroad,/Which meets all motion and becomes its soul,/A light in sound, a sound-like power in light,/Rhythm in all thought, and joyance every where— . . ." (*See also* Synaesthesia.)

For both writers, pantheism was a particularly appealing means of representing reality. But only a little can be safely asserted about that initial juncture of greatest mutual influence and interaction, beginning with the Alfoxden period. First, Wordsworth's early mystic experiences in the Lake District, which he later recorded and interpreted (as his own childhood in *The Prelude* and as the childhood of the pedlar or wanderer in *The Pedlar*, *The Ruined Cottage*, and *The Excursion*) give credence for some sort of spiritual consolation satisfied, for a time at least, by the ideals of the One Life. Second, what Coleridge was working through at this time—professionally and theologically as he considered the Unitarian ministry and philosophically through his studies of German thought—also accords with Pantheism. Pantheism was a convenient handle, thereby, for certain esthetic, intellectual, and imaginative concerns.

John Toland, an Irish free-thinker of the early 18th century, is generally given credit for at least popularizing if not inventing the term "Pantheism" in a 1705 essay. Toland's notions were that God and nature are the same, that the many are one and the one many, a sentiment Shelley articulates much later at the end of *Adonais* (1821): "The One remains, the many change and pass;/Heaven's light forever shines, Earth's shadows fly;/Life, like a dome of many-coloured glass—/Stains the white radiance of Eternity,/Until Death tramples it to fragments." (*See also* Neoplatonism.) Pantheism at times enters into the platonic dialogue concerning illusion versus reality in which reality is the substantial totality of an integrated universe, illusion being the human perception of difference, division, alienation, and death.

Pantheism is, therefore, a mystical apprehension of the utter indivisibility, dependence, and interpenetration of God and the world, God and nature, God and humanity. It is an idealistic philosophy that comes to English literature by way of German philosophy. (*See also* Berkeley's Idealism, German Idealism, Kant.) It offered a philosophy to buttress the intertwined ideas of creativity, divinity, and the imagination that undergird Romanticism, a philosophy that sought to account for the creative intelligence, but at the expense of a unique and separate personal identity, which was finally too high a price to pay for those initially most attracted to it. (*See also* Imagination.)

Laura Dabundo

Works Consulted

McFarland, Thomas. *Coleridge and the Pantheist Tradition*. Oxford: Clarendon, 1969.

Piper, H.W. *The Active Universe*. London: Athlone, 1962.

Stallknecht, Newton P. *Strange Seas of Thought: Studies in Wordsworth's Philosophy of Man and Nature*. Bloomington: Indiana UP, 1966.

Wordsworth, Jonathan. *The Music of Humanity*. London: Nelson, 1969.

———. *William Wordsworth: The Borders of Vision*. Oxford: Clarendon, 1982.

Pantomime

In their 18th-century form, the pantomimes begin with a brief opening scene, often (though not always) gloomy in tone, in which a motley collection of characters, often drawn from literature or folklore (Faust, Merlin, and John Bull appear together in one opening), speak rhyming lines of dialogue, often lampooning contemporary political figures. Harlequin appears among these characters, and, in the loosely constructed plot that follows, things always begin to look bad for him, whether he is being chased by an irate father or ascending a mock-epic funeral pyre. A supernatural figure—generally a fairy queen—steps in to save him, and, with a wave of her wand, the opening gives way to the "harlequinade."

The harlequinade is an extremely physical romp carried out by masked stock characters who are of such great antiquity as to be archetypes: Harlequin, Pantaloon, Columbine, and Clown. All of these characters have their stock masks and costumes and have existed for centuries in the Italian *commedia dell'arte* and, possibly even earlier, as part of the Roman Saturnalian festivals. The plot of the harlequinade is simple and always the same. Harlequin carries off Columbine from the house of her father Pantaloon. Pantaloon chases Harlequin. Pantaloon's servant, the Clown, pretends to be helping Pantaloon, but is in fact on the side of the lovers. Apparently bungling, he throws many obstacles in Pantaloon's way. Harlequin, meanwhile, is aided by the power of his magic bat, a wooden stick or club associated with his character. This bat has the power to transform things into people, people into things, and things into other things, creating great opportunities for stagecraft.

Until the late 18th century, the opening had little or no connection with the harlequinade. Its characters served simply as a slightly dull foil for the exuberance of Harlequin and his companions. The well-known playwright R.B. Sheridan was apparently the first to link the two parts of the pantomime in his four-act *Robinson Crusoe*, produced on January 29, 1789. A great success in its day, the play combines serious and comic incidents and connects the harlequinade characters with the story of Robinson Crusoe. Although it was not evident at the time, this unification of the pantomime marked the beginning of a greater focus on narrative openings and the dwindling of the role of the ritualistic harlequinade.

Nevertheless, the harlequinade survived for many years, perhaps reaching its height during the career of Joseph Grimaldi, the most famous of British pantomime performers, who rose to popularity in the 1806 Boxing Day pantomime *Mother Goose*. Grimaldi's great talent was to invest the clown with a personality that transcended the stock tricks and business, so that the audience followed his adventures with sympathy and interest, as well as laughing at his antics. Grimaldi's tremendous popularity brought the role of Clown into greater prominence in British pantomime, eclipsing the role of Harlequin. The original "Joey the Clown," Grimaldi was a sufficiently prominent figure for the already famous Charles Dickens to edit *Memoirs of Grimaldi* in 1838. Worn out by the extraordinary physical demands of his art, this prince of clowns died in 1828.

For much of its existence, pantomime was considered too light an entertainment to stand on its own and was served up to the insatiable theatergoers of the time as dessert after an evening of serious drama. Yet, in spite of its overt frivolity, or perhaps because of it, the pantomime seemed to have a stimulating and liberating effect on the minds of generations of children and on many artists. Dickens frequently acknowledged his continuing fascination with pantomime, and it is perhaps not surprising that Keats came up with the idea of negative capability while walking home from a Christmas pantomime. (*See also* Negative Capability.) This odd, ritualistic "feast of fools" was an event that might, after all, greatly appeal to those who are "capable of being in uncertainties, mysteries, doubts, without any irritable reaching after fact and reason." (*See also* Theater.)

Andrea Rowland

Works Consulted

Disher, Maurice Willson. *Blood and Thunder*. London: Muller, 1949.

— — —. *Clowns and Pantomimes*. New York: Blom, 1968.

Eigner, Edwin. *The Dickens Pantomime*. Berkeley: U of California P, 1989.

Grimaldi, Joseph. *Memoirs of Grimaldi*. Edited by "Boz." London: Bentley, 1838.

Sand, Maurice. *The History of the Harlequinade*. New York: Blom, 1915.

Wilson, A.E. *King Panto*. New York: Dutton, 1935.

Parliament

During the Regency period, the parliament of Ireland was dissolved and Ireland and Great Britain were joined as one country. The Act of Union with Ireland (1801) was prompted by fears of a French invasion. To make the union with England more palatable to Irish Catholics, Pitt planned to extend them political rights in the British Parliament. Viewing Catholic Emancipation as a violation of his coronation oath, George III dissolved Pitt's ministry in 1801. (*See also* Pitt, William.)

Granting political rights to Irish Catholics was part of the larger issue of parliamentary reform that had been brewing since the time of John Wilkes and was not achieved until 1832, with the passage of the Reform Bill. Three separate periods of the reform movement can be detected. In the time of Wilkes, parliamentary reform was advocated by a coalition of Whig landlords and London merchants opposing the tax policies of George III. As the movement for reform entered its second phase (1806–19) and became more popular, prominent Whigs, such as Lord Brougham and Sir Samuel Romilly, found other causes to support, fearing that domestic unrest might lead to outright revolution. In its third phase, culminating with the passage of the Reform Bill in 1832, the movement for reform was led by industry leaders who wanted to lower the price of bread. Moderate reform was conceded by the Whigs to avoid radical reform or universal suffrage. (*See also* Reform Bill of 1832.)

Byron entered the reform movement in its second phase, when the Nottinghamshire weavers smashed looms in order to protest the fact that mechanical inventions were displacing them from their jobs. In conjunction with the moderate Whig Lord Holland, Byron presented his bill in the House of Lords on February 27, 1813, and managed to change the penalty for framebreaking from a capital offense to a misdemeanor. (*See also* [The] Luddites.) His other parliamentary activities were also typically Whig, though Byron was far to the left of the Whigs in his support of popular movements: he argued for an extension of the franchise for Catholics on April 21, 1813, and on June 1, 1813, he presented Cartwright's petition for reform of Parliament.

Shelley's attitude toward reform is well represented by pamphlets he wrote in 1817. In *A Proposal for Putting Reform to the Vote,*

Shelley argues that reform should take place in two stages to avoid revolution: first, the franchise should be extended to the middle class and then universal suffrage could be achieved. He demands annual parliaments and calls for a coalition among radical and moderate reformers in order to achieve their aims. In *A Philosophical View of Reform*, he views the English reform movement as a stage in the evolution of the spirit of liberty.

During the Regency period, members of Parliament were also preoccupied by the need to fund the Napoleonic Wars. After Napoleon's surrender in 1815, a postwar depression ensued that fueled political unrest. To meet the demands of irate farmers, it became necessary to introduce a Corn Bill in 1815 that would regulate the price of wheat. (*See also* Corn Laws.) Opposed to the demands of the agriculturalists were the industrialists, who needed a low price of bread in order to feed the workers who manned their factories. As soldiers returned from the Continent, unemployment became rampant, resulting in massive demonstrations in 1816, 1817, and 1819. The Liverpool administration advocated repressive legislation, such as the Coercion Acts (1817) and the Six Acts of 1819, to contain the growing unrest.

During this period, the Tory Cabinet passed the Sturges Bourne Acts (1817), which reduced funds available to the poor, and the Act of 1819, which restricted child labor to 12 hours a day. In 1820, members of Parliament became occupied by the Prince Regent's attempts to obtain a divorce from Queen Caroline. Sympathy for the Queen tended to strengthen the Whig alliance with the people and to weaken the radical cause by diverting the people's attention from the cause of human suffrage to the pageantry of monarchy. (*See also* Burke, Edmund; Censorship; Combination Acts; Currency Question; Fox, James Charles.)

Jonathan Gross

Works Consulted

Cameron, Kenneth. *Shelley: The Golden Years*. Cambridge: Harvard UP, 1974.

Dawson, P.M.S. *The Unacknowledged Legislator: Shelley and Politics*. Oxford: Clarendon, 1980.

Erdman, David. "Byron and the Genteel Reformers." *PMLA* 56 (1941): 1065–94.

Halevy, Elie. *The Liberal Awakening: 1815–1830*. Trans. E.I. Watkin. New York: Smith, 1949.

Pastoralism

The pastoral has a long history, going back to Theocritus, the father of pastoral poetry, and continuing through Virgil, Sidney, Spenser, Milton, Pope, and Wordsworth. The mainstay of the pastoral is the contrast between the simple, virtuous, happy country and the corrupt, complex city. By the 19th century, the form had become rather standardized, with idealized shepherds living a simple, happy, virtuous, uncorrupted life in the country. Implicit is the contrast with the city, which is always a malignant influence.

Overall, the Romantics rejected the pastoral as a genre, with the exception of Wordsworth, who wrote two great pastorals, *The Ruined Cottage* and *Michael*. Though varying from the form featuring typical idealized pastoral shepherds, Wordsworth's two poems are probably the culmination of the pastoral tradition.

In *Michael*, Wordsworth depicts a shepherd over 80 years old; his wife Isabel, who is about 20 years younger; and Luke, the son of their old age and the joy of both their lives. Michael is exceptionally strong and capable, his mind is still alert, and he is attuned with nature. To pay off a note that threatens his ownership of his property, Michael arranges for Luke to become an apprentice in town to repay the money, after which he is to return to inherit Michael's land. Soon after Luke leaves, however, he begins to slip morally, a decline that continues until he becomes so corrupt that he is forced to flee the country, thereby destroying the happiness of old age for Michael and Isabel. The central symbol of *Michael* is a pile of unhewn stones, originally intended as a sheepfold and as a covenant for Michael and Luke, which is never completed. Wordsworth contrasted the idyllic, happy, sincere, simple life of the country with the depravity of the city. The story of Michael is poignant and moving.

Another superb example of both the pastoral and of Wordsworth's skill is *The Ruined Cottage*. It is the story of Margaret, a simple countrywoman, married to Robert, whom she loves above all else. They have two children, but war and disease conspire against their happiness, and Robert deserts Margaret and his two small children. Wordsworth focuses throughout the poem on Margaret's cottage, which becomes a symbol of her psychological state. It is first a happy home, loved and well kept. The story is told to a traveler (possibly a young Wordsworth) by an old pedlar who sees in the remnants of a ruined house (just four walls now stand) the story of Margaret, whom he has visited through the years. Progressively, the cottage deteriorates and decays, as does the surrounding land, mirroring Margaret's mental collapse and failure. Eventually, Margaret's child dies of neglect, and soon, Margaret also.

Families are destroyed in both *Michael* and *The Ruined Cottage* as a result of the intrusion of the world. Two idyllically happy families are represented at the beginning of the poems, and at the end the only remains are natural monuments to

their lives, which yet have the capacity to evoke poetic commemoration and honor. (*See also* Poetry.)

Shirley Laird

Works Consulted

Cullen, Patrick. *Spenser, Marvell, and Renaissance Pastoral*. Cambridge: Harvard, 1970.

Greg, Walter W. *Pastoral Poetry and Pastoral Drama*. New York: Russell, 1959.

Heath-Stubbs, John. *The Pastoral*. London: Oxford, 1969.

Sambrook, James. *English Pastoral Poetry*. Boston: Twayne, 1983.

Peacock, Thomas Love

(1785–1866)

One of the most fascinating if underrated 19th-century figures, Thomas Love Peacock is perhaps less known as a writer than he is as the (sometime) father-in-law of novelist-poet George Meredith and an intimate of the Shelley circle during the mid-1810s. This crabbed, crotchety, and intensely opinionated pedant was also broad and expansive in his interests and literary allusions. Ideas flowed as tirelessly from him and his *roman à clef* characters as artful dodges from an unconscionable street sharper or charitable acts from a confirmed do-gooder.

Peacock, an only child, was born in Weymouth, Dorsetshire. His father, a glass merchant, died when he was very young. For the next few years, he and his mother, Sarah Love Peacock, lived with her parents in the Surrey village of Chertsey. Peacock's maternal grandfather, a lively and colorful retired naval officer, made so strong an impression on Peacock that he appeared in fictional guise in one of Peacock's seven short novels. But a far stronger impression was made on the boy by his intelligent and energetic mother, to whom he remained deeply attached until her death in 1833. Peacock's literary career began with her strong encouragement and astute guidance, which she continued to offer him as long as she lived. In light of the esoteric erudition that later characterize Peacock's fictional works, it is much to his credit that his formal education extended only from his seventh to his 13th year, when he attended the Englefield House School.

Next followed five or six years as a clerk in London, during which time he read the classical writers. He also submitted a prize-winning essay for a contest conducted by a magazine for children and began writing poems in an attempt to become a poet. These early efforts, crude and amateurish, continued after his London clerkship and featured such subjects as the ancient Syrian city of Palmyra (now in ruins), medieval monks deep in their cups, and the mighty River Thames. Peacock's self-education, planned or unplanned, continued apace: extensive reading and travel—the latter included walking tours throughout Great Britain and a one-year tour (from 1808–1809), as captain's clerk aboard the H.M.S. *Venerable*. In 1809, while he was on a walking tour in Wales, he met Jane Gryffydh, who later became his wife. Her cultural background appealed to Peacock; among the languages he employed in his literary pursuits throughout the rest of his life—including Latin and Greek, Italian and French—was Welsh.

One of the most formative influences on Peacock's thinking and his literary career was his meeting with the tempestuous, brilliant youth Shelley (almost seven years Peacock's junior) in 1812. This led to Peacock's becoming a familiar figure in the "smart set" of opinionated freethinking dilettantes serving as satellites of the maritally troubled, guilt-ridden poet who had defied canons of temporal and religious authority. By such acts as his trumpeting of atheism and his discarding of his pregnant wife Harriet to enter into an adulterous relationship with Mary Godwin, Shelley was at once a self-propelling scandal and a magnetic attraction to certain intellectually raffish types, such as Thomas Jefferson Hogg and J.F. Newton. Peacock, so different from Shelley in temperament and critical judgment, remained close to him until Shelley and his second wife (Mary Godwin) left England permanently in 1819. But the character of Shelley, with superadded quirks and crotchets, plays a role in several of Peacock's conversational novels.

In 1819, when he was well launched on a serious literary career—poems and two of his novels had already been published—Peacock accepted an appointment in the East India Company. He remained there for the next 37 years, arising from a modest post in the Examiner's Office to Chief Examiner in 1836, a position he held until his retirement. Some of the philosophical notions that turn up, not always favorably, in his novels, seem to derive from influential thinkers he knew during his service in the East India Company. Among them were the leaders of the Utilitarian movement, which advocated political and socioeconomic reforms, predicated on the principle of self-interest: Bentham (Peacock's regular dining companion for a time) and James Mill and his son John Stuart Mill—both were also employees in the East India Company (James Mill was Peacock's boss). The year after Peacock began his service with the East India Company he married his Welsh sweetheart Jane Gryffydh. Also in 1820, he produced the remarkable half-satirical essay *The Four Ages of Poetry*, which confirmed Peacock as humorous foil of the Romantics.

According to Peacock on literary history, classical poetry passed through four ages. From an iron age of warriors, heroes, and gods intervening in their battles, poetry passed into a golden retrospective age (Homeric), adorning and exaggerating the glorious past. Following that, when men had become civilized, was the silver age (Virgilian), during which the poetry recast and polished earlier literature or originated new forms: comic, satiric, or didactic. The brass age was poetry's second childhood: a regression to the crudities of the iron age, combined with an attempt to restore the golden age by an appeal to nature. Then came the dark ages, followed by the "four ages" of modern poetry, covering the period from the medieval minstrels and troubadours to Wordsworth and his nature poetry. Peacock asserted here that at present a poet, living among civilized folk, is half-barbarian, dwelling in the past, with an outmoded way of thinking. Shelley's famous manifesto, *A Defence of Poetry* (1821), was intended as a corrective to Peacock's essay.

In 1849, Peacock's daughter Mary Ellen, widowed not long after her first marriage in 1844, married George Meredith, a man younger than she and just beginning a literary career. Their incompatibility and her adultery brought the marriage to a tragic end and presaged her demise as well. Meredith made use of this experience in his poetic sequence "Modern Love" (1862) and in novels, such as *The Ordeal of Richard Feverel* (1859) and *The Egoist* (1879). Critics have found a more Peacockian influence on Meredith's novels in the importance he placed on conversational settings and ideas as opposed to plot and possibly also in the philosophy of comedy he developed in his essay *On the Idea of Comedy, and of the Uses of the Comic Spirit* (1877).

An important reason for the protracted neglect of Peacock's novels is their esoteric and antique subjects, covering much of what was known and thought by the well-read, the well-educated, and the practical-minded men and women of Peacock's day. Moreover, it is not easy to identify and appreciate the connection between characters in the novels and real-life counterparts. While one can hazard a list of actual models for the characters in five of the novels, the identifications remain precarious, finally, because of the difficulty of achieving a sufficient degree of certainty.

Peacock's five conversational novels, like the two others, are enlivened by humorous effects (e.g., caricature, word play, absurdity of plot, lurking irony, farcical commotion, character-defining names, and travesty of ideas) and a sprinkling of songs and poems. Moreover, the novels evoke at least two important features of ancient Greek traditions: (1) the *symposium*, a rousing feast where delectable food, wine, and ideas are made available to intellectual guests, who are inclined toward revelry and argumentation; and (2) *gamos*, the union of the sexes (nuptial announcement or wedding) that concludes a comedy in the classical tradition and that may be accompanied by a burst of spirited merrymaking (*komos*).

Headlong Hall (1816) concerns houseguests spending Christmas with the bookish Welsh squire Harry Headlong. Among the guests are Foster, a "perfectibilitarian"; Escot, a "deteriorationist"; and Jenkison, a "status-quoite" (likened to Shelley, Peacock, and Thomas Jefferson Hogg, respectively). Joined, *inter alia*, by Panscope (Coleridge possibly), Gall (perhaps Jeffrey), a phrenologist named Cranium, a "scientific" musician named Chromatic, and several female relatives, they take up topics of the day: what is progress and is it good or bad, can humans be continually improved, and landscape design. As a result of this gathering, affinities develop and four marriages result.

The humor of *Melincourt* (1817) is at least as extravagant. The symposium subjects include the relationship between higher apes and humans, the problem of poverty and overpopulation, voting rights and political corruption, chivalry, and literary criticism of poetry. Behind these round-table discussions is a flimsy love story about a marriageable young heiress in Westmorland at about the end of the Napoleonic era.

Nightmare Abbey (1818) is steeped in the annals and the intellectual currents of the English Romantic period, with emphasis on Shelley and his two wives and Byron and Coleridge. The setting is the family manor of Christopher Glowry, a Lincolnshire squire. His eccentric son Scythrop (strongly suggesting Shelley) is the most prominent figure of fun in this amusing book.

Crotchet Castle (1831) contrasts past and present by having a house party take a boat trip from the imitation-castle villa of a Scotsman named Crotchet in a valley of the Thames, via (medieval) Oxford, to a Mr. Chainmail's imitation 12th century castle in (ancient) Wales. Peacock's strong dislikes are evident: reckless financial speculation, educational and other reforms, paper currency, Oxford as an educational institution, the Society for the Diffusion of Useful Knowledge, The *Edinburgh Review* and writers for periodicals like it, Scotsmen, and prominent Parliamentarian and reformer Brougham—currently the Lord Chancellor. The romantic plot here is more fully developed than was the case with the earlier novels.

In *Gryll Grange* (1861), Peacock continues his much earlier attack on Brougham and his educational reforms and voices new antipathies: competitive examinations for admission to the professions, and the National Association for the Promotion of Social Science. Indeed he seems to have set himself against the progressive spirit of the times.

Peacock's two remaining novels—*Maid Marian* (1822) and *The Misfortunes of Elfin* (1829)—may well appeal to a more specific audience than that of his other works: an audience geared to old legends of swashbucklers, fair maidens, ongoing battles between the men of the court and outlaws or rebels, complicated by the involvement of the Church. Yet in the reworked Robin Hood story of *Maid Marian* and the farrago of Welsh legends, some newly translated and specially prepared for the occasion, the author is the satirical, song-writing, word-playing Peacock still, ever capable of a sudden bit of whimsy or an offhand political commentary. (*See also* Brougham, Henry; Satire.)

Samuel Irving Bellman

Works Consulted

Butler, Marilyn. *Peacock Displayed*. London: Routledge, 1979.

Dawson, Carl. *His Fine Wit*. Berkeley: U of California P, 1970.

Mills, Howard. *Peacock*. Cambridge: Cambridge UP, 1969.

Percy, Thomas
(1729–1811)

Thomas Percy, Bishop of Dromore, in Ireland, was responsible for a work that changed English literature, *Reliques of Ancient English Poetry*.

Born in 1729 in Shropshire, Percy was the son and grandson of grocers. They spelled their name "Piercy" or "Pearcy." Later, Percy conformed the spelling of his name with that of the aristocratic house of Northumberland, to whom he dedicated his major work. After attending the local grammar school, Percy matriculated at Christ Church, Oxford, where an unremarkable performance but a facility for languages garnered a B.A. and an M.A. by 1753. He also received a D.D. from Emmanuel College, Cambridge, in 1770.

For 29 years, Percy served as parish priest to at first one and then a second living in Northamptonshire. He married Anne Gutteridge (or Goodriche) with whom he had six children and 47 years of happiness. At a time when absentee rectors were common, Percy lived in his vicarage and took his parish duties seriously, although he was frequently in London and devoted much of his time to literary matters.

Percy's first literary venture was the translation from the Portuguese of a Chinese novel, *Hau Kiou Choaan*, published in 1762, matters Oriental being then much in vogue. (*See also* Orientalism.) But almost immediately, impressed by Macpherson's Gaelic poetry, he shifted his interest to the historical and European, translating and publishing five Icelandic poems.

But more important was the more substantial work that was occupying his energies. Percy claimed to have rescued a 17th-century manuscript of even older poems from being used to kindle the fire of his neighbor Humphrey Pitt. Thereupon, he launched a search for other ancient manuscripts, which he collected, edited, sometimes modernized (to the contempt of Johnson and others), and published as his *magnum opus* in 1765 (with a second edition two years later, a third in 1775, and a fourth, edited by his nephew in 1794, who defended his uncle against charges of forging the originating manuscript). The book caused great excitement and spurred antiquarian interest. (*See also* Antiquarianism.)

Percy published, originally, about 180 full or partial poems, including romances, histories, ballads, and songs, both lyrical and satirical. He also anthologized broadside as well as folk material, and his second-largest source of material was a collection of broadsides gathered by Samuel Pepys. Percy suffered some conflict over his work. While he worried about its gravity and suitability, particularly for a cleric, he also was torn between the desire to preserve the texts, although multiple versions of the same work at times confounded him, and the impulse to improve their clarity and readability. Thus, he compromised the scholarly value of his project, though its literary merit was incalculable. For examples, Percy drew attention to the character of the minstrel (who preserved the oral tradition of the bard) whom Percy saw as the source of the ballad, as opposed to the poetry written expressly for the broadside press, or the communally derived, collectively authored ballad. Additionally, his collection restored emotion and the supernatural to poetry banished previously by Neoclassicism.

Percy also edited *The Household Book of the Earl of Northumberland in 1512* (1768), another antiquarian volume, and in 1770, *Northern Antiquities*, a translation of more ancient Icelandic poems.

Meanwhile, he contributed to biblical scholarship. In 1778, he became Dean of Carlisle and, in 1782, Bishop of Dromore, in Ireland, a post he held for 29 years. Once again, he occupied his diocese and ministered faithfully to its inhabitants. His eyesight began to fail in 1804; he was blind by the time he died, two years after his wife, in 1811. Both were buried in his cathedral.

Laura Dabundo

Works Consulted

Davis, Bertram H. *Thomas Percy: A Scholar-Cleric in the Age of Johnson*. Philadelphia: U of Pennsylvania P, 1989.

Dictionary of National Biography, *s.v.* "Percy, Thomas."

Fowler, David C. *A Literary History of the Popular Ballad*. Durham: Duke UP, 1968.

Friedman, Allan B. *The Ballad Revival: Studies in the Influence of Popular on Sophisticated Poetry*. Chicago: U of Chicago P, 1961.

Gaull, Marilyn. *English Romanticism: The Human Context*. New York: Norton, 1988.

Hodgart, M.J.C. *The Ballads*. London: Hutchinson U Library, 1962.

Wheatley, Henry B. *Reliques of Ancient English Poetry . . . by Thomas Percy, D.D.* 1886. New York: Dover, 1966.

Peterloo

Peterloo is the name given by popular satirical indignation to a large and important gathering of reform-minded and radical workers, together with many women and children, held on August 16, 1819, at St. Peter's Field in Manchester. The gathering was brutally dispersed by military forces, ordered into action by an alarmed magistracy. Eleven participants in the gathering were killed and about 400 were more or less severely wounded. Many on both sides were veterans of the Battle of Waterloo fought four years before. Peterloo, in which British military might was unleashed on British citizens, seemed a perversely ironic commentary on that historic triumph. Almost immediately, the action at St. Peter's Field was called the Peterloo Massacre. Shelley's poem *The Masque of Anarchy* castigates the government's role in provoking it.

Home secretary Lord Sidmouth had appointed the Waterloo veteran General Sir John Byng the Commander of the Northern Districts in 1816, making him in effect the chief of law enforcement in this increasingly industrialized district. Byng's predecessor, Thomas Maitland, was approbated by the government in 1812 for his decisive shattering of the Luddite rebellion, which he had accomplished through the public hangings of 17 men. Sidmouth's informers thought that a similarly firm hand would soon be needed because the causes of discontent that had led to the Luddite uprisings had exacerbated over time. In the years following Byng's appointment, radicals and agitators for reform held mass meetings, marches, and demonstrations, gave speeches, gathered in correspondence clubs, and printed broadsides, newspapers, and pamphlets. In the mushrooming industrial centers of the Northern District, the workers' growing awareness of their disenfranchisement and oppression provided the audience and the impetus for these activities, and many of the chief figures in the movement were drawn from the workers' ranks. Their rulers and employers viewed their discontent and calls for reform with responses ranging from callous indifference to alarm verging on panic.

Bills outlawing public gatherings that the magistracy thought seditious, especially the mass meetings and correspondence clubs of the workers' movement, ensued. These measures were passed in February 1817; and in March, Sidmouth engineered the suspension of habeas corpus. In Manchester, on March 9, 1817, the magistrates, constables, and their spies observed without immediate interference a large and unruly demonstration, the beginnings of what became known as the Blanketeers' March, which was followed by yet more mass meetings and petition drives at St. Peter's Field the next day. When Byng, who was on the scene, thought the situation had gone far enough, he ordered the Dragoons to disperse the large crowd. Scores were arrested, but almost miraculously, there were only a few injuries and one death. This successful experiment in crowd control must have given Byng and his subordinates confidence in their procedures.

The years that followed provided many opportunities for similar repression of workers' demonstrations—arrests for sedition on the information of spies and police actions against mass meetings. As the demonstrations of the summer of 1819 grew in size and frequency, a plan to hold a gigantic mass meeting at St. Peter's Field took shape among the workers' leaders. It was to be addressed by Henry Hunt, a well-known radical orator. The authorities kept careful track of this development, determined to make a stern example, and Byng massed all the force he could in Manchester and the surrounding districts—a sizable force of some 20 troops of cavalry and about as many companies of infantry. These were commanded by Byng's deputy Guy L'Estrange, except for a troop of Manchester yeomanry and the Manchester constables under the direct command of the local magistrates.

In the days before the meeting, workers, many of them women, and their families, attired in their best clothes and carrying signs and banners, marched in from the outlying towns. On the day of the meeting, some estimates number the crowd on St. Peter's Field at 150,000—the largest gathering of industrial workers ever held. The troops were ranged in readiness on side streets, and, shortly after Hunt had begun his oration, the signal was given to move out. The resulting cavalry charge on the defenseless crowd was devastating; many more were wounded by being trampled by the horses or by the frightened demonstrators than were cut down by slashing sabers. The field was quickly cleared, and the fleeing citizenry was pursued through the streets of the town.

The organized mass rebellion that the government expected Peterloo to provoke never occurred. Indignation and outrage among the workers caused by the massacre were widespread, and some among the so-called respectable classes joined in calling for the punishment of those responsible. Protest meetings were held, but for the time being, the workers' will to resist was broken. Some pressure was mounted on the government to relieve those injured and to indict those responsible, but little came of it except for more reactionary measures from the Cabinet, especially the so-called Six Acts, which gave almost unlimited police powers to the Home Secretary and his delegates. In part because of Peterloo and its disappointing aftermath, the Establishment's grip on the working class became firmer and agitation for reform did not effectively regroup until 1832. (*See also* Lower Classes, [The] Luddites, Parliament.)

Kenneth Watson

Works Consulted

Marlow, Joyce. *The Peterloo Massacre*. London: Rapp, 1969.

Read, Donald. *Peterloo: The "Massacre" and Its Background*. Manchester: Manchester UP, 1958.

Reid, Robert. *The Peterloo Massacre*. London: Heinemann, 1989.

Thompson, E.P. *The Making of the English Working Class*. New York: Random, 1966.

White, R.J. *Waterloo to Peterloo*. New York: Macmillan, 1957.

Phrenology

The science of phrenology, now rejected, emerged between 1796 and 1805 from the laboratory of Viennese physician and anatomist Franz Joseph Gall (1758–1828). Phrenology literally means "discourse on the mind," but as a science it purported to be a universal system of understanding human psychology. Divining human character from physical appearance had been an ancient pursuit, going back to the classical physiognomy of Aristotle. Physiognomists studied all the human features from head to toe to determine signs of character.

Gall's influential contribution to unraveling human psychology was twofold. First, his science embraced the rationalist spirit of the 18th century. He spurned the metaphysical nature of physiognomy attempting instead to proceed empirically from careful dissection of brain tissue. Second, Gall's focus was specific to the human brain and skull. He posited that each section of the brain controls human emotion and character and that the skull's shape corresponds to these sections. The brain, argued Gall, is a collection of interrelated organs arranged in a three-tiered structure. The lower organs house humanity's instincts; the middle regions contain emotional propensities; the top and foremost organs preserved human reason and spirituality. Since the contour of the skull reflects one's allotment of instincts, propensities, and intelligence, careful measurement of the skull illuminates one's total human nature, or "mental faculties." Gall detected 27 distinctive mental faculties, which he classified into two categories: (1) feelings and propensities and (2) knowing and reflecting faculties. Convinced he had discovered a completely scientific understanding of human psychology, Gall named his new science "craniology."

Because Gall rejected a metaphysical approach to his studies, religious authorities, fearing his materialism, pressured the government to force him from Vienna. In 1805, Gall went into exile in Paris; he was accompanied by his devoted student Johann Caspar Spurzheim (1776–1832). In Paris, Gall was enthusiastically received, and his lectures and medical demonstrations, well attended. He continued to study

brain tissue, following the brain's own structure in his dissections, convinced that the key to human psychology was in this structure.

Spurzheim, eager to establish his career and to win converts, left Paris for London in 1814. If he had hoped for a reception equal to that in Paris, he was disappointed. Powerful journals, like the *Edinburgh Review* and the *British Quarterly*, vociferously opposed phrenology. The medical community was divided in its appraisal of the new science. Followers of Sir Charles Bell, whose *New Idea of the Anatomy of the Brain* (1811) began the unraveling of sensory and motor nerves, held phrenology in contempt. Still, phrenology found a large and faithful following in Britain. Spurzheim's emphasis on the essential relationship between the physical and the moral and his contention that phrenology could improve humankind appealed greatly to a reformist generation. Spurzheim taught many how to locate the mental faculties (he expanded Gall's 27 to 35), how to decipher the brain's structure, and then how to interpret individual character from measured and observed data.

By 1823, the *Phrenological Journal and Miscellany* began publication and local societies proliferated. Spurzheim promoted phrenology with a near religious fervor. Crossing the Atlantic to win American disciples, he died suddenly in Boston, at the beginning of a hectic lecture tour. His final mission marked the ascendancy of phrenology, for Spurzheim appeared a martyr to many. Inspired by his example, some of his devoted friends took up the cause.

As a science, phrenology enjoyed its heydey in the early Victorian period. The phenomenally successful publication of George Combe's (1788–1858) *The Constitution of Man* (1835) signaled a growing interest in "head-reading." Among the most famous believers were Hegel, von Bismarck, Marx, Balzac, the Brontës, Eliot, Whitman, and Queen Victoria. Its obvious applications to educational, public health, and penal reforms urged some converts to seek practical uses for this new psychology. Spurzheim's brand of phrenology was never wholly deterministic; he held that self-improvement was possible once one gained a knowledge of one's mental faculties. In an age that codified progress, the promise of widespread correction proved irresistible (though the phrenology of Combe denied the possibility of improvement for African, Asian, and Mediterranean peoples).

Phrenology succeeded for a time because it synthesized scientific method with a progressive theory of human psychology. Phrenology's exact measurements and link to anatomical dissection gave it an aura of certitude; its promotion of individual and social reform gave it the luster of philosophy. It was systematic, all-encompassing, and simple. Two important forces led to its demise. British religious authorities, Anglican and Dissenting alike, united to oppose its rationalism and materialism (America, unencumbered by hegemonic religious leaders, embraced it longer). In the authorities' view, it was decidedly unChristian. But science provided the strongest arguments against phrenology's system. As medical scientists examined the brain in more detail, they were able to disprove phrenology's main premises: that each mental faculty's organ varies in size, that size itself determines one's allotment of a given faculty, and that all these organs affect the skull's shape.

Nonetheless, phrenology, especially Gall's version, provided three important directions for modern science. First, the modern paradigm of the cerebral localization of functions originated in the work of phrenology. Second, phrenologists helped establish psychology as a biological science. Finally, phrenology's naturalistic approach influenced the development of evolutionary biology, physical anthropology, and sociology.

Susan Naramore Maher

Works Consulted

Cooter, Roger. *The Cultural Meaning of Popular Science: Phrenology and the Organization of Consent in Nineteenth-Century Britain*. New York: Cambridge UP, 1984.

Davies, John D. *Phrenology: Fad and Science; a Nineteenth-Century American Crusade*. Hamden: Archon, 1971.

De Giustino, David. *Conquest of the Mind: Phrenology and Victorian Social Thought*. London: Croom, 1975.

Erickson, Paul A. *Phrenology and Physical Anthropology: The George Combe Connection*. Halifax: St. Mary's U, 1979.

Stern, Madeleine B. *Heads and Headlines: The Phrenological Fowlers*. Norman: U of Oklahoma P, 1971.

Young, Robert M. "Franz Joseph Gall." *Dictionary of Scientific Biography*. Vol. 5. New York: Scribner's, 1981: 250–56.

[The] Picturesque

Writing to Sir Joshua Reynolds in 1791, Gilpin declared, "With regard to the term *Picturesque*, I have always myself used it merely to denote *such objects, as are proper subjects for painting*." This statement sounds much like remarks by Addison, who, at the beginning of the 18th century, approved of nature as it conforms to art, or by Pope (to Joseph Spence) that "[a]ll gardening is landscape painting." Yet the similarities are deceptive, for Gilpin's painterly qualities were specifically contrast, irregularity, roughness, variety, novelty, and a mixture of light and shadow. Burke discusses many of these features in *Philosophical Enquiry into the Origin of Our Ideas of the Sublime and*

Beautiful (1757) but dismisses them as ugly. (*See also* Burke, Edmund; Landscape Painting; [The] Sublime; Topographical and Travel Prints.)

Burke's work nonetheless remains important in the development of the picturesque aesthetic. Though in many ways faithful to Neoclassicism, he defined sublimity and beauty emotionally rather than intellectually with rules that deviated from early 18th-century gardening, painting, and architecture, which sought to please through conscious evocation of classical models and moral messages. Gilpin's six volumes of tours—beginning with *Observations on the River Wye* (1782) and his essay *On Picturesque Beauty* (1792)—seek a middle category between Burke's extremes of the limitless and the obscure (sublime) and the smooth, polished, and confined (beautiful), hence, the picturesque.

Like Burke, Gilpin regarded picturesque qualities as inherent in objects rather than in the observer. But while he spoke of nature, he thought of art, specifically the paintings of Lorrain, Poussin, Salvatore Rosa, and Gaspard Dughet. The English on the Grand Tour had long admired their work and bought examples. (By the early 19th century, they had brought home some 80 Claudes and 100 Rosas; between 1711 and 1759, about 300 Dughet landscapes, some copies to be sold in England, while engravings even furthered their popularity.) Gilpin fostered this taste and extended it to tourism and landscape gardening. Whereas in the late 17th and early 18th centuries, provincials traveled to see London, in the latter half of the 18th century Londoners sought remote locations that Gilpin and other writers of tour guides indicated were similar to the landscapes of Claude and the Italians. Wordsworth's original (e.g., 1793) visit to Tintern Abbey was probably inspired by such books, as

was Turner's to the Lake District. The three oils Turner exhibited in 1798 that resulted from this excursion (i.e., *Morning Among the Coniston Falls, Cumberland*; *Dunstanburgh Castle, N.E. Coast of Northumberland*; and *Buttermere Lake*) recall the picturesque mode of Gilpin and Lorrain.

Uvedale Price and Richard Payne Knight extended Gilpin's ideas by focusing on the observer not the object seen. For Price, picturesque scenes please because they inspire certain associations— Allison's 1790 *Essays on the Principles of Taste* also stresses the association of ideas. Knight went further, defining the picturesque as "that kind of beauty which belongs exclusively to the sense of vision, or to the imagination, guided by that sense." Price at Foxley, Herefordshire, and Knight at Downton laid out estates on the model of the picturesque, as did Scott at Abbotsford and Thomas Hope at Deepdere, thereby offering an alternative to the landscaping of "Capability" Brown and his successor, Repton. (*See also* Nash, John.) The vogue for the picturesque encouraged local-color writing, such as the poetry of Clare; many of Wordsworth's early works, such as *An Evening Walk* and *Descriptive Sketches* (both published in 1793) and *The Ruined Cottage* (written from 1797 to 1799), were composed under the same impulse. Christopher Hussey provides a long list of topographical painters (including Constable, Gainsborough, and Turner) who were similarly influenced. Price also saw in pure light and color a picturesque quality that may well have affected Turner's later work and that of the Impressionists, even though they rejected much of the genre painting that they regarded as the essence of the picturesque.

The picturesque should not be equated with a love of nature unimproved. In his

Letters on the Scenery of Wales, R.H. Newell complained, "Nature's compositions are seldom complete or correct," echoing an observation of Gilpin's. The picturesque remained tied to Neoclassicism in its search for an abstract ideal, in its use of art to improve nature, and in its appeal to an educated elite that could make the proper painterly associations. Yet the movement fostered a greater appreciation for a new category of landscape, encouraged new forms of writing, painting, and gardening; and, in Knight's appeal to the mind's eye, coincided with Romanticism's emphasis on the imagination. Because the antiquity and irregularity of Gothic architecture appealed to the picturesque sensibility, the new aesthetic furthered the revival of medievalism as well. In short, it taught people to see, and so to think, in a new way. (*See also* Gothicism, Medievalism, Painting.)

Joseph Rosenblum

Works Consulted

Andrews, Malcolm. *The Search for the Picturesque: Landscape Aesthetics and Tourism in Britain, 1760–1800*. Stanford: Stanford UP, 1989.

Brennan, Matthew. *Wordsworth, Turner, and Romantic Landscape: A Study in the Traditions of the Picturesque and the Sublime*. Columbia, SC: Camden, 1987.

Hipple, Walter John, Jr. *The Beautiful, the Sublime, & the Picturesque in Eighteenth Century British Aesthetic Theory*. Carbondale: Southern Illinois UP, 1957.

Hussey, Christopher. *The Picturesque: Studies in a Point of View*. London: Putnam's, 1927.

Piranesi, Giovanni Battista

(1720–78)

Architect, etcher, stage designer, furniture and interior designer, and amateur archaeologist, Giovanni Battista Piranesi was born in Venice, but the city with which his name is inextricably linked is Rome. Settling in Rome in 1740, he set about capturing both the ancient and the modern city in his hundreds of etchings.

A strong Romantic flavor pervades Piranesi's vision of ruined Roman monuments, his nostalgia for the greatness of Roman antiquity producing etchings that are picturesque and poetic. (*See also* Antiquarianism, Classicism.) From 1745 onward, he published *Vedute di Roma* (Views of Rome), dramatic pictures of the ancient city that established his great popularity. More than any other artist, he shaped the mental image of Rome held by most people. The 137 drawings are studies in light and shade. While his representations of Roman architecture were always faithful, he altered the scale to make these majestic monuments appear more colossally proportioned than they were. Walpole commented that Piranesi's vision of Rome was even grander than Rome at the height of its glory, but this was in keeping with Piranesi's violently pro-Roman, anti-Greek sentiments, which he championed in the 1761 *Della magnificenza ed architettura de' Romani* (On the Magnificence and the Architecture of the Romans).

Another famous series of plates produced by Piranesi is the *Carceri d'Invenzione*, surreal pictures of imaginary prisons. Its fearful, disturbing images inspired the landscape in Beckford's Gothic novel *Vathek* (1786).

Only one of Piranesi's architectural designs was ever constructed, but his influence was felt in architecture, painting, stage design, and literature. Long after his death, his *Vedute* continued to be published, giving people who had never traveled to Rome their clearest image of the monuments that are its glory.

Linda Jordan Tucker

Works Consulted

Chilvers, Ian, ed. *The Concise Oxford Dictionary of Art and Artists*. New York: Oxford UP, 1990.

Hind, Arthur M. *A History of Engraving & Etching: From the 15th Century to the Year 1914.* New York: Dover, 1963.

Murray, Peter and Linda. *A Dictionary of Art and Artists.* Baltimore: Penguin, 1965.

Watkin, David. *A History of Western Architecture.* New York: Thames, 1986.

Wittkower, Rudolf. *The Pelican History of Art: Art and Architecture in Italy, 1600–1750.* New York: Penguin, 1973.

Pitt, William

(1759–1806)

William Pitt, the younger, was British Prime Minister (1783–1801, 1804–06) during the French Revolution and Napoleonic Wars and strengthened the office of Prime Minister during his tenure. (*See also* Parliament.)

Pitt began his political career as Chancellor of the Exchequer under Lord Shelbourne in July 1782. During this time, he improved the government's credit through sound budgetary measures and sent Wiliam Eden to negotiate a commercial treaty (1786) with France, thereby liberating Anglo and French trade from prohibitory duties.

Pitt was selected to be Prime Minister by George III after the defeat of Fox's East India Bill in the House of Lords (December 1783). As Prime Minister, Pitt ended England's diplomatic isolation and weakened French influence by a defensive alliance with Prussia and Holland (1788). Through the Nootka Sound dispute (1790), he stopped Spanish ambitions on the western seaboard of North America, making possible the westward expansion of Canadians to the Pacific.

In February 1793, Pitt led England in its alliance with the crowned despots against Republican France. During wartime, Pitt suspended the Habeas Corpus Act and restricted the right of public meet-

ing. Confronted by shortages in the British Army and Navy, Pitt oversaw the use of press gangs, a practice by which British citizens were captured aboard ships and forced to serve in the war. He advocated the Union of Ireland and Great Britain to ensure British security against French invasion, but he was forced to resign in 1801 when King George III and members of his cabinet refused to grant political rights to Irish Catholics.

Pitt's second ministry was hampered by the King's refusal to allow Fox in the cabinet. Leading the House of Commons and conducting the war, Pitt was forced to combat the Foxite Whigs and the Grenville group that remained in opposition. He achieved a heralded naval victory at Trafalgar (1805), which ended the invasion threat and ensured Britain's naval supremacy. After his death in 1806, Pitt became the spiritual leader of the Tory party, which held power for the next 25 years.

Jonathan Gross

Works Consulted

Barnes, Donald Grove. *George III and William Pitt, 1783–1806.* New York: Octagon, 1965.

Ehrman, John. *The Younger Pitt: the Years of Acclaim.* London: Constable, 1969.

Jarrett, Derek. *Pitt the Younger.* New York: Scribner, 1974.

Reilly, Robin. *William Pitt The Younger.* New York: Putnam's, 1979.

Poetry

Poetry in the Romantic age is complex, ambitious, boldly innovative, and lyrical. It also offers simplicity of feeling through ballads, songs, and hymns. Romantic poetry takes its beginnings from such forms as Burns's *A Red, Red Rose*, Chatterton's *Bristowe Tragedie*, Cowper's *Olney Hymns*, and Scott's *Minstrelsy of the Scottish Border*.

Blake's *Poetical Sketches*, with songs like *My silks and fine array*, carry an Elizabethan spirit into the age, and his *Songs of Innocence and Experience* bring pastoral innocence into encounters with ironic disillusionment. Blake's songs are major achievements in tone, subject, and theme, as are the ballads of Wordsworth and Coleridge in their "experiments" of 1798 and 1800. Lyrical expressions of strong feeling about common experience, as in *The Last of the Flock*, are complemented with narrations of uncommon events in *The Rime of the Ancient Mariner*. (*See also* Lyric, Metrical Theory and Versification, Pastoralism, Puns.)

Keats's ballads extended the form in a unique direction, while Shelley made brilliant adaptations of both ballad and hymn. Keats's *La Belle Dame Sans Merci* extends the ballad from Blake's horrific *Grey Monk*, Scott's rendition of *Lenore*, and even Coleridge's *Ancient Mariner* into the realm of psychological probing that characterizes Romantic poetry at its best. Shelley's ballads move differently, toward the poetry of working people in *The Mask of Anarchy*, which turns the medieval form into an ironic ballad of rebellion. Shelley also used the hymn in strikingly different ways. Because the hymn has a convention of appeal from low creature to high creator, it assumes a humble tone: however, Shelley challenges that assumption and disturbs that tone in such poems as *Hymn to Intellectual Beauty*. (*See also* Ballads.)

Romantic poetry is ambitious to modify classical forms for modern experience. Such are the sonnets and stanzaic verses of various kinds, including the odes. In the immediate background lay the poetry of Collins and Gray, but beyond was the mighty achievement of Milton. Blake's unusual experiments in form include his odelike *America, A Prophecy* and *Europe, A Prophecy*, which recompose Milton's *Ode on the Morn-*

ing of Christ's Nativity. Cowley also gave models for irregular verse of high purpose. Coleridge wrote several odes, from the regular Pindaric *Ode to the Departing Year* to the irregular *Dejection: An Ode*. Wordsworth's most universally famous poem may be his *Ode: Intimations of Immortality from Recollections of Early Childhood*. It is not, however, his only ode, and neither is the irregular Pindaric his only kind, because his *Ode to Duty* is a firmly executed example of the Horatian, or homostrophic, ode.

Great as the odes of Coleridge and Wordsworth are, they do not exceed in excellence the odes of Shelley and Keats, which deepen epistemological questioning and heighten subjective themes of the age. Poems such as *Ode to a Nightingale* and *Ode on a Grecian Urn* continue to fascinate and joyfully surprise with innovative structures and styles of verse and language. So too do Shelley's odes, especially *To a Skylark*, his pastoral and elegiac ode *Adonais*, and most famously his *Ode to the West Wind*, which combines *terza rima* with a sequence of sonnets to serve themes of natural process and visionary energy.

Blake worked briefly with the sonnet, as in the boldly unrhymed *To the Evening Star*. While Coleridge's sonnets recognize a popular form, they do not achieve the excellence of sonnets by Wordsworth and Keats, whose mastery intimidates rivals. In exquisitely shaped responses to a beautiful evening by the seaside or to an early morning in London, in rousing calls for liberty, Wordsworth used the sonnet as Milton had: to solemn purposes with spiritual potency. Wordsworth also set his sonnets in sequences, in *The River Duddon* and *Ecclesiastical Sonnets*. Though Milton also provided models for Keats, after Leigh Hunt, Shakespeare's version offered a greater challenge, and so Keats made a distinctive turn to the Shakespearean shape, coming to sharp points of insight with the rhyming closures of *On Sitting Down to Read King Lear Once Again* and *When I have fears*.

The achievement of Milton set a standard of excellence for Romantic poetry in the sonnet and the ode, but the chief and highest aim of poetry in the age was to create a modern epic: one that would continue, not displace, the short epic of *Paradise Regained* and the long one of *Paradise Lost*. (*See also* Epic.) Thomson's *Seasons* was a wildly popular derivative of the Miltonic epic; Young's *Night Thoughts* was an influential contribution; and Cowper's *Task* was an entertaining entry. However, none of these realized the lyrical, visionary epic that Blake and Wordsworth created. Taking on the adversarial spirit of Milton, Blake rewrote Milton's epics in two complete poems, *Milton* (1809) and *Jerusalem* (1820), and one incomplete, *The Four Zoas* (Vala). These are poems of thundering blank verse, biblical in rhythm and subject, with symbolic narratives of visionary proportion. As a painter and engraver, Blake complicates his poems with visual as well as verbal metaphors. (*See also* Milton.)

Wordsworth's epic impulse was purely verbal, but his task was the same as Blake's: to recover Miltonic form as a vehicle for Romantic imagination. Wordsworth wrote blank-verse accounts, in Miltonic style, of his growth as a poet. This was to be a preliminary apologia for the great epic of his time, urged on him by Coleridge, to be called *The Recluse*. While he did not complete that ambitious project, Wordsworth did invent a new epic form with *The Prelude* (in three versions, 1798, 1805–06, and 1850). The child and poet as hero on romantic quest, through searching self-examination and international recreation, gave to Wordsworth's epic a vigorous spirit of renovation. The younger poets of the age did not live to benefit from the model of *The Prelude*, but Keats read *The Excursion* (an installment of *The Recluse*) as one of the finest achievements of the time. Keats apprenticed himself by writing an epic, in rhymed couplets, based on Endymion's love for the goddess of the moon, but Keats yielded to the Miltonic spirit in his unfinished *Hyperion* and *The Fall of Hyperion*. The first is modeled on *Paradise Lost*; the second is a dream vision, modified by the example of Dante's *Divine Comedy*, though in strong blank verse.

Epic impulse produced much fine, perhaps the best, poetry in the age, but it took odd directions. One was verse narrative which mixed, or competed with, prose fiction and romantic epic. Such poetry often found immediate popularity from readers accustomed to verse from Dryden's *Absalom and Achitophel* to Crabbe's *The Borough*. Romantic verse narratives, however, swerved from that line, bent by Spenser's *Faerie Queene* and certain Italian chivalric tales. In this genre, Byron set the mark for distinction, though he had able predecessors in Chatterton, Scott, and Coleridge and able competitors in Shelley, Keats, Clare, and Hunt.

Wordsworth tried his hand at verse narrative, and he succeeded with *Margaret, or The Ruined Cottage*, though his success is less for narrative than for meditative reflection; other tales, like *Michael* or *The White Doe of Rylstone* (with its Spenserian cantos in irregularly rhymed octosyllabic verse) succeed more from handling of language than of story. *Lamia* and *The Eve of St. Agnes* by Keats and *The Revolt of Islam* by Shelley are arguably better than Wordsworth's narrative poems.

Keats's poems, the one in couplets imitating Dryden and the other in Spenserian stanzas, show mastery of versification as well as economy (and rich ambiguity) of narration. Shelley's romantic epic, however, has little virtue of economy in storytelling, though it also shows a mastery of the Spenserian stanza for character analysis and symbolic expression of a revolutionary theme. Shelley, more than Keats or Wordsworth, believed the Spenserian form was an invitation to elaboration of incidents and luxury of language, which may explain the prolixity of his poem. That he could practice economy of expression, even in elaborate narrative verse, is shown by his *Witch of Atlas*, surely benefiting from the wonderful example set by Byron in the same stanza form of ottava rima for *Don Juan*.

No poet of the age was better at telling stories in verse than Byron, not even Scott, who surrendered the competition to do his major work in the Waverley novels. Byron made all verse forms serve his great talent, for Gothic mood or Mediterranean gaiety. He was instantly famous with his Spenserian *Childe Harold's Pilgrimage* and his Oriental tales of *The Giaour* and *The Bride of Abydos* in octosyllabic couplets. But *Don Juan* is the poem that guarantees his fame as a major poet of the age. Putting his satiric skills to narrate the picaresque adventures of Don Juan, Byron gives the Romantic hero a dose of modern medicine, in a stanzaic verse he learned from reading Italian epic romances. Like much ambitious poetry of the age, *Don Juan* is an open-ended expression of life in all its variety, and so it does not end, it is merely interrupted.

Byron may also have set the mark (with *Manfred* and *Cain*), though not for highest distinction, in that very special mode of Romantic poetry, the closet drama, with its untheatrical form of dramatic lyric, which would culminate in the monologues of Browning and drive on to reappear in dramatic poems by Auden, such as *The Sea and the Mirror*. Others who took the drama from the stage to the mind, in the manner of *Manfred* and *Prometheus Unbound*, were Beddoes and Southey, but it is to Shelley's great dramatic poem that modern interest turns. Taking the ancient and mythic story of Prometheus, Shelley unbinds the Greek god to express Romantic aspiration; the poem is a drama of the mind in the act of finding itself, through sympathetic imagination, liberated to creative vision. This is a demanding poem, at times intensely lyrical, at times densely symbolic, but always richly figurative and superbly ironic, as it challenges the visions and verse of Aeschylus, Dante, and Milton. (*See also* Mental Theater.)

A unique achievement of Romantic poetry is a product of innovation, experiment, and historical/philosophical reorientation. This is the poetry of self-reflection and psychological romance, sometimes called the dramatic monologue, in which the "self" is the subject, theme, protagonist, and speaker. With roots deep in literary history, such poetry turns from a survey of landscape (or other external object, scene) to analysis of self in reflection. Coleridge set the standard for this Romantic mode, giving priority to the self alone, generating flights of imagination through an interior space and time, until external setting is transformed by energy of imaginative vision. Such a poetic experience questions the source of value and, more radically, the grounds for knowing reality. (*See also* Conversation Poems.)

Romantic poets made the dramatic monologue the primary verse mode of modern poetry in English. Wordsworth's *Tintern Abbey* is a near perfect realization of this kind of poem, though Coleridge's *Frost at Midnight*, Byron's *Prisoner of Chillon*, Shelley's *Mont Blanc*, and Keats's odes constitute worthy examples as well. Speaking is a search for self in which language constructs the subject of observation, as Wordsworth does when he describes a scene of the Wye River valley, using metaphors that connect observer with observed, as Keats does when he contemplates an ancient Greek urn, though using metaphors to sever rather than to bind the artist with his art. Poetry of the age draws strength from dialectical fusions of natural uncertainties with artful ambiguities. (*See also* Frame Narrative.)

Richard D. McGhee

Works Consulted

Abrams, M.H. *Natural Supernaturalism: Tradition and Revolution in Romantic Literature*. New York: Norton, 1971.

Bloom, Harold. *The Visionary Company: A Reading of English Romantic Poetry*. Ithaca: Cornell UP, 1971.

De Man, Paul. *The Rhetoric of Romanticism*. New York: Columbia UP, 1984.

Langbaum, Robert. *The Poetry of Experience: The Dramatic Monologue in Modern Literary Tradition*. New York: Norton, 1957.

Polidori, John William

1795–1821)

Had John William Polidori not introduced the vampire into the English Gothic novel by writing *The Vampyre* (1819), his name would be only a footnote to Byron's biography, but in addition to *Frankenstein*, *The Vampyre* was the result of Byron's proposal that he and his guests write ghost stories while at Villa Diodati in June 1816.

Born in 1795 in London, Polidori earned a medical degree from the University of Edinburgh at the astonishing age of 19. In 1816, he became personal physician and traveling companion to Byron when the poet went into voluntary exile on the Continent. With precocious intellect and some desire for literary fame of his own, Polidori was pleased to travel with Byron and was offered a substantial fee from Byron's publisher, John Murray, to keep a journal of Byron's travels. That journal was not published until 1911, when Polidori's nephew, William Michael Rossetti, edited the diary that Polidori's sister, Charlotte Lydia Polidori, had expurgated because of some "improper" passages. Unfortunately, after copying Polidori's diary, she destroyed the original.

After Byron settled in Geneva, with Mary Godwin, her half-sister Claire Clairmont, and Percy Shelley as neighbors, the Shelley entourage frequently visited Byron's rented villa. In response to their many conversations on ghostly phenomena and stories, the group decided to write original Gothic stories, but only Mary Shelley's and Polidori's ever reached publication.

Apparently Byron had little use for "Polly dolly," as he not too affectionately referred to Polidori, because he dismissed him from service in 1816. Although Byron repeatedly made fun of the doctor, they remained on fairly friendly terms and met again in Milan, where Byron helped Polidori out of legal difficulties, and later Byron recommended him to John Murray, asking Murray to help the doctor find a publisher.

When Polidori published his short Gothic novel, *The Vampyre*, in 1819, it was attributed to Byron by the publisher Colburn and became instantly successful. Although Polidori objected to the attribution and Byron repudiated the work, sending his own fragment upon which the concept of *The Vampyre* was based to his publisher, Byron's fame had already carried *The Vampyre* to literary success, with translations in German, French, and Spanish, as well as pirated editions appearing in America. Actually the fragment and the novel are quite dissimilar, although the core of mysterious death, promises of secrecy, and strange powers is within Byron's fragment. Polidori's tale focuses on the sinister vampire Lord Ruthven (a name borrowed from Lady Caroline Lamb's notorious novel *Glenarvon*, based loosely on Byron) and his relations with Aubrey, a younger, innocent man, whose beloved Ianthe becomes the vampire's victim. The overtones of Polidori's relationship with Byron are obvious.

Returning to England and continuing to work as a physician, Polidori nevertheless still sought literary recognition. The same year as he released *The Vampyre*, he also published *Ernestus Berchtold, or the Modern Oedipus* (with echoes of *Frankenstein*'s subtitle "The Modern Prometheus") and *Ximenes, The Wreath, and Other Poems* and, in 1820, *The Fall of the Angels*. Apparently his income as physician and writer was insufficient for his gambling debts because Polidori poisoned himself in his own dwelling in 1821. But his vampire story saved his name from obscurity. Perhaps his appreciation for Gothic literature was inherited by his sister's children, Christina and Dante Gabriel Rossetti. (*See also* Vampire.)

Karen McGuire

Works Consulted

Bleiler, E.F. "Introduction to *The Vampire*." *Three Gothic Novels*. New York: Dover, 1966.

Dictionary of National Biography, s.v. "Polidori."

Harson, Robert R. *A Profile of John Polidori with a New Edition of The Vampyre*. Diss. Ohio U, 1966.

Marchand, Leslie A. *Byron: A Biography*. New York: Knopf, 1957.

Rossetti, William Michael, ed. *The Diary of Dr. John William Polidori, 1816, Relating to Byron, Shelley, etc.* 1911. Folcroft, PA: Folcroft Library Editions, 1975.

Poole, Thomas
(1765–1837)

Thomas Poole's most notable role in the history of English Romanticism was his close friendship with Coleridge. They met in 1794 when Coleridge and Southey visited the village of Nether Stowey during a walking tour.

Poole offered his patronage to Coleridge. Besides providing financial support, he also became a mentor and a paternal figure for the poet, who admired Poole's steadiness which contrasted with his own extremist tendencies. Coleridge even relocated from Bristol to Nether Stowey and became Poole's neighbor. There, he tried his hand at a rustic, agricultural existence.

Poole was a self-taught intellectual, a well-to-do tanner, and citizen of Nether Stowey who held politically liberal views. He never married; instead he committed himself to philanthropic and community projects and business. Before taking over his family's tanning concern, he worked as a common laborer. He became a competent manager and a caring employer, established men's and women's benevolent societies, and built a school.

Although he never attended university, Poole had a passion for self-improvement and was fascinated by men he regarded as possessing genius. He accumulated a solid library and formed a book club, lending texts to Coleridge and listening to the poet's comments about them. He also attempted to write poetry. Coleridge, in turn, benefited immensely from Poole's suggestion that he begin a new project: the systematic writing of his autobiography in the form of letters addressed and sent to Poole. These writings helped generate memories and ideas that Coleridge developed in later works.

As their correspondence and friendship evolved, there were some strains—as when Poole bungled an attempt to save Coleridge's marriage and (perhaps out of jealousy) charged that Coleridge had begun to hero worship his friend Wordsworth. However, as Coleridge's marriage further disintegrated and drug and alcohol abuse increased, Poole continued to provide support.

Poole also carried on an extensive correspondence with Coleridge's wife Sara, for whom he became a confidante, and he took a fatherly interest in Coleridge's son Hartley.

Anne T. Ciecko

Works Consulted

Coleridge, Samuel Taylor. *Collected Letters of Samuel Taylor Coleridge*. Ed. E.L. Grigg. Vols. 1–6. Oxford: Clarendon, 1971.

Coleridge, Sara. *Minnow Among Tritons: Mrs. S.T. Coleridge's Letters to Thomas Poole*. Bloomsbury: Nonesuch, 1934.

Doughty, Oswald. *Perturbed Spirit: The Life and Personality of Samuel Taylor Coleridge*. Toronto: Associated UP, 1981.

Holmes, Richard. *Coleridge: Early Visions*. London: Hodder, 1989.

Weissman, Stephen M. *His Brother's Keeper: A Psychobiography of Samuel Taylor Coleridge*. Madison: International UP, 1989.

Poor Law of 1834

The Poor Law Amendment Act of 1834 was the most far-reaching poverty legislation in England since the 1601 Act established parish relief by means of tax levies. To alleviate the old system's inadequacy in the face of increased population, the new law established the national Poor Law Commission. The Commission was authorized to group hitherto-independent parishes into unions, each having its own board of guardians under the Commission's central authority. The law met with some resistance, particularly in the North, where it was attacked as dictatorial in its meddling with local affairs and insensitive in its treatment of the poor. The "New Poor Law," as it came to be known, discouraged the practice of outdoor relief (direct handouts) for the able-bodied poor, instead promoting the workhouse test as more efficient at identifying the truly needy. In 1842, the passage of the Outdoor Labour Test Order flatly prohibited boards of guardians from furnishing relief to able-bodied poor outside the workhouse, but the measure was not regularly enforced.

The idealistic Tory legislators who constructed the workhouse scheme envisioned a stringent yet clean, disciplined, and orderly environment designed to improve as well as house those who found themselves there. In reality, the dreaded "Tory Bastille" effectively split up families by segregating men, women, and children. Furthermore, the inmates' inability to come and go at will made it impossible for them to find gainful outside employment. If the board did, against custom, offer outdoor relief as an alternative, the case had to conform to the test of "less-eligibility"; that is, the recipient had to do work that was hard, repetitive, and unprofitable, thus discouraging him or her from seeking relief unless absolutely necessary. Honest laborers and their families, it was thought, would do almost anything to avoid the ministrations of the Poor Law. In the workhouse too, the principle of less-eligibility governed the diet and occupation of the inhabitants; theoretically, they were to be maintained at a standard of living lower than that of the average local laborer. Despite the Poor Law's emphasis on the workhouse, however, only 10% to 20% of England's paupers ever occupied one by the mid-19th century. Local boards of guardians found ways around the strict application of the regulations. For example, because the definition of "able-bodied" was vague, the boards had some latitude in the granting of outdoor relief. This frustrated one of the law's essential motivations: the desire for a uniform national system to deal with pauperism.

Although the New Poor Law was based on a theoretical distinction between honest poverty and idle pauperism, one of its great failings was its practical inability to separate the willing-to-work from the shiftless, a particular problem during periods of mass unemployment. In another failure of discrimination, the workhouse also lumped the able-bodied together with children, the old, and the sick; critics of the law felt that the application of less-eligibility to the latter groups was inhumane. Protest throughout the 1840s and 1850s inspired modifications of earlier rules: pauper schools were established for the education and training of workhouse children, and a medical service was staffed for the aged and ill. Workhouses nonetheless remained harsh and depressing places, but egregious horrors tended to have local rather than systemic origins. The basic structure erected by the New Poor Law proved durable, for it survived with several changes for more than a century.

Sue Petit Starke

Works Consulted

Brundage, Anthony. *The Making of the New Poor Law: The Politics of Inquiry, Enactment, and Implementation, 1832–1839.* New Brunswick: Rutgers UP, 1978.

Fraser, Derek, ed. *The New Poor Law in the Nineteenth Century.* London: Macmillan, 1976.

Henriques, Ursula R.O. *Before the Welfare State: Social Administration in Early Industrial Britain.* London: Longmans, 1979.

Knott, John. *Popular Opposition to the 1834 Poor Law.* London: Croom, 1986.

Rose, Michael E. *The English Poor Law, 1780–1930.* Newton Abbot: David, 1971.

Porter, Jane
(1776–1850)

Jane Porter, sister of poet and novelist Anna Maria Porter, is known primarily as a writer of historical novels. Her first novel, *Thaddeus of Warsaw*, published in 1803, was a highly successful account of a young nobleman who was an exiled member of the family of the king of Poland. The novel's popularity led to nine editions of the book by 1810. The work is an example of the early historical novel, written prior to the more well-known novels of Scott, who instituted and personalized the genre.

With a woman named Luckie Forbes, the young Scott visited the Porter home frequently. They entertained the family with fairytales and stories of the borders, to which Porter was always indebted. As a girl, she had read Spenser's *Faerie Queene*, Sydney's *Arcadia*, and tales of chivalry, from which she acquired her love of romance.

Porter's second novel, *The Scottish Chiefs*, was written within a year and published in 1810. It, too, met with great success. A romance based on the life of William Wallace, a Scottish patriot whom she had heard about from Forbes, it followed the events of his life to his execution and culminated in the Battle of Bannockburn. Translated into German and Russian, the novel won European fame and was condemned by Napoleon. It was reprinted nine times between 1816 and 1822 and is one of the few historical novels prior to *Waverley* that have survived.

Porter wrote two plays: *Egmont, or the Eve of St. Alyne* and *Switzerland.* The latter, produced on the stage in 1819 with Kean in the lead, was a failure, and it closed after only one performance.

The work that followed the plays was the three-volume *Duke Christian of Luneburg, or Traditions of the Harz* (published in 1824); it was suggested by George IV and dedicated to him. In 1831, *Sir Edward Seaward's Narrative* was published. As an account of his Caribbean exploration, it was purported to be taken directly from Seaward's diary, but, because historical novels are a combination of history and imagination, it was widely believed, then as now, that Porter fictionalized much of the *Narrative*, including the Caribbean islands. Even so, Porter regarded her work seriously and believed the use of her literary talents to be religious as well as creative obligations.

Other works by Porter include the following: *The Pastor's Fireside*, published in 1815, which deals with the later Stuarts; *Sketch of the Campaign of Count A. Suwarrow Ryminski* (1804); and a preface to *Young Hearts, by a Recluse* (1834). With her sister Anna Maria, she wrote and published *Tales Round a Winter Hearth* (1826) and *The Field of Forty Footsteps* (1828). She contributed works to many periodicals, and several unpublished works were lost through a sale in 1852.

Porter died in 1850 at her brother's home in Bristol, England.

Karla Alwes

Works Consulted

Dictionary of National Biography, s.v. "Porter, Jane."

Drabble, Margaret, ed. *The Oxford Companion to English Literature*. Fifth ed. Oxford: Oxford UP, 1985.

Porter, Jane. Introduction. *The Scottish Chiefs*. Chicago: School Library Association, 1831.

Price, Richard

(1723–1791)

Richard Price served as a Unitarian minister for more than 50 years in London, Hackney, and Stoke Newington, but he is best remembered for his moral philosophy, which was held in disdain by most English. His Dissenter beliefs made him the victim of discrimination in England and might have shaped his conviction that freedom comes from the individual, not from the government.

Price held that humans can choose their own fates by being able to observe ethics impartially but are held within the boundaries established by God. As a result, he believed society, which possesses both positive and negative ethics, is basically good. Out of this grew his belief that citizens should be free to follow their own moral wills, not the government's. He felt that any freedom the government offers must come from the people. He became an early supporter of the American Revolution (and later the French Revolution).

Price's *Observations on the Nature of Civil Liberty, the Principles of Government and the Justice and the Policy of War with America* was published in early 1776. Condemning the British resistance to independence in the American colonies, it roused fervor on both sides of the issue. Price wrote that the English should be concerned about the liberty of their American cousins because what happened in America affected liberties in England and ultimately the world. Therefore, he felt, the English should support the Americans' desire to establish their own government because the Americans should have the same privileges as the English who had created a government in England. In addition, Americans were unique individuals on another continent and of another community and should have the freedom to make their own moral judgments and decide what constitutes liberty.

Price was also an exemplary mathematician who was made a fellow of the Royal Society in 1765. A paper he presented in 1771 established the framework for present-day life-insurance policies. He was consulted by both William Pitt, the

Younger, and Benjamin Franklin on fiscal issues for both England and the new United States.

Jo Ann Ferguson

Works Consulted

Agnew, John P. *Richard Price and the American Revolution*. Urbana: U of Illinois, 1949.

Bonwick, Colin. *English Radicals and the American Revolution*. Chapel Hill: U of North Carolina, 1977.

Cone, Carl B. *Torchbearer of Freedom: The Influence of Price on Eighteenth Century Thought*. Lexington: U of Kentucky P, 1952.

Cua, Antonio S. *Reason and Virtue: A Study in the Ethic of Richard Price*. Athens: Ohio UP, 1966.

Plumb, J.H. *England in the Eighteenth Century*. Baltimore: Penguin, 1972.

Williams, E.N. *Life in Georgian England*. New York: Putnam, 1967.

Priestley, Joseph

(1733–1804)

A prolific and versatile theologian, scientist, educator, and political commentator, Joseph Priestley began life as the eldest son of cloth dressers. Born in 1733, in Fieldhead, Yorkshire, he was reared in an industrious Dissenting community close to the textile center of Leeds. Priestley's mother died in childbirth when he was age 6, leaving Jonas Priestley to cope with six children. In 1742, Priestley's wealthy, childless aunt, Sarah Keighly, adopted him and brought him to her husband's estate, Old Hall, Heckmondwike, for his upbringing and education within the Presbyterian tradition.

Priestley was an independent, intelligent child, and his aunt determined early that a career in the Presbyterian church would best suit his talents. Priestley thought highly of his aunt, and though she was a confirmed Calvinist, she was never rigidly doctrinaire in her dealings with others. At Old Hall, Priestley met many of the day's leading Dissenters and heretics, participating in their discussions. No doubt the Keighlys' home was a stimulating environment for such a promising child. Priestley attended local parish schools; his aunt supplemented his education with tutors; and Priestley directed much of his education, particularly between his 16th and 19th years when ill health postponed his entry into college.

In his teens, Priestley rejected the doctrine of predestination and proclaimed that salvation is available to all; soon after he also rejected the idea of the Trinity. At a young age, he was already making grave spiritual decisions and surveying critically the orthodoxies around him.

Thanks to his aunt, Priestley's early education was thorough. Besides learning Calvinist doctrines, he studied classical (Hebrew, Greek, Latin, Chaldee, Syriac) and modern languages (German, French, Italian), natural philosophy, and mathematics, his weakest subject. His education at Daventry Academy (1752–55) familiarized him with many Dissenting opinions and enabled him to organize his own thoughts effectively. Logic and metaphysics played an important part in his academy education; at Daventry he also received his first formal scientific training. It was here that Priestley accepted the heresy of Arianism (i.e., that Jesus Christ had not existed coeternally and timelessly with God but had been created by God). The humanity of Christ became a principal theme in Priestley's theology. Upon reading Hartley's *Observations on Man* (1749), Priestley enthusiastically accepted the theory of association and Hartley's reduction of all mental phenomena to physical explanations. Priestley avowed himself "a confirmed necessarian" and from that point followed a philosophical line that was at once rationalist, utilitarian, and mechanistic. He emphasized the primacy of fact and thus spent his life attempting a synthesis between his scientific and rational observations and his devotion to the idea of a revealed religion.

Priestley's liberal religious views impeded his ministerial career. His first office, at Needham Market, Suffolk, where he entered the ministry in 1755, was unsuccessful. His rejection of the atonement, of the inspiration of the sacred text, and of God's intervention into the individual soul did not win him many allies. He moved on to Nantwich in Chesire (1758–61), but poverty hampered his living, and a school he proposed failed to materialize. In 1761, he left the ministry to pursue teaching, having accepted a post at the Dissenter's Academy in Warrington (1761–67). There, he taught languages, oratory, and civil history and policy and in his spare time published volumes on the principles of education and pedagogy. His fellow tutors shared his religious biases, so Warrington proved a happy place for him. Moreover, his marriage to Mary Wilkinson in 1762, daughter of the renowned ironmaster Isaac Wilkinson, added considerably to his contentment.

In these fruitful years, he first met Benjamin Franklin, who became a lifelong friend, and pursued scientific investigations. He received a fellowship in the Royal Society in 1766. The following year, he wrote the successful *History and Present State of Electricity* and began a series of biting political tracts that placed him among the most controversial polemicists of his day. His *Essay on the First Principles of Government* (1768) provided Bentham with his infamous equation, "greatest happiness of the greatest number" and, more important, articulated Priestley's firm belief in individual rights and a curtailed role for the state. Educational reform also claimed

Priestley's attention, and his ideas were forcefully argued in *Essay on a Course of Liberal Education* (1765).

Priestley left Warrington in 1767 to return to the ministry. His new appointment, at Mill Hill Chapel, Leeds, was fortunate, and at this post his creative energies exploded. Adjoining the Chapel was a brewery. By experimenting with the "fixed air" (carbon dioxide; gases were then called "airs") that rose up from the fermenting beer, Priestley created soda water, the first carbonated beverage, considered medicinal in his day. This discovery prompted the Royal Society to honor him with the Copley Medal in 1773. Priestley continued to delve into religious controversy, publishing essays and tracts on contested subjects, from the reasoning of St. Paul to such diverse issues as family prayer, church discipline, and the Last Supper. At Mill Hill, he took an important spiritual step, accepting Socinianism, the forerunner of Unitarianism. A disciplined writer, he produced numerous volumes, including a second scientific history, *History of Optics* (1772).

Once more he left the ministry, this time to act as librarian for William, Earl of Shelburne. Between 1773 and 1780, Priestley oversaw the Earl's library and devoted all his spare time to chemical experimentation. Though Priestley was an orthodox chemist, he was remarkably gifted as an experimenter and observer. During these years, he described, isolated, and identified ammonia, sulfur dioxide, nitrous oxide, nitrogen dioxide, and silicon tetrafluoride. Unquestionably his most important discovery was oxygen (then called "dephlogisticated air"). Priestley's investigations helped establish the experimental techniques of pneumatic chemistry. Though an advocate of the now disproven phlogiston theory of combustion, Priestley's position in the forefront of 18th-century chemistry is indisputable. Traveling on the Continent with the Earl of Shelburne in the summer and fall of 1774, Priestley met Antoine Lavoisier, co-discoverer of oxygen and scientific rival, and the Abbe Boscovich; he also resumed his friendship with Franklin, but the American Revolution prevented significant collaboration. Among the important volumes he published during this decade were *Experiments and Observations on Different Kinds of Air* (1774–77) and *Disquisitions Relating to Matter and Spirit* (1777). Though science overshadowed theology during this decade, Priestley had not forgotten his resolve to combine scientific materialism with biblical revelation.

Priestley's last ministerial post in England was at the New Meeting Congregation, in Birmingham (1780–91). Birmingham, an active community for Dissent and science, suited him admirably. He was a member of the Lunar Society, a group of formidable amateur and professional scientists that included Erasmus Darwin, Matthew Boulton, James Watt, and Josiah Wedgwood. Priestley's active interest in political and religious controversy inflamed political conservatives in the city. His *History of the Corruptions of Christianity* (1782) and *History of Early Opinions Concerning Jesus Christ* (1786) did little to appease the authorities. In 1791, on the anniversary of the fall of the Bastille, a mob descended on Priestley's church and home, destroying both, including all his books, writings, scientific equipment, and written results.

The Priestleys fled Birmingham to London, and in 1794, fearing their safety, Priestley and his wife set sail for North America to join their sons in Northumberland, Pennsylvania. Priestley was feted in the infant republic, and while visiting Philadelphia he was received by Washington

and offered a professorship at the University of Pennsylvania. He participated in Franklin's Philosophical Society and enjoyed the city's cultural advantages. But Priestley favored family over fame and joined his sons in Northumberland, 160 miles northwest of Philadelphia, then a rugged five days' journey to the fork of the Susquehanna River. The Priestleys commenced building a house (now a historical site), but Mary Priestley died before its completion. The new home contained a lab comparable to the one Priestley lost in Birmingham, and during his final years he experimented for the greater part of each day. It was here that Priestley completed his last great investigation of carbon monoxide. He died quietly, surrounded by his devoted family, in 1804.

Susan Naramore Maher

Works Consulted

Davis, Kenneth S. *The Cautionary Scientists: Priestley, Lavoisier, and the Founding of Modern Chemistry.* New York: Putnam, 1966.

Gibbs, F.W. *Joseph Priestley: Adventurer in Science and Champion of Truth.* London: Nelson, 1965.

Hiebert, Erwin N., et al. *Joseph Priestley: Scientist, Theologian, and Metaphysician.* Lewisburg: Bucknell UP, 1980.

Schofield, Robert E., ed. *A Scientific Autobiography of Joseph Priestley, 1733–1804.* Cambridge: MIT UP, 1966.

———. "Joseph Priestley." *Dictionary of Scientific Biography.* Vol. 11. New York: Scribner's, 1975.

Primitivism

Primitivism emphasizes the superiority of past ages over contemporary culture or asserts the value of simple ways of life identified with ancient societies, pastoral utopias, and primal modes of thought and feeling. This cluster of ideas becomes particularly important in the 18th and 19th centuries with the rise of historicist social theories, the gradual urbanization of European life, and a new emphasis on stages of human development.

The desire to return to earlier ways of life and thought was a reaction to Enlightenment ideas about progress. A longing had been expressed earlier for the return to a Golden Age, but increased awareness of existing "uncivilized" cultures was combined with 18th-century skeptical historicism to produce widespread primitivist speculation. Voyages of discovery led to interest in societies that existed without the benefits of modern civilization. Rousseau's noble savage was echoed in Diderot's account of native life in Tahiti, *Supplement au voyage de Bougainville* (1796). African tribes, North American Indians, and Oriental cultures all figured in European attempts to romanticize non-western societies.

Romantic primitivism also represented a psychological desire to see individuals governed by natural laws and thus not subject to sin and guilt. Goethe ascribes a preference for Homer, fairytales, and the pastoral to his young Werther in *Die Leiden des jungen Werthers* (1774), while elevating women, children, and rustics because of their intuitive and powerful emotions. Schiller praises Greek poetry and celebrates childhood for its naive idealisms. Wordsworth's early poems speak for children and rustics, while at the same time adopting a loosely pagan linking of the natural and spiritual worlds.

Primitivism had an equally pervasive influence on Romantic poetic theory. Wordsworth and Shelley followed Rousseau and Herder in arguing that primitive languages are more immediate, and thus more poetic, than modern tongues. Rousseau identified such poetic power in so-called savage and Oriental forms of speech and writing. Romantic critics argued over the relative merits of primitive

verbal spontaneity and civilized poetic rules. At the same time, a wide variety of primitive writing was produced or rediscovered. Percy collected *Reliques of Ancient English Poetry* in 1765. Scott published *The Lay of the Last Minstrel* in 1805. Such traditional works as the Eddas, the *Neibelungenlied*, the *Chanson de Roland*, and the *Bhagavad Gita* were all recovered or translated. Macpherson and Chatterton wrote primitivist forgeries under the names Ossian and Rowley, respectively. Burns, Clare, and Barnes produced rustic peasant and dialect poems.

Romantic classicism and Orientalism can also be seen as forms of primitivism. Keats's Endymion and Hyperion, Byron's Oriental heroes, Shelley's Prometheus, and Blake's unfallen Albion all suggest returns to earlier intuitive and imaginative modes of being. English and European writers developed enthusiasm for Greek antiquity and the Middle Ages as well as for non-Western cultures and the Celtic fringes of Europe. Victorian medievalism, Yeats's use of Irish myth, and Eliot's anxieties about modern civilization all derive from the idealizations of Romantic primitivism. (*See also* Antiquarianism, Gothicism, Medievalism, Orientalism/Exoticism.)

Ashton Nichols

Works Consulted

Boas, George. *The Cult of Childhood*. London: Warburg Institute, 1966.

Boas, George, and A.O. Lovejoy. *Primitivism and Related Ideas in Antiquity*. Baltimore: Johns Hopkins UP, 1935.

Fairchild, H.N. *The Noble Savage*. New York: Columbia UP, 1955.

Torgovnick, Marianna. *Gone Primitive*. Chicago: U of Chicago P, 1990.

Said, Edward. *Orientalism*. New York: Pantheon, 1978.

Whitney, Lois. *Primitivism and the Idea of Progress*. New York: Octagon, 1934.

Prometheanism

Prometheanism refers to the surge of interest in the myth of Prometheus during the Romantic period, culminating in such works as Mary Shelley's *Frankenstein* (subtitled "The Modern Prometheus"), Byron's *Prometheus* and *Manfred*, and Shelley's *Prometheus Unbound*. The Romantics were attracted to several elements in the myth of Prometheus—his creation of humankind from clay (in some versions of the myth); his role as benefactor of the human race; his cruel punishment, suffered while chained to a rock; and his unwavering defiance of Zeus's authority.

In their rewriting of the myth, the Romantics produced two different interpretations of the Prometheus figure. In one interpretation, Prometheus represents the heroic individual who maintains a mastery over himself despite the debilitating effects of pain, despair, and guilt. This Promethean capacity to endure interminable suffering and yet remain defiant and proud becomes a prominent characteristic of the Byronic hero. The other interpretation, developed by Shelley in *Prometheus Unbound*, recognizes in Prometheus the exemplary revolutionary who champions the oppressed and refuses to succumb to ruthless tyranny. In an age when revolution and its attendant Prometheus, Napoleon, failed to dislodge the old order, Prometheus remains for Shelley a symbol of hope for the eventual overthrow of oppressive systems.

The primary classical source for the myth, Aeschylus's *Prometheus Bound*, was much criticized during the 18th century for its seemingly uncontrolled diction and loose structure, but critical opinion began to change after the first English translation appeared in 1773; within a few decades, it was heralded as one of the masterpieces of Athenian drama. By 1825, there were seven editions of Aeschylus's collected works and 14 editions of individual plays. It was in this atmosphere of heightened interest in Aeschylus and *Prometheus Bound* that Shelley and Byron, the two Romantic poets most often associated with Prometheanism, were educated. The first work Shelley was instructed to read when he arrived at Oxford was *Prometheus Vinctus*; Byron relates that during his school days at Harrow *Prometheus Bound* was one of the plays read three times a year, and for his first English verse exercise he translated a chorus from the play.

Influenced by Byron and Shelley and the current interest in Prometheus, Mary Shelley incorporated elements of the myth in her novel *Frankenstein* (1818). Victor Frankenstein is a "modern Prometheus," as the subtitle denotes, because he discovers how to fashion a living being out of inanimate clay, the assembled parts of dead bodies. After Frankenstein brings his creature to life, however, its ugliness disgusts him and he abandons it, failing to minister to it as Prometheus does to mankind in the original myth. Although the creature manages to educate itself to some degree, it feels such bitterness toward its creator that it takes revenge by murdering those who are most dear to Frankenstein. In this reworking of the myth, Frankenstein aspires to the status of Prometheus but falls short because of his inability to shoulder the responsibilities of a creator.

What attracts Byron to the figure of Prometheus is not his power to create but his power to endure suffering. In his first significant reference to Prometheus in *Ode to Napoleon Buonaparte* (1814), Byron asks whether Napoleon, after being exiled to Elba, will be able to endure his defeat and humiliation nobly, like a Prometheus. Two years later in his short poem *Prometheus*,

Byron explicitly equates the sufferings of Prometheus with the human condition. Prometheus, he contends, is an emblem of humanity who is part divine and can foresee eventual mortality, but who is also endowed with the spirit and will to defy fate, transforming death into a victory.

This Promethean attitude of endurance and defiance receives its fullest expression in *Manfred*, published the year after *Prometheus*. The first reviews of *Manfred* linked it to the Faust legend, but Byron insisted that Aeschylus's *Prometheus Bound* was the main literary influence. Like *Prometheus Bound*, *Manfred* is set in a wild, mountainous region, and the action consists almost entirely of speeches, as Manfred struggles to understand and endure his destiny of grief and pain. Manfred differs from Prometheus in that his suffering is not punishment for helping humankind, but the result of guilt for destroying his relationship with Astarte, the one person he had loved. At the end of the drama when demons come to drag Manfred away to his death, he turns them back, proclaiming the independence and immortality of the mind and its power to requite itself for good or evil. In *Manfred*, Byron locates the Promethean struggle within the human psyche; Manfred is both tormenter and defiant sufferer, enduring his own self-inflicted punishment of guilt.

In the major Romantic work on the Prometheus myth, *Prometheus Unbound* (1820), Shelley returns to the original mythic material and rewrites the lost ending to Aeschylus's trilogy in which Prometheus is finally freed. Shelley's interest is in the larger political dimensions of the myth, the struggle between the forces that would liberate the human race and those that would oppress it. Although Shelley retains much of the traditional Prometheus story—Prometheus as bene-factor of humankind, as sufferer, as rebel against tyranny—he rejects the traditional ending in which Prometheus and Jupiter are reconciled. Shelley's Prometheus remains in implacable opposition to Jupiter, yet Shelley is also careful to show that Prometheus's opposition is rooted in his high moral character rather than in stubborn pride—the satanic element that motivates Byron's Promethean characters. The central action of the drama is Prometheus's retraction of the curse he had spoken earlier against Jupiter. By withdrawing the curse, Prometheus puts into motion the forces of destiny, represented by the character Demogorgon, who topples Jupiter from power. In the new Promethean age that follows, Shelley envisions all forms of oppression fading away and humankind living in a state of utopian harmony.

Paul M. Wiebe

Works Consulted

Clubbe, John. "'The New Prometheus of New Men': Byron's 1816 Poems and *Manfred*." *Nineteenth-Century Literary Perspectives: Essays in Honor of Lionel Stevenson*. Ed. Clyde de L. Ryals. Durham: Duke UP, 1974: 17–47.

Curran, Stuart. "The Political Prometheus." *Studies in Romanticism* 25 (1986): 429–55.

Robinson, Charles E. *Shelley and Byron: The Snake and Eagle Wreathed in Flight*. Baltimore: Johns Hopkins UP, 1976.

Small, Christopher. *Ariel Like a Harpy: Shelley, Mary and Frankenstein*. London: Gollancz, 1972.

Thorslev, Peter L., Jr. *The Byronic Hero: Types and Prototypes*. Minneapolis: U of Minnesota P, 1962.

Prophecy and Apocalypse

With the advent of revolutions in America and France, late-18th-century England inevitably saw the close of the century in apocalyptic terms, with two general responses defining the poles of reaction. As reflected in Hazlitt's *The Spirit of the Age*, revolt and reaction were those poles, and as M.H. Abrams has indicated,

Hazlitt's contention was that the poetry that typified Romanticism sprang from and toward revolution and reaction.

The prose works of the times mirror these poles; Burke's *Reflections on the French Revolution* strongly reacts against events in Paris, while Paine's *Rights of Man* and Wollstonecraft's *A Vindication of the Rights of Men* champion the social upheaval let loose during the French Revolution. However, both interpretations of historical events adopt apocalyptic language as the linguistic ground from which to argue, and this appropriation is most especially true of certain poets; it is in the poetry, rather than the prose, that the fullest extent of biblical influence—as repository of symbols, as alternative poetic tradition, and as paradigm of revolt—can be most profoundly felt.

This inclination of both rebels and reactionaries to "read" historical events in apocalyptic terms has its ontology partially in increased scrutiny of the Bible generally and the writing prophets of the Hebraic tradition, specifically during the mid-18th century. The rediscovery of the prophets played a crucial role in the Romantic appropriation of biblical poetics, for the writing prophets seemed to embody a key Romantic rediscovery: the individual inscribed within cultural parameters is alienated from self and society in the process. The strong social consciousness of prophets, like Isaiah, Ezekiel, and Jeremiah, fueled by a desire for justice, is married to the mode of conveyance itself, biblical poetics, and these forms are appropriated and transmuted by poets and writers in the period.

Critics of the Bible, most particularly Robert Lowth in his *34 Lectures on the Sacred Poetry of the Hebrews* (delivered over a decade and published in 1753), found its "origin and first use of poetical language

...to be traced into the vehement affections of the mind," a position that illuminates the curious blend of personal intensity and social consciousness characteristic of Romantic poetry. More specifically in relation to Romantic poetry, looking anew at Bible poetry provided the means for escaping classical rules of poetry-making. The Hebraic tradition, the originary source of all Western concepts of apocalypticism, offered imaginative freedom by providing a poetic antecedent to the classics that yet contributed to them.

Certainly, Blake is the most vocal in his valorization of "The Old & New Testaments [as] the Great Code of Art," yet the conclusion to *The Prelude*, as announced in its Preamble, testifies to Wordsworth's sensitivity to his role as a poet-prophet: "Prophets of Nature, we to them will speak/ A last inspiration." Coleridge's *The Rime of the Ancient Mariner* situates the myth of the Wandering Jew as its central unifying trope, a symbolic gesture reflecting Coleridge's ability to read Hebrew and appropriate the Bible's stylistic and semantic horizons directly. Byron's 1815 collection of poems, *Hebrew Melodies*, reflects his concern to embrace Hebraic concepts, settings, and rhythms, while the impact of the Bible and prophecy on Shelley can be most literally felt in his *Defence of Poetry*, where "a poet is a prophet, not because he predicts the future, but because he 'participates in the eternal, the infinite, and the one.'"

The rhetorical power of the prophets also has a strong satiric edge focused both on the future as on the present. This edge of prophetic discourse is omnipresent in Blake's *The Marriage of Heaven and Hell*. Early in the work, Blake's exuberant citation of Isaiah provides the form for *The Marriage*, and in one "Memorable Fancy" the narrating persona of the work dines with the prophets Isaiah and Ezekiel, who repeatedly link poetic genius and prophetic utterance. Yet Blake's *Marriage* and subsequent illuminated prophecies also draw heavily on Revelation, with Blake's works manifesting the alpha and omega of biblical prophetics. The satiric element of prophecy is equally present in a work like Byron's drama *Cain*. Although initially condemned as sacrilegious, the work can be read in terms of the Protestant tradition, where Byron shuns exegesis to confront the text purely.

Once the French Revolution failed ideologically, sinking into terror and tyranny, Romantic poets took an inward turn based on the belief that social revolution was doomed to fail if it was not accompanied (or perhaps preceded) by a mental evolution, a revolution in being initiated by beings. Within Romantic criticism this inward turn has been characterized by what Abrams calls "the apocalypse of imagination," in which transformation is to occur, not within public human, but rather within a history of a single individual's mind, a movement from active political engagement to the imagination. Biblical poetry also offered English Romantic writers a way to interpret historical events as interlaced with mental functions, with exterior and interior phenomena mirroring one another. "I assert poets to be prophets in the gross sense of the word, or that they can foretell the form as surely as they foreknow the spirit of events . . . which would make poetry an attribute of prophecy, rather than prophecy an attribute of poetry," as Shelley's *Defence* puts it.

Poetry infused with the spirit of prophecy (the Hebrew word *ruach* can equally be interpreted as "wind," "spirit," and "breath") also provided what many critics believe to be the primary pattern of imagery for Romantic poets, where the wind functions as symbol for the inspiration or in-spiriting of the poet. The transference of this biblical ethos to nature can be most clearly felt in Shelley's *Ode to the West Wind*, where the wind becomes "The trumpet of a prophecy" capable of rousing the slumbering souls of mankind to an appreciation of beauty and an appetite for justice. This type of inner transformation speaks to the internalization of apocalyptic expectation, with messianic expectation assumed by the individual visioning seer; poetry is the vehicle for the dissemination of inner realization, spreading outward from within rather than the reverse, which was what the failed revolution in France seemed to promise.

Mark Lussier

Works Consulted

Abrams, M.H. *Natural Supernaturalism: Tradition and Revolution in Romantic Literature*. New York: Norton, 1971.

— — —. "English Romanticism: The Spirit of the Age." Ed. Harold Bloom. *Romanticism and Consciousness*. New York: Norton, 1970: 91–119.

Drury, John, ed. *Critics of the Bible, 1724–1873*. New York: Cambridge UP, 1989.

Jemielity, Thomas. "Prophets or Projectors? Challenges to Credibility in Hebrew Prophecy." *Studies in Eighteenth-Century Culture* 18, 4 (1988): 445–78.

Hoagwood, Terence Allan. *Prophecy and the Philosophy of Mind: Traditions in Blake and Shelley*. University, AL: U of Alabama P, 1985.

Roston, Murray. *Prophet and Poet: The Bible and the Growth of Romanticism*. Evanston: Northwestern UP, 1965.

Schneidau, Herbert. *Sacred Discontent: The Bible and Western Tradition*. Berkeley: U of California P, 1977.

Tannenbaum, Leslie. *Biblical Tradition in Blake's Early Prophecies*. Princeton: Princeton UP, 1982.

Wittreich, Joseph Anthony, Jr. *Angel of Apocalypse: Blake's Idea of Milton*. Madison: U of Wisconsin P, 1975.

Publishing

In the 19th century, color printing, inexpensive bindings, and octavo volumes were replacing the engraved, leather-bound quartos of the 18th century. From 1790 to 1830, the aquatint was the most popular means of book illustration. Lithography, invented in 1798 by Aloïs Senefelder, was costly enough to be limited to map printing and expensive editions. In 1836, chromolithography, which replaced the 1835 Baxter process of using engraved wood blocks of color on copper plates, increased the illustrators' range of colors and, ultimately, made lithography a less complicated and more exciting printing tool. Although wood engraving was on the decline, Bewick's works were sought for commercial printing, of stationery for instance, and his cuts for the popular *History of British Birds* were considered exceptional. In the early part of the century, steel and stipple engraving were also practiced.

Most books were printed on the iron hand-press known as the Albion, which replaced the wooden printing press of the 18th century. The Albion, used until the advent of mechanized printing, was considered easy to operate because a screw, instead of counterweights, raised and lowered the platen; hence, no special training or skills were required. By 1792, printers, such as Vincent Figgins, began to use "New Style" type faces, which, among other alterations, discarded the long "s" of the 18th century's type fonts. In 1803, Bryan Donkin completed the first paper-making machine for the Fourdinier brothers, which is still in use today with some changes. Although the Fourdiniers declared bankruptcy not long after the machine was operating, Donkin led the paper-making industry on the Continent until his death in 1855. And the dust jacket, which did not

become a standard feature of a book until the 1870s, began appearing in the early 1820s when cloth was substituted for leather bindings, especially when publishers elected to bind a press run identically, called edition binding.

In 1814, a new copyright law was passed in England. It extended the protection period for an author's work or bookseller's property from 14 to 28 years or until the author's death if he or she were alive when the 28 years expired. These provisions were modified in the 1842 Copyright Act, which extended the length of the copyright to 42 years or 7 years after the author's death. While later revisions of the law diminished its significance, the 1814 and 1842 Copyright Laws retained the importance of copyrights registered by booksellers in Stationers' Hall.

The formation of collectors in groups, such as the Roxburghe Club (1812), was also important to book publishing in the early 19th century. Black-letter press books, finely printed and bound books of any sort, and the publications of private presses were preserved by such men as Thomas Dibdin, whose 1809 *Bibliomania* spawned much interest in collecting books of historical and artistic value. Francis Douce, after three years with the British Museum, turned in 1811 to book collecting, bequeathing his manuscript and black-letter collections to Oxford's Bodleian Library in 1834. Another important collector was Richard Heber, who said, "No gentleman can be without three copies of a book, one for show, one for use, and one for borrowers." His immense library was sold in lots in London, Paris, and Ghent, from 1834 to 1836.

Booksellers—such as John Murray, who offered binding as one of his customer services—profited from the collectors' activities in the period. Murray, whose trade began in earnest in 1768, was the son a Royal Marine who had sold his commission to go into the book trade. The Murray house, which is still in business, founded the *Quarterly Review* in 1809 and was the chief publisher of Byron's works.

From 1790 until 1810, the Minerva Press flourished, led by William Lane, who founded his trade in 1770. The Minerva Press specialized in inexpensive editions, especially of novels, for circulating libraries. Another important figure in London publishing was James Lackington, who invented the practice of remainder sales in 1793. He was so successful that by 1798 he was retired, although he lived until 1815. Lackington's trade gave rise to the prosperous wholesaling business of Simpkin and Marshall, which flourished from 1814 until 1941 as the major suppliers of books to urban and provincial stores.

It was against the tide of falling prices and cheap editions that the Longman house stood under the management of Thomas N. Longman, nephew of the founder, Thomas, who started his London trade in 1724. T.N. Longman brought in six nonfamily members as partners between 1794 and 1826 and held weekly "Literary Meetings" on Saturdays. Thomas Moore was Longman's leading pre-1850 author but it also published Wordsworth, Coleridge, and Southey. In 1798, Longman purchased Joseph Cottle's Bristol trade, Cottle having published the *Lyrical Ballads*. Longman became copublisher of the *Edinburgh Review*, with Archibald Constable in 1802, acquiring full publishing rights in 1826. In the 1820s, the firm spent nearly £5,000 on newspaper advertisements, and at least half its list sold for more than 10 shillings. A sampling of Longman's publications include Moore's *Lalla Rookh*, Bowdler's *Family Shakespeare*, Edmund Malone's *Shakespeare*, and Chamber's *Cyclopedia*.

Other notable English publishers were John Nichols, who issued the *Gentleman's Magazine* in the period; Taylor and Hessey, the publishers of Keats and The *London Magazine*; Edward Moxon, Charles Lamb's publisher; William Blackwood and Sons, famous for *Blackwood's Magazine*, the early works of Scott, and the novels of Ferrier; and Godwin, who specialized in children's books.

Beverly Schneller

Works Consulted

Briggs, Asa, ed. *Essays in the History of Publishing in Celebration of the 250th Anniversary of the House of Longman, 1724–1974*. London: Longmans, 1974.

Feather, John. *A Dictionary of Book History*. New York: Oxford UP, 1981.

Oliphant, Margaret. *Annals of a Publishing House: William Blackwood and his Sons, Their Magazine and Friends*. 1897. 3 vols. New York: AMS, 1974.

Smiles, Samuel. *A Publisher and His Friends. Memoir and Correspondence of the late John Murray*. 2 vols. London: Murray, 1891.

Puns

The English Romantic poets did not use puns as frequently or with the variety with which Shakespeare, Milton, and the Elizabethans used them, but the Romantics used them nonetheless.

Thomas Hood has been described as a punster without equal in the language. Typical of his puns are those in the first two stanzas of *Faithless Nelly Gray, A Pathetic Ballad*:

Ben Battle was a soldier bold,
And used to war's alarms;
But a cannon-ball took off his legs,
So he laid down his arms.

Now as they bore him off the field,
Said he, "Let others shoot,
For here I leave my second leg,
And the Forty-second Foot!"

There is humor and exuberance in such puns, and Hood maintains this playfulness throughout this poem and in many others. But Hood was not a major Romantic poet, and his work falls late in the Romantic era, making him a transitional figure into the Victorian period.

Of the major Romantic poets, only Byron writes much humorous poetry, and he, too, uses puns for their witty effect. In *English Bards and Scotch Reviewers*, for example, he ridicules Bowles's use of ringing bells in his couplet: "Ah! how much juster were thy Muse's hap,/ If to thy bells thou would'st but add a cap!" Byron is suggesting that Bowles deserves a jester's cap and bells. Not only is there a pun on bells, but juster suggests jester.

Such poems use what modern readers regard as puns, but to the Elizabethans puns were serious poetic devices that could be used to convey deep meanings without comic intent. Milton, a highly serious poet, often uses puns to show the derivation of words, perhaps under a Platonic belief that etymology gives insight into the true nature of things. William Empson's *Seven Types of Ambiguity* examines many such uses of puns and points out that puns largely vanished from English literature in the 18th century as poets aimed at clarity and univocality of meaning. In fact, Coleridge defended Shakespeare's use of puns against the attacks of Johnson and others.

Although the use of puns for serious purposes in Romantic poetry has been neglected by critics, some of the major poets (probably reflecting the influence of Milton and Shakespeare) do so. Blake uses such punning names as Urizen (your reason) and Urthona (earth owner) in his prophetic works, and his chimney sweepers cry "'weep! 'weep" in plying their trade. And the sinister implications of the third

stanza of *The Ecchoing Green* are deepened by a pun in the line "Round the laps of their mothers," in which "laps" may be read as "lapse" or "fall," a central theme in Blake.

Keats, too, uses puns rather frequently, especially in his odes, where he seems to delight in language with the same gusto as the Elizabethans. He puns on "brede" (breed) and "overwrought" (worked over, overexcited, and over reached) in *Ode on a Grecian Urn*. He puns on "ear" in the word "endear'd" and puns on "mourn" (morn), "bourn" (born), and "borne" (born) in *To Autumn*. In *Ode to a Nightingale*, the word "tread," can be read as "copulate": "No hungry generations tread thee down."

Despite claims that puns in Wordsworth are rare, critics have identified passages in which they are clearly functional. There is the pun on "tidings" (tidal flows or greetings) in *The Excursion*, puns on *glare* and "lustres" (chandeliers or those who lust) in *The Prelude* as well as on "urn" in diurnal in *A Slumber Did My Spirit Seal*. Puns may be the key to some hidden eroticism in Wordsworth. Wordsworth may have used such recurring puns as "muse" (to think deeply and to create poetry), as in *A Night-Piece*, and "repose" (to rest and to pose again), as in *Tintern Abbey*.

Of the other major Romantic poets, neither Shelley nor Coleridge used puns extensively. Although Coleridge defended Shakespeare's use of puns—finding them appropriate to character, passion, and the powers of association—his defense is questionable, and perhaps Coleridge really did not approve of punning in serious contexts.

Although puns went out of fashion in the 18th century in serious literature, some of the major Romantic poets—notably Wordsworth, Keats, and Blake—were following the Elizabethans and Milton in reviving them for serious purposes. (*See also* Poetry.)

Walter S. Minot

Works Consulted

Alden, Raymond M. "The Lyrical Conceits of the Elizabethans." *SP* 14 (1917): 129–52.

Barnet, Sylvan. "Coleridge on Puns: A Note on His Shakespeare Criticism." *JEGP* 56 (1957): 602–09.

Burke, Kenneth. *A Grammar of Motives*. Berkeley: U of California P, 1969.

Caviglia, Ann Marie. "A Very Rare Wordsworthian Pun." *TWC* 4 (1973): 158–59.

Empson, William. *Seven Types of Ambiguity*. 3rd ed. London: Chatto, 1953.

Harding, Eugene J. "A Possible Pun in Keats's 'Ode to a Nightingale.'" *KSJ* 24 (1975): 15–17.

Hartman, Geoffrey. *The Unmediated Vision*. New Haven: Yale UP, 1954.

Kneale, J. Douglas. *Monumental Writing: Aspects of Rhetoric in Wordsworth's Poetry*. Lincoln: U of Nebraska P, 1988.

Mahood, M.M. *Shakespeare's Wordplay*. London: Methuen, 1957.

Minot, Walter S. "Wordsworth's Use of *diurnal* in 'A Slumber Did My Spirit Seal.'" *PLL* 9 (1973): 319–22.

Minot, W.S., John I. Aides, and Gordon K. Thomas. "Notes on Wordsworthian Puns." *TWC* 5 (1974): 28–32.

Murray, Roger. *Wordsworth's Style: Figures and Themes in the Lyrical Ballads of 1800*. Lincoln: U of Nebraska P, 1967.

Reid, J.C. *Thomas Hood*. London: Routledge, 1963.

Ricks, Christopher. *Milton's Grand Style*. Oxford: Clarendon P, 1963.

Thomas, Gordon K. "The Lapful of Pleasures." *Unicorn* 2 (1973): 22–23.

Wolfson, Susan J. *The Questioning Presence: Wordsworth, Keats, and the Interrogative Mind in Romantic Poetry*. Ithaca: Cornell UP, 1986.

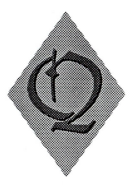

The *Quarterly Review*

The *Quarterly Review*, founded in 1809, published well into the 20th century. Its heyday was during the first few decades of the 19th century, when it was at the center of literary, religious, and political issues of its day; the stands it took on those issues were almost uniformly conservative, High Church, and Tory. (*See also* Journalism, Publishing.)

The great Whig publication, the *Edinburgh Review*, had been in existence since 1802, and its power over public opinion was growing apace. Although Scott had printed articles in the *Edinburgh* (though its politics differed from his own), in 1807, when Jeffrey printed pieces critical of the war with France and calling for peace at any price, Scott became exasperated. In a letter that year, he lists his complaints about the *Edinburgh*'s liberal stands on issues like the war, Catholic toleration, and British (as opposed to Scottish) national pride. The last straw for Scott came soon after: Jeffrey printed an unfavorable review of Scott's *Marmion*. Scott broke off relations with Jeffrey and began work on setting up a rival publication.

Scott worked with the London publisher John Murray, who was eager to challenge the increasingly powerful Scottish publisher Constable; Constable's *Edinburgh Review* gave his business a prestige and power that a mere publisher of books could not hope to match. The inner circle that formed the *Quarterly Review*, then, consisted of Scott and Murray, George Ellis, Croker, and, soon Southey. Scott was certainly the most important writer the new project could boast, but he was not interested in being an editor. That job fell to Gifford, who held the post from 1809 to 1825; after Gifford, Murray gave the job to Lockhart, Scott's son-in-law, who held it until 1853.

The *Quarterly Review* was set up specifically as an organ for anti-Whig politics and aesthetics. As such, it had almost immediate success, for its circulation figures soon rivaled the *Edinburgh*'s. But it was never as spectacular a publication as its rival: Gifford's editorial skills and erudition simply could not compete with Jeffrey's intellectual range and rhetorical power. Overall, the same contrast can be made between the two reviews: the *Edinburgh* made news, the *Quarterly* more soberly—sometimes stodgily—defended its position.

The *Quarterly* emphasized political, religious, and social topics more than its rival did, albeit giving some attention to literary matters. It published negative reviews of Keats, Shelley, Hunt, and Lamb—as would be expected from a journal with such a political mission. But these reviews, though often caustic by modern standards, did not reach the heights (or depths) of vituperation that Jeffrey and others achieved in the *Edinburgh*. Gifford set a tone of Tory respectability for the new magazine, and though he followed a policy of strict anonymity for his contributors (as did Jeffrey), overall his contributors did not use anonymity to make violent personal attacks. There are exceptions. Croker wrote a well-known savage review of Keats's *Endymion* in 1818, which contributed, many felt at the time, to the young poet's death. His scathing review of Tennyson in 1832 is usually considered the cause of that poet's 10-year silence. Nonetheless many of Gifford's writers were in the government or closely associated with it (even the free-swinging Croker was a secretary to the Admiralty), and this also contributed to the magazine's more political slant.

In literary matters, the *Quarterly* was often surprisingly liberal and seemed more open to innovation—unlike the *Edinburgh*, which consistently championed poets who wrote in Pope's mode (e.g., Crabbe and Campbell) and derided those, like Wordsworth, who did not. Scott's pres-

ence had much to do with this, and the more extreme young Romantics, like Shelley and Keats, were not well received by the *Quarterly* (Byron was often praised, but this was no doubt due in part to his aristocratic status). Most often, literature was seen through the filter of politics, and the stance of the author determined whether the review would praise or damn the work—hence, avant-gardism in literature could be acceptable if it were combined (as in Scott and middle to later Wordsworth and Southey) with political conservatism.

The *Quarterly Review* quickly became an established presence on the literary scene. But some conservatives felt that it was too mild-mannered to compete effectively with the splashier *Edinburgh*, and this led to the founding of *Blackwood's Edinburgh Magazine* in 1817—a far more freewheeling kind of project than the *Quarterly* ever dreamed of being. But even though the *Quarterly* was somewhat restrained in an unrestrained age, it found its place and was an important voice during the first few decades of its life.

Raymond N. Mackenzie

Works Consulted

Amarasinghe, Upali. *Dryden and Pope in the Early Nineteenth Century: A Study of Changing Literary Taste, 1800–1830*. Cambridge: Cambridge UP, 1962.

Buchan, John. *Sir Walter Scott*. New York: Coward, 1932.

Graham, Walter. *English Literary Periodicals*. New York: Thomas Nelson, 1930.

Lockhart, John Gibson. *Narrative of the Life of Sir Walter Scott, Bart., Begun by Himself and Continued by J.G. Lockhart*. London: Dent, 1909.

Radcliffe, Ann Ward

(1764–1823)

Ann Ward Radcliffe, the most popular British novelist of the last decade of the 18th century, published five Gothic romances in her lifetime: *The Castles of Athlin and Dunbayne* (1789), *A Sicilian Romance* (1790), *The Romance of the Forest* (1791), *The Mysteries of Udolpho* (1794), and *The Italian or the Confessional of the Black Penitents* (1797). In 1826, a sixth romance— *Gaston de Blondeville: Or the Court of Henry III Keeping Festival in Ardenne*—was published posthumously along with a memoir of Radcliffe's life commissioned by her husband and written by Thomas Noon Talfourd. (*See also* Novel.)

Little is known of Radcliffe's life prior to her marriage at Bath in 1787 to William Radcliffe, a journalist who later owned the *English Chronicle*. What is known is that her father was a haberdasher and her family moved in 1772 to Bath, where she seems to have obtained a typical education for young ladies of the middle class: a smattering of art, literature, and music with some exposure to aesthetics and ethics. After her marriage, she took up writing as a hobby to occupy herself when her husband's professional obligations kept him away from home for long periods of time. Shy and reclusive, Radcliffe initially had no intentions of publishing her work but finally did so at the urging of her husband.

Her first effort, *The Castles of Athlin and Dunbayne*, is an almost unreadable short romance, but in it she established the conventions for her next four—increasingly successful—novels. Although her style is turgid and the action disjointed and confusing, the basic outlines that dominate her later and more mature work are present: the delicate heroine, gentlemanly hero, scheming villain, gloomy setting, frequent apostrophes to nature, and explained supernatural (Radcliffe's method of explaining apparently supernatural events in natural terms).

Her second book, *A Sicilian Romance*, shows a marked advance in technique and is much more readable. Her natural descriptions are less extraneous and are used not just as a backdrop to the action but also as a source of religious solace to the frightened heroine, reminding her of God's greatness and power. In addition, the explained supernatural is used more effectively to advance suspense by creating mysteries that are not resolved until late in the tale.

It is her third novel, *The Romance of the Forest*, that brought Radcliffe the critical acclaim that her first two efforts had not. This underrated work merits more critical attention than it has received: the plotting is tighter and more logical than in the other works; the characterization, although still weak, is more psychologically complex; and the Gothic elements—the isolated forest setting, a mysterious manuscript, and the apparently supernatural occurrences— are integrated more effectively into the action.

The popularity Radcliffe gained by the publication of her third romance was enhanced greatly by the appearance of her fourth—*The Mysteries of Udolpho*—for which she was paid the then-unheard-of sum of £500. *Udolpho* has been in print continually since its publication in 1794 and is paradigmatic of the sentimental tale of terror, forming a model even today for the kind of fiction produced by such best-selling authors as Victoria Holt and Phyllis Whitney. Although the style remains turgid and the characterization weak, *Udolpho* shows a vast improvement in Radcliffe's suspenseful use of apparently supernatural events and in her colorful deployment of vivid nature scenes.

Udolpho has always been Radcliffe's most popular romance, but *The Italian*—for which she was paid a precedent-setting £800—is artistically her most successful work. For the first time, she devotes as much attention to the hero as to the heroine, physically separating the two and alternating between their adventures until they are eventually united in the inevitable happy ending. In this work, the nature descriptions are shorter and less intrusive, and the apparently supernatural events are more frightening and their natural ex-

planations, more believable, than in previous works.

Radcliffe's final romance—the posthumous *Gaston de Blondeville*—was written solely for her husband's entertainment and is of little artistic merit, although it is of some interest to students of Radcliffe, since it is her only attempt to employ the "actual" supernatural.

In spite of her stilted style and her use of sentimental stereotypes, Radcliffe exerted an enormous influence on Romanticism in general and on many of the more talented writers who followed her, including "Monk" Lewis, Coleridge, the Brontë sisters, Maturin, Dickens, and Poe; numerous minor 19th- and 20th-century Gothicists also owe a debt to her groundbreaking work. The addition of terror to the established sentimental novel gave a new dimension to fiction, and the use of the apparent supernatural to explore the psychology of fear influenced the development of the psychological novel and led to the use of the ambiguous or ironic supernatural by such major Romantic figures as Poe and Hawthorne. However, Radcliffe's major contribution to literature was her extensive use of natural settings. Nature descriptions had virtually disappeared from poetry in the 18th century and had never become a part of the evolving novel, but Radcliffe changed all that with her frequent, and often lengthy, descriptions of scenery, which she used for a variety of purposes. Unique in prose fiction were her use of nature to arouse pleasing emotions in her characters; to create an atmosphere appropriate to scenes of action, romance, and suspense; to induce the heroine's religious awe at the greatness of God and thereby to soothe her troubled mind; to reveal character; and to objectify the character's emotional states. Her use of nature, introduction of apparently supernatural events, and emphasis on feeling make her work a paradigm of Romantic fiction.

When she died at age 59 in 1823, not having published for the last 26 years of her life, it was rumored that her long literary silence was due to her having been driven mad by an overactive Gothic imagination. To correct that rumor, her husband commissioned Talfourd's memoir, which was published with *Gaston de Blondeville*. It revealed the mundane truth of the matter: Radcliffe ceased publishing because her sensitive and retiring nature could not bear the constant public attention paid her by her host of literary admirers. She chose retirement over fame. (*See also* Gothicism.)

John A. Stoler

Works Consulted

Cottom, Daniel. *The Civilized Imagination: A Study of Ann Radcliffe, Jane Austen, and Sir Walter Scott.* New York: Cambridge UP, 1985.

Kiely, Robert. *The Romantic Novel in England.* Cambridge: Harvard UP, 1972.

Murray, E.B. *Ann Radcliffe.* New York: Twayne, 1972.

Smith, Nelson C. *The Art of the Gothic: Ann Radcliffe's Major Novels.* New York: Arno, 1980.

Stoler, John A. *Ann Radcliffe: The Novel of Suspense and Terror.* New York: Arno, 1980.

Raeburn, Sir Henry

(1756–1823)

Sir Henry Raeburn was perhaps the best known Scottish artist in the 19th century. Born in Stockbridge, into a family of well-to-do mill owners, Raeburn left school at age 15 and was subsequently apprenticed in 1773 to a goldsmith. He showed an interest in painting, however, and by age 21 was an established portrait painter in Scotland. In fact, Raeburn was one of the first painters to make a business of his art, regularly painting businessmen and members of nobility.

Raeburn's finances were stabilized by his 1778 marriage to the wealthy widow of Count Leslie. He lived very well on her money, including building a large gallery where his paintings were displayed.

His early style was more akin to that of Reynolds than to any Romantic painter, but as he aged, his work took on an unusual lighting quality, strong and vigorous, with interesting compositions not generally found in previous portraiture. This different view of light is said to date from his two-year sojourn in Rome. Raeburn's portrait business flourished on his return. His *Sir John and Lady Clerk of Penicuik* (1790), which illustrates his use of light, is often called one of the finest portraits of the Romantic period. The composition is informal and set outdoors rather than in the usual stiff, indoor tableaux.

Raeburn also differed from the traditional portrait painters in that he believed in painting individuals, rather than a type or a glorification of the social position of the individual. Critics have noted Raeburn's efforts to capture the truth of the personality as revealed to the artist. Certainly, the evidence of this attitude toward individuality is clear in the portraits.

The portraits of children show movement from the stiffer work of Reynolds into the freedom of the Romantic era as well. They are not posed, well-mannered children, but natural, playing children, which reflects Raeburn's understanding of his subject in an era when children were generally to be seen and not heard.

Raeburn was admitted to the Royal Academy in 1815, which is interesting in light of the fact that he rarely visited London. He also received far-flung honors from Florence and from North Carolina. He was knighted by George IV during the

King's visit to Edinburgh in 1822. In 1823, just two months prior to his death, he was appointed King's Limner in Scotland.

Linda A. Archer

Works Consulted

Bury, A. "Raeburn." *Connoisseur* 150 (1962): 251.

Cummings, Frederick J. *Romantic Art in Britain: Paintings and Drawings, 1760–1860*. Philadelphia: Philadelphia Museum of Art, 1968.

Irwin, Francina. "Early Raeburn Reconsidered." *Burlington Magazine* 115 (1973): 239–44.

Piper, David, ed. *The Genius of British Painting*. New York: Morrow, 1975.

[The] Real Language of Men

"The real language of men" is a phrase used by Wordsworth to describe a new emphasis in poetic diction. The phrase appeared first in the 1800 Preface to *Lyrical Ballads* and was repeated in the 1802 "Appendix on Poetic Diction." The idea conveyed by the phrase gave rise to debates throughout the century about the value of naturalness in poetic language, the dangers of Neoclassical artificiality, and the possibility of ever achieving a "real" language within the carefully structured verbal forms of poetry. Wordsworth himself was not as true to this ideal of language "really used" as is often supposed, although many of his poems strive for a directness and simplicity that seemed revolutionary long after their first publication. (*See also* Literary Criticism and Literary Theory; Organicism.)

Coleridge, in *Biographia Literaria* (1817), criticized Wordsworth's statements about diction, claiming that every person's language varies widely and that Wordsworth should have called the language he was seeking "ordinary." Wordsworth's verbal directness, however, like Coleridge's own poetic practice, suggests important modifications of 18th-century ideas that described

poetry as the adornment of thought. The Romantic model of verbal organicism sees a poem not as complex figures of speech used to make ideas more ornate but as a version of the reality it sets out to describe. Romantic poems often strive to reproduce actual emotions and passions rather than employing the erudite allusiveness of much Neoclassical diction. Coleridge's conversation poems employ a different kind of real language than Wordsworth's lyrical ballads to contribute to this development. Poems by Cowper, Burns, and Clare also present appeals to various forms of real language.

Wordsworth's emphasis on real language was based not so much on a defense of the rustic and simple as on a theory about the origins of poetic language. He argued, as had Rousseau, that the earliest poetry was presented in the language of ordinary conversation, close to the power of the experiences it described. On this model, ornately poetic language emerged only later, as words were employed to distance events and objects by way of figurative tropes. Poetry, in the wake of the artifices of Neoclassicism, needed to be composed of more permanent and communal forms of verbal exchange.

Wordsworth's emphasis on real language, and its concurrent suggestion of the importance of spoken words, has had a significant influence on subsequent poetry. Shelley, in his Preface to *The Cenci*, cites his own use of "the familiar language of men" to evoke readerly sympathy. Browning's diction owes part of its roughness and harshness to his effort to reproduce spoken language in poetic texts. The energy of Dickinson and Whitman, the vigor of Hopkins and Yeats, and the directness of vast amounts of 20th-century verse all owe something to Romantic emphasis on natural organicism in literary language. Wordsworthian ideas about diction anticipate ordinary language philosophy, emphasis on the speech-act, and pragmatic theories of meaning. The idea of a real language also reminds one that all language is social, the product of a culture spoken and written by real men and women.

Ashton Nichols

Works Consulted

Barfield, Owen. *Poetic Diction: A Study in Meaning*. Middletown, CT: Wesleyan UP, 1973.

Ferguson, Frances. *Wordsworth: Language as Counter-Spirit*. New Haven: Yale UP, 1977.

Greenbie, Marjorie Barstow. *Wordsworth's Theory of Poetic Diction*. New Haven: Yale UP, 1917.

Rehder, R. *Wordsworth and the Beginnings of Modern Poetry*. London: Croom, 1981.

Ward, J.P. *Wordsworth's Language of Men*. Brighton, Sussex: Harvester, 1984.

Reconciliation of Opposites

The concept of the reconciliation of opposites permeates all of Coleridge's thought. Coleridge first uses the phrase in a discussion of the ideal poet, contending that the ideal poet brings about a "balance or reconciliation of opposite or discordant qualities" when his imagination works on the subject and the object to produce a new unity. In *Biographia Literaria*, he states that the imagination synthesizes the opposite or discordant qualities "of sameness, with difference; of the general, with concrete, of the idea with the image; the individual, with the representative; the sense of novelty and freshness, with old and familiar objects. . . ." He recognizes the creative power of the poet as he synthesizes his subject and his object as analogous, however dim, to the creation of the universe.

As the poet synthesizes his experiences into a new unity, the movement is circular;

in a letter to Cottle (1815), Coleridge uses the Hermetic image of the *ouraboros*, the "snake with it's Tail in it's Mouth." But the new unity is not the same as the original experience; rather it is more—a combination of both the subject and the object but at a higher level. In a letter to C.A. Tulk (1818), Coleridge comments on Tulk's use of another image for the synthesized unity of polarities: marriage or bisexual reproduction. The male and female come together in a creative union through which a child is produced. The child is neither the male (thesis) nor the female (antithesis) but a unique combination of both (synthesis), who then becomes a part of the next cycle of life as either the thesis or antithesis. Coleridge compares the synthesizing function of the poet to the plant in nature. "The organic form," he writes, "is innate; it shapes as it develops itself from within, and the fullness of its development is one and the same with the perfection of its outward form."

In Coleridge's aesthetic theory, the reconciliation of opposites results in beauty, whether of sound or sight. In art, he states, the picture cannot be mere copying (*natura naturata*); it must represent the essence (*natura naturans*). The artist reconciles the external with the internal; the external real with the internal and actual. Similarly, the concept of the reconciliation of opposites is integral to Coleridge's epistemology. "All knowledge," he writes, "rests on the coincidence of an object [nature] and with a subject [mind]." Knowledge then becomes self-knowledge, for only in the act of reconciling the object and the subject or mind are the subject and object identical. The mind or spirit must become an object to itself so that it can reconcile the infinite (spirit) with the finite (object) into a union of both. He concludes that "[i]n the existence, in the reconciling, and the recurrence of this contradiction consists the process and mystery of production and life."

Coleridge's epistemology is inextricably tied to his theology. God is absolute unity from which all things, including man, come and to which all seek to return. The finite self or sum or I am thus seeks to know or find itself in the absolute or infinite I am. Since, in Coleridge's view, evil consists of fragmentation or division of the finite self, redemption results from the reconciliation of the parts to the One. The function of the secondary imagination is to replicate the creative power of the indwelling spirit of God or the primary imagination. In all of his thought—esthetic, theological, epistemological, moral—Coleridge seeks the reconciliation of opposites or disparate elements to produce "multëity in unity."

Martha Watson Bargo

Works Consulted

Abrams, M.H. *The Mirror and the Lamp: Romantic Theory and the Critical Tradition.* New York: Oxford UP, 1953.

———. *Natural Supernaturalism: Tradition and Revolution in Romantic Literature.* New York: Norton, 1971.

Hill, John Spencer. *Imagination In Coleridge.* Totowa, NJ: Rowman, 1978.

Reform Bill of 1832

Until the Age of Romanticism, the British Parliament had undergone no major changes in its electoral structure since the reign of Charles II (1660–85). By the 19th century, population had more than doubled, and the new industrial economy was causing a major shift from country to city, yet the traditional landowning, aristocratic control continued. As a result, the new manufacturing centers, such as Leeds, Manchester, and Birmingham, had no parliamentary representation. Early 19th-cen-

tury electoral districts (boroughs) did not reflect existing conditions.

Three major events occurred in the summer of 1832 that greatly encouraged the movement for reform: the unpopular George IV died, the last great agrarian uprising in England occurred, and a series of revolutions started on the Continent. The king's death required new elections, and the returns reflected the growing feeling that parliamentary reform was necessary to prevent further disturbances or even a revolution. When the very conservative Prime Minister, the Duke of Wellington (*See also* Wellesley, Arthur) adamantly refused to consider any changes, his support in Parliament collapsed, and he resigned in 1830.

A government was formed by the aristocratic Whig Lord Grey (1764–1845); it received radical support because the new cabinet was united on parliamentary reform. However, Grey's first bill passed Commons by one vote. Because of this weak showing, Parliament was dissolved in April 1831, and new elections were called. A greatly strengthened Whig majority was returned.

The second attempt passed Commons but suffered defeat in Lords. Serious political disturbances followed in many parts of the country. After extensive political maneuvering and the new ruler William IV's reluctant promise to create sufficient peers to force passage through Lords, the upper house approved the third bill in June 1832, and it received the royal signature three days later.

The Reform Bill of 1832 added about one-half million new voters, but its most important result was the redistribution of seats in the House of Commons. Some 56 boroughs (one having cows for constituents) with two representatives each were eliminated, 30 boroughs lost one of their two members, 22 new electoral districts with two members and 20 with one member were created, and some 65 new seats were distributed among the shires.

The bill did not mean that Britain had become a democratic country, nor did it mean that the modern political party structure had developed, but it did indicate that King and Lords could no longer oppose the will of the House of Commons on major issues. It also meant that the important industrial figures would probably be elected to Parliament and assume positions of leadership. Passage of the bill had an additional and rather interesting result: the people began to take a much greater interest in politics. Debates in Parliament had become a spectator sport. (*See also* Parliament.)

K. Gird Romer

Works Consulted

Arnstein, Walter L. *Britain Yesterday and Today: 1830 to the Present*. Boston: Heath, 1966.

Gash, Norman. *Politics in the Age of Peel: A Study in the Technique of Parliamentary Representation, 1830–1850*. New York: Longmans, 1953.

Longford, Elizabeth. *Wellington*. New York: Harper, 1970.

Moore, David Cresap. *The Politics of Deference: A Study of the Mid-Nineteenth Century British Political System*. Hassocks, England: Harrester, 1976.

Woodward, Sir Llewellyn. *The Age of Reform, 1815–1870*. Oxford: Clarendon, 1962.

Ziegler, Philip. *King William IV*. New York: Harper, 1973.

Regency

Strictly speaking, one uses the term "English Regency" to refer to the period when George III became irreversibly mad and England was ruled by a regent, his eldest son, George, Prince of Wales. The Regency ended in 1820, when George III died and his son was crowned George IV. The term "Regency" also refers to a style of clothing, architecture, art, and manners that were influenced by the tastes of the regent and the upper class. Arbiters of taste—the *ton*, fashionable aristocrats led by the Prince Regent—set the pace in the enjoyment of the latest in art, design, and fashionable entertainment. Fortunes were gambled away on the turn of a card. The latest fashions were imported from France, although France and England were at war. High-waisted muslin dresses in the Empire style replaced the stiff brocades and stays of the 18th century. Men gave up satin coats, knee breeches, and silk stockings for knitted trousers and tail coats. Wigs and hair powder were given up for more natural styles. Regency architecture ranged from the lavish Oriental designs favored by the Prince Regent when he built the Pavilion at Brighton to chaste and formal Grecian facades of Adam.

Appearances were important to the upper classes during the Regency. Young women were expected to adhere to a strict code of social behavior in order to land eligible husbands. For upper-class women, marriage was the only acceptable choice; single women became paid companions, governesses, or unpaid family drudges, unless they inherited wealth in their own right. Young men were also to adhere to a code of behavior: all must show *bottom*, a particularly English attitude which meant they must display cool unconcern, whether setting their horse at an impossible jump or gambling away a huge sum.

Social activities were a way of life during the Regency. Both upper-class and upper-middle-class men and women spent almost all their time pursuing entertainment, which was possible because they employed armies of servants. Popular activities included the theater, the opera, and concerts, picnics, parties, balls, and extended visits at great estates. The men also enjoyed prizefights, cockfights, racing, fox-hunting, and shooting. The more athletic women rode horseback, but the majority walked and sketched. A double standard was part of Regency life: while the Regency bucks were profligate, women were censured if they strayed. Probably the best contemporary picture of Regency manners and attitudes among the upper middle class can be found in the novels of Austen.

For almost half of the Regency period, England was at war with France. England's greatest military hero, the Duke of Wellington, was a notable example of Regency style. The final battle of the Napoleonic Wars was also fought during the Regency period. Many middle- and upper-class families lost sons, husbands, and brothers in the carnage at Waterloo. The war also brought poverty, discontent, and death to the lower classes.

The Regency was a time when the English upper classes were still immensely rich and content. It was a time of leisure — with horses and stagecoaches, not yet steam. England's ruler during this period was a product of his times. By 1811, Prince George was no longer a floridly handsome youth but rather a corpulent and dissipated man, mercilessly satirized by cartoonists. Although warm hearted and emotional, he spent his youth estranged from his father, mainly due to his own indiscretions. He secretly and illegally married the actress Mrs. Fitzherbert, but was encouraged by his father to wed the dirty and uncouth Caroline of Brunswick. He stayed with her long enough to father one child, Princess Charlotte, who was, by all accounts, a lively and lovable child who died tragically young. Locked in an unpleasant marriage and isolated from the political sphere, the Prince spent his money on elaborate and often beautiful buildings, which included the Pavilion at Brighton,

Carlton House and Regent's Park in London, and the Royal Lodge at Windsor. He also spent lavishly for the finest furnishings for his residences, for extravagant dinners, and for his middle-aged mistresses, whom he loved sincerely. Unfortunately, this extravagance was paid for largely by the middle class at a time when many of the working class were near starvation. Although George IV had virtues, he came to rule too late in his maturity, after participating freely in the most profligate society of modern times. The English people and even his friends eventually rejected his weaknesses and prodigality. (*See also* Lower Classes; Napoleonic Wars; Royal Family; Wellington, Arthur.)

Elsa A. Nystrom

Works Consulted

Halévy, Elié. *A History of the English People in the Nineteenth Century, England in 1815.* New York: Barnes, 1961.

Hibbert, Christopher. *The English, A Social History, 1066–1945.* New York: Norton, 1987.

Laudermilk, Sharon, and Teresa L. Hamlin. *The Regency Companion.* New York: Garland, 1989.

Plumb, J.H. *The First Four Georges.* Boston: Little, 1956.

White, R.J. *Life in Regency England.* New York: Putnam, 1963.

Religion

The transition from the Age of Reason to the Age of Revolution was the harbinger of momentous changes in religious sentiments in England. It was particularly noted for the drive toward religious emancipation, which had a significant effect on the relation between church and state. Traditionally, the Anglicans of this period were considered staunch conservatives, who jealously guarded the rights and privileges that Erastianism fostered. The Established Church was heavily entangled with partisan politics, and the episcopate was primarily regarded as a reward for political services not as a field for pastoral oversight. The value of the sees varied enormously, from £7,000 per annum at Canterbury to £450 at Bristol. Negligence was not uncommon, and the incumbents of parishes were inadequately supervised. The parishes were poorly endowed: over 5,500 livings in the 18th century (more than one-half the total) were worth less than £50 per annum; in the most extreme case, the poorest was valued at £1 1s. Pluralism was not uncommon—even among high-ranking clergy: valuable deaneries (e.g., St. Paul's, Westminster, Christ Church) were usually held by bishops appointed to poorer sees (e.g., Bristol, Rochester, Oxford). The bishops were the foremost representatives of the "High Church" tendency within Anglicanism, which was motivated more by politics than by theology. (*See also* Church of England, Sabbatarianism.)

The conservatism pervading the upper levels of the Anglican hierarchy set the tone for attempts at political and religious reform that affected all denominations under the British Crown. It affected the reform of Parliament; the freeing of nonconformists, Roman Catholics, and Jews from the civil and religious disabilities under which they genuinely suffered; the abolition of the slave trade; and the reform of the Church of England itself. This was a gradual process, which took about a century to complete (1760–1860).

Not all Anglicans were content with the state into which their church had fallen. Foremost among these were the Methodists and their acknowledged leader, John Wesley (1703–91). A committed Anglican throughout his life, he experienced a conversion in 1738, which incited him to pursue a life of evangelistic work. He organized a body of lay pastors, and together

they embarked on a mission of itinerant preaching, which extended to every corner of the British Isles; Wesley himself covered some 5,000 miles annually. Established Churchmen were often hostile, but these field preachers were greeted with enthusiasm by the general public. Contrary to Wesley's wishes—but as a logical conclusion to his vision—a system and spirit independent of the Church of England grew within the ranks, and by the time the first Methodist minister was ordained in 1784, the "Connexion," as it was known, was showing increasing signs of becoming an independent church. By the time of Wesley's death, Methodism and Anglicanism were following very different paths; by the beginning of the 19th century the separation was complete.

Traditionally, Methodists have been actively concerned with evangelism and social welfare. However, their greatest and most lasting contribution to the common heritage of Christendom was in the field of hymnody. Charles Wesley (1707–88, brother of John) wrote hymns to support the efforts of Methodist preachers; he was the most prolific hymn-writer in the English language, with over 6,500 compositions to his credit. His treatment of his subject is the clearest evidence of the growing influence of Romanticism on religious expression in this period: the emphasis on the personal rather than the public (as in "Jesu, Lover of my soul"), the distant rather than the easily tractable, and the imaginative as opposed to the rational. The reputation that Methodists enjoy for a certain vitality in their singing derives from the emphasis that they have always placed on hymns as an integral part of public worship. (*See also* Hymnody.)

Because of their Anglican origin, Methodists were not hampered by the restrictions affecting the nonconformists, which included Congregationalists (or Independents), Baptists, Presbyterians, Unitarians, and Quakers. The members of these communions numbered about 250,000 during the latter half of the 18th century and were consigned to a "backwater" national life. Many were active in business—particularly the Quakers, and they also played important roles in science and invention. They were helped in the 17th century by the Act of Toleration (1689), which acknowledged their right to exist and worship as they wished. They were hindered, however, by the Test Act (1673), which required all holders of office under the Crown to receive the Eucharist according to Anglican usage, to take the Oaths of Supremacy and Allegiance to the King, and to make a declaration against transubstantiation.

They were further restricted in access to higher education because of the peculiarly Anglican oaths required, and so alternative facilities were provided through the Dissenting Academies. These institutions probably provided the best education available in England in the 18th century, because the curriculum was flexible and included subjects that were neglected elsewhere, such as science, geography, and modern languages. They were the only institutions of higher learning open to nonconformists until the opening of the nondenominational University of London in 1828 (the same year in which nonconformists were formally admitted into Parliament).

For Roman Catholics, the problems of toleration by the establishment were more complicated. Throughout the 18th century, they were a small and dispirited minority, totaling no more than 1% of the population. Attempts were made to improve their position through the Catholic Relief Acts (1778, 1779), which enabled them to own landed property and by which priests ceased to be persecuted; however, the passage of this law prompted riots in London and Edinburgh (the Gordon Riots). In 1791, further respite was granted: Roman Catholic worship and schools were tolerated, and certain legal and military posts were opened to them. But the stiffening of English conservatism, precipitated by the French Revolution, resulted in a fear of further tampering with the established legal bulwarks. The government managed to hold off until 1829, by which time the pressure for reform had mounted greatly; the Catholic Emancipation Act passed in that year allowed Roman Catholics to sit in Parliament and to occupy almost all military, judicial, and administrative offices under the Crown. This event clearly marked the end of the old ideal that church and state in England were one society.

Religious reform did not end there. The Jews, who had not been allowed to reside in England from 1290 to 1656, did not enjoy the full benefits of British citizenship: they were the only significant minority not to be granted admission to Parliament. During the second half of the 18th century they—like the nonconformists—had contributed greatly to England's prosperity. Although they were granted full participation in the financial transactions that accounted for Britain's great industrial strength and imperial power, there were certain aspects of life in which they were held in an inferior state—particularly in admission to public office. The leading members of the Anglo-Jewish community (including Nathan Mayer Rothschild and Moses Montefiore) saw nonconformist and Roman Catholic emancipation as a signal to begin their own campaign for the removal of disabilities. In 1833, 1834, and 1836, bills to this effect were passed in the

House of Commons; but they were defeated in the House of Lords, largely through the efforts of the Anglican bishops, still clutching at outdated principles of the constitution. Finally, in 1858, Lionel Nathan Rothschild took his seat in Parliament; thus ended the campaign for religious emancipation that characterized this period. (*See also* Brothers, Richard; Colquhoun, Janet; Irving, Edward; Southcott, Joanna.)

Leon B. Litvack

Works Consulted

Bossy, John. *The English Catholic Community, 1570–1850.* New York: Oxford UP, 1976.

Cragg, Gerald R. *The Church and the Age of Reason, 1648–1789.* Baltimore: Penguin, 1966.

Davies, Rupert E. *Methodism.* London: Epworth, 1976.

Holmes, J. Derek, and Bernard W. Bickers. *A Short History of the Catholic Church.* New York: Paulist, 1984.

Norman, Edward. *Church and Society in England, 1770–1970.* Oxford: Clarendon, 1976.

———. *The English Catholic Church in the Nineteenth Century.* Oxford: Clarendon, 1984.

Rupp, E. Gordon. *Religion in England, 1688–1791.* Oxford History of the Christian Church. Oxford: Clarendon, 1986.

Salbstein, M.C.N. *The Emancipation of the Jews in Britain.* Littman Library of Jewish Civilization. Rutherford, NJ: Fairleigh Dickinson UP, 1981.

Vidler, Alec R. *The Church in an Age of Revolution, 1789 to the Present Day.* Baltimore: Penguin, 1961.

Revett, Nicholas

(1721–1804)

A major contributor to the Greek Revival style of architecture in the middle to the late 18th century in England, France, Germany, and even the United States, Nicholas Revett began his career by first studying painting in Rome in 1742. Although a native of Suffolk, he was influenced by the new science of archaeology resulting from the Pompeii, Paestum, and Herculaneum excavations between 1736 and 1756. These Italian sites, especially Paestum, were very accessible for Western Europeans in the mid-1700s to view and to admire Greek architecture. (*See also* Architecture.)

Revett and Stuart, a painter-architect friend, visited Venice around 1750 and then Greece, via Pola, between 1751 and 1754. A story is told that the "Athenian" Revett was seized by corsairs during his later wanderings in Greece and finally released after paying a ransom. He returned to London in 1755.

By the middle of the century, Revett's architectural career had been launched. His ambitious few years in Greece, measuring and examining the ruins of Athens, produced the first volume of *Antiquities of Athens* (folio) in 1762, from which reproductions of Attic and Cycladic monuments captured the hearts of the British. This work was a joint endeavor with Stuart. The second edition appeared in 1788, the year of Stuart's death; the third edition in 1794 was edited by W. Reveley, and the last one was published after Revett's death in 1816 (by J. Woods). These beautiful engravings demonstrate the nobility, purity, and simplicity of Greek Doric architecture. The finished products based on these designs exemplified the Neoclassical principles of a severe or oversimplified architecture with columns supporting real entablatures, for instance (or with true structural, not merely ornamental, elements).

This Greek Revival period, a reaction to Rococo and the Late Baroque styles, lasted into the period of the Regency (1811–20). (*See also* Classicism, Hellenism.) It even had a dramatic influence on mid-19th-century American architecture. Especially in the West and in the South, a

Neoclassical-type of architecture was perfect for a warm southern climate and its affinity for classical elements, such as porticoes and porches.

Revett was also influenced by his stay in Asia Minor between 1764 and 1766, and he later produced his famous drawings for *Antiquities of Ionia* (1769–97). Other significant works by the artist-turned-architect include the Doric porticoes at Trafalgar House (c.1771) and Ayot St. Lawrence Church (1788), both copied from the Temple of Apollo at Delos. He also designed the Ionic and Doric porticoes and two temples in West Wycombe Park (c.1766). He died in London in 1804, but his architectural products maintained the heightened enthusiasm for Greek art and culture both in England, Western Europe, and parts of the United States.

Constance Pedoto

Works Consulted

Bryan, Michael. *Bryan's Dictionary of Painters and Engravers*. 5 vols. London: Bell, 1903–05.

Hartt, Frederick. *Art: A History of Paintings, Sculpture, and Architecture*. New York: Abrams, 1976.

Osborne, Harold, ed. *The Oxford Companion to Art*. Oxford: Clarendon, 1970.

Sturgis, Russell. *Dictionary of Architecture and Building*. New York: Macmillan, 1902.

Reynolds, John Hamilton
(1794–1852)

John Hamilton Reynolds is remembered for his friends rather than his works. Born in 1794 to George Reynolds, a schoolmaster, and his wife Charlotte Cox, he attended Shrewsbury School. Originally, Reynolds had determined to be a surveyor, but he accepted a post as clerk in an insurance office and simultaneously set about writing verse. Encouraged by a family friend, Reynolds had a remarkably early start to his career, publishing his first volume of verse at age 19. *Safie* (1813), which imitates Byron's Oriental tales, was a considerable, though short-lived, popular success, and it drew praise from Byron. Reynolds published another book the next year; *The Eden of the Imagination* (1814) imitates the early Wordsworth. It was not popular, but Wordsworth thought well of it. *An Ode* (1815), on the overthrow of Napoleon, was quickly forgotten, but Reynolds's *The Naiad and Other Poems* of the same year was favorably received.

Reynolds's critical career also began early. He became editor of the *Champion* in 1815. There, he published his own verse, as well as that of Keats and Cowden Clarke. Though he gave up his *Champion* editorship to pursue a career in law, his periodical talents came in increasing demand. Through the early 1820s, he wrote for *The Yellow Dwarf*, the *Scots Magazine*, and *Blackwood's*. He became a mainstay, along with Hazlitt and Lamb, of the *London Magazine*.

Reynolds had a particular talent for light verse. Perhaps his most famous work is his parody of Wordsworth's *Peter Bell*, which he wrote in a day, after seeing an advertisement for the genuine article. He succeeded in having it published anonymously before the real *Peter Bell* came out. Complete with absurd footnotes, it is a well-targeted parody of the Wordsworthian style, particularly of its prose. Reynolds wrote a comic opera, *One, Two, Three, Four, Five; By Advertisement* (1819) and published *The Fancy* in 1820. Both achieved popularity. In 1822 he married Eliza Drewe. He also collaborated on a volume of comic *Odes and Addresses* (1824) with his friend and brother-in-law, Thomas Hood.

Reynolds's early publishing successes and his own good nature drew him into Keats's circle. He was an early friend of Benjamin Bailey and Charles Duke and was introduced to Keats by Leigh Hunt in

October 1816. Reynolds quickly realized Keats's genius and proclaimed Keats's superiority to his contemporaries in his *Champion* review of *Poems* (1817). Reynolds and Keats quickly became literary comrades and sent verse to each other for emendation; Keats addressed a verse epistle to him and as well some of his most significant letters. In return, Reynolds contributed his knowledge about the realities of publication to Keats. He also had a little to do with the revising of *Endymion* and convinced Keats to drop his first, bellicose draft of the preface. It was Reynolds, too, who proposed that the two collaborate on a set of verse translations from Boccaccio. Keats's contribution was *Isabella*. Reynolds appears to have become distanced from Keats just before Keats's death, due perhaps to tensions between his own sisters and Keats. To the end of his life, however, Reynolds was devoted to Keats's memory.

After his initial successes, Reynolds's life became an accelerating series of disappointments. His last volume of serious verse, *The Garden of Florence* (1821), was not enthusiastically received, and he wrote verse only intermittently after this disappointment. His periodical contributions became increasingly journalistic after 1825. A few theatrical efforts met with only limited success. Reynolds was not successful in his legal work, either, and his finances grew desperate, culminating in bankruptcy in 1838. Plans to write a biography of Keats came to nothing, though he did assist Milnes in his efforts to do so. Dismissed from his editorship of *New Sporting Magazine* in 1840, Reynolds accepted a minor legal post on the Isle of Wight. Turning to alcohol for comfort, his health declined, and he died in 1852. His tombstone identifies him as "The Friend of Keats." (*See also* Satire.)

James Najarian

Works Consulted

Gittings, Robert. "The Poetry of John Hamilton Reynolds." *Ariel* 1 (1970): 7–17.

Jones, Leonidas. *The Life of John Hamilton Reynolds*. Hanover: UP of New England, 1984.

Richardson, Joanna. *Letters from Lambeth*. Woodbridge: Boydell, 1981.

Ricardo, David
(1772–1823)

The political economist David Ricardo was born in London in 1772. The child of Sephardic Jewish parents (his father was raised in Amsterdam and his mother in England), religion was important in his early life. As part of his informal early education, he seems to have briefly attended, a Jewish school in Amsterdam, where much of his father's family remained. His father, an affluent stockbroker, took Ricardo into his business at age 14. At 21, Ricardo married Priscilla Ann Wilkinson, a Quaker; as a result of the marriage and of his own decision to become a Unitarian, Ricardo's ties with both his family and his father's firm were severed. By that time, however, Ricardo had established good relationships with members of the Stock Exchange. He became a stockbroker— highly successful and wealthy by age 26.

After reading Adam Smith's *Wealth of Nations*, Ricardo abandoned his scientific hobbies in order to devote his attention to political economy. In a growing circle of friends, which included James Mill, Malthus, Bentham, and Thomas Thornton, Ricardo found a forum for discussion of economic and social theories. His first tract, *The High Price of Bullion, a Proof of the Depreciation of Bank Notes* (1810), was written in response to the depreciation of the pound, which Ricardo attributed to the lack of a gold standard. As a "bullionist," he believed that the supply of paper money should not exceed the metallic standard. He elaborated on his views in *Proposal for an Economical and Secure Currency* (1816), in which he proposed that the standard should be gold ingots (sometimes called "Ricardoes") rather than coins. His experience with the overproduction of paper money was firsthand; the excess of paper money meant that profitable loans could be made to the government, and Ricardo did very well on a loan he made to the government shortly before Waterloo.

In 1815, Ricardo published the *Essay on the Influence of a Low Price of Corn on the Profits on Stock*. He argued that the effect of the Corn Laws, which were being advanced by the powerful landowner interests, was to sustain high tariffs on the importation of grain, resulting in an increase in value of even marginal farmland. His theory, presented more extensively in his celebrated *Principles of Political Economy and Taxation* (1817), contended that wages do not drive prices up but that prices are due directly to the quantity and quality of the land available. Thus prices, in general, are determined by the cost of the food that is raised at the greatest expense. In his belief that landlords were motivated entirely by self-gain and returned little to society, Ricardo opposed Malthus, who viewed landlord farmers more positively.

Ricardo's "iron" law of wages stated that in the event that wages increase above subsistence levels, the laboring population will increase to a level where it will not be able to demand high wages, and it then will, again, decline in number. Wages will, therefore, stabilize at subsistence levels. He thus opposed the Poor Laws, since he believed that subsidies would, in the long run, benefit only the rich, who continue to collect profits no matter what the wage. Ricardo observed that the value of commodities was proportional to the amount of labor required to produce it. This theory was important to the emergence of a group called "Ricardian Socialists" and to the works of both Marx and Engels.

Ricardo also expressed concern, in an 1820 article in the *Encyclopaedia Britannica*, about national debt and advocated that governments should pay expenses immediately rather than deal with them through costly loans. In his *Plan for a National Bank* (1824), which eventually resulted in the Banking Act of 1844, he urged that an independent set of commissioners should take over, from the Bank of England, the responsibilities of issuing paper currency and managing the national debt.

In spite of Ricardo's antipathy toward landowners as a class, he became a substantial landowner himself. After retiring from the Exchange, he purchased Gatcomb Park, his country estate. From 1820 to 1823 he served as MP for Portarlington, an Irish borough that he had bought. In the House of Commons, his laissez-faire politics were clear; he spoke persuasively on behalf of free trade and voted consistently against taxes.

Ricardo's influence was profound on classical economics; his theories were widely advocated after his death by such writers as De Quincey. Ricardo's analytical methodology, which relied heavy on abstractions and modeling, was an important new approach in political economy. Although he and Malthus were opposed on many issues, they shared what might be called a pessimism about the economic progress of society.

Alan Rauch

Works Consulted

Blaug, Mark. *Ricardian Economics: A Historical Study*. New Haven: Yale UP, 1958.

Deane, Phyllis. *The State and the Economic System*. New York: Oxford UP, 1989.

Gootzeit, Michael. *David Ricardo*. New York: Columbia UP, 1975.

Heilbroner, Robert L. *The Worldly Philosophers*. 5th ed. New York: Simon, 1986.

Hollander, Jacob Harry. *David Ricardo: A Centenary Estimate*. 1910. New York: Kelley, 1968.

Niehans, Jürg. *A History of Economic Theory*. Baltimore: Johns Hopkins UP, 1990.

Paul, Ellen Frankel. *Moral Revolution and Economic Science*. Westport, CT: Greenwood, 1979.

St. Clair, Oswald. *A Key to Ricardo*. New York: Kelley, 1957.

Thompson, Noel. *The People's Science*. Cambridge: Cambridge UP, 1984.

Weatherall, David. *David Ricardo, A Biography*. The Hague: Nijfoff, 1976.

Robinson, Henry Crabb

(1775–1867)

Henry Crabb Robinson, whose life spanned the entire period of English Romanticism and a good part of the Victorian era, was acquainted with most of the important literary figures of his time and wrote about them in his voluminous *Diary* (1811–67). He was a friend of Coleridge, Lamb, and Southey and an intimate and traveling companion of Wordsworth, who dedicated to Robinson his *Memorials of a Tour to Italy*, the poems commemorating the journey they took together in 1837. He knew Goethe, Schiller, and others prominent in German literary circles and was an enthusiastic and knowledgeable promoter of German literature and thought in England. Goethe and Wordsworth were the poets whose genius he most admired and for whom he was a staunch apologist. Robinson's record of conversations with them and with Blake, whose work he also championed, is an invaluable source in the literary history of the age.

Robinson, called "Crabb" by his friends, was born at Bury St. Edmunds. Deprived of a public school education because his parents were Dissenters, he attended his uncle's academy at Devizes for a brief time and then was articled at age 15 to an attorney at Colchester. Literature interested him more than law, and during this period he began assiduously reading and keeping a diary (a pocket-diary, not the famous one of 1811)—two activities that became lifetime habits. One book from this period that had a profound influence on Robinson, as it also did on Wordsworth and Coleridge, was Godwin's *Political Justice*. It prompted one of Robinson's first articles, published in the *Cambridge Intelligencer* in 1795 and determined thereafter his idea of justice.

Between 1796 and 1800, Robinson divided his time between London and Bury, making desultory efforts to become a lawyer while weighing the possibilities of a literary career. He felt acutely his lack of a university education, and in 1800, with no other suitable prospects before him, he went to Germany to study and to travel. He remained in the country for five years, during which he became educated in German philosophy and literature not only by studying these subjects at the university in Jena, where he enrolled as a student, but also by meeting many of the contemporary artists and thinkers—among them Goethe, Schiller, Herder, Schelling, and Schlegel.

Two years after his return to England, Robinson was hired to report for *The Times* on the Napoleonic Wars and became the first British foreign correspondent. Following this stint as a journalist, he took up the study of law in earnest and was admitted to the bar in 1813. He practiced law for 15 years, earning a sufficiently comfortable income to retire in 1828 at age 53. Afterward, he traveled extensively, read omnivorously, and socialized frequently with his literary friends.

Of Robinson's record of all these pursuits in the *Diary*, his account of the books he read and the writers he knew remains of most interest today. Having been an early admirer of the *Lyrical Ballads*, which he said revolutionized his literary taste, he tended to be an appreciative yet not undiscriminating reader of Wordsworth's poetry. He did not share Goethe's high regard for Byron's verse, but he did concur with Lamb about Keats's poetic promise. An inveterate fiction reader, he kept up with and commented extensively in his journals on Scott's novels, as well as those of such later writers as Dickens and Thackeray.

Although Robinson felt that he was not particularly endowed with the "Boswell faculty," he did have a facility for capturing the essence of a conversation and for providing this as a means of insight into character. His interviews with Blake in 1825, in which he elicited the poet's sentiments on art and religion, are particularly illustrative of his ability to illuminate the writer through his words. In other instances, he brings Coleridge to life as both a person and a poet in his detailed report of that great talker's public and private discourses. Robinson also revealed important aspects of the quarrel between Wordsworth and Coleridge, including his own role in effecting a reconciliation. According to his *Diary* entries in May 1812, it was Robinson who played the part of peacemaker and go-between, even to the point of drafting a portion of the conciliatory letter that Wordsworth sent to Coleridge.

During his retirement, Crabb Robinson—sociable bachelor and avid student of the arts—was very fittingly instrumental in the founding of the Athenaeum Club and University College, London. In a fresco at the college, the diarist is pictured surrounded by more than 30 of his distinguished friends. It was largely to them that he owed such fame as he had; their debt to him was for the patient preservation of their words and deeds for posterity.

The last entry in Henry Crabb Robinson's *Diary*, dated January 31, 1867, reflects his reading of Matthew Arnold's *The Function of Criticism at the Present Time* and the thought that he might help Arnold understand Goethe's poetry. Robinson died a few days later in 1867, and was buried at Highgate Cemetery.

Guin A. Nance

Works Consulted

Baker, John Milton. *Henry Crabb Robinson of Bury, Jena, The Times and Russell Square*. London: Allen, 1937.

Morley, Edith J. *Crabb Robinson in Germany, 1800–1805*. London: Oxford UP, 1929.

———, ed. *Henry Crabb Robinson on Books and Their Writers*. 3 vols. 1938. New York: AMS, 1967.

———, ed. *The Correspondence of Henry Crabb Robinson with the Wordsworth Circle*. 2 vols. Oxford: Clarendon, 1927.

———, ed. *The Life and Times of Henry Crabb Robinson*. 1935. New York: AMS, 1970.

Robinson, Mary

(1758–1800)

Acclaimed as the English Sappho for her poetry and known as "Perdita" for her most famous dramatic role, Mary Robinson achieved prominence in her time as both author and actress. Between 1775 and 1800, she produced several volumes of poetry, earning the praise of Coleridge, who promoted her work to Southey. During the 1790s, she also published a succession of best-selling novels; the first, *Vancenza, or The Dangers of Credulity*, sold out in a day. (*See also* Satire.)

Through the benefaction of David Garrick and Richard Sheridan, Robinson made her acting debut in 1776 as Juliet at the Drury Lane Theatre, where for four seasons she was a popular attraction in a variety of roles. It was as Perdita in *The Winter's Tale* that she enchanted the young Prince of Wales (later George IV), who courted her as "Florizel" and subjected her to public scandal when he rejected her for another mistress.

Now more notable for her royal liaison than for her literature, Robinson was born in Bristol, the third child of Mary (Seys) and John Darby, a whaling captain who had been born in America. She began her education at the school in Bristol run by More's sisters and continued it at various schools in London, where her mother moved after Darby deserted the family.

At age 15, and while a student at Oxford House, Robinson was introduced to Garrick, who was sufficiently impressed with her beauty and talent to share the stage with her as Cordelia to his Lear. These plans for her debut failed to materialize when, a few months later, she married Thomas Robinson, an articled clerk considered by her mother to have good financial prospects. Soon after, his profligate ways landed him in debtor's prison, where Mary accompanied him with their infant daughter Maria. During this confinement, she returned to her childhood interest in writing poetry; fittingly, captivity was one of her themes. Through the patronage of the Duchess of Devonshire, she published her first collection, *Poems*, in 1775.

After the scandal caused by her affair with the Prince Regent, Robinson abandoned the stage and devoted herself to writing. In addition to novels and poetry (which she published under such pseudonyms as Laura Maria, Tabitha Bramble, Daphne, and Echo), she wrote plays and pamphlets. Her essay, "Thoughts on the Condition of Women, and on the Injustice of Mental Subordination," was written with the encouragement of Godwin, who approved of her social philosophy.

Robinson died at age 42, having been paralyzed from the waist down for the last 17 years of her life. Writing to Maria Robinson after her mother's death, Coleridge expressed his admiration for both Robinson's talents and her "heart."

Guin A. Nance

Works Consulted

Griggs, Earl Leslie. "Coleridge and Mrs. Mary Robinson." *Modern Language Notes* 45 (1930): 90–95.

Luria, Gina. Introduction. *Walsingham, or, The Pupil of Nature*. By Mary Robinson. New York: Garland, 1974: 5–9.

Molloy, J. Fitzgerald. Preface. *Mrs. Mary Robinson, Written by Herself*. By Mary Robinson. London: The Grolier Society, 1894: vii–xvii.

Robinson, Mary. Preface. *The Poetical Works of the Late Mrs. Mary Robinson*. London: Phillips, 1806: i–xvii.

Rogers, Katharine M. *Feminism in Eighteenth-Century England*. Urbana: U of Illinois P, 1982.

Rogers, Samuel

(1763–1855)

Samuel Rogers was once regarded as one of the leading poets of his generation. Byron ranked him one place below Scott and well above Wordsworth and Coleridge in his pantheon of living poets. Other judges were less generous, but Rogers was generally admired as a poet of talent and taste. Today, his verse is seldom read, and he is known almost exclusively for his caustic wit and famous breakfasts, as a connoisseur of art, but above all, as an associate and generous benefactor of some the leading literary figures of the early 19th century.

Born in London, the son of a Cornhill banker, Rogers was educated privately and, having rejected the Presbyterian ministry, joined his father at the family bank. His early reading included Johnson, Goldsmith, and Gray, who remained his models throughout his life. In 1781, he contributed essays to the *Gentleman's Magazine*. The following year, he wrote an unacted opera. At age 23, he published at his own expense an *Ode to Superstition* (1786), which sold 20 copies over four years. In the summer of 1789, Rogers, following the example of Johnson and Gray and inspired by the picturesque narratives of Gilpin, toured Scotland, keeping a detailed journal in which he compared his observations of landmarks with those of Gilpin. A Welsh tour two years later showed him using a personal picturesque vocabulary, but like Gilpin, Rogers remains a product of the Age of Reason and seems incapable of bringing to life the picturesque scenes he so ably describes.

This inability to go beyond his Neoclassical models in picturesque description is apparent in Rogers's best-known volume, *The Pleasures of Memory* (1792), which was heavily indebted to Goldsmith's *Deserted Village* and *The Traveller*. Despite its shortcomings, it caught the taste of the day and went through 15 editions by 1806. Byron maintained that the poem contains not a single vulgar line. On his father's death in 1793, Rogers inherited the family's share in the bank and with his newfound wealth began to cultivate the friendship of leading Whig statesmen, including Fox and Sheridan, and prominent radicals, such as Horne Tooke, Samuel Parr, Paine, and Priestley. He also bought paintings and sculpture and took advantage of the Peace of Amiens in 1802 to ogle the looted Italian art at the Louvre. In 1803, Rogers built himself a fine new house in St. James Street, Westminster, hiring Stothard and Flaxman to help decorate it. With many of his former banking duties now handed

over to a younger brother, Rogers was able to devote himself almost entirely to his poetry, connoisseurship, and society. His four-hour literary breakfasts became famous.

In 1804, an eight-year friendship came to an end with the death of Gilpin, whose influence on the young and impressionable Rogers was substantial. With Gilpin's passing, Rogers's life entered a new phase, which was given a fresh impetus through the poet's first meeting with Wordsworth and Coleridge, also in 1804. Coleridge instantly disliked him, but among Wordsworth, his sister Dorothy, and Rogers there grew an intimacy which, sustained by a regular correspondence, lasted for over 50 years. Rogers became a fervent Wordsworthian (though with reservations) and helped the poet obtain his Distributorship of Stamps. His reservations were such, however, that in 1826 he offered to edit a selection of Wordsworth's verse—an offer the poet politely declined. By 1842, Wordsworth's poetic style had altered sufficiently to suit Rogers's taste, and he declared every line of *Poems Chiefly of Early and Late Years* to be "pure gold."

Rogers first met Byron in 1811. The younger man ranked Rogers's work above his own, praised him in *English Bards*, and throughout his life regarded Rogers's verse as a healthy antidote to the wrongheadedness of the Lake School. Rogers in turn was intrigued by Byron and tried to imitate his style in *Jacqueline* (1814), a poem that shared the same volume as Byron's *Lara*. But Byron's pathological (and self-confessed) jealousy of Rogers showed itself in a virulent squib, published in 1833 as "Question and Answer," which poked fun at its victim's personal appearance and reputation as a poet and probably became known to Rogers during Byron's lifetime. Rogers's esteem for Byron fell mightily in Italy during a tour of 1822 to 1823, when the pair cavorted and swapped scurrilous gossip. Rogers, to his credit, never published a word against Byron.

In Italy, Rogers also met Shelley, whom he respected but never read. Keats, who had died a year earlier, does not merit a mention in Rogers's correspondence. Indeed, Rogers's tastes were essentially unadventurous, although Crabb Robinson's complaint that Rogers had no relish for any modern book seems an overstatement. He was steeped in the Neoclassicals but had no fuddy-duddy prejudices against contemporary writers. He was, for instance, an admirer of Beranger and Lamartine, met the latter but considered him affected. He was an early admirer of Goethe, but later turned against *Faust* and *Wilhelm Meister*. His tastes in art were equally eclectic. Visitors to his home marveled at the walls crowded with paintings of the highest excellence. He was a patron of Flaxman and collected work by Chantry; Turner he ranked above Lorrain and Poussin and censured the Art Union for encouraging mediocrity.

The brief *Human Life* (1819) probably contains the best of Rogers's work, although *Italy* (1830) turned out to be his biggest financial success. The work had originally appeared in two parts in 1822 and 1828—the first prompted by a tour in 1815, the second by that of 1822. Neither part sold, but when combined in one volume and reissued in lavish format with steel engravings by Turner and Stothard, *Italy* became one of the publishing coups of the century. With it, Rogers at last threw off the albatross-like influences of Goldsmith, Pope, and Cowper, and the poem's unforced colloquial style and many charming descriptive passages impressed many—including the young Ruskin, who found it an inspiration. Its wide popularity was such that it is hard to view Lady Blessington's description that "it would have been dished were it not for the plates" as anything but the product of malice.

Despite his success, Rogers's rank among his contemporaries in the Romantic age is probably lower than that of any other major figure, and it has been said that few other poets of equally modest endowments labored with such fastidious care to elevate mediocrity to something like distinction. But if his verse can be ignored, it would be foolish to deny him his rightful position as the premier patron and literary host of his age—a personality, more generous than sharp-tongued, who dominated 50 years of English letters right up to his death in 1855.

R.M. Healey

Works Consulted

Barbier, Carl Paul. *Samuel Rogers and William Gilpin*. New York: Oxford UP, 1959.

Clayden, P.W. *The Early Life of Samuel Rogers*. London: Smith Elder, 1887.

———. *Rogers and His Contemporaries*. 2 vols. London: Smith Elder, 1889.

Hale, J.R. *The Italian Journal of Samuel Rogers*. London: Faber, 1956.

Hill, Alan G., ed. *The Letters of William and Dorothy Wordsworth, 1821–1834*. 2 vols. Oxford: Clarendon, 1978–79.

Marchand, Leslie, ed. *Byron's Letters and Journals*. 12 vols. Cambridge: Belknap, 1982.

Marrs, Edwin W., ed. *The Letters of Charles and Mary Anne Lamb, 1796–1817*. 3 vols. Ithaca: Cornell UP, 1975–78.

Morley, Edith J., ed. *Henry Crabb Robinson on Books and Their Writers*. 3 vols. London: Dent, 1938.

Roberts, R. Ellis. *Samuel Rogers and His Circle*. London: Methuen, 1910.

Rosetta Stone

In the 18th and 19th centuries, there was a great interest in antiquities and a desire for more knowledge about ancient Egyptian history, religion, and art. (*See also* Antiquarianism, Orientalism.) When Napoleon made his expedition to Egypt in 1799, he took along scholars to study and catalog the relics. They discovered much, but the prize was undoubtedly what came to be called the Rosetta Stone. (*See also* Napoleon, Buonaparte.)

In 1799, at Rashid ("Rosetta"), near Alexandria, an officer in Napoleon's expedition found an irregularly shaped black basalt tablet. It was approximately 3.5 feet tall by 2.5 feet wide and bore hieroglyphics in three different types of characters, one of which was the ancient Greek alphabet. The other two were Egyptian hieroglyphics and a form of cursive Egyptian hieroglyphics called "demotic" script. After its discovery, the stone was made available to scholars interested in deciphering it. Their work laid the foundation for the later translation of Egyptian hieroglyphics.

English physicist Young was responsible for some of the earliest scholarly work done on the Rosetta Stone. He corrected the long-held but erroneous belief that hieroglyphs are symbols and realized that the direction in which figures faced determines the direction in which they are to be read. Nonetheless, he made mistakes in his work which prevented him from completely deciphering the tablet. That achievement was earned by Frenchman Jean-François Champollion. (*See also* Young, Thomas.)

In 1822, after many years of labor on the tablet, Champollion succeeded in fully translating it when he made his breakthrough discovery that hieroglyphs constitute a phonetic, syllabic, and alphabetic writing system, and he correctly determined the phonetic values of the signs. The key to his success lay in his determination that signs within a cartouche, an oval figure, spell the name of Ptolemy. Ptolemy's name appears in another bilingual relic, which helped to verify Champollion's finding. His study of Coptic, a form of ancient Egyptian written in Greek letters (with special signs created for sounds not used by the Greeks), aided his work.

Champollion determined that the text of the stone was a decree from Ptolemy V Epiphanes, which dealt with tax exemptions for priests and the establishment of a temple cult in Memphis.

When the French were defeated at the Battle of the Nile in 1801, the Rosetta Stone fell into the hands of the British. It is now exhibited at the British Museum.

Linda Jordan Tucker

Works Consulted

Francis, Sir Frank, ed. *Treasures of the British Museum*. London: Thames, 1971.

Greaves, Richard, *et al. Civilizations of the World: The Human Adventure*. New York: Harper, 1990.

Rowlandson, Thomas
(1757–1827)

Watercolorist, illustrator, and caricaturist, Thomas Rowlandson was one of the most prolific and popular artists of the late 18th and early 19th centuries. The extent of his work, which runs to several thousand drawings (widely scattered in public and private collections) and an equal number of prints, has never been comprehensively determined or methodically studied.

Rowlandson was born in London in 1757. His father was a cloth merchant who went bankrupt soon after his son was born and later became a printseller and publisher. The family was helped out by the father's brother, James Rowlandson, and his wife, Jane Chevalier, of French Huguenot descent. Through his aunt, Rowlandson became familiar with the French colony in Spitalfields—he learned to speak French fluently—and later inherited, and squandered, a large legacy from her. He went to school at the Soho Square Academy and was admitted to the Royal Academy Schools in 1772. He spent six years there, a precocious and highly talented student. He exhibited publicly for the first time in 1775.

Though he had training as a portrait painter, on leaving the Royal Academy he quickly established a reputation for pen-and-watercolor sketches and caricatures. He applied his fluent style to a wide range of social subjects—elegant spas and public meetings places, men's and women's fashions, military reviews, maritime scenes, coaching, field sports and rural pleasures, professional types and street people, gambling and dissipation; and he was repeatedly drawn to certain themes—age and youth, love and courtship, marriage and adultery, affectation and mortality. With equal ease, he depicts the buxom lubricity of young women and the gouty grotesqueness of old men; he delights in the exuberance of crowds and relishes the comedy of sexual voyeurism and innuendo. Notable designs that reflect his range and themes include *Vauxhall Gardens*, *Skating on the Serpentine*, *Greenwich Hill*, *The Swing or Rural Sports*, and the *Exhibition "Stare" Case, Somerset House*. In his political satires, he maintains an equally prolific output. Remaining nonpartisan, he responded to the major events of his day, domestic and foreign, and caricatured the leading participants.

Rowlandson attracted patrons for his drawings and enjoyed long and friendly relations with two of them. Henry Wigstead, amateur caricaturist and Bow Street magistrate, supplied him with many ideas and sketches, which Rowlandson then brought to completion. He also traveled widely with Wickstead, producing sketches based on these journeys to illustrate texts by his patron, for example *An Excursion to Brighthelmstone* (1790) and *Remarks on a Tour to North and South Wales* (1800). Matthew Mitchell, a Cornish squire and London banker, was equally generous in his patronage, and with him Rowlandson traveled in England and on the Continent.

Rowlandson also produced many prints for the commercial market. He worked mainly for the printsellers William Humphrey and Samuel William Fores and then in the last decades of his life, for Rudolph Ackermann. Book illustration had always been one aspect of his work; under Ackermann's guidance, it became a principal focus. In collaboration with Auguste-Charles Pugin, he illustrated the three-volume *Microcosm of London* (1808–10), and with William Combe, who wrote up the text to his designs, the three celebrated comic tours of Dr. Syntax. The first was *The Tour of Dr. Syntax in Search of the Picturesque*, published in 1809 in Ackermann's *Poetical Magazine* and in 1812 in book form. It is a burlesque on the cult of the picturesque that centers on the eccentric, clerical pedant Syntax, which was then expanded into the broader humor of the sequels, *The Second Tour of Dr. Syntax in Search of Consolation* (1820) and *The Third Tour of Dr. Syntax in Search of a Wife* (1821). The collaboration between Rowlandson and Combe also produced *The English Dance of Death* (1815–16), *The Dance of Life* (1817), and *The History of Johnny Quae Genus* (1822). For Ackermann, Rowlandson perfected what had always been his favored print medium, the aquatinted etching.

The quality of Rowlandson's work in his later years varies considerably. The delicacy and exactness of much of the illustrative work contrasts with the careless crudity of the numerous journeyman caricatures he produced for Thomas Tegg, for many of the designs of Henry Bunbury or George Woodward. But Rowlandson's work, whatever its quality, was in constant demand; his style is unmistakable: at its best it combines the playful spirit of the rococo and the earthy vigor of caricature. Rowlandson died in 1827.

Jonathan E. Hill

Works Consulted

Falk, Bernard. *Thomas Rowlandson: His Life and Art*. New York: Beechhurst, 1957.

Grego, Joseph. *Rowlandson the Caricaturist*. 2 vols. London: Chatto, 1880. New York: Collectors Edition, n.d.

Hayes, John. *Rowlandson: Watercolours and Drawings*. New York: Phaidon, 1972

Paulson, Ronald. *Rowlandson: A New Interpretation*. New York: Oxford UP, 1972.

Stephens, Frederick George, and Mary Dorothy George, eds. *Catalogue of Political and Personal Satires Preserved in the Department of Prints and Drawings in the British Museum*. 11 vols. London: Trustees of the British Museum, 1870–1954.

Royal Family

The British royal family moved from the Georgian age to the Victorian age during the Romantic period. The Georgian age began in 1714, when a prince from the small German state of Hanover replaced the last Protestant Stuart; it lasted until 1830. The political turmoil of the 17th century had resulted in an act of Parliament stating that the King of England must be a Protestant. Thus, the English Catholic princes of the Stuart family were rejected because of their religion. Twice, in 1715 and 1745, the Stuart pretenders attempted to depose the Hanoverians who now ruled England, but the rebellions always failed, although some support for the romantic Stuarts lingered. The British Whig party strongly supported the House of Hanover, and the harsh suppression of the Jacobite Rebellion in 1745 finally crushed active support for the Stuart cause.

The first of the Hanoverian kings, George I and George II, knew little of English customs and politics, and the cabinet and Parliament gained in power as a consequence. When George III became King in 1760 he was young, ambitious, and determined to rule independently. Despite this intention, his reign was fraught with problems, which included the Seven Years War and the American Revolution a few years later. The French Revolution brought further problems, and the rise of Napoleon forced England into a another deadly struggle with France, its long-time rival. Thus, George III was unpopular early in his reign; many blamed him for the loss of the American colonies and for other problems at home and abroad.

The first two King Georges were lusty men who had many mistresses, but George III also had a highly developed sense of duty, devoting himself to his family and to being a king, although he had married the dull and homely, by all accounts, Charlotte of Mecklenburg, with whom he produced 15 children. George III was the only member of the Hanoverian dynasty who remained faithful to his wife.

George III loved his sons and daughters but often had trouble with them. He kept his daughters strictly confined, but his sons were often in the public eye. Thoroughly anglicized, the royal princes were difficult characters, prodigal and profligate, and sometimes unstable to the point of madness. To the British populace, their crude appetites and brutal habits made the aging George III seem a paragon of virtue in comparison, who gained in popularity as he grew increasingly more frail in the 1780s.

The Hanoverians were notorious for having poor relationships with their heirs, and George III was no exception. In 1788, he lapsed into madness and seemed near death. The Prince of Wales and his supporters gathered to wait for it. The unnatural eagerness of the Crown Prince further increased public sympathy for George III and hatred for him and his brothers. Although the King never completely recovered, he lived until 1820, in his final years both mad and blind. His eldest son, the Prince of Wales, acted as regent during the last nine years of his reign.

Crowned at age 58, George IV, once floridly handsome, was now corpulent and dissipated. His unfortunate marriage, to the unpleasant Caroline of Brunswick, warped his life and encouraged further profligacy. (*See also* Brougham, Henry.) Their union produced only one child, the lively and beloved Princess Charlotte, who unfortunately died in childbirth at age 19.

George IV had waited too long to become king, and those years had not been well spent. Although he had ability, he was hated by the people and died a bitter and disappointed man. He was succeeded by his brother William, the Duke of Clarence, one of the more presentable sons of George III. "Sailor Billy" had a respectable but undistinguished naval career but a disreputable private life. After living with Jordan, the actress, for many years and fathering her 10 children, he realized only a legitimate child could inherit the throne. He discarded his mistress and married Princess Adelaide. Two brothers also rushed into marriage for the same reason; none of the seven royal princes, now middle-aged, had a living legitimate child. When Princess Victoria was born in 1819, her parents, the Duke and Duchess of Kent, won the race to produce a legitimate heir to the British throne.

Early on the morning of June 28, 1838, the 19-year-old Princess Victoria awoke to the sound of cannons fired to honor her coronation day. Reigning until her death in 1901, she restored public respect for the Royal Family as the Victorian age became a symbol for middle-class morality and the virtues of domestic felicity. (*See also* Napoleonic Wars, Regency, Upper Classes.)

Elsa A. Nystrom

Works Consulted

Briggs, Asa. *The Making of Modern England, 1784-1867, The Age of Improvement*. New York: Harper, 1960.

Durant, Will and Ariel. *The Age of Napoleon*. New York: Simon, 1975.

Halévy, Elié. *A History of the English People in the Nineteenth Century, England in 1815*. New York: Barnes, 1960.

Hibbert, Christopher. *The English: A Social History, 1066-1945*. New York: Norton, 1987.

Plumb, J.H. *The First Four Georges*. Boston: Little, 1975.

Shearman, Deidre. *Queen Victoria*. New York: Chelsea, 1986.

Russian Romanticism

Russian Romanticism is roughly contemporaneous with the major Western European movements, beginning in the early 1800s and lasting until the ascendancy of Realism in the 1840s. Indeed, there is much in common between Russian and European Romanticisms. The major Romantic genres (e.g., the ballad and the elegy) are well represented, as are the most popular themes: the Russians, too, are preoccupied with graveyards, magic, and the fantastic; they express the supernaturalism of the Gothic and the primitivism of Ossian; they write of political issues, of urbanization, of social revolution, and of nature. Yet there is a special problem at the heart of Russian Romanticism —

a contradiction between European influence and the heightened values of originality and nationalism that this influence carried. The Russian Romantics were painfully aware that the need to borrow from Western Europe conflicted with the need to develop a legitimate national literature of their own.

Russian Romanticism grew from this very conflict. Though the Russians uniformly rejected 18th-century Neoclassicism, they were otherwise split in two. Out of the Sentimentalism of the 1790s—centered around N.M. Karamzin (1766–1826)—came the *Arzamas* circle, a group devoted to the Westernization of Russia and the modernization of its language. To another circle—that of A.S. Shishkov (1754–1841)—this meant "Frenchification" and the embrace of European decadence; the Shishkovites instead promoted the value of an intrinsic Russian culture. The most important writers of the 1810s—V.A. Zhukovsky (1783–1852) and K.N. Batyushkov (1787–1855)—were members of the *Arzamas* circle. Zhukovsky, a poet and translator whose work set standards for 19th-century poetry, is generally regarded as the founder of Russian Romanticism. His highly successful 1808 translation of Bürger's *Lenore* presented a challenge to the conservative Shishkov circle. In 1815, P.A. Katenin (1792–1853) responded with his own translation of *Lenore*—colloquial and significantly retitled *Olga*—which began a polemical "battle of the ballad" that would run throughout the late 1810s.

It was Zhukovsky, too, who set the tone for the early 1820s with his translation of Byron's *The Prisoner of Chillon* (1821). This struck the ear of Russian Romanticism's greatest poet, A.S. Pushkin (1799–1837), who followed almost immediately with his poem, *The Captive of the Caucasus* (1822),

thereby initiating in Russia a vogue of Byronism. In the 1820s, the center of Russian letters shifted to Pushkin, a former member of the *Arzamas* group, who now led his own circle: the *Pushkin Pleiade* (as they later came to be known) included Zhukovsky, E.A. Baratynsky (1800–44), the "hussar poet" D.V. Davydov (1784–1839), and, later in the decade, another of Russia's great writers, N.V. Gogol (1809–52). In the 1820s, Pushkin produced such works as *Eugene Onegin* (written, 1823–31) and *Boris Godunov* (1825, published 1831). Pushkin was also involved, at least peripherally, in another group, the Civic, or Decembrist, Romantics, who advocated the inseparability of literature and politics; it produced passionate poetry written in a spirit of protest and included Katenin, as well as K.F. Ryleev (1795–1826), V.K. Kyukhelbeker (1797–1846), and A.A. Bestuzhev (1797–1837). Finally, the early 1820s saw the rise of the *Wisdom Lovers*, a group of metaphysically inclined "Russian Schellingians" who argued for the inseparability of literature and philosophy.

In the later 1820s, following the failed Decembrist Revolt of 1825, the literary world again changed shape. Decembrist Romanticism all but disappeared, and Pushkin's group became known as the Literary Aristocrats, dedicated to Western influence and standards of good taste. By the 1830s, they were polemically engaged with a group of Literary Plebeians—a group, largely of literary journalists, that promoted popular standards for literature. This movement included Bestuzhev (later a popular novelist under the name of Marlinsky) as well as the notorious journalist F.V. Bulgarin (1789–1859). In 1829, partially under the influence of Scott's Waverley novels (translated in the 1820s), Russian literature shifted largely to prose.

The Plebeian writers contributed Bulgarin's *Ivan Vyzhigin*—a forgettable novel that became Russia's first "best seller"—along with a flood of second-rate "Russian Walter Scotts," who rushed to gratify the nation's newfound craving for historical novels. The Literary Aristocrats also turned to prose: by 1829, Pushkin was writing the fiction that occupied his later years; M.Y. Lermontov's (1814–41) stories began to appear in the early 1830s, as did Gogol's. Among the historical novels of the 1830s appear Gogol's *Taras Bulba* (1835) and Pushkin's *The Captain's Daughter* (1836), two of the period's great works. Other major works of the decade include Pushkin's *Tales of Belkin* (1830) and *The Queen of Spades* (1833), and Gogol's comic play *The Inspector General* (1836). Though largely unnoticed, Russia poetry continued in these years. Pushkin's narrative masterpiece *The Bronze Horseman* (1833) is from the 1830s, as is most of Lermontov's best poetry. Also working at this time, though not appreciated until the 1850s, was F.I. Tyutchev (1803–73), a meditative, metaphysical poet who spent much of his life in Germany under the influence of German Romanticism.

The last works of Russian Romanticism are among its greatest. Only in the 1840s are Gogol's collected *Petersburg Tales* and *Dead Souls* (both 1842) published; and Lermontov's *The Hero for Our Time* appears in 1841. By this time, however, the great age of Russian Realism was approaching. The influential critic V.G. Belinsky (1811–48)—who rose initially among the Literary Plebians—now called for "Naturalism" and ushered in the realistic novel. Yet, as recent studies have shown, Russian Romanticism remained a strong presence in the "romantic realism" of writers like Dostoevsky, and all later Russians felt its influence. Significantly, this influence is also felt in Western Europe; particularly through the works of its three giants—Pushkin, Gogol, and Lermontov—Russian Romanticism succeeded in raising Russian literature for the first time to world status.

John Axcelson

Works Consulted

Leighton, Lauren G. *Russian Romanticism: Two Essays*. The Hague: Mouton, 1975.

Mirsky, D.S. *A History of Russian Literature: From Its Beginnings to 1900*. New York: Vintage, 1958.

Terras, Victor, ed. *Handbook of Russian Literature*. New Haven: Yale UP, 1985.

Tschizewskij, Dmitrij. *On Romanticism in Slavic Literatures*. The Hague: Mouton, 1957.

Sabbatarianism

Sabbatarianism refers to any religious movement that has as its goal the pure and strict observance of Sunday, the Christian Sabbath. In particular, it refers to certain groups that, from the late 15th to the late 19th centuries, attempted to restrict and to ban the performance of certain activities on the Sabbath. Most of these groups took literally the laws of the Old Testament regarding the Sabbath as a divinely ordained day of rest. By restricting all activity marked by work or pleasure, they worked to ensure that the English Sabbath would imitate the Jewish Sabbath. Because of the Evangelical Revival of the late 18th and early 19th centuries, by 1850 such Sabbatarian groups had succeeded in having legislation passed that forbade business meetings, sporting events, and theatrical performances from being held on Sundays.

The impulse toward Sabbatarianism may be traced to the English and Scottish Reformation of the 16th century. In 1595, Bound's *True Doctrine of the Sabbath* proposed that the English Sabbath be strictly observed according to the laws of the Old Testament. When James I issued *Book of Sports* (1618)—which allowed sporting events to be held on Sundays—the Sabbath question took on political as well as religious overtones. The controversy reached its height in 1677, when the Puritan Parliament passed the Sunday Observance Act, marking the English Sunday as a divinely, and legally, ordained day of rest. By 1780, various Sabbatarian societies sought legislation that would abolish Sunday trading, close Post Offices, and halt rail service as well as secure laws that would make it illegal to charge admission to places of entertainment on Sundays.

Henry L. Carrigan, Jr.

Satanism

"Satanism," in the Romantic sense, refers to a variety of literary and cultural phenomena. In a famous and provocative attack on the "Satanic school" of Byron and Shelley in the Preface to *A Vision of Judgement* (1820), Southey first described the poetry of his contemporaries as "satanic"—that is, impious and morally depraved. To many scholars of Milton in this century, "satanist" has referred pejoratively to Romantic critics of *Paradise Lost*, particularly Blake and Shelley, whose interpretations appear to glorify the character of Satan. Today, however, "Romantic Satanism" has lost much of this opprobrium and has considerably widened its range of reference. It has gained an almost facile explanatory power among critics who invoke it in discussions ranging from the psychopathological and protodecadent aspects of authors like Byron to the general theme of individualism, self-assertion, and sublimity in Romantic literature.

The Romantic perspective on Satan is so complicated and qualified that no writer of the age could be considered a true "Satanist." No one individual thoroughly idealized Satan or identified this closely with the figure: there was no "Devil's party" in the Romantic era. Nevertheless, many Romantic writers and artists were absorbed with the myth of Satan: the persistent fascination with the Devil evident in their work amounts to Romantic myths of Satan. In new or renovated guises, the figure of Satan looms large in the writings of Blake, Byron, and the Shelleys and appears in the work of many other English and continental writers, painters, and popular artists. Nearly rivaling Prometheus as the most characteristic mythical figure of the age, Satan assumes a prominence in the Romantic era never exhibited before or since.

The Romantic conception of Satan is largely the legacy of 18th-century English culture. In it, the myth of the adversary lost its religious authority and was reconstituted in the heroic, humanized, and sublime figure of Satan, represented in the contemporary criticism and illustration of *Paradise Lost*. Writers in the Romantic age further transform Satan from the traditional author of evil into a flexible symbol with functions ranging from exploring metaphysical rebellion, ethical transvaluation, and political revolution; to dramatiz-

ing human psychology and evil (often through the vehicle of the demonic *Doppelgänger*); to producing such literary effects as irony and satire. Among Romantic writers, Milton's Satan is typically reenvisioned as an unstable, radically ambiguous figure: an image of expanding consciousness, human desire, and rebellion, the Romantic Satan may alternately be a tragic figure, a tyrant, or a mocking voice of skepticism and irony. This Janus-figure constitutes the core of Romantic myths of Satan, embodied in several imaginative adaptations or displacements of Milton's Satan in the works of Blake, Byron, and the Shelleys.

Blake's satanic mythmaking falls into two overlapping phases: one transforms Satan into an image of desire; in the other, Satan is a myth of restraint. In the first, Blake introduced and develops satanic embodiments of the liberating, apocalyptic capabilities of humankind: the "voice of the Devil" in *The Marriage of Heaven and Hell* (1790–92) is Blake's mouthpiece for ethical transvaluation and the metaphysics of energy and the fiery, revolutionary figure of Orc in *America: A Prophecy* (1793), *Europe: A Prophecy* (1794), and *The Song of Los* (1795). The second phase begins in *The Book of Urizen* (1794). There, Blake introduces a new and antithetical satanic figure: as a conflation of Milton's God the Farther and Satan, Urizen combines the roles of tyrant, demiurge, and usurper. He attempts to tyrannize the "Eternals" by enslaving their energy to moral laws and by confining it within matter. After briefly introducing Satan as a surrogate for Urizen in Night VIII of *The Four Zoas* (c. 1797–1806), Blake makes him a mythic figure that comprehends the multiple forms of spiritual error that inhibit apocalypse in the major prophecies: the Selfhood, the Covering Cherub, and the Spectre of

Albion in *Milton* (c. 1804–08) and *Jerusa-lem* (ca. 1820). In his last illuminated book, *The Ghost of Abel* (1822), Blake identifies Satan with the bloodthirsty, accusing Elohim who demands the death penalty for the first murderer.

In his quasiautobiographical represen-tation of Satan, Byron appropriates and transforms two aspects of the myth: the rebel angel and the tempter. Emerging in the verse tales, the figure of the rebel angel focuses Byron's moral and metaphysical rebelliousness for the first time in the recast third act of *Manfred* (1817). There, Byron articulates the hero's independence of the powers of heaven and hell by adapting Satan's "the mind is its own place" speech (*Paradise Lost*), thus transforming the myth of Satan into a vehicle of the Romantic values of defiance and absolute moral and metaphysical autonomy. The other dimen-sion of Byron's myth of Satan first appears in *Cain: A Mystery* (1821); as an ambiguous reconception of Milton's Satan, the dra-matic character Lucifer possesses a di-vided mythic identity, comprising the con-tradictory roles of the rebel angel and the cynical Mephistophelean tempter. That is, Lucifer initially establishes himself as Cain's mentor in metaphysical rebellion, angrily declaiming against Jehovah's cosmic tyr-anny; yet Lucifer simultaneously destroys Cain. By mocking the futility of his postlapsarian existence, Lucifer drives Cain to the despairing rage that brings on the murder of Abel. *The Deformed Transformed* (1824) presents a similarly split satanic figure, the enigmatic "Stranger," who of-fers the suicidal protagonist supernatural assistance without demanding his soul; at the same time, his running commentary on life relentlessly punctures Arnold's aspira-tions and pretensions.

Shelley's fascination with envisioning cosmic, theomachic battles creates a double myth of Satan resembling Blake's: on one hand, he transfers diabolic imagery from his Gothic juvenilia to his first major po-ems, demonizing the God of Christianity in *Queen Mab* (1813) and *Laon and Cythna* (1818). But in the same works, by grafting satanic attributes onto other mythological figures, Shelley also begins to fashion what becomes a succession of heroically satanic antagonists to the tyrant-God. He blends Milton's Satan with Ahasuerus (*Queen Mab*) and introduces the Luciferean Spirit of Good in Canto One of *Laon and Cythna*. After this point, Shelley's myth of Satan darkens: although his boldest idealization of the fallen archangel appears in the essay *On the Devil and Devils* (1819). This does not carry over into his two major plays of the same period, *Prometheus Unbound* and *The Cenci* (1820). In both, the grafting of sa-tanic traits onto the protagonists produces the conspicuous and problematic residue of hatred, pride, and thirst for revenge in the regenerated Prometheus and the moral ambiguity of Beatrice Cenci's murder of her father, the domestic surrogate for God in *The Cenci*.

Frankenstein (1818) was published be-fore the major "Promethean" writings of Byron and Shelley were conceived, but Mary Shelley's novel can be viewed as a darkly satanic countermyth and palinode to their conception of the Romantic Prometheus. Victor Frankenstein's Promethean aspirations propel him along a satanic path of transgression, alienation, and destruction, while his creature's aban-donment and quest for revenge are mod-eled explicitly on the characterization of Milton's fallen angel.

Of the satanic figures among these writ-ers, only Blake's Orc and Shelley's Prometheus liberate and redeem (and even these are problematic); the others are dark, fragmented, or otherwise ambiguous mythic characters. The personifications of desire and rebellion seem inevitably to shade off into a more negative figure, and Satan consequently suggests an abortive mode in Romantic mythmaking. This is partly because of the inherent limitations of a traditional mythological figure: although dead for religious purposes, the myth of Satan nevertheless represents recalcitrant raw material for the project of fashioning new protagonists as the vehicles of new values, energies, and ideas. That is, a satanic identity tends to pull any unconventionally conceived character back into the Christian frame of reference, inhibiting the impulse to idealize and thoroughly renew the figure of Satan.

Contemporary history, too, certainly exerted pressure to darken the myth of Satan: the portentous, menacing energies and actions of major military and political figures (like Napoleon) were widely interpreted through the lens of demonic mythology. Satan represents an experimental figure in Romantic myths, most effective when he subverts, defies, or overthrows ideologies and value systems; he is less capable of transforming or renewing them.

Peter Schock

Satire

Satiric writing flourishes when sharply defined political and cultural controversies rage, as England, between the French Revolution and the passage of the Reform Bill, seems to demonstrate. At that time, hundreds of skillful verse and prose satires appeared, commenting on contemporary authors or politicians, burlesquing the Prince Regent's behavior or the fads of London society, condemning English "Jacobins," and calling for parliamentary reform.

Satiric poets distinguished for either their contemporary reputation or the craft of their work include (besides Byron) Wolcot ("Peter Pindar"), Gifford, Mathias, George Daniel, Moore, and Sir Charles and Lady Morgan. In this satiric poetry, certain subgenres can be isolated, such as the review of the literary world—examples include *Modern Poets, a Satire* (1791); Mathias's *The Pursuits of Literature* (1794–97); Thomas Dutton's *The Literary Census* (1798); Byron's *English Bards and Scotch Reviewers* (1809); *Modern Poets: A Dialogue in Verse* (1813); Daniel's *The Modern Dunciad* (1814); *Sortes Horatianae: A Poetical Review of Poetical Talent* (1814); *Tears of the Novel Writers, or, Fiction's Urn, a Satirical Poem* (1814); Leigh Hunt's *The Feast of the Poets* (1814); "Peter Pepperpod's" *The Literary Bazaar; or Poet's Council* (1816); *Poesy: a Satire* (1818); *The Press, or Literary Chit-chat* (1822, perhaps by James Harley); and "The Dunciad of To-Day" (1826), which has been attributed to Benjamin Disraeli.

The Baviad (1791) and *The Maeviad* (1794), Gifford's satires on the "Della Cruscan" poets, and Byron's first major satire, *English Bards*, employ harsh rhetoric, drawn from Juvenal and Charles Churchill (1731–64), which many contemporary satirists favored. Personal attacks on individual writers, like Gifford's mudslinging *Epistle to Peter Pindar* (1800) and Hunt's more clever *Ultra-Crepidarius: A Satire on William Gifford* (1823), illustrate how satires that apparently concentrate on the literary scene have political subtexts.

Political satire abounded, not only the many short pieces appearing in newspapers, but volume-length works as well. The well-known parodies of such poets as Southey, Erasmus Darwin, and Richard Payne Knight that appeared in the Pittite *Anti-Jacobin* newspaper of 1797 to 1798 satirize their perceived "Jacobinical" tendencies. Eaton Stannard Barrett's *All the Talents* (1807, signed "Polypus") was the most widely read of the works concerning the Whig ministry of 1806 to 1807. While they may lack literary pretensions, *The Political House That Jack Built* (1819, illustrated by Cruikshank) and the other pamphlets of verse that publisher Hone aimed at a popular audience amid the unrest of the late Regency reveal how satirical expression contributed to public debate on England's leaders (satiric texts dealing with royalty and politics often shared traditions of representation with the graphic satires being produced by such brilliant artists as Cruikshank and Gillray).

The Mohawks (1822), attributed to Sydney Owenson, Lady Morgan, and her husband Sir Charles, is a witty, angry satire on the Tory ministry and its press hirelings, employing the *ottava rima* stanza and the informal diction of Byron's *Beppo* (1818) and *Don Juan* (1819–24) for a scathing and direct attack on the political establishment.

The two most notable authors of verse satires on politics and royalty are Wolcot and Moore. Writing under the pseudonym "Peter Pindar," Wolcot was one of the most popular satiric poets between the 1780s and the early 19th century because of works like the mock-heroic poem *The Lousiad* (1785–95), which tells of George III's overreaction to finding a louse on his plate. Wolcot's other targets include the Royal Academy and Johnson's biographers, the latter being the subject of *Bozzy and Piozzi; or the British Biographers: A Town Eclogue* (1786), in which Boswell and Hester Lynch Thrale Piozzi contend for the privilege of writing Johnson's life. (Several other poets also wrote satires on the Royal Family using the "Pindar" pseudonym or a close variant of it.)

Moore's *Intercepted Letters: or, The Twopenny Postbag* (1813) and *The Fudge Family in Paris* (1818) are fictitious collections of letters that explore the injustices inflicted by the nation's Tory leaders; no less a personage than the foreign minister, Lord Castlereagh, was irritated by how Moore treated the Holy Alliance and the government's policies toward Ireland in *The Fudge Family*.

Poets wrote satires on the fashions of the day: *Modern Manners* (1793) by "Horace Juvenal" (Mary Robinson); Thomas Beck's *The Age of Frivolity* (1806); Croker's *The Amazoniad: or, Figure and Fashion* (1806); and Henry Luttrell's *Advice to Julia* (1820). Lady Anne Hamilton's *The Epics of the Ton: or, The Glories of the Great World* (1807) provide a series of generally unflattering character sketches of the nation's elite men and women. Not all satiric poetry was as harshly condemnatory as Gifford's or as bitter as the Morgans'; there were also numerous light, comic satires in the tradition of Christopher Anstey's *New Bath Guide* (1766), characterized by conversational language and such comic forms as anapestic couplets and awkward rhymes: John Cam Hobhouse's *The Wonders of a Week at Bath* (1811), N.T.H. Bayly's *Epistles from Bath* (1817), *Rough Sketches of Bath* (1817), and *Parliamentary Letters* (1818), and Hood and John Hamilton Reynolds's *Odes and Addresses to Great People* (1825). Luttrell's *Advice to Julia* and Byron's later satires have ties to this kind of benign satire, in which human error elicits laughter rather than disgust.

The period also saw significant prose satires, in addition to the novels that merely possess some satirical elements (such as Austen's) to concentrate on texts in which the satiric mode predominates and that depend on established traditions of prose satire. The period's most accomplished writer of Menippean satirical narratives was Peacock, whose six novels are indebted to Petronius, Lucian, and Voltaire; his characters represent positions on pressing issues in culture and politics, and they devote much time to discussion and debate. Isaac D'Israeli's *Flim-Flams! or, The Life and Errors of My Uncle, and the Amours of My Aunt!* (1805), a text with obvious similarities to *A Tale of a Tub* and *Tristram Shandy*, attacks excesses in science and scholarship. His son Benjamin Disraeli's *The Voyage of Captain Popanilla* (1828) is a fantastic voyage satirizing trends in British politics and culture, such as Benthamite utilitarianism, the colonial system, and the vogue for books dealing with fashionable life. Some effectively satirical prose narratives work by way of parody: Beckford's *Modern Novel Writing: or the Elegant Enthusiast* (1796) and *Azemia: A Descriptive and Sentimental Novel* (1797–98) burlesque prevalent styles in fiction, and Edward DuBois's *The Travels of St. Godwin* (1800) parodies William Godwin's *St. Leon* (1799) in order to attack that author's social doctrines.

The most obvious impediment to exploration of these texts is their rarity: important satiric works, such as Daniel's *Modern Dunciad* and the Morgans' *Mohawks*, have not been reissued since the early 19th century and can be found in only a few research libraries, although there are 20th-century editions or published photoduplications of the works of Byron, Gifford, Peacock, Bayly, Moore, Hunt, and Disraeli.

The uncertainty surrounding the authorship of the many anonymous and pseudonymous texts is comparably intimidating. The greatest difficulty, nevertheless, is intrinsic to the study of satire: reconstructing the contexts of individual satiric texts. To appreciate much satire from the 1790s, for example, requires a sense of how many Britons saw their values being challenged or threatened by factors that sometimes are superficially incommensurable: the events in France, movements like feminism, and literary modes like the Gothic.

Gary R. Dyer

Works Consulted

Beaty, Frederick L. *Byron the Satirist*. De Kalb: Northern Illinois UP, 1985.

Butler, Marilyn. *Peacock Displayed: A Satirist in His Context*. London: Routledge, 1979.

Carnochan, W.B. "Satire, Sublimity, and Sentiment: Theory and Poetics in Post-Augustan Satire." *PMLA*, 85 (1970): 260–67.

Carretta, Vincent. *George III and the Satirists from Hogarth to Byron*. Athens: U of Georgia P, 1990.

Hopkins, Kenneth. *Portraits in Satire*. London: Barrie, 1958.

Jackson, J.R. de J. *Annals of English Verse, 1770–1835: A Preliminary Survey of the Volumes Published*. New York: Garland, 1985.

Lockwood, Thomas. *Post-Augustan Satire: Charles Churchill and Satirical Poetry, 1750–1800*. Seattle: U of Washington P, 1979.

Rickword, Edgell, ed. *Radical Squibs and Loyal Ripostes: Satirical Pamphlets of the Regency Period, 1819–1821*. Bath: Adams, 1971.

Wardroper, John. *Kings, Lords, and Wicked Libellers: Satire and Protest, 1760–1837*. London: Murray, 1973.

Scott, John
(1784–1821)

John Scott is best known as the editor who first published Lamb's Elia essays and writings by other leading figures in the Romantic movement, including Hazlitt, Clare, "Barry Cornwell," Wainewright, and John Hamilton Reynolds. He is also remembered as a protagonist in a bitter literary controversy that led to the duel in which he died. (*See also* Essay; Journalism; Lockhart, John; Publishing.)

Born the son of an Aberdeen upholsterer, Scott showed an early ability for observation and imaginative description, and while at Aberdeen Grammar School, where Byron was a fellow pupil, he imbibed a love of literature. After leaving Aberdeen's Marischal College without a degree, he spent six years as a bank clerk in Glasgow, leaving in 1803 to enter the War Office as a temporary assistant clerk, a post held by Leigh Hunt at the same time. During this period, Scott began to write sporadically and considered becoming a playwright. Instead, in 1807, he became editor of the *Statesman*, a mildly radical evening paper, which John and Leigh Hunt had founded the previous year. Late in 1808, Scott left for the equally radical *Censor*, but after less than a year found a more congenial position as editor of the newly founded *Drakard's Stamford News*, the brainchild of radical Stamford grocer and versifier Octavius G. Gilchrist. Scott, with Gilchrist's moral and financial support, made *Drakard's* into a leading radical voice that campaigned for, among other causes, electoral reform, abolition of slavery, Catholic emancipation, the liberalization of the criminal laws, and freedom of the press.

In 1813, Scott returned to London as editor and owner of *Drakard's Paper*, modeling his new venture on the Hunts' *Examiner*. *Drakard's Paper* was renamed *The Champion* in 1814, and, as such, published early works by Thomas Barnes, who later became one of the *Times*'s greatest editors; dramatic and fine art criticism by Hazlitt; and irregular pieces by Lamb. *The Champion* was also enthusiastic about Walter Scott's first novel, *Waverley*, and the novels of Austen. John Scott had published two reformist pamphlets while editor of the *Stamford News*, but, in 1815, produced the full-length book *A Visit to Paris in 1814*—a

largely hostile record of his impressions of the postwar city—it ran to five editions.

A life-long admirer of Wordsworth, Scott first met the poet in 1815 at Haydon's studio, where he was sitting for a cast. Thereafter, the two became friends. Haydon, who persuaded Scott to take up the issue of the Elgin Marbles in the *Champion*, probably convinced Scott to recruit for his staff the precocious John Hamilton Reynolds, who gradually took over much of his editor's workload. In 1816, the product of a second continental tour, *Paris Revisited in 1815*, appeared; it was as well received as the first travel book had been, reaching four editions. Encouraged by this success, Scott turned to epic poetry, but the projected 1,800-line celebration of Waterloo was never completed, probably to the relief of many of his friends. Yet Scott was not finished with poetry. In 1816, he left with his family for a third continental tour. Devastated by the death of his son Paul in Paris, he quickly composed *The House of Mourning* (1817). The publication of this long poem greatly helped his finances, but critics were justifiably lukewarm. Scott's publishers discouraged him from attempting anything similar; Keats considered the poem vile.

Scott remained abroad, with occasional visits home, until 1819. The book about France, Switzerland, and Italy that he had left England to research was still incomplete, and by 1817 he had given up control of *The Champion*. He had also failed to land a lucrative post as dispatch writer for the East India Company and had instead been appointed editor of Baldwin Cradock and Joy's projected *London Magazine*. Intended to be a miscellany with a strong literary flavor, the *London* was a Whig and metropolitan alternative to the Tory *Blackwood's Magazine* conducted from Edinburgh by Lockhart and Wilson. The first issue appeared in January 1820, and contained work by, among others, Octavius Gilchrist, Horace Smith, Hazlitt, "Barry Cornwall," Wainewright, and Bernard Barton. Scott was contracted to contribute 48 of its 120 pages. Reynolds soon joined the others; and Lamb made his debut in August 1820. Though his tastes in poetry were unadventurous—he revered Wordsworth but had little taste for Shelley and Keats—Scott was a genuinely gifted editor. Few in his profession could, for instance, have handled such an eccentric maverick as Wainewright. Unfortunately, the pugnacity that had assured his success proved at last to be a fatal flaw.

Scott, late in 1820, decided to return the abuse heaped on Leigh Hunt and other "Cockneys" by the *Blackwood's* men over the years. He dubbed *Blackwood's* the "Mohock Magazine" and condemned Walter Scott (Lockhart's father-in-law) for using his influence to get John Wilson his professorship of moral philosophy. Battle ensued after events were set in motion that culminated in the hot-tempered Scott agreeing to fight a duel with Jonathan Christie, Lockhart's friend and agent. The opponents' first shot went wide, and at this point the duel should have been called off. But due to a mix-up between the seconds, Christie fired a second time, wounding Scott mortally. He died ten days later in a nearby tavern surrounded by his family and friends. He was 36.

R.M. Healey

Works Consulted

Jones, Leonidas M. *The Life of John Hamilton Reynolds*. Hanover, NH: UP of New England, 1984.

———. "The Scott-Christie Duel." *Texas Studies in Literature and Language* 12 (1971).

O'Leary, Patrick. *Regency Editor: Life of John Scott*. Aberdeen: Aberdeen UP, 1983.

Scott, Sir Walter
(1771–1832)

Sir Walter Scott's stature in Romanticism is colossal, yet anomalous. Both acclaimed for innovative genius and accused of narratological simplicity, Scott remains an enigmatic monument. Vanguard poet, iconoclastic novelist, pioneering critic, editor, biographer, and antiquarian, Scott in his life and works almost defies assessment in compass and singularity. Surely, however, his decisive legacy emanates from his sophisticated integration of traditional cultural antiquities into contemporary literary form. (*See also* Novel.)

Scott was born in 1771 into the ebullience of Enlightenment Edinburgh and to the comfortable middle-class circumstances of his lawyer father's home. Partly because of ill health, Scott spent much of his youth in the rural regions surrounding Edinburgh and in the Border country where he delighted both in the oral traditions of the region told to him by relatives and local folk and also in the printed ballads of Percy's *Reliques of Ancient English Poetry*. After attending Edinburgh High School, he matriculated at the University of Edinburgh to study classics, being called to the bar in 1792 after a supplemental course of legal studies. As an advocate, Scott mixed with the professional and literary classes in Edinburgh, and his interest in German literature inspired him to publish translations of Bürger's *Lenore* and *Der Wilde Jäger* (1796) and Goethe's *Götz von Berlichingen* (1979).

Two years after his marriage in 1797 to Charlotte Carpenter, Scott was appointed sheriff-depute of Selkirkshire in the Borders. There, assisted by John Leyden, James Hogg, and others, he collected from oral informants the folk songs and ballads that constituted most of his *Minstrelsy of the*

Scottish Border (1802–03), a three-volume, densely annotated collection that bespoke its editor's scholarly command of regional history and traditional culture. The *Minstrelsy* was an immediate success, and its publication established a new and important reputation for Scott, in poetic and antiquarian circles, which was sustained for 30 years. (*See also* Antiquarianism, Ballad.)

In 1805, his first original work, *The Lay of the Last Minstrel*, introduced a fresh poetic flavor to an audience still digesting Wordsworth and Coleridge's revolutionary *Lyrical Ballads*. *The Lay* takes the form of a ballad epic, focusing on heroic events of the English-Scottish Border's historical past through the traditional storytelling prism of the minstrel of the title—a methodology that echoes the *Minstrelsy*'s ballads and anticipates Scott's Waverley novels' purview and construction. The approach and success of *The Lay* were effectively duplicated in *Marmion: A Tale of Flodden Field* (1808) and *The Lady of the Lake* (1810), two more ballad epics straddling, respectively, the historical kingdoms of Scotland and England and the division between Highlands and Lowlands. Already, Scott was programmatically and sequentially exploring cultural history and geography—era by era, region by region— through time and space, an approach that again anticipates his Waverley novels project.

His career to date had brought sufficient wealth and fame that in 1812 Scott began planning the construction of Abbotsford, a stately Border country mansion that became his pride, joy, and, in part, ruin. Scott's poetry never again reached the popular or critical heights of *The Lady of the Lake*, and although the later verse romances of *Rokeby* (1813), *The Bridal of Triermain* (1813), *The Lord of the Isles*

(1815), and *Harold the Dauntless* (1817) met with some success, it was clear to Scott that his poetic career would not be like Byron's meteoric ascent.

Scott's career as a novelist began auspiciously in 1814 with the anonymous publication of *Waverley*, a fictional treatment of the historical events surrounding the 1745 Jacobite Rebellion led by Charles Edward Stuart. Subtitled "'Tis Sixty Years Since," *Waverley* reconstitutes history in the fictionalized context of the Scottish Highlands and among the clans and warrior-chief followers of the Young Pretender. Scott thus romanticizes both time and place in *Waverley*, yet carefully infuses both with realistic detail—an approach to novel writing that was to become the anonymous signature of "The Great Unknown."

Waverley's best-selling success was quickly and plentifully followed by a succession of novels set in historical Scotland and composing Scott's finest and most original achievement. *Guy Mannering* (1815) and *The Antiquary* (1816) were followed by *The Black Dwarf* and *Old Mortality* (1816). The series of important Scottish novels then continued with *Rob Roy* (1817), *The Heart of Midlothian* (1818), *A Legend of Mon-trose* (1819), *The Bride of Lammermoor* (1819), *The Pirate* (1821), and *Redgauntlet* (1824). Each of these novels, together with the stories in *Chronicles of the Cannongate*, first series (1827), is situated principally in a particular region of Scotland and from the mid-17th century to the late-18th century, a historical and geographical span that allows Scott to explore the distinctive role played by traditional culture within larger historical events. Throughout this remarkable series of novels, Scott's program is to clash, then reconcile local cultural contexts with larger historical events. (*See also* Bonington, Richard Parkes; Nationalism; Turner, Joseph Mallord William.)

Before his Scottish novel output was over, Scott began to feel that although its scope was rich to mine, it could not be sustained indefinitely, and so he pushed his fictional focus further back in time and expanded it to include England as well as Scotland. This second historical avenue of exploration began with *Ivanhoe* (1820), a tale of Saxon-Norman intrigues (principally among King Richard I, his brother John, Robin Hood, and Ivanhoe), and progressed most notably through *Kenilworth* (1821), *The Fortunes of Nigel* (1822), *Quentin Durward* (1823), *The Talisman* (1825), and *Woodstock* (1826). Again, although now viewing a more distant past and farther-flung settings, Scott's method was to trace both continuity and change over both time and place by focusing on the clash of competing cultural traditions.

While the success of this widened fictional focus reenergized Scott's writing and for a time alleviated some financial difficulties arising from early business failures and major expansion of the Abbotsford estate, it could not avert the ultimate collapse of his costly investment in the troubled printing and publication businesses of Ballantyne and Constable. In 1826, he was declared bankrupt, agreeing under the conditions of creditor settlement to pay off his debts by continued writing. From this point on, Scott wrote under the compounding pressure of deteriorating health with a discipline and fortitude described movingly in his *Journal*, begun in 1825 and kept until his death in 1832. Although the novels of this period—*The Fair Maid of Perth* (1828), *Anne of Geierstein* (1829), *Count Robert of Paris* (1831), and *Castle Dangerous* (1831)—are not considered among his best, their sales, together with those of collected editions ultimately, balanced his financial affairs upon settlement of his estate.

The extraordinary industry that char-acterized the length of Scott's career also produced significant expository works that included critical editions of Dryden (1808) and Swift (1814), lives of James the First (1811) and Napoleon Buonaparte (1827), a history of Scotland (1829–30), and an epistolary treatise on demonology and witchcraft (1830). Scott's renown, however, is fastened properly to his poetic and fictional works, which, though diverse, disclose an integral artistic mission to fuse the modes of oral tradition and literature.

It is evident that in his *Minstrelsy of the Scottish Border* and in the long narrative poems of his early career Scott was at pains to delineate and preserve certain items of traditional cultural expression. The copious but fragmented notes that accompany these works, however, point both to his artistic inclination to elaborate on such items and to the correlated restrictions of the poetic form. His switch to the novel form, with its special freedoms for development of character and narrative context, permitted Scott ultimately to dramatize, through juxtaposition, the historical conflict—even competition—between traditional or folk culture and mainstream or high culture.

In his novels, Scott imbues this conflict with significance and intensity through an imaginative but meticulously authentic representation of traditional texts, textures, and contexts. Tangibly real in its live, culture-based processes while often essentially romantic in its themes and concerns, folk narrative and its narration thus constitute simultaneously both fact and fiction. Scott comprehensively exploits this fertile fusion of Romanticism and realism, establishing in the process folk culture's artistic versatility and stature as a credible counterpart to purely literary art.

In harnessing the muse of tradition to speak and sing through his characters,

Scott thus follows both in the wake of MacPherson and Burns and in the slipstream of Wordsworth and Coleridge. Scott has, however, less in common with his English Romantic contemporaries than with the grand-scale regional fiction of such writers as Hardy and Faulkner. Like them, he goes beyond mere preservation of folklore to artistically deploying it in dynamic, meaningful relation to the more dominant cultural constructs. A resolute champion of the individual and of the culturally disenfranchised, Scott's most enduring legacy is one of liberal compassion and vast humanism.

Jack Truten

Works Consulted

Anderson, W.E.K., ed. *The Journal of Sir Walter Scott.* Oxford: Clarendon, 1972.

Brown, David D. *Walter Scott and the Historical Imagination.* Boston: Routledge, 1979.

Goslee, Nancy Moore. *Scott the Rhymer.* Lexington: U of Kentucky P, 1988.

Grierson, Herbert John Clifford, ed. *The Letters of Sir Walter Scott.* London: Constable, 1932.

Johnson, Edgar. *Sir Walter Scott: The Great Unknown.* New York: Macmillan, 1970.

Kerr, James. *Fiction Against History: Scott as Storyteller.* New York: Cambridge UP, 1989.

Lascelles, Mary. *The Story-Teller Retrieves the Past.* Oxford: Clarendon, 1980.

Lockhart, J.G. *Memoirs of the Life of Sir Walter Scott, Bart.* Edinburgh: Cadell, 1837–38.

Millgate, Jane. *Walter Scott: The Making of the Novelist.* Buffalo: U of Toronto P, 1984.

Mitchell, Jerome. *Scott, Chaucer, and Medieval Romance.* Lexington: U of Kentucky P, 1987.

Parsons, Coleman O. *Witchcraft and Demonology in Scott's Fiction.* Edinburgh: Oliver, 1964.

Reed, James. *Sir Walter Scott: Landscape and Locality.* New Jersey: Humanities, 1980.

Wilt, Judith. *Secret Leaves: The Novels of Sir Walter Scott.* Chicago: U of Chicago P, 1985.

Sculpture

The arrival in 1802 of 15 crates containing almost all of the Parthenon sculpture into Plymouth harbor marked a dramatic change in the tradition of sculptured art in England. England's increasing popularity with the Turks after Napoleon's defeat in Egypt (1801) allowed the Earl of Elgin, ambassador to Constantinople, to attain permission to excavate and even export Greek antiquities. The additional 1803 importation of the Elgin Marbles enhanced, both in England and on parts of the Continent, a minor renaissance of classical sculpture and architecture. Lord Elgin's interest in antiquities abroad coincided with increasing public interest among the English in sculpture. The later purchase of the Parthenon friezes was symptomatic of England's changing views toward private collecting. The Romantic period underwent not so much a clearly delineated change in sculpture as it did a subtle but perceptible change in artistic sensibilities. (*See also* Elgin Marbles.)

At the beginning of the 19th century, a dramatic increase in public support of sculpture supplanted private patronage, a crucial event in the history of English sculpture. Between 1802 and 1812, approximately £40,000 of public funds had been allotted by Parliament for national monuments memorializing military champions and statesmen, in addition to the large sums spent by the Corporation of London and by subscriptions raised in cities throughout England. By 1830, the money increased significantly. Prior to the 19th century, sculpture had been a status symbol in aristocratic and middle-class homes and gardens. Practical considerations, such as overcrowded family chapels and the cultural changes brought about by the

Napoleonic Wars, caused private patrons to forgo additional elaborate memorials. Bust monuments remained popular, and less frequently patrons commissioned a standing figure. Even the number of commissions for large compositions with several figures interacting, formerly commonplace in village squares and churches throughout the country, largely declined.

As early as 1773, Sir Joshua Reynolds and others of the Royal Academy attempted to obtain permission to adorn St. Paul's Cathedral with sculptures in the tradition of Westminster Abbey. Both the Dean of St. Paul's and the Bishop eventually came to an agreement that made the cathedral a showcase of some of the period's finest work. In a precedent-setting move, all designs had to meet the approval of the Committee of the Royal Academy. The academy elected a separate committee—consisting of the architects Sir Robert Smirke, James Wyatt, and George Dance; the painter James Barry; and two of the century's most distinguished sculptors, Thomas Banks and John Bacon, the Edler. Strife between church leaders and committee members and concern among government officials (including Prime Minister Henry Addington) that the academy should allocate public money led Parliament, eager to accelerate the dedication of monuments promoting British valor, to appoint its own committee. In 1802, the Treasury organized the Committee of National Monuments, later dubbed "the Committee of Taste," composed of seven men, none of whom were artists. Their responsibilities included allocating funds, selecting designs and sculptors, and determining the project's size. Scholars assume that the committee's influence was minimal, although the precise effect it had on the period's most significant compositions is unclear.

Just after the middle of the 18th century, the impact of Neoclassicism began to be felt on English sculpture, having already influenced both architecture and painting. Because the credo of the Neoclassicists called for a return to the purest styles of antiquity and especially to that of the Greeks, it rejected baroque and rococo. Greek originals of the finest quality, however, were nearly nonexistent or unavailable for study either in England or on the Continent. The most important artists and writers had not yet visited Greece, and the Napoleonic Wars helped further to isolate Europe and, more specifically, England. Although Neoclassical views had mostly been based on lesser Greek artifacts circulated out of Italy, many of which later proved to be second-rate imitations, a more subtle influence governed the outcome of Neoclassicism in England. In perhaps an unconscious turn from the rationalism of the 18th century, the disciples of this new school combined their enthusiasm for Greek sculpture with a passion for sentiment, in part, the fertile ground from which the Romantic movement later sprung. Additionally, some scholars believe that a nostalgic view of the past inheres in Romantic ideology.

Sculpture in England not only lagged behind sculpture on the Continent, it also lagged behind the other fine arts. Because the veneration of classical arts had been more persistent in England in the second quarter of the 18th century than anywhere on the Continent, Neoclassicism in England lacked the novelty that enhanced its popularity elsewhere in Western Europe. Moreover, the combination of the antique and the baroque developed as early as 1720 by Louis François Roubiliac in his classical busts, Michael Rysbrack, and Peter Scheemakers dictated English taste in sculpture for much of the century. Near the end of the century, however, English sculpture entered a transitional phase at the hands of a young generation of sculptors, among whom Sir Richard Westmacott and Francis Chantrey are the most prominent. Nowhere in Europe was sculpture influenced by such crosscurrents of style. Often a wide range of disparate elements informs the sculpture of the late 18th and early 19th centuries, while no eclectic school as such ever solidified. Sculptors of the time experimented widely, influenced at once by the persisting imprint of the baroque, the reserved grandeur of Renaissance painting, the slowly emerging Neoclassicism, the picturesque movement, and, significantly, the closely associated rustic genre, a precursor to Romanticism, found in the animal paintings and sculpture of George Garrard, the stable scenes of Morland, and the naturalistic animal sculptures of Anne Seymour Dramer. Like rustic, the term "picturesque" described more a movement of taste than any clearly delineated aesthetic category. The picturesque, the last anticlassical movement before Romanticism, celebrated the free inventions of sculpture, the asymmetry of art and architecture, and the painterly. (*See also* Picturesque.)

Not until Neoclassicism arrived on the scene as the leading school did the eclectic tastes of early 19th-century sculptors largely disappear. But the Romantic influence remained. England's 1816 purchase of the Parthenon friezes made available for the first time in Western Europe an important, verifiably authentic, Greek collection. Firsthand study of the friezes led to questions about the ideas and concepts that previously governed classical art and provided new dimensions to the concept of nature. In his autobiography and miscellaneous writings, the painter Haydon captured for the entire art community of En-

gland the Romantic fascination and overtones associated with the Elgin Marbles when he said they projected nature as the basis of all. Their presence provided new impetus specifically in the world of sculpture.

Francis Chantrey (1781–1841), in his memorials to Generals Hoghton, Bowes, and Cadogan, pursued the Attic artist's motif in the Parthenon frieze of covering the ground of his compositions with fallen and overlapping figures, staggered profiles, one behind another. The influence of the Elgin Marbles can be seen in William Theed's composition of *Hercules Taming the Thracian Horses* (c. 1816) in Buckingham Palace, and in the monument to General Sir William Ponsonby (1816–20), begun by Theed and completed by Edward Hodges Baily.

John Bacon (1740–99), Thomas Banks (1735–1805), and Flaxman long remained three of the 19th century's most influential sculptors. Although much of Bacon's career evidences stagnation through repetitious sculptures, he produced some of the period's most stunning works. His masterpiece, at London's Guy Hospital, is the *Monument to Thomas Guy* (1779); it depicts two life-sized figures framed by an ebony marble arch. The elegantly dressed Thomas Guy, founder of Guy's Hospital, grasps the hand of a half-naked ailing man, whose legs break through the plane established by the arch. The gracefully linked hands and the intensity of two men's shared gaze draw the sculpture together, while poignantly betraying the Romantic sentiment of the time. Southey, England's Poet Laureate, lauded Banks as one of the best sculptors England ever produced, if not one of the most neglected. Often proclaimed his best work for its graceful movement and pastoral beauty, the *Monument to Mrs. Hand* (1785) depicted the death of the young Mrs. George Hand in the arms of her grieving husband. Of the three sculptors, only Flaxman rose to international fame. His design and execution of the *Monument to the 1st Earl of Mansfield* (1795–1801) became the first free-standing or "insulated" monument in England. Unlike traditional monuments with a collection of figures built out of a central pyramid, his monument comprises independent figures, self-sufficient in form and balance.

Sir Richard Westmacott (1775–1856), the son of sculptor Richard Westmacott, the Elder, and Chantrey are both sculptors of merit and influence. Although Westmacott had every advantage of parentage, wealth, and education in Rome, in the final analysis Chantrey proves the more enduring artist. Born to a family of modest income and almost entirely self-educated, Chantrey rose through the ranks to a high position among England's elite artists. His *Monument to David Pike Watts* (1817–26) captures his keen awareness of human behavior and reserve of sentiment that popularized his work. Only the dress of the kneeling and grieving daughter, boldly contrasted with the contemporary dress of the dying father, reveals Chantrey's fondness for classical elements. Westmacott's *Monument to the 7th Earl of Bridgewater*, probably inspired by the pastoral settings of Florentine Renaissance art, portrays a young mother cradling an infant in her lap under the insistent and tender gaze of a boyish father. The old shepherd figure and dog in the background add to the family composite an agrarian sentiment, popularized by such writers as Wordsworth.

Recent assessment of England's late 18th- and early 19th-century sculpture reveals its rich and diverse origins. Having developed in a milieu of revolution and isolation, its eclectic nature resists easy analysis. A sign of the ongoing influence of the period's sculptors, however, can be found in the Victorian habit of using their work as models.

Gregory S. Jackson

Works Consulted

Boase, T.S.R. *English Art, 1800–1870.* Oxford: Clarendon, 1959.

Burke, Joseph. *English Art, 1714–1800.* Oxford: Clarendon, 1976.

Gunnis, Rupert. *Dictionary of British Sculptors, 1660–1851.* London: Odhams, 1953.

Roston, Murray. *Changing Perspectives in Literature and the Visual Arts: 1650–1820.* Princeton: Princeton UP, 1990.

Whinney, Margaret. *Sculpture in Britain: 1530 to 1830.* 2nd ed. Rev. by John Physick. London: Penguin, 1988.

———. *English Sculpture, 1720–1830.* London: HMSO, 1971.

Sentimentalism

Manifested in mid-18th-century theology, literature, and critical thought, Sentimentalism is a cultural movement based on the notion of the primacy of emotion and innate moral sentiment. The term is used interchangeably with "sensibility" and "sentimentality" to denote indulgence in feeling and sympathy.

Reacting against Enlightenment emphasis on reason, Sentimentalism originally incorporated the Cult of Sensibility (1740s–70s), which was based on sentiment—the belief in innate virtue and social benevolence as evidenced by displays of feeling. However, sentiment deteriorated into artificial sentimentality. In the 1780s to 1790s, when Sentimental literature became extravagant to the point of evoking excessive emotionalism (sensibility) rather than moral reflection (sentiment), the term was used pejoratively. Today, the flexible term suggests overreaction, vulgar feeling, tender feeling, and humanitarianism.

Sentimentalism developed from such

philosophical tracts as the second Earl of Shaftesbury's *Characteristics* (1711), Hume's *Treatise of Human Nature* (1740), Adam Smith's *Theory of Moral Sentiments* (1759), as well as Rousseau's *La Nouvelle Heloise* (1761) and *Emile* (1762), all of which postulated that sympathy (altruism) was a natural impulse to ensure social harmony. Exploiting domestic situations and the rhetoric of virtue, much Sentimental literature attracted a middle- and upper-class readership that indulged in feelings of moral superiority and joyous benevolence resulting from their compassion for others less fortunate.

Even though Henry MacKenzie's *The Man of Feeling* (1771) demonstrates the archetype of the ultrasensitive hero too refined for coarse society, Sentimentalism is particularly ascribed to women, thought to be endowed with finer sensibility. As in Richardson's classic novels *Pamela, or Virtue Rewarded* (1740) and *Clarissa* (1748), which established the Sentimental formula of persecuted innocence, the female body simultaneously is an object of male passion as well as an indicator of female virtue. Inherent in Sentimental literature is the belief that the body is the vehicle by which virtue and sympathy manifest themselves. Sensation filters its way through one's person through dramatic gestures, looks, sighs, tears, easy illnesses, spasms, swoons, and other physical exhibitions of extreme emotion. The finer the sensibility, the more dramatic the display of feelings. Ultimately, in both men and women, the body became susceptible to disease, hysteria in women and melancholia in men, even to the point of suicide, as in Wolfgang von Goethe's *The Sorrows of Young Werther* (1794), and pathetic death, as in *Clarissa* and *The Man of Feeling*.

Sentimentalism affected most literary genres. Reacting to the aristocratic mode of Restoration theater, Sentimental drama was largely melodramatic pathos dealing with social problems, and middle-class audiences tearfully took to their handkerchiefs for Richard Cumberland's tragedies *The Mysterious Husband* (1783), *The Captive* (1790), and *The Jew* (1794) and Colley Cibber's comedies *The Careless Husband* (1704) and *Apology* (1740).

As demonstrated in early ballads, devotional and meditative verse, and poems of personal yearnings, Sentimental poetry became maudlin, obsessed with death. Edward Young's *Night Thoughts* (1742–46) and Thomas Gray's elegies exalt melancholia and the poet's isolation. Such stress on personal introspection, passion, and the sublimity of feeling rather than on rational thought attracted Romantic poets who believed poetry excited the passions. Later, Romantic poets themselves sentimentalized sensitivity as the supreme quality of the artist.

Primarily, Sentimentalism patterns the development of the novel, from Richardson's epistolary formats to Sterne's *A Sentimental Journey* (1768) and *Tristram Shandy* (1767) and Goldsmith's *The Vicar of Wakefield* (1766) to Austen's *Sense and Sensibility* (1811), which mocked sentimental overreaction in the drawing room. Sentimental fiction became so popular mid-century that lending libraries multiplied rapidly. Sentimental novels were marked by stock characters (a chaste maiden under siege by an artful rake, avaricious parents, and faithful servants), histrionics, and unrealistic rhetoric to heighten human action and feeling. When fostering emotion, rather than instruction, became the true purpose of Sentimental fiction, many women, especially young girls, were warned to avoid reading novels, considered evil influences on young girls' minds and moral aptitude, swaying young minds and hearts to excesses of emotion, instability, and way-wardness rather than to moral rectitude and duty as was their original intent. Sentimental novels were attacked as amoral, anti-Christian, and overly sexual. *The Curse of Sentiment* (1787) and *The Illusions of Sentiment* (1788) warned against sensibility. Fiction writers such as Wollstonecraft, who wrote *Mary, A Fiction* (1788), attacks sensibility in *A Vindication of the Rights of Woman* (1792).

Considered pre-Romanticism by some critics, Sentimentalism attracted Romantic poets with the idea that the artist has superior sensibility. The man of feeling in Sentimental literature becomes the sensitive individual in Romantic fiction. Celebrating feelings of both joy and misery, Romantic writers are concerned with many of the antirational underpinnings of Sentimentalism but not with its moral didacticism. Romantics emphasize the imagination and independence, not moral instruction for social concerns.

Norma B. Goldstein

Works Consulted

Brown, Herbert Ross. *The Sentimental Novel in America, 1789–1860*. Durham: Duke UP, 1940.

Kaplan, Fred. *Sacred Tears, Sentimentality in Victorian Literature*. Princeton: Princeton UP, 1987.

Kelly, Gary. *English Fiction of the Romantic Period, 1789–1830*. New York: Longmans, 1989.

Mullan, John. *Sentiment and Sociability, The Language of Feeling in the Eighteenth Century*. New York: Oxford UP, 1988.

Todd, Janet. *Sensibility, An Introduction*. New York: Methuen, 1986.

Weissman, Judith. *Half Savage and Hardy and Free, Women and Rural Radicalism in the Nineteenth-Century Novel*. Middletown: Wesleyan UP, 1987.

Shakespeare

Romantic poets and critics looked into Shakespeare and saw themselves. With pleasure and delight, they found in Shakespeare not an Elizabethan playwright but the quintessential Romantic poet. Such unreserved reverence for the Bard had not always been the case. Though critics of the 17th and 18th centuries deeply admired Shakespeare, they insisted on his shortcomings: he violated Aristotle's rules; his plots were sloppy and haphazard; his language was excessive and uncontrolled; his humor was gross and unseemly; historical and geographical inaccuracies abounded. He was envisioned as an untutored genius living in a rude and barbarous age, excelling in genius but lacking in judgment, creative but undisciplined, a child of nature ignorant of the rules of art. Efforts were made to correct and improve Shakespeare's works. In his edition of the plays, Pope excised lines and passages he found objectionable, suspecting Shakespeare could not have written them. Such dramatists as Dryden and Tate even rewrote certain plays, *Troilus and Cressida* and *King Lear*, respectively, in order to bring them into line with the Neoclassical taste for a transparent moral order and poetic justice.

In the Romantic age, however, the reputation of Shakespeare underwent a radical change. He was reenvisioned not merely as the child of nature but as a deliberate and disciplined artist—a conception that has tended to prevail ever since.

The Romantic reassessment of Shakespeare was spearheaded by the German critic Schlegel. In opposition to the prevailing Neoclassical literary standards, Schlegel argued in his *Lectures on Dramatic Art and Literature* (1809–11) that artistic and literary standards are not fixed or absolute but relative to historical circumstances. Schlegel claims there have been two major artistic periods—Classical and Romantic. Each period in Schlegel's view is quite different but artistically equal. Classical art and literature are characteristically pagan, worldly, finite, and ideal, while Romantic is Christian, otherworldly, infinite, and mystical. The Pantheon represents one kind of achievement, Westminster Abbey another. Likewise, Sophocles, might express the highest standards of Classical drama, but nonetheless Shakespeare expresses the highest attainment of the Romantic. Schlegel creates an aesthetic of artistic relativism which, in effect, liberates Shakespeare from two centuries of Neoclassical constraints, thus opening the way for a fundamental reevaluation of Shakespeare.

For Schlegel, Shakespeare's violation of Aristotelian unities indicates not artistic failure but greater genius, since such unities would be quite inappropriate to express the more expansive and mystical orientation of Romantic culture. Moreover, while Neoclassical critics saw Shakespeare as a genius lacking judgment, Schlegel rejects the very distinction between genius and judgment, arguing, on the contrary, that any true genius would necessarily contain judgment within itself. In other words, creativity is not opposed to rules of order but creates its own rules and appropriate order. Schlegel describes genuine art as shaped by "organical form"—an innate and natural artistic order that emerges from within the work itself. Ideal literary forms, for Schlegel, must be analogous to forms in nature, such as plants and flowers, that exist in infinite variety and yet are nonetheless exquisitely formed and orderly. (*See also* Organic Form.)

But for Coleridge, more than Schlegel, Shakespeare does not merely imitate organic forms but looks so deeply into the essential principles of nature that his works become almost pure expressions of nature itself. Two centuries earlier, Ben Jonson had praised Shakespeare as "not of an age,

but for all time," but Coleridge perceives the timelessness of the Bard in far more insistent and philosophic terms. Coleridge describes Shakespeare as having an oceanic mind that contains all that nature contains, only in Shakespeare nature is presented as more unified and comprehensible. Shakespeare presents pure and refined truth, free from the dross of history and untainted by the circumstances of Elizabethan dramatic production. Shakespeare becomes for Coleridge not just a consummate poet but a divine prophet of eternal truth.

As a spokesman for the essential and stable truths of nature and the human heart, Shakespeare becomes for Coleridge a voice with godlike and unerring status—virtually incapable of error or even anything less than perfection. Like the divine mystic in *Kubla Khan*, Shakespeare had "drunk the milk of Paradise," and the milk of Paradise is always pure and untainted. If faults appear in the texts, they are for Coleridge the chimerical effects of the reader's failure to understand or the botched results of inept copyists and publishers.

While Neoclassical critics had praised Shakespeare for his mimetic ability to present faithfully the observed patterns of human behavior, Coleridge emphasizes Shakespeare's imaginative power to render transcendent nature, nature beyond the particulars of the observable world. Keats was apparently likewise impressed with Shakespeare's nonmimetic art—in his edition of Shakespeare, the plays of fairies and spirits, *Midsummer Night's Dream* and the *Tempest*, are the two plays most thumbed.

Lamb, in his essay *On the Tragedies of Shakspeare Considered with Reference to their Fitness for Stage Representation* (1811), applies Coleridge's principles to the question of Shakespearean stage productions. Lamb concludes that the plays are not fit for staging, or, more precisely, the stage—any stage—is unfit for the plays. Like Coleridge, Lamb sees Shakespeare's works as expressions of a platonic realm of supreme and transcendent truth. Thus, any staging of the plays—with tangible actors and particular costumes and settings—would inevitably corrupt and degrade their sublime nature. As Coleridge insists the plays transcend the circumstances of history, Lamb insists the plays transcend the material conditions of the stage. Even the most skilled actor is for Lamb an annoyance and distraction from the ethereal qualities of the plays. Not only are fairies difficult to portray on stage, but human characters, such as Hamlet and Lear, express sorrows too profound and passions too volcanic for the inadequate performances of flesh-and-blood actors. Stage representations of Shakespeare are necessarily and inevitably misrepresentations. The only fitting theater for Shakespeare is the theater of the mind, where an idealizing and Romantic imagination can envision the plays in their appropriate sublimity. (*See also* Mental Theater.)

Stephen J. Lynch

Works Consulted

Badawi, M.M. *Coleridge: Critic of Shakespeare*. Cambridge: Cambridge UP, 1973.

Drakakis, John, ed. *Alternative Shakespeare*. London: Routledge, 1985.

Eastman, Arthur M. *A Short History of Shakespearean Criticism*. New York: Norton, 1974.

Foucault, Michel. *The Order of Things*. New York: Pantheon, 1971.

Schoenbaum, S. *Shakespeare's Lives*. Oxford: Clarendon, 1970.

Shelley, Mary Wollstonecraft Godwin
(1797–1851)

Daughter of two famous people, Mary Wollstonecraft and William Godwin, and mistress and later wife to another, Percy Bysshe Shelley, Mary Shelley has until fairly recently been obscured by her family, by her affiliation with the Byron-Shelley circle in Europe, and by the popularity of her most famous work, *Frankenstein: or, the Modern Prometheus* (1818). (*See also* Novel.)

Until mid-20th century, Mary Shelley was of interest mainly to scholars interested in the Byron-Shelley circle. Furthermore, because of negative comments made in 1878 by Trelawny, a friend of the Shelleys, early biographies of the Shelleys suggest that she was merely her husband's devoted pupil. In fact, the standard life, *Mary Shelley* (1938) by Rosalie Glynn Grylls, did not examine Mary Shelley's life after Percy Shelley's death. In the last half of the 20th century, however, scholars have begun to take Mary Shelley seriously. Furthermore, she is an important Romantic who survived into the Victorian age and, therefore, enables readers to see how the Romantic movement evolved into Victorianism.

Because of her pregnancy, Mary Wollstonecraft married William Godwin in March 1797; and Mary, who was named for her mother, was born in August 1797. Eleven days later Wollstonecraft died of septicemic fever, leaving Godwin responsible for Mary and her illegitimate three-year-old half sister, Fanny Imlay, and leaving Mary ultimately to feel responsible for the first of many deaths.

As a toddler, Mary accompanied Godwin and Fanny to meet Godwin's famous friends; and her fiction often features daughters who admire their fathers.

However, when she was age 4, Godwin married Mary Jane Clairmont, who had two children—Charles and Jane (later known as Claire), who accompanied Mary and Percy when they eloped and who later bore a daughter, Allegra, to Byron.

Because there were few good schools for girls and because Godwin had been influenced by Wollstonecraft's views on education, Fanny, Mary, and Jane were educated at home where Mary studied history and literature, both classical and contemporary; French; Latin; geometry; geography; natural history; and art and where she met many of Godwin's acquaintances, including Wordsworth, Coleridge, Davy, and Maria Edgeworth. At age 10, she published her first work, an expanded version of a popular comic song, "Mounseer Nong Tong Paw" about a provincial Englishman who goes to France and misunderstands the language. She also did copying and proofreading at her father's publishing company, M.J. Godwin & Co.

Mary Godwin and Percy Shelley first met in 1812, but living with the Baxter family in Scotland as she was from 1812 to 1814 prevented a close acquaintance until May 1814. They became lovers in June 1814, although Shelley was married to Harriet Westbrook, who had borne him one child and was pregnant with another. Believing in free love, Mary Godwin and Percy Shelley expected William Godwin and Harriet Shelley to consent to their union; Mary Godwin was surprised at her father's opposition.

Promising initially to accept her father's wishes, Mary Godwin changed her mind when Percy Shelley threatened suicide; and the two, accompanied by Mary's stepsister Jane Clairmont, left for France. Mary Godwin was already pregnant with the first of their four children. Despite his liberal sentiments, William Godwin refused

to reconcile with his daughter until Harriet Shelley's suicide permitted the marriage. By that time (December 30, 1816), Mary Godwin had borne Percy Shelley two children, a girl who died unnamed and a son named William Godwin. Clara and Percy Florence were born after the marriage, but only Percy, who inherited the Shelley title and fortune, survived to adulthood.

With her husband, she studied the major English poets: Spenser, Shakespeare, Milton, Coleridge, Wordsworth, Byron, and Southey, as well as the poetry of the Bible. Other reading included *The Canterbury Tales*, Godwin's *Life of Chaucer*, Beckford, Richardson, "Monk" Lewis, Scott, and Radcliffe, as well as Goethe and Schiller in translation and Voltaire, Rousseau, de Stael, and classical writers in the original.

Sometimes regarded as the first science-fiction novel, *Frankenstein* is Mary Shelley's first mature work. Its origin is well known because of the introduction that she wrote for the 1831 edition. While the Shelleys and Clairmont were living near Geneva in 1816, they often joined Byron and Polidori, Byron's personal physician and traveling companion, to discuss mesmerism, electricity, and galvanism and whether science would soon unlock the riddle of life. One evening, the group gathered to read aloud *Fantasmagoriana*, a German book of ghost stories, and Byron suggested that each write a ghost story. Only Mary Shelley and Polidori (whose *The Vampyre* was published in 1819 and erroneously attributed to Byron) completed their stories (*See also* Polidori, John William.)

Shelley completed *Frankenstein* at the end of 1817, and it was published in March 1818. Its publication was followed by tragedies within the Shelley household: Clara's death in 1818 and William's in 1819; a miscarriage in June 1822, which almost caused Mary Shelley's death; and finally Percy Shelley's drowning in July 1822.

Frankenstein was enormously popular from the beginning. On July 20, 1823, Richard Brinsley Peake's adaptation, *Presumption; or, The Fate of Frankenstein*, was performed at the English Opera House, and a second edition of *Frankenstein* appeared in 1823.

On August 25, 1823, Mary Shelley returned to England, where she continued to help her father until his death in 1836. She also wrote, edited, and attempted to placate her father-in-law, hoping that he would offer assistance to her remaining child. Percy was educated at Harrow and at Trinity College, Cambridge, and married Jane St. John on June 24, 1841. His mother moved in with the newlyweds in July and lived with them (now financially independent because of Sir Timothy's death in 1844) until she died, apparently of a brain tumor, in 1851.

Although Mary Shelley is best known for *Frankenstein*, she published five other novels during her lifetime: *Valperga: Or, the Life and Adventures of Castruccio, Prince of Lucca* (1823), *The Last Man* (1826), *The Fortunes of Perkin Warbeck, A Romance* (1830), *Lodore* (1835), and *Falkner. A Novel* (1837). She also wrote a novella of father-daughter incest, *Matilda* (written 1819–20 but not published until 1959), literary biographies, an unfinished memoir of her father, travel books and short biographies, stories, essays, reviews, and poems. Moreover, scholars can study her husband's work because she gathered and edited his unpublished poems and prose pieces, published his complete works, and explained his character: *Posthumous Poems of Percy Bysshe Shelley* (1824); a four-volume collection, *The Poetical Works of Percy Bysshe Shelley* (1839); and *Essays, Letters from Abroad,*

Translations and Fragments, By Percy Bysshe Shelley (1839; second edition, 1841).

Carol A. Senf

Works Consulted

Gilbert, Sandra, and Susan Gubar. *The Madwoman in the Attic: The Woman Writer and the Nineteenth-Century Literary Imagination*. New Haven: Yale UP, 1979.

Levine, George, and U.C. Knoepflamacher, eds. *The Endurance of Frankenstein: Essays on Mary Shelley's Novel*. Berkeley: U of California P, 1979.

Moers, Ellen. *Literary Women: The Great Writers*. Garden City, NY: Doubleday, 1976.

Sunstein, Emily W. *Mary Shelley: Romance and Reality*. Boston: Little, 1989.

Shelley, Percy Bysshe
(1792–1822)

Typically seen as a great lyric poet of the Romantic Age, Percy Bysshe Shelley should be viewed in the wider context of the esthetic, intellectual, political, and social revolution of the times. From his juvenilia to his mature poetry, he habitually wrote with a comprehensive and critical perspective on human history. Childhood environment and early schooling, under the conservative eye of his father, were unquestionably significant in the formation of his antiestablishment, rebellious, and liberal attitudes. In 1810, the year he entered Oxford, he published two Gothic novels, *Zastrozzi* and *St. Irvyne, or The Rosicrucian*, and two volumes of "graveyard" verse, *Original Poetry by Victor and Cazire* and *Posthumous Poems of Margaret Nicholson*, all containing adolescent themes of supernatural destruction, social rebellion, and sentimental romantic love. However, except for their relationship to the Gothic tradition, these sensationalistic works give but slight indication that a major Romantic writer was forming a unified perspective out of which his mature poetry, drama, and essays would come.

After six months at Oxford, Shelley and his friend Hogg were expelled from the university for writing and publishing a short pamphlet entitled *The Necessity of Atheism*. This event launched Shelley toward an independent career of study and writing that continued until his death. A hasty and ill-fated marriage to Harriet Westbrook (1811) lasted harmoniously for two years, the young couple moving from one place to another in England, Scotland, Ireland, and Wales, while Shelley continued writing and became involved with radical political agitation. In 1812, Shelley met Godwin, a progressive humanitarian thinker and author of *An Inquiry Concerning Political Justice*, and his daughter Mary, the child of Mary Wollstonecraft, author of *Vindication of the Rights of Woman*. Over the next two years, the philosophical basis for Shelley's revolutionary thought was established, primarily through his study of the writings of Godwin, Hume, Paine, Plato, Rousseau, Voltaire, and Wollstonecraft.

As early as *Queen Mab* (1813), Shelley comprehensively surveys the disastrous scene of Western history. In the poem, he employs a dramatic visionary mode that reveals the systematic scheme of oppression and exploitation that tyrannical thought and policy have visited on Europe. Combining radical philosophical ideas from the 18th-century Enlightenment and a serious revolutionary zeal, the poem calls for a total transvaluation of existing governmental, religious, and social codes. Increasing intellectual maturity led Shelley beyond the merely lurid stage of his "Gothic period" into the formative power behind the Romantic imagination, although he relies on Gothic atmospheric imagery and thematic conventions throughout his mature poetry.

A major emotional upheaval also occurred in Shelley's life around this time (1814), when he fell in love with Mary Wollstonecraft Godwin. Deserting his wife Harriet, he eloped to the Continent with Mary and her stepsister Claire Clairmont, who was pursuing Byron. For these young people, the years 1814 to 1817 were wrenching, anxiety-ridden, and filled with emotional, financial, and family conflicts, which ultimately resulted in Harriet's tragic suicide, the marriage of Mary and Shelley shortly thereafter, and their being denied custody, by the English courts, of Shelley's and Harriet's two children (1817). Shelley continued to write regularly during this difficult period, publishing the essay *A Refutation of Deism* (1814) and composing a number of minor lyrics (1814–15). In the face of great personal adversity, his writings manifest a determined energy that eventually produces substantial works in 1816, such as *Alastor*, *Hymn to Intellectual Beauty*, and *Mont Blanc*. Critics and scholars now see these works as the distinct beginning of his mature thought and the entrance to his deepest philosophical poems.

Alastor, a long narrative poem focusing on the growth and demise of the visionary ideal, depicts the life of a young poet as seen through the eyes of a mature poet, one who is simultaneously sympathetic and critical of the former's imaginative excesses. By seeking the platonic good, true, and beautiful in all phenomena, the young poet begins a complex search for the secrets behind his mental and emotional responses to the world in which he finds himself. Unfortunately, his praiseworthy quest soon turns into a most destructive curse, for he falls deeply in love with his own self-image while undergoing an extraordinary narcissistic dream vision. He projects the seductive maiden of his refined imagination into his actual world, thereby ignoring the reality of human love that is offered to him and seeking instead a phantom object of desire. His frenzied journey through foreign lands and wilderness ultimately brings him to a lonely, desperate death, where his only and final consolation is the abiding and soothing forces of nature and the elegiac voice of the older narrator poet.

In the preface to *Alastor*, Shelley described the poem as an allegory of the human mind caught in a vicious obsession with the conflict between the real and the ideal, the actual and the imaginary. This quest-curse motif used regularly in his early Gothic writing continues in most of the later major poems. Understandably, the poem has been read by some critics as a metaphor for Shelley's own life up to age 24.

Unlike *Alastor*, which ends with a dire warning against extreme romantic idealism, *Hymn to Intellectual Beauty* and *Mont Blanc* conclude with quite different visions. These major poems of 1816 incorporate powerful affirmations of creative and metaphysical experience. *Hymn to Intellectual Beauty*'s urgent search for esthetic self-understanding results in the poet's deep, calm dedication to the art of poetry and its ability to carry refined truth into human life. In *Mont Blanc*, the poet's vision is raised above the purely phenomenological, quotidian factors in existence to the snow-covered summit of the mountain, inducing reality and imagination to perform an "interchange" whereby the two become one. What is remarkable in all three of these poems is Shelley's developing mythopoeic potential: they mark the route toward the great poems in the last five years of his life.

The year 1816 was important in another major respect, for Shelley met Byron, one of the best-known literary figures of the day. In Switzerland, along the shores of Lake Geneva, the two poets exchanged revolutionary thoughts, and Byron encouraged the younger poet to develop his radical views, both in poetry and prose. Later, they planned to join the liberal editor Leigh Hunt and others to publish an antiestablishment journal that would attempt to undermine the existing conservative and tyrannical social structures in European society. But Shelley's premature death put an end to their plans. Meanwhile, however, he continued to write a series of inflammatory prose and poetic works that were designed to provoke a hostile response from church, state, and genteel society and a positive reaction from progressive thinkers and the underprivileged. But his words fell on blind eyes and deaf ears. In 1817, he wrote and published two essays, *A Proposal for Putting Reform to the Vote* and *An Address to the People on the Death of Princess Charlotte*, and a long narrative poem, *The Revolt of Islam*, all of which had little effect, except to further Shelley's growing sense of despondency over the seeming impossibility of significant social change. (*See also* The *Liberal*.)

Ignored by the reading public and the critics, shunned by family and friends, Shelley, Mary, and their children William and Clara left England permanently and traveled to Italy, living at various locations there from 1818 to 1822. Within little more than a year after their departure, both children died, throwing the unfortunate parents further into despair but also increasing their individual (and cooperative) literary ventures. Originally begun during their second trip to the Continent in 1816, Mary finished and published her extraordinary novel *Frankenstein* (1818), while Shelley completed *Rosalind and Helen* and started *Julian and Maddalo*, "Euganean Hills," and *Prometheus Unbound*.

The remaining three and a half years of Shelley's life were extremely productive, filled with poems and essays of such artistic and intellectual genius that a sympathetic reader can only wonder at his expanding literary power. In 1819, he completed *Prometheus Unbound, The Cenci, Peter Bell the Third, Julian and Maddalo, The Mask of Anarchy, Ode to the West Wind,* and the essay *A Philosophical View of Reform.* Restricting attention to the challenging lyric drama *Prometheus Unbound* and the horrifying tragic drama *The Cenci,* one can argue that they are not only Shelley's most profound works but also intimately linked by the moral paradigms each projects.

Beginning in defiance and hate, Prometheus's rebellion against the omnipotent and destructive tyrant Jupiter turns into an act of universal forgiveness that finally permits love to overthrow the forces of evil. As a cosmic metaphor, one that incorporates esthetic, ethical, and philosophical truths, the play can be read as the struggle every individual might experience with his or her inner being in the search for personal self-understanding, an ultimate subjective value for Shelley. On the other hand, the forces of good, represented by Prometheus, Asia, and Demogorgon who resist and eventually overcome the agents of evil symbolized by Jupiter, Mercury, and the Furies, broaden the play's scope to a metaphysical level of universal revolution in which humankind will be free from all forms of tyranny and oppression and exist in a perfectible world of peace and harmony. In such an edenic state, love would be the ruling force and only human indifference to it or rejection of it could once again release Jupiter's forces of hate.

Contrary to Shelley's greatest hopes, *The Cenci* is a "sad reality" that mirrors history's pattern of evil overcoming good.

Here one sees how oppression, exploitation, violence, and destruction turn human life into a graveyard of perverted virtue in which the micro- and macrocosmic good, truth, and beauty become evil, untruth, and deformity. The utterly vile actions of her father, which include rape, incest, and the total debasement of his own daughter, cause Beatrice to change from a paragon of innocence, inspiration, and strength into an avenging demon of hate. She has her father murdered, lies to church authorities about her role in the crime, and ignobly tries to defend her actions. Ironically, she becomes the self-image of Count Cenci's ghastly evil, and if the world is guided by manichaean divine forces of right and wrong, Beatrice certainly chooses representative acts to honor the latter god. In this horrible reversal of the good, the reader's burdensome task is to condemn her but also feel overwhelming sympathy for her at the same time. Thus Beatrice and Prometheus, Shelley's most powerful champions in the confrontation with evil, stand forth as universal but opposed archetypes of potential response to the profound ills that could attack each individual and every society.

Other noteworthy poems of that year, *England in 1819, Ode to the West Wind,* and *Song to the Men of England,* compare favorably with the odes and poems of 1820 — *To a Skylark, To Liberty, To Naples, The Sensitive Plant, The Witch of Atlas,* and *Swellfoot the Tyrant.* All continue Shelley's intense commitment to the exploration of issues related to mythopoeic vision and radical social change, reflecting his attempt to balance Romantic idealism with a rigorous skepticism. Ranging from the beautifully lyric to the bitterly satiric, these works fit solidly into a Shelleyan vision that projects both a heartfelt subjective joy and an objective agony over the condition of humanity. The deaths of the Shelleys' two children, Clara and William, in 1818 and 1819, respectively, were obvious grounds for increasing despair, but this parental sorrow was somewhat mitigated by the birth of Percy Florence (1819) and Mary's and Shelley's increasing authorial vitality, in spite of other domestic disruptions.

Many biographers and critics have commented on Shelley's complicated, unorthodox love affairs. Besides his elopements with Harriet and Mary, which did result in marriage (a minor contradiction for a "revolutionary" who did not believe in that institution), indications of serious emotional entanglements with Claire Clairmont, Teresa Viviani, and Jane Williams created further tension through the years up to 1821 and 1822, years that led Matthew Arnold to exclaim later, "What a set!" Unquestionably, *Epipsychidion* can be seen as Shelley's "fictionalized love biography," an idealized personal and poetic apologia that accounts for the enormous complexity behind outward expressions of love, not merely for one person, but potentially many others. Also in 1821, Shelley wrote *A Defence of Poetry, Adonais*, and *Hellas*, a range of works that proclaims the poet as seer, the "unacknowledged legislator," and the authentic revolutionary who leads the human imagination toward the recognition of its deepest inner identity and its greatest individual and collective good.

As his life drew to a tragically premature close, Shelley continued his intense search for the fitting expression of the overriding truths of his time in relation to historical context. *Charles the First* and *The Triumph of Life* (1822), both unfinished works, hauntingly remind the reader of Shelley's fragmented but paradoxically coherent life and work. Like his other revolutionary poems, *Charles the First* attacks the corrupted core of arbitrary rule and evil government. Equally significant, a poem like *The Triumph of Life* reveals another central concern for Romanticism: how can subjective consciousness confront the ambiguous nature of human experience, labor through its personal self-deceptions, and still avoid the curse of "the Chariot of Life?" In the poem, the young visionary poet must learn to see past the dark grave of Rousseau's terrible mistakes and avoid the pitfalls of his inferno. On the far side of human failing, opposite Rousseau and other historical dignitaries, stand the luminary figures of Socrates and Christ, radical symbols of wisdom and love. Only such virtues can save humanity from its ingrained narcissistic temptations and raise it to the Romantic realm of an imaginative truth beyond skepticism—the "deep truth" for those whom Shelley calls "Immortals."

Although his restless visionary quest to inspire others to challenge and struggle against despotic, tyrannical powers that control or extinguish human dignity and freedom was never successful and hardly recognized during his lifetime, except by a limited circle of friends, he determinedly continued that admirable pursuit until death overtook him. Clearly, Shelley's intellectual grasp of the major forces that shape human destiny, for good or for evil, was remarkable, leading such a noted interpreter of history as Karl Marx to place him in the first rank of those poets who have fought for the cause of justice and humanistic socialism. Even Wordsworth thought highly of Shelley's artistry, his craftsmanship, but, unlike Marx, he surely had serious reservations about the younger poet's political and social views.

A month short of his 30th birthday, Shelley drowned in a sailing accident during a violent storm off the coast of Italy. With a friend, Edward Williams, he perished after a visit to greet Leigh Hunt at

Leghorn, a meeting that was to have been the origin of a revolutionary literary publication for all of Europe. Buried in the Protestant Cemetery just outside the walls of ancient Rome, Shelley leaves an astonishing legacy of usually difficult, obscure, and problematic writings that are also esthetically refined, intellectually challenging, and strangely inspirational. On his tombstone, Mary, Byron, and other friends placed the inscription "Cor Cordium," or "Heart of Hearts," a fitting memorial that reverberates throughout Shelley's poetry and prose. (*See also* Androgyny; Censorship; Classicism; Epipsyche; Incest, Mavrokordatos; Mental Theater; Necessity; Neoplatonism; Poetry; Prometheanism; Satanism; Smith, James and Horace; Synaesthesia.)

John V. Murphy

Works Consulted

Bloom, Harold, ed. *Percy Bysshe Shelley: A Collection of Critical Essays*. New York: Chelsea, 1985.

Cameron, Kenneth Neill. *The Young Shelley: Genesis of a Radical*. New York: Macmillan, 1962.

Clark, Timothy. *Embodying Revolution: The Figure of the Poet in Shelley*. New York: Oxford, 1989.

Dawson, P.M.S. *The Unacknowledged Legislator: Shelley and Politics*. New York: Oxford, 1980.

Everest, K. *Shelley Revalued: Essays from the Gregynog Conference*. Totowa, NJ: Barnes, 1983.

Foot, Paul. *Red Shelley*. London: Sidgwick, 1980.

Gallant, Christine. *Shelley's Ambivalence*. New York: St. Martin's, 1989.

Hoagwood, Terence Allan. *Skepticism and Ideology: Shelley's Political Prose and Its Philosophical Context from Bacon to Marx*. Iowa City: U of Iowa P, 1988.

Hodgart, Patricia. *A Preface to Shelley*. New York: Longmans, 1985.

Holmes, Richard. *Shelley: The Pursuit*. London: Weidenfeld, 1974.

Leighton, Angela. *Shelley and the Sublime*. New York: Cambridge, 1984.

Webb, Timothy. *Shelley: A Voice Not Understood*. Atlantic Highlands, NJ: Humanities, 1977.

Sherwood, Mary Martha
(1775–1851)

Mary Martha Sherwood was a prolific and popular writer of religious tracts and children's stories. Born in 1775, at Stanford, Worcestershire, Sherwood was the second child of George Butt, D.D., and his wife Martha. She received her education at home and at the Abbey school at Reading, where she studied Latin and composed stories and plays. (*See also* Children's Literature.)

Sherwood's first published story was *The Traditions*, which appeared in 1794. When her father died in 1795, mother and children moved to Bridgnorth, where Sherwood continued to write stories with a strong religious motif, designed to influence the morals of the poor. In 1803, she married her cousin, Captain Henry Sherwood. A child, Mary Henrietta, was born in 1804.

Sherwood accompanied her husband when he was sent to India and while there continued to write stories and involve herself in works of charity, including the founding of an orphan home at Kidderpur. In 1814, she wrote *The Infant's Progress*, and shortly after she composed the enormously popular *Little Henry and His Bearer*. This sentimental tale, published in 1815 by the American Tract Society, is the story of Little Henry, an infirm orphan child whose Christian piety eventually effects the conversion of the heathen "bearer" Boosy to Christianity. The story went through over a hundred editions by 1884 and was as popular as *Uncle Tom's Cabin*, evidenced by its translation into French, German, Hindustani, Chinese, and Sinhalese. The story may have been influential in Herman Melville's composition of *Typee*. In 1815, Sherwood published *The Indian Pilgrim*, a Hindustani version of *Pilgrim's Progress*.

The Sherwoods returned to England and settled at Wick, with a family that eventually included their five children and three adopted orphans. Sherwood's charitable works and the writing of religious tracts and tales continued throughout her lifetime. Perhaps her best-known work, a collection of moral tales known as *The History of the Fairchild Family, or The Child's Manual*, appeared in 1818. A second volume was published in 1842 and became an immediate best seller; other editions followed through 1889. In addition to its wide influence on young readers of the 19th century, the work was influential in Dickens's creation of Pip in *Great Expectations*.

Sherwood wrote over 95 tracts and tales, pious in tone and designed to influence the moral character of young people, including *The Monk of Cimies*, *The Nun*, *Henry Marten*, and *The Lady of the Manor*. She died in 1851, two years after her husband.

Louise Flavin

Works Consulted

Bryant, John. "'Little Henry,' and the Process of Composition: A Peep at the *Typee* Fragment." *Melville Society Extracts* 67 (1986): 1–4.

Chaney, Lois. "Pip and the Fairchild Family." *Dickensian* 79 (1983): 162–63.

Sherwood, Mary Martha. *The Life of Mrs. Sherwood, Chiefly Autobiographical*. Ed. Sophia Kelly. London: Darton, 1857.

Siddons, Sarah

(1755–1831)

One of the greatest actors in the history of English theater, Sarah Siddons dominated the early Romantic stage from the time of her second performance in London in 1782. She excelled in tragedies and serious dramas, and her characterization of Lady Macbeth introduced innovations to the role that contemporary actors still retain (the mimed hand washings, the white nightgown, imitation of somnabulist behavior). Idealized by writers such as Hazlitt and Baillie as the epitome of Romantic womanhood—Joshua Reynolds called her "some grand Idea of the Tragick Muse"—Siddons's impulse to render certain characters more vulnerable and accessible has until recently been underappreciated. In her extensive notes on playing the characters of Lady Macbeth and Queen Katharine, for example, she reveals her dissatisfaction with generalized acting and her sensitivity to the limitations imposed on the woman who acts. (*See also* Theater.)

As a woman performer of the late 18th and early 19th centuries, Siddons should have occupied a somewhat precarious social position, but the fact that she was a devoted mother of five kept at bay much of the scandal other actresses attracted. Because her attractive, less talented actor-husband, William, was sometimes profligate, envious of her success, and irritated by her erratic health, Siddons bore the burden of supporting her children economically and spiritually. In her reminiscences of 1831, she recalls that she was too busy to do much else but act and mother; thus, her reputation easily survived the sniping of Catherine Galindo, for example, who in 1809 published accusations of an alleged affair between Siddons and Galindo's husband; Siddons also seems to have been unfazed by complaints that her offstage manner was arrogant and aloof.

Her life was not without drama, however: she outlived three of her children and her brother, the famous actor Kemble, and also suffered the emotional vicissitudes of Sir Thomas Lawrence's friendship. For years attracted to Siddons, he became engaged to both her daughters on separate occasions, wrecking the family's peace. In 1784, she was hissed off the London stage because of unsubstantiated rumors about her refusal to perform the obligatory actor's benefit while in Dublin the summer before. For these reasons, the tone of Siddons' memoirs, written in the last year of her life, is melancholy and restrained.

Siddons was the eldest child of strolling players, Roger and Sarah Kemble, who put her on the stage when she was an infant. Her first theatrical success occurred when she performed Ariel in *The Tempest* at age 13. In 1773, she married William Siddons, to whom her parents objected because he was an actor. Their first child, Henry, was born the following year, and Siddons established the pattern of most of her pregnancies, performing until delivery and returning to the stage before she was fully recovered. One month after her daughter, Sarah Martha, was born in 1775, Siddons left the provinces for London where David Garrick had engaged her to act. She debuted as Portia to his Shylock, but in this and other roles she met with lukewarm reviews, and her contract at Drury Lane Theatre was not renewed. For five years, she underwent an apprenticeship in regional theaters in Liverpool, Manchester, York, and Bath, performing an enormous number of parts and refining her craft in front of difficult audiences, conditioned as they were to glib, and primarily comedic, entertainment. Siddons learned to hold a crowd before returning to Drury Lane, in 1782, for her second London debut, a triumphant performance of the title role in *Isabella*. In 1785, she acted Lady Macbeth for the first time, a part with which she was henceforth associated and which she had been studying since she was 20.

Between 1782 and 1802, Siddons played approximately 70 different roles, among them Volumnia in *Coriolanus*, Mrs. Haller in *The Stranger*, Elvira in *Pizarro*, Zara in *The Mourning Bride*, and Jane in *De Montfort*. In 1806, Siddons moved from the Drury Lane company to Covent Garden, where Kemble was actor-manager. There, Siddons acted until her formal retirement in 1812, bowing out memorably as Lady Macbeth. Two years later, Edmund Kean introduced a more naturalistic style of acting. Her last appearance on stage was at a benefit in 1819 playing the role of Lady Randolph in *Douglas*. She was buried at Paddington Churchyard in 1831.

From annotations to some of her greatest performances, her letters, and journals of the period, Siddons the actor emerges: graceful in movement, mobile in face, with a clear voice that vibrated with melancholy, shunning stage tricks and artificial behavior, psychologically credible, and capable of memorizing parts quickly and retaining them. Her methodology consisted of studying some roles for years, making detailed notes about her characters' histories. Siddons also believed that staying in character off stage and listening to the parts of the play that would affect her character on its next entrance were the means with which to create coherence and intensity. Her remarks on Lady Macbeth are especially interesting for revealing her subtextual performance. Siddons describes Lady Macbeth as an early 19th-century woman, emotionally and financially vulnerable because she is dependent on her husband's social and personal identity; her ambitious aims can be accomplished only through the cultivation of a sexually attractive, charming persona. Against the traditional portrayal of Lady Macbeth as a fiendish *la belle dame sans merci*, Siddons set her conception of the heroine as physically fragile, inconsistently compassionate, and ruled by repressed ambition.

Aside from her acting notes, occasional verses, epilogues, and prologues, and her slim volume of reminiscences, Siddons published an abridged version of *Paradise Lost* in 1822 from the text she read to her children, focusing on the story of Adam and Eve. Her early admiration of Milton was as great an influence on her acting career as was Shakespeare.

Catherine Burroughs

Works Consulted

Boaden, James. *Memoirs of Mrs. Siddons*. 2 vols. London: Colburn, 1827.

Campbell, Thomas. *Life of Mrs. Siddons*. 2 vols. New York: Harper, 1834.

Fitzgerald, Percy. *The Kembles*. London: Tinsley, 1871.

French, Yvonne. *Mrs. Siddons: Tragic Actress*. London: Cobden, 1936.

Jenkin, Fleeming, ed. *Mrs. Siddons as Lady Macbeth and as Queen Katharine*. New York: Columbia UP, 1915.

Kelly, Linda. *The Kemble Era*. New York: Random, 1980.

Mackenzie, Kathleen. *The Great Sarah: The Life of Mrs. Siddons*. London: Evans, 1968.

Manvell, Roger. *Sarah Siddons: Portrait of an Actress*. New York: Putnam, 1971.

Siddons, Sarah. *The Reminiscences of Sarah Kemble Siddons, 1773–1785*. Ed. William Van Lennep. Cambridge: Widener Library, 1942.

Skepticism, Humean

As an extension of Berkeley's subjective idealism, the skepticism of David Hume (1711–76) is predicated on the philosophical belief that because there exist no logical arguments that can overcome all doubts, no knowledge is possible. Though the young Hume had hoped his *Treatise of Human Nature* (1739), the original delineation of his theory, would make him the Isaac Newton of philosophy and psychology, it was not until the publication of his more popular *An Enquiry Concerning Human Understanding* (1748) that he gained a wide audience for his philosophy.

Strongly influenced by Locke, Hume ruthlessly carries the empiricist methodology of his predecessor to its skeptical conclusion. Using what is commonly referred to as "Hume's fork," Hume begins with the assumption that all knowledge is based either on reason (relation of ideas) or on experience (matter of fact). He then demonstrates that all ideas, complex as well as simple, are derived from impressions, and even complex impressions must be reduced to aggregates of simple experiences. This means that all knowledge must, of necessity, derive from logical relationships among simple experiences, specifically, causation, induction, and belief in an external world. These three interrelate to form the epistemological base, for belief in an external world rests on principles of induction which, in turn, rely on the theory of causation. From his examination, Hume concludes that all assertions of causation rest on *a priori* experiences, not on reason; that all induction is based on the erroneous projection that supposed cause-and-effect relationships of the past will obtain in the future; and reason is incapable of verifying the existence of anything not directly experienced. Therefore, one cannot prove anything about reality, for one can only know one's own association of ideas. Hume's conclusion is consistently skeptical: though an explanation undoubtedly exists, it cannot be known. Yet, Hume remains jolly and concludes his *Treatise* with a cheery recognition of the pleasure and comfort of ordinary pastimes. (*See also* Berkeley's Idealism, Commonsense Philosophy.)

Sheila A. Spector

Works Consulted

Beauchamp, T.L., and A. Rosenberg. *Hume and the Problem of Causation*. New York: Oxford, 1981.

Flew, Antony. *David Hume: Philosopher of Moral Science*. New York: Blackwell, 1986.

Fogelin, R.J. *Hume's Skepticism in the* Treatise of Human Nature. Boston: Routledge, 1985.

Hall, Roland. *Fifty Years of Hume Scholarship: A Bibliographical Guide*. Edinburgh: Edinburgh UP, 1978.

Hume, David. *Enquiries concerning Human Understanding and concerning the Principles of Morals*. Ed. L.A. Selby-Bigge. 3rd ed. Oxford: Clarendon, 1975.

———. *Essays Moral Political and Literary*. Ed. E.F. Miller. Indianapolis: Liberty Classics, 1985.

———. *A Treatise of Human Nature*. Ed. L.A. Selby-Bigge. 2nd ed. Oxford: Clarendon, 1978.

Norton, David Fate. *David Hume: Common-Sense Moralist, Sceptical Metaphysician*. Princeton: Princeton UP, 1982.

Strawson, Galen. *The Secret Connexion: Causation, Realism, and David Hume*. Oxford: Clarendon, 1989.

Wright, John P. *The Sceptical Realism of David Hume*. Minneapolis: U of Minnesota P, 1983.

Slavery

Slavery involving Africans dates back to antiquity, but the three ventures of Sir John Hawkins in the 1560s are generally considered the first successful British slaving voyage. On Hawkins's first expedition in 1562, he captured over 300 Blacks. Soon the number of Blacks in England rose steadily, particularly in London, Liverpool, and Bristol. Most of the slaves, however, were brought to work on plantations in the New World.

The British began to expand their empire considerably in the 17th century. White indentured servants initially tended the cotton and tobacco crops; however, in 1640, sugar cane, a crop that requires a large number of workers, began to be grown. Over 150,000 slaves were imported to Barbados and Jamaica between 1663 and 1711. The Royal African Company was formed in 1672 in an attempt to control the trade, which reached its peak in the 18th century.

The years between 1787 and 1838 were marked by a keen interest in social and political reform, which is manifested in the movement toward abolition, first of the slave trade in 1807, then of slavery itself in 1833. Some critics see the antislavery movement in England as being driven by purely virtuous motives; others, as motivated by economic, not humanitarian, factors. The latter believed that although slavery was becoming less profitable, the Industrial Revolution was based on capital acquired from the slave system. However, slavery in Great Britain did not end simply because of humanitarianism or economic reasons but rather because of a variety of changing developments.

There was much support for abolition in philosophy, literature, and art. Many of the 18th-century French *philosophes*, such as Montesquieu, Rousseau, and Voltaire, had denounced slavery. Montesquieu's *L'Esprit des Lois* (1748) in particular had a strong impact on the British, including Burke, whose *Sketch of a Negro Code* (1792) supported a gradual abolition. Others influenced by the French include Adam Ferguson, James Beattie, and William Blackstone.

Proponents of the 18th-century notion of the noble savage tended to sympathize with Blacks, albeit often depicting them in a stereotypical manner. Examples include Aphra Behn's novel *Oroonoko* (1688), Thomas Sotherne's stage adaptation of *Oroonoko* (1696), Thomas Day's poem, *The Dying Negro* (1773), and Cowper's *The Negro's Complaint* (1788).

The Romantics continued this favorable if condescending treatment. Such writers as Coleridge, Wordsworth, Byron, and Shelley sympathized with Blacks, as did many lesser-known figures, including James Montgomery in *Poems on the Abolition of the Slave Trade* (1809). Perhaps the most famous work to 20th-century readers is Blake's poem *The Little Black Boy*.

Artists also contributed to the abolitionist cause. Blake's illustrations for John Gabriel Stedman's *Narrative of a Five Years' Expedition against the Revolted Negroes of Surinam* (1796), Fuseli's painting *The Negro Revenged* (1806–07), and Turner's *Slavers Throwing Overboard the Dead and Dying— Typhoon Comin On* (1840) serve as examples of works that depict antislavery sentiment. The emblem of the movement, in fact, was Josiah Wedgwood's cameo, "Am I Not a Man and a Brother" (1787).

Religious groups also played a major role in the abolitionist movement. With their beliefs in an inward light, equality, and brotherly love, the Quakers on both sides of the Atlantic, led by John Woolman and Anthony Benezet, pressed for abolition. Though the Quakers were a small group, they influenced many non-Quakers, such as John Wesley, the founder of Methodism, who wrote *Thoughts upon Slavery* (1771).

Benezet also influenced the Evangelical Granville Sharp, one of the members of the Society for Effecting the Abolition of the Slave Trade. Sharp, a lawyer, challenged the legality of slavery in the *Somerset* case of 1772. James Somerset, a slave, was taken from the West Indies to England, where he escaped, was subsequently recaptured, and was about to be returned to the West Indies until Sharp intervened. Lord Mansfield, the most famous judge of his day, ruled that a master's colonial rights could not be exercised and ordered Somerset discharged. Mansfield's decision was often taken as meaning that slavery was abolished in England, but he simply decided that a slave master could not forcibly remove a slave from England.

Mansfield also was the judge in an influential 1783 case. The captain of the slave ship *Zong,* claiming a water shortage, ordered 132 sick slaves to be thrown overboard. Although Sharp was unsuccessful in prosecuting those who threw the slaves overboard, the publicity surrounding the case aroused much sympathy for the abolitionist cause.

Another Evangelical who was a member of the Society for Effecting the Abolition of the Slave Trade was Thomas Clarkson, described by Coleridge as a "moral steam engine." He tirelessly traveled to gather evidence against the slave trade, speaking to over 20,000 seamen in compiling his *An Essay on the Impolicy of the African Slave Trade* (1788).

The most famous abolitionist was Wilberforce. He first wrote against the slave trade when he was age 14, and after his spiritual conversion to Evangelicalism, he devoted his life to the slaves' cause. The friend of Prime Minister Pitt and many other powerful persons, Wilberforce's name became synonymous with the antislavery movement. (*See also* Brougham, Henry; Fox, James Charles; Wilberforce, William; Wright, Frances.)

While the work of people such as Sharp, Clarkson, and Wilberforce has often been acknowledged, little attention has been paid to the struggles of Blacks to free their race from bondage. Free Blacks, such as Olaudah Equiano and Ottobah Cugoano, played a significant role in the abolitionist movement. Equiano (also known as Gustavus Vassa) was brought as a child to England from Africa. His *Interesting Narrative of the Life of Olaudah Equiano, or Gustavus Vassa, the African, Written by Himself* (1789) is an early example of the slave narrative, an autobiography that vividly displays the horrors of slavery. Equiano was also involved in the Sierra Leone plan, which attempted to repatriate ex-slaves in Africa. Cugoano, another eloquent voice against slavery, wrote *Thoughts and Sentiments on the Evil and Wicked Traffic of the Slavery and Commerce of the Human Species* (1787).

The opponents of abolition were numerous and well-organized. There were several attempts to justify the trade on moral and religious grounds, including George Turnbull's *Apology for Negro Slavery* (1786). Most defenses of the slave trade depict Blacks as subhuman to justify their mistreatment. Perhaps the best example is Edward Long's *History of Jamaica* (1774). Opponents of abolition claimed that slavery had always existed in Africa, ignoring the important differences between African and European slavery. They maintained that slaves were introduced to civilization and Christianity. Advocates of slavery felt that slaves were better off than the English factory workers. They claimed that Blacks were unproductive and would be unable to survive without the discipline of slavery. One writer reasoned in 1789 that overpopulation in Africa meant that servitude was actually preferable.

The most compelling argument was that Great Britain depended economically on the slave system. Great Britain was the leading slave-trader in the 18th century, and slavery was seen as necessary for the plantation system to survive. Planters had strong support in such port cities as London, Lancashire, Bristol, and Liverpool, cities that garnered profits from the trade, and the planters had strong political support, including that of Henry Dundas (Viscount Melville), the Duke of Wellington, and King George III. (Moreover, the trade was said to be a "nursery" for sailors.) Stephen Fuller, a Jamaican planter and leader of the Society of West India Planters and Merchants, counted on this economic interest when he said in 1787: "The stream of popularity runs against us; but I trust nevertheless that common sense is

with us, and that wicked as we are when compared with the abolishers, the wisdom and policy of this country will protect us."

The abolitionists' most common strategy to overcome such powerful opposition was an attempt to win over public support. To this end, they issued thousands of books and pamphlets and gathered hundreds of petitions. The major piece of legislation passed in the 1780s and 1790s was the Slave Trade Regulating Act (Dolben's Act) in 1788, which limited the number of slaves that could be carried according to the tonnage of a ship.

The increasing bloodiness of the French Revolution and the slave rebellion in St. Domingue (present-day Haiti) in 1791 further divided Britain over abolition. Britain lost over 40,000 soldiers in St. Domingue fighting the slaves who were led by Toussaint Louverture, but many hated him and saw abolitionists as being dangerous radicals. (*See also* Toussaint Louverture.)

In the increasingly conservative political climate of the 1790s, several motions to end the trade were defeated between 1791 and 1802. Furthermore, attempts for international abolition were stymied because of the wars with France.

The abolitionist cause, however, made some gains. The Slave Carrying Bill of 1799, building on Dolben's Act, further reduced the number of slaves that could be transported. More important was the agreement, worked out by Lord George Canning and Wilberforce, to limit the African slaves that could be imported to newly conquered Trinidad and Dutch Guiana by convincing planters from the older colonies that they would be facing increased competition if new land opened up for slaves.

Pitt died in early 1806. Although he had been considered a champion of the abolitionists, Pitt often hesitated to act against what he felt was the popular interest. The Talents Ministry (led by W.W. Grenville and Charles J. Fox) that replaced him was more unswerving in its desire to end the trade. This support made it easier to pass the Foreign Slave Bill (1806), which destroyed almost 75 percent of the trade. The final step in ending the trade, the Abolition Bill, became effective May 1, 1807. Grenville claimed, after its passage, that Parliament had "performed one of the most glorious acts that had been done by any assembly of any nation in the world."

After the trade was abolished, Great Britain quickly established punishment for those who illegally sold slaves. Captured ships were forfeited, and a fine was levied for every captured slave. In 1811, slavers risked transportation as well. Despite these laws, the trade flourished.

Britain tried to establish an international agreement to end the trade. The African Institute was formed shortly after slave trading was made illegal in Britain, and Clarkson, one of its officers, spent numerous hours speaking with foreign ministers about the matter. In the Treaty of Ghent ending the War of 1812, America and Britain agreed to try to suppress the trade on a worldwide basis. Although Britain made agreements with several nations, including Portugal and Spain, in attempts to end the trade, the difficult task was often left to the Royal Navy.

The abolition of the trade also did not have the desired effect of helping slaves' conditions. Wilberforce said ending the trade would give "the death-blow" to slavery. However, for many slaves, conditions actually worsened after the abolition of the trade. The elderly and women, for example, were forced to do work that would not have been required of them earlier. (*See also* Humanitarianism.)

By the 1820s, many people became convinced that emancipation was necessary. Thomas F. Buxton, replacing the aging Wilberforce as head of the movement, unsuccessfully introduced a bill in 1823 to abolish slavery. Appeals were made demonstrating popular support. The Anti-Slavery Society published close to three million tracts between 1823 and 1831. Women played an increasingly important role at this time. Abolition was, in fact, one of the few areas in which women were allowed to express a political voice. There were a number of women's antislavery organizations, and women helped raise funds and obtain names for petitions (one petition in 1833 contained over 350,000 women's signatures). Women often comprised the bulk of members at meetings, so much so that it could be noted in 1833 that there was an "unusually large proportion of men" present at one session.

The slaves played a large part in obtaining their liberation as well. The daily resistance of the slaves (e.g., by sabotage and theft) crippled the slave system by making it less profitable. Many became runaways, some setting up their own communities. There were almost constant rebellions in the British West Indies, perhaps the three most significant occurring in Barbados (1816), in Demerara (1823), and in Jamaica (1831). The Jamaican rebellion (also called the Baptist War) involved over 60,000 slaves; 540 slaves and 14 whites died. Sam Sharpe, the Black Baptist preacher who led the rebellion, was executed, but the rebellion created much support for the abolitionist movement. White missionaries returning from Jamaica, such as William Knibb, reported the harsh conditions used to repress the rebellion.

When the Whigs, the staunchest supporters of abolition, regained office in 1830, it seemed clear that victory of the antislavery forces was near. Early in 1833, more than 1.5 million people signed petitions to abolish slavery. The planters and their supporters finally conceded, and on march 25, 1833, the Emancipation Act received the Royal assent. The act declared "that slavery shall be abolished throughout British Colonies, on, from and after the First of August, 1834." Over 750,000 slaves were freed. The slave owners were compensated for the loss of their slaves, and a six-year transitional period of apprenticeship was agreed to (shortened to August 1, 1838). However, a large illegal slave trade with Cuba and Brazil, which did not abolish slavery until many years later, continued.

Louis J. Parascsandola

Works Consulted

Anstey, Roger. *The Atlantic Slave Trade and British Abolition 1760–1810*. Atlantic Highlands, NJ: Humanities, 1975.

Craton, Michael. *Sinews of Empire: A Short History of British Slavery*. Garden City, NY: Anchor, 1974.

Davis, David Brion. *The Problem of Slavery in the Age of Revolution. 1770–1823*. Ithaca: Cornell UP, 1975.

Mannix, Daniel P., and Malcolm Cowley. *Black Cargoes: A History of the Atlantic Slave Trade, 1518–1865*. New York: Viking, 1962.

Reynolds, Edward. *Stand the Storm: A History of the Atlantic Slave Trade*. London: Allison, 1985.

Walvin, James. *England, Slaves and Freedom, 1776–1838*. Jackson: UP of Mississippi, 1986.

Smith, Charlotte Turner

(1749–1806)

Charlotte Turner Smith was a highly respected poet and novelist. She repopularized the sonnet with her collection *Elegiac Sonnets* and contributed to the development of the novel, influencing Radcliffe and Scott with her extensive descriptions of nature and sensitive depictions of character.

Born into the landed gentry, Smith had an affluent upbringing in London and at the family seats near Guildford, Surrey, and at Bignor Park, Sussex. Raised by her aunt after her mother's death in 1752, Smith attended schools in Chichester and London. In 1765, she married 23-year-old Benjamin Smith, the son of a wealthy West Indian merchant. She regretted this early marriage because Smith was an adulterous and abusive husband, who squandered both of their fortunes. His father tried to put money in a trust for Smith's children (12 in all), but litigation over the estate, begun in 1776, went on for 30 years. In 1783, Smith accompanied her husband to debtor's prison for seven months.

While in debtor's prison, Smith tried to publish her poems to raise funds. William Hayley allowed her to dedicate the book to him, and she printed it at her own expense. *Elegiac Sonnets* (1784) was a great success and grew from about 20 sonnets to over 90 in the ninth edition (1800). Smith's sonnets, half of which are in the Shakespearean form, influenced the Romantic revival of the sonnet and were celebrated and emulated by Bowles, Wordsworth, and Coleridge. Most of her sonnets are meditations on nature, though she includes several based on Petrarch's sequence and on Goethe's story of Werther.

Smith often presents a solitary speaker who looks to nature for some reflection of the speaker's inner state. Melancholy, anguish, and frustration are the chief emotions, and the natural elements provide sympathetic correspondence. For example, the speaker in *To the Moon* takes refuge in the benign serenity of the night sky, and in *Written in the Churchyard at Middleton in Sussex*, she gazes enviously on the human bones that have been whitened by the wild blast of the sea. The poetry becomes more political in later pieces, such as *The Sea View*, in which a shepherd's view of nature is ruined when he sees the mangled bodies of wartime casualties floating in the ocean.

In 1785, the Smiths escaped to Normandy to flee creditors. In 1787, on their return to England, they separated, though Benjamin continued to harass his wife for money until his death in 1806.

Smith translated two works from the French, *Manon l'Escaut* (1785) and *Romance of Real Life* (1787), before she tried novel writing. She had immediate popular and critical success with her first novel, *Emmeline, or the Orphan of the Castle* (1788), an absorbing story, praised for its characterizations and natural scenery. Smith wrote 10 novels over 10 years: *Emmeline* (1788), *Ethelinde* (1789), *Celestina* (1791), *Desmond* (1792), *The Old Manor House* (1793), *The Banished Man* (1794), *The Wanderings of Warwick* (1794), *Mrs. Montalbert* (1795), *Marchmont* (1796), and *The Young Philosopher* (1798).

Writing in the tradition of literature of sensibility, Smith makes innovative use of concepts of the sublime and the picturesque to describe her characters' experience of nature. Her primary concern is with realistic human problems, though Gothic settings, castles, and imprisonments provide episodic interest. Many of Smith's heroines are orphans, whose marginal status interferes with their prospects for happiness; and many of her heroes are well-bred but poor, dependent on financial windfalls. In her censure of primogeniture, arranged marriages, and the English legal system, Smith dealt with subjects that she knew all too well.

Her late novels deal more directly than the earlier ones with contemporary politics. Like Wollstonecraft, whom she admired, Smith asserted women's right to speak about public issues. *Desmond*, her only epistolary work, shows Smith's support for the French Revolution, while in *The Banished Man* she condemns the tyranny of Jacobinism.

A devoted mother interested in children's education, Smith wrote six instructive books for young people, which included *Rural Walks* (1795) and *The Natural History of Birds* (1807). Although positive in tone, informative, and moralistic, they did not achieve the popularity of her sister Catherine Ann Dorset's whimsical *The Peacock "At Home"* (1807).

Before her death, Smith was completing *Beachy Head with Other Poems* (1807). The 800-line title poem, written in blank verse, contains one section that makes a remarkable companion piece to *Tintern Abbey* and even echoes its language, as Smith recalls her happy childhood in the south of England where she became a worshiper of nature. Full of botanical and zoological details, her descriptions in *Beachy Head* have more specificity than Wordsworth's, though she lacks his confident persona, and writes more about hermits than herself.

Smith was an accompanied stylist, whose versatility enabled her to range from biting satire to evocative meditation. She preferred to think of herself as a poet and insisted that she wrote novels only to earn money to support her children. Fortunately, her skill and talent matched her determination and industry, and she produced a valuable collection of works in both genres.

Deborah Kennedy

Works Consulted

Ehrenpreis, Anne Henry. Introduction. *The Old Manor House*. By Charlotte Smith. London: Oxford UP, 1969.

Fry, Carroll Lee. *Charlotte Smith, Popular Novelist*. New York: Arno, 1980.

Hilbish, Florence May Anna. *Charlotte Smith, Poet and Novelist (1749–1806)*. Philadelphia: U of Pennsylvania P, 1941.

Stanton, Judith Phillips. "Charlotte Smith's 'Literary Business': Income, Patronage, and Indigence." *The Age of Johnson* 1 (1987): 375–401.

Smith, James

(1775–1839)

Smith, Horace (born Horatio)

(1779–1849)

The brothers James and Horace Smith were two of the better-known literary amateurs of their day. Their fame rested largely on the immensely popular volume of verse parodies, *Rejected Addresses*, they coauthored in 1812, although Horace also produced many novels, several burlesques and farces for the stage, and a major poem, *Amarynthus* (1821).

Sons of a London solicitor, Robert Smith, James and Horace were educated in nonconformist institutions until they were age 17. At Chigwell School, New School, and Alfred House Academy, they studied modern and classical languages, drawing, and mathematics, among other practical subjects. After completing school, James became a clerk in his father's firm (1791) and was admitted as an attorney to King's Court seven years later. He took over the firm in 1832, the year his father died. Leaving Alfred House Academy in 1796, Horace secured a clerkship in a London counting house and by 1812 had worked his way into the London Stock Exchange, where he became a shrewd speculator. After meeting Percy Shelley at Leigh Hunt's home in 1816, Horace befriended the poet and brought his sound business sense to the management of Shelley's financial affairs.

With the publication of *Rejected Addresses*, which went through 19 editions and sold thousands of copies in the first 30 years of its existence, the Smiths became celebrities. Although both were established writers by this time—James, a regular contributor to the *Monthly Mirror* and the *London Review*, and Horace, the author of several novels—it was for *Rejected Addresses* (originally published with James's *Horace in London*) that the Smiths were known.

The *Addresses* began as a private joke between the brothers and a friend, Charles William Ward, the Secretary of the Drury Lane Theatre. After a fire destroyed the theater in 1809, it was rebuilt, and, as part of its reopening ceremony in 1812, a contest was announced soliciting dedicatory verses for the new theater. The selections committee was dissatisfied with all of the submissions (the Smiths' among them), and eventually engaged Byron to write the address that was delivered on opening night. Nevertheless, James and Horace began to send Ward amusing parodies of the poems actually submitted by obscure poetasters (one Dr. Busby being the most obscure) and by the best-known writers of the day, including Coleridge, Wordsworth, Crabbe, Scott, Southey, "Monk" Lewis, Cobbett, and Byron. On Ward's recommendation, the 21 verse parodies were collected into a volume and, after an initial rejection, were published and favorably received in both the *Edinburgh Review* (November 1812) and the *Quarterly Review* (September 1812). In general, the Smith's "victims" received the send-ups in good humor. On being introduced to James, George Crabbe is said to have taken the parodist's hands and exclaimed in a laugh," Ah! my old enemy, how do you?"

Although James confined his literary efforts after *Rejected Addresses* to contributions primarily to *New Monthly Magazine*, Horace retired a wealthy man from the

Stock Exchange in 1821 and embarked on a leisurely literary career. Married twice, both times against his father's wishes, Horace associated with many of the most famous figures of the day, from Shelley, Southey, and Scott to Thackeray, a frequent visitor to Smith's home in Brighton. From this residence in Brighton, the younger Smith brother wrote historical novels between 1826 and 1846, publishing them at the rate of nearly one a year. The most successful of these (and a work Scott admired) was the first, *Brambletye House* (1826), set in Cromwellian and Restoration England. His minor successes as a novelist, however, never unseated his reputation as the author of the *Addresses*.

After several debilitating bouts of gout over many years, James died in 1839. And a decade later in 1849, Horace followed, after a short decline.

John F. McElroy

Works Consulted

Beavan, Arthur H. *James and Horace Smith: a Family Narrative.* London: Hurst, 1899.

Hayward, Abraham. "James Smith." *Biographical and Critical Essays.* Vol. 1. London: Longmans, 1858.

Holmes, Richard. *Shelley: the Pursuit.* New York: Penguin, 1987.

Smith, Horace. *Amarynthus.* Introduction by Donald H. Reiman. New York: Garland, 1977.

Smith, Horace and James. *Rejected Addresses and Horace in London.* Introduction by Donald H. Reiman. New York: Garland, 1977.

Smith, Sydney

(1771–1845)

Famous for his polemical writings, letters, and bons mots, Sydney Smith was born in 1771 to Robert Smith and Maria Olier. His mother was of Huguenot extraction. Smith was educated at Winchester School and in 1789 entered New College, Oxford. Though he wanted to study for the bar, his father was unwilling to support him financially. Without much enthusiasm, Smith entered the clergy. In 1794, he was ordained to the curacy of Nether Avon, Salisbury Plain. The squire took a liking to the young curate and appointed him tutor to his eldest son. Although Smith and his charge had originally planned to go to Weimar, the political situation in Europe prevented them, and the pair settled in Edinburgh instead. There, Smith married Catherine Amelia Pybus in 1800.

The intellectual climate in Edinburgh at the time was fertile, and in 1802, Smith, with Jeffrey and Brougham, founded the *Edinburgh Review*. It quickly became the most influential and the most honest review in the country. In 1803, Smith moved to London, where the fame of his wit and good humor increased. He preached at the Foundling Hospital, and his lectures on moral philosophy at the Royal Institution were crowded with listeners. Smith was a rarity in his own day: a Whig clergyman espousing unpopular political views. He was most well-known for his support of Catholic Emancipation. In 1807, he anonymously published the *Peter Plymley Letters*. The *Letters* supported Catholic Emancipation with such vigor and eloquence that they made Smith permanent and powerful enemies, who retarded Smith's rise in the church and prevented him from ever getting a bishopric. Smith's writing for the *Edinburgh Review* was mostly on political and social questions, and while the subjects of these essays have diminished in significance, the appeal of Smith's style has not. His sermons, too, are readable.

After Pitt's death, a brief Whig ministry allotted Smith the living of Foston-le-Clay in Yorkshire. In 1808, however, the Tories passed the Clergy Residence bill, and Smith was forced to remove himself from London to Yorkshire. Though Foston had not had a resident clergyman since the reign of Charles II, Smith accepted his fate gracefully. With the help of Queen Anne's Bounty, he built himself a comfortable parish house to replace the hovel in which he had been intended to live, invented small conveniences to make life happier and farming easier—a chimney, a universal back-scratcher for all sizes of livestock—rented out garden plots at a pittance so that his parishioners could supplement their spare diets, and preached to, supported, and medicated to his flock. In turn, he was beloved.

Smith continued to write for the *Edinburgh Review* and to support Catholic Emancipation, and he befriended the Whig nobility of the north of England, among them Lord Grey and Lord Carlisle. Although he never received the bishopric so many thought he deserved, Smith's position gradually improved. In 1823, the Duke of Devonshire loaned Smith the living of Londesborough in Yorkshire until his own son should come of age in 1832. In 1828, a coalition ministry gave him a canonry at Bristol, and Smith was able to exchange his Yorkshire living for one closer to that city. In 1831, he accepted a canonry at St. Paul's. Already a leading reviewer, Smith became a leading raconteur and dinner guest once he moved to London. When Roman Catholics were emancipated in 1829 and the Reform Bill was passed in 1832, the battles of Smith's polemical career were largely won. The death of his younger brother Courtenay in 1839 made Smith a rich man, able to take a house in Grovenor Square. He conducted his cathedral business faithfully and continued to write polemical works until his death in London in 1845.

James Najarian

Works Consulted

Bell, Alan. *Sydney Smith: Rector of Foston 1806–1829.* York: St. Anthony's Press, 1972.

Epstein, Joseph. "The Mere Common Sense of Sydney Smith." *New Criterion* 83 (1989): 9–20.

Pearson, Hesketh. *The Smith of Smiths.* London: Hamish Hamilton, 1934.

Society for the Suppression of Vice

The Society for the Suppression of Vice was the principal institution through which members of the Evangelical and Methodist movements sought to control what they perceived as the moral degeneration of English society. Working chiefly through the courts, the Society aimed to stifle such activities as Sabbath breaking, country sports, and nude bathing, and members of the Society often brought indictments against writers and publishers who produced licentious or blasphemous materials. The Society thus functioned as an arbiter of public behavior and public speech, a censor of sorts that influenced the social practices and public discourses of early 19th-century England.

Though not specifically recognized as the Society for the Suppression of Vice until the early 1800s, the organization began in 1787 when Wilberforce convinced George III to issue a proclamation condemning drunkenness, obscenity, blasphemy, and other forms of morally questionable behavior. Such Royal proclamations about moral laxity were common in the 18th century, but rarely were they taken seriously as guidelines for public behavior, let alone as legally binding on all British subjects. Immediately after the 1787 pronouncement, however, Wilberforce established a "Proclamation Society" that proceeded with some vigor to enforce the King's will.

During the anti-Jacobin fervor following the French Revolution, the activities of the Society began to take on a more distinctly political cast. While the Society still targeted its lawsuits against blasphemy and obscenity (there were over 600 successful prosecutions for Sabbath breaking between 1801 and 1802), such immorality had come to be associated with the radical community. Moral turpitude was seen not merely as a lapse in Christian virtue, but also as a sign of political insurrection. Consequently, most radicals objected to the Society's activities, despite the fact that they were often aligned in their political positions on such issues as the abolition of the slave trade and relief for the economic distress of the lower classes.

The attitude of the Tory government toward the Society was more ambivalent. On the one hand, the government saw the Society as a useful ally in its fight to control the antigovernment discourse of the radicals. On the other hand, the Society's insistence on a pious, well-regulated life carried across class divisions and threatened the amusements of the wealthy and powerful (e.g., Sunday card parties and adultery) as well as those of the poor and disenfranchised. Furthermore, the conservative ruling class often found the religious enthusiasm of the Society distasteful compared with the more staid English church.

In the 1820s, and especially after the passage of the Reform Bill of 1832, the influence of the Society began to wane. In effect, the Society passed its duty of moral vigilance on to the various disciplinarian groups of Victorian England.

Kyle Grimes

Works Consulted

Halévy, Elié. *A History of the English People in 1815.* 1924. London: Ark, 1987.

Owen, John Beresford. *The Eighteenth Century: 1714–1815.* New York: Norton, 1974.

Thomas, Donald. "Press Prosecutions of the Eighteenth and Nineteenth Centuries: The Evidence of King's Bench Indictments." *The Library.* 5th ser. 33 (1977): 315–32.

Thompson, E.P. *The Making of the English Working Class.* 1963. New York: Vintage, 1966.

Wickwar, William. *The Struggle for the Freedom of the Press, 1819–1832.* London: Allen, 1928.

Southcott, Joanna

(1750–1814)

A farmer's daughter and domestic servant from the West Country of England, Joanna Southcott was one of a number of self-proclaimed prophets popular in the country during the 18th and 19th centuries. Basing her prophecies on the Book of Revelation and often presenting them in mystic, rhymed verse, she preached that the Last Judgment, announced by a series of catastrophes, was at hand. From this destruction of the world, a new Messiah would appear to restore the earth to the faithful. (*See also* Religion.)

Southcott recorded her first divine communications in 1792. Her popularity began to grow rapidly in 1801 when news of her prophecies reached London and when her first pamphlet, *The Strange Effects of Faith*, was published. In 1802, she moved to London, where she met with followers and published her works in numerous inexpensive booklets which were sold throughout the country. During 1803, she traveled in Western and Northern England, delivering her message and identifying the redeemed. The proof of salvation given to believers was a paper signed by Southcott and closed with a seal she had found years earlier. As many as 100,000 of her followers, known as "The Sealed People," were given these signs of redemption.

A second climax in Southcott's popularity occurred in 1814, when she announced, at age 64, that she was pregnant, chosen by God to give birth to Shiloh, His Son. For several months, public attention focused on her, with newspaper stories on her health and songs composed in her honor. When she died in the last week of 1814, her disciples, expecting her to awaken, kept her body warm for several days.

Although she described signs of divine intervention and the utopia promised to the elect quite vaguely, Southcott's message was popular with England's poor. It appealed to their political frustrations, offering them the vision of a God who would destroy their enemies and deliver them into paradise. Southcott's prophesies did not, however, inspire people to social action; in fact, she preached against faith in political salvation, arguing that universal peace would arise only through the abolition of sin, not through revolt against kings.

Her influence lasted long after her death. In 1825, two men each claimed to be Shiloh but were dismissed as frauds by the leader of the Southcottians, John Wroe. Various offshoots of Southcott's cult experienced waves of popularity until the end of the 19th century. Evidence of her fame beyond her circle of religious followers can be found in the work of major writers. Blake, for instance, wrote a poem about her, *On the Virginity of the Virgin Mary and Johanna Southcott*, and Dickens used her as a sign of the times at the beginning of *A Tale of Two Cities*. Mention of her also appears in the correspondence of Southey, Keats, and Byron.

Susan Meisenhelder

Works Consulted

Garrett, Clarke. *Respectable Folly: Millenarians and the French Revolution in France and England*. Baltimore: Johns Hopkins, 1975.

Gaull, Marilyn. *English Romanticism: The Human Context*. New York: Norton, 1988.

Harrison, John F.C. *The Second Coming: Popular Millenarianism, 1780–1850*. New Brunswick: Rutgers, 1979.

Johnson, Dale A. *Women in English Religion*. New York: Mellen, 1983.

Thompson, E.P. *The Making of the English Working Class*. London: Gollancz, 1963.

Southey, Caroline Anne Bowles
(1786–1854)

Caroline Anne Bowles Southey wrote and published both prose and poetry but is perhaps best known as the second wife of Robert Southey. Born in 1786, at Lymington, Hants, she was the only child of Captain Bowles of the East India Company, who taught her to write and to fish before he died while she was quite young. Her mother's family was descended from the French-speaking aristocracy of Jersey. Until her marriage to Southey in 1839, Caroline Bowles lived at her family's Buckland cottage in Hampshire.

Bowles was a gentle woman of character. As a young woman, she allowed her mother and uncle to persuade her to turn down a marriage proposal from a now anonymous suitor, apparently a man in the military. On her mother's death in 1816, she was left without income. Colonel Bruce, an adopted son of her father, offered his support, suggesting both that she become his adopted sister and that she accept the gifts (such as a large white donkey) he was determined to lavish upon her. Bowles successfully resisted these offers but was finally persuaded to accept an annuity of £150. In the meantime, Bowles had decided to make her living as a writer.

In 1818, she sent the poet Southey a letter describing her rather secluded life; she enclosed a copy of her narrative poem

Ellen Fitzarthur and asked for comments. Southey's reply was encouraging, and they established a correspondence that lasted some 20 years and culminated in marriage. The tone of their letters is warm and supportive; both Bowles and Southey were respectful of each other's work. Southey, noting her interest in storytelling and love of the English forest, suggested, in a rather flirtatious letter to Bowles in 1823, that they collaborate on a long poem about Robin Hood. They began work on the poem at Bowles's Buckland cottage, but the poem was never finished.

Southey visited Bowles throughout the years of their correspondence, finding her secluded home an ideal place to write. In an 1831 letter to Margaret Holford Hodson, Southey describes a typical writing visit to Bowles: he devotes himself to writing for 11 days, seeing no one but Bowles and going out only for a long walk with Bowles and her Shetland pony before dinner.

Bowles also found the relationship conducive to her writing. Though she published in *Blackwood's Magazine* and the annuals, most of her work was received in book form. Her volumes were moderately popular and generally well-reviewed. Narrative in approach, her poetry and her prose often dealt with elements of pathos. *Ellen Fitzarthur,* published by Longman in 1820, was followed by *The Widow's Tale, and Other Poems* (1822); *Solitary Hours* (1826); *Tales of the Moors* (1828); *Chapters on Churchyards* (1829); *Tales of the Factories* (1833); *Selwyn in Search of a Daughter* (1835); and *the Birthday* (1836). In his review of *The Birthday,* Henry Nelson Coleridge (Coleridge's nephew and son-in-law) compares Bowles's poetry to Cowper's in its diction and attention to rural themes.

Southey's first wife, Edith Fricker, died in 1835, after a long decline into senility. Southey was devastated and turned to Bowles for comfort; they were engaged in 1838 and married in 1839. Unfortunately, Southey was in failing health, a fact Bowles tried to keep from general knowledge. But the changes soon became noticeable: he had difficulty sustaining conversations, no longer kept up his correspondence and, by 1840, could not recognize friends such as Wordsworth. To compound the pain of the situation for Bowles, Southey's children blamed her for his decline. Cuthbert Southey's collection of his father's letters carefully omits the lengthy correspondence Southey had with Bowles.

After Southey's death in 1843, an exhausted Bowles returned to Buckland cottage in Lymington. She published the incomplete *Robin Hood* with some of her previously unpublished poems, but she did not write anymore. She was granted a £200 Civil List pension by Queen Victoria in 1852 and died two years later. Her correspondence with Southey was finally collected and edited by Edward Dowden in 1881.

Kit Ayars

Works Consulted

Bernhardt-Kabisch, Ernest. *Robert Southey.* Boston: Twayne, 1977.

Courtney, Janet. *The Adventurous Thirties.* London: Oxford UP, 1933.

Curry, Kenneth. *New Letters of Robert Southey.* New York: Columbia UP, 1965.

———. *Southey.* Boston: Routledge, 1975.

Dowden, Edward. *Southey.* New York: Harper, 1902.

Jerdan, William. "Robert Southey." *Men I Have Known.* London: Routledge, 1866.

Symons, Arthur. *The Romantic Movement in English Poetry.* New York: Dutton, 1909.

Southey, Robert

(1774–1843)

Robert Southey is known as the author of *The Three Bears* and as the target of Byron's vicious satire. In his time, he was known as a literary journalist, historian, biographer, and Poet Laureate. While at Oxford, in 1793, Southey began his first major poem, *Joan of Arc*, shortly before meeting Coleridge. This poem imitated classical epics, boldly featuring a heroine with Catholic faith and French nationalist fervor. In 1794, he and Coleridge planned their American Pantisocracy, a utopian community of liberal life-style. Southey's political radicalism motivated his dramatization of *Wat Tyler* and his share in Coleridge's drama *The Fall of Robespierre*. Leaving Oxford without taking a degree in 1794, he returned to Bristol, where he secretly married Edith Fricker in 1795. He and Coleridge lectured on history and politics in Bristol, but they quarreled over Pantisocracy and went their separate ways.

Southey lived with his uncle in Portugal in 1795 and 1796, and again in 1800; these visits provided material for his Letters from Spain and Portugal. Though lacking Coleridge's imaginative subtlety, he shared an enthusiasm for lyrical poetry, and he composed most of his lyrics between 1794 and 1800, while under Coleridge's immediate influence. Southey experimented with a variety of lyrical forms, from sonnets and ballads to odes, inscriptions, and eclogues, on subjects ranging from natural phenomena to tales of terror and the suffering of abandoned mothers. Unlike Coleridge, however, Southey turned scenes of nature into occasions for moralizing, as in *The Evening Rainbow*, with its "arch of promise," or *The Holly Tree*, viewed "with curious eyes."

His interest in myth drove Southey in the main direction of the Romantic movement, toward visionary grandeur if not transcendental achievement. Realizing that constraints of history limited inventive freedom in *Joan of Arc*, he turned to exotic religious myths for materials with which to experiment in Romantic epic. His first completed poem of this kind was *Thalaba The Destroyer*, published in 1801 just before his return from Portugal. A narrative in 12 books of irregular, unrhymed stanzaic verse, its young Moslem hero, Thalaba, resists many temptations in questing for vengeance against underground powers of evil; he passes all tests, descends and destroys his enemies, then receives his reward in paradise. Thalaba's trials have archetypal significance, inspiring the imaginations of Shelley and Keats.

Southey, however, lacked faith in the freedom of imagination, and so his poems fail to lift vision to heights of understanding human history or to plumb its depths for insight into human character. When he turned to explore evil in *The Curse of Kehama*, he was unable to enter spiritual corruption as a state of the individual soul. Meanwhile, he continued with the poem whose subject had preoccupied him since his youth, the story of the Welsh hero *Madoc*, published in 1805 (after Southey and his wife Edith had made their home for life at Keswick, in the Lake District). This poem of blank verse narrates, on the model of *The Aeneid*, adventures of the historical Madoc in Wales (Part I) and in Aztlan (Part II). Southey mixes historical epic with religious myth in this story of Welsh struggles for freedom and Christian missions to civilize the Aztec Indians of America. Then, he finished his poem of Hindu myth, *The Curse of Kehama*, begun in 1801 and published in 1810; it shows effects from Southey's sufferings at the time, when his mother and infant daughter died.

Southey's Romantic epic was concerned with heroic struggles against the evils of mortality. The hero of this poem, also structured in imitation of the *Aeneid*, is a middle-aged father, Ladurlad, cursed to eternal exile by the powerful, godlike Rajah, Kehama. Ironically, Ladurlad's curse is also a blessing of spiritual strength, which finally prevails over the evil ambitions of Kehama.

That Southey could not execute his conception of evil was a mark of his limited contribution to the Romantic movement, more effectively continued by Southey's great literary enemy, Byron, and more subtly initiated by Coleridge. When Southey rewrote his Portuguese epic, *Roderick, The Last of the Goths* (1814), he converted the villainous Roderick into a heroic protagonist, as Southey himself was converted from revolutionary republican into establishment monarchist. Evil is simplified even more in his poetry after he became Poet Laureate in 1813, including his infamous *Vision of Judgment* in 1821, vindicating the monarchy of George III and inspiring Byron's glorious mockery of both the mad king and laureate Southey.

Poet though he was, Southey's most accessible writing today is his prose, of which he produced a great variety. He did not complete his plan to write a history of Portugal, but he did publish a history of Brazil in 1810, and he wrote a *History of the Peninsular War* (published 1822–32). Still interesting are his books on English society, beginning with *Letters from England by Don Manuel Espriella*, in 1807, and concluding with *Sir Thomas More: or, Colloquies on the Prospects of Society* (1829). The first imitates Goldsmith's *Citizen of the World*, with observations made by a foreign visitor; the second explores opportunities for irony in a dialogue with Thomas More, Utopian visitor from the past. These books develop Southey's growing distrust of democracy, disdain for capitalism, and disgust with immorality. Indeed, immorality subverted the heroic career of Lord Nelson, whose biography Southey published in 1813.

In what was to be the crowning achievement of his life's work, Southey published *The Doctor, &c.* in 1834, the year Edith was moved to a mental asylum and barely four years before Southey's own mental health gave way. Begun in 1813, *The Doctor* is an encyclopedia of fact and fiction in the manners of Sterne, Rabelais, Montaigne, and Burton. It is the "story" of Dr. Daniel Dove, Southey's ideal figure of the past. It is a whimsical, yet often tedious, collection of anecdotes, sketches, and pedantry whose humor is in its ambition to tell it all. More and more Southey's imagination became captive to the past, turning his vision backward to oppose urgencies of the present, but to his credit, Southey brought the values of his past to bear as a critique on faults of his present. (*See also* Lake School, Nationalism, Satire.)

Richard D. McGhee

Works Consulted

Bernhardt-Kabisch, Ernest. *Robert Southey*. Boston: Twayne, 1977.

Carnall, Geoffrey. *Robert Southey and His Age: The Development of a Conservative Mind*. 1960. Oxford: Clarendon, 1960.

Curry, Kenneth. *Southey*. Boston: Routledge, 1975.

———. *Robert Southey: A Reference Guide*. Boston: Hall, 1977.

Spanish Romanticism

The Romantic movement entered Spain in the 1830s with the return of the liberals who had been exiled during the reign of Fernando VII. The movement represents a rejuvenation in Spanish literature. Following a particularly sterile literary period, Neoclassicism, the themes and ideals of

Romanticism provoked a reevaluation of classical Spanish works of the medieval age and 16th- and 17th-century works, products of Spain's "Golden Age." Although the works produced during the period contain all the characteristics of the Romantic mode with the addition, in its final stages, of a traditional Roman Catholic element, in general, the movement was most influenced by French Romanticism.

Romanticism was particularly suited to the Spanish national character; however, its success was brief. By 1850, the realistic movement had already taken root as the prevailing literary mode. After this date, Romanticism continued to be the dominant characteristic of the work of the poets Gustavo Adolfo Bequer and Rosalia de Castro, whose poetry continued to influence 20th-century Spanish writers.

Among the leading figures of Spanish Romanticism are the playwrights and poets don Angel de Saavedra; dugue de Rivas, whose drama *Don Alvaro, or the Force of Destiny* introduced the movement in 1835; Juan Eugenio Harzenbush, author of *Los amantes de Teruel* (1837); and Jose Zorilla, who wrote a Romantic drama, *Don Juan Tenorio* (1844), based on the Don Juan theme. The poetry of Jose de Espronceda represents the most varied and complete production of the period. Spain did not produce works in prose comparable to the great historical novelists. However, the interest in local color that formed part of the Romantic movement occasioned the "costumbrist" movement, which consisted of short scenes dealing with local customs that were published in newspapers and magazines. The most representative author of this movement was Mariano Jose Larra.

Lynn Fedeli

[The] Spirit of the Age

The English Romantic period, conventionally set between the publication of *Lyrical Ballads* in 1798 and the death of Scott in 1832, has been variously described as an age of revolution and a time of transition, as an era of coherence and an epoch of contradiction. Each is an accurate yet limited depiction; for, like the concept of Romanticism itself, this period of literary history has evoked and evaded attempts to distill from its several complex features a single unifying definition. Late 18th- and early 19th-century reviewers, confronted with new modes of verse that departed from the Neoclassical models, tended to recognize poetic originality as the hallmark of the age. At the same time, they conceded the lack of commonality among those poets often regarded as the most innovative "master-spirits" of the day (Wordsworth, Byron, and Scott by some accounts). Likewise, the poets, none of whom claimed either to be a "Romantic" or part of a school of poetry, thought of themselves as individual voices in what became one of the greatest eras of lyricism.

Yet poets and reviewers alike recognize in the times a palpable atmosphere, an intellectual and creative current, that sparked writers dissimilar in literary intent and doctrine. Shelley found in this "spirit of the age," as he called it in *A Defence of Poetry*, the galvanizing energy that was bringing about a rebirth of English literature. Both he and Hazlitt, whose *The Spirit of the Age* (1825) suggested various facets of the period through a series of contemporary portraits, linked this distinctive spirit with revolutionary and renovating change. The source and emblem of the change they located principally in the French Revolution, which Hazlitt regarded as the primary impetus for Wordsworth's poetic revolution.

Among the Romantic poets, only Wordsworth had firsthand experience of the French Revolution. He was 19 years old when the storming of the Bastille occurred; at 20, he was in France, his hopes fixed on the Revolution as the herald of a new and regenerated age. Yet for the other Romantic writers as well, both those of Wordsworth's generation and those such as Byron and Shelley who came later, the French Revolution exerted a powerful influence as an indication of the political, social, and poetical freedom that was possible once the strictures of convention are removed. Despite its failure to achieve the initial high promise of social and political reform, the Revolution became an augury of a new order that, with differing manifestations, most of the major Romantic poets envisioned imaginatively in their work. (*See also* French Revolution.)

Out of this prevailing *Zeitgeist* of revolutionary change emerged the shifts in perspective and poetic practice that set the writers of this age apart from their Neoclassical predecessors. These shifts, which were in some ways the culmination of a transition in thought that had been taking place since roughly 1750, changed many of the fundamental ideas about such matters as nature, poetry, and the poet. Whatever, for example, their disagreements over the value inherent in nature as opposed to that imparted to it by human imagination (a point of opposition between Blake and Wordsworth especially), the Romantics all rejected the 18th-century notion of nature as mechanistic and static and found agreement in conceiving of it as an organic process. (*See also* Organic Form.) This dynamic model of order in the universe was paralleled in aesthetics with a new dynamic vision of the possibilities and pur-

poses of poetry. (*See also* Poetry.) Where the Neoclassical writers had found comfort in conformity to prescribed artistic standards, the Romantics were energized by diversity and the freedom to forge new modes of individual expression. For several of them, poetry took on an oracular office, becoming a kind of secular gospel, and the poet was regarded as having a priestly or prophetic role in the perceptual regeneration of a fallen world. (*See also* Prophecy and Apocalypse.) Thus the idea of a social revolution achieved through political avenues gave way to the conception of a spiritual revolution made possible through mental means—through the power of the mind and the medium of poetry.

However else it may be described, Romanticism is fundamentally a way of seeing, a perceptual vantage point. During the late 18th and early 19th centuries in England, the writers that came to prominence within a vortex of extraordinary change caught the spirit of possibility and promise inherent in an age of revolutionary ferment. Out of this context, they shaped individual visions that spoke in varying ways of the indomitability of the human spirit and a world made new through the imagination.

Guin A. Nance

Works Consulted

Abrams, M.H. *The Correspondent Breeze: Essays on English Romanticism.* New York: Norton, 1984.

— — —. *Natural Supernaturalism: Tradition and Revolution in Romantic Literature.* New York: Norton, 1971.

Clubbe, John, and Ernest J. Lovell, Jr. *English Romanticism: The Grounds of Belief.* DeKalb: Northern Illinois UP, 1983.

Gaull, Marilyn. *English Romanticism: The Human Context.* New York: Norton, 1988.

Johnston, Kenneth R., Gilbert Chaitin, Karen Hanson, and Herbert Marks, eds. *Romantic Revolutions: Criticism and Theory.* Bloomington: Indiana UP, 1990.

Prickett, Stephen, ed. *The Romantics*. New York: Holmes, 1981.

Rosso, G.A., and Daniel P. Watkins, eds. *Spirits of Fire: English Romantic Writers and Contemporary Historical Methods*. Rutherford: Fairleigh Dickinson UP, 1990.

Wordsworth, Jonathan, Michael C. Jaye, and Robert Woof. *William Wordsworth and the Age of English Romanticism*. New Brunswick: Rutgers UP, 1987.

Spontaneous Overflow of Powerful Feelings

When Wordsworth writes in the Preface to the second edition of *Lyrical Ballads* (1800) that all good poetry is the "spontaneous overflow of powerful feelings," he is articulating a basic tenet for the 19th century in poetry. Refuting Neoclassical empiricism and rationalism as the means of knowing both the external and internal landscape, his philosophy declares the poet to be a person of exceptional "organic sensibility" who has thought long and deeply about the relationship between his feelings and his thoughts. If, according to Wordsworth, thoughts represent past feelings, and feeling are modified and directed by thoughts, then his concept of the interplay between the two is yet another example of his belief in the connectedness of all sentient things. His tenet reiterates the Romantic faith in organicism (as opposed to mechanism) by affirming the harmony of the inward and outward as they are shaped by the mind of the poet into poetry. This process occurs by means of the poet's own mind synthesizing the outer (nature) with the inner (the individual mind). The powerful feelings are generated by the poet's sympathetic response to nature's power to terrify, awe, and heal. (*See also* Literary Criticism and Literary Theory.)

Each of the poems, then, has a purpose that, like nature, ministers to the heart of readers. In the Preface to the edition of 1800, Wordsworth declares even more straightforwardly that the purpose of these poems is to show the way in which feelings and ideas are associated in a state of excitement. The purpose is not always clear to the poet in the beginning stages of composition, but "habits of meditation" have so informed and "regulated" his feelings that his descriptions of the objects that excite his strong feelings naturally carry with them a purpose. The poet worthy of the name of Poet has contemplated the relation of feelings and thoughts and because he has done so repeatedly, he will be "connected with important subjects," and the description will incite a fellow feeling in the reader. The means by which he attains this end are, in Wordsworth's own words in the 1800 Preface, "various": by tracing the "maternal passion" in its subtlety of feeling, as in *Idiot Boy* and the *Mad Mother;* by viewing the final struggle of the human being as death approaches, as in the *Forsaken Indian;* by showing the "perplexity and obscurity" with which children view death; and by showing the strength of "fraternal" or "moral attachment" when it is early associated with the beauty of nature, as in *The Brothers* or *Simon Lee.* The poet then creates in the reader a heightened moral sensation.

Clearly it is by choice of subject that Wordsworth imparts to the reader the connection that nature and humanity share. Of equal importance to the poet and the craft of poetry is the focus Wordsworth has on style. The "spontaneous overflow of powerful feelings" on the part of the reader is a result of the poet's purpose, a purpose achieved most specifically through the language of the poetry. The language is concrete; "personifications of abstract ideas rarely occur." Also important as a fundamental part of Wordsworth's new credo is the poet's announcement in these Prefaces that he vows to imitate and adopt "the very language of men." And finally, he states that he has been true to his subject with no "falsehood of description." As a result, he has created language in the poems that, with the exception of the meter, differ in no real respect from the language of good prose.

Wordsworth, like Coleridge, sees association as an emotional process rather than as a rational or intellectual process. Ideas or images associate or are connected by the feelings that run through them. Nature in its infinite breadth and depth stirs the divine in the poet, thus enabling him to take the "spontaneous overflow of powerful feelings" and to recollect them "in tranquility" so as to minister to the soul of humanity in the form of poetry. (*See also* Associationism, Emotion Recollected in Tranquility, Empiricism, Organic Form.)

Paula P. Yow

Works Consulted

Rader, Melvin. *Wordsworth: A Philosophical Approach.* Oxford: Clarendon, 1967.

Spots of Time

A supreme aspect of Wordsworth's faith is his belief in the creative nature of the human mind. His monumental poem, *The Prelude*, is now considered the fundamental philosophical statement of the poet's belief that the free and creative character of the human mind can add an "imperishable increment of power" to life. If imagination is once active and if the faculties are exercised with both strength and freedom, then the power of the human mind to hear these voices of sensory experience and to perceive these natural objects acutely encourage the "unfolding" of the intellect that Wordsworth chronicles in Book XII of *The Prelude*.

In moving away from the associationism of Hartley, Wordsworth's philosophy incorporates the belief that the creative mind grows in stages. As the subtitle of *The Prelude, Or the Growth of A Poet's Mind*, suggests, the intellect unfolds. The first stage, that of childhood, is the animal stage. The second stage is one of sensation, or sensual pleasure, that in Wordsworth's words, "craves combinations of new forms" that Wordsworth in his own life sought in his many walking tours. In this second stage of sensation, the inner faculties are still asleep, yet the mind is constantly perceiving and recording natural images. These two preliminary stages culminate in the final stage when the inner faculties open to aesthetic pleasure.

The "spots of time" that Wordsworth writes about in Book XI of the 1805 edition or Book XII of the 1850 edition of *The Prelude* hold for the mind that eternal power that adds to life. This power is embraced in the growth of the poetic mind in the second stage, where the senses dominate. The poet writes that "There are in our existence spots of time,/which with distinct pre-eminence retain/A vivifying [renovating] Virtue. . . ." By describing the Virtue as *vivifying* in the early edition of the poem, he conveys the idea of the quickening, the enlivening, the renewing of that portion of the poet's sensibility that is attuned to the beauty and pleasure of the "sensations" that the mind perceives. The substitution of the word *renovating* for *vivifying* illustrates the growth of Wordsworth's philosophy into a vision of the interactive, organic power of the poetic mind as the mind incorporates the "renovating" virtue that combines the restorative powers of nature with the "creative soul" of the poet. Hence, the real subject of the poem, that the poet is a human speaking to humanity, is further elucidated by the power and virtue that result from the poet's powers of recollection to inform his sensitivity and creativity.

A major tenet of Wordsworth's philosophy that the "mind is lord and master" and "outward sense" but the "obedient servant of her will" is illustrated by the examples in Book XII of *The Prelude* that the poet calls up of his own "spots of time." He remembers that as a child he rode toward the hills with "an ancient servant of [his] father's house" and that when he somehow became separated from his companion, he dismounted and walked on the stony moor to happen upon a bottom where a murderer had been hung in iron chains. The gibbet, the bones, and the iron case were gone, but on the turf the murderer's name was carved, still visible after many years. The child fled the sight to climb the common and see a "naked pool" and near it a girl with a pitcher on her head, struggling against the wind. It was, he writes, "an ordinary sight," but to a child lost and terrified by the vision of death pictured on the dreary landscape, the sight of the girl with her "garments vexed and tossed" by the wind took on significance as a "beacon crowning the lone eminence." Yet on the "melancholy beacon" fell a "spirit of pleasure" coupled with the "golden gleam" of youth. So, the poet concludes, "feeling comes in aid of feeling," and to have once been strong is to hold forever this power that renews and restores. The "hiding places of man's power" open, and when age dims physical sight, these "spots of time" can nonetheless be recalled as the "spirit of the Past/For future restoration." (*See also* Associationism, Organic Form.)

Paula P. Yow

Works Consulted

Rader, Melvin. *Wordsworth: A Philosophical Approach.* Oxford: Clarendon, 1967.

Stothard, Thomas
(1755–1834)

Probably the most popular and prolific illustrator of his times, Thomas Stothard executed a wide variety of art forms, from landscape, sculpture, and history painting to ceramics, silverwork, and book illustration. His decorative style and sentimental subjects appealed to a broad range of his contemporaries. He is perhaps now best known for his close association with Flaxman and Blake. Together, these three friends developed a reduced linear style to amplify the emotional resonance of their art. They also were among the first artists of note to become involved in the newly developing manufacture of mass-produced art commodities, such as illustrated books, ceramics, and silverwork.

By utilizing new techniques of production, such as the division of labor and specialization, several entrepreneurs began to turn out mass-produced luxury objects directed to a new and lucrative market. Stothard's success lay in his ability to adjust to the diverse commercial demands of these new areas of art production. Although Stothard's market-conscious attitude formed the basis of his prolific employment, financial success, and popularity, it was not incompatible with his identity as a venerated professional artist and Royal Academician. Nor did his affiliation with several radical political organizations, particularly in his youth, affect the general spread of his fame and rise of his prices.

Stothard was able to accommodate the diverse demands of both manufacturers of art commodities and individual, private patrons because he functioned as a specialist. In this role, he could readily adapt his designs to a wide variety of markets. For example, he would use a design produced for silver or for book illustration as the basis for a self-contained painting. His designs were interchangeable, fulfilling the requirements of both his commercial employers and his private patrons. Stothard's work was not adversely affected by his adoption of various industrial practices, because he, unlike many later artists, was still able to master the multifarious skills utilized in art production in the years around 1800. His diverse commercial activities are indicative, however, of the transformation of the artist's function in an industrial society.

Shelley M. Bennett

Works Consulted

Bennett, Shelley M. *Thomas Stothard, The Mechanism of Art Patronage in England circa 1800.* Columbia: U of Missouri P, 1988.

Bray, Anna Eliza. *The Life of Thomas Stothard, R.A. with Personal Reminiscences.* London: Murray, 1851.

Coxhead, A.C. *Thomas Stothard, R.A.* London: Bullen, 1906.

Stuart, James

(1713–88)

James Stuart began his career as a fan painter, employed by Louis Goupy. Born in England in 1713, by 1742 Stuart was in Rome, but not until nine years later did he join Revett on an important expedition to Athens to study architecture, a hitherto unexplored source of architectural inspiration.

Returning to London in 1755, the two men collaborated on a volume called Stuart and Revett's *Antiquities of Athens,* published in 1762. The immediate influence of the work was small, though today it ranks—along with Wood's *Ruins of Palmyra* (1753) and Adam's *Palace of Diocletian at Spalatro* (1764)—as one of the three most important architectural travel books of the century.

Upon his return to London, Stuart found a patron in Admiral Lord Anson, who employed him to design several large London homes, including Mrs. Montagu's in Portman Square (later called Portman House, destroyed by fire in 1941) and Lord Anson's home in St. James's Square. In these two homes, Stuart introduced what he then called an Athenian order.

While still a painter and a young man, Stuart is believed to have studied the Raphael *loggie* and Giulio Romano's work, because in designing parts of the Spencer House, he employed a similar example of this type of elaborate decoration. The interior of the Chapel at Greenwich Hospital, reconstructed following a fire in 1779, is acclaimed to be Stuart's most remarkable work; however claims to this work have also been made on behalf of William Newton.

Stuart is remembered most for *Antiquities of Athens,* which opened up a great new field of interest to future architects and designers. In his day, the book contributed in an important way to the fashionable trend known as "Greco-gusto." In 1788, Stuart died, having grown irresponsible and intemperate in his later years, an isolated, enigmatic figure, whose career hardly did justice to the enormous talent he possessed.

Marilyn Jean Clay

Works Consulted

Myers, Bernard, ed. *McGraw-Hill Dictionary of Art.* London: McGraw, 1969.

Summerson, John. *Georgian London.* London: Pleiades, 1945.

[The] Sublime

The "sublime" is perhaps the most important and certainly the most controversial aesthetic term in the 18th and early 19th centuries. It is usually juxtaposed, by way of contrast and definition, to the category of the "beautiful" or, less frequently, of the "picturesque." "Sublime" is derived from Longinus, an obscure Greek writer of probably the first century, author of *Peri Hypsous, On the Sublime*. Longinus was first translated into English in 1652, but only achieved real popularity when Boileau's translation became available in English (1736). The term denotes a certain emotive force of language in literary productions, token not of mere technical expertise or observation of the rules of composition but of a supposed greatness of soul in the author. The concept of the sublime thus became closely involved with that of "genius" and was especially associated with Milton's *Paradise Lost* and the Old Testament. It was often defined in terms of its effects—of awe, or a "pleasing fear"—and imaged in terms of a flight or an elevation or an expansion of the mind.

The *rhetorical* sublime, briefly described above, is often distinguished by historians from the *natural* sublime in recognition that many critics, such as Addison, Akenside, Baillie, Burke, Gerard, Hume, and Reid followed Longinus in analyzing sublimity as a response to natural landscapes, especially landscapes that comprised an image of vastness, whether in power or physical extent. With modern critics the term "Romantic sublime" has entered critical currency. Broadly speaking, one may take the term's distinctiveness from a tendency from the late 18th century to attribute the emotions of awe, astonishment, and elevation associated with the sublime less to the nature of its object and more to the supposed discovery of unknown, possibly transcendent, aspects or powers in the perceiving consciousness itself. A useful schematization of this tendency, which finds its most influential statement in Kant's *Critique of Judgment* (1790),

appears in Coleridge's lines written after first hearing the poem by Wordsworth that was later to be known as *The Prelude*: "power streamed from thee, and thy soul received/The light reflected, as a light bestowed." One consequence of this focus on the activities of the perceiving mind is that objects obviously grand or stupendous are no longer necessary to trigger the sublime experience. Wordsworth in particular is notable for linking sublime processes of thought with the apparently trivial or everyday. Coleridge explicitly defines the sublime in terms of the human mind's ability to perceive any entity in the capacity of a symbol of the infinite.

The sublime is thus preeminently a moment of interpretation. Its effect is associated with the breakdown or overwhelming of received and familiar modes of perception or representation (e.g., a tiny flower suddenly takes on a vast significance). The breakdown induces a crisis that is understood in terms of the impingement of another, often transcendent, order of being. Reference to this order is taken to resolve the sense of the collapse of limits, rendering it cause for celebration. Any sublime moment, then, if it is to be more than a moment of crisis and a breakdown in understanding, demands some notion of the beyond to provide what might be termed a second-order level of meaning. This demand for some sort of credible God term, inherent as it is to the structure of the sublime, also renders it an object of both suspicion and linguistic self-consciousness in a poet such as Shelley, in whose poetry the sublime coexists with an intense metaphysical skepticism.

The sublime forms part of the recurrent concern with issues in the philosophy of perception to be found in Romantic poetry. As a putative overcoming of dualism, it is sometimes imaged in terms of a secular redemption or, especially among the second generation of Romantic poets, by images of sexual union. The sublime is thus a discourse of boundaries and limits; it is liminal rather than mystical, its most suitable emblem the line of the horizon itself. Dialectically, it may become an endorsement of the very limits it purports, momentarily, to transgress and often finds its counterpart in writing of intense alienation. Hence also the distrust of received accounts of the sublime to be found in the visionary poetry of Blake or, conversely, Keats's skepticism of the sublime's implicit repudiation of the natural world. However, what the sublime crisis may be taken to mean varies greatly from poem to poem. Indeed this question itself is one of the major characteristics of Romantic poetry, concerned as it often is with the processes and making of meaning.

Timothy J.A. Clark

Works Consulted

De Bolla, Peter. *The Discourse of the Sublime: Readings in History, Aesthetics and the Subject.* Oxford: Blackwell, 1989.

Ende, Stuart E. *Keats and the Sublime.* New Haven: Yale UP, 1976.

Hertz, Neil. *The End of the Line: Essays in Psychoanalysis and the Sublime.* New York: Columbia UP, 1985.

Leighton, Angela. *Shelley and the Sublime: An Interpretation of the Major Poems.* Cambridge: Cambridge UP, 1984.

Modiano, Raimonda. "Coleridge and the Sublime: A Response to Thomas Weiskel's *The Romantic Sublime.*" *The Wordsworth Circle* 9 (1978): 110–120.

Monk, S.H. *The Sublime: A Study of Critical Theory in Eighteenth-Century England.* 1935. Ann Arbor: U of Michigan P, 1960.

Twitchell, James B. *Romantic Horizons: Aspects of the Sublime in English Poetry and Painting, 1770–1850.* Columbia: U of Missouri P, 1983.

Weiskel, Thomas. *The Romantic Sublime: Studies in the Structure and Psychology of Transcendence.* Baltimore: Johns Hopkins UP, 1976.

Wlecke, Albert O. *Wordsworth and the Sublime.* Berkeley: U of California P, 1973.

Sunday-School Movement

Because there was no system of national or popular education in 18th-century England, few children attended elementary school. The rural masses, which formed about two thirds of the population, were predominantly illiterate, and the Bible was a neglected book. The poor conditions of the working classes and their children aroused the sympathy of Robert Raikes, a printer and publisher from Gloucester. Raikes's initial efforts were to secure a reform in the conditions of jails and prisons, rendering the life of a prisoner at least endurable. Failing in this endeavor, he began a new experiment, the modern Sunday School, which swiftly gained a place among the most important of modern religious-educational institutions.

Raikes's first school, Sooty Alley, opened in 1780, in the kitchen of a home adjacent to his residence. The children met in the morning, and on Sundays they returned for instruction after church. Good behavior was rewarded by Bibles, testaments, books, games, shoes, and clothes. The school mistress, who had primary responsibility for the students, was paid about a shilling a day.

Once Raikes was satisfied that his scheme had passed the experimental stage, he made it public. He explained his plan to Wilberforce and John Wesley, who were enthusiastic. Notices of his experiments were published in local periodicals, thus making his movement widely known throughout Great Britain.

From the first, Raikes applied a voluntary principle in his classroom. Paid mistresses and masters were at first necessary, but they gradually disappeared. Much of the teaching was done by monitors, older students who acted as teachers to the younger ones. This feature of wholly volunteer instruction and management made Raikes's system unique and adapted the Sunday School to the needs of poor communities and parishes, thus aiding in its remarkable spread throughout Great Britain. (*See also* Education; Lancaster, Joseph; Trimmer, Sarah.)

The Bible was the center of the Sunday-School curriculum. Other books included *The Sunday Scholar's Companion, A Copious School Book,* and *A Comprehensive Sentimental Book,* the last containing the alphabet, spelling, moral and religious lessons, and stories and prayers. Raikes's use of the Bible as the primary textbook distinguished his Sunday-School movement from earlier sporadic schools. It was a practical revolution in the system of instruction and gave much popularity to the plan.

Although there was some opposition to the Sunday-School movement, primarily by the nobility who feared the consequences of educating the poor, for the most part, the Sunday-School movement was widely supported. It found advocates among Dissenters and churchmen alike and progressed so rapidly that the Queen gave it royal favor by sending for Raikes in order to hear his story firsthand.

Five years after Raikes organized his first Sunday School, William Fox, a London merchant, conceived of his own plan for a Sunday School Society. The first full name was "The Society for the Support and Encouragement of Sunday Schools in Different Counties of England," but as the work extended to Wales, Ireland, and the British colonies, the name was changed to "The Society for the Support and Encouragement of Sunday Schools throughout

the British Dominions." It was popularly known by the shorter title of "The Sunday-School Society."

The method of the Society was to lease rooms or buildings in villages where the poor needed instructions, hire teachers, and maintain schools under rules adopted by the Society. The Society provided Bibles, testaments, and other needed books for the pupils and had each school inspected by competent visitors. The proceedings of the Society were subject to the approval of a general committee composed of 24 persons, one half of whom were from the Church of England, and the other half from Dissenting denominations. In 27 years, it formed 3,370 Sunday Schools.

Both Raikes's Sunday Schools and the Sunday-School Society were chiefly philanthropic organizations. Gradually, however, the Sunday-School system began to emerge into a wider movement for religious education. On July 13, 1803, the London Sunday-School Union was formed. The chief purpose of the Sunday-School Union was to improve Sunday Schools and thus promote some system in religious education. W.F. Lloyd, who had achieved success in Sunday-School work, became secretary of the Union in 1811. Under his leadership, the Union came into greater prominence and wider usefulness. His periodical, *Teacher's Magazine,* attained a high rank with educators for several years.

The work of the Sunday-School Society and the London Sunday-School Union was carried on by the Church of England Sunday-School Institute, formed in 1843, and the Wesleyan Sunday-School Union, formed in 1875. What unifies these different Sunday Schools is the belief that education should embrace the whole person and that physical, intellectual, and religious training are all necessary to Christian education. Voluntary instruction, the use of the Bible as a textbook, and the economical character of the Sunday-School movement made for its widespread growth in Great Britain and elsewhere.

Mary Susan Johnston

Works Consulted

Armytage, W.H.G. *Four Hundred Years of English Education*. Cambridge: Cambridge UP, 1970.

Briggs, Asa. *The Making of Modern England, 1784–1867: The Age of Improvement*. New York: Harper, 1960.

Halévy, Elié. *A History of the English People in the Nineteenth Century: England in 1815*. Vol. 1. New York: Barnes, 1961.

Harris, Ronald W. *Romanticism and the Social Order, 1780–1830*. London: Blandford, 1969.

Lawson, John, and Harold Silver. *A Social History of Education in England*. New York: Methuen, 1973.

Rice, Edwin Wilbur. *The Sunday School Movement and the American Sunday-School Union*. Philadelphia: American Sunday School Union, 1917.

Wardle, Addie Grace. *History of the Sunday School Movement in the Methodist Episcopal Church*. New York: Methodist Book Concern, 1918.

Supernaturalism

It is a critical axiom that cultural periods acquire much of their shape by reacting against their immediate predecessors; certainly Romanticism's most salient features—its emphasis on emotion and introspection, its celebrations of the "common" and the natural, its interest in revolutionary change (and its attendant dislocations)—all distinguish it from the more formalist, urban (and urbane) rationalism of much Neoclassical literature. Romantic interest in the supernatural is likewise a central feature of the period's response to Neoclassicism and its privileging of realism and became as well an important tool in the Romantic investigation of the human condition and human potential in an age of sweeping changes.

Although Romantic supernaturalism is very much the product of a particular historical moment, it spoke to its age by drawing heavily on a variety of prior forms and practices. Gothic novelists and Romantic poets alike turned to Shakespeare and Elizabethan revenge tragedies for ghosts and the atmosphere of guilt and hidden crimes; burgeoning interest in rural folk culture, particularly British balladry and folklore, introduced new realms of supernatural fable and imagery. The period's interest in travel literature supplied a ready fund of foreign locales, while the elegiac meditations of the graveyard poets were rich sources of mood and setting; the popularity in England of German *Sturm und Drang* literature (with its valorization of intense emotion, defiant individualism, and social marginality) and the fantastic tales of Hoffmann, Tieck, Bürger, and others created an interest in the nonrational that whetted the appetite of the English reading public.

While these and other sources of Romantic supernaturalism are fairly easy to determine, much more complex is the matter of why literary supernaturalism came into such vogue in this particular period.

Gothic fiction is generally recognized as beginning with Walpole's *The Castle of Otranto*, published on Christmas Eve in 1764, but the genre achieved its enormous popularity not until some 30 years later, not coincidentally (most scholars believe) at approximately the same time that the Terror in France was reaching its most horrific pitch. Gothic fiction provided a perfect medium to address those concerns raised in England by the French Revolution; Gothicism's frequent reliance on Continental settings, Roman Catholic institutions and practices, and beleaguered nobles in half-ruined castles provided a literary form well able to articulate revolutionary anxieties while displacing them sufficiently (often through historical distancing) to render them palatable. (*See also* Gothicism.)

Another revolution of sorts was also under way at the time, one with powerful implications not only for supernaturalist fiction but for all of Western culture. The publication of such works as Wollstonecraft's *Vindication of the Rights of Woman* (1792) fueled a debate about gender role and privilege that continues today, and while few works of Romantic supernaturalism are regarded as unqualifiedly "feminist" by modern standards, many Gothic novels, by focusing on the persecution and pursuit of innocent young heroines by villainous men, do raise compelling questions about women's lack of access to various forms of power and about the implications of Western culture's paradigms of gender identity and construction.

Questions of identity and self are significant parts of the entire Romantic context. The waning influence of Christianity in the Western world led many Romantic writers to ask searching questions about the nature of selfhood and the relation of the individual not only to society but to the transcendent. As Western metaphysics began to postulate an increasingly remote divine, reexaminations of spirituality and transcendent possibility became a major part of Romantic literary endeavor, and the supernaturalist literature of the time participated fully in this project. Indeed, some scholars have found a sense of the numinous or spiritual dread to be a definitive characteristic of Gothicism. The responses of various writers to these metaphysical anxieties differed greatly. Radcliffe, whose *The Mysteries of Udolpho* (1794) was perhaps the single most popular Gothic novel, wrote works that found consolation in moral virtue, piety, and rationalist principles; such writers as Lewis,

whose novel *The Monk* (1795) was perhaps the most notorious Gothic fiction, were less confident of the orderly workings of a benevolent divine providence. Regardless of their ideological or metaphysical persuasion, however, Romantic writers found that supernaturalism provided an adaptable language that permitted incisive consideration of the political, spiritual, and psychological (particularly sexual) ramifications of these ongoing reassessments of individual identity.

Writers traditionally labeled "Romantic" also relied on many of these same sources and impulses: Coleridge drew heavily on ballad tradition for *Christabel* and *The Rime of the Ancient Mariner*; Southey borrowed from Continental literature, while Scott mined the riches of Scottish history and legend; Keats recounted a haunting from Boccaccio, and Byron turned the Faust myth into a compelling poetic drama. But these (and many other) borrowings from the past spoke very much to the present, for in the hands of the Romantics, supernaturalism generally forsook the cloak of horror it had been given by Gothic fiction and became more concerned with investigating the possibility of transcendence.

So powerful was the lure of supernaturalist imagery that even Wordsworth, whose Preface to the *Lyrical Ballads* makes plain his interest in everyday occurrences and his repugnance toward the excesses of Gothic fiction, found room in some of his mature poetry for supernaturalist or Gothic elements. Although Wordsworth, unlike Burns, never celebrated superstition as a vital element of rural imaginative life, he did rely at times on superstitious belief and supernatural innuendo as means of considering the role and power of the imagination and of the human relationship to the suprarational; *The Thorn, Goody Blake and*

Harry Gill, Hart-Leap Well, and *The Danish Boy* all rely, to some degree, on supernaturalism or superstition. *Peter Bell* is an important text in the tradition of Gothic or supernaturalist satire, a genre that flourished in the later years of Gothicism's popularity. The most famous Gothic satire is Austen's *Northanger Abbey.*

The explicit division of labor in the *Lyrical Ballads* left the overtly supernatural to Coleridge; *The Rime of the Ancient Mariner, Christabel,* and *Kubla Khan* (collectively known as "the mystery poems") are the supernaturalist works for which he remains most famous. Employed to examine, among other things, complex psychological states and the relationship of the individual to society, these works are a high-water mark of Romantic supernaturalism.

While Shelley's millennial optimism found expression in works often reliant on a modified classical mythology, among his first publications are the traditional (indeed, derivative) Gothic novels *Zastrozzi* (1810) and *St. Irvyne* (1811). While Gothic elements are evident in mature works such as *The Cenci* (1819), Percy Shelley's repudiation, recounted in his *Hymn to Intellectual Beauty,* of Gothic horror for modes more congenial to his transcendent optimism is representative of the relationship between Romantic and Gothic supernaturalism. The earlier visionary poet Blake likewise found Gothic supernaturalism unsuitable for his poetic project.

Keats, with his strong interest in romance, found supernatural imagery congenial, but consistently used it to support his optimistic aesthetics. Conversant with Gothic fiction but apt to treat it with an amused if affectionate irony, Keats employed supernaturalism, in works such as *The Eve of St. Agnes, Lamia,* and *La Belle Dame sans Merci,* as another way of conducting his investigations into human tran-

scendent capability, a project that occupied much of his attention in the great odes.

Byron's ironic pessimism made him more amenable to Gothic elements, but his most famous supernaturalist work, *Manfred,* makes clear that these elements hold no terror. Ending in an act of heroically defiant solipsism, the poem glancingly recognizes some of the power of Gothic gloom but refuses to acknowledge it as a final assessment of the human condition. It is telling that Byron began what many scholars believe would have been the first vampire novel in English, but abandoned it after only a few pages. Byron's traveling companion and physician, Polidori, would go on to borrow Byron's idea and turn it into *The Vampyre,* published in 1819.

Byron's aborted novel had its origin in one of the key events of Western supernaturalist literature. In the summer of 1816, Byron was living next door to Percy and Mary Shelley on the shore of Lake Geneva; a period of wet weather was passed in the reading of ghost stories, ending in a challenge for each member of the group to write a supernatural tale. Byron and Percy Shelley quickly abandoned their projects while Polidori eventually produced the English language's first vampire novel, but by far the most famous result of this challenge was Mary Shelley's *Frankenstein,* begun that summer when she was 18 years old and published two years later. The daughter of Wollstonecraft and Godwin, himself the author of the semi-Gothic novels *Caleb Williams* (1794) and *St. Leon* (1799), Mary Shelley incorporated into her tale of "the modern Prometheus" many of the principles of her father's liberal political philosophy, particularly the belief that social and familial circumstances are largely responsible for human behavior. Her novel also reflects many of her mother's feminist principles, earning it an important place in the tradition of feminist fiction, and its reliance (although tangential) on science and technology have led many scholars to identify *Frankenstein* as the beginning point of science fiction.

The work of these and other writers makes clear that the Romantic period is a crucial one in the history of literary supernaturalism. It synthesized a variety of predecessor forms and produced a new supernaturalist genre, the Gothic, that ably addressed many of the sociocultural anxieties of the age. And although this particular form of Romantic supernaturalism soon disappeared—Maturin's *Melmoth the Wanderer* (1820) is generally taken to be the swan song of classic Gothic fiction—its impulses and imagery did not. Romantic and Victorian writers developed new forms with large debts to the Gothic: detective and mystery fiction, the modern romance, science fiction, and horror. Romantic supernaturalism enabled superficially escapist fiction to engage in legitimate sociopolitical commentary; it provided a psychological lexicon a century before Freud; it permitted examination, in popular form, of metaphysical issues of foundational—and continuing—importance to Western civilization. For all of its associations with casual titillation, vicarious thrills, and lowbrow culture, Gothic and Romantic supernaturalism is now recognized as a major cultural element in its own historical moment and as the immediate predecessor of a vital and valuable part of modern literary endeavor.

Jack G. Voller

Works Consulted

Carter, Margaret L. *Specter or Delusion? The Supernatural in Gothic Fiction.* Ed. Robert Scholes. Ann Arbor: UMI, 1987.

Birkhead, Edith. *The Tale of Terror: A Study of the Gothic Romance.* 1921. New York: Russell, 1963.

Day, William Patrick. *In the Circles of Fear and Desire: A Study of Gothic Fantasy.* Chicago: U of Chicago P, 1985.

DeLamotte, Eugenia C. *Perils of the Night: A Feminist Study of Nineteenth-Century Gothic.* New York: Oxford UP, 1990.

Ellis, Kate Ferguson. *The Contested Castle: Gothic Novels and the Subversion of Domestic Ideology.* Urbana: U of Illinois P, 1989.

Fleenor, Juliann E., ed. *The Female Gothic.* Montreal: Eden, 1983.

Haggerty, George E. *Gothic Fiction/Gothic Form.* University Park: Pennsylvania State UP, 1989.

Heller, Terry. *The Delights of Terror: An Aesthetic of the Tale of Terror.* Urbana: U of Illinois P, 1987.

MacAndrew, Elizabeth. *The Gothic Tradition in Fiction.* New York: Columbia UP, 1979.

Punter, David. *The Literature of Terror: A History of Gothic Fictions from 1765 to the Present Day.* New York: Longmans, 1980.

Summers, Montague. *The Gothic Quest: A History of the Gothic Novel.* 1938. New York: Russell, 1964.

Varma, Devendra P. *The Gothic Flame.* London: Barker, 1957.

Swedenborgianism

Emanuel Swedenborg (1688–1772) was a Swedish scientist, engineer, mystic philosopher, and theologian. The son of a bishop, Swedenborg received extensive scientific training in France, England, and Holland, before returning to Sweden to take up an appointment as an assessor at the Swedish Board of Mines in 1716. He made innovations in contemporary engineering practices, and his work in metallurgy and biology represented significant advances in those fields. Swedenborg also published treatises in cosmology and mathematics. However, after undergoing a spiritual crisis in early 1745, he believed that he had been given a mission by God to interpret the Scriptures and to describe his own experiences in what he claimed to be the world of angels and spirits. He subsequently published, in Latin and frequently anonymously, 30 volumes, including the eight-volume *Arcana coelestia* (1749–56).

Swedenborg's religious thought is unorthodox. Rejecting traditional ideas about the trinity, sin, atonement, and eternal punishment, he developed a system that resembles Neoplatonism in Christian dress: he believed that the physical world is a reflection of the spiritual world, for example, and he explained this in terms of his doctrine of correspondence. He also believed that heaven and hell refer to inner, psychological states.

Swedenborg never preached a sermon or founded a sect. But he acquired followers nonetheless, and a decade after his death Swedenborgian societies were being founded in England, organized principally by Robert Hindmarsh, a Methodist. The first General Conference of the New Jerusalem Church took place in Great Eastcheap in London in April 1789. This meeting was attended by Blake, who is one of the signatories on the conference resolution. In the United States, Swedenborg's doctrines arrived in the late 1780s, and a society of the New Jerusalem Church appeared in Baltimore, Maryland, in 1792. John Chapman ("Johnny Appleseed") distributed the Swedenborg message through the Midwest. In 1817, the General Convention of the New Jerusalem met in Philadelphia. The Swedenborgians still exist today, although as a religious movement their numbers have always been small.

Swedenborg's influence has been profoundly felt in literature. During the late 1780s, Blake was a thoroughgoing Swedenborgian. He owned and annotated Swedenborg's *Divine Love and Wisdom,* and Swedenborgian ideas can be discovered in the *Songs of Innocence* (1789). Blake was intrigued by Swedenborg's declaration that a new age had begun in the spiritual worlds in 1757—the date of Blake's birth. How-

ever, by the time Blake came to annotate Swedenborg's *The Wisdom of Angels concerning Divine Providence,* in about 1790, his attitude to the Swedish seer had become far more critical. And in *The Marriage of Heaven and Hell* (1790–93), Blake turned against his former mentor, satirizing him mercilessly. The title is an allusion to Swedenborg's *De coelo* (1758), which is known in translation as *Heaven and Hell.* Blake objected to what he perceived to be Swedenborg's theological orthodoxy and his conventional morality. But Blake later referred favorably to Swedenborg in his poem *Milton,* and Swedenborg's influence runs deep throughout Blake's work: his term "Divine Humanity," for example, is taken directly from Swedenborg.

In the United States, Swedenborg was well known to the Transcendentalists. In the late 1850s, Walt Whitman attended Swedenborgian meetings in New York and read his works extensively, although not uncritically. Ralph Waldo Emerson included an essay on Swedenborg as a mystic in *Representative Men* (1850), and the journals of Henry David Thoreau contain many references to Swedenborg. Nineteenth-century French literature also owed a debt to Swedenborg, particularly in the work of Hugo, Lamartine, Sand, and Balzac, the last most notably in *Séraphita* (1835). Symbolist poets, such as Baudelaire, were attracted to the Swedenborgian idea of correspondences, as were Strindberg and Yeats.

Bryan Aubrey

Works Consulted

Block, Marguerite. *The New Church and the New World: A Study of Swedenborgianism in America.* New York: Holt, 1932.

Jonsson, Inge. *Emanuel Swedenborg.* New York: Twayne, 1971.

Paley, Morton D. "'A New Heaven is Begun': William Blake and Swedenborgianism." *Blake: An Illustrated Quarterly* 50 (1979): 64–90.

Raine, Kathleen. *Blake and Tradition*. 2 vols. Princeton: Princeton UP, 1968.

Swedenborg, Emanuel. *The Universal Human and Soul-Body Interaction*. Ed. and trans. George F. Dole. New York: Paulist, 1984.

Synaesthesia

Synaesthesia is the rare phenomenon in which a stimulus, such as sound, evokes an additional response in an unrelated sense such as smell, taste, touch, or vision. A certain note on the scale, for instance, might cause the listener to see a color in addition to hearing the sound. Such blendings of sensory impressions enable one to speak of loud colors or cool sounds.

Attuned to perception and consciousness, several Romantic poets employed synaesthesia as a literary device, though writers as far back as Dante had also used it poetically. While Wordsworth's poetry was greatly concerned with sensation and consciousness and Keats's poetry was also highly sensory, the two poets who most used synaesthesia were Shelley and Coleridge.

From his earliest writings, but to an even greater degree later, Shelley frequently employed synaesthesia as an instrument for expressing some transcendental state and for evoking the idea of a mystical merging with a perfect, fully integrated cosmic ideal. He often equated moral and sensory discernment, so that a harmonious blending of sensory experience becomes a sign of a greater spiritual harmony. *Alastor, Prometheus Unbound, Adonais,* and *Epipsychidion* are particularly rich sources of synaesthetic images. Similarly, the proto-pantheistic creed of Coleridge's early poetry-making days derived in large measure from an aesthetic that celebrated merged sensory impressions.

Two brief examples from Romantic poetry illustrate the use of synaesthesia. In Shelley's *To a Skylark*, the notes of the bird's song are likened to the phosphorescence of the glowworm, the sweet fragrance of a rose, and bright drops of rain. In Coleridge's *The Eolian Harp*, an awareness of the unity of "the one life within us and abroad" emerges for the speaker from the music of the harp, a music that he describes as "a light in sound, a sound-like power in light." (*See also* Camelion Poet; Egotistical, or Wordsworthian, Sublime.)

Linda Jordan Tucker

Works Consulted

Mahoney, John L. *The English Romantics: Major Poetry and Critical Theory*. Lexington: Heath, 1978.

Noyes, Russell, ed. *English Romantic Poetry and Prose*. New York: Oxford UP, 1956.

O'Malley, Glenn. *Shelley and Synesthesia*. Evanston: Northwestern UP, 1964.

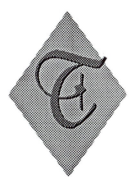

Taylor Family

Ann (1782–1866) and Jane Taylor (1783–1824), two sisters originally trained as engravers, are credited with being the first English authors to write exclusively for children. Their joint productions, *Original Poems for Infant Minds* (1804–05), *Rhymes for the Nursery* (1806), and *Hymns for Infant Minds* (1810) were enormously popular: *Original Poems* went through some 50 editions in England and was translated into German, Dutch, and Russian; *Hymns* went through nearly 100 editions in England and America. Though many of their poems are too didactic for modern tastes, some have entered into the oral tradition, including *Twinkle, Twinkle Little Star*. (*See also* Children's Literature.)

The Taylors came from a talented family: their grandfather engraved plates to illustrate Goldsmith's *Deserted Village* and Richardson's *Sir Charles Grandison*, and their father engraved plates for Boydell's Bible and *Shakespeare*. When the engraving market collapsed, their father became an Independent minister, first at Colchester and then at Ongar in Essex. He taught his six surviving children at home and superintended their engraving. The girls were precocious and vivacious. They wrote plays and verses and formed their own literary group, The Umbelliferous Society."

Ann was the first to publish. An election song she wrote privately for family and friends was printed in 1797, and a poetical solution of a puzzle in *Minor's Pocketbook* won first prize in 1799. She became a regular contributor and then editor for Darton and Harvey. Jane's first poem, *Beggar Boy*, was printed in the *Pocketbook* in 1804. At first, "Nancy" and "Jenny's" parents did not favor their writing, which was done early in the morning and late at night. But when the girls' collections of verses began to make money—the Taylors were some of the few poets who did make money—the parents and brothers began to publish, too. Their father wrote textbooks, especially on biography; their mother wrote books of advice and manners; one brother wrote humorous tales for children, while the other, the most intellectual of the family, wrote philosophical and religious works, as well as executing designs for his father's and his sisters' books. The Taylor family was used by Sir Francis Galton as an example in his theory of distribution of intellectual capacity in his *Hereditary Genius* (1869).

Though their verses are collected together, the sisters wrote the poems separately, as is occasionally noted by an "A" or "J" which follows the verse. Since original publication, however, the authorship has been confused. Jane is most famous for *The Star*, *The Cow and the Ass*, and *The Violet*, her poems generally display an interest in nature and speak about kindness to animals. *I Love Little Pussy* has also been attributed to her. Ann is the author of *Dance, Little Baby* and *Meddlesome Maddy*; her interest lies more in people and their behavior. Jane's work was admired by Robert Browning and Scott and frequently parodied (by Lewis Carroll for example).

Ann W. Engar

Works Consulted

Armitage, Doris Mary. *The Taylors of Ongar*. Cambridge: Hoffer, 1934.

Delamar, Gloria T. *Mother Goose From Nursery to Literature*. Jefferson, NC: McFarland, 1987.

Johnson, Edna, *et al. Anthology of Children's Literature*. Boston: Houghton, 1959.

Opie, Iona and Peter, eds. *The Oxford Dictionary of Nursery Rhymes*. Oxford: Clarendon, 1951.

Taylor, Isaac. *The Family Pen*. London: Jackson, 1867.

Taylor, Jane

(1783–1824)

Jane Taylor composed significant serious poetry in addition to her widely read pieces for children that were published with those of her older sister Ann. Jane was born in 1783 in London to an engraver, who later became a Dissenting minister, and his wife Ann, who was to follow their children into authorship.

Reared in Lavenham, Suffolk, and in Colchester, Jane began to write stories and poems at an early age. Jane began contributing to the annual *Minor's Pocketbook*, in 1804. The two volumes of *Original Poems for Infant Minds* (1804–05), by "several young persons"—Ann and Jane, with contributions by their brother Isaac and Adelaide O'Keefe—achieved tremendous popularity, going through dozens of editions over the following decades. The sisters followed *Original Poems* with other works including *Rhymes for the Nursery*, which contains Jane's *The Star*, familiar as "Twinkle, Twinkle, Little Star." In 1811, she and her family moved to Ongar, Suffolk, and the next year Jane went with Isaac to live in Southwestern England, where in the absence of a Dissenting congregation she attended both Methodist and Anglican services.

In 1813, the sisters' collaboration was dissolved by Ann's marriage to Joseph Gilbert, like their father a nonconforming minister. The first book entirely of Jane's composition, the didactic *Display: A Tale for Young People*, was published in 1814 and went to 11 editions. In 1816, appeared her *Essays in Rhyme, on Morals and Manners*, a collection of poems aimed at mature readers that combine satirical character sketches with calls to both intellectual rigor and religious faith. She continued writing for young people: from 1816 to 1822, she contributed to *The Youth's Magazine* the essays and poems that in 1824 were published in collected form as *Contributions of Q.Q.* In 1816, she returned to the family home in Ongar, where she and her mother began their novel *Correspondence Between a Mother and Daughter at School* (1817).

Jane developed breast cancer in 1817, and in her final years devoted herself increasingly to religion. She died in 1824. *Memoirs and Poetical Remains of the Late Jane Taylor*, edited by Isaac, appeared in 1825. There are numerous later editions of her works.

Gary R. Dyer

Works Consulted

Curran, Stuart. "The I Altered." *Romanticism and Feminism*. Ed. Anne K. Mellor. Bloomington: Indiana UP, 1988: 185–207.

Dictionary of National Biography, *s.v.* "Taylor, Jane."

"Jane Taylor, 1783–1824." *The Feminist Companion to Literature in English: Women Writers from the Middle Ages to the Present*. Ed. Virginia Blain, Patricia Clements, and Isobel Grundy. New Haven: Yale UP, 1990.

[Taylor, Isaac.] "Memoirs." *Memoirs, Correspondence, and Poetical Remains, of Jane Taylor*. Vol. 1 of *The Writings of Jane Taylor*. 5 vols. Boston, 1832.

Taylor, John

(1781–1864)

Hessey, James Augustus

(1785–1870)

The publishing firm of John Taylor and James Augustus Hessey lasted only 20 years, but at its dissolution in 1826, Taylor and Hessey had known, encouraged, defended, and published some of the most brilliant writers ever: Keats, Lamb, Hazlitt, De Quincey, Coleridge, Carlyle, and Clare, among others. (*See also* Publishing.)

Taking his early training at James Lackington's ("Temple of the Muses") publishing company, Taylor learned how a publisher could meet the increasingly diverse demands of a new reading public, Although he quit the firm after only four months, he had met Hessey there, and a lifelong friendship had begun. In 1806, they formed their partnership as publishers and booksellers at 93 Fleet Street, learning in their first years even more about the trade, as well as establishing themselves as fair and reputable businessmen.

In 1817, John Hamilton Reynolds introduced them to Keats, and shortly after, they decided to publish Keats, convinced that he was a genius. In fact, as letters show, Taylor's own ideas about art's autonomy and the authenticity of the imagination in revealing an otherwise invisible reality paralleled Keats's in many ways. These foci, moreover, created numerous occasions on which Taylor struggled between his role as a publisher, one who makes his living by uniting artist and public, and his role as a sympathizer and patron of the artist.

Keats's association with Taylor and Hessey did not end with his death in 1821. Indeed, he became a kind of touchstone genius through which their work as publishers can be seen. They had found in Keats a genius in the ongoing state of developing negative capability, and through his struggles with the public and with what it meant to be an artist, they had become aware of how moral, social, and political issues are intrinsically involved with the public's reception of literature. Such is the case with their purchase of the *London Magazine* in 1821, a publication through which they introduced such writers as De Quincey, Hazlitt, and Lamb. The venture ended in 1825, but within four years, Taylor, as editor, and Hessey, assisting managerially, witnessed the enormous success of De Quincey's *Confessions*, in 1822, and the decided failure of Lamb's *Elia* essays. There are several reasons why one work finds popularity and another does not, but by 1825, Taylor was seriously worn out and had turned from promoting poetry and imaginative literature to science, perhaps in an effort to keep up with the times.

The partnership dissolved in 1826, although the friendship remained. There was, it seems, a new London and an antipoetic climate. In spite of their awareness of the changing times, Taylor and Hessey believed that they had played a part in preserving works of imagination for future generations.

Jo-Anne Cappeluti

Works Consulted

Barnard, John. *John Keats*. New York: Cambridge UP, 1987.

Bate, Walter Jackson. *John Keats*. Cambridge: Belknap, 1963.

Chilcott, Tim. *A Publisher and His Circle: The Life and Work of John Taylor, Keats's Publisher*. Boston: Routledge, 1972.

Rollins, Hyder Edward, ed. *The Keats Circle: Letters and Poems of the Keats Circle*. 2nd ed. Cambridge: Harvard UP, 1965.

Telford, Thomas

(1757–1834)

The canal era in England began in the late 18th century and culminated in 1830. It was short-lived, but its effects were long reaching. During the Industrial Revolution, more expedient methods for shipping iron and coal were sorely needed. In an experiment to transport coal more efficiently, the Duke of Bridgewater had the first canal completed in 1761 in Manchester. The immediate result was that the cost of coal in Manchester was cut in half. Other ironmasters soon began to press Parliament for canal construction as well as much-needed major road improvement.

Born in Eskdale, Scotland Thomas Telford had his own ideas regarding the construction of all-weather roads and contributed as well a wealth of ideas regarding canal construction. During his lifetime, Telford engineered the construction of new canals in England as well as major bridges, harbors, docks, and waterways.

President of the Society of Civil Engineers in London, Telford was the surveyor of the London-Holyhead road and architect of the beautiful Menai Strait suspension bridge, a bridge connecting the Island of Anglesey and the mainland of Gwynedd County in Wales. He also engineered Ellesmere Canal, which connects the Mersey, Severn, and Dee Rivers in England.

As a young man, Telford apprenticed as a mason, but later, his experiments with cast iron pointed him in the direction of suspension bridges. By 1825, he was regarded as an expert in his field and was consulted on numerous major continental works. An impressive career followed in which he engineered several exquisitely beautiful suspension bridges. Among his important works are Conway Bridge, castellated to blend with Conway Castle, using an elegant iron suspension; St. Katherine's Docks (1819–26); Pony y Cysylte Aqueduct; Hardcastle Tunnel (1824–27); Holyhead Road (1817); and the Caledonia Canal in Scotland. (*See also* Industrial Revolution; MacAdam, John Loudon.)

Marilyn Jean Clay

Works Consulted

Ashton, Thomas. *The Industrial Revolution, 1760–1830*. New York: Oxford UP, 1948.

Schultz, Harold. *History of England*. 2nd ed. New York: Barnes, 1971.

Thomson, David. *England in the Nineteenth Century*. London: Cape, 1950.

Textual Supplements

Literary texts have been supplemented throughout history, but the Romantics made particularly extensive use of elements appended to areas outside of the text. These components—what Gérard Genette refers to as the "paratexte"—can consist of prefaces, dedications, manifestoes, title pages, letters, epigraphs, introductions, advertisements, all forms of titles, notes, illustrations, marginalia—essentially anything that is separated from the text proper but somehow connected with it.

Significantly, the Romantics anticipated critical developments in the second half of the 20th century in this regard as they broadened the notion of the text to include elements that had previously been relegated to an exterior status. In this sense, the margins of the text expand to the point that they figuratively dissolve. Moreover, the Romantics prefigured another component of later critical theory though their intense preoccupation with the inadequacies of language. After all, an adequate language would logically need no additional commentary. But the Romantics viewed language as an extremely unreliable medium, and perhaps nothing better illustrates this than their many attempts to direct the readers' interpretation of their primary texts.

The Romantics' supplements assume a wide range of forms: Blake's illustrations published with some of his works function to complicate—rather than to simplify—the act of reading; Coleridge added marginal glosses in 1816 to his *The Rime of the Ancient Mariner* (first published in 1798) to create another layer of textual commentary and thus expand the range of narrative voices in the poem; and when large numbers of Keats's personal letters began to appear in print at the middle of the 19th century, his reputation changed considerably, since the letters provide a great deal of insight into his theories on poetry.

Wordsworth's Preface to *Lyrical Ballads* is arguably the most famous example of the Romantic's endeavors to supplement their works. Initially appearing as a short advertisement to the collection of poems, the Preface grew extensively as Wordsworth altered it several times when new editions of the volume were published. Because the Preface includes comments on the plan behind the poems in the volume, principles of poetic composition, the role of the poet, and the state of modern poetry, the Preface had an immense influence on readers' interpretations of these "experiments" by Wordsworth and Coleridge. Wordsworth also dictated notes for many of his poems to a family friend, Isabella Fenwick, in 1842 and 1843, and these famous comments—now referred to as the Fenwick Notes—have similarly acquired the status of substantial prefatory guides to his works.

Maria Edgeworth's novel *Castle Rackrent* (1800) features a lengthy Preface that praises "the prevailing taste of the public for anecdote" as "an incontestable proof of the good sense and profoundly philosophic temper of the present times." Through this Preface, Edgeworth attempts to elevate the genre of the "plain unvarnished tale" that had been "censured and ridiculed by critics who aspire to the character of superior wisdom." Her readers, accordingly, could feel justified in enjoying her anecdotal novel through the authorial sanction she provides in her opening gambit which assuaged their uneasiness with such reading fare.

Mary Shelley also made calculated use of such supplements in the 1817 Preface (written by her husband Percy) to her novel *Frankenstein; or, The Modern Prometheus* (1818). The relatively brief Preface establishes an intriguing mood for the reader by speculating on the eerie subject matter that follows. Like advertisements to the film treatments of Frankenstein's monster that appeared much later, the Preface lures readers with commentary on the ways that the novel "affords a point of view to the imagination for the delineating of human passions more comprehensive and commanding than any which the ordinary relations of existing events can yield."

In a passage that links this Preface to numerous others, Shelley describes the romantic setting in which the novel was written. Although this is a curious development, it reveals a distinct characteristic of Romantic literature: the creation of author-reader empathy. Along with this understanding of the circumstances under which a work was composed, comes (or so the Romantics hoped) a greater competence for interpreting the author's general message.

While Wordsworth and other Romantics use this strategy frequently, Percy Shelley offers possibly the most engaging example of compositional setting with his Preface to *Prometheus Unbound* (1820). Shelley describes the setting as "mountainous ruins" featuring "flowery glades, and thickets of odoriferous blossoming trees" which "extended in ever winding labyrinths upon . . . immense platforms and dizzy arches suspended in the air." This intensely sensuous description, along with Shelley's other elaborate comments on the poem, such as its characters, function as a detailed preparation for pleasurable reading—an effect the Romantics as a whole tried to create for their readers.

In his famous long prefatory note to *Kubla Khan: Or, a Vision in a Dream. A Fragment* (1816), Coleridge goes so far as to, presumably, fabricate a compelling story of the poem's genesis through a drug-related experience in order to appeal to the readers' attraction to the unusual. This paratexte (along with the titles) allows Coleridge to create a dream-vision economy for the poem which, in turn, grants considerable license for vivid imagery as well as provides an explanation for the poem's alleged lack of completion.

Well-known for his exciting adventure tales, Scott extended his knack for such narratives into his substantial introductions, prefaces, and notes to his novels and poems. He tried to accommodate his readership by including anecdotes regarding composition, pertinent historical background, his own actual experiences, and even his own efforts to adjust to his immense fame and the surprising difficulties it created for him.

This widespread use of supplements by the Romantics was not allowed to flourish without a satirical backlash of some kind, and Byron provides possibly the most humorous example of this through an unincorporated preface to *Don Juan* (1818–23). He spends more than two pages ridiculing Wordsworth's prefatory technique and argues that if readers are willing to accept Wordsworth's directions for reading his poems they will likewise accept his egregiously ridiculous description of the poem's narration.

Byron by no means spurned textual supplements and, in fact, used them as much as any of the other Romantics. He realized, as did the others, that this device offers considerable potential for influencing the ways that readers interact with their texts—which may explain why he decided not to incorporate this particular preface into the poem.

Scott Simpkins

Works Consulted

Edgeworth, Maria. *Castle Rackrent*. New York: Norton, 1965.

Genette, Gérard. "The Proustian Paratexte." *SubStance* 27 (1988): 63–77.

Mileur, Jean-Pierre. *Vision and Revision: Coleridge's Art of Immanence*. Berkeley: U of California P, 1982.

Rzepka, Charles J. *The Self as Mind: Vision and Identity in Wordsworth, Coleridge, and Keats*. Cambridge: Harvard UP, 1986.

Shelley, Mary. *Frankenstein; or, The Modern Prometheus* (1818 Text). Ed. James Reiger. New York: Bobbs, 1974.

Simpkins, Scott. "The Reader and the Romantic Preface." *Rocky Mountain Review of Language and Literature* 44 (1990): 1–2, 17–34.

Watson, Kenneth. "Coleridge's Use of Notes." *Romanticism Past and Present* 6 (1982): 2, 11–22.

Wolfson, Susan J. "Keats the Letter-Writer: Epistolary Poetics." *Romanticism Past and Present* 6 (1982): 2, 43–61.

Theater

The Romantic theater was varied and vital, and its dramatic literature, generically eclectic. Because many playscripts of the period (other than closet plays) were closely allied to their production, one cannot be swayed by some Romantic critics' insistence on dichotomizing theater and drama. Few plays from the Romantic era have been canonized for ongoing literary analysis, but this does not mean the Romantic period lacked rich theatricality. (*See also* Mental Theater, Pantomime.)

For most of the era, the Romantic playhouse consisted of a large apron that extended beyond the proscenium doors and over the pit. Gradually, the forestage was cut back until it emerged only an inch or two past these doors and the actors were absorbed into the stage picture. Drury Lane Theatre abandoned the stage doors in 1822, but most actors continued to deliver their major speeches downstage center, with a deferent "chorus" of so-called minor players hovering behind them in symbolic postures.

Romantic staging was representational not realistic. As visual spectacle escalated, the stage machinist became more prominent in the production design: in addition to detailed scene painting by such talents as Philippe Jacques de Loutherbourg, gauze was introduced to the set, along with panoramic devices, trapdoors, limelight, and stage fires. In 1817, Covent Garden and Drury Lane installed gas lighting to replace candles and oil lamps, while the lights in the auditorium chandelier burned throughout the play until 1850. So important was the visual aspect of Romantic theater that demand for a genre called "dog drama" arose in 1803 when a dog named Carlo was trained to "rescue" a child from a large pool of water at Drury Lane; in the same vein, in 1811 Covent Garden presented *Blue-Beard*, complete with live horses on stage.

By contrast, the era's costuming was rather modest, an amalgam of contemporary and period clothing. Its eclecticism reflected the potentially liberating spirit of much of Romantic theater; not until an 1823 to 1824 production of *King John* was an attempt made to produce faithfully the costume of an historical period.

One of the remarkable features of Romantic playhouses was their size. Drury Lane and Covent Garden—the only theaters licensed to perform the legitimate, or spoken, drama—could each seat approximately 3,000 people. It is ironic that these theaters maintained a monopoly on the spoken word while, increasingly, their offerings depended less on what could be heard than what could stun the eyes of those in the far-distant galleries. The Haymarket, a Royal theater that performed in the summer season when Drury Lane and Covent Garden were dark, was considered an intimate space because it sat only 1,500 people. Understandably, Kean was said to have given his best performances here.

Fiercely competitive, Drury Lane's and Covent Garden's histories paralleled each other during the Romantic period. Christopher Wren had designed Drury Lane in 1674, and it was rebuilt in 1794 under the management of Kemble, who inherited the managerial mantle from David Garrick and Richard Brinsley Sheridan. After the theater burned in 1809; it was redesigned to be even larger when it reopened in 1812. Covent Garden, rebuilt in 1792, burned in 1808 to reopen in 1809 under the management of Kemble, who in 1802 had left Drury Lane. Upon reopening, Covent Garden became the scene of the Old Price riots, the most famous theatrical protest of the period. To protest the increase in ticket prices and in the number of private boxes, audiences demonstrated at the theater for 67 nights (between September and December 1809), with the result that Kemble was compelled to reduce both the number of boxes and the performances' prices. Historians cite this protest as the most dramatic indicator of London playhouses' increasing democratization. These protests did not secure Royal patronage or coax the defecting aristocracy back from the King's Opera House, where ballet and opera were undergoing a golden age. Not until mid-century did Queen Victoria's patriotic sentiment for English theater announce to the aristocracy that it was again respectable to go to the theater.

Respectability was less an issue for the middle- to lower-class audiences; they were more concerned with the relevance of the material being performed. As bastions of England's canonized drama, Drury Lane and Covent Garden did not generically experiment, as did the "minor theaters." The minor theaters were relatively free to ignore tradition and offered a more popular fare, which addressed social and political subjects. In 1789, for example, Sadler's Wells offered the topical *Gallic Freedom: or Vive La Liberte*, about the storming of the Bastille; this theater came to specialize in nautical dramas of English naval battles, with real tanks of water on the stage. Although hampered by the Licensing Act of 1737, the minor theaters created extravaganzas, spectacles, and a variety of other dramatic forms. They skirted the restrictions on presenting legitimate drama by devising burlettas (i.e., dramatic narratives studded with songs, dancing, recitative, and other distractions) in order to belie comparison with the "legitimate" plays from which the burlettas' plots were sometimes borrowed.

Audiences so enthusiastically supported minor theaters that Drury Lane and Covent Garden lost money during the period. In the 1790s, an average of 1,500 people attended each Royal theater, not enough to make playwrighting lucrative or to support the large company of actors retained to perform the wide-ranging repertory. Late 18th- and early 19th-century audiences insisted on their right to participate in the performance by clapping in the middle of a soliloquy when an actor delivered a pleasing interpretation (a "hit"), booing and hissing at an actor if he or she had somehow violated their sense of morality, approving or disapproving the repetition of a new play when the manager stepped before the curtain at the play's end to "give out" the drama. These audiences ate, drank, threw objects, and solicited prostitutes (who were allowed to operate from saloons and lobbies in the legitimate theaters, until William Charles Macready dispelled them in 1842). Between 1763 and 1765, Garrick had abolished the practice of allowing members of the audience to sit on the stage, but the barnlike auditoria seem not to have hindered the Romantic audience from active involvement in the performance (when it interested them). While social classes were generally separated by the structure of the playhouse—aristocracy and upper middle classes in boxes, middle classes in the pit, and working classes in the galleries—the Romantic theater was becoming a place to mix. The downward trend in ticket prices during the first two decades of the 19th century, the half-price tickets offered at 9 p.m., and a repertoire increasingly responsive to the middle and lower classes all reflected and encouraged a more democratic theater.

The variety of dramatic genres suggests this opening up of the Romantic playhouse. Alongside a conservative impulse that harkened back to traditional dramatic models (classical Greece, Shakespeare, Jacobean tragedy) ran a revolutionary urge: the successful playwrights were the adaptors who could explode generic boundaries. Sheridan produced a huge hit with his version of a Kotzebue play, called *Pizarro* (1799), and novels by Radcliffe, Godwin, Mary Shelley, Scott, Walpole, Lewis, Henry Mackenzie, and Clara Reeves (among others) were frequently adapted. German and French plays were modified for English audiences, along with English Restoration drama, Shakespeare's romances, and his better known tragedies. The Gothic tragedy, or Gothic thriller, with its despairing hero, castles, dungeons, and physically frail but enduring heroine, was the dominant form between 1800 and 1830, inspired by Walpole's unacted *The Mysterious Mother* (1768). Richard Cumberland, Bertie Greatheed, James Boaden, Henry Siddons, Baillie, Maturin, Coleridge, R.L. Sheil, Henry Hart Milman, and Percy Shelley either created or adapted dramas in this mode. After Thomas Holcroft's *A Tale of Mystery* in 1802, melodrama proliferated, an admixture of English and German dramas and Guilbert de Pixérécourt's French boulevard melodrama. Each of the Romantic poets and some women playwrights revived verse drama; Shelley's *The Cenci* (1819) is the most anthologized. In addition to J.S. Knowles's popular *Virginius* (1820), Hemans wrote *The Vespers of Palermo* (1823);

Mitford, *Rienzi* (1828); and Baillie, over 25 plays.

Aside from these types of dramas, there were five-act comedies, burlettas, farces, burlesques, the extravaganzas of L.R. Planché, spectacles, farcettas, comediettas, light operas, 18th-century sentimental comedy, and pantomime—the period's most popular form.

Increasing interest in character psychology was tied both to the star system of acting and to the burgeoning corpus of theatrical criticism. The Romantic period has frequently been called the Age of the Actor, the description of a performance enduring beyond the role itself. Once an actor achieved success in a role he or she became, in effect, entitled to that part throughout a career. The actor also became associated with roles that were similar in type and the style required to perform them: thus, Kemble and Siddons acted primarily drama and tragedy—"the Kemble school" of acting connoting a statuesque, classical formalism—while Kean was considered the embodiment of Romanticism (spontaneous, instinctive, emotional) after his debut in 1814 as Shylock. Like Napoleon—the short man who made good—small-framed Kean captured the imagination of a generation of critics, especially Hazlitt and Keats, who wrote *Otho the Great* (1819) with Kean in mind. Shelley created the role of Beatrice Cenci for Eliza O'Neill, debuting as a compelling Juliet the same year as Kean. To fashion roles specifically for well-known actors—Jordan in comedy, Eliza Lucy Bartolozzi (Madame Vestris) in burlesque, and Grimaldi the great clown—was a common practice, and aside from perpetuating hierarchical ensembles, it encouraged critical discussion about the relationship between the actor's personality and characterization.

The cult of the individual actor also partially indicates why so much theatrical criticism emerged during this time. In London, periodicals, such as the *Dramatic Censor* (1800-01) and the *Theatrical Reader* (1805) were designed to focus on issues of performance. The minute details of an actor's performances were exhaustingly analyzed, fostering a sporting atmosphere that portrayed actors as fair game for a frequently ill-informed reviewer who pitted one performance, style, or theater against another.

Contributing to this competitive atmosphere was the fact that only two theaters in London were licensed to perform spoken drama. In response to Fielding's satirical dramas, the 1737 Licensing Act authorized Covent Garden and Drury Lane—the theaters for which William Davenant and Thomas Killigrew had obtained patents from Charles II to perform plays—to do "the drama." This influential legislation also established the position of Lord Chamberlain and his Examiner of Plays, charged with approving (i.e., censoring) a play's political, sexual, and religious content. During the Romantic period, John Larpent and George Colman, the Younger, consistently excised references to political events. The only significant challenge to the monopoly of the Royal theaters occurred in 1787 when John Palmer tried to open the Royalty Theatre near the Tower of London; the patent theaters' swift legal action ensured that instead of performing spoken plays, Palmer's theater could feature only music, dancing, and dumb show; it folded at season's end. Theater bills to propose the establishment of a third Royal theater met with defeat in 1808, 1810, and 1813. In 1832, convinced that English drama had declined, Parliament appointed the Select Committee on Dramatic Literature, chaired by Edward Bulwer, to investigate,

among other things, the effects on Romantic theater of the century-old Licensing Act. While a Dramatic Performance Bill to license any theater to play spoken drama was defeated in 1833, 10 years later the Theatrical Regulation Act ostensibly abolished theatrical monopolies. The position of Lord Chamberlain, however, endured until 1968. (*See also* Dibdin, Charles.)

Catherine Burroughs

Works Consulted

Booth, Michael, ed. Prefaces. *English Plays of the Nineteenth Century*. 5 vols. Oxford: Clarendon, 1969.

Booth, Michael, Richard Southern, Frederick and Lise-Lone Marker, and Robertson Davies, eds. *The Revels History of Drama in English (1750–1880)*. Vol. 6. New York: Harper, 1975.

Cave, Richard Allen, ed. *The Romantic Theatre: An International Symposium*. Totowa, NJ: Barnes, 1986.

Cox, Jeffrey. *In the Shadows of Romance: Romantic Tragic Drama in Germany, England, and France*. Athens: Ohio UP, 1987.

Donohue, Joseph. *Dramatic Character in the English Romantic Age*. Princeton: Princeton UP, 1970.

———. *Theatre in the Age of Kean*. Totowa, NJ: Rowman, 1975.

Evans, Bertrand. *Gothic Drama from Walpole to Shelley*. Berkeley: U of California P, 1947.

Fletcher, Richard. *English Romantic Drama, 1795–1843: A Critical History*. New York: Exposition, 1966.

McKenna, Wayne. *Charles Lamb and the Theatre*. New York: Barnes, 1978.

Nicoll, Allardyce. *A History of Late Eighteenth-Century Drama: 1750–1800*. Cambridge: Cambridge UP, 1927.

———. *A History of Early Nineteenth-Century Drama: 1800-1850*. 2 vols. Cambridge: Cambridge UP, 1930.

Otten, Terry. *The Deserted Stage; The Search for Dramatic Form in Nineteenth-Century England*. Athens: Ohio UP, 1972.

Watson, Ernest B. *Sheridan to Robertson; A Study of the Nineteenth-Century London Stage*. Cambridge: Harvard UP, 1926.

Thomson, George

(1757–1851)

The musicologist and musical editor George Thomson was born in Fife, Scotland, and educated in Edinburgh. From 1780 to 1830, he was employed as a government clerk in Edinburgh. He sang and played the violin as a member of the Edinburgh Musical Society.

From 1791 to 1841, Thomson was preoccupied with publishing modern accompaniments for Scottish folksongs and poems. He first contacted the Viennese composers Joseph Haydn and Ignaz Pleyel following their visit to London in 1791. Haydn and Pleyel agreed to compose piano accompaniments to the folksongs and other lyrics that Thomson culled from earlier publications. The result was the first volume of Thomson's *Select Collection of Original Scottish Airs*, with arrangements by Haydn and Pleyel and lyrics mainly by Burns. It was published at Thomson's expense in Edinburgh in 1793.

In succeeding years, Thomson enlisted other prestigious continental composers, including Leopold Kozeluch (from 1797), Beethoven (from 1803), Carl Maria von Weber (from 1825), and J.N. Hummel (from 1826). To these he later added the London composer Henry Bishop. Altogether, Haydn contributed 187 settings to Thomson's editions; Beethoven, 126 settings. Thomson's practice was to supply the composer with the melody line of a traditional folksong, which the composer was to embellish with harmonies, usually in the Viennese style. Unfortunately, fearing that his composers might preempt his volumes by publishing unauthorized editions of the songs in their own countries, Thomson was seldom willing to send them the actual lyrics to which their accompaniments were to be united in print. Only rarely did his composers see the words to which they composed their music.

Thomson was equally ambitious in enlisting contemporary poets for his project. As well as Burns, he attracted Hogg, Scott, Baillie, Moore, Campbell, Opie, Grant, and many lesser-known writers. Even Byron, on account of his half-Scottish ancestry, was included. The poets, using the same original folksongs that had been shown to the composers, were expected to compose new lyrics. Thomson completed the process by combining the modern poetry with the modern music.

Thomson's edition of the *Select Collection of Original Scottish Airs* extended to five volumes. In 1841, a sixth volume was added, and the work as a whole was retitled *The Melodies of Scotland*. The volumes were large, lavish, and beautifully printed. Thomson also produced two somewhat similar collections of *Welsh Airs* and *Irish Airs*. These two latter collections are of less interest, although the Irish volumes contain Byron's lyric *The Kiss, Dear Maid, Thy Lip has Left*. A selection of the more popular songs from the Scots, Irish, and Welsh collections, embellished with engravings by contemporary artists, was published in six smaller volumes in 1822 to 1824. The poems set to music by Beethoven include Byron's *Away ye Gay Landscapes* and Hogg's *Highland Watch*. A few of the other lyrics are Burns's *Should Auld Acquaintance* and *Catherine Ogie*, Scott's *The Dying Bard to his Harp*, Moore's *When Damon Languish'd at my Feet*, and Byron's *I Saw Thee Weep*.

Thomson's editions represent a highly innovative attempt to combine the poetry and music of the Romantic age. The volumes were extremely popular among genteel audiences in their day. They helped to spread an awareness of Romantic art across national boundaries. Perhaps better than any other work of their time, they illustrate the fashion for drawing-room entertainments.

Thomson's work has certain limitations, however. The lyrics are often bowdlerized, or "improved," to make them acceptable in genteel circles. His composers had little knowledge of Scottish music or Scottish poetry or language. With their tameness, bowdlerizations, and Viennese harmonies, the *Scottish Airs* is insufficient in both Scottish spirit and artistic integrity. Beethoven's settings (for which he received one guinea apiece) are workmanlike and inferior to his other compositions. Haydn was pleased to accept Thomson's money, but he sometimes apparently arranged for one of his students to compose the accompaniment. Although Thomson's attempt to wed Romantic poetry with Romantic music is highly pleasing, it never approaches the profounder sense of union found in, for example, Blake's combination of poetry and engraving.

During his later years, Thomson came under fire for his financial treatment of poets. However, posthumous critics have dismissed these charges as groundless. His correspondence with contributors shows that Thomson was both fair and generous. Writing in 1833, Hogg gave a reasonable assessment of his friend's strengths and weaknesses, describing Thomson as "a kind open hearted fellow, who entertains literary and musical people most liberally": "but then he is the most troublesome devil to write songs for that ever was created, for he is always either bothering one with alterations, or else popping them in himself."

Thomson's editions are a significant and worthwhile experiment in combining different art forms and different national cultures. As often happened in Romantic art, the aspiration is somewhat greater than the actual achievement. Perhaps Thomson's highest accomplishment lay in the financial and personal encouragement he offered to so many contemporary composers and poets. (*See also* Hymnody, Music.)

David Groves

Works Consulted

Fiske, Roger. *Scotland in Music: A European Enthusiasm.* New York: Cambridge UP, 1983.

Hadden, J. Cuthbert. *George Thomson, the Friend of Burns; His Life and Correspondence.* London: Nimmo, 1898.

Johnson, David. *Music and Society in Lowland Scotland in the Eighteenth Century.* London: Oxford UP, 1972.

The Letters of Beethoven. Ed. Emily Anderson, 3 vols. New York: Macmillan, 1961.

The Letters of Robert Burns. Ed. Roy G. Ross. Oxford: Clarendon, 1985.

Thomson, James
(1700–1748)

Although the dates of his life coincide almost exactly with the Neoclassical period of English literature and most of his work adheres to Neoclassical literary principles, James Thomson is best known for two works that exerted a profound influence on budding Romanticism in the 18th century: *The Seasons* and *The Castle of Indolence.*

Thomson was born in 1700, in Ednam, Scotland. Intending to emulate his father, a clergyman, he entered the College of Edinburgh in 1715 to study for the Presbyterian ministry, but he gave up those plans in 1725 and moved to London to begin what became a highly successful literary career. During his lifetime, he published, in addition to *The Seasons* and *Indolence*, several well-received minor poems, most notably *A Poem Sacred to the Memory of Sir Isaac Newton* (1727), *Hymn on Solitude* (1729), and *Rule, Brittania* (1740), the latter of which appeared in *Alfred: A Masque* (written with David Mallet and Thomas Arne) and remains today a popular patriotic song. Like most Neoclassicists of his day, Thomson saw tragedy and the epic as the highest forms of literary art and consequently he tried his hand at both, producing the epiclike *Liberty* (1735–36), a ponderous blank verse failure of over 3,000 lines, and five Neoclassical tragedies: *Sophonisba* (1730), *Agamemnon* (1738), *Edward and Eleonora* (1739), *Tancred and Sigismunda* (1738), and the posthumous *Coriolanus* (1749). These plays all closely adhere to the rules and conventions of Neoclassical drama and so, while moderately popular in their own day, are today of only slight historic or scholarly interest.

Thomson's greatest achievement, and one which links him to the nascent Romantic movement, is *The Seasons*. The original version of *Winter* was published in 1726 and was followed by *Summer* (1727) and *Spring* (1728). In 1730, the entire *Seasons*, including *Autumn*, was published. However, Thomson continued to revise and expand the work for the next 15 years. For example, the first published version of *Winter* consisted of 405 lines, but by 1746, it had grown to 1,069 lines. The other sections of the poem also were expanded over the years, although not to the same extent.

Because of the extensive revision and expansion of *The Seasons*, it became an eclectic hodgepodge of almost everything in which the author had an interest: current events, prison reform, condemnation of hunting, philosophic speculation, recent scientific experiments and discoveries, praise of the simple rural life, and scenes of natural description, among many other topics. The nature of Thomson's additions to the poem reveals a movement away from the Neoclassical and toward the Romantic. For example, Thomson added many Gothic, sentimental, rustic, and descriptive passages. Moreover, at points—unfortunately, all too few—he avoided the stultifying Miltonic poetic diction that dominates 18th-century blank verse and that Wordsworth attacked in the Preface to the *Lyrical Ballads*. Because of the poem's immense popularity, these infrequent but startlingly vivid passages reached a wide audience and showed the way to a new poetic language suited to the subjects of emerging Romanticism.

Thomson contributed to the 18th century's growing interest in Spenser, a poet revered by the Romantics, with his Spenserian imitation, *The Castle of Indolence* (1748), the last poem he published in his lifetime. This work, along with Shenstone's *The Schoolmistress* (1742), represents the apex of the Spenserian revival. Although the heavy moralizing of Canto II is not very successful, Canto I captures the sensuous, dreamy atmosphere of Spenser which the Romantics so admired. The poem is an important road sign on the highway from Neoclassicism to Romanticism.

Thomson died suddenly of a fever in 1748.

John A. Stoler

Works Consulted

Campbell, Hilbert H. *James Thomson*. Boston: Twayne, 1979.

Cohen, Ralph. *The Art of Discrimination: Thomson's The Seasons and the Language of Criticism*. Berkeley: U of California P, 1964.

———. *The Unfolding of the Seasons*. Baltimore: Johns Hopkins UP, 1970.

Grant, Douglas. *James Thomson: Poet of "The Seasons."* London: Cresset, 1951.

McKillop, Alan D. *The Background of Thomson's Seasons*. Minneapolis: U of Minnesota P, 1942.

Spacks, Patricia Meyer. *The Varied God: A Critical Study of Thomson's The Seasons*. Berkeley: U of California P, 1959.

Tighe, Mary Blachford
(1772–1810)

Known today for the possible influence of her poetry on that of Keats (an influence the importance of which is questioned in recent Keats biographies), the Irish poet Mary Blachford Tighe was famous in the Romantic period for her long poem *Psyche; or, The Legend of Love* (1805), an allegorical retelling of the story of Cupid and Psyche which recasts the Greek myth in Renaissance, Gothic, and Romantic conventions. During Tighe's lifetime, which was shortened by the consumption under which she was already suffering during the poem's composition, *Psyche* was published only privately, in an edition of 50 copies, none of which is apparently still extant. Moore wrote a poem in its praise, *To Mrs. Henry Tighe on reading her Psyche* (1802), and it received a great deal of critical approval upon posthumous publication.

Besides its value as elegant, polished verse and as an erotic variation of the epic quest theme, *Psyche* is fascinating as a study of sex roles and role reversals. The myth itself is a sort of Cinderella story in reverse—an observation made easier by Tighe's Gothic context. Other examples of such reversals occur in the details. Dawn is female throughout, but the figure of Morn is a male. The Lamialike figure of jealousy is again male—though this image recalls the fact that, although Milton's Sin is such a female figure, his male devils become snakes, too, in the end. Miltonic echoes are as insistent here as Spenserian

ones, in fact, and Byron is foreshadowed as strikingly as Keats. The storm at sea in Canto V, for example, looks modestly forward to that in *Don Juan* and lands Psyche near the cave occupied by the Haideelike Patience. Both Tighe and Byron are clearly using Homer's Nausicaa for their model, and the Romantic figures that result are interestingly similar.

Tighe wrote sonnets and other poems, which were published with her allegory. The manuscript of an unpublished novel called *Selena*, said to be autobiographical, is in the National Library of Ireland.

John Anderson

Works Consulted

Bate, W. Jackson. *John Keats*. Cambridge: Belknap, 1963.

Blain, Virginia, Patricia Clements, and Isobel Grundy, eds. *The Feminist Companion to Literature in English*. London: Batsford, 1990.

Todd, Janet, ed. *British Women Writers*. New York: Bedrick, 1989.

———. *Dictionary of British and American Women Writers, 1660–1800*. Totowa, NJ: Rowman, 1984.

Weller, Earle Vonard. *Keats and Mary Tighe: The Poems of Mary Tighe with parallel passages from the work of John Keats*. New York: Century, 1928.

Tipu Sultan
(1750–99)

One of the most colorful and calumniated among the Muslim rulers of India, Tipu Sultan was the son of Hyder Ali, an unlettered soldier of fortune, who had risen from the ranks to become the commander of the army of Mysore. Fakr-un-nisa, Hyder Ali's second wife, when pregnant, had visited the *Dargah* (tomb) of Tipu Mastan Aulia to pray for safe delivery of a son, whom the grateful parents named after this Sufi saint.

By 1761, Hyder Ali had become *de facto*

master of Mysore, though a scion of the Wodeyar dynasty was the titular ruler. Unlike his father, therefore, Tipu received an eclectic education and grew into an urbane youth, versed in several languages, including French. At age 18, as an envoy to the Nizam of Hyderabad, Tipu scored a diplomatic coup by turning a sworn enemy into an ally, but the fickle Nizam soon developed cold feet and went over to the British. Tipu, who now received baptism on the battlefield, forced the British forces to abandon Mangalore without a fight and again proved his mettle against the Marathas. The British forces under Colonel Baillie were also worsted, and Tipu followed it up with a spectacular victory over the army under Colonel Braithwaite at Kumbakonam near Madras. Indeed, but for the untimely death of his father, which afforded the British a fortunate respite, Tipu could well have altered the course of Indian history.

When he took over as ruler at age 32, in 1782, Tipu was hemmed in by enemies on all sides. Dauntlessly, the Sultan led his forces to Bednur, forcing Colonel Mathews to capitulate and making the Governor of Madras, Lord McCartney, conclude the treaty of Mangalore in March 1784.

The only dissonant element in this success story was Tipu's inability to subdue the intrepid Coorgi Highlanders. Unquenchable in their ardor for freedom, notwithstanding ruthless suppression, like the Nairs of Kerala, they were a persistent thorn in his flesh until his fall in 1799.

The Marathas, who were equally unreconciled to his rise, made Tipu's action against the Hindu principality of Nargund the pretext to renew hostilities, providing the Nizam an opportunity to fish in the troubled waters. Tipu not only compelled his foes to retreat but, in a series of brilliant maneuvers, forced them to sue for peace. To his adversaries' surprise, Tipu offered them most magnanimous terms, insisting only on recognition of his sovereign status. Tipu then sent emissaries to the Mughal emperor at Delhi; to the Caliph, then at Constantinople; and to the French court. The French mission fueled fears in the minds of the British that he could be the nemesis of their imperialistic designs. Lord Cornwallis, the Governor General, therefore, while subtly egging on the Nizam, made overtures to the Peshwas and the Scindhias to join the Grand Alliance against this "common enemy of all mankind," which precipitated the third Anglo-Mysore war. After initial success, Tipu was vanquished and compelled to sign the humiliating Treaty of Seringapatam in 1792.

He then launched a diplomatic offensive to mend fences, both with the Peshwa and the Nizam. However, the foolhardy legation to the French governor of Mauritius, which resulted in the inconsequential Malartic Proclamation, was deemed sufficient provocation to Cornwallis's successor, Lord Wellesley, to plan Tipu's extirpation. Wellesley ordered the British armies under Generals Harris and Stuart and his brother, Colonel Arthur Wellesley (first Duke of Wellington), to march into Mysore and besiege Seringapatam. Whether through perfidy, weakness of the defending forces, or both, the Sultan perished in the thick of battle on May 4, 1799, when his capital fell to the invading hordes.

It may be said on unimpeachable evidence that Tipu was neither the bloodcurdling tyrant portrayed by the British nor the paragon of virtue depicted by court chroniclers, but a complex, mercurial character, who envisioned ideas far in advance of his times. Institution of declaration of assets by public servants, relatively humane treatment of prisoners of war, and establishment of a Court of Appeal, comprising both Hindu and Muslim judges, were some of the startling measures initiated by him. His correspondences with the Hindu savant, the Shankracharya of Sringeri, his letter to the Archbishop of Goa to depute priests for his Christian subjects, his liberal endowments to temples, apart from his galaxy of ministers, headed by the Brahmin, Purnaiah, amply illustrate his secular credentials. His personal library at Seringapatam, despite despoliation at British hands, proves his insatiable quest for knowledge. (*See also* Hastings, Warren.)

D.C. Saxena

Works Consulted

Bowring, Lewin B. *Haider Ali and Tipu Sultan.* Dehra Dun: EBD, 1969.

Fernandes, Praxy. *Storm Over Seringapatam.* Bombay: Thacker, 1969.

Forrest, Denys. *Tiger of Mysore: The Life and Death of Tipu Sultan.* London: Chatto, 1970.

Murthy, H.V.S., and R. Ramakrishnan. *History of Karnataka.* New Delhi: Chand, 1977.

Tooke, John Horne

(1736–1812)

As notorious a radical as he was renowned a linguist, John Horne Tooke was born in Westminster in 1736. His father, John Horne, was a poulterer. John Horne Tooke, who adopted the surname of his supporter William Tooke, was a political radical who created a philosophy of language based on etymology. Comprising an elaborate system, Tooke's major works illustrate a belief in language as a context of intellectual history rather than of a philosophical issue.

Tooke's early life evidences his diverse talents. In 1754, he entered St. John's College, Cambridge, where he gained knowledge of many languages, contributing to his fascination with etymology. He began a legal career at the Inner Temple, and, forced by his father to take Holy Orders, was ordained a priest in 1760. After he made several tours of France, he threw himself into the political turmoils of England.

As an associate of Paine, Tooke was tried for treason as a conspiratorial genius of the democratic movement. His encounters with the law often regarded questions of language. In 1777, he was tried for sedition for a pro-American Revolution statement. Confined to the King's Bench Prison, Tooke published his first comments about language, *A Letter to J. Dunning.* (His first publication, a strictly political pamphlet, was *The Petition of an Englishman*, which appeared in 1765.) In this letter, as his trial made clear, Tooke attempts to show that the meaning of words is integrally connected with law and justice, discussing the disagreement in terms of language theory. Since his conviction hinged on a verbal statement, Tooke's appeals led to a discussion of grammar, expounded at great length in his major work. However, the *Letter*, according to Coleridge's 1830 comments in *Table Talk*, contains the germinal content of his later work and expounds Tooke's characteristic doctrines.

The trials affected Tooke's reputation and potential, for in 1779, 1782, and 1794, he was denied admission to the bar, despite his being eminently qualified. In 1794, he was tried for high treason for his part in the democratic societies. Although he was acquitted, the notoriety of the trials overshadowed his career. (*See also* Frend, William.) He lost bids for a seat in Parliament in 1796 and 1801, thereafter retiring to his home in Wimbledon. Plagued by gout and other minor diseases, Tooke died at home in 1812.

Tooke's philosophical and philological reputation rests primarily on his massive work *The Diversions of Purley* (1786, 1798). Tooke brought out a second volume in 1805 and was reportedly working on a concluding, third volume, but in 1812, months before his death, he burned the manuscripts. Written over some 30 years, *The Diversions of Purley* defies ready categorization. Tooke argues for studying language not in relation to other disciplines (notably philosophy) but in relation to its own changing history, primarily through etymology. The *Diversions of Purley*, in the form of a debate between three participants, allows Tooke to refute objections of his companions. This dialogic form is appropriate, since Tooke consistently presents his ideas in opposition to others, notably philosophical linguists James Harris and Lord Monboddo.

Although the rise of continental philosophy contributed to a fall in Tooke's reputation, as evidenced by the publication in 1824 of John Fearn's *Anti-Tooke*, Tooke shares some of the goals of the early Romantic movement in England, such as the refutation of class division and the emphasis on language's connection with real people in real situations. His work was widely read and debated between 1798 and 1805 (there are over 200 pages of critical reviews of Tooke in the *Monthly Review* and *Monthly Magazine*). Notably, Hazlitt, in *Spirit of the Age*, praises Tooke for his demythologizing of words, treating words like a chemist. Finally, regardless of the critical defects of his works, Tooke's exhaustive etymologies, especially of Anglo-Saxon origin, continue to inform and interest linguists and to illustrate, as Olivia Smith has argued, the connection between political and linguistic change.

Lisa Plummer Crafton

Works Consulted

Aarsleff, Hans. *The Study of Language in England, 1780–1860*. 2nd ed. Minneapolis: U of Minnesota P, 1983.

Dictionary of National Biography, s. v. "Tooke, John Horne."

Land, Stephen K. *From Signs to Propositions: The Concept of Form in 18th Century Semantic Theory*. New York: Longman, 1967.

Smith, Olivia. *The Politics of Language, 1791–1819*. Oxford: Clarendon, 1984.

Stephens, Alexander. *Memoirs of John Horne Tooke*. 2 vols. 1813. New York: Franklin, 1968.

Topographical and Travel Prints

By 1821, so related a writer for the *Quarterly Review*, "every nook in our island has now been completely ransacked and described by our tourists and topographers." Indeed, so great was the passion in Great Britain during the late 18th and the early 19th centuries for touring, especially to locales identified as picturesque, and for recording what was seen in words and images, that it provoked satire, not just in Rowlandson's *The Tour of Doctor Syntax, In Search of the Picturesque* (1812) but also in a comic opera, *The Lakers* (1798).

Rowlandson's barbs notwithstanding, the picturesque impulse, which may be loosely characterized as an aesthetic preference for the rough and irregular, the ruined and the neglected, and the singular and the evocative, did much to stimulate tourism and topographical art, inspiring Englishmen and -women to discover their native land as well as its historical edifices. And this desire to see the picturesque English countryside, not to mention its towns and its architectural antiquities, especially its medieval ruins, in turn set scores of publishers, writers, and artists to the task of meeting the demand of prospective travelers, whether they actually intended on a journey or preferred one taken vicariously through books and prints.

Artists and publishers of prints about 1800 had a sizable repertory of printing techniques, and new ones, such as lithography, also soon became available. Copper engraving, mezzotint, and etching were commonplace, with etching about to undergo a notable revival in the prints of Cotman. Likewise current were soft-ground etching and aquatint, the latter popularized by the prolific printer and bookseller Ackermann, whose shop, the Repository of Arts, opened in the Strand in 1795. Lithography was the principal innovative printing technique introduced during the first quarter of the 19th century, and after its invention in 1798 by Aloys Senefelder (1771–1834), it was widely used by, among others, Charles Joseph Hullmandel (1789–1850), especially after the early 1820s. Other printmaking techniques, in particular wood-engraving and steel-engraving, were more often employed to make inexpensive reproductions of paintings, illustrations for books, and pictures for the newly created popular press, like *Punch* or the *Illustrated London News*. Alone or in combination, engraving, etching, and lithography were used to produce illustrated travel books and thousands of topographical images, many of which depicted the countryside, the towns, and the antiquities of the British Isles.

The late 18th-century vogue for travel, created in part by the publication of tour guides, led to the publication of additional guides and countless plate books, some of which no doubt were purchased by those desirous of the satisfaction of travel without its attendant uncertainties. Parts of the British Isles rediscovered or discovered for the first time by these travelers were the Wye Valley, Wales, Yorkshire, the Lake District, and the Scottish Highlands. One early guide to picturesque tourism of this sort was Gilpin, whose *Observations on the River Wye, and Several Parts of South Wales* first appeared in 1782 with his sketches reproduced by etching and aquatint. Gilpin's Wye guide, which not only was often reprinted but which had circulated in manuscript form for over a decade prior to its publication, was no exception, and a host of contemporary writers and artists similarly invited their compatriots to sample the pleasures of tourism. Set within this tradition must therefore be one of the most famous English tour books, Wordsworth's *A Guide Through the District of the Lakes in the North of England* (1835). And, for those whose taste for travel in England had been sated by the numerous guides and collections of plates, there was always David Roberts (1796–1864), whose drawings of the Near East were lithographed and published in *The Holy Land* (1842) and *Egypt and Nubia* (1846).

The English countryside attracted a host of artists, and printmakers reproduced their views using virtually every available technique. Over such lesser figures as the prolific John Britton, whose *The Beauties of England and Wales* appeared in 18 volumes and with some 684 engraved plates between 1801 and 1816, or R.G. Reeve, whose aquatints after drawings by William Westall and Samuel Owen appeared in a *Picturesque Tour of the River Thames* (1828), Constable and Turner, both of whom published volumes of landscape prints. Constable's *Various Subjects of Landscape, Characteristic of English Scenery* (1833) was executed in mezzotint by David Lucas under the close supervision of the artist. Throughout his artistic life, Turner involved himself in numerous projects to have his paintings and watercolors reproduced as prints, including the *Liber*

Studiorum (1807–19), the *Picturesque Views in England and Wales* (1827–38), and the 40 views contributed to W.B. Cooke's *Picturesque Views on the Southern Coast of England* (1814–26).

Unlike most contemporary landscape painters, the makers of topographical prints did not ignore the Industrial Revolution. An aquatint of Philippe Jacques de Loutherbourg's *Iron Works, Colebrook Dale* appeared in his *The Romantic and Picturesque Scenery of England and Wales* (1805), while the transformation of the countryside by the construction of the railroad was lithographed by John Cooke Bourne in *Drawings of the London and Birmingham Railway* (1839), and this new means of travel was celebrated in the same author's *History and Description of the Great Western Railway, Including its Geology, and the Antiquities of the District Through Which it Passes* (1846).

The townscape received much the same attention. John Britton, for example, published *Picturesque Views of the English Cities* (1826–28), illustrated with engravings after drawings by George Fennell Robson and woodcuts, and *Picturesque Antiquities of English Cities* (1830). But by far the outstanding examples of townscapes were those of Ackermann and Thomas Shotter Boys. Of Ackermann's many color-plate books, the best known are *The Microcosm of London, or London in Miniature* (1808–10), with aquatinted plates after drawings by Rowlandson and Augustus Pugin (1762–1832); *A History of the University of Cambridge* (1815); and *A History of the University of Oxford* (1814). Boys's townscapes are important not just as works of art but as historical documents, for they were, to use his words, "drawn from nature," and they reflect accurate representations of urban life during the first half of the 19th century. His *Picturesque Architecture in Paris,*

Ghent, Antwerp, Rouen, &c. (1839) also marked an event in lithographic printing; it was printed by Charles Hullmandel using the process of chromolithography, which Boys claimed to have invented. But the process was laborious and expensive, so his 26 lithographed *Original Views of London as it is* (1842) and his *A Series of Views of York* (1841) were later colored by hand.

The extraordinary interest of the public and of artists and print sellers in the antiquities and ruins of England, while by no means novel—for William Dugdale's *The Antiquities of Warwickshire Illustrated* had been published over a century earlier in 1656—produced nevertheless an outpouring of images of cathedrals, parish churches, and ruined abbeys. The *Antiquities of Great Britain* (1807) offered, for example, 84 plates engraved by William Byrne, 52 after drawings by Thomas Hearne, while Francis Grose's *The Antiquities of England, Wales, Scotland, and Ireland* (1773–91) contained over 1,000 engravings. In 1822, Charles Hullmandel began publication of *Britannia delineata: Comprising Views of The Antiquities, Remarkable Buildings, and Picturesque Scenery of Great Britain*; although only the 24 colored plates for Kent were lithographed, Hullmandel had succeeded in recruiting James Duffield Harding, Samuel Prout, and William Westall for the project. John Britton's *The Architectural Antiquities of Great Britain* (1807–26) and the *Cathedral Antiquities* (1813–35) together held over 650 plates. And Cotman recorded venerable secular and ecclesiastical buildings in his too little known *The Architectural Antiquities of Norfolk* (1818) and *Architectural Antiquities of Normandy* (1822). By the late 1830s, the taste for such volumes had hardly abated, and Joseph Nash (1808–78) issued his lithographed *Architecture of the Middle Ages* in 1838.

The proliferation of these images points to the passionate interest in pre-industrial England at a time when the Industrial Revolution was at hand. Further, both the content of these prints and the effects the artists sought to achieve in them have important counterparts in contemporary literature and intellectual movements. Sadly, this flourishing of printmaking soon ended, all but eliminated by cheaper processes for the mechanical reproduction of images like steel-engraving and wood-engraving, by the invention of photography, and, above all, by the development of techniques for the rapid and inexpensive reproduction of photographic images during the second half of the 19th century. Never again would artistic prints and plate-books of such quality be produced for a mass market. (*See also* Panorama, Picturesque, The Sublime.)

Robert W. Brown

Works Consulted

Abbey, John Roland. *Scenery of Great Britain and Ireland in Aquatint and Lithography, 1770–1860, from the Library of J.R. Abbey: A Bibliographical Catalogue*. London: Curwen, 1952.

———. *Life in England in Aquatint and Lithography, 1770–1860, from the Library of J.R. Abbey*. London: Curwen, 1953.

———. *Travel in Aquatint and Lithography, 1770–1860, from the Library of J.R. Abbey*. London: Curwen, 1956–57.

Andrews, Malcolm. *The Search for the Picturesque. Landscape Aesthetics and Tourism in Britain, 1760–1800*. Stanford: Stanford UP, 1989.

Klingender, Francis D. *Art and the Industrial Revolution*. Ed. and rev. Arthur Elton. 1968. London: Paladin, 1972.

Lister, Raymond. *Prints and Printmaking. A Dictionary and Handbook of the Art in Nineteenth-Century Britain*. London: Methuen, 1984.

Rare and Valuable Colored Plate Books and an Extensive Cruikshank Collection from the Library of the Late Sir David Lionel Goldsmid-Stern Salomons, Bart. New York: American Art Association, Anderson Galleries, Inc., 1930.

Russell, Ronald. *Guide to British Topographical Prints*. Newton Abbot: David, 1979.

Shanes, Eric. *Turner's England. A Survey in Watercolors*. North Pomfret: Trafalgar Square, 1990.

Tooley, R.V. *English Books with Coloured Plates, 1790 to 1860. A Bibliographical Account of the Most Important Books Illustrated by English Artists in Colour Aquatint and Colour Lithography*. Rev. ed. Folkestone, Kent: Dawson, 1979.

Twyman, Michael. "Charles Joseph Hullmandel: Lithographic Printer Extraordinary." *Lasting Impressions. Lithography as Art*. Ed. Pat Gilmour. London: Alexandria, 1988: 42–90.

———. *Lithography, 1800–1850: The Techniques of Drawing on Stone in England and France and Their Application in Works of Topography*. London: Oxford UP, 1970.

Toussaint Louverture

(1743–1803)

Former slave, man of property, revolutionary, general, dictator, Toussaint Louverture remains as elusive a figure today as he was to his contemporaries. Physically, he was small and unattractive. He commanded by the sheer force of his personality. (*See also* Slavery.)

According to tradition, Toussaint was born into slavery in 1743 on the sugar plantation known as "la plantation Bréda." He was freed in 1776 and soon became a landowner and, according to some sources, a slaveowner as well. Not much is known about Toussaint during this period except that he learned to read and write and that he was sober, hard-working, prosperous, and well-respected. No records remain to indicate what his political opinions were prior to the beginning of the slave insurrection in August 1791. Toussaint was not one of the original leaders of the rebellion, and the exact point at which he joined the insurgents is unclear. The first time that his name appears in the record alongside the names of the initial leaders is 4 December 1791. From that point on, until his arrest and deportation to France in 1802, he was a central figure in the colony.

Although events in France provided a catalyst for the revolt, the exact cause is not clear. Apparently the Blacks, Toussaint included, believed that King Louis XVI wished to free them and that the "republicans" did not. As a result, the rebels wore the white cockade, proclaimed their allegiance to the Crown, and established control over the north and west of the colony. Formal abolition of slavery by the Convention of 4 February 1794 merely recognized a *fait accompli.* By that year, Toussaint had emerged as the leader of the Blacks, allied himself with the French Republic, and been appointed "colonel and commander of the western theater." Although he rarely shared his thoughts, it is generally agreed that, by 1794 to 1795, he had also concluded that the Blacks should ultimately control the island, that, even more so than the Whites, the "gens de couleur" were their enemies, and that complete independence from any European power should be their ultimate goal.

To accomplish this, Toussaint made himself indispensable to a succession of White governors sent from France, managing to force those whom he did not like to leave and generally acting with complete autonomy. He simply ignored directives from France when it suited his purposes. He signed a secret accord with the English without the knowledge of the government in France and conducted negotiations with the Americans. Consequently, by December 1800, the Blacks, under Toussaint, controlled the island. In February of the following year, Toussaint convened a constitutional convention. On 3 July 1801, he approved the constitution that gave him the title of "governor for life." This was followed by a joint decree by Toussaint

and the colonial assembly that transformed the island into an "associated state," in effect declaring their independence from France. The now governor for life continued to consolidate his power and to eliminate all political and military rivals. Napoleon responded by sending an army commanded by General Leclerc to take the situation in hand.

Toussaint refused Leclerc's summons, was declared an outlaw, continued to resist the French, suffered a series of defeats, and finally capitulated. Stripped of his rank of lieutenant-general, he retired to one of his plantations, where he remained until being accused of conspiracy by Dessalines and other Black generals and arrested on 7 June 1802. Leclerc ordered him deported to France, where he was imprisoned at Fort le Joux until his death in 1803. He did not live to hear the news that Dessalines had proclaimed "Hayti" independent on 1 January 1804.

Toussaint was a study in contradictions. As Wordsworth wrote: "Though fallen thyself, never to rise again,/Live, and take comfort. Thou has left behind/Powers that will work for thee. . . ." Always more Royalist than republican, possessed of unlimited self-confidence yet fearful of his personal safety, austere in his personal habits but lavish in his entertainment, vain, autocratic, sensitive to his lack of education and anxious that his government not be seen as unlettered or provincial, shrewd, intelligent, absolutely indefatigable, he was by all accounts an extraordinary individual. His contemporaries either admired or hated him; there was no middle ground. To posterity, however, he was the architect of Haitian independence, which ensured Black control of the island and a permanent end to slavery.

Elaine McAllister

Trelawny, Edward John

(1792–1881)

The writer and adventurer Edward John Trelawny was born in 1792, possibly in Cornwall. After a rebellious childhood, during which he was thrown out of school for attacking the headmaster and then setting fire to a room, he was sent to sea at age 12. Although in *Adventures of a Younger Son*, his semiautobiographical novel, he claimed that his years as a sailor were filled with sanguinary exploits, in reality his naval experience was undistinguished. During an assault on Java in 1811, Trelawny was wounded, and he resigned from the navy in the following year, still a midshipman.

After a failed marriage and a period of depression, Trelawny began the imposturing that was to go on for the rest of his life. He gave himself the rank of captain and developed fantasies about his naval career based, to a large extent, on his reading of Byron's Eastern tales, particularly *The Corsair*. He also became a great admirer of Shelley's radical early poem *Queen Mab*. In January 1822, he joined Byron and Shelley in Pisa to help them design sailboats, and, in fact, designed the overmasted vessel that later capsized with Shelley aboard. To the circle at Pisa, Trelawny was an extremely Byronic figure, possibly more so than Byron himself, and Percy and Mary Shelley seemed to have accepted at face value the extravagant tales that Trelawny told them about South Sea adventure.

After Shelley's drowning, Trelawny presided over his cremation, and, when Byron proposed that Trelawny accompany him to Greece to support the Greek struggle for independence, Trelawny quickly agreed. Unfortunately, Byron died at Missolonghi in April 1824. Trelawny obtained lodgings in Florence and began to write down the tales with which he had regaled the Pisan circle some years before. *Adventures of a Younger Son* was published anonymously in 1831 and became an instant success. In *Adventures*, Trelawny's unnamed protagonist deserts the navy and joins a French privateer, and the two sail across the Indian and South Pacific Oceans, going from one violent scene to the next. The "younger son," whom the reading public identified as Trelawny, is murderous and callous, but his thirst for freedom and his tragic love for his child bride Zela are among his Byronic virtues. *Adventures*, which features a fast-paced narrative and exotic locales, captivated several generations of 19th-century readers, who believed every word of it. In fact, until Lady Anne Hill used Trelawny's naval records to prove the book fiction in 1956, *Adventures* was considered an autobiography.

In 1858, Trelawny capitalized on his relationships with Byron and Shelley with *Recollections of the Last Days of Shelley and Byron*, reissued in slightly different form as *Records of Shelley, Byron, and the Author* in 1878. Although distorted by Trelawny's adulation of Shelley and jealousy of Byron, these works provide a fascinating account of the Pisan circle and Byron's fatal trip to Greece. Trelawny died in 1881, having outlived nearly everyone who could contradict his misrepresentations.

William D. Brewer

Works Consulted

Hill, Anne. "Trelawny's Family Background and Naval Career." *Keats-Shelley Journal* 5 (1956): 11–32.

St. Clair, William. *Trelawny: The Incurable Romancer*. New York: Vanguard, 1977.

Trelawny, Edward John. *Adventures of a Younger Son*. Ed. William St. Clair. London: Oxford UP, 1974.

— — —. *Records of Shelley, Byron, and the Author*. Ed. David Wright. New York: Penguin, 1973.

Trimmer, Sarah Kirby

(1741–1810)

One of the most prolific children's authors in English, Sarah Trimmer was also one of the most active influences in late 18th-century education. Her development of and work with charity schools provided full-time education for the children of the poor. Her essays and treatises on Christian education, her children's stories, and her spelling books were well known and influential, and they underscored her moral views and practical theology. (*See also* Children's Literature.)

Born into the middle-class family of Joshua and Sarah Kirby, Trimmer moved with her family to London in 1756, where her father taught the Perspective to the Prince of Wales (later King George III) and the Queen. Her family's friends included Johnson, Hogarth, Reynolds, and Gainsborough. Trimmer met her future husband James Trimmer at Kew, married at age 21, and spent the next 23 years raising and educating her 12 children. Her husband died in 1792, and 9 of her children outlived her.

It was when she was educating her own children that Trimmer began to write and publish her exemplary tales and moral lessons. In such works as *Fabulous Histories* (1786), widely known as *The History of the Robins* and *An Easy Introduction to the Knowledge of Nature* (1790), she showed children how to live a good life and how to treat animals humanely. The everyday problems of children were illustrated in these works, and out of this practical experience with her own children came Trimmer's desire to instruct and amuse a wider audience.

After a friend suggested that she write down her stories, Trimmer began to take her writing seriously. Her first periodical, *The Family Magazine* (1788–89), was a monthly aimed at servant children. Its instructive tales were meant to improve the mind and to teach these children how to grow and lead good lives. Some of the stories from the magazine were later published as *Instructive Tales* (1810).

Trimmer's growing interest in instructing the poor and her ideas on education soon found a natural outlet. She was one of the first to recognize the value and importance of newly established Sunday Schools, and, in 1786, Trimmer established such a school at St. George's Church in Brentwood, which lasted two years. (*See also* Sunday-School Movement.) She strongly believed in the values these schools taught and their insistence on the moral duty of industry. One of the first to establish church-based education for the poor, Trimmer was soon writing about her experiences and instructing other educators, and even Queen Charlotte visited her in 1786.

Sarah Trimmer's works on the poor and in church education include *The Oeconomy of Charity* (1787), *Reflections upon the Education of Children in Charity Schools* (1797), and *Essays on Christian Education* (1802–06). Believing in the value of work and economy, she founded a trade school for girls in 1787. In fact, her desire to educate girls and to value them as learners was ahead to its time. She believed that girls were to be prepared not only for a life of fashion or family. She taught them academic skills, morality, as well as how to be physically fit.

Her lifelong belief in morality led her in June 1793, to form a connection with the Society for Promoting Christian Knowledge. For her students, she wrote and developed textbooks and spelling books, but she could also be very strict in her views. For her second periodical, *The*

Guardian of Education (1802), she screened or censored material she thought unfit.

Trimmer's other activities included visits to the sick and poor and helping with soup kitchens that sprang up in the 1790s. Such concern and compassion were returned after her death by the poor people of Brentwood, who paid to erect a monument to her. Trimmer's legacy is certainly in her pioneer work in education. Called a reactionary and revolutionary in her time, she has also been called the founder of today's comprehensive education. She is remembered not only for her moral tales and the creation of practical guides to learning, but also for how her sense of duty led to the education of a generation.

Gary Kerley

Works Consulted

Dictionary of National Biography, *s.v.*, "Trimmer, Sarah."

Jones, M.C. *The Charity School Movement.* Hamden, CT: Archon, 1964.

Meigs, Cornelia. *A Critical History of Children's Literature.* Rev. ed. New York: Macmillan, 1969.

Schlueter, Paul, and Jane Schlueter, eds. *An Encyclopedia of British Women Writers.* New York: Garland, 1988.

Silver, Harold. *The Concept of Popular Education.* London: MacGibbon, 1965.

Todd, Janet, ed. *British Women Writers: A Critical Reference Guide.* New York: Continuum, 1989.

Yarde, Doris M. *The Life and Works of Sarah Trimmer.* Bedfont: Honslow and District History Society, 1972.

Turner, Joseph Mallord William

(1775–1851)

The art of Joseph Mallord William Turner is considered by many to be an art of extremes. Although his talent was early recognized by the art establishment, and he sold many conventional paintings, his later work was experimental in nature. *The Burning of the Houses of Parliament* and *The Fighting Temeraire Being Pulled to its Last Berth* are indicative of the transition period in Turner's work before he became completely obsessed with the interplay of color and light. Most of his later works, such as *Snowstorm* and *Rain, Steam and Speed*, were considered, during his lifetime, to be dabs, definitely incomplete. (*See also* Landscape Painting.)

Turner's father, a barber, recognized the monetary value of his son's talent when Turner was a young child, exhibiting and selling his son's work to help support the family. Turner's art was acknowledged as being of a very high quality for one so young, and he followed, at extremely young ages, the traditional steps of an accepted English artist.

Turner entered the Royal Academy in 1789, receiving free tuition, at the age of 14. His work was saluted by critics fairly early in his lifetime, and as a result Turner rapidly received commissions which increased yearly. Among the patrons awarding these commissions were such highly placed individuals as Lord Egremont, the Bishop of Ely, and Lord Malden.

Most of Turner's early work consists of watercolors and some engravings. In 1796, though, Turner began experimenting with oil as a medium. His first oil to be exhibited at the Academy, *Fisherman at Sea*, was shown that same year. It is obvious from this painting that Turner was already experimenting with light in the effects he paints of the moonlight on the water. He was always more concerned, even in his landscapes, with the effect of light on objects than he was with the objects themselves.

In 1799 at age 24, two years older than Constable when he entered the Academy as a student, Turner was made an associate member. In 1802, he became a full member at 26, which was the earliest possible age. At this time Turner was delving somewhat into the picturesque—Beckford's Fonthill Abbey provided inspiration for some of these paintings.

Turner spent the summer of 1802 traveling on the Continent, spending much time in galleries studying European painting. While visiting Switzerland, he did some 400 sketches, including designs that later evolved into oils, such as *Falls of Reichenbach 1804* and *Upper Falls of Reichenbach*. These paintings, while containing some traditional landscape elements, are wild, Romantic, and painterly in both subject and style.

Since his financial state was very secure after his return, Turner built an addition onto his house—a gallery. Thus, in 1804, Turner did something unheard of in England. He began exhibiting his own paintings in his own gallery. This was a somewhat lucrative venture, though many saw it as unacceptably self-serving.

Turner was also hired as a lecturer on perspective at the Royal Academy. He held this position from 1806 to 1837, even though he was reportedly a disaster as a teacher and delivered his lectures only 12 times in 31 years. These lectures were said to be extremely dull, although the visual aids were considered quite good. Part of the problem seems to have been that Turner was an educated painter, well read and very knowledgeable about his art, and therefore his lectures tended to be too difficult for the students to understand.

Turner's visit to Italy in 1819 was a turning point in his career. He was struck with the quality of light in the Mediterranean and fell permanently in love with the peculiar illustration of this effect in Venice. He painted a series of paintings at all of his Italian stops: Florence, Rome, Naples, and Milan, but the most significant are his

Venetian paintings. He uses these colors, light affects, and scenes until the end of his life.

In 1831, Cadell, the publisher, asked Turner to do the illustrations for a new volume of Scott's poems which was to be published. Scott did not like Turner, and Turner did not want to go to Scotland for the job, but the book did manage to come together, and something else as well. During this journey in the North, Turner produced *Staffa. Fingal's Cave*, which perfectly captures his sensibility. This painting was also the first of Turner's work to make its way to the United States.

Following the Scott illustrations, Turner entered into what could be termed a literary period. He worked on pictures for two volumes of Rogers's poetry, *Italy* in 1830 and *Poems* in 1834. At the same time as the Rogers *Poems*, Turner was illustrating Byron's poems for the latest Murray edition. This was an interesting assignment, because Turner was an avid reader of Byron and had earlier (1832) exhibited a painting entitled *Childe Harold's Pilgrimage—Italy*. The final poetic illustrations Turner did were for Campbell's collected poems in 1837. From that point on, Turner left illustration behind. He had found the problems with transferring his particular style to the more rigid form of engraving much too frustrating. (*See also* Topographical and Travel Prints.)

Returning semipermanently to the medium of oil in 1838, with *The Fighting Temeraire*, Turner infuses the light he became enamored with in Venice into an English setting to emphasize his point that the glory of the old warship, even in its final hours, was much more than what ugly, industrialized tugs and steamships could hope to attain. The effect of the golden light focused on the ship is similar to that used in *The Burning of the Houses of*

Parliament, a swirling vortex out of which arise somewhat indistinct, but still recognizable, shapes. (*See also* Bonington, Richard Parkes.)

His work habits and painting style were the topic of many jokes and caricatures in magazines and newspapers, since he tended to finish his paintings on the day prior to exhibition. The general pattern was for the artists to be allowed into the exhibits the day before opening to put a last coat of varnish, if necessary, on their works. Turner generally appeared with all of his painting supplies and actually finished the pictures while they were hanging there. He felt that he could not actually finish the painting properly until he saw it in exhibition surroundings.

Turner's death in 1851 clearly signaled the death of the Romantic movement in British painting. He was buried in St. Paul's Cathedral, but the real drama did not lie in his death, nor did Turner's memory fade immediately. His will was a major source of contention, since he disinherited his relatives in favor of founding a home for impoverished male English artists. This segment of the will was reversed by the courts, although the nation did inherit the entire artistic legacy—around 350 paintings and nearly 20,000 watercolors and drawings. Turner's wish for a separate gallery to house his works, however, was not granted until 1987, over 130 years after his demise.

Linda A. Archer

Works Consulted

Clark, Kenneth. *The Romantic Rebellion: Romantic versus Classical Art*. New York: Harper, 1973.

Paulson, Ronald. *Literary Landscape: Turner and Constable*. New Haven: Yale UP, 1982.

Reynolds, Graham. *Turner*. New York: Abrams, 1969.

Utilitarianism

In broad terms, utilitarianism is a moral or ethical theory that judges actions according to their consequences. Thus, an act is judged to be right or good if its consequences are in some way beneficial and wrong or bad if they are not. Modern utilitarian theory further distinguishes act utilitarianism and rule utilitarianism. The former focuses on particular actions and consequences; the latter draws general rules for classes of actions. While there are precursors to utilitarian ethics in the hedonism of Epicurus; in the moral theories of Richard Cumberland (1631–1718), which equate moral goodness with happiness; and in the ethics of Paley, utilitarianism received its chief impetus from the British philosopher Bentham and his disciples James Mill (1773–1836) and Mill's eldest son, John Stuart Mill (1806–73).

Bentham, who John Stuart Mill paired with Coleridge as possessing the two seminal minds of the age, originally trained for the law. He quickly became concerned that the law and legal institutions appealed too often to what he termed "legal fictions," abstract principles that were obscure and even contradictory with no clear

foundation in reality. He became a leader of a group of reformers known as the "philosophical radicals" and later the "English Utilitarians," which included James Mill, Godwin, Ricardo, and others. Playing on the etymology of radical (in Latin, *radix* means root), they proposed to trace the law to its roots, founding it on a clear, objective basis. With this in mind, they were active in the support of the reform bills of the 1830s. (*See also* Jeremy Bentham.)

Bentham's chief theoretical work, *Introduction to the Principles of Morals and Legislation* (1789), attacks the then-prevailing notion of moral intuitionism, the belief that absolute moral principles are intuitively self-evident. Instead, he argues, all moral principles emerge from the interaction of two principles, the association of ideas and "the greatest happiness" principle. The association of ideas, deriving from Hartley, Hume, and ultimately Locke, contends that ideas and sensations are mechanically linked with each other by association in the mind. In this way, an idea might evoke an absent sensation that has been associated with it. The "greatest happiness" principle asserts that human behavior is governed by pain and pleasure and that the greatest good is that which promotes the greatest pleasure. Bentham synthesized these to form his principle of utility: that which promotes pleasure or diminishes pain is good and that which does the opposite is bad. Moral principles and the laws and institutions that derive from them, therefore, may ultimately be reduced to an association of ideas with pain and pleasure. Taking this a step further, Bentham contends that the notion of community is a "legal fiction." When an institution aims for the welfare of the community, it is really aiming for the benefit of the majority of the individual members who compose it—the greatest good for the greatest number. This, Bentham concludes, is the true objective foundation of law.

To provide an objective means of judging the merits of an action, Bentham devised what he termed an hedonic calculus. He proposed to analyze the pain and pleasure of an act by assigning numbers to various quantitative aspects of pain and pleasure, such as their endurance, intensity, and inevitability. If the final ratio favors pleasure, the act is judged beneficial, if pain, then detrimental.

James Mill, philosopher, historian, and political economist, was one of Bentham's chief disciples. Trained in divinity, Mill abandoned his calling because of moral doubts and a loss of faith. Turning to a career in letters, he earned a place in the East India Company with his *History of India* (1817). During this period, he also became a defender of Benthamite principles. His most important work was his *Analysis of the Phenomena of the Human Mind* (1829), an attempt to provide a psychological basis for utilitarianism. Mill elaborated Hartley's associationism, arguing that the entire content of the mind is the result of the passive accumulation of composite ideas.

The association of ideas with sensation is crucial to Mill's theory of education. If the content of the mind is predicated on a passive association of ideas, the object of education is to ensure that the proper associations are made. This became the basis for the rigorous intellectual training that Mill gave his eldest son, described by John Stuart Mill in his *Autobiography* (1873).

John Stuart Mill was one of the most influential and important British philosophers in the 19th century. While his father's educational program had him reading Greek at age 3, it also left him emotionally crippled. After a severe depression in 1826, the young Mill began to look beyond the Benthamite orthodoxy to the philosophies of Saint-Simon and Coleridge. Only after his father's death did Mill blossom as an independent thinker, making important contributions in logic, economics, the philosophy of science, and political reform. He remained, however, a utilitarian, developing its doctrines in books such as *Utilitarianism* (1863), *An Examination of Sir William Hamilton's Philosophy* (1865), and the posthumous *Three Essays on Religion* (1874).

Mill's philosophy began from a position of radical empiricism. His *System of Logic* (1843) goes so far as to argue that even so-called deductive reason is itself predicated on inductive inference. Following both Bentham and his father, he accepted the associationist account of mental life. He contends, however, that the mind plays an active synthetic role. The content of the mind, he suggests, is qualitatively different from the quantitative aggregation of its ideas. This informed his contribution to utilitarian ethics. While Bentham focuses on the quantitative nature of pain and pleasure, Mill makes a qualitative distinction between higher and lower pleasure. Where Bentham remarked that push pins are preferable to poetry if push pins give greater pleasure, Mill responded, "It is better to be Socrates dissatisfied than a pig satisfied." Thus the "greatest happiness" principle was modified to the greatest sum of the *higher pleasure.*

Thomas L. Cooksey

Works Consulted

Anschutz, R.P. *The Philosophy of J.S. Mill.* Oxford: Clarendon, 1953.

Bowring, John, ed. *The Works of Jeremy Bentham.* 11 vols. New York: Russell, 1962.

Copleston, Frederick, *Modern Philosophy: Bentham to Russell.* Vol. 8 of *A History of Philosophy.* Garden City, NJ: Image Books-Doubleday, 1962.

Halèvy, Elié. *The Growth of Philosophical Radicalism.* Trans. Mary Morris. Clifton, NJ: Kelley, 1972.

Harrison, Ross, *Bentham.* Boston: Routledge, 1983.

Lyons, D. *Forms and Limits of Utilitarianism.* Oxford: Clarendon, 1965.

Mazlish, Bruce. *James and John Stuart Mill: Father and Son in the Nineteenth Century.* New York: Basic, 1975.

Mill, James. *Analysis of the Phenomena of the Human Mind.* 2nd ed. 1869. New York: Kelley, 1967.

Ogden, C.K. *Bentham's Theory of Fictions.* London: Keagan, 1932.

Packe, Michael St. John. *The Life of John Stuart Mill.* New York: Macmillan, 1954.

Robson, John M., ed. *Collected Works of John Stuart Mill.* 32 vols. Toronto: U of Toronto P, 1963.

Ryan, Alan. *The Philosophy of John Stuart Mill.* London: Macmillan, 1970.

Stephen, Leslie. *The English Utilitarians.* 3 vols. 1900. London: London School of Economics and Political Science, 1950.

Vampire

A blood-sucking revenant, the vampire returns from the grave to destroy the lives and frequently the souls of its victims. Although both male and female vampires destroy their victims, the male generally uses force to dominate victims while the female (also known as a lamia) relies on seduction.

The vampire occurs in the myth and folklore of most cultures and also in Greek and Roman literature but does not appear in modern literature until the Romantic period had given sophisticated readers a taste for mysterious and supernatural subjects. (*See also* Supernaturalism.) Although male vampires share some characteristics of the Gothic villain, the earliest literary vampires occur in poems with medieval or classical settings. For example, *Lenore*, written by Gottfried August Bürger in 1774 and translated into English by William Taylor in 1797, tells of the undead Wilhelm who returns from the Crusades to carry Lenore to the grave. Because of Taylor's translation and Scott's adaptation, which appeared anonymously in 1797 as "William and Helen" in *The Chase and William and Helen*, English Romantics quickly became familiar with the vampire and made use of it.

The most famous examples, *Christabel* and *La Belle Dame Sans Merci*, both use medieval settings. *Christabel* is especially interesting because Coleridge, who situates the lamia from classical literature in medieval times, is the first English writer to feature a female vampire. He wrote Part I in 1797 and Part II in 1800, and, though he often announced plans to complete the poem, he published all that there ever was to be of it in 1816. At that point in the plot, both the motherless Christabel and her father Sir Leoline have been seduced by the beautiful Geraldine, though Christabel has also seen Geraldine's secret and been struck dumb by the experience. Beginning with A.H. Nethercott's classic study *The Road to Tryermaine*, most critics have focused on the dangerous sexuality of Coleridge's lamia.

Other poems, including Goethe's *The Bride of Corinth* (1797), which was taken directly from Phlegon of Tralles, and Keats's *Lamia*, which originated in a story by Philostratus, adapt the classical lamia figure, a seductress who eventually destroys her male victims. *Lamia*, written in 1819 and published in 1820, presents the vampire as extraordinarily attractive, perhaps even as the poem's heroine. When she falls in love with a young Corinthian, Hermes transforms her into a beautiful woman, and she and Lycius live happily in her palace. The callow Lycius invites his friends to a wedding feast. An uninvited attendant, his old mentor Apollonius, recognizes her as a lamia and calls her by name. With that, her beauty withers, she and her palace vanish, and Lycius dies of grief. The poem, unlike earlier Romantic poems, clearly alters the source material and is often interpreted in terms of Keats's persistent interest in the relationship between the ideal and the real.

Somewhat less well known in this vein, Southey relied on folklore. In *Thalaba the Destroyer* (1797), an art ballad that refers to a number of superstitious beliefs, Southey includes an elaborate prose explanation that traces the beliefs in Hungary, Greece, and Turkey.

While most vampires in early Romantic literature clearly reveal their origins as either folklore or classical literature, one obvious exception stands out. Two engravings (plates 6 and 33) in Blake's *Jerusalem* (published 1804–20) use the vampire bat to symbolize the Spectre, the figure in Blake's mythology that represents destructive forces that prevent human beings from achieving their full creative potential.

Later, Romantics move farther from myth and folklore. One significant change occurs in the works of the second generation of Romantics, including Polidori, Byron's personal physician and the writer who introduced the vampire to English fiction. Although Keats focuses on the seductive lamia figure, Shelley, Byron, and Polidori combine the vampire from folklore with the Byronic hero. As Mario Praz points out, the title characters in Byron's *The Giaour* (published 1813), *The Corsair* (published 1814), and *Lara* (also published in 1814), are Byronic heroes who share the vampire's love of darkness, hypnotic powers, and obsession with the destructive side of love, and *Manfred* (published 1817) features a preternaturally strong man who, like the vampire, is condemned to live. (*See also* Byronic Hero.)

Shelley's *The Cenci*, written between 1818 and 1819 and published in 1819 and 1821, uses the vampirelike Count Francesco Cenci to explore such taboo subjects as incest and atheism, as well as the way that evil affects hitherto innocent individuals.

Finally, with Polidori, the vampire makes the transition to fiction. Although Byron, Polidori, and the Shelleys agreed to write ghost stories, only Polidori and Mary Shelley produced complete stories: Mary Shelley wrote and published *Frankenstein*; Byron published a "Fragment"; and Polidori transformed his employer into the prototypical male vampire, Lord Ruthven, an evil nobleman who destroys those who come in contact with him.

Polidori's *The Vampyre*, which was erroneously attributed to Byron when it was published in *The New Monthly Magazine* in 1819, was adapted to the French stage by Charles Nodier and just as quickly adapted for the English stage by James Robinson Planche as *The Vampire, or, The Bride of the Isles*. Although Planche objected to being required to use Scottish costumes, which were owned by the Lyceum Theatre, the play opened in August 1820. The play is famous for introducing "the vampire trap," a piece of stagecraft that enables an actor to disappear almost instantly under the stage. In 1829, Planche was given the opportunity to produce a more authentic adaptation, which he set in Hungary. Nonetheless, the original adaptation was popular and continued as a stock piece throughout the 19th century.

Carol A. Senf

Works Consulted

Nethercott, A.H. *The Road to Tryermaine*. 1939. rpt. New York: Russell, 1962.

Praz, Mario. *The Romantic Agony*. 1933. New York: Oxford UP, 1970.

Summers, Montague. *The Vampire: His Kith and Kin*. 1928. New Hyde Park, NY: University, 1960.

Twitchell, James B. *The Living Dead: A Study of the Vampire in Romantic Literature*. Durham, NC: Duke UP, 1981.

Vegetarianism

Records of lively debates concerning what constitutes the proper diet of humanity can be found in the memoirs, poetry, novels, essays, and periodicals of the Romantic period. For some Romantic reformers, poets, and fictional characters, vegetarianism was the chosen diet. Their arguments against meat eating addressed moral, ascetic, health, ecological, aesthetic, and physiological concerns. Their theories display millennial fervor, mirror the Romantic interest in classical authors, and syncretize vegetarian beliefs with standard Romantic themes.

The word "vegetarian" was not coined until 1847; during the Romantic period those who abstained from eating animals were known, perhaps condescendingly, as Pythagoreans (from Ovid's description of Pythagoras's speech against flesh eating in *Metamorphoses*), more rarely as Tryonists (after 17th-century vegetarian writer Thomas Tryon), or simply as followers of the vegetable diet. Byron refers to keeping "to Pythagoras" in one of his letters.

Historians, such as Keith Thomas and James Turner, posit the 1790s and the beginning of the 19th century as a pivotal time for agitation on behalf of animals and see vegetarianism as the most serious challenge to the status quo. The practitioners of Romantic vegetarianism were involved with radical politics and other unorthodoxies; they linked their dietary position with these reforms. Political ills of the day—from slavery to Robespierre's bloody rule—were traced to the moral evil that meat eating introduced to the world. Many optimistically believed that the widening of human rights would soon include the recognition of the rights of animals.

To vegetarian writers of this time, all things Romantic led to vegetarian issues: the Golden Age was vegetarian; Prometheus's discovery of fire is the story of how humans came to eat meat; the trees in the Garden of Eden represented not good and evil but flesh eating and vegetable diet. Shelley, perhaps the most famous vegetarian of this time, proposes the vegetarian interpretations of Prometheus and Adam and Eve in his essay *A Vindication of Natural Diet*, which also appears as one of his notes to *Queen Mab*. Alastor's "bloodless food," the bloodless banquet in *The Revolt of Islam*, as well as *On the Vegetable System of Diet* and a section of *A Refutation of Deism* reflect Shelley's continuing interest in this issue.

John Oswald, whose 1791 book *The Cry of Nature; or, An Appeal to Mercy and to Justice, on Behalf of the Persecuted Animals*, inaugurates the humanistic arguments on behalf of animals in the Romantic period, lost his life in France in 1793, fighting for the Jacobins at the battle of Pont-de-Cé. It is thought that the antihunting leader of the military volunteers in Wordsworth's *Excursion* is based on Oswald. Other vegetarians of this time include Scottish philosopher Adam Ferguson; Yorkshire printer George Nicholson, whose publications include *On the Conduct of Mind to Inferior Animals* (1797) and *On the Primeval Food of Man; Arguments in Favour of Vegetable Food* (1801); John "Walking" Stewart; Republican publisher and founder of *The Monthly Magazine*; Sir Richard Phillips, who published *Golden Rules on Social Philosophy; or, a New System of Practical Ethics*, including "The Author's Reasons for not eating Animal Food" (1826); antiquarian Joseph Ritson, whose vegetarian writings greatly influenced Shelley's *An Essay on Abstinence from Animal Food as a Moral Duty* (1802); Dr. William Lambe, a physician whose books about curing cancer and other diseases encouraged a vegetarian regimen, for example, *Reports on the Effects of a Peculiar Regimen on Scirrhous Tumours and Cancerous Ulcers* (1809); author John Frank Newton, friend of Godwin and Shelley, who wrote *The Return to Nature; or, a Defence of the Vegetable Regimen* (1811); inventor and one of the founders of the Society for the Prevention of Cruelty to Animals, Lewis Gompertz, who wrote *Moral Enquiries on the Situation of Men and Brutes*; and William Cowherd, founder of the Bible Christian Church, a branch of Swedenborgianism which was vegetarian, and included as followers parliamentary reformer Joseph Brotherton and his wife, vegetarian author Martha Brotherton, who wrote *Vegetable Cookery* (1821).

Discussions of the vegetarianism of such authors as Shelley, Ritson, and Phillips are found in the memoirs and reminiscences of their Romantic acquaintances: Godwin on Ritson, Thomas Jefferson Hogg and Peacock on Shelley, and Cobbet and George Borrow on Phillips.

Pythagoreans were discussed with contempt in the pages of *The Political Herald and Review*. Still others, such as the writers of *The Anti-Jacobin*, lampooned vegetarians, showing them to be eccentric and cranks. Peacock humorously depicts the vegetarian view of Prometheus in the character of Mr. Escot, the deteriorationist, in *Headlong Hall*. Cutlet, a sentimental butcher who reads Joseph Ritson's *Essay on Abstinence*, appears in Lamb's *The Pawnbroker's Daughter*, and *Dinner by the Amateurs of Vegetable Diet* (1821) parodies Shelley's first vegetarian essay.

Other fictional depictions treated the issue more seriously: M. Ruffigny in Godwin's *Fleetwood* adheres to a vegetarian diet, as does the Monster in Mary Shelley's *Frankenstein*.

Carol J. Adams

Works Consulted

Bronson, Bertrand H. *Joseph Ritson: Scholar-at-Arms*. Berkeley: U of California P, 1938.

Clark, David Lee. "The Date and Sources of Shelley's *A Vindication of Natural Diet*." *Studies in Philology* 36 (1939).

Erdman, David. *Commerce des Lumières: John Oswald and the British in Paris, 1790–1793*. Columbia: U of Missouri P, 1986.

T.H. "Pythagorean Objections against Animal Food." *London Magazine*. (1825): 380–83.

Thomas, Keith. *Man and the Natural World: A History of the Modern Sensibility*. New York: Pantheon, 1983.

Turner, James. *Reckoning with the Beast: Animals, Pain and Humanity in the Victorian Mind*. Baltimore: Johns Hopkins UP, 1980.

Ventriloquism

Though the English Romantics preferred to see the creative mind as an aeolian harp, they were often acutely aware that the more accurate image might be that of the ventriloquist. Indeed, the double character of the imagination leaves it open to charges of solipsism and duplicity: The poet who claims both to perceive and to half create the world is vulnerable to a comparison with the ventriloquist who projects his own voice onto a dummy world.

In recent times, this possibility has been explored most vigorously by Edward E. Bostetter, whose controversial book, *The Romantic Ventriloquists: Wordsworth, Coleridge, Keats, Shelley, Byron* (1963), in many ways initiated the modern skeptical critique of English Romanticism. Bostetter wonders whether the Romantic poets were not guilty of wish fulfillment and concludes that this is indeed the case: "The poet became in reality the divine ventriloquist projecting his own voice as the voice of truth." Suspicious of Romantic affirmations, Bostetter finds a poetry of increasing doubt—marked by the poet's ever-growing, uneasy realization that his affirmations are unrealizable. This awareness led to a series of unfinished—indeed unfinishable—poems, and ultimately drove the poet into a solitude of the psyche. Wordsworth and Coleridge, unable to maintain their illusions against an intractable reality, withdrew into traditional orthodoxies; similar disillusionment led Keats and Shelley to take refuge within a solipsistic fantasy life. According to Bostetter, only Byron was able to escape these debilitating effects—and this because he embraced ventriloquism and exploited it comically.

Bostetter's ground-breaking critical example has influenced succeeding generations of scholars. Tilottama Rajan has called him a "proto-deconstructionist," and indeed, though Bostetter lacks a specifically deconstructionist or Marxist vocabulary, the spirit of his hard-nosed demystification of Romantic self-representations inhabits the work of many later skeptics. Jerome J. McGann, for example, has developed further the positive aspects of Byron's self-conscious ventriloquism. McGann sees ventriloquism in Byron's unique ability to layer several different voices within a single passage—the one an ironic supplement to the other. Thus, McGann uses ventrilo-quism as a metaphor to describe not the poet's delusion or duplicity but rather his ironic dialogism: Byron's double-voicedness lies in his sophisticated ability to deepen and problematize his language by projecting within it the disruptive voices of satire. Even modern optimists recognize the importance of Bostetter's work on ventriloquism. Though for M.H. Abrams, Bostetter's insistent focus on Romantic self-delusions represents a "literary Manichae-ism" that is opposed in principle to impure affirmations, he nonetheless acknowledges the value and necessity of such critiques: they focus concern on the richness of Romanticism and its many-layered attitudes and stances. Indeed, those critics who yet affirm the professed values of Romanticism can no longer ignore the presence and dark implications of Romantic ventriloquism; rather, they now point to the poet's own awareness of the problem and to the form of his complex solution.

John Axcelson

Works Consulted

Abrams, M.H. *Natural Supernaturalism: Tradition and Revolution in Romantic Literature.* New York: Norton, 1971.

Adams, Hazard. "Edward E. Bostetter (1914–1973)." *The Wordsworth Circle* 4 (1973): 160.

Bostetter, Edward E. *The Romantic Ventriloquists: Wordsworth, Coleridge, Keats, Shelley, Byron.* Seattle: U of Washington P, 1963.

McGann, Jerome J. "Byron, Mobility, and the Poetics of Historical Ventriloquism." *Romanticism Past and Present* 9.1 (1985): 67–82.

Rajan, Tilottama. *Dark Interpreter: The Discourse of Romanticism.* Ithaca: Cornell UP, 1980.

Visionary Landscape Painting

The English tradition of visionary landscape portrays Edenic shadows. As practiced by Palmer and the "Ancients"—Calvert, Richmond, Linnell, and others—visionary landscape holds the

Miltonic view expressed in *Paradise Lost* that the earth is "but the shadow of Heav'n, and things therein/ Each to other like more than on Earth is thought." The work of these artists during the late 1820s and early 1830s attempted to express the countryside's mysticism or at the very least convey the glimpse of eternity that, to use Palmer's phrase, results from drawing aside "the fleshly curtain." The consequence of this approach is that visionary landscape often seems transcendental. Its scenes appear visitable only in the imagination; its beauty depends on physical inaccessibility. Yet the Shoreham group (the Ancients) based their work on actual English scenes. Palmer's art was especially committed to particular study and accurate images even though they might be altered in the final works. Visionary landscapes are not dream scenes but ones perceived through the heightened senses and memories of the observer. They often resemble the effortlessness of childhood perception.

The Ancients favored the well-tended countryside around the village of Shoreham in Kent, where Palmer lived from 1826 until the early 1830s and where he gathered a circle of artists who would visit and work in the village. Shoreham is not sublime or picturesque but agriculturally rich—a rounded, lush place which has the village church as its common spiritual focus. Harmony, fertility, and bounty permeate the visionary landscapes depicting the area. Harvest moons, cottage roofs, farmers, and plump, placid sheep and cattle are set amidst the ripe, swollen, dense forms of hills, fields of wheat, and trees.

Blake and Linnell shared the conviction that all aspects of landscape (form, moods, light, effects) assume metaphorical significance: the subject always implies more than just itself. Both artists understood

visible nature to be a reflection of the spiritual world perceived through the imagination. This orientation toward the visionary underlies the "poetical landscapes" Linnell painted during the 19th century—art that intended to use all its resources to produce spiritual perceptions. Palmer's own transformation as an artist occurred between 1822 and 1824, when he came under the influence of Blake and Linnell and developed a concentrated, linear style and shaped his own belief that paradise could be seen in nature but experienced only in the mind's "Valley of Vision."

Turner, the quintessential Romantic artist, evoked a spiritual quality in many paintings, but his hazy treatment is at variance with the specificity of Blake, Linnell, Calvert, and Palmer, visionary landscape's leading exponent. (And Blake is, rather, a figurative artist; his landscapes are rudimentary.) Turner's distrust of nature becomes associated with what he called the "Vegetative Eye," the eye that looks directly on things, uninformed by anything spiritual. Palmer was struck with the intensity and detail in Blake's work and his emphasis on imaginative discernment. By applying these attributes to landscape, Palmer created a view of the pastoral as holy through an accumulation of minute, spiritualized particulars. This sense of the miniature and the sacred irradiates both Blake's work and the landscapes of Palmer and the Ancients. Their art reworks an inherited Christian tradition—but one overlaid with personal experience and a more creative spirit. The Shoreham painters cultivated an informed vision, touched, as Coleridge says in *Dejection: An Ode*, by "the passion and the life whose fountains are within." Thus, rather than literal transcriptions of nature, these landscapes are elastic. They are imbued with religious meaning, charged with intense emotion, and portray a responsive nature.

The sense of mystic vision extends even to the mediums used and their handling. For instance, in some of his illustrations Palmer mixed sepia and gum to produce a warm brown and then varnished them, thereby producing a translucent, antique quality. At other times, he worked with a mixture of watercolor, pen, tempera, and varnish, which gives his work the luminosity of stained glass. The result is a highly sensuous surface the lines of which possess a moral dimension while simultaneously receiving its charge from Biblical tradition and erotic energy.

D.C. Woodcox

Works Consulted

Binyon, Laurence. *The Followers of William Blake*. New York: Minton, 1925.

Crouan, Katherine. *John Linnell: A Centennial Exhibition*. New York: Cambridge UP, 1982.

Grigson, G. *Samuel Palmer: The Visionary Years*. 1947.

Richards, B.A. "Visionary Landscape." Unpublished Manuscript. 1989.

Vaughan, William. *Romantic Art*. New York: Oxford UP, 1978.

Vulcanism

Vulcanism, or "plutonism," developed in the late 18th century as a reaction against Neptunism, or "geognosy." Abraham Gottlob Werner (1750–1817), the charismatic spokesman of Neptunism, held that the earth's rocks of all sorts precipitated from a primordial ocean in stages each marked by its own "cataclysm"; such cataclysms were responsible both for the earth's varying stratified mineral composition and for such topographical features as valleys, formed by the violent run-off of the sea. The Vulcanists, in contrast, distinguished igneous from sedimentary rocks and held that regular, rather than cataclysmic, liftings of the sea floor by subterranean heat produced the present rocks, while the regular action of erosion produces topographical features. This emphasis on cyclical rising and eroding rather than on onetime catastrophes has led historians of science increasingly to give up the term "Vulcanism" in favor of "Uniformitarianism." (*See also* Burnet, Thomas.)

The pioneer Vulcanist was James Hutton (1726–97), whose work entered the professional mainstream through accounts and amplifications by his mathematician friend John Playfair (1748–1819). Hutton began his scientific career as a medical student whose interests were more chemical than physiological. Financial success through a chemical enterprise in producing sal ammoniac allowed him to purchase a farm and follow an interest in agriculture, which was to remain with him to his death. Biographers suggest, quite plausibly, that Hutton's attention to erosion came as much from his careful attention to agricultural land management as from an intellectual interest in Horace-Bénédict de Saussure's (1740–99) accounts of fluvial deposits from Mont Blanc's streams. These two influences, along with Hutton's own constant geological fieldwork, combined to create a vision of a landscape regularly draining to the sea, while marine fossil deposits ashore suggested a sea regularly rising to become land.

Hutton's conclusion from this vision of balanced erosion and land building was presented in a 1785 "Abstract of a Dissertation read in the Royal Society of Edinburgh . . . concerning the System of the Earth, its Duration and Stability." (The published form of this paper was not discovered until the 1950s, and its printed dissemination and impact in Britain and abroad still remain unclear.) Hutton's first widely distributed publication was *Theory of the Earth; or an Investigation of the Laws observable in the Composition, Dissolution, and Restoration of Land upon the Globe* (1788), a view elaborated in the *Theory of the Earth: With Proofs and Illustrations; in Four Parts* (Parts 1 and 2, 1795; Part 3, posthumously, 1899). In both of these books, Hutton augments his primary observation of erosion and resurfacing: subterranean heat and expansion lift marine sediments, the "vulcanism" in Vulcanism. For Neptunists, modern volcanoes are a local, recent anomaly; for Vulcanists, they evidence the regular displacement from the hot "mineral realm," where heat also fuses the minerals of igneous rocks and contributes to metamorphosis. Given the importance of heat to the Vulcanists, Hutton not surprisingly devoted speculative energy to the nature of heat itself in *Dissertations of Different Subjects in Natural Philosophy* (1792) and his final book, *A Dissertation Upon the Philosophy of Light, Heat, and Fire* (1794).

Hutton's 1788 book produced sharp criticism. His model of indefinitely long geological cycles drew attacks from a coalition of Neptunists and Christian diluvialists, like Jean André de Luc (1727–1817) and Richard Kirwan (1733–1812). The bulk of their public attacks amazingly suggests that erosion never occurs and that the soil and rocks are in a constant state. John Playfair's 1802 consolidation of Hutton's work and confirmation of river-valley erosion established Hutton's view as recognizably superior to that of his critics.

Although his geological timetable provoked Christian literalist attack, Hutton was a religious thinker and often concluded his geological writings with a statement on Vulcanism as a sign of God's design. Three years before his death, he published in three volumes *An Investigation of the Principles of Knowledge* (1794), which proposes nature as a "machine" subordinate to God's "wisdom"—a wisdom, however, that humankind can approach only through careful study of the machine.

Abidingly accepted into the scientific canon through Charles Lyell's *Principles of Geology* (1830–33), the Vulcanists did not have the direct effect on their Romantic literary contemporaries that Werner and the Neptunists had. Hutton also did not achieve the status of literary-scientific essayist in his own right, as Darwin would; in spite of such interesting attempts as Donald M. Hassler's to see Hutton's thinking as "poetic," his prose style receives universal blame as an impediment to the point that, without Playfair's summary, Hutton's ideas might have been lost.

In addition to the reprintings of Hutton's major geological writings, Edward Battersby Bailey's *James Hutton—The Founder of Modern Geology* provides a blow-by-blow paraphrase, with generous quotations, of Hutton's major books and papers. (*See also* Geological Sciences.)

William Crisman

Works Consulted

Bailey, Edward Battersby. *James Hutton—The Founder of Modern Geology*. New York: Elsevier: 1967.

Chorley, Richard J., *et al. The History of the Study of Landforms, or the Development of Geomorphology*. Vol. 1. New York: Wiley, 1964.

Geike, Archibald. *The Founders of Geology*. New York: Macmillan, 1905.

Gillispie, Charles Coulston. *Genesis and Geology: A Study in the Relations of Scientific Thought, Natural Theology, and Social Opinion in Great Britain, 1790–1850*. Cambridge: Harvard UP, 1951.

Hassler, Donald M. "The Scottish Reasoning of James Hutton: Poet in Spite of Himself." *Studies in Scottish Literature* 21 (1986): 35–42.

Ospovat, Alexander M. "Romanticism and German Geology: Five Students of Abraham Gottlob Werner." *Eighteenth Century Life* 7 (1982): 105–16.

White, G.W. Introduction. *System of the Earth, 1785. Theory of the Earth, 1788. Observations on Granite, 1794.* By James Hutton. Darien, CT: Hafner, 1970.

Wade, Thomas

(1805–1875)

Although a minor figure, Thomas Wade is interesting as a poet whose work reflects both the continuing aspirations and the declining force of Romanticism between 1820 and 1840. Born in Suffolk, Wade came to London at an early age and published in 1825 *Tasso and the Sisters*, a collection of verse which shows the influence of Shelley, Byron, and Moore and which was favorably reviewed in the literary press.

For the next few years, Wade turned his attention to the drama, producing a tragedy, *Woman's Love* (1828), and a farce, *the Phrenologists* (1830). Both plays were successful on the stage, but in late 1830, Wade outraged his audience with his tragedy, *The Jew of Arragon*, which presented its Jewish characters as sympathetic heroes subjected to Christian persecution.

In 1835, Wade produced his first significant volume of verse, *Mundi et Cordis Carmina*. In this collection, Wade shows both his characteristic strengths and weaknesses. There are moments of real poetic power, but there is much that is mannered

and clumsy. Shelley's influence is pervasive but is as often stifling as inspiring. This volume also shows Wade experimenting, often successfully, with different forms of the sonnet, a practice that he continued throughout his long career. *Mundi et Cordis Carmina* was attacked by the reviewers, and Wade protested in a broadside sonnet addressed "To Certain Critics" in which he presents poets as "chosen reeds" through which "The Universal Pan" makes music.

In the late 1830s, Wade issued several poems in pamphlet form which contain some of his best verse. In 1837 appeared *The Contention of Love and Death, Helena*, and *The Shadow-Seeker*. In 1839, Wade published *Prothanasia and Other Poems*. Although these works met with little success, and the original pamphlets are now exceedingly rare, the poems contain interesting and troubled reflections on central Romantic themes. In *The Contention of Love and Death*, the possible immortality of the creative mind is debated rather inconclusively. *Helena* owes much to Keats and also raises disturbing questions about the Romantic imagination. *Prothanasia* is indebted to Shelley's *Alastor* and dramatizes the dangers of spiritual questing, while *The Shadow-Seeker* laments the difficulty of finding the image of the ideal in the physical world.

After 1839, Wade largely turned from poetry to a more or less successful career in journalism. He continued to write sonnets and contributed short poems to periodicals but never produced another collection of verse.

Among Wade's shorter poems the most interesting are *The Coming of Night* and *The Winter Shore*, both of which hymn in blank verse a nature that seems both sublime and dying, and several of his sonnets, in which nature, transcendent spiritual power, and creative genius are treated with a strange combination of skepticism and lyrical enthusiasm. Wade's work is too often diffuse and derivative, but his poetry and his contribution to Romanticism deserve to be better known.

Phillip B. Anderson

Works Consulted

Bernard Quaritch Catalog 1087: The English Romantics.

Bloom, Harold. *The Visionary Company.* Ithaca: Cornell UP, 1971.

Elton, Oliver. *A Survey of English Literature: 1830–1880.* 2 vols. New York: Macmillan, 1929.

Nicoll, W.R., and T.J. Wise, eds. *Literary Anecdotes of the Nineteenth Century.* New York: Dodd, 1895.

Wainewright, Thomas Griffiths
(1794–1847)

Artist, art critic, and poisoner, Thomas Griffiths Wainewright was called the "genius" of the *London Magazine* by Lamb and achieved minor notoriety in Regency Britain more for his criminal activities than for his literary talents. Wainewright donned a number of masks for the influential magazine, including Cornelius Van Vinkbooms, Egomet Bonmot, and his most characteris-

tic persona, Janus Weathercock. His career in Britain was terminated, however, when he fled the country bankrupt and under suspicion for forgery and murder in 1831.

With both parents dying during his infancy, Wainewright was raised by his maternal grandfather, Dr. Ralph Griffiths, publisher of the *Monthly Review*. He was educated at Charles Burney's academy, knew Fuseli and Flaxman, and studied at the studio of Thomas Phillips. He was a skilled draughtsman as well as a fairly acute art critic, and between 1821 and 1825, he exhibited some five works at the Royal Academy, specializing in watercolors and crayons. But it was for his work for the *London Magazine* that he was best known.

Wainewright cultivated and represented a Regency archetype: the dandy dilettante. To a great extent he was a prose portraitist and proselytizer for this subclass, which plausibly includes Byron, the young Disraeli, Beau Brummel, and Scropes Davies, to name a few. One of his articles, "Dogmas for Dilettantes," amounts to a manifesto for what Hazlitt acerbically called "The Dandy School."

Nevertheless, Wainewright was friendly with and admired by Hazlitt, Lamb, De Quincey, Cunningham, and Hood. His frivolous and fantastic *roué* narrative poses counterbalanced the sober analyses of John Scott (the editor of the *London* until his death in a duel) and the curmudgeonly prose of Hazlitt, and complemented the whimsical Elia persona that Lamb developed. In fact, Wainewright often referred to Hazlitt and Lamb in his essays and published a long narrative about the death of Elia after Lamb prematurely killed off his persona in 1822. In dinner conversations with many of the *London* contributors, and in print, Wainewright suggested essay ideas; one such suggestion eventually resulted in Lamb's essay "Poor Relations."

The last Janus Weathercock paper appeared in January 1823, when Wainewright declared he was "steadfast for lack of oil," and indeed Wainewright was constantly in deep financial troubles caused by a slim annuity and an extravagant life-style. In 1826, he forged a note against his trust fund, and two years later he became ominously desperate. He apparently poisoned (presumably with strychnine), in succession, his uncle, his wife's mother, and his wife's half-sister. When the insurers refused to pay out a policy on the last's life, Wainewright fled to France; he returned in 1837, was convicted, and eventually was transported to Australia, where he died in 1847.

Wainewright was caricatured by Dickens and Bulwer Lytton and studied by Oscar Wilde; he was extensively discussed by Victorian criminologists. He is probably best remembered, like the *New Yorker*'s "man-about-town," as the vivid image of both an important magazine and a unique social type.

Joel Haefner

Works Consulted

Curling, Jonathan. *Janus Weathercock: The Life of Thomas Griffiths Wainewright, 1794–1847*. London: Nelson, 1938.

Dictionary of National Biography, *s.v.*, "Wainewright, Thomas Griffiths."

Graham, Walter. *English Literary Periodicals*. New York: Nelson, 1930.

Haefner, Joel. "The Two Faces of the *London Magazine*." *Charles Lamb Bulletin* 44 (1983): 69–81.

Riga, Frank P., and Claude A. Prance. *Index to the London Magazine*. New York: Garland, 1978.

Wainewright, Thomas Griffiths. *Essays and Criticism by Thomas Griffiths Wainewright*. Ed. W. Carew Hazlitt. London: Reeves, 1880.

Walpole, Horace
(1717–97)

Born with the proverbial silver spoon in his mouth, Horace Walpole came into the world in 1717, the third son and youngest child of Catherine Shorter, who came from a wealthy merchant family, and Sir Robert Walpole, who was to serve as Prime Minister under the first two King Georges and who became the first Earl of Orford. In some ways, Walpole typifies the upper-class literary dilettante of his age, moving in the best social circles, sitting in the House of Commons, involving himself in the major social and political issues of the day, and trying his hand at a variety of literary endeavors, including the establishment of an important printing press on his Strawberry Hill estate. But Walpole was more than the stereotypical effete, upper-class snob as he is so often depicted. For example, his early and strong moral opposition to slavery and his sympathy for the American colonists' struggle for independence are more in tune with the later Romantics than with many of his upper-class contemporaries. (*See also* Gothicism, Novel.)

In literature, Walpole's attitudes and achievements are fairly typical for the wealthy dilettante of the period. He tried his hand at verse; satire; biography; histories of literature, art, and politics; periodical essays; and letters (then considered a legitimate and important literary form). Outside of his letters, which are among the best of the century, these efforts are for the most part undistinguished and infused with Neoclassical literary principles. However, Walpole became an important factor in the emergence of Romanticism when he created the first Gothic novel, *The Castle of Otranto*, in 1764. He followed that influential work with a minor, but no less Romantic, creation, a blank verse tragedy, *The Mysterious Mother*, in 1768.

The latter is superior artistically to *Otranto*, but it had not so great an influence on later writers. The play centers on a double incest theme: the protagonist, Edmund, has a sexual encounter with his mother, although at the time he is unaware of her identity; this union produces a child whom, 16 years later, Edmund meets, falls in love with, and marries. When the truth is finally revealed, his mother kills herself, the girl is banished to a convent, and Edmund goes off to war as solace for his misery. The play is gloomy, unremittingly tragic, but Walpole still is able to build suspense gradually to the climax. Its Gothic devices, passion, and sensationalism make it a thoroughly Romantic production in a period that was still predominantly Neoclassical. (*See also* Incest.)

Otranto is much the same kind of work. Although poorly written with a confusing plot, it lays the foundation for future Gothic romances. Manfred, the villain of the piece, lusts for the frail Isabella, formerly betrothed to his recently deceased son. Enter the hero, Theodore, who loses his own love, Matilda, to the blade of Manfred but who saves Isabella and marries her. Due to the popularity of Walpole's romance, the persecuted maiden theme, which Walpole seems to have borrowed from Richardson's *Pamela* and *Clarissa*, becomes the major plot for almost all of the 18th-century Gothic romances that followed and remains today centrally important to the genre. Walpole also employs the Gothic devices that eventually became the defining conventions of the genre: a castle with secret passages set in a gloomy wood, mysterious events and noises, supernatural occurrences, a noble hero raised as a peasant, extremely punctilious female characters who weep and faint incessantly, and

a towering and enigmatic villain who poses a sexual threat to the heroine. He borrowed these devices from works as various as those of Shakespeare and Richardson, but he combined them and introduced them into prose fiction to create the Gothic romance, which continues to be one of the most popular forms of fiction.

Although he became the fourth Earl of Orford at age 74, Walpole never sat in the House of Lords, preferring to spend his last years at Strawberry Hill, entertaining and writing letters. He died quietly in 1797, and was buried beneath the church on his estate. (*See also* Antiquarianism.)

John A. Stoler

Works Consulted

Evans, Bertrand. *Gothic Drama from Walpole to Shelley*. Berkeley: U of California P, 1947.

Kallich, Martin. *Horace Walpole*. New York: Twayne, 1971.

Ketton-Cremer, R.W. *Horace Walpole*. London: Duckworth, 1940.

Lewis, W.S. *Horace Walpole*. New York: Pantheon, 1961.

— — —. *Rescuing Horace Walpole*. New Haven: Yale UP, 1978.

Mehrota, K.K. *Horace Walpole and the English Novel*. Oxford: Blackwell, 1934.

Varma, Devendra. *The Gothic Flame*. London: Barker, 1957.

Watt, James

(1736–1819)

James Watt was born not far north of Glasgow in the village of Greenoch, Scotland, in 1736. His father was a merchant who had gone bankrupt so Watt was on his own at an early age. At age 19, the mechanically oriented Watt went to London to apprentice himself to an instrument maker, but because he had always had a weak constitution, after only a year his health forced him to return home. Several faculty members at the University of Glasgow had been impressed with Watt's abilities; he received the job of instrument maker for the college.

In 1764, Watt was asked to repair a Newcomen steam engine, an engine that was used to pump water out of mines. The machine was named for Thomas Newcomen (1633–1729), a merchant who became interested in the problem of water in the mines and developed what he called a "fire and air" engine to solve the problem. The term "steam engine" first appeared in print in 1719. The steam section of the Newcomen machine was composed primarily of a cylinder open at the top containing a piston, a boiler underneath, and a cold-water container. Steam entered at the bottom of the cylinder forcing the piston up; the steam was then stopped by closing off the boiler; an injection of cold water cooled the steam; and gravity forced the piston down. This created a pumping action, but alternately heating and cooling the cylinder made the process very slow and required large amounts of steam and fuel.

Watt began by studying the properties of steam. He decided two conditions had to be met before an economical condensing steam engine could be developed. First, the temperature of the condensed steam had to be as low as possible, and, second, the cylinder needed to be the same temperature as the steam. In the Newcomen engine, these conditions were impossible to meet.

One Sunday afternoon while strolling in Glasgow Green, Watt visualized a solution. If the steam could be condensed in another container rather than the cylinder, both of his preconditions could be met. Many problems remained to be solved, but the idea of the separate condenser worked very well.

In 1769, Watt obtained a patent for his machine. He did not have sufficient capital to continue his experiments so he found a partner in John Roebuck, founder of the Carron iron works. But Roebuck's business failed, and, to earn a living, Watt turned his attention to surveying. He was outstanding at the job and even invented a micrometer for measuring distance; however, his interest in the steam engine remained. After gaining the support of Matthew Boulton, of Birmingham, the two men established the company of Boulton & Watt and began to manufacture engines in 1775.

Watt felt the engine had greater potential than merely pumping water. In 1781, he received a patent on his method for converting the reciprocating motion created by the piston to the rotary motion necessary to operate machinery. He also developed a system of valves which allowed steam to enter the cylinder only during the early part of the piston stroke. Still later, he developed methods to control the speed of the engine. The later inventions along with his original ideas greatly reduced fuel consumption and made the steam engine capable of powering all kinds of machines, thus encouraging the development of the factory as well as various forms of transportation. Watt's primary problem was that he never admitted the value of high-pressure steam, which is one of the key principles of modern engines.

When his patents expired in 1800, Watt turned the business over to his son James and retired to his home near Birmingham, where he devoted his attention to mechanical ideas. His last work was a machine for duplicating sculpture.

Watt was married twice and had a number of children, most of whom died young. His first wife was Margaret Miller, a cousin, and his second was Anne Macgregor.

Watt died in 1819, and is buried at the parish church in neighboring Handsworth.

K. Gird Romer

Works Consulted

Ashton, T.S. *The Industrial Revolution, 1760–1830*. New York: Oxford UP, 1969.

Mantoux, Paul. *The Industrial Revolution in the Eighteenth Century: An Outline of the Beginnings of the Modern Factory System in England*. Rev. ed. London: Cape, 1928.

Strandh, Sigvard. *A History of the Machine*. New York: A & W, 1979.

Watts, Alaric Alexander
(1797–1864)

Alaric Alexander Watts was a minor poet and prominent editor of the popular English gift-books during the 1820s and 1830s. Numbered among his friends were such luminaries as Scott, Southey, Coleridge, Wordsworth, and Mary Shelley.

Born in London, Watts was raised by his mother after his parents' bitter divorce during his childhood. After completing his education at Power's Academy at Ashford, he held various tutoring and clerking jobs, before becoming subeditor of the *New Monthly Magazine* in London around 1818. The following year, he oversaw the failed production of Maturin's tragic play *Fredolpho*. He was also a contributor to the *Literary Gazette*, and through that popular publication, he made the acquaintance of many literary figures of the day. In 1822, he became editor of the *Leeds Intelligencer*, leaving it three years later to become editor of the Manchester *Courier*, all the while writing both poetry and prose. A volume of his poetry, *Poetical Sketches*, printed privately in 1822, earned him a reputation as a poet.

In 1824, Watts established and edited the popular *Literary Souvenir*, an annual publication of poetry, short stories, memoirs, and art. Introduced into England in 1811 by London publisher and bookseller Ackermann, these miscellanies, known as annuals, souvenir books, and gift-books, were enormously popular during the 1820s and 1830s. Inspired by German literary almanacs, the ornamental books were sold in huge quantities as Christmas and keepsake gifts, principally for middle- to upperclass women. Along with the *Literary Souvenir*, other popular annuals were *Forget-me-Not*, *Friendship's Offering*, *The Amulet*, and *The Anniversary*. Taking themselves seriously, they stressed middle-class values and served moral lessons in an often treacly sauce of sentiment. Contributors to these volumes were both renowned and aspiring writers and artists, though most serious writers scorned the books. Both Wordsworth and Southey wrote and spoke disdainfully of them, yet contributed to them, as did Scott, Coleridge, and Shelley.

Watts took pains to solicit work from the best writers and artists for the *Literary Souvenir*, and, finding this type of work more suited to his tastes than editing a newspaper, he resigned the editorship of the *Courier* and took on full proprietorship of the *Souvenir* in 1826.

Meanwhile, Watts continued to write and publish poetry in *Poetical Album* (1828), *The Laurel*, and *The Lyre* (1829; reprinted together in 1867). He also helped to establish the newspaper *Standard* (1827) and founded the *United Service Gazette* (1833), both minor provincial publications.

As the *Literary Souvenir*, which in 1836 had been renamed *The Cabinet of Modern Art*, began to decline in popularity, Watts found himself trying to shore up his assorted troubled publications, and he became involved in litigation with his partners in the *Gazette* and others. In 1850, he went bankrupt. However, also in 1850, an edition of his collected works, *Lyrics of the Heart*, was published and became popular in England and America for quite some time. Watts took a minor civil service job in a tax office and continued to engage in literary pursuits until his death in 1864. Among them, in 1856, he edited the first issue of *Men of the Time*. In it, the article on Watts was considerably longer than that on Tennyson.

Linda Jordan Tucker

Works Consulted

Bennett, Betty T. *Mary Diana Dods, A Gentleman and a Scholar*. New York: Morrow, 1991.

Dictionary of National Biography, s.v., "Watts, Alaric Alexander."

Jack, Ian. *English Literature: 1815–1832*. Oxford: Clarendon, 1963.

Watts, Alaric Alfred. *Alaric Watts: A Narrative of His Life*. 2 vols. London: Bentley, 1884.

Webb, Cornelius

(1789–?)

The role of Cornelius Webb in the Romantic movement is minor if singular. In the October 1817, issue of *Blackwood's Magazine* appeared the following lines by Webb over what appeared to be a description of the favorite topics of conversation among the literary disciples of Leigh Hunt at Hampstead: "Our talk shall be (a theme we never tire on)/Of Chaucer, Spenser, Shakespeare, Milton, Byron,/(Our England's Dante)—Wordsworth—Hunt, and Keats,/The Muse's son of promise; and of what feats/He yet may do." These lines, or some of them, were repeated above later *Blackwood* articles ridiculing "The Cockney School," and "Corny" Webb along with "Johnny" Keats and other "Cockneys" became regular butts of the *Blackwood's* men. Keats had cause to regret the literary activities of Webb, whom he

mentions just once as a "poetaster—who unfortunately was of our party at Hampstead," and it was once believed to be tragically ironic that Keats and John Scott—two key figures in the Romantic movement—died prematurely as an indirect result of Webb's muse.

Born sometime in 1789, in London, the son of William Webb, Cornelius appears to have been a precocious versifier who published poems from at least 1813 in journals that included *The Gentleman's Magazine*, the *New Monthly*, and both Gold's and Baldwin's *London Magazines*. Two early collections of verse—*Heath Flowers* (1817) and *The Reverie* (?1818)—were advertised but cannot now be traced, although the former was reviewed in April 1817. However, the privately printed *Sonnets, Amatory, Incidental and Descriptive* (1820) was widely and enthusiastically reviewed, one critic ranking the sonnets above those of Wordsworth in minute finishing. This friendly reception prompted the Olliers in 1821 to bring out a follow-up volume of twice the length; but *Summer, an Invocation to Sleep; Fairy Revels; and Songs and Sonnets* was more coolly received. Some of the last poems Webb wrote in this period appeared in another Ollier venture, *The Literary Pocket Book*, edited by Leigh Hunt which, when it came out in late 1821, gave the *Blackwood's* men another opportunity to bait the Cockneys, though by now the old enmity had somewhat waned.

Also, by this time, critical discouragement and doubtless financial insecurity, not to mention the tragic deaths of Keats and Scott, for whose fate Webb might have felt partially responsible, forced the young writer to turn to prose, and journals like the *Literary Gazette*, the *New Monthly*, *New European*, and *Gold's* were glad to print his essays, tales, and sketches. However, one old standby, Taylor and Hessey's *Lon-*

ðon Magazine, which under Scott had welcomed Webb, now preferred the likes of Hazlitt, Lamb, and De Quincey, and new editor Taylor announced that he had eight guineas worth of Webb material unused.

Webb's first prose collections, *Posthumous Papers, facetious and fanciful, of a Person lately about Town* (1828) consisted mainly of magazine articles, and again the superlatives flowed from the reviewers' pens. To the *Athenaeum*, Webb's book was full of grave beauties and one particular tale, "A Story of the Old Time in Italy," was quoted from as having almost no rival. Such absurdly exaggerated praise can be easily dismissed, and it is more interesting to note that Douglas Jerrold, a writer of infinitely greater talent than Webb, based one of his many plays on one of these "posthumous" sketches entitled "Two Eyes between Two: a Tale of Bagdad."

The panegyrics heaped on *Lyric Leaves* (1832), the first volume to bear the name of Webb (which he now spelled Webbe), surpassed anything that had gone before and has been rightly denounced as illustrating the astonishing vagaries of book reviewing. Compared with Robert Browning, whose debut volume *Pauline* had appeared at about the same time, Webb had a meager talent, and his verse, much of the early published work being collected in *Lyric Leaves*, exhibits all the faults of Hunt and Keats at their weakest moments. And yet, the *Examiner* and *Spectator* ignored Browning while recommending Webb as a true poet. Similarly, Tennyson's *Poems* (1833) was widely censured for its affectations, and the *New Monthly*, while attacking him for imitating Keats and Shelley, felt *Lyric Leaves* to be "full of beauty and promise."

In his defense, it may be said that while Webb's verse is too often flat and prosy, his best prose sketches are frequently spirited and well observed. The cameos in *Glances at Life in City and Suburb* (1836) drew admiration from old *Blackwood's* enemy Lockhart, who compared Webb to Lamb and Goldsmith. The *Athenaeum* saw in him the spirit of Dickens, a not unjust comparison. A volume of similar sketches, *The Man about Town*, appeared in 1838, and Webb also contributed two papers to Kenny Meadows's *Heads of the People* (1840–41).

In 1836, Webb maintained that for many years he had been the final corrector of the *Quarterly Review* proof sheets. It is not known when he gave up this work, but by early 1845, the year in which his last book, a second series of *Glances at Life*, came out, he was freelancing as a proofreader and was depressed and in penury. In a series of letters to a printer friend, he predicted that unless help came soon he would "either be in a strait jacket; the Thames, the Garette [sic] or the Insolvent Debtor's Court." He had verses and epigrams to sell, but any employment "a cut above beating of carpets and carrying of bones to a bear" would do. Meanwhile the critics continued to be enthusiastic.

Webb's financial plight worsened, and by 1847 he was, according to his own testimony, comfortably ensconced as a Poor Brother in the Charterhouse, a charitable institution in London, where fellow distressed writers included J.A. Heraud, William Thomas Moncrieff, and William Wickenden. In 1852, Webb was still at the Charterhouse, and it was probably here, in some security, though with little dignity, that he ended his days.

R.M. Healey

Works Consulted

Cross, Nigel. *The Common Writer: Life in Nineteenth Century Grub Street*. New York: Cambridge UP, 1985.

Green, David Bonnell. "Four Letters of Cornelius Webbe." *Notes and Queries* (Jan. 1958): 40–41.

Healey, R.M. "The Other London Magazine: Gold's and its contributors." *Charles Lamb Bulletin* n.s. 61 (1988): 155–64.

Marsh, George L. "A Forgotten Cockney Poet — Cornelius Webb." *Philological Quarterly* 21 (1942): 323–33.

Webbe, Cornelius. *Sonnets: Summer: Joseph and his Brethren.* 1820. Introduction by Donald H. Reiman. New York: Garland, 1978.

Wedgwood

The Wedgwood firm was the leading pottery manufacturer in Britain in the second half of the 18th century. Much Wedgwood pottery shows the influence of the Neoclassical revival in art that began in the 1760s. The Wedgwood family was also prominent in Dissenting circles and developed friendships with several notable figures of the period, including Erasmus Darwin, Priestley, Wright, Watt, Godwin, Davy, Coleridge, and (later) the Carlyles.

The Wedgwoods had been potters for several generations in the district around Stoke-on-Trent, but the first potter of distinction was Josiah Wedgwood (1730–95). He was said to have ceased formal schooling at age 9. At 14 he was apprenticed for five years to his elder brother, Thomas Wedgwood (1717–73), who had inherited the family business. At the end of this period when Thomas declined to take him into partnership, Josiah first went into partnership with other master potters, then set up his own business in 1758. He had already begun experimenting with new methods of glazing and firing, an activity that he continued until his death and that resulted in notable improvements in the quality of the ware he was able to produce. The success of his business led him to establish an enlarged factory in 1769 and to build a new village for his workers, which he called Etruria in homage to the classical styles of pottery that he was making. Also in 1769, he formed a partnership with Thomas Bentley, an influential Liverpool merchant. Artists such as Flaxman and Stubbs were employed to make new designs. In addition to producing pottery for Queen Charlotte (his cream service became known as Queen's Ware), he developed a thriving export trade. He was active in promoting the Trent-Mersey canal; when completed in 1777, the canal ran past his factory. He was elected a member of the Royal Society in 1783.

Among Josiah's six children, Josiah Wedgwood II (1769–1843) was primarily responsible for carrying on the potteries at Etruria. Susannah (1765–1817) married a son of Erasmus Darwin and was the mother of Charles Darwin (1809–82), the naturalist. Tom Wedgwood (1771–1805), who was plagued by illness from his early twenties and died at age 34, was an original thinker, experimenting in psychology and chemistry; he is claimed to be the first photographer. At Cote House near Bristol, the house of his brother John, Tom met Tom Poole, Beddoes, Davy, Coleridge, and other members of the Bristol radical circle in 1797; in September of that year, he visited Wordsworth at Alfoxden, apparently to interest Wordsworth in a scheme for a new form of education (which Wordsworth probably had in mind when criticizing such schemes in Book V of The Prelude). Tom later spent time with Coleridge in Wales and the Lake District and appears to have influenced Coleridge's early philosophical and scientific thinking. In 1798, when Coleridge was about to accept the Unitarian ministry at Shrewsbury, the brothers Tom and Josiah gave Coleridge an annuity of £150 a year so that he could devote himself to poetry and philosophy (Josiah's half was discontinued in 1811). Coleridge wrote a short eulogy of Tom in *The Friend* (1809).

Among the third generation, the youngest daughter of Josiah II, Emma Wedgwood (1808–96) married her cousin Charles Darwin; Josiah's son Hensleigh (1803–91), who became a distinguished philologist, married Frances, daughter of the politician and historian Mackintosh. Frances was a close friend of Jane Welsh Carlyle until the latter's death in 1866. The pottery firm continued under the management of direct descendants of the first Josiah Wedgwood until 1968.

David S. Miall

Works Consulted

Litchfield, R.B. *Tom Wedgwood: The First Photographer*. London: Duckworth, 1903.

Wedgwood, Barbara and Hensleigh. *The Wedgwood Circle: 1730–1897*. Westfield, NJ: Eastview, 1980.

Wills, Geoffrey. *Wedgwood*. New York: Hamlyn, 1980.

Wellesley, Arthur (First Duke of Wellington)

(1769–1852)

Arthur Wellesley was born in Dublin, Ireland, in 1769. He was the son of Garret Wesley (sic), First Earl of Mornington. Wellesley was sent to Eton, then to a military college at Angers, France, but in neither case was there any suggestion of his future importance. He was commissioned ensign and entered the army in 1787. For the next nine years, he served in several positions and campaigns in England and Europe.

In 1796, Wellesley was promoted to colonel and in 1797 arrived in India, where he remained for the next eight years. The most important boost to Wellesley's military career occurred when his older brother Richard, Second Earl of Mornington (1760–1842), arrived as governor-general. It was sometime shortly before this that "Wellesley" was adopted as the proper spelling of the family name. During this period in India, the future "iron duke" made his reputation. Wellesley returned to England in 1805, and, in 1806, married Kitty Pakenham.

In the spring of 1808, revolts against Napoleon broke out in the Iberian Peninsula. Wellesley was placed in temporary command of an expeditionary force sent to Portugal. He became commander of what became called the Peninsular Army in 1809. In a major victory at Talavera, he defeated the forces of King Joseph of Spain (Napoleon's brother) and was made Viscount Wellington of Talavera. Wellington's conduct of the war was masterful on both offense and defense. He became Earl Wellington in 1812, and field marshall in 1813, after his victory at Vitoria. By the end of the year, the French had been driven out of Spain; the Peninsular War was formally ended 10 April 1813 at the Battle of Toulouse. Napoleon had abdicated on the 6th. On 3 May 1814, Arthur Wellesley was created the Duke of Wellington by a grateful nation.

The Duke was appointed ambassador to the French court, but apparently he did not realized the deep feelings the French retained for Napoleon. On 5 February 1815, Wellington was named plenipotentiary to the Congress of Vienna, where he served with the British Foreign Secretary Lord Castlereagh. The appointment was short-lived because on 20 March Napoleon entered Paris, and the "Hundred Days" began.

Wellington was given command of the army in the Netherlands. With essential assistance of the Prussian Marshall Blücher, he defeated Napoleon at the Battle of Waterloo. The Duke later said that he had taken more care with this battle than any other in his career, a revealing statement since the best estimates are that he fought some 30 of them during his military career. Wellington crossed the frontier into France on 21 June; Paris surrendered on 3 July; and Napoleon was exiled to St. Helena on 7 August. The allies made Wellington commander of an occupation army, a position he held until the occupation of France ended in 1818.

In 1818, general became politician and diplomat. He served in the cabinet of Lord Liverpool (1770–1828) as Minister of Ordinance until Liverpool's resignation in 1827. He attended the Congress of Verona (1822), where he unsuccessfully opposed armed intervention in Spain. He failed to moderate Tsar Nicholas's demands against the Turks during the Greek revolt of 1826.

Wellington became Prime Minister in 1828. During his almost two-year term, the cabinet had to face two major problems. First was the question of Catholic Emancipation in Ireland. Wellington was not happy with the idea but realized such an act was the only way to prevent rebellion. The other problem concerned parliamentary reform, which he consistently and adamantly opposed (*see also* Reform Bill of 1832). On 15 November 1829, he was forced to resign.

Until 1846, when he gave up partisan politics, Wellington served unselfishly where he was needed. He had relinquished command of the army when he became Prime Minister; he resumed command in 1842 and held that position for the rest of his life.

Wellington had assumed the position of elder statesman and national hero. The people forgot his political conflicts and remembered his military victories. Respect gradually turned into veneration, some-thing the caustic Wellington frequently found ridiculous. He died in 1852 at age 83 and was buried in St. Paul's in London.

Wellington was energetic and attentive to detail; he could work unbelievably long hours; his courage was remarkable; and his sense of duty was unwavering. As a politician, his views were narrow and high Tory; his loyalty was to the monarch. He had little knowledge in such fields as economics. As a military leader, he was an aloof man who separated himself from his men, although the idea that he thought all of his troops the "scum of the earth" is certainly an exaggeration. His men trusted and followed him because he won battles and they knew he would not sacrifice their lives needlessly. The lower ranks have the ability to describe a respected commander in a few words. Their name for Wellington says it all: "the long nosed bastard what beats the French."

K. Gird Romer

Works Consulted

Keegan, John. *The Mask of Command*. New York: Viking, 1987.

Longford, Elizabeth. *Wellington*. London: Weidenfeld, 1969–72.

Woodward, Ernest Llewellyn. *The Age of Reform, 1815–1870*. 2nd ed. Oxford: Clarendon, 1962.

West, Jane

(1758–1852)

A prolific writer whose published works span more than 40 years, Jane West wrote plays and conduct books, translations and scriptural essay, but she is best remembered for her shorter poetry and her novels. Within the genre of the novel, West was remarkably versatile; her works include novels of antisensibility, *The Advantages of Education* (1793) and *A Gossip's Story* (1797); a historical novel, based on the Civil War *The Loyalists* (1812); a historical romance, *Alicia de Lacy* (1814); and an Evangelical novel, *Ringrove* (1827). Her poetry, though tending toward conventional subjects and extended length, for example, *The Mother: A Poem in Five Books* (1809), can be fluent and witty, especially when cast in the iambic tetrameter couplets for which she demonstrates a particular affinity.

In all of her work, poetry and prose, West explicitly subordinates art to the morality prescribed by her conservative politics. This politics is itself often made explicit, as in her *Elegy on Edmund Burke* (1797), and is still more often strongly implied, as when she makes a Jacobin philosopher (whose rhetoric resembles that of Godwin's *Political Justice*) into the rapist-villain of her novel *A Tale of the Times* (1799).

Self-educated and the wife of a yeoman farmer, West always cultivated a personal image—consistent with her political views, though rather inconsistent with the formidable volume and success of her literary output—of herself as housewife and mother, busy with cooking and sewing, and only occasionally writing for recreation. When she wrote to Bishop Percy in 1800 to ask for a favorable notice to readers, she based her appeal on the need to provide for her three sons. The Bishop was happy to give this recommendation, and West, in her turn, dedicated her conduct book *Letters to a Young Man* (1802) to him. By this time, the Queen, too, had become aware of West, whose novels had been recommended to her Majesty, again by a bishop. Her books were soon being published in many editions, and in Ireland and America as well as England. As is often true of women writers of the time, the exact nature of West's social and economic positions, unclear even to her contemporaries, has

become more so with scholarly neglect and the passing of time.

John Anderson

Works Consulted

Blain, Virginia, Patricia Clements, and Isobel Grundy, eds. *The Feminist Companion to Literature in English.* London: Batsford, 1990.

Lonsdale, Roger, ed. *Eighteenth-Century Women Poets.* New York: Oxford, 1990.

Todd, Janet, ed. *British Women Writers.* New York: Bedrick, 1989.

———. *Dictionary of British and American Women Writers, 1660–1800.* Totowa, NJ: Rowman, 1984.

Wilberforce, William

(1759–1833)

William Wilberforce, British philanthropist and abolitionist, dedicated his life to freeing the slaves. He entered politics at age 21 and served in the House of Commons for Hull, Yorkshire, and Sussex. He was a member of the Clapham Sect, an influential group of Evangelical social reformers in London, and religion was the pivotal force in his life. His campaign against slavery arose out of what he felt were the two great objects that God had put before him: "The suppression of the slave trade and the reformation of manners." (*See also* Society for the Suppression of Vices.)

Wilberforce was born in Yorkshire in 1759, the son of a wealthy merchant who enjoyed the privileges and advantages of financial ease. As a young boy, he lived with relatives in London and was exposed to the vital Evangelical religion which had first been preached by John Wesley and George Whitefield. His mother removed him from this atmosphere when he was age 11, but it nevertheless played a formative role in his life.

Wilberforce's time at Cambridge and his early years in the Parliament showed no sign of the seriousness that later marked his life. He was able and popular, attended races and balls, and enjoyed life in the circle in which he had been reared.

The turning point of his life occurred in 1784, when he converted to Evangelicalism. His conversion was not marked by a sudden crisis, but was so complete a transformation that his former life appealed to him no longer. He briefly abandoned his political life for one of religious contemplation and wrote a major handbook of Evangelicalism.

By 1786, Wilberforce, then age 27, resumed his legislative tasks, but with a new interest in problems of large humanitarian significance. His religious and moral interests, his training, and his genius as an orator and parliamentarian were becoming apparent to Abolitionists in England and made him an obvious leader in the antislavery movement.

On May 12, 1789, Wilberforce opened up the question of the slave trade before the House of Commons. He met the general claim that slavery was a long-established custom by citing facts as to the actual trade itself. He based his warfare against the slave trade on evidence and made real the harsh conditions of the slaves. His campaign was aided by a growing abolitionist movement, the members of which lectured to packed lecture halls throughout Great Britain, and returning Methodist and Baptist missionaries offered first-hand accounts of the conditions of slaves in the West Indies. In addition to these lectures, millions of tracts and pamphlets were published, women's antislavery societies were established, and the issue even began to appear in children's books and magazines. Above all, the antislavery movements expressed itself in terms of religion.

Nevertheless, within Parliament Wilberforce met with opposition. In 1791, Parliament voted that all antitrade evidence should be heard again and, in 1792, voted to remove the slave trade only gradually. Thus, the work of Wilberforce lasted nearly 20 years. There had to be three readings of his bill before abolition finally prevailed in 1807. In 1823, he sponsored the establishment of the Anti-Slavery Society, but ill health forced him to relinquish leadership of the emancipation crusade to Sir Thomas Fowell Buxton. Wilberforce died just one month before final passage of the act of Parliament that abolished slavery throughout the British Empire. (*See also* Slavery.)

Mary Susan Johnston

Works Consulted

Brown, Ford K. *Fathers of the Victorians: The Age of Wilberforce.* Cambridge: Cambridge UP, 1961.

Coupland, Reginald, Sir. *Wilberforce: A Narrative.* Oxford: Clarendon, 1923.

Furneaux, Robin. *William Wilberforce.* London: Hamilton, 1974.

Hayward, Jack Ernest Shalom, ed. *Out of Slavery: Abolition and After.* Totowa, NJ: Cass, 1985.

McConnell, John Francis. *Evangelicals, Revolutionists and Idealists: Six English Contributors to American Thought and Action.* New York: Kennikat, 1972.

Pollock, John Charles. *Wilberforce.* London: Constable, 1977.

Warner, Oliver. *William Wilberforce and His Times.* New York: Arco, 1962.

Wilkie, Sir David

(1785–1841)

David Wilkie was instrumental in establishing the importance of "subject," or anecdotal, painting, a pictorial form that elevates the story and its moral lessons as primary elements of fine art. A well-known Scottish-British genre and portrait painter, Wilkie first studied art in Edinburgh. His father, the Rev. David Wilkie, was a minister of Cults in Fifeshire where he was born, and his mother, Isabella Lister, was the daughter of a farmer at Pitlessie. Stories are told that Wilkie's first means of communication was drawing and that, at the village school of Pitlessie, he often drew pictures of peers as payment for pencils and marbles. At age 14, however, he studied seriously at the Trustees' Academy in Scotland's capital city, returning, though, in 1804 (at age 18) to Cults, where he executed his famous *Pitlessie Fair* (1804).

The next year, at age 20, Wilkie entered the Royal Academy in London (1805) and soon began to exhibit his paintings there. His *Village Politicians* was a huge success at the Academy showing of 1806, later entering the personal collection of the prominent judge Lord Mansfield. His earliest works (before 1825) are executed, in terms of subject matter and technique, in the Dutch manner of David Teniers, the Younger, and Adriaen van Ostade (17th-century Dutch/Flemish realists). The colors are used more thinly than in the middle period of his paintings between 1811 and 1820. Other significant early works would include *The Blind Fiddler* (1807) and *Rent Day* (1808), paintings commissioned by Sir George Beaumont and Lord Mulgrave, respectively. Wilkie's early style raised genre painting in Great Britain to that of historical painting, as demonstrated by *Chelsea Pensioners Reading the Gazette of the Battle of Waterloo* (1822), executed for the Duke of Wellington. It was a tremendous success, attracting huge audiences, because it elevated domestic elements over historical and brought fine art to the middle class.

Important paintings of Wilkie's strongly Dutch/Flemish-influenced middle period include *The Village Festival* (1811); *Blindman's Buff* (1812–13); *The Letter of Introduction* (1814); and *The Penny Wedding* (1818), which he painted for the Prince

Regent and which hangs in Buckingham Palace. *Reading the Will* (1820), another important work of this period, was completed for the King of Bavaria.

In the mid-1820s, Wilkie began to suffer health problems—provoked most likely by the death of his mother in 1824 (his father had died in 1812)—and, after making a few trips back and forth to Scotland in 1822, he decided to travel as a cure. He went to Germany, Italy, Austria, France, Switzerland, and Spain (where he was greatly influenced by Velázquez and Murillo). After he returned to England in 1828, his style became bolder and incorporated stronger colors with a larger scale. Although his works were considered less strong and robust than those of Hogarth, they are characterized by a spontaneous gaiety and much humor in combination with a looser or less detailed style and less pictorial truth. Frequently, too, he utilizes historical subjects and executed several portraits of royalty. An example of this style is *The Preaching of Knox Before the Lords of the Congregation, June 10, 1559* (1832). Wilkie's career peaked as the Painter in Ordinary to King George IV in 1830 and with his nomination for the Presidency of the Royal Academy. In 1836, he was knighted.

Wilkie was also known as the type of artist traveler who captured the true spirit of the great British Empire: its taste for exotic scenery, architecture, and social customs. In fact, motivated by health problems again, he journeyed to the East in 1840. He painted the Sultan's portrait in Constantinople; then he left for Smyrna, Rhodes, and Beirut to Jerusalem. He intended to return home through Alexandria, Malta, and Gibraltar; however, he became ill on the steamer while leaving Malta. He died in 1841 and was immediately buried at sea within the sight of

Gibraltar. His death is commemorated in a famous painting entitled *Peace: Burial at Sea, The Death of Sir David Wilkie* (1842), ironically painted by his chief rival at the Royal Academy, Turner. He left an unparalleled legacy of paintings and etchings on the beauty of the domestic and peasant life.

Constance Pedoto

Works Consulted

Bryan, Michael. *Bryan's Dictionary of Painters and Engravers*. 4th ed. Vol. 5. London: Bell, 1903–05. 5 vols.

Mullins, Edwin, ed. *The Arts of Britain*. Oxford: Phaidon, 1983.

Osborne, Harold, ed. *The Oxford Companion to Art*. Oxford: Clarendon, 1970.

Rothenstein, John. *An Introduction to English Painting*. London: Cassell, 1965.

Williams, Helen Maria

(1762–1827)

Helen Maria Williams had a long and prolific career as a writer: she was a celebrated poet, an influential translator of works of French literature and history, and an important chronicler of the French Revolution.

Born in London, in 1762, Williams was the daughter of Charles Williams, an army officer from Wales, and of Helen Hay Williams, originally from Scotland. After the death of Charles Williams in 1769, the family, who were strong Dissenters, moved to Berwick-on-Tweed. Their friend Dr. Andrew Kippis, a well-known London minister, helped Williams to publish her first poem, the long ballad *Edwin and Eltruda* (1782). Following its success, the family returned to London, where Williams published her two-volume *Poems* of 1786. This collection, which included several sonnets, odes, and the 1,500-line *Peru*, secured her reputation as a bright young poet of the

1780s. During that time, Williams's poetry was highly praised in reviews and by such readers as Hester Thrale Piozzi, Hayley, and Burns, who was particularly impressed with her *Poem on the Bill Lately Passed for Regulating the Slave Trade* (1788). A major poet in the school of sensibility, Williams wrote antiwar poetry replete with scenes of familial grief and suffering.

Liberal sentiments ran high in the 1780s, and Williams's poetry appealed to the taste of a majority of the reading public. She welcomed the French Revolution and moved to France in 1792, where she remained most of her life. But English support for the French Revolution waned through the 1890s. Her friend Anna Seward pleaded for her to return to England, and Laetitia Matilda Hawkins condemned Williams's unfeminine foray into politics. Williams suffered misogynist attacks in the British press due to her Girondist beliefs and her romantic relationship with John Hurford Stone. However, she remained committed to the cause of liberty, raised two nephews who became prominent Protestant leaders in Paris and Amsterdam, and made her home a gathering place for liberal intellectuals. Among her many English and American visitors were Rogers, Joel Barlow, Catherine and Thomas Clarkson, Crabb Robinson, and Lady Morgan.

Williams's initial visit to France in July 1790 resulted in the publication of the first of several books on that country. *Letters written in France, in the Summer 1790, to a Friend in England* gives a first-hand account of the Fête de la Fédération and tells the pathetic story of her friends the Du Fossés, whom she had met during their exile in England. Her story of them, which Wordsworth uses in *Vaudracour and Julia*, was reprinted eight times over the next year. It was far more successful than her only novel *Julia* (1790), which combines sensibility and Republicanism in the story of a love triangle. The second volume of *Letters from France* (1792) is jubilant in tone, filled with street scenes, anecdotes, and gossip related by many well-connected friends.

The tone changes dramatically in the next volume, which opens with a letter dated January 25, 1793, four days after the execution of Louis XVI. Williams bemoans the end of the golden days of the Revolution and castigates Robespierre. Her coverage of the campaign of 1792 includes anonymous letters with detailed accounts of the Austro-Prussian war, probably written by Stone and Thomas Christie. In the fourth volume, she goes on to discuss the King's trial, and she reproaches Burke and the British press for their prejudiced reports.

The fifth and sixth volumes deal with the Reign of Terror. Williams and her family were arrested October 11, 1793, and spent two months in prison, first in the Luxembourg and then at a convent in Fauxbourg St. Antoine. After their release, they returned to Paris, where Williams's sister Cecilia married Madame du Fossé's cousin, Athanase Coquerel, in March 1794. To avoid arrest as a Girondist, Williams went to Switzerland from June to December 1794, later producing the two-volume *A Tour in Switzerland* (1798). The last two volumes of *Letters from France* conclude with the establishment of the Directory in 1795. Narrating the fall of Robespierre, Williams observes that "men are monsters when they have unlimited power, whether wearing imperial purple or a red jacobin cap."

When Cecilia Coquerel died in 1798, leaving two sons, Athanase, Jr.(1795–1868) and Charles (1797–1851), Williams became a second mother to them. She raised them in the Protestant faith, and later Athanase Jr. served as the pastor for a Reformed Church in Amsterdam and then in Paris, and Charles founded the *Annales protestantes* in 1819 and the *Revue Britannique* in 1825. As the boys grew up, finances were strained because the family possessions and Williams's pension had been confiscated in England when the family emigrated to France. While Stone and her brother-in-law Athanase Coquerel pursued publishing, Williams wrote another book on France, *Sketches of the State of Manners and Opinions in the French Republic, towards the close of the 18th Century* (1801). Lord Nelson's annotated copy still survives. *Sketches* contains the democratic tale "History of Perourou; or the Bellows-Mender," often reprinted on its own and later adapted for the stage as *The Lady of Lyons* (1838) by Edward Bulwer-Lytton.

Despite these successes, Williams's livelihood was threatened when she met with Napoleon's disapproval. In 1802, he had her imprisoned for 24 hours because he objected to what seemed to be anglophile sentiments in her verses on the Peace of Amiens. Then in 1803, Williams published *The Political and Confidential Correspondence of Louis XVI*, based on letters that were later found to be forgeries. Concerned that the unfavorable letters would provoke a Bourbon reaction, Napoleon had the police seize 5,000 copies of the English and French editions. Facing financial ruin, Williams defended her work, and the legal proceedings were dropped, though she still faced vilification from Bernard de Moleville, in his *Refutation of the Libel on the Memory of the Late King of France* (1804).

The 19th century began rather inauspiciously for Williams, and other than a poem to her nephews published in 1809, no original works again appeared until 1815. Instead, she worked on translating, having had considerable success in 1795 with her English edition of Bernardin de Saint-Pierre's *Paul and Virginia*. In 1814, she published translations of Alexander de Humboldt's work, including the first two volumes (five others would appear by 1829) of his and Aimé Bonpland's *Personal Narrative of Travels to the Equinoctial Regions of the New Continent, during the Years 1799–1804*.

Once Napoleon was no longer a threat to her, Williams published her book on the Hundred Days—*A Narrative of the Events which Have Taken Place in France from the Landing of Napoleon Bonaparte on the First of March, 1815, Till the Restoration of Louis XVIII* (1815)—lauded in the *Quarterly Review*. Some of the events she discusses are the possession of Lyons, Napoleon's forced abdication, and the divestment of the Louvre. She also mentions the active role of women in French politics, noting, for example, the courageous acts of the daughter of Louis XVI, the Duchess of Angoulême. Williams ends the book with a tone of weariness, hoping that after "the political convulsions which have devastated Europe, . . . the long profaned but ever-sacred name of liberty will become the order of the day of the nineteenth century." A resurgence of the White Terror after the Restoration made liberty, or the lack of it, again her theme in her last book on France (1819), which includes a short history of Protestant persecution.

In 1820, Williams met Wordsworth, who had written his first published poem in her honor—*Sonnet On Seeing Miss Helen Maria Williams Weep at a Tale of Distress* (1787). In response, she remarked, "with how much pleasure I left politics, the laws of election, and the charter—to take care of themselves, while I was led by Mr. Wordsworth's society to that world of poetical illusion, so full of charms, and from which I have been so long an exile."

Williams's last publication, *Poems on Various Subjects* (1823), contains poems that span her career, the 40 years in which she risked her life to work for her religious and political ideals. After living a short time in Amsterdam with her nephew, she returned to Paris, where she died in 1827. She was buried in Père-Lachaise near her mother and John Hurford Stone.

The compassion and idealism that made her an exemplary poet of sensibility in the 1780s soon led Williams to shift from poetry to the more practical medium of prose. Her eyewitness accounts of the French Revolution and its aftermath reached a wide audience. As one of the few women to publish political and historical writing during the Romantic period, she was a revolutionary in many senses of the word.

Deborah Kennedy

Works Consulted

Adams, M. Ray. "Helen Maria Williams and the French Revolution." *Wordsworth and Coleridge: Studies in Honour of George McLean Harper*. Ed. Earl Leslie Griggs. Princeton: Princeton UP, 1939.

Todd, F.M. "Wordsworth, Helen Maria Williams and France." *Modern Language Review* 43 (1948): 456–64.

Todd, Janet. "Williams, Helen Maria." *A Dictionary of British and American Women Writers, 1660–1800*. Totowa, NJ: Rowman, 1985.

Woodward, Lionel D. *Hélène-Maria Williams et ses amis*. Paris: Librairie Ancienne Honoré Champion, 1930. Geneva: Slatkine, 1977.

Willing Suspension of Disbelief

"Willing Suspension of Disbelief" is a phrase introduced by Coleridge in his *Biographia Literaria* to describe an intellectual process of reader response to highly imaginative poems, a response that precludes skepticism or disbelief when the characters and action presented are not wholly in accord with the natural order.

The reader believes in the supernatural elements of a poem, at least within the context of the work, because the poet presents them with poetic truth. (*See also* Literary Criticism and Literary Theory.)

Coleridge uses the phrase when discussing the original plan for *Lyrical Ballads* (1798) and, in particular, how his poems in that collection differ from those of Wordsworth. Explaining that while Wordsworth's poetry presents nature as it appears in ordinary life to the sensitive and creative mind of the poet, his own, he writes, presents nature as modified by the imagination so that supernatural events can be included. Coleridge maintains that these supernatural events or effects are to seem as real in his poetry as they do to those who believe, at particular times and for whatever reasons, that they experience such supernatural intervention in their own lives. Thus, Coleridge reveals his endeavor to embellish nature in *The Rime of the Ancient Mariner* and *Christabel*, poems that charm the reader with their mysteries: angelic spirits, the curse, the glittering or evil eye, the powers of witchery, the beneficence of God when all of his creatures are revered.

The expression "willing suspension of disbelief" has proved useful subsequently in critical discussions of drama and fiction as well as of poetry. It has been applied in the 20th century not only to supernatural events but also to other elements of plot development that, on reflection, would seem improbable, possibly even impossible.

Mary D. Zoghby

Works Consulted

Coleridge, Samuel Taylor. *Biographia Literaria*. 2 vols. London: Oxford UP, 1907.

— — —. *The Rime of the Ancient Mariner*. New York: Collier, 1902: 67–82.

— — —. *Christabel*. New York: Collier, 1902: 83–96.

Wilson, John (Christopher North)
(1785–1854)

Eclipsed by the dazzling array of stars on the Romantic firmament, John Wilson occupies a tenuous foothold in the English literary pantheon. The indifference to his corpus, marked by an impressive range of interests and indubitable intellectual vigor, may be accounted for by the coexistence of the excellent with the execrable, often hand in hand with capricious misjudgments, which make a dispassionate appraisal of his writings difficult.

John Wilson, better known as Professor Wilson, or Christopher North (his pseudonym), was born in 1785, at Paisley, a Scottish version of Sleepy Hollow. His father was an affluent manufacturer, but it was his mother who instilled in him a deep sense of piety. Wilson's childhood gave little evidence of precocity, and he engaged in the usual boyhood pastimes. After initial schooling in his birthplace, Wilson was sent as a boarder to the academy run by a clergyman, Dr. Joseph MacIntyre of Glenorchy. This was followed by a short spell at the University of Glasgow, during which he corresponded with Wordsworth and became his ardent acolyte. (*See also* Essay, Journalism.)

It was as an alumnus of Magdalen College, Oxford, however that Wilson gave indications of his multifarious interests and accomplishments, climaxed by the Newdigate Prize for Poetry. But despite intimacy with the leading lights of the Romantic movement, who were his neighbors at Elleray in the Lake District, Wilson's poetic output lacked fervor, and both *Isle of Palms* and *City of the Plague* evoked little interest, unjustly ascribed by Jeffrey to the influence of the "pond poets."

The launching of *Blackwood's Magazine*, in 1817, enabled the flowering of his talents as a prose writer. Mingling criticism with biography in his outpourings on myriad subjects, alternating gaiety with gravity, irradiating his musings and perceptions with a genial wit and humor, Wilson had his readers almost eating out of his hands. His collected essays in *Noctes Ambrosianae* enjoyed a wide readership, though the sequel to it, *Recreations of Christopher North*, rather unaccountably flopped.

As a unknown entity, prior to achieving journalistic renown, Wilson had been persuaded by friends like Scott to seek election to the Chair of Moral Philosophy at Edinburgh, in 1820. Despite denunciation in the *Scotsman*, he confounded the skeptics by emerging triumphant over Sir William Hamilton. Wilson's meticulously prepared lectures may have enhanced his professional popularity, but his professorial meditations, published as *Lights and Shadows*, have not found favor with posterity.

His reputation rests, not on *Essays Critical and Imaginative*, printed posthumously in four volumes, which exclude virtually all that is regarded as significant, but on *locus critici* embodied in an insightful article for the *Edinburgh Review* on the fourth canto of Byron's *Childe Harold*, an essay on Spenser, and *Specimens of British Critics*. The essay on Spenser is regrettably marred by a meandering examination of the first book of the *Faerie Queene*, while the title of *Specimens* is grossly misleading, in that Dryden and Pope receive almost exclusive attention and even Chaucer is given short shrift. Indeed, it may be argued, not entirely without justification that Wilson's essay on Wordsworth, eulogy of Macaulay's *Lays*, and disparaging examination of Tennyson's early poems, in Vol-

umes 1 and 2 of his *Essays*, are superior paradigms of his critical explorations.

Besides prolixity, Wilson's tendency to dilate on the irrelevant and immoderation in apportioning praise and blame are flaws that detract considerably from the value of his work.

D.C. Saxena

Works Consulted

Gilfillan, George. *A Gallery of Literary Portraits*. New York: Dutton, 1927.

Saintsbury, George Edward Bateman. *A History of Criticism and Literary Taste in Europe from the Earliest Text to the Present Day*. Edinburgh: Blackwood, 1949.

Wilson, John. *Essays Critical and Imaginative*. London: Blackwood, 1856–57.

———. *Specimens of British Critics*. Philadelphia: Carey, 1846.

Wise Passiveness

"Wise passiveness" is the state of soul celebrated by the character of William in Wordsworth's poem *Expostulation and Reply*. William, having been berated by Matthew (often thought to represent Hazlitt) for his dreaminess and lack of studious attention as he sits on an "old grey stone" and criticized for his inattention to the wisdom communicated by books, offers a Wordsworthian, perhaps even a larger Romantic reply. On the one hand as he recreates a morning by the Esthwaite Lake, "When life was sweet, I knew not why," he describes the powerlessness of eye and ear in the presence of nature. On the other, eschewing a kind of tyranny of the senses, he reaches out to describe the nature around him with its power to "impress this mind of ours" and teaches Matthew that we can nourish the mind and spirit "In a wise passiveness." In *The Tables Turned*, the companion poem, William takes the initiative, going on the offensive with Matthew and urging him to put aside his books and his general busyness, to let nature "with its world of ready wealth" teach and provide in a single encounter a sweeter lore than the collected wisdom of the past.

Wise passiveness, far from a state of lethargy or a philosophy of anti-intellectualism, is a condition necessary for interaction with the life-giving powers of nature. It is drastically different from the activity of the "meddling intellect," which, in analyzing and dissecting, loses sight of the beauty and wholeness of nature. It is at odds with the image of the mind as a passive recipient of the data of sensation and of nature as the static, machinelike model of Newtonian physics, wondrous in its order but separate from human beings.

Nature is a sacred place in which human beings achieve not only wisdom but holiness. It is a living, dynamic force, God's hieroglyphic, His book. And men and women must read in that book, not compulsively and not simply with the outward eye, but also with the inward eye, which restrains, calms, understands. With the intimidation of physical things at bay, an inner peace dominates, and memory plays its role, perhaps the role envisioned by Wordsworth in his celebrated definition of poetry as a spontaneous overflow of feeling, but essentially of that feeling recollected in tranquility.

Wise passiveness, has larger implications than the personal. It offers in a sense a new and Romantic epistemology, unlike that of Enlightenment rationalism, a trust in the inner life as a source of knowledge, a joy in the pleasures of communion between the active mind and the life-giving forces of nature.

John L. Mahoney

Works Consulted

Hartman, Geoffrey. *Wordsworth's Poetry, 1787–1814*. Cambridge: Harvard UP, 1987.

Perkins, David. *Wordsworth and the Poetry of Sincerity*. Cambridge: Harvard UP, 1964.

Salvesen, Christopher. *The Landscape of Memory: A Study of Wordsworth's Poetry*. Lincoln: U of Nebraska P, 1965.

Watson, J.R. *Wordsworth's Vital Soul: The Sacred and Profane in Wordsworth's Poetry*. Atlantic Highlands, NJ: Humanities, 1982.

Woodring, Carl. *Wordsworth*. Boston: Houghton, 1965.

Wolcot, John ("Peter Pindar")
(1738–1819)

John Wolcot, who wrote under the pseudonym "Peter Pindar," was the most popular verse satirist of the last two decades of the 18th century and the beginning of the 19th century. Born in 1738, in Dodbrooke, Devonshire, he did not devote his energies to poetry until he was in his 40s. In 1767, upon receiving his medical degree from the University of Aberdeen, he became the physician of Sir William Trelawney, governor of Jamaica. In 1769, he returned to England to be ordained an Anglican priest so that he could accept an ecclesiastical living in Jamaica; however, he returned to find that the position he had expected was not available, the incumbent having recovered from his illness.

After Trelawney's death in 1773, Wolcot went back to England, practicing medicine in Cornwall until he moved to London in 1781 as the sponsor of the young artist John Opie. He had been writing poetry for some time and began to receive notice with his *Lyric Odes to the Royal Academicians* (1782) and *More Lyric Odes to the Royal Academicians* (1783), for which he adopted the pseudonym "Peter Pindar."

Over the next few decades, he produced over 60 books of satirical verse, dealing with such prominent figures as Pit the Younger, Sir William Chambers, More, Boswell, Hester Lynch Thrale Piozzi, Paine, Sir Joseph Banks of the Royal Society, poet laureates Thomas Warton and Henry James Pye, and the King: *The Lousiad*, the five cantos of which were published from 1785 to 1795, relates in mock-epic fashion the story of how George III, upon discovering a louse on his plate, ordered that the cooks' heads be shaved.

Both the large number of piracies of Wolcot's works and his many imitators (e.g., "Paul Pindar") attest to his popularity. In 1800, Wolcot came to blows with Gifford after an exchange of insults in print, and in 1807, he was sued for "criminal conversation" (adultery), but won the case. He died in 1819 and at his request was buried in St. Paul's Church, Covent Garden, next to another author of comically satiric poetry, Samuel Butler, the author of *Hudibras*.

Wolcot's poetry is characterized by its playful tone and the poet's self-dramatization, and he excels at mock-heroic and mock-odal verse, far more than any of his contemporaries. His most memorable writing is found in the works dealing with George III, in which he exploits for humor the King's stutter and low tastes. Wolcot's influence can be seen in some of Byron's and Moore's satires.

Gary R. Dyer

Works Consulted

Carretta, Vincent. *George III and the Satirists from Hogarth to Byron*. Athens: U of Georgia P, 1990.

Dictionary of National Biography, *s.v.*, "Wolcot, John."

Hopkins, Kenneth. *Portraits in Satire*. London: Barrie, 1958.

Lockwood, Thomas. *Post-Augustan Satire: Charles Churchill and Satirical Poetry, 1750–1800*. Seattle: U of Washington P, 1979.

Vales, Robert L. *Peter Pindar (John Wolcot)*. New York: Twayne, 1973.

Wollstonecraft, Mary
(1759–97)

One of the leading radical writers of the late 18th century, Mary Wollstonecraft is best known for *Vindication of the Rights of Woman* (1792). In this book, Wollstonecraft embraced the egalitarian ideals of the French Revolution and boldly called for full civil and political rights for women. Although her work was censured by many, its influence on other radical thinkers and feminist writers—from Percy Bysshe Shelley to Virginia Woolf—has been profound.

Born in London in 1759, Wollstonecraft was the second of seven children and the first daughter of Edward John Wollstonecraft and Elizabeth Dickson, an Irishwoman. Although her grandfather, a master weaver, trained her father for the same profession, Edward Wollstonecraft lost his inheritance through a series of failed ventures as a gentleman-farmer. Already volatile and tyrannical, Wollstonecraft's father was abusive when drinking. Her mother, in turn, neglected Wollstonecraft and lavished attention on the family's eldest son. To escape this domestic unhappiness, Wollstonecraft left home at age 19, determined to support herself.

After a succession of unsatisfactory jobs—as a lady's companion in Bath, a teacher at a girl's school in Newington Green, and a governess to aristocratic children in Ireland—Wollstonecraft, with the help of the publisher Joseph Johnson, took the uncommon step of establishing herself in London as a professional writer. Johnson, whose authors included Erasmus Darwin, Maria Edgeworth, and, later, the young Wordsworth, had already published Wollstonecraft's educational work, *Thoughts on the Education of Daughters* in 1786. After she began working with him, he went on to publish her book for children, *Original Stories from Real Life* (1787) and her first novel, *Mary, a Fiction* (1788), which was based on an early friendship.

In 1788, Wollstonecraft began to write reviews for Johnson's progressive magazine, *The Analytical Review*, a job that exposed her to a broad range of contemporary intellectual debates and brought her together socially with leading radical writers and artists, including Paine, Barbauld, Fuseli, Blake, and Godwin. In this environment, she developed her political radicalism, articulated in *A Vindication of the Rights of Men* (1790). Published five weeks after the appearance of Burke's *Reflections of the Revolution in France*, this work was one of the first of the more than 30 responses to Burke in a pamphlet war that also included Paine's *Rights of Man*. In her book, Wollstonecraft argues that it is precisely the old order of hereditary property and monarchical and church authorities which Burke wants to uphold that is disruptive to society. Property and its inheritance, she maintains, give some men a false power by granting them wealth and prestige they did not earn by their own merit and labor. Conversely, men who possess talent and virtue but no property often suffer a low status. For Wollstonecraft, this arrangement of hierarchies in society is clearly not rational.

Wollstonecraft had an uneasy relationship with the role for women writers during her day. Exploring the evolution of powerful feelings or the farthest reaches of the imagination might be considered ideal occupations for male poets like Wordsworth and Blake, but a woman was most acceptable as a writer if she kept her domestic priorities clear. In line with her role as enlightened educator of her children and civilizing agent of her husband, she might write conduct books, religious tracts, educational works, and fiction, the latter preferably with a moral to teach proper behavior. With *Thoughts on the Education of Daughters* (1787), Wollstonecraft had begun her writing career within the prescribed mode. Yet, this early educational work contains hints of the staunch feminist Wollstonecraft became. For although she makes clear that the purpose of girls' education is to prepare them for the duties of wife and mother, her attitude toward the matrimonial state is pessimistic. She argues that girls should be taught stoicism: intellect, religion, and an independent character would help them live with the misfortunes they are likely to encounter in marriage.

By the time Wollstonecraft wrote *Vindication of the Rights of Woman* in 1792, she had combined her radical politics with a tradition of feminist protest that had already been well articulated during the Enlightenment. Women had been excluded from the ideal of enlightened reason; to be female was to possess sensibility, instinctual receptivity, nurturing protectiveness, and childlike fancy. But this notion of an innate female nature had been challenged by the English feminists Mary Astell and Catherine Macaulay, who argued that women could exercise reason as well as men if they were properly educated. Thus, Wollstonecraft inherited from Enlightenment feminists a commitment to women's equality based on their capacity for rational thought.

One of the arguments central to *Vindication of the Rights of Woman* is that women are socially produced; the over-refinement, obsession with appearances, and perpetual seductiveness that writers like Rousseau attributed to the essential natures of women are in fact the products of a false education. For Wollstonecraft, false education produced in the condition of women a whole set of unnatural inversions: outward appearance is developed at the expense of reason and understanding; reputation is favored over genuine modesty; over-refined sensibility usurps physical and mental strength; and deceit and cunning replace real affection in women's relations with men. Finally, just as she locates disorder within existing social structures in *A Vindication of the Rights of Men*, here Wollstonecraft argues that the very exclusion of women from legitimate rights in the social contract make of women the disrupters of civil society that they are feared to be: women excluded from the contract are also not bound by it and often become social outlaws.

Wollstonecraft had seen this double bind at work in the unfortunate marriage of her younger sister Eliza. Rather than rely on her brother for financial support, Eliza, at age 19, had married Meredith Bishop, a man whose domineering nature and irrational jealousy made her as miserable as her father had. While nursing Eliza through a postpartum breakdown, Wollstonecraft became convinced that her sister would never fully recover and retain her health unless she left the marriage. In early 1784, at Eliza's insistence, both women secretly left Bishop's house and went into hiding, a step for which neither had any legal protection, since husbands had absolute rights to their wives' persons, property, and children. Although Bishop finally agreed to the separation, friends shocked by the bold action shunned the Wollstonecraft sisters. Years later, Wollstonecraft recounted the

incident in her last novel, *Maria or the Wrongs of Woman* (1798), in which she argues that when women find themselves victimized by unjust laws that uphold a man's right to abuse them, they have the right to appeal to their own sense of justice and act accordingly.

In her own life, Wollstonecraft was rarely afraid to break with social conventions. Thwarted by Fuseli and his wife when she proposed living with the couple to continue her platonic relationship with the painter, she left London in December 1792, and set out alone for Paris to observe the French Revolution first-hand. Once there, she fell in love with an American author and speculator, Gilbert Imlay, with whom she had a child, Fanny. When the Gironde government fell and it was no longer safe for foreigners in Paris, Wollstonecraft and Imlay moved to the French village of Neuilly and then on to Le Havre. There, amid considerable personal danger, Wollstonecraft wrote *Historical and Moral View of the Origins and Progress of the French Revolution* (1794). On two occasions, when Imlay tried to leave her and when she discovered him living in London with another woman, Wollstonecraft attempted suicide. As part of her recovery, Wollstonecraft journeyed to Scandinavia as Imlay's business envoy, writing her celebrated collection, *Letters Written during a Short Residence in Sweden, Norway, and Denmark* (1796).

Having freed herself from this painful love affair, Wollstonecraft, now a famous writer, resumed her life in London. In 1796, she married the celebrated radical philosopher William Godwin, author of *Political Justice* (1793) and *Caleb Williams* (1794). The relationship was happy, but ten days after giving birth to her second daughter, Wollstonecraft died of puerperal fever. This daughter, Mary later married

Percy Bysshe Shelley and wrote the novel *Frankenstein*.

Determined that Wollstonecraft's life and work should not be forgotten, Godwin published her *Memoirs* in 1798 and inadvertently unleashed a feminist backlash. The public disclosure of her relationship with Imlay, her suicide attempts, and her conception of Godwin's child before marriage outraged an increasingly conservative English public. Wollstonecraft and other women writers associated with her were vilified in works like Richard Polwhele's poem *The Unsex'd Females* (1798), and well into the 19th century her life and work were seen by many as a threat.

Kathryn Kirkpatrick

Works Consulted

Brody, Miriam. Introduction. *Vindication of the Rights of Woman.* By Mary Wollstonecraft. New York: Penguin, 1975.

Ferguson, Moira. Introduction. *First Feminists: British Women Writers, 1578–1799.* Ed. Moira Ferguson. Bloomington: Indiana UP, 1985.

Ferguson, Moira, and Janet Todd. *Mary Wollstonecraft.* Boston: Twayne, 1984.

Godwin, William. *Memoirs of the Author of Vindication of the Rights of Woman.* London, 1798. Rpt. in *Feminist Controversy in England, 1788–1810.* Ed. Gina Luria. New York: Garland, 1974.

Sunstein, Emily W. *A Different Face: The Life of Mary Wollstonecraft.* New York: Harper, 1975.

Wordsworth, Dorothy

(1771–1855)

Dorothy Wordsworth's magnetic presence can be found in William Wordsworth's poems — as muse, as mystical spirit, and as beloved companion of memory and the present moment. She is the listener addressed in *An Evening Walk* and the subject of *To My Sister*. She is mentioned in *To A Butterfly*, where she seems to inhabit the butterfly's spirit, and celebrated for her sensitivity, tenderness, and inspiration in *The Sparrow's Nest* and *On Nature's Invitation Do I Come*. *Tintern Abbey* significantly recognizes her as the protector and preserver of the poet's memories, as the one person who can share the blessings of nature and through whose spirit make nature more revered and more humanly resonant. As inestimable companion and as source of inspiration, she appears in *The Prelude*. According to some critics, the five *Lucy* poems may reveal the poet's fear of his sister's departure or death and his achievement of consolation as he sees her fused with the landscape. *Lucy Gray or Solitude* derives from a story told to Dorothy Wordsworth about a child lost in a snowstorm, and, much affected by the story, she related it to her brother. A number of other Wordsworth poems are based on incidents or descriptions she recorded in journals. *Beggars, Resolution and Independence, Alice Fell,* and *I Wandered Lonely As a Cloud* have prose counterparts in *The Grasmere Journals* (1800–03). *To a Highland Girl, Stepping Westward,* and *The Matron of Jedborough and Her Husband* are subjects described in Dorothy Wordsworth's *Journal of the Scottish Tour* (1803). *The Alfoxden Journal* (1798) includes a description of the sky later adapted in both *Peter Bell* and *A Night Piece.* A variant also appears in Coleridge's *Dejection: An Ode.*

Dorothy Wordsworth's observations were important to her brother (and, in a lesser way, to Coleridge) for awakening him to subjects and scenes he may otherwise not have attended. Moreover, she provided her brother with the physical comfort and psychological support necessary for his genius to emerge and develop and made it possible for him to find another self through the self she gave him.

Dorothy Wordsworth is known to have contributed descriptions to Wordsworth's

Introduction to *Select Views of Cumberland, Westmoreland and Lancashire* (1810) by the Rev. Joseph Wilkinson; and her *Excursion up Scawfell Pike* was used—abridged and altered—as the opening chapter to Wordsworth's *Guide to the Lakes* (1822), which later included her *Tour of Ullswater* as an Appendix (1825). In the 1815 edition of Wordsworth's poems, several of Dorothy Wordsworth's poems appeared: *A Cottager to Her Infant, A Sleepless Baby* (the last two stanzas added by Wordsworth), *Address to A Child During a Boisterous Winter Evening*, and *The Mother's Return*. The 1842 edition of Wordsworth's poems replaced these poems with a single one of Dorothy Wordsworth's entitled *Floating Island*. Dorothy Wordsworth's other poetry—verse for children, poems celebrating events or describing landscapes, elegiac poems, and the more personal poems that she composed during her illness—have only recently been made available. Yet, she wrote few poems (31 recently identified), and her only prose works, perhaps even her journals, are written less out of artistic compulsion than to fulfill another's need or to answer a social commitment. In *A Narrative Concerning George and Sarah Green of the Parish of Grasmere*, she solicits support for the recently orphaned children whose tale she sympathetically narrates. While *Mary Jones and her Pet-Lamb* (composed about 1820) may reveal her fears of being deprived of familial support and her need for love and stability, the work is basically a tale related to amuse a child.

It is her journals that are known for the many entries that suggest the sources for Wordsworth's poems, establish the dates of their composition, and relate his methods of writing and his disposition during that process. The journals also allow the reader to enter the daily lives of the Wordsworths and their circle, as well as to

follow their travels. They significantly contribute to the reader's understanding of the first quarter of the 19th century. Dorothy Wordsworth reveals the struggles and surprises travelers face in seeking transportation, finding appropriate guides, securing food and shelter, and locating sites. The reader sees detailed landscapes, architecture distinct to a region, and differing costumes and national character. The English countryside is recreated, too. *The Grasmere Journal*, which intimately reveals Dove Cottage and its surroundings, also shows her brother's dedication to his art, her determination to provide for his genius, and their domestic occupations and almost daily walks. Certainly that best known of her journals conveys the mutual love and respect between sister and brother and reveals their common interests. Several entries have particular psychological interest, especially those recognizing the fearful tension Dorothy Wordsworth experienced at her brother's impending marriage, later the apparent harmony that the three Wordsworths achieved.

Born in 1771, in Cockermouth, Cumberland, Dorothy Wordsworth was just a year and nine months younger than William, the only daughter among four boys. Their father was an attorney, an agent to Lord Lowther, who owned the Cockermouth estate, where the family lived. His wife, Ann (neé Cookson) died in 1778, but fortunately before her death, Ann Wordsworth had arranged a home for her daughter with a cousin, Elizabeth Threlkeld, whom Ann had known well in childhood. Thus, at Halifax with her capable and affectionate Aunt Threlkeld (and a lively household of nieces and nephews for whom Threlkeld was guardian) Dorothy lived for nine years, until at age 16 when she was directed to live with her Cookson grandparents at Penrith.

In 1783, Dorothy's father had died; at that time two uncles were appointed guardians of the five children and oversaw the disputed finances arising from the unwillingness of Lord Lowther (created Earl of Lonsdale in 1784) to pay the debts that John Wordsworth had incurred on his behalf. In 1784, Dorothy was removed from a school in Hipperholme, where she had boarded for three years, to a local school in Halifax, which she attended until she was age 15. As a matter of economy, her guardians determined that on reaching age 16, Dorothy could be of service to her grandparents. Meanwhile, from the time she had left home at age 6 until she arrived in Penrith, she had not seen her brothers. (No arrangements had even been made for her attend her father's funeral.) The joyous reunion with her four brothers and the special companionship she found with William were the only bright moments in the gloomy household where her grandparents monitored her behavior and disapproved of her interests in books and learning. At Penrith, though, she met the congenial Peggy and Mary Hutchinson (later Wordsworth's wife), orphans like herself.

Through the efforts of a more understanding Cookson uncle, in 1788, Dorothy left the stultifying atmosphere of Penrith for Norfolk, where she remained at Forncett Rectory, until 1794. She taught at the Sunday School and was nurse and supervisor to the Cookson children. Only occasionally did she meet with her brothers. In 1793, Dorothy learned of William's liaison with Annette Vallon and the birth of their child and wrote sympathetic letters to the Frenchwoman and sought to mediate between her uncle and her brother, who was, however, forbidden to visit Forncett. Yet Dorothy, determined to be united with her brother, traveled to Halifax in 1794 to see him. After that, except for occasional journeys, they remained together until William Wordsworth's death.

In 1795, with a legacy William Wordsworth had received, he and his sister settled in Racedown, Dorsetshire, where she tended Basil Montagu, the 2-year-old child of a friend. From there the Wordsworths moved to Alfoxden in Somerset to be closer to Nether Stowey, home of their new friend Coleridge. In these two critical years, 1795 to 1797, critics believe that Dorothy gave William the consolation and conviction he needed to retain his poetic spirit, the sympathy, assurance, and regard for nature that enabled him to grow poetically.

With Coleridge, the Wordsworths departed for Germany in 1798. The Wordsworths stayed in Goslar, a sordid and decaying town where they found themselves virtually isolated from society.

On December 20, 1799, seven months after their return from Germany, the Wordsworths arrived at Dove Cottage (known then as Town End), Grasmere. The Wordsworths, later joined by Mary Hutchinson Wordsworth, occupied Dove Cottage until 1808.

But before William Wordsworth's marriage to Mary, in 1802, Dorothy Wordsworth and her brother traveled to Calais for a month with Annette Vallon, and William Wordsworth's daughter Caroline. Back in England, they stayed in London, where Dorothy Wordsworth was reunited with her other brothers and where she met Charles and Mary Lamb, who became lifelong friends.

In 1803, Dorothy Wordsworth toured Scotland with Coleridge (who accompanied the Wordsworths for a time). Among other places, they visited Dumfries, the home of Burns, then recently deceased, and Lasswade where they met Scott, who became a friend. For her first Scottish journal, Dorothy took no notes, recalling all the events from memory and writing most of the journal during the winter to 1803 to 1804, completing the work during the spring of 1805.

With the removal of the Wordsworth family—including three small children—from Dove Cottage to Allan Bank in 1808, Dorothy Wordsworth, always burdened with endless household tasks, found herself deluged by new responsibilities. She set about sewing mattresses, installing windows, cooking, washing, cleaning, and ploughing; in addition, because Mary Wordsworth was indisposed, she cared for the children. Later, after the birth of a second daughter, Mary needed Dorothy Wordsworth's nursing. The family again moved, in 1810, to the Rectory, where the fifth child was born, with Dorothy Wordsworth again managing house and children, as well as providing care for the mother and infant. During 1810 to 1812, Dorothy Wordsworth's life was circumscribed by household obligations. In the summer of 1812, while she was alone in supervising the children, their parents having to attend to affairs away from home, Catharine, a chronically ill child, suffered convulsions and died in her aunt's arms. Thus, Dorothy Wordsworth had to console the other children, plan the funeral, and observe the painful social interchanges and the religious ceremonies.

In 1814, the Wordsworths moved to Rydal Mount, the last house they occupied. Dorothy Wordsworth continued her long-term duties, contributing to the maintenance of the household and serving as copyist and proofreader of her brother's poems. (The extent of her labors as Wordsworth's amanuensis is particularly evident from one instance; in 1804 before Coleridge sailed for Malta, she copied ap-

proximately 8,000 lines of his poetry for him.) In the more comfortable circumstances of Rydal Mount, especially after the poet became Distributor of Stamps for Westmorland in 1813, Dorothy Wordsworth's responsibilities eased. She renewed her interest in church matters and became an advocate of the Tory cause, most vocally in 1818 when the Lowther family sought a parliamentary seat from Westmorland. That same year, with a painter friend, Miss Barker, who lived nearby, she climbed Scawfell Pike and recorded the experience in a short journal.

In 1820, Dorothy, William, and Mary Wordsworth and two others traveled through France, Belgium, Germany, Switzerland, and the Italian lakes, crossing the Simplon Pass to Paris. During this tour, Dorothy Wordsworth delighted in reliving some of the scenes her brother had visited in 1790. In France, she was finally able to visit her niece Caroline, whose marriage she had missed. Now four years married, Caroline Baudouin had two daughters, the first named for her aunt, Louise Dorothée. Unlike the 1803 journal, the *Tour of the Continent* journal was based on voluminous daily note-taking.

On her return to England, following her pattern, Dorothy Wordsworth cared for anyone who needed her services. In 1821 and 1822, she nursed Mrs. Quillinan of Rydal, first after the birth of her second child and later after an accidental burning. Like her niece, in 1812, Mrs. Quillinan also died in Dorothy's arms, and Dorothy Wordsworth again—Mr. Quillinan being absent—arranged the funeral and settled financial matters. (Quillinan married William Wordsworth's daughter Dora, in 1841.) In 1822, with Mary Wordsworth's sister Joanna Hutchinson, Dorothy Wordsworth toured Scotland again. The journal of this visit is especially interesting in describing how two unattended women traveled through a frequently rugged and uninhabited country at a time when women traveled seldom and rarely by themselves.

In her 50s, Dorothy Wordsworth continued to be an indefatigable walker and traveler, bustling with energy and warm enthusiasm, delighting in people and social occasions but also in reading. In 1828, she went to the Isle of Man, recording this visit in a short journal. When later that year her nephew, John Wordsworth, needed support during his first curacy, she traveled to Whitwick, a poor industrial area, where she kept house, helped compose sermons, and visited members of the parish. In 1829, in the midst of her many activities, she developed a serious illness from which she never recovered, presenile dementia, most probably. From 1830 to 1835, she experienced shorter and shorter remissions, until she was entirely debilitated. At Rydal Mount, Sarah Hutchinson (Mary's sister) was Dorothy Wordsworth's constant companion until Sarah died in 1835.

Earlier that same year Dorothy Wordsworth's personality drastically changed. The slender and meticulous woman became obese and unkempt; the once considerate and sensitive adult became a petulant and demanding child, often abusive and even violent. All her life she had acted with clear purpose, but now she engaged in meaningless and repetitive activity, although she retained her enthusiasm for poetry, remaining capable of reciting her brother's poems. Moreover, she composed her own poetry. Nor did her sensitivity for others ever completely disappear; her letters from this period clearly reveal an awareness of others. Yet, she was mostly reduced to living inside her own vagrant thoughts, too distracted to read books and too overwrought to meet

people, an invalid who could experience nature only when she was wheeled into the Rydal garden. In that condition, she was lovingly cared for by the Wordsworth family until her death in 1855, having been tended by her sister-in-law for the five years since William Wordsworth's death.

Marilyn Jurich

Works Consulted

Alexander, Meena. *Women in Romanticism*. Totowa, NJ: Barnes, 1989.

Darlington, Beth. "Reclaiming Dorothy Wordsworth's Legacy." *The Age of William Wordsworth*. Eds. Kenneth R. Johnston and Gene W. Ruoff. New Brunswick, NJ: Rutgers UP, 1987.

De Quincey, Thomas. *Literary Reminiscences*. New York: Hurd, 1876.

De Selincourt, Ernest. *Dorothy Wordsworth, A Biography*. Oxford: Clarendon, 1965.

Ellis, Amanda M. *Rebels and Conservatives: Dorothy and William Wordsworth and Their Circle*. Bloomington: Indiana UP, 1967.

Gill, Stephen. *William Wordsworth, A Life*. Oxford: Clarendon, 1989.

Gittings, Robert, and Jo Manton. *Dorothy Wordsworth*. New York: Oxford, 1987.

Gunn, Elizabeth. *A Passion for the Particular, Dorothy Wordsworth: a Portrait*. London: Gollancz, 1981.

Homane, Margaret. *Women Writers and Poetic Identity: Dorothy Wordsworth, Emily Brontë, and Emily Dickinson*. Princeton: Princeton UP, 1980.

Lee, Edmund. *Dorothy Wordsworth: The Story of a Sister's Love*. New York: Dodd, 1887.

Legouis, Emile. *The Early Life of William Wordsworth, 1770–1798: A Study of the Prelude*. Trans. J.M. Matthews. New York: Russell, 1965.

Levin, Susan M. *Dorothy Wordsworth and Romanticism*. New Brunswick, NJ: Rutgers UP, 1987.

Maclean, Catherine MacDonald. *Dorothy and William Wordsworth*. New York: Farrar, 1972.

Moorman, Mary, ed. *Journals of Dorothy Wordsworth*. New York: Oxford UP, 1988.

Quiller-Couch, Sir Arthur. *Studies in Literature*. Cambridge: Cambridge UP, 1930.

Woof, Pamela. *Dorothy Wordsworth, Writer.* Grasmere: The Wordsworth Trust, 1988.

Wordsworth, William
(1770–1850)

Introduction

William Wordsworth, regarded by Matthew Arnold as the greatest English poet after Shakespeare and Milton, was Poet Laureate from 1843 to his death in 1850. His major publications include *Lyrical Ballads* (1798), a collaboration with Coleridge containing such poems as *The Rime of the Ancient Mariner* by Coleridge and *The Thorn, Tintern Abbey*, and (in the second edition of 1800) *There was A Boy, Nutting, Michael*, the *Lucy* poems, and the famous preface by Wordsworth; *Poems, in Two Volumes* (1807), which included the great *Ode: Intimations of Immortality*; and *Poems* (1815), which exhibited Wordsworth's new arrangement of his many lyrics and also contained the long preface and essay supplementary on imagination and fancy. It is an irony of literary history that Wordsworth's unquestionably greatest poem, his 14-book autobiography *The Prelude, or Growth of a Poet's Mind*, was not published until after his death in 1850, thus placing what is now regarded as the quintessential Romantic text in the middle of the Victorian period.

Born and raised in the Lake District in the north of England, Wordsworth claimed that he grew up under the influence of natural objects that awakened and strengthened his imagination. Orphaned by age 13, he went to St. John's College, Cambridge (1787–91), where he received his B.A. after completing the requisite European tour with a friend. It was during this tour in 1790 that Wordsworth first became exposed to the French Revolution, still in its early stages, and to the sublimities of the Alps. Wordsworth poetically recounted the experiences of his Alpine journey throughout his career. It was also in France, when Wordsworth returned the following year, that he had a love affair with Annette Vallon, who later bore a daughter, Caroline. The emotional significance of Wordsworth's sudden paternity, in the apocalyptic context of the French Revolution in 1791 to 1792, and the war between England and France that began in 1793 and lasted for the next 22 years (with the exception of the brief peace of Amiens in 1802–03), has probably been underestimated. The very fact that Wordsworth had had an illegitimate child was not publicly known until the 20th century. Wordsworth sympathized deeply with the French Revolution and thus faced serious emotional conflicts not only when his country went to war with France but when the Revolution itself failed. Wordsworth returned from France in 1792, and, after some wandering and uncertainty regarding his vocation, settled in the Lake District again to become a full-time poet.

Life and Works

Wordsworth was born in Cockermouth, where his father was law-agent for Sir James Lowther, the principal landowner in that part of the Lake District. William was the second child and son in a family of four boys and a girl. In 1778, when he was age 8, his mother, Ann Cookson Wordsworth, contracted pneumonia and died. Consequently, the children were scattered, and Wordsworth and his sister were separated for nine years. (*See also* Wordsworth, Dorothy.)

About a year later, William and his older brother Richard, destined for a legal career, were enrolled at the old, established grammar school at Hawkshead, in the Lake District, boarding with Ann Tyson, who became a second mother to her charges. The school itself was quite good, and Wordsworth's five years there were well spent, providing him with a solid grounding in the classics, mathematics, and science, all central to the Hawkshead school's mission as preparatory for Cambridge. Wordsworth was, additionally, particularly benefited by schoolmasters who took especial interest in his reading and literary progress.

At St. John's College, Cambridge, Wordsworth was a lackluster student. After his father died, his guardians intended that he take Holy Orders and then assume an appointment held by a Cookson relative. Instead, Wordsworth saw these years of presumptive study as his dedication to the poetic vocation, partly inspired, ironically, by two collegiate absences, summer walking tours with a college friend, one through Wales and one through France. These vacations animated his poetry for years: Mt. Snowdon in Wales contributes the concluding scene in *The Prelude*, for which the French Revolution is the crisis and the *cri de coeur*.

At age 23, Wordsworth published two poems, *An Evening Walk* and *Descriptive Sketches*, which established him as a poet in the 18th-century tradition of poetry based on place—locodescriptive or topographical verse. Though Wordsworth later consciously turned away from the style of his 18th-century predecessors, announcing his new approach in the Preface to the second edition of *Lyrical Ballads* (1800), the influence of this tradition remained in Wordsworth's poetry in both direct and displaced ways. Clearly, it found expression in Wordsworth's *Guide to the Lakes* (1810), a work that surpasses the standard travel book for tourists. But what distin-

guishes Wordsworth's adaptation of this and other literary conventions from earlier examples is his emphasis on psychology and language, whereby landscape is not described for its own sake but for what it can reveal of the mind of the poet. To take the case of *Lyrical Ballads*, one discovers in the title a hybrid genre, implying both narrative incident (ballad) and personal meditation (lyric); the result is, as Wordsworth argues in his Preface, a style of poetry in which feeling is more important than action. To the extent that there is any narrative action at all, it is meant to throw into relief the particular emotion created in the minds of the narrator and the reader.

By thus challenging conventional literary expectations through the subordination of incident to feeling, Wordsworth made it clear that he was moving in a new direction in poetry, not just in terms of genre, but also of style. He wished to reject many of the stock devices used by contemporary poets, such as personification of abstract ideas, Gothic or supernatural themes, falsely ornate diction, and tortured syntax. The language Wordsworth chose to use in *Lyrical Ballads* was, he claimed, the common language really spoken by men and women; and the reason he deliberately chose such language was that it represented a conscious turn away from the artificial diction of many 18th-century poets toward a more natural and permanent style of poetry. Though Wordsworth's theory of language does not necessarily apply to all the poems in *Lyrical Ballads*, and even less to some of his later poems as an ideological announcement, it parallels contemporaneous political movements, such as the French Revolution, that likewise emphasized a democratic interest in the common person. Wordsworth's choice of subjects—abandoned women, idiot boys, and later discharged soldiers, beggars, and pedlars—similarly illustrates his social concern. Furthermore, the idea of poetry as a social act of communication is expressed in his definition of the poet as "a man speaking to men": the poet differs not in kind from other people, but only in the degree to which he expresses the imagination; Wordsworth's definition thus retains the 18th-century interest in the character and talents of the poet. Poetry, which speaks a common language to a common audience, is seen as arising naturally and organically from within the poet; it becomes expressed as "the spontaneous overflow of powerful feelings" that stem from a habitual process of imaginative reflection. Coleridge later disputed Wordsworth's theory and its relevance to his practice in the *Biographia Literaria* (1817), arguing that Wordsworth's language was not really the language of everyday life, but a purified form of it. Other critics have similarly questioned how the theory fits the practice, but the fact remains that Wordsworth's preface constitutes an important document in the history of literary criticism, preparing the way for the modernist idiom. (*See also* Emotion Recollected in Tranquility, Real Language of Men, Spontaneous Overflow of Powerful Feelings, Wise Passiveness.)

The year 1792 found Wordsworth in London, uncertain what to do professionally but very much caught up in political affairs. He traveled some through the British Isles, including places, like Salisbury Plain and Tintern Abbey, that later became resources for his poetry. In 1794, William Calvert, a Hawkshead friend, offered him and his sister Dorothy a residence called Windy Brow, a farmhouse in Keswick back in the Lakes. It was the start, with one interruption, of their living together for the rest of their lives. Another life-changing juncture occurred in London

in 1795, when Wordsworth met Coleridge, and both of their lives, as well as their poetry and the course of English literature, were altered forever. Shortly thereafter, Dorothy and William Wordsworth took up residence in Racedown Lodge in North Dorset, a home made possible by the will of Raisley Calvert, brother of the school friend, whose dying days Wordsworth tended. As tenants, Wordsworth and his sister took care of little Basil Montagu, motherless child of a friend. They learned child-rearing while Wordsworth worked on his poetry.

Coleridge, meanwhile, was living with his wife in Nether Stowey, in the West Country and, in mid-1797, enticed Dorothy and William to settle nearby in Alfoxden House. This was to be the scene of the poets' year of most intense collaboration and cooperation, the location for the writing of the *Lyrical Ballads*, as well as much else.

Before the volume was published, however, the three had set sail for Germany. Dorothy and William spent a cold, lonely and impoverished winter in Goslar, while Coleridge was studying elsewhere. After they returned to England in 1799, the Wordsworths joyfully established themselves again in the Lake District in Grasmere, while the Coleridges moved into Greta Hall, in nearby Keswick, which eventually became the home of Southey and of Coleridge's family, if not of himself. The Wordsworths stayed in Dove Cottage through William's marriage in 1802 to Mary Hutchinson and the births of three of their five children, three sons and two daughters (1803 and 1810). Also in 1802, claims on behalf of John Wordsworth against the Lowther estate were settled in the Wordsworths' favor. Moreover, Wordsworth's previously ever-impecunious situation continued to improve through his friendship with Sir Henry Beaumont and his political appointment, in 1813, as Distributor of Stamps, in effect a tax agent, in Westmorland and portions of Cumberland, coincident with the move of the Wordsworths to their final home, large, comfortable Rydal Mount, near Rydal Water.

But there were hardships, too, which left their traces in Wordsworth's poetry, particularly the deaths from 1805 through 1812, of his seaman brother John and his children Catherine and Thomas.

In his preface to *The Excursion* (1814), Wordsworth announced that he was embarked on a huge poetic project entitled *The Recluse*, of which the nine-book *Excursion*, and other blank-verse long poems, such as *Home at Grasmere* and *The Tuft of Primroses*, were only fragments. The architectural figure that Wordsworth used to characterize this project was a Gothic church, with its antechapel, main church, and smaller oratories as allegorical components of his oeuvre. The introductory movement of this enormous structural design is his poem *The Prelude*, autobiographical and preparatory in its confirmation of the poet as a chosen spirit capable of accomplishing the epic tasks before him. *The Prelude* in its literary form adopts the conventions of classical epic, though in a radically transformed way: the invocation of the muse, for example, becomes the poet's opening address to the gentle breeze that fans his cheek; the descent to the underworld becomes Wordsworth's experience in the French Revolution. While the immediate influence on *The Prelude* in terms of genre is most obviously Milton's *Paradise Lost*, it is clear from Wordsworth's numerous echoes that he also has Homer and Virgil, not to mention Shakespeare, in mind. Critics have pointed to the shape of the 14-book version of the poem (the first edition of

1850) as resembling the structure of a 14-line sonnet: the first eight books, or octave, move from the poet's childhood to his experience in London; the first tercet of the sextet (Books 9–11) recounts Wordsworth's involvement in France; and the final tercet (Books 12–14) reascends from the depths of the disastrous failure of the French Revolution to the apocalyptic restoration of Imagination. Viewed in this way, the conventionally epic qualities of the text appear contained by lyric form; *The Prelude* thus becomes a lyrical epic, just as Shelley's *Prometheus Unbound* is "a lyrical drama."

The history of *The Prelude* is complicated, involving almost half a century of composition and revision. Wordsworth's letters reveal that he began the poem in Germany in October 1798, as home thoughts from abroad. From the beginning, and throughout Wordsworth's life, the poem was often called simply "the poem to Coleridge"—Wordsworth's wife gave it the title of *The Prelude* for its posthumous publication—because Coleridge, or an imaginative version of him, was the original intended reader. Coleridge is addressed explicitly at crucial points in the text and finally attains the status of a "joint labourer" by the end. The earliest draft of the poem begins abruptly with a question—"Was it for this . . . ?"—that provides no referent for either "it" or "this." What follows this opening, hastening literally *in medias res*, is the sequence of childhood memories that were later worked into the first book of the full-length poem, as well as other important episodes, such as those portrayed in *There Was a Boy*, published in *Lyrical Ballads* in 1800, but afterward included in Book V of *The Prelude*. The recollections of childhood that structure Book I form the ground of Wordsworth's "rigorous inquisition" of his abilities, implicitly affirming the "genius, power,/Creation and divinity itself" of the poet. Wordsworth's "heroic argument" thus seeks to surpass Milton's great argument in *Paradise Lost* by creating a mythology of imagination in place of Christian doctrine. The boldness of Wordsworth's attempt to usurp divinity itself by locating it in the creative imagination denotes the impulse of Romanticism generally and again distinguished Wordsworth from his 18th-century predecessors. (*See also* Imagination.)

The concept of imagination is of particular importance to Wordsworth, who attempted at length to distinguish it from the lesser power of fancy in his 1815 preface to *Poems*. Arguing that both powers are creative, Wordsworth maintained that imagination is a sublime faculty of the mind that confers, abstracts, and modifies the properties of existence in a powerful and enduring way, while fancy is able to work only with limited objects and for temporary effects. Wordsworth's examples of imagination indicate that this faculty of mind is intimately connected to the rhetorical use of language; thus the conferring, abstracting, and modifying powers of imagination are seen to be the effect of rhetorical figuration (e.g., metaphor and metonymy). Coleridge disagreed with Wordsworth's elevated opinion of fancy, saying that Wordsworth mistook the operation of fancy alone for the cooperation of fancy and imagination. What was at stake in this disagreement, and in the larger elevation of imagination in Romanticism generally, was the poet's claim to godlike power, authority, and creativity.

Imagination is the theme of *The Prelude*, as Wordsworth says at the end of the poem, though the way that he illustrates the theme is through autobiographical narrative based on memories and anecdotes rather than on explicitly philosophical ar-

gument. Those moments that best demonstrate the mind's power are called "spots of time": typically based in childhood, they often involve traumatic or otherwise memorable experiences which, when recalled later in life, function as a source of power able to restore the poet spiritually. Two particular episodes that Wordsworth recounts as spots of time occur in Book XII—the gibbet scene, in which the poet as a young boy encounters the place where the corpse of a murderer was hung in chains; and the Christmas holiday scene, in which Wordsworth's father suddenly dies, leaving the poet an orphan. Both involve separation, death, guilt, and eventually restoration, which demonstrates that to an extent "the mind is lord and master," it appears that the point of the spots of time has to do with the ability of the mind to interpret experience, to imagine it, to structure it, and to return to it as a creatively formative moment in the development of the self. The spots of time, which are not limited to the episodes in Book XII but are scattered throughout the poem, usually place the poet in an unexpected encounter with something outside himself—another person, a natural object, or a text—in such a way that the encounter reflects profoundly and self-consciously on the poet himself, at once revealing and putting in question aspects of the self as it is rhetorically constructed in the text. (*See also* Spots of Time.)

Structurally, the central episode in this regard is Wordsworth's crossing of the Simplon Pass in the Alps in Book VI. While on a literal level, the journey is misdirected (Wordsworth actually gets lost), on an allegorical level, the error can be read as demonstrating that the poet really cannot miss his way because that way is mapped out providentially, as he had claimed at the beginning of *The Pre-*

lude. The poem comes to a halt, as Wordsworth celebrates an interpretive power of the mind, which he calls imagination. Similarly, in the final book of *The Prelude*, Wordsworth climbs Mount Snowdon at night in hopes of seeing the sun rise; what he experiences instead is the naked moon. Again, the indirection is interpreted positively, as an emblem of the creative mind. Yet on other occasions, the hermeneutics of encounter point to ironies and aporias within Wordsworth's text. When he sees the blind beggar in Book VII, for example, the effect is similar to that of the spots of time; the poet encounters otherness, yet that otherness tells him everything he could know about himself. The label on the beggar's chest both repeats *The Prelude*'s genre of autobiography and calls into question the possibility of autobiography through the blindness of the beggar and his written label. *The Prelude* thus questions itself.

As examples of Wordsworth's formal and stylistic range, his epic achievements in *The Prelude* and *The Excursion* should be set beside the hundreds of sonnets that he wrote after having been inspired by reading Milton's sonnets in 1802. Wordsworth's sonnets, built largely on the Italian model, cover a variety of topics in both private and public voices—for example, the death of his daughter Catherine (*Surprised by Joy—Impatient as the Wind*) and contemporary political matters (*Poems Dedicated to National Independence and Liberty*). Wordsworth also produced a number of sonnet sequences—for example, *The River Duddon, Ecclesiastical Sonnets*, and *Sonnets Upon the Punishment of Death*—as well as numerous individual sonnets on occasional topics. (*See also* Milton.)

Other minor genres that Wordsworth elevated to major importance include the Romantic ode—his *Intimations of Immortal-*ity (1807) stands as the foremost example of the sublime ode—and also the epitaph and its related form of the inscription, popular in Renaissance and 18th-century literature. Wordsworth wrote three essays on the genre of the literary epitaph, arguing that many poets had abused or degraded the form; what was needed was reeducation in proper epitaphic style and feeling. Wordsworth's theorizing about epitaphic inscription is important today for the issues it raises about textuality (e.g., poetic voice, the death of the author, speech versus writings), but moreover for its directing the reader to the presence of epitaphic figuration in Wordsworth's poetry. The pattern of Wordsworth's encountering a literal or figural grave, as in the spots of time, for example, recurs throughout his works, and points to a larger phenomenological structure in which the poet repeatedly confronts past or proleptic versions of himself even as his language encounters its own textuality in rhetorically reflexive or self-conscious ways.

Wordsworth criticism has suffered from the bias that anything written by the poet after 1807 is inferior and not of critical interest. Recently, that opinion has begun to disappear, and critics are now reading the late works to study the development of Wordsworth's style, his changing relation to politics and history, or his achievement in specific genres, such as the ode or the sonnet. At the same time, there is continuing interest in the early Wordsworth, as editors and critics reconstruct the manuscripts to trace the evolution of the poetry.

Wordsworth succeeded Southey as Poet Laureate in 1843, his nation's tribute to its greatest poet after Chaucer, Spenser, Shakespeare, and Milton. (*See also* Associationism, Androgyny, Incest, Lake

School, *Lyrical Ballads*, Mental Theater, Poetry, Toussaint Louverture.)

J. Douglas Kneale

[LD]

Works Consulted

Abrams, M.H., ed. *Wordsworth: A Collection of Critical Essays*. Englewood Cliffs: Prentice-Hall, 1972.

Gill, Stephen. *William Wordsworth: A Life*. Oxford: Clarendon, 1989.

Hall, Spencer, with Jonathan Ramsey, eds. *Approaches to Teaching Wordsworth's Poetry*. New York: MLA, 1986.

Hartman, Geoffrey H. *The Unremarkable Wordsworth*. Foreword by Donald G. Marshall. Minneapolis: U of Minnesota P, 1964.

———. *Wordsworth's Poetry, 1787–1814*. New Haven: Yale UP, 1964.

Johnston, Kenneth R. *Wordsworth and The Recluse*. New Haven: Yale UP, 1984.

Kneale, J. Douglas. *Monumental Writing: Aspects of Rhetoric in Wordsworth's Poetry*. Lincoln: U of Nebraska P, 1988.

Liu, Alan. *Wordsworth: The Sense of History*. Stanford: Stanford UP, 1989.

Moorman, Mary. *William Wordsworth: A Biography*. 2 vols. Oxford: Clarendon, 1957–65.

Onorato, Richard. *The Character of the Poet: Wordsworth in* The Prelude. Princeton: Princeton UP, 1971.

Wright, Frances

(1795–1852)

Frances Wright was born into a tradition of radical liberalism and intellectual rigor. Her father was a firm supporter of Paine, whose *Rights of Man* he distributed in a cheap version during 1794. His family was prominent in Glasgow intellectual circles; James Mylne, Wright's great-uncle, held a professorship of moral philosophy at the University of Glasgow for more than 40 years. Her mother's family was more conservative, although a great-great-aunt, Elizabeth Robinson Montagu, "Queen of the Blues," was one of the most famous and gifted Bluestockings of the time. When Wright's parents died in 1798, she and her younger sister Camilla were sent to her maternal relatives in London—a grandfather and an 18-year-old aunt. In 1806, as the result of a large inheritance, Wright's aunt moved the family to Dawlish on the Devonshire coast. There, she surrounded her nieces with servants and comforts, determined to bring them up as proper British ladies.

Wright, however, refused the role of gentlewoman, upset and disgusted by the social inequalities she saw around her and the unconcern evinced by her grandfather and others. She was inquisitive in her lessons, surprising and disconcerting tutors with her penetrating questions and impatience with equivocation. Already she displayed her conviction that women deserved as stringent an education as men, and when she could not find intellectual satisfaction in the classroom, she turned to self-education. At age 16 or 17, she read Carlo Botta's *Storia della guerra dell'independenza degli Stati Uniti d'America* and first learned of the country the democratic principles of which seemed so clearly to put into practice her own theories of liberal equality. In 1813, at 18, Wright left her aunt's home and returned to Scotland with her sister, thus effecting her first triumph of will over custom. In Glasgow, the sisters lived with the Mylne family, allowing Wright the opportunity to mix in liberal society. Her main course of study was of the United States, with which she was fascinated. It became her goal to visit what she saw as the land of perfect liberty.

During the three years she stayed in Scotland, Wright also expanded her learning in other directions. She studied Greek philosophy and became a disciple of Epicurus, whose practices of toleration, self-discipline, and social generosity, as well as the admittance of female scholars, were especially attractive. To express her admiration, she wrote *A Few Days in Athens* (published 1822), a defense of Epicurean principles, in which a young man, Theon, believes an unsubstantiated attack on Epicurus, later meets the philosopher, and becomes converted to his views. The tale contains a self-portrait of Wright, a female student named Leontium, who is tall, noble, learned, admired, and often called on to settle disputes or answer questions. Wright's own favored position in Glasgow's intellectual community suggests the general accuracy of this description, although it also displays the active self-confidence that would often put off those more used to the decorously silent proper lady. Also during the Glasgow years, Wright wrote plays and poetry; *Thoughts of a Recluse* is a long poem she worked on throughout her life. Semiautobiographical, it is Byronic, cynical, angry, and called unpublishable by a friend concerned that its pointed politics would risk libel. The only surviving play from this time is a verse tragedy, *Altorf*, describing the Swiss quest for freedom from Austrian tyranny during the 14th century.

In 1818, Camilla and Wright decided to visit America and made their plans known only to Rabina Millar, who had become a close friend and mother-figure. Overcoming all last-minute objections, they set sail in August and landed in New York on September 2, 1818. Having agreed to correspond with Millar in a series of letters designed for publication, Wright carefully crafted her responses to America's still new atmosphere of liberty and equality. The result, published in 1821 in London upon her return, is *Views of Society and Manners in America*. Extremely enthusiastic, the letters deal ably with such subjects as the position of women and the working

class, Quakerism, abolition, Niagara Falls, Congress, the Federal Party, the climate, Philadelphia, and much more. The volume was an immediate best seller, widely admired in both Britain and the United States. Although some conservative presses ridiculed her fervent esteem and others dismissed it, many politically liberal men took notice of the work and the author. Wright had allowed the book to be published "By An Englishwoman," but her work behind the scenes soon made her authorship known. Bentham sought out her acquaintance because of his enjoyment of *Views* and his agreement with its political and social stance, as did Lafayette. Wright maintained long and affectionate friendships with both; indeed, her second voyage to America was in the company of Lafayette, although family objections prevented their sailing together. Through these two men, Wright came into contact with James Mill, Francis Place, George Grote, Benjamin Constant, Augustin Thierry, and others.

During her first visit to America, Wright's play *Altorf* was produced in both New York and Philadelphia. In New York, it ran a successful three performances to great acclaim and widely favorable reviews; interestingly, reviewers assumed the anonymous author to be not only American but a man. The Philadelphia performance coincided with the advertisement of an American edition of the play in 1819. This publication was remarkable in that it included not only Wright's name but a potentially inflammatory Preface denigrating the British stage and valorizing American receptiveness. The play was published in London in 1822, dedicated to Millar, with a new and less troubling Preface. Also in 1822, both the French version of *Views* and a second English edition came out, this time bearing her name, substantially unrevised despite recommendations to lessen her adulatory tone.

In 1824, Wright traveled to the United States a second time, determined to add her voice to those few protesting slavery (practically her only criticism of America in *Views* concerns slavery). She published a pamphlet in 1825 called *A Plan for the Gradual Abolition of Slavery in the United States without Danger of Loss to the Citizens of the South* and attempted to prove her ideas by buying a tract of land in Tennessee and settling a small group of slaves to work toward their liberty. Although her project failed (chiefly due to the inept managing and indiscretion of those she had left in charge), she remained enthusiastic. Until her death, she concentrated on improving the lives of all oppressed populations, including Blacks, workingmen, and women. She lectured widely on such topics as federally sponsored education for all, workers' and women's rights, abolition, and birth control and was one of the first to use the term "humankind." She was both adored and execrated by American society. In 1848 her last piece was published; *England the Civilizer* was an apocalyptic description of egalitarianism initiated mainly by women.

Jacqueline Labbe

Works Consulted

Boyer, Paul S. "Frances Wright." *Notable American Women, 1607–1950, A Biographical Dictionary.* Ed. Edward T. James. Vol. 3. Cambridge: Harvard UP, 1971: 675–80.

Eckhardt, Celia Morris. *Fanny Wright, Rebel in America.* Cambridge: Harvard UP, 1984.

McFadden, Margaret. "Frances Wright." *An Encyclopedia of British Women Writers.* Ed. Paul Schlueter and June Schlueter. New York: Garland, 1988: 489–90.

Waterman, William Randall. *Frances Wright.* New York: AMS, 1967.

Dictionary of National Biography. s. v. "Darusmont, Frances."

Wright, Joseph
(1734–97)

The artist universally known as "Wright of Derby" was born and educated in that city (which still possesses a wonderful collection of his canvases). After being apprenticed to the portraitist Thomas Hudson, Wright worked there for many years, interrupted only by occasional visits to Liverpool or London. In addition to his work as a portrait painter, Wright also produced memorable subject studies related to the scientific interests of Erasmus Darwin and the Birmingham group known as "The Lunar Society." Wright's unique contribution to their investigations lay in his concern with light. He concentrated on scenes lit by firelight or candles and created a succession of masterly studies in *The Gladiator* (1765), *The Orrery* (1766), *The Air Pump* (1768), and *The Alchymist* (1771). He also produced fine studies of Derbyshire scenery in the Dales and at Matlock, which capture the new interest in picturesque travel of that time.

In 1773, Wright went to Italy, and his two-year stay culminated in the painting of two remarkable night pieces in the mode of sublime terror: *An Eruption of Mount Vesuvius* and *The Girandola at the Castle of St. Angelo at Rome*, exhibited in 1776. He settled at Bath, but failed to establish himself as a portraitist there and increasing ill health gradually affected the quality of his later work.

Wright's undoubted masterpieces are the succession of historical and scientific candle- or firelit pieces that he painted in his Derby years. He is among the first English painters to show a scientific curiosity, and the new factories and furnaces of the early Industrial Revolution are also among his subjects. He was a portrait painter of rare accomplishment, and his night scenes of moonlit rivers, valleys and mountains look forward to the poetic intensity of nature presentation which was to characterize the approaching Romantic age.

William Ruddick

Works Consulted

Nicolson, Benedict. *Joseph Wright of Derby: Painter of Light*. London: Routledge, 1968.

Egerton, Judy. *Wright of Derby*. London: Tate Gallery, 1990.

Klingender, F.D. *Art and the Industrial Revolution*. London: Carrington, 1947.

Young, Thomas
(1773–1829)

Thomas Young, physician, physicist, and Egyptologist, was born in 1773, in Milverton, Somersetshire. A precocious, serious, and austere child, Young was deeply impressed by the strict regimen of the Quaker faith of his family. It is often said that Young had read the Bible through twice by age 4 and could recite Goldsmith's "Deserted Village" at age 6. Young, though not much interested in modern literature, had a facility for languages and quickly became accomplished in Greek, Latin, Hebrew, Italian, and later several Middle Eastern languages. Following the advice of a wealthy uncle, later his benefactor, he pursued his interest in medicine in London. His interest in the physiology of the human eye led to his memoir on the curvature of the crystalline lens, which was published in the Transactions of the Royal Society in 1792. After being elected a Fellow of the Royal Society, Young pursued his career in medicine while under the patronage of the Duke of Richmond. In 1795, he attended the University of Göttingen and received his degree as Doctor of Physic, Surgery, and Midwifery.

Degrees in medicine at Cambridge followed, and in 1803, at age 30, he received his M.D. From 1801 to 1803, Young was Professor of Natural History at the Royal Institution. From 1804 on, he maintained a private practice in London and was elected physician to St. George's Hospital in 1811. Young served as foreign Secretary to the Royal Society from 1803 until his death in 1829.

Perhaps Young's most significant contribution to physics was his double-slit experiment which, by demonstrating that two adjacent sources of light both reinforce and cancel each other (interference), laid the foundation for wave theory. His findings, later supported by Fresnel and Poisson, gained him the enmity of Lord Broughham who, in the *Edinburgh Review*, took issue with him for questioning Newton, who advocated a strictly corpuscular theory of light. As a physician, Young's interest in what is now called physiological optics led him to describe the principles of depth perception and astigmatism. He also formulated a theory of color perception, based on separate nerves that respond to red, green, and violet, which was fully developed by Hermann von Helmholtz. Young's scientific interests were diverse;

he is known for one of the earliest descriptions of capillary action and is considered the first to have used the term energy as a physical concept. The phrase "Young's modulus," which refers to Young's description of a body's resistance to elongation under stress, is still widely employed.

In spite of his considerable contributions to physics and optics, Young is best remembered for his efforts to translate the Rosetta Stone. Although efforts to interpret hieroglyphics had been made, Young was the first to publish, in an anonymous article in the *Encylopaedia Britannica* (1819), a comparison of the stone's various texts. Young identified the hieroglyphics in ovals as royal names and established that the demotic inscription had symbolic as well as alphabetic characters. His work on hieroglyphics was influential, though, as his correspondent Champollion demonstrated, it had some limitations. Young's hiero-glyphic research continued until his death when he was preparing an Egyptian dictionary. (*See also* Rosetta Stone.)

In an era of polymaths, Young was widely respected by his Romantic peers in England and abroad; Helmholtz considered him one of the finest English scientists. "It was," according to Humphry Davy who knew Young well "difficult to describe what he did not know."

Alan Rauch

Works Consulted

Oldham, Frank. *Thomas Young, F.R.S.: Philosopher and Physician*. London: Arnold, 1933.

Peacock, George. *The Life of Thomas Young*. London: Murray, 1855.

Tyndall, John. "Thomas Young." *New Fragments*. New York: Appleton, 1897: 248–306.

Wood, Alexander. *Thomas Young, Natural Philosopher, 1773–1829*. Cambridge: Cambridge UP, 1954.

Wortham, John David. *The Genesis of British Egyptology*. Norman: U of Oklahoma P, n.d.

Index

A

Ackermann, Rudolph, 1–2. *See also* Rowlandson, Thomas; Topographical and Travel Prints; Watts, Alaric Alexander.

Adam, Robert, 10–11. *See also* Regency.

Aikin, John. *See* Aikin, Lucy; Ballad; Barbauld, Anna Letitia; *The Monthly Magazine; and British Register.*

Aikin, Lucy, 2

American Romanticism, 2–4

Ancients, The, 4–5. *See also* Blake, William (as engraver); Linnell, John; Palmer, Samuel; Visionary Landscape Painting.

Anderson, Robert. *See* Campbell, Thomas.

Androgyny, 5–7. *See also* Swedenborgianism.

Annuals. *See also* Hemans, Felicia; Hogg, James; Hood, Thomas; Landon, Letitia Elizabeth; Mitford, Mary Russell; Watts, Alaric Alexander.

Anticatholicism. *See* Gordon Riots.

Antiquarianism, 7–10. *See also* Ballad; Chatterton, Thomas; Gothicism; Hellenism; Macpherson, James; Percy, Thomas; Primitivism; Rosetta Stone.

Antislavery. *See* Slavery.

Anxiety of Influence. *See* Influence, Anxiety of.

Apocalypse. *See* Prophecy and Apocalypse.

Applied Arts. *See* Decorative Arts.

Architecture, 10–12. *See also* Decorative Arts; Domestic Architecture; Nash, John; Regency; Revett, Nicholas; Stuart, James.

Arne, Thomas, 395

Arnold, Samuel, 395

Arts and Crafts Movement. *See* Decorative Arts.

Ashe, Andrew, 396

Associationism, 12–14. *See also* Bentham, Jeremy; Education; Literary Criticism and Literary Theory; Necessity, Doctrine of; Priestley, Joseph; Skepticism, Humean; Spontaneous Overflow of Powerful Feelings; Spots of Time; Utilitarianism.

Astronomy. *See* Herschel, William.

Attwood, Thomas, 395

d'Aubisson, J.F., 216

Austen, Jane, 14–18. *See also* Education; Gothicism; Hamilton, Elizabeth; Irony; Literary Criticism and Literary Theory; Medievalism; Murray, John, Publishers; Novel; Satire; Scott, John.

Autobiography and Confession, 18–20. *See also* Natural Supernaturalism.

Ayrton, W. *See* Music.

C

H

M

N

O

Q

R

Y